THE FRENCH FOREIGN LEGION

A Complete History of the Legendary Fighting Force

Douglas Porch

HarperPerennial
A Division of HarperCollinsPublishers

A hardcover edition of this book was published in 1991 by
HarperCollins Publishers.

First HarperPerennial edition published 1992.

DESIGNED BY BARBARA MARKS
MAPS BY PAUL PUGLIESE

The Library of Congress has catalogued the hardcover edition as follows:

Porch, Douglas.
    The French foreign legion / Douglas Porch.—1st ed.
        p.   cm.
    Includes bibliographical references and index.
    ISBN 0-06-016652-5
    1. France. Armée de terre. Légion étrangère—History.
I. Title.
UA703.L5P67 1991   90-55834
355.3′59′0944—dc20

ISBN 0-06-092308-3 (pbk.)

92 93 94 95 96 AC/MB 10 9 8 7 6 5 4 3 2 1

For Olivia

CONTENTS

Illustrations follow page 344.

GLOSSARY

ALE	*Archives de la Légion étrangère, Aubagne*
Armée d'Afrique	French army units regularly stationed in North Africa
Armée Coloniale	White and native units which normally served in the French colonies other than North Africa
ALN	*Armée de libération nationale*
Armée Métropolitaine	French army serving in metropolitan France
BEP	*Bataillon étranger parachutiste*
BLE	*Bataillon de Légion étrangère*
Bled	Algerian hinterland
BSLE	*Bureau des statistiques de la Légion étrangère*
Chasseurs d'Afrique	Light cavalry raised for service in North Africa
DBLE	*Demi-brigade de Légion étrangère*
DCRE	*Dépôt commun des régiments étrangers*
DFL	*Division française libre*
DMI	*Division de marche d'infanterie*
FFL	*Forces françaises libres*
FLN	*Front de libération nationale*
GM	*Groupe mobile*
Infanterie de Marine	Troops under command of the French navy which were shifted to the army in 1900 and became the *Armée Coloniale*
Pieds noirs	North Africans of European extraction
REC	*Régiment étranger de cavalerie*
Régiment étranger	Foreign regiment
REI	*Régiment étranger d'infanterie*

REP	*Régiment étranger parachutiste*
RMLE	*Régiment de marche de Légion étrangère*
RMVE	*Régiment de marche de volontaires étrangers*
SHAT	*Service historique de l'Armée de terre*
SIL	*Service d'immatriculation de la Légion*
Tirailleurs algériens	Algerian Rifles
Tirailleurs sénégalais	Senegalese Rifles
Tirailleurs tonkinois	Tonkinese Rifles
TOE	*Théâtre d'opérations éxterieures*
zouaves	Corps formed in 1831 in Algiers from the *zouaoua* tribe. It gradually evolved into an entirely French force although its uniforms were modeled on North African dress.

PREFACE

"THE FRENCH, BEING a thrifty and practical people, have always been eager to let any available foreigners assist them in any necessary bleeding and dying for *la Patrie*," writes American historian John Elting at the beginning of a chapter on the *régiments étrangers* in his massive study of the Napoleonic army. "From the Scots who rode with Joan of Arc to the Foreign Legion at Dien Bien Phu, the foreign soldier, idealistic volunteer or hard-case mercenary, is an integral part of the French military tradition."[1] This book is a study of some of those foreigners in French service—the French Foreign Legion from its inception in 1831 to the departure from Sidi-bel-Abbès in 1962. The attractions of writing such a book are obvious. While many national armies contain or have contained regiments or units with long and, at times, even heroic pasts, none has captured world imagination in quite the same fashion, or to such a degree, as the Legion. No corps is so surrounded by romance, by legend, by mystery.

Why this should be so is not difficult to discover. The Foreign Legion was and continues to be unique in our age—a multinational, polyglot force made up of men, some of whom were on the run from the law or had in some other way reached the end of their tether, some of whom simply wished to push life's experience to the very brink of endurance and beyond, cast out upon the diverse and distant lands that once comprised the French colonial empire. The men and the settings have combined to make the history of the Legion one of unparalleled exoticism, pathos and drama.

But while this may explain the attractiveness of the subject for the historian, it does not in itself justify yet another history of the Legion. Indeed, a moderately diligent English-speaking reader with access to a public library should be able to locate one or two books that tell the familiar stories of the stubborn defense of Camerone, of Tuyen Quang or of Dien Bien Phu. Not surprisingly, the classic histories of the Legion are in French. Some of the nineteenth-century histories such as General Grisot's *La Légion étrangère de 1831 à 1887,* or Bernelle and de Colleville's *Histoire de l'ancienne Légion étrangère,* have stood the test of time and have become important sources for historians of the early Legion. In our own century, General Paul Azan's *La Légion étrangère en Espagne, 1835–1838,* published in 1907, and A.-P. Comor's history of the 13ème DBLE in World War II have offered excellent studies of those periods of Legion history.

Nor has the Legion's special recruitment and psychology escaped the notice of authors. As early as 1864, French writer Antoine Camus defined the Legion mentality in *Bohèmes du drapeau,* an exercise repeated by G-R Manue and Ferri-Pisani in the years between the two world wars. In *The White Kepi,* published in 1956, American author Walter Kanitz, who in 1939–40 served in a unit of French foreign volunteers (RMVE), made a very original attempt to get at the "truth" of the Legion through a thematic exploration of the attitudes and experiences of legionnaires. Since the nineteenth century, the Legion, too, has taken steps to adjust its methods of leadership to the special psychology of legionnaires. Recent editions of the quasi-official *Livre d'or de la Légion étrangère* contain a chapter on the *"psychologie du légionnaire."* And in 1951, the Legion even published a manual written by Legion captain Henri Azam, *La Légion étrangère: Ses régles particulières,* designed to instruct its cadres in the delicate responsibility of drawing the most from their men. The problem posed by these exercises in the definition of a legionnaire psychology is that it is difficult to detect the point at which truth merges into myth.

I believe that there is room for a book on the Legion that links its combat performance to its recruitment, training, rituals, and special social environment. My claim for the originality of this work is based upon the questions it poses, the forgotten or neglected episodes of Legion history that it reveals, the extent of its documentation, and its attempt to define the frontiers between the myths and realities of Legion history. For the author, the accomplishment of this task has required several summers spent combing archives in France for undiscovered documents, diaries and memoirs, pulling from more accessible sources material that has eluded other authors, and consulting often excellent monographs and theses, many of which have yet to be folded into any general history. This study does not pretend to be an exhaustive history of the Legion—that would be quite impossible! The Legion forces selectivity simply because it has been in existence for too long, fought in too many places, and is a subject too rich in human drama for any student of its past to claim totality for his work. However, its basic premise is that without an understanding of why men volunteered for the Legion, what psychic income they drew upon being initiated into its peculiar mysteries and *esprit,* and the stages of development and levels of growth in the career of a legionnaire, then the litany of heroic acts that makes up most Legion histories are rather like reading a book of crime fiction in which the motive for the murder is never revealed. A history of the Legion is also a history of a portion of the European working class in the nineteenth and twentieth centuries, one which a Marxist historian might claim had slipped through the fingers of the "capitalist revolution." It is often, but not invariably, a chronicle of dropouts, of misfits, of refugees, of men commonly regarded as out of place in normal society. What this book hopes to explain is how they fought so well, and why this class of man needed to bury himself in an army to find self-expression. In many respects, the Legion offers a mirror image of its society, a comment upon Europe's norms and values and France's attitudes toward foreigners, a place where men were able to find something that civilian life failed to provide them. In this respect, the book hopes to suggest that military history has broader implications than many historians have so far been willing to attribute to it.

The peculiar psychology and motivations of these apparently enigmatic fighting men have exercised a fascination since the nineteenth century. Before 1914, the *1ᵉʳ étranger* was known as the *"1ᵉʳ mystérieux."* French journalist Lucien Bodard found legionnaires to be virtually the only truly inscrutable race planted among a human Indochinese landscape that he otherwise deciphers with remarkable sensitivity. As legionnaires at Cao Bang, the post at the extreme end of the deadly Route Coloniale 4 that paralleled the Chinese frontier in Tonkin, prepared to receive the Viet Minh onslaught in October 1950, ". . . they looked perfectly happy," he quoted a French administrator as saying. "And yet, these fellows behind the machine guns are under sentence of death already, condemned to be swept away by the Viet wave whenever Giap gives the order and his tens of thousands of regulars sweep forward. Their cheerfulness filled me with pity; but with admiration too. For after all, they really had no hope, with nothing but one little airfield as their only link with the rest of the world."[2]

Perhaps the greatest paradox of the Legion is how an elite unit has come to be fashioned out of material regarded as unpromising. One of the general assumptions of modern military history has been that conscripts, or at the very least national forces, are superior in most respects to those composed of mercenaries. Perhaps I should pause at this moment to explain what is meant by my reference to the Legion as a mercenary force. My Legion friends object strenuously to this appellation, and their case is a good one. The first and most obvious connotation of *mercenary* is one who exchanges military service for cash. The "cash nexus" is what distinguishes a mercenary from a mere professional soldier. While many legionnaires no doubt enlisted in the past to have regular meals, the desire for material gain was seldom a primary, or even secondary, reason for enlistment. On the contrary, the overwhelming majority of recruits never thought to ask how much they were to be paid, and it came as a great shock to some of them, like the German-American Erwin Rosen, who enlisted before World War I, to discover how scandalously low Legion wages actually were, certainly lower than for professional French soldiers in other units. Only in very recent years, and perhaps also traditionally in Indochina where they qualified for extra "colonial pay," have legionnaires received anything resembling a fair wage. Indeed, the abysmal pay of the legionnaire was a persistent source of problems for the Legion. But when this was pointed out, the government argued (unconvincingly!) that to pay legionnaires a fair wage would open them to charges of being mercenaries. Therefore, harsh administrative logic decreed that the virtue of the legionnaire, as well as that of France, was somehow redeemed by his impoverishment.[3]

However, in other ways the Legion does meet the criteria for a mercenary force, the most obvious being that the legionnaire is compensated in ways other than cash payment, and ways that were honored in an exceptionally masculine, perhaps also in an exceptionally working class, environment. The future German writer Ernst Junger, who joined the Legion in 1913, had no doubts that he was serving in a mercenary force, "even though the pay was in counterfeit coinage: The promise of the extraordinary."[4] The legionnaire is also a soldier hired into foreign service, notwithstanding the large numbers of Frenchmen who have served in the Legion. The Legion also demonstrates certain dysfunctional traits commonly associated with mercenary forces, namely a high desertion rate. Finally, the Legion has consciously cultivated an attitude of professional detachment that distinguishes it from other troops made up of men who fight for a cause. Indeed, as will be demonstrated, men who joined the Legion out of the idealistic motives of serving France, democracy or to fight fascism were made to feel very much out of place in the Legion.

And here the problems of explaining Legion performance begin. The word *mercenary* has acquired an unflattering connotation in both English and French because it suggests someone incapable of elevated sentiments such as loyalty to a cause but who acts only in his own interests. Traditionally, mercenary forces were often little more than congregations of ruffians with soldierly skills. For this reason, many societies have found mercenaries to be unsteady, even dangerous, foundations upon which to rest the fortunes of the state. Some Muslim dynasties preferred a system of military slavery over that of hiring mercenaries because slaves were easier to acquire, proved more loyal, and, because of their servile status and youth, adapted more readily to new military techniques and innovations than did mercenaries.[5]

In the West, the prejudice against mercenaries runs at least as far back as the end of the Feudal Age, when the expansion of the cash economy allowed the Italian city-states to hire *condottieri* to put muscle into their foreign policies. The result, according to Machiavelli, among the first Western writers to call for conscript armies, was a disaster: "The present ruin of Italy is the result of nothing else than reliance upon mercenaries," he wrote in the fifteenth century. After describing pitched battles among *condottieri* bands in which the only men killed were those unfortunate enough to be pitched from their horses and suffocate in the mud, he gave a comprehensively damning appraisal of their fighting abilities: "They are disunited, ambitious, without discipline, disloyal, overbearing among friends, cowardly among enemies; there is no fear of God, no loyalty to men."[6] And while most kingdoms relied upon mercenaries in the centuries between Machiavelli and the French Revolution, they did not always earn the praise even of the great captains whose reputations were built upon their blood. King Gustavus Adolphus, whose mercenary armies ravaged Germany in the Thirty Years' War, saw them as "faithless, dangerous and expensive," and took good care to keep them away from his native Sweden.[7] A master warrior of the eighteenth century, Frederick the Great of Prussia, was of the opinion that his men had "neither courage, nor loyalty, nor group spirit, nor [spirit of] sacrifice, nor self-reliance." They were capable only of a primitive *Korpsgeist,* and "[because honor has no effect on them] they must fear their officers more than any danger." He conceded that an army recruited among patriotic citizens would be infinitely more resilient, more adaptable and cheaper than his own, but he was unwilling to redistribute political power in the way that an armed citizenry would have demanded. So mercenary armies survived, not because they were militarily efficient, but because they provided the foundations of royal absolutism.[8]

In France, the employment of mercenaries dated from the twelfth century, when King Philippe Auguste resolved to acquire a force more dependable than the feudal levies who were obliged to remain under arms for only forty days. He instituted a system of payment in lieu of service for his knights, the income from which was in turn invested in the hiring of *routiers,* or "free companions." The practice of employing mercenaries grew during the Hundred Years' War between France and England in the fourteenth and fifteenth centuries. Many of these mercenaries were foreigners—when in 1439 France created fifteen companies to form the nucleus of a standing army, two of them were Scots. Attempts to form a national infantry in the form of *francs-archers*—bowmen who were called "franc" because they were exempt from paying taxes—between 1448 and 1509 foundered, causing the kings of France to rely upon mercenaries and foreigners to fight for them. And while the size and power of France meant that her government was not held hostage to turbulent mercenaries as were the small and fragmented states of Italy in Machiavelli's day, the cost of mercenary troops meant that they frequently went unpaid or were disbanded and thrown upon the countryside, which gave them a bandit reputation. This unsavory image deepened in the eighteenth century, when a growing nationalist sentiment, the French defeats in the Seven Years' War (1757–63), and growing calls for political reform that accused royal authority of resting upon the bayonets of its troops, especially of its foreign troops, increasingly called the practice of hiring foreign soldiers into question. At the same time, the growth of similar sentiments elsewhere gradually reduced the number of foreigners available for recruitment. Switzerland remained the exception to this general rule. There poverty, tradition and government encouragement continued to hemorrhage men into the armies of foreign monarchs.[9]

Nevertheless, when the French Revolution erupted in 1789, foreigners were well represented in the French army, making up perhaps a quarter of its strength. Most of them were to be found in the eleven Swiss regiments whose recruitment was fairly strictly controlled by *capitulations* or agreements between the King of France and various cantons. Twelve of ninety-one non-Swiss regiments in the French line infantry were also foreign regiments.[10]

When the Revolution broke out, the foreign regiments proved most loyal to royal authority, which hardly increased their popularity with reformers. From its earliest days, the Constituent Assembly called for the abolition of foreign units in the French army. This was finally achieved on July 21, 1791, after soldiers of the former Nassau Regiment, a German unit, grown weary of constant harassment from French civilians, tore all their distinctive insignia from their uniforms and "declared that they are French, and that they wish to serve as French."[11] Only the Swiss units, covered by an ancient and special treaty, survived until August 20, 1792, when popular hostility caused them to be disbanded.

From a historical perspective, then, the introduction of conscription by the French Revolution that was called for in 1790 and definitively organized in 1798 is seen as a great step forward in the evolution of military organizations, allowing the creation of homogeneous armies based on the cheap supply of patriotic manpower, clearly superior to their more expensive predecessors in which loyalty to the organization was low, desertion rates high, discipline draconian, and tactical and operational possibilities limited. Citizen armies expressed national purpose and fought for national goals, which made them, potentially at least, at once more forceful and more flexible instruments in the hands of energetic and innovative commanders. Nor were they as likely to threaten the integrity of the state.

This is not to say, however, that foreign soldiers disappeared from the Revolutionary armies—quite the contrary. The National Assembly was torn between the need to keep the army both well-disciplined and loyal, goals which in the midst of the Revolution were not always compatible. Political agitation, resignations, mutiny and desertion had disorganized much of the old Royal Army, while patriotic volunteer and national guard battalions called up to defend *"la patrie en danger"* when France and Austria went to war on April 20, 1792, broke and ran at the first sight of enemy cavalry. This poor performance, combined with the capitulation of Longwy and Verdun to the invading enemy armies in September, which placed Paris in danger, caused the government to enlist between three and four thousand well-disciplined Swiss troops released from service in French units barely a month earlier.[12] Likewise, French propaganda that called for soldiers in enemy ranks to "embrace liberty" presented the Revolutionaries with the problem of what to do with those, mainly Dutch and Belgians, who rallied to their cause. On August 1, 1792, a *légion franche étrangère* was created, followed in September by a *légion germanique* for Prussian and Austrian deserters.

The proliferation of foreign units in the French army grew in the period of the Directory (1795–99), which even signed a new *capitulation* with Swiss authorities in 1798 allowing them to recruit soldiers in the Helvetian cantons. Napoleon made extensive use of foreign and allied troops, organizing Italian and Polish auxiliaries during his Italian campaign of 1796–97, and Copt and Greek legions during his invasion of Egypt. *Bataillons étrangers,* which eventually became *régiments étrangers,* were organized from 1802 to incorporate foreign deserters, prisoners and other odds and ends out of place in French line regiments. These were true foreign legions in which Napoleon was careful to mix nationalities in the battalions. However, he must have thought them of uneven quality, for they were assigned secondary, often coastal defense, roles or garrison duties in Holland, Spain and Italy for most of their existence. After 1805, the number of foreign troops in the *Grande armée* increased substantially as Napoleon's conquests brought more and more of Europe under his control and as allied and vassal states were prevailed upon to contribute men to the French army. Between a third and a half of Napoleon's army that invaded Russia in 1812 was made up of foreigners, many of whom, like the rest of that army, failed to return. But their stock dropped rapidly when Saxon units deserted during the battle of Leipzig, followed by the defection of the Bavarians and mutinies in other German units. Many of the foreign units were dissolved in November 1813, leaving only Swiss, Poles and three *régiments étrangers.*[13]

So while legislators and most theorists continued to favor conscription in some form or another after 1789, this brief sketch demonstrates that the traditions of mercenary service survived the Revolution. In fact, it can even be argued that the Revolution gave the mercenary tradition a new lease on life in France, for by making France into the homeland of the Revolution, it virtually guaranteed that generations of Europe's politically repressed would make for Paris. Some of these refugees would be forced to resort to military service, only to discover legal barriers that kept them out of French line units. The problem for the French army was to discover ways to transform these refugees and other foreigners into efficient soldiers. Outside of France, Swiss mercenary units continued to be counted in the Prussian army until 1848, that of Naples until 1861, and in the Papal forces until 1870, with the Pope's Swiss Guard surviving to our own day.

Historically, however, the view that mercenaries could be made to

perform efficiently, and in certain conditions more efficiently than conscripts, found its strongest proponents among French colonial soldiers,
who faced essentially two problems: those of power projection and adaptability. Even under the *ancien régime,* colonial expansion met indifference
and even hostility in France, and found favor with only a few ministers
such as Richelieu and Colbert. Voltaire could dismiss cession of Canada to
the British in 1763 as the trifling loss of "a few acres of snow." The
disastrous French expeditions to Egypt (1798–1801) and Saint-Domingue
(1801–1808), as Haiti was then known, did little to contribute to the
general popularity of foreign adventures in the French government and
public opinion. Even the acquisition of Algiers in 1830 was often regarded
by the July Monarchy (1830–1848) as an embarrassing legacy of the fallen
Bourbon Restoration (1815–1830). The brutality of the conquest, the lack
of economic viability of the French empire and the ever-present menace of
a German attack after 1871 caused many to regard colonial expansion as
a useless and even dangerous distraction that weakened France's position
in Europe and even threatened to draw her into a war against her
interests.[14] Therefore, in the minds of many Frenchmen, the empire remained the domain of *têtes brûlées,* wild adventurers, marginal or ill-
adjusted social elements.

This was to have consequences in military terms. Between the fall of
Napoleon in 1815 and the Franco-Prussian War of 1870–71, France practiced a form of modified conscription, with recruits selected by an annual
lottery. The relatively small size of the army, which meant that only a few
of the young men eligible were conscripted each year, the fact that those
who had drawn a "bad number" could pay someone to serve in their place,
and the fact that service was seven years with a high percentage of reenlistments, made distinctions between conscripts and professional soldiers
academic. While units like the Foreign Legion, *zouaves* and *Chasseurs
d'Afrique* were created especially for service in "Africa," as Algeria was
then known, and specialized units of *Infanterie de marine* manned other
far-flung French possessions, the main task of conquering Algeria in the
1830s and 1840s fell to French line regiments.

This changed after 1871, when the French army expanded enormously to meet the military challenge of a united Germany. Conscription
was broadened, the possibility of purchasing a replacement eliminated,
and service time eventually reduced to two years. From this time, the
"Metropolitan Army" largely composed of conscripts was regarded by
the French public as a force to be used for home defense. When the Third
Republic dispatched some line regiments from western France to help in
the conquest of Tunisia in 1881, there was a public outcry. As a result,
French governments were reluctant to send troops and often even to provide cash for colonial conquests. Therefore, French officers were forced
to recruit an army on the cheap to expand the boundaries of empire and
to garrison lands already conquered. This meant creating an army spe-

cially tailored for colonial service—combinations of European professionals and native levies.

The second complaint against conscripts in the colonies was that they adapted badly to the rigors of service there. Despite the reluctance to employ French conscripts in imperial expeditions, units of the 19th Army Corps in Algeria, *zouaves* and *Chasseurs d'Afrique* which contained conscripted North Africans of European extraction and Jews with a smattering of metropolitan French conscripts, continued to be used in colonial expeditions, as was the *infanterie légère d'Afrique*, the penal *Bataillons d'Afrique*, more commonly known as the *"Bats d'Af,"* made up of conscripts who, because of a prior criminal record, were deemed unworthy to serve with honest Frenchmen. A small number of conscripts also were present in cavalry, engineer, artillery, transport and veterinary units used abroad. But because these conscripts belonged to the *Armée d'Afrique* and because of the small numbers involved, no one protested their use in the colonies. Conscripts, albeit voluntary ones, were included in the Madagascar expedition of 1895 and in the 1900 China expedition with unhappy results, their youth and lack of acclimatization being blamed for their high mortality rates.

Another, unspoken, objection to conscripts among colonial soldiers was that they inevitably brought more scrutiny to bear on the conduct of colonial operations from politicians of the Third Republic. Also, colonial theorists like the future Marshal Hubert Lyautey argued that colonial service was a special calling whose requirements were very different from those of European warfare. Like many French colonial officers, Lyautey believed that the importation into the colonies of inappropriate European military methods and of a "metropolitan mentality" had been the source of many disasters. His arguments, laid out in a celebrated article entitled "Le rôle colonial de l'armée" published in the prestigious *Revue des Deux Mondes* in 1900, was instrumental in persuading the French parliament to pass a law creating a separate colonial army in that year. In fact, the 1900 law simply streamlined the French imperial military organization to the point of taking the *troupes de marine* away from the French navy and attaching them to the army under their new title of *troupes coloniales*. It also included provisions allowing units of the *Armée d'Afrique*, including the Legion and the *tirailleurs*, technically part of the metropolitan army, to be used in colonial possessions outside of North Africa.[15]

The existence of this separate "two-army" tradition in France was in no way unique in this age—British forces included many colonial regiments as well as the celebrated Indian Army. The Dutch colonial army was created in 1830, while the Spanish kept colonial garrisons in Cuba, Puerto Rico and the Philippines until 1898, and in 1920 created their own Foreign Legion modeled in part on the French Legion, but trained more specifically for combat in the mountainous Rif. Yet, on the European continent in an era of large national armies, the mercenary tradition remained a minority one, and the tradition of foreign white mercenaries one close to extinction. A handful of European officers like Charles "Chinese" Gordon found employment in the armies of oriental potentates; the Dutch hired about a thousand foreigners for their colonial army at the turn of the century, mostly Germans but also, until he deserted, the French poet Arthur Rimbaud; and foreign immigrants furnished many soldiers for the U.S. Army. However, it was in the French Foreign Legion that the venerable and virtually extinct tradition of white mercenary service survived in its most robust form.

And given the poor reputation of such soldiers, even in the eyes of their eighteenth-century commanders, the Legion would seem to have offered little promise of the elite performance which its historians claim for it. The image of the Legion as popularized in the years between the world wars by such books and films as *Beau Geste* is of a mongrel unit recruited among the scrapings of humanity, perhaps even among the criminal classes, but also containing a fairly sizable contingent of "gentlemen rankers" who fled into the Legion to escape a dark past or out of a desire for adventure. This heterogeneous collection of men was denied any of the motivations commonly thought essential for modern fighting men—patriotism, a desire to defend family and homeland, the certainty that one's national cause is righteous and, lastly, the crutches of a language and national character, even of a shared sense of humor, so essential in carrying men over the rough spots. That the Legion is presumed to have fought so well appears to defy common sense.

THE COMMON ASSUMPTION has been that the Legion was able to function, like those armies of Frederick the Great, because of discipline so draconian that a sergeant of the Legion made Captain Bligh appear indulgent by comparison. Unit cohesion was guaranteed by fear of punishments long outlawed in Europe, if indeed they had ever existed there, and by the sheer remoteness of the Legion's garrisons. General Duchesne's well-known admonition to his legionnaires during the Madagascar expedition to "march or die" seems to sum up rather neatly the conditions of service, except that it might be amended to read "march *and* die"! In this world of desperate and brutalized men, desertion, the running sore of the Legion, offered the only escape from the evil conditions in which legionnaires were forced to live—better risk decapitation at the hands of marauding Arabs or drowning in the Suez Canal than continue an existence which was only one notch above that of a penal colony. In any case, in the public view at least, the only thing worse than fighting against the Legion was to fight for them.

In summing up the problem from the Legion point of view, Captain Morin de La Haye went a long way toward confirming the popular view of Legion service: "Given the heterogeneous elements which we recruit from all over for the Legion, the fabrication of the soldier is particularly delicate there," he wrote in 1886.

The legionnaire in no way resembles the good little French soldier who only wants to accomplish his service with no fuss and then return home. The man who enlists in the Legion often has a military vocation. But he is sometimes a déclassé, an adventurer, someone made bitter by life, a bandit. In the Legion we get everything. In the companies which have a strength of three to four hundred men, one finds a mixture of ex-officers, ruined gentry, anarchists and freed convicts. One must knead this human capital so as to give it worth as an engine of war. We do this through a training system pushed to its maximum intensity.

The men, isolated in the posts of the Sud Oranais such as Géryville, Thiaret, Méchéria, constantly practice maneuvers, marksmanship; we push them to the limit.

In the beginning this system produces vague impulses of revolt. Refusal to obey, desertion, cases for court martial occur daily; men shoot at their officers, others look to unhorse them; in the Legion, the officer must expect everything. The human beast shows his teeth and is brought to heel only through the use of fists.

At certain times we carry out forced marches. We leave for the south. Everyone must keep up. The man who remains in the rear risks death by starvation or being taken by Arab dissidents. After these marches, the number of stragglers is considerable: One must be strong to endure. This is the Darwinist survival of the fittest applied to the troops.

It seems unlikely that troops treated in this way could be capable of anything but mutiny. But Morin de La Haye disagreed: "The training and education of the legionnaire are therefore very hard," he continued.

But they produce surprising results. In several months, one has a solid troop, maneuverable, admirably practiced in shooting and marching, and entirely in the hands of its leaders. The men obey not with submission, but with spirit and assiduity. One would say that the constant exercise of the will of the leader works on them like a hypnotic suggestion. One sees in the eyes of the soldiers that they are attentive to orders, proud to maneuver well, and conscious of their worth. It is superfluous to dwell upon the amount of work one must require of the instructors to obtain this result. They carry it out with zeal, even fanaticism, in the expectation of campaigning with the men that they prepared for this end.[16]

The apparent paradox in this brief explanation of the evolution of the legionnaire from rebellious recruit to proud soldier is that conventional wisdom would appear to doubt that such poor material and such brutal training methods could produce an elite fighting force. Of course, this is not to say that heterogeneous, even press-ganged, forces in the ancient mold did not on occasion rise to superior levels of performance—one only has to think of the armies of Frederick the Great or Wellington, or the British navy in the Napoleonic Wars. But, generally speaking, there is just so much that severe discipline, rigorous training, tight leadership and perhaps the desperation of circumstance can do to improve the performance of "the scum of the earth enlisted for drink." And even if these forces are capable of flashes of heroism, they lack the inner strength to sustain them through prolonged adversity. After all, one is unlikely to *"faire Camerone,"* that is, fight almost to the last man as did a group of legionnaires at the Mexican village of Camerone in 1863, if there is the slightest possibility of a viable alternative. Riffraff commonly behaves like riffraff given half a chance, which is one reason why most nations have chosen to fight their wars with conscript armies, at least since the Franco-Prussian War of 1870–71 made them virtually mandatory.

All of this suggests several possibilities. The most obvious is that the performance of the Legion was perhaps less consistently inspirational than Legion lore would have one believe. This has not been my conclusion. The Legion has never lacked for courage, although I believe I can show that it has been plagued by endemic problems, namely desertion, which could on occasion prove very disruptive. Nor has the Legion been immune in conditions of prolonged conflicts from what modern military observers call the "curve of combat efficiency," which dictates that the accumulated stress of battle leads to a progressive deterioration of performance.[17]

Therefore, while recognizing in full the potential for exaggeration, even for mistaken assessment, it seems logical to conclude that critical reports were drawn up in good faith and reflect an honest perception of conditions in the Legion at a particular time.

But if Legion performance has generally lived up to its press notices, then there appears to be something exaggerated or left out of Morin de La Haye's description—perhaps recruitment to the Legion has been of a higher quality and service and discipline less brutalizing than has been commonly supposed. Or perhaps the act of enlistment was not necessarily one of desperation, but a search for something that conventional society, even conventional military society, could not provide—risk; glory; a tough, quasi-outlaw image; and a quest for the assurance, in an incongruous way the stability, that only a strict hierarchy and a rough and ready justice could provide. A third possibility might be that, while the Legion merited in full its unsavory reputation, it discovered ways to minimize its handicaps, or even to transform qualities that would be liabilities in conscript armies into strengths. It is just such questions that this book will seek to answer.

There are many dangers awaiting a historian of the Legion, not the least the enormous mystique of that corps. No force has been so much the object of mythmaking as the Foreign Legion, a process that began even before the Geste brothers decided to try their luck at soldiering. However, this accretion of myth has been one of the major impediments to a serious study of the Legion as a fighting force, and helps to account for the fact that works on the Legion often seem to lurch between popular hagiography and eulogies to its heroism, and condemnations of the Legion as a brutal, quasi-criminal institution, unworthy of a nation with pretensions to civilized values.

While the encrustation of myth provides one of the main impediments to understanding the Legion, it also furnishes one of its most irresistible attractions. Of no element is this more true than of recruitment. The identity of legionnaires has always been shrouded in mystery, and intentionally so. Part of the romanticism of the Legion rests on its tradition of asylum and its laws of silence, both reinforced by the *anonymat*—the Legion policy of adopting a false identity upon enlistment that was built into Article 7 of the ordinance of March 10, 1831, that founded the corps. The *anonymat* has caused people to build great legends about the Legion.[18] Indeed, it has caused legionnaires to build great legends around themselves—Antoine Sylvère, who enlisted under the name of Flutsch in 1905, noted that once even the familiar bearing of a name had been abandoned by men already disoriented by life, legionnaires set about conjuring up a past out of their fantasies and failures.[19]

The task of the historian is to get as close to the truth as his documentation and historical imagination will allow. Even this cursory introduction will alert the reader that, in the case of the Legion, this can be no easy task. Despite the often harsh realities of service, mystery is at the very heart of the Legion. It was created by the circumstances of its early years, nurtured as the very essence of its personality, reinforced by certain regulations tailored specifically for the corps, and jealously guarded by those who have successfully gained admittance to its inner fraternity. To study the Legion, then, is to open oneself to problems beyond the standard range, difficult enough in themselves, of those that confront the historian who attempts to divine the motives and actions of men long dead. It is in reality to break a code, to explain the men whose experiences have often burst the normal confines of human activity. It is also to explain the rules and social rituals of this curious freemasonry whose continued existence is in itself a social, political and military statement that cannot be ignored. The Legion forms an important part of France's military self-image, but not a central part. The Legion does not so much run against the current of history; it defies it. To explain this defiance, and why, on balance, it has been a story of remarkable success, is the task of this book.

ODE TO A MERCENARY ARMY

These, in the day when heaven was falling,
  The hour when earth's foundations fled,
Followed their mercenary calling
  And took their wages and are dead.
Their shoulders held the sky suspended;
  They Stood, and earth's foundations stay;
What God abandoned, these defended,
  And saved the sum of things for pay.

                                    A. E. Housman

Chapter 1

"LE PLUS BEAU CORPS DE FRANCE"

THE FRENCH FOREIGN LEGION was created by King Louis-Philippe on March 10, 1831. The stilted official prose of the royal ordinance of that date directed that a legion of foreigners aged between eighteen and forty years be recruited for service in the French army. When a bill to create a foreign legion had been originally presented to the Chamber of Deputies in February, it stipulated that these foreigners could serve only outside of France, a provision that found its way into the law voted on March 9, 1831. Although this proviso had been dropped from the final text of the law signed on the following day, it was nonetheless clear that one of the purposes of the new Legion was to clear France of foreigners. While in theory a number of options for foreign assignment were open which included Guadaloupe and Martinique, the French garrisons in Greece or at Ancona in Italy, in 1831 the most likely destination was Algiers.

Official documents usually give little away. But this one speaks volumes both about the state of France in 1831 and about the relationship between that country and the corps of foreign soldiers it had called into being. The revolution which in July 1830 toppled the Bourbon Restoration rekindled hopes among many European liberals and nationalists that the new regime would take up the crusade to spread liberty and equality throughout Europe, as France had done between 1789 and 1815. Many of these men flocked to France, encouraged by the unilateral renunciation by France of the extradition treaties with other European governments signed in the shadow of the reactionary Congress of Vienna of 1815. This hope also set off a series of minor detonations throughout Europe—in Italy, the German States, Poland and in what came to be Belgium. Spain already seemed to exist in a permanent state of civil war. However, with the exception of the independence movement in Belgium, none of these revolutions enjoyed the success of Paris's *Trois Glorieuses,* as the three "glorious" days of the July uprising had come to be called. After an initial period of surprise, the princes of Europe almost everywhere had restored the reign of order.

Defeated, many of the unsuccessful revolutionaries fled toward France, which, until deposed by Russia's October Revolution of 1917, served as the homeland of the Revolution. They were joined by other foreign immigrants who came into France for personal or economic reasons and who, without resources, became vagabonds, delinquents or even contributed to the considerable political turmoil of the period. Many of the soldiers from the Swiss regiments disbanded in 1830 had also failed to return home. For Louis-Philippe, France's new constitutional monarch, this invasion was unwelcome. Enough homegrown revolutionaries existed in Paris, Lyon and other French cities who wanted to lead the revolution of 1830 toward what they believed should be its natural conclusion—a republic. In the opinion of the Citizen King, they needed no reinforcements.

The idea of employing the French army to absorb, and therefore tame, these revolutionaries had come about in the previous year. In August 1830, a retired cavalry captain named Gauthier suggested in a letter to the war minister, General Etienne Gérard, that agitation would continue in Paris until those who had participated in the July Revolution had been rewarded with military commissions. The idea was taken up by the government, which eventually reserved two sublieutenancies and four sergeant slots in each regiment for men who had distinguished, or claimed to have distinguished, themselves on the July barricades.[1] What proved a partial solution to the problem of local revolutionairies might also be applied to that of the influx of foreigners into France.

The Legion, and many of her historians, like to see the 1831 ordinance as the continuation of France's long reliance on foreign troops. But it is equally possible that without the circumstances of the moment, the tradition of a foreign corps might have been as much a casualty of the July Revolution as was the Restoration. However, when Louis-Philippe turned his attentions to those who swarmed into France quite literally from all directions (many of the Poles who came in 1832 arrived by boat), he discovered that the proposed remedy of incorporating foreigners into the army had hit a snag—it was illegal, and with good reason.

The 1830 revolution had been an expression of French nationalism as well as a demand for liberal reform. Frenchmen who had been raised to the very summit of glory by Napoleon discovered their national prestige much diminished under the restored Bourbons. Waterloo had brought the impossibly corpulent Louis XVIII to the throne, who was succeeded in 1824 by his brother, Charles X. They cut a sorry figure in France. The dynamism that had helped Henri IV and Louis XIV to transform France into a modern and powerful state in the sixteenth and seventeenth centuries had been bred out of these later Bourbons. Reactionary, still brooding about the fate of their brother Louis XVI and his wife, Marie-Antoinette, at the hands of the Revolution of 1789, they were, in the eyes of many of their countrymen, kings who owed their throne to foreign bayonets and who, in return, appeared to bend those energies left them toward keeping France a second-class power to serve the interests of Metternich, the Austrian chancellor and grey eminence of Restoration Europe, and the English.

As was traditional with regimes whose power was not based upon the consent of the governed, the Restoration relied in part on pampered guards regiments and foreign mercenaries to enforce their authority—in this case six regiments of Swiss and the *régiment de Hohenlohe*, into which foreigners of all nationalities were recruited. The Swiss Guards in particular had become hated symbols of royal authority. As opposition to the Bourbons grew after 1827, fights between the Swiss and Parisian workers were reported in July 1827 and June 1828. In October 1829, police reported that groups of Swiss Guards from Paris's Babylone barracks frequently mistreated civilians there. Nor were the Swiss popular in the army. In the first place, they earned double and in some ranks even triple the pay of their counterparts in French regiments. And quite apart from manning the hardship garrisons of Paris, Versailles, Saint-Cloud and Fontainebleau, Swiss officers occupied one rank above the equivalent command position in a line regiment, positions often acquired, it was openly charged, through court intrigue rather than ability.

Not surprisingly, resentment against the Swiss ran high in the army, as when, in November 1828, a full-scale regimental fight broke out between the Swiss and the 2nd Grenadiers at Versailles. This resentment was matched in the population and found full expression in the 1830 Revolution, when the fury of the crowds was especially directed at the Swiss. By Friday, July 30, the fourth *glorieuse*, with the insurgents already in control of Paris, the Swiss were deserting in large numbers, and their colonels began to solicit safe-conduct passes out of the country for their troops from the Provisional Government, no doubt acutely conscious of the massacre of Swiss soldiers following their attempt to defend Louis XVI against a Paris mob on August 10, 1792.[2]

The Revolution of 1830 was taken as an excuse for a general military housecleaning. All guards regiments were abolished, a step seen by many soldiers as one of the greatest accomplishments of the July Revolution, for it ended the most flagrant examples of favoritism and returned the French army to the egalitarian principles of 1789.[3] Foreigners were also shown the door: Article 13 of the Charter, which served the July Monarchy as a constitution, read, "No foreign troop can be admitted into the service of the State, except under a [special] law." On August 14, 1830, the Swiss regiments were disbanded, a process that was complete by the end of September. With the Treaty of Lucerne of April 24, 1831, France renounced her *capitulations* with the Swiss Republic.

But if the Swiss were roundly disliked, the attitude toward that other regiment of foreigners, the Hohenlohe, was less well-defined. Unlike the Swiss, the Hohenlohe was a curious artifact rather than the hated symbol of a fallen regime. Created on September 6, 1815, under the title of *Légion royale étrangère,* the unit's original purpose had been to enlist those soldiers in Napoleon's *régiments étrangers* who still wished to serve France. The regiment's patron and honorary colonel was a naturalized Frenchman, the Prince of Hohenlohe-Waldenburg-Bartenstein, whose name was assigned to the regiment in February 1821. Created Marshal of France and Peer of the Realm in 1827, Hohenlohe died in 1829. However, his regiment was in no way the object of favoritism as were the Swiss. After occupying a series of dreary provincial garrisons throughout the Restoration, in July 1830 the regiment found itself in Marseille, ironically, perhaps, in occupation of Fort Saint-Jean at the entrance to the old harbor, one of the forts that in later years would become the staging point and the first experience of Legion life for so many men bound for Sidi-bel-Abbès. The presence of a regiment of foreign mercenaries seems to have passed virtually unnoticed in a town that had become one of the major depots for the expeditionary force sent to attack Algiers in May 1830, except perhaps for the public concerts of the regimental band that had received rave reviews from the opposition newspaper, *Le Sémaphore.*

Like all provincial towns, Marseille was forced to await events in Paris rather than participate in the movement that would settle the political fate of France. In the days before the telegraph, news traveled slowly. That of the July Revolution reached Marseille only on August 2, by which time Charles X was on his way into exile. There were rumors that the Hohenlohe commander, Colonel Pozzo di Borgo, attempted to raise his regiment against the orders on August 4 to replace the white flag of the Bourbons with the tricolor of the Revolution. But if true, the revolt came to nothing. Hohenlohe was fêted by the newly formed Marseille National Guard, and on August 22 the new division commander, Lieutenant General Delort, declared that by their conduct the soldiers of Hohenlohe had earned the right to be "naturalized Frenchmen" and promised to replace the "H" on their shakos with a number. However, this local enthusiasm for the Hohenlohe was not shared by the new government, which seemed undecided, even confused, about its fate. On December 12, it ordered the Hohenlohe to prepare to embark for "Castle Morea," near Patras, where a French garrison was supporting Greeks fighting for independence against Turkey. Then on January 5, 1831, in a rapid about-face, it ordered the regiment disbanded. Those soldiers who wished to continue in the French army—presumably those eligible for French nationality—were incorporated into the 21st Light Infantry Regiment.[4]

Therefore, it would appear that the tradition of foreign troops in the service of France had been broken, both by law and in the spirit of Frenchmen, by the Revolution of 1830. When a new recruitment bill was passed on March 21, 1832, Article 2 declared that "no one will be admitted to serve in the French forces if he is not French," an obvious indication that the existence of the Legion was ignored by the lawmakers even a year after its creation. However, there is a second and perhaps even more venerated tradition in France at least since 1789—that of offering asylum to foreign refugees, especially to those escaping political repression. And it is to this tradition, rather than to that of hiring foreign mercenaries, that the *Légion étrangère* appears to owe its existence. The Foreign Legion was created in response to a short-term refugee crisis, a crisis that was contributing to the political turmoil in France and costing the French government a considerable amount of money in subsidies to foreign refugees.[5] While it is true that the mercenary tradition, which was alive and well in Prussia, Naples and the Papal states, as well as being part of France's very recent history, offered an obvious solution to this crisis, the Foreign Legion was not conceived as a corps that would "continue the traditions" of the Swiss and the Hohenlohe regiment.

On February 26, 1831, the War Minister ordered a depot established in Langres in eastern France to receive "refugees and foreign deserters." But when "foreign workers employed in France and non-naturalized soldiers from the *régiment de Hohenlohe*" requested admittance, they were turned away. "I do not think that the creation of this depot has as its goal recruitment of this nature," wrote the general commanding the 18th Military Division.[6] The evidence that, in the view of the government, the Legion was only a temporary expedient, a corps raised to funnel undesirable foreigners from the frontiers to Africa, is almost overwhelming. In 1834, a year before the Legion was handed over lock, stock and barrel to Spain, General Voirol, commander-in-chief in Algiers, wrote to war minister Marshal Nicolas Soult to suggest that if enlistment in the Legion were raised from three to five years, the unit's military performance might improve. However, Soult replied that the military efficiency of the Legion was of little interest to him: "As the Foreign Legion was formed with the only purpose of creating an outlet and giving a destination to foreigners who flood into France and who could cause trouble, we have no need to consider your suggestion," he wrote on February 14. "The government has no desire to look for recruits for this Legion. This corps is simply an asylum for misfortune."[7]

To be sure, the precedent of foreigners in the service of France made the establishment of a foreign regiment in 1831 an unextraordinary, if an unfashionable, event in an era that was moving toward national armies. The Legion was the illegitimate child of the July Revolution, an embarrassment, at once acknowledged and shunned, whose meager patrimony was to be the right to die for France in the wastes of her empire. Its very name suggested all that was unfamiliar, unknown and distrusted, the very antithesis of the citizen, the compatriot, the comprehensible. Throughout the first decades of its existence, the Legion was to be largely friendless, the few men who would speak up for it like social workers pleading the case for the homeless and the needy, and with about as much success. France regarded it as a dumping ground for undesirables, a repository for the destitute, an attitude reinforced by the Legion's geographic isolation from France. As a consequence, the high command was seldom to understand the Legion, seldom entirely to trust it. The very nature of its primary purpose as a quasi-social service, and almost by default as a military organization, meant that too often they would regard it as something created to be sacrificed, perhaps even squandered, rather than a military instrument to be nurtured, honed and led.

While the older Legion histories give the impression that the organization of the corps was a fairly smooth process, the archives tell a different story. By 1831, foreigners were arriving in droves. The commander of the 5th Military Division reported on March 5, 1831, that "The number of foreign deserters arriving in Strasbourg increases with each day and might become considerable."[8] Those arriving at Langres, most "in a complete state of destitution," had quickly swamped the capacity of the 385-man barracks, so toward the end of March the government ordered the depot shifted to Bar-le-Duc, a town that straddles the Ornain River about 150 miles east of Paris, over the "lively" protests of the prefect, the chief administrative officer of the *département*.[9] Depots were also established in Auxerre in Burgundy to accommodate Italians, and at Agen in the southwest for Spanish refugees.

On paper, at least, this unsolicited recruitment drive had paid great dividends: by July, Bar-le-Duc served as the garrison for 1,164 "legionnaires."[10] Alas, all was not well with the new corps. As any unit knows, and as a new unit discovers to its peril, although recruits are often easy enough to come by, the art of transforming them into soldiers resides in its cadres. However, experienced officers and noncommissioned officers (NCOs) were in fairly short supply in 1831. The July Days of 1830 had set off an unbelievable turmoil in the army. Some officers had resigned out of loyalty to the Bourbons, part of the "internal emigration" that witnessed the self-exile of a number of aristocrats to their provincial estates. Others had been forced into retirement against their will by jealous colleagues and subordinates eager for advancement. Delegations of NCOs formed in many regiments to present inspecting generals with lists of "reactionary" and "Carlist" (a name given to followers of the deposed Charles X) officers whose removal they demanded. Indeed, so common had these political denunciations become that popular humor suggested, "A Carlist is someone who has a job that someone else wants." The number of officers lost to the army temporarily or forever in this way is not known, but forty-four of sixty-four infantry regiments and five of twelve dragoon regiments saw their colonels sent into retirement.

Replacing them was another matter. In many cases, NCOs were commissioned as second lieutenants following the Revolutionary practice of "careers open to talent," which merely served to encourage further denunciations of superiors. But the government also turned to the *demi-soldes*—ex-Napoleonic officers placed on "half-pay" (hence the name) by the Bourbons in 1815—to solve their command crisis. Eight hundred and thirteen infantry officers and 455 cavalry officers were called out of retirement.[11] It is likely that this government action was motivated in great part by a desire to curry favor with a group that was considered notoriously Bonapartist during the Bourbon Restoration.[12] If so, it backfired both militarily and politically. Of course, at least one of these *demi-soldes*, Thomas Bugeaud, would stake out a brilliant, if bloody, career in the army. But most proved to be an embarrassment: Poured into uniforms that had not seen the light of day since Waterloo, their attempts to shout half-remembered or archaic commands produced chaos on the parade ground, a potentially fatal confusion in an era when close-order drill *was* tactics. Furthermore, their enthusiasm for the July Revolution often got the better of their common sense, and in the view of future Legion colonel and Marshal of France Certain Canrobert, they too often proved to be poor disciplinarians.[13] Lastly, the return of these Imperial veterans with a crushing advantage in seniority actually produced mutinies among men who saw the possibilities of promotion within their lifetime disappear over the horizon.[14]

Therefore, it is within this context of political and military turmoil that the Legion's novice attempts to organize must be understood. The desperate shortage of officers and the rather unattractive prospect of serving in a regiment of refugees made officers, especially good officers, hard to come by. While French officers appear to have regarded the nomination of foreign officers to staff positions in the Legion as an affront, nomination to command positions in the Legion was regarded by French officers as a punishment, especially as by oversight or design their names had been removed from the seniority list.[15] It was a complaint that was to continue in the Legion's early years, and one registered by the inspecting general of the 6th Battalion at Bône in Algeria in 1833: "Today as officers are sent into the Foreign Legion as a punishment, they serve reluctantly, are humiliated to be there and look for any way to return to France. Several have very bad records and those good officers are upset to have comrades of this ilk."[16]

Those who did land in the Legion too often comprised a catchbag of *demi-soldes,* foreigners or men who lacked the ability or the connections to find better employment. The Legion's first commander, the Swiss Baron Christophe Antoine Jacques Stoffel, complained in June 1831 that "Among the 26 officers who are here, only eight are competent at their job. The others have been retired from the service for a long time, are foreigners or from the cavalry. It is of the utmost urgency that we be sent good line

officers who can speak German."[17] One of these officers, Second Lieutenant Mathieu Galloni d'Istria, earned the unenviable distinction in an August inspection report as "the worst officer in the army."[18] Stoffel also
complained in that same month that his chief administrative officer "seems
to have a talent to disorganize everything."[19] The government began combing the country to find foreign officers willing to take posts in the Legion.
Although a large number of refugee Spanish officers lived in France, generals and prefects who interviewed them reported that they would fight
"only to defend the liberty of their country."[20] Only six Spaniards took up
the offer to serve in the Legion as officers, all of whom had resigned by
1834. In the end, 107 foreigners, mostly Swiss, German and Polish, would
serve as officers in the Legion by 1835.[21]

In such a heterogeneous command in such turbulent times, conflicts
were almost inevitable. Those that struck the infant Legion were perhaps
unexceptional, but they certainly helped to get the regiment off to an
interesting start. Stoffel himself was part of many of his unit's problems. In
August, the inspecting general suggested diplomatically that the Swiss was
perhaps not the right man for such a command: "This colonel seemed to
me a man of integrity, loyal, gifted with too much kindness, zealously
active and capable," he reported on August 22. "But he lacks military
practice, above all command experience as he has only served as a staff
officer. He knows neither the regulations nor the ordinances. . . . But, I
repeat, he is an estimable man who works and is interested, and who soon
will be competent. As he becomes better known, he is loved, appreciated
and given credit . . ."[22]

Stoffel's difficulties were not entirely of his own manufacture. His two
battalion commanders, Majors Clavet Gaubert and Salomon de Musis,
nurtured their own ambitions and "were not pleased when he arrived,"
according to the inspecting general. "It is certain that he was badly received
by them and that on the day of his arrival these two officers said publicly
before the troops that M. Stoffel was ignorant, inept, and not worthy to
command them." With any luck, the soldiers did not understand these
denunciations. However, if these fledgling legionnaires could not trust their
ears, they could believe their eyes, especially when the colonel passed in
review at the head of one of his battalions with "a woman disguised as a
man" marching at his side. "Obliged, therefore, to appeal to the honesty
and the *délicatesse* of this senior officer, he confessed that it was indeed a
woman," the inspecting general continued. "I gave him a formal order to
get rid of her immediately, and he assured me on his honor that he would
do so. I took measures to see if my orders would be carried out."[23]

However, the true strength of a unit resides with its NCOs. Alas, those
of the Legion were not bad, they were simply nonexistent. Although an
appeal went out to French ex-NCOs to come out of retirement and join the
Legion, very few if any appear to have done so.[24] Therefore, NCOs were
selected from among the number of German university students who were

to be found among the refugees at Langres because of "their knowledge and their social position."[25] However, Clavet Gaubert complained in May that "The NCOs and the corporals whom we have provisionally chosen are that in name only. They do not wear, nor can they wear, distinctive marks of rank. They have no confidence in themselves. They are without authority and cannot act against their subordinates, some of whom cannot forget that they were NCOs in the foreign regiments from which they have come."[26]

Part of the problem may have been caused by the social divide that existed between the German students, some of whom had been named as corporals, and the rest. "Social position" may have been a positive disadvantage when dealing with the sort of characters who crowded into the Legion depots, who were already demonstrating egalitarian, not to say proletarian, tendencies that would set the tone in barracks. Major Clavet Gaubert wrote the war minister on July 11, 1831, that the German students exhibited "exaggerated pretensions. . . . But it became impossible for me to accustom them to live in common with the deserters most of whom were given to stealing and debauchery." So he formed the university students into two separate companies. However, later, "when we proceeded to the election of NCOs, several refused the promotion which they merited so as not to leave their comrades." Their real motivation soon became clear: they hoped to be designated as the two elite companies of grenadiers and skirmishers contained in each line battalion, but which were only permitted in the Legion from April 1832. "Once we even saw grenades and hunting horns on the shakos of several of them, which we obliged them to take off immediately," Clavet Gaubert assured the war minister.[27]

If the German students were groping for an *esprit de corps,* many of the new recruits appeared to offer poor material from which to fashion a regiment. Clavet Gaubert complained in May that the obvious problems of attempting to control nine hundred men with twelve officers and a smattering of NCOs were complicated by the selection of Bar-le-Duc as the site for the regimental depot. Although Bar-le-Duc could claim to be the birthplace of Napoleonic marshal Oudinot, in 1831 it was a modest little town with much to be modest about. Like many of the towns of eastern France that depended on textiles, Bar-le-Duc was in the grip of a recession. The peasants who drifted to town to escape rural poverty exacerbated the unemployment problem, creating groups of idle and disaffected men. It was for this reason that the prefect of the Meuse protested so vehemently against the addition of dispossessed and perhaps politicized foreigners to this already volatile situation.

Bar-le-Duc may have been chosen over a larger garrison town like Metz or Strasbourg because it was thought to be a quiet backwater where these men would be kept well out of harm's way until they could be shipped out of the country. But it had one enormous disadvantage—barracks space was woefully inadequate. Therefore, the army was forced to billet the soldiers in private homes, which made them almost impossible to control: "In fact, the dispersion of the men in the houses of the inhabitants and in a town without gates or walls means that there is no way to establish a guard or patrols," Clavet Gaubert complained. Nor had the government furnished them with the accoutrements of military life: "Neither arms, nor equipment, nor uniforms to maintain, from which results idleness which favors the natural tendency of the Germans for drink."[28] Stoffel agreed. The army had not created a regiment, but merely a holding pen for foreign undesirables. Give them a flag, a band, create elite companies of grenadiers and skirmishers, make them "proud to wear the uniform"—then, Stoffel insisted, the Legion could become *"le plus beau corps de France."*[29] All of these requests were met in 1832.

In fact, the poor organization of the Legion was a major impediment to the creation of anything resembling a harmonious regiment. On the contrary, it contributed substantially to a cycle of indiscipline and insubordination that was contained only with difficulty. The basic problems began with poor and perhaps even dishonest accounting methods. In the nineteenth century, individual units had far more control over their own accounts than do modern armies. This was an outgrowth of the pre-1789 system of the "regimental chest," from which all troop needs were met. To the regimental and company sergeant-majors fell the responsibility for keeping check on the *masse individuelle* or basic allocation of money given to each soldier for his uniform, equipment, soap, polish and food.

Ensconced amidst his numerous ledgers in a small, poorly lighted room, the sergeant-major tried to balance his books, stopping the pay of men in prison or the hospital or charging torn or lost equipment against accounts. Once his calculations were made, the money was counted out to the lieutenants or corporals, men responsible for purchasing the food for their sections and giving the unspent money to the soldiers. Needless to say, the possibilities for corruption in all this were immense, as were the possibilities for misunderstanding. In August, Stoffel complained that he had been obliged to give over the command of companies to second lieutenants who "spent the pay of their men. Then the sergeant-majors and sergeants, most of whom do not understand the French language, and nothing at all of accounting, contributed a great deal to the confusion because they did not keep an exact register of the equipment which they distributed."[30]

Quite naturally, irregular or even nonexistent pay could hardly have improved the temper of the troops, many of whom were frequenting local cafés and selling their food or shoes and underclothes to buy drink. The command reacted by holding back their pay to replace the equipment or by sending them to prison for indefinite periods. The prefect complained that the local jail contained up to fifty-six legionnaires per cell, many of whom had simply been forgotten by the sergeant-majors, who neglected to provide money for them to eat, as the jail was not responsible for feeding military prisoners.[31] By mid-May, the "tendency to insubordination and indiscipline" had reached crisis proportions, with rumors of a general revolt circulating in the companies. Clavet Gaubert and Salomon de Musis assembled one hundred National Guards who, during noon roll call, watched over the assembled legionnaires while police arrested several ringleaders and led them off to jail.[32] Also in May, twenty soldiers were arrested to break up a "desertion plot," only for it to be discovered that they had yet to sign their enlistment papers and therefore could not be court-martialed.[33] Stoffel feared that when the army tried to move the legionnaires toward the ports of embarkation and Algeria, they would simply "melt en route."[34] His fears proved exaggerated, and few legionnaires seized the opportunity to escape during the march between Bar-le-Duc and the south coast.[35] The prefect of the Meuse and the mayor of Bar-le-Duc must have breathed a sigh of relief when, on November 25, the Legion depot in their town closed its doors and transferred to Toulon.[36] The transfer of the Legion to Toulon and then to Algiers was a gradual process, however, for the depot of the Spanish battalion at Agen remained open until 1832 because of a lack of Spanish recruits.

In 1831, THEREFORE, the Legion saw for the first time the country that for the next 130 years was to be at once its spiritual home and the crucible that would forge its unique character. From the troopships, Algiers appeared wildly exotic, a fortress town plucked from the Middle Ages, a northernmost outpost of Africa that clasped the rugged Barbary Coast. The tricolor proclaiming French occupation curled and snapped above the round bastion that anchored the crenellated outer wall of the harbor. However, the domes, minarets and whitewashed houses, a chaos of cubes brilliant in the autumn sun, that spread up the hill beyond were defiantly African.

Nor did the city's exoticism diminish upon closer inspection. The Belgian Louis Lamborelle described the city he saw when, in 1841, he disembarked with a contingent of Legion recruits: "There we were in the middle of the Arab town," he wrote. ". . . Moors, Arabs, Jews, bedouins from the plain in their white burnouses . . . some wearing turbans, others a haik tied around their heads by a camel rope. . . . Some walked silently and majestically. Others lay like wild beasts at the foot of a boundary-mark. Still others gravely smoked their pipes in doorways of the houses. Some Moorish women, covered from head to foot by a large white wrap which only let you see the pupil of an eye, were already going to the baths followed by their slaves."[37] The sergeant led the recruits through the city gate of the Bab-Azoun and, shouting "Balek! Balek!" ("Make way! Make way!"), forced his way through the Berber market which crowded outside the gate.

The road to Mustapha, where the Legion had installed its headquarters in a country palace confiscated from the Dey of Algiers, ran for about three miles through a string of suburbs sprinkled over a pleasantly hilly countryside. And as barracks went, it ranked among the best: "The entrance

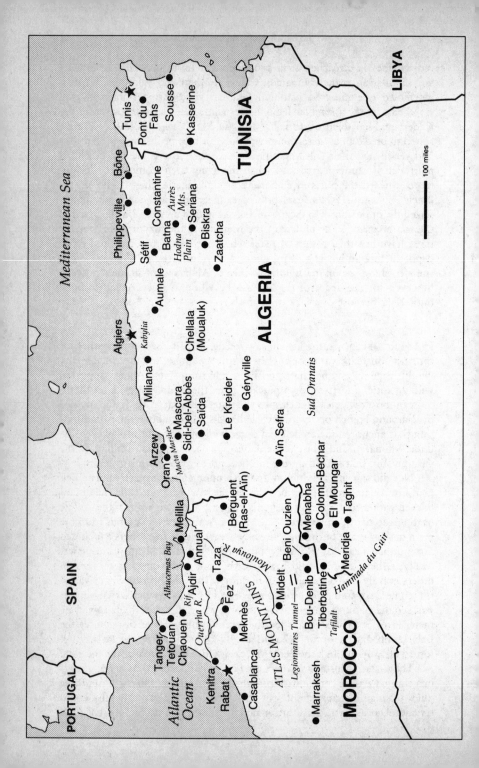

hall was entirely covered in marble, of which the alternate black and white squares formed a gigantic chess board," Lamborelle recorded. "In the middle was an admirably worked fountain, from which a single spray of water fell into an agate basin. All of the buildings equalled this magnificence. The doors especially were remarkably worked, made up of a myriad of small pieces of wood, the rarest and most precious varieties, artistically brought together in a mosaic which was truly the work of a grand master." The rooms had been cleared of furniture so that the legionnaires could sling their hammocks.[38]

However, in 1831 Algiers, which had been seized by the French barely a year earlier, was in a great state of disrepair, as it had been partially destroyed and thoroughly pillaged in the invasion. Already cosmopolitan in an Oriental sort of way, this erstwhile outpost of the Turkish empire now folded a layer of Europeans into a social mélange which already included most examples of *Homo africanus*. And what Europeans! General Pierre Berthezène, who commanded the Occupation Division of around fifteen thousand men in 1831, complained to the war minister of "The vagabonds that Spain, Italy and above all Malta has vomited onto these coasts. I can still add, and there are not just a few of them, those who have come from France and whom you have sent us."[39]

Berthezène did not have the Legion in mind when he wrote those lines, not yet, anyway. This particular invective was directed at the corps of "Parisian Volunteers . . . the scrapings of the streets of Paris . . . given over to dissolution and debauchery," who had already justified in full their nickname of "French Bedouins."[40] These Parisian Volunteers, who were not necessarily Parisians, also traveled under the name of *"Volontaires de la Charte"*—Volunteers of the Charter. The unit was soon dissolved, with some of its members placed into the newly formed *zouaves,* and others contributing to the formation of the 67th Infantry Regiment. Berthezène had early on grasped his fundamental problem—how to reconcile the task of colonization and military efficiency with that of, in the words of his predecessor in Algeria, Marshal Bertrand Clauzel, acting as a repository for "all who live in misery and can upset the tranquility and public repose."[41]

The French soon discovered that most of the units created for service in Algeria in 1831–32 would be the source of considerable discipline problems. The *zouaves,* whose military reputation eventually served as a model for many units in the American War Between the States, had a rocky start, as did the *Chasseurs d'Afrique,* which was created in November 1831. After two 1834 mutinies, several *chasseurs* were executed and six officers cashiered by courts-martial. The Legion was also a source of concern for the authorities. In January 1832, the commanding general in Algeria, René Savary, the duc de Rovigo, ex-minister of police under Napoleon, distributed the Legion in small detachments throughout the town because, in their case, ". . . it would take only one drunken binge to touch off an insurrection."[42] The general inspecting the Legion complained in 1834 that, in their haste to speed undesirable foreigners out of France, mayors and recruiting officers were enlisting men who were "visibly" infirm.[43] However, the need to provide a receptacle for undesirable foreigners remained one of the most potent arguments for keeping the Legion in existence. In April 1836, for instance, General Joseph Bernelle, eager to create a Legion cavalry, wrote to his superiors that by sending him Polish refugees with experience in that arm, the government would at once rid France of "agitated and turbulent elements" while "uniting under strict discipline and for active service men whom it already pays to do nothing."[44]

But were the men of the Legion as bad as all that? In 1831, the Legion had been organized into national battalions of Swiss and Germans, Italians, Spanish and Poles, although these categories were never watertight. For instance, many if not most legionnaires in the 6th Dutch–Belgian Battalion, formed in 1833, were in fact Germans who had deserted over the Belgian frontier and were subsequently guided to France. The Belgians who joined were young, many drawn by "the attraction of the African adventure."[45] The inspector of the 3,168 legionnaires stationed at Mustapha on December 1, 1832, was of the opinion that the 87 French had joined for rapid promotion and the 94 Swiss were "zealous," most being from the Swiss regiments of the Bourbons, while the 571 Italians were aloof and "jealous." The 98 Belgians and Dutch and 19 Danes and Swedes got high marks, as did the 85 Poles, rated as "good and brave soldiers." The 10 Englishmen were "little known." However, the 2,196 Germans did give cause for concern: "many are deserters or political refugees, medical students, lawyers or solicitors, of a disquieting imagination. These must be continually watched." What a far cry from eighteen months earlier, when these students were selected as NCOs and even had pretensions of forming elite companies![46]

So what had happened? The disappointed idealism of the 1830 revolutions, the dashed hopes that the *trois glorieuses* would spark the "liberation" of Europe must have played a part. Men who enlisted out of revolutionary fervor could hardly have been delighted at being exiled to Africa as undesirables. Yet this could not have been the full story, for the Poles, for instance, established an excellent reputation in Algiers and subsequently in Spain, although hatred of Russia was undoubtedly at the top of their political agenda. Of course, it may have been that most of the Poles were soldiers by profession, as the 1831 rebellion against Saint Petersburg was essentially a military one. The Legion was also exhibiting a martial dislike of intellectuals, preferring men with lesser expectations to those whose critical attitudes too easily led to disaffection. Rovigo suggested that the Legion's problems lay essentially with "a hundred or so bad subjects, deserters of various armies, who require close watching" and who should be released from service. But these men were in the Legion precisely because they did require "close watching."[47]

Despite the fact that the Legion was given its first regimental banner by a royal ordinance of November 9, 1831, a regimental spirit was slow to develop among men who did not speak French, many of whom had no previous military experience. The fact that the Legion, which eventually grew to seven battalions, was fragmented and often assigned to the least desirable, most disease-ridden posts or given useless or often futile tasks to perform hardly improved spirits. The real key to performance, Rovigo believed, lay with the officers: "A leader who knows how to handle these men can soon create an *esprit de corps*."[48] For, despite their disparate and troubled backgrounds, or perhaps because of them, most legionnaires responded well to two things: first, officers who took an interest in them, who nurtured their self-respect, a role model who must be a soldier's soldier, and one who was ever sensitive to their very acute sense of justice and human dignity. Second, they needed an institution with which they could identify, one that gave them both the pride and perhaps also the forced discipline that was lacking in their personal lives. Of course, the second largely followed from the first, especially in the French army, which lacked the tradition of a strong corps of NCOs to be found in the British or Imperial German armies.

The problems of recruiting good officers at Bar-le-Duc followed the Legion to Algeria. Not all officers were bad, of course. The abolition of the Royal Guards regiments in the 1830 Revolution created a thirst for elite units in Algeria, which the Foreign Legion helped to satisfy. One of the Legion's early commanders, Colonel Michel Combe, was one of the French army's most ardent supporters of light infantry, whose ideas contributed to the formation of the *Chasseurs à Pied,* a light infantry unit.[49] A number of foreign officers sought entry into the Legion, including, in 1834, 227 Polish refugees in London. But while the Legion undoubtedly counted officers of worth, it is difficult to escape the conclusion that the quality was uneven. General Voirol complained in 1833 that French officers in the Legion frequently resorted to sarcasm or "injurious or disdainful expressions" that pushed the legionnaires to "resistance and insubordination."[50] It is probable that the German students especially were offended by this behavior and showed it. But the poor attitude of too many officers had devastated morale. On January 1, 1834, Voirol reported that regimental pride was nonexistent, drunkenness endemic, the turnover of troops too great, and that no one wanted to reenlist once their three years' service was completed.[51]

Conditions of service must also have played a fundamental role in the Legion's morale problems. The sad truth was that things were not going well for the French in Africa. The troops of the original expeditionary force sent out in the summer of 1830 to administer a lesson to the Dey of Algiers, who had had the temerity to strike the French consul with a fly whisk, were thoroughly demoralized and eager to get home. Low morale was due in part to the political turmoil in France, to the continued fallout of the Revolution, to the often acrimonious debates that split the Assembly over what to do with Algiers now that it had been conquered, and to the utter lack of enthusiasm among the French people for the Algerian enterprise. The military situation in Algiers also contributed to low spirits. The soldiers who originally had been bivouacked outside the town in early 1831 were pulled inside the walls for security. This had transformed Algiers into a besieged town, so Rovigo had hit upon the solution of building a series of blockhouses at strategic approach points to permit a bit of breathing space. However, this too caused problems. At best, duty in these small outposts was tedious, at worst lethal.

To their credit, legionnaires fought honorably in these early engagements. Two companies were engaged on April 7, 1832, in the unit's first action. On May 23, 1832, a detachment of twenty-seven legionnaires and twenty-five *Chasseurs d'Afrique* under Major Salomon de Musis were attacked near the Maison Carrée, which protected the eastern approaches to Algiers. The Major urged his legionnaires to hold on while he disappeared with the cavalry to find help, leaving them under the command of the Swiss Lieutenant Cham. The legionnaires, hardly familiar with African warfare, shot a first volley at the approaching Arabs and then broke for a small wood a short distance away. Having broken ranks, a fatal mistake in conditions when volley firing was the best guarantee of defense, the legionnaires were surrounded, and killed or captured. The prisoners, including Lieutenant Cham, the first Legion officer to die in combat, were massacred one by one as they refused to abjure Christianity and adopt Islam. Only legionnaire Wagner, a Saxon, agreed to accept Islam and was spared. In the camp of his new masters, where he was now employed as a slave, Wagner met five deserters from the Legion who were also subsequently killed when they too attempted to escape to Algiers. Wagner eventually managed to flee and after thirteen days made his way to the Maison Carrée, where his battalion was drawn up to hear his story and learn the hard lessons of desertion. Salomon de Musis was transferred to the penal *infanterie légère d'Afrique* in disgrace, and died in 1836 in an Arab ambush.[52]

But an enemy by far more ubiquitous, persistent and deadly than the Arabs, and one that mercilessly stalked legionnaires, was disease, "fever," a term used in those days of imprecise medical science to cover typhoid, pneumonia and, most commonly, malaria. (The great cholera epidemic that ravaged Algiers and other North African towns in 1834–35 was called by its proper name.) Between 1831 and 1835, 3,200 legionnaires, or about one-quarter of strength, either died or were released as too debilitated to serve because of disease. In July 1833 alone, 1,600 of 2,600 legionnaires of the Algiers garrison were in the hospital, not a tantalizing prospect in an era when Algerian hospitals were little more than primitive sheds for parking the sick. The old saw that legionnaires only entered the hospital to die was no mere boast. It reflected the reality of a situation of near-criminal neglect, of hospitals without beds, where the ill were placed in hammocks or simply deposited on a layer of straw in requisitioned houses, under tents or crude lean-tos opened to the four winds. Sanitary facilities and running water were virtually nonexistent, and the sick had to ask permission to hobble into town, if they were able, to take a bath. However, most scandalous were the constant complaints of hunger among the sick, who had to spend their own money, do odd jobs around the hospital or, in extreme cases, even sell parts of their uniforms, often to the kitchen staff, to feed themselves. Such was the case of legionnaire Pregno who, suffering from dysentery, was forced to spend his savings and then sell his shoes, collar and gaiters to buy the special food prescribed by the doctor. Pregno was fortunate—he was given only two months' prison by a court-martial that recognized his dilemma. But military judges, who were usually prepared to admit drunkenness as an extenuating circumstance in breaches of discipline, with Dickensian logic too often dismissed justified cases of hunger as an insufficient reason for selling pieces of the uniform.[53]

What was Rovigo prepared to do about this? The short answer is, not much. In partial mitigation, it should be pointed out that he was in good company. In the first decade of the Algerian occupation, few senior officers seemed overly concerned about the deplorable conditions in which their soldiers lived. It would take the dynamic General Bugeaud, appointed governor-general in 1840, to jack up a slothful and even dishonest military administration and create service conditions approaching something in which human beings might reasonably be expected to exist. Rovigo placed the blame for the Legion's high mortality rate on the exceptional intemperance of its soldiers. This was certainly a contributory factor. He declared war on the numerous cabarets and wine merchants which, along with dishonest land speculation, seemed to be the only business ventures that had so far flourished in Algiers.[54] However, the real problem, as he knew full well, was that the Legion was set tasks in those areas around Algiers considered the least healthy, and where men left for more than three days almost invariably succumbed to "fever"—guard duty at the Maison Carrée or draining the marshes of the Mitidja, the plain that stretches east and south of Algiers behind the Sahel Hills. For instance, of forty legionnaires sent to the Maison Carrée in 1834, all were hospitalized within a month.[55]

Of course, someone had to do these jobs. But why so often the Legion? Rovigo insisted that the Legion's public works projects in the Mitidja were a spontaneous initiative, and that its two battalion commanders were "impassioned for this idea" of using legionnaires as colonizers.[56] But there was more to it than that. Rovigo, in contrast to his predecessor Berthezène, was a staunch advocate of military colonization as a way to disarm critics in France who clamored for an end to the North African adventure.[57] The Legion's officers must have known how to make themselves, and their unit, agreeable to the commander-in-chief. There is nothing intrinsically suspicious about a military unit volunteering for tasks that help to accomplish the mission. And all units, not just the Legion, were required to participate in public works projects. When in 1835 a battalion of the Legion was excused from road-building duties because of a high number of hospitalizations, they took it as a slight on their ability to perform.[58] Also, it is fair to add that the Legion's officers did attempt to mitigate the noxious effects of these pestilential garrisons somewhat. For instance, when the 6th Battalion, advertised as a low-country unit but in fact overwhelmingly German, melted like spring snows while holding the fort at Bône, it was suggested that they be replaced by the more resilient Spaniards. However, the high command reasoned that the sight of the handful of healthy legionnaires marching out of town would virtually finish off the majority of the suffering, so the rotation was abandoned.[59] Eventually, some of these garrisons would be handed over to native Algerian troops. However, the conclusion that the healthy garrisons were reserved for French troops while the Legion, considered expendable, was assigned the rest is difficult to escape.[60]

The tedium of manual labor, perhaps the obvious distaste of many French officers for their foreign troops, and the reality of service in Africa, which meant that a legionnaire was far more likely to perish miserably from disease than go out gloriously, must have scorched many romantic visions of adventure. In most cases, this simply translated into low morale. Occasionally, however, soldiers preferred to opt out before their contracts reached full term. In North Africa, this was a rather desperate alternative, for it meant desertion to the enemy, always a risky business. Not surprisingly, perhaps, the problem was most troublesome at the insalubrious Maison Carrée, where the El-Ouffia tribe offered sanctuary to any legionnaire who cared to come. When, for instance, on April 6, 1832, Sergeant Muller of the 3rd Battalion and a comrade were promised by two "bedouins" that "we would be well treated and that we would no longer have to work," they tipped off Major Salomon de Musis. On April 7, these "deserters" were shadowed into the mountains by a substantial French force. However, after the women had cut off their buttons and exchanged their uniforms for Arab burnooses, "I started to be afraid," continued Muller. "We mount our horses. Seeing that the detachment was not coming, I take a bedouin by the foot. I throw him to the ground. I turn my mule around. I want to rejoin the encampment. The detachment arrives, fortunately." It certainly did. The Arabs left seventy dead, including two Legion deserters, and the Legion took home ten thousand francs worth of prizes, which were distributed according to rank.[61] The extent of desertion in the Legion before 1835 is unknown. But Rovigo complained in May 1832 of Legion deserters inciting their comrades to join them, "by writing that they will have, like them, a horse, money and women."[62]

As has already been made clear, the Legion's first years in Algeria were more often spent in the hospital or building roads than in combat. This was probably just as well. Until 1840, the French relied principally upon heavy columns launched from their few coastal enclaves into the hinterland to crush the Algerian resistance. This operational approach worked only when the Algerians decided to accept battle, which increasingly they did not. Their preferred method of operation was to allow the French to exhaust themselves in the struggle to push their artillery and supply wagons through the parched, roadless *bled,* as the North African hinterland was called, and then to attack the demoralized columns once they turned for home. This was a marvelous tactical approach, for it denied to the French their superiority in firepower and discipline while exploiting the superior mobility and resilience of the Arabs. The native resistance retained the advantage of surprise and was able to control the level of its casualties.

Nor was it evident that the Legion was any more prepared to confront the Arabs in combat than was the rest of the French army. A tactical approach that emphasized close-order drill and volley firing with relatively short-range muskets was more appropriate to the battlefields of Napoleonic Europe than for the type of war the French encountered in Africa, one of ambush and surprise where individual audacity and initiative counted for more than the ability of men to act as automatons, in choreographed unison like some well-rehearsed stage act. Perhaps General Voirol was paying the Legion a splendid compliment in 1833 when he wrote that it was "better at war than on the exercise field."[63] Already in 1831 Berthezène had complained that the Legion was poorly trained,[64] a fault which was probably remedied only slowly given the lack of enthusiasm of many officers, the constant turnover of men, the large numbers in the hospital and the fact that the Legion spent most of its time building roads.[65]

Yet the role of an army is to fight, and in June 1835, three companies of the 4th Battalion, made up of Poles, and the 5th Battalion, mostly Italians, of the Legion under Lieutenant Colonel Joseph Conrad were part of a column commanded by General Camille Trézel dispatched against Abd el-Kader, who was preaching resistance to tribes in the east near Oran. At five o'clock on the morning of June 26, Trézel organized his column, made up of three-and-one-half battalions of infantry, four squadrons of *Chasseurs d'Afrique,* a small amount of artillery and a large convoy, in a square with the Poles in the lead and two squadrons of cavalry and the Italians on the left flank, and directed it through the "forest" of Muley-Ismael, a large copse of jujube, lentisk and tamarind trees, spread over a series of small hills that rose up between the wadis of the Sig and the Treblat. As the column followed a shallow ravine that wound through the thinly wooded hills, Arab skirmishers began firing on the *avant-garde* and the flanks. The 4th Battalion moved forward in a line to clear the skirmishers from the column's front, only to be attacked by a larger number of Arabs and driven back. With the convoy seriously threatened, the *Chasseurs d'Afrique* charged, only to have its colonel shot down. In the confusion, a bugler blew the retreat, which caused the considerable convoy to do an about-turn. The 5th Battalion counterattacked on the flank with a battalion of the 66th Infantry Regiment, driving away the Arabs who had already reached the wagons. By midday, Trézel's column had fought its way out of the forest onto the plain. Two of the wagons were so damaged that they had to be burned, while those carrying the tents were unloaded to accommodate the wounded, who numbered 180. The bodies of fifty-two dead were left behind.

On the 27th, Trézel camped beside the Sig while he attempted unsuccessfully to negotiate with Abd el-Kader. On the morning of June 28, he moved toward Arzew across the broad plain, the convoy organized in three files, the three companies of the 4th Battalion of the Legion on the right flank and the 5th Battalion on the left. Large numbers of Arab horsemen shadowed the lumbering column but remained at a respectful distance. At two o'clock in the afternoon the column reached a point where the track ran between the Macta marshes on the right and the hills of the Muley-Ismael forest to the left. It was at this narrow defile that Abd el-Kader chose to attack. Arabs, mounted and on foot, threw themselves at the front of the column as others blasted away from the underbrush on the left. The 5th Battalion was ordered to hold the enemy at a respectful distance but to remain close to the convoy. Although the legionnaires of the 5th Battalion carried out the order, it was done at a considerable cost, for they remained in an exposed position while the enemy shot at them from the underbrush. To end this difficult situation, Lieutenant Colonel Conrad, whom General Trézel subsequently described as "having a lot of energy and spirit, but little reflexion,"[66] led his men in an attack that pushed the assailants back into the trees. There, however, the legionnaires ran into a wall of fire that drove them back in confusion, causing elements of the 66th Infantry in the rear guard to panic also. Worse, the retreat uncovered the left flank of the convoy. The confusion was increased by the fact that the Arabs had set fire to some of the vegetation, which swathed the battlefield in smoke. The companies were cut off, scattered, and panicked. Conrad ordered the three companies of the 4th Battalion who were guarding the wounded to rally to him, and eventually collected his legionnaires behind the safety of a small hill.

General Trézel gave Conrad the lion's share of the blame for causing the defeat at Macta. When Trézel rode up from the rear guard, he discovered that Conrad "and a large number of officers wanted to pass this river (Macta) at a ford and march to Mostaganem. It was a mad scheme already underway which I halted only with difficulty," Trézel wrote. Worse, however, Conrad's action had uncovered the column. Without protection, the drivers cut their traces and rode off on their mules, perhaps following the example of much of the cavalry, which, Trézel complained, he only saw again when he reached the sea. Others drove their wagons into the marshes, only to bog down to the axles before they had gone more than a few yards. The Arabs had seldom had it so easy, and it was almost at leisure that they shot down the fleeing drivers, finished off the wounded who in their helplessness screamed for aid, and stole whatever took their fancy.

In the rear guard, the soldiers of the 66th whose commanding officer had been killed panicked and joined other French soldiers who were wading into the marshes. Trézel led a charge of two cavalry squadrons that had not deserted to reach the convoy, or what remained of it. Protected by a few steady infantry units, mainly Legion and penal *Bataillons d'Afrique,* and the artillery, which had maintained its discipline and protected its cannon, Trézel was able to lead his soldiers to Arzew on the Mediterranean, constantly shadowed by Arab horsemen, who, however, elected not to attack. When the exhausted column heaved up at the coast, it counted about 300 wounded, including Legion second lieutenant Achille Bazaine, destined to become French commander-in-chief in the Franco-Prussian War, 62 dead, including two Legion officers abandoned on the field of battle, and 280 missing. The infantry was taken off to Oran by ship while the cavalry, reenforced by friendly tribal levies, returned by land.[67]

French morale was seriously battered by the Macta debacle. The government ordered the Oran garrison to remain on the defensive, and mutual accusations and recriminations broke out among various corps. The Legion was not spared. Macta had brought out rivalries between the Polish and Italian battalions, each of whom accused the other of incompetence, so that the Legion commander, Colonel Bernelle, decided to amalgamate the largely segregated battalions into nationally mixed ones.[68] This step may also have been forced upon him by the fickle nature of national recruitment, which made it impossible to maintain a national battalion at strength. Already, in 1834, complaints had been voiced that the absence of Spanish recruits, caused by the outbreak of the Carlist Wars in that country, might force the amalgamation of the battalions.[69] Of equal significance, at least in the short run, was the fact that the amalgamation order reached the Legion on August 17, 1835,[70] the day it disembarked at Tarragona. The Algerian adventure was suspended so that the Legion could participate in a campaign which would very nearly become its last—Spain.

Chapter 2

"BETWEEN POLITICS, DIPLOMACY AND THE CANNON" — THE LEGION IN SPAIN, 1835-1839

IN 1835, THE LEGION was handed over to Spain. A harsh fate in the best of times, this was especially so in the early decades of the nineteenth century when Spain was what she would again become in 1936—a turbulent power vacuum that tempted the nations of Europe to intervene. The grand era of the Spanish Hapsburgs, when New World bullion fueled a foreign policy whose dynamism made Europe tremble, was well and truly past. Shattered by the Napoleonic invasion of 1808, which touched off a war of unimaginable savagery, stripped of most of her empire by the colonial rebellions of the 1820s, Spain by the 1830s was an exhausted country, and one barely recognizable as European, justifying in full the popular observation that "Africa begins at the Pyrenees." In the absence of a strong government, the regionalism and deep social and political divisions that were never far beneath the surface had begun to reassert themselves. Madrid, once a political and cultural capital of world-class status, was reduced to a quaint backwater, a fortress city from which successive governments attempted to impose order on a mosaic of peoples all demonstrating an innate genius for creating chaos. However, foreign statesmen continued to view Spain's endless and dreary quarrels, her chronic and bloody instability, as a battleground of international ideology and national prestige. The specifically local nature of the disputes within this imperfect nation-state, Spain's traditional preference for anarchy over centrally imposed order and her desire to be left alone by the outside world were subtleties lost on the political generation of the 1830s, as they were a century later. However, in this case, the Legion was to pay the price for this political misperception.

This particular chapter in the ongoing Spanish civil war opened in 1833 when a series of uprisings against the "liberal" government of Isabel II erupted in Castile, Navarre and the Basque provinces in favor of the late King Ferdinand VII's brother, Don Carlos. Smaller Carlist guerrilla bands materialized in Aragon, Catalonia and Valencia. The stakes, both ideological and strategic, were crystal-clear to the governments of Europe. Britain, France and Portugal feared the success of a reactionary, proclerical rebellion in Spain, which would damage their prestige and threaten their interests. In April 1834, the four governments formed the Quadruple Alliance, which was a diplomatic triumph for Isabel II but of little practical value in quelling her domestic disturbances. However, further afield, there were a number of governments that preferred reaction for its own sake. The conservative Italian states of Turin and Naples recognized Don Carlos outright. Austria, Prussia and Russia found the man congenial but for the moment withheld diplomatic recognition.

The war against the Carlists did not go well for the government. The rebellion found the bulk of the Spanish forces preoccupied with disorder in Portugal. The remainder were set to catch the elusive guerrilla bands in Castile and Navarre, which at the time appeared to pose the more immediate threat. However, this dispersion of force allowed the rebellion in the remote, mountainous Basque country of the north to put down firm roots. There the combination of a traditional, largely self-sufficient society with its own language, led by a class of landowners and priests deeply suspicious of the liberal Madrid government, and a leader of genius in General Tomás Zumalacárregui soon made the three Basque provinces and much of western Navarre an inhospitable area for the government.

In July 1834, Don Carlos slipped out of his English exile, traveled in disguise through France and appeared in the rebellious Basque country to take command. By the spring of 1835, Zumalacárregui had defeated every general Isabel had sent against him, raised a force of thirteen thousand men largely through conscription and was virtually inviolate in his mountain fastness. Don Carlos had established a court which, though rustic, bore enough resemblance to the real thing to invite diplomatic recognition—and hard cash—from the well-disposed powers of central and eastern Europe. A catchbag of French legitimists and other conservatives and even a Prussian general appeared to offer their services to the rebellion. Madrid was on the verge of panic, fearing that if the Carlist forces broke south across the Ebro they would touch off a general rebellion that would shake Madrid to its very foundations. In May 1835, Isabel appealed to her allies for something more substantial than moral support.[1]

The reaction in France was at first cool. The king, Louis-Philippe, was just beginning to feel secure on his throne and was not eager to risk it, and European peace, with an untimely intervention in yet another Spanish

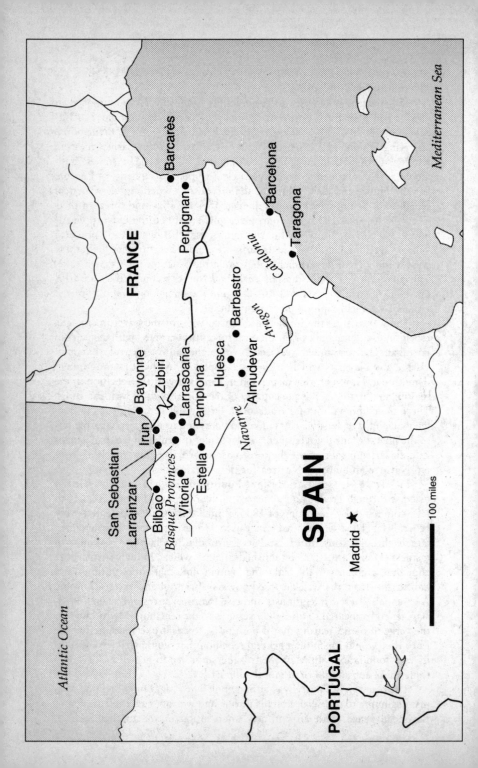

quarrel. The ex-war minister, Marshal Soult, had experienced firsthand the dreadful fighting of the Peninsular War under Napoleon and warned his countrymen against stirring up the Spanish "hornet's nest" once again. Austria, Prussia and Russia also opposed French intervention. However, no one was prepared to confront Adolphe Thiers, the young firebrand journalist whom the 1830 Revolution had catapulted into the political imperium. As minister of the interior, on June 6, 1835, he persuaded his colleagues in the government to dispatch the Foreign Legion to Spain to aid the constitutional government there. Louis-Philippe gave his assent two days later, and on June 28 a convention between the governments of Spain and France ceded the Legion to Madrid. On the following day, by royal ordinance, the Legion ceased to be part of the French army.

Left to his own devices, Thiers would no doubt have done more to aid the Spanish constitutionalists, especially after he became prime minister in February 1836. Thiers saw the Spanish conflict as the vehicle for the "renaissance of French diplomacy," a way in which France could begin to reassert influence on the world stage, which she had failed to do since Waterloo. He also argued that in her delicate internal state, France could not tolerate the establishment of a conservative Carlist monarchy, which would transform Spain into "the Vendée of Europe," a reference to the pro-Bourbon rebellions that plagued western France following the revolutions of 1789 and 1830. However, the clincher was the decision by Britain and her Portuguese ally to raise volunteers for Isabel's beleaguered government. Thiers was loath to see French influence in Madrid eroded to the advantage of London. To force his points home, he threatened to resign unless he got his way. Louis-Philippe decided that Thiers would do less damage inside the government than in opposition and gave in. However, Thiers could not ignore altogether the opinion of Soult, who reminded him in January 1837 that by sending soldiers to Spain, "it is impossible to place French troops in a more equivocal situation."[2]

The nature of this political compromise demonstrates in part how the Legion survived infancy against the odds. By sending the Legion, France could affirm diplomatic support short of a binding commitment. If things turned sour in Spain, Paris would not confront the difficult problem of extracting her forces while at the same time struggling to save face, for, after all, wars are often easier begun than terminated. Once France turned over the Legion, its fate would be in Madrid's hands. For its part, Isabel's government may have preferred French support to come in the form of regular regiments. But this simply was not realistic given the political situation in Paris. And besides, the Legion offered tangible evidence of French interest, with no strings attached. A substantial commitment of French forces most certainly would have required more French interference in the political and military affairs of Spain. But the Legion was a different matter—it was a gift, a disposable item, and so appealing to the politicians and diplomats precisely because it was expendable. Already, in 1834, the

439 Spaniards of the 4th Battalion of the Legion had been sent to Oran, from whence they were shipped to Spain at the request of the Spanish government, an indication that even then the French government had envisaged employing the Legion in the Iberian peninsula.

The news of this little bargain was badly received in the Legion. But was the French government really being unfair? Its attitude was that legionnaires were mercenaries, after all, men hired to do the government's bidding. And besides, what difference should it make to them for whom they fought, so long as they were paid? (The fact that the Spanish seldom were to pay them was not factored into the argument.) There are historians who argue that this transfer of the Legion to Spain was perfectly in keeping with the fairly common practice of "loaning" troops to foreign governments in need of professional military expertise.[3] However, two things must be said: First, the Legion was not loaned, but handed over lock, stock and barrel. In fact, the word "cession" does not appear in the official agreement between the two governments, but was used in a letter of July 2, 1835, by the war minister, Marshal Nicholas Maison. Minutes of a meeting on July 27 between the two governments prior to signing the accords on the following day speak of the "delivery" of the Legion to Spain, as if it were so much merchandise. It was precisely this absence of precision that subsequently would allow both governments to shirk responsibility for the Legion's welfare.

Second, if the legionnaires were mercenaries in the general sense that they were soldiers in the service of a foreign government, it is equally apparent that they did not view themselves simply as guns for hire. For them, the Spanish bargain was a breach of faith. One officer wrote from North Africa that many would have been willing to go to Spain as part of the French army, but not in Spanish service: "All the officers and, in general, all the soldiers are furious," *zouave* Captain Demoyen wrote on July 17, 1835. "The foreign officers say that they came to serve France and not other countries."[4] Paris was informed that "almost all officers refused to follow the corps to Spain" and that "the soldiers of the Legion were pushed to desert, or to join Abd el-Kader, or to rebel so as not to embark."[5] The government at first threatened, and then wisely backed off, sending two officers from the ministry to explain that by going to Spain, the Legion was actually serving the interests of France. All legionnaires of foreign nationality were obliged to depart for Spain. Foreign officers might refuse, but lost their employment. Those French officers who still refused to be convinced were allowed to transfer to other regiments, unless they had joined the Legion straight from civilian life, in which case it was to civilian life that they returned. Those officers who agreed to go to Spain were rewarded with promotions for remaining with the Legion. "These promotions produced the desired effect," the report to the war minister concluded.[6] While these promotions, handed out on July 22, 1835, and made official on November 6, were approved by the French government, Paris subsequently refused to recognize promotions and decorations earned in Spanish service, or to credit these officers with seniority acquired in Spain upon their return to the French army.[7]

However, in the short run, the turmoil over the transfer of the Legion to Spain may have helped solve some of its military problems. As has been seen, inspecting generals in Algeria had given the Legion generally low marks. Under Colonel Bernelle, things had undoubtedly begun to improve. However, Macta had exposed yawning gaps in cohesion and tactical expertise, not just in the Legion, but throughout the *Armée d'Afrique*. The first thing the Spanish controversy did to improve this state of affairs was to allow the departure of a number of officers who, for whatever reason, had no desire to go to Spain. The fact that eighty-five men below the rank of major were promoted would seem to suggest that the number of officers asking for other assignments or simply resigning their commissions was fairly high.[8] The 123 officers who remained probably formed as heterogeneous a crowd as the 5,000 men whom they were to command— Napoleonic veterans, *demi-soldes*, officers of the ex-Royal Guard and Swiss regiments, ex-NCOs and a smattering of officers picked up from the dissolved *Volontaires d'Isabelle*, a collection of soldiers of fortune come to serve the constitutionalist cause. Thirty-eight foreigners were also to be found among the officers,[9] as well as a number of naturalized Frenchmen. And the percentage of foreign officers probably increased after September 1836, when the Legion had obviously been forsaken by the French government and many French officers began to return home. For instance, in December 1838, thirty-four of sixty-three officers remaining in the Legion were foreign; some of them had been promoted through the ranks.[10]

Among these men were certainly officers of quality. Several, including Bernelle, Jean-Louis Baux and Captain Hippolyte Renault, were to finish their careers as generals, and one, Second Lieutenant Achille Bazaine, as a Marshal of France. Several held decorations earned in Algeria, including Lieutenant Colonel Conrad, Italian majors Raphael Poerio and Sebastiano Montallegri, Polish major Thadée Horain, and Italian captain André Ferrary, as well as Bazaine. German sergeant G. von Rosen found the Italians and Germans among the officers a fairly common lot, but thought the aristocratic Poles very distinguished. And while he recorded complaints against individual officers and criticized the tendency of his compatriots to be a trifle brutal, on the whole he classified his superiors as "very good men."[11] The reports on the officers drawn up in 1838 when the Legion was in desperate condition give an unflattering and perhaps not an altogether unbiased assessment of some of them. Nevertheless, of 129 officers listed upon whom there is complete information, 60, or almost half, were rated as good or excellent, and another 49 received mixed reviews, often because they were too old for active service or deficient in administration. Only twenty were rated as frankly bad, charged with things like excessive brutality, drunkenness, lack of courage or shirking responsibility generally, or, in the case of Second Lieutenant Jacques Touflet, "born to be an artist." Nor do these assessments appear to reflect a national bias, for each category is almost equally divided between French and foreign.[12]

The second thing that improved the cohesion and consequently the efficiency of the Legion was Bernelle's decision to abandon the fairly homogeneous national battalions in favor of nationally mixed units. The reason usually given for this decision has been the rivalries and recriminations after Macta, which dangerously divided the Legion along national lines. However, Macta must simply have been the event that finally pushed the high command to undertake a reorganization which was in the interest both of administrative efficiency and of discipline. While German recruitment to the Legion was to remain fairly consistent for over a century, the availability of other nationalities for service was too unsteady to make national battalions the basis of Legion organization. By 1834, the outbreak of the Carlist wars had already begun to dry up the numbers of Spaniards available for service, prompting a call for the amalgamation of the battalions,[13] while Germans far outnumbered lowlanders in the 6th "Belgian-Dutch" Battalion.[14] It was simply more efficient to distribute men according to need rather than have some battalions periodically swollen by political events in Europe's far corners, only to shrink to insignificance after a few years.

But the question of administrative convenience pales in comparison to that of discipline. When, in future years, the Legion was inundated with men of one nationality, it was courting trouble, perhaps serious trouble in times of political tension or military reversals. A concentration of nationality facilitates the growth of a clannish spirit, even of a rival nationalism, which makes it more difficult, if not virtually impossible, to foster a common *esprit de corps*. Common cultural and linguistic bonds might preempt the creation of a regimental personality and a sense of unit solidarity. At its worst, national homogeneity might give rise to a sense of resentment, a feeling of exploitation that could, and on occasion did, bubble over into indiscipline or even mutiny, which officers, confronted by a sullen mass of men whose language, values and sensitivities they imperfectly understood, were poorly equipped to deal with because they commanded Poles or Spaniards or Italians rather than legionnaires. This attitude probably contributed to the Legion's low ratings in the first four years of its existence.

In short, Bernelle realized that, unlike a national force, whether conscript or professional, which depends for cohesion on common bonds of culture and citizenship, a mercenary unit draws its strength from its heterogeneous character, that homogeneity actually threatens it. This rule was not necessarily hard and fast. As will be seen, Bernelle violated his own principle to raise a unit of Polish lancers for use in Spain. But in all likelihood he did this because he needed cavalry quickly and did not have time to train it, preferring to call upon the Poles, who had great experience as cavalrymen. Also, in 1840, the Legion would make up a battalion out of the numerous Carlist refugees who poured into France in 1839–40, and between 1855 and 1859 attempt to recruit a Swiss Legion. This system was resurrected in the first year of World War I. But, after 1835, the Legion preferred to mix its nationalities rather than concentrate them. At certain periods, however, as immediately following the two world wars, its recruitment was so overwhelmingly German that this was effectively impossible.

Of course, heterogeneity is not enough in itself to keep a corps whose only commonality is its very diversity marching in one direction—"divide and rule" may work as a system of imperial administration, but it offers a less satisfactory basis for military performance. The cohesion of this newly ordered corps in Spain seems to have been assured in part by its very foreignness, the fact that it was the "French corps" in the midst of the Spanish army, and therefore felt it had a reputation to uphold—indeed, the *Légion étrangère* is often referred to as the *Légion française, division auxilliaire française* or even the *Légion algérienne* in contemporary accounts.[15] Also, unlike North Africa, where individual battalions and companies were spread piecemeal over the countryside, the Legion for the first time was serving as a coherent unit, with its own artillery and eventually its own cavalry. This contributed to a spirit of self-sufficiency, practically of being a separate army.

The Legion's sense of identity also appears to have been reinforced by an acute perception of serving the constitutionalist cause against the forces of reaction. The temptation to conclude that this was the natural consequence of the wholesale recruitment of political refugees is almost overwhelming. However, the history of the Legion suggests that it managed to retain an apolitical character at least until the 1930s. As an institution, the Legion's success lay in great part in its ability to transform often highly politicized recruits into soldiers prepared to serve any cause. Many legionnaires certainly retained their own beliefs, often on the extremes of the political spectrum, which was precisely why they were in the Legion in the first place. The job of the Legion was to turn these men into professional soldiers, not commiserate with their political misfortunes.

However, evidence suggests that in Spain, the political commitment to the constitutionalist cause served as a unifying factor for the Legion. This came about in part by default—Spanish priests, overwhelmingly favorable to the Carlists, revived fears of the French that dated from the Napoleonic invasions of 1808–13, and advertised the legionnaires as men without religion who were not above eating children. This was to result in a cool, not to say hostile, reception in the north. But more importantly, most officers had remained with the Legion because they had been convinced that by serving Isabel they were serving French interests. "When we consented to come to Spain, it was with the positive intention to support and defend a constitutional government in Spain, in harmony with our own . . . ," Bernelle wrote. His officers agreed that "they were fighting in the name of France and of constitutionalist Europe." This sentiment of serving a political cause had filtered down to the ranks, to the point that Legion sergeant-major Émile Hippolyte Bon even composed a "Song of the French Legion in Spain," which announced to these "noble outlaws, enemies of tyrants" that "Liberty has opened to you other fields/ Where the cannon of a free people peals." Apparently this composition was sung by "the beautiful and harmonious German and Italian voices" upon disembarkation in Spain.[16]

Alas, Spain was also to demonstrate to the Legion, as it was to make clear to those legions of international volunteers who flocked there a century later, that political ideology was an inadequate basis for military cohesion in the confused circumstances of civil war. A political situation that appeared to those north of the Pyrenees to be a clear-cut struggle between constitutionalists and reactionary royalists took on an altogether more murky and sinister aspect as soon as one stepped ashore on the Iberian Peninsula. Disembarking legionnaires at Tarragona were greeted by enthusiastic crowds shouting: " 'Long live liberty! Long live the French!' Sometimes 'Long live the Queen,' but only rarely," Captain Abel Galant noted. "That surprised us." That evening, Bernelle led his officers out of the local theatre after "seditious shouts" were heard in the audience to demonstrate to the agitators "that they could expect nothing from the French troops because our watchword was 'Isabel II and the Constitution.' "[17] However, this demonstration of political factionalism worried Bernelle enough for him to write to Paris for instructions on how to act in a political crisis: "If the government were replaced by despotism or republicanism, I know what I would do as an individual. But as commander of a corps composed mostly of Frenchmen or men who have adopted France as their fatherland, should not the French government give me instructions which would direct me in a difficult situation?"[18] But, as the Legion was to discover to their immense bitterness, the French government was to remain deaf to their calls for guidance, and for help in the precarious situation into which they had been cast.

VITORIA AS THE legionnaires saw it in the first days of 1836 was not an impressive town. Hunkered across the road that paralleled a tributary of the Ebro River as it snaked northeast toward Pamplona and San Sebastian, Vitoria appeared bleached of color, as gray as the leaden sky that hung upon the snowcapped mountains which dominated it to the north and east. But to soldiers covered with mud and soaked to the skin after nine days of marching over impossibly rugged terrain in the dead of winter, even this ragged burg must have appeared a welcome sight, enough of a morale booster to allow legionnaires to pull themselves together for what Abel Galant described as "an almost triumphal entry."[19]

Triumphal or not, to those who cared to look carefully about them, the atmosphere was almost poisonous. The town was largely empty of local men, many of whom were away in the mountains fighting with the insurgents. The women, almost Arab-like in their black dresses, shawls and heads swathed in scarves, collected around the fountains in tight conclaves, casting suspicious glances at the legionnaires, whose reputation as cutthroats and outlaws had preceded them. Later, legionnaires would turn this to psychological advantage before battle, wiggling their fingers like horns on their foreheads to announce to the enraged Carlists opposite that they had been cuckolded.[20]

But the coolness of the local population was not the only factor calculated to put the French in a bad mood. After five months in Spain the Legion counted nine actions to its credit, the most important in Catalonia, where two companies of legionnaires held the village of Senahuga, near Lérida, against a four-day Carlist siege. Upon arrival at Vitoria, the proud but already bedraggled Legion was greeted by General Sir George de Lacy Evans, commander-in-chief of the British Legion, and his brilliantly presented staff. If Legion officers detected a certain indefinable smugness in the demeanor of the British, they were probably not imagining things. Evans in particular had already met the French at Vitoria in 1813, where as a lieutenant he had commanded several cavalry charges that had consummated the rout of Marshal Jean-Baptiste Jourdan's army, capturing numerous prisoners, an artillery piece and a chest of money in a victory that had driven Napoleon's forces back across the Pyrenees. He had subsequently earned the plaudits of his commanders for exceptional bravery at Bayonne, Toulouse and Waterloo. For this, and perhaps also in grateful memory of the Anglo-Spanish alliance against Napoleon, Evans had been given the rank of lieutenant general by Isabel's government, while the Legion's Bernelle was a mere brigadier in Spanish service.[21] And if this were not insult enough, the French officers quickly discovered that their wealthier British counterparts had already snapped up the town's best accommodation, such as it was.[22]

However, Vitoria was the front line in the war against the Carlists, and it was here that the Legion assessed the strategic situation they faced at the opening of the spring campaign season of 1836. The government's strategy of scattering forces to deal with brushfire guerrilla wars everywhere had allowed the Carlists to carve out a de facto kingdom in the three Basque provinces and western Navarre. When, in 1835, Madrid at last decided to attend to this most important center of the rebellion, they were dealt devastating defeats by the brilliant Zumalacárregui, who confidently took them on in open combat. By June 1835, beleaguered government garrisons held tenuously to the larger towns, while the Carlists roamed at will in the countryside.

Then the government got a break—Zumalacárregui, an exceptional commander in the open field, was forced against his better judgment by Don Carlos to besiege Bilbao. It proved a disastrous mistake. Don Carlos argued that the capture of a significant town that he could then use as a capital would boost his cause both at home and abroad. Also, Bilbao was a seaport, which would give him access to arms without having to run the gauntlet of French frontier patrols on the Pyrenees. While these were two good reasons for doing the wrong things, Don Carlos ignored two important factors. First, his movement was an overwhelmingly rural one that had little support in the larger towns and cities, least of all Bilbao. Second, his troops, while excellent guerrilla fighters, lacked the skills and elaborate equipment to carry out a complicated siege operation. Most disastrous of all for Carlist aspirations, while in the trenches Zumalacárregui sustained a very minor leg wound which, thanks to the incompetence of his surgeons, resulted in his death. The siege of Bilbao collapsed in June, and in July, Zumalacárregui's less able successor, General Moreno, lost the Battle of Mendigorría.

Therefore, in the summer of 1835, the momentum of the Carlist insurrection had been contained. But the insurgents still counted considerable strengths. Their army of around thirty thousand men was not well trained by classical military standards, but these tough peasant soldiers showed initiative and were excellent skirmishers. They enjoyed the support of the population, which guaranteed them a virtually inexhaustible supply of manpower, access to the local food supply and an excellent intelligence network, something denied to the government. The remote, mountainous and largely roadless terrain provided a virtually inviolate sanctuary from which to operate.

Yet the Carlists had weaknesses, and they were fairly substantial ones. On the basic military level, they suffered greatly from an almost total lack of artillery, as well as shortages of arms, ammunition and shoes, although this was offset in part by similar deficiencies on the government side. Legion Second Lieutenant Jean-Jacques Azan complained that combats were broken off and retreats ordered "because of a lack of munitions. It's something which happens continually in Spain because of poor administration and the generals' lack of foresight." Azan also noted that his opponents were tactically naive, especially in the sort of positional war they now chose to fight: "If their military genius had equaled their courage," he wrote in December 1836, "I think that the Legion would have had it."[23]

The greatest Carlist weakness was the defensive strategy they now adopted. On the face of it, a defensive strategy might have great appeal in the short term if it could force the government to attack the insurgents on ground favorable to themselves. However, as a long-term strategy, it was a formula for defeat. Zumalacárregui had realized that an aggressive strategy capitalized on the superior mobility of his forces to keep the government off balance with surprise attacks. It also allowed the Carlists to keep the military initiative, giving the impression of progress, which further tarnished the image of the government beyond the rebellious provinces. As Zumalacárregui might have been able to predict, the morale of Carlist soldiers began to erode once they were set defending fixed positions. And although Carlist columns twice broke out south of the Ebro, once marching to the very walls of Madrid itself, without the impression of the backing of a dynamic mass movement, shadowed by government forces who could not crush them but who could keep control around the fringes, local populations were dissuaded from offering active support. The Carlists were forced back, their tails between their legs, into their northern bastion. Denied any prospect of ultimate success, the Carlists fell to quarreling among themselves, and by 1840 the movement had collapsed from its own internal divisions.[24]

In other words, time was on the government's side. The death of Zumalacárregui, the Carlist defeat of July 1835 at Mendigorría and their failure to spread the rebellion into Catalonia had stretched them to the limit. All the government need now do was follow a strategy of patient containment, taking care not to forfeit a victory that could come to them only in the fullness of time. Deprived of hope, the Carlist cause would grow increasingly anemic, weaken and die. Nor was the government in a position to pursue a more aggressive military strategy. Simmering discontentment in other parts of Spain, as well as the unstable political situation in Portugal, forced Madrid to spread its troops thinly throughout the country. The forces it could spare for the Basque provinces were not substantially greater than those commanded by the Carlists, a vital consideration, as substantial numerical superiority would be required to crack Carlist control of the highlands. And many of these government forces would be tied down defending towns, and therefore unavailable for offensive operations.

Nor was the quality of Isabel's army above suspicion. Most Spanish officers were more expert at *pronunciamentos* than in leading frontal assaults on enemy positions, and factionalism within the army was to produce several important mutinies. French Major Renaud de Vilback reported to his superiors in France that "The (Spanish) army has neither magazines, nor money, nor resources of any sort, and even when it would have defeated, destroyed the Carlists, it will find itself even weaker when confronted by a new enemy of the Queen which is already at work."[25] Desertion to the Carlists was commonplace, especially among the Queen's elite Royal Guards, which had supplied the insurgents with much-needed military skills. Those who remained were demoralized and terrified by the horrible retribution handed out by the ferocious Basques to wounded and captured government soldiers. They, in turn, took out their fears and frustrations upon the population, which drove even more people into the Carlist camp.[26]

It was precisely this situation that the intervention of the Quadruple Alliance was meant to repair. Alas for Isabel, support from her allies proved a disappointment. The British Legion had been raised in indecent haste and thrown untrained into Spain, a collection of "six or eight thousand ragamuffins" according to one British observer, whose lack of discipline and military skill would not weigh heavily in the military balance. Because the arch-Tory Duke of Wellington opposed the Whig policy of intervention, officers of the regular British army boycotted Evans, forcing him to recruit four hundred officers from among a rabble of mercenaries and men who had seen no service whatsoever. Nor did Evans, a man whose bravery as a subaltern was beyond question, demonstrate obvious qualities of leadership. Thin, with a full head of unruly hair, deep-set eyes and a furrowed face, he was celebrated for his volcanic temper. He had left the army after Waterloo and owed his command to his radical political views and his reputation as an outspoken opponent of Wellington's military policies, rather than to any demonstrated talent for command. Spanish Prime Minister Mendizabal called Evans "a man of mighty intentions and small performance," although it probably would have taken a magician rather than a general to transmogrify the British Legion into something resembling a military force, even without the added difficulties of Spanish incompetence and ill will.

But while Evans's biographer gives him fairly high marks for transforming the British Legion into an effective fighting force, this was not achieved overnight. On the contrary, the thrashing handed to Evans's forces at Oriamendi just south of San Sebastian, where the panic of the 1st Battalion of the British Legion sparked off an ignominious rout, did much to revive flagging Carlist fortunes in the early months of 1837. The British Legion redeemed its military reputation somewhat in May 1837 by the capture of Irun on the French frontier. But while Evans insisted that he had "struck a mortal blow to the Carlist cause," the fact remained that the town was lightly defended, making it rather easy pickings for Evans's ten thousand men supported by Royal Marines and British naval artillery. The victory was also tarnished by the fact that, once through the breech, the British Legion threw themselves into an orgy of rape and pillage that was contained only with difficulty. When Evans attempted to turn his victory to political advantage in the parliamentary elections of 1837, his Tory opponents nicknamed him "Count I-run."[27] The British Legion never played anything more than a marginal role in the Carlist War, and though allowed to waste away through disease, desertion and neglect, given its composition it is unlikely that it could ever have had a decisive impact on the campaign.

This left the French Foreign Legion. It had at least two advantages over its British counterpart. First, it was a force in being, rather than one recruited in haste on the streets of London. Second, it had effective leadership, officers who, despite their diverse origins, were experienced commanders, and none more so than the commander, Joseph Bernelle. Like Evans, Bernelle was a veteran of the Napoleonic Wars. However, unlike his highly politicized British counterpart, Bernelle was a soldier and no more. Enlisting in 1801 at the age of sixteen and leaving the army only briefly during the Bourbon Restoration, the fifty-year-old colonel already counted thirty-two years of service by 1835, when the Legion disembarked in Spain.

He had served with Napoleon's armies in Italy, Illyria, Dalmatia, Germany and France, remained in service under the Restoration and, in 1833, had become colonel of the Legion. Bernelle was perhaps the ideal Legion commander, especially in this troubled early period of its history. A well-proportioned man with dark, slightly receding hair, Bernelle's arched eyebrows, mustache and goatee and well-drawn jaw suggested a character of great resolution. This was no illusion. He was a strict disciplinarian, too strict for the liking of many legionnaires who preferred his less austere, German-speaking subordinate, Lieutenant Colonel Joseph Conrad. In fact, one of Bernelle's first acts upon arriving in Spain was to introduce caning into the disciplinary code under the pretext that it was permitted in the Spanish army. Nor did he hesitate to order up firing squads for offenses which, in peacetime, were considered relatively minor ones. Officers usually escaped with sentences of fortress arrest, but enough of them were punished to stir up resentment over Bernelle's Bligh-like tendencies.[28]

Despite his lack of popularity, the Legion greatly benefited from Bernelle's leadership. His firm hand and his policy of nationally mixed battalions went a long way toward settling down a corps that had experienced serious discipline problems in North Africa. He also saw immediately that the Legion's effectiveness would be increased, and its dependence upon the elusive Spanish somewhat lessened, by the addition of an under-strength regiment of Polish lancers (which he persuaded the Spanish minister in Paris to pay for), a battery of artillery and an ambulance section, thereby making it a relatively complete division.[29] But Bernelle had his faults, ones that deepened the gulf which, from the beginning, divided him from his command. In the first place, he loved ostentation, brilliant uniforms and an entourage of chattering staff officers, some of whom were members of his close family. And while some of this may have been necessary to maintain the dignity of his position in Spanish eyes, to the rough-hewn men of the Legion, such displays made Bernelle appear arrogant and artificial. In fact, it was Bernelle's tendency to carry the family atmosphere of the Legion too far that really annoyed his officers and caused comment among the men. The inclusion of cousins and nephews on his staff was one thing. But when he allowed his wife to follow him on campaign, that was going too far. The rather dour Madame Tharsile Bernelle was frequently to be seen sitting on horseback, the scarf of an aide-de-camp around her waist, imperiously giving orders to everyone in sight. The legionnaires called her Isabel III, and worse, and saw her as her husband's *éminence grise,* the source of every arbitrary promotion or punishment.[30]

But for the moment, the Legion's problems remained beneath the surface, too unimportant to influence performance in the early months of 1836. The Legion was undoubtedly the most disciplined and efficient force on either side of this sad war. However, it was too small to sway the balance in what had become a military stalemate. The government's approach was generally sound, maintaining a line of small garrisons running from north of Pamplona to Vitoria designed to prevent a Carlist breakout. However, from time to time, strategic requirements or government pressure on its generals for a more aggressive military posture caused the constitutionalist forces to come out of their lines, usually without result. Such was the case in January 1836 when General Cordova launched an offensive into the Arlaban Mountains, which controlled communications between Vitoria and Bilbao on the northern coast. The Legion participated in this expedition, which saw the government troops advance up the valley only to withdraw when cold, fatigue and hunger forced them on January 18, 1836, to relinquish the heights they had conquered on the previous two days. Carlist pressure in Navarre combined with Bernelle's desire to unite his scattered battalions caused the Legion to be transferred to Pamplona in February.

PAMPLONA IS THE first city which, in calmer times, a traveler through the western Pyrenees encounters in Spain. The road from southern France climbs gradually through a well-watered land of oak and spruce forests and meadows that in spring and summer are thick with flowers or haystacks in rows as regimented as the slopes allow. As the craggy, snow-covered peaks loom closer, the valleys narrow, the villages of slate-grey houses wedged along the mountain torrents become rare and the trees give over to an abrupt, often fog-shrouded landscape of rock and grass, whose only inhabitants are sheep and smugglers. Even today, one might have to wake up the solitary gendarme whose white stone house and barrier sit small and forlorn at the top of the border pass. The contrast as one descends the Spanish side is stark. The mountains act as a barrier to the rain-laden clouds that blow off the Bay of Biscay, so the southern slopes are drier, less verdant, clothed in scrub rather than in the magnificent forests and rich meadows of the north. Poor houses and small plots of cultivated land crudely carved between a shallow, muddy river and a cliff of bush and boulder fight for space at the bottom of steep valleys. As the land opens out, it becomes more Mediterranean, gradually changing color from green to grey to light brown as the fields become larger, more regular, planted in ripening wheat or vines. Eventually, one descends into a broad and fertile valley, in the middle of which appears astride a circular hill the ashen citadel of Pamplona.

After the rather Spartan regimen of Vitoria and its environs, Pamplona seemed to the legionnaires an oasis of tranquil urbanity, where life carried on almost as normal in the heart of a hostile and war-torn land. Jean-Jacques Azan especially appreciated its civilized atmosphere, its "beautiful main square, the middle of which is ornamented by a fountain which gives abundant water. It possesses magnificent promenades and a superb church with a modern entrance," and compared it to a stage set for an opera with a medieval theme.[31] But the Legion was to have little time to savor Pamplona, for it was dispatched up the valley of the Arga, which flows south out of the Pyrenees to occupy the garrisons of Larrasoaña and Zubiri. This was difficult and dangerous duty. To remain within the small posts and blockhouses that studded the valley was to yield the countryside to the insurgents. However, to venture into a countryside teeming with rebels was to risk ambush by an enemy superior in number and local knowledge. This hard lesson was learned on March 6, when a company of the Legion deployed at the village of Leranoz near Zubiri in a fairly routine operation to provide protection for fifteen Spanish soldiers sent to cut hay. When Leranoz proved to be occupied by the Carlists, the Legion moved in to clean them out. Suddenly they found themselves surrounded with what Bernelle claimed to be four companies of enemy soldiers. One of the elite companies was sent to rescue their comrades and cut their way into Leranoz with a bayonet charge, only to find themselves entrapped in turn. The two companies organized a defensive position and fought off attacks for three hours until nightfall, when the Carlists lifted their siege. The Legion lost one sergeant and eight troops in the skirmish, two of whom had been captured and shot outright. Bernelle placed Carlist losses at twenty.[32]

Leranoz proved to be only an *hors d'oeuvre* for a more substantial combat that occurred almost three weeks later. At five o'clock on the morning of March 24, the 4th Battalion of the Legion marched out to occupy the heights overlooking Zubiri to provide security for troop movements in the valley between Zubiri and Larrasoaña. The weather was dreadful, and the legionnaires of the *avant-garde,* blinded by hail and snow, climbed the slopes with difficulty. Suddenly the trailing battalion heard the ragged detonation of an ambush. As the isolated point company tried to regain their composure, they were assailed by a troop of Carlist cavalry. Ex-Swiss Guard Sergeant Samuel-Benoît Berset rallied his section despite receiving at least twenty wounds and fought off the attackers while Bernelle sent the 5th Battalion at the run to turn the Carlists on the left. Afterwards, Bernelle complained bitterly that the failure of the Spanish to move around to the right as ordered to encircle completely the insurgents, together with the absence of the Spanish division that was supposed to be in reserve, cheated him of a more complete victory. But as it was, the Legion had a profitable morning. The appearance of the 5th Battalion created a panic among the attackers. Thirty surrendered outright, while the rest fled down a narrow ravine "in such disorder that it suggests the most complete defeat and demoralization," Bernelle wrote. One hundred thirty Carlist bodies, including several officers, were left behind, and Bernelle estimated the total Carlist casualties at two hundred. For its part, the Legion lost forty killed and thirty-two wounded.[33]

But this was not the last word on this skirmish near Zubiri, known as the Battle of Inigo or Fernandorena. The high number of legionnaires killed was the direct result of the Carlist practice of shooting enemy wounded. Bernelle also discovered the charred bodies of five Legion captives among the carnage, so he ordered the immediate execution of his thirty Carlist prisoners. This was to cause ructions in France when it was learned that Bernelle was offering no quarter. But Paris failed to understand that this war in Spain had more in common with the sort of conflict being fought in North Africa than with a European conflagration in which the laws of humanity were usually respected. The Legion had rapidly been introduced to the dark side of warfare south of the Pyrenees. Atrocities in the early phases of the war had provoked the disgust of Europe, so that British Viscount Eliot, Wellington's emissary to Spain, had managed to arbitrate a treaty between the two sides that prohibited the murder of prisoners and created a framework for their periodic exchange. However, the Carlists claimed that the Legion as a foreign corps was not covered by the Eliot Treaty and proceeded to treat legionnaires who fell into their hands with great savagery.

One such distasteful incident occurred in April 1836, when Bernelle dispatched Corsican legionnaire Simonetti, "an astute and clever man," across Carlist lines to pose as a deserter. After eight days in the hills, Simonetti returned to identify the location of the Carlist camp. A punitive force of sixty legionnaires supported by three companies fell upon the unsuspecting Carlists, capturing Jules Garnier, a Frenchman in Carlist service, a sergeant and three soldiers, and killing a Legion deserter. This skirmish proved a bitter one for the Legion. "Several riflemen who wandered away from the line and having been wounded out of view of their comrades, remained on the battlefield at the mercy of the enemy," read Bernelle's April report. "[They] were treated in such a way that the very memory makes me tremble in horror. Two of these brave men were found at the end of the action and taken to the ambulance. They had their lips cut, their cheeks slashed with a sword or a knife, the skin of the forehead peeled off and their eyelids ripped off. However, they were still alive!"[34] Jules Garnier was more fortunate. So impressed was Bernelle by his contrition that he not only pardoned him, but also asked that he be allowed to join the Legion.[35] Under pressure from France, Bernelle ceased to execute prisoners. But his gesture was not reciprocated by the Carlists, so in a short time the butchery began anew.

Eighteen thirty-six was to be a busy year for the Legion. The Carlists continued to pressure the government all along the line from Zubiri to Larrasoaña. On April 25, Bernelle sent out a company to cut down a small pine forest infested by snipers who kept up a constant harassing fire on an outlying blockhouse. Attacked, the legionnaires withdrew, but the next morning dawn revealed the heights of Tirapegui, which dominated Larrasoaña, crowned by what was estimated to be three thousand five hundred Carlist soldiers. Bernelle set out a screen of three Legion companies with strict orders not to attack. They disobeyed him, and soon Bernelle was forced to come to their rescue with five hundred men and four cannon. The fight lasted six hours: "The enemy with his numerous forces, five times greater than our own, wanted to overwhelm our position," Bernelle reported. "Three times we fought them off with our bayonets. Our soldiers, mixed up with theirs, showed . . . great courage. The ravine from which the rebels emerged was covered with their dead. Their losses must have been considerable." Isolated legionnaires were surrounded and massacred, and even Bernelle was slightly wounded on the arm. At seven o'clock, the Legion withdrew by echelons into Larrasoaña with twenty dead and seventy wounded. Carlist losses were reckoned to be three times greater, around eighty dead and two hundred wounded.

Despite this relative success, Bernelle was furious. The courage of the Legion had been beyond question. But war was an intelligent game, not something to be rushed at like the French knights at Agincourt. While he praised the heroism of men like Corsican second lieutenant Ascagne-Alcide Ferrandi who, isolated with a small number of soldiers, was massacred, he condemned his lack of caution. "He misunderstood his duties as an officer, that of obedience," Bernelle wrote, and sacrificed himself as well as some of his men needlessly. He castigated the impetuosity of his officers and NCOs who, though covering themselves with honor, had allowed a greater victory to slip away. "Our soldiers [were] carried away by their usual ardor and did not listen to the voices of their officers," he complained. No military organization can function without courage. However, courage alone is no substitute for the intelligent conduct of war. Bernelle admitted that the battle had been indecisive, but he believed that the Legion had demonstrated its decisive combat superiority over the enemy.[36]

Despite the general unpopularity of Bernelle among both contemporaries and historians, it is difficult not to admire his period of command. He used the Legion wisely throughout the summer of 1836, not risking ambitious operations that would waste its strength for small strategic gain. Yet at the same time he kept his corps active, maintaining its morale and fighting edge, unlike Evans, who allowed the British Legion to waste away from inactivity or pitched it into operations beyond its skills and capabilities. On August 1, Bernelle inflicted a major defeat on the Carlists at Zubiri with little loss to himself. He kept a notoriously difficult corps in line with firm discipline, and took steps to give it as much operational autonomy as possible through the creation of a cavalry and artillery. Indeed, it is possible to argue that the Legion was actually stronger in August 1836 than it had been a year earlier, more battle-hardened and even more numerous—replacements had far exceeded the 117 men killed in battle and the 380 who had died from wounds or disease, or who had been shot or imprisoned.[37] And despite letters to the war ministry from subprefects on the French side of the Pyrenees asking what to do with Legion deserters who walked in from Spain, desertion appears to have been kept well under control.[38]

But the Legion's situation began to deteriorate rapidly in August and September 1836. The elements of this decline were already present even before cataclysmic events in France and Spain decided the fate of the Legion. First, the confused status of the command arrangements exacerbated the divisions within the officer corps occasioned by Bernelle's strict command methods. Despite the varied origins of the Legion officers, there is no evidence that these conflicts broke down along political or social lines. One was a member of Bernelle's (or was it Madame Bernelle's?) magic circle, or one was not. The man who captured the leadership of the anti-Bernelle party was the second in command, Joseph Conrad. The conflict was a natural and altogether predictable one, as the two men possessed completely incompatible personalities. While Bernelle was dignified, aloof, ostentatious, Conrad was hearty, down to earth, a man of simple tastes. Where Bernelle stressed discipline and control, Conrad was a warrior's warrior, fiery, impetuous, always in the forefront of any attack, which had won him praise, decorations, admiration and several wounds since he had come out of Saint-Cyr as an infantry subaltern in 1808. Legionnaire G. von Rosen described him as "a small man with large shoulders, around fifty years old, with a handsome German face. His attitude and manner were truly military. He wore a full beard which gave him a really martial air, and usually wore a small round red cloth skullcap with gold trim, without visor, which he traded against his will on holidays for the tricorn which Bernelle had imposed upon all officers."[39]

The real sticking point between Bernelle and Conrad was the undue influence of Madame Bernelle in the affairs of the corps. In January 1836, following operations in the Arlaban, Conrad tried to do something about it by promoting his own choices to fill vacancies in the ranks, claiming this as his right as colonel of the regiment. Bernelle, a brigadier, was technically in command of the "division" of the Legion. Not surprisingly, Bernelle rejected this spurious reasoning, and when the war minister in Paris decided in Bernelle's favor, Conrad resigned and returned to France in February. The disappearance of the popular Conrad and the obvious discord in the officer corps could not but be felt further down in the ranks, and contributed to Bernelle's decision to resign in August 1836.[40]

If Bernelle had to fight both the Carlists and his own officers simultaneously, he also was locked in combat with the French and Spanish high commands, a fight he was destined to lose. For while the Legion was fighting well, even brilliantly, in the summer of 1836, it was operating on an increasingly short string. Perhaps it was the date that caused the brooding exiled general to explode, but on July 14, Bernelle dispatched a long screed to the war ministry in Paris in which he enumerated his complaints: the reintegration into regular regiments of all officers who had refused to follow the Legion to Spain in 1835 and even of those who had resigned in Spain "after having done everything to convince their comrades and their subordinates to follow their example"; the indifference of the French government to the massacre of Legion prisoners by the Carlists; the refusal of the French government to honor his proposals for promotions and decorations of officers and legionnaires; inadequate policing of the frontier, which allowed a continued supply of arms and recruits to reach the enemy; the absence of replacements from France; and finally the criminal neglect of the Legion by the Spanish government, which paid, fed and supplied them at irregular intervals, if at all. Paris replied in conciliatory terms, but the pressures of the past year proved too much for Bernelle. As the government had not kept its word, he considered himself released from his. He quit, and twelve officers resigned with him.[41]

It may have been that Bernelle's precipitous resignation was meant to forestall his relief. Bernelle's divisive command methods, and especially the conduct of his wife, who was rumored to be showing more than ordinary interest in a Polish officer in the corps whom she insisted on accompanying to the battlefield, had been brought to the notice of Thiers. Already in July, the prime minister had toyed with the idea of replacing Bernelle with General Thomas Bugeaud or Marshal Bertrand Clauzel.[42]

The resignation of Bernelle in itself need not have produced immediate consequences. But with his departure, Legion morale began to unravel and performance seriously to decline. The first indication that all was not well in Spain occurred on August 16, when a Spanish military rebellion forced Isabel to accept a more liberal constitution, considerably to the left of that favored by France. The reaction of Paris was not long in coming. The liberal revolution in Spain simply reinforced the desire of King Louis-Philippe to have done with the whole Iberian mess. Don Carlos, if not yet a spent force, had been contained. Events in Madrid no longer posed any direct threat to France, which made further intervention unnecessary. Besides, the king had become increasingly annoyed with his prime minister, Thiers, who had begun to raise a replacement corps at Pau near the Spanish border whose numbers he had secretly swelled beyond those authorized by the king, agitated for General Bugeaud to take command and even announced to the press that they would soon march to Isabel's aid. That was simply too much. On August 25, Thiers tendered his resignation and was replaced on September 6, 1836, by the anti-interventionist Count Louis-Mathieu Molé. The "auxiliary corps" at Pau was marched off toward Algeria, and the Legion was well and truly marooned in Spain.[43]

The wound was a mortal one. But life remained yet in the Legion. Before he retired, the war minister, Marshal Maison, had named Colonel Jean-Louis Baux, called Lebeau, to replace Bernelle. Lebeau came with the highest recommendations of Bugeaud, perhaps because, like him, he had been a *demi-solde* for the fifteen years of the Restoration. But more than that, the fifty-six-year-old Lebeau had a distinguished military record going back to the Revolution and the Empire. He had been in the thick of the fight, with a wound to prove it, at Waterloo. He also enjoyed a well-deserved reputation as a talented tactician. Alas, Lebeau, although an officer of exceptional ability, was the wrong man for this job. Intellectual, incorrigibly modest, he lacked the panache and commanding presence to impose himself upon a polyglot, multinational regiment. Lebeau cut an awkward, disheveled figure in this monosyllabic world in which gesture, attitude and stylish appearance counted for so much. And how could it have been otherwise when his uniform consisted of an old cape, a pair of britches that barely covered his knees, shapeless boots from which protruded a pair of impossibly long spurs, and an outsized hat that looked as if it had been purchased from a traveling circus?

Quite frankly, Lebeau appeared to be intimidated by his legionnaires, and with good reason, for they were in a foul mood. Most were existing on a short ration of poor-quality bacon that had put many in the hospital, and the only thing regular about their pay was that it was constantly in arrears: "In the middle of so much discontent, I am always afraid that I may lose control," he wrote to France. "I will hold on, but if you only knew what sort of men these are! Otherwise they are very courageous."[44]

Lebeau's lack of confidence may well have affected his performance. On September 14, the Legion joined with Spanish forces to attack the heights above the town of Estella southwest of Pamplona, which were strongly held by Carlist forces. Legion losses were light despite a fairly vigorous use of the bayonet. Below sat the town, which served the Carlists as a capital, in an extremely vulnerable position. Amazingly, the constitutionalists withdrew on the very threshold of what could have been an important victory, perhaps because they lacked ammunition, but the reason is not entirely clear.[45] What was clear, however, was that Lebeau had had enough, discouraged by the poor condition of his corps for which he was blamed, the growing discord in the officer corps and the "surprising, incomprehensible" abandonment of the Legion by the French government. In November, barely three months after assuming command, he followed Bernelle over the Pyrenees to France.[46]

Now, at last, the Legion acquired the commander whom they had so long admired, Joseph Conrad, but in conditions that could hardly have been worse. Hunger was so great that "eight officers of the Legion reported to the hospital yesterday to *eat*," reported Major Jean-François de Cariès de Senilhes. "One cannot have an idea of their misery."[47] Soldiers asked to be freed from their contracts, and Conrad, eager to get rid of useless mouths, often allowed them to go on condition that they renounced all claims to back pay and indemnities. Others began to desert, some to the Carlists, "and the Queen will find them as relentless against her cause as before they were her warm partisans," wrote French general Jean Harispe, commander at Bayonne and in close touch with the Legion, in a prophetic message. Indeed, according to Major de Senilhes, desertion, especially desertion to the enemy, was the result of their loss of faith in the constitutionalist cause rather than the harsh conditions of service per se: "Yesterday, there were threats in the cantonments from entire companies to leave with arms and baggage," he reported in December 1836. The Legion had been bivouacked for too long in the midst of a pro-Carlist population and were beginning to realize the futility and hopelessness of the whole Spanish mess: "When the insurrection has become second nature and when it is sustained by an entire population, it is not an extra effort without antecedents and isolated from its consequences which can destroy the [enemy] army," he continued. "A victory over this can only modify the elements which sustain it, and it will soon reproduce itself in another form or around other ideas."[48]

In fact, what surprised de Senilhes was how well Conrad "has maintained [the Legion] until now as a regular organization and in a condition which still imposes the terror of its arms on the enemy."[49] How indeed? The departure of the less dedicated officers and men may have acted as a bond to those who remained, whose shared hardships strengthened the sense of comradeship. Also, the fact that between three and four hundred men each month were eligible for liberation from February 1837 on may have encouraged many to wait out their enlistment contracts rather than run the risks of desertion. Nevertheless, the losses had been substantial. In January 1837, an attempt by sixty legionnaires to desert *en masse* was prevented at the last minute, "and they are encouraged by a good number of officers who are completely disgusted and demoralized," de Senilhes reported, two of whom Conrad had locked up for "uttering opinions subversive to order and discipline."[50] In the first week of February, 161 legionnaires deserted, including a sergeant-major, four sergeants and nine corporals. So bad had desertions become that Conrad considered pulling his soldiers out of Zubiri because its proximity to France tempted his exhausted legionnaires to make a break for the frontier.[51]

In early February 1837, the Legion numbered 239 officers and 3,841 men,[52] substantially down from a peak strength of 298 officers and 6,134 men and probably reflecting a loss of about 37 percent.[53] And the situation would only get worse. In August 1835, six Legion battalions had arrived in Spain, reinforced by a seventh battalion in 1836. By the end of 1836, the Legion still counted six battalions. However, by March 1837, it was capable of putting three in the field, by April only two, and by June only one Legion battalion remained. In July 1837, the journal *Le Siècle,* quoting Spanish sources, claimed that the Legion in Spain had lost 1,510 men, or one quarter of its original strength of around 6,000 men, through desertion, while 1,376 men, about twenty-three percent, had been released from service, and 875, or 14 percent, had died in battle or of disease.[54] The days left when the Legion would remain militarily effective were limited. If it was to be used, it had to be used before its troops melted away completely.

Yet another reason why the Legion maintained its combat effectiveness despite adverse conditions became apparent on March 21. In the course of a series of seemingly pointless promenades up narrow river valleys, Conrad was ordered to occupy Larrainzar, a village that stood at the foot of a steep wooded hill about twenty miles north of Pamplona in the valley of the Ulzama. The Legion occupied Larrainzar at eight o'clock on the evening of March 20 after a difficult march in appalling weather: "Those unfortunate ones who could not follow died," wrote Jean-Jacques Azan. "In the night, the peasants brought in frozen soldiers."[55] At dawn on March 21, Conrad sent his first battalion to secure the high ground above the town while the remainder of his two battalions, which formed the rear guard of the twelve-thousand-man column, awaited the order to continue toward Pamplona. At ten o'clock, just as the rear guard was about to follow the torrent of retreating Spanish troops, those in the town heard an explosion, followed by a ragged volley of returned fire in the wood above them.

Conrad immediately ordered his men up the hill. The second battalion moving up the steep slopes soon mingled with the first battalion, whose soldiers had been driven off the crest by the Carlist attack. Perhaps it was from these legionnaires in retreat that they learned that a company under Captain Johan Albrecht Hebich had been abandoned at the summit. The second battalion, followed closely by the third, moved to the rescue, bodies bent forward against the mountain and the hail of musket balls fired by the insurgents above. But no insurance salesman would have touched Hebich at that moment despite the rescue attempt, for his position appeared utterly hopeless. His company was surrounded by an estimated two battalions of Carlists, and their defensive position was no more than a few tree trunks hastily arranged around the stone foundations of a tumbled-down mountain barn. However, the Carlists were soon forced to acknowledge that in Hebich they had taken on the wrong man.

The forty-four-year-old Württemberg native was a soldier of the sort who craved action and was prepared to go anywhere to find it. By the time the Napoleonic wars had come to an end, Hebich already counted several wounds received fighting for and against France. But even a commission in the Württemberg cavalry was not enough to keep him home. In 1820 he traveled to Greece, where he was again wounded several times in the independence wars. In 1823, he came to France. How he lived is not clear, but he did establish contacts with the Orleans family, who, in 1831, secured a commission for him in the Legion. Hebich's record in the Legion was abysmal. He established a reputation as vulgar and insulting even in a corps that placed little value on social refinements. "He is excessively drunken, without any dignity," his superior Colonel Combe wrote of him in 1832. "He is brutal beyond belief, unjust to his inferiors, arrogant and vulgar toward those above him. He insults and provokes all with whom he comes into contact. He is profoundly ignorant for his position, listless, lazy, always claiming to be ill when asked to perform the smallest service, even refusing to do it. He is unworthy in every way to be counted as a French soldier."[56] In 1833, Hebich came within an ace of expulsion by an army board, saved no doubt by his royal connections. After that, he calmed down somewhat, but continued to drink heavily and in 1836 was punished with thirty days prison by Bernelle for threatening a sergeant with his saber. Nevertheless, he received grudging admiration for his unquestioned bravery, and at no time more so than on March 21, 1837.

The case of Hebich is interesting beyond the scope of his acts at Larrainzar, for while he was certainly atypical of the officer corps of the Legion, his type was a fairly common one in the ranks—violent, drunken, headstrong, lazy, impossible to control in the garrison. But in a firefight, men like Hebich almost made one feel sorry for the enemy. Abel Galant, who wrote a chronicle of the Legion in Spain, thought him magnificent in the face of what looked like certain death, holding off repeated charges for at least two hours in his primitive redoubt. Conrad's battalions struggled up the mountainside to discover Hebich standing on a stone in the middle of his improvised fortress directing the fire of his men. He had lost seven legionnaires, but at least three times that number of Carlist corpses lay around the barn.

But the rebels were everywhere. The legionnaires charged and drove them into the forest, where they were at a decided disadvantage against an enemy who knew well every fold and wrinkle in the terrain and who were more at home in the irregular skirmishing that now ensued. "We crossed a ravine without looking to see if we were supported," Azan wrote. "We were surprised and on the point of being taken prisoner. Without keeping our heads, we would not have been able to withdraw. By luck, a drummer was with us. I told him to beat a charge, and this saved us: The enemy thought our battalions were near, and fled. This gave us time to cross the ravine and rejoin our column which was retreating."[57] Theirs was a mistake that Bernelle had criticized at Tirapegui, and one brought on by a combination of excessive ardor, the difficulties of controlling battle in the wooded, hilly terrain, and perhaps also by contempt for the enemy. It is also likely that the Carlists, realizing that they were no match for the better-disciplined Legion in the open, tried to draw them into situations where the individual fighting skills of the mountain men could be turned to advantage. By the time the Legion reached the valley and the sanctuary of Larrainzar, it counted nineteen dead, including four officers; five officers were wounded, as were fifty-four legionnaires and NCOs.[58] Nor was the retreat to Pamplona an easy one: "We marched and fought without letup," wrote Lieutenant Jean Bamberg, a German serving with the Legion, "because the battalions of the Legion were vigorously and closely followed."[59]

After Larrainzar, the Legion deteriorated rapidly. Conrad was forced increasingly to resort to the firing squad to discourage desertion: "It is painful to think that, while we do not keep our promises to these brave men, we hold them religiously to theirs," he wrote.[60] Morale plummeted and Conrad hesitated to appear before his men, "because I no longer know what to reply to their well founded and just reclamations which assail me from all quarters, which remind me of the often repeated and never kept promises which I never ceased to make."[61] Desertions and departures reduced the Legion to two battalions, two cavalry squadrons and an artillery battery. Officers were driven into debt simply to eat, and Conrad was even forced to sell his horse after he went five months without pay: "I really don't know how all this will finish," he wrote to General Harispe at the end of March.[62]

It all finished, more or less, in the early summer of 1837. An army under Spanish General Iribarren, of which the Legion was part, had spent much of the month shadowing a Carlist army as it moved west into Catalonia. On May 24 at five o'clock in the evening, the government forces were drawn up on a range of low hills before the town of Huesca. The Carlists obviously believed that it was far too late in the day to fight, for their officers had begun to hand out lodging billets. According to Bazaine, as the Legion watched the enemy nonchalantly preparing to settle down for the night, several of Iribarren's staff officers arrived shouting: "The Legion forward! The Legion forward!"

It is not entirely clear why Iribarren decided to give battle at Huesca. His decision might have been one of impulse, as his troops apparently were calling for a fight, and the Carlists seemed poorly prepared to receive an onslaught. However, Iribarren's attack at Huesca made little sense, either strategically or tactically. Strategically, his objective should have been to block the Carlist advance into Catalonia. To do this, he should have selected a strong defensive position, like the one he was in, and forced the rebels to attack him. Defensive battles are easier to control and usually inflict a greater number of casualties on the enemy. Tactically, it made little sense to attack, for the day was already well advanced and the battle was bound to be overtaken by nightfall, when the individual fighting skills of the Carlists would give them the edge. Also, even if the Carlists seemed half-asleep, they still occupied strong defensive positions in the gardens around Huesca and in the town itself, which would have to be taken in brutal street fighting.

Should Conrad have questioned the order to attack? Almost certainly, as commander of a foreign division it would have been his right. Given Iribarren's poor record as a commander, it should have been Conrad's duty, for it was the height of folly to sacrifice what was left of his corps in a hazardous frontal assault that could bring no substantial strategic gain. But this was not Conrad's style. Nor, probably, did a man of such aggressive temperament wish to avoid battle. Conrad threw his troops into the walled gardens and orchards before him and drove almost to the gates of Huesca itself. Caught off guard, the Carlist soldiers were badly cut up. But soon realizing that the Legion, typically left dangling without support from its Spanish allies, was dangerously far forward, the enemy swarmed out of the town and took up defensive positions behind the walls on the Legion flanks. Iribarren sent a battalion to reinforce Conrad, but the enemy was by now far too numerous and well entrenched. "More than 600 men were shooting at us as at a target," Galant recorded. The Carlists took advantage of the twilight and the enormous amount of dust and smoke to attack the government troops to the left of the Legion, who inexplicably had failed to move to Conrad's aid. In this attack, Iribarren was mortally wounded leading his cavalry in a countercharge. Despairing of support, Conrad ordered a retreat: "It was executed in step, ordered and without haste, carrying a good third of our wounded with us. . . . The enemy followed, but at a respectful distance," Galant wrote.

However, at one o'clock in the morning, when the Legion reached its bivouac in the village of Almudevar, it could take account of the extent of the catastrophe: "Almost half our officers were put *hors de combat* [and] we lost nearly 500 men in this fatal day," Galant wrote. In fact, although Galant as usual overestimated Legion casualties, reality was bad enough— between 350 and 400 legionnaires *hors de combat,* including 28 officers, of whom four were dead. And if this were not loss enough, a further one thousand legionnaires, their enlistments run out, were marched toward Pamplona.[63]

It is difficult to know how much fight was left in the Legion after Huesca. Perhaps none at all had it not been for the extraordinary circumstances of its final battle only a few days later. Don Carlos led his army west from Huesca marching toward Catalonia and, he hoped, rapturous popular acclamation. On June 2, the Carlist troops were preparing their noon meal at Barbastro, a small town of narrow streets, grey stucco houses and red-tiled roofs that caps a hill next to the Vero River, when the new Spanish commander, General Marcelino Oraa, attacked out of the west with eighteen thousand troops. As at Huesca, the Carlists rallied from their initial surprise and counterattacked. Probably more by chance than by design, they fell upon the flank of Oraa's first line, which fled through the olive groves that covered the hills to the west of town. Conrad and the Legion, which occupied the flank of the second line, suddenly saw the enemy loom up before them through the olive trees. There was a pause, a moment of utter stupefaction, for as the musket balls clipped twigs over their heads or kicked up chunks of desiccated earth around their feet, they realized that before them in ranks as serried as the broken terrain and wood allowed stood many of their ex-comrades.

Desertion to the enemy, while not a great problem for the Legion in their first year in Spain, became more serious after September 1836. The Carlists began to make a concerted effort to exploit the obvious disaffection in the ranks of their most redoubtable opponents, and with some success. The Carlist legion that filed through the groves around Barbastro on that June afternoon numbered around eight hundred men. It was undoubtedly their presence that stimulated the badly suffering Legion into one final effort. Baron Wilhelm von Rahden, a German officer serving with the Carlists, witnessed the battle: "I have never seen during my very full military career—neither before nor after—the spectacle of a melee as bloody as this one," he wrote. "The soldiers recognized each other during the combat. They called out their names and their nicknames, in French or in German, approached each other as friends, spoke, asked questions, and then killed each other in cold blood."[64]

The Legion occupied the extreme right of the constitutionalist line. To their left, the Spanish troops broke under the ferocity of the Carlist onslaught. What happened next is best described by Bazaine: "Our troops hesitated, confusion began to appear in our ranks," he wrote to General Harispe. "[Conrad] believed that by setting an example through his own courage, he could rally them. He went well to the front of the skirmish line, placed his cap on the end of his cane, and shouted: 'Forward!' But the men, seized by panic, did not hear his voice. They continued to flee. . . ." A bullet in the forehead brought Conrad to the ground. "His body almost fell into the hands of the enemy. But thanks to the help of an officer and four courageous NCOs and soldiers of the Legion, I got him onto my horse and across the battlefield. However, as we were outflanked on our left, I needed a half-hour to get his body out of danger."[65] The Legion, disheartened, demoralized, leaderless, fled from the smoldering olive grove following the retreat of General Oraa's troops. But it was no disgrace, only the last straw.

Some saw in Conrad's solitary charge a willful suicide brought on by his sense of shame and personal responsibility for the agony of his corps. Perhaps, but it is equally true that the low state of Legion morale, especially since Larrainzar, had forced him to take risks: "After the battles of 20, 21 and 22 March, I could only acquit myself with honor by exposing myself continually to set the example, for already the officers and soldiers were no longer the same," he had written to General Harispe on April 29.[66] Had he lived he might have consoled himself with the certainty that he had decimated the Carlist legion—only 160 of the 800 men had survived the battle unscathed, and the Carlist legion was disbanded a few weeks later. The Duc d'Orléans, the eldest son of Louis-Philippe and heir to the French throne, assumed responsibility for Conrad's two sons, who were placed in a military college, while his widow was given a pension by the king.[67]

The Carlist War sputtered on for another two years, but the Legion's contribution to it was much diminished. Under the command of Lieutenant Colonel André-Camille Ferray, the Legion, or what was left of it, fought a victorious action at Astrain in Navarre on September 10, 1837, against three Carlist battalions. Of 350 men who took the field, 100 were officers. The understrength regiment of Polish lancers was reduced to two squadrons when, on June 20, 1837, it was incorporated directly into the Spanish army with which it fought until disbanded in September 1838. Perhaps the greatest success story of the war was the Legion artillery and sapper units created by Bernelle. The artillery battery, which included 37 legionnaires, would fight with the Spanish virtually until the end, only disbanding on April 1, 1839. It earned the praise of its hosts, while the sappers, originally raised by Bernelle to act as a personal guard, were revived in the twentieth century when, wearing beards and leather aprons and carrying axes, they were given the task of leading every Legion march. When, in January 1839, the Legion was finally repatriated to France, it contained 63 officers and

159 NCOs and legionnaires, and an indeterminate number of their women and children.[68]

Divisions in the rebel ranks as well as the sheer desolation the war had brought on the northern provinces eventually splintered the rebel effort. In August 1839, one of Don Carlos's principal commanders arrested and shot four rival generals and then, in August, signed an armistice on favorable terms. In mid-September, the Pretender fled into France at the head of twenty thousand supporters and into the arms of the French police. Six thousand rebel diehards fought on until they too crossed the Pyrenees into exile in May 1840. "The arrival of the Carlists was a veritable exodus," wrote Captain Certain Canrobert, future Marshal of France who was stationed in Perpignan near the Spanish frontier. "Several of the battalions were more or less intact: the men had white, blue or red berets, capes and tunics with military buttons and all sorts of trousers. Some wore sandals. Others marched barefooted and even barelegged. Women, children, old people followed the soldiers, Lord knows in what rags and in what misery."[69] Pragmatic to the last, the Legion even recruited a battalion from among their old enemies.

If there was a lesson in all of this for the Legion, it was succinctly put by Abel Galant: "Each time that a military force unfortunately finds itself placed between politics, diplomacy and the cannon," he wrote in 1842, "it must be sacrificed."[70] And because it was a foreign force, the Legion, like a destitute relative dependent upon the charity and continued goodwill of more fortunate relatives, would find itself placed in this equivocal position more often than most. In these conditions, the challenge of maintaining a high level of performance in the face of official indifference and neglect was no less daunting. But institutional memory was short. Indeed, January 1839 closed the records on what was already being called the *ancienne Légion*.

However, if the "old Legion" had been sacrificed in Spain, a new Legion, inadvertently almost, had been resurrected by an ordinance of December 16, 1835. While the government dithered over whether to commit this new force to Spain, on June 7, 1836, the war minister, seeking to avoid the problems that had surrounded the "delivery" of the Legion to Spain the preceding year, stipulated in the enlistment contract that each legionnaire must be prepared to "follow the Legion or each detachment of the Legion anywhere that the government will judge convenient to send it." When Thiers resigned in 1836 over Louis-Philippe's refusal to reinforce the Legion in Spain, this "new Legion" was dispatched to Algiers where, by 1839, it had already earned the praise of one officer who was to rise to great prominence in the military history of France—the future Marshal Achille Leroy de Saint-Arnaud.

Chapter 3

THE
"NEW LEGION"

At the very moment that the Foreign Legion appeared destined for destruction in Spain, the unstoppable flow of refugees into France combined with the manpower needs of the Algerian generals to give the Legion experiment a new lease on life. On December 16, 1835, Louis-Philippe created a *nouvelle légion* whose purpose was to supply recruits to the Legion in Spain. In August 1836, a battalion of legionnaires—the last to be cast into the Iberian maw—was dispatched under Conrad. By late November, another eight-company battalion of foreigners had been recruited, according to inspection reports largely among Dutchmen. But France had now washed her hands of the Spanish intervention and so directed this new Legion to Africa.

On December 15, 1836, this new Legion set foot upon the southern shore of the Mediterranean, where it became part of the 2nd Brigade, whose duty was to ensure the tenuous security of the Mitidja plain behind Algiers. But punitive raids into the mountainous Algiers hinterland against elusive tribesmen proved frustrating, especially for the Legion, which appears to have been recruited in haste and poorly trained. Its new commander, Major and future general Alphonse Bedeau, discovered that many of his legionnaires simply were not up to the rigors of campaigning in the African climate, and that of a paper strength of 1,600 men, only 1,200 or 1,300 were fit for service.[1] In France, recruitment of the Legion continued, so that by September 1837 a second battalion was in existence, which allowed the army to give the Legion an organization identical to that of a French regiment.

The treaty of Tafna signed between the French and resistance leader Abd el-Kader brought a temporary peace to the eastern Oran region by the summer of 1837, while operations around Algiers, though cumbersome, had pushed the tribes back into their mountains. This left the French free to settle a score with Ahmed, the Bey of Constantine. And a heavy score it was. In November 1836, the French had marched a column of 8,700 troops to the very gates of Constantine, only to be repulsed before a city that proved far more difficult to take than, in their overconfidence, they had supposed. But French embarrassment had turned to disaster as they struggled back to the coast at Bône through appalling weather. They had been harassed as far as Guelma by the Algerians, elated and emboldened by the humiliation they had just inflicted on what many still considered, despite Waterloo, to be Europe's premier army. And humiliation it was—most of the baggage train had been lost or thoroughly pillaged even before the siege was abandoned. Some of the soldiers had not been informed of the retreat and many of the wounded had been left to their fate on the battlefield, while a thousand others had perished in the hospitals in the days following the retreat, 108 of them in an accidental explosion.

The governor-general, Marshal Clauzel, just before he lost his post as a result of the debacle, insisted that the honor of French arms be avenged. It was in part to compensate for the losses suffered in this first siege of Constantine that the *nouvelle Légion* left Pau on December 5, 1836, bound for Algeria. One historian of French expansion in Algeria, Charles-André Julien, saw in the second siege of Constantine the beginning of a pattern that would become an all too familiar one during the next 130 years of French colonialism—French soldiers pushing the bounds of empire ever outward amidst the ignorance and indifference of French public and political opinion. "Molé [the prime minister] had no policy," Julien wrote, "and General Baron Bernard, the war minister . . . had no personality."[2]

Clauzel's successor, General Count Charles Denys de Damrémont, was taking no chances this time. On October 1, 1837, he marched out of his camp at Medjez-Amar, eight miles southwest of Guelma, at the head of a 20,400-man force that included a large battalion of military engineers commanded by Lieutenant General Rohault de Fleury and a substantial siege artillery directed by General Sylvain-Charles Valée, aging, stiff, severe, but considered the first artilleryman of France. When, on October 5, the French column arrived on the plateau of Mansoura before Constantine, they realized that their commander could not be accused of bringing a hammer to crush a fly. One look at the citadel set upon a huge outcropping of stone in the uplands of eastern Algeria was enough to ruin the week of even the most optimistic military engineer. "The oriental fairies could not imagine a more precipitous and inaccessible fortified town than Constantine," the expedition's surgeon major wrote. "Sitting atop a single rock whose cliffs are sheer and of an immense height, at the foot of which flows the Rummel. It seems to defy man to attack it."[3] Constantine was approachable only from the southwest across a narrow neck of land called the Coudiat-Aty. Otherwise, the Rummel had sliced a deep gorge that shaped an impregnable peninsula of stone around the city. Nor, obviously, had the return of the French eleven months after their unsuccessful siege caught Constantine by surprise. The walls were crowded with Kabyles, fierce hill people determined to resist the French, and their commanders, Bey Ahmed and his adjutant Ben Aïssa, had even conjured up an artillery of their own—sixty-three cannon competently served by Turks. Substantial groups of Berbers also lolled about on the surrounding hills ready to pounce upon any attackers who became careless.

The French manhandled their seventeen guns onto the Coudiat-Aty and began to throw up siegeworks about four hundred yards from the wall. On October 7, an Arab attack was repulsed. Two days later, the French opened their bombardment. On the 11th, the Algerians launched several attacks on the French saps, one of which was opposed by two companies of legionnaires who, General Valée reported, ". . . attacked the enemy with the greatest resolution: the Arabs were bowled over and pursued, swords in their kidneys, as far as the escarpments which cut the terrain at this point permitted. [The enemy] left many dead. For our part, we had several men killed among whom we have to regret Captain Marland: 14 men were wounded, among them Captain Raindre who had a leg shattered and Captain MacMahon, aide-de-camp of the Governor General, who was wounded by a bullet."[4]

The French had constructed more batteries in the night and continued to pound the outer wall, seeking to silence the Turkish cannon. Only on the 11th could Valée begin to concentrate upon creating a breach. "By the evening, the breach was clearly visible," he wrote. But the wall proved more resilient than he had imagined. "Its thickness was 1 meter 40 centimeters, but it was built against some old buildings that added considerably to its thickness. The facing of the wall was constructed of very hard limestone blocks."[5] This was of more than mere academic interest—the solidity of the walls combined with the harassing fire of the Turkish guns, which obliged the French to give more attention than planned to counter battery fire, meant that the provision of two hundred shots per cannon might prove inadequate. And the supply depots were too far away to repair the miscalculation.

As was customary in siege operations, when the wall was breached a messenger was dispatched (in this case "a young Arab from the Turkish battalion") to invite the town to surrender and therefore avoid the subsequent horrors of street fighting and pillage. He is reported to have returned with a defiant message: "If the Christians lack powder, we shall send them some; if they have no more biscuits, we will share ours with them; but, as long as one of us lives, they will not take Constantine." "Those are brave people," Damrémont is reported to have said. "The affair will be even more glorious for us!"[6] Valée gives a more laconic version in his official report: "[The messenger] returned the next day without having been mistreated, but brought a verbal response from the inhabitants which announced their intention to be buried among the ruins of the town."[7]

Throughout the night of October 11–12, the French worked to build more batteries closer to the wall, but not without opposition: "The enemy who discovered probably because the moon was bright the operation which we were preparing, directed a violent musket fire at us which obliged us to abandon our work momentarily."[8] The defenders who watched from the surrounding hills swarmed as if to attack, but seeing the French in their trenches preparing to receive them, they wisely reconsidered. At 8:30 on the morning of the 12th, Damrémont went forward to inspect the breach and was blown away by a Turkish cannon ball. Command fell to Valée: "[I] ordered all the means to terminate promptly the operation," he wrote. He redoubled the fire of his guns, which silenced the Turkish batteries—"Even the musketry ceased to be heard"—so that his siege mortars could continue to enlarge the breach. At 3:00 in the afternoon, an emissary came out of the town to ask for a truce. Valée, suspecting correctly, no doubt, that the defenders were attempting to stretch out the siege until the French ran out of food and munitions, replied that negotiations could only follow a surrender. He ordered his batteries to fire at irregular intervals throughout the night to disrupt attempts to repair the breach. At 3:30 on the morning of Friday October 13, two captains crept to the wall and returned to report that the breach was wide enough to fit twenty-five men attacking in line, and that no attempt had been made to repair it.[9]

By 7:30 that same morning, Legion lieutenant Achille de Saint-Arnaud had already spent three and one-half hours hunkered down behind the most advanced line of guns, barely one hundred yards from the breach: "The noise of the artillery was deafening, one blast following upon another," he wrote to his brother. "The shells and musket balls of the Arabs passed overhead or next to us, showering us with fragments of rock or earth."[10] But he was not frightened, or, rather, his obvious nervousness was that of impatience rather than fear. Saint-Arnaud was stoking himself up to do something that would be judged either completely foolish or completely sublime, for he was well aware that this was perhaps his last chance to salvage what, so far, had been a career of embarrassing mediocrity.

Of course, no one can control his own birthday. It was sheer bad luck that Saint-Arnaud's career came on line in 1815 just as a quarter-century of European warfare ended abruptly and spectacularly at Waterloo, for he was just the sort of impulsive young man whom Napoleon might have chosen to lead his hussars in some madcap *mêlée* with the enemy. Typically, the sort of juvenile flamboyance that might have earned for him admiration on the battlefield landed him in deep trouble in peacetime. Saint-Arnaud's aristocratic lineage secured for him a sublieutenancy in the king's exclusive *garde du corps*. But his *petit bourgeois* pocketbook meant that attempts to keep pace with the extravagant life-style of his wealthy contemporaries soon plunged him into impossible debt and forced his resignation in 1817, not yet twenty years old. The following year, a place was found for him in a line regiment, but his tempestuous nature was ill-suited to the dull routine of provincial garrison life. Indeed, he seemed ill-suited to army life in general—by 1820, he was again a civilian after he attempted to provoke a duel with a superior officer, strictly against regulations. He drifted to Greece in 1822, but found life as a mercenary among the Greek independence fighters little to his liking. He accepted an offer of a sublieutenancy in a detachment destined for Martinique, but neglected to appear at the unit's departure and instead offered his resignation, an act that ignited a family quarrel after which even his mother would not let him in the house. Subsequent attempts, and one can imagine that they were fairly frantic ones, by his family to get the Bourbon government to take him back came to nothing.

The Revolution of 1830 offered Saint-Arnaud, like so many others, a second chance. In February 1831, at the age of thirty-three, he was again a sublieutenant, but this time determined "to obliterate this past which I would not buy back at any price."[11] Saint-Arnaud had undergone, quite literally, a change of heart. Barely two months into his new assignment with the 64th Infantry Regiment at Brest, he met Laure Pasquier, the daughter of a retired naval commander, whom he soon married. In December 1831, he became a lieutenant. But he soon discovered that, despite zealous service, years were easier lost than regained. The final blow came in the spring of 1836 with the death of his young wife. A thirty-eight-year-old lieutenant, a widower with two small children, his life a tissue of failure, Saint-Arnaud did a perfectly logical thing—he volunteered for the Foreign Legion.

Now, almost a year after he reported to the *nouvelle Légion* at Pau, he at last had been brought face-to-face with his opportunity: "At Constantine," he had decided, "I will get myself killed or I will make up for lost time and get noticed."[12] Valée signaled the start of the attack. The siege guns shifted their fire beyond the breach. Lieutenant Colonel Louis de Lamoricière rose up and led his three hundred *zouaves,* forty sappers and two elite companies—*voltigeurs* [skirmishers] and grenadiers—of the 2nd Light Infantry Regiment toward the yawning gap in the wall. Within seconds they were swarming over the breach. The plan called for the second wave, of which Saint-Arnaud and his legionnaires were part, to surge forward as soon as the first attack had fought its way through the breach and into the town. But from his position, Saint-Arnaud could see that they were stuck—the bombardment had failed to destroy a second curtain wall that held Lamoricière in the breach while, from all sides, the defenders poured a deadly fire into them. The shout went up for ladders. To Saint-Arnaud, it seemed an eternity before sappers ran forward with them, as well as ropes and sacks of powder. Then he heard a terrific explosion—just as the French prepared to scale the wall, the Turks blew a mine that toppled it onto the attackers. Forty Frenchmen were buried under the debris, including the battalion commander of the 2nd Light Infantry. Lamoricière was badly burned.

Although Valée's report makes no mention of it, Saint-Arnaud reckoned that at this point the assault was within an ace of failure: "Those who escaped, half burned, wounded, disfigured, their clothes in tatters, ran out of the breach shouting: 'Look, friends, comrades, don't attack! Run! Everything is mined. You will be blown up like us!' Our soldiers hesitated and looked toward their officers," Saint-Arnaud wrote to his brother. Because the lack of artillery ammunition made a second attempt impossible, at least in 1837, the French had only one option opened to them. History credits Colonel Michel Combe, ex-colonel of the Legion and commander of the second wave, and Major Alphonse Bedeau of the Legion with hurling their troops into the balance at this critical moment. Saint-Arnaud, with typical absence of modesty, recorded that it was a spontaneous and simultaneous initiative on the part of several officers, including himself: "Anyone might have done it, but it took initiative, and at the moment when an exploding mine always makes one suspect a second, it required audacity to charge into certain danger."[13]

"The progress of [our] troops in the town became more rapid after the wall collapsed despite the resistance of the enemy," Valée reported.[14] Saint-Arnaud agreed that the defenders had made a serious tactical error in blowing down their own defenses. But for those on the inside, including Saint-Arnaud and his hundred legionnaires, the most murderous part of the operation was just beginning. He later admitted that he was "carried away" and completely "forgot himself" as he charged into the streets of Constantine,[15] most of them mere alleyways where the roofs of the houses were so close that only a sliver of sky was visible above the men who struggled in the semitwilight below. Saint-Arnaud ordered his men to follow as he threw himself at a battery to the left of the breach: "The Turks defended themselves with desperate courage. They fired and we killed them while they were reloading: What admirable soldiers! Our bayonets did not leave one alive. We did not take prisoners."[16]

They then moved toward the sound of the fighting when some sappers came to ask him to remove a barricade that was holding up progress. Saint-Arnaud rushed to a narrow street crowded with legionnaires and soldiers from the Bataillon d'Afrique, all leaderless and in a state of great agitation, so great in fact that they did not notice that they were trampling the body of a captain of engineers who had already been killed by fire from the barricade. Saint-Arnaud took time to notice that the obstacle that blocked the street only a few yards away was "artistically constructed: doors, beams, mattresses, nothing was lacking." He placed some of his best marksmen in the houses that overlooked the street, took sword in hand, and sprinted forward, followed by a jostling queue of soldiers. "I threw myself on the barricade which I crossed by falling on the other side. . . . There, on the ground, I was happy to hear the soldiers shout furiously: 'Help the Captain! Help the Captain! He's wounded, on the ground!' " However, he was not wounded but up like a flash carving his way through the defenders.[17]

Soon, however, enemy fire became so intense that all progress was brought to a halt "by a rolling cross fire which destroyed anyone who tried to get across. The soldiers refused to go forward." The fire was coming from a house which, Saint-Arnaud subsequently discovered, was a barracks. By now, most of the French troops were so jumbled together that it was a motley of regiments under five or six officers that stormed the building: "What a scene, brother, what carnage!" Saint-Arnaud wrote. "The blood flowed down the steps. . . . Not a cry, not a complaint escaped from the dying men. We killed and died with this hopeless rage that makes you grit your teeth and consigns the cries to the bottom of the soul. . . . Very few of the Turks looked to escape, and those who withdrew took advantage of every nook and cranny to fire upon us."[18]

The fall of the barracks ended the last organized resistance in Constantine. Finally, the son of a sheik arrived to surrender. "The Arabs ran in every direction shouting: 'Semi! Semi!' to stop the fighting."[19] But not before Colonel Combe was mortally wounded. Saint-Arnaud stood next to him as the first bullet struck: "A simple nervous shudder betrayed his suffering. He began walking toward the breach when he was struck by a second bullet, which produced the same reaction. Without a complaint, without uttering a word, he continued to walk toward the breach."[20]

With a handful of men, Saint-Arnaud plunged into the back streets: "It was a great imprudence," he admitted, "[because] we had not taken a twentieth of the town when it surrendered." But after an initial panic at the sight of his force, the Arabs rushed forward to kiss his clothes and show their submission. Not all accepted defeat and occupation so easily: "Near the Casbah . . . we discovered an awful spectacle," he wrote. "Around two hundred women and children lay broken on the rocks which enclose the town on this side. The Arabs . . . attempted an impossible escape through these precipitous ravines. Terror hurried their steps and made them even more uncertain, and quite a few women, quite a few children perished in this horrible way."[21]

Near the breach, the army was dissolving into chaos: The soldiers who had not taken part in the attack began to flood into the town and pillage everything in sight. Despite the fact that General Joseph Rullière "shouted at the pillagers, threatened to take the most severe measures ... nothing stopped the soldiers. ... The pillaging ... soon spread to the officers and when we evacuated Constantine, as usual the richest and most abundant part of the spoils had been accumulated by the army command and by the staff officers."[22] And there was much to pillage; so confident had the inhabitants been of a successful defense that they had taken no steps to hide valuables: "Everything was pillaged, nothing was respected. The soldiers found coffers full of money."[23] Soon, the French camp resembled a huge market where Jews appeared to buy up many of the most valuable pieces from the ignorant soldiers for a few worthless Turkish copper rubles used by native children in their games. The pillaging was stopped only after three days, and the task of burying the dead in a huge common grave outside the town began. Saint-Arnaud was more than a little bitter that his legionnaires, as well as other corps who had taken part in the storming of Constantine, were ordered to bivouac on the Coudiat-Aty while the staff officers moved in to occupy the most sumptuous houses in town.

Saint-Arnaud's reputation has suffered at the hands of historians, who have tended to see him as someone so churned by ambition that he was willing to do almost anything to advance his career—such as turning out the French parliament on December 2, 1851, in a *coup d'état* that brought Louis-Napoleon Bonaparte to power as Emperor Napoleon III and subsequently resulted in the exile of some of his most illustrious colleagues in the *Armée d'Afrique*. It might be tempting to see Saint-Arnaud's performance during the storming of Constantine as one of the first documented instances of his willingness to build a future on the dead bodies of his legionnaires. After all, Saint-Arnaud did win his "cross" of the Legion of Honor, and Bedeau a promotion to lieutenant colonel, while most of the crosses awarded to his legionnaires were wooden ones. Of a Legion battalion five hundred men strong that marched to Constantine, Major Bedeau had selected one hundred to participate in the second assault wave, of whom twenty-one were killed or wounded. But while one could argue that the legionnaires were exploited for the ambitious ends of their officers, this does not get us very far when we attempt to explain Legion performance. The only evidence we have of what Saint-Arnaud's legionnaires thought of his mad dash through the streets of Constantine comes from the man himself. But the indications are that even he was slightly amazed by their enthusiastic reaction: "My soldiers have declared me brave at the top of their voices," he told his brother, "and even though I did not spare them, for of fifty who were with me, ten are dead and eleven wounded."[24] At one point, a legionnaire named Keller threw himself between Saint-Arnaud and some Turks and paid for it with his life: "The poor boy died for me, because the bullets were aimed in my direction."[25] Such things do happen in combat, especially if the officer is popular. The German Clemens Lamping, who enlisted in the Legion in 1840, found his comrades "for the most part brutal and undisciplined, but ready to encounter anything. They form a band who, under an energetic leader, might do great things."[26] What Saint-Arnaud's experience would seem to suggest is that popular, intrepid, even reckless officers did have the ability to galvanize their legionnaires into extraordinary performance. Saint-Arnaud's legionnaires followed him precisely because he did not spare them.

Constantine does not appear to have been the first time that this new Legion had been noticed after an exceptional combat performance. Saint-Arnaud wrote to his brother in May 1837 that a recently completed expedition ". . . has brought us [the Legion] a great advantage . . . that of making ourselves better known. On the days of the 29th and the 30th [April], the Legion gloriously took its place in the ranks of the army. We received our baptism of fire, and all the regiments who seemed to distance themselves from our *foreignness,* today come up and fraternize."[27] One of the great puzzles of the Legion, however, one of the apparent contradictions that has made the Legion so inexplicable to many, French commanders not the least, is how a force capable of putting on so formidable a performance in battle could display such deplorable garrison manners. The problem for the historian is how to reconcile the obvious bravery of the Legion under fire with inspection reports of the period, most of which were so unfavorable that they led many to wonder if the Legion were worth preserving at all.

As SAINT-ARNAUD SUGGESTED, the foreignness of the Legion was certainly an impediment to its acceptance as a credible fighting unit by the French high command, especially in an era when the French regarded themselves as Europe's best soldiers. As has been seen, the Legion as constituted in 1831 was seen basically as a temporary expedient, a short-term response to a refugee crisis. Shoved off to Spain, the experiment was believed to be at an end. However, the refugees continued to arrive, while Algiers required troops, so the experiment gained a new lease on life almost as soon as it was abandoned. The end of the Carlist War in Spain in 1840 and the arrival of large numbers of refugees over the Pyrenees again reinforced the Legion. French officers might not be expected to bestow anything more than grudging respect upon this corps of mercenaries: "The elements which make up the Foreign Legion are such that one cannot hope that the *esprit de corps* is as uniform there as in a French corps," the Legion's inspector, Lieutenant General Count Alphonse d'Hautpoul, declared in 1841. "Nevertheless, the 1st Regiment has been in existence for several years. It has had several honorable actions of which the memory flatters the corps and have given birth to a love of the flag among officers and NCOs."[28]

D'Hautpoul's observations, while perhaps patronizing, cannot be discounted as mere prejudice or xenophobia, for the evidence suggests that the Legion in this period had serious discipline problems. This was in part a temporary phenomenon that resulted from the rapid expansion of the

Legion to six battalions. Many of the new recruits were Carlist refugees, rustic and unruly recruits who, grouped in separate units, proved difficult to control, especially by cadres who were often hastily assembled from the castoffs of other units.[29] Yet one of the difficulties for the historian is to reconcile many generally favorable comments on the discipline and *esprit de corps* in the Legion recorded by many of the inspecting generals with the long list of problems that they then cite.

All soldiers might on occasion be expected to display high spirits, even unruliness, in barracks. But it was clear that Legion behavior, together with that of the penal *Bataillons d'Afrique*, was often noteworthy: "Discipline must be severe and prompt as infractions are numerous and serious," d'Hautpoul continued. "Drunkenness, selling equipment, acts of insubordination, desertion to the enemy, these are the principal faults which one recognizes among soldiers of the Legion."[30] In fact, the problems enumerated by d'Hautpoul were all of a piece. From its earliest days, observers had noted the Legion's weakness for alcohol: "The excesses of drink are more frequent in the Legion than in French regiments," Brigadier General Dampierre observed in his November 1838 inspection.[31] In the previous year, General Joseph Rullière had attributed the drunkenness of the Legion to excessively strict discipline that "by brutalizing them produces a sort of inertia." Then they would sell pieces of their equipment or uniforms to get money for drink, "on the pretext that this is the only way to get out of the barracks and escape a discipline which is too rough."[32] And, of course, once in the bars and wine shops that abounded in Algeria they could fall victim to unscrupulous merchants who would encourage them to drink more than they could possibly afford and then connive with a civilian "client" who would offer to buy parts of their uniforms to extricate them from their embarrassment. As a result, it was not an uncommon sight in the 1830s to see groups of legionnaires returning to barracks without shoes, shirts or even trousers, but always wearing their high shakos, for this piece of equipment found no buyers on the outside.[33] It is for this reason that the inspector of the 1st Regiment in 1843 recommended a closer "surveillance in their conduct out of barracks."[34]

The extent of the insubordination mentioned by d'Hautpoul is more difficult to assess, although inspectors' comments could reasonably lead one to believe that the Legion existed virtually on the brink of mutiny. Brigadier General Dampierre reported in November 1838 that the officers were trying to "banish in the Foreign Legion the serious infractions which darken the reputation of this corps."[35] In October 1840, Lieutenant General Jean-Paul Schramm reported that disobeying NCOs was a common cause of punishment,[36] while in November 1845, the future Marshal of France Jacques César Randon congratulated the colonel of the 2nd Regiment on the fact that only sixty-five legionnaires had been condemned to "severe penalties" in that year, substantially down from previous years.[37]

Why was discipline such a terrible problem for the Legion? Unlike the situation only fifty years later, when memoirs of legionnaires produced a minor boom in the publishing industry, very few legionnaires in the 1830s and 1840s took the trouble to record their years of service, a poor record of literary output explained in part by the fact that less than half of them could read and write.[38] Therefore, unlike the years before World War I when the Legion again passed through a serious discipline crisis, we seldom hear their side of the story, not the least in inspection reports because, according to Clemens Lamping, "The whole affair is . . . a mere formality. The two gentlemen walk through the ranks, look at reports, and ask here and there a soldier whether he has any complaints to make: after which they get into their carriage, complimenting the Commander in the most flattering terms, on the admirable condition of his regiment. Reclamations made by the soldiers are satisfied in the most summary manner by arrest for groundless complaints. There is unfortunately often cause enough for complaint in all the regiments, but the means of appeal are so complicated that a soldier has the greatest difficulty in making his grievance known. Any commissioned or non-commissioned officer who ventured to assist him would never be forgiven, and must give up all hopes of advancement as long as he lives. Nothing is so odious to the French as a *réclameur* [complainer]."[39]

What has survived are the viewpoints of officers, too many of whom, unfortunately, tended to regard the legionnaires as scum unworthy of humanitarian treatment. The future Marshal François Certain Canrobert, who in 1840 helped to organize the battalion of legionnaires formed among Carlist refugees, condemned "These soldiers of the Foreign Legion, the rejects of the armies of Europe, often assassins and thieves, deserters without scruple who tomorrow become the worst enemies of yesterday's comrades."[40] The future Marshal of France and President of the Third Republic, Patrice MacMahon, recorded that Legion colonel de Sénilhes was convinced that his legionnaires could be kept in line only with "the menace of the cell and of prison."[41] Brigadier General Thierry, who inspected the 1st Regiment in 1844, thought that even this was not enough: "The police and the discipline are severe," he reported. "But the means of repression spelled out in the regulations are insufficient for the type of man who makes up this corps."[42] In this, he simply echoed the view of Lieutenant General François-Marie-Casimir de Négrier, who reported in 1842 that "The inspection of the punishment records proves that there are a large number of NCOs and soldiers upon whom the ordinary disciplinary sanctions no longer have any effect."[43]

Perhaps it is this view, apparently widespread among Legion officers, that such extraordinary men required extraordinary punishments that caused some of them to resort to excessive brutality. Even Saint-Arnaud, whose concern for his men is obvious in his letters and whose affection for them apparently was reciprocated, was guilty of running his saber through the chest of a Spanish legionnaire who was "murmuring and swearing in the ranks."[44] When Lieutenant Colonel Patrice MacMahon's baggage disappeared on campaign, a zealous captain dropped the suspect, a Legion private, down a well, suspended only by ropes tied to two fingers: "After several immersions, the legionnaire, half drowned, finally admitted where he had hidden the remainder of the loot," MacMahon remembered.[45]

Such excessive measures did not pass entirely without comment in the army. In 1842, even the war minister, Marshal Soult, wrote to the governor-general of Algeria, General Thomas Bugeaud, to complain of excessive punishments in the discipline sections of the Foreign Legion, ". . . of a rigorous disciplinary regime, which submits them to the privations of insufficient food, hard and often unjust corporal punishments. This magistrate adds that even taking into account the exaggerated nature of these complaints, the court martial, without going beyond the bounds imposed upon them by a wise and discreet reserve, is obliged to recognize through the depositions even of the NCOs who are charged with the surveillance of the discipline section, that bread and water, *the whip and the cane* are the means employed to correct insubordination and resistance among the disciplinary soldiers. The result is a system of repression which is altogether alien to our French values." So shocked were the military judges by revelations of conditions within the Legion discipline section that they refused to condemn soldiers who had escaped from it for desertion.[46]

Such treatment was not only inhumane, it also undermined military efficiency: "The officers of the *Bataillons d'Afrique,* the discipline companies and of the Foreign Legion all think that if they were not armed with exceptional powers, they would cease to be obeyed and would be assassinated by their soldiers," wrote a French visitor to Algeria in the 1840s. "We understand perfectly the requirements of this discipline, in the middle of such heterogeneous and dangerous elements as those which make up certain regiments, and in a country where war is continuous. We know that normal discipline would be inadequate in such conditions; that one requires there, as in the navy, special repressive measures, and an iron discipline must keep insubordination in check. But, if it is true that things have reached the point to which we have alluded [a reference to severe punishments], is it not evident that discipline would be maintained in the face of the rights of humanity, at the expense of the dignity and the morals of the army? Tortures like those which one inflicts demoralize the soldier, and develop in him deplorable habits which he acquires from this type of half-savage war which one must make in this country."[47]

It is certainly possible, likely in fact, that the Legion contained a number of men who were absolutely impervious to discipline, even of the most rigorous sort. However, it is equally possible that officers and NCOs overreacted to the incorrigible behavior of a few legionnaires by making an excessive and even arbitrary discipline the rule for the entire corps, which was perceived by the rank and file as an injustice. In other words, the strict, even harsh discipline that characterized the Legion in this period actually produced more discipline problems than it cured. And the most serious manifestations of those discipline problems were mutiny and desertion.

Mutiny, or even collective indiscipline, has not been a frequent occurrence in the history of the Legion. However, to occur, it required at least one essential prerequisite—a concentration of men of one nationality. In October 1840, Lieutenant General Schramm repeated the rule laid down by Bernelle five years earlier: "The mixing of men of all nations in the same company prevents national coteries, and serves to create emulation among the men in combat or on marches," he wrote.[48] It was wise advice, which had been ignored in March of that year with disastrous results.

In 1839, the exodus of the defeated Spanish Carlists toward France began. Most swarmed on Perpignan in southern France, where a vast refugee camp had been set up to accommodate them on the garrison drill field. There the government fell back upon the by now familiar expedient of offering enlistment in the Foreign Legion as a means of clearing France of some of these refugees while at the same time providing soldiers for Algeria. A 4th Battalion of the Foreign Legion was officially organized at Pau from these men on October 1, 1839, and its three companies arrived in Algiers in March 1840. The five other companies necessary to bring the battalion to full strength were subsequently organized in Algiers. A 5th Battalion was created at Perpignan on August 28, 1840, and by mid-September it numbered almost six hundred men. Canrobert, who helped to organize the 5th Battalion, believed that many of his men were common criminals, although it is possible that the brutal character of the mountain war they had been fighting for five or six years meant that they simply behaved that way. At the same time, he acknowledged their previous service: "Many were wounded," he wrote, "several badly." Among them was a deserter from the old Foreign Legion in Spain who acted as an interpreter so that training could begin. "These new soldiers, brigands or smugglers, gave me some tough times," Canrobert remembered. "I had to watch them closely. Every day at muster, at least three sorts of crimes committed by one of them was brought to my attention: a theft, a rape or a murder. But I also had some good men . . ."[49]

These Carlist battalions proved to be unhappy experiments. In March 1840, thirty Spaniards of the 4th Battalion plotted to murder all of their officers save three and desert to the Arabs. In the end, only one lieutenant was wounded in the escape. Eight of the mutineers were captured and shot. However, the rebellion was much discussed in the *Armée d'Afrique,* where it was taken as proof that the Legion was not to be trusted. Even Saint-Arnaud, who should have known better, as he was charged with writing the report ("I gave a dramatic turn to the events which pleased everyone"), was mortified: "What confidence can we have in such men?" he wrote to his brother. "We no longer have the enemy to fear, but our own men who assassinate us in the course of duty, who murder our honor by abandoning a post which was confided to us. . . . I am deeply grieved . . ." More to the point, he believed the reputation of the Legion to be irreparably damaged. "The blow, which caught me by surprise, is crushing because I can foresee all the consequences. The Legion is compromised. The fruits of our combats, our watches, our fatigues, perhaps annihilated. Four years of pain, of abnegation and of devotion struck off the calendar of our future. Despite this, I am facing up to the storm. I raise the morale of others. I give strict orders. I take terrible measures, but it is necessary [this is when he stabbed the muttering Spaniard]. . . . I do not fear for myself. . . . But this lost prestige, this handsome reputation of the Legion tarnished by a hundred miserable men. That is what makes me cry like a baby."[50]

While Saint-Arnaud admitted subsequently that the incident in the 4th Battalion blew over fairly rapidly, discipline in the 5th Battalion also appeared to be shaky. "The hope that I placed in the Spanish battalion has unfortunately not been realized," the battalion commander, Major de Lioux, wrote on November 29, 1840. "Hardly had they arrived [in North Africa], than 44 men went over to the enemy with arms and baggage. An officer also disappeared. He left with the funds of the company which he commanded. The Marshal [Valée] immediately ordered the departure of the battalion for Bône." The colonel of the 53rd Infantry Regiment refused to allow the Spanish legionnaires to stand guard duty and considered disarming them. "I kept them for two days as prisoners in my camp," he reported. "Fortunately, they did not take it into their heads to revolt."[51]

This mutiny of 1840 serves to point up the second problem of the Legion—desertion. The mutiny and mass desertion in the Spanish battalions were certainly the result of a combination of exceptional circumstances that included national homogeneity and the fact that they had all been recruited from a defeated army that had its own way of doing things. As Canrobert suggested, they may also have been from the start an exceptionally bad lot, and they had been in the Legion for too short a time (only a matter of weeks) to have absorbed any regimental loyalty. Yet desertion was hardly a new phenomenon in the Legion. On the contrary, inspecting generals had complained since 1831 that desertion and the Legion were inseparable, and as has been seen, desertion from the Legion in Spain became a serious problem after the summer of 1836. The problem was inherited in full measure by the new Legion organizing at Pau, which lost 14.6 percent of its strength to desertion in 1836. According to the inspecting general, the new corps "conserves a tendency to desertion, and the selling of uniforms to get money to buy disguises so they can better avoid the police. The nearness to the frontier, the provocations of Spanish agents have done much to contribute to this state of affairs."[52] Statistics for the period show that desertion posed a significant problem for the Legion, but not a catastrophic one:[53]

Year	Number of Deserters	Strength	Percentage
1836	105	719	14.6
1837	226	2,095	10.8
1838 (Nov)	221	2,743	8.0
1839 (Oct)	232	2,850	8.1
1840 (Oct)	283	4,150	6.8
1841*	292	2,779	10.5
1842 (Nov) 1st reg.	291	2,436	11.9
1843 (Nov) 1st reg.	292	2,482	11.8
1844 (Nov) 1st reg.	287	2,764	10.4
(Sept) 2nd reg.	151	2,726	5.5
1845 (Sept) 1st reg.	199	3,129	6.3
(Nov) 2nd reg.	184	3,285	5.6

* 1841 figures taken from January 1842 report.

Three points should be made about these figures. First, it is not clear if they are complete. The Legion was fragmented into many small garrisons, and inspecting generals may not have had information on all of them. Second, these figures may not represent the real extent of *attempted* desertions. Regulations required a soldier to be absent for six days before he was listed as a deserter. And in Algeria, it might be very difficult for a deserter to avoid detection for a week. Third, while these figures might not have shocked the Duke of Wellington, 11.1 percent of whose infantry regularly took "French leave" in this period,[54] it did indeed scandalize French officers unused to watching substantial numbers of their troops *filer à l'anglaise*. For instance, the 2nd Light Infantry Regiment, which fought beside the Legion at Constantine, rarely counted more than three desertions a year between their arrival in Algeria in 1835 and their departure for France in 1841. In 1837, the year of Constantine, no soldiers deserted. The following year, only one soldier deserted, no soldiers were sent to discipline companies and only two corporals were broken for drunkenness. In 1839, the regiment had a clean slate in Algeria, although there were desertions from the regimental depot in France, presumably among new conscripts.[55] Even the *zouaves*, who were founded at the same time as the Legion and had many organizational problems as it was gradually transformed from a native regiment to one made up exclusively of Frenchmen, recorded a maximum desertion rate of 8 percent in 1838. However, by 1839 its rate had fallen to 2 percent and remained infinitesimal after that.[56]

The question of desertion will be treated more fully in a later chapter. However, in the absence of legionnaires' opinions on desertion, officers in the 1830s and 1840s advanced two theories about its causes. The first was that desertion sprang from unjust and arbitrary discipline. This was the view of General de Négrier, who, writing of the Legion discipline section, condemned ". . . the means which we could not effectively refuse to recognize as altogether alien to our customs, and which the barbarous employment would not even be justified by happy results, because the consequences of such a system would be to increase the number of deserters, and could successively serve as an excuse before a court martial."[57] Count Pierre de Castellane, son of General Victor de Castellane, who commanded the Army of Observation at Perpignan, reckoned that discipline in a normal Legion unit was severe enough: "It takes an iron hand to bend such diverse elements into the same mold," he wrote in 1845. "Also discipline knows no indulgences. Misfortune upon he who disobeys! The court martial is without mercy and justice is prompt."[58]

The view that brutality was a prime cause of desertion in the Legion and that it could be reduced substantially through more humane and sensitive treatment was endorsed by MacMahon. "To command his men, my predecessor believed it necessary to employ exclusively the tough approach," MacMahon wrote. "Rarely did he speak to them without bullying them, calling them by the least flattering names and menacing them with the cells and with prison. For this reason, he had acquired no moral influence upon them and desertions under his command were very frequent. I adopted a completely opposite approach during my command. When I spoke to the men, I let on that I believed that only their desire to fight had caused them to leave their countries, and I never suggested that I doubted their honesty. In this way, I acquired a real influence over them and I seldom had any serious discipline problems."[59] The inspection report for the 2nd Regiment supports MacMahon's version of events: Henri d'Orléans, the duc d'Aumale, complimented MacMahon on building an *esprit de corps* and noted that desertions had almost been cut in half under his command.[60] But it is entirely possible that some officers with difficult or abrasive personalities were intentionally sent to the Legion.[61]

The second, equally plausible, explanation put forth for desertion was that many legionnaires were inherently unstable men, perpetually on the move, who thought nothing of changing sides even in the middle of a campaign: "As the Foreign Legion is made up of deserters from other armies, it is quite normal to see them change sides at the drop of a hat," wrote Canrobert, expressing an exaggerated but widely held view on the origins of legionnaires. "As a drunkard will always be a drunkard, so a deserter moves shamelessly and for the most petty of pretexts from one army to another."[62]

A third explanation for desertion, which was seldom mentioned directly, might be a feeling of injustice at the often unnecessarily rigorous conditions of service imposed on the Legion. The high sickness rates that put large numbers of legionnaires in the hospital and which was directly attributable to the unhealthy garrisons—like the Maison Carrée—that they were forced to occupy must have caused resentment. It was common knowledge that the Legion often drew the least salubrious garrisons. This might have caused some men to flee the prospect of a slow death in the hospital. On the other hand, it is also possible that a low desertion rate corresponded with a large number of hospitalizations. Statistics are fragmentary, but when desertion rates were lowest, the numbers of men in hospital or listed as suffering from "fever," as in the 1st Regiment in 1839 and 1840 and in the 2nd Regiment in 1844 and 1845, were extremely high.[63]

Yet desertion was not an option to be undertaken lightly. The major difficulty with desertion in Algeria was that there were few places to desert to. A man walking to Algiers, Oran or Bône, especially if he was wearing a uniform or part of a uniform, would quickly be apprehended. Even if he exchanged his uniform for civilian clothes, he might be stopped by authorities and asked for his passport, which was required even for internal travel. This left desertion to the enemy. The leader of the Algerian resistance, Abd el-Kader, offered sanctuary to French deserters, although his amnesty was not always honored by his supporters, who had a disconcerting tendency to submit any soldier who fell into their hands to the death of a thousand cuts. But even if a deserter reached the Emir's camp with his head still on his shoulders, life there did not always live up to expectations. The Frenchman Marius Garcin, who served Abd el-Kader as his armaments advisor, wrote that Legion deserters, mostly Germans and Italians

arrive with joy in their hearts, come to offer their services to the sworn enemy of the French. But fifteen days do not go by before they are torn by terrible regrets. They would give up half of their life if they could return to their flag. Several told me that if it were simply a question of five years in chains, they would return tomorrow, but there is no longer time. Most enlist in Abd el-Kader's militia. Several prefer the artillery. Others just wander from tribe to tribe, earning a living as practitioners of the medical arts, about which they know nothing. A few escape via Tunis or Morocco, but most die miserably, or are assassinated during their travels.[64]

Saint-Arnaud interviewed an Italian who deserted for six months before returning to the Legion: "[Abd el-Kader] does not pay his troops, he feeds them badly, clothes them in rough garments, but he has an army," he was told. "He has two regular battalions made up of French and foreign deserters commanded by a deserter, an artillery corporal. He also has a regular [cavalry] squadron."[65]

According to Count Pierre de Castellane, Legion deserters who turned themselves in did not invariably face a harsh punishment. "About two months ago, two deserters came in, one from the *zéphirs* [the penal unit] and the other from the Foreign Legion," he wrote in 1843.

The latter one is named Glockner. He is a Bavarian, son of an ex-war contractor in French service, nephew of one of the most prominent military people of Bavaria. His story almost reads like a novel. He first entered the military college of Munich, then following several thoughtless acts was sent to a regiment of Household Cavalry. But his ardent imagination, his love of adventure was soon to draw him to new follies. He deserted and went to France. Having received a cool reception, like all deserters, he was enlisted in the Foreign Legion. Hardly had he arrived in Africa than his deception was even more cruel. And, always drawn toward the desire for the unknown which tormented him, one morning he went over to the Arabs. He remained there for three years. . . . He returned to us like the prodigal son, bemoaning his indiscretions, weeping for his family, for his father especially, and asking for the favor to be enlisted as a French soldier. When we spoke to him of returning to the Legion: 'Oh! No, I beg of you, don't send me to the Legion,' he replied. 'Send me into a French regiment, in your zouaves whose name is known throughout Europe. I will not disappoint you.' We enlisted him as an Arab.[66]

Not all deserters were smitten with remorse or allowed to perish anonymously in the *bled*. One of the most celebrated deserters of this period was a Frenchman named Moncel, a Hercules of a man who terrorized his comrades as much as the enemy. After having been punished by his superior for slaughtering wounded Arabs, he deserted to the enemy and conspired to draw his ex-comrades into an ambush from which few escaped. Among the bodies was discovered that of the offending superior, completely stripped, with "2 novembre 1836 Moncel" carved on his chest. Despite his fierce hatred of the French, Abd el-Kader found Moncel to be something of a liability and conspired with the chief of the Arab bureau—created to govern the tribes under French jurisdiction—at Blida to betray him to the French, who took him to Algiers and shot him, swearing and threatening to the very last. Canrobert claims that Moncel was a Legion deserter.[67] His interesting life and almost majestic death makes him entirely worthy of that great corps. Alas, by the autumn of 1836 when Moncel was carving insults in his ex-sergeant's chest, the Legion had been out of Algeria for over a year. Moncel was, in fact, a deserter from the *spahis*, a regiment of native cavalry.

All of this might suggest that many, if not most, of the Legion's discipline problems might be traced to poor or tactless leadership rather than to the incorrigible nature of the legionnaires. This was the opinion of Lieutenant General Schramm, who, in October 1840, praised the combative qualities of the Legion, the "glory" that they had won during the last expeditions, and wrote that it "takes second place to no other corps in bravery and in resolution."[68] Perhaps he was referring to the Legion's performance in the Mouzaia pass in May 1840, or in the Bois des Oliviers in June of that year. But more likely Schramm was referring to the siege of Miliana, when a battalion of the Legion, one from the 3rd Light Infantry Regiment, forty-five artillerymen and a detachment of engineers held off thousands of Arabs throughout the brutal summer of 1840. A burning sirocco out of the Sahara drove temperatures to 120 degrees as the French troops struggled to repulse repeated Arab attacks against the crumbling fortifications. The garrison was so decimated by disease brought on by fetid water and strict rationing, which soon limited them to one meal per day, that the colonel ordered dummies made that were dressed in the uniforms of the dead and placed on the walls to give the impression of strength (an act which perhaps inspired P. C. Wren, the author of *Beau Geste*). When the Arabs began to count the graves, he had several dead placed in each hole, but the rotting corpses soon pushed up the ground. By October 4, when a relief column under General Nicolas Changarnier finally reached Miliana, only 600 of the original 1,232 men in the garrison remained alive, and of these only 150 were capable of fighting. The soldiers were emaciated, barely able to stand, and some actually died on guard duty. So bad was their state that two months later only seventy of those rescued had survived, including Captain Bazaine, who had already fought with the Legion through the Spanish campaign. Only twenty-five legionnaires had deserted during the siege.[69]

Indeed, the uneven quality of Legion leadership offers one possible explanation as to why a corps that performed so well in battle labored under such a poor reputation among officers in the *Armée d'Afrique*. For beneath a crust of officers of incontestable worth—MacMahon, Saint-Arnaud, Bazaine, Bedeau, Collineau, Vinoy, Espinasse, Mayran, Lacretelle, Luzy-Pélissac, Mellinet, d'Autmarre, all future generals—who, in the opinion of Clemens Lamping, ". . . look upon [the Legion] as a short cut to advancement,"[70] inspecting generals in the 1830s suggested that many of the rest were little better than average. The main complaint leveled against the officer corps of the Legion was that many were too old for active service. Of course, this was true of the entire French army, which was fairly top-heavy with Napoleonic veterans, most of whom mercifully began to disappear in the 1840s. Canrobert argued that a concentration of older officers was fatal to performance in the harsh campaign conditions of Algeria: "One cannot stress enough . . . the importance of having young officers on campaign. . . . Under an energetic and brilliant leader, the least acclimatized troops are capable of heroism. Under tired leaders, the best soldiers are like a herd being led to the slaughterhouse. They are ready to die if they don't run, but incapable of virile acts."[71]

The Legion owed its good battle performance, as at Constantine, essentially to the fact that both officers and soldiers were rigorously selected. Those left behind were accused of being bad administrators, having "little education," or "lacking command experience."[72] In addition, as a general rule officers in this period took little interest in the welfare of their troops.[73] And while this may have been less important in more homogeneous corps, in a unit as diverse as the Legion, many of whose soldiers had been cast adrift by life and who as a consequence were disoriented and psychologically fragile, it could prove disrupting indeed.

But the complaints did not stop there. Lieutenant General Schramm reported that the professional knowledge of Legion officers was "very weak. They hardly concern themselves with their theory. They are very backward in the study and application of military regulations." Several, he claimed, had backgrounds that were *"peu honorable."*[74] In their defense, it must be said that the army in Algeria had a very practical orientation and was little concerned with mastering the sort of theoretical war that preoccupied officers in France. Also, a fair percentage of the officers were foreigners and therefore less well grounded in French military practice. For instance, the 2nd Regiment in 1844 contained thirteen captains, seven lieutenants and four second lieutenants of foreign nationality.[75]

One of the more serious charges leveled at the officer corps of the Legion was that they failed to supervise the NCOs, a complaint that would continue to be voiced, not least by legionnaires, throughout much of the Legion's history. Inspecting generals found many Legion NCOs drunken, poorly trained, too old, sometimes sent into the Legion from other units as a punishment, and even capable of "exploiting the soldier for their own pleasures and unbridled passions."[76] The lack of supervision and the often indifferent quality of the cadres was bound to be felt further down in the form of poor training. In 1840, Schramm declared that training was so neglected in the Legion that "They are barely even shown how to fire their rifles, because there is no [basic] training camp."[77] Lamping confirmed Schramm's accusation—upon enlistment, "I was asked whether I knew how to load and fire, and on my replying in the affirmative, I was, without further question, transferred to the third battalion of the Legion. . . ."[78]

Therefore, the Legion in 1840, like much of the French army in North Africa, appears to have been sifting for a purpose and a direction. The absence of any coherent strategy of conquest on the French side, of any clear mission to rally spirits and channel energies, translated into poor training, often limp leadership and a general deficiency of morale in Legion units scattered over Algeria in isolated posts in which sickness and desertion rates were high. And this at a time when its adversaries appeared to be more than holding their own, and in some areas even growing stronger. It was clear that the French needed to take a new direction; otherwise, their African enterprise would prove a stagnating and expensive one. That new direction would be provided by General Thomas Bugeaud.

Chapter 4

LA CASQUETTE
DU PERE BUGEAUD

AFTER A DECADE in North Africa, the French occupation was in a perilous condition. Despite individual successes like the creation of the zouaves and the Legion, the French had failed to adapt their military system to the demands of North African warfare. Under the dynamic leadership of Abd el-Kader, the North African resistance had turned their traditional hit-and-run attacks, ambushes or even sieges of isolated French garrisons into a fairly coherent strategic system. At first the French adapted poorly to what was, for them, a new form of warfare, by scattering their forces in out-posts such as Miliana where they could be isolated and overwhelmed, or where they dropped like flies from disease. Then, in 1840, things began to change.

The nomination of Thomas Bugeaud as governor-general in 1840 was to alter radically the way the French army did business in Algeria. Fifty-six years had done little to soften Bugeaud's almost permanent look of stern determination. A strong chin, a square Roman nose, a face cratered by smallpox and a pair of stern blue eyes set beneath bushy brows made him look, Saint-Arnaud believed, as if he had been "carved in granite."[1] An occasional smile and a bald crown with a border of white hair that still contained traces of its original red were the only features that hinted at a milder, almost grandfatherly quality, which Clemens Lamping recognized when Bugeaud inspected the Legion in 1841: "[He] was very gracious," Lamping wrote.

He appears to be about fifty, and has an air of great determination and
coolness. He is of middle size and strongly built; his face is much sun-burnt,
but pleasing; and he would be taken for a younger man than he is, did not
his snow-white hair betray his age. Bugeaud is a man of restless activity,
and keeps everyone alert by his continued presence. At three every morning
he gives audience, to which all who have any complaint are to be admitted.[2]

If Bugeaud looked as if he had raised bluntness to the level of a moral principle, this was no exercise in role playing. He was no pampered political general, but a man who had seen life from the bottom. The French Revolution had destroyed his childhood, scattered his family and confiscated his inheritance. Because he was an aristocrat—albeit a backwoods one—officials of the Terror had imprisoned him before he was ten. He never lost those rustic qualities bequeathed to him by his early education, which consisted largely of hunting, fishing and exchanging blows with peasant lads in his native Périgord in southwestern France, qualities tempered to steely hardness by his years campaigning against *guerrilleros* and Wellington's redcoats in Spain. In 1815, Colonel Bugeaud was denounced for having rallied to Napoleon during the Hundred Days and retired from the army. Therefore, he turned to practice that other passion of his life, farming. A pioneer in agricultural experimentation, he never ceased to preach that "After God, your wife and children, it is clover you must adore." And even as governor-general in Algeria, he continued to repatriate money from raids to Périgord for agricultural improvements.[3] Reintegrated into the army with his rank of colonel in September 1830, he was promoted brigadier general (*maréchal de camp*) on April 2, 1831, soon after which he was elected to the Chamber of Deputies.

Bugeaud's strong opinions, usually expressed in a "corporal's language," and volcanic temper were bound to make him the focus of controversy. One of his first soldierly duties was to guard the duchesse du Berry, mother to the Bourbon pretender to the throne, who was arrested and confined in a chateau at Blaye near Bordeaux after she attempted to raise a proroyalist rebellion in western France. This task caused him to be both belittled by the left and excoriated as a renegade by aristocratic supporters of the Bourbons. However, by undertaking this politically unpopular task, Bugeaud confirmed his usefulness to King Louis-Philippe and assured his future under the new regime. Ironically, during the 1830s Bugeaud was also one of France's most outspoken opponents of the adventure into which France had plunged in Africa—ironic not only because he condemned an enterprise with which his name was later to be most closely associated, but also because on this issue he made common cause with the liberals, whom he despised. The extreme left especially never forgave Bugeaud his harsh repression of the April 1834 insurrection in Paris, which resulted in the massacre of several innocent civilians by soldiers in the rue Transnonain, an incident immortalized by French artist Honoré Daumier in a popular lithograph. *"Massacreur de la rue Trans-nonain"* was one of the epithets Bugeaud was awarded by his enemies on the left, and not necessarily the most unflattering. But Bugeaud was not the sort of man to take an insult lying down—he demanded satisfaction when a popular young liberal deputy, Charles Dulong, had the effrontery to call him a "jailer" during a parliamentary debate in 1834. As the offended party, Bugeaud exercised his option to put the first shot cold-bloodedly into the brain of his unfortunate adversary, who never recovered from his coma and died several hours later. After this, his detractors usually preferred to express their uncomplimentary opinions anonymously or in private.[4]

And well they might! Canrobert wrote that Bugeaud's reputation had preceded him when he arrived in Algeria for the first time in 1836. However, nothing had prepared them for the scene he pitched when, in the middle of a route march, a courier arrived with a packet that included a newspaper with an article critical of Bugeaud. The general halted his troops, drew the entire division into one vast square, and, placing himself in the middle, "walked backwards and forwards, livid and trembling with rage, shouting a string of oaths and insults. Then he started to read some lines from a newspaper article in which he was called a hard and boastful leader, as incompetent and cowardly before the enemy as he was brave with words. . . . Without pausing for breath, he raised his head: 'Which one of you is the depraved person,' he said, 'who is the scamp, who is the animal!'—I leave out the most vulgar—'who dared to write such a piece on me? I'm sure he's among you. . . . Identify yourself! He won't find his general before him, but a man, his equal, named Bugeaud, who will run him through with his sword!' " Everyone watched this astounding performance in stupefied silence, not sure whether it was a joke or whether their commander had reverted to the state of a semidemented sergeant-major. After a very long silence, Bugeaud launched into a brief diatribe against journalists and then ordered the march to resume.[5] In fact, Bugeaud's little performance was less absurd than it seemed. In the volatile atmosphere following the 1830 revolution, some officers had denounced their superiors in anonymous articles in opposition newspapers. No doubt Bugeaud sought to discourage similar excursions into the world of hackery by officers in his command.

Bugeaud's objections to France's invasion of Algeria were twofold and reflected his major interests in life: "I can tell you," he explained before his parliamentary colleagues, ". . . after having seen Algiers, that it is worthless, both for crops and for war, and that sooner or later, we shall have to leave it whether we like it or not."[6] He was correct, of course, but about a century off in his calculations. As a farming man, he believed that "The Regency is not cultivatable," although later as governor-general he was to do his best to encourage European settlement and even a "model farm" manned by ex-soldiers who had stayed on as colonists.[7]

However, it was his views on war that were of immediate interest to the Legion. As a soldier, he recognized the remarkable similarity between the military problem the French faced in Algeria and that which he had witnessed in Spain between 1808 and 1814: How does a modern army encumbered with all of the impedimenta required for a campaign in Europe manage to fight efficiently in a roadless, waterless terrain against a mobile, elusive enemy? He provided part of the answer in 1836 when sent with a division to reinforce the French camp at Tafna, which had been besieged by Abd el-Kader. Canrobert was present when the general called the officers into his tent and lectured them on their mistakes: "You drag thousands of wagons and heavy artillery with you which slows your movements," he told them. "Rather than surprise the Arabs with rapid, offensive marches, you stay on the defensive, marching slowly. Your enemies follow you and attack at their convenience. All this is going to change!" After explaining how he had operated against Spanish guerrillas in Aragon, he laid down his new order of battle: "To begin with, no more heavy artillery, no more of these heavy wagons, no more of these enormous forage trains. . . . The convoys will be on mule back and the only cannons permitted will be light ones." Despite the heat, when he emerged from Bugeaud's tent Canrobert felt as if he had just stepped out of a cold shower. The overwhelming opinion among the officers was that, by abandoning his heavy artillery, Bugeaud had just set out a recipe for collective suicide. After a private conclave, the officers sent their most senior colonel to talk some sense into the newly arrived general. Bugeaud sent him packing.[8]

It proved a wise decision. Only a few days later, Bugeaud surprised the Emir with the flexibility of his newly mobile columns, feinting up a heavily defended gorge and then moving by a more circuitous route onto a plateau above the Sikkak River. When Abd el-Kader recovered enough to attack, Bugeaud formed his division into a V, confusing the Arabs, who were accustomed to attacking simultaneously the front and rear guards of the etiolated French columns. The Arabs were repulsed by massed infantry fire rather than by heavy artillery—he had introduced them to an old trick used by harassed French troops in Spain, which consisted of cutting a musket ball into four parts and ramming it down the barrel on top of the already introduced ball to create a sort of small-arms "grapeshot," very useful against an enemy that liked to work in close, at knife-point. Bugeaud then ordered his men to drop their packs and counterattack, driving a large number of Arab soldiers over a bluff to their deaths in the Sikkak River below. Another five hundred, cornered at the foot of a rock outcropping, surrendered, the first time the French had bagged so many POWs.[9]

When, in 1840, Bugeaud apparently underwent a change of heart and returned as governor-general, he transformed his tactical success on the Sikkak into a strategic system. At the same time, his victory in 1836 had taught Abd el-Kader the futility of assailing massed French firepower. If anything, the Emir became even more elusive, refusing battle on anything other than his own terms. Therefore, Bugeaud found that he could no longer count on the Arabs to attack him. He had to make his columns even more mobile, more rapid, able to exist for days on short rations while they climbed into the desiccated hills of Algeria in search of the enemy. If the Algerians refused to fight, then he would make war on their livelihoods— the *razzia,* a form of basic economic warfare that assumed that even an Arab would submit when he could no longer eat. The entire *Armée d'Afrique* was obliged to adapt to these new methods. It would be a difficult transition, not the least for the Legion.

The French system before Bugeaud consisted of scattering forces in fixed garrisons surrounded by blockhouses. In 1842, Louis Lamborelle, a legionnaire from Belgium, found that half of his battalion remained in Bougie housed in wooden sheds waiting to rotate every fourteen days or so with the other half, which guarded the outlying blockhouses.[10] Lamping described these blockhouses as usually two-story affairs constructed of oak planks sent from France and thick enough to stop a musket ball, assembled on high ground around the main coastal towns. The larger ones were surrounded by a ditch and wall, and might have "two cannons and some wall pieces, which are of great service." Combat usually consisted of the natives shouting "a torrent of friendly epithets, such as 'hahluf' [swine], etc., which is quickly followed by a shower of balls. We are no less civil in our turn, allowing them to approach within a short distance, when we treat them to a volley of musketry and a few discharges from the field pieces; whereupon they usually retire somewhat tranquillized but still vehement in abuse. We of course have much the best of it behind our walls and ditches, but from time to time some of us are wounded or killed." More determined attacks might require the use of grenades: "I need not add that on these occasions every one does his duty," concluded Lamping, "for each fights for what he values most, namely his head."[11]

However, the outcome might be quite different if the North Africans were able to ambush a party outside the blockhouses, as happened to a group of legionnaires in May 1841 near Algiers. Lamping's company, marching to the sound of the guns, arrived too late:

... [T]heir bodies still lay as they fell, side by side, and there was not one among them that had not received several wounds. The number of dead and wounded horses scattered around showed how bravely they had fought. The Hadjutes had, as usual, carried away their fallen comrades. Of the fifty soldiers who had left the blockhouse one only escaped who, having been wounded at the beginning of the fight, had fallen among some thick brushwood, where he had lain concealed . . . [and] thus been a spectator of the whole of this horrid scene, and had been forced to look on whilst the Hadjutes massacred his comrades and finally cut off their heads, which they bore away as trophies hanging to their saddle bows. . . . During the whole *way home I did not hear a single song nor one coarse jest, of which there were generally no lack; even the roughest and most hardened characters were shaken by that which they had just seen. Every one reflected that the fate of their comrades might one day be their own.*[12]

The siege of Miliana demonstrates just how dreadful life could become in one of these posts. And while Miliana was perhaps a particularly grisly example, even in posts that were not under constant threat of attack existence was barely tolerable. Poor, not to say inedible, rations meant that soldiers usually preferred to forage for roots, and put dogs, cats and even rats in the cooking pot rather than rely on the bacon distributed by the *intendance,* which provoked violent diarrhea. And while accounts of life in these isolated garrisons in the 1830s and 1840s are scarce, those that exist for later periods suggest that these outposts were also torn by human conflict brought on by boredom—fighting, insanity, even suicides, self-mutilation and homosexuality.

When he arrived in Algeria in 1840, Bugeaud found the army wasting away. In December of that year he questioned the official statistics, which put the number of deaths among the soldiers for 1840 at eight thousand. This, he insisted, could only refer to the province of Algiers, excluding Constantine and Oran. A few days later, Soult agreed that the sanitary state of the army in Algeria was "truly disastrous."[13] This was apparent to Lamping when he visited a comrade in a military hospital only to find "a host of ghostlike beings crawling slowly along in their grey capotes and white night-caps . . . their glazed eyes looked sadly out of their sallow emaciated faces, all of which bore traces of misery, and most of melancholy and homesickness. . . . Several times I heard the mournful exclamation, *'Ma belle France!'* Poor devils! Many of them will never see fair France again."[14]

Bugeaud's plan was to get his troops out of these pestilential posts and put them on the road, a plan that had the full backing of War Minister Soult: "The war against the Arabs cannot be conducted as it would be in Europe," he wrote to Bugeaud in January 1841. "The poor results of the regular military operations have demonstrated this conclusively. Therefore, place the troops under your command according to the system which is most likely to break all resistance and pacify the country as quickly as possible."[15] On the face of it, this was all to the good, if for no other reason than it would improve the health and morale of the soldiers. The obvious question to ask, however, is, How well was the Legion able to adapt to this new way of warfare?

The "new Legion" had grown steadily since the first battalion arrived in Africa in 1837. By December 30, 1840, it numbered five battalions and was large enough for the government to order the Legion split into two separate regiments on that date. The 1st Regiment of the Foreign Legion was stationed in the province of Algiers, and from 1843 extended its activity into the hinterland of Oran to the west. The 2nd Regiment remained in Constantine province in the east. Despite the fact that national battalions had been abandoned in principle, in practice the two regiments developed distinctly different characters, with the 1st Regiment composed of a majority of "men of the North," while the 2nd Regiment specialized in Mediterranean recruits. Until the Crimean campaign of 1854, the two regiments were to lead an almost totally separate existence. Both were kept about equally busy in their respective spheres of operation until the surrender of Abd el-Kader in 1847, after which the 2nd Regiment in the Constantinois saw the bulk of the action, fighting twenty-seven engagements between 1847 and 1852, compared to only one major action in Algeria and three in eastern Morocco in 1852 for the 1st Regiment.[16]

Despite the growth and reorganization of the Legion, its new commander-in-chief behaved like a man who had just taken delivery of a consignment of damaged goods. In an 1842 report never before reproduced, Bugeaud complained that the Legion was so inefficient that it should be abolished: "The principal cause for worry is in the Foreign Legion," he wrote to Soult on June 18.

I seize this opportunity, Monsieur le Maréchal, to tell you that, in my opinion, the Foreign Legion will never offer a force upon which we can count. It has some very good officers and a few good NCOs. But the composition of the soldiers is detestable—one can count on them neither in a serious combat, nor for sustained marches. They fight badly; they march badly; they desert often. They try whenever the opportunity presents itself, and sell to the enemy their arms, their munitions, and their uniforms and equipment. The first regiment seems better than the second, and one was even unhappy with it around Mascara. I took with me a battalion made up of elite companies, and I was quite satisfied with them. But these companies were select, made up of only the healthiest men. And, despite this, they marched less well than the others.

I seriously believe, Monsieur le Maréchal, that we should cease to have such soldiers in Africa, for they are more expensive than French regiments, and they are far from projecting the same image. There is not one general officer who does not prefer to march with two of our good battalions than with five of the Foreign Legion. This troop is therefore more costly than the others because twice the numbers offers fewer guarantees.

Therefore, I propose that the Foreign Legion no longer be recruited, and successively to combine one battalion with another, then one regiment with the other, and eventually disband this regiment once its strength is too small to maintain it. The officers will be gradually reassigned in the army, or retired, or mustered out on medical grounds. Unless, however, the spirit of the 1st regiment changes under the beneficial command of Colonel Despinoy, or through a more scrupulous recruitment, because it would be less numerous. Keeping only one regiment would assuredly be enough.[17]

Of course, Bugeaud was never a man to mince words or nuance his views. However, it is patently clear from his report that he considered the Legion deficient in at least two categories essential to his new style of warfare—marching and fighting. It must be said that life under Bugeaud was no bed of roses. The rigors for Europeans of campaigning in a land as harsh as that of North Africa were daunting. Canrobert mentions that when Bugeaud launched his forces on the relatively short marches that preceded the Battle of the Sikkak River, he was forced to shed two regiments newly arrived from France simply because they could not keep up.[18]

When he returned in 1840, things if anything got tougher, because he was now commander-in-chief in Africa and therefore able to implement his system countrywide. And because the native resistance now had to be avidly pursued, often for great distances, Bugeaud made no concessions to his troops: "If we allow ourselves to be dominated by the very natural desire, very good in most cases, to save the troops, we would rarely arrive at good results," he wrote. ". . . If we hunt and ruin Abd el-Kader, our infantry and our cavalry will have plenty of time to recuperate."[19] The future general Charles-Nicolas Lacretelle, who joined the Legion as a second lieutenant fresh from Saint-Cyr in 1843, was certain that he marched at least 250 days a year: "My life in those days was that of all troop commanders, walking a lot, without seeing much or rather without understanding much of what I saw," he remembered. "Usually when we arrived in a town or made camp, the first thing that was said to us was that we were leaving at dawn."[20]

Louis Lamborelle recounted that Bugeaud's infantrymen were said to require "the thighs of a buck, the heart of a lion . . . and the stomach of an ant." While Bugeaud ordered much to be carried on muleback, mules were relatively scarce beasts in Algeria, so the "soldier camels" shouldered the rest, and that could be substantial: cartridge belt and a rigid rectangular leather pack containing eight days' rations, forty bullets, spare boots, shirts, underwear and socks, sewing and musket-cleaning kits, fork, several knives, at least two spoons, boot polish, soap and whatever condiments were required for the cooking. Outside the pack hung a groundcloth, sheepskin, tent half, liter canteen, tin cup and "a chamberpot in which the soldier cooked his supper."[21] To this already substantial load, one must add a musket, bayonet and often sticks, which were picked up en route for the evening campfire and placed on top of the pack. Most soldiers also carried a walking stick, which served three purposes: to help climb steep hills; when placed beneath, to support the pack during halts on the march (throwing off the pack or lying on the ground to take the weight off the shoulders was the sign of a raw recruit); and as a tent pole.[22]

Thus equipped, the soldiers marched out of their garrisons, usually before dawn. Hardly had they departed than bugle calls ordered a halt so that the tail of the column could catch up before it lurched off again. Once on the road, marching discipline relaxed, so that the soldiers were allowed to talk, sing, smoke or exchange friendly banter with the officers, some of whom were on horseback, most of whom walked beside their troops, collars open, heads covered with a white hood or a handkerchief dangling behind their *képi*. The general led the column, followed by the cavalry. A company of sappers came next, leading mules laden with their tools. Then came a portion of the infantry, followed by the artillery, their mountain guns lashed onto the backs of stolid mules; the ambulance flying a red flag; and the convoy carrying the regimental baggage and supplies, which usually included a small herd of cattle to be consumed during the march, all under the watchful gaze of NCOs. More infantry closed the march, followed by the rear guard accompanied by mules carrying *cacolets*—metal stretchers introduced in the 1840s to carry sick and wounded.[23]

If the march was a long one, a pause of an hour and a half would be ordered at midday, the *grande halte* when the soldiers would brew up coffee. However, in arid regions where water was scarce, dry soldiers' biscuits might be crumbled in the grounds and the coffee "eaten." By afternoon, heat and fatigue had usually drained the men of all energy except that required to complain. "This heat takes away all appetite," Lamping wrote, "and one longs for nothing but a shady tree and a gushing fountain. All else is vain." If the column encountered a stream, the troops dissolved into a jostling mob: "General orders and sentinels are of no avail; what is punishment or even death to the soldier at this moment! He would rather die by a bullet than by thirst."[24]

After what seemed an eternity, the column heaved up at a spot where a staff officer accompanied by several Arab irregulars had traced out a camp—a square with the infantry in double file beside their arms on the outside, the cavalry, artillery and baggage in the middle. The soldiers were ordered to break ranks, and everyone scattered to their tasks. Each squad sent a man to fill the water bottles at a muddy well and another to build a fire to brew up the coffee—if, that is, it had not been "eaten" at midday—and others began to set up the three-man tents. One man was sent to collect the squad's meat ration, which was distributed by an NCO who, his back turned to the assembled soldiers, pointed to a ration composed ideally of 320 grams per man and shouted, *"Pour qui?"* (For whom?) A soldier claimed it and took it back to his camp, where the pot full of rice, onions and bacon was already boiling over the fire. If there was no water, the rations were fried in beef or lamb fat. The beef, freshly killed, was too tough for immediate consumption. It was usually boiled all night and consumed before departure the next morning. Sometimes, if food was scarce, the soldiers were forced to experiment. Lamborelle found that coagulated beef's blood spread on a dry biscuit made a passable meal, while experienced soldiers were able to identify wild carrots and potatoes, or leaves and herbs from which a passable salad could be concocted.[25] "We cannot be accused of gluttony, at any rate," Lamping insisted.[26]

Once the evening "soup" was consumed, the soldiers had a brief moment to play cards or lotto, to wash or repair clothing or clean their weapons, before the first watch was set out and taps sounded—"Those savage, sharp notes thrown out into the silence of the camp had something of the sublime," Lamborelle wrote.[27] Lamping remembered the hyenas whose "hoarse croaking bark" was "my regular lullaby."[28] Each battalion sent a company to man the outposts, where the practice was to light a fire and then withdraw to observe if anyone came between them and the flame.

Less sublime was reveille, when bugles and drums strategically placed among the tents would drive even the heaviest sleeper into the open. If the commander were in a cheerful mood, he would order the band to play popular dances while the troops bolted down their breakfast of meat that had been stewing all night, struck their city of tents, and frantically searched for stray pieces of equipment in the half-light of dawn. The corporals called the roll in each squad and, the report sent up the chain of command, the march resumed, the band playing "La casquette du père Bugeaud," a song allegedly made popular in the *Armée d'Afrique* by the *zouaves* after Bugeaud rushed from his tent during a night alert wearing his cotton night cap.[29] The verses were left to the imagination of the troops, but the refrain was sacred: "*As-tu vu la casquette, la casquette, as-tu vu la casquette du père Bugeaud?*"

It all sounds like good clean fun, a sort of July Monarchy version of Boy Scouting. In fact, this sort of campaign life called for enormous stamina, which many men did not possess. If, for instance, the French column were hot on the trail of an Arab force, the pace could be unrelenting. Lacretelle said that his legionnaires sometimes pursued the enemy so closely that "the dung from their horses was still steaming."[30] If the march were pressed, many simply could not keep up, especially if they were suffering from fever or diarrhea. In January 1842, General d'Hautpoul complained that enlistment standards were too low and that many legionnaires lacked the ability to carry out long marches. General Fabviez repeated the complaint in November of that same year, adding that the government should stop enlisting men whose only qualification for the martial life was their status as political refugees who might trouble the public order in France.[31] General Randon made the same point in 1845.[32] Nor were the soldiers the only ones to fall by the wayside. Lacretelle noted that "*les fatigues*" of campaigning in North Africa were such that two of the three classmates who had volunteered with him for the Legion from Saint-Cyr in 1843 had died within a year.[33]

Night alerts, which were frequent, or, in the south, the braying of camels shattered the short nights of men already exhausted after a hard day's march. The south was especially dreaded because of thirst, ". . . that horrible fever which overwhelmed me for several hours," Lamborelle wrote. "I was not only thirsty in my mouth and in my throat. My entire body was thirsty. The only thing I swallowed was air which heated up passing through my mouth and burned my gullet. I fell down and lay behind a sand dune. I saw death as the only solution to my physical suffering, when a friend (should I say a brother?) appeared at my side. . . . [He] put his last mouthful of water to my lips. Then he got me up with several encouraging words which are never lost on a soldier. I got up with his help. He took my pack on his back, and I was able to rejoin my company."[34]

If any legionnaires were tempted to malinger, they might be dissuaded by a visit to the surgeon. MacMahon's doctor in the 2nd Regiment in 1843 was a Pole named Ridzeck, "a good warrior but a mediocre doctor," who systematically bled to death seventeen men suffering from heatstroke. "Realizing that his method was not working, he took an ax and split open the skull of one of the dead to understand the cause of the problem." According to MacMahon, Ridzeck had better success subsequently using ether to treat sunstroke, but his reputation could hardly have encouraged business.[35]

This interminable marching, day after blistering day, tormented by heat, hunger and thirst, all in pursuit of an evasive foe, eventually took its toll. Lamping claimed that "The troops were so thoroughly disheartened" during these marches "that many of the soldiers destroyed themselves for fear of falling into the hands of the Bedouins." Still others ". . . begin as usual to invent the most extraordinary theories, some asserting that the General has sold us to Abd el-Kader." Most, however, grew ". . . indignant . . . and railed at the cruelty of the General, who they said sacrificed his men to a mere caprice. . . . I several times heard the exclamation, 'I wish that the Bedouins would grow out of the ground by millions and put an end to us all.' The fatigues and hardships of this kind of war at last produce perfect indifference to life, which becomes a mere burden."[36] One French sergeant-major serving in the 1st Battalion of the 1st Regiment of the Legion in 1843 contemplated "putting an end to a life which is made up of deceptions, boredom, privations and misery, but more than once when I was about to put an end to myself, one thing held me back; it's that I have always heard that only a coward puts an end to life." Nevertheless, he reported that the Legion offered a demoralizing existence: "Since I came to this damned Africa, I have been constantly outside," he reported. ". . . I spent six months continually outside and always marching in the greatest heat and, apart from a few Bedouins which we skewer with our bayonets because they are not worth a bullet, we rarely have the opportunity to fire our weapons. The life in Africa today is limited to fatigues, to miseries and to privations, but no more fights. The Arabs [are] too weak and deprived of their resources, because do you think that we are going to leave them a moment's peace?"[37]

Bringing the enemy to battle was the great problem of these expeditions. Sometimes the columns were detected early, so that they would be harassed from dawn till dusk by swarms of horsemen: "It is no joke to be firing in all directions from sunrise to sunset, and to march at the same time, for we seldom halt to fight at our ease. The General only orders a halt when the rear-guard is so fiercely attacked as to require reinforcement." The litters were soon filled with wounded. The provisions were redistributed among the men to free more mules. "In the end, however, both men and mules are dead beat, and every one must shift for himself. It requires long habit, and much suffering, before a man can bear to see his comrades butchered before his eyes without being able to help them."[38]

By far the most successful operations were those that maintained a degree of secrecy. Dawn was the best time to attack, for after sunrise the Arabs would see the dust of the approaching column and scatter. But their camps were usually too far away to reach in a single night march, while the horses of the cavalry were often too exhausted to play their vital role in an attack.[39] After days of climbing and descending mountains, fighting their way through scrub, following false trails or bursting into Arab campsites only to find them deserted, the men often could hardly walk: "We went forward with difficulty by jumping on the balls of our feet, because we could no longer put pressure on the whole foot," Lamborelle wrote.[40]

However, sometimes the signs that the enemy was close were unmistakable—an abandoned animal, thick smoke on the hillside at dawn. Then, "all tiredness disappeared as if by magic."[41] All the infantry who had managed to keep up were gathered together for the attack by officers whose hoarse orders *"Serrez! Serrez!"* ("Close up! Close up!") were passed down the line. The cavalry and the *goumiers,* irregular native horsemen, were sent along the ridge line to block the only escape route. Two-thirds of the infantry were deployed as skirmishers, the rest held in reserve. "Strict orders had been given to kill all the men and only to take the women and children prisoners," Lamping wrote.[42] At a signal, the infantry moved forward, bursting through the hedge of prickly pear that surrounded these villages: "Cries of alarm are shouted, shots are exchanged, terror spreads through the valley," Lamborelle recounted. "Women, men, children flee toward the only exit which the terrain offers them, but they find the chasseurs [d'Afrique] and the *goums.* Bullets fly in all directions, the sabers of the cavalry kill a large number of the enemy. A hundred or so bodies are stretched out on the ground. The herds, the women and children are thrown back toward the infantry, and the entire razzia is reunited in the center of the valley."[43] Lamping's legionnaires butchered every man who "reeled half awake out of their huts . . . no one escaped death."[44]

The soldiers helped themselves to anything in the camp—heavy silver jewelry, knives, clothes, muskets still warm from combat—while the prisoners looked on, the men (if any had survived) proud and menacing, the women exhausted, the children confused. "That did not bother us," Lamborelle wrote of these *après razzias.* "We worried little about politics. So long as the herd was gathered up, we were satisfied."[45] Indeed, food was the primary preoccupation of the raiders. Not only did the *razzia* deprive the natives of their livelihood and force them to submit; it also allowed the French to survive on campaign and, if successful, to have a little extra when the spoils were distributed. One French general, Louis de Lamoricière, insisted that his troops exist almost exclusively on the spoils of their campaigns, which provided an extra incentive to mobility and combativeness.

However, the soldiers often had to move quickly, as the noise of battle inevitably alerted the countryside, which rallied to dispute the departure of the French: "We were forced to retreat in such haste that we left the greater part of the cattle behind," Lamping wrote. "The fire of the companies we had stationed in our rear with the field pieces at last gained us time to breathe. We however had but few killed and wounded."[46] But the effort was worth the hardship, according to Lamborelle: "That evening after an extraordinary distribution of sheep had been made to all companies, we celebrated our victory with a great feast, in which quarters of mutton, plates of brains and roast lamb were devoured."[47] If the raid had been made on a village or on a semipermanent camp, the soldiers would prod the ground with their bayonets looking for the secret silos in which the Arabs hid their grain. The finder would be rewarded with ten francs, and the *intendance* would be able to make a supplemental distribution of wheat that evening.

Then the long march back to base began. This was the most difficult part of the operation, for the captured herds had to be controlled, the Arabs prevented from escaping, the women guarded against "the excesses of victory" and the footsore children sometimes carried. It was not always possible to distinguish victor from vanquished in this multitude. When Lamping's battalion limped into Blidah after one such *razzia,* ". . . many a one who would long since have been given over by the physicians in Europe still crawled in our ranks. Our shoes and clothes were in rags; many even had wound pieces of ox hide about their feet in default of shoes. . . . All the people of the town . . . lifted up their hands in amazement at our deplorable appearance; and it was only on comparing ourselves with these sleek and well-fed citizens that we perceived how wild and wretched we looked, and that our faces were dingy yellow, and our bodies dried up like so many mummies . . . not even Shylock himself could have cut one pound of flesh out of the whole column."[48] One may well imagine that the appearance of a battalion of the 1st Regiment, which returned from an expedition in June 1841, was similar to that described by Lamborelle: "Last night at six o'clock I returned [to Douéra] with my battalion after a long and rather difficult expedition," wrote Swedish major Westée. "The soldiers, with neither coats nor blankets, suffered horribly from an almost continual rain and the glacial cold of the Atlas and the valley of the Chéliff. We were not lucky enough to hear a shot fired in anger, but we did at least do immense damage to the emir [Abd el-Kader] by destroying his depots."[49]

Once back in garrison, the sheep were sold and the profits distributed among the soldiers according to rank—at least, that was the theory. "But the common soldiers complain, and perhaps not quite without reason, that the higher powers are apt to keep the lion's share for themselves."[50] Then, for two days, discipline relaxed: "No roll calls, no chores, no guard duty. All the men were brothers. In town one only met soldiers of every arm who embraced and who rolled under the tables after having spent on one meal the forced economies of several months."[51]

Bugeaud's methods of warfare were ultimately successful. But their brutality generated heated controversy in France, and found critics even in the *Armée d'Afrique*. There is no evidence that sympathy for the natives ever kept the Legion from its duty. On the contrary, there was little love spared for the North Africans, who fought "like jackals. . . . There is everything to fear from these barbarians who never spared the lives of their prisoners," according to Lamborelle. "And even when they were vanquished, we had to be careful. Often, when he saw he was going to be taken, the Arab held out his musket, the barrel forward, to a soldier who grabbed it. He then pulled the trigger. The ball mortally wounded the soldier and the prisoner was free." Even the prospect of imminent death offered no release for the soldier from the fear of their diabolical vengefulness: ". . . in the midst of the savage cries which he hears, he is pursued by the image of his mutilated body, his head a bloody trophy for the barbarians whom he is fighting."[52]

Given this attitude, how prisoners were treated depended on a number of things: the length and toughness of a campaign, how many men had been lost and whether any stragglers had died in atrocious circumstances at the hands of the Arabs or any bodies had been mutilated. Above all, the behavior of the victors depended upon the officers. In the native corps especially, where the prospect of pillage and worse was institutionalized as a recruiting pitch, excesses were regarded as almost the normal consequence of an operation, essential for the morale and self-esteem of the Moslem soldier. Lamborelle insisted that no such excesses were committed by the Legion: "I repeat, these men are as good as they are brave." But, he continued, "It is up to their leaders to develop their sentiments of generosity."[53] Even these hardened campaigners could not be oblivious to the destruction they wrought, to the livelihoods—and lives—shattered in these *razzias*. Lamborelle claimed that the prisoners were the first concern of the command on the return to garrison: "Several tents were immediately put up for the prisoners. We lit fires, and distributed food. Everyone, officers and soldiers, came from everywhere or formed a silent and sympathetic circle around the captives. Pity for the vanquished is the first glory of the victor."[54] Lacretelle remembered that once during a return from a successful *razzia*, an Arab emerged from the undergrowth and hurled a large stone at the colonel just as a legionnaire shot him. As the wounded Arab lay on the ground, a *goumier* came up to ask if he wanted to die. He then shot him in the head. Lacretelle concluded that the Arab had lost his family in their raid and no longer had any desire to live: "The act of desperation of this Arab, who came voluntarily to be killed, caused us much sadness. . . . The colonel ordered the march to resume and each of us continued lost in his silent reflections."[55]

BUGEAUD'S WISH OBVIOUSLY did not come true. The Legion was not abolished, and this for several reasons. First, it served the needs of France, which required a place to send her political refugees, guests who had overstayed their welcome and other social encumbrances. Second, it served the needs of Algeria, which required soldiers. But there is a third reason why the Legion survived attempts to disband it that has been ignored by historians, which is that it was able to adapt successfully to Bugeaud's strategic system. How did it accomplish this? The indications are that the Legion actually improved as a fighting force in the mid-1840s. Just as the routine of fixed posts devastated morale, so the ambulatory life in the open air was a first step toward restoring it. Even if legionnaires did not have to fight—and many, perhaps most, *razzias* actually struck into thin air—the very march itself would create problems to confront, challenges to surmount, create an atmosphere of real soldiering. No one said it was easy, but the real enemy of morale, and consequently performance, especially for the Legion, is not hardship, but boredom. So Bugeaud contributed toward the salvation of the Legion at the very moment he was recommending its abolition.

And because the Legion was actually doing something other than quietly coming apart at the seams in garrison, other things began to fall into place for it. First, the quality of Legion leadership improved, both because the corps could now attract the sort of officer interested in the active, outdoor life with its perils and promotion, and also because those good officers already with the Legion—and even Bugeaud admitted that they were not in short supply—now found an opportunity to exercise their leadership talents. In 1841, Bugeaud complained that "the colonels of the Foreign Legion have fallen short of my expectations."[56] The following year, he obviously placed his hopes for the resurrection of the 1st Regiment on the appointment of a new colonel. Apparently he was not disappointed. General Fabviez, who inspected the 1st Regiment in November 1842, reported that "This corps had fallen into a very bad state under poor leadership. It is visibly improving under its new colonel."[57] The arrival of MacMahon as colonel of the newly created 2nd Regiment in early 1843 went a long way toward solving the leadership problems there.

The prospect of action also began to draw in a better class of subaltern, continuing a trend that began perhaps as early as 1836. When Lacretelle went on his last school holiday before leaving Saint-Cyr, he met a general recently returned from Algeria who asked him which regiment he intended to choose upon graduation. When the cadet stated his preference for the dragoons, the senior officer—obviously a wise man—objected that the glorious days of the cavalry were finished, and suggested that an officer with a future selected Algeria and the infantry, "where he will find for a long time yet, opportunities to distinguish himself, in the Foreign Legion especially, because it is never spared and it is sent on all the operations." When Lacretelle returned to school for his final term and announced his decision to join the Legion, "My comrades were greatly surprised. . . . At Saint-Cyr we had never heard the Legion spoken of. We did not even know that it existed."[58] And this was more than a decade after the corps had been founded.

A final element that helped to solidify the officer corps, according to the duc d'Aumale, was an ordinance of February 18, 1844, ". . . which gives the right to command in the Legion to the most senior officer irregardless of origin. [This] has ended these violent arguments of principle, based on national sentiment and pride."[59] Perhaps, but this ordinance also stated that of two officers of equal grade, the one serving *à titre français*— that is, as a regular French officer—always had command over one serving *à titre étranger*—a foreigner in French service—whether a real foreigner or a Frenchman serving in that category. In September 1845, Brigadier General Thierry announced that "The general aspect of the 1st regiment of the Foreign Legion is extremely satisfactory."[60]

Other factors also helped firm up regimental control and strengthen discipline. First, Bugeaud's system allowed battalions to be united rather than scattered about in various posts where the command often exercised its influence with difficulty.[61] Second, it appears that the creation of the 2nd Regiment in 1840 created a shortage of NCOs in the Legion, which was only gradually rectified.[62] But a third and crucial factor was the change in life-style that occurred in 1842. The best of the Legion commanders, like MacMahon and Alphonse Bedeau, who held various command positions in the Legion between 1836 and 1839, realized that "with good officers, this band fights admirably. It can be led by appealing to its honor."[63]

Life on the march required officers to lead by example, a factor that was of dramatic importance in a democratic army like that of France in which an officer was not automatically given respect because of his upper-class social status, as in the more aristocratic armies of Great Britain or Imperial Germany. Lamborelle found that the officers acquired enormous authority over the rank and file by the simple fact that they shared their hardships on campaign: "The officer sees the soldier as a companion in danger and glory rather than as an inferior," he testified. "His greatest preoccupation is to spare his men unnecessary fatigue and privations. In a country where rations are lacking, he does not hesitate to help his soldiers out, advancing them money so the pot will not be empty. In return, the soldier is grateful. He is not only devoted to his officer, but more, he has a filial respect. In combat, he never abandons his officer, watches out for him, will sacrifice himself to protect him, to save him, to make sure he does not fall into the hands of the enemy if he is wounded. In camp, he keeps his fire going, looks after his horse, his mule. If he finds some game, some fruit, he shares it."[64] Lamborelle was no doubt speaking only of popular officers, and of those soldiers closest to them. But the sentiment is probably not overstated given those qualifications.

The marching and combat that now became part of the daily life of the *Armée d'Afrique* also introduced an element of competition that stimulated regimental pride as well as a healthy competitive spirit among the various nationalities of legionnaires. In 1840, General Schramm was of the opinion that "As for an *esprit de corps,* there is none, or very little."[65] But the seeds of a regimental spirit had been planted and, ten years after the formation of the Legion, were beginning to take root, not surprisingly, as part of an oral tradition whose custodians were the old veterans: "In the evenings, our sergeant talked of his campaigns," Lamborelle wrote of his first months in the Legion. "He was an old Africa hand who had been in the regiment since its formation. During the fifteen days I was with him, he told me in great detail of all the campaigns in which the Legion had taken part. He was at the Mouzaia Pass, at the Battle of Macta, the storming of Constantine where he was part of the assault column commanded by Colonel Combe. He told us of the heroic death of this brave man who, wounded by two musket balls, still had the strength to walk with the slow steps of a dying man toward the duc de Nemours and to say to him in a calm and firm voice these sublime words: 'My Lord, I am mortally wounded, but I die happy, for I have seen a splendid day for France. Alas, those who survive me are happier, for they can speak of victory.' "[66] It was a somewhat imaginative version of the death of Combe, but that is hardly the point. Or rather, that is precisely the point, for these heroic accounts of the regiment's past served as a bond for the present and a standard to emulate in the future.

And that standard was maintained on March 15, 1844, when the duc d'Aumale personally led a charge of a *bataillon de marche* made up of the elite companies of the 2nd Regiment against the fortified village of M'chouneche in the Aurès Mountains after several attacks by line regiments failed to reach the walls. So impressive was the courage of the legionnaires in their successful storming of M'chouneche that Aumale asked his father, King Louis-Philippe, to reward the regiment with its own standard.[67] Such events, which were quickly incorporated into regimental lore, were especially important to legionnaires because, according to Colonel de Villebois-Mareuil, who commanded the 1st Regiment in 1895, "His tendency is to dramatize, to drape everything in legends. To the stark truth which bores him, he prefers his invention which is amusing. He develops a passion for it and will not give it up until, absorbed in his own story, little by little he begins to believe it is part of his own past."[68]

Regimental pride led naturally to an individual pride. At its origins, it was rooted in nationalism, which, as Schramm believed, "serves to create emulation among the men in battle or on the march."[69] National diversity served to unite the Legion rather than divide it so long as the units were kept heterogeneous, for just as no legionnaire wanted his regiment thought a weak link in the *Armée d'Afrique,* likewise no one wanted to disgrace his country. Lamborelle saw an exhausted legionnaire perish from heatstroke rather than report to the ambulance. And after one action, he boasted that "The Belgians of the Legion proved once again that they were worthy of the reputation for courage that they knew how to conquer in the *Armée d'Afrique.*"[70]

By general consent, the Spaniards usually reaped the highest praise as marchers: "The Spanish, while weak in appearance, give away nothing in this respect to the Belgians and Germans," Randon wrote.[71] Even the Carlists appeared to have lived down their deplorable reputation by 1844, when General François du Barail advanced the opinion that "In Africa, the Spaniards are more or less at home. The climate and to a certain point the habits and manners of the countries are similar. These Carlists, used to fatigue and the dangers of war, were for our Foreign Legion an almost inexhaustible source of recruitment. Tireless marchers, of an absolute sobriety, they were the true elite soldiers and became, in addition, upon their liberation the solid elements of colonization."[72] MacMahon praised the Germans in his command, "most of whom were very energetic veterans, who marched well, but as skirmishers they were far from equalling the Spaniards. These were the true soldiers of Africa, nimble, intelligent, inexhaustible marchers and enormously brave. In the summer if we crossed a stream, their comrades would stop, plunge their heads in the water and drink unimaginable quantities. Several times I saw in such cases Germans die on the spot. As for the Spaniards and the Turks, they would not even stop but merely scoop up a little water in the hollow of their hand."[73]

Randon rated the Italians at the bottom of the Legion's roster of nationalities,[74] but MacMahon found that forty Englishmen who had deserted to the Legion from Evans's British Legion in Spain ran the Italians a close second: "They were good fellows, but incapable of supporting the long marches if they did not get supplemental rations," MacMahon wrote. "Often, after four days, they had eaten up their eight days' rations and we were obliged to reprovision them or see them fall behind." MacMahon decided to demonstrate the dangers of falling out on the march. "The first time I saw them lying by the roadside, I sent out twenty *spahis* [native cavalry]. Disguised as [Abd el-Kader's] horsemen, and shouting at the top of their lungs, my cavalrymen shot at the English taking care not to hit them. As they did not want to lose their heads, they decided to rejoin the column. The next day, I wanted to do the same thing, but they had discovered the trick and shot at the spahis without bothering to move."[75]

Stronger *esprit de corps* improved performance, Lamborelle argued, because courage was inseparable from the milieu, an *esprit de corps* developed gradually in the soldier until it became virtually a reflex: "There is a strange observation to make," he wrote, "and that is by daily growing accustomed to danger, a man imperceptibly comes to play with death as easily as if it were a game of cards. I refer to those who have been in combat, [that] the heart grows used to peril, as the ears become accustomed to the noise of a fusillade. Courage is also a little a question of habit, and often one does not find it in himself on the first day. One must not forget either that he has an older brother who is called: The sentiment of honor and duty."[76]

The Legion had fought some honorable actions between 1837 and 1841 that had demonstrated that the corps had potential as a military unit. By moving it out of its static positions, Bugeaud allowed it to realize that potential to a much greater degree after 1842, especially as it fought often as *bataillon de marche* with elite companies. However, this still does not tell us how good it actually was, or resolve complaints about poor training or its inability to march. The answer is that the Legion was probably as good as it had to be. One of the advantages of Bugeaud's system, and one reason why it was so well adapted to his military instrument, was that the level of training and military skill required in Algeria was not as high as a European regiment would be expected to attain. The Legion did not need to be drilled to parade-ground perfection to carry out a *razzia,* so the problem of poor training was minimized. What was required was the ability to undertake brutal marches. While no statistics exist for this period on the attrition rate on the march, one can assume, judging by the complaints, that it was fairly high. But the important thing is that, in the end, this did not matter because enough men got to the point of conflict to keep the Legion effective against an opponent often taken by surprise, who sought first to protect his family and property, and who had poor collective discipline. And even if these marches were costly in manpower, it made little difference, for there were plenty of replacements.

So while commanders sometimes complained that Legion recruits were unpromising material from which to fashion warriors, the point is that the supply was virtually inexhaustible, so long as political upheaval made France a preferred place of exile, and so long as urban overpopulation made Algeria and the Legion a potential social safety valve. So the recruitment of many men who fled into the Legion for want of an alternative actually became a strength, for it solved the problem that often troubles professional military organizations, especially in wartime—that of finding cheap and plentiful replacements. One of the results was that the Legion may have been no *Wehrmacht,* but then in the conditions of colonial warfare it did not have to be.

The 1840s appear to have been critical years in the history of the Legion, perhaps among the most important. The *razzia* was hard, dirty, unspectacular work in which battle honors were more rare than sober legionnaires on Saturday night. But battle honors would come. The essential accomplishment of these years is that the Legion had begun to forge a collective spirit that was to carry it into mid-century and beyond. In short, despite the disappearance of the "old Legion" in Spain and attempts by Bugeaud to extinguish the "new" one virtually in its cradle, it had survived childhood. At the same time, it was already apparent to those who cared to look closely that the Legion required special handling—it was a unique corps with a distinct personality and quite separate leadership requirements. Those officers who assumed that legionnaires were simply stateless brutes and proceeded to treat them accordingly obtained poor results. "One must, to lead them, mix firmness with affection, a severe discipline but which one knows at certain times how to relax," Lamborelle recommended.[77] Also, the Legion could not be allowed to molder in garrison, where the least attractive aspects of its personality tended to gain the upper hand. If the conditions of sensitive leadership and action were met, the Legion was capable of demonstrating a determination and resilience that in this period could make it as good as the best in the *Armée d'Afrique*. And in 1849 it would require all the reserves of energy and courage it possessed to meet one of its most grueling challenges—the siege of the desert fortress of Zaatcha.

Chapter 5

ZAATCHA

THE NAME ZAATCHA elicits only the faintest echo in modern histories of the Legion. In 1849, this desert village marked the southernmost penetration of the French in eastern Algeria. Anyone staring south from the fringes of the oasis complex crowded with date palms into the savage immensity of the Sahara must have wondered if the French could, or should, go any further. Indeed, they would soon have cause to wonder if their conquests had taken them too far already. By mid-century, the Tell, as the coastal highlands were called, had been "pacified." But the journey south from Constantine had not yet been deprived of interest, for the inhabitants still retained their attachment to many of those practices that gave North Africa its flavor of perilous exoticism. Important visitors could still be greeted by village chiefs offering a "diffa"—a wooden bowl filled with meat and cous-cous, a semolina of wheat that was a staple of the Maghreb (the coastal highlands of Tunisia, Algeria and Morocco)—as a mark of respect. But isolated travelers might still be murdered, or at the very least robbed, if nightfall caught them outside one of the small posts and way stations constructed at intervals along the route.

The track wound south out of the high country around Constantine until it reached Ain M'lila, where the rivers and wadis that had slashed meandering courses out of the mountains spilled over a flat plain to form a *sebbka*, or shallow salt lake, which, in summer, evaporated like a mirage. Figures who might have plodded out of Biblical scenes, leading camels or mules that swayed beneath outsized sacks of grain or dates, often surmounted by a woman who quickly covered her face at the approach of strangers, followed paths worn through the bluish salt fields. Over this dazzling plain, which resembled a Siberian steppe in mid-winter, aquatic birds circled seeking puddles that the summer sun had yet to reclaim.

Batna appeared as an oasis of civilization amidst this blasted landscape of almost lunar severity. Constructed as a base of operations at the foot of the Aurès massif, it had already lost that "biscuitville" quality that stamped so many European settlements in Algeria, so-called because crates used to transport dry military biscuits served as the primary building material. On the contrary, many of the buildings had been fashioned from the wood of venerable cedars felled in the mountains to the south. The town was surrounded by a wall that, if not up to European specifications, at least prevented surprises by the turbulent hillsmen of the Aurès. The presence of soldiers had spawned a respectable commerce of small shops, and even a public bath. In the autumn of 1849, the military had also spawned something else—an inordinate number of ambulances carrying sick and wounded from Zaatcha.

If the road from Constantine to Batna was moderately insecure, Europeans who wished to follow the track south toward the Sahara could do so only in military convoy. The square vestiges of Roman camps, once outposts for the extinct city of Lambaesis, presided from ragged knolls over the track that stretched southwest from Batna through a wild plain. Soldiers fixed their packs onto the backs of mules (strictly against regulations) and trudged forward into a landscape of increasing savagery. The spahis on flank guard seemed too close in to screen a serious attack. The column halted every hour to close up, and forded the Wadi Tamarisk, a favorite place of ambush, with great caution. The plain began to undulate like a calm sea expecting a tempest, and then disappeared altogether into a chaos of rocky outcroppings and frugal vegetation, which in turn rose into mountains of somber stone. Eventually, the trail caught up with the El Kantara River, a clear torrent that toiled and twisted southwest as if eager to escape the tormented peaks through which it ran until it plunged into a defile between two pink hills—the Kantara Gorge, called "the mouth of the desert" by the Arabs. It was through this crevice that the traveler caught his first glimpse of the Sahara, an immense speckled plain that stretched southward until it merged with the horizon.

The transition from the Tell to the desert is as spectacular as it is abrupt. The naked, rose-colored ridges of the Aurès loom like a fortress wall over the northern limits of the Sahara, which, by desert standards, are rich and well watered. The trail winds out of the Kantara Gorge and soon enters an oasis of greenery: high date palms screen the sun to allow fruit trees and gardens of melon, cucumber and other vegetables, irrigated by a complex network of small water channels, to grow in the shade beneath. Villages of sun-dried bricks, some resembling medieval fortresses, lie half-hidden in the foliage. The track skips from oasis to oasis across elevations of stone and sand until it reaches the largest oasis, that of Biskra. In 1849, Biskra counted over 100,000 date palms that clung to the wadis and watercourses that slithered out of the Tell until they disappeared into the salt-flecked Chott Melrhir.

Twenty-five miles southwest of Biskra, on the fringes of the depression of the Chott Melrhir, lay the small oasis of Zaatcha, an extraordinarily quaint but seemingly insignificant settlement half-lost amidst the date palms of the Tolga oasis complex. Zaatcha was not on any main road—the track that went southward from Biskra to Touggourt, Ouargla and the Sudan beyond missed it altogether. Indeed, one would have needed a guide with fairly extensive local knowledge to find the place at all. However, in 1849 this apparently unimportant speck on the map of the Sahara managed to stop a modern European army dead in its tracks and detonate a crisis that rippled as far away as Paris itself.

Not only did Zaatcha become one of the most arduous campaigns of a very arduous conquest of Algeria, but it also would appear on the face of it to have been one of the least necessary, or at the very least the most avoidable, for by 1849, French "Africa" (Algeria did not yet officially exist) had been to all intents and purposes "pacified." Of course, there remained a few corners here and there to tidy up, like the mountainous and ever-defiant Kabylia to the east of Algiers. But Abd el-Kader had surrendered in 1847, and after having been fêted in Paris, was placed under house arrest in Toulon and then Pau before being interned in the gilded cage of the Château d'Amboise. In October 1852, he would be dispatched to exile in Egypt and eventually Damascus, from which he was never to return to North Africa.

The second most tenacious Arab leader, Ahmed Bey, who had defied the French at Constantine, in 1848 had exchanged the exciting life of a resistance chief for a pension and suitable accommodation for himself and his substantial number of wives and concubines in Algiers. In 1844, the French had reached Biskra, and so crossed the threshold of the Sahara. There seemed little point in going any further: The desert tribes, small and poorly organized, posed no threat to French control of the Tell. There was nothing in the Sahara worth taking, either economically or strategically. There is no evidence that Paris, or any other European government for that matter, wanted the Sahara. Besides, as the French were to discover to their cost, the conquest of the world's least hospitable desert would require substantial modifications in force structure, which meant, among other things, that they must master the camel—a beast as truculent and defiant as any of the human variety that were to be encountered in Algeria. The conquest of the Sahara would have to await another, later epoch.[1]

So why Zaatcha? In analyzing this, we are limited by the evidence, which comes exclusively from the French side. However, to believe their case, one must be prepared to accept rather uncritically the notion that great events must have great causes. For General Émile Herbillon, whose controversial handling of the siege of Zaatcha let him in for enough criticism to force his disguised retirement in 1850, those causes were essentially two. The first was the very insecurity of their conquest. To the French, Algeria appeared to have been temporarily subdued rather than mastered. The population, diverse though it may have been, was a volcano seething with explosive potential, a permanent conspiracy of fanaticism plotting the destruction of their temporary masters, a collection of combustible material awaiting the spark that would ignite it into life. Zaatcha—that small blue-green speck in a sea of sand—was that spark. No matter that a general in the War Ministry in Paris eating his morning croissant over a map of Algeria might miss it if the smallest crumb landed 230 degrees southwest of Biskra, Zaatcha would become the holy cause for which the Algerian masses were waiting, the signal for the uprising that would hurl the French back into the sea. If even French soldiers were prepared to admit that their rule was tolerated rather than welcomed (and how could they deny it?), then it must be true.

And like every colonial general worth his salt, Herbillon transferred the blame for the revolt back to the homeland. This was his second point—the Revolution of 1848, which in February overthrew the July Monarchy and ushered in the turbulent period of the Second Republic, offered the natives the spectacle of a disordered and leaderless France. Quite naturally, they were quick to take advantage of this perceived weakness: "The news of our political dissensions was carried to the population by the . . . Biskris," Herbillon wrote. "In the towns, they had witnessed the public demonstrations and carried away the impression that a profound dissention divided the masses. Upon returning home, they recounted with oriental exaggeration, the scenes which impressed them and said that the fall of military power and its replacement with civilian power was certain. In this they were supported by the Jews of Constantine who were dangerous emissaries, commercial travellers of false information. These tales were avidly listened to by the people of the Sahara whose sentiments of hatred were stoked and who saw in these events the imminent fall of our power and our force."[2]

French officers make a desperate plea for this view in all of their letters and reports preserved in the war archives. For instance, Captain Edouard Collineau of the 2nd Regiment wrote that the natives had taken note of the diminished strength of the garrisons and, "While they did not understand the exact significance [of the events in France], they think that they can take advantage and that awakens hopes among them which were only dormant."[3] French historian Charles-André Julien, admittedly no admirer of French colonialism in North Africa, disputed the contentions of the soldiers that the Zaatcha revolt sprang directly from political events in France. In the first place, he notes, the charge that the 1848 Revolution created an impression of division and weakness as far as Algeria is concerned is incorrect. On the contrary, the Second Republic ended all speculation about a French pullout from Algeria by proclaiming Algeria to be an integral part of French territory. Second, the native resistance had been well and truly beaten by almost a decade of Bugeaud's *razzias,* and in the eighteen months between the February Revolution of 1848 and the rebellion at Zaatcha in the summer of 1849, Algeria, apart from a few isolated mountain areas that required attention, had remained calm.[4]

Of course, it is nonetheless true that despite the bloody repression of the June Days of 1848 that ended the cycle of revolution, political debate remained intense in France, as did international tensions in Europe—for instance, in 1848 Canrobert accepted the colonelcy of the 2nd Regiment of the Foreign Legion with great reluctance because he believed this would cause him to miss the European conflagration he thought imminent: "For forty-eight hours I thought of resigning," he wrote. "I no longer wanted Algeria. I dreamed of shots fired in Germany or Italy. I too wanted to go there."[5] However, even Pierre-Napoleon Bonaparte, who briefly joined the Legion at Zaatcha, stayed long enough to realize that the 1848 Revolution was not a primary cause of the rebellion.[6] Indeed, if the situation in the south of Constantine Province was as tense as some officers claimed, then all the more reason to tread cautiously. But that, apparently, is not what they chose to do.

The sad fact was that Arab fanaticism and French irresolution and instability played only walk-on roles in this great drama. Zaatcha was to a large extent a mess of the army's own making, in which a poorly implemented military strategy completed a series of events that betrayed the military's insensitivity to local issues. The origins of the Zaatcha affair can be traced directly to the appointment of Captain Charles Gaillard de Saint-Germain to command the oases of the northern Sahara centered upon Biskra soon after the French reached them in 1844. Like most of these Arab Bureau postings, that occupied by Saint-Germain required enormous tact, sensitivity to local customs and beliefs, and a generous dose of political wisdom. Alas, Saint-Germain's strengths were those of a combat soldier, not of a local politician. The general practice in those regions administered by the army was to name a *caïd,* or native chief, favorable to French interests and then watch him like a hawk while he managed local affairs. However, Saint-Germain preferred a more direct management style, which quite naturally undermined the influence of the French-appointed *caïd.*

What might have simply been poor politics turned to disaster in 1848 when Saint-Germain, now a major in the 2nd Regiment of the Foreign Legion, decided to raise money to build a fortress at Biskra by declaring everyone equal before taxes and increasing the annual contribution per date palm from fifteen or twenty to perhaps as much as fifty centimes. In this way he raised 120,000 francs, a by no means insubstantial sum for one of the world's most impoverished regions.[7] No one enjoys paying taxes, especially a people for whom they had been virtually unknown before the arrival of the French. The inhabitants deeply resented the fact that the tax fell on all trees, not just those that bore dates. This was simply bad politics, which became disastrous because the French were too thin on the ground in Biskra to keep control by themselves.

The first inkling the French had that the natives might be growing restless occurred on May 16, 1849, when another Legion officer attached to the Arab Bureau, Second Lieutenant Joseph Seroka, heard rumors during his rounds of the oases that Bouzian, once *caïd* of Zaatcha, was stirring up ill feeling against the French. When his claims that the Prophet appeared regularly to him met with skepticism, Bouzian promised that Mohammed would send a sign: the next day, he announced that during the night the Prophet had come to shake his hand, and as proof he pulled up the sleeve of his burnoose to reveal a green hand. When the *caïd* of the small oasis of Liouach complained to Seroka that Bouzian had begun to make inroads among his followers, the lieutenant decided to investigate. On the 18th, he rode into Zaatcha to find Bouzian sitting alone in the main square of the small, fortified village. Seroka ordered him to mount a mule. As he was about to comply, Bouzian's rosary broke (Seroka believed this to be intentional), and he stooped down and began to gather up the beads. Impatient, Seroka ordered two of his spahis to seize Bouzian. By this time, however, a crowd had gathered that moved to Bouzian's defense. A scuffle broke out, shots were fired, and Seroka and his spahis bolted for the gate without Bouzian.[8] A second force of twenty spahis and thirty *goumiers,* or irregular auxiliaries, was dispatched to bring in Bouzian, only to find Zaatcha bolted against them.[9]

Having failed to nip the rebellion in the bud—on the contrary, the bungled police work had only served to publicize it—the French found their alternatives limited in the short term. Most of the troops were occupied in pacifying the Collo Mountains in the extreme north of Constantine Province, so the Arab Bureau sent the Sheik El-Arab to blockade Zaatcha with his retainers. This proved to be a mistake, as even the future commander of the siege, General Herbillon, admitted—the Arab sheik used the opportunity "to carry out some personal vengeance. . . . In any case, there were too many shared interests, too much in common between [the Sheik] and the inhabitants for this isolation to be anything but illusory."[10] For his part, Saint-Germain did not appear too alarmed by the events at Zaatcha, a complacency for which Herbillon took him to task.[11]

In Herbillon's view, Saint-Germain failed to realize that a number of tribes, especially the Ouled-Sahnoun, "turbulent cutthroats" who occupied the Hodna plain to the northeast of Zaatcha and who were ready to throw in with the "party of disorder" at the drop of a hat, were watching this example of French inaction against Bouzian with great interest. So great was the impact of the apparent French paralysis before Zaatcha that the Ouled-Sahnoun, estimated at fifteen hundred strong, audaciously attacked the *smala,* or extended family, of Si-Mokran, the *caïd* whom in 1844 the French had placed in charge of the Hodna region. More insulting, however, was the fact that this attack took place at the Wadi Barika, about fifty miles northwest of Biskra, where the *smala* was camped beneath the very walls of the fortress Saint-Germain was constructing with the aid of a small detachment of Legion laborers drawn from the 4th Company of the 3rd Battalion. The skirmish roared back and forth in the noisy, dusty, chaotic, but surprisingly (at least to outsiders) bloodless manner of these traditional North African encounters for some time, until the attackers imprudently made a rush at the legionnaires who, until then, had been mere spectators. One volley threw the Ouled-Sahnoun into precipitous retreat. However, as they fled through the trees, they destroyed what they could of the intricate network of irrigation channels.[12]

For Herbillon, the link between the attack at Barika and the defiance of Bouzian at Zaatcha was obvious—if the French anywhere showed weakness or hesitation, they opened themselves to revolt everywhere. Yet the connection between the two events appears far more tenuous. If, for instance, this was part of a giant desert conspiracy, then why was Bouzian not in the forefront of the Barika skirmish? The attack of the Ouled-Sahnoun seems to have stemmed from entirely separate grievances. Even Herbillon admitted that Si-Mokran had been a disastrous appointment: "The descendant of a family of *marabouts* [religious leaders], [Si-Mokran] was not a warrior, and therefore was held in low esteem by the Arabs of the great tents," he wrote. "He did not know how to recruit supporters, and had even created animosity through his avarice and his immoral life." Already on several occasions the French had had to rescue him from the consequences of his unfortunate decisions by sending troops.[13]

The second hint that the Ouled-Sahnoun were motivated by something other than religious fanaticism or French weakness comes from piecing together other trifles of evidence that suggest that the French occupation of the oases had done much to upset the traditional economic balance of the region. Herbillon explained that the Ouled-Sahnoun grew grain in the Hodna, which they exchanged for dates at Biskra.[14] According to Pierre Bonaparte, one of Saint-Germain's innovations had been to encourage the Biskris to plant their own grain. This well-intentioned reform had met with great success, so great, in fact, that it had served to cut the Ouled-Sahnoun out of a market vital for their existence, severing the economic links between the Hodna and the oases.[15] This probably explains why the retreating Ouled-Sahnoun took out their fury on the irrigation system.

All of this would suggest that poor and insensitive military management had set off a series of separate detonations that, in the mind of the soldiers, had coalesced into a single conspiracy against French rule. Their reflex was to fall back upon force, rather than seek to manipulate and compromise, as the war minister, Joseph Rullière, wished them to do: "War may bring victories," he wrote to the governor-general of Algeria on August 22, 1849, "but only politics can assure lasting conquests."[16] Alas, this was advice whose destiny was too often to be ignored in North Africa. The military reflex was too ingrained in the *Armée d'Afrique,* the sense of insult too highly developed to allow such behavior to go unpunished. There was no time now to lament past errors, or to undertake the slow and pains-taking task of rebuilding confidence. For French officers, the submission of the native population was only tactical, based upon local wisdom, which dictated that one must "kiss the hand which you cannot cut off." No Moslem could accept in good conscience the domination of these "foreign dogs." The best course, the only course for the French, was to bring out the big stick.

And in 1849, despite much whimpering among the apologists for Zaatcha, that stick was a fairly formidable one as blunt instruments go. Eight years or so of quick marching around Algeria under the direction of Bugeaud had transformed the sluggish garrison army of 1840 into an aggressive and offensive-minded force. The *Armée d'Afrique* was still de-ficient in cavalry and therefore could never really succeed in matching the Arabs in mobility. But whatever was humanly possible to accomplish on foot, they could accomplish, and sometimes more.

That said, Zaatcha caught the Legion, especially the 2nd Regiment, which undertook the siege, at a particularly awkward moment. The 1848 revolution that ushered in the Second Republic revealed the ambivalent attitudes to the Legion both in France and in Europe. All legionnaires who counted five years' service were invited to apply for French nationality, which many did. The 1st Regiment, which had already begun to settle in at the site of Sidi-bel-Abbès south of Oran in the east, was little affected by political events. As a gesture of the fraternal solidarity of peoples, Paris ordered that all Polish legionnaires who so wished could terminate their enlistment contracts. Only 23 chose to do so, 17 of whom returned within a month. The 2nd Regiment was harder hit. While few Poles chose to abandon its ranks, a request from the Piedmontese ambassador to free his nationals from the Legion caused a hemorrhage of Italians out of the 2nd Regiment. So, on the eve of the campaign, the regiment had been deprived of 618 men, almost a battalion's worth of strength.[17]

Despite this handicap, the Legion counted upon the quality of its lead-ership to make up its manpower deficit. To succeed in a troop command, especially of a troop like the Legion, required the toughness of a prison guard, desperate ambition and a touch of madness. All of these qualities were present in the commander of the Batna subdivision whose task it was to sort out the Zaatcha mess—Jean-Luc Carbuccia. Carbuccia was a Cor-sican, "from one of the best families in Bastia" according to Pierre-Napoleon Bonaparte,[18] which presumably he meant as a compliment. As will be seen, opinion on Carbuccia was sharply divided. A Legion colonel who was considered one of the most dynamic officers in Algeria, Carbuccia had already earned a certain notoriety by his (unsuccessful) experiments with organizing a camel corps, and by setting his legionnaires to carry out excavations at Lambaesis. During these excavations, he had inscribed upon a tombstone of a Roman legionary, "Colonel Carbuccia [of the IInd Foreign Legion] to his colleague in the IIIrd Roman Legion."[19] French writer Camille Rousset wrote that despite his obvious energy, Carbuccia "rightly or wrongly was thought by the troops to be unlucky in war."[20]

Carbuccia was now about to achieve what many must have thought would be infamy by marching a column composed of 600 legionnaires, 400 soldiers of the penal *zéphyrs,* a nickname given to the *bats d'Af,* 250 horsemen and a few odds and ends into the Hodna plain. The Hodna was not quite the Sahara, but in July the French troops might be excused if they failed to distinguish the subtle differences between the Sahara and what a geographer would call the "pre-Sahara." Marching around the desert in the height of summer is not everyone's idea of a holiday. It is hot—very hot—with the thermometer sometimes reaching 140 degrees Fahrenheit at midday. In that sort of weather, a man needs all his energy just to breathe. But perhaps because he was prepared to execute the unexpected, Carbuccia surprised the Ouled-Sahnoun camped at Metkouak on the Hodna plain on the morning of July 9. As *razzias* went, Carbuccia's was a model of its kind—a predawn attack that produced utter panic. Women, children and the old were killed in their own stampede to escape, while the soldiers collected two thousand camels and twelve thousand sheep.[21]

The *razzia* of the Ouled-Sahnoun offered a powerful demonstration of French force, and one that produced political results. The tribes in the Hodna region, impressed by Carbuccia's athletic performance, came in to ask for the *aman,* or pardon, which was usually accorded after the supplicating tribe paid an appropriate fine in sheep and camels, and turned in all their muskets. The Zaatcha rebellion was now placed in quarantine. There was no immediate danger of it spreading to the north (if indeed there ever had been). Even the most paranoid of soldiers must have admitted that. Bouzian was a local phenomenon whose command of an insignificant oasis could do nothing to threaten the French grip on southern Algeria. Let the bad blood, distrust and family rivalries that were endemic in the oases, and perhaps the ultimate threat of French retaliation, do their work. Left alone, Bouzian's rebellion was bound to fade away. However, patience was not Carbuccia's strong suit. Hardly pausing to recuperate from his storming of the Hodna, he delivered his substantial booty to Biskra and turned his column toward Zaatcha.

Had the legionnaires of Carbuccia's column been normal tourists, the oasis they spied at five o'clock on the morning of July 16 would certainly have appeared inviting. The deep blue-green of the date palms spread somberly over a khaki countryside temporarily softened by the rose-colored light of dawn. To these experienced soldiers, it could hardly have seemed to offer a military obstacle of great consequence, much less be the focus of an insurrection which threatened French control of Algeria itself. Indeed, they must have wondered what all the fuss was about. Zaatcha was merely the principal settlement in a tiny oasis complex that consisted of two blobs of greenery that sat like paint splattering on a sandy canvas. The larger of the two green patches was shaped like a human heart. It clustered along a wadi that ran for about a mile and a half north to south and measured about a mile across. The northern quadrant contained Zaatcha, a small village whose wall and moat gave it the appearance of a medieval fortress in miniature. A single gate led out of the town through the palms to the west. Three hundred yards to the south of Zaatcha in the midst of gardens and palm trees lay Lichana, an entirely separate, unfortified collection of square houses constructed from sun-dried brick. To the west, separated from the principal oasis by a narrow channel of sand, was the smaller oasis of Farfar, which measured about a mile in length and barely three-quarters of a mile across.

There is no evidence, however, that Carbuccia had a clear notion of the geography of the place. Indeed, the war minister later criticized him for having failed to carry out a proper reconnaissance.[22] From his position to the northeast of the oasis, all he could see was a forest of date palms that hid even the minaret of the mosque of Zaatcha, barely three hundred yards from the edge of the vegetation. What was plainly visible was the *zaouia*, or monastery, which sat on the northeastern limit of the oasis. Nor is it clear that he had a plan of attack. Herbillon claimed that Carbuccia believed that the mere appearance of the French force fresh from thrashing the formidable Ouled-Sahnoun, combined with a little selective felling of the date palms upon which the economy of the oasis depended, a traditional tactic in the northern Sahara, would suffice to force a submission.[23]

In short, Carbuccia was overconfident. But then why should he not be? He was a man at the height of his powers and energy. He commanded a force that had just scored a brilliant victory over one of the most feared tribes in southern Algeria, and in the process had demonstrated remarkable resilience and prowess in a season when sane men slept during daylight hours. Furthermore, oasis dwellers were held in low esteem as fighters by French and nomad alike, no more than a collection of pusillanimous gardeners whose primary concern was to protect their date palms. In this respect, the French were to fall victim to their own prejudices and stereotypes.

Yet there were at least two factors that should have caused Carbuccia to act with less haste. The first has to do with that tattered cliché that those ignorant of history are condemned to repeat it. This was never more true than on July 16, 1849. Zaatcha had achieved a great deal of regional celebrity in 1831 (or 1833—the sources disagree), when it successfully resisted a siege laid against it by the Bey of Constantine.[24] Therefore, the memory, and precedent, of a successful resistance might serve to make many Zaatchans confident that they could repeat the glories of the past.

The second cause for pause lay in the fact that Carbuccia's force was not designed for static siege operations. Indeed, the Legion, like the entire *Armée d'Afrique*, had been transmogrified under Bugeaud into a stripped-down force whose strength lay in its mobility. The expertise gained in launching devastating *razzias* against nomads or attacking mountain villages could not easily be transferred to the Sahara, at least as long as the oasis dwellers insisted on remaining behind their walls. The war minister was quite clear about this: "The attack of an oasis cannot be treated in the same way as the attack on a mountain position," General Rullière reminded Carbuccia, a trifle too late, in August.[25]

In Carbuccia's defense, two things may be said. First, the oases had not proved particularly difficult to control in the past. According to one author, the mere appearance of French troops before an oasis "larger than Zaatcha" in 1847, combined with selective pruning of the date crop, had worked to bring the inhabitants to their senses with a minimum of bloodshed.[26] Second, Carbuccia gives a slightly different version of events of July 16 than does Herbillon, his superior who was not present. The colonel claimed that he did not plunge headlong into the oasis immediately upon arrival looking for a fight. On the contrary, he was attacked by the inhabitants of Zaatcha, who surged out of the trees led by "the sherif" (presumably Bouzian), but who were easily dispersed by a few bursts of artillery. This had a salutary effect, and the *"djemmas,"* or councils, of several oases came forward to request the *aman*. Carbuccia then marched his troops past the northern edge of the Zaatcha oasis to Farfar, which also requested the *aman*. As it was stunningly hot, with a wind out of the south that was like the breath of a blast furnace, Carbuccia ordered his men to wait out the heat of the day in the shade of Farfar. But just as they were settling down, firing broke out. "Full of ardor, our soldiers, forgetting that they should rest, ran at the enemy," Carbuccia reported. "We chased them out of the gardens. Soon the entire column was engaged, but the commander of the column, mounting on horseback, brought back the soldiers whom the engagement had made very animated." Some did not turn back before they reached the walls of Zaatcha, which they announced had been heavily fortified. The French had five killed and twelve wounded in this opening skirmish.[27]

What to do now? For Carbuccia, the choice was obvious. "In this critical moment," Herbillon wrote, "this senior officer [Carbuccia], counting upon the prestige of our arms, upon the enthusiasm which animated his troops, and the quality of the officers, believed that the best course of action was an all out attack, a retreat being too risky."[28] In many respects, this made sense. Audacity, especially in North Africa, often carried the day against an enemy whose morale and discipline might splinter under pressure, but who also became emboldened at the slightest sign of weakness or hesitation in their enemy. On the other hand, there were other factors that argued against a *coup de main*. In the first place, there were the disturbing reports that Zaatcha was heavily fortified. Second, the troops must have been worn out after their night march, a fatigue rendered almost insupportable by the suffocating heat. Carbuccia gave his men time to eat, and at two o'clock in the afternoon marched them out of Farfar to retrace their steps across the griddle of sand and stone around the northern edge of the Zaatcha oasis, while a feigned attack by his *goumiers* distracted the rebels to the west.

The colonel stopped his troops on the northeast side of Zaatcha astride the track that led to Biskra. His artillery began a slow bombardment while he organized his legionnaires and zephyrs into two columns of 450 men each. At four o'clock, after a brief speech "to each column about the glory of their predecessors," Carbuccia launched them at the oasis. The legionnaires under Saint-Germain moved through a small breach in a garden wall made by the artillery. The scenery changed instantly from one of an uninterrupted view of nothing much clear to the horizon to a tangle of foliage and mud walls. The legionnaires wandered about in confusion for some time, following a tortuous path that eventually brought them to the north face of Zaatcha. That was about as far as they got. The fire coming out of the village was murderous. Especially annoying was that belching from the triangular holes that pierced the wall close to ground level, originally constructed as ventilation shafts but which now did double duty as gunslits. At this point, it should have become obvious that Zaatcha would require the attention of something that packed more punch than a group of lightly armed infantrymen. Nevertheless, the legionnaires rushed the walls, only to be stopped dead in their tracks by the moat of stagnant water.

AFTER LOSING FOUR OFFICERS and quite a few soldiers, Saint-Germain ordered the troops back to a less exposed sector while the artillery was ordered up to create a breach. Here the French learned another important lesson. At the best of times, their light field guns would have had their work cut out for them breaching a wall of dried mud. Now they discovered that the Zaatcha defenses rested upon a solid foundation of large stones, which they surmised must have been part of earlier Roman fortifications. As night was falling, Saint-Germain asked for permission to retreat, as did the second column of zephyrs, whose experiences at another part of the wall had been virtually identical. As Carbuccia regrouped his forces on the plain, he realized that he had had a bad day—31 of his men were dead, including 14 legionnaires, and fully 117 were wounded, 71 of them from the Legion. Carbuccia sat for three days contemplating Zaatcha before decamping on the night of July 19 for the march back to Biskra.[29] The Arabs saw him off with joyful singing.

When the war minister, General Rullière, received news of Carbuccia's failure, he was livid, and utterly rejected the colonel's contention that his attack, though unsuccessful, had terrified the Arabs: "I believe that [the Arabs] are too intelligent not to see in this event a partial defeat, and that their ardor and confidence in the oases will grow very substantially," he wrote to the governor-general on August 10. "The victory songs which the inhabitants were singing testify that the Colonel has undergone, unnecessarily, a serious setback for our troops. It is up to you, General, to moderate the ardor of this colonel whose judgement and intelligence have sometimes been sacrificed to an excessive ambition."[30] However, Rullière agreed that the mistake could not be left unrepaired, especially as news of the French setback was common gossip as far away as the Kabylia. He also agreed that revenge must await cooler weather. His only caution—just do not botch the operation this time![31]

That, however, was an order not easily carried out. Herbillon complained that the apparent inactivity of the French in the late summer caused other tribes, most notably those in the Aurès Mountains to the northeast of Biskra, to take heart. There, "a mob of disorderly, worthless vagabonds and fanatics" bullied a most placid holy man named Abd el-Hafid into leading them "to exterminate the Christians." The unhappy Hafid, caught between his religious duty to lead a holy war and his basic cowardice, tipped off Saint-Germain, who had 350 legionnaires rushed in from Batna. At noon on September 17, Saint-Germain received word that the attackers were camped on the Wadi Seriana. Where this camp is located is not entirely clear. Contemporary French maps list Seriana well to the southeast of Biskra, in the lowlands near the Chott Melrhir. But this location could not fit the description of the fight that took place there. According to the battle report, the Arabs were encamped further north, at a point about sixteen miles east of Biskra where the river flows out of the Aurès Mountains onto the Saharan plain.[32] There they sat for the moment, probably gathering support in the Biskra oases before launching an attack, perhaps upon Biskra itself. Saint-Germain decided to preempt them—he gathered up his legionnaires, a sprinkling of *spahis* and about two hundred *goumiers* and marched in broad daylight to the Seriana, where he arrived about four-thirty in the afternoon.

The native force, estimated at between four thousand and five thousand men, was camped upon the site of an oasis whose palm trees had been felled in an earlier tribal conflict. Of course, the tribal coalitions that collected under the leadership of a holy man, and that when they were substantial enough were called *harkas*, were not formal military organizations. They usually included women and children, as well as flocks of goats and camels, which often grazed at a substantial distance from the main camp. It seems improbable that the French could have approached Seriana undetected—at the very least the dust thrown up by the approaching column would have given them away. More likely the rebels placed their faith in the force of their numbers. "We were faced with a solidly established enemy," wrote Captain Collineau of the sight that confronted the Saint-Germain column at Seriana. "The positions occupied by the sherif caused us a disagreeable surprise. But, it was too late to retreat. . . ."[33] Saint-Germain followed the classic *razzia* tactic of marching his infantry in line straight at the camp while he led the *goumiers* around the left flank to cut off the camp from its line of retreat into the mountains. The result was a rout. The Legion drove the defenders into the wadi, and then climbed the east embankment to attack the small hill where Hafid and six hundred of his supporters had rallied for a final stand. The Legion gave them a volley, and they bolted for the hills, running as best they could the gauntlet of Saint-Germain's horsemen. About two hundred failed to make it, while many of the rest, including Hafid, escaped only by leaving everything behind, including most of their clothing—the field was littered with burnooses jettisoned by men desperate to shave critical seconds off the Saharan sprint record. The victors collected large numbers of horses and mules, two hundred muskets, and enough clothing to start a mail-order business. Unbelievably, given the enemy carnage, the Legion had not suffered a scratch—almost. Among the three dead on the attacking side lay Saint-Germain, two bullet holes in his head. It was only fair. The whole sad business had been largely his fault anyway. But his death was much regretted in the French army. The Legion marched back to Biskra, leaving the *goumiers* to pillage the camp.[34]

The success at Seriana, which followed closely that of early July against the Ouled-Sahnoun, suggests that the Legion had reached an impressive peak of fighting fitness by 1849, perhaps one of its most brilliant, which has not been generally acknowledged. It also serves to reinforce the view that the strength of the *Armée d'Afrique* as refashioned by Bugeaud in the 1840s lay in its mobility. The trouble is that neither Herbillon nor Carbuccia, nor their superiors, seem to have drawn the proper conclusions from this. The first would seem to be a rather obvious military one—that a force trained and equipped for mobile warfare might be expected to perform less well in siege operations.

The second, political conclusion would appear to follow logically from the first—why risk a defeat, or at the very least a disproportionate commitment of forces, by besieging a strongly held fortress obviously determined to hold out, which could throw doubt on the solidity of French arms? Locked into his lair at Zaatcha, Bouzian was a formidable opponent. But those who wished to join the dissidence beyond those walls could be in no doubt that they risked the wrath of the Legion. The French, through the mobility of their forces, as stunningly demonstrated in the Hodna and at Seriana, were perfectly capable of isolating Zaatcha and preventing the contagion from spreading. They could have cut off Zaatcha and Bouzian by increasing patrols in the oases, organizing an economic boycott and bribing away support. Eventually, Zaatcha would have fallen like ripe fruit into their hands, without the enormous investment in men and materiel that a prolonged siege would obviously require. But Herbillon never for a moment seems to have to considered this more patient strategy. Rather, he complained that Seriana had failed to produce the expected political results. Many of the oases "remained in a sort of doubtful neutrality, and those who were in revolt took no steps to submit."[35] There was only one way to deal with this sort of problem as far as the French soldiers in Algeria were concerned, and that was a thumping demonstration of French power. Herbillon requested reinforcements, and the governor-general ordered him and Carbuccia south to deal with Zaatcha once and for all.

If the future campaign produced anxiety in Paris, this was because the potential for damage was so great, both in Algeria and in France, not to mention Zaatcha. The war minister, an experienced Algeria hand, demonstrated in full that paranoia common to the colonial breed when, on September 4, 1849, he wrote to the governor-general that ". . . a large setback in the Constantine Province would compromise the security of all of Africa [meaning, of course, French North Africa]." Nor had he changed his mind three weeks later when he cautioned that another failure before Zaatcha, or even an incomplete victory, "established on bad foundations"—that is, without appropriate political consequences to guarantee the results obtained—would mean that "a spring insurrection is imminent."[36]

Bad news from Algeria would also rattle a government whose stability was precarious. The bloodily suppressed June Days of 1848 had temporarily put an end to the riotous behavior of the Parisians. But the shaky Second Republic had yet to establish a solid political base in the country. The last thing the government required was a lengthy military campaign that would focus yet more discontent, provide yet more ammunition for their opponents, especially if things deteriorated rapidly in North Africa. For this reason, Rullière wrote to the governor-general that he must choose his commanders with great care, ". . . not only from the point of view of war, but also with an eye for the general political situation and the government of the Arabs. . . . The further they are away from the center of government, the more you must take their personal qualities into consideration."[37]

It was precisely these "personal qualities" that preoccupied Rullière. Administrative logic dictated that the command of the expedition fall to General Herbillon as chief of Constantine Province, seconded by Colonel Carbuccia, commander of the Batna subdivision that included Biskra and Zaatcha. But Rullière had little confidence in either man, and, as it turned out, with good reason. The first, and perhaps most important, quality of a good commander in this era when disease claimed far more soldiers than did bullets was to get his men to the battlefield in fairly good shape. Apparently on this score Herbillon's record was a blemished one. Patrice MacMahon, who had campaigned with Herbillon in the 1840s, noted that he ran up high sickness rates among his troops because he chose his campsites badly, near rivers where the temperature variation between day and night was substantial, and also, no doubt, because these lowlands were malarial. Wise commanders, according to MacMahon, camped on high ground, even if it lacked shade and water.[38] But Herbillon did not learn his lesson, for as the troops assembled at Biskra in September 1849, fully 300 were in the hospital, while in the Legion alone 444 men were reported unfit for service. Herbillon blamed the stagnant water and "the lack of cleanliness in and around the camp. The men throw their trash anywhere they find a hole or a fold of earth."[39]

Nor was Rullière willing to place confidence in the command qualities of either man: "I repeat, I do not believe General Herbillon and Colonel Carbuccia capable of successfully conducting these operations," he continued.[40] Worse, the individual shortcomings of the two men were magnified tenfold when they were placed in tandem. In Rullière's opinion, Herbillon "is not in a state to lead this operation. . . . *He is extremely irresolute and will not make decisions.*" [Italics in original.] One of the *Armée d'Afrique*'s young prodigies, Louis de Lamoricière, who was to be exiled to Rome after President Louis-Napoleon Bonaparte proclaimed himself Emperor Napoleon III on December 2, 1852, suggested assigning another general to him, ". . . to compensate for his weakness . . . [but] today even you admit the inadequacy of this precaution because General Herbillon does not necessarily listen to the opinions of his equals in rank."[41] And, as was to become apparent as the operations progressed, he was to prove a poor planner.[42]

Herbillon's irresolution meant that he was bound to be dominated by his headstrong subordinate, Carbuccia, for whom Rullière obviously had no great affection.[43] Algerian Governor-General Viala Charon's view of Carbuccia differed little from that of Rullière. "I followed [Carbuccia] throughout his career and I always found him the same," he wrote to General Jean-Jacques Pélissier when he learned of Carbuccia's death at Gallipoli, a staging point for the Crimean expedition, in 1854, "looking for popularity at the expense of the dignity of man, and often implacable with the weak and servile in the presence of the powerful. He drew Herbillon into more than one mistake at Zaatcha. . . ."[44] In early September, Rullière told the governor-general to select one of the *Armée d'Afrique*'s stellar commanders, like Pierre Bosquet or Saint-Arnaud, to command the expedition. On September 22, he placed the earlier suggestion in stronger terms, by informing Charon that the president of the Republic and the council of ministers "invited" him to choose another commander. But, as often happened in colonial affairs, orders from Paris could be conveniently ignored or arrive too late to be executed. The colonies were a law unto themselves.[45]

At eight o'clock on the morning of October 7, 1849, Herbillon arrived before Zaatcha with 4,493 men, about 1,000 of whom were Carbuccia's legionnaires, and eleven artillery pieces served by 300 artillerymen. This army established its base on a small hill called the Coudiat-el-Meida, about 550 yards to the northeast of the oasis edge. From this small promontory the soldiers could look out over Zaatcha, to Farfar and the Tolga oasis beyond. In the midst of his army, Herbillon must have looked the very picture of confidence—his slender frame, his tunic with great gold epaulets, the beard that surrounded his mouth, and the kepi tilted rakishly over his right ear made him look younger than his fifty-five years. And, on the face of it, he had no reason to worry. After all, his force was almost a quarter as large as that sent against Constantine in 1837, and Zaatcha was a mere fly-speck compared with what had been one of the greatest, and most formidably bastioned, cities in North Africa.

But in his memoirs, Herbillon confesses that he was far from confident. In the first place, he claimed, his force, though substantial, was simply too small to besiege the entire oasis.[46] This was a red herring. He never needed to seal off the entire oasis. Lichana and Farfar were not in revolt, only Zaatcha, which was a postage stamp of a place that could have been ringed fairly easily by earthworks. The sapper colonel attached to the expedition proposed to approach Zaatcha from three directions—from the *zaouia* [monastery] to the northeast, from Lichana to the south, and from Farfar to the west. Herbillon rejected this sensible solution: "With so few people, to divide our efforts from the beginning, was to be weak at all points, to expose our flanks to attacks of the rebels and to throw ourselves open to all their enterprises which, by harassing our troops, would have excited the audacity of the Arabs even more."[47]

Now, while dividing one's force in the face of the enemy is not a tactic recommended by most staff colleges, and one that certainly brought on the demise of Custer at the Little Big Horn and Lord Chelmsford at Isandlwhana in 1879, Herbillon's troops, if so divided, would not have been out of touch with each other, but close enough to offer mutual support if attacked. If Herbillon really feared this as a possibility, he could easily have organized mobile groups, fire teams that could have rushed to any portion of the trenches in danger. But neither the trenches nor the French base camp ever came under serious threat. In 1865, the French were able to surround and successfully besiege Oaxaca, a Mexican town of twenty-five thousand inhabitants built partially on hills, with a force of essentially equal size.

And this exposed the second fatal weakness in Herbillon's logic. The Arabs had no interest in coming out of Zaatcha. They wished to fight a defensive battle, force the French to attack them. The only time they seemed prepared to sacrifice this substantial tactical advantage, apart from occasional raids on the trenches, was when the French began to cut down their date palms. But Herbillon's decision was final: "All our efforts should therefore concentrate on one point, and after mature reflection, the general decided that the trench depot would be established at the *zaouia*. . . ."[48] The results of this decision were not difficult to predict—Zaatcha was allowed to resupply and reinforce each night because the critical west face of the town, which contained the gate and the road out, were never invested. Therefore, at the outset Herbillon sacrificed a weapon vital to the success of so many sieges—starvation. And while the Arabs could draw on an almost inexhaustible supply of fresh manpower from the outside, Herbillon had virtually drained the garrisons of Constantine Province and had to beg fresh forces as casualties, disease and the climate took their toll. There is some indication that Herbillon believed a decisive demonstration by his force would persuade the Arabs of the futility of resistance. But, if true, he was destined for disappointment, for things began to go wrong from the very beginning. In what was to become a too familiar accusation during the course of the siege, Herbillon blamed his initial setbacks on Carbuccia, who was ordered to seize the *zaouia* with the infantry, which included six hundred legionnaires. The commander insisted upon the limited nature of this operation to his subordinate: "Colonel Carbuccia was given a formal order not to go beyond the houses grouped around the minaret and, above all, not to pursue the Arabs into the gardens which were unknown to us," he wrote. "This order was passed on and repeated several times orally to the troops." This done, the artillery opened fire, collapsing several walls. The Arabs scattered and the troops seized the *zaouia* almost without resistance. In fact, so effortless was this opening attack that, ". . . in the heat of the action, officers and soldiers totally forgot [their orders] and pushed into the gardens where the Arabs, hidden behind the walls, directed a murderous fire at them. Many of them, marching blindly, even got to the crenelated walls of the village, where several were killed." Although the blame for this *fuite en avant* (forward flight) was laid at the feet of the *Chasseurs à Pied* and the *zéphyrs*, rather than the Legion,[49] the result was the same. Realizing the danger, the soldiers began what Herbillon described as a "precipitous flight," which stopped only when they reached a small "mountain gun" whose rapid fire kept the pursuing Arabs far enough away to allow them to rally.[50]

This opening action of the second siege of Zaatcha by the French exposed the shortcomings of Herbillon's approach. The first was that he had underestimated the skill and determination of his adversaries. He admitted that he had hoped the seizure of the *zaouia* would deflate their will to continue.[51] In fact, he had handed them at the very least a moral victory at this critical opening stage—how could they not be encouraged at the sight of the mighty *Armée d'Afrique* fleeing through their gardens, leaving behind quite a few of their twenty-five dead and dragging sixty-seven wounded with them in retreat? "The cadavers of our soldiers produced the greatest enthusiasm among them," Herbillon admitted. "Bouzian proceeded to announce [the defeat] in the neighboring oases by sending as trophies clothes stripped off them. This spectacle was visible proof, strong medicine which increased the numbers of his partisans (some from as far away as the Tell) and encouraged those already with him."[52] Needless to say, had the oasis been invested completely, Bouzian would neither have been able to get out to announce his victory, nor those tempted to support him to get in.

The second aspect of this opening action that bode ill was that it raised serious questions about Herbillon's control of his own troops. Why, if they had received repeated orders to limit their advance, did they continue? Was this lapse of discipline an exceptional case caused, as Herbillon claimed, by the passions of the moment? Or did it betray other, more fundamental shortcomings, like an institutionalized ardor that bordered on recklessness, useful perhaps in a *razzia,* but a positive hindrance in a controlled operation like a siege? Or was it more willful, a reaction by ambitious officers against their commander's well-established reputation for hesitation, caution, indecision, an act of collective indiscipline? Whatever the reason, it was a cause for worry. It suggested that the *Armée d'Afrique,* while tough and resilient, had not developed the discipline, coordination and skill in minor tactics required for an offensive siege. It also hinted that Herbillon did not have a firm grasp on his command. In Algiers, fears were soon expressed that Herbillon, despite his good qualities, was "not up to it." Colonel Borel noted that "It's a great pity that such a forthright man, so loyal, so attentive, so up to date on the affairs of the Province [of Constantine], capable of undertaking everything, is now lacking in self-confidence, in *élan* and initiative. It's a pity, but lacking that, can one command?"[53]

If proof were needed that the failure of the first attack was not a fluke, it was furnished on the following day. On the morning of October 8, a battery established just within the oasis behind the *zaouia* began to bombard the town barely one hundred yards away. While clouds of dust and smoke were clearly visible from the French positions, the effects of the bombardment were hidden by the palm trees. A battalion-sized reconnaissance of Algerian *tirailleurs* was ordered forward to see if a breach had been created. Incredibly, given the experience of the preceding day, they too decided they could take the town singlehanded, and rushed the walls, from which they were bloodily repulsed with seven dead and forty-three wounded. Herbillon must have been struck by a strong sense of *déjà vu* when he saw them rush back, causing panic among the soldiers, who abandoned the most advanced positions in the gardens, which had to be retaken the next day.[54] Clearly, Herbillon had serious difficulties with what a modern officer would call "command and control."

He was also going to have serious problems creating a breach. The *tirailleurs* reported that the bombardment had made little impact on the lower, stone section of the walls.[55] But surely Carbuccia's experience in July should have told him that the walls would be difficult to breach. This was the view of the war minister, who, on November 10, announced it "unthinkable" that after the July 16 experience Herbillon had neglected to include incendiary shells in his inventory, because "they would certainly have produced a great effect in Zaatcha and Lichana."[56]

Herbillon also noted that no wailing or death dirges had been heard from Zaatcha of the sort that normally followed combat with the Arabs. He took this to mean that the dead on the Arab side had all been outsiders who had no women to mourn them.[57] This might have been true. Equally possible is that Arab losses had so far been very light. In any case, his insistence that the resistance of Zaatcha beyond that normally expected of desert Arabs sprang directly from the presence of "fanatical" outsiders betrays a confusion bordering upon incompetence. If this were true, then why had he not taken steps to seal off the town from the outside?

On the morning of October 9 began the tedious business of constructing saps that snaked out from the *zaouia* toward Zaatcha barely 250 yards away. It also proved to be a difficult and dangerous business. The Arabs, not notable as marksmen in normal times, managed to sow confusion with highly accurate sniper fire directed especially at the artillery batteries at the moment of unmasking. The chief sapper was critically wounded. Herbillon attributed this unaccustomed accuracy to the presence of ostrich hunters among the defenders.[58] Workers in the trenches were harassed by large stones thrown into the heads of the saps and by the occasional raid, one of which was vigorously repulsed by a company of Legion grenadiers on October 10.[59]

By October 11, the sap had reached the south wall of Zaatcha, where the artillery had succeeded in reducing the corner tower to rubble. Until then, Herbillon had believed that the arrival of the sap at the moat would "suffice to force the inhabitants, who in all probability did not wish to expose themselves to a final assault, to surrender. On the contrary, the besieged only became more entrepreneurial, more audacious and more stubborn in their resistance which continued to increase the closer we came to the village."[60] Therefore, he pushed a sap toward the northeast angle of the wall to open a second breach, harassed every step of the way by Arabs who knew the oasis well enough to spring surprise attacks or who, lighting huge bonfires in the night, exposed the saps to a plunging fire from the walls. And while the French toiled away at this exhausting work, each night they could hear the firing and ululations of the women that announced the arrival of fresh contingents. The Arabs appeared to be growing in strength and audacity, despite the arrival of 1,512 French reinforcements on October 12, which brought French numbers to around 6,000. To drive home their will to resist, the Arabs coordinated attacks on both the saps and the French camp on the night of October 13, which, if not particularly effective, at least demonstrated a robust morale.

The trench work continued at a snail's pace. On the south face, the French had reached the moat that surrounded the walls. The wall was badly enough damaged to storm, but attempts to pass bricks and debris from the *zaouia* to hurl into the moat snagged on the accurate fire from the village, which killed several sappers. On the right, the trench crept forward only a yard or two each day, hampered by Arab countermeasures, by the difficulties of cutting palm trees to shore up parapets, and by the time taken to fabricate the *gabions,* portable wicker earthworks, to protect the workers in the trenches. By the 18th, Herbillon had become worried by reports of unrest in the Tell caused by the slow progress of the siege. The government even passed on a report that the Italian freedom fighter Garibaldi planned to travel to Zaatcha to lead the resistance, although why Arabs supposedly locked in a Moslem holy war would have turned to a Christian for leadership is not entirely clear.[61]

Herbillon admitted that the fragile political situation in Algeria, rather than the progress of the siege, caused him to order an attack for October 20.[62] He called a war council, which concluded that if the south wall were sufficiently damaged to attack, the northern sap was still twenty-two yards away from the moat, which, unfilled, offered a water obstacle nine yards wide. An enterprising captain of engineers suggested that a wagon be pushed into the moat to serve as a bridge for the attackers. Only the colonel of the 43rd Infantry Regiment, whose soldiers would be expected to charge over this makeshift bridge, expressed reservations. The rest unanimously agreed that even if the plan failed on the north face, it would provide the diversion needed to get Carbuccia and his legionnaires safely into the town from the south.[63]

At five-thirty on the morning of October 20, the artillery opened fire, gradually increasing in intensity. A battalion of *tirailleurs* screened Lichana to prevent surprises from that quarter, while cavalry and *goumiers* policed the western approaches. On the left, where the Legion was expected to carry the honors of the day, the word was given to attack. Unfortunately, the wall the sappers had constructed to protect the head of the trench refused to collapse to allow the attack to begin. When eventually it was destroyed, the rubble was so encumbering that the legionnaires could file out only one by one into a murderous fire. The light company managed to occupy the breach, but at great cost.

Ten legionnaires climbed onto the roof of a house just inside the wall, but when it collapsed, the attackers spontaneously fled back across the moat into the sap, according to Grisot because the tower's collapse exposed them to the full force of the garrison's fire.[64] "This retrograde movement resulting from natural instincts, would probably not have happened if these two companies had been supported when they arrived on the breach which they sought to hold," Herbillon believed.[65] On the other hand, Herbillon appears to be responsible in part for his lack of support, which sprang from a tactical problem he had not yet solved. He was later criticized for attempting to storm Zaatcha with what amounted to less than two understrength battalions.[66] However, his problem was that while his army was substantial, there were just so many troops he could fit in a small sap or use to attack a small breach without causing impossible chaos.

The Legion's retreat was covered by a company of *Chasseurs d'Afrique,* fortunately, because the Arabs followed them to the sap itself. This, Herbillon believed, was the moment to counterattack, and he faulted Carbuccia's decision not to do so: "This unexpected news caused the greatest surprise and destroyed the confidence which we placed in the attack on the left."[67] But, in Carbuccia's defense, it is not clear that he had any troops capable of counterattacking at that moment.

The attack on the right was equally unsuccessful. The wagon that was supposed to serve the 43rd as a bridge flipped into the moat, causing the conscripts to wade through five feet of water and then climb a wall that had been only partially destroyed. They clung to the breach for two hours and suffered 17 killed and 80 wounded before being ordered to retire. For its part, the Legion counted 13 dead and 40 wounded. In all, the failed attack had cost the French 45 killed and 147 wounded.[68] Herbillon blamed Carbuccia for the failure, and the war minister concurred: "I agree with you that Colonel Carbuccia's attack on the left was not as energetic as that of the 43rd," he wrote to the governor-general. "It had greater advantages, a better prepared path, and it got less far and held less well. However, in such a difficult operation, I have no thought of assigning from such a distance the slightest blame." He reiterated his view expressed in September that the French should move against those things the oasis dwellers valued most—their water and their palm trees.[69]

Only now did Herbillon begin, it seems, to take account of his difficulties, and they were many—too few engineers, too little siege equipment, no grenades, an artillery that was too light to breach the walls and ammunition much of which, dating from the siege of Constantine twelve years earlier, too often declined to detonate. The destruction it had caused had made problems worse, for it simply created more piles of rubble behind which the defenders could hide. Casualties and sickness were reducing his numbers. He was also forced to admit that he had underestimated his opponents, and recognized that his measures, rather than undermining their will to resist, had actually stiffened it.[70] Nevertheless, all of his officers save one were for abandoning several of the gardens to reduce the extent of their front and pursue the siege. The one dissenting voice, Herbillon noted with apparent surprise, was Carbuccia's: "His insistence on this point opened my eyes and I could see in him only bad intentions, even more when I heard that, during a dinner, he was not afraid to rejoice at my failure of 20 October," Herbillon wrote.[71]

The sluggish progress of the French before Zaatcha had not gone unnoticed among the Algerians, although their restlessness was far from the brewing general revolt Herbillon feared. Its manifestations were rumors of seditious talk in tribal councils and an increase in brigandage, especially against convoys traveling between Batna and Biskra. It was one of these convoys that brought in the new commander of the 3rd Battalion of the Legion, Pierre-Napoleon Bonaparte. His presence added one of the more bizarre twists to the Zaatcha episode, and would help both to strain relations between Herbillon and Carbuccia almost to the breaking point as well as draw the siege into the political debate in France. Pierre-Napoleon, son of Lucien Bonaparte, who had served his brother as president of the council of five hundred during the Directory in 1799, was born in 1815 in Italy, where his father had fled into exile. Like his first cousin Louis-Napoleon, in 1848 Pierre had returned to France from the exile imposed upon all Bonapartes after Waterloo to trade upon the prestige of his name to get elected to the Constituent Assembly as a representative for Corsica on May 7, 1848. Eager to associate himself with the military glory of his illustrious house, he was named a major in the 1st Regiment of the Foreign Legion on April 19, 1848, by virtue of the fact that he had held this rank in the army of New Granada (Colombia) in 1832 when he was seventeen years old.

He certainly regarded this as an intermediate step to rank in a regular French regiment, for he petitioned the Assembly on May 17, 1849, to be integrated into the army as an officer *à tître français*. Perhaps some important people, including his cousin Louis-Napoleon Bonaparte, president of the Second Republic, suggested that his case might be strengthened if he actually bothered to appear for duty with the Legion, which he had yet to visit. Even though an officer in the 1st Regiment, he was given a command in the 2nd Regiment, which was part of Herbillon's column. Pierre-Napoleon's account is somewhat different. He claims that he solicited a posting in the Zaatcha operation, and was promised the command of an "elite unit." However, upon arrival in Algeria, he was informed that, as he was not a French citizen but a Roman by birth, he could serve only in the Legion with a foreigner's commission. This distressed him acutely, both because his Frenchness had been called into question and because he apparently believed the Legion insufficiently elite.[72]

The closer Bonaparte came to Biskra, the more the romance of Africa began to give way to the realities of a stymied siege. As the convoy filed through the Kantara Gorge and onto the Sahara plain, it was shadowed at a respectful distance by Algerians who on occasion rushed about in a "fantasia" of galloping, shouting and firing into the air, but who otherwise kept a respectful distance. Still, it was amusing, and concentrated the minds of the muleteers who, for once, ceased complaining and worked with something approaching efficiency. Biskra was otherwise—a collection of miserable oases organized around Saint-Germain's fortress, which was filled with sick and wounded from the siege. The track from Biskra to Zaatcha followed the foot of the Saharan Atlas, which rose like a somber fortress to the north, while to the south an unending plain stretched off to the horizon, broken only by an occasional cluster of date palms that sat, scorched and bedraggled, between the folds of low dunes.

The increasing bleakness of the land provided an appropriate introduction to the French camp, which was arranged in lines across broken terrain, the tents of the officers and the ambulance pitched on rocky outcroppings that protruded above the canvas shelters of the soldiers. About four hundred yards to the southwest was a spring that gushed abundant but virtually undrinkable water. Two hundred yards beyond that, the oasis began. Bonaparte could hardly believe that this was what had held up the army for so long: "Zaatcha is nothing, when all is said and done, but a miserable village which is hardly fortified," he wrote. He entered the "trenches" for a closer look, and followed their meandering path along bits of wall shored up by palm trunks, past gun loops that allowed the French to reply to the harassing fire of Arab blunderbusses, until he could glimpse the breach in the south wall. It still contained a corpse, "completely naked, swollen, blackened," lying beneath an enormous beam.[73]

Since the failure of the October 20 offensive, the French had busied themselves in two activities—extending their trenches and felling date palms. The two activities were not unrelated, as the tree trunks reinforced the saps. But the felling of the date palms was also meant to bring economic pressure on the defenders, who it was hoped would surrender rather than see their livelihood irrevocably destroyed. Rullière had suggested on September 22 that the weakness of an oasis lay in its two

vulnerable points . . . the palm trees and the water. These are the indispensable conditions of their existence. They are the only wealth of the country. The destruction of the palm trees will have more effect in an oasis than the death of a man. It is therefore in their interests that one must menace them. I do not suggest total destruction, which on the contrary one must avoid as much as possible. But it will be useful to make them fear it and even to begin to do it . . . to bring the inhabitants into submission.[74]

This seemed like sensible advice. However, in this case it did not appear to work. The French maps show two principal springs—Aïn Meioub close to the French camp, to which the Arabs would have had no access, and Aïn Fouar, whose streams flowed past Zaatcha itself. There is nothing in the documents that suggests that the French ever attempted to cut off Zaatcha from its water supply. In any case, as the Zaatchans were free to come and go after dark through the west gate, presumably they could resupply at will. There is no evidence that lack of water was a factor in Zaatcha's downfall.

As for the date palms, it is certain that the defenders did make an effort to protect them. But it is not clear whether they did so to salvage their economic livelihood, or because French palm-cutting parties proved to be tempting targets. If, as Herbillon claimed, many of the defenders were outsiders, then presumably they were indifferent to the economic pressures of palm cutting, and simply preferred to hit the French when they were out in the open and preoccupied with other things. And here the French seem to have demonstrated a remarkable lack of tactical imagination. For if the felling of date palms did not bring on surrender, at least it brought the defenders into the open where the superior discipline of the Europeans should have given them a decisive advantage. But instead of using this opportunity to lay traps and ambushes for the Arabs, the French allowed themselves to be surprised.

The inexperienced Bonaparte learned of the lethal nature of tree cutting on October 25, when he was put in charge of a party of two hundred legionnaires and two hundred *zéphyrs*. He marched his men out to the palm trees with the band in front, and almost immediately lost two legionnaires to snipers. He then set his men to work felling trees, guarded only by a small post of *zéphyrs*. The work began unhindered, the silence broken only by the hollow sounds of the axes upon the resilient tree trunks. Unseen, the Arabs crawled forward through the debris of the oasis. A sizable group suddenly rushed the guard post, and, according to Pierre-Napoleon, overwhelmed them. Bonaparte first saw Arabs, isolated or in small groups, appear here and there. Suddenly a large mass moved up a ravine to attack. A number of officers fell, and "many soldiers gathered round them, some carried them to the rear. Others, as often happens in these cases, probably to escort them."[75] He placed himself at the head of twenty-five grenadiers of the Legion and held back the attack long enough for the rest to rally, aided by another small group of legionnaires led by a sergeant, who also stood firm. The French lost six killed and twenty-two wounded.[76]

The arrival of Bonaparte allowed Carbuccia to make a public display of his Bonapartist sentiments. According to Herbillon, Carbuccia "only saw in Pierre Bonaparte an instrument which could help him advance and acted toward this. . . ."[77] Carbuccia welcomed Bonaparte with a dinner in the saps, where the officers ate while sitting cross-legged on rugs and the Legion band played "patriotic airs." After the colonel toasted the president of the Republic, the band struck up the *"Marseillaise."* This infuriated the Arabs, who fired their blunderbusses, bringing down a shower of lead through the date palms. Others shouted insults across the trenches at Carbuccia, whom they knew by name as head of the Batna region. The Legion was also a special target of insult by Arabs who, Bonaparte believed, must have been to Algiers, because they shouted in French: *"Bataillon di juifs!"* *"Cochons, juifs!"* (Battalion of Jews! Jewish Pigs!) They also pushed donkeys into no-man's land in the hope that the French would come out to get them and thereby offer themselves as targets. Instead, the French simply shot the donkeys themselves. These festivities were punctuated by a mortar which fired an hourly round. All in all, despite the distractions and "the execrable odor of corpses," Bonaparte passed a capital evening's entertainment.[78]

Whatever their attractions, however, the delights of Zaatcha were insufficient to hold Pierre-Napoleon, who announced to Herbillon barely five days after his arrival that pressing legislative matters in Paris required his attention. Herbillon suspected that Carbuccia had pressed him to return so that he could denounce the conduct of the siege in France. He also believed that Pierre-Napoleon lacked the stomach to sit out a siege whose end was not in sight. Herbillon tried to talk Bonaparte into staying—an extraordinary statement as he was, after all, Bonaparte's commanding officer. But the cousin of the president was not to be dissuaded, so "wanting to avoid jeers and shelter the great name of Napoleon from ridicule," Herbillon gave Bonaparte the mission of reporting the difficulties faced by the French before Zaatcha to the governor-general and requesting reinforcements.[79]

However, rather than pay a visit upon the governor-general, Pierre-Napoleon avoided Algiers altogether and caught a boat for France directly from Philippeville.

Herbillon for once had seen clearly that Bonaparte's departure was bound to cause problems. According to the war minister, the slowness of the siege, combined no doubt with news of the failure of the October 20 assault, "has agitated public opinion."[80] The enemies of President Louis-Napoleon Bonaparte were too numerous and too suspicious of his intentions (and with good reason) not to exploit this golden opportunity to attack him through his cousin. A Bonaparte fleeing his army! This was a chance too good to pass up. Even before Pierre-Napoleon's boat docked in Marseille, many were saying that he had fled the final assault, which promised to be murderous, and that he feared contracting cholera. Pierre-Napoleon replied rather weakly that there had been no cholera at Zaatcha when he was there. This did not stop General de Castellane from noting in his diary that "War is not to his taste, or so it seems."[81] But the charge stuck. Abandoning armies in distress seemed to be a family trait—after all, Pierre-Napoleon's uncle had left two armies behind, one in Egypt and the other in Russia, nor had he exactly lingered after Waterloo to put things in order. On November 19, Pierre-Napoleon was stripped of his majority in the Legion for deserting his post. He demanded a parliamentary debate on the issue, which was held three days later. The new war minister, Count Alphonse d'Hautpoul, said that had Herbillon not given Bonaparte a letter to carry to the governor-general, then the ex-major would surely have been court-martialed. In his defense, Bonaparte moved that all representatives be allowed to be in the Assembly when voting was taking place, a motion unanimously rejected.[82] Never mind! Pierre-Napoleon was to get his revenge on December 2, 1851, when cousin Louis-Napoleon ordered the army to flush out the National Assembly, and a year later to the day proclaimed himself Emperor Napoleon III.

Bonaparte's disgrace was also bound to be that of Carbuccia, at least temporarily. On November 8, a column of 1,200 *zouaves* under Canrobert arrived at Zaatcha, driving before them three thousand sheep and goats gathered in *razzias* on the way south. At first they were a welcome morale booster in a French camp demoralized by lack of progress, inadequate food and incessant rains. But the joy soon turned to horror when it was realized what they brought with them: Two days out of Aumale, a new settlement about one hundred miles south of Algiers, severe diarrhea and vomiting, unmistakable signs of cholera brought on by infected food and water, began to appear among Canrobert's *zouaves*. The dry climate accelerated the dehydration that brought on kidney failure and death: "We spend our evenings burying bodies," Canrobert wrote.[83] Soon all of the horses were laden with soldiers, something that could not escape the attention of the Algerians, who began "to follow the column like jackals, looking to harass stragglers and to cut the throat of isolated soldiers." Each day their numbers grew until one morning Canrobert discovered a compact mass obviously intent on disputing his passage through a defile. As his horses could carry no more wounded, which a battle would inevitably produce, Canrobert opted for a different stratagem: Approaching the Arabs, he shouted, "You hear me? Know that I carry the plague with me. If you block my passage, I will throw myself on you." The Arabs scattered quickly.[84]

So, too, did the Legion. The arrival of reinforcements was the signal for the departure of Carbuccia and his legionnaires, who, on November 10, marched out toward Biskra. While they were assigned to escort convoys through the Kantara Gorge, they missed the final act of the siege of Zaatcha, which, predictably, was a bloody one. The honors of the day went to Canrobert and his *zouaves,* who charged the breach where, over a month earlier, the 43rd had lingered for two horrible hours. Once inside the town, all resistance was extinguished within an hour by *zouaves* who simply massacred everyone in sight. Canrobert claimed that he was so overwhelmed by the losses in his regiment that he left his men to their revenge and went back to his tent to sleep. When he awoke, the head of Bouzian was grimacing from atop a pole outside his tent.[85]

Herbillon argued in his memoir on Zaatcha that the result was to produce "a terrible effect on the spirit of the Saharans" and consolidate the French conquest in the south of Constantine Province.[86] Others, however, saw Zaatcha as one of the great tragedies of the conquest of Algeria, the ruined oasis as a monument to an unimaginative policy that favored force over diplomacy. "I am afraid to say that the glory of the vanquished eclipsed that of the victors," wrote the French consul in Tunis, Péllisier de Réynaud, citing the orgy of rape, murder and destruction carried out by the *zouaves* upon the captured fortress as especially sickening.[87] Zaatcha also appears a monument to a misconceived and wasteful military strategy. Julien's estimate of 1,500 French dead and wounded "without counting the victims of cholera" as against 800 Arabs appears exaggerated. Official figures, including those for Carbuccia's July attack, while they do not include those lost to disease, list 193 killed and 804 wounded, many of these latter only bruised or "concussed" by stones and spent shot.[88] Still, by the standards of Algerian warfare, this was an enormous, and unnecessary, loss of life. In the view of Canrobert, "The siege of Zaatcha was one of the toughest campaigns of the African war. The army—for a real army was employed—lost a quarter of its strength."[89] Its length, the climatic conditions, and the toll in human life, both French and Arab, makes the siege of Constantine in 1837 appear as a relatively surgical operation by comparison.

How does one rate the performance of the Legion at Zaatcha? One has already noted that the expedition, from the beginning, was underequipped. Too much of the strain of the siege fell upon the ordinary soldiers. Still, Herbillon cites two incidents when the Legion fell back a trifle too quickly— from the breach on October 20, and during the palm-cutting episode.[90] Of course, even he lay the main blame for the failure of the October 20 assault on the lack of reinforcements, while the collapse of the tower exposed the attackers to a murderous fire. It is also fair to point out that the south breach, at the time considered the most practicable, was never successfully stormed. As for the palm-cutting episode, the combination of surprise, the fact that the soldiers were scattered and vulnerable, and the lack of adequate protection explains a momentary tendency to flee. Of course, all the troops involved briefly faltered, not merely the Legion. Again, this appears to be a failure of command, which neglected to anticipate an attack and take adequate measures to defend against it, even to turn it to the advantage of the French.

Pierre-Napoleon Bonaparte noted that the Legion counted only one officer per company.[91] The shortage of officers created a vacuum that often left the soldiers leaderless in critical moments. The quarrels at the top, especially the friction between Carbuccia and Herbillon, could not go unnoticed further down. Likewise, Herbillon's reputation as a commander of more than ordinary mediocrity must have decreased the confidence of the rank and file, especially as the progress of the siege was so slow as to be imperceptible. Herbillon complimented his men: "This unfortunate affair nevertheless reflected the greatest honor upon the troops," he wrote.[92] And so it did. It would have been asking too much of the Legion, or of any corps, to compensate entirely for the serious shortcomings of the command. Alas, that task would too often fall to them in their history.

Chapter 6

"CORPS SANS PASSE ET SANS AVENIR": THE LEGION, 1850-1859

ORAN IN MID-CENTURY was one of the most bizarre towns in a very bizarre land. Its buildings, built in every conceivable architectural style, climbed the steep sides of a narrow ravine that opened to the sea. "Everywhere there are ramps, everywhere stairs, never a flat piece of ground," wrote Louis de Massol, a Belgian who came to the Legion in 1852.[1] The fortress of Saint-Grégoire stood sentinel above the town, while below a garden planted with lemon, orange and fig trees followed the bottom of the ravine to the Château of Santa-Cruz on the seafront. Despite the fact that Oran's twenty-five thousand inhabitants, divided almost equally among Spaniards, Arabs or Berbers, and Jews, seemed to be constantly in motion, the town had yet to acquire the air of prosperity that it was to possess by the century's end. On the contrary, to those arriving on the weekly packet from Marseille, Oran appeared distinctly down at heel.

Fifty miles to the south of Oran lay Sidi-bel-Abbès. The trip there from Oran took approximately ten hours, not because the roads were especially bad, but because the coach stopped frequently at roadside inns where travelers spilled out to drink absinthe and *"champoraux,"* an Algerian cocktail of sugar, coffee and throat-scalding brandy. Fights among the inebriated passengers at these halts were fairly frequent. They lengthened the journey still more, but added interest to what was otherwise a rather tedious trip.

The arrival at Sidi-bel-Abbès was an agreeable surprise. The road climbed steadily through an empty, desiccated countryside sprinkled with dwarf palms and other stunted bushes, until it leveled off onto a plain. There, in the middle of a patchwork of green, irrigated gardens and golden fields of wheat, rose up the walls of the town. When Second Lieutenant Charles-Jules Zédé, fresh from Saint-Cyr to take up his first posting with the 2ᵉ *régiment étranger,* saw "Bel Abbès" in 1857, it was already losing its frontier roughness. The last attack on the town had occurred in 1845, when fifty-six Ouled-Brahim disguised as beggars had infiltrated the settlement while most of the garrison was out on patrol and opened the gates to their brothers outside. The outlying units had been drawn back by the sound of the guns to restore order. From January 1, 1848, the town became the center of a military subdivision whose commander was also the colonel of the 1st Regiment of the Foreign Legion. A year later, Sidi-bel-Abbès was incorporated by order of the president of the Republic, Louis-Napoleon Bonaparte.

A decade later, the town was gradually taking on the air of a settled community. Almost half of the town's population were Spaniards, who ran the bars that in the evenings filled with legionnaires, or who otherwise made their living from the garrison. An Arab shanty that was off-limits to legionnaires (the prohibition was seldom respected) had already grafted itself onto the European settlement. There, legionnaires might wander the teeming streets at dusk (it was not wise to go alone) to buy a lamb kebab prepared by men squatting before charcoal braziers, follow an Arab woman through a door and up dark stairs or, if the soldier had it in mind to desert, exchange his uniform for a suit of civilian clothes. Periodic sweeps by patrols would scatter the soldiers down dark alleys and cul-de-sacs. Sidi-bel-Abbès was hardly paradise, but it offered the advantage of allowing legionnaires to earn extra money in off-duty hours by working for the townsfolk. Already a small but fairly prosperous community of retired legionnaires had formed.

The spread of cultivation into the surrounding plain had helped to reclaim the marshes that had made Sidi-bel-Abbès such an unhealthy place in the 1840s—in 1846, for instance, 146 legionnaires in the garrison had died of disease. The Legion cultivated its own large garden beyond the walls, but even here the vine had yet to make its appearance and would not do so until the 1870s, when the phylloxera epidemic temporarily wiped out the French wine industry, and when enough wealth had been accumulated to allow farmers the luxury of waiting four years for the first crop.[2]

By mid-century, the Legion had survived its adolescence, but its future was far from secure. In 1850, French military opinion was divided on its usefulness. Some even regarded the Legion as a national embarrassment— it was one thing to organize penal battalions like the *zéphyrs* for French delinquents, but why should the army be required to absorb the refuse of Europe as well? It had already been written off once in Spain, and had been tolerated during the 1840s because the French command needed all the rifles it could muster in Algeria. However, by 1850 the conquest of what was to become Algeria was virtually complete from the Mediterranean to the Sahara, with the exception of the mountainous Kabylia. North Africa, where so many brilliant careers had been made in the 1840s, now became a military backwater, allowing the French to reduce the garrison of occupation. What would the role of the Legion now be?

"They are talking of abolishing the Legion," the future general Edouard Collineau wrote on September 8, 1851. "In that case, where shall I go?"[3] By early 1852, however, the immediate future of the Legion appears to have been secure, for the new governor-general of Algeria, General César Randon, suggested a reorganization of the *Armée d'Afrique* that would increase the Legion to three regiments, one stationed in each of the three provinces of French North Africa.[4] And while the third regiment was not created, on May 10, 1852, representatives from the two Legion regiments were present in Paris to receive the eagles distributed to all regiments to replicate those carried by the units of the First Empire, an indication that the danger had passed for the moment.

The next two decades of its history would present the Legion with some serious challenges, however. It had made its reputation (such as it was) as a colonial force. The question was, How well would a force trained essentially for the conditions of Algerian warfare adapt to the set battles and bitter sieges of the Crimean campaign of 1854–56, and to the classic battles of the Italian campaign of 1859? At the same time, it must not lose its colonial touch, for it would help to shore up Louis-Napoleon's ill-fated Mexican adventure of the 1860s, where again it would come within a whisker of being left behind by the French government. Finally, in the Franco-Prussian War of 1870–71, where it would serve on French soil in violation of the law of March 9, 1831, an unhappy year capped by the "Bloody Week" of May 1871 in which perhaps as many as twenty-five thousand members of the Paris Commune were massacred by French soldiers, the Legion was thrust into the cauldron, and the historical controversies, of a French civil war. Adaptability and military efficiency might not guarantee the survival of the Legion, but its failure to rise to new challenges in the next two decades could certainly place its future in doubt.

Given the restricted esteem in which the Legion was held in this period, its prospects did not appear secure. Despite the fact that it had been the object of some flattering remarks from senior officers, the Legion seemed to exist on the margins of the *Armée d'Afrique,* a situation little changed from the previous decade when legionnaire Clemens Lamping complained that few officers ". . . had the courage to protect the interests of the Foreign Legion against the French general officers."[5] "It is distressing to think that this regiment which for so long has rendered such services to France, alternatively as a fighting regiment and as a colonizing one, is so little favored by successive war ministers," de Massol lamented in 1852,[6] even though the war minister at the time was none other than Saint-Arnaud.

It was a complaint that would follow the Legion through much of its history. In 1854, when the Englishman William Stammer inquired of a French general about enlisting in the French army for the Crimean campaign, he was told that the only regiment open to him as a foreigner was the Legion, which he could not recommend—"Poor devils!" he was told. "They have all the fighting and no glory."[7] In 1863, Legion lieutenant Diesbach de Torny complained that there was little of either to be had in the lethal duty of escorting convoys through the yellow-fever-infested lowlands behind Veracruz, Mexico, which had been assigned to the Legion precisely because its soldiers were considered "the pariahs of the army." When the French commander in Mexico, General Elie Frédéric Forey, was asked to transfer the Legion, which was melting away from disease, to the more salubrious highlands, he is alleged to have exclaimed, "What! . . . Those rogues, that rabble of the Legion isn't dead yet?"[8] "I had to leave the foreigners, in preference to the French, in a position where there was more sickness than glory to acquire," Forey admitted.[9] All of this caused French writer Antoine Camus, who paid an extensive visit to the *Armée d'Afrique* in the 1860s, to label the Legion as the French army's orphan regiment, "a corps without a past and without a future."[10]

Clearly the image of the Legion as an assemblage of cutthroats, deserters and adventurers was a serious stumbling block to its acceptance as a unit equal to others. Officers with more traditional attitudes found it difficult to imagine how a collection of mercenaries recruited from the scrapings of humanity, disciplined in a way that revolted many of the most hardened veterans and whose soldiers were prepared to desert at the drop of a hat could possibly be taken seriously as a fighting unit. And they had a point. Even Lamping admitted that, "Like all hirelings, our corps has much of the character of Wallenstein's [a celebrated commander of Catholic forces in the Thirty Years' War] camp."[11] But the Thirty Years' War had ended more than two centuries earlier, and many officers might have been forgiven if they believed that "hirelings" had no place in a modern army whose *esprit de corps* should be based upon patriotism.

The sort of unit that Zédé discovered at Sidi-bel-Abbès in 1857 sent cold shivers down his spine—"The Legion was then permeated with the wreckage of [Europe's] vanquished parties," he wrote, which included both Spanish Carlists and Parisian revolutionaries of 1848 who enlisted under strange names like Têtu (stubborn). There were also the defrocked bishop of Florence, a descendant of an Eastern European royal family and a Hungarian general who had chosen the wrong side in 1848. Most of Europe's nationalities were represented, "and even a Chinese who looked strange with his pigtail hanging from beneath his kepi. . . ."[12] It was commonly assumed that hunger, or some other personal misfortune, rather than a vocation for soldiering had driven them into the Legion.[13] William Stammer noted that his messmates were so poor that ". . . the breaking of a clay pipe was regarded as an irreparable calamity."[14]

How was the army to make soldiers out of such unpromising material?

The task was generally perceived to be a difficult, and some thought an impossible, one. Even Antoine Camus, who believed the Legion to be much misunderstood, conceded that a whole category of legionnaires could be characterized by "daily rebellions against certain military practices which irritate them in the extreme."[15] It is quite possible that these "rebellions" stemmed from the fact that legionnaires, most of whom counted prior service and had a greater experience of the world than did many of their French counterparts, resented many of the disciplinary regulations and practices designed for an army of conscripts in their early twenties. It is equally possible that many legionnaires had acquired habits and attitudes that ran counter to any sort of discipline at all.

The worst offenses occurred during the four yearly periods when legionnaires were paid whatever was left of their quarterly uniform allowance of thirty-five francs. When this occurred, Sidi-bel-Abbès usually dissolved into an alcoholic orgy that lasted until the money ran out.[16] Following these drinking sprees the retribution was distributed to those who were drunk on duty, who drew their bayonets in the course of a fight, those accused of theft or who sold equipment to prolong their celebrations—the worst offenders were dispatched to the discipline sections in the *bled,* as the Algerian hinterland was called, while the guard rooms of Sidi-bel-Abbès filled with soldiers who forfeited their pay until the Legion was reimbursed for the missing pieces of uniform.[17]

Discipline in isolated garrisons or on campaign might be more rough and ready. Some might be trussed up and placed in *cacolets*—metal stretchers lashed on muleback used to carry wounded—which made for a very uncomfortable journey. But the favorite rural punishment in this period was the silo. These were grain cellars dug into the ground by nomadic North Africans, which the *Armée d'Afrique* quickly discovered served admirably as bucolic jail cells. In the French camp at Gallipoli at the beginning of the Crimean campaign, the prisoners were confined in this manner during the day, and at night brought out to gather up the corpses of soldiers who had died from cholera. When the men in the silos began to protest and to insult their superiors, a channel was dug to the sea to let in water: ". . . Homeric shouts, some bravos were followed by swearing," Legion captain Paul de Choulot recounted.[18] Not one of these men perished from the cholera epidemic, and when the disease had run its course, their punishments were lifted.[19]

The problem for French commanders was that these rigorous disciplinary methods possibly caused as many problems as they controlled. The difficulty is apparent in the inspection report of the *1er étranger* in 1861. General Ulrich denounced a discipline that was "severe, often too rigorous, for coercive means forbidden by the regulations and by the sentiment of humanity" were inflicted upon the soldiers. For starters, "Major Aubry ordered a man who was merely suspected of theft tied up and exposed to the sun for nine days." On the other hand, he conceded that "Misdemeanors, serious infractions are very frequent and denote an advanced state of demoralization." The question, of course, was how one could expect this conglomeration of outlaws to perform: "A regiment which counts 648 deserters, in which one does not dare hand out the munitions which each soldier must carry, in which only one pair of shoes per man can be distributed lest they sell them, is far from being a disciplined regiment," he believed. "It is unworthy of confidence, perhaps even dangerous."[20] It is possible that the personality of Colonel Antonio Martinez, a courageous soldier but a poor administrator, contributed to the unit's problems.

The enigma of the Legion was that, despite its reputation for occasionally getting out of hand, those who served with it spoke very highly of its *esprit de corps* and combative qualities. Zédé may be accused of bias when he remembers of his regiment in the period between the Crimea and Mexico: "Perhaps there has never been a corps with more pride in itself than the 2*e* *étranger*. We showed with pride the flag covered with glorious inscriptions, we spoke with enthusiasm of the illustrious men who sprang from our ranks: Marshal Saint-Arnaud, Marshal de MacMahon, Marshal Bazaine . . . and so many others of slightly less renown. . . . The curious thing was that the regiment, which formed a compact unit because of an *esprit de corps* which bordered upon fanaticism, was composed of the most diverse elements."[21] Diesbach de Torny wrote of the barracks square at Sidi-bel-Abbès decorated by the legionnaires in August 1863 with inscriptions of the regiment's past victories. When the colonel appeared and questioned why one of the signs had been left blank, he was told, "That's the place to inscribe the Mexican campaign. And everyone began to shout: 'Let's go to Mexico!' "[22]

SWORDS WERE NOT carried by legionnaires in North Africa, so even the dullest soldier realized that their distribution could mean only one thing—that the Legion was about to travel. The ritual of departure was fairly well established: The colonel assembled the regiment for a "short but vibrant speech." Enthusiasm was instantaneous. Officers repaired to the mess to clamor for champagne, which most could not possibly afford, while the soldiers paraded through the streets beating on their mess tins with tent poles. Merchants immediately descended on the barracks in an attempt to collect their unpaid debts. Lieutenants were obliged to exchange their horses (strictly against regulations) against the two pack mules permitted on campaign, while the troops stuffed their kits into impossibly small, and impossibly heavy, knapsacks. When, at last, the preparations for departure were complete, the regiment was drawn up. The colonel cried "en avant," the band struck the first chords of the popular song "Artilleur de Metz," and the troops swung onto the road running north to Oran and adventure beyond.[23] In the 1850s, that adventure was to be had in the Crimea and in Italy.

*   *   *

FRENCH PARTICIPATION IN the Crimean War of 1854–56 may be remembered by American and British readers, who usually associate that war with Florence Nightingale, the news dispatches of William Russell, and the Charge of the Light Brigade, as a remote event. But it was important both for France and the Legion. The origins of the Crimean intervention can be traced to Russia's continued pressure to expand into the Balkans and toward the Mediterranean at the expense of the decaying Ottoman Empire. In 1853, Russian Emperor Nicholas I moved his troops into the Danubian principalities of Wallachia and Moldavia (later known as Rumania). Great Britain, who opposed Russian access to the Mediterranean because it would threaten her strategic route to India, had been a traditional supporter of Turkey. What France sought to gain from a war with Russia is less obvious. Because France was one of the protectors of the Holy Places in the Ottoman Empire, it is often assumed that Louis-Napoleon declared war to court French Catholic opinion. But the issue of the Holy Places had been settled before war was declared. And while in the short term the war did rally opinion on both left and right for a crusade against Russia, popular, especially Catholic, support for the war proved fickle. Louis-Napoleon's real motive appears to have been diplomatic—by joining in an alliance with Great Britain, he could split the entente of the conservative powers, Russia, Austria, and Prussia, and allow himself more scope to realize future diplomatic ambitions. As a consequence, France and Britain declared war on the tsar on March 27, 1854.

The decision to send the Legion to participate in the Crimean campaign of 1854–56 was a controversial one. Many generals, including Saint-Arnaud, were opposed to it, believing it imprudent to strip Algeria of white troops while the conquest of that land was still so recent. However, despite the best efforts of Saint-Arnaud's *aide-de-camp*, Colonel Louis Trochu, Napoleon III took the decision to dispatch the Legion to the Crimea on May 10, 1854. "The two regiments of the Foreign Legion have joined us in Gallipoli," Major Renson, a staff officer in the *Armée d'Orient*, wrote on July 9, 1854. "It's a mistake. They should have stayed in Africa where they were very useful." Renson attributed the presence of the Legion to a *"coup de Corse"* of General Jean-Luc Carbuccia, who had recovered nicely from his "disgrace" at Zaatcha, thanks to his confirmed Bonapartist opinions and his Corsican origins. Renson believed that Carbuccia had used his contacts with the royal family to persuade the Emperor to send his old corps, arguing among other things that the presence of the Legion might stimulate desertion among Poles serving in Russian ranks.[24]

On May 10, 1854, both regiments of the Legion received orders to furnish two battalions each for a Legion infantry brigade, while a third battalion provided by the *1er étranger* stationed at Gallipoli would act as the brigade depot. The charm that Gallipoli appeared to possess when approached from the sea after a long voyage quickly vanished upon disembarkation. What seemed to be an attractive collection of gray houses that followed the curve of the hillside on the European shore of the Dardanelles proved upon closer inspection to be a labyrinth of narrow streets running between shabby wooden buildings, all of which were filthy enough to disgust even soldiers accustomed to Algeria. The filth no doubt contributed to the cholera epidemic that broke out in the town, one that killed Carbuccia and over two hundred legionnaires.

Because the Legion had not been included in the original war plans, it was kept for a time at Gallipoli. Eventually, a *bataillon de marche* made up of eight elite companies was organized to strengthen the division of General Canrobert, which had been severely weakened by cholera. On August 25, General Canrobert, ex-colonel of the *2ᵉ étranger,* inspected the battalion personally. On September 14, this battalion disembarked with much of the rest of the expeditionary force at Calamita Bay in the Crimea. On the 19th, the combined Anglo-French army began to march in the direction of Sebastopol over a slightly undulating plateau. By the end of the day, the Russian positions on the heights above the Alma were visible in the distance.

By seven o'clock on the morning of September 20, the French army was drawn up in two lines facing west, the sea and the Allied fleet to their left, the English army on their right. The legionnaires brewed coffee while they waited for the English to move into line. At eleven-thirty in the morning the two Allied armies moved forward, across the Alma River and toward the heights occupied by the Russians. Canrobert ordered the troops to shed their backpacks and sent the Legion forward with two artillery batteries to occupy the heights. In skirmishing formation, the legionnaires began exchanging shots with the Russians barely three hundred yards away, a fight that lasted for three hours until, at five-thirty in the evening, the Russians retired. The Legion was ordered back to the banks of the Alma, where they collected their packs and made camp. The battalion counted sixty casualties, including five officers wounded.

The failure of the Allied commanders to take advantage of the Russian defeat to seize Sebastopol condemned them to a lengthy siege. In October, the elite battalion that had fought at the Alma was disbanded and integrated into the remainder of the Legion, which arrived from Gallipoli to form a brigade commanded by newly promoted Brigadier General Achille Bazaine. The new arrivals could not have been reassured by the scene that greeted them in the Crimea. The Legion camp was sited on a bleak plateau overlooking the Strelitzka Bay, a land of abandoned farms squared and cut by dry stone walls, once the protection for fruit orchards and vineyards that were soon enough sacrificed to the army's need for firewood. From their camp, the legionnaires, whom the Russians soon nicknamed "leather bellies" because of the cartridge pouches they wore suspended from around their necks in the "African" manner, could make their way to the siege works that now encircled Sebastopol. The winter would be a calvary for the Legion, as it was for all Allied troops. Working in deplorable conditions, dodging mortar and artillery shells lobbed at the trenches, the legionnaires pushed the earthworks toward the Russian walls, fighting mud, cold, snipers, dysentery and cholera. The fatigue of the day was redoubled at night, when half the men remained on alert while the other half tried to sleep in the relative safety of scrapes hollowed out in the sides of the trenches. On November 5, a surprise Russian sortie left three Legion officers and forty-three legionnaires dead and wounded a large number of others before a counterattack drove them back to their walls. This was followed on November 14 by a violent storm, which flooded the trenches and destroyed the shelters behind the lines. After that, the legionnaires took greater care to anchor their tents. But the rigors of the winter that a thin layer of canvas did little to diminish, the siege operations that kept men continually outside and the shortage of firewood led to many cases of frostbite, despite the arrival of more suitable winter clothing in December.

The Russians were not content to conduct a passive defense, but skillfully harassed the Allies with raids, ambushes, countermines and frequent bombardments. 1855 opened with a determined Russian assault on the siege lines held by the 2nd Battalion of the *2e étranger,* which was vigorously repulsed on the night of January 19–20, in the words of one Spanish sergeant, "like a hammer smashing butter on an anvil."[25] This was followed by other large-scale raids in February and March, the result of which was to leave a large number of unclaimed cadavers between the lines. So highly valued were the warm Russian boots that legionnaires were more than willing to run the risks and endure the discomfort of a night excursion into no man's land to strip a body, especially as the Russian soldiers were in the habit of tying their purses around their legs.

The Legion celebrated the arrival of spring with a night attack on a central fortification of the Russian defensive lines whose mortars rained down serious harassing fire on the French trenches. At eight-thirty on the evening of May 1, six elite companies taken from the *1er* and *2e étrangers* jumped off and seized the bastion with a bayonet attack. Colonel Viénot arrived with the remainder of the *1er étranger* and fought off repeated Russian counterattacks, while other legionnaires working under the direction of French military engineers worked to link the captured bastion to the French lines. Dawn found the Legion firmly in possession of the Russian redoubt and eight mortars. Among nearly one hundred Legion casualties was fifty-one-year-old Colonel Viénot—the Legion barracks at Sidi-bel-Abbès and subsequently Aubagne were baptized with his name. The following day the Russians again attempted to retake their lost bastion, to no effect. On May 3, a truce was declared so that the two sides could collect their dead. French and Russian officers exchanged courtesies and cigars in no-man's land until bugle calls announced the resumption of hostilities.

Not content to accept the loss of their battery, the Russians began to push forward a counterfortification along a ridge line between a cemetery and the sea designed to dominate the French trenches. On May 22, the Legion participated in a two-pronged attack to seize the Russian position. At nine o'clock in the evening, the two battalions of the *2ᵉ étranger* and one of the 98th Infantry Regiment left their trenches, flopped on their stomachs to allow the Russians to shoot off their muskets and then moved by the right flank to take an outer line of defenses. They then held on for dear life as three Russian battalions counterattacked until well into the night. Their losses were five Legion officers and thirty-four legionnaires killed, eight officers and 174 men *hors de combat*.

A SECOND GROUP on the right composed of three battalions of legionnaires and *Chasseurs à Pied* were assigned the more difficult mission of taking the main Russian position. They succeeded, but lost it to a strong Russian counterattack. The artillery on both sides then got into the act. Over the next two days, the position changed hands five times before the French finally claimed it, but at the cost of over two hundred casualties for the Legion. When on May 23 a truce was declared to collect the dead, it required five hours to complete this grisly task, the bodies already swollen and blackened by the heat. This was the final substantial Legion participation in the war. When on September 8, 1855, the main Russian battery at Malakoff fell to a French assault, thus opening Sebastopol to the Allies, the Legion's contribution was one hundred volunteers who carried ladders. The remainder of the war was spent building trenches until, on March 2, 1856, the firing of cannon announced that peace had been signed. On April 13, a large review was held in the presence of French commander-in-chief Pélisser and the Russian General Luders to honor the cemetery of Legion dead and to announce that, to compensate the Legion, Louis-Napoleon offered French nationality and a transfer to French regiments to all who desired it. This was done in great part as a budgetary measure. However, this did not mean the abolition of the Legion. In response to the call by war minister Marshal Jean-Baptiste Vaillant for "the requirement to conserve a corps able to receive those who come from foreign countries," the organization of the *1ᵉʳ* and *2ᵉ régiments étrangers* was confirmed by decree.[26] By July, the Legion had been united at Sidi-bel-Abbès. In all, the legion lost 12 officers killed and 66 wounded in the war, while 1,625 legionnaires were killed or wounded.

The Crimean campaign was important for the Legion in at least two respects. First, it was the first time that the two foreign "legions" fought as a unit, which was an important beginning in the formation of a communal unit mentality. This coincided with the end of the first quarter-century of the Legion's history, when the old generation who had been with the unit from its earliest days disappeared definitively, to be replaced by a new crop of leaders. Second, the Crimean campaign gave the Legion, as well as the entire *Armée d'Afrique,* a double vocation, that of fighting in France's European wars as well as in her colonial ones. Over time, the sentiment that France's greatness rested primarily upon her colonial achievements would take hold in her soldiers overseas, and cause them increasingly to see themselves as an important element in the defense of France, even an essential one. That sense of constituting a vital component in France's defense was only increased in 1859, when the Legion was recalled to Europe to fight with the French army against the Austrians in Italy.

IN MANY RESPECTS the Crimean War prepared the way for French intervention in Italy by weakening Russia and creating mistrust between Saint Petersburg and Vienna, the two powers that had most seriously attempted to uphold the status quo that emerged from the 1815 Congress of Vienna. Each now distrusted the ambitions of the other in the Balkans, the flourishing of a rivalry that would eventually provide a pretext for World War I. Louis-Napoleon's desire to challenge Austrian control of Lombardy and Venetia was curiously hastened by an attempt on his life by an Italian nationalist, Felice Orsini, on the evening of January 14, 1858, as the emperor was making his way to the Opera. For a variety of reasons, which included an emotional attachment to the cause of Italian unity, the desire for Imperial glory to reinforce the popularity of his regime, a bid to appear as the champion of the "modern" cause of the consolidation of nations and the more concrete prospect of acquiring Nice and Savoy for France, in July 1858 Louis-Napoleon concluded a secret pact with the prime minister of Piedmont, Camillo di Cavour. In April 1859, the cunning Cavour tricked Austria into a declaration of war, and French troops rushed to his aid.

The first regiment of the Legion was poorly prepared to undertake this campaign. Understrength, the government had shifted it to Corsica in April 1859 in the hope that it would attract enlistments from Italians eager to fight for the unity of their nation. When, in the following month, it was shifted to Genoa, the *1er étranger* counted barely six hundred men and was brigaded with the *2e étranger,* which arrived directly from Oran. On June 4, 1859, after a series of marches and reconnaissances, the two armies met before the town of Magenta.

The countryside that stretched away before the small town of Magenta was typical of that of the Lombard plain—a level carpet of orchards and vineyards segmented by walls, lanes and hedgerows. However, the legionnaires who stood gazing upon it in the gentle heat of June 1859 were not seduced by its pastoral beauty. If the broken nature of the terrain removed the threat of a cavalry attack, it offered a perfect series of strong points and lines of resistance for a determined infantry. For most of the morning, the legionnaires had advanced, seeing nothing of the Austrians but straining beneath the weight of their heavy blue overcoats and knapsacks surmounted by a tent half, pole and cooking equipment. At midday they halted to await the arrival of the rest of the corps. The red tile roofs and warm ocher walls of Magenta were visible a mile and a half away through the foliage.

The cavalry screen of the *7e Chasseurs à cheval* passed through their ranks moving toward the rear, driven in by three columns of advancing Austrians. Captain Rembert of the *1er étranger* was the first to spy the white coats of the enemy across the vineyards. Impulsively he shouted a command to attack. The Austrians, momentarily taken aback, quickly recovered their composure when they realized that Rembert's Legion company was heavily outnumbered. At this moment, Colonel Louis de Chabrière, commanding the *2e étranger,* ordered his men to down packs and charge, just as he pitched from his horse—dead. The line of legionnaires and *zouaves* heaved forward in a piecemeal fashion as each section discovered an opponent to his front. In the confusion of walls, vineyards and smoke, the Austrians began to withdraw, firing as they retreated. Zédé's company pursued, climbing over walls, stepping past the bodies of dead *zouaves,* until halted by Lieutenant Colonel Antonio Martinez. The captain of the grenadier company that Martinez had deployed as skirmishers to cover his front returned to report Austrian troops filing out of Magenta. Martinez ordered a charge, and legionnaires and *zouaves* cheered, leveled their bayonets and rushed forward. "The Austrians hardly resisted but surrendered *en masse,*" Zédé wrote, "and we were furious to see the officers ride away with their flags. Only one was captured, and that was by the *zouaves.*"[27]

As the 2nd Corps of legionnaires and *zouaves* stood poised to storm the town, MacMahon arrived and, as he trotted past the Legion, uttered the statement that today adorns the wall of almost every Legion bar: *"Voici la Légion! L'affaire est dans le sac!"* ("The Legion is here! The affair is in the bag!") But the affair was far from being in the bag. The easy part of the battle was over. Magenta remained in the hands of the Austrians, who were now represented by the Croatians, soldiers who specialized in shooting the wounded and who singlehandedly might have inspired the Geneva Convention of 1864, and by their crack Tyrolean mountain troops. As legionnaires and *zouaves* waited impatiently for the orders to storm the town, the Imperial Guard was ordered into line. The reaction of the hardened veterans of Africa to the arrival of the pampered Parisian household troops was predictable: "The Guard! Get them out of here! Let them go stand guard at Saint-Cloud! The chambermaids of the Tuileries [Palace] will be too sad if they get hurt!"[28]

The 2nd Corps was drawn up into serried ranks. To their front, the Austrians organized their artillery and infantry behind a railway embankment that formed a convenient breastwork in front of the town. "The charge was spontaneous," Zédé wrote. "The hurrahs, the cries of *En avant!* were shouted, *zouaves* and legionnaires hurled forward. Neither cannon nor the volleys of the Austrians could stop them and this torrent rolled toward Magenta carrying all before it." However, like a wave breaking over a sea wall, the French attack shattered as it slapped against the Austrian defenses. In fact, two attacks failed, with heavy losses, before the French finally succeeded in breaking into the town. "From this moment, all was disorder and confusion," Zédé continued. "Everything dissolved into desperate struggles among small groups." Several officers were killed, including General Espinasse, an ex-Legion officer, shot down as he led a charge. Martinez, his face covered with blood after a bullet took away his left eyelid, directed his troops to break down doors and charge up stairs. Fires broke out in the disputed houses, adding smoke to an atmosphere already suffocating with heat, dust and powder. Prisoners, when there were any, were gathered in the church on the square. The fighting died out only at dawn on June 5.

The officers attempted to re-form the regiment, but that proved impossible. The victorious soldiers intended to celebrate, and had lost little time in breaking into the wine cellars and smashing open the casks. The cellars soon became flooded with wine, and the men so drunk that more than one survivor of the Battle of Magenta was found in the morning floating face down, drowned in wine. The scene in the streets of Magenta was a mixture of tragedy and farce—Zédé found it impossible to distinguish the dead from those who were merely dead drunk. One could walk from one end of the town to the other without once setting foot on the ground, so thickly lay the corpses of men and horses and the inert forms of inebriated soldiers: "One heard nothing but the moans of the wounded," Zédé remembered. Soldiers moved about stripping the dead of their boots, uniforms and ammunition, so that before long many of the bodies lay "in a state of nature." The next day they were pitched unceremoniously into a common grave.[29]

Wounded soldiers wandered about searching for an ambulance. Polish legionnaire M. Kamienski, his arm shattered by a musket ball, spent the night on the ground next to three other wounded soldiers. The next morning, one of them told him to follow the railway tracks to the dressing station: "As for me," the soldier said as he rolled a cigarette, "I'm going to die here without bothering."[30] It was probably just as well. Zédé discovered the spectacle at the dressing station to be "lamentable. The railway station, where the hospital had been established, overflowed with unfortunates laid out on the bare earth. During the entire night, the doctors had only their medical bags which they carried with them, no linen for bandages, no chloroform. . . . They could do little more than give water to the wounded." The *2e étranger* had lost four officers killed and 250 men killed or wounded.[31] The Legion's casualties included Kamienski, who perished a few days later of blood poisoning.

On June 7, the Legion marched into Milan to a triumphal welcome by Italians delighted to be liberated from the Austrian yoke. "Our camp was invaded by a population drunk with joy. Our soldiers were showered with food and wine, and taken into the houses where they were fêted endlessly."[32] Exuberance, even Italian exuberance, had its limits, however. The officers of the Legion succeeded in capitalizing upon the delirium of the moment to entice some Italians to enlist. However, by the time they reached Genoa for reembarkation, most of the new recruits had vanished.[33] Following a final, bloody and confusing battle at Solferino, the Emperor concluded a surprise peace with Austria on July 12. Cavour was disappointed that France's rapid conclusion of hostilities denied him a full victory—he was able to seize Lombardy but not Venetia. But Louis-Napoleon had been genuinely upset by the deficiencies of the French army, had begun to glimpse the dangers a unified Italy posed for France and was further dissuaded by the mobilization of Prussian forces along the Rhine. For its part, the Legion for the first time participated in the victory parade in the French capital, a recognition of its role in the campaign.

THE VERY LEAST that one can say about the performance of the Legion at Magenta was that it fully matched that of the other French corps, like the elite *zouaves*. The *2ᵉ étranger* was in the thick of the fight, and by all accounts acquitted itself with great courage. The obvious question to ask, especially given the fact that so many officers had gone on record as having a poor opinion of that corps, is, How did they do it? Was Magenta perhaps a fluke? The short answer is that it was not. The Legion added considerably to its battle honors in the 1850s—the elite battalion of the Legion maintained its discipline during the Battle of the Alma in 1854, when the first line of French troops rushed spontaneously at the Russian lines. The *2ᵉ étranger* carried the honors of the day during the difficult Kabylia campaign of 1857. The fierce tribesmen who occupied the mountains to the east of Algiers were among the last to submit to French rule. Their stone villages, which clung to the ridges of their desiccated mountains, offered natural fortresses, which had to be taken one by one. In June 1857, a large number of Kabyles had concentrated at Ischeriden, a small village built upon the edge of a steep ravine. On the hills that dominated the village, the resistance had organized a series of defensive walls. Early on the morning of June 24, after a preliminary artillery bombardment lasting almost an hour, the French launched an attack by the *zouaves* and the 54th Infantry Regiment. The dissidents allowed the attackers to advance within a hundred yards before opening a heavy fire, which stopped the French dead in their tracks. While the 1st Battalion of the *2ᵉ étranger* rushed to reinforce the *zouaves* and the 54th, the 2nd Battalion downed packs and marched against the right flank of the Kabyle positions. Without firing a shot, the legionnaires advanced upon the entrenchments despite heavy fire until they crossed the low stone wall and went to work with their bayonets. Taken from the flank, the Kabyle position unraveled.[34]

Ischeriden helped to bring the Legion to public notice because the battle was covered by the popular French magazine *L'Illustration*. Specialists began to consider the Legion a serious military rival to the elite *zouaves*, known as "the world's premier soldiers," and a healthy competition grew up between the two units, who were often brigaded together until 1870. Likewise, Zédé recorded that military opinion at the close of the Italian campaign credited the bravery of French soldiers, including legionnaires, for salvaging some rather lackluster generalship.[35] Clearly, the Legion had discovered some way to transform their apparent liabilities into assets.

The first place to look for an answer, perhaps, is in the quality of Legion recruitment. The notion that those who joined the Legion did so as absolutely the last resort when all of life's other possibilities had been closed off was the contemporary one. When William Stammer presented himself at the Legion recruitment bureau in 1854, his request to enlist was greeted with disbelief:

How was it that I, a man with money in my pocket, a good coat on my back and, it is with diffidence that I say it, an extremely good address, could voluntarily enter such a regiment was beyond their comprehension. I think that the younger and more romantic employés in the office inclined to the belief that I had been thwarted in love, and had joined the Legion in the hopes of being killed on the field of battle, whilst the older hands shrugged their shoulders and muttered, "Poor fellow, he is an Englishman, and must certainly be half-witted."[36]

When Zédé boarded the ship for Mexico with his legionnaires, the captain, who knew Zédé's brother, also a naval officer, ". . . confessed to me his apprehension at having on board, for a long voyage, such bandits as the legionnaires, and he was surprised to see me in such company." When the ship reached Martinique, the legionnaires were confined to the fortress under armed guard by nervous local officials who feared that they might run amok.[37]

But not everyone shared this view of *Homo legionis*. Antoine Camus argued against the belief that most recruits were driven to the Legion by hunger. Certainly, many came in need or because of a downturn in their personal circumstances, but there were far easier ways of earning a living. No, men were drawn to the Legion by the attractions of regimental life, by "the thirst for the struggle . . . [by] the secret desire to receive their baptism of fire among the world's premier soldiers." Many of these men were "ignorant," "rough," "taciturn" and might even become rebellious when pressed too hard by military discipline.[38] But Camus clearly believed that Legion recruits were not "the scum of the earth enlisted for drink," but men who had professional potential.

Of course, this might not always be the case. In wartime especially, when the demand for bodies was strong, the doors of the recruitment bureaus might open rather more widely than usual. For instance, the competition for recruits was keen during the Crimean War, when both the British and French sought to entice Swiss into their armies. Although the British appeared to gain the upper hand by offering an enlistment bonus of 150 francs, compared to twenty francs held out by the parsimonious French, 1,600 men were eventually incorporated into the short-lived *IIe Légion étrangère* (1855–56), which was made up of two infantry regiments and a bataillon of *tirailleurs*. In 1856, these men became the *1er régiment étranger*, which was often referred to as the "Swiss" until its dissolution in 1861. This short-lived experiment was the last time that the Swiss, so long associated with the military history of France, were incorporated into a separate unit by a French government. But the war minister complained that many of them were underage and undersized. For their part, the Swiss took offense at this unseemly competition to entice their young men abroad as mercenaries, and in 1859 passed a law forbidding Swiss to serve in foreign armies.[39]

However, the point to make is that, with the possible exception of the Mexican campaign, recruits to the Legion in this period may not have been as devoid of military potential as contemporary inspection reports and contemporary prejudice might suggest. Certainly the Legion formed a heterogeneous, even a motley, collection of men, most of whom were foreign, of dubious backgrounds, who spoke French badly and whose motives for enlistment were open to question. But one may concede, if merely for the sake of argument, that the potential for producing a quality unit might just exist. The next obvious question to ask is, how did the Legion attempt to do just that?

In any modern unit, the foundations for performance and *esprit de corps* are laid on the exercise field. In the Legion, as in other armies during this period, training consisted primarily of drill. William Stammer drilled in the morning and in the afternoon, and apart from barrack details was otherwise free to wander into town.[40] Corporal Fijalkowski followed a similar routine in 1859: "To keep us occupied, we have three hours of exercises twice daily, roll call at 11 o'clock, to which we must bring a well cleaned piece of equipment, and details . . ." However, the *Armée d'Afrique* must have been doing something right, for when he reached Italy, Fijalkowski noted that ". . . the regiments coming from France suffer much more than us."[41] When the Belgian Eugène Amiable reached Mexico after training at the temporary Legion depot at Aix-en-Provence, he found that he was poorly prepared to confront the first three-day march: "I was so exhausted that I could hardly feel my legs," he wrote. But he soon got used to it. Later, when his unit was given additional training, he believed that ". . . three quarters of the men did not need it: many being officers of different nations."[42] But, on the whole, the Legion does not seem to have placed much emphasis on training. Louis de Massol noted that training was often neglected in barracks,[43] while Zédé was frequently sent out with his company on "colonization projects" during which training was entirely neglected. In any case, Zédé believed that six shots fired in target practice was sufficient for legionnaires. And perhaps it was, for during the Battle of Magenta his men fired only nine shots each on average.[44]

Rigorous training does not appear to have been the source of the Legion's battlefield success. Nor could the *esprit de corps* described by Zédé and Diesbach de Torny have been even in part the product of the pay and conditions of service, which were desperately inadequate. Legionnaires were paid barely enough to live on: "As for the small pleasures," wrote Fijalkowski, "we are paid 7 sous [1 franc 40 centimes] every five days, out of which we furnish our own shoe polish and soap. That is why we hardly make economies."[45] And while they might be able to earn extra money in Sidi-bel-Abbès by working in town, on campaign, especially in Mexico where the cost of food was high, soldiers might virtually starve to death— Amiable paid 15 centimes for a tortilla in Mexico, and on a very thirsty march claimed to have been charged sixty-five centimes for a glass of water.[46] Not surprisingly, the commander-in-chief in Mexico, ex-Legion officer Achille Bazaine, provoked howls of protest from the Belgian and Austrian contingents serving Emperor Maximilian when he reduced them to the same pay as the French troops.[47] After years of such poor treatment, it is no wonder that the Legion found the fifty centimes a day the Versailles government paid their troops during the siege of the Commune in 1871, together with the daily ration of wine and brandy (double ration when fighting), a real morale boost.[48] De Massol complained that the Legion was the lowest-paid unit in the French army simply because no one took an interest in them,[49] a rather curious observation as the Legion ostensibly was paid the same as French recruits.

Nor, for soldiers, did the Legion necessarily offer a stepping-stone to better things. On the contrary, Fijalkowski, who had completed his secondary education—quite rare for a common soldier—complained that the better men in the company found promotion blocked by French NCOs sent from other regiments, often as a punishment, and by favoritism: "Daily I hear my comrades complain and regret having enlisted, because they are not promoted ...," he wrote. He was told that his best hope was to become a naturalized Frenchman and transfer to a line regiment.[50] But while the lack of promotion may have discouraged some of the more ambitious recruits, Camus was of the opinion that most foreign legionnaires were illiterate or spoke such poor French that they could never aspire to rank.[51] De Massol painted a very bleak picture of the Legion in garrison: "Discipline, training, military spirit ebb away each day," he wrote. "The officer vegetates, the NCO languishes, the soldier suffers and is bored." In fact, so bored did legionnaires become that they intentionally sought admission to the discipline company where "... he never has to drill, to stand guard, to train."[52]

This would seem to suggest that Legion morale was fragile in the extreme. In fact, many of these descriptions may lead one to wonder how the Legion kept from falling apart altogether. But could things really have been as bad as all that? Legionnaires admitted that they made terrible garrison troops. But even if it is fair to point out in the way of mitigating circumstances that all soldiers tend to lose their edge in barracks, one must concede that the Legion's lapses into alcoholism and indiscipline in garrison bordered on the heroic. But how reliable an indicator is this that Legion morale was necessarily fragile? Perhaps alcoholism and indiscipline might be a sign of high morale, a way of keeping one's aggressive instincts sharp when there is no fighting to do. In that case, there would not necessarily be a contradiction between the claims of Zédé and Diesbach de Torny that regimental pride based on the Legion's battle honors and the number of its officers who had achieved stellar rank was high, even "fanatically" so, and inspection reports that concluded that, based on garrison statistics, the Legion was on the verge of revolt. Or, at the very least, in the view of General Ulrich, who inspected the 1er étranger in 1861, a regiment ". . . that is nothing more than an amalgamation of all the nations of Europe, does not have nor can it have an *esprit de corps*."[53]

But even if we assume that Legion morale was fragile, that the quality of its recruitment was uneven and that its multinational character made it difficult to meld such disparate elements into a unified force, how could the Legion maximize its—apparently limited—assets? One way lay in the regimental structure of the period, which required that each regiment produce picked companies of grenadiers and *voltigeurs,* or light troops, the remainder being assigned to line companies, *compagnies du centre,* as the French called them. In this way the Legion was able to select and group its most motivated and skilled soldiers under its most dynamic officers. This paid enormous dividends in the Crimea, for instance, where Marshal Saint-Arnaud formed a *bataillon de marche* from the elite companies of the two Legion regiments. It was this *bataillon d'élite* that kept its discipline at the Alma, which prompted General Canrobert to call upon his "brave legionnaires" to "serve as an example to the others." Elite companies also carried out most of the assaults assigned to the Legion on important objectives during the dreadful winter siege of Sebastopol.[54] The grenadier company of the 2e étranger led the assault on Ischeriden and distinguished itself at Magenta.[55]

In 1868, elite companies were dissolved in the French army because the increased firepower of modern weapons had made the specialized functions of grenadiers and skirmishers obsolete. This also appeared to be a victory for those who argued that elite companies hurt the overall performance of a unit because they siphoned off and concentrated the best talent to the detriment of the rest of the regiment. Their loss was regretted as well, because those serving in elite companies lost the extra pay that went with the assignment.[56] After 1870, the Legion continued the practice of forming *bataillons de marche*. However, the criticism leveled at these was that, unlike the old elite battalions made up of established companies, the new organizations, while also made up of picked troops, broke up the standing companies and therefore had to reforge a unity among officers and men who were largely unknown to each other.

A second way in which the Legion was able to confound its critics was by turning the heterogeneous origins of its soldiers to its advantage. While French line units recruited the bulk of their soldiers through a national lottery in which all twenty-year-old males were required to participate, the Legion took virtually anyone who walked through the door of the recruiting bureau. While most of them would not be shortlisted for *Who's Who,* they were generally older men—the average age in the 1860s was between twenty-eight and thirty-two years[57]—whose experience and diverse backgrounds the Legion was able to draw upon in times of need. The Legion has always maintained that the heterogeneous origins of its soldiers was especially useful for tasks of colonization, such as construction or agriculture. And while there is no evidence that the backgrounds of legionnaires were more diverse than those of line soldiers in this period, it is certainly possible that they were more experienced at their former professions, young conscripts hardly advancing beyond the stage of apprentice before their call-up, if indeed they had acquired any skills at all.

However, what probably did distinguish the Legion from line infantry regiments in this period was the number of ex-soldiers, often deserters, in its ranks. For instance, of five hundred men who joined the Legion between 1868 and 1870, fully seventy-four, or 14 percent, listed their professions as *"ex-militaire"* or *"ex-officier."*[58] As has been shown, the large number of former soldiers with experience in arms other than the infantry who served with the Legion in Spain allowed Conrad to create a light division that included cavalry and artillery. This sort of flexibility was not demanded of the Legion in Algeria because the French possessed their own cavalry, and because artillery was virtually useless there. Nor were flexibility and adaptability much in demand in the set-piece European battles that the Legion fought in this period. However, in Mexico the diverse nature, and the military nature, of Legion recruitment allowed them to modify their force structure to meet new tactical situations.

Chapter 7

MEXICO,
1863-1867

MEXICO WAS NOT a success for French arms. However, better political management might have salvaged some advantage for France out of an adventure Napoleon III appears to have entered into rather impetuously, with an inadequate grasp of the complexities of Mexican politics. As the political and military situation in Mexico deteriorated for the French, especially after the summer of 1865, the Legion's operational flexibility was severely tested, as was its discipline and morale. If some Legion officers began to draw parallels between Mexico and the ill-fated Spanish venture of 1808–14 under Napoleon I, it was because for them the two countries had more in common than a language.

The Mexican campaign was at once the Legion's salvation while at the same time it almost produced its eclipse, at least temporarily. In 1861, the *1er régiment étranger* was dissolved, and on December 16 of that year the war ministry suspended enlistments in the *régiment étranger* (ex–*2e régiment étranger*) for an indefinite period. On December 30, 1861, a ministerial note allowed all legionnaires who were foreigners with one year's service remaining of their two-year enlistment to return to civilian life.[1] Clearly the government seemed intent upon reducing Legion strength substantially. Mexico reversed this policy and allowed for the rapid expansion of the Legion—on March 22, 1864, enlistments were once again accepted for the corps.

One of the reasons for the *volte-face* of the French government toward the Legion was that, as in Spain in 1835, Paris began to envisage a central role for the Legion in its Mexican policy. The genesis of that role stretched back to January 1862, when the courts of France and Austria began negotiations to create a throne in Mexico for the Archduke Maximilian. One of Maximilian's conditions for acceptance was that he be given a body of at least ten thousand soldiers recruited in Europe to form the nucleus of a future Mexican army.

The political difficulties for Napoleon III of handing over a corps made up of Frenchmen were obvious. In September 1863, Napoleon III proposed to bequeath the Foreign Legion to Maximilian, at least for a certain period. It is likely that the idea originally was that of Bazaine, who was preparing to take over command of the French expeditionary corps in Mexico, and who had participated in the earlier Spanish experiment. The Convention of Miramar, signed on April 10, 1864, stipulated that the Legion would remain French so long as French troops continued to occupy Mexico, and then would pass under the authority of the Mexican government. A critical difference between Miramar and the Franco-Spanish accord of 1835 was that the Legion officers would retain their normal right to promotion in the French army. Vacancies created by the progressive departure of Europeans from the corps would be filled by Mexicans. The plans to raise the Legion to a strength of eight battalions continued until December 13, 1866, when Napoleon III, under threat of war with the United States, decided to repatriate the Legion to France with the remainder of the French forces.

Despite the enthusiasm of the departure from Sidi-bel-Abbès, and a monotonous but otherwise pleasant crossing, the first views of Mexico conjured up a deep sense of foreboding in some. Standing at the ship's railing, Charles Zédé saw "A muddy coast devoid of vegetation signposted with the carcasses of wrecked ships. On our right, a small island upon which sat the dilapidated fortress of San Juan de Ulla; on the left, the Isla de los Sacrificios, absolutely arid, but covered by a multitude of crosses indicating the graves of our sailors, victims of the insalubrious climate." Indeed, the place reeked of death—vultures circled overhead while large sharks, clearly visible beneath the surface of the water, shadowed the ships: "On land and on sea, these disgusting animals seem to stalk you like a prey."[2] The view once ashore was equally depressing. Veracruz was hardly more than an agglomeration of low houses that shouldered up to an inadequate harbor, "depressing and dead," wrote Diesbach de Torny, "wide streets with grass growing in them and few inhabitants." Virtually the only amusement was to watch the incredibly voracious vultures eat the rubbish that was thrown out into the streets or feed on the carcasses of animals, and even men, that were found floating in the harbor each morning.[3]

To legionnaires, there seemed to be nothing worse than Veracruz. But there was—the tropical lowlands behind Veracruz, which immediately became the Legion's theater of operations. To them fell the task of escorting supply convoys along the primitive roads that ran west through the lugubrious bush toward the highlands beyond. It was loathsome and dangerous

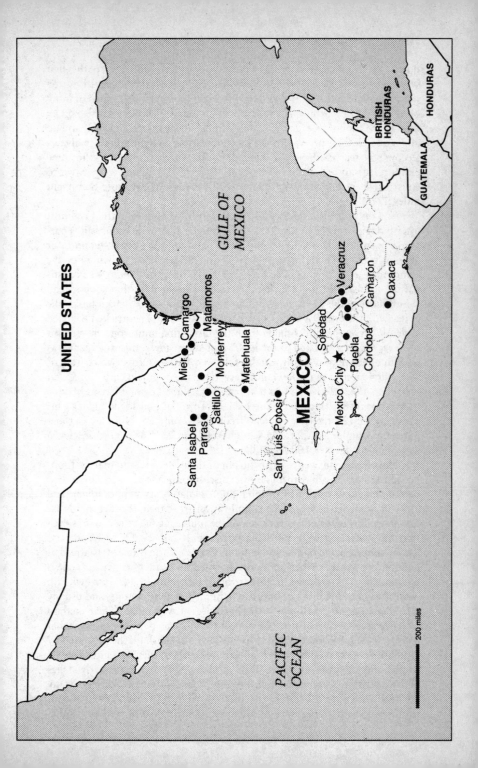

duty. The wagons were too heavy for the roads, little more than paths, that were rutted and slashed by deep ravines, called *barrancas,* carved out by the torrential rains. "These [marches] are terribly tiring, privations of food, of clothes," Diesbach de Torny wrote in his diary. "We sleep for five or six days at the foot of trees in the water. Almost always torrential rain, and no change of clothes, no way to get dry. Impossible to light a fire . . . always sleeping in wet clothes. The next day, the march resumes in the same clothes. It is an ordeal that few people realize."[4] Marching from dawn to sunset in these conditions, a convoy could seldom cover more than eight miles.[5]

Not only did the terrain and climate prolong these journeys almost interminably, but they caused excessive fatigue and made legionnaires particularly susceptible to the second great scourge of the coast—*vomito,* or yellow fever. Even the newest arrival quickly became familiar with the symptoms of the disease. The first sign of the onset of *vomito* was constipation, followed by a headache, then cramps in the neck that soon spread to the entire body. Then the vomiting began, dark blood "which looks like coffee with the grounds suspended in it," wrote Zédé. The stricken were fed olive oil while "poultices made from the disgusting mud from the streams of Veracruz were applied to the legs." Not surprisingly, this treatment was seldom effective and death usually followed within six to twelve hours.[6] These first months in the lowlands devastated the original Legion force that arrived in 1863. Zédé claimed that one-third of the Legion force in Mexico perished in 1863.[7] However, Diesbach de Torny put his losses higher—his company of 124 men was quickly reduced to only 25, while in October 1863 he complained that 109 legionnaires had died of *vomito* in eleven days, while a further 160 were ill.[8]

The obvious answer to the problem of the *vomito* was to march troops as quickly as possible through the disease-ridden coastal plain to the healthy highland town of Córdoba, approximately sixty miles inland and 2,800 feet above sea level. The complication arose from the fact that Mexican guerrillas repeatedly struck out of the jungles against the convoys. Not that the Mexicans were particularly intrepid soldiers. On the contrary, legionnaire Amiable had a low opinion of them: "The Mexican is afraid of gunfire," he wrote. "When he shoots, he turns his head. One of their volleys discharged at 30 feet never frightens you. If one is hit, it's just bad luck. We have always said that ten of ours can fight fifty of these bandits, and usually give them a good thrashing."[9] Diesbach de Torny agreed: "Their method is to flee as soon as they fire," he wrote. "They come back later to see what damage they have done and to strip the dead and finish off the wounded by mutilating them horribly. Like all cowards, these men are cruel."[10] Of course, the Mexican resistance to the French, especially in the early stages of the intervention, was very much of the "come as you are" variety. Many of them were indeed bandits, and the rest, though perhaps extremely patriotic, were little more than ill-organized guerrilla bands formed around highly independent leaders who on occasion might be persuaded to join forces with other bands to mount a large raid. So long as the odds could be kept at five to one, then, barring surprise, it was not much of a contest. But what if the Mexicans could increase the odds to twenty to one?

At seven o'clock on the morning of April 30, 1863, Captain Jean Danjou, a hero of the Crimea who had lost a hand when his musket had exploded during a topographical expedition in Algeria and who carried a wooden one in its place,[11] ordered his reconnaissance team of sixty-two legionnaires and three officers to halt near the small village of Camarón, about fifty miles southwest of Veracruz. They had been searching the countryside west of Palo Verde for signs of Mexican guerrillas since one o'clock in the morning, but so far had found none. Now it was time for coffee. Sentinels were set, wood gathered and the fires lighted. Before the coffee could be drunk, however, the lookouts signaled Mexicans to the west. Danjou ordered the fires doused. His legionnaires took up their arms. The Mexicans soon appeared, mounted on horseback. Danjou formed a square on some open ground. The Mexicans attacked. Danjou waited until they were within one hundred yards before he unleashed a volley that shattered the charge. While the Mexicans reorganized, he moved his square one hundred yards to the east onto a small rise surmounted by a hedge of cactus to await a second, more tentative charge, which was easily repulsed.

Danjou ordered his troops into the Hacienda de la Trinidad, a square-walled farmyard that stood about two hundred yards east of Camarón along the road to Palo Verde. This fortress—for that was what it was to become—was about fifty yards square. The ten-foot-high wall was pierced by two doors and a third opening that obviously had once been an entrance. A string of rooms occupied the north face. Danjou set about shoring up the defenses, a task the Mexicans did not disturb. However, the problem for Danjou was that even if the Mexicans could not see in, he could not see out. Sergeant Morzicki, son of a Polish officer who had taken refuge in France, was hoisted onto the roof of the north face. He reported sombreros as far as the eye could see. Furthermore, they appeared to be well armed, and were dismounting and taking off their spurs. Time passed. The legionnaires were out of water and the heat was oppressive. Finally a Mexican came forward waving a white handkerchief. He pointed out that the French were hopelessly outnumbered and suggested that they surrender. Danjou refused. Corporal Louis Maine, one of the survivors, explained why: "As the enemy had shown neither infantry nor artillery, we could defend ourselves for a long time against cavalrymen no matter how numerous. It was not with their short carbines without bayonets that they could overwhelm a company of the Legion behind walls." Danjou obliged his men to raise their hands and swear that they would defend themselves to the death.[12]

According to Maine, things held together fairly well at first. Attempts by the cavalrymen to get into the farmyard were thwarted with little difficulty, and it appeared that the Mexicans had little stomach for a fight to the finish. However, around midday two things occurred that altered the situation. Danjou, who had been circulating in the yard with a cavalier disregard for his own safety, was struck in the chest by a bullet and killed. Worse, the Mexicans were reinforced by three battalions of infantry. By two o'clock in the afternoon, pockets of surviving legionnaires pressed hard against the walls to avoid the plunging fire that had transformed the central courtyard into an abattoir. The building on the north face had caught fire, which swathed the farmyard in smoke asphyxiating enough to leave the devil himself gasping for breath, adding considerably to the torment of thirst. "Hope no longer existed," Maine recounted. "Still, no one thought of surrender."

By late afternoon, "There was only five of us left: Second lieutenant Clément Maudet, a Prussian named Wenzel, Catteau, Constantin and me," testified Maine.

We held the enemy at a distance, but we could not hold out much longer as our bullets were almost exhausted. Soon, we had only one each. It was six o'clock and we had fought since the morning. "Ready . . . fire!" said the lieutenant. We discharged our five rifles and, he in front, we jumped forward with fixed bayonets. We were met by a formidable volley. Catteau threw himself in front of his officer to make a rampart with his body, and was struck with 19 bullets. Despite this devotion, the Lieutenant himself was hit with two bullets. Wenzel also fell, wounded in the shoulder, but he got up immediately. Three of us were still on our feet, Wenzel, Constantin and I. . . . We were about to jump over the Lieutenant's body and charge again, but the Mexicans surrounded us with their bayonets at our chests. We thought we had breathed our last, when a senior officer who was in the front rank of the assailants ordered them to stop and with a brusque movement of his saber raised their bayonets which threatened us: "Surrender!" he told us. "We will surrender," I replied, "if you will leave us our arms and treat our lieutenant who is wounded." He agreed. He offered me his arm, gave the other to the wounded Wenzel and they brought a stretcher for the Lieutenant. We arrived behind a small rise where [Mexican] Colonel Milan was. "Is this all that is left?" he asked when he saw us. And when told yes, "These are not men. They are demons."[13]

Diesbach de Torny was with the first French troops to reach Camarón on May 2 to find that the bodies of legionnaires had been left to the vultures, "so that one could not recognize the poor unfortunates who after such brave conduct were left for two days to these ignoble animals."[14]

The defense of El Camarón, or Camerone as the French called it, was an inspiring example of heroism and courage, which, as will be seen, came to form the central myth of the Legion. However, when viewed in another light, it suggested that the French might have some strategic problems in

Mexico that might prove insurmountable. The overriding problem was a political one. French intervention in Latin America was one of Napoleon III's long-held ambitions. Even before he became emperor, he dreamed of extending French influence into Central and South America to thwart the expanding Protestant and Anglo-Saxon culture of the United States. He was encouraged in these ambitions after 1860 when the victory of Benito Juárez in the Mexican civil war caused a number of conservative Mexican exiles to seek asylum in Paris. There they were able to gain the ear of the French emperor through his wife, Eugénie de Montijo, of Spanish origin and very pious, who held that it was the duty of the Catholic states of Europe to protect the Church wherever it was menaced in the world. As the Second Empire depended in large measure upon Catholic support, the sentiments of the empress were of more than casual interest. They were given a sharper focus, however, when Juárez defaulted on his international loans. Important French financial interests led by the Duc de Mornay utilized the mendacious reports of the French representative in Mexico, Dubois de Saligny, to persuade Napoleon III that the population desired nothing more than liberation from the tyranny of Juárez and his Liberals.[15]

French intervention in 1862 reopened the civil war that had been won by Juárez and the liberals. Obviously, conservative and clerical interests rallied to the French as saviors. This in itself might not have proven fatal—certain areas of the country were deeply conservative, plenty of Mexicans were prepared to switch allegiance, or to serve both sides simultaneously for that matter, and the Juaristas were too weak to put up an effective military resistance, at least initially. French forces drove Juárez into the north and early in 1865 pushed what remained of the standing Mexican army over the border into Texas.

However, Louis-Napoleon made two miscalculations that were to prove fatal to the French cause in Mexico. First, he hoped for a Confederate victory in the War Between the States. But no sooner had Robert E. Lee surrendered at Appomattox in April 1865 than Washington turned her attentions to the problem of French intervention to the south. By the summer of 1865, Juárez had begun to receive arms and even American volunteers, which gave his cause the military muscle, as well as the diplomatic support, that it had lacked. Within the space of a few months, the apparently strong French position had been seriously eroded, giving the political, as well as the military, initiative to Juárez.

Louis-Napoleon's second political mistake was to arrange for the Austrian Maximilian to rule Mexico as emperor. This was a serious miscalculation for two reasons. First, by placing a foreign sovereign on the Mexican throne, the French bestowed upon Benito Juárez and his liberals the aura of patriotic resistance. The corrupt and often vindictive conservatives who supported the new emperor were now viewed as pawns of foreign interests. In fact, to some French minds the situation seemed hauntingly similar to the fanatical resistance encountered by Napoleonic armies in Spain, and this concern was encouraged by an early defeat of French arms before Puebla in 1862, a Mexican victory that is still celebrated today as a national holiday. When in 1864 Zédé met some Juarista officers who had been taken prisoner, he found that "They were inspired by an exalted patriotism like that of the Spaniards who have a hatred of all that is foreign. . . . From that moment, I had doubts about the success of our intervention . . . "[16]

Nor did Maximilian prove to be an astute politician. He made virtually no attempt to win over the vast Indian population of Mexico, but became a de facto prisoner of the conservatives, whose interests lay in oppressing and exploiting them. He dissolved the military commission directed by the French that aimed to construct an Imperial army, and with it went virtually any hope of establishing an effective military force capable of defending his throne once the French departed. One of the plans called for the ranks of the Legion to be filled with Indians, both as a political appeal to this important population and as a way to provide the nucleus of a Mexican army built around the Legion. This showed an imaginative use of the Legion as a political as well as a military instrument, and two companies of Indian legionnaires were raised. However, these units became so depleted by desertion that the experiment was abandoned. Why? No hard evidence exists for the Mexican case, but attempts in later years to use the Legion as the nucleus of locally raised forces also proved disappointing for a variety of reasons. The legionnaires, while technically proficient, had a very special *esprit de corps* and disciplinary methods that transmitted poorly to units whose soldiers did not share the Legion's mercenary outlook. It is also possible that the Legion accepted such duty with bad grace, regarding it as an unwelcome distraction. One can only suppose that these Indians adapted badly to the Legion's military culture, or that they were fundamentally out of sympathy with the imperial regime. Maximilian also lifted the French blockade of Mexican ports, which allowed the resistance to import substantial quantities of American surplus arms virtually unhindered, as well as volunteers who flooded into Mexico as "immigrants."[17]

This deteriorating political situation could not help but affect military operations. Camerone was but a foretaste of the problems that would increasingly confront the French. For after a few successful sieges of major towns held by liberal forces, as well as a drive in the northern states that in the summer of 1865 shoved Juárez into Texas, the French distributed their army, which never amounted to more than thirty thousand men including Belgian, Austrian and even an Egyptian detachment, in small detachments to hold the countryside they had won.

And here the problems began. The Mexicans were extremely fond of horses—indeed, the standing joke among French officers (if a joke it was) was that Maximilian, who seldom left his palace, was the only man in Mexico who did not ride a horse. Legionnaire H. Spinner put his finger on the problem when, after toiling over mountain roads in pursuit of the "bandits," he found that "These centaurs, one hundred times faster on their horses than we infantrymen on our legs, had disappeared."[18] Not only could they disappear when attacked, they developed the disconcerting habit of reappearing at inopportune moments, concentrating their forces on isolated garrisons or convoys. In fact, Mexico looked like a series of little Camerones waiting for a place to happen. "We march, march without stopping," wrote Diesbach de Torny in February 1864.

We enter the villages without firing a shot, [but] we do not have the men to hold what we take. . . . All the troops which retreat before our army reform in the tropical lowlands in guerrilla bands strong enough to give us serious worries. We are too weak to pursue, [we] are like prisoners in the posts which we occupy, just happy enough to hold on. Now that they know our weakness, they come shoot at us in broad daylight, something they would not have done before. . . . Even though we are victorious, we cannot travel without fighting, every day assassinations and stagecoaches stopped. . . . Send forty men alone, they will be massacred by the small bands of four to five hundred men who come out of nowhere and who are elusive, protected by the inhabitants of the towns and the countryside who keep them abreast of what we do.[19]

It became obvious as early as 1863 that the French must do something to counter the superior mobility of the enemy. Their first excursion into the realm of counterguerrilla warfare was an unorthodox one, organized by a freelance soldier named Charles-Louis Dupin. Dupin's career had begun brilliantly—a graduate of the elite *École Polytechnique* in 1834, he had joined the infantry and distinguished himself in Algeria and Italy. However, something went terribly wrong during the China expedition of 1860, when, it was rumored, Dupin had been cashiered for selling articles pillaged from the summer palace. In 1862, he appeared in Mexico and offered his services to his former comrades, who set him to organizing a force of irregulars to beat the jungle behind Veracruz. Zédé described Dupin as a "small, bald old man, with a long white beard, a hook nose and lively eyes. A well-educated man, he had the polished manners of a duelist. He was blessed with an unbelievable constitution and was marvelously coordinated in physical exercises. But, he possessed all the vices except drunkenness. He was a valorous soldier and wise leader. His troop was perfectly designed for the task which it had been assigned—hunting guerrillas."[20]

Zédé's assessment of Dupin was accurate—he was an upper-class thug utterly wanting in morals. However, to speak of a "design" when referring to Dupin's force is perhaps an overstatement. On paper Dupin's little army might look impressive—a battalion of five hundred men, two to a horse, capable of marching about sixty miles in twenty-four hours. To this were joined two squadrons of 150 horsemen each, two light cannons, and an ambulance. However, by the colonel's own admission, his force made the Legion look like a collection of choirboys: "One cannot claim that each nation sent its most praiseworthy representatives," Dupin wrote of his multinational force, in a remarkable unpublished personal memoir that is preserved in the French war archives. "Almost all these men had left their countries to pursue a fortune which constantly eluded them. Discipline was unknown in this troop. Officers, NCOs and soldiers got drunk in the same tavern and soon the wine or the brandy would establish a fraternity and an equality among them which usually, between ten o'clock and midnight, would finish by an exchange of blows and other similar caresses." Their uniforms were torn and soiled, and one-third of the troops had no uniforms at all. Their armament was heterogeneous. "If this forced had marched through the boulevards of Paris," Dupin admitted, "one would have thought it was an ancient band of thieves exhumed from the back streets of the city."[21] Zédé insisted that Dupin's force was recruited from "soldiers liberated from the army in Mexico who had acquired a taste for the country. The majority were ex-soldiers of the Legion."[22]

The limitations, and especially the drawbacks, of such a force are fairly obvious. Dupin claimed great success for it, especially in gathering intelligence, the lack of which was to plague French operations throughout Mexico. Later on, the "counterguerrilla" force was attached to many French columns in the north. However, reading his memoir, it is clear that Dupin's principal activity lay in churning the countryside to burn farms, hold mayors and other prominent citizens to ransom and torture anyone who fell into their hands, not so much to get intelligence on rebel movements, but rather to extract information about hidden valuables. "From this moment, work is stopped and the country is given over to famine for a year. This, combined with the recent conquest of Mexico City, helped convince the inhabitants to submit," Dupin concluded, prematurely, in the summer of 1863.[23]

Amiable admitted that the Mexicans lived in great fear of Dupin.[24] Dupin argued that his brutal reputation was greatly exaggerated, and that whatever his faults, one must realize the brutal environment in which he was forced to operate: "I've hardly sent a dozen bandits to another world, and in this, I have done good work, because these rogues would probably have already killed more than thirty honest folk," he wrote to his niece in February 1864. "If you knew how much I have aged since I came to this awful country. Everyone thinks I'm 60 when I'm hardly 49."[25] While it is certain that Dupin's force often behaved in no worse a fashion than some of his Mexican opponents, it is unlikely that his terror tactics did more in the long run than increase the number of Mexicans determined to resist the invader. Apparently both Maximilian and French commander Achille Bazaine realized this, and sent him packing. But the elegant Dupin managed to convince Napoleon III that he was doing great work in Mexico, so the emperor returned him there, where he remained until the last troops were evacuated in 1867. Napoleon subsequently reintegrated him into the French army with the rank of major, but he died the following year, some believed from poisoning.[26]

Dupin's was an interesting if somewhat irregular and inadequate response to the guerrilla problem. A second option was to recruit the guerrilla bands for the government, and Bazaine attempted to do this. However, most operated on their own account, often in the name of both sides, were more interested in terrorizing and pillaging a territory than in serving the government, were impossible to coordinate for any sort of strategic operation and quickly became a political embarrassment. In short, they were more trouble than they were worth.[27]

For this reason, it was soon apparent that the Legion too needed to acquire mobility, more mobility even than in Algeria, if it was to hold its own against the mercurial Mexicans. As early as October 1863, a *"compagnie franche"* was formed from one hundred Legion volunteers considered the most able marchers.[28] But although this light company continued to function throughout the Mexican occupation, it could only be a halfway solution. What the Legion needed was cavalry, and in April 1864 a "company of mounted partisans" was formed in the 1st Battalion to act, according to the regimental history, as "dragoons."[29] However, the real break for the Legion came with the fall of Oaxaca in February 1865. When the garrison surrendered, the French collected so many horses that they were able to develop their mounted forces substantially, according to Zédé, by calling principally upon German ex-cavalrymen.[30] Not all were so experienced, however. Amiable claimed that he volunteered for this new formation because he believed a horseman would be spared the "dragging about and carrying his own baggage." However, he quickly discovered that his horse had a mind of its own—he fell off fully five times on his first patrol and was left so far behind that, had his company not stopped in a village to bake bread, he might never have caught up.[31]

Nor was life among the "partisans" one of great ease. Amiable found that he was constantly on the move, sometimes spending ten days without taking his boots off, his feet becoming so swollen that he could hardly feel them. In areas where there were few wells, men drank filthy, stinking water from stagnant pools only after the horses and mules had been watered. The only advantage—and it was a substantial one—of the mounted forces was that one seldom went hungry, as the inhabitants usually fled at the mere sight of them, leaving their pigs and chickens behind.[32] While these cavalry formations were often used as convoy escorts or integrated into the "mobile columns" that Bazaine used, on the Algerian model, in Mexico, they did on occasion operate independently. Their most notable success came in November 1865, when a squadron of Legion cavalry operating with a "mobile column" dispatched to relieve the siege of Monterrey caught up with the retreating Mexicans, killing 112 of them.[33]

But there were other victories—in January 1866, Major Gustave Saussier surprised a Mexican band near Saltillo, killed forty of them and wounded one hundred, while capturing eighty-seven horses. On March 2, a small force made up of mule-mounted legionnaires and Mexican auxiliaries covered about sixty miles in thirteen hours to attack a rebel band near Monterrey, killing about thirty of them. In June, Saussier's legionnaires, escorting a convoy near Monterrey, inflicted about fifty casualties on the enemy.[34]

Yet the Legion cavalry, or that raised by other contingents like the Belgians, could never be a war winner. There were simply too few of them—240 officers and men in September 1866[35]—to be able to operate safely beyond infantry support. One of the problems was the lack of mounts—horses sent from France often broke their legs during transit in rough seas and had to be killed. This meant that the strategic effect of the sort produced by cavalrymen like J.E.B. Stuart, Bedford Forrest or Phil Sheridan at that very moment north of the border was simply beyond their means. In North America, specialists had concluded that the era of cavalry had passed, and that mounted infantry made the most effective troops. In the War Between the States, mounted infantry was especially effective for the South as an adjunct to defensive warfare. It allowed rapid concentration of troops and devastating raids, obliging generals like Ulysses Grant to expend large numbers of troops to guard his communications—for instance, at Vicksburg, two-thirds of the Union forces were guarding communications so that one-third could undertake the siege.

In Mexico, the advantages of mobility lay with the Mexicans. Their men were virtually born on horseback. Furthermore, the strategic situation favored them, for the French were drawn deep into Mexico and scattered in isolated garrisons that were especially vulnerable to mobile forces which could concentrate and disperse at will. In Mexico, the Legion cavalry became a sort of fire brigade, rushing about the countryside to rescue French garrisons in distress. For instance, in March 1866, a force of Legion cavalry rescued 44 legionnaires and support troops besieged for five days in a church at Parras, north of Mexico City.[36] In July 1866, 125 legionnaires barricaded themselves in a farm near Matehuala and fought off over 500 Mexicans for two days until relief arrived.[37] On December 12–13, 1866, a group of 50 legionnaires were surrounded and were saved in the nick of time by mobile troops.[38] Such incidents were fairly commonplace in 1866. As long as the legionnaires could reach a defensible position, the Mexicans seldom had the skill, or the stamina, to triumph.[39] However, if caught in the open, it might be another matter. The worst defeat suffered by the invaders was inflicted on a combined Austro-Mexican force on June 14, 1866, when a convoy they were escorting was attacked and overwhelmed at Camargo across the river from Rio Grande City, Texas, on the American frontier. Among the attackers, led by the Juárist chief Escobedo, were a large number of American blacks liberated from the Federal army. The 300 Austrians fought bravely, but their defense was compromised by two battalions of their Mexican allies who managed to change sides in the midst of the fray, and they were forced to surrender. The Mexicans collected over 1,000 prisoners, eight cannon and three hundred wagons.[40] This offered proof that the French could only react to events rather control the pace of the war. Their cavalry could not give them the strategic initiative.

Of course, even without the creation of these mobile forces, the Legion could always rely on the superb marching ability of its soldiers, which remained impressive. The Mexicans thought the Legion mad for marching in the impossible heat of midday. Indeed, their concern was such that even one of Diesbach de Torny's Mexican prisoners suggested that "You'll kill yourself in this country." And while Diesbach de Torny put on a brave front—"We French don't keep hours. . . . When we're thirsty, we sing!"— he admitted secretly that the Legion in Mexico was maintaining, quite literally, a killing pace.[41] For instance, the legionnaires who marched from San Luis Potosí to relieve the siege of Matehuala in late March 1866 made the normally ten-day journey in less than half that time, averaging almost five miles an hour despite resistance from the Mexicans. Many men simply could not keep up. "As for myself," wrote Amiable of this grueling march, "my tongue was down at least to my feet, but I kept going, knowing what awaited stragglers."[42] But by punishing the infantry in this way, the Legion probably lost in firepower what it gained in mobility, especially as the veterans of Africa were replaced after April 1864 by recruits hastily trained at the temporary Legion depot in Aix-en-Provence.

That the Legion was able to achieve as much as it did in Mexico was probably due to the quality of its officers. In common with other regiments, especially those in Algeria, it was largely a celibate group—Zédé noted that only four officers in the regiment were married, almost all of whom occupied administrative positions.[43] In many respects they were as diverse as the troops they led. Zédé found that the foreign officers at Sidi-bel-Abbès counted the Spaniard Lieutenant Colonel Antonio Martinez, who "spoke a quite extraordinary French," and a Prussian Second Lieutenant Ernst Milson von Bolt, who would fight the French in 1870. The Legion also served as a refuge for those whose families were in political disgrace, like the son of Marshal Bourmont, the man who had deserted Napoleon on the eve of Waterloo, who needed to maintain a discreet existence during the Second Empire.[44] Others, like the Swiss Diesbach de Torny, were impoverished aristocrats who lived by their sword.[45] A few like Zédé had excellent prospects but chose the Legion because they sought action. However, many more joined because they lacked the credentials for success in other, more prominent corps, "where one succeeds only through contacts with powerful superiors whom one must always please."[46]

So, despite their heterogeneous origins, the Legion officer corps was a distillation of men who craved action, eschewed comfort and had little to lose but their reputations in the eyes of their fellow officers. Add to this the conscious cultivation of a macho image expected of officers whose troops, by common consent, were little better than jailbait, and the inevitable result was an atmosphere of uncommon aggressiveness in the mess. Zédé confirmed that the Legion officer corps was "a violent milieu."[47] "We fought for the pleasure of fighting," Charles Clemmer discovered when he joined the Legion in Algeria. "Without rime or reason, we intentionally sought a quarrel with people we did not even know, whom we had never seen. Anything served as a pretext in the bars and cabarets: a song begun at another table, a glass of wine poured 'en quarte,' that is to say the hand turned to the right, a gesture, a look, was interpreted as requiring a duel." One evening while dining in a restaurant, a man came to his table and drank his glass of wine. After a moment of surprise, Clemmer suggested that if he wanted a glass, he should be happy to buy him one. The officer then began to insult him so that he broke a bottle over his head. Four days later (presumably after the man had sufficiently recovered), they fought a duel.[48]

Incorrigible duelists, nicknamed *"buveurs de sang,"* or "blood drinkers,"[49] were in fairly plentiful supply in the French army of the Second Empire. So common were duels among officers in this period that dueling probably produced the highest number of casualties among officers after enemy bullets. Two captains in Zédé's regiment were killed in duels by fellow officers, while a third lost an arm to a saber. Lieutenant (later general) Lambert was wounded in the chest by the saber of Lieutenant Bournhommet. However, though victorious, the unfortunate Bournhommet was cashiered from the regiment "for having hesitated to cross steel with Lambert."[50] Even Lieutenant Evariste Berg, who had miraculously survived Camerone in 1863, fell victim the following year to a duel.[51]

The argument in favor of dueling was that it preserved high standards of honor in the army, both among officers and soldiers, so long as certain minimum rules were respected—an attempt to legislate those rules for the French army in 1848–49 failed. The first was that duels must be fought among men of equal rank, although Clemmer reckoned that if officers and NCOs did not fight each other often, it was simply because they did not frequent the same bars.[52] Officers were also prohibited from fighting civilians of inferior social position, although given the low social position of most officers the cutoff point must have been fairly obscure. Last, regulations required that a doctor and a "master of arms" must be present. In the cavalry, the master of arms decided if the pretext were sufficient for a duel. But the French never went as far as the Prussians, for instance, who required that all quarrels be submitted to a regimental honor council, which decided if a duel were warranted. On the contrary, virtually any pretext was sufficient, and any man who hesitated to take up a challenge, like poor Bournhommet, risked disciplinary action and disgrace.[53]

One need only find a few examples to demonstrate that the need to demonstrate aggression, rather than to defend honor, was more often than not at the origins of these duels. On the trip from France to Mexico, Legion officers were forbidden to come into the wardroom outside of meal times. When one of the Legion's future battalion commanders, Captain Alexis Hubert de La Hayrie of the *zouaves,* wandered in during a prohibited hour to get a glass of water, he was placed under arrest by the ship's second in command. De La Hayrie accepted the punishment because, he said, they were on shipboard, but added that he intended to kill the naval officer as soon as they set foot on shore.[54] It is certainly possible that the captain's order excluding army officers from the wardroom may have been inhospitable. It may even have smacked of snobbery. However, perhaps the officers in his command preferred not to frequent men who had the disconcerting habit of threatening death to anyone in a blue suit who looked at them sideways. A duel between Diesbach de Torny and a fellow captain who had tricked him into dancing with an unattractive and heavy-footed Mexican woman was avoided only because no swords were available and it was felt that pistols were a trifle too final given the nature of the dispute.[55] In August 1866, twenty-one Belgian officers sent their cards to an equal number of French, mostly Legion, officers at San Luis Potosí after the Frenchmen made unflattering comments about Belgian courage and, at the suggestion of Legion captain Auguste Ballue, proposed that they be excluded from the officers' mess.[56]

Duels, therefore, became the vehicle through which officers sought to validate their personal bravery, to keep their aggressive instincts honed, to demonstrate to themselves and to those about them that they were warriors, fearless, even careless for their personal safety, prepared to take on any enemy or, for that matter, any friend. The aggressiveness of Legion officers, and especially of the battalion commanders—Gustave Saussier, Alexis de La Hayrie, and Paul-Amiable de Brian—formed one of the great strengths of the corps in Mexico.[57] Time and again they pushed their men to the very brink of endurance, and beyond. Without them, the Legion might never have been able to achieve the mobility and striking power they demonstrated in Mexico, all by applying Bugeaud's dictum that once the enemy is destroyed, then the troops "will have all the time they need to rest."

However, aggressiveness, especially when it was confused with honor, could have baleful consequences, as was demonstrated at the hacienda of Santa Isabel on March 1, 1866. In the second week of February, the 2nd Battalion of the Legion under de Brian chased a group of Mexicans out of the small town of Parras, about sixty miles east of Saltillo, Coahuila. His orders were to remain in Parras long enough to organize a local defense force but, according to the official report, not to venture out of Parras. In late February, a band of 1,200 horsemen under the Mexican chief Trevino eluded Legion cavalry near Saltillo, and on February 28 joined another group of seven hundred rebels at the hacienda of Santa Isabel, about ten miles north of Parras. "Convinced that the French garrison at Parras, whose strength he knew, would not hesitate, despite its numerical inferiority, to attack, he decided to wait in an advantageous position," reads the French report. "He made an intelligent choice in Santa Isabel."[58]

Santa Isabel was a fairly typical Mexican farm utterly devoid of architectural distinction. A slab of crumbling masonry laid along the road running north from Parras through a dessicated plain, Santa Isabel appeared to be a fairly straightforward place to attack, except from the west, where it backed against a high, boulder-strewn hill. There is no evidence, however, that de Brian was actually aware of this. The report subsequently faulted him for, among other things, failing to make a reconnaissance. Whatever knowledge he had of Santa Isabel must have been gleaned from some of the four hundred Mexicans whom, together with three stripped-down companies of legionnaires numbering 185 officers and men, he led out of Parras after dark on the night of February 28, 1866.

In assuming that the French would attack him, Trevino showed remarkable insight, as well as an ability to turn one of the Legion's strengths—its aggressiveness—against it. Paul-Amiable de Brian de Foussières Fontèneuille was not a man who could pass up a scrap. Joining the *2e étranger* straight out of Saint-Cyr in 1849, de Brian had earned the coveted *Légion d'honneur* by 1851 for bravery against the Kabyles. Wounded and promoted to captain in the Crimea, he had fought in Italy and Algeria before coming to Mexico with the 62nd Infantry Regiment in 1863. However, he lost little time in searching out his old regiment, which he rejoined as a battalion commander in March 1864. "My orders are not to come out," he is quoted as saying in the official report. "But I cannot allow the enemy to come insult me at three leagues from Parras without dishonoring myself." Obviously, for de Brian combat was simply another duel from which one could not back off without losing face. He might also have assumed that the Mexicans, even if superior in number, would turn tail in the face of a vigorous French assault, as they had so often done in 1864 and 1865.

The column marched at a fairly leisurely pace, as the major was in no hurry to arrive before dawn. However, at three o'clock in the morning, they were fired upon by Trevino's sentries about eight hundred yards south of the hacienda. De Brian deployed his troops, one company of legionnaires to the left of the road, one company to the right of it, while the friendly Mexicans were in the center. The third Legion company was kept in reserve. He ordered everyone to lie down. The defenders continued desultory fire, but in the darkness they did no damage. He gave orders that everyone march forward on signal, and then took up his position with his Mexicans on the left, probably because they were in greatest need of leadership.

Just before dawn, the bugle blew the charge and the line of attackers rose up and jogged toward the hacienda, which could have been nothing more than a dark silhouette in the distance. Things began to go wrong almost immediately. On the left, the charge of the company of Legion *voltigeurs* was stopped dead by a *barranca* that ran like a deep dry moat between them and their objective. This forced them to slide to the right to join the other troops attacking up the road. There, however, all was confusion. The linear attack had disintegrated into a jumble of men, legionnaires and Mexicans, running up the road toward the farm. By the time everyone had covered the eight hundred or so yards between the attack line and the walls of Santa Isabel, they were little more than a disorganized mob of men heaving for breath, "the officers no longer know their soldiers, the soldiers are no longer with their officers."

Now, just as the eastern sky was beginning to throw a little light on the battlefield, de Brian began to appreciate the strength of Trevino's position. The attackers were now fired upon by swarms of riflemen from the top of the hacienda wall, in some places twenty feet high, and from the crown of the hill to their left, which rose 130 feet out of the plain. It took no genius to realize that if they were to survive, the French must seize the high ground. Spontaneously, the legionnaires abandoned the wall and began scaling the hill under heavy fire. De Brian went down barely thirty feet up the slope, as did several other men. But as the wave of legionnaires approached the summit, the rebels could be seen drifting to the rear, despite attempts by their leaders to beat them back into line.

Then, just as the French appeared to be within an ace of success, a curious incident happened that turned a merely bad morning into a disastrous one. From the hacienda, a voice shouted in French, "Retreat!" The order was repeated several times. The legionnaires began falling back down the hill, their numbers reduced to around ninety. At this point, a large number of Juarista cavalry galloped from behind the hacienda. This spectacle was more than the Mexican cavalry that had accompanied de Brian could stand, and they opted to live to fight another day. The rest was sheer butchery. Trevino unleashed the thousand horsemen whom he had gathered behind the hacienda, who swept down the road and cut in behind the retreating French. In twos and threes, the legionnaires attempted to defend themselves, but without much success. De Brian was killed while he was being carried down the road by a Legion sergeant. All the wounded on the slope were finished off, as was the doctor who had brought the ambulance to the wall of the hacienda. Those who were able threw themselves into a *barranca* that paralleled the Parras road to escape the rebel cavalry. There they were organized by a Sergeant Desbordes into two lines and began to walk down the canyon. But they were able to travel only four hundred yards before they hit a cul-de-sac. Mexicans crowded on the lip of the *barranca* to shoot down on the French. When the fire of the legionnaires discouraged many from showing their heads, they began to pelt them with stones and shout that they would bury them alive. After an hour of this, Desbordes surrendered his 82 survivors, 40 of whom were wounded. The Legion lost 102 officers and men dead. One straggler had escaped.[59]

Amiable, who was sent to rescue the 44 legionnaires and 26 soldiers from the transport corps who subsequently held out for five days in the

Parras church, visited Santa Isabel a few days after the battle. "The spectacle before our eyes was awful," he wrote. ". . . We buried at least 200 men of our legion. . . . We dug ditches three yards deep and four yards across and put twenty cadavers in each. Several had already been buried; their hair and parts of their clothes came out of the earth. It stank. The ground in many places was full of dried blood, which formed large pools. I was sick for several days . . ."[60]

Santa Isabel did have one curiously face-saving footnote for the Legion. The Legion prisoners were taken to a remote desert camp not far from the American border where, under the command of German sergeant Fiala, they overpowered their guards and escaped across the Río Grande. Somehow they made their way to New Orleans and caught a boat to Veracruz, where they reported for duty. Marshal Bazaine decorated Fiala, and upon his retirement from the Legion, he was made custodian of the château at Pau near the Pyrenees. Fiala's story is all the more remarkable as he was one of the few legionnaires to leave the United States for Mexico. Unfortunately for the Legion, the traffic was usually in the opposite direction.

Desertion, of course, has from the earliest days been associated with the Legion. No desertion figures exist for the Crimea or Italy, although the Italians who joined the Legion in Milan in 1859 managed to disappear before the regiment re-embarked for North Africa.[61] Nevertheless, the Legion's reputation for taking French leave was alive and well in the 1860s. General Ulrich complained in 1861 that 648 men had deserted the *1er étranger* in Algeria, a whopping 22 percent, which is all the more astounding as Algeria was a very difficult place to desert from. Once the Legion reached Mexico, however, it appeared as if desertion might become a hemorrhage that would seriously undermine its combat effectiveness. The inspector of the *régiment étranger* in Mexico in 1863 noted that, although morale was high, "desertions have unfortunately been too numerous since its arrival in Mexico." Yet there was no great cause for worry, as those who had left were merely *"des misérables."*[62] Therefore, desertion might be beneficial if it allowed the Legion to eliminate a small number of unenthusiastic soldiers.

In 1864, General Brincourt reported 404 desertions in a corps of 3,471 men, a desertion rate of 11.6 percent, which had been about normal for the 1830s.[63] Once the Legion was able to shed its reluctant elements, desertion rates appear to have dropped to more manageable levels—6 and 5.8 percent for 1865 and 1866, respectively. However, these figures must be opened to question, for complaints about Legion desertion redoubled in these years: "In the expeditions in the North [of Mexico], the number of desertions multiplied to the point that they became a real plague," wrote General Félix Douay in 1866. "Twice on the banks of the Rio Bravo, they took on the character of a defection."[64]

General Castelnau believed that

*The régiment étranger is well beneath the quality of the old Foreign Legion.
A good percentage of the men who make it up today only enlisted for a free
trip to America, and as soon as they have the opportunity, one sees them
desert en masse. When the régiment étranger occupied Matamoros in 1865,
and when it operated in 1866 near the frontier of the Rio Grande, there
were up to 80 desertions in a single day. Isolated cases of desertion are in
any case constant there, not only during marches but also in garrison, and
even in Mexico City.*

Especially troubling, however, was the large number of legionnaires
going over to the enemy: ". . . each guerrilla band counts several deserters
from the *régiment étranger* in its ranks," Douay reported.[65] The rebel
leader Porfirio Díaz even had formed a separate corps of three hundred
French deserters, most of them legionnaires, which gave a good account of
itself.[66] The Belgian consul in Mexico reported that ninety-three legionnaires deserted during the expedition to Mier on the American frontier in
June 1866, while the French vice-consul in Galveston complained that
European deserters were flooding into Texas.[67] General Daudignac recorded that entire squads of legionnaires were deserting with arms and
baggage on the road out of Veracruz because they believed the United
States to be only two or three days' march away, which probably prompted
the September 1866 complaint by an English observer that deserters from
"those irregular regiments which are formed from the refuse of France and
Europe" had been committing atrocities on the road between Mexico City
and Veracruz.[68]

To be sure, the Legion could claim no monopoly on desertion. Médecin
major Jules Aronsshon noted that "On our side, we have seen corps where
desertion has cleared out the ranks promptly. Thus, in the Legion, one
deserts in groups of twenty, thirty at a time." But he also cited trouble in
other units, including the *zouaves*, and with Austrian and Belgian forces.
"Odd sort of campaign, don't you think?" he concluded.[69]

Obviously, Maximilian's troops were experiencing discipline problems
as early as 1865, and it would only get worse, especially in the Legion. The
above anecdotes also suggest that, perhaps for the first time since Spain,
desertion from the Legion was serious enough to undermine its combat
efficiency. "As long as we are ten to twelve days' march from the frontier,
they will only leave in small bands," General Douay wrote to his brother
from San Luis Potosí on February 2, 1866. "In almost all the units, they
leave in twos with arms and baggage when they are on guard in the advanced posts. But they have long distances to cover. Several have been
taken and shot, which keeps most of the others in line. I don't know what
will happen when they only have a few kilometers to cover to reach
safety."[70]

The obvious question to ask, then, is, Why were legionnaires deserting
in such large numbers? As already suggested, the official explanation was

that these deserters had enlisted in the Legion with that very purpose in mind. Bazaine believed that "a good many of them enrolled in the corps [Foreign Legion] to get a free trip, but it will cost them dearly if caught,"[71] an assertion repeated by French historian Pierre Sergent.[72] Therefore, the problem of Legion desertion in Mexico appears to have been considered both by officers at the time and historians since as an exceptional phenomenon, attributable to the fact that many recruits simply joined up for the ocean voyage. Of course, it is fair to point out that the Legion had (and has) a vested interest in propagating this view, as other explanations might suggest that the Legion might be unsuitable for certain types of operations.

So, was the inordinate amount of Legion desertion in Mexico simply a product of a short-term influx of would-be immigrants? Of course, it is always possible that some men saw enlistment as a cheap ticket to the New World. But there were far easier ways to get to the United States than enlisting in the Foreign Legion—after all, tens of thousands of impoverished immigrants did it every year. With the War Between the States raging, even if a man of military age could not get assisted passage from the American consul in any European port city (which is by no means certain), he found instant employment once setting foot in North America where the war had created an acute labor shortage and where a quarter of the 2 million white troops in Union Armies were made up of immigrants. If, as General Douay claimed, two-thirds of the Legion in 1866 were Germans,[73] it may have been that they were simply too broke, too lazy or not allowed by French frontier police to go further without enlisting. However, a more likely explanation seems to be that these deserters had enlisted in the Legion and then had second thoughts about military life, or that, once in Mexico, they seized the opportunity to desert without much premeditation.

The archives of the temporary Legion depot at Aix-en-Provence suggest that, rather than being eager to get to Mexico to desert, Legion recruits were eager to desert *before* they could be sent to Mexico. Serious problems obviously had been brewing for some time before they finally erupted in the spring of 1865, for on March 29, two hundred legionnaires rioted after five of their number were arrested.[74] The cause of the trouble is not apparent from the report, but morale was obviously low, for two days later the general commanding at Marseille suggested that Legion replacements for Mexico be sent via Toulon on the Mediterranean coast rather than marched across the country to Saint-Nazaire on the Atlantic, because "the men only want to desert and that, on the road from Aix to Saint Nazaire, they will probably seize the first opportunity to evade the surveillance."[75]

On April 11, the 4th Corps again complained that "The foreigners enlisted in the Legion in general do not want to embark for Mexico and to avoid it use all means at their disposal. A rather large number call upon either their families or the Minister of Foreign Affairs to cancel their contract." The general warned that men should not be excluded from the regiment for indiscipline, for this would simply encourage other men to

misbehave so that they could become civilians once again. Many legionnaires deserted to Marseille, where they enlisted in the Pontifical forces or
the American army, "which is being recruited clandestinely. . . . I profit
from this opportunity to call the attention of Your Excellency to the paltry
help such *poor elements* will give to the government of the Emperor of
Mexico."[76] The following day, the general at Marseille noted that the
announcement of a draft for Mexico invariably produced a wave of desertions at Aix—twenty-four on April 12 alone.[77]

The growing unpopularity of the Mexican War in France might also
have cooled the original military enthusiasm of some recruits. Town–
garrison relations at Aix deteriorated seriously due to the growing unpopularity of the war and the problems caused by the unenthusiastic
legionnaires. The downward slide was apparent in January 1865, when
three legionnaires offered to treat the clients of a local bar to a spectacle of
"prestidigitation." The locals were sent out to collect a number of articles,
"such as dresses, shawls, jackets, coats, dresses, rings, money, eggs, vegetables, etc.," which were then taken into a back room to be "prepared" by
one of the legionnaires prior to the act. By this time, "a numerous public"
had gathered, according to the *Messager de Provence,* which reported the
event. After a rather long wait, the legionnaire failed to reappear, so his
two colleagues disappeared into the back room to hurry him along. By the
time a Parisian could have recited the Edict of Nantes from memory, these
good citizens of Aix finally realized that they had been duped. Few legionnaires had ever been provided with such a bountiful means of desertion—
"You are mystified and robbed!" concluded the *Messager de Provence.*[78]

By summer, relations had hit rock bottom. Fights between legionnaires
and townsfolk appeared to be such a principal evening pastime that the
Messager de Provence demanded the soldiers be stripped of their bayonets,
which gave them an unfair advantage in these encounters. The minister of
the interior sent along a petition signed by the local population requesting
the removal of the Legion from Aix to his colleague in the War Ministry.[79]
It did not happen. Even as late as February 1867, Louis Aubin, a "land-
owner" at Aix, wrote directly to Emperor Napoleon III to complain that
legionnaires were "breaking into houses in the country, stealing men's
clothes, to dress in mufti so they can desert, which happens every day. They
drink, eat and, when they find nothing to eat, or drink, and nothing of
value, they break everything up."[80]

The conclusion suggested by all these troubles at Aix is that most
recruits did not view the Legion as a form of assisted passage to the New
World. If ever this had been their intention upon enlistment, they quickly
regretted their decision and sought to bail out before they reached the ports
of embarkation. Reluctant recruits may also have contributed to what
some saw as the declining performance of the Legion in Mexico. It is
certain that the end of the War Between the States in April 1865 saw the
tempo of combat increase in Mexico, and that most of these engagements

were victorious ones for the Legion. Nevertheless, this provides an inadequate indication of performance, as the Mexicans, like most guerrilla forces, were not interested in dominating the battlefield in a traditional European sense, but concentrated upon harassing actions. The growing desertion rate would seem to indicate that the heart had gone out of the French effort generally, and that this was felt acutely in the Legion. "When we leave, [Maximilian] will only have the support of the Foreign Legion and the Cazadores," General Douay wrote on September 27, 1866. "The Legion, made up of rather mediocre troops who are quick to desert, is still under strength. . . . More, most of the officers of the Legion serving *au titre français* have asked to leave Mexico the day that our flag is lowered, and it is impossible to leave them after the departure of the Marshal [Bazaine] and of the national troops."[81]

The waning enthusiasm of the legionnaires, rather than the premeditated desire to travel at French government expense to Mexico, appears to have been the cause of the numerous desertions in Mexico. Many no doubt enlisted on a whim, in the belief that soldiering was a life of romantic adventure, and were bound to be in for a rude shock when confronted with the harsh realities of Legion life. The shock was increased by the 1864 decision to raise the enlistment in the Legion from two to five years, where it has remained ever since. Of course, the infusion of large numbers of new recruits into a military force at war always brings problems of integration in its wake. However, these problems especially affected the Legion, which depended upon a rather long socialization process during which regimental loyalty would gradually supersede parochial and potentially divisive nationalism among heterogeneous recruits. The temporary depot at Aix fulfilled this socialization function poorly, in part because responsibility for the care of Legion recruits fell upon the shoulders of the 7th Infantry Regiment stationed in Aix.[82] As the Legion expanded from three to six battalions for the war, other regiments no doubt seized the opportunity to unload unpopular or inefficient officers and NCOs into these new formations. Moreover, while the Crimean and Italian campaigns were relatively brief and popular, Mexico appeared to present the possibility of an almost endless military commitment, which served to lower the war's popularity in France, which must also have played a part in lowering morale in the Legion.

The nature of the war in Mexico also placed particular strains on Legion morale and efficiency. In the first place, the Legion may not have been able to reforge the unity and *esprit de corps* it had exhibited at Sidi-bel-Abbès in 1863. Much of the original force was destroyed by the *vomito*. From mid-1864, many of the replacements, all of whom came from Aix, were of dubious value. Nor did the contingent of old Legion hands exist to initiate them into the rituals and lore of the regiment, thereby speeding their integration by developing regimental pride. The lack of homogeneity of the Legion could be extended to the government forces in general, a motley collection that included not only the diverse units—Arab, French and foreign—of the *Armée d'Afrique,* but also Mexicans, Belgians, Austrians and even a unit of Egyptians. Friction, duels and a general lack of cooperation were fairly frequent among them. Santa Isabel probably provided the most spectacular failure of such a combined Legion-Mexican operation. But there were others, in particular in June 1866 when the Franco-Belgian convoy marching from Monterrey to Mier failed to support a convoy of Austrians and Mexicans that was attacked and destroyed near Matamoros. The failure of the French to run to the rescue was put down to low morale in the French camp.[83] However, had the Matamoros convoy been composed of Frenchmen, they almost certainly would have been supported.

But these large operations aside, much of the Legion was scattered about in small, isolated garrisons. This undoubtedly had several effects. As in Algeria before the arrival of Bugeaud, discipline and morale were no doubt harder to maintain in these small detachments, isolated from the main body of troops and feeling very vulnerable indeed, especially as the Mexicans were more agile and far better armed, and therefore more dangerous, than the Algerians had been in the days of Algerian conquest. Furthermore, scattering troops about in penny packets violated the principle upon which the efficiency of the Legion, as well as that of other corps, had been based—namely, rigorous selection. In Mexico, the Legion was not always permitted the luxury of leaving its least able soldiers behind and operating with picked troops. So while its mobile corps might continue to perform credibly, its garrison troops could lack initiative and élan.

All or some of these factors may have set legionnaires to thinking of alternative careers. As in Algeria, virtually the only option open to many deserters in Mexico was to defect to the enemy. But unlike Algeria, desertion to the enemy was a fairly risk-free option in Mexico. Furthermore, it might even be an attractive one: "What is very clear is that the profession of guerrilla is one of the most lucrative in Mexico," war minister Marshal Randon wrote to Bazaine, "and that the leaders of bands are never bothered about finding soldiers and money—two elements of a war in which the Mexican government is in default."[84] Indeed, in the spring of 1865, the Legion sought to dry up a potential source of guerrilla support as well as solve its own recruitment problems by enlisting Confederate soldiers who had sought asylum in Mexico. The idea was dropped, however, when only one came forward, and even he insisted on a six-month trial period.[85]

The Mexicans sensed early on that the dubious loyalty of legionnaires to their cause and to their corps might be exploited, and began to encourage desertion. Diesbach de Torny began shooting Mexicans for encouraging desertion from his company in early 1864.[86] Amiable reported that Mexicans had fair success encouraging desertions around Monterrey, until a legionnaire denounced the principal agent, who was shot.[87] As has been seen, French deserters, many but not all from the Legion, were to be found in many Mexican bands.[88] Indeed, General Daudignac discovered an old legionnaire at Sidi-bel-Abbès in 1895 who had served with the guerrillas in Mexico, but who was incapable of remembering whether he had fought for or against the French.[89]

The risks of desertion may have increased from October 1865, when Maximilian, probably prompted by Marshal Bazaine, ordered all captured partisans to be shot.[90] Some credited this order with the increasing viciousness of the war, although the fact that the Mexicans were becoming better armed, and no doubt more aggressive, may also have been a factor. When, on July 3, 1866, a large group of Mexicans withdrew after a two-day attack upon two Legion companies near Matehuala, they reportedly left behind ten dead and thirty wounded, two-thirds of whom, according to the French divisional order, "have been recognized as miserable men who left the French ranks to fight against their old comrades. No one can ignore that, in all of their engagements with us, the Mexicans force the French deserters to march before them by beating them. This is the way that these unfortunates pay, in an ignoble death, the price of their crime."[91] This may have been true in a few instances. However, there is no evidence that this was liberal policy or practice. On the contrary, it is far more likely that the army wished deliberately to paint a black picture of the fate of deserters by distortion or deliberate falsehood. In any case, it seems fairly clear that desertion to the enemy in Mexico was a viable option for the disgruntled.

A second way in which Mexico, especially northern Mexico, differed from Algeria was that the United States actually offered somewhere to desert to, without having to worry about an inhospitable reception from the enemy. This meant that a campaign in the northern states of Mexico particularly provoked a hemorrhage of desertion serious enough to threaten Legion efficiency.

Last, it was becoming increasingly clear that the war was unwinnable. It took no Napoleon to realize, especially after the Union victory of 1865, that no matter how well they fought, victory must elude them because Washington now actively aided the Juaristas. The Imperial forces were too few, and attempts to create a viable Mexican force had collapsed. Even Mexican officials and soldiers who supposedly supported the government defected to the liberals at the first opportunity. American "immigrants" flooded in to aid the Juaristas. Furthermore, the feeling was strong among Legion officers, at least, that they were backing the wrong horse. Zédé called the whole business *"une mauvaise affaire,"* and while it did not prevent the Legion from fighting hard, the enemy was given "the esteem merited by a party which defends the liberty of its country" against foreigners and priests, whom the legionnaires, not religious men as a rule, despised. The sentiment was unanimous that Maximilian should abdicate and that the French should leave.[92] "Let's try to leave before the house falls in on us," Legion officers said openly, according to Major Clemmer. "There is no longer any point in trying to hold it up."[93] Diesbach de Torny, never a barrel of laughs at the best of times, quickly soured on the Mexican adventure, declaring that "There is enough here to put one off the profession." As early as 1864, he condemned "This damned war. . . . This damned country."[94]

Many officers, like Diesbach de Torny, resigned or transferred out of the Legion, to get out while the gettin' was good. Of one hundred officers in the *régiment étranger* in 1863, sixteen died during the campaign. Thirty-one of the original one hundred still remained with the unit in 1867, including Saussier, Zédé and Giovanielli, all future generals. The remainder had transferred out, often as the result of a promotion, which usually required a change of corps.[95] Of course, resignation is the officer's option. Soldiers can only serve out their enlistment, or desert. Many of those officers who remained probably allowed discipline to relax. French General Thoumas noted a certain *laissez-aller* in the Legion, symptomatic of deteriorating discipline. He complained that officers—and even NCOs—were riding horses, contrary to regulations, and dressed in sombreros and *"costumes de fantaisie."* "Gambling caused many victims among the officers and *l'aguardiente* [alcohol] ravaged the soldiers," he noted. He blamed the relaxation of discipline on the "dispersion of troops" in isolated garrisons.[96]

The increasing violence of the war from the summer of 1865 on lowered morale further.[97] Furthermore, the Prussian victory over the Austrians at Sadowa in 1866 fell like a thunderclap over the army in Mexico. American diplomatic and military pressure, the deteriorating military situation in Mexico and the war's increasing unpopularity in France combined with the worsening diplomatic situation in Europe to cause the French government to decide on a withdrawal in late 1866. The Belgian government also called its troops home, and they left with the first group of departing French troops in January 1867. As France too began to introduce military legislation to strengthen her army, French officers must have feared that they might be forced to sit out the next European conflict, with all of its attendant promotion and glory, in a Latin American backwater.

The combination of low morale, declining discipline and the proximity of the American frontier led to a large number of desertions from the Legion in August 1866. On August 12, the Legion entered the town of Mier, abandoned in haste by the frightened inhabitants, and began to pillage. "This pillage was the most productive of all Mexico," Amiable recounted. "We discovered gold and silver hidden everywhere. For my part, I discovered an old sock hidden in the trunk of a tree containing five American ounces, about 800 francs, as well as a clock and a pair of dueling pistols which I sold at Monterrey, and from which I feasted with my cousin." For a week, the soldiers wandered the streets taking anything they fancied: "Several of them picked up a fortune. My captain resigned on our return: which led us to believe that he feathered his nest at Mier."[98] The Mexicans shot at them from the hills above the town, but no one paid any attention. This is when ninety-three French soldiers, their finances now in good order, decided to opt for American citizenship. Worse, according to Douay, was that those legionnaires who deserted from Mier in June 1866 were among the best: "[The column from Matamoros] had to come back quickly because already 89 soldiers of the Legion, and the best soldiers [all elite, artillerymen above all] seeing American territory near, deserted," he wrote on July 9, 1866. "It's around a tenth of the infantry [of the column] and that gives you some idea of what we can expect of these troops."[99] After eight days, those who remained loaded their wagons with loot and made their way slowly south.

The Mier column offers perhaps the most spectacular example of declining performance. The sack of Mier and the large number of desertions that followed were denounced as a "deplorable" lapse of discipline by Belgian colonel Alfred Louis Adolphe Graves van der Smissen. Belgian captain L. Timmerhans agreed, adding that "this troop was considered with reason in normal times to be well disciplined and courageous under fire." Obviously, for Timmerhans, as well as for many others, one suspects, 1866 in Mexico did not qualify under any definition of "normal times." But something had clearly snapped, because on the return trip to Monterrey, the Legion hardly bothered to chase the Mexican resistance that lined their route: "To run after these bandit chiefs," Amiable admitted, "was a vain exercise."[100]

Of course, it may be useful to place Legion indiscipline and desertion in Mexico in perspective. The Legion certainly did a better job of assimilating its heterogeneous soldiery than did that other great Foreign Legion of the period, the U.S. Army. So bad were the desertions from the U.S. Army in the Mexican War of 1845 that Santa Anna was able to form an entire brigade of renegade Irishmen who had crossed over the lines. The Union Army counted fully 201,000 desertions in the War Between the States and desertions in the postwar decades ran close to one-third of strength.[101]

After the tremendous frustrations of the Mexican campaign, Napoleon III's December 1866 order to repatriate all French troops, including the Legion, must have come as a relief. The battalions of the Legion were pulled in toward Mexico City, from which they marched to Soledad to board trains that carried them quickly through the jungles to Veracruz to avoid the *vomito*. At Veracruz each of the six battalions camped only one night before embarking for home. By the end of February 1867, the last troopship that would repatriate the Legion to Algeria had slipped away from the lugubrious Mexican coastline. Some 1,918 officers and legionnaires had perished in Mexico, 1,601—83 percent—victims of disease.

Chapter 8

THE FRANCO-PRUSSIAN
WAR AND THE COMMUNE

THE LEGION'S ALGERIAN homecoming was not a happy one. On April 4, 1867, the government ordered the Legion reduced from six to four battalions, which resulted in the immediate disbandment of the Legion artillery and engineering units, and the transfer of 84 officers and by July 387 NCOs and corporals out of the regiment. In August, Paris ordered further reductions to slash the force from 5,000 to 3,000 men, so that French legionnaires were sent to regular units and almost 1,000 foreigners had their enlistment contracts unilaterally terminated. What remained was scattered among isolated posts in eastern Algeria, where they were set building posts and roads.

What was depressing duty at the best of times was made even more onerous as 1867 was a crisis year in Algeria, when a poor harvest pushed up the price of food beyond the means of many Arabs to pay for it. Typhus soon joined the starvation that was killing the native population by the thousands. The high price of food required legionnaires, especially in the southern posts, to survive on the hardtack and poor-quality meat provided by the French supply corps, which, when added to the exhausting labor and absence of a strongly centralized command in these isolated posts, lowered morale still further. Soon inspecting generals reported a resurgence of the Legion's "deplorable tendency toward drunkenness," which, as in the past, was financed by the selling of equipment. And if this were not bad enough, a serious cholera epidemic soon broke out in the garrisons.

By the end of 1867, the Legion had been reduced to three thousand men, but the survivors had begun to look back upon the Mexican years with deep nostalgia, an attitude the remainder of the decade did nothing to alter. General Grisot, who lived these years with the Legion, spoke of the "*lourd ennui*" and "fatigue" of life in these isolated Legion posts, where conditions were primitive, where the nearest source of firewood was often eight miles distant, where a few vegetables coaxed by dint of great effort from the unyielding soil or a skeletal chicken were received in the mess with almost religious awe.

The only distractions were provided by periodic scrambles to intercept elusive bands of raiders who darted into French territory from Morocco. But these outings usually caused far more damage to the Legion than to the Moroccans: One column returning to Géryville after a demonstration of force in April 1868 was caught by bad weather in the mountains and forced to abandon most of its equipment after the camels died of fatigue. The legionnaires fashioned footwear out of animal skins and marched on. Many died of misery and fatigue. When the column reached Géryville, casualties in the Legion included nineteen suicides and a company commander who had been seized by Arabs when he wandered away from the column and had been tortured to death. An expedition to punish dissidents in the Djebel Amour north of Géryville in February 1869 collapsed when the Legion column, already on the verge of starvation because the supply corps failed to supply it with meat, was caught in a series of terrible snowstorms that forced it back to base empty-handed.[1]

In this context, news of the outbreak of war between France and the German states in July 1870 should have been greeted with positive joy by legionnaires. Initially, however, life for the Legion actually got worse. As the 1831 law founding the Legion also prohibited its use in metropolitan France, two battalions were sent to replace the *zouaves* at a place the Arabs called El-Hasaiba—The Damned—because it was malarial. Soon graves of legionnaires sprouted next to those of the *zouaves* in the garrison cemetery.

However, the government's reluctance to use the Legion in the war against Germany was quickly overtaken by events. The first was that large numbers of foreigners, especially Irishmen, were expected to offer their services to France. This caused Napoleon III to order the formation of battalions of foreign volunteers separate from the Legion to serve for the duration of the war. But the expected bonanza of volunteers failed to live up to predictions, so on August 22, the one battalion of foreign volunteers that had been organized at Tours became the 5th Battalion of the *régiment étranger*. Nearly five hundred Germans enlisted as volunteers for the duration of the war, as did some Belgians who were sent to Algeria after the Belgian government objected to its citizens being used in the conflict.[2] On September 1, a decree called into being a 2ᵉ *régiment étranger*, but the rapid pace of the war consigned this order to oblivion, as it did other legalistic quibbles about using the Legion in France. In October, after the main French armies had been beaten and surrendered at Sedan and Metz, Napoleon III captured and sent into an English exile, and the Third Republic had been declared on September 4, two of the four Legion battalions stationed in Algeria arrived in France, minus their Germans, who remained behind.

By that time, the 5th Battalion had already fought an honorable, and very costly, action at Orléans. At two o'clock on the morning of October 11, the battalion had been caught up in an attack by Bavarian units. The battalion commander was killed in the eight hours of bitter house-to-house fighting that ensued. Dispersed, many of the legionnaires had not received the order to disengage and withdraw across the Loire River. At the end of the day, the battalion had taken 600 casualties and left behind 250 prisoners.[3]

That this Legion battalion had fought so well surprised many, for its organization had been plagued by difficulties. It was a very large and unwieldy battalion of 1,350 men, and as usual for the Legion, it was a very heterogeneous crowd that included many Poles, Swiss, Belgians and even a number of deserters from the German forces.[4] While this was nothing new for the Legion, the problems were compounded by the extreme shortage of regular officers to staff the raw levies being called up by the republicans to continue the war that had been so badly mismanaged by the Empire. Many of the Legion's officers were snapped up for other duties, their places often taken by foreigners whose military credentials were insufficiently scrutinized by a government fighting with its back to the wall. One of the better officers was the future Peter I of Serbia, an ex-cadet at Saint-Cyr. On the lower end of the competency scale was an Irishman named Kirwan who came to France at the head of 100 Irish volunteers to form an ambulance corps, but, sensing the rapidly deteriorating French position, offered to take up arms. Grisot complained that Kirwan spent most of his time writing newspaper dispatches. Other temporary Legion officers included a lieutenant who defected to the Prussians, a Spanish major who deserted with arms and baggage and a Turk who was relieved after a month after he got into several fistfights with his legionnaires.

On October 19, the two battalions sent from Algeria joined the remnants of the 5th to become part of the Army of the Loire. But by that time the French were in serious difficulties. A revolution in Paris on September 4, 1870, had overthrown the Empire. The new Third Republic struggled manfully to carry on the war amidst the utter chaos of defeat. German armies besieged Paris and had pushed south to the Loire River, where the French had organized a defense with a ragtag collection of soldiers left in Africa and volunteers, both French and foreign. Like other units, the Legion was plagued by the almost total absence of military expertise. Combat, a confusing experience at the best of times, was rendered even more difficult to control, so that even fairly minor skirmishes could prove very costly. While the newly organized 5th Battalion had fought very well at Orléans, subsequent performance was less inspiring. Discipline began to collapse as the distribution system broke down, and soldiers foraged for food and clothes in the bitterly cold winter of 1870–71, or turned to the numerous alcohol merchants who shadowed the lumbering French armies. Several legionnaires were shot after lapses of discipline, but this did little to stop the rot.

In early December a second battle was fought at Orléans. As in the earlier October encounter, a number of legionnaires scattered in houses were lost when they failed to get news of the French withdrawal. Many of the 210 men who failed to answer roll call in the 1st and 2nd Battalions on the night of December 3–4 had perished from cold, hunger and fatigue after three nights of sleeping in the snow. As the Legion fell back in the middle of a disorganized French army on the night of December 4–5, some settled into houses along the route of march, where they were captured by the advancing Germans. By the next morning, the regiment reckoned that it had lost half its strength. On the 10th, the remnants of the three battalions were formed into a single *bataillon de marche*.

On December 18 the Legion received a reinforcement of two thousand young soldiers, most of them Bretons who had never fired a rifle, which brought the one-thousand-man regiment to three thousand. "We reorganized the cadres with the old troopers, with anyone who could wear stripes," wrote Grisot. "But the recruits preferred to listen to the old soldiers, rather than to the newly formed cadres."[5] Discipline was poorly maintained throughout the army, with soldiers squandering munitions on hunting expeditions—an occupation that also caused continuous alerts as units confused the execution of a rabbit with a Prussian attack—selling provisions and cutting down fruit trees. In the train stations, soldiers cut off from their units pillaged and stole from their comrades.

This *laisser-aller* in the army in general was bound to prove contagious. The situation in the Legion was hardly improved when on January 19, 1871, the paymaster was killed and the company chest that contained 4,341 francs captured by the enemy. And if this were not bad enough, on that very night a German reconnaissance party surrounded and captured an entire Legion company as it sat, sentinelless, calmly warming itself around a roaring fire. This occurred in part because the lack of mobility among the French obliged them to camp on their forward positions rather than retire to the rear, leaving advance posts to screen their cantonments. German campfires were almost never visible from the French lines.

The major problem was the lack of discipline: "The young soldiers, Bretons for the most part, fought among themselves rather than help each other out," Grisot complained. But he believed that the men of the *régiment étranger* were less demoralized than those of other regiments. For this reason, the Legion, though inexperienced, managed to seize the heights above Sainte-Suzanne near Montbéliard in the Franche-Comté from the Germans in mid-January.[6] "We advanced under a hail of shells," one Legion officer wrote. ". . . The Prussians fled in all directions." But the next day, the enemy returned in strength and the French withdrew. "Our men no longer have shoes," the same officer reported. "Many have frozen feet and food is lacking."[7] The death rate in the aid stations was considerable.

Such was the situation when the French government threw in the towel and signed an armistice in January. However, the cessation of hostilities did not affect the *armée de l'Est,* to which the Legion had been transferred, which remained on a war footing until March 1. Even the scrupulous Grisot confessed that such was the confusion of this year that Legion losses were impossible to estimate. In mid-March, 415 men from the conscript "class" of 1863, and those who had enlisted "for the duration of the war"—presumably most of the foreigners enlisted in France—were released. Leave was distributed liberally which reduced numbers still further.

This was the situation on March 27, 1871, when the Legion was ordered to join the army of Versailles, which was organizing to fight the Parisian insurrection known as the Commune, ignited on March 18 when the conservative government of Adolphe Thiers had attempted to disarm the national guardsmen who had been defending the French capital against German forces. What is not clear is how many of the 66 officers and 1,003 legionnaires who entrained for Paris were foreigners. As has been seen, in December 1870 the regiment had been composed of at least two-thirds French conscripts. Furthermore, on April 20, it received a reinforcement of six officers and 370 conscripts from two French line regiments.[8] Therefore, the *régiment étranger* that participated in the siege of Paris, after several hard months of campaigning in France when it lost twelve of its officers and received large transfusions of Frenchmen, was very different in composition from the hardened mercenaries of the *Armée d'Afrique.* The Foreign Legion had never been less foreign.

The legionnaires arrived at Versailles, the royal village that had become the seat of the new Republic, on April 1 and camped along the boulevards that fed into the stately Avenue de Saint-Cloud. By April 4, they had joined the troops besieging Paris, and by the 15th had begun fighting their way through Neuilly on the western fringe of the city. Sniping from the houses, from behind the stone walls of the gardens and from behind barricades thrown across the narrow streets, the Communards defended themselves tenaciously. But the legionnaires noticed that orders by Communard officers to counterattack the besiegers usually provoked bitter quarrels in the rebel ranks, so that their assaults were seldom serious. The greatest threat was that posed by the Communard artillery, which constantly pounded the besiegers. However, the effectiveness of the Communard artillery was somewhat compromised by its predictability—never opening before 9:00 A.M. and taking a prolonged lunch break. At 4:00 P.M., "the absinthe hour," firing again ceased until after dinner, when it was only desultory. On the 19th, the Legion was pulled out of line after a dawn attack surprised and carried three Communard barricades and captured three cannon. But veteran legionnaires noted that their losses after four days in line, which included 3 officers and 15 legionnaires killed and 9 officers and 102 legionnaires wounded, were higher than during the battle of Magenta in 1859.

Despite fairly high casualties, Legion morale was maintained at a high pitch by the generous pay and ample provisions lavished upon them by the Versailles government, and by frequent periods of rest behind the lines. By the third week in May, the Versaillais were squeezing the defenders seriously. The Legion entered the city, large sections of which were on fire and masked by smoke, from the northwest through the Porte Maillot on May 25.[9] The legionnaires were under strict orders not to drink at the wine merchants' shops after a corporal died from poisoned alcohol. On May 26, a company of the Legion attacked a barricade near the Porte de la Villette, captured ten cannon, and shot four men captured there upon the order of the captain. On the 27th, the Legion seized the Buttes Chaumont after house-to-house fighting, and on the 28th descended into the working-class district of Belleville, where a large number of prisoners were taken on the barricades. Although neither Grisot nor any other historian mentions it, many of these prisoners were shot out of hand. The regimental diary reads: "Unfortunately, it was necessary that the punishment fit the crime, and in the afternoon a large number of executions were carried out." On May 30, "the morning was spent burying the bodies of the *fédérés* [as the Communards were called] shot the 28th and 29th."[10]

The Legion's participation in the brutal suppression of the Commune, in which, by conservative estimates, around twenty-five thousand Communards were killed, has formed one of the most controversial aspects of its history. Indeed, in 1976 the French Communist Party proposed the abolition of the Legion precisely because, they charged, the mercenary legionnaires had played a leading role in the bloodshed of the Commune. However, in its defense, two things must be said. The first is that passions were running very high in France in the late spring of 1871, following a humiliating defeat at the hands of the Prussians. Even the Legion's diarist felt the need to justify the execution of Communard prisoners: "The tricolor had probably replaced forever the infamous red flag whose triumph of several days stupefied Paris and all of France by its monstrous crimes carried out in the shadow of this flag," he wrote, citing "pillage, assassinations, horrible immolations of our most precious monuments and the pulling down of the Vendôme column."[11] Second, it would be wrong to interpret the suppression of the Commune as the importation of some sort of African barbarity into France by the mercenary soldiers of Algeria. It was a purely French affair, a civil war that had flared up periodically since 1789, of which the Commune was merely the final bloody episode. The vast majority of the executions were carried out by regiments of French conscripts, not African mercenaries.

Still, the episode did not serve to enhance the reputation of the Legion. Even Grisot admitted that the regiment met hostility from the European inhabitants of Oran, normally people who voted for the left, when it disembarked in June 1871.[12] For the moment, the right held political power in France for a series of complicated reasons emanating from the war. However, the left-wing republicans under Leon Gambetta were slowly making a comeback, and in 1879 would capture both houses of parliament and force the resignation of the conservative president, ex-Legion colonel Patrice de MacMahon. A thorough reform of the French army based upon republican principles of universal conscription, the duty of every man to fight in defense of his country, was high on their agenda. There was little room in the intensely patriotic ideology of these men for a mercenary corps that appeared to be a dinosaur of a bygone age. Worse, it had participated in the suppression of the Commune, a movement that some on the Left, revivified by the amnesty of the Communards granted in 1880, had already promoted into the pantheon of revolutionary movements, to rank just one step below the storming of the Bastille. By the 1870s, the Legion had acquired a past, even if some of the legionnaires preferred to forget their individual pasts. The question was, did it have a future?

Chapter 9

THE
INITIATION

IN 1871, THE Legion may be said to have entered what in retrospect appears to have been its golden age. During the forty-three years between the Treaty of Frankfurt, which ended the Franco-Prussian War, and the assassination at Sarajevo that inaugurated World War I, it was in the forefront of the great burst of imperial expansion that took the French flag deep into Indochina, Africa, Madagascar, and Morocco. The Legion's participation in these expeditions lifted it from relative obscurity to become one of the most celebrated, if most controversial, regiments in the French Army. There were at least two reasons for this: First, the Third Republic proved reluctant to risk its new "metropolitan" army of short-service conscripts in perilous imperial adventures. Therefore, unlike the conquest of Algeria, which had been undertaken in the main by numbered French regiments, imperial expansion in the Third Republic would fall almost exclusively to colonial units raised specifically for that purpose. Therefore, the Legion would form a conspicuous component in many of these well-publicized ventures.

A second factor that contributed to the Legion's higher profile, if not increase in stature, was the growing national tensions that steadily created the climate in which Europe prepared for war. Hardly had the final shots of the Franco-Prussian War been fired off than the ambiguous attitude of the French government toward the Legion surged to the surface. In July 1871, Paris ordered that the six battalions of the Legion (the 1st, 2nd, and 5th of the *régiment de marche* in France, the 6th Battalion in formation at

Dunkirk, an autonomous company serving with the II Army of the Loire and the 3rd and 4th Battalions in Algeria) be reduced to four. Furthermore, enlistments in the Legion were to be limited to men from the provinces of Alsace-Lorraine—taken from France and integrated into Bismarck's Reich—to Swiss and to Frenchmen with an authorization from the War Ministry. This measure, designed principally to eliminate the large number of Germans who traditionally enlisted in the Legion, was lifted only in 1880. Even so, this directive appears to have been almost totally ignored by recruiting sergeants, for when J. N. Gung'l, a Frenchman of Hungarian extraction, joined the Legion in 1872, he was surrounded by Poles, Belgians, Italians and a large number of German deserters still wearing their old uniforms, all of whom were presumably declared honorary Alsatians for the occasion.[1]

IF THE ATTITUDE of the French government toward the Legion was ambiguous, that of the Germans was definitely hostile. The large numbers of Germans serving in the Legion made it a special target of pan-Germanist propaganda as World War I approached. These writings sought to portray the Legion as a quasi-criminal institution, a military underworld of brutalized and desperate men, whose very existence was an affront to modern civilization, not to mention Germany, whose sons sweated and died in the service of the enemy. Such accusations quite naturally tickled many Frenchmen, especially sensitive to any slight on the prestige of the Grand Nation, into frenzies of rebuttal. The end result was that the Legion was increasingly brought to public notice.

Even before World War I, a popular image of the Legion as a refuge for those in trouble was beginning to take shape—the German-American Erwin Rosen, who enlisted in 1905, was told by a German that every tramp "always talked about the Legion. All the other Germans on the road wanted to enlist in the Legion."[2] After 1918, with the publication of such books as *Beau Geste,* the Legion suffered a veritable explosion of publicity, to the point that it changed the very character of the corps, according to the French writer Antoine Sylvère, who had served before 1914: "The short term enlistments, bonuses, the publicity brought about by the parades in Paris and the popular songs soon brought in men very different from those I had known," he wrote, "who were often confused with the *joyeux* [*Bat d'Af*], and who one never saw on leave in France where, it must be admitted, they would have been unbearable."[3] But this plethora of publicity did little to settle the basic debate about the character of Legion. On the contrary, it became increasingly difficult to separate the myth of the Legion from the reality, a problem that persists down to our own day.

So where does the truth lie? The question is not merely an academic one. For the Legion was charged with two separate, perhaps contradictory, tasks by the French government. On one hand, it served as a release valve for social, and even political, tensions, absorbing the unemployed (and the unemployable), the troublemakers and the penniless foreigners who might make mischief. At the same time, it had to be militarily efficient. The question is, how could the Legion remain in the military game after being dealt a hand that can only be described as a busted flush? To answer this question, we must discover first who these men were, how they came to the Legion, their motivations and expectations and, lastly, how the Legion processed and prepared them for service.

ENLISTMENT OFTEN TOOK place in a dingy room of an official building in Paris, or in one of the French provincial towns, especially those near the German or Belgian frontiers. The Englishman Frederic Martyn, who enlisted in 1889, found the colonel to whom he spoke at the recruiting depot "a peculiar sort of recruiting officer" because "his manner was dissuasive instead of the opposite,"[4] an experience shared by many recruits, who were often told to go "reflect" for twenty-four hours. The Irishman John Patrick Le Poer, sixteen, a runaway and utterly broke, had to insist that he be allowed to join to a sergeant who finally relented, muttering "poor devil."[5] An underage Ernst Junger refused to be dissuaded by a recruiting officer who told him that there was much fighting in Africa—"This was naturally pure music for my ears, and I hastened to reply that I was in search of a dangerous life."[6] The French colonel who gave Martyn his contract explained the Legion's caution: ". . . the life will not appeal to any one who does not love the soldiering trade for its own sake," he said. "There are many, too many, who join the Legion with no sort of qualification for a soldier's life, and these men do no good to themselves or to France by enlisting."[7]

The army's enlistment priorities may not have been those of the French gendarmes, however. Martyn met two fellow recruits who "told me an extraordinary story of their having been arrested on a trumped-up charge by the French police, and been given the choice between going to prison and joining the Legion. I couldn't reconcile this tale with the recruiting officer trying to dissuade me from joining, and I don't believe it now, but I am bound to say that I heard much the same thing from others later on."[8] Rosen met a black American legionnaire who told him a similar story of his arrest after a fight in a Paris restaurant: "They did done tell me, it was penitentiary or Legion." Nor was the American consul any help. "Take yer medicine, says he. Which I did—taking the Legion."[9] The French jurist Charles Poimiro challenged German critics in 1913 to prove their charge that French frontier police forced German nationals who had wandered over the border to join the Legion, but believed that, in any case, this was better than allowing them to beg and steal in France.[10]

After a fairly perfunctory medical examination at the end of which only those obviously agonizing in the final stages of consumption were rejected, the recruits were presented with a contract. Few bothered to read it (perhaps because they could not) before signing. One who did, Erwin Rosen, discovered that it contained "a great many paragraphs and great stress was laid on the fact that the 'enlisting party' had no right upon indemnification in case of sickness or disability, and no claim upon pension until after fifteen years of service."[11] He signed nonetheless.

The recruits were given a third-class ticket to Marseille and a small sum of money for food during the trip before a corporal marched them to the station. Le Poer's corporal amused himself by recounting harrowing stories about the Legion, but the young Irishman chose to believe that he was making them up.[12] The newly minted legionnaires traveled unescorted, although Rosen believed that their tickets, stamped "Légion étrangère" in bold red letters, were an invitation to supervision by the conductor.[13] When Le Poer's group got down at a stop to buy some food, they were surrounded by a curious crowd who believed that they were criminals, which included a woman "rather pretty, around thirty years old, who seemed to be as frightened as if she were in the presence of cannibals from the Congo."[14]

Fort Saint-Jean, an ancient gray fortress, squats on a rocky promontory at the entrance to Marseille's old port. The recruits were led down from the station in the brilliant Mediterranean sunlight, along the Canebière, Marseille's main thoroughfare, bustling with gesticulating Frenchmen, skirting the western edge of the rectangular harbor basin where elegant yachts were moored alongside tramp steamers, fishing boats and exotic levantine sailing ships. They negotiated their way among barrels, sacks and boxes in the process of being shifted and pulled by perspiring Frenchmen and impassive Arabs. Junger's corporal escort made a brief detour through the narrow back streets populated by drunks and prostitutes to fill his water bottle with dark Algerian wine before leading his charges over a drawbridge and between two sentries to be swallowed up by the sinister fortress. If none had had an inkling during their walk that this would be their last contact with European civilization for some time, perhaps forever, they could be under no illusion once through the gates that they were now on the threshold of Africa—the courtyard was crowded with spahis, *zouaves, tirailleurs,* legionnaires returning from leave and even some delinquents bound for the *Bats d'Af* awaiting the next packet to Algeria.

The stopover at Fort Saint-Jean could last up to ten days, a tedious confinement during which permission to go into town was usually denied, especially to foreigners. The time was spent staring over the battlements to the Château d'If, standing on an island just off the coast, and the blue sea beyond, or gazing for hours at the square yellow buildings of Marseille and the barely controlled chaos of the harbor below, over which presided the bleached promontories of the Chaîne de l'Étoile. Those with money discovered quickly enough that one could drink in the canteen for what on the outside would be considered knockdown prices. Those who had no money had to improvise—one of Rosen's companions swapped his boots for four liters of wine.[15] The moment of departure could evoke mixed feelings: Junger and his new friends "spoke a little of Africa and Indochina" before going to sleep on deck.[16] Martyn, usually fairly upbeat, felt a sharp pang of regret as their ship sailed past the British Mediterranean fleet festooned with Union Jacks: "I felt that I had wilfully thrown away my birthright," he remembered. "I was a despicable renegade."[17] Joseph Ehrhart, an orphan who had been disowned by the rest of his family, was acutely aware that in the crowd that had come to see his ship off, "to us legionnaires, no one waved goodbye. The shores of France grew hazy and, in spite of myself, I felt apprehensive. 'Will you see France again?' I thought. 'What is waiting for you out there?' "[18]

Spirits lifted somewhat at the sight of Africa. In the first light of dawn, Junger could barely make out the "confused silhouettes of mountains emerging from the obscurity. . . . At last the sun rose from the sea behind us and revealed a range of powerful summits which in the light took on hues of deep red. At their feet, the sea was bordered by the low white houses of a town."[19] Oran appeared quite suddenly between a narrow gap in the cliffs, "as if from a conjurer's box . . . a maze of flat-roofed houses on hilly ground," according to Rosen.[20] A sergeant came on board, marched to the bow and shouted, *"Légionnaires à moi!"* The recruits were led through a city that, to the surprise of some, appeared far more European than African.

The stay at Fort Sainte-Thérèse, the Legion's uncomfortable depot in Oran, was usually mercifully brief. However, Ehrhart might have made his Legion career in Oran when the commander, discovering his proficiency in French, offered to make him a secretary and see that he was promoted: "I thanked him and refused," he wrote. "I wanted to travel, really know the Legion, see combat and if possible become an NCO. . . . I wanted to be a real legionnaire. I was enthusiastic. He let me follow my destiny."[21]

It was at Oran also that recruits were often asked to select their regiment. Flutsch chose the *2e étranger* at Saïda because he had been profoundly impressed by a legionnaire from that regiment. "I don't know why," wrote Ehrhart, "but I had a preference for the 1st Regiment at Bel Abbès,"[22] perhaps because he had heard that most of the combat drafts were taken out of the *1er étranger*. But the decision was often an arbitrary one, taken by men of the same nationality or by a group who made the voyage from France together, and was often a mere formality as the sergeant's obligation to fill vacancies in both might cause him to ignore preferences.[23] The recruits were soon herded aboard the narrow-gauge trains of the West Algerian Company, which chugged south at a pace "which could almost be beaten for speed by a bicycle ridden by a cripple,"[24] through a fairly prosperous countryside of isolated farms and small villages nestled among fruit orchards, vineyards and fields of wheat. At the frequent stops in the small red stations, the trains were assaulted by Algerians wearing wide-brimmed straw hats not unlike Mexican sombreros and offering green figs, oranges, dates, melons and tobacco for sale. The corporal in charge of the Italian Aristide Merolli's contingent, absolutely refused to allow his men off the train at these stops for fear they would desert: "You'll do it in your trousers!" he shouted.[25]

The tattered, disheveled and sometimes by now half-dressed recruits eventually arrived at their destinations. Sidi-bel-Abbès, home to the 1st Regiment of the Legion since 1875 when the *régiment étranger* had left Mascara, had added layers of sophistication since its establishment in the 1840s: a public garden, a theater and a tree-lined street whose many bars catered to legionnaires. In the Jewish quarter, merchants did a brisk business changing the banknotes of most of the countries of Europe sent to legionnaires by their families, or dealing in secondhand clothing. Across the parade ground and behind the mosque lay the *"village nègre,"* in whose narrow alleys illuminated by torches black, Arab and even European prostitutes well past their prime called to passing legionnaires from low, darkened doorways. The air was heavy with the smell of Arab cigarettes and of meat grilling on the charcoal braziers set out in the streets.

"In the midst of these miserable women moved the scum of the population of Sidi-bel-Abbès," wrote Rosen. "There were negroes in ragged linen coats who in daytime carried heavy burdens on their backs and spent their evenings regularly in the village nègre. Spanish laborers chattered and gesticulated with the Spanish girls. It was the meeting-place of the poor and the wretched, a corso of humanity at its worse."[26] Ehrhart recorded that, for a legionnaire without money (which was most of them), there was nothing to do but attend the twice-weekly concert in the public gardens given by the Legion band: "Every Saturday evening, arm in arm and singing, we followed the band at a quick march."[27]

Saïda was similarly devoid of mystery, hardly more than an overgrown village in the highlands of the Tell, arranged around a main square that was usually filled with an Arab market, over which presided the town hall, constructed in the incongruous style of a medieval French fortress.

At either destination, however, the reception was identical. Assembled at the railway depot, they walked through the town behind the immaculately turned out regimental band to the barracks, where they were greeted by shouts of *"Les bleus! Les bleus!"* ("The recruits! The recruits!") from legionnaires who spilled into the courtyard. "Anyone from Frankfurt . . . from Strasbourg . . . from Leipzig?" Sometimes old friends met, especially the *"cheval de retour"* or "returned horse"—ex-legionnaires who had sampled the delights of civilian life and found them wanting. But usually one was content to find someone from home who could give them news.[28] During the decade of the 1870s, the colonel of the regiment, Marquis Amédée de Mallaret, might also inspect the new arrivals. Poorly rated as a disciplinarian, Mallaret nevertheless possessed an elephantine memory. Gung'l saw him squint at a recruit who bore a decorous Polish name, "and tell him in a tone which invited no reply: 'You served in the regiment in 1866, as a Belgian, under such and such a name.' Having made this observation, the matter was forgotten. In the Legion, one created no difficulties about papers."[29]

The new recruits were issued their kit and sent for another medical examination, which, in Martyn's case, ". . . consisted merely of the doctor asking me if I was all right and cautioning me to be careful in my dealings with the opposite sex."[30] Then they were distributed among the barracks rooms, where the old soldiers could initiate them in the basic skills of their trade. The German Jean Pfirmann was handed over to his "double" by the section corporal: "Here is the recruit," the corporal said. "See to it that he becomes a good legionnaire."[31]

There was one more formality to accomplish—as legionnaires were not permitted civilian clothes, these must be got rid of. "Would you like me to sell your clothes for you?" Martyn was asked. "I shall get a better price than you would, perhaps."[32] Rosen accepted the offer of his sergeant to act as a go-between, and was just as happy that he did not have to deal with a raucous "riff-raff" of Arabs, Spaniards and Jews who stripped the legionnaires of their civilian clothes for a fraction of their value.[33] Aristide Merolli, who decided to conduct his own negotiations, was taken into a courtyard to confront ". . . a howling mob of Arabs in dustcoats and Jews dressed like Europeans or with a turban *à la polonaise,* who ran at us, deafened us and annoyed us with noise and gesticulations, tore our clothes from us, felt them, smelled them, hurled them back, disdainfully, and threw out an offer which we found insulting. Nevertheless, for a modest sum, a few francs, all our belongings were snapped up by the rapacious men and the crowd recovered its calm. The satisfied faces of these buyers confirmed that we had made a bad deal."[34] Ehrhart's new comrades threw his clothes over the barrack wall to a legionnaire who soon returned laden with cigarettes and bottles of wine.[35]

It was at this moment, the fatigues and upheaval of the journey to Algeria behind them, that many could begin to take stock of the service for which they had volunteered five years of their lives. Junger, to take but one example, immediately realized that he had been cast into a "mixed and questionable" society: a small Italian who constantly chewed garlic and with whom he could communicate only in sign language; an Austrian with a low-class Viennese accent forced to flee his country after trying to murder a rival for his girlfriend's affections; a massive German, ex-circus actor, whose party piece was to chew and swallow his wine glass ("But once you had seen this two or three times," recorded Junger, "it got boring."); two Frenchmen, one of whom was the section corporal; a rather shifty Spaniard whose family lived in Sidi-bel-Abbès; two Germans who were inseparable; two Dutchmen, one of whom had lived in Borneo and the other of whom frequently wrote letters "in the laborious manner of children" to his fiancée, who apparently already had waited ten years for his return; and, lastly, a rather elegant but aloof Pole who, it was rumored, had fled into the Legion after being caught with his hands in the company till.[36]

Legionnaires obviously comprised a fairly heterogeneous collection of humanity. But who were these men? The question is not an easy one to answer, as legionnaires not only enlisted under false names—the *"anonymat"*—but also conjured up false pasts to match. When Ehrhart's recruiting sergeant asked him if he preferred to enlist under his real name, or borrow a name and nationality, he asked the advice of an old legionnaire, who told him to retain his real identity if he had nothing to hide: "In the Legion, no one concerns himself with what you may have on your conscience," he was told.[37] However, others like Flutsch, who did have something to hide, or who simply wanted a fresh start in life, preferred more imaginative options. This practice was both respected and even encouraged by the Legion as part of its romanticism and tradition of asylum. Indeed, it may be more important to know who they were not, or who they pretended to be. For, as has been noted, the *anonymat* has caused people to build great legends around the Legion.[38] What has been less apparent, perhaps, is that it caused legionnaires to build great legends around themselves: "With complete bad faith, I constructed for myself a past as I would have dreamed it to be," Antoine Sylvère confessed, "that of the son of a rich farmer, happy owner of at least twelve cows, destined for a life of abundance and of study. As I had to justify my flight, I did not hesitate to kill off my father and remarry my mother to an absolutely insupportable man. The only truth which ended the story was the affirmation that I was happy in the Legion and had not the slightest desire to leave."[39] One of Rosen's companions, a German named Muller, gave his name as von Rader and "declared that his father was the Chancellor of the German Supreme Court and that he himself was by profession a juggler and lance-corporal of marine reserves. And the colour-sergeant put it all down in the big book without the ghost of a smile."[40]

But outside the Legion, the *anonymat* gave birth to at least two legends, both of which proved useful recruitment tools. The first, which was current almost from the first days of the corps' creation, portrayed the Legion as a band of outlaws, an asylum for men on the run from the law. This was certainly true, as the Legion itself admitted. During morning muster, pictures of fugitives might on occasion be circulated by the sergeant as part of a police inquiry. But Luc Dangy insisted that no one would have identified the culprit even had he been standing in the front rank.[41] Flutsch, who fled into the Legion to avoid prosecution for embezzlement, and Junger discovered that men who had had minor scrapes with the law were a fairly common commodity in the Legion.

To be sure, any army might offer a convenient asylum to men in legal difficulty, not the least the British army, according to Frederic Martyn: "Personally, if I wished to hide from the police of this or any other country, when they wanted badly to find me, I should be very careful indeed to keep away from the Legion," he maintained. "I rather fancy that it would be safer to try to get into the Metropolitan Police."[42] But opinion was unanimous that professional criminals would not find a home in the Legion. Even the Swiss Leon Randin, who condemned the Legion as human exploitation on a grand scale, admitted that hardened criminals would find the life uncongenial,[43] a view supported by the Legion commanding general in the 1930s, Paul Rollet.[44] Nor might the Legion offer them an inviolate sanctuary—on his way back to France to face trial after he confessed to his own crimes, Flutsch was accompanied by a legionnaire of one week being extradited to Germany to stand trial for murder.[45]

Yet the "outlaw" myth was important, for it drew to the Legion men for whom the attractions of serving in such company were irresistible, men perfectly qualified to serve in more "respectable" military organizations. However, as will be seen, the *anonymat* also offered the disadvantage from the Legion's viewpoint of permitting bad soldiers, even deserters from the Legion, to re-enlist without having to produce the service record that might have caused them to be rejected.

The second great myth depicted the Legion as a band of romantic outcasts, a refuge for Europe's Beau Gestes, men of good family and education who after being jilted or enduring some other downturn in their affairs sought to bury their misfortunes, and themselves, in the Legion. This image of the Legion was well established at least by the 1850s.[46] However, by the turn of the century some authors claimed that the Legion had assumed a definite middle-class character. The most extreme statement of this view came from the French writer Georges d'Esparbès, who, after listing the rather modest professions of legionnaires enlisting in 1885 and 1898, dismissed them as fabrications,

> . . . *attributable to imagination, to untruth. Many of these vultures transformed themselves into sparrows to get into the barracks unnoticed: the engineer enlisted as a mechanic, the financier as bookkeeper, the architect as a worker, the solicitor as office worker, the factory owner as an operative, the count passes for a horse trainer, the intellectual for a gardener, the polytechnicien for a blacksmith, the philosopher for a farmer or the salesman for a valet de chambre. The column reserved for those "without profession" numbers 112, and obviously overflows with ex-officers, doctors, teachers, priests, lawyers: it is the statistics of Misfortune which hide there.*[47]

This view was supported by others who wrote on the Legion before World War I, including the journalist Hubert-Jacques and Colonel Gaston Moch.[48]

However, Aristide Merolli, a legitimate member of the middle classes who threw up a promising but tedious prefectural career in Italy to join the

Legion in 1910, in which he rose to the rank of captain, identified four basic recruitment categories:

1. *The miserable, without work who prefer to enlist rather than beg and sleep under bridges. 2. Those who seek adventure, generally the very young. 3. Deserters. 4. Adventurers who come to forget their mistakes or who would like to be forgotten by society. Romantic heros spring up sometimes, and it is these cases, purely exceptional, which give rise to the legend that kings having lost their thrones, bishops who misplaced their miters or generals who lost their stars make up the majority of legionnaires.*[49]

Of course, the *anonymat*, reinforced by the reluctance of some legionnaires to discuss their true pasts and their tendency to invent imaginary ones, encouraged this image. Yet the belief that the Legion offered asylum to rich or famous men bestowed both glamor and mystery upon the corps and allowed its members to lay claim to special status in the army. Rosen was told that a member of the Prussian royal family had died fighting for the Legion in the 1880s: "The 'royal prince of Prussia' is part and parcel of the unwritten history of the Legion, told from légionnaire to légionnaire, and I have often wondered how much truth there may be in the legend," he wrote. "Very likely the man of Saïda had been a German aristocrat, the black sheep of some good family, and in the course of time and telling the Legion had made him a royal prince of Prussia."[50] Le Poer, Rosen, Martyn, Junger, even Flutsch, all encountered legionnaires whose bearing, manner or unexplained sources of revenue indicated that they had been men of condition before coming into the Legion. However, discretion often prevented them from asking questions. On the other hand, there were plenty of legionnaires willing enough to tell their life story over a liter of cheap Algerian wine. And d'Esparbès to the contrary, legionnaires appear to have demonstrated a marked preference for social promotion rather than modesty. This was especially true of those who claimed to have been officers or NCOs before coming into the Legion. For instance, Protestant pastor J. Pannier, who served in Tonkin in 1900, was startled when a legionnaire appeared before him in the uniform of a German cavalry lieutenant, threw off his cloak and said: "I want you to see that I am not mad, and for you to know who I am. Here is my card."[51]

So much for the place of the *anonymat* in the creation of the Legion's public image. What has been almost totally ignored by historians is the role of the *anonymat* in the socialization process of the legionnaire. What the Legion offered its recruits was the possibility of a completely fresh start in life, with a slate wiped clean of past sins. "I don't want to know what you have done," Ehrhart's colonel explained to the new arrivals. "That is why a legionnaire, even an ex-convict, can become an NCO, be decorated, even be awarded the *Légion d'honneur*, if he shows himself worthy." And when his conscript military record listing numerous stays in the guardhouse was forwarded to the Legion, his captain told him, "All that is in the past. It doesn't interest me. What counts is what you do here."[52] The adoption of a new name and past not only meant that history could not catch up with one, but it also, eased the psychological transition between the past and the new existence. "The idea that a new life is possible is very attractive to him," Junger wrote, especially to those men who did not know what they wanted: "When all is said and done, no one is so easily led as he who does not know what he wants."[53] Legionnaires became actors, men who lived behind a mask that increasingly became indistinguishable from their true identity. But actors require a stage. That was provided by the corps, and a heroic one it was, too. Their new existence, their new identity, became tightly bound to that of the regiment. In this way, the heroic deeds of the Legion were especially important because they strengthened and validated the personal identities of the legionnaires in a world where fiction and reality were not always easy to distinguish.[54]

All military organizations seek to impress their novitiates with the heroic deeds of past generations as part of their adaptation to a new military life. However, this formed an especially important part of induction into the Legion. Much, perhaps most, of this indoctrination was unofficial. For instance, Flutsch delighted in hearing stories of bar fights that pitted legionnaires defending the honor of their corps against a motley of soldiers from other regiments. "Flory's eyes sparkled as if he could imagine the barroom where 20 drinkers were making fun of the Legion." But for Flutsch these were more than mere accounts of low brawls. These stories and the man who told them, the uneducated Flory, exemplified for him the best of the Legion—rough and uncultured but with a "sort of innate grandeur," indomitable spirit and integrity that prepared legionnaires "to accomplish some sublime and immense sacrifice."[55]

The theme of the supreme sacrifice was also strongly emphasized in the official indoctrination process. Martyn's contingent was taken into the *"salle d'honneur,"* which at Sidi-bel-Abbès was a separate building with a suitably impressive entrance. The walls of the large room were covered with portraits of past Legion heroes and canvases of battle scenes. An NCO recounted the battle of Camerone and concluded by saying, "Soldiers of the Legion, remember the third company of this regiment and Camaron when it comes to your turn to fight." Martyn confessed to being "profoundly impressed." But his comrade Petrovski was enthusiastic: "What a regiment!" he exclaimed on leaving the building, "What men!"[56] Ehrhart, too, was awed by the commemoration of Camerone at Sidi-bel-Abbès, which he witnessed in 1906: "When they blew the retreat," he wrote, "more than one legionnaire had tears in his eyes. I had been a legionnaire for only a short time, [but] I was moved and my thoughts were for all of those unknown men who died so that this flag would always fly proudly."[57] By the time Aristide Merolli arrived at Saïda in 1910, the list of battle honors had lengthened considerably since Martyn's day. He and his fellow recruits listened to them with "profound emotion," as well as to the war stories of the veterans, "a thousand dizzying episodes of audacity and cold courage" that made them eager to complete training and get on with their own *"belles aventures."*[58]

Furthermore, as will be seen, the *anonymat* became an important ingredient in the Legion's battle performance. Men who could claim, or imply, that they had previous military experience might be promoted more rapidly to corporal or section leader. But more, even if they did not seek promotion (and many did not), it could give men a moral ascendancy and influence over their fellow soldiers in a unit that before 1914 was desperately short of cadres. One of the results might be the creation of parallel hierarchies in some instances. As will be seen, these parallel hierarchies encouraged by the *anonymat* could cut both ways, to increase performance in combat or to encourage indiscipline and even desertion, depending upon the disposition of the "natural" leader.

So while there were certainly *Beau Geste* types in the Legion, they made up only a minuscule minority. Leon Randin was probably generous to them when he wrote in 1906: "Whatever is said, the unfortunate victims of life, those defeated in 'the struggle for life,' are more numerous in the Legion, despite the popular legends which claim that most of legionnaires are fallen princes or sons of ruined families. Take one hundred of these unhappy soldiers, and you have a maximum of twenty or thirty scatterbrains or 'déclassés' and seventy or eighty victims that misery or hopelessness have thrown into the chasm of the Legion."[59] For Ehrhart, an orphan dismissed at age twenty-two from the French army with a very undistinguished service record, the Legion was a last resort. "What am I to do?" he asked. "My uncles and my aunts want nothing to do with me. I am on my own. I have no trade, no civilian clothes, no money. I am completely destitute." After sleeping rough and trying to pick up some money carrying bags in the train station, he tried to enlist in the French marines. "A lieutenant questioned me about my military record and told me that he saw the Foreign Legion as my only option. I accepted. I had no choice."[60] Flutsch's comrades, with two exceptions, were very modest fellows indeed. A striking illustration of the social recruitment of the Legion occurred with the arrival at the Sidi-bel-Abbès and Saïda train stations of the weekly draft of filthy, ragged recruits, who were greeted by an immaculately turned out Legion contingent led by the band.

Commanders of the famous Spanish *tercios* under Philip II actually sought to enlist gentleman rankers, called *particulares,* because it was believed that they set an example of courage for the lower-class recruits.[61] Those members of the middle class who enlisted in the Legion, however, were usually more trouble than they were worth. One of the results of the myth of the Legion as an exile for jilted middle-class males was that it encouraged some men of a more dramatic disposition, like Erwin Rosen, to make for the Legion as soon as life's prospects began to look a little bleak.

"These women! these women!" Martyn was told by the medical officer in the process of his induction physical. "What fine recruiting-sergeants they are! How many engagements in the Legion would there be, I wonder, if it wasn't for women?"[62] Of course, the number of enlistments provoked by broken love affairs was probably infinitesimal, although Martyn believed that they made up "a fairly numerous class."[63] However, from the Legion's point of view, the image of their service as a sort of romantic holiday from the pressures of life was not healthy. For while the numbers of middle-class recruits were limited, some of them served to give the Legion a bad name, because the realities of Legion life almost never lived up to their romantic expectations. As a consequence, their books about the Legion often take on the tone of exposés, litanies of the horrors of Legion life, or a sort of *leçon morale* directed at the rudderless or the suicidally romantic. When one examines the nature of Legion life, it is easy enough to understand why this was so. For the middle-class recruit had to come to terms not only with the transition from civilian to military life, and a rather special military life it was, too. But there was also the added shock of being thrust into an overwhelmingly working-class milieu, a rough and ready world stripped bare of the courtesies and deference that they had grown to consider a normal part of everyday existence.

The first problem faced by every recruit was the growing realization, perhaps not entirely apparent at the moment of enlistment, that five years of one's life had been signed away. Gung'l was struck by a wave of melancholy a few days after his enlistment: "The novelty had worn off," he wrote. "The fatigues of the job began to weigh."[64] Those who joined on a lark like Frederic Martyn or in a moment of despair like Rosen realized soon enough that they had made a mistake: "I stared at the immense gravel-covered barrack yard and its scrupulous cleanliness, at the immense buildings and their naked fronts, at the bare windows," Rosen remembered. "Why, this must be a madhouse and I—surely I must be a madman, who had to live for five years (five years said the contract) in a place like this."[65]

Nor was this despair alleviated by the realities of a military existence, which required the recruit to forfeit autonomy, individual pride and class status to a collective *esprit de corps*. Rosen was warned ". . . to have your feelings frozen into an icebox. Don't let anything bother you. No use getting mad about things here. Just say to yourself: 'C'est la légion.' "[66] "To be a good soldier," wrote Charles des Ecorres, who joined the Legion in 1872

one has to leave his personality at the barracks gates, become wax which receives all impressions, put his tongue in his pocket, hide the resentment in his eyes, have legs of steel to run like a deer when summoned by the sergeant, take without wincing all the snubs, and despite all that display everywhere a finesse *and a superior intelligence.*[67]

Middle-class recruits were not the only ones to feel that life in the Legion fell short of their expectations. Foreigners who joined for patriotic reasons, especially those from Alsace-Lorraine, the French provinces amputated by Bismarck in 1871, also felt their moral commitment to France scorned by a regiment that failed to live up to their ideal, a problem that was to recur in both world wars. For the idealistic Francophile Lionel Hart, born on the Ile Maurice of British parents, who joined the Legion in 1883, a service in which rough discipline substituted for moral incentives was one long torment.[68]

Patriotism was not high in the legionnaire's system of values to say the least. When Private Silbermann arrived at the 2e *étranger* at Saïda in 1891, he was told that while legionnaires would die to the last man to defend the regimental standard, ". . . you mustn't speak to them of patriotism; they wouldn't understand."[69] Dangy agreed that patriotism was not fashionable in the Legion: Legionnaires were soldiers, "and only that. They don't give a damn about anything which doesn't concern their bellies or their pockets. When they are no longer happy with the grub or the pay, you'll see them make a scene. Then they will go see if the food is better with Menelik or in the Spanish Legion."[70] Flutsch's corporal explained that the Legion's banner bore the inscription *"Valeur et Discipline,"* rather than *"Honneur et Patrie,"* which decorated regimental flags in the regular army, "so as not to exclude a certain number of men who have led an irregular life" but who, "despite their past mistakes remained worthy of bearing arms."[71] But *"Valeur et Discipline,"* once the device of Napoleon's *Grande Armée* as well as that of the Second Empire, was also calculated not to offend men, many of whom were, after all, foreign mercenaries, by asking them to fight in the name of a "Fatherland" that was not their own.

The nationality of the legionnaire had always been as much subject to fantasy as his name. Between 1831 and 1881, Frenchmen were allowed to enlist in the Legion with special authorization of the war ministry. After 1881, they might enlist in the Legion if they had satisfied their service obligations in the regular army and in the reserves. All this did, however, was to drive those Frenchmen who wished to enlist but who could not produce the necessary papers to claim foreign nationality. Flutsch, to give but one example, enlisted as a Luxemburger although he was a native of Auvergne. Charles des Ecorres, who joined in a spasm of patriotic enthusiasm after watching the famous Longchamps review of 1871, which announced the rebirth of the French army, was of the opinion that ". . . it is raining Parisians in the Legion," many of whom were ex-Communards who had fought against the French army, and the Legion, in 1871.[72] "GM" noted that from 1881 it had become possible for Frenchmen to enlist legally,[73] a situation that had been regularized and facilitated in 1892 when, to increase recruitment, Frenchmen who had completed their military service were allowed to join *"à titre étranger."*[74] In 1897, Frenchmen formed the largest single national contingent in the 1er *étranger* if Germans and Alsace-Lorrainers "or those claiming to be such" were counted separately.[75] And there were probably a substantial number of French to be found among the 1,007 Belgians, 573 Swiss and 106 Luxemburgers.

All of this would seem to suggest that the Legion faced an uphill struggle in its attempt to meld this jumble of nationalities, disenfranchised workmen, love-shocked bourgeois, men who fled into the Legion one step ahead of the law, the romantically naïve whose illusions would puncture with the first week of basic training and those who had simply lost all hope into something resembling a military unit. And with some they no doubt did—Rosen, for instance, was obviously a lost cause from day one and would eventually desert, for the Legion had nothing to offer him but a constant reminder of his own stupidity. And, as has been seen, the middle class and the patriotic might also be in for a letdown, unless they could adjust their expectations. To this one might add some of the rejects from other corps, or even those refused reenlistment in the Legion but who, upon their return to France, had joined under a false name and who obviously could not adjust to military life.

But the situation was not as hopeless as all that: "The Legion was not a dung heap," Flutsch wrote, with a peasant's sense of nuance.

It was a compost heap in which one found all sorts of human specimens— inveterate drunkards, delinquents who could not feel free for a day without doing something to be returned to prison, old soldiers who, kicked out of la Coloniale [the French marines] after numerous punishments for drunkenness and despite their ten or twelve years of service, come to complete the years which would give them the right to a pension of forty sous [8 francs] a day. On top of these were a number of serious men of incontestable human worth. This milieu obviously had nothing in common with an educational institution. For me, it was salvation, and I would be the last one to slander it.[76]

To critics like Leon Randin who charged that the Legion was "a speculation in human misery," preying upon workers thrown out by unfair employers and army deserters, victims of European militarism,[77] the Legion countered that they offered rehabilitation to those like Flutsch for whom enlistment was "a total renaissance: the complete effacement of the past and entry into a new life."[78] Five years in the Legion allowed a man to think through his problems, get back on his feet, and reconquer his self-esteem, often in battle. Legion service may have been purgatory, but it was a purifying one that saved the sinful, reformed the fallen and made honest men of vagabonds and bandits—"a physical hell," the saying went, "but a moral paradise."

Therefore, it is quite clear that the redemptive qualities of Legion service were established in the popular mind well before World War I. It was also well established in the official mind: ". . . The Legion must offer to men of white race the delicacies of adventure," wrote General Trumelet-Faber in 1912.

To those who have the vocation of reiter or landskneckts [mercenary formations in early modern Europe] which they cannot realize in their countries; to those who hide a heavy past and who, struck with remorse, want to follow an esteemed and useful profession; to foreign deserters who we must get away from the frontiers and even to French deserters who under a false name want to prepare their rehabilitation; to the vanquished of life who have failed in unfortunate enterprises and who no longer have the courage to confront the problems of existence. To all of these categories, the Legion can offer, with an honorable asylum, the possibility of satisfying either their tastes or their needs, and finally, while serving the cause of civilization, the promise of a modest future with a pension.[79]

But not all came to the Legion in search of asylum or redemption. On the contrary, there were those perfectly capable of holding down good jobs in civilian life. "I couldn't get used to stupid civilian life again," Dangy was told by a recruit. "I need to be here. So, one day when I was fed up, I signed on for five more."[80] One of the men who accompanied Flutsch on the ride from Oran to Saïda insisted that "I got good wages . . . I knew my trade" in civilian life. But he found it impossible to save money and was constantly in trouble for unpaid bills. "So I said to myself, 'Shit, I'm tired of living like this. You can't take care of yourself, Lécrivain. You've got to enlist in the Legion. That way you'll walk a straight line." [81] Two of Flutsch's friends, the obviously well-educated Baudry and Noblet, confessed that, in civilian life, they "always had the impression of being outside humanity. . . . In the Legion, we have been manual laborers without qualifying as déclassés, as failures."[82]

All of this might mean not only that the level of recruitment was not entirely hopeless from a military point of view. Even men who came into the Legion after having made a mess of things in another regiment, like Ehrhart and Flutsch's acquaintance Vittini, often did so resolved to make a better job of it the second time.[83] But more important, it suggests that most Legion recruits shared at least one common trait—they had failed to discover real satisfaction outside the Legion. Therefore, they might be inclined to seek a niche within a group that offered them increased self-esteem, or one that allowed them to submerge their self-doubts and failures beneath a general devotion to the corps. Ehrhart, for instance, encountered a legionnaire in the 2e étranger, an ex-convict, across whose forehead was tattooed *"Je t'emmerde"* (roughly translated, "F—— Off!") and *"Ni Dieu Ni Maître"* ("Neither God Nor Master"). "What do you expect me to do on civvy street with a mug like mine?" he asked Ehrhart.[84] The task of the Legion was to discover ways to integrate and socialize its recruits, as well as to train them to respectable levels of military efficiency.

*   *   *

"Au jus! Au jus!" The "juice" in this case was coffee black enough to stand a spoon in. The legionnaires rolled over and reached for the tin mugs that hung on hooks at the head of the bed, which the duty soldier filled from a large jug. The first rays of the Algerian sun filtered through the barracks windows—*"Le-e-vez-vous donc!"* ("Get up!") the corporal, sitting up sleepily in his bunk, shouted. Anyone desiring to visit the eight taps that lined the entrance hall on the ground floor rushed to stake his claim on the limited facilities. The thirty minutes of pandemonium preceding the morning muster had begun—soldiers swept under their beds with brooms made from palm leaves, rolled and folded their blankets and mattress, dusted and dressed. The sergeant passed through the room to check the order. At 6:00 A.M., the barracks square was crowded with ranks of legionnaires in their white linen suits, blue sashes, knapsacks, cartridge-belts buffed to brilliance and rifles. The morning formalities completed, the recruits were marched to the drill field.

In Sidi-bel-Abbès, the training ground was known as the "plateau," an open space surrounded by olive trees and red African oaks near the *village nègre*. The legionnaires filed down the street between the barracks and the training field, past donkeys laden with goods, veiled women and half-naked children who imitated the steps of the marching soldiers while shouting things in Arabic, possibly insults, which usually provoked a volley of stones from the squad corporal. The first week was spent largely in introducing soldiers to the basics of the trade, a task complicated by the fact that many recruits spoke no French, so that some basic terms—general orders, guard regulations, rifle parts—were repeated until mastered, or possibly even explained in German. Martyn believed that the language problem was not critical in the training phase because the Legion contained a number of good linguists.[85] Merolli's instructor also periodically stopped to allow those who spoke "German, Italian, Sanskrit and Chinese" to explain what he had said.[86] But off the drill field, the Legion was largely a mosaic of self-contained linguistic enclaves. For instance, Flutsch discovered that one of his first fatigue parties was composed mainly of Germans who spoke no French—"A Belgian and three Alsatians were the only ones with whom I could have a conversation"—and called the Legion a silent world punctuated by periodic binges of drunkenness.[87] As no formal instruction in French was given, legionnaires developed their own basic vocabulary for international communication. Anton Premschwitz was of the opinion that the French of the Legion would be "incomprehensible" to anyone schooled in the language of Molière and Racine.[88] Roger de Beauvoir found that legionnaires "managed to make themselves understood by speaking I don't know what sort of salami which conforms to their own idiom, which would make the Arabs laugh if Arabs ever laughed. Very few legionnaires ever bother to learn French, which makes leadership rather difficult."[89] Le

Poer noted that while French was the language of command, "every battalion, every company, I might almost say every squad, had its own peculiar idiom," adding that "Goddam" [sic] was the only English word included in the Legion lexicon.[90] One Legion expression, *"Allez, schieb' los!,"* which loosely translated means "Get a move on!," had passed into the vocabulary of Algeria to the point that even the Arabs used it.[91]

THIS LACK OF language ability was to be important. For not only did it mean that Legion training was essentially practical, thereby often causing veterans to contrast it to what many believed to be the excessively theoretical training they had received in the metropolitan army, but it also required officers to lead by example. Merolli's lieutenant earned enormous respect by demonstrating every movement of drill, boxing, gymnastics, and so on, punctuated by the phrase *"Faites comme moi"*—"Do as I do." "We wanted to do as well as he, so that our troop would become the image of its leader."[92] So, in this relatively silent world, gesture, example, even imagery and symbolism took on enormous importance.[93] It required Legion officers to be men of physical presence, theatrical inspiration, and prepared to lead from the front.

As in most armies, drill occupied much of the first days: "Formation of a line, a column, going from column to line, from line to column, etc.," wrote Flutsch of these exercises. "Of course, the novices could not follow the movements, but there were always enough old soldiers so that one pulled by the arm and the other pushed from behind, and they were shoved into the place where they should be."[94] The second week emphasized physical training—gymnastics, boxing and running—as well as visits to the rifle range. "In the form of a wide square, we went round the drill-ground, five minutes, ten minutes—un, deux, un, deux—always in sharp time," wrote Rosen. "The corporal, a splendid runner, ran at the head. . . ." Breath came in short fast gasps, eyes burned, hearts pounded until the corporal shouted *"A volonté!,"* the signal for a final sprint.[95] In the pauses between exercises, the soldiers, their uniforms soaked with perspiration, stood around in the hot sun smoking until the corporal finished his cigarette, walked two hundred yards and shouted, *"A moi!,"* initiating another cycle of sprints. The soldiers were marched back to the barracks for the eleven o'clock *"soupe"*—a monotonous stew of macaroni, potatoes or whatever garden vegetables were in season, served with gray French army bread. The old legionnaires occupied the limited seating in the barracks room, while the recruits ate standing up or sitting on their beds. In the summer months, training was usually suspended in the hot hours of the day, when men lay on their bunks in the suffocating barracks in fitful sleep. The afternoons might be filled with instruction in hygiene and basic first aid, or preparation for inspection. However, much of it was occupied by fatigue duties, the hated *corvée*.

As in most armies, the *corvée* ran the gamut from peeling potatoes to general duties around the barracks. However, unlike other regiments (or so Rosen claimed), the Legion often offered its soldiers to the municipality, individual farmers or even other regiments as cheap labor. Rosen condemned this practice, not because the work was difficult, but because he found it demeaning to perform low-order manual tasks while "the loafing Arab rabble prowled around and made jokes at our expense."[96] However, it is more likely that other legionnaires with less pride were more willing to undertake such work, for the simple reason that the regimental fund only retained half the wage, the legionnaire receiving the other half. Flutsch worked all day digging up roots only to earn "four or five sous" (about one franc).[97]

Legionnaires were willing to undertake such unrewarding work for the simple reason that they were so badly paid. Legion pay was low—indeed, scandalously low, about five centimes (one cent or a halfpenny) per day in an era when an American private was paid twenty-five cents a day and a British soldier at least a shilling, which was about the same. Rosen believed that he had been "disgracefully swindled." He claimed to have encountered all vices in the Legion save one—gambling, for the simple reason that legionnaires had nothing to wager.[98] Of course, poverty is in many respects a relative concept. But a daily pay that bought nothing more than a box of matches, and which even the Arabs scorned, was clearly inadequate, as even many officers conceded. In 1905, the Infantry Director wrote that "the pay of the legionnaire, when he is a young soldier, is so low that he hesitates to buy a stamp to send a letter."[99]

"Money is a thing of immense value in the Foreign Legion," Rosen wrote, because there was so little of it.[100] Old legionnaires at Sidi-bel-Abbès and Saïda examined the weekly draft of recruits for those sheep who had not been completely shorn. They might be invited to the canteen for a little friendly advice about how to get on in the Legion—at their expense, of course. The proceeds of the sale of civilian clothes, though modest enough under normal circumstances, could fund an evening's libations when a *sou* (twenty centimes, or about four cents) bought a litre of wine. Rosen claims to have witnessed some old soldiers in Sidi-bel-Abbès steal a recruit's equipment and then sell it back to him for five francs.[101]

Nor were legionnaires above writing home, exaggerating the difficulties of service, in the hope of eliciting a small contribution toward their well-being: ". . . His descriptions of famine and hardship are most moving," Rosen wrote. "They must be very hard-hearted people indeed who do not acknowledge the receipt of such a letter with a small postal order. Then there is joy in the land of Sidi-bel-Abbès. For a day, or a few days, or even a week, the prodigal son with the postal order lives like a king. He has his boots cleaned for him and would not dream of making his own bed as long as his money lasts."[102] This was called having one's *truc*, or "thing," done for him. It was not resented so long as the unofficial servants were chosen from the patron's own squad, but on the contrary was regarded as a method of wealth distribution.[103]

Ehrhart found that legionnaires, himself included, frequently sang in the cafés, in the streets, or even begged to get money for drink, "but he mustn't be caught." His colonel was scandalized when he discovered that veterans were selling their decorations to finance their evenings on the town—he called a quick inspection and retained the pay of any decorated legionnaire who could not produce his medals until they could be bought back.[104] Others might make money at such highly prized skills as tattoo artist.

At five o'clock in the evening, a second *"soupe"* was served, identical to the first, after which the legionnaires were "free" until the "all in" at nine in the evening. Those with money might rush into town where cafés sold wine by the hour rather than by the glass, or drift into the canteen for a few liters to recover from the terrors of the day. Most, however, took one of their two white linen uniforms to the washhouse to beat, pummel and brush it to the standard of cleanliness upon which the Legion insisted. Like most things in the Legion, Rosen especially detested this obligation. However, this was one of the most pleasant parts of the day for most, a sort of social hour during which news and gossip were exchanged in an especially leisurely manner, as uniforms left untended on the line to dry had the disconcerting habit of vanishing into thin air. The American-born Maurice Magnus complained that the Legion's attention, almost obsession, with cleanliness did not extend to corporeal hygiene. Each squad was allowed only one shower a week, which was often sacrificed to training or fatigue duties, which made for strongly smelling barracks rooms.[105]

Then came the *astiquage*—the rubbing and polishing of the cartridge belt with melted wax until it shone to brilliance, a task that took up to two hours each evening. Growing impatient with this tedious process, and failing to identify it as a totem, or act of subordination, of the sort required by all armies, Rosen chose to paint his belt. The corporal "almost fainted" when he saw it.

He tore the belt out of my hand, and in a fit of rage ran round to all the men's rooms, to show the other corporals what horrible things happen in this sinful world. A painted cartridge-belt! The old soldiers of the companies came running up and with many "merdes" and "noms d'un chien" surveyed in petrified astonishment the greenhorn who had been so audacious as to attempt to supplant the sacred "astiquage" of the Legion by painting![106]

As the nine o'clock "all in" approached, groups of legionnaires, many of them the worse for wear, could be seen making their way back to the barracks. At Sidi-bel-Abbès, the sergeant of the guard usually closed the large gates, leaving only a small sallyport open. "One could watch the drunken legionnaires stop several meters from the small door, then take aim to try to get through without bumping into something," Ehrhart wrote. Those who missed "or who raised a ruckus" were thrown into the guard room. "I saw a legionnaire brought back in the costume of Adam!"[107]

Even for those who got into their rooms unhindered, this might be a tense moment, as Flutsch discovered when one of his fellow recruits who had drunk too much, a Corsican named Vittini, made the desperate mistake of talking back to a corporal: "The reply was immediate and decisive," Flutsch remembered.

Two seconds later, Vittini, dazed by a head butt right in the face, sat on the floor leaning against the table. The Corporal, taking him by the shoulders and drawing him up, threw him down on his stomach. Holding him down with his knee, he grabbed a fist full of hair, and hammered his face on the flagstones, ignoring the cries of his victim. . . . I saw Vittini, his face completely masked in blood which flowed from his nose, his mouth, his forehead. . . . "Warning to you new boys who don't yet know how to respect a corporal in the Legion," [said the corporal.] "This is the first lesson."

The unfortunate Corsican was then dragged off to the cells, "leaving behind him a trail which was still visible in the corridor eight days later, when he was released."[108]

So far the Legion's training regimen appeared to be fairly mild, almost easy. Martyn believed that "He would be a lazy man indeed who could find anything to complain of in that first week's training," which was "a bed of ease" when compared to that of the British cavalry. The "running drill" which occupied the second week "was a trifle harder. . . . [but as] the pace was no faster than our 'double', I cannot see that it could possibly do any healthy man the slightest injury."[109] But by the third week, life for new recruits became more interesting.

The Legion's pride, as has been seen, lay with its marching ability. Recruits began by undertaking short marches with diminished loads. Junger found this stage of training fairly pleasant, although he could not fail to note the incongruous spectacle of marching through an African landscape with a French regiment singing German marching songs.[110] Ehrhart, too, found this aspect of training very enjoyable: "I liked trotting through the countryside in the mornings," he remembered. "The band—drums, bugles, fifes—often played, or sung marches in German and in French. Life was good, and I did not regret having come to the Legion."[111] However, both distance and weight were gradually increased, until twenty-mile marches in full kit became fairly standard, a task made more onerous by the heavy hobnail boots issued to every legionnaire: "When we had got to this stage I cursed the day I enlisted," Martyn remembered, "and I fancy most of the others were doing the same."[112] The German Raimund Anton Premschwitz could not believe the amount of equipment he was expected to pack into his knapsack. Even after the veterans helped him organize his kit (". . . they don't work for nothing and I had to pay a liter of wine"), it appeared to him as an "unspeakable monster."[113] Martyn reckoned that he had between seventy and eighty pounds on his back.[114]

However, these were merely the hors d'oeuvres for longer marches, alerts or maneuvers. Bugles blasted *"Aux armes!"* in the dead of night. The barracks immediately shook into an uproar as corporals walked through their rooms shouting: *"Faites le sac! En tenue de campagne d'Afrique!"* ("Make up packs! Campaign uniform!") Men hurriedly assembled their effects by lantern light while the wildest rumors circulated about rebellions in Morocco or among tribes in the south. However, the distribution of blank cartridges gave away the game—just another training exercise. With disappointed shouts of *"Merde!"* the legionnaires slipped down to the barracks square. The companies formed up and exited the barracks square in columns four abreast. The band struck up "Le Boudin," which resounded off the houses of the still-dark streets. Sleepy and disheveled heads appeared from behind half-opened shutters and small groups of dark figures gathered on street corners to watch the Legion file out of town.

At this stage, the marchers were fairly lighthearted. The band turned back once open country was reached, leaving the legionnaires to entertain themselves: *"Le sac, ma foi, toujours au dos!"* ("My pack, by faith, always on my back!") one legionnaire chanted, provoking general mirth. Some joked; the young legionnaires questioned the veterans about the destination. The reply was usually that the length of the march would be determined by the rank of the commanding officer: "Tell you what, Dutchy," Rosen was told by an American legionnaire. "If the old man himself [the general] has got up in the middle of the night you may send your little legs a message to get ready for a lot of work."[115] Soon enough, the chatter died away to be replaced by the heavy tread of boots. The pack straps began to cut into the shoulders, while the arm whose hand clutched the rifle strap felt as if it were being attacked by a swarm of fire ants. At the first halt, the novices threw off their packs, while others simply flopped down on their backs without removing their loads.

After a rest that seemed to have lasted seconds rather than minutes, the march resumed. The effort to regain one's feet was intense. The cold dawn soon gave way to a progressively hotter morning. Recruits wondered if anyone could be suffering as intensely as they. The legs seemed as if they had no blood left in them, and the slightest bump or jolt from a comrade was like being broadsided by a sledgehammer. Anyone who attempted to fall out was shouted back into line. If that failed to work, then the soldier might be tied by the shoulders to a pole jutting from the baggage cart, which forced him to march or be dragged along over uneven ground. The air boiled in the lungs, faces wore a mask of white dust and the legionnaires leaned forward into any rise in the ground, their breaths coming in short bursts until the summit was passed and the road slipped downward into a shallow valley. Finally, when it seemed as if further progress was beyond human endurance, someone mercifully shouted: *"Halt! Campez!"* Arms were stacked, sacks thrown to the ground and the tent supports and covers were extracted. The corporal of each section stepped out of line and held a tent pole high above his head to mark the tent line for the company. The legionnaires buttoned their tent sections together, and in seconds a suburb of canvas sprawled over what before had been a plain of white sand.

There was little time to relax: the soil was stripped into narrow trenches for cooking, potatoes peeled, coffee ground, wood gathered, baggage unloaded and sentries set out. In desert areas, each member of a section was required to contribute a half-liter of the two liters of water that he had been given in the morning for the *soupe* and coffee. Those who had consumed their water ration on the march might be given a handful of rice or macaroni in its precooked state.[116] By seven o'clock in the evening the camp was a litter of slumbering soldiers, their rifles tied to their wrists or bound together and fixed to the wrist of the corporal sleeping in the tent as a precaution against marauding Arabs. At two o'clock the following morning, the camp sprang to life amidst the confusion of whistles and shouts. "If one could not find his pack, another his strap, a third his blanket, etc.," wrote Premschwitz, "the best thing was that everyone had a rifle which did not belong to him—in the darkness, one simply took what was to hand."[117] Flutsch jumped into formation stuffing extraneous pieces of equipment into his pockets: "I must look stupid," he said to a veteran. "Don't worry. You are not by yourself," came the reply. "No one will make fun of you. This is not *la biffe* [the French infantry]. In the beginning, only those who have served in Africa can make out. And not even all of them! . . . The tirailleurs and the Bat d'Af are never in such a hurry."[118]

And so it went on, day after grueling day, until the column reached Géryville or some other distant garrison, usually after a week of marching. When one legionnaire fell out on the march and dragged into camp an hour late, Lionel Hart's sergeant punished him with the crapaudine, a particularly harsh punishment which will be described later.[119] Premschwitz complained that so many legionnaires fell out on one winter maneuver, exhausted not only by the march itself but also by their inability to sleep at night while shivering from cold beneath the one inadequate blanket issued to them, that the route was lined with soldiers crowding around tufts of alfa, which they set alight for warmth. It was four days before all of them wandered into camp.[120]

Nor did it do any good to appeal to the doctor—on the contrary, it could be positively dangerous. When Rosen complained of stomach cramps on the march, the surgeon dismissed him with a preemptory "on the march there are no sick men," and he narrowly escaped punishment for shirking.[121] Ehrhart, who had a bottle broken over his head in a bar brawl between French and German legionnaires, and no doubt suffering from a mammoth hangover, went to the doctor on the following morning to escape a scheduled march. "His diagnosis was to write in his notebook, 'Seven days prison.' . . . During my seven days' punishment, the lump [on my head] disappeared." He also admitted that legionnaires were masters at simulating conjunctivitis or in working up a sore using matches and a knife.[122]

To outsiders, indeed to legionnaires, these training exercises and the punishments for those who could not keep up might have appeared unnecessarily harsh. However, even Rosen conceded that, given the dreadful conditions in which the Legion was frequently forced to campaign, where "separation from the troops means death," strict march discipline was vital.[123] A veteran explained to Flutsch that on campaign a man who dropped out was simply disarmed and left to try his luck with the enemy.[124]

These marches developed more than stamina, however. They became a test of individual pride: "A man who chokes because he's hurting is like one who doesn't want to fight—you despise him," Flutsch was told.

You walk with your shoes full of blood and when you arrive, you will do the fatigues like everyone else and you go to bed at the same time as the others. No one will compliment you for it. You will be a real legionnaire, like the others. When they put you with another on campaign, he needs to know that he is with a man without having to look at your face and he needs to know that you will do your job.[125]

Individual pride was reinforced by national pride, the reluctance to have one's nation thought of as a weak link: When one of Flutsch's friends came down with dysentery on the march, he simply carried on with "the faucet running" because *"Je suis un Gaulois!"*[126] Nor was this sense of national pride confined to the French.

Legion training was not uniformly praised. In 1881, Captain Jean-Louis Armengaud complained that he received a reinforcement of two hundred Legion recruits "who are hardly trained, and whose instruction will have to be completed at Ras-el-Ma" before they could be thrown into battle.[127] Of course, this may have been exceptional due to the Bou-Amama revolt of that year. However, Flutsch was dispatched to Géryville after only twelve days' training at Saïda.[128] Premschwitz followed a seven-week instruction course at the turn of the century, while in 1910 Merolli remained thirteen weeks at the depot at Saïda, although his sergeant promised early release for those obviously proficient in their new trade.[129]

CRITICISMS OF LEGION training were essentially two. The first concerned the quality of Legion NCOs. The importance of the "firm but fair" training sergeant who serves as a role model for recruits, helping them to make the transition from civilian to soldier, has frequently been noted.[130] Some, at least, felt that Legion NCOs relied more upon brutality than leadership. Jean Pfirmann discovered upon enlisting in 1887 that "We had some instructors whose morality was not exactly irreproachable. They came to the Foreign Legion to escape a sentence in the Bataillons d'Afrique. After training, some of them had been promoted. But they sometimes lacked mercy, and we found them very tough." However, the colonel removed all NCOs with a disciplinary record from the training cadre. "The purge was complete, and for us, life got better."[131] Premschwitz found the training NCOs swelled with self-importance and generally insulting, a defect that was not remedied by Legion officers who were conspicuous by their absence.[132] Merolli was a trifle more indulgent: "Among the NCOs, only one was really impossible and of a brutal intransigence," he wrote.[133]

The shortage of good NCOs was a major weakness of the Legion, as even Legion colonel de Villebois-Mareuil admitted in 1896.[134] The problems of recruiting good NCOs were many. In the first place, many of the best men, those for instance who had been officers in a foreign army, had come to the Legion on sabbatical from the responsibilities and competitiveness of life and did not seek command positions. Also, peer pressure might cause potential NCOs to prefer to remain with their friends, especially when they realized that the task of a corporal who lived with his section and yet was responsible for maintaining discipline, often with his fists, was generally regarded as the most difficult—and the most lonely—job in the Legion. Lionel Hart found that the corporal was ". . . the dog of the company. He is on call day and night. He serves at the whim of the sergeant, who abuses him, and he must be on good terms with the soldiers who try to escape fatigues."[135] Pfirmann discovered that it required much tact to be a corporal when there were often men of superior education in his squad. "It is also right to insist that these men of superior background rarely ridicule a corporal," he wrote. "Their good education prevents them." Authority might also be compromised by national divisions—for instance, the German Pfirmann had difficulty making two French veterans of the Franco-Prussian War who "affirmed that it was very humiliating for a French soldier to be commanded by a German" carry out his orders.[136] Becoming an NCO required that one go through special classes and pass examinations. This made promotion difficult for foreign soldiers whose command of French was inadequate—Pfirmann was surprised when he graduated number thirty-three of one hundred "student-corporals" "despite my inferiority in French."[137] As the best soldiers were often to be found among the foreigners, the Legion perhaps failed to take full advantage of a valuable source of leadership.[138]

And units were often reluctant to send their best troops to the "student corporal section" because they would lose them.[139] While promotion appears to have been fairly rapid during the 1880s, when the Indochina campaign required great numbers of soldiers, it slowed down considerably toward the end of the century, so that only in one's second period of enlistment might a corporal's stripes become a possibility.[140] Many did not care to wait that long. For those who were ambitious, the pay and promotion prospects were infinitely superior in *la coloniale*, causing a hemorrhage of many of the best soldiers and sergeants into that service.[141] Nor was the recruitment of NCOs helped by the ease and frequency with which they might be broken back to the ranks, as typified by the reminder offered by officers that stripes were not awarded, but were merely "on loan."

The result was an NCO corps that was at best uneven, in which "chance has played such a role in their investiture that they do not all possess, it must be admitted, the presence which commands authority."[142] But how important was this to training? While in the years preceding World War I General Hubert Lyautey complained that the absence of NCOs had diluted training in the Legion,[143] the truth is that this was probably less important than in other corps, because of the large number of ex-soldiers who were to be found among the new recruits. The *anonymat* that encouraged parallel hierarchies also made up in part for the lack of a formal hierarchy by providing role models and unofficial leadership (some of which, it must be admitted, might not always have been constructive). Lastly, the emulation and competition among the various nationalities, not to mention the fact that for many the Legion represented the last throw of the dice with which they had to succeed or fail utterly, made the absence of a formal hierarchy less important.

A second training deficiency related to the inadequacy and shortage of NCOs, according to Martyn, lay with the fact that the depot companies were too large and unwieldy, so that "recruits are not looked after and supervised in the way that is necessary to the proper education of a recruit."[144] Sidi-bel-Abbès and Saïda not only offered basic training, they were also centers that filtered men coming and going from postings in the Far East, Madagascar, Morocco or one of the numerous garrisons in the Sud Oranais (southwestern Algeria). In this constantly fluctuating mass of men, the authority of the command was even less than in a detached company. And it was here that unsuspecting recruits might fall under the influence of the undesirable elements shed by the field companies. They befriended a disoriented youth, drinking at his expense until his money ran out, "then incite him to sell his equipment for a few *sous* to a Spaniard or a Jew, to get some money to go AWOL where he perverts him completely," Captain Abel Clément-Grandcourt complained in 1910. "Admit it, the number of young soldiers who are spoiled in the beginning and from then on are only jail bait is large, very large."[145]

The problem seems to have become more acute after the turn of the century, when the government adopted a deliberate policy of sending many soldiers of the *Bats d'Af* into the Legion. Flutsch was cautioned on the dangers of basic training: "In Saïda, there are men who come in from the discipline companies or the penitentiary," he was warned.

*They've got some filthy habits. . . . They'll be nice chaps. They'll help you
out. They will do jobs for you and then try to take you off somewhere, and
even if you hold your own, you can be badly hurt. So at Saïda, don't make
friends. Say that you are big enough to look after yourself, and if they insist
tell them to bugger off and be ready to smash them. It's not the same in the
companies. We know each other and everyone is more or less alike. If trash
like that gets in by chance, he is soon sent back where he came from. But
Saïda is the headquarters and there a youngster has to be careful.*[146]

In 1906, War Minister Eugène Etienne ordered that new recruits must be
kept for at least six months in a training company "as far as possible from
the depot," a method already applied in the *Bataillons d'Afrique*. But he
conceded that "the moral amelioration of legionnaires . . . will take a long
time."[147]

However, these defects, while serious, were not critical. Dangy discovered that "The commanders count on the initiative of their men and upon
the experience of the veterans to perfect the acquired knowledge."[148] But
the real strength of Legion training lay with the fact that it concentrated on
the essentials. Rosen waxed almost rhapsodic about Legion training: " 'Being practical' was the leading principle of the whole training." He found the
instructors very helpful. "We were obliged to work hard, but never had the
feeling of being bothered with anything unnecessary. It was practical work,
the reason for which every one understood."[149] The Legion did not measure up to Germanic standards of drill, according to Premschwitz: "We
marched in the streets with much noise, and paraded effortlessly to the
great satisfaction of our commanders," he wrote of a July 14, 1898, parade
at Sidi-bel-Abbès.

*But even so, we did not keep in step and the alignment was bad. The
parade is the least worry of the French gentlemen. It is always piteously
carried out. This was hardly surprising, because one could not find the time
to bother with something which is considered a nonsense. Here the essential thing is to know bayonet drill, boxing and gymnastics. This is how one
forms an accomplished soldier.*[150]

It must be conceded that one school of thought would argue that this
neglect by the Legion of drill and other ritualistic aspects of soldiering
calculated to build morale and inculcate instinctive obedience must lower
efficiency: "Not only does [drill] make men look like soldiers," writes
English historian Richard Holmes, "but, far more important, it makes
them feel like soldiers."[151] But this simply was not the style of a corps that
was, after all, a colonial and not a continental force. While European
regiments were usually tightly knit organizations ruled with a rod of iron
by a strict and omnipresent hierarchy, the Legion appears to have been
largely a self-regulating world in which discipline "was a collective act

where the judgments of the community were the most redoubtable," according to Flutsch.[152] In the absence of a more formalized organization, recruits were brought into contact with those who stood at the epicenter of Legion culture—the old sweats who had learned to "think Legion." This translated into a *"je m'en foutisme"* ("I don't give a damn!"), a refusal to be rattled, a *"calme colonial"* in the face of the inevitable adversities, large and small, of Legion life, a serenity of mind achieved only by those who had acquired the habit of experiencing life exclusively in Legion terms.[153]

The result was the ironic and perhaps contradictory one that, while Legion punishments were more frequent than in other regiments, Legion discipline was less formal, even relaxed. Luc Dangy, who enlisted in the Legion at eighteen but who was obliged upon reaching his twentieth birthday to transfer to a metropolitan regiment to do his military service, found the transition a difficult one: "The principal cause of my failures came from the fact that I had been a legionnaire," he wrote. "I was used to a certain liberty in an organization which was special, which banished the small vexations, the little troubles, the little stupidities of military life, and I could not accept that in France these were exploited on an industrial scale." While in the Legion the old soldiers showed the newcomers the ropes, in France those in their second and third years of service terrorized the *"bleus."* While the Legion hierarchy was inspired by a large dose of common sense, officers in France lacked tact, imposed a depressing discipline, were like "prefects in a school . . . despotic functionaries. . . . You have to believe that they sought out every possible way to bother the soldier." They even forbade putting hands in pockets: "Well, in the Legion one could put his hands in his pockets, even if it were 100 degrees in the shade." Compared to the Legion, the metropolitan army was a perversion of military life: "I, who had been a good legionnaire [four days prison in two years], became a bad soldier."[154]

A system that emphasized physical toughness, emulation and peer pressure rather than formalized discipline and drill probably appealed more to the mature, experienced soldier, as well as to the man who might have found it difficult to fit into a more formal military environment. In this way, the contradictions of the "good fighter bad soldier" were minimized. "The Legion understands its soldiering business," Rosen wrote. "One must admit that."[155]

Legion training stressed the development of individual initiative, according to Rosen, and nowhere was this more evident than in field training.[156] Flutsch agreed and described an experience in which a group of recruits was placed in charge of a private who claimed to have served as an adjutant (sergeant-major) in the marines, and told to attack a hill. The ex-adjutant deployed his troops, ordered two imaginary volleys and then stormed the slopes *à la bayonette.* The training sergeant gathered everyone about and complimented them on their courage. The bayonet attack was especially impressive, he said, a worthy subject for a painting, for which he even suggested a title, *"La prise du mamelon vert"* ("The Storming of the Green Knoll"), an allusion to an episode during the Crimean War. Unfortunately, "in a real action, you would all be dead. Now, nothing is as inoffensive as a dead man. Personally, I would far rather fight five thousand dead men than ten determined live ones." He then made them repeat the maneuver using the cover of the terrain and more direct individual fire. Once this had been accomplished successfully, he cautioned his men against the attitude, common in other corps, that branded those who sought cover as cowards:

That which in la biffe *would be judged dishonorable is highly honorable here because it is practical . . . don't hesitate to lower your head, throw yourself on your belly when you are under precise fire. In this way, you will remain alive to shoot in your turn, in this way, you will form the Legion, the most dangerous troops in the world for the enemy. . . . Always remember, in the Legion we don't fight like the knights of the Middle Ages. We fight as dirty as possible. The enemy doesn't like that. But, then, he's the enemy and we don't have to be particularly nice to him.*[157]

In the Legion, as in any army, one trained to fight. However, in the Legion, one also fought to train. Life in the Legion, especially for new men, or men assigned to a new unit within the Legion, was like a perpetual series of challenge rounds. Single combat was folded into Legion culture as a necessary requirement for personal respect. In the fifteen or so years immediately following the Franco-Prussian War, fighting was ritualized in the form of dueling among soldiers. However, this was officially discouraged, and gradually fell from fashion, to be replaced by an atmosphere in which, according to Dangy, "Violence reigns as mistress. . . . In this reunion of individuals of all sorts, pusillanimity is a defect which puts a man at the mercy of his companion," he wrote. "One must dominate, never retreat, face up always, which offers proof that one is as good as anyone, only this will get you respect."[158] Le Poer discovered that "It was necessary to fight a little at the beginning to assure one's rights and obtain an equitable share in the distribution of food and other things. But once one had proved himself, things went smoothly."[159]

ROSEN WAS HORRIFIED by the atmosphere of pervasive violence: when a larger man provoked him by sitting on his newly made bed, he had no choice but to descend into the barrack yard to settle accounts. Although Rosen complained that legionnaires "can't box like Christians" but instead "roll around like pigs," by Legion standards his fight was merely a polite little scuffle, even though he managed to prevail in the unequal contest only by banging his assailant's head on a stone: "Parbleu, that was a good idea with the stone," his opponent said after he had picked himself up off the ground. "Eh, you'll be a good legionnaire very soon. We men of the Legion quarrel often, but at heart we're comrades."[160]

Fighting appears to have been more pervasive in the Legion than in other corps. One reason was that it was tacitly encouraged because it was taken as a sign of masculine aggressiveness: "When we got into a fight, it wasn't like here, it caused a lot of problems," Flutsch was told by an ex-marine. "In the Legion, they don't bother you about that . . ."[161] The international character of the corps also contributed to these intramural contests: "Because the Legion is French, and Germans are the most numerous, the differences of race come back to this Franco-German antagonism," wrote legionnaire Jean Martin.

The majority of Russians or "candle-eaters," the Poles, and in general those from northern and central Europe are with the Germans. The Latins, the Belgians are francophile. The British, when there are any, don't give a damn. One mustn't think that this makes for perpetual conflict, but it gives rise to niggling problems, to preferences of NCOs for their nationals, and on payday, often fights between drunken legionnaires which have no other cause.[162]

Violence also offered a way to control regimental thugs, the *"caïds, who think that with a good blade and the skill to use it they can always give orders."*[163] Flutsch witnessed the fate of a new transfer, a giant of a man named Leborgne, who attempted to terrorize his section: "[Leborgne] charged," he recorded.

The ex-sailor dropped down in a quick movement, to simulate a head butt, rose up and threw two fists forward, powdering the eyes of Leborgne with a double jet of sand which he picked up during his first feint. Leborgne swore and lowered the head, just enough to receive a terrible kick in the face, which put him on his backside. A second kick, more violent, threw him backwards. In the blinking of an eye, Van Lancker was on him and with hard kicks of his hobnailed heels in his face, forced his head into the gravel. . . . The ex-sailor continued to roll over his adversary who no longer reacted with kicks. He began to work him over in detail, on the ankles, the knees, on the tibias, with angry and destructive relentlessness. After breaking the ribs in passing, he stretched out the inert arms to smash the hands, the elbows, the forearms. "Don't kill him completely," Garrigou warned. "No fear", Van Lancker said. "I've done enough so he won't bother us any more."[164]

If violence formed a rite of passage in the Legion, the validation of one's worthiness to qualify as a bona fide legionnaire, it also served as a way to promote collective loyalty and unit cohesion. Sections were willing to go to almost any lengths to promote solidarity: Corporal John Le Poer agreed to turn a blind eye when his comrades wanted to teach an Austrian in their section a lesson. But when the lesson turned to tragedy, he helped them arrange a cover-up by sticking a knife in the cadaver and throwing it over the wall to make it appear as if the unfortunate victim had been killed by natives. "I was sure at least that none of my men would try to shoot me in the back when we were next in combat," he reasoned.[165] Le Poer recounted that quarrels between men of different sections could set off collective feuds that outclassed that of the Hatfields and McCoys in lethality.[166]

Sectional loyalty might be affirmed in other ways, especially on payday or during the *"cuite de la quinzaine"*—literally the fortnightly drunk—when the wine purchased on payday was consumed in a matter of minutes. Then entire sections might join in combat against other sections with picks and shovels, the results of which, as Flutsch discovered, might be at least as damaging as a relatively warm skirmish with marauding Arabs.[167] Le Poer's company got into a pitched battle with another Legion company, an epic fight that he claimed left twenty dead and had to be broken up by two squadrons of *Chasseurs d'Afrique*.[168]

However, the fact that life in the Legion was often like a perpetual Olympic boxing final without referees or even rules must not be taken to mean that it teetered on the brink of complete disintegration. On the contrary, once they stepped beyond the barracks gates, "without questioning, legionnaires grouped together against the others," wrote Jean Martin. "This was because, while we were admired for our toughness and our renown by men of other arms, we felt by their attitudes that we were still for them outlaws, even in Africa where they lived next to us."[169] The Legion's unwritten code required all of its members to come running when the shout of *"à moi, la légion"* issued from any bar or back street, no questions asked. In the tribalized society of Algeria, where Frenchmen, Spaniards, Maltese, Italians, Jews and several varieties of Arab and Berber, not to mention the miscellaneous collection of regiments that called itself the *Armée d'Afrique*, coexisted in an uneasy relationship, fights were not only frequent, they seemed (to legionnaires at least) to be a perfectly normal activity. "The legionnaires, who regard themselves as superior, deeply despise the natives, and treat them with less respect than dogs," wrote Raoul Béric in 1907. "They take pleasure in bumping them in the streets of the town and insulting them in every language of Europe," which led to frequent fights.[170] The contempt that legionnaires showed the inhabitants was also extended to other regiments, especially the penal units, perhaps because they were so often confused with them in the popular mind: "But if a dispute arises between a battalion of *zéphyrs* and another of the Foreign Legion," Le Poer wrote with only slight exaggeration, "there is but one way of restoring order—call out the cavalry and the guns."[171]

Dangy believed that "if violence is not always necessary, it is always useful."[172] For if fighting among legionnaires validated personal courage, fighting between legionnaires and Arabs, Spaniards or soldiers from "the French army" helped to reinforce corps solidarity. Furthermore, violence against the outside, non-Legion world became a sort of defiance of conventional social norms from men who had never found satisfaction in conventional society. In its extreme and least attractive manifestations, it almost became a revenge upon a disdainful world.

The fact that legionnaires were generally believed to be criminals—an impression their leisure-time activities did little to dissipate—caused them to be shunned on the outside. Rosen noted that at Sidi-bel-Abbès even the women drew their skirts close around them when they passed a legionnaire in the streets.[173] Ever the gallant Italian, Merolli asked a Spanish girl to dance at a *bal populaire*, only to find himself immediately surrounded by her brothers. In his opinion, it was this civilian

disdain which prevents legionnaires from finding outside the barracks, the softness of a friendship or the charming and graceful smile of a woman, which causes them to adopt this independent and off-hand manner with civilians, an artificial attitude which would melt like snow with a friendly handshake or kind word.

This forced isolation also helped to explain "the inclination of legionnaires toward drunkenness."[174] Nor, as Martin suggested, was this disdain confined to civilians. Charles des Ecorres was amazed when, during the Bou Amama insurrection of 1881, the colonel of a line regiment forbade his conscripts to have any contact with legionnaires with whom they were sharing a bivouac.[175] Le Poer found that "French regulars and even the native Algerian corps had more scorn than sympathy for us. It is true that we paid them back in kind."[176]

Legionnaires obviously led a very lonely life. In military terms, the fact that the Legion was at once despised and feared was not altogether a bad thing, for it created a sort of negative integration, a solid front against the outside world. It led to the external manifestations of pride such as impeccable dress (another manifestation of group superiority and "narcissism"), marching ability and ferocity in combat, whether in bar fights or against the enemies of France, for which the Legion was famous. It also perhaps helped to counter those characteristics of the Legion that might otherwise have caused divisiveness and undermined an esprit de corps. National divisions, especially in an era of high patriotism, offered perhaps the greatest threat. However, the "us against the world" attitude also helped to force a cohesion among men whom Dangy insisted were by nature "aggressive loners,"[177] Hamlets without their Ophelias, and in a society whose motto, Raoul Béric believed, was "every man for himself."[178]

This, then, was the Legion's initiation. Though some sniffed at the quality of Legion training, the truth is that it was probably as good as it had to be. The legionnaire was not called upon to fight an enemy with the military skill of a European opponent. The primary quality of a legionnaire was endurance, the ability to march miles, under a blistering sun, with little food and water. And that requirement was well catered for in Legion training. The absence of more formal drill and discipline helped to assimilate a heterogeneous and largely unorthodox soldiery who might have rebelled at more formalized training. Regimental pride, a product in great part of the social atmosphere of the Legion, and the general perception of that corps on the outside as hovering on the fringes of the criminal classes, sort of *Bat d'Af* with funny accents, did the rest. It left a residue of pent-up hostility and aggressiveness that made legionnaires like chained dogs ready at any moment to be unleashed. The danger, of course, was that aggressive behavior produced by esprit de corps and high morale might slip over into indiscipline, individual or even collective, that the chained dogs might slip the leash.

Yet these great tensions of Legion life had another advantage, for they allowed the Legion to shift quickly to a wartime mentality, to make with relative ease the psychological leap from peace to war because the behavioral requirements for each were not substantially different. In 1885, the action was to be found in Tonkin.

Chapter 10

INDOCHINA —
THE INVASION

DESPITE AN IMAGE that inextricably binds the Legion with North Africa, it was Indochina that provided both its most popular garrison and ultimately its calvary. After 1883, the Legion burst the narrow confines of its North African existence, which had contained it for over a decade, to join in the Scramble for Africa and the French expeditions in the Far East, an extension of tasks that required tripling Legion strength from a modest four battalions in the summer of 1883 to a dozen by the turn of the century.

The history of the French penetration of Indochina is fairly complex, but the ingredients were typical of French imperialism, including fear of British colonial rivalry, the desire to tap the reputedly rich markets of China's Hunan province via Tonkin, pressure by the French Catholic Church to protect their missionaries and, above all, the presence of a handful of French officers ambitious to advance their country's future there and not content to wait upon events. In the 1840s, the French had begun to cast about for a base in the Far East to offset that of the British at Hong Kong. Their chance came with the outbreak of the Second Opium War in 1857, during which a combined Anglo–French force occupied Canton and in 1860 Peking. As the Catholic Church was one of the pillars of Napoleon III's Second Empire, the French seized the opportunity offered by the concentration of military force in the Far East to chastise the Annamese—the contemporary term for Vietnamese—for their persecution of Catholic missionaries. They bombarded Da Nang in 1858 and seized Saigon in 1859, which the Annamese signed over to them in 1862. In 1867 the French took the rest of Cochinchina, the southernmost province of Annam, and declared it a French colony.

The advance of the British into Burma kindled fears among some Frenchmen that perfidious Albion was about to open a southern route into Hunan. The exploration of the Mekong River by young French naval lieutenant Francis Garnier in 1866–67 proved that to be a dead end. However, in 1873, French trader and arms merchant Jean Dupuis proved the Red River to be navigable from Hunan to the Gulf of Tonkin. Furthermore, he had discovered that in Hunan salt fetched thirty times its Hanoi price. However, problems arose when the Annamese pointed out that the exportation of salt from their country was illegal. Not to be deterred, Dupuis mobilized his small army of Chinese thugs, captured the chief of police in Hanoi, seized a dozen river junks filled with salt and prepared to tow them up the Red River by steamboat. The Annamese attempted to negotiate an end to the crisis. But in June 1873 Dupuis's patience cracked—he seized a portion of Hanoi, ran up the French colors and sent word to Admiral M. J. Dupré, the governor-general in Saigon, that either France back him or he would call on the English.

Of course, Dupré knew that Dupuis was only making empty threats. Besides, he had formal orders from Paris not to intervene in Tonkin. However, Dupré hoped that by ending the increasingly bloody confrontation in Hanoi he could persuade the Annamese government in Hue to recognize officially the aggrandizement of French control of Cochinchina in 1867, while heading off any competition by European rivals. Therefore, he sent none other than Francis Garnier with 180 men to Hanoi to extricate Dupuis from the difficulties of his own making. It proved to be a serious mistake. Once in Hanoi, Garnier and Dupuis discovered that they were two of a kind—Garnier began to issue proclamations declaring the Red River open to commerce and in November stormed the Hanoi citadel. Urged on by Christian missionaries, he proceeded to impose his rule in the Red River Delta. However, Garnier was killed in December leading what amounted to a single-handed bayonet charge against a force sent to recapture Hanoi. Dupré ended the crisis by signing a treaty with Hue in March 1874, which gained recognition for Cochinchina as well as established French concessions in Haiphong and Hanoi.

The 1874 treaty was fraught with complications. Annam was nominally a vassal state of China. The Chinese regarded Indochina, and especially the northern province of Tonkin, as vital to the security of their southern frontier. However, the French interpreted the treaty to mean that Chinese suzerainty was at an end. Continued frustration over the failure to open the Red River, and the insecurity of the small French garrisons at Haiphong and Hanoi, caused Saigon to dispatch fifty-five-year-old naval captain Henri Rivière to Tonkin with 233 French marines and Annamese auxiliaries to reinforce the French concessions there in March 1882. If the French had wanted history to repeat itself, then they could not have contrived a more congenial set of preconditions. Despite formal orders to the contrary, Rivière stormed the Hanoi citadel. A French fleet sailed to his rescue, but in May 1883 Rivière was killed when his force, ignoring the most elementary notions of security, was ambushed outside of Hanoi.

When news of the events in Hanoi reached Paris, the Chamber of Deputies voted five and one half million francs to support operations in Tonkin and earmarked reinforcements of three thousand men for the Far East, promising that "France will avenge her glorious children."[1] A French fleet sailed up the Perfume River and seized two forts that guarded access to Hue. They then forced the Annamese to accept a treaty of full protectorate. In December 1883, a French force, which included one battalion of the Legion, captured strategic Son Tay on the Red River. This caused the Chinese to reinforce Bac Ninh, correctly thought to be the next French target. However, after desultory resistance, the poorly disciplined Chinese abandoned Bac Ninh on March 12, 1884. In May 1884, the Chinese agreed to withdraw from Tonkin.

The war appeared to be over. However, in June, when a French force was dispatched to occupy Lang Son, the last substantial town in Tonkin before the Chinese frontier, they were stopped thirty miles south of their objective by a Chinese garrison near the small town of Bac Le. What happened next depends upon the version one reads. One sympathetic to the Chinese claims that their commander explained that he realized that France and China were now at peace, however, he had received no orders to withdraw. He asked the French to wire to Beijing for instructions on his behalf. The French commander, Lieutenant Colonel Alphonse Dugenne, gave the Chinese one hour to clear off. When they did not, he attacked, but was repulsed with twenty-two dead and sixty wounded.[2] Dugenne, and later official French propaganda, advanced the claim that they were treacherously ambushed at Bac Le. Whatever the case, this time France, under pro-colonialist prime minister Jules Ferry, intended to make a better job of it. The French prepared a full-scale invasion, one that included the Legion.

The problem for the French was how best to bring about a decisive victory over China. They decided to divide their forces, one group striking at Formosa while a second would reinforce Tonkin. It proved to be a costly and nearly disastrous decision. After bombarding Fuzhou on the Chinese mainland, and thereby eliciting a declaration of war upon France by China, the French under fiery Admiral Amédée Anatole Courbet landed a force on the northern coast of Formosa near Chi-lung in October 1884. It was hard to see what the French hoped to achieve by an invasion of Formosa. The island was far from Beijing. And while it is true that Courbet seized the coal fields of northern Formosa, the coal was low grade and its loss of little value to China. Apparently Paris felt that a campaign on the mainland of China was too risky and so settled for a peripheral operation more easily supported by the navy.[3]

The Formosa action of 1884–85 is one of the little-known campaigns

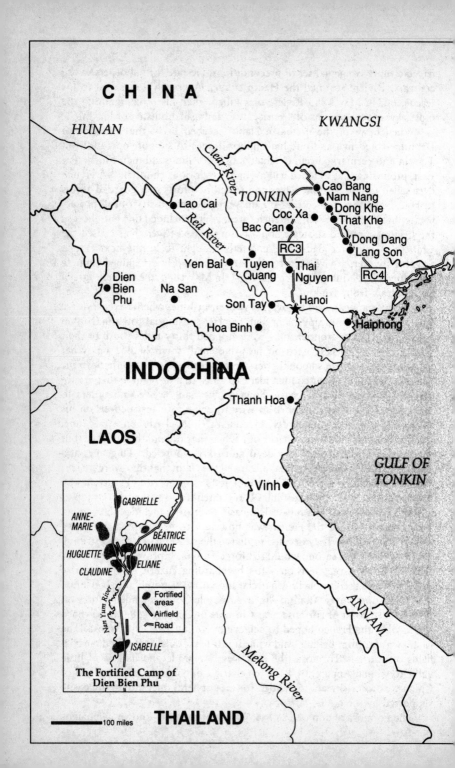

CHINA

HUNAN

KWANGSI

Clear River

Lao Cai

TONKIN

Cao Bang
Nam Nang
Dong Khe
That Khe

Coc Xa

Bac Can

Red River

Dong Dang
Lang Son

RC3

Yen Bai

Tuyen
Quang

Thai
Nguyen

RC4

Dien
Bien
Phu

Na San

Son Tay

Hanoi

Haiphong

Hoa Binh

INDOCHINA

Thanh Hoa

LAOS

GULF OF
TONKIN

Vinh

ANNAM

GABRIELLE

ANNE-
MARIE

BÉATRICE

HUGUETTE

DOMINIQUE

CLAUDINE

ELIANE

Nam Yum River

Fortified
areas
Airfield
Road

ISABELLE

The Fortified Camp of
Dien Bien Phu

Mekong River

100 miles

THAILAND

of the Legion, and with good reason—it got nowhere. The Chinese had anticipated the attack, and stiffened their garrison with twenty thousand soldiers, over three times the number the French would bring against them. The French got ashore with a ridiculously small force of 1,800 men and, after a hard struggle, seized the heights above Chi-lung. However, they were repulsed at Tan-shui twenty miles along the coast. The monsoon broke over this condition of stalemate, turning the French camp into a morass through which cholera raged. The Formosa invasion, meant to bring pressure on the Celestial Empire, soon had the French squirming in discomfort—their army was melting away from disease, and their front line was so porous and poorly manned that the Chinese would creep between the outposts at night to exhume and decapitate the bodies of dead French soldiers.[4]

In January 1885, with the garrison at Chi-lung down to six hundred men, reinforcements were landed, one of whom was Lionel Hart. He discovered the town to be hardly more than a pile of cinders in an amphitheater of mountains whose heights were occupied by the enemy. The marines and *joyeux* welcomed the legionaires, but "they are all very pale and very tired."[5] With these reinforcements, the French launched offensives in late January to disengage Chi-lung and, in March, pushed to the outskirts of Tan-shui. However, it was clear that Formosa was a dead-end theater, that the French had nothing to gain from persisting there but more casualties and a diversion of scarce resources. The real decision had to be sought in Tonkin.[6]

The situation in Tonkin was far from reassuring. Although nine thousand French troops occupied it in the spring of 1884, a garrison that would eventually grow to forty thousand by the summer of 1885, they were on the strategic defensive. Quite apart from the Chinese buildup over the border in Kwangsi, troops that already had begun to infiltrate south, the French faced another, more persistent enemy in Tonkin—the Black Flags. The Black Flags took their name from the fact that each section, and each officer, carried a black flag. The result was that their lines were so festooned with standards that one legionaire preparing to attack the fortress of Bac Ninh in March 1884 was moved to declare, "Look. . . . They've done their washing. It's hanging out to dry."[7]

The French referred to them as pirates, which they certainly were—most were Chinese who drifted south because of poverty or after the failure in 1864 of the Taiping rebellion against the Chinese government. But they were more than that. Organized by an intelligent but illiterate Chinese named Liu Yung-fu, the Black Flags dominated the upper reaches of the Red River from their base at Lao Cai on the border with Yunnan. Despite their semi-brigand status, they enjoyed official relations with both the Vietnamese and Chinese governments—the Vietnamese recognized them because they controlled the primitive and predatory *montagnards* populations, who were not ethnic Vietnamese, to the northeast of the Red River

Delta, while the Chinese saw them as an extra measure of Chinese control in Tonkin. L. Huguet, a marine officer, described the Black Flags as very well armed with Remingtons, Spencers, Martini-Henrys and Winchester repeaters.

Their uniform(!) is made up of a jacket and light trousers of blue wool. Their legs from the bottom of the knee to the ankle are protected by cloth bands of the same color. As for their headgear, it varies enormously. Most often it consists of a large hat with a wide brim, sometimes doubled inside with a piece of fabric like the rest.[8]

The French spent most of the spring and summer of 1884 securing the Tonkinese delta and moving into the highlands as far as Tuyen Quang on the Clear River. The Chinese and the Black Flags had three primary strengths—they were very numerous; they were much better armed than were the French, whose 1874 model single-shot Gras rifles gave them a lower rate of fire; and they were expert at building defensive fortifications. So impressive were their fortifications that Western wisdom assumed that they must have had European help. After viewing one such fortress, which was made up of a series of palisades separated by open ground and trenches filled with bamboo spikes, Martyn was of the opinion that "a company of Royal Engineers could not have made a better job of it." His fellow legionnaires believed that an Englishman by the name of "Sir Collins" had directed its construction.[9] Furthermore, these fortifications were often surrounded by bush of such density that the attacking force might have to hack a path to it and then emerge one by one into open ground before deploying for an attack, a lengthy and extremely lethal process.

However, the French criticized the strategy of the Chinese and Black Flags as timorous and unimaginative. Huguet, who fought on the Red and Clear Rivers, found that the enemy "are past masters in the art of moving earth. That which makes their strength is also their weakness. Used to the shelter of deep trenches where they burrow like moles, they lack the daring to march and manoeuvre in open country." Their insistence on fighting from prepared defensive positions meant that they rarely ambushed advancing French columns often strung out along narrow jungle paths: "In such places our small troop would have been infallibly destroyed if we had encountered a few audacious enemy," Huguet believed. "Fortunately for us, the Black Flags did not know how to profit from the abundant advantages which the exuberant tropical vegetation offered them." As for the Chinese regulars, he found them individually courageous, but their tactic of passive defense was "even less comprehensible given the fact that they benefited from superior numbers. In truth, if they had been more flexible, Tonkin would not belong to us."[10] Dick de Lonlay, who participated in the Lang Son expedition, was of the opinion that in the open field the Chinese lacked "unity of direction, cohesion." Their fortifications, while well built, were usually badly sited. "Our troops are fighting against men who are sufficiently disciplined, battle-hardened, but who are almost always badly led," he concluded.[11]

A strategy of occupying defensive positions deep in the country and forcing the aggressive French to come to them might have worked well, especially given the desperate logistical problems that the French encountered in Tonkin. However, the Chinese seldom demonstrated the tactical skill required to capitalize on their superior firepower. Although they possessed artillery, they seldom used it. They were also miserable marksmen: "The Chinese . . . never put the rifle to the shoulder as Europeans do when about to fire," wrote Le Poer.

Instead, they tuck the rifle-butt into the armpit and try to drop the bullet, as it were, on the attacking party. They cannot well do this until the attack comes within five hundred yards of the defence, nor can they do it when the enemy is within two hundred yards of their line . . . as we closed with the bayonet and were practically at point-blank range, the Black Flags wavered and fired at the sky rather than at us.[12]

Everyone agreed that the Chinese tended to become a bit windy when the French got close enough to skewer them. However, their fortifications could break the momentum of an attack, so that both sides might fire at each other through holes in the bamboo palisade until the French could blast their way in using dynamite or their light artillery. Then the Chinese would flee, abandoning their fort. This was perhaps because they tended to place their best troops in the front line, and when these suffered heavy casualties (which they invariably did) or were broken, those in the second echelon tended to take to their heels.[13] In any case, the French seldom had enough troops to surround these fortresses and cut off the retreat, so the Chinese, while badly mauled, simply retired to another defensive position, and the process began again.

The Tonkin campaign of 1884–85 was to become one of the most controversial of French imperial campaigns between the Commune and the outbreak of World War I. The fact that it came perilously close to complete disaster derailed the brilliant parliamentary career of Jules Ferry, while it generated a controversy over the retreat from Lang Son in the French army that still has yet to be resolved. The Ferry government's aggressive colonialism, combined with the leadership of two of the French army's most dynamic colonial officers, Generals Louis-Alexandre Brière de l'Isle and François de Négrier, and the relative ease with which a small number of French troops had attacked and overwhelmed strongly held defensive positions like that of Bac Ninh in March 1884, was to have potentially disastrous consequences for the campaign the French fought during the winter of 1884–85. Above all, it gave the French enormous confidence in themselves, and of no corps was this more true than of the Legion.

General de Négrier especially became something of a cult figure in the Legion after he led them against the 1881 Bou Amama rebellion in Algeria. A.-P. Maury described him as "severe especially with drunks and the undisciplined, but he was fair and he looked after us like a father. When we met, he questioned us with affability and interest." Needless to say, Négrier's popularity paid dividends on operations—when Maury's company was dispatched to take a village, "we went and took it as he ordered, without hesitation or waiting. We were his Legion. He counted on us. We had to prove that we were worthy of his affection and of his esteem."[14] When in March 1885 Bôn-Mat's legionnaires were ordered to invade China and attack a fortified Chinese position containing an estimated twelve thousand to fifteen thousand men with only three thousand, they saw nothing strange about it: ". . . We were so used to winning that everything seemed possible to us," he wrote. "Because Maulen [Vietnamese for "Quick," the nickname given to Négrier by his soldiers and the natives] led us, whose name alone was worth several battalions, and because it flattered our ego to go on an excursion on Chinese territory."[15]

The willingness of the French to attack also was linked with the savage nature of the conflict. "The Chinese have put a price on our heads," even the Christian Lionel Hart recounted. "They dig up our dead, cut their heads off, and put them on the end of their lances or on their flagpoles, and show them to us while laughing from their fortifications. Sometimes one recognizes the face of a friend, and, turning away from this sickening spectacle, we swear vengeance."[16] Le Poer, too, reported that the sight of comrades who had fallen out on the march, only to be killed and mutilated by the Black Flags, drove the legionnaires into such a frenzy of vengeance that in the next action they slaughtered all their Chinese prisoners.[17] A.-P. Maury agreed that his legionnaires took no pity on the Chinese after they received a basket containing heads and a letter explaining, "*Voilà!* This is how all French will be treated."[18]

A final factor in the audacity and vigor of the French campaign was the officer corps. Officers in this period got mixed reviews from legionnaires. Martyn and Bôn-Mat appear to have enjoyed cordial relations with their officers. Maury, too, praised his lieutenant in Indochina, who failed to break him when he was discovered asleep on guard duty during the precipitous retreat from the Gates of China, but instead listed a lesser offense on his record.[19] Others, however, found them severe and disdainful. Lionel Hart believed that "Our superiors admire us as soldiers, but despise us as individuals. They make us understand this often. For them, we are just rabble and cannon fodder. They do not know us personally."[20] Charles des Ecorres, who served in the 1870s but who did not go to Tonkin, believed that officers merely saw legionnaires as stepping-stones for their own ambitions:

The Legion has always been a formidable arm in the hands of an ambitious commander. They have nothing to fear, no criticism, no one is interested in these pariahs of all races who come to get holes in their hide for France. So, get on the road and watch out! One marches, one sweats his guts out. The plain is peopled with cadavers and the officer gets his promotion which he grandly merits.[21]

The problem of arrogant, indifferent, even brutal officers was not a new one in the Legion—Le Poer complained that any officer who showed concern for his troops risked derision by his fellow officers.[22] Nevertheless, logic would seem to dictate that an openly expressed disdain of officers for their troops, if widespread, must undermine efficiency: Captain G. Prokos, who studied Legion operations in Tonkin very closely, insisted that successful officers "led their men as friends, as true collaborators whom he must, above all, make interested in the success of the enterprise." Otherwise they fell out on the march, and he was soon left with "a small core of disheartened men who only continued to follow from a spirit of discipline or pride."[23]

Obviously, as has been noted, all officers who led legionnaires did not fall into the unpopular category—even a rather sour Le Poer confessed that he became friends with his captain in Tonkin after the officer had shown great consideration for his dying friend Nicholas.[24] Others may have been distant, even abrupt, but this leadership style was perhaps better accepted in an era when social distinctions and deference were assumed to be normal, especially among those of a working-class background, from which the majority of legionnaires were drawn.

It is also possible that legionnaires took such attitudes more or less in stride because the combative qualities of their superiors far outweighed their character defects. Even if officers were gruff, legionnaires, even fairly cynical ones, appeared to respond well to leaders who were tough, brave and above all competent. Le Poer discovered that legionnaires were left in no doubt about ". . . how little he cares for their comfort" and were angered by the tendency of the officers "to swear at the sick, to sneer at the wounded, to order the dead to be thrown any way into a trench, and to abuse the burial party because they did not cover the carcasses quickly enough." What was more, this attitude of contempt actually discouraged some of the best men from seeking promotion—his aristocratic Russian friend Nicholas, for instance, turned down a battlefield promotion to corporal because ". . . the idea of one who had commanded a company accepting the control of a squad and receiving curses and abuse from the company officers when a soldier got into trouble was not to be entertained for a moment." However, he had to concede that their physical courage was beyond reproach: "Our officers fought like devils," he wrote. "Truth to tell, though we did not like them, we could not help admiring their courage in a fight."[25]

Nor was the question of whether or not to follow an officer, popular or unpopular, one up for discussion in the Legion: "The column goes to ground, flat on the earth, awaiting the order, the supreme order," Carpeaux recorded.

All eyes are on the enemy, but all thoughts are on the captain! They counsel him, implore him, supplicate, order him depending on the force of their energy. Everyone feels death, there, very close. Everyone wants to avoid it, to flee it. But no one dares to run, preferring to be killed rather than be treated as a coward. . . . But the captain remains standing up and still undecided. This is a superb opportunity for him to get noticed, to be decorated. To turn back is to lose his cross [of the Legion of Honor].[26]

Carpeaux's observation also serves to underline the further point that personal pride played a large part in the Legion's fighting prowess. And while this is true for all forces, in the Legion this personal pride was reinforced by the fact that, in addition, one wanted to disgrace neither his squad nor his nationality, much less besmirch the reputation of the Legion itself. Lastly, the effects of poor leadership, when it existed, might be minimized by the existence of a parallel hierarchy in many squads. This was a product both of the romantic reputation of the Legion as a haven for gentlemen down on their luck and of the *anonymat,* which allowed men to embellish, or invent, pasts of such distinction that they gained a social ascendancy in their squads. Le Poer insisted, no doubt with exaggeration, that ex-officers virtually abounded in the Legion, that the authorities realized this and were careful to assign no more than one per squad. "Every one of them was a second corporal, so to speak, and really, to take the case of the man I knew best, Nicholas was far more respected amongst us than our authorized superior, and the corporal was well aware of the fact as we," he wrote. "Well, these were the leaders."[27] They might be a force for good or evil—indeed, Le Poer claimed that Nicholas contrived a massacre of Chinese prisoners to avenge one of their mutilated comrades that their superiors were powerless to stop. But when such men existed and were well disposed, they might, on occasion, provide an element of leadership and cohesiveness to counter the effects of indifferent officership.

In sum, these first relatively facile victories, together with the desire to avenge deaths and mutilations at the hands of a barbarous enemy and a spirited, ambitious officer corps willing, even eager, to take risks, caused the French commanders to underestimate their enemy, to fail to notice improvements in enemy forces, and ultimately to overreach themselves. The French were overconfident, and with good reason, as even Le Poer believed: ". . . In the first place, the generals and the other officers firmly believed that the Black Flags and their allies would never be able to stand up against either our rifle fire or our charge. . . . In the second place, we soldiers had learned to depend implicitly on our commanders. They had led us so well that we had as much confidence in their foresight and military skill as they had in our courage and steadfastness."[28] It was a characteristic that was to mark the fighting in Indochina even after 1885—Martyn, speaking of an unsuccessful attempt to seize a fortress despite repeated attacks (unsupported by artillery), put them down ". . . to the fact that the French officers persistently refused to recognize the military ability of these pirate commanders, and consistently under-estimated the fighting power of their men."[29]

Had the French been more attuned to the intricacies of Chinese politics, they might have noted in the early autumn of 1884 that the Chinese and Black Flags appeared prepared to take the strategic offensive. In October 1884, Liu Yung-fu's Black Flag, reinforced by a contingent of Yunnanese troops, settled in around the town of Tuyen Quang, which lay on the Clear River in the highlands northwest of Hanoi. In mid-November, a column of seven hundred legionnaires and marines under Lieutenant Colonel Duchesne made their way up the Clear River supported by three gunboats. "From a tourist point of view, the valley of the Clear River is really magnificent," Huguet found, high wooded mountains through which a river of limpid water sometimes rushed and foamed between granite cliffs, or meandered through broad valleys planted with fields of maize. However, from a military point of view the abrupt terrain and dense jungle afforded ample opportunities for ambush.

Six miles short of Tuyen Quang, the column fought its way through an enemy position after the Legion outflanked a Chinese line established along a fortified ridge. After a rest, the column set out again: "An absolute silence, strange, unusual settled down over this dismal landscape, and froze the hearts of the most courageous," Huguet remembered. "In spite of ourselves, one felt impregnated with the horror which oozed from this funereal countryside . . ." Every eye was peeled for ambush. The trail disappeared into a narrow gorge, and became very muddy, and night was fast approaching. The bugler of the *avant-garde* blew the opening chords of the "Boudin," the Legion march that was gaining in popularity in the corps since first being introduced during the Mexican campaign. In the distance, the call was answered. Even a marine like Huguet was relieved. Soon Vietnamese bearing torches arrived to light the way to Tuyen Quang.[30] On November 23, the column departed without incident, leaving a garrison composed of two companies of legionnaires, a company of *tirailleurs tonkinois* (Tonkinese rifles), and other odds and ends including 32 artillerymen, a few engineers, a doctor and a Protestant pastor—a grand total of 619 men, 390 of whom were legionnaires, and thirteen officers under the command of Major Marc Edmond Dominé of the *Bat d'Af*. The curtain of Black Flags closed once again around Tuyen Quang.

The French had not been idle elsewhere, however. In October, they had driven the Chinese out of the country from Bac Ninh to Bac Le, and might have pushed north to Lang Son had not the demands of Tuyen Quang, the lack of reinforcements and the insistence of the war minister in Paris that operations be restricted to the delta not prevented it. However, the replacement of the war minister, which coincided with the arrival of reinforcements including two battalions of legionnaires in January 1885, allowed the French commander, General Brière de l'Isle, to launch his forces north to clear the "Mandarin Road," hardly more than a track running from Hanoi through Lang Son to the "Gates of China," once and for all. On February 3, 1885, the column composed in all of twelve battalions of around nine thousand men set out under a gray drizzle. As the column filed out of the delta and entered the rather desolate-looking mountains, Bôn-Mat for one had a sense of foreboding:

"... One felt that the task would be difficult, that we marched toward the unknown, and, instinctively, we looked behind us to look once more upon this plain.... We only knew the delta, rich and populated, abounding with resources of all sorts, the Tonkin where one lives, where one plays. We were going to find the Tonkin where one suffers, where one dies.[31]

Barely two days into the mountains, the advancing column encountered strongly held Chinese positions—"each valley is barred by a trench; each peak is crowned by a fort; it's an inextricable jumble of fortifications," wrote Bôn-Mat.[32] At first the French stormed them head on, but the cost was substantial. One Legion company lost one-third of its force and all of its officers in this first combat, so that the command of the company fell to the sergeant-major. After this experience, it was discovered that a simple flanking maneuver often sufficed to send the Chinese scurrying to cover their line of retreat.[33] After three days of fighting, Bôn-Mat's legionnaires moved into the abandoned forts, ignoring the Chinese corpses lying about, collapsed onto the straw beds and barely had time to eat a biscuit before falling asleep. However, they were up early, for "if the Chinese abandoned their forts, they left their fleas ..."[34]

On February 9, the march continued northward beneath a lowering sky. The Chinese offered only delaying actions, but the track became a quagmire, and the revictualing convoy often arrived late at night only after a difficult march by torchlight. At nine o'clock on the morning of February 12, the column came in sight of strong Chinese positions organized in depth along the heights at Bac Viay, the last stop before Lang Son. A strong artillery barrage drove the Chinese from their first lines, and the fortresses on the hilltops held long enough to permit the rest to escape. The road to Lang Son lay open, but at a cost of well over two hundred casualties, so many in fact that they could not all be evacuated. The French attempted to pursue, but without success: "The Chinese carries his rifle and cartridges," read the battalion diary. "Our infantryman has the pack which weighs him down."[35] Only harassing fire greeted the French as they marched along the river road on February 13. The mountains fell away, the river made a sharp bend to the right, and suddenly Lang Son appeared barely a mile away.

In 1885, Lang Son was a square walled citadel about 425 yards on each face, enclosing some brick pagodas, a few huts, a mirador and much empty space. Most of the population occupied the village of Ki Lua, which stood about three-quarters of a mile north of Lang Son. The few flags flying from the ramparts disappeared as the French approached, and within minutes a tricolor spanked the air above the battlements. On the 23rd, the French marched out to drive the Chinese from Dong Dang, a small settlement that stood ten miles north of Lang Son at the head of a narrow valley that ran to the Gates of China. After a fairly typical combat during which the Chinese were driven from their forts perched on mountain peaks, they fled up the rough track that threaded between high cliffs to the Gates of China, leaving a wake of abandoned equipment.

Lyautey, who visited Lang Son and the Gates of China in 1894, found that it reminded him of the Kabylia in Algeria, a land of naked and savage mountains, whose cliffs and pinnacles were crowned with fortresses. The menacing head of a tiger chiseled in the rock beside a narrow defile indicated the entrance to the gates.[36] In 1885, the defile had been fortified and provided with a stone entrance, which the French proceeded to blow up, using the enormous quantities of powder abandoned by the Chinese in their retreat. General Brière de l'Isle left General de Négrier in command and marched off to look after the other pressing problem, Tuyen Quang.

The siege of Tuyen Quang is ranked in the annals of the Legion heroics only slightly below that of Camerone, and rightly so. However, the strategic role played by Tuyen Quang in the French campaign of conquest is unclear. Grisot claimed that Tuyen Quang formed a "barrier" against the advance of the Yunnan army.[37] In one sense, the prolonged resistance of Tuyen Quang tied down large numbers of Black Flags and Yunnanese regulars who might have caused the French great embarrassment elsewhere. However, the failure of the Chinese to operate against the delta while Brière de l'Isle was heavily engaged in the north probably had more to do with a lack of any coordinated Chinese strategic plan than with the resistance of the Legion at Tuyen Quang itself. For after all, Chinese who invested Tuyen Quang in December 1884 could easily have bypassed the fortress by going down the Red River, or by surrounding the garrison with a small holding force while the bulk of their army operated elsewhere, especially after February 1885 when Brière de l'Isle launched his operation toward Lang Son. In all probability, the Chinese saw Tuyen Quang as a vulnerable target and decided that there they might inflict upon the French a defeat of proportions significant enough to create at least psychological damage.

So if the military significance of Tuyen Quang is unclear, its symbolic importance became immense. And all the more so because the place was virtually undefendable—a square each of whose walls measured three hundred yards built on the banks of the Clear River. The fortress was dominated by a number of wooded hills. Captain Champs, a sergeant-major in 1885, was of the opinion that if the Legion had been sent to garrison Tuyen Quang, "then the post wasn't worth much."[38] But the legionnaires and *tirailleurs tonkinois* defended it for three months with a dogged tenacity that suggested that they valued their reputations, and their lives, even if the place was a strategic backwater.

On January 16, the Chinese began to dig their lines of investment around the garrison, which were complete by the 20th. On the night of January 26–27, a mass of Chinese charged through the Annamese village 400 yards from the garrison, set it alight and then surged toward the French positions. The warm reception they received from the legionnaires drove them back in confusion: "We must have killed more than a hundred," the Protestant chaplain Th. Boisset wrote in his diary, "and the cannonade does not seem to be finished yet."[39] This convinced the Chinese to begin more methodical siege operations. Soon trenches began to snake toward the French positions, despite the best efforts of the garrison's four light cannon to dispute their progress. The Chinese objective was a blockhouse that stood on a small mole 350 yards from the southwestern angle of the French position. When it became obvious to the French that the Chinese had driven mine shafts beneath the blockhouse and were prepared to blow it up, they pulled in the garrison on the night of January 30, and then destroyed the fortification with their artillery.

The Chinese continued their siege with admirable, if unsettling, persistence. During the day they made fascines—bundles of sticks used to shore up parapets—and kept up a constant sniping on the garrison that caused one or two casualties each day. At night they pushed their saps relentlessly forward, while bombarding the garrison with a constant, casualty-producing fire. For their part, the French worked feverishly to shore up their positions, but were hampered by the fact that the garrison counted only twenty-nine shovels. On February 3, an Annamite crept out to take news of the garrison's predicament to Hanoi, but Boisset speculated that the operations around Lang Son might prevent a relief from being sent.[40] To prevent surprise attacks, the French lowered lanterns from the wall at night. So close were the approach trenches that some enterprising legionnaires snagged a Chinese flag using a cord with a noose tied to the end of a bamboo pole.

On February 8, as the officers dined, a shell burst on the roof of their mess, scattering debris over the plates, the infallible announcement that the Chinese had received artillery.[41] While at first the firing was badly regulated, gradually the enemy gunners became more expert and their shells began to slam into the pagoda that Marc Edmond Dominé, the garrison commander, used as a command post, and hit the shacks that housed the troops, causing casualties. In the early hours of February 12, the Chinese blew a mine beneath the French defenses and a Forlorn Hope—The party sent to seize and hold the breach—rushed forward. A rapid French response killed between thirty and forty of the advance party, which convinced the assault columns waiting in the saps to postpone their attack. Hardly minutes passed when a second mine blew. A Chinese appeared to plant a flag in the breach, only to be shot down by the legionnaires who, brought forward by cries of *"aux armes!,"* rushed to the defenses. Three subsequent assaults were repulsed, but at a cost of five legionnaires killed and six wounded. The next day, a sortie by the garrison drove the Chinese out of their most advanced saps and allowed the legionnaires to destroy some of the approaching earthworks. But the relief provided by this small success quickly evaporated when it became apparent that the Chinese had added heavy mortars to their siege batteries.

At six o'clock on the morning of February 22, the Chinese sent up a din of trumpets and shouts from their trenches. Anticipating an explosion, Captain Catelin of the Legion began to pull his men back from the positions he knew to be mined. Seconds later, the first of three mines was exploded by the Chinese, the second of which killed a Legion captain and the last of which collapsed almost sixty yards of wall. Groups of defenders kept up a hot fire while their comrades worked feverishly for four hours to repair the damage caused by the mines. They succeeded, but at the end of the day the Legion counted one officer and four legionnaires dead, and one officer, three NCOs and thirty-seven legionnaires wounded.

On the following day, another Chinese assault was repulsed. On the 25th, the deadly Chinese tactic was repeated—a mine blew, followed by an assault that obliged a number of legionnaires to keep the assailants at bay while their comrades worked to repair the damage. Four more legionnaires perished and another twelve were wounded. At eleven thirty in the evening of February 27, more mines exploded, followed by an assault on three different points of the defenses. The Chinese swarmed on the breaches, waving their black flags and hurling grenades and satchels of powder. "For nearly 30 minutes, the fighting continued hand-to-hand on the breaches, the combatants separated only by the bamboo palisades which crowned the defenses," Dominé wrote in his diary.[42] By dawn, repeated attacks had been driven off, but the Legion had lost another three dead, including an officer, and nine wounded.

The garrison's situation was desperate. Only 180 rifles were in working order to defend a perimeter 1,200 yards long, 120 yards of which had been destroyed by mines. On March 1, the garrison heard firing to the south and suspected that it was a relief force. But Dominé's troops were too exhausted to mount a breakout. When Chinese firing redoubled on March 2, many must have feared that they might be overwhelmed before the relief could arrive.

In fact, the Chinese firing had masked their withdrawal. On March 3, the garrison woke up to discover that the Chinese had decamped in the night.[43] The reason soon became clear—that very afternoon, the relief column, which had left Lang Son on February 16, stumbled up the track along the Clear River after fighting a desperate action at Hoa Moc against a blocking force that cost more killed than had perished in the entire siege—indeed, Hoa Moc was the most murderous battle fought by the French in Tonkin since their 1883 invasion. For many in the relief force, the sight of Tuyen Quang was a sobering one: "All the approaches [to Tuyen Quang]—churned, blasted, lamentable—were covered with corpses and the carrion rotted in the air," Huguet complained. "The pestilential emanations of all of these putrid corpses turned your stomach . . ."[44] "What a spectacle! What desolation! What ruin!" exclaimed Boisset when he emerged from the citadel to walk over a battlefield littered with abandoned weapons and tools of the siege, and furrowed with almost six miles of trenches. "Our liberators cannot believe their eyes."[45] So impressive was the defense of Tuyen Quang that the government ordered the publication of Dominé's journal in the *Journal officiel,* while a separate edition was printed and distributed to garrison libraries throughout France and the colonies. But France's, and the Legion's, trials in Indochina had only begun.

Chapter 11

"A SECOND
FATHERLAND"

"MORE THAN ALGERIA, Madagascar or the [Western] Sudan, Indochina is for [legionnaires] a second fatherland," wrote Captain, and ex-legionnaire, Louis Carpeaux. "Its strange calm infiltrates in their blood with the malaria itself, and they can no longer rid themselves of the nostalgic visions of sun splashed rice paddies."[1] "Believe me, there are few people who, digging into their memory, will come up with better souvenirs," wrote L. Huguet, a marine officer who served with the Legion during the conquest of Tonkin in 1883–85.

For me, these moments are unforgettable, these magnificent November nights on the Clear River, in an incomparable landscape! . . . The soft light of the moon would reflect off the beautiful fanpalm leaves. The continuous murmur of insects in the sleepy atmosphere in which a transparent vapor seemed suspended. A hundred feet away, the dark shadow of a massif of bamboos would be lighted by the gleam of a small fire against which would be silhouetted, in various poses, the men on guard. Further away, at the top of a mirador, the linh *[soldier] stands immobile. At its base, the European sentinel marching backwards and forwards probing with his eyes the surrounding hills. . . . A small boy surreptitiously slipped beneath the blanket of a soldier after devouring his rice cake, while a little way off a group of coolies were talking, while passing around the same rustic pipe.*[2]

Yet these nostalgic images of Indochina could hardly mask the fact that it was a desperately unhealthy place, where, when there was not a cholera epidemic, "dysentery is queen and malaria king."[3] "Few of us came back to that barracks again," Frederic Martyn wrote of his draft of legionnaires sent from Sidi-bel-Abbès to Tonkin in 1889. "Probably more than half 'settled down' for ever in the jungles, swamps, and burial grounds of Indo-China, while many more became so broken in health that they were discharged as being unfit for further service without returning to the Legion's headquarters."[4] Legion Sergeant Ernest Bolis, who went to Tonkin in the 1890s, soon found that of the original 116 men of his company, only 17 remained, the rest having died or been invalided home.[5] Death was so common among the large military garrison of Son Tay that one visitor charged in 1889 that "every year all the corpses are exhumed and thrown into a communal grave, the crosses and inscriptions disappear. One must not enlarge the cemetery."[6] Between 1887 and 1909, only 271 legionnaires died in combat in Indochina, while fully 2,705 perished from disease.[7]

Despite the lethality of the place, there was no shortage of legionnaires eager to volunteer for the Far East. "Most of our leisure was spent discussing avidly our chances of being sent to the Orient," John Le Poer remembered. "Life, we believed, could not be as monotonous in Tonkin— there were frequent battles there, and, more, there was the powerful attraction of being able to pillage surreptitiously, after battles or skirmishes."[8] The promise of combat was no doubt a great draw, as was the simple desire to move on, to "see some country"—"I am tired of soldiering here [Algeria]," Le Poer's friend told him. "Why should I not see the world?"[9] "The prospect of living in the bush in Tonkin, of confronting danger, filled me with joy," wrote legionnaire Jean Pfirmann of his 1888 selection.[10]

But above all, the quality of life was perceived to be better. Even anti-Legion writer Leon Randin found the legionnaires in Tonkin more mellow than in Algeria, less intemperate, less racist, less inclined "to play the hardened veteran." Discipline, too, he believed to be more relaxed, the NCOs less brutal, and the officers "suddenly adopt the unusual attitudes of older brothers."[11] In 1903, General Bertrand, commander of the 3rd Infantry Brigade in Algeria, noted that legionnaires sought service in Tonkin because one year there counted double for pension purposes. They also qualified for the "colonial pay" regularly given to marines abroad but denied to legionnaires in Algeria, because it was considered part of metropolitan France. The worst punishment that could be inflicted upon a legionnaire in Algeria, he believed, was to remove him from the list for Tonkin.[12] In 1909, General Hubert Lyautey reported that Legion garrisons must be retained in Indochina because the possibility of service there was *the* great enlistment draw,[13] which was certainly true in the case of legionnaire Joseph Ehrhart, who reenlisted for five years just to get to Tonkin. When he heard of his selection, "I couldn't sit still . . . I was mad with joy, I did a cartwheel, I walked on my hands, I no longer knew where I was!"[14]

For legionnaires, men for whom life was largely devoid of comforts,

Indochina was not only exotic, it also came as close to *la dolce vita* as most of them would ever get. The newly arrived Ehrhart, billeted in the marine barracks at Hanoi, was amazed when a group of marines walked into their dormitory followed by a posse of "boys" who gathered up their dirty clothing and cleaned their rifles. He later discovered that, as might be expected, the Legion's rules were somewhat stricter, but nevertheless a far cry from the life-style of North Africa—as Annamese (as the Vietnamese were then called) were not allowed in the rooms and *never* given weapons, legionnaires had to carry their dirty uniforms to the ground floor to be washed, and clean their own rifles. "Boys" also served them in the refectory, and even washed the uniforms of those in the punishment cells.[15]

Without a doubt, the greatest benefit of life beyond Suez was the relative abundance in Indochina of women—the *congaï,* literally "young girl" in Vietnamese, whose presence made even the most remote Legion garrisons so much more livable than in Algeria. It was hardly love at first sight, however. European soldiers were initially put off by women who constantly chewed (and spit) betel nuts and painted their teeth black. But they could often be induced to give up one, or both, of these habits. Not surprisingly, the prettiest girls fell to the officers.[16] "There wasn't much to do [in Indochina]," Ernst Junger was told by an old legionnaire in 1913. "We spent a lot of time stretched out on our beds daydreaming. When the heat of the day was passed, we would go to the Annamese village, have our clothes washed, and everyone had his Annamese mistress."[17] There was even a commerce in these girls, with a departing soldier able to resell his *congaï* to a new arrival—sometimes at a profit!

The widespread practice of keeping Vietnamese mistresses was not without its dangers, however. Some feared that the girls served as enemy spies and agents.[18] But this appears seldom to have been the case. As will be seen, Viet Minh attempts to use *congaï* as agents between 1946 and 1954 foundered on the twin rocks of the loyalty of those women willing to sleep with French soldiers, and the "bourgeois morality" of those who were not. The problem of the *congaï* was not that they were likely to conspire against France, but rather the more obvious one that their very presence served as a conspiracy against military discipline. Joseph Ehrhart discovered that in Tonkin, "Despite the colonial pay, I was not rich, and I did not want to follow the practice of certain legionnaires who sold their wine ration at each meal to keep their congai, usually one who cared nothing for them." He eventually succumbed, however, and the combination of his tendency to linger beyond evening muster with his "co," and the jealousy of a corporal eager to send him to the cells so that he could advance his own courtship, eventually led to Ehrhart's unsuccessful attempt at desertion, which almost earned him an extended stay in a discipline company.[19] However, the *congaï* could also prove immensely loyal, even vital, to the French war effort—Bôn-Mat's squad would virtually have starved on the parsimonious rations of the intendance during the grueling Lang Son campaign of 1885 had not his enterprising *congaï* made heroic efforts to obtain extra food for them.[20]

The availability of women was not the unique attraction of Indochina. There was yet another—opium. Of course, it must be remembered that in the nineteenth century opium was thought to provide certain medicinal benefits. Also, efforts to prevent its use among Europeans in Indochina were complicated by the fact that the refinement and sale of opium eventually became a government monopoly, from which the French colonizers derived fully one-third of their tax receipts in Indochina by the time of World War I.[21] The extent of its use is difficult to determine. It is possible that, like the use of drugs in the United States and Europe in our own day, smoking opium began as an novel amusement among the upper echelons of Europeans abroad and gradually spread downward. The first to introduce opium into the forces may well have been naval and staff officers, those most in touch with civilian colonial society in which it was fairly frequent to organize an opium corner in the sitting room.

There is no evidence that opium displaced the traditional penchant for alcohol in the Legion, although legionnaires had to abandon wine and absinthe, too expensive in the Orient, in favor of rice wine, the noxious, highly intoxicating *choum-choum,* which sold for thirty-five centimes a liter. But Junger was told that smoking opium was common in the Legion: "There was not much surveillance," an old legionnaire recounted. "In our post, almost everyone smoked, despite formal orders to the contrary. It was the custom of the country."[22] In Tonkin, Silbermann was at first impressed by the friendliness of the locals, until he realized that they wanted him to bring soldiers to their opium dens to smoke at two sous (forty centimes, about eight cents or sixpence) a pipe.[23] And at least one man in Bôn-Mat's squad in 1884 quickly discovered a taste for "pulling on the bamboo," which eventually led to his being passed over for promotion.[24] A visit to an opium den was one of the first items on Ehrhart's agenda upon reaching Hanoi.[25] In 1891, the Catholic Church in Indochina condemned the abuse of opium and decreed that only repentant addicts could receive the sacraments. In 1907, the French government, worried by the spread of opium dens from Indochina to port cities in France, forbade any government official from smoking, while in 1912 Paris newspapers began a press campaign "against the progress of opium addiction among officers of the navy and colonial troops." However, while addiction was officially frowned upon, "Sunday smoking" continued to be tolerated until World War II.[26]

As a consequence of the plethora of volunteers, the Legion could afford to be fairly selective about whom they sent to Indochina, at least after the initial conquest of Tonkin in 1883–85. Competition to be included in the draft was keen. When in 1889 Frederic Martyn saw that the call for volunteers excluded those with less than nine months' service and any punishments, "I hardly thought it worth while to ask for my name to be put down on the list in the face of this restriction."[27] But he was taken nonetheless. Ernest Bolis was rejected as too young—the more mature soldiers were thought better to resist the rigors of the climate—but he successfully appealed to his superiors to be included.[28] In 1906, legionnaire Lucien Jacqueline was left behind because his teeth were bad.[29]

The departure of a Tonkin draft was always the occasion for celebration. At the farewell review at Sidi-bel-Abbès, Bolis swelled with pride: "I admired with pleasure the old soldiers among us, faces bronzed by the sun, made thin by their labors, their tough, even slightly savage, exteriors ... their worn kepis pulled down over faces sporting large beards, their foreheads furrowed from grimacing at peril."[30] Martyn marched out with the admonition of his colonel to "remember the glorious traditions of the Legion," and the *zouave* band saw them off at the quay in Oran with the "Marseillaise," "a rattling war-song" and "patriotism-reviver" that was bellowed enthusiastically by all troops on board.[31]

Once out of sight of land, however, the elation of departure quickly subsided, especially in rough seas. Lionel Hart found the hold of the *Canton* fetid and crammed full of bunks: "There are impossible scenes when, at night, the swells provoke violent seasickness," he wrote. "Then the groans and sometimes disputes break out among the poor unfortunates who, despite their precautions, vomit on each other.... The scene loses nothing of the picturesque."[32] But morale and the sense of expectation usually remained intact, at least as far as the Suez Canal.

Port Said lay simmering on a coast as white as a snowfield at the entrance to the canal. The spectacle of Egyptians surrounding the ship with a flotilla of small boats to sell fruit, trinkets or tobacco must not have appeared overly exotic to men coming from Algeria.[33] However, even the dullest private could not help but notice that he was on the edge of a frontier—tropical whites appeared and, for legionnaires, the kepi was replaced by a high, rounded pith helmet. But this frontier was as much a psychological as a geographical one, for beyond lay the East, peopled not with Arabs filled with sullen pride, but by brown masses whose individualism seemed irretrievably lost in the sheer magnitude of their misery. With each port of call, the apparent subservience of these malingering multitudes, their seeming willingness to be dominated or bought, reinforced the sentiment of racial and cultural superiority among Europeans so that by the time they set foot in Indochina, they were already well on the way to acquiring a colonial mentality.

In 1884, the Suez Canal, opened only fifteen years earlier, was a trench barely one hundred yards wide flanked on the west by a large levee that for some miles separated it from the Manzala Lake, while to the east the Sinai extended bleakly to the horizon. The ships were forced to sail very slowly, and even to tie up at night, while every five miles small settlements housing European employees of the canal company sat like emerald islands in a khaki sea. However, deserting legionnaires invariably added interest to what otherwise might have proved a rather dull interlude. After two legionnaires splashed to freedom on Martyn's ship, marines were placed around the decks to prevent further escapes. However, one night a third legionnaire crept down the rope securing the ship to the bank: "Having got so far he was taken with a severe attack of funk, and, not being able either to go forward or to come back, was constrained to call for help," wrote Martyn. "He was evidently under the impression that we were in the River Nile, for when I and many others, ran up to the bow in response to his frenzied screams he was yelling 'Crocodile! Crocodile!' with all the power of his lungs."[34]

This tradition of desertion in the Suez Canal was evidently established by the first drafts sent out to Indochina. While the regimental diary of the 3rd Battalion of the Legion, which passed through Suez in 1884, makes no mention of desertion,[35] Lionel Hart, a member of the 4th Battalion, whose *Canton* was one of a convoy of four troopships bound for the Orient, claimed that they were "sowing deserters" as they sailed through the canal, one of whom reached the shore under a hail of bullets from fifty-six guards, and who retained the presence of mind to shout back, *"Je ne suis pas mort!"* ("I am not dead!") This produced two results: the first was that, "when, on the bridge, the major believes he sees something in the water, he grabs the rifle from the sentinel's hand and fires." The second was that all legionnaires were confined below decks, which virtually produced a mutiny:

. . . a terrible uproar began—animal cries, the most bizarre singing, the most obscene insults against the officers, the bloodiest threats, the most infernal row, everything that a thousand demons can invent of shouting and noise, all the tumult that you can imagine, broke out all at once in this small hold, where a thousand men found themselves quartered. A ladder broken, the officers insulted, four men placed in irons, this was the final result of this unbelievable scene which lasted from six o'clock in the evening until one o'clock in the morning.[36]

Silbermann's ship shed seventeen deserters going through the canal in 1895,[37] while Lieutenant Colonel Albert Ditte reported that the governor-general of Madagascar, General Joseph Gallieni, was furious when, in 1900, as tensions with Britain over the Fashoda crisis were still running at full flood, sixty Legion reinforcements jumped ship in the canal, a fact he put down to their unwillingness to face a European opponent.[38]

The tradition remained alive and well into the twentieth century. In 1913, Junger's old veteran explained to him that the canal was "the place where it's easiest for you to escape. All you have to do is to fall in the water, and you are in a neutral country. About fifteen men got through the nets, and one of them didn't know how to swim and went down for the third time. Then they lined up on the shore, saluted politely, and buggered off."[39] The English writer Evelyn Waugh discovered on a trip through the canal in

1930 that the lower decks contained a contingent of legionnaires bound for the East,

> ... mostly Germans and Russians; in the evenings they formed into little groups and sang songs. They had a band of drums and mouth-organs which came up to play in the first-class saloon on the evening of the concert. The drum was painted, with the device "Mon Jazz". Two of them climbed through a porthole one night in the Suez Canal and escaped. Next day a third tried to follow their example. We were all on deck drinking our morning aperitifs when we heard a splash and saw a shaven-headed figure in shirt-sleeves scrambling up the bank behind us. He had no hat and the sun was at its strongest. He ran through the sand, away from the ship, with gradually slackening speed. When he realized that no one was pursuing him he stopped and turned round. The ship went on. The last we saw of him was a figure stumbling after us and waving his arms. No one seemed the least put out by the occurrence.[40]

These desertions in Suez were more of an embarrassment for the Legion than a serious reduction of strength. Silbermann was of the opinion that most of the deserters had volunteered for service in the east precisely so that they could desert. And, as in Veracruz in 1863, "the officers didn't care," he believed. "They were even happy to get rid of them."[41]

Once out of Suez, everyone began to feel the full force of the monotony of the forty-day voyage. A fairly strict military routine was maintained—reveille, formations, inspections, guard duty. "It's not much, but at sea this produces a profound tedium and puts nerves on edge," Lionel Hart wrote to his mother,[42] especially in the oppressive heat south of Suez. There was little to do but scrub the decks, watch dolphins, play cards, tattoo each other with needles and india ink or organize national choirs. "The worst part of the voyage was while we were going through the Red Sea," John Le Poer recorded. "There one loathed his morning coffee and growled at his evening soup. The dull, deadly, oppressive heat in that region almost killed us. We lay around, unable almost to curse, and the soldier who finds himself too weak to do that, must be in a very bad way indeed."[43]

The arrival at a landfall like Aden, Colombo, or Singapore for recoaling momentarily plucked everyone from his torpor. Here those so inclined who had missed the opportunity to desert in the canal might seize a second chance. In Singapore, a Bulgarian on Le Poer's ship stripped to his underwear, blacked his skin with coal dust, and joined a line of coolies coaling his ship. No one noticed that he was rather large for a Chinese until he walked down the gangplank, threw away his basket and sprinted down the dock.[44] The diary of the 3rd Battalion records that four legionnaires escaped during coaling at Singapore, while three more jumped overboard as they were leaving the harbor: "They were not hit by the bullets," the diary records laconically. "We continued on our way."[45]

Not all were so lucky. Martyn saw two German legionnaires make a dash for the gangplank at Singapore,

. . . thinking, probably, that the sentries would not shoot to hit, even if they fired at all. If the sentries had been legionnaires this belief would have been justified, for a legionary would never hit an escaping comrade if he could help it, though he would be sure to carry out his orders scrupulously by firing at him. The marine sentries, however, had no particularly kind feeling towards legionnaires, for soldiers of the ordinary French regiments appear to think that "legionary" and "pig of a Prussian" are almost convertible terms, and they obeyed their orders to the letter, killing one and seriously wounding the other.

The incident caused such bad blood between the Legion and the marines that they had to be confined to opposite ends of the ship for the remainder of the voyage.[46] Legionnaire Jean Pfirmann also reported that in Indochina, even in the hospital to which he had been confined, "the marines did not get on with the Legion, and on the slightest pretext, a quarrel began which threatened to degenerate into a fight. The legionnaires often sang in German," he continued. "Immediately the marines protested and forbade the legionnaires to sing."[47]

Le Poer confirmed the rather ambivalent attitude of most legionnaires toward desertion. Despite a strict cordon of *joyeux* of the penal battalions, an Italian legionnaire managed to slip undetected into Singapore harbor. Unfortunately for him, he was plucked out of the water by the boat of the French consul, who returned him to the ship bound hand and foot. "How the commandant cursed him," wrote Le Poer, "how the Frenchmen [*joyeux*] smiled and jeered; how we, his comrades, felt sad that our worthy comrade should have been caught almost on the threshold of liberty! *Camaraderie* overcame all other feelings, and we pitied the poor wretch, for we guessed that a court-martial would have little mercy on a soldier, especially a soldier of the Legion, captured in the act of deserting from his company while on the way to the seat of war." According to Le Poer, the incident had two results: first, it brought the strained relations between the *Bat d'Af* and the Legion, who seemed to have reversed roles as jailer and jailed, to a head. "The commandant was lucky in two respects—the voyage to Saigon was short, and a French war vessel accompanied the transport. Had there been twenty days' voyage without an escort the decks would have been washed red with blood. . . ." Second, Le Poer claimed that the commandant (major) was killed in a skirmish soon after his arrival in Tonkin, shot in the back, Le Poer suggested, by Italians in his own battalion.

As no Legion major in Indochina died of anything, much less a bullet in the back, between 1883 and 1887, Le Poer's story appears to be based upon rumor or wishful thinking. But even if the story of the major's execution were untrue, Le Poer's point was that the officer had deeply offended the legionnaires' sense of dignity.

After all, is it not bad enough for an officer to punish a man or to get him punishment? Why should he swear at the poor devil and abuse him as if he had no spirit, no sense of shame, no soul? Any man will take his punishment fairly and honestly, if he believes that he has deserved it; no man will stand abuse without paying in full for it when he gets his chance, for abuse is not fair to the man who is waiting for his court-martial. But all, or nearly all, officers are either fools or brutes.[48]

Saigon, which had been in French hands since 1859, was seldom more than a brief port call for the Legion, whose ultimate destination was Tonkin. The troopships threaded their way through the Bay of Along, whose islands of weathered rock rose out of the sea like so many tortured shapes, until the engines were shut down in the midst of a muddy harbor. As Haiphong lay twenty-eight miles and two sandbars up the muddy waters of the Cua Cam estuary, some captains preferred to transfer the troops to small river boats for the six-hour trip. Otherwise, one had to take on a pilot and wait for high tide.

Like Calcutta, Haiphong was an entirely colonial creation, and in 1884 not a particularly impressive one at that. The 1874 treaty between France and the Annamese throne had conceded a small piece of spongy ground to the French to be used as a naval revictualing station. Obviously, the Vietnamese did not think that they had given away much, and at first view they appeared to be correct. Here the French had constructed a dock, houses for the consul and the navy commissioner, a customs post, a naval magazine, and a small barracks. Once the visitor had seen these official buildings, the few whitewashed houses, two "hôtels-restaurants" and a warehouse or two, and, of course, visited the cemetery, which was reached by walking along a dike and where the water table was so high that burials there appeared to strike a compromise between a service at sea and one on land, Haiphong held no further secrets. Lyautey, who saw Haiphong in 1894, called it "a town in a swamp,"[49] and most people found the view over a flat, marshy countryside, broken only by distant clumps of bamboo that denoted the presence of a village, profoundly depressing, especially when the country was swept by the monsoons or lay simmering beneath a blanket of humid heat. The region was infested with Chinese pirates who derived their principal income by kidnapping women and children for sale in the ports of southern China. Of course, the town was to grow in size and sophistication with the progress of the conquest of Tonkin until it became a major port city. However, Lyautey believed that, for soldiers at least, the barracks at Haiphong—"A pile of ruins in a marsh, where like prisoners the men are stacked on camp beds, with only one blanket, without light, without air. It's unhealthy and it stinks."[50]—made a poor first, and last, impression of Tonkin.

The voyage from Haiphong to Hanoi offered a nautical challenge reserved only for experienced captains. In 1894, Lyautey made the trip up the Cua Cam, across the Bamboo Canal to the Red River and Hanoi in fifteen hours. However, the commercial service took two days, perhaps because the small river steamer towed a junk, presumably reserved for native passengers, in its wake. Perhaps, also, because any encounter with one of the numerous mudbanks required the captain to await the next tide to float free. Lyautey, typically enthusiastic about anything colonial, was transported by the spectacle of light green rice fields stretching to the horizon, the clusters of coconut palms, and the thatched villages hidden behind their bamboo hedges, ". . . busy, noisy, sweating life and fecundity. . . . It's a dream to slide this way on a true estuary, as sinuous as a stream, through a vast plain where thousands of beings, yellow and hunched over, swarm like insects in the light."[51]

Unlike Haiphong, Hanoi was an established town when the French obtained the right to install their cantonment there in 1874. The initial French presence consisted of a small fortress garrisoned by two hundred French marines, which was more like something out of the Wild West than the Orient—a square of pointed stakes about seven feet high built next to the Red River, which, at Hanoi, was about eight hundred yards wide. A few houses had been put up around it, together with a tiny hospital and a requisitioned Chinese house that served as the Residency. During the 1870s, the insecurity of the area was such that the first French representative hightailed it back to Saigon after a few nights in Hanoi. However, by 1881 the locals had more or less ceased to shout insults and take potshots at the French after dark, which allowed the embryo of a colonial society to develop there. Life was cheap, servants plentiful, and, if Hanoi lacked the sophistication of Saigon, at least it offered a *frisson* of frontier savagery that included pagodas, pirates, lepers and mandarins, whose official processions of guards, scribes and flagbearers periodically hurried through the streets, preceded by a servant beating a tambourine to shoo traffic out of the way. Bôn-Mat, who disembarked in Hanoi in 1884, declared it *"une jolie ville"* built around a lake whose focal point was the Pagoda of the Great Buddha, situated in an arbor of pine trees and whose marble steps led down to the water's edge. He especially enjoyed Hanoi's Chinatown, a separate walled section of narrow paved streets, brick houses and small shops "where a demi-obscurity constantly reigns, [and where] riches are piled up, some true marvels."[52]

Hanoi quickly learned that the arrival of a boatload of legionnaires was likely to disturb the city's imperial dignity. Like most legionnaires, A.-P. Maury instantly discovered a taste for oriental cuisine: fish, shrimp, rice, crab and pork. "We quickly took to this food," he wrote. "We bought it from the natives, or we took it by force," when they refused to take French money.[53] However, the evident zeal with which Martyn's companions set out to sample the local vintages was probably more typical: "The bulk of our party . . . were . . . painting the town a brilliant vermilion," he recorded. "The men had been making a first trial of shum-shum, a potent rice spirit, and hundreds of them were riotously drunk. A fair number of them had to be carried to the barracks and tied up when they got there to prevent them committing murder." Obviously the high command had to get them out of town, and promptly shipped them up the river for two weeks of acclimatization training, which consisted mainly of wading through rice paddies.[54] Protestant pastor J. Pannier, sent to Tonkin in 1901, reported that newly arrived drafts of legionnaires were regularly confined to barracks in Hanoi after their long sea voyage lest they run amok.[55]

BY MARCH 1885, the French had been remarkably successful in Tonkin (if less so in Formosa)—with hardly more than a relative handful of troops, they had driven the Chinese off the Mandarin Road and broken the siege of Tuyen Quang, thereby achieving their immediate strategic objectives. This battlefield success had apparently convinced the emperor to sign away all claims to Tonkin,[56] so that rumors of imminent peace had even reached French troops in the field. Now was obviously the time for the French to adopt a defensive strategy to secure what they had won. Besides, they had other reasons to exercise caution. While the Black Flags and Yunnanese troops had been cleared from Tuyen Quang, they had retired in good order, and still held the upper reaches of the Red River in considerable force. The Kwangsi army had been driven out of Tonkin, but lurked just on the north side of the Gates of China. Négrier had been left at Lang Son with a garrison that probably numbered less than five thousand men, in part because Brière de l'Isle needed them for Tuyen Quang, but basically because that was about the maximum number that even the parsimonious French intendance could support logistically.

To be fair, the problems of supply were immense. Originally, eight thousand coolies and eight hundred small horses had been collected to support the expedition. But even though the distance between Hanoi and Lang Son was only about eighty-five miles, the Mandarin Road was hardly a superhighway, and a coolie could carry an absolute maximum of sixty pounds. This in itself would have made resupply a ponderous process. However, it was further complicated by the fact that the coolies, who were forced labor, tended to desert at the first opportunity, *en masse* if possible, and could not be replaced. A report of March 18, 1885, complained that coolies were difficult to recruit and retain because of the sinister reputation of upper Tonkin, because they were badly treated by Europeans, and because the Chinese tended to massacre any coolies they captured.[57] Ammunition was in short supply. But equally as bad, French rations, which usually amounted to little more than hardtack and macaroni, were distributed only every other day, while on the off day they dined on the rice and tea left behind by the Chinese.[58] This could only increase the fatigue of the troops, who had already fought a series of battles: "After fifteen months of a campaign like this," wrote Bôn-Mat, "I had just about had enough." (Indeed, it was here that his *congaï* saved the day, and made a substantial profit, by frequent trips back to the delta for supplies.)[59]

Another reason for caution resided in the fact that, while the French had won the victories, Chinese tactics were improving: Bôn-Mat found that, "over the past year, there has been a remarkable progress on the part of their commanders in the employment of their forces. Instead of a pure and simple defensive, they are beginning to know how to maneuver and, for the first time, at Dong Dang their fire forced our artillery to change positions." The battle of Hoa Moc, though a French success, came perilously close to falling into the category of a Pyrrhic victory—it had been the most costly of the campaign so far, with 76 French killed and 408 wounded,[60] many of whom did not survive the trip back to base. Of course, these numbers may seem trifling, especially when compared with the far greater losses inflicted upon the Chinese. But it created a steady rate of attrition, especially when combined with losses caused by disease and climate, which the French could make up only with difficulty. On the other hand, manpower was the least of the worries of Chinese commanders. Le Poer found the Chinese regulars from Kwangsi the most impressive he had met in Tonkin: "When the fight was going on we were surprised at the gallant manner in which our foes stood up against us," he wrote. "After a time, when more than once we had hurled them back with the bayonet, we recognized that we were dealing with the most formidable force that we had yet encountered. They gave us bullet for bullet, thrust for thrust. They were good men, and when the bayonets crossed they fought quietly and earnestly, and died without a murmur, almost without a groan." He believed that a real weakness of the Chinese soldier was a sort of fatalism that often caused him to give up at critical moments, especially when confronted by a bayonet charge. "But in the firing they more than held their own, they were more numerous, their ammunition was evidently plentiful, and, to tell the plain truth, in spite of our bayonet charges they fairly shot us off the field."[61]

For all of these reasons, then, what happened next provides one of the most unexpected, and from the French point of view one of the most disastrous, episodes of the campaign. It is also one of the most puzzling because, in the words of British sinologist Henry McAleavy, "the usual French explanation of their retreat from Langson imposes in parts a severe strain on our credulity."[62] The first weeks of March on the frontier were fairly quiet. From the French post of Dong Dang, across a plain of rice paddies from the Gates of China, the Chinese could be observed fortifying two positions on their side of the border, beyond which it was reckoned that an army of forty thousand Chinese were encamped. Early on the morning of March 22, a Chinese force attempted to surprise Dong Dang, but was easily repulsed. Whether it was this attack that jolted de Négrier into action, or, as French historian Philippe Franchini believes, a wire from Ferry ordering him to "strike a blow" to get the negotiations with China off dead center,[63] the general decided upon an offensive. He assembled three thousand men, including legionnaires, for an attack on the Chinese army, which was organizing a fortified camp at Bang Bo inside China itself.

In retrospect, de Négrier's decision to launch an offensive into mainland China, against a force that outnumbered his own by at least twelve to one, appears suicidal. What is more, he seriously miscalculated the effect of his invasion on the Chinese army, whose soldiers were incensed and who swore a solemn oath to drive the foreigners from their sacred soil or die in the attempt.[64] Nor do the political risks of failure appear to have been taken into account, for they could easily have strengthened the Chinese hand at the peace negotiations as well as shatter the fragile support for the war in Paris. Nevertheless, de Négrier argued that the Chinese buildup across the border, far from requiring caution, obliged him to attack; otherwise he would face a repeat of the siege of Tuyen Quang with the difference that, at Lang Son, a successful rescue might be written out of the script.

In his deposition of April 1885, de Négrier admitted that he had full knowledge of the Chinese buildup across the frontier: "The cavalry patrols and the reconnaissances of officers who continually covered the country reported from 15 March a progressive augmentation of Chinese forces," he reported.[65] Indeed, that is precisely why he decided to attack. (In fact, de Négrier makes no mention of a wire from Ferry ordering him to undertake some spectacular action to jolt the Chinese into ceding Tonkin.) "The Chinese tactic consisted lately of maintaining close contact, to construct as closely as possible to the adversary, a fortified camp in front, then to act against the lines of communication, by pushing gradually one or several corps which would dig in as they advanced," Négrier continued. "The necessity to distance the enemy from the line of communication linking Langson with the rear obliged the occupation of Dong Dang."

However, when the Chinese began building two forts in front of Dong Dang, "the command confronted an alternative—either evacuate Dong Dang immediately or to give this post a little air. To evacuate Dong Dang would bring the enemy directly to Langson, and, from then . . . [the Chinese] could act against the line of communications, and compromise the supply of Langson. Given the small number of forces at our command, a passive defense, which obliged us to guard a number of points, must be ruled out. One would, in effect, have been obliged to cover consecutively Langson and the line of communications to Dong Sung. It seemed preferable to unite all the available forces in one mass and to attempt to punch through the enemy line by attacking one of the points in this line." When the Chinese attacked Dong Dang on the night of March 21–22, "the general resolved immediately to profit from the moral effect produced by this defeat, to attack Bang Bo [the Chinese camp] with all his forces."[66]

This offensive looked at first to offer a repeat of the other successful French actions—after an attack up the steep slopes against one of the two forts that dominated the valley by two French battalions and one of *tirailleurs tonkinois* stalled, the Legion assaulted it head on and succeeded. After a brief artillery bombardment, the Chinese abandoned the second fort. The French filed through the Gates of China into Kwangsi province. A second line of fortresses was taken, yet in the distance a third fortified line was clearly visible. A large Chinese force appeared and attempted to envelop the French right wing, but were driven off by artillery. Night fell, and the French camped on their positions, fairly content, one suspects, with the day's work.

When, around eleven o'clock on the morning of March 24, the fog cleared, they could look out over a landscape of rocky peaks and narrow valleys, in which Chinese fortifications figured prominently. The French began their usual, now almost routine, business of fortress-taking, hampered somewhat by the poor distribution of artillery munitions, when, about three o'clock in the afternoon, they were counterattacked by a Chinese force that Bôn-Mat put at between twenty-five and thirty thousand men. The first inkling that legionnaire A.-P. Maury had that the tide of battle had turned against him was when his company noticed the battalion of the 143rd Regiment leap out of a captured Chinese fort and run down the hill. "Our captain looked on the other side of the mountain to find out the cause of this retreat and to assess our position," he wrote. The reasons were immediately clear: "Clouds of Chinese sprang up from all sides. They were ten meters from the summit which we occupied. 'Fire! Fire!' cried the captain. 'They are there, three feet away!' "[67] The great retreat had begun.

The French began to fall back, the Legion holding the rear, from hill to hill toward the Gates of China, surrendering the hard-won forts to frontal assaults or Chinese threats against the single line of retreat. Even worse, ammunition was beginning to run low: "Our ranks are cut down, our bullets are running out," Maury recorded. "I had only two . . . I thought I would not escape alive from such a combat. . . . Of 90 men, only 27 were left."[68] "Shot at from the front and from the flanks, we took a murderous fire and high casualties," wrote Bôn-Mat. ". . . The wounded, those too tired to keep up were left behind never to be seen again."[69] "My one object at that time was to get away," Le Poer wrote. "I had no desire to fall, wounded or unwounded, into my pursuers' hands."[70] As night came, the French filed back through the Gates of China and rallied at Dong Dang. The Chinese did not pursue.[71]

The next day the French sat at Dong Dang. Strong parties were sent out to search the battlefield for missing soldiers: "We brought back a dozen, but far more numerous were those whom we found executed and odiously mutilated," remembered Bôn-Mat.[72] The 2nd Battalion of the Legion reported one captain and nine legionnaires killed, fifty-two wounded and two missing from the previous day,[73] although the regimental history appears to understate the true number of casualties. De Négrier ordered his battered troops to fall back on Lang Son. When, at seven o'clock on the morning of March 28, a substantial column of Chinese festooned with banners marched down the Mandarin Road and assaulted Lang Son, the Legion had been strengthened by the arrival of almost 1,700 replacements. This added considerable strength to the defense, which was able repeatedly to repulse the Chinese attacks during a long day of fighting. At dusk, the Chinese fell back toward Dong Dang: "One must admit, however," noted the Legion's diarist, "that the retreat was orderly and that the Chinese manoeuvred well."[74] But there was far worse news when the French came to count the day's casualties—General de Négrier had been gravely wounded in the chest around three-thirty in the afternoon. Command had passed to the commander of the *régiment de marche d'infanterie de ligne*, composed of three battalions of metropolitan infantry, Lieutenant Colonel Herbinger.

On the face of it, Herbinger's elevation to the command of the brigade should have caused few problems. A native of Alsace graduating first in his class from Saint-Cyr in 1861, Herbinger was considered one of the French army's coming officers. His record combined battlefield experience in Mexico, the Franco-Prussian War and the Commune with an academic knowledge that caused him to be named to the prestigious post of professor of tactics at the French war college, the Ecole Supérieure de Guerre. Herbinger was summoned in late afternoon from an outlying village that one of his battalion had been defending, informed of de Négrier's condition, and told that, as the next highest ranking (the two other battalion commanders were majors, and Négrier had undertaken the campaign without a colonel as second-in-command), he was now in charge. He called a conference of his officers, and announced that Lang Son was to be abandoned that very night, and that the force would fall back on the delta as quickly as possible. What could not be carried was to be destroyed, which was virtually everything.

This order produced indescribable confusion: "An unbelievable spectacle awaited us," wrote Bôn-Mat as his legionnaires fell back through Lang Son. "Barrels of wine and tafia, cases of biscuits and meat, sacks of coffee, flour, open, gutted, overturned, lay over the floor." Some of the legionnaires were unable to resist the opportunity for a free drink, so that

drunkenness would soon lay out several. In the town, there was chaos, and it seemed that this decision to leave Langson had unsettled everyone. Here, one threw the artillery pieces into the water, as we had neither coolies or mules to transport them, despite the protestations, the supplications of the commander who promised to have his men drag them. Further on, the brigade chest, which contained perhaps as much as six hundred thousand francs which arrived two days ago, was also sacrificed. It would have been easy to save this money by giving a few pieces to each man. In the citadel, we opened the boxes of cartridges and threw them in the lakes.[75]

(This was all recovered in 1945, when the lakes were dragged for materiel thrown in after the Japanese takeover of Indochina in March of that year produced an almost identical panic.)

In his subsequent court-martial, Herbinger claimed that he had not distributed the money among the soldiers because they were already loaded with cartridges, and because it would have caused further disorders as so many of them were drunk: "Lieutenant colonel Herbinger cites the 2nd Battalion of the Legion as being particularly drunk."[76] Legion Major François Georges Diguet vehemently denied that any more than fifteen to twenty of his men were drunk, "and this because he had not been informed that the barrels of tafia had been abandoned by the intendence without taking the precaution of breaking them open, and because the sutlers gave the alcohol which they could not carry in the precipitious flight to the men."[77] Maury's group stayed sober enough to chop down the flagpole at the top of the citadel, and then helped themselves to bullets. "Then we opened the trunks. Those of the recently arrived officers were full of clothes, shoes, etc. We had to abandon almost everything. . . . We were upset. In the streets, on the road, where we marched quickly, we met several soldiers, lying on the ground, completely drunk. We disarmed them and abandoned them." The officers were apparently furious at Herbinger's decision. One, Major Servière of the *Bat' d'Af*, offered to hold Lang Son single-handed.[78] "Let no one run away with the idea that we simple soldiers did not feel the sting of defeat," wrote Le Poer of this retreat from Lang Son. "Indeed, we felt it, and sorely too."[79]

The French retired back to the delta with no serious mishaps—the Chinese shadowed their retreat, but offered little more than harassing fire. Nevertheless, the strategic situation for the French was fairly desperate. The Chinese had their tails up, fully twenty thousand Annamese volunteers had flocked to the Chinese banner after de Négrier's defeat and the Kwangsi army had begun preparations to attack Bac Ninh. To the northwest, even after the relief of Tuyen Quang, the Yunnanese troops and Black Flags retained the strategic initiative, and Annamese were also streaming in from the country around Hung Hoa and Son Tay to join them. So while Chinese losses had been high, so were the numbers of their replacements. Faced with a renewed and vigorous revival of Chinese military fortunes, the French would find it virtually impossible to sustain a long and unpopular war in faraway Tonkin, especially after Ferry's Indochinese policy had been discredited and his government tumbled.[80] However, despite their resounding success, on April 4 the Chinese signed a cease-fire, the preliminary step to the Treaty of Tientsin in June, which ended Chinese claims upon Tonkin once and for all. This apparently inexplicable Chinese surrender was due to a combination of factors, which included ignorance of the military situation in Tonkin, fear of a war with Japan over Korea, and an uprising in Chinese Turkestan.

However, the major fallout from the retreat from Lang Son was felt in Paris, not Tonkin. News of the retreat fell like a thunderclap on the Chamber of Deputies, where the president of the council of ministers, Jules Ferry, asked for two hundred million francs in extra credits to prosecute the war against China. The right abused him for sending troops with insufficient support, while the left, led by the fiery and intemperate Georges Clemenceau, accused him of nothing less than high treason. With those in the Chamber of Deputies shouting "Ferry Tonkin!" while the crowds without hurled less flattering denunciations, the Ferry government perished in a hostile vote of 308 to 161. The ex-prime minister escaped by a side door, his political career shattered. And for the first time in the history of the Third Republic, a government was toppled over its policy of colonial expansion.

Yet the story was not yet finished. The army in Tonkin required a scapegoat, someone to blame for the dramatic reversal of fortunes. Not surprisingly, the popularity of de Négrier and his glorious wound deflected the wrath of the officer corps from the general and his controversial order to invade China to the unfortunate Herbinger and his precipitous but far more logical decision to avoid entrapment in Lang Son. A court-martial, in a bizarre decision that seemed to foreshadow the "guilty, but with extenuating circumstances" verdict of Captain Dreyfus's 1899 trial, declared Herbinger incompetent to command, but recommended against his dismissal from the army. They need not have bothered, for he died a broken man in 1886.[81]

De Négrier's reputation survived his defeat at Bang Bo intact. The news of the Chinese sellout at Tientsin provoked a palace revolution in Hue. A conflict between French and Annamese forces caused the fourteen-year-old king to place his treasury on a white elephant and flee to the mountains to organize resistance against the French. The French merely named a replacement and split the Empire of Annam into three territories of Tonkin, Annam, and Cochinchina. Cambodia had been a French protectorate since 1863, and Laos was incorporated into French Indochina between 1893 and 1896.

The Pacification of Upper Tonkin

The role of the Legion in Indochina was far from over, however. "Now that France has Tonkin," observed one British diplomat, "all she has to do is conquer it."[82] This would not prove an easy task for several reasons, the first, of course, being the obstinate refusal of the enemy to concede defeat. Although the Chinese regular forces had withdrawn, the Black Flags still lurked beyond the delta in the Tonkinese highlands, where they were to pose the major, and persistent, military problem that the French were to face in Indochina into the twentieth century. Unfortunately, de Négrier's example of indiscipline made the French parliament deeply reluctant to vote funds for further action in Indochina. Therefore, the subsequent campaign was hampered by limited forces, and forces with limited means, as well as by colonial officials who often suspended operations, or limited their scope, to maintain the fiction for the benefit of French parliamentary and public opinion that Tonkin was pacified.[83]

Jean Pfirmann got a shock when he arrived in Tonkin in 1888, to discover that

the men there did not have the martial air common to legionnaires. Without their uniform, one easily would have taken them for brigands. Each one had a rifle without a bayonet or a sling. He possessed neither belt nor cartridge pouch, but carried six packets of bullets in the pockets of his tunic. We frowned to see such a penury of materiel and munitions. . . . We were not at ease. When you do not feel a bayonet at the end of the barrel of your rifle, you believe yourself half disarmed.[84]

The French were also forced to adapt to new forms of warfare that would be quite unlike the set-piece clashes of forces, relatively familiar to French officers, that characterized the campaigns of 1883–85. Now began the slow work of pacification, small-unit actions against pirate redoubts planted deep in the tropical highlands.

The inaccessibility of these pirate bases posed the second problem. "Try to fancy geraniums, fuchsias, and such like flowers, thirty feet high and with trunks twice the thickness of a man's body," Martyn wrote of the forests in which the Legion operated.

Imagine, multiplied a hundred thousand times, the scent of an old-fashioned flower garden thickly planted with stocks, wallflowers, pinks, mignonette, carnations, and any other sweet-smelling flowers that come into your mind. Picture gigantic flower-trees whose blossoms start the day a pure white and then change from this successively to the palest of pale pinks, and every other shade in the gradations of red until at sunset the flowers are a deep rich crimson. Palms, bananas, magnolias, frangipannis, shaddocks, and every other tropical tree that you can call to mind, with a great many others that you have never heard of, were to be found there, covered with ivy and climbing plants of all descriptions until the whole was one glorious tangle of scent and colour.[85]

Legion Sergeant Louis Carpeaux found the expeditions through these forests, where the jungle canopy was filled with monkeys, where the sound of mountain cascades thundered in the distance and where one often emerged on rock outcroppings that presided over cloud-filled valleys, almost overpowering: "The pirate is indispensable to the savage poetry of this splendid nature," he wrote.

He binds the heart in a state of perpetual emotion which makes one better feel the beauty of the landscape. The effect was so impressive that the column, like an immense reptile, slithered noiselessly through the somber bamboo or above the sunlit clouds. Even the legionnaires, despite their skeptical nature, avoided speaking, conquered by the mysterious charm which enveloped them.

He conceded, however, that as campaigning country it left much to be desired: "What creates the *thrill* in this land is that one can never see what is in front of him."[86]

Most of the remaining problems, logistical and tactical, would follow naturally from the very nature of the country. One solution, of course, was simply to leave the pirates alone in the sparsely occupied, inhospitable and fever-infested mountains. However, their devastating raids on villages in French-controlled areas ruled out that option. Therefore, columns had to be organized to ferret them out of their highland lairs, and here the problems began. The columns were usually made up of legionnaires or marines and *tirailleurs tonkinois,* and therefore were called *"panachées"* or "shandy" columns. This mix was justified tactically because it was thought to combine the solidity of white troops with the availability, mobility and adaptability of native levies. Not everyone was enthusiastic about this practice, however. Mixed expeditions were thought to lack cohesion, and commanders, because they held the Annamese in low esteem, reserved the tough fighting—and the high casualties—for the Europeans.[87] Carpeaux attributed their elevated casualty rates to the pith helmet, believed essential protection against sunstroke east of Suez, but unpopular among legionnaires because it offered distinguishable targets to Chinese marksmen.[88]

For legionnaires, the *tirailleurs tonkinois* appeared to be a military manifestation quite different from the exotic, but nevertheless recognizably virile, native military formations in North Africa. Indeed, most European newcomers found it difficult at first glance to distinguish the sex of the Vietnamese, so alike were they in dress, hairstyle, and in the fact that both men and women chewed or smoked. On their first night out in Hanoi, Martyn and his Russian friend "were waited on by a clean handy native, whose sex we could not agree upon. He, or she, had a rather pleasing face and wore a chignon, so Petrovski addressed it as 'my dear' and proceeded to chuck it under the chin on the sly, which seemed to amuse it very much." However, they were alerted by the hilarity which their conduct provoked at a neighboring table that the waiter was, in fact, a male. "After that, Petrovski guarded against further mistakes by treating all Annamites as men until the contrary was proved."[89]

The apparently feminine appearance of the Vietnamese men caused legionnaires to nickname the *tirailleurs tonkinois* "young ladies," no mere slur, according to Major Chabrol, who campaigned in Upper Tonkin, but a symptom of a fairly serious misapprehension, as on operations it created "a rapprochement favorable to immoral acts, because of the effeminate appearance of the Annamite."[90] Carpeaux's fellow legionnaires called the *tirailleurs tonkinois "les bouzous"*[91]—monkeys—a less flattering name, perhaps, but at least one calculated to cause fewer problems in the field between the Annamese soldiers and sex-starved legionnaires. However, on operation this condescension often turned to admiration at the ease with which the Annamese negotiated the jungle trails, so that Carpeaux's legionnaires began to refer to them as "centipedes."[92]

Martyn found the *tirailleurs* "all very companionable," but nevertheless

a very comical figure until one gets used to him. He wears a chignon, on the top of which is perched a lacquered hat very much like a dinner plate in shape. This is fastened on by red ribbons which pass round the top of the hat and under the chignon, the effect at first sight being very ludicrous indeed. It is beneath the dignity of these warriors to carry anything beyond their arms and ammunition, so our column presented the strange spectacle of natives of the country loafing along at their ease while we Europeans were loaded up like peddlers' asses.

Martyn rated those recruited from the upper Tonkin very highly indeed, but believed those from the delta to be "mere dummies, of no more military value than a Bengali baboo."[93] Silbermann complained that the *tirailleurs* always slept on guard duty and that it took them ten minutes to turn out for an alert.[94] Lyautey observed in the 1890s that desertion was a real problem among the *tirailleurs tonkinois,* a phenomenon which he put down to the fact that the old Gras rifles with which they were armed were mere pop guns compared to the modern weaponry of the pirates.[95]

These columns therefore presented a strange appearance to anyone educated to European warfare. A *tirailleur* usually served as a "point," followed at fifty yards by a "cover point" of four *tirailleurs* and a corporal. However, the main job of the *tirailleurs* was to guard the coolies, no easy task as most had been recruited by force and sought the first opportunity to escape. Bôn-Mat wrote that the coolies in his column had to be "guarded like prisoners." But still so many fled that the order was given to fire on any who attempted to escape: "This measure could, at a distance, seem barbarous, [but] it was justified by the circumstances and indispensable for the survival of the column," he claimed.[96] Half of the coolies in Carpeaux's column slipped away at night. Therefore, the captain demanded replacements from the headman of the nearest village, who gave them a number of women to carry the baggage.[97]

Nor were coolies, who could carry a maximum load of about thirty-five pounds, particularly efficient, especially when compared with the mules used in North Africa but that proved less adaptable in the mountainous terrain of upper Tonkin. Sometimes the coolies could not carry that very effectively—A.-P. Maury reported that those wounded who were able preferred to walk because the coolies so frequently dropped the bamboo stretchers that carried casualties.[98] The presence of so many human porters also made the column slow and difficult to control, and forfeited any element of surprise the French might hope to achieve.[99] Pfirmann found the tendency of the coolies to bolt for the bush at the first report of a rifle a special nuisance as, after combat, the legionnaires were left without tools to bury the dead and to construct bamboo stretchers for the wounded, whom they had to carry themselves.[100]

Next in the column might come the artillery. Opinion upon the worth of artillery in upper Tonkin was divided. One of the great drawbacks of artillery was that its presence required yet more porters—forty per piece! The guns were lashed to frames made of two large pieces of bamboo tied together in an X. "Sooner or later the bamboos break, sooner or later the porters fall and roll with the piece over a precipice or into an arroyo," wrote Carpeaux, who, while admitting that columns could sometimes be immobilized by artillery, still thought artillery useful because the pirates feared them.[101] Le Poer disagreed: "[Guns] are worse than useless to small parties on the trail of the enemy or holding some out-of-the-way position which may have to be abandoned at a minute's notice. . . . We were quite confident that we could maintain our ground with the rifle alone."[102]

In a *panachée* column, the Legion might be given the rear guard. Martyn discovered that this position was often shared by the wives of the *tirailleurs tonkinois*, a length of bamboo over one shoulder balanced by an iron cooking pot on the front and the husband's kit dangling on the rear: "The ladies evidently preferred our company to their own, and no matter how much we hunted them on they would always drop back again until they were just in front of us," he wrote. "When we addressed any remark to them they would smile and show their beautiful black teeth, throwing back some repartee that caused intense amusement to the other women, and would probably have amused us also if only we could have understood it."[103]

Not surprisingly, the French discovered that such columns did not work well. Poor or nonexistent intelligence meant that they wandered the jungle trails for days in sweat-soaked uniforms, fighting mosquitoes, passing the isolated graves of those who had preceded them and, usually in a state of advanced depression, camping at nightfall in an abandoned pagoda whose walls were covered with graffiti written in many of the languages of the Legion, all without locating an enemy. "Despite our marches and countermarches along the river or in the forest, the bandits continued to terrorize and pillage the poor natives in the region," Pfirmann remembered. "And often, after many nights spent in the unhealthy and humid forest, we had to return to the fold without having seen the shadow of a Chinese."[104] Villages or pirate redoubts that the French did discover were often abandoned. When any action did occur, it was initiated by the pirates on their terms.

The greatest danger was that the cumbersome, etiolated columns would be ambushed. Carpeaux's column was sent into one such trap by the same village headman who had given him the women porters. The captain, realizing that the headman was under threat, rejected demands that he be decapitated and only flogged him, perhaps a misplaced act of kindness as a guide later tipped off the pirates of a planned French attack.[105] Fortunately for the French, these ambushes were seldom very costly because the pirates "limit themselves to firing from distances which are more or less murderous."[106] Nevertheless, these halfhearted skirmishes often created pandemonium, with coolies fleeing in all directions and soldiers firing wildly at puffs of smoke in the foliage or at straw hats, which the Chinese liked to attach to branches and move with strings. "I was shot at and I shot back at some smoke," one of Flutsch's comrades answered when asked if he had fought in Tonkin. "The pirates aren't like Moroccans, you never see them. You know that they are around the place where we are sent to be seen. From time to time they fire on us, the column deploys and finds sweet bugger all."[107]

After 1891, the French altered their methods somewhat. Under the influence of Governor-General Antoine de Lanessan, four military territories were created along the frontier with China, each under the command of a colonel who began a slow, progressive conquest of his theater. This required the French to reduce the number of their troops committed to static defense in small posts, either by closing the posts down altogether or by turning them over to armed partisans.[108] Colonel Joseph Galliéni, who arrived in Tonkin in October 1892 to take command of one of these territories, revived the old North African technique of columns converging simultaneously from different directions upon known pirate lairs. He enjoyed a certain success with this tactic, with one group fixing the fortress in front while a second flanked it. But the problems of coordinating movements with columns without liaison, over terrain so difficult that precise timing was difficult to achieve, with unreliable guides, while the pirates would often escape once their position was outflanked, requiring a vigorous pursuit, limited the benefit of this technique.[109] Lyautey, who seconded Galliéni in these operations, also complained that plans were compromised by rivalries among French officers "haunted by the idea that everyone thought only of *stealing* the affair from the other, each manoeuvering to escape the control of the Colonel, to pull off a *coup de main*, and then cover himself with a *fait accompli*."[110]

However, the worst feature of these lengthy columns was the strain they placed upon the legionnaires who made up their main striking force. Despite efforts to reduce their enormous load to a tent half containing several essentials rolled and tied over the shoulder, a rifle and 144 bullets, "it's still too much," Carpeaux insisted. After several days of slashing one's way through thick forests, wading rivers, climbing peaks, falling down, sleeping rough in wet clothes, "there were those who lay down, absolutely refusing to get up even when one spoke to them of pirates. . . . 'I don't give a damn! *Gottfordom!* . . . Let them cut my head off! . . . At least it will be finished!' That was their response." At first, columns would halt until the men could be persuaded to move on or be collected by coolies with bamboo stretchers. When one legionnaire collapsed motionless in Carpeaux's column, his feet were burned with matches in an effort to prod him into action, until it was realized that he was dead.[111] But as this attention to the salvation of each fallen legionnaire slowed the columns, the officers eventually ordered them disarmed and left behind. "The Black Flags . . . may get you if they like," Le Poer's captain told him when he became too ill to march, "but they sha'nt have your arms or ammunition."[112] Not unnaturally, some legionnaires, even those close to complete collapse, still retained enough desire for survival that they threatened to kill anyone who attempted to deprive them of their weapons: "I worked by persuasion," Carpeaux remembered. "I sat next to the poor exhausted legionnaire. We sighed, vomiting in chorus. Then, when he least expected it, I took his rifle and I gave it to my boy, who was furious at having to carry it."[113]

In the evening, the corporal often sent some men back to look for stragglers, but if they discovered anything at all, it was usually the mutilated, decapitated bodies of their comrades. "The worst thing about Tonkin," Flutsch was told,

was that the Legion organized light columns: nothing but a canteen, a haversack and some bullets. There were no wagons, so if there were sick or wounded, it was awful. It was often in the worst spots where, if we left a chap, we would find him butchered by the pirates who came to play at cutting him up or to stick a pug up his ass until it came out his shoulder. Now, we didn't approve of that. So when there was one who was on his last legs, we gave him a drink of tafia and then we said: "Now it's your last mouthful." We would stick the barrel in his mouth and pull the trigger. Then we could go off with a clear conscience.[114]

Le Poer believed that his captain really had no option but to strip dying legionnaires of their weapons.[115] Not only did it deny weapons to the enemy, but also the sight of the mutilated bodies or heads of these legionnaires, which his captain forced everyone to look at, served to discourage straggling and stoke a desire for revenge. Carpeaux believed that the pirates missed a trick by failing to capitalize on the excessive fatigue of the legionnaires: "If they had made war to fight, we were so exhausted that they could have massacred all of us," he claimed. He also observed that of fifty legionnaires who set out on an operation, barely ten were in a fit state to fight when they reached the objective.[116]

It was clear that the system of large columns sent on extended operations, quite apart from their vulnerability and the fact that they forfeited surprise, therefore allowing the pirates to escape, was extremely costly in manpower, especially Legion manpower. Major Chabrol was of the opinion that these large columns were "necessarily sterile if the instrument meant to carry them out is worn out after fifteen days." Smaller columns shorn of all but a few coolies operating for five or six days, he argued, would be far more profitable, for the men could be pushed to the brink of endurance and "they can recuperate and eat better when they return [to base]."[117] Carpeaux believed that this unacceptable attrition of legionnaires even before they could be brought into combat caused Galliéni to alter radically the French strategy in upper Tonkin.[118] That was probably part of the motivation for his shift to the *"tâche d'huile"* techniques for which he became celebrated in colonial military circles—that is, the establishment of a series of small posts which, acting aggressively, would eventually spread to control the surrounding countryside like an "oil spot." It was also apparent, as Bugeaud had discovered a half-century earlier in Algeria, that he needed to control the population if he was to deprive the pirates of a livelihood. Smaller columns offered the added advantage of transforming operations into small local affairs that escaped attention in Hanoi and allowed colonial administrators to perpetuate the fiction that Tonkin was pacified.

The key to the success of this new tactic appears to have been the emplacement of posts within close striking distance of the pirate hideouts. Nevertheless, these methods were not invariably successful. Carpeaux, who participated in several operations in 1894–95 near Lao Kay, suggested that these smaller operations, while perhaps more rapid and less exhausting, were also less popular among legionnaires because they increased the risk of ambush and especially of capture, a fate dreaded by all legionnaires. The absence of coolies to increase mobility also appears to have revived the heavier loads.[119] Furthermore, while the French columns were certainly more rapid, they seldom appear to have been very secret—the pirates were able to collect intelligence in French posts by mingling with the population on market days (indeed, Carpeaux recognized the corpse of a man from whom he had purchased a chicken after an attack on a pirate fortress), threatening or bribing guides, or simply placing sentinels or dry bamboo, which crackled underfoot, or pointed stakes along the approach paths that the French invariably took.

The presence of *congaï* in the French posts, Prokos believed, invariably compromised security and made advanced planning incompatible with secrecy. The most successful operation he witnessed was carried out by eighteen legionnaires who, without warning, were awakened by their captain in the dead of night, marched for five hours and struck a pirate fortress at dawn. Nevertheless, even when surprise was complete and damage inflicted on the foe, many French officers were reluctant to pursue a fleeing enemy either because their soldiers were already exhausted or because they were content with a limited success.[120] The pirates, usually operating in groups of five or six with two coolies to carry weapons, ammunition or wounded, shattered and reunited like fragments of mercury, and if seriously pressed could always find sanctuary in China.

Indeed, operations close to the Chinese frontier always ran the risk that the local pirates might be seconded by Chinese soldiers. When on August 23, 1892, the commander of the post of Phuc Hoa, near Cao Bang, fell into a formidable ambush, the only exit open to him was to lead what was left of his ninety-one-man force, which included twenty-seven legionnaires, across the frontier into China to seek the shelter of the Chinese frontier post of Bo Cup. The Chinese commander reluctantly offered the French troops asylum. Hardly had a few minutes passed than the reason for his hesitation became obvious—the gates opened to allow the return of a large number of his troops, their faces and hands black with powder, two or three of whom approached the lieutenant in charge of the legionnaires to express their surprise at seeing him alive and to compliment him upon his bravery.[121]

When Colonel Galliéni, who commanded the 2nd Military Territory at Lang Son between October 1892 and the summer of 1896, complained to the Chinese commander of the military region across the frontier, the picturesque and venerable Marshal Sou, about the raids and incursions of Chinese troops into Tonkin, he was told, "I am terribly sorry, but I can do nothing. My troops are impossible, no discipline. How can I control them? Even so, if you can catch any of my soldiers causing problems, don't hesitate, I pray you. Shoot them! And shoot them without a trial!" Of course, no Chinese troops were ever caught. So Galliéni's solution was to replace the well-mannered marines in the frontier posts with legionnaires, who soon gave the Chinese a dose of their own medicine by raiding four villages in China. When Marshal Sou protested, Galliéni apologized profusely: "Those soldiers are foreigners," he told the Marshal. "Unfortunately they have no discipline. So, how can I control them? If you catch them, don't hesitate, I pray you, and shoot. Shoot without a trial." This response earned the highest compliment from Sou, that Galliéni was worthy of having been born a Chinese. Needless to say, Galliéni had no further problems with Chinese incursions.[122]

The operations gradually applied extra pressure on the pirates at a time when the security provided by French posts for the Annamese and *montagnards* populations allowed them to sever their links with the pirates, with whom they had no linguistic or political ties, and remove the threat of reprisals. Carpeaux believed that the policy of offering twenty piastres for the head of a pirate enjoyed great success. So many heads were brought in that he wondered "if to earn 20 piasters, the *nhaqués* [peasants] didn't settle a few scores among themselves." These heads, displayed upon posts, together with those of pirates captured and publicly decapitated before the assembled village, were hideous, but effective, propaganda for French rule. They also provided some distraction for legionnaires—one payday, Carpeaux saw one drunken legionnaire throwing rocks at a grisly head and shouting, "Come down from your bamboo, you good for nothing!"[123]

By the end of 1897, a combination of French pacification techniques, the legalization of the opium trade, and improved diplomatic relations with China, which sought to cut off the flow of pirates from the north, had succeeded in ending much of the turmoil in Tonkin. Nevertheless, success could never be complete because the difficulty of controlling the vast, inaccessible reaches of Tonkin with a relatively small number of troops, because of continued turmoil in China, and because the market in China for slaves, buffalo and especially opium, which the pirates brought up from the south, often with the connivance of corrupt Chinese officials, remained buoyant. For these reasons, the peace in upper Tonkin was always fragile. 1901 witnessed a revival of Chinese incursions, as did 1914, while the pirate De Tham operated there with some success between 1908 and 1910. The relative triumph in Tonkin owed much to the stamina of legionnaires, and to a certain extent to their ability to adapt to jungle conditions. But the pirates were not a formal military opposition in the classical sense, in that they were essentially bandits who sought to live to fight again another day. After the regular Chinese troops had withdrawn in 1885, the Annamese population slumped into a political indifference shaken only by the Japanese victory over the Russians in 1905, which sent a signal throughout Asia and beyond that the whites were not invincible. Political indifference in Indochina was not necessarily a condition that would last forever, however. This does not seem to have worried the confident colonialists at the turn of the century, in part because imperial wisdom considered the Vietnamese to be poor soldiers. A half-century later, however, the French would be forced to revise their opinions.

Chapter 12

"THEY FOUGHT LIKE UNCHAINED DEMONS" — THE LEGION IN DAHOMEY

THE TWO MAJOR campaigns to conquer Dahomey (modern Benin, which occupies the western frontier of Nigeria on the Gulf of Guinea in West Africa) and Madagascar appear to have been tailor-made for the Legion, even though, as in the case of Tonkin, they were plucked from their familiar North African setting and deposited in parts of Africa normally reserved for the French marines. For colonial commanders, the Legion provided a repository of troops eager to take up the challenge, trained to accept hardship, and whose sacrifice, if events took an unexpected turn for the worse, would raise hardly a murmur of protest in France. These campaigns also appeared to offer a challenge that the Legion was ideally equipped to handle. The relatively small numbers of legionnaires involved—a battalion plus reinforcements in each case—permitted commanders the luxury of taking the field with the cream of their soldiers.

In perhaps one important respect, these campaigns offered a challenge unworthy of the Legion—the Dahomans, although courageous, adapted badly when challenged by a modern army, while the Malagasies were not even courageous. Yet the difficulties of terrain, disease and the inability of the French to work out suitable logistical support transformed both campaigns into tests of endurance, litanies of sacrifice, which ranked them among the most arduous of expeditions. Therefore, this chapter will remain faithful to one of the themes of this book, which has been to consider the history of the Legion not simply as a series of vigorously heroic acts, but rather to place its performance within the context of the command and logistical environment in which it operated. These campaigns also allow a better appreciation both of the role reserved for the Legion in France's imperial military system and its contribution to the success of those expeditions.

The selection process for these expeditions followed what was, by now, a fairly familiar pattern in the Legion. Since December 1884, the Legion had been comprised of two regiments, the *1er étranger* with its headquarters at Sidi-bel-Abbès and the *2e étranger* at Saïda. Each regiment was asked to furnish four hundred men to make up an eight-hundred-man *bataillon de marche.* Frederic Martyn, repatriated to Sidi-bel-Abbès after contracting blackwater fever in Tonkin, found Algeria "pretty comfortable generally, but the monotony of the life soon began to oppress me again, and I was thinking of putting it to Petrovski that we would do well to volunteer again for Tonkin." The two men were dining in town on one July evening in 1892 when they read in the *Echo d'Oran* that a Legion battalion was to be sent to Dahomey. "We made short work of the remainder of the dinner," rushed back to the barracks, and the next morning volunteered "with nearly every man in the depot" for Dahomey. Martyn believed that they owed their selection to the fact that they had seen service in Tonkin, and that they knew the designated battalion commander, Major Marius-Paul Faurax.[1]

The situation in the *2e étranger* was similar. When news of the expedition arrived in Géryville, all the officers of the second battalion volunteered. To escape from his *embarras du choix,* the colonel designated the most senior captain, lieutenant and second lieutenant, who then proceeded to select their company: "The men chosen with extreme care form a remarkable force," wrote Lieutenant Jacquot in his diary. "A good number of them have already seen action in Tonkin. All are robust, full of ardor, dream only of bumps and bruises, and, in a word, are delighted to give up the monotonous and too regular life of the barracks to run through the bush."[2]

In fact, this method of forming regiments or battalions *"de marche"* from volunteers was not uniformly praised in the Legion throughout the 1890s. A major objection might be termed a philosophical one. The practice that treated the Legion regiments as "reservoirs from which one draws men as needed, completely ignores the moral force, the esprit de corps which provides the cohesion and the unity of the company," one officer wrote, "important factors for the leader and which one tries so hard in France to create and maintain." It was infinitely preferable, some officers believed, to send constituted companies, using volunteers simply to replace men too young or unfit to campaign.[3]

However, with the exception of the 1893 Siam crisis, when an established Legion company was sent to the Far East as part of a *bataillon de marche* of four companies, the Legion practice was to create new formations for each expedition, for several reasons. The most obvious advantage of this system was that it allowed a unit to campaign with its best elements: "Of all things I . . . consider it to be essential that the very best men in our army should alone be employed in such a war," the commander-in-chief of the British forces from 1895 to 1901 and experienced colonial hand General Viscount Garnet Wolseley wrote of "savage warfare."

Call for volunteers, and take 100, or perhaps 200 men out of as many battns. as may be necessary to make up the number of men required, select the best offrs. from each battn. to command their own men, and then select from the army generally the best F.Os. and regtl. staff. With battns. formed in this manner, your loss will be much less than if so many battns. are taken because they are 1st. on the roster, and the war will be brought to an end in a much shorter space of time.[4]

Wolseley's advice was easier to implement in the French army than in his own, for the regimental system was simply not as sacred there as in the British forces. While there had been an emphasis upon the development of a regimental spirit in the metropolitan French army after 1871 with the establishment of regimental histories and *salles d'honneurs* in each regiment, the transfer of personnel among the army's many numbered regiments gave the French forces a national flavor and discouraged the creation of "prestige" regiments of the sort that existed in Britain or Germany. In the colonies, the sense of regimental affiliation was stronger. But even there, in both the French marines and the Legion, the regiment was essentially an administrative unit that mothered numerous companies scattered over the countryside, and even over the world. The standard practice when called for a campaign was to form companies, such as those furnished by the Legion in the Western Sudan in 1892–93 and in 1894 in the Sudan and Guinea, battalions or even regiments *de marche* from among select volunteers.

In many respects, this made good sense, both militarily and administratively. Militarily, it is altogether likely that a system that was desirable in other units, especially in those containing conscripts who could not be sent against their will on imperial expeditions, became virtually a requirement for the Legion in this period because it counted a greater percentage of discipline problems, alcoholics or men whose employment posed political problems than did the French marines, or even a French line regiment. This was because the Legion had become, in part, a dumping ground for problem soldiers from other corps. However, the Legion's real disadvantage in this respect was that it had fewer places to hide its problems. As will be seen, a few might be retained in the depot companies at Sidi-bel-Abbès or Saïda, or exiled to an auxiliary service in some remote garrison in the south of Algeria. Yet the Legion lacked the panoply of administrative and service units, available to regular French regiments, that could serve as repositories of reluctant or incapable warriors. Therefore, selection formed an essential component of Legion effectiveness.

However, while the desire to go to war with the best soldiers may have motivated some commanders to retain the volunteer system, politics and the public image of the Legion also appear to have been a major concern of the war ministry, which, in 1894, argued that

Without overlooking the disadvantages of the unités de marche, *it is noticeable that the Legion companies contain a large number of men from Alsace-Lorraine. The dispatch to the colonies of constituted companies has as a consequence the serious disadvantage of furnishing a pretext for the rumors spread in Alsace-Lorraine that soldiers of the Legion are exposed to particular dangers and thus in this way to reduce one of the principal sources of Legion recruitment. For, it would be very difficult to send off a constituted unit while eliminating men from Alsace-Lorraine because of their origins.*[5]

In other words, the Legion may have been an *"unité de sacrifice,"* but some legionnaires were obviously considered more expendable than others.

However, the debate was not simply over how the Legion was to be packaged in these colonial expeditions. Some Algerian commanders argued that they should not be sent at all, that the Legion was simply too small to hold the fort in North Africa *and* loan battalions to the marines for colonial expeditions. From an administrative viewpoint, it was difficult to transfer entire companies from Algeria, where commanders objected that garrisons were already dangerously overstretched. If an entire company were taken away from a garrison, it might be impossible to find another to take its place. Therefore, it was probably easier to bleed units for soldiers than to transfer them wholesale.

Yet, according to the commander of the 19th Army Corps in Algeria on the eve of the Dahomey expedition in 1892, "bleeding" did not solve the basic problem of the lack of manpower. Requests for Legion reinforcements for Dahomey and the Western Sudan would

more or less exhaust all their vital forces. As a result, these regiments will be unable for an undetermined period of time, not only to satisfy the demands of Tonkin but also to assure the security of our frontier in the Sud Oranais, where they are the most solid troops. Furthermore, in the event of mobilization, it will be impossible to form the two battalions of 1,000 men which the Legion must furnish to the mobilized 19th corps.[6]

This advice was ignored, and Legion units continued to conquer and to provide permanent garrisons for areas outside of North Africa because colonial soldiers preferred not to count exclusively upon native troops for the conquest and maintenance of the empire. While native troops had many qualities—endurance, adaptability and few logistical needs—they were believed to lack the solidity of white troops. Legionnaire Henri Paul Lelièvre may be accused of prejudice when he insisted that he admired the courage of the Senegalese *tirailleurs* in Dahomey, but that they had been recruited in haste and poorly trained. "They lacked one thing, discipline," he wrote.

There is no way to make a Senegalese do what he doesn't want to do. They have no respect for their leaders, whom they treat as equals. Also, during combat, [the leader] has all he can do to keep them on line, because they were mediocre. These tirailleurs always wanted to charge the enemy with the bayonet. . . . We sometimes took losses because of their errors. . . . They advanced and got in front of the Legion companies. This kept us from firing while they attracted the fire of the enemy.[7]

Lieutenant Colonel Albert Ditte explained the quasi-official attitude to native troops to an audience at the French war college in 1905: While he cautioned that military virtues were not the exclusive preserve of Europeans, ". . . the inconvenience of native troops lies in the confidence that one can have in their fidelity to the national flag. This is precisely why the employment of Europeans [in colonial expeditions] is indispensable."[8]

Therefore, discipline was fragile because the political reliability of native troops was suspect. When this suspicion of disloyalty was combined with a lack of discipline, the potential for disorder was obvious. Lieutenant Colonel Jean-Louis Lentonnet, an officer of the Algerian *tirailleurs* who participated in the Madagascar expedition as part of the *régiment d'Algérie,* stated the problem more bluntly. Strict discipline with native troops was essential, he believed, because "it is a small step from scrounging to brigandage. The light column [in Madagascar] is a real Tower of Babel, where the French are in a minority. What would happen to us if the authority of the officers was no longer obeyed?"[9] This was not mere paranoia or racism, for pillage and especially the capturing of slaves was so much a part of the French military system in Africa, especially in the Western Sudan, that many campaigns there probably owed their inspiration at least as much to Attila the Hun as to Napoleon. "Basically there was little difference between a *sofa* [African warrior] and a [Senegalese] *tirailleur,*" writes the Canadian historian A.S. Kanya-Forstner.

The prospect of plunder was the principal reason why the latter served the French, and the regular distribution of captives was the most efficient way to secure his continued loyalty. That female prisoners were euphemistically called épouses libres *did not make them any less a form of payment. When [the governor general of the Western Sudan] tried to stamp out the practice [in 1894] by punishing some of the officers responsible, the main concern*

*of his military commanders was to prevent the news from reaching the
tirailleurs lest they be encouraged to desert.*[10]

Even the Legion slipped effortlessly into this local custom when it
campaigned in the Western Sudan. For instance, in July 1894, when the
French sacked the village of Bossé in the Mosi territory of West Africa, the
1,200 captives were distributed as slaves to the victors, with the legionnaires on the expedition given first pick just after the officers.[11] Lieutenant
Charles Mangin, destined to be one of France's most distinguished generals
in World War I, was given thirty days' detention in October 1894 for
having distributed slaves among his servants and interpreters.[12] The primary danger posed by pillaging, at least from the viewpoint of the French
officers, was that it could easily dissolve the fragile notions of discipline
among the native soldiers. Therefore, white soldiers were included in these
expeditions to ensure that discipline was maintained as much as for their
fighting qualities.

In 1894, officers even experimented with using legionnaires as cadres
for black troops, an experiment which, in the opinion of Lieutenant Mangin, was unsuccessful: "Of 20 men from the Legion, 14 were casualties,"
Lieutenant Mangin wrote after the action at Bossé. "Despite this, the impression of everyone was that the legionnaire is useless when he is isolated
in the midst of natives and that this idea of '*encadrement*' of Sudanese
troops by the Legion is a great mistake. . . . This magnificent troop must
operate with its own cadres. To disperse it is to destroy it to no benefit."[13]
So while French military power abroad relied upon a heterogeneous soldiery, and even boasted of the virtues of this system, it is clear that the
officers did not entirely trust it—an ironic conclusion in many ways, as the
most notorious case of military indiscipline in Africa, the revolt of the
Voulet-Chanoine expedition of 1898–99, occurred when white officers
mutinied against French government authority.[14]

So white troops were considered an essential ingredient in French im-
perial expeditions because they were disciplined and reliable. The question
then became, where were they to be recruited? The metropolitan army in
France was one source of white manpower. As has been seen, numbered
French regiments had provided the mass of troops for the conquest of
Algeria in the 1840s, and had even participated in the Mexican expedition.
Yet with the end of the Franco-Prussian War and the extension of conscription in France, it became more difficult for the government to cast
conscripts into campaigns of imperial expansion. Opponents of colonial
expansion argued that these expeditions abroad were a distraction that
took French manpower away from the critical frontier with Germany.
Also, as will be seen in Madagascar, the dispatch of metropolitan units,
even when composed of volunteers, on these often lethal colonial campaigns was political dynamite. Conscription had even turned once elite
units of the *Armée d'Afrique*, like the *zouaves* and the *Chasseurs d'Afrique*,

into pale imitations of their metropolitan counterparts. This basically left only three professional white infantry units more or less available on demand for service abroad—the penal *Bats d'Af,* the *troupes de marine* and, finally, the Legion. Besides, campaigns, especially those in Tonkin, continued to provide a great recruitment draw for the Legion, while it is also possible that the army used the Legion as a means to keep a presence in these domains normally reserved for the navy and *armée coloniale.*[15]

While volunteers for these expeditions were plentiful, legionnaires were not unaware of the risks they ran. As Martyn marched out of the barracks gate on the way to Oran to the strains of the Legion march, "I thought of the lively lot that had marched with me behind that tune on the former occasion, and wondered if I should again be one of the lucky few to return undamaged, finally coming to the conclusion that the odds against me were much greater than when I set out for Tonkin." When the train left the Sidi-bel-Abbès station, only to stop after fifty yards and reverse back beside the quay, "Many of the superstitious legionnaires looked upon this as a bad omen and openly expressed their regret at having volunteered for the job."[16] However, their regrets vanished when they reached Oran and were fêted for four days by the population, all of which reminded Martyn of Rudyard Kipling's poem "Tommy Atkins,"[17] and led him to conclude cynically that "the French people love a legionary—when they want him." Nevertheless, when the transports *Mytho* and *Ville de Saint-Nicolas* pulled away from the Oran docks on August 7, 1892, no legionnaire had taken advantage of the four days of festivities to desert.[18]

The seventeen-day voyage from Oran to Cotonou on Africa's Slave Coast was uneventful. On the 23rd, the ships came in sight of land—a long bar of sand that stretched away toward the east, dotted with palm trees and the low huts of an occasional village—which was the signal for a last-minute frenzy of clothes-washing and a general mucking out of the quarters. The ships soon dropped anchor off the town of Cotonou, whose wharf jutted two hundred yards into sea, and began the slow process of disembarkation by lighter and native canoe, a task that the Atlantic swells transformed into a test of athletic skill. "The clumsy or the fearful have to be careful, for not only do they risk crushing a limb between the lighter and the metal pilings of the wharf, but if they lost their grip on the rope [ladder], it would be very difficult to save them because of the state of the sea and the presence of sharks," wrote Lieutenant Jacquot. ". . . Some men are so terrorized that we are obliged to put them in a basket and hoist them onto the platform . . ."[19] Martyn, too, declared that the landing was carried out "in the exciting and haphazard manner peculiar to the surf-bound West African coast."[20]

However, the relief of a successful disembarkation was quickly replaced by disappointment at the appearance of Cotonou: "I imagined a small town or at least a large village," wrote legionnaire Lelièvre, who instead found a settlement consisting of the aforementioned wharf, six or seven huts, a "factory" that traded in almonds and palm oil for shipment to Europe, a blockhouse, a small military hospital, the house of the French resident and a few wrecked native canoes on the beach.[21] Therefore, it was with few regrets that the soldiers, once they collected their rifles and ammunition, clambered aboard native canoes or small French river gunboats for the twenty-mile trip across Lake Nokoué and into the mouth of the Ossa River to Porto Novo.

Porto Novo, the staging point for the expedition, was the chief city of the Tofa kingdom, a French protectorate at war with its more powerful neighbor to the north, King Behanzin.

At Porto Novo, the disembarking legionnaires were greeted by the Tofa sovereign. "The monarch came and looked on quite affably while we were marched in," Martyn wrote, "and didn't seem at all put out when we laughed at him. . . . He had on a French naval officer's cap, and a richly embroidered frock coat, but nothing else whatever . . ."[22] The "barracks," large hangars covered with palm leaves that sheltered rows of camp beds of local confection, were comfortable enough. However, apart from a small European quarter, the town was a squalid labyrinth of mud-walled, palm-thatched houses separated by narrow lanes teeming with naked children, pigs, chickens and most forms of household rubbish, settled upon marsh ground beside a lagoon. "Add to this that the natives have the detestable custom of burying their dead beneath the floors of their huts, and you will no longer be surprised of the frequency in this town of fevers and pernicious diseases," opined Jacquot.[23] In Porto Novo, light tropical uniforms and pith helmets were distributed to the legionnaires, as well as porters to carry their supplies: "We were told that all were volunteers, and therefore we must go gently with them so as not to put it into their heads to desert," Lelièvre recorded. "We were told that the blacks were always slow to obey, but if one used persuasion they would do everything asked of them. . . . I had no trouble recognizing the one assigned to me . . . he was blind in one eye, and so I could always locate him in the column."[24] Then they were sent to catch up with the bulk of the expedition made up of marines and Hausa and Senegalese *tirailleurs,* who had preceded them.

The expedition was commanded by Colonel (later general) Alfred-Amédée Dodds, a mulatto from Saint-Louis-du-Sénégal, who had graduated from Saint-Cyr and spent his entire career in the French marines. "His face reveals this intelligence of mulattoes," one of his officers recorded, "lit by large eyes showing a great softness."[25] The objective of the French column was the city of Abomey, about eighty-five miles north-northwest as the crow flies from Cotonou. Dodds had rejected a direct march on the capital, preferring to travel up the Ouémé River, which ran north from Porto Novo, and then to march the forty miles overland from Paguessa to take Abomey from the southeast. While this route virtually doubled the distance from the coast to Abomey, it offered several advantages—it avoided the marshes that a direct overland approach would have encoun-

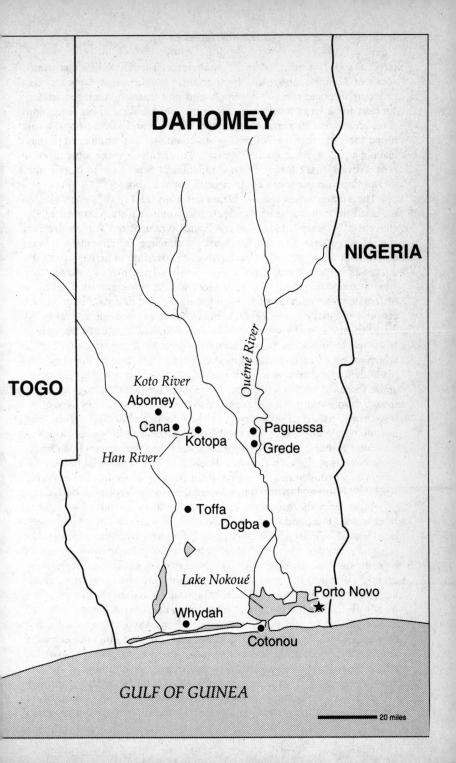

tered, as well as turning Behanzin's main forces, thought to be concentrated south of Abomey. Above all, the river route would reduce French dependence upon porters, facilitate supply and give Behanzin gunboat artillery support for a large portion of his expedition. He divided his forces into three groups of 800 men each by mixing his white and native troops, giving him a force of around 2,700 men, with about an equal number of porters, leaving a reserve of around 900 men at Porto Novo. At the same time, he sent a diversionary force of two companies of Senegalese to march from Grand Popo on the south coast directly toward Abomey.[26]

The French estimated the Dahoman army at 12,000 "men," which included the contingent of female warriors quite naturally known to Europeans as Amazons. However, the French writer Alfred Barbou declared this a vast overestimate, claiming that the standing army numbered about 4,500, including 800 Amazons, capable of expanding to perhaps 10,000 if a *levée en masse* were declared.[27] Nevertheless, by African standards, they were a formidable force, and none more so than the Amazons. This corps of female warriors had been organized in the first half of the nineteenth century, originally from non-Dahoman captives, to provide a loyal bodyguard for the king. However, they had participated in most of Dahomey's wars and by mid-century had become one of his most prestigious units, which meant that many of the kingdom's most important families began to place their daughters in it. The attraction of service with the Amazons, apart from the military prestige, lay in the fact that Amazons were extended most of the privileges accorded to the king's wives: They lived in the large royal palace at Abomey, had their food prepared for them, and anyone who met them on the road had to make way for them. However, they were forbidden relations with men other than the king on punishment of death. But as the king already possessed a fairly substantial harem, this rule in effect condemned them to a life of chastity, a condition they shared with the Legion and that perhaps contributed to the ferocity of both units.

Apart from the Amazons, the Dahoman army contained a standing force of two thousand to three thousand male warriors directed by a special class of military chiefs. In wartime, numbers were expanded by the obligation of all free males to serve. Each soldier carried his own provisions on campaign, usually enough to last about two weeks. Tactically, the army usually went into battle in an arc formation, the most important chiefs fighting on the right wing while the lesser chiefs fought on the left. Each wing was divided into two divisions and each division into several units led by the village war chiefs. By African standards, the Dahoman army was tactically elaborate, able to fire by ranks, offer covering fire, form extended lines from deep columns and undertake flanking movements.[28] However, although around two thousand rifles had been purchased through German arms dealers by 1891, the majority of Dahoman soldiers still fought with blunderbusses, bows and arrows and short swords. And, despite these tactics, it was an army whose main purpose was not to fight pitched battles, but to undertake slave raids on the frontiers of the empire and, in this way, to force villages to accept Dahoman suzerainty. It was an army that had already begun to fall behind its better-armed opponents in Africa, especially the Hausas. Its shortcomings against the French had already been demonstrated in 1890, when they had been repulsed before Cotonou with heavy losses.[29] This should have caused the Dahomans to reassess both their strategy and their tactics before they undertook a major campaign against the French. However, as these battlefield maneuvers appear to have been deeply bound up with the Dahoman social structure and court ritual, it would have required a political revolution to change them.

King Behanzin did not have a good press with the French, in part because his regime, a fairly tyrannical and militarized one, practiced polygamy, ritual sacrifice and cannibalism, hardly the sort of thing to win him many friends even on the anti-imperialist left. They also complained that their subsidies, paid to buy his friendship, had instead been invested in Winchesters and Franco-Prussian War vintage *chassepots,* with which Behanzin had replaced about half of the muskets carried by his troops, 400,000 rounds of ammunition, five "machine guns" (in fact, old French *mitrailleuses*) and six Krupp cannon purchased from German merchants of death in Togo. Furthermore, he had employed these weapons in the attack upon Cotonou in 1890. And while the French had been obliged to digest this unneighborly act and sign a peace treaty with Behanzin in October 1890, basically because the government felt that their parliamentary majority could not survive a war in Dahomey, colonialists in France and Africa were itching for an opportunity to reopen hostilities.

That opportunity came on March 27, 1892, when Dahoman soldiers fired upon the French gunboat *Topaz* as it ventured up the Ouémé into Dahoman territory. The fact that the French resident was on board was deemed to be sufficiently insulting to launch an invasion of Dahomey. In fact, the situation was far more complicated than the French, posing as protectors of the Tofas, cared to concede. Until the 1880s, Abomey had controlled all of the territory running to the coast. However, the French began to demand that Cotonou be handed over to them, claiming this as her right based upon trade treaties concluded in 1868 and 1878. In truth, the clauses upon which French claims to Cotonou rested were the forgeries of French merchants. As these clauses did not exist in the Dahoman texts, Abomey quite naturally rejected them.

The dispute became more aggravated when the French extended their protection to the Kingdom of Porto Novo, which had been a Dahoman tributary since the 1820s. In 1889, the aggressive colonial minister Eugène Etienne sent Dr. Jean Bayol, a navy doctor fanatically devoted to French expansion in Africa, to Abomey to demand that Cotonou be handed over to the French. When he met with refusal, he occupied Cotonou, incarcerated the Dahoman governor, and annexed a large block of territory to the west of Lake Nokoué that included the old slave trading station of Whydah. This was a major strategic and economic blow at Dahomey, for it completely severed the Dahomans from their coastal outlets through which they shipped palm oil, their only cash crop, upon which they depended to support their large army. The French then tried to force the king of Dahomey to renegotiate his tariff agreement, which provoked the attack on Cotonou, which was successfully repelled by the garrison of Senegalese troops.[30]

As usual in matters of colonial expansion, the skirmish quickly outgrew the confines of a local dispute when Berlin protested that the French were attempting to expand their sphere of influence in violation of standing treaties. The explanation for the outrageous French behavior toward the Dahomans, and for the German response, can be found in France's strategic designs in Africa, rather than in any deep desire to corner the palm oil market. The colonialists in Paris had caught a bad case of the jitters because they feared that the Bight of Benin would become a southern front through which the Germans in Togo might advance upon the fabled city of Timbuktu, already targeted for annexation by the French. Meanwhile, the British, already active north of Lagos, would be the first to reach Lake Chad, a land believed so bountiful that French propagandists were already touting it as a potential "French India."[31] Therefore, the conquest of Dahomey, Paris hoped, would sever the ambitions of her imperial rivals in the Western Sudan, while opening a southern approach to support her own expansion westward from Senegal into the Niger basin.[32]

On September 1, the Legion marched north out of Porto Novo along a trail that led through a palm forest and past villages surrounded by fields of potatoes and maize. However, the relative pleasantness of the countryside and the friendliness of the blacks who sold fruit and chickens to the passing troops could not mask the difficulties of campaigning in the tropics. "One hour we would be struggling through a mangrove swamp, and the next forcing our way through tall grasses that reached well above our heads and chopping our way through thick bush," Martyn remembered of this early march. "We carried nothing except our arms and 150 rounds of ammunition per man, and even this light load was as much as we could struggle along with."[33] "The heat is suffocating," Jacquot recorded on September 2, "and our men, although lightly loaded, sweat profusely, so we can hardly advance two miles an hour."[34] For Lelièvre, the march was made especially painful by small insects that had penetrated the skin of his feet, which a local black had to extract with a needle.[35]

And so the march continued for over a week, up before dawn to consume the obligatory draught of quinine, check ammunition and then march north along the east bank of the Ouémé River, stopping at ten o'clock for breakfast, then continuing the march until around four o'clock in the afternoon, when camp was made by forming a square, clearing fields of fire in the bush (a process that usually brought out an army of ferocious ants) and slaughtering a cow for supper, which brought down a flock of vultures from the sky who became more and more persistent as the march progressed.[36] On September 5, Jacquot's company hitched a ride upriver on pirogues dragged by French gunboats. By September 11, the first troops arrived on a piece of high ground overlooking the Ouémé across from the small village of Dogba. Here Dodds decided to establish a camp to regroup the entire expedition before pushing further north.

At five o'clock on the morning of September 19, all the drums, fifes and bugles of the column banged and blew a wake-up call that even the soundest sleeper could not ignore. The men of two of the groups crawled from their tents arranged along the faces of the square encampment (the first group had been dispatched north on the preceding day). Lieutenant Jacquot was hardly awake when he heard shots barely one hundred yards away. He did not have time to finish dressing, but found his revolver and looked for his legionnaires,

who are already running toward us their rifles in hand, some in their undershorts, others with their shirts on. It doesn't matter, they are there, and when Major Faurax comes up less than two minutes later, we have already opened fire on a numerous enemy whose ranks appearing at the edge of the wood fortunately are stopped by the abatis which forms an obstacle between the forest and this side of the camp.[37]

Frederic Martyn had "been fumbling and groping around to get ready for our march" when he heard shots and saw the marine pickets come "bounding into camp with thousands and thousands of black shadows close at the men's heels—the Dahomeyans had surprised us."[38] Men were running in all directions, snatching rifles from the stacks in front of the tents, "it didn't matter which one," according to Lelièvre, and firing into the jungle on the east face of the camp.[39] Legionnaire J. Bern found the tide of attackers rolling out of the jungle in the half light of dawn "truly impressive" and believed that "with troops less steady than the marines and our brave legionnaires, I don't know what would have happened. The least hesitation and all might have been lost. Fortunately, everyone did his duty."[40]

"As fast as we could ram the cartridges in and loose off we fired into the moving black shadows and saw them topple over like corn falling under the sickle," Martyn wrote.[41] When Lelièvre joined the firing line, the Dahomans were barely ten yards away, "kneeling or sitting on wooden stools which they brought with them."[42] "The infantry fires violent salvos," wrote Jacquot, "the artillery shoots canister at barely 100 yards, while the gunboat *Opale* joins in by sprinkling the woods with small shells from her Hotchkiss which pass whistling over our heads."[43] Martyn's group launched the first of several charges at those in front of them,

ramming our bayonets into their bodies until the hilt came up against the flesh with a sickening thud, and then throwing them off to make room for

*another, like a farm laborer forking hay, until we had to clamber over dead
and dying men piled two or three high to get at the living. For the moment
there was no question of those of the enemy who were receiving our special
attention running away. They couldn't run away, for the great mass behind
was pushing them on to our bayonets. It was a terrible slaughter.*[44]

Lelièvre agreed that the slaughter was terrible and desperately one-
sided, largely because the attackers were such poor shots, "for, despite the
rain of bullets which covered the camp, we only counted four dead and
several wounded," most of them caused by snipers placed in treetops.[45]
Martyn agreed that, the snipers apart, "in general the enemy were wretched
shots, which was in part explained by the fact that they rested the butt of
the rifle on the thigh when firing, so that the bullets for the most part
passed over our heads."[46] Despite their poor marksmanship, they had
managed to kill the Legion battalion commander, Major Faurax. And no
one doubted their courage. "The enemy ripostes with an unbelievable energy," Jacquot found. "Bullets and canister do not cause him to retreat an
inch and without a doubt if the abatis had not been there he would have
thrown himself on our bayonets. For two hours the fight continues, the
firing slackening from time to time only to begin almost immediately with
new intensity."[47]

After nine o'clock, the fighting died away. Dodds, fearing that the
Dahomans were merely regrouping for another attack, ordered the artillery
to fire into the forests. Then the line advanced into the jungle, only to find
that the enemy had decamped: "We can now visit the scene of the combat
in security, where 130 or 140 corpses are stretched out, for, one must say
it, the wounded Dahomans are considered as corpses," wrote Jacquot. "We
do not have the means to treat and save them and they are finished off
where they lie. The Lebel bullets have done wonders. We find blacks who,
hidden behind enormous palm trees and believing themselves safe, have
been shot through despite their cover. These wounds are awful . . ."[48]
Lelièvre discovered the ground to be covered with bodies of

*large men of ferocious aspect, covered with hideous wounds and bathed in
blood. Some lack a head and others a leg. I saw several with their heads
split open . . . [by] artillery fire. . . . The wounded who we finished off died
courageously, one of whom had his two legs broken and who had been
taken to the colonel to be interrogated and who refused to talk. Several,
realizing that they were taken, did themselves in.*[49]

A reconnaissance carried out by Jacquot's company discovered thirty more
bodies abandoned by the retreating Dahomans "that our porters dragged
by the feet back to the bivouac."[50] The bodies, together with a large
number of weapons, were collected by the porters into a large pile and
burned.

The French estimated that they had been attacked by a force of four to five thousand, which, rumor had it, had set out to bypass them and strike at Porto Novo, but which instead had been lured into an attack upon what they believed would be an easy target. They had been allowed to approach so closely to the camp because the sentinels at first believed them to be porters on their morning *"promenades hygiéniques."*[51] The next day, the positions of the French camp were strengthened and christened Fort Faurax, in memory of the dead Legion major. But not before an emissary from Behanzin arrived to ask for peace, and to threaten that "the shark who will eat the French" would soon arrive with twelve thousand men and artillery. He also asked for the bodies of several chiefs killed in the assault. "In the way of reply, we took him to the place where his comrades had been burned," wrote Lelièvre. "He was very frightened, believing that we were going to throw him on the ashes." Dodds sent him away with a message to the effect that if "You are the shark who eats the French, then I am the whale who eats the shark."[52] Perhaps it escaped his attention that whales do not as a rule dine upon sharks, but then Behanzin's command of this aspect of natural history was probably no greater than that of the French colonel.

The march resumed up the east bank of the river, slowly, because of the need to carve a path for the artillery through the thick bush, and because of the requirement, insisted upon by Dodds since Dogba, that a trench be dug each evening along the four sides of the camp. Rain fell in buckets, men collapsed on the march and "each night found us utterly exhausted," said Martyn,[53] a situation that was hardly improved by the order to double pickets and the requirement that all soldiers "stand to" in the trenches each morning.[54] "Nothing is more tiring than a night of guard duty in these tropical countries," wrote Lelièvre, who complained of the enervating watch tormented by mosquitoes, distracted by fireflies and frightened by the cries of howling monkeys and nightbirds, while all the time fearing that an attack would find the sentries caught in a crossfire.[55] On September 28, the French gunboats were ambushed unsuccessfully while carrying out a reconnaissance up the river, while on the night of September 30–31, the French camp was briefly, and harmlessly, bombarded by Dahoman artillery from the opposite bank. All of this led Dodds to believe that the Dahoman army was massing at the Tohoue ford, where he planned to cross over the river. Therefore, on October 2, while continuing a reconnaissance up the left bank calculated to deceive the enemy into thinking that he was proceeding northward toward the ford, Dodds quickly shifted a contingent over the river by gunboat and pirogue to establish a bridgehead on the west bank south of the ford. Caught by surprise, the Dahomans could not oppose Dodd's move to the right bank of the Ouémé.

Once across, the French continued their march up the right bank toward the village of Paguessa, but not before Dodds had ordered a substantial reduction of the baggage train to save the porters, whose numbers were diminishing.[56] On the morning of October 4, Dodds set out at six o'clock, marching in two columns, one following a path along the river while the one on the left made its way with difficulty through high grass. About a mile and a half north of the village of Grede, a well-laid ambush broke upon a newly arrived squadron of Sudanese spahis at the head of the column. The horsemen were retreating in some haste when the next unit in the order of march, a company of Hausa riflemen, took a broadside from the high grass, and according to Martyn, "retired to the rear without stopping to make further enquiries."[57] The marines and Senegalese bore the brunt of the attack, with some of the Legion companies too coming on line. Lelièvre found that "their fire was much better directed than at Dogba," especially that of the snipers in the trees, who managed to fell three French officers. However, the projectiles of their Krupp guns passed overhead to crash harmlessly into the jungle behind.[58]

The battle developed into the kind of slogging match seen at Dogba, with the French drawn up in defensive squares supported by small eighty-millimeter artillery served by French sailors firing volley after volley into waves of attacking Dahomans often led by the Amazons. "The uniform of these female warriors was a sort of kilted divided skirt of blue cotton stuff," Martyn recounted.

This garment barely reached to the knees. It was supported at the waist by a leather belt which carried the cartridge pouches. The upper part of their bodies were quite nude, but the head was covered with a coquettish red fez, or tarboosh, into which was stuck an eagle's feather.... These young women were far and away the best men in the Dahomeyan army, and woman to man were quite a match for any of us.... They fought like unchained demons, and if driven into a corner did not disdain the use of their teeth and nails.[59]

Indeed, one marine grabbed an Amazon thinking no doubt that he would claim her as a prize. But she bit his nose with such ferocity that only when mortally wounded by an officer who ran her through with his saber could she be induced to let go.[60]

"All of a sudden, the bugle sounded 'cease fire,'" Lelièvre wrote. "... The Dahomans probably believed that our silence meant that we were out of ammunition and charged again (for, during the combat, they retreated a little), screaming. Then we opened up all along the line with salvos."[61] A company of the Legion was ordered to outflank the Dahoman line on the left. "We had not begun our fire when 300 or 400 Dahomans emerge out of the high grass right in front of us," Jacquot wrote. "Surprised to find troops at a point they believed unoccupied, they do a quick about face and flee for their lives in front of our bayonets, not without leaving several behind."[62] The gunboats on the Ouémé moved up beyond the left flank of the Dahomans, firing first upon their reserves, clearly visible in clearings along the river, and then opened a flanking bombardment of their main battle line. The Dahomans fled northward at about ten o'clock.

The battlefield, as at Dogba, was a tangle of carnage. The high grass, which barely two hours before seemed impenetrable, had been trampled flat. Jacquot estimated that two hundred Dahomans lay dead, including thirty Amazons. "But it is not possible to evaluate exactly the losses of the enemy, as they usually carry away as many of their dead and wounded as they can," he wrote. "But without exaggerating a great deal, one can augment the number of victims left on the field by two-thirds."[63] Lelièvre discovered that their ambush consisted of a series of well-concealed fortifications made of tree trunks, which apparently they had foolishly abandoned to fight in the open against the superior firepower of the French. "All around and inside these defenses [were] dead," he recorded.

Entering one of them I found three Dahomans of which one was still breathing. (I finished him off with my bayonet.) Among these dead, many Amazons. . . . I was surprised to see that most of them were very young girls, hardly formed. However, among them were some old women with flaccid breasts. . . . Two lying next to each other seemed to me to be mother and daughter.

The ground was also covered with fetishes, which, in this case, had decidedly failed to work.[64] As at Dogba, the corpses were gathered in a pile and incinerated.

On October 5, Dodds sent out scouting parties toward the direction of Abomey. "The party I was with scoured the country until late in the afternoon without seeing any Dahomeyans except a dead one here and there—evidently wounded men from G'bede [Grede] who had struggled on until they had dropped and died," wrote Martyn.[65] However, others discovered that the Dahomans held a bridge that crossed a tributary of the Ouémé. A violent rainstorm caused Dodds to postpone his departure until the 6th, when the French once again began their slow movement forward, part of the men keeping watch while the other group slashed a broad path through the foliage.

About two o'clock in the afternoon, Jacquot was sitting in his tent with another officer, reading the newspapers brought in by the post the day before, when he heard several shots followed by an intense fusillade and the pounding of cannons. He hardly had time to look up when a bullet whistled into his tent and ripped into the newspaper he held in his hands. Throwing it to the ground, he rushed out to discover that the Dahomans had decided to make a fight for the bridge over the small stream. It was not a serious one, however, probably because they wished to escape with their guns, with which, Martyn believed, they might have done substantial damage from their fortified positions on the far side of the bridge had they chosen to make a stand.[66] A bayonet charge by the Legion cleared the bridge of defenders. A group of Amazons also broke cover and fled before Jacquot's company,[67] a sign perhaps that Dahoman morale had begun to suffer after two stiff battles. Still, the Dahomans left behind ninety-five dead, while the French losses were six killed and thirty-three wounded, almost as many as the eight killed and thirty-five wounded on the 4th.

As the French passed through the Dahoman camp, they discovered that the Africans had abandoned a large amount of ammunition and supplies in their precipitous retreat.[68] Lelièvre found four prisoners, including an Amazon, tied up in front of Dodds's tent: "The Amazon was very sweet and could have been no more than fifteen years old. She smiled when we caressed her. We put a bucket of water next to her and brought her some food. After being interrogated by the Colonel, and despite their protestations of innocence, they were all shot."[69]

The most difficult phase of the campaign now began for the French as they moved away from their supply line on the river and struck out overland toward Abomey through about sixty miles of thick, unmapped bush. The trail the French followed toward Abomey was decorated with fetishes and broken by prepared ambush sites. Dodds organized his force in three parallel columns flanked by cavalry. However, only the center column marched on the trail, while those on the flanks had to cut their way through the jungle and scrub: "From 8 o'clock in the morning the firing begins and the combat continues until nightfall against a numerous and tenacious enemy, which harasses us, who charges us with the greatest courage."[70] Nevertheless, the Africans' courage often evaporated when confronted by a Legion bayonet charge, which invariably sent them into headlong retreat. The Dahomans were also frustrated by Dodd's marching order, which though slow and fatiguing for the Frenchmen protected his convoy, usually the most vulnerable section of a column.

Yet the French were also suffering. The constant fighting took a small but mounting toll of casualties, while the retreating Dahomans filled in their wells, forcing the French to collect rain water to drink. On October 13, "when we reached the place where it was decided to camp for the night every one was so utterly exhausted that we pitched ourselves on the ground and went to sleep in the open, without troubling to eat or to pitch our tents," Martyn wrote. As a consequence, they were drenched by a night rain, which at least "provided us with satisfaction for our devouring thirst."[71]

On October 14, the French met their most serious test since Dogba. The main trail to Abomey led through the village of Kotopa, which the Dahomans had fortified with defense lines three deep, before it descended to the Koto River. On the low heights beyond the Koto, the defenders had sited their artillery. To avoid having to attack Kotopa, which, Dodds calculated, would cost him heavily, he ordered his artillery to bombard it while he bypassed the village to the north, marching toward a ford over the Koto that his guides believed to be upriver. At eight-thirty in the morning, his troops cut their way out of their bivouac through a tangle of bush and vines. "The heat is overwhelming and our canteens are soon empty," Jacquot recorded. "So we give a great sigh of relief when we emerge upon a vast plateau where we see several hundred yards away the somber line of foliage through which runs the Koto."[72]

As Dodds hurried his square toward the river, the Dahomans on the far side realized they had been outflanked and began to throw artillery shells in his direction, most of which declined to explode. However, when the square approached the Koto, it ran smack into a jungle so impenetrable that Dodds halted it and sent out reconnaissance parties to locate the ford. As the exhausted soldiers brewed up coffee and awaited orders to move, the Dahomans gradually invested his square so that by mid-afternoon he was forced to withdraw to higher ground, where he settled down for the night. "The night is calm, but our spirits are not," Jacquot wrote. "We are in an impasse whose outcome is unknown to us. An inextinguishable thirst keeps us awake all night, which we spend pacing the camp."[73]

On the 15th, the Dahomans attacked the French bivouac, and were repelled with great losses. But the French camp was short of water, the aid station filled with exhausted soldiers, and the convoys from the rear met increasing resistance. An attempt to take the porters under the guard of a company of Senegalese to the Koto to fetch water collapsed when the Dahomans attacked, creating panic among the porters, who dropped their receptacles and fled back to the safety of the French square. A Legion company had to rush to the aid of the hard-pressed Senegalese and lead them back to camp. On October 16, Dodds pulled back from the river and reestablished his camp on the site of that of the 13th.

This stage in the campaign was baptized the "Camp of Thirst" by the French. Lips blackened and cracked, tongues became swollen and men fought to drink from small pools of filthy water. Martyn estimated that 20 percent of the Europeans were suffering from dysentery.[74] On October 17, Dodds sent to the rear a convoy of 200 wounded guarded by two companies of native troops. The French now numbered only 53 officers, 1,533 men and around 2,000 porters. The outcome of the campaign appeared to be in doubt.

However, the Dahomans too were suffering desperately. Not only had their losses on the battlefield been substantial, virtually destroying the Amazons as a fighting force, but an epidemic of smallpox had broken out among the survivors. Furthermore, the Yoruba slaves whom the Dahomans impressed to work their palm oil plantations seized the French invasion and the preoccupation of Behanzin's army to revolt. Indeed, one African historian has estimated that the marauding bands of Yorubas did far more damage to the Dahoman war effort than did the French, especially because they destroyed and disrupted the Dahoman food supply and brought Behanzin's army to the very verge of starvation.[75]

Furthermore, in carrying out his tactical retreat of October 16, Dodds had merely sought to place himself in a better position to attack. Reinforcements of two Senegalese companies brought the column strength to 69 officers and 2,001 men, which Dodds reorganized into four groups of one Legion company and two native ones each, three of which were supported by two artillery pieces each. (The marine companies had melted away from fatigue.) He also reorganized his support services, which had suffered desperately from the diminished numbers of porters. Many had no doubt fallen out from the same fatigue as had affected the soldiers. Others had deserted, like the thirty porters who scurried away from a water party led by Jacquot on October 21.[76] But mistreatment had also taken a toll—Martyn saw one faltering porter skewered by a spahi. However, when he reported this mistreatment to an officer, "all I got from him was a half jocular remark to the effect that the Spahis were queer cattle, and that I had better leave them alone."[77]

On October 23, an emissary from Behanzin arrived before the French camp to ask for peace. Dodds demanded that the Dahomans abandon their defenses on the Koto, which on October 25 they refused to do. On October 26, Dodds formed his men in a square and moved to cross the river, fighting their way through trenches that the investing Dahomans had dug around the French bivouac. However, to avoid the heavily defended main path to Abomey, Dodds took his square into thick brush south of the road and crossed a river. Only on the 27th did the French discover that the river they had crossed was not the Koto, but one of its confluents, the Han River. As Dodds pondered his next move, another emissary from Behanzin arrived and offered to abandon the Koto. Dodds recrossed the Han River, burned Kotopa and then crossed the Koto against only light opposition.

On November 2, Dodds took up his march again, after rejecting negotiations with several emissaries because, he believed, Behanzin simply sought to gain time to raise reinforcements for his army.[78] Beyond the Koto, the forest thinned out and the country took on a more civilized appearance, despite the fact that the villages were deserted. Still, Dodds's desire to keep his forces in a defensible square and to avoid marching along the path where the Dahomans had set up their defensive works made the advance heavy going. A Dahoman defense was broken before the village of Ouakon, but not before Lieutenant Jacquot was wounded. Early on the morning of November 3, the Dahomans mounted a frontal assault upon the French camp that, once again, was bloodily repulsed. Although the fighting died away before noon, they returned on the following morning. The French moved toward Cana, one of the royal cities of Dahomey, which the Dahomans defended with "a tenacity greater, if that is possible, than in the preceding combats. In particular, a band of around 300 soldiers held off all attacks and left the greater part of their numbers dead on the field."[79]

This proved to be the final combat of the campaign. Behanzin opened negotiations with Dodds, who handed him a list of demands that included a war indemnity of fifteen million francs, the establishment of a French protectorate, a French occupation of Abomey, three of his principal counselors handed over as hostages and that Behanzin surrender all of his artillery and two thousand repeating rifles. When, on the 15th, Behanzin returned with only two cannon, a *mitrailleuse,* one hundred rifles, five thousand francs and two "unknowns" as hostages, the French concluded that the king "only looks to trick us and gain time." They broke off negotiations and marched on Abomey barely ten miles away.[80] However, when the French entered it on November 17, it was little more than a smoldering ruin. Dodds, now a general, ordered Behanzin deposed. The ex-king took refuge in the north of the country and gathered the remnants of his army. Realizing that he could not win a military contest with Dodds, he repeatedly tried to gain French recognition for a Dahoman state in the north. Dodds resolutely refused, appointed a brother of Behanzin as king, and in 1894 covered the north with troops. Along with a few resolute supporters, Behanzin was hounded from village to village, fed and protected by his subjects, until he was run to ground by Dodds, who exiled him first to Martinique, then to Algeria, where he died in 1906.

On the surface, at least, it appears that the French were remarkably successful, and remarkably lucky. For the modest outlay of 11 officers and 70 soldiers killed, and 25 officers and 411 men wounded, they had seized Dahomey. Although the number of those stricken by sickness multiplied these figures fivefold, the bill was well within the French capacity to pay. Without a doubt, the Legion had proved the most solid unit—by common consent they fought better than the native troops, while their losses to disease and fatigue of about 35 percent of strength were nonetheless lower than those of the marines, who by mid-October had ceased to exist as a fighting force.[81] Nevertheless, the inability or unwillingness of the French to develop the individual skills of the soldiers to allow them to adapt better to the conditions of jungle warfare was, as in Tonkin, again apparent—whereas Dodds did for a time abandon his march along the main trail to Abomey, he continued to employ regimented European formations in terrain better suited for more flexible, individual tactics. This had contributed to the confusion and fatigue of his march, as well as to his initial inability to break through on the Koto. But while, as has been seen, some attention was given in Legion training to these individual tactics of fire and movement, in Dahomey they were not applied.

In one sense, it is difficult to argue with success. But the campaign, while fairly rapid, had hardly been a pushover. By mid-October, the French were suffering terribly. The marines had suffered horribly, while the Legion, although still very much an effective fighting force, had been weakened by disease and fatigue. Dodds required early success, for by December the dry season meant that the Ouémé was no longer navigable, while the diminishing number of porters would have made it impossible to sustain even a small force that far from the coast.[82] Therefore, the Dahomans should have sought to prolong the campaign, not win it outright. Had they not flung themselves into premature assaults upon French squares but instead enticed the invaders toward Abomey, allowing fatigue and disease to take their toll while concentrating their energies upon supply lines, or in ambushes and night attacks to force the French to spend days marching in fatiguing squares and nights in sleepless alert, then they might have had greater success. After all, in mid-October the French lacked the offensive power to break the Dahoman lines on the Koto, even though they were held by a half-trained, poorly armed and half-starved army that had suffered nothing but devastating defeat since the beginning of the campaign.

So the French won a fairly quick victory, in part because Dodds organized his campaign well, because his supply lines were short, but above all because his enemy made costly mistakes. This is not to say, however, that the outcome might have been very different had Behanzin made certain strategic adjustments (even had that been possible), for his problems were fairly major ones. Given the fact that the Dahomans traditionally saw war as a sporadic activity consisting of little more than a series of raids that aimed to capture slaves rather than kill opposing troops, they sustained their campaign remarkably well, especially given the overwhelming superiority of French firepower. After the failure of their surprise attack at Dogba, they adopted a defensive strategy, which, as has been seen, caused the French great problems at the Koto River. However, they never abandoned their costly tactical rigidity, nor did they think through the implications of increased firepower, both their own and that of the French. For instance, although some of their troops were armed with modern weapons, they continued to use them as if they were muskets, running forward, firing, and then retiring to reload.

Behanzin's attempts to negotiate with the French were dismissed as ploys to gain time to recruit more soldiers and to prolong the campaign into the dry season. In fact, they were probably sincere bids to end hostilities and preserve something of Dahoman independence. The misunderstanding more likely arose from a cultural difference between Western and African notions of how a war should end—Behanzin believed that he was merely being asked to pay tribute in the African manner, while the French wanted complete surrender and disarmament. While Behanzin turned over a few weapons as a token of surrender, it was virtually impossible for him to meet Dodds's demands that he hand over all of them because many were in the hands of chiefs who would not give them up, or to pay a large indemnity in cash that he did not possess. It is also likely that he sent two "unknown" hostages rather than three of his closest counselors because they fully expected the hostages to be ritually sacrificed. After all, that is precisely what the Dahomans did with their hostages.[83]

The anthropological subtleties of the native cultures that they set out to conquer were of far less interest to French soldiers than were the lessons to be drawn from a campaign, especially one as successful as that of Dahomey. And those lessons were fairly straightforward. First, organize the invading force in the proportions of one-third white troops drawn preferably from the Legion or the marines and two-thirds native troops. Second, avoid wear and tear on the infantry as much as possible. This meant having well-organized logistics. In tropical climates, limit the soldier's load to his rifle and ammunition. This was generally the practice in Tonkin, and one that Dodds used in Dahomey. In areas without roads, advancing columns should use river transportation whenever possible, or depend upon porters and pack animals. Third, against poorly armed and organized native forces, mobility was more important than firepower. Light columns that moved toward a strategic objective as quickly as possible enjoyed the best chance of success.

These seemed to be perfectly logical conclusions to draw, ones tested to an extent in Tonkin and confirmed in Dahomey. Unfortunately for the Legion, most of these lessons were ignored, or badly applied, three years later when France invaded Madagascar. For this reason, to those looking back in the aftermath of the Madagascar expedition of 1895, Dahomey appeared to offer a textbook example of a successfully, even a brilliantly, conducted operation. Madagascar, by contrast, was a disaster, the blame for which was laid squarely at the feet of a series of bureaucratic decisions taken by men unfamiliar with colonial conditions. Yet these adverse circumstances once again tested the Legion's discipline and stamina, as well as its worth as an element of imperial conquest.

Chapter 13

"MARCH OR DIE!" — THE LEGION IN MADAGASCAR

THE MADAGASCAR EXPEDITION of 1895 was the most disastrous colonial campaign of the Third Republic. Orchestrated by a number of interests, which included a clutch of deputies from the island of La Réunion intent upon annexation and Catholics who had never pardoned the Hova monarchy its 1868 conversion to Protestantism, the expedition got off on the wrong foot from the very beginning. This need not have been the case, for two months before October 1894, when the French took advantage of a rebellion against Hova rule over the island to present the Malagasy prime minister with a proposal to establish a French protectorate, an interministerial commission had been hard at work planning a military expedition in anticipation of a Hova refusal. So, when in November 1894 it was made official that Madagascar would be forced to accept a French protectorate at the point of a bayonet, military preparations were already well advanced.

Alas, this did not guarantee their efficiency. The source of the problems, the critics believed, stemmed from the decision to confide the expedition to the army rather than to the marines, which won the Madagascar contract simply because they had underbid the navy for the honor of attacking the "Red Isle" by thirty million francs.[1] Although army units had been present during the conquest of Tonkin, and the Legion continued to serve there, army officers had had little experience in colonial campaigning since Mexico. The French foreign minister at the time of the decision to invade Madagascar, Gabriel Honotaux, later excused the mistakes of the war ministry, whose "organization is not made for that, which does not have the necessary contacts with the colonial world so that from one day to the next it can recruit from all over the globe the means which it needs."[2] Due to lack of experience, the army desperately underestimated the requirements of the Madagascar expedition, which helped to explain their low bid.

Nevertheless, it would be unfair to argue that the experience of other colonial campaigns was totally ignored by the committee that met in August 1894 to draw up a plan of campaign. Nor was their plan necessarily a bad one. In one month, representatives of the ministries of war, the navy, the colonies and the foreign office manufactured an invasion blueprint that, they believed, would require twelve thousand men to overcome a semi-organized Hova army of forty thousand. The objective of the operation was Antananarivo (Tananarive), the capital of the Hova people who dominated the northern half of the island, situated in Madagascar's mountainous interior. Majunga on Madagascar's west coast was chosen as the port of entry. Not only did it offer a large harbor, but also it stood at the mouth of the Betsiboka River, which, when combined with its tributary the Ikopa, provided a navigable route about 160 miles deep into the Hova heartland. Estimates put the number of porters and mule drivers required to support them for the remaining distance to Tananarive at eighteen thousand to twenty thousand. However, it was reckoned that this number could be reduced to five thousand by using the *voiture Lefèbre*—two-wheeled metal wagons invented in 1886, which came in kits and weighed about five hundred pounds when assembled.[3] A final, and ultimately extremely controversial, decision taken by the committee was to depend essentially upon white troops, many of them from metropolitan units, to furnish two-thirds of the combatants, thereby reversing the proportions of white and native troops used in Dahomey. Worse, many of these white troops would come out of metropolitan units, which were neither experienced nor acclimatized to campaign conditions outside of Europe.[4]

Knowledgeable marine officers criticized this plan almost immediately. Leaving aside for the moment the heavy dependence upon white troops, something that flew straight in the teeth of conventional colonial military wisdom, their objections were essentially two: The first was that Majunga was simply too far from Tananarive, and possibly on the wrong side of the island. The use of other ports on the east coast of Madagascar as a staging area, in particular the commercial port of Vatomandry through which most of the supplies including weapons arrived for Tananarive, would have cut the distance the invaders marched by two-thirds. A combination of Vatomandry and, say, Tamatave or Andevoranto might also have allowed the French to use separate columns to converge from different directions upon their objectives. The second objection was that the invasion force, which, excluding reinforcements sent later, eventually numbered almost fifteen thousand fighting men and seven thousand porters, was simply too large and too heavy. While the Hova army appeared formidable on paper, there were probably no more than ten thousand of them able to bear arms. A light force of five thousand fresh colonial troops, shorn of the impediments of heavy artillery and wagons included by the committee, and backed by eight thousand mules and porters, could make quick work of the Hovas.[5]

As will be seen, many of these criticisms were proved correct by events. However, the committee invasion plan was not foreordained to near disaster. Many of the problems were not so much with the plan as with the plan's execution. After all, Madagascar was a far larger country than Dahomey and its government was far more sophisticated than that of Behanzin, although the veneer of civilization reflected in the quasi-European aspect of its capital and the Christianity of its Hova inhabitants was a very thin one. Its army, even if not up to European standards, possessed some modern weapons and counted foreign mercenaries, particularly English officers, in its command. Furthermore, the mountainous interior offered many opportunities for even a half-trained force to make heroic stands in high passes and narrow defiles. It was perhaps acceptable for headstrong colonial officers to count upon a large degree of incompetence in their enemy when making campaign plans. But this was a more dangerous assumption to make from the vantage point of Paris, even if the Hovas proved feckless and incompetent beyond the wildest imaginations even of marine officers. The greatest mistake of the committee, however, was not in their choice of Majunga or in the numbers they dispatched to Madagascar. Rather, it lay with their failure to factor the problems of execution, what German military philosopher Carl von Clausewitz called "friction," into their calculations.

From the sea, the Madagascan landfall at Majunga appeared inviting in April 1895, especially after days spent on transports that now smelled strongly of manure and human negligence, and where even the food had taken on the flavor of soot and coal dust. A spit of sand that separated the Indian Ocean from the Bay of Majunga, about five miles wide at its entrance, led from the water to the European quarter, a tiny grid of streets bearing names far grander than the modest architecture of the wooden houses shaded by large mango trees that bordered them appeared to merit. Behind this small concession to order, a modern chaos of native huts spread to the foot of a beautifully wooded hill, whose low summit was crowned by a small fort, crumbled and blackened by the naval bombardment it had suffered on January 15, 1895.

When Captain Emile Reibell invoked officer's privilege to flee his stinking ship ahead of the general disembarkation, he quickly discovered two of the reasons why Madagascar would prove to be a tough nut to crack. His first night on shore, spent in a deck chair that he unfolded on the beach, was a torment of swarming insects.[6] The fact that some of these insects were the cause of "fevers," and therefore constituted enemies far more lethal than most colonial opponents (especially the Hovas) was at that very moment in the process of being discovered. Nevertheless, even the dullest commander abroad had known for years that low swampy terrain was unhealthy and should be crossed as rapidly as possible.

The reason why the expedition's commanding general, Charles Duchesne, had not moved quickly into the relatively healthy highlands became Reibell's second discovery—all was confusion at Majunga. Engineers building a wharf into the ocean soon struck a coral reef that made the approach of large ships impossible, so that the process of unloading became lengthy and tedious. Worse, the Bay of Majunga, which stretched fifty miles to the mouth of the Betsiboka River and which appeared to be a haven of safety to mapbound Parisians, proved to have a swell that would swamp the rivercraft that had been unloaded in pieces and assembled on the Majunga beach. Therefore, the river support system upon which the French had counted to take them deep into the island was scratched from the beginning. Duchesne's next option to move his expedition forward was to turn to porters. However, this proved impossible, essentially because the planners had skimped on this requirement to save money. Frantic efforts to recruit porters from as far away as Indochina collected only 1,400 men, mostly Somalis from the African mainland. Virtually the only successful recruitment of porters was carried out in Algeria by Major François Lamy, a *tirailleur* officer, who produced 3,500 volunteers, mainly highland Kabyles, by March. When news of the expedition's logistical difficulties became known, and especially the failure of Indochina to deliver on its promise of 2,000 porters, a further recruiting drive in Algeria netted 2,000 men, mostly the flotsam of Algerian cities and therefore less handy than the Kabyles. These, together with a few Sakalave tribesmen recruited locally, produced 7,715 "auxiliaries" to support an invading army of 658 officers and 14,773 troops.[7]

While small, this proportion of porters was not substantially different from the numbers projected by the planning committee. Rather than carry goods themselves, however, as was the practice in the remote areas of Indochina and Dahomey, the role of these auxiliaries, especially those from Algeria, was to conduct the Lefèbvre wagons pulled by mules. For experienced colonial soldiers, the decision to include two thousand of these wagons in the provisions of the expedition had been a curious one. Of course, the original purpose had been to employ them at the end of the river network to support the final push toward Tananarive. Perhaps the ministry denizens in Paris had envisioned the Lefèbvre wagons lumbering like Conestogas across the clean Madagascan highlands. But now they had to be used in the tropical lowlands. However, here it was quite obvious that they could not advance without a road. So General Duchesne ordered his troops to build one.

The initial reaction of the Hova government to the French invasion appeared to be a sort of agitated apathy, a fact that the Englishman E. F. Knight put down to the fact that the French had bribed many of the court

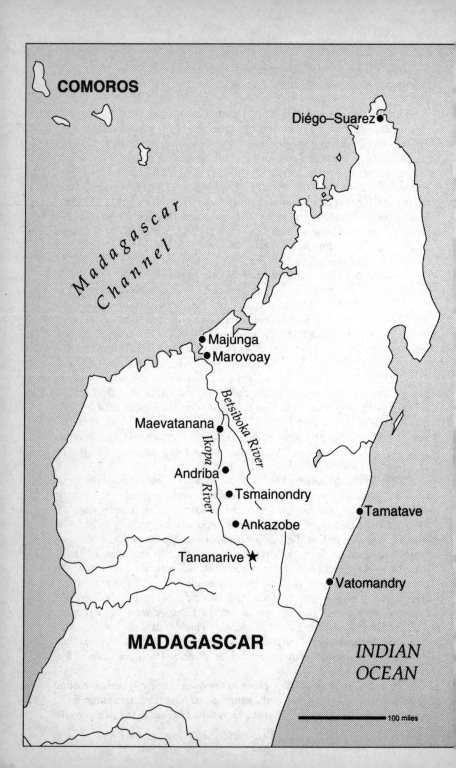

into a state of, if not outright treason, at least one of cautious procrastination.[8] An army was mobilized, which included veterans of the war with the French ten years earlier and younger conscripts, and installed in a large camp outside of Tananarive. "They were a ragged lot, and discipline there appeared to be none," Knight wrote.

When paraded before the PM or some other great man, they used to raise cheers and brandish their arms, while their officers waved their swords with ridiculous gestures and simulated the slaughter of the foe. These were practically the sole manoeuvres, for the drill their European officers had taught them was now neglected as foreign trickery unworthy of Hova warriors.[9]

Apart from a royal guard armed with Remingtons, about half the army carried rusty Snyders. However, only ten to fifteen bullets had been issued per soldier on the pretext that as each bullet would "kill a man," stocks were then more than adequate to deal with the French. The rest of Her Majesty's Forces were armed with muskets and even bows and arrows. "Soldiering in Madagascar for a native was a calling devoid of allurement," wrote the Englishman Bennet Burleigh, who covered the war from Tananarive for the *Daily Telegraph*. "There was no commissariat, no pay, no outfit except a rifle, a few rounds of ball cartridge, and a bit of calico."[10] Indeed, robberies carried out by unpaid, starving soldiers became a real nuisance in the capital.[11]

As the French forces disembarked at Majunga from January to April and advanced inland, the morale of the Hova army, already fragile, eroded further. The Legion contribution to the expedition consisted of a *bataillon de marche* of eight hundred men drawn equally from the two Legion regiments, which were organized into a *régiment d'Algérie* with two battalions of Algerian *tirailleurs*. On May 2, 1895, Marovoay, a town at the mouth of the Betsiboka, was attacked by a French force. Despite strong fortifications, and the fact that they outnumbered the French, the Hovas fled after a bombardment by French gunboats, but apparently not before killing their commander, whom they accused of treason.[12] When on June 9 a battalion of the Legion participated in the capture of Maevatanana, a town on the Ikopa River, from an enemy that bolted so quickly that the legionnaires were unable to cut off their flight, morale plummeted in Tananarive. One Hova soldier told E. F. Knight that at Maevatanana he had been frightened by the "invisible death. . . . 'There was no smoke,' he said. 'There was scarcely any noise, and yet our men fell in hundreds. We believe that there was magic in it.' "[13]

Yet this gloom turned to the brightest optimism when it was learned that Duchesne had stopped his advance to build a road. Knight reported that even the Hovas could not understand why the French did not advance beyond

*sickly Maevatanana. We heard that their men were dying like rotten sheep,
that their transport had completely broken down, and that they were altogether in terrible straits. We were at a loss to understand how any sane
general could keep his force so long in the deadly lowlands instead of
pushing on, without delay, at any cost, to the healthy highlands, which
were but a few day's march distant.*[14]

How, indeed! Each morning at six o'clock the soldiers took up their
shovels, which they had christened "rifle model 1895," and began leveling
the hard red clay into a roadway three meters wide that ran along the right
banks of the Betsiboka and Ikopa Rivers. At ten o'clock work was suspended during the heat of the day, and then resumed until five-thirty in the
evening. Lieutenant Langlois found that his legionnaires, often working up
to their waists in the swamps of the Betsiboka, quickly became depressed:
"Nothing is more enervating, discouraging than these long days, these
interminable evenings spent in the rot of the swamps," he wrote in June,
"in the middle of the slime, beneath a terrible sun, always surrounded by
the same yellow, rocky countryside, always sent to sleep by the plaintive
cries of stray dogs." Furthermore, the logistical system had virtually broken
down, so that legionnaires lived virtually by slaughtering stray cattle left
behind by the inhabitants. Still, this was insufficient to sustain men engaged
in heavy roadwork. Malnutrition, when combined with low morale, hastened death: "Many men are dying at Tsarasotra," Langlois reported a
month later. "All day our men make crosses, dig graves, and every evening
it is always the same funereal and lugubrious alignment of white cadavers.
Nevertheless, we have grown used to these macabre spectacles, and we live
almost indifferently next to that which, two months ago, would have had
us all crying."[15] "Our men are terribly fatigued," Lieutenant Colonel Jean-
Louis Lentonnet of the *régiment d'Algérie* recorded in his diary on June 11.
"The fevers strike down more each day. If this goes on much longer, no one
will be spared."[16] This was no exaggeration. Brigade aid stations and field
hospitals allocated to the expedition, calculated on the basis of 1,500
casualties, proved to be desperately inadequate, in part because the budget
director believed that medical services were an area in which he could make
savings.[17] They soon filled to overflowing with soldiers racked with malaria and dysentery. "Still the roadworks," Lentonnet catalogued on June
15. "We can no longer count the victims. And for what? To drag behind us
the Lefèbvre wagons. Whomever decided to send them to Madagascar is a
real murderer. The cemeteries are filling up. When are we going to march
forward?"[18]

But Duchesne persisted, and persisted. The obvious question to ask is,
why did he not look at other options? For instance, from the beginning,
when it became obvious that his river support system would not work, he
might have shifted his force by transport to the east coast, where as early
as December 1894 the French navy had established a base at Tamatave. A

second option would have been to hold his troops at Majunga or even at
the substantial French naval base of Diégo-Suarez at the northern tip of the
island until the problems of river supply could be sorted out, which they
were, at least in part, by July through a combination of requisition and
improvisation. "How many lives would have been saved if this system had
functioned from the 15th of April, as it was supposed to!" wrote Reibell.[19]
A third option would simply have been to organize a light force sooner,
using the Algerian porters and their mules as logistical support.

Yet he selected none of these options. Perhaps he felt constrained to
follow the ministry plan, or felt the river route too insecure or uncertain to
supply his army.[20] As a veteran of the Second Empire who had fought in
the costly conquests of Tonkin and Formosa, Duchesne simply accepted
lack of food and high losses to disease as a normal part of campaigning.
Nor was he alone: Silbermann was as horrified as his colonel when, during
the 1900 China expedition, a group of young marines came to complain
about the lack of food. "We had no right to complain," he believed, "for
we were all volunteers and when you go on campaign, you don't go to a
banquet."[21] It may also have been the case that tenacity and willpower,
considered essential military virtues, in Duchesne's case, as well as that of
his chief-of-staff, General de Torcy, suffocated imagination and flexibility
of mind. Langlois described Duchesne as "a little taller than average. His
body, a trifle stooped, testifies to the fatigues endured in Tonkin and Formosa. What is immediately striking is his profoundly energetic and tenacious expression. One immediately feels in the presence of an iron will."[22]
In any case, Duchesne's conduct of the Madagascar campaign did not hurt
his career, for he became a member of the *Conseil supérieur de la guerre*,
reserved for the most senior generals.

Unfortunately, Duchesne's iron will proved more durable than the bodies of his soldiers. By August, the work camps along the Betsiboka and the
Ikopa were fringed with forests of crosses and peopled with men emaciated
by dysentery and malaria, who "no longer have the strength to go to the
Latrine," wrote Legion Lieutenant Langlois. "They are living putrescence,
real moribunds."[23] Officers who once attempted to encourage faltering
soldiers with a word or a drink from their canteen now did neither: "The
heart grows hard, [and] in the end one passes by with indifference, head
low, before the victims of fatality," wrote Reibell.[24] By the end of the
month, Langlois complained that Legion companies, normally two hundred strong, had been reduced to "seventy or seventy-five men. Entire units
have disappeared."[25] In fact, the Legion, although badly off, still had 450
of its original 800 men able to answer roll call on September 1.

Other units had fared far worse—the 200th Infantry Regiment, formed
of conscripts, most of whom had been drawn by lot from twelve designated
metropolitan infantry regiments, had virtually ceased to exist. Of 800
Chasseurs à Pied recruited in part among French Alpine troops, only 350
were able to hold a rifle, barely. Yanked from their worksite and thrown

into an attack against Hova positions on June 30, a great many men simply fell exhausted on the ground. "Half of the unit had to be evacuated," wrote Reibell, "and the rest is anemic, spent, can never, with the exception of a few men, press on."[26] Engineering units, used to build, or rather attempt to build, bridges over the swamps had been destroyed—when Duchesne saw ten soldiers led by three officers marching back from a bridge worksite, he is alleged to have shouted, "That's a lot of officers for so few men!"[27] That, however, was what remained of a company of engineers. Only 20 of the original 150-man contingent of *Chasseurs d'Afrique* were able to mount a horse. The 13th Marine Infantry Regiment, 2,400 strong when they disembarked at Majunga in March, was reduced to 1,500 men.

As the Dahomey campaign had shown, by far the most resistant troops were the native formations. The ragged but resistant *régiment colonial* formed of Hausas and Malagasies and volunteers from the island of La Réunion counted only 600 casualties, most of them Réunionais. The prize for resistance, however, went to the Algerian *tirailleurs,* who had lost only 450 of their original 1,600 men.[28] Reibell reported that the general staff was singing the praises of the Algerians.[29] It was a pity that they had not included more of them in their plans. And despite the praise lavished upon the Algerians, Lentonnet complained that the Legion was repeatedly favored over his Algerians in the distribution of supplies, which "produces a bad impression in our ranks."[30]

However, if the Algerian *tirailleurs* were winning the praises of the staff, the Algerians recruited to work as mule and wagon drivers soon found themselves bearing the brunt of the blame for the poor conditions on the march. This was in part a logical extension of their association with the Lefèbvre wagons, which the men had come to see as the symbol of their misery and the cause of so many deaths among their comrades. Langlois's legionnaires nicknamed them *"La Fièvre"* (fever) wagons, and greeted their arrival in camp with "the most unanimous and energetic shouts and catcalls. We hate them, these miserable vehicles. . . . Some soldiers even spit on them, as if [the wagons] could understand and suffer from the abuse with which they are covered."[31]

They also began to hate those who looked after them, a tendency that was encouraged, according to Reibell, by some staff officers who cited deliberate sabotage by the Kabyle conductors for the expedition's difficulties rather than their poor planning and organization. The Kabyles were accused of stealing supplies destined for the front and even of making the return trip of the evacuated soldiers piled in the bins of the Lefèbvre wagons so miserable that many died.[32] No doubt some of these accusations were true. However, it was obvious that the logistical planning of the expedition had been so haphazard as to be almost criminally negligent. As demonstrated in Tonkin and Dahomey, porterage was a crucial element in the success of a campaign, as critical as the combative qualities of the troops. In Dahomey, Dodds had assembled 1,858 porters for a force of

1,366 men, and given strict orders that they "be treated without brutality," be paid regularly and carry no more than thirty kilos.[33] Each soldier was assigned a porter who carried his pack. And while these orders were not always followed to the letter, especially as the campaign became more difficult and more porters attempted flight, at least they sustained the Dahomey column well in the opening weeks, when it virtually destroyed the Dahoman army.

By contrast, in Madagascar the requirement for porters and drivers had been desperately underestimated, so that, even with the Lefèbvre wagons, soldiers had to carry their own packs, which added to their fatigue. Furthermore, planners had placed the Algerian porters and drivers low on their priority list—even on the ship out from Algeria, Reibell discovered that desperately inadequate arrangements had been made to feed the Kabyles. Once on shore, they had been expected to work all day and then virtually fend for themselves. "The Kabyles, who have been worn out and abused, are at the end of their tether," Reibell recorded in September. "The hospitals refuse to receive them on the pretext that there is no room. No one looks after them even though they have the worst job to do. They leave before first light and arrive at the staging hut after midnight, battered, lacking food, sores on their feet and legs."[34] "Among these poor, ragged, pitiful devils, I was amazed to see a child perhaps ten years old at the most," Legion Lieutenant Langlois wrote in August. "Like his comrades, he bravely led his mule, stretching out his little legs to follow the animal."[35]

Even Duchesne began to realize that, despite the arrival of reinforcements, his force was wasting away to the point that soon it would be incapable of combat. According to his report to the French parliament, on August 4 he took the decision to create a light column to press forward to Tananarive. Nevertheless, this column could not be created, he believed, until the road had reached Andriba, which would serve as the staging area for the projected offensive.[36] In early September, the road, such as it was, was declared complete, and the light column began to form at Mangasoarina on the plain of Andriba. Three hundred fifty tons of supplies were collected there, and reinforcements, including 150 legionnaires, joined the force: "The most impressive of all these relief detachments was that of the Legion," Reibell, who had seen them disembark at Majunga in mid-August, wrote.[37] When, on September 12, Langlois witnessed the review of the men, including a battalion of the Legion, whom Duchesne had selected for the light column, he was less impressed. There, surrounded by the naked red mountains of Madagascar, 1,500 men stood to attention,

so dejected, so depressed, so pale, that one would have believed them more dead than alive. Their clothes were in rags, their boots in pieces, their helmets, too large for their emaciated heads, fell to their shoulders, covering almost entirely their yellow faces where only eyes the color of fever seemed to exist. And they seemed so pathetic, so poor, so miserable, that unconsciously tears came to the eyes.[38]

On September 14, the light column left Andriba. In the van was the *régiment d'Algérie,* made up of two battalions of Algerian *tirailleurs* and a battalion of the Legion. A second group had at its nucleus the aptly named *régiment mixte,* which contained a battalion of the 13th Marine Infantry Regiment and some Malagasies and Senegalese. In the rear, the remnants of the 200th Infantry Regiment and some more Africans and marines guarded the convoy. In all, 4,013 soldiers led by 237 officers and followed by 1,515 mule drivers and 2,809 mules left for Tananarive.[39] Some pessimists were already calling this march "the suicide of General Duchesne," but Langlois's legionnaires were already dreaming of the riches to be found in the capital.[40] Nevertheless, it was apparent as the column made its way off the plateau of Andriba and up the narrow valley of the Mamokomita that the countryside of rocky, naked slopes rising to jagged summits would be difficult enough to march through, much less fight over if a determined enemy chose to defend it. Therefore, it was with great relief that the column, after a march of seven miles, arrived at the foot of Mount Tafofo at the end of the Mamokomita defile to find it undefended.

The view from the summit was glorious—three large mountain massifs separated by valleys whose floors, made green by marshes, cacti and mango trees, contrasted with the stark, boulder-strewn slopes. However, hardly a mile and a half away a Hova army was in the process of throwing up fortifications along a ridge line near the village of Tsmainondry, which blocked the column's projected line of march up the Firingalava valley. At dawn on the following morning, Duchesne launched his troops into the attack. The task of the Legion was to carry out a frontal assault, wading through the marshes that covered the valley floor and attacking up the slopes, while other units flanked the positions. However, hardly were they through the marshes than the Hova artillery opened up. Fortunately, few of their shells exploded. The legionnaires began to fire on the offending batteries from over two thousand yards away, inaccurate from such a great distance, but enough to send the Hova troops dressed in their white lambas, a shawl-like garment, scattering like the flocks of aquatic birds that the legionnaires had raised while wading through the marsh. "One of the defenders, probably believing that his resistance had been sufficient, got up, looked around, and bolted off with no self respect," wrote Langlois.

The entire trench, worried, became agitated. Two or three other men got up, looked about, and . . . , like their comrade, took French leave. That proved too much for the delicate morale of the intrepid warriors of Ranavalo. As one man, like those jack-in-the-boxes pushed out on their springs, they suddenly surged out of the back of the parapets and disappeared rapidly down the thousands of ravines which furrowed the terrain, throwing away their

arms so as to run faster. We saluted this grotesque flight with the most en-
ergetic catcalls.[41]

Yet the undignified retreat of the Hovas before Tsmainondry, while
gratifying, simply allowed the French to march on to the next, and many
believed the most formidable, obstacle of the campaign, the Ambohimenas
mountains. The route of the column climbed the valley of the Firingalava
river, wading through torrents that spilled down mountainsides so steep
that only with difficulty could the mules be kept from tumbling into the
water below. The fatigue of the men was obvious, and a wake of stragglers
trailed behind the advancing French who, on the 17th, could see the great
mass of the Ambohimenas, which lay across their path in the distance.
Duchesne made camp to allow the remainder of the plodding column to
catch up, and on the 18th ordered a night march to approach the Hova
defense lines. The men ate their meager rations and then bent into a path
that led straight up the mountainside. "The men . . . advanced with great
difficulty," according to Langlois. "We were obliged to use clubs to make
these poor feverish men march. We struck them with a heavy heart, but
absolutely convinced that our duty and their interest commanded it. All
who remained behind are lost men."[42]

When dawn broke, the Hova fortifications were visible atop the high
ridge to the front. The *régiment d'Algérie* was given the task, once again,
of mounting a frontal assault, while the *régiment mixte* climbed the mountain to turn the Hova positions on the flanks. As the legionnaires approached, puffs of black powder smoke appeared from the heights, but the
defenders were firing from a distance too great to cause any damage. The
Hova artillery soon joined in, but it shot badly. Even though the legionnaires and *tirailleurs* were still over a mile away, the line of Hovas in their
white lambas lower down the slopes rose up and began grappling their way
toward the fortifications on the summit, sowing panic. Duchesne ordered
his legionnaires and *tirailleurs* forward toward groups of men milling
around some of the fortifications that had yet to be abandoned, when the
appearance of the marines and Malagasy *tirailleurs*, recruited among Sakalave tribesmen, traditional enemies of the Hovas, on the ridge to their flank
precipitated a complete panic. "Despite the fact that our troops were beginning to become accustomed to the speed with which the Hovas ordinarily break off the combat," Duchesne reported, "they had the profound
surprise to see them abandon completely their formidable positions and
beat a retreat along the entire front."[43]

The French now stood on the threshold of the Hova heartland. From
the naked heights of the Ambohimenas, they could look out over a spread
of plateaus covered by a checkerboard of rice paddies and small villages
surrounded by hedges of cactus. All that lay before them now was a few
days of hard marching. According to E. F. Knight, the Malagasy
commander-in-chief had told his prime minister that "I can do nothing. My

men will not stand. They run away as soon as they perceive that two or three of their friends have been killed. Nothing will stop them." An English officer trying to put some backbone into the Hova army told him that, in their panic to get away from the French attack on the Ambohimenas, fully 300 soldiers had tumbled over a precipice and been killed. Soldiers had bribed their officers to run away "so as to have an excuse for saving their own skins," which had reduced the army, which had numbered around 7,000 on September 12, to 1,313 starving men by September 23. To be fair to the Hovas, on the Ambohimenas their soldiers probably had shot up what little ammunition they had been given while the French were still well out of range. The Hova government was calling up miserable peasants and even prisoners, who passed through the streets of Tananarive shackled by the neck, to carry out a last-ditch defense of the capital.[44]

However, the ability of the French to take advantage of Hova confusion and demoralization was impaired by their own condition, which verged upon utter collapse—the light column was barely in a fit state to lurch forward, much less administer a knockout punch. Langlois believed that the mere effort to climb the Ambohimenas had cost the attackers a tenth of their strength. Patrols sent out returned only with corpses already stiff with death, victims of the night cold of the mountains, or exhausted by the intense heat of the day. Several had obviously committed suicide. Indeed, suicide had already manifested itself in the Legion—on September 3, Langlois's company had marched out of camp past the body of one of their soldiers who had hanged himself from a mango tree. In the wee hours of the morning of September 21, a legionnaire shot himself through the head with a bullet that then pierced the colonel's tent, narrowly missing him. On the following day, a second man in his company shot himself just before dawn: "Our excellent paymaster . . . is of the opinion that the men are intentionally killing themselves just to force him to write out the death certificates, a work which he claims to detest," wrote Langlois.[45] Lentonnet noted on July 27, even before the light column set out, that "Suicides are very rare in the regiment of Algerian *tirailleurs*. But they are more frequent in the Legion. In three days, there have been no less than six legionnaires who have killed themselves. Yesterday, one hanged himself, another blew his brains out." On September 21 he again recorded that "suicides are more and more frequent in the Legion, which is becoming demoralized."[46]

Langlois agreed that morale was seriously low: "In the silent camp, the men seem discouraged and without energy," he wrote. "It is the first time since the beginning of the campaign, that I have noticed such an utter demoralization."[47] Low morale, a great danger in any unit, was thought especially serious in the Legion. Legionnaires, because of their pasts, were believed to be psychologically fragile, apt to give themselves over to expressions of despair, of which suicide was one. It is possible, as some believed, that for many legionnaires enlistment had been an alternative to suicide. Raimond Premschwitz and Flutsch both admitted that they had considered it, and that the Legion, for them, had been an option of last resort.[48] Frederic Martyn also recommended it for those who were contemplating suicide, because "it may possibly introduce you to a zest of life that you have never felt, and in any case you can commit suicide just as well in Algeria, you know, as you can in London."[49] But service as an antidote to suicide might not work in every case. Jacques Weygand, who commanded a Legion cavalry squadron in the 1930s, believed legionnaires particularly susceptible to "crises, whims and depression." However, the theory, in any case, was that the active life of the Legion kept these under control. Suicide, like desertion, hit its peak in calm garrisons where "they must look themselves in the mirror, and it's not happy." For this reason, Legion officers were always careful to keep their men busy and occupied, to prevent unconstructive brooding over the past, "to distract their men, to tear them from the mortal prostration which grips the best ones."[50]

Therefore, two perceptions seem prevalent about suicide in the Legion. The first is that the Legion had a relatively high suicide rate, at least higher than that of other corps. The second is that suicide appeared to occur more frequently in garrison because legionnaires, predisposed to depression in conditions of enforced boredom and inactivity, rose to the occasion when confronted with the challenges of a campaign. Neither of these is possible to resolve with any certainty. French historian Bernard Savelli concluded in his thesis on the Legion in Tonkin before World War I that suicides in the Legion at that time averaged only three or four a year, and the rate was no higher than those of other corps, including the Algerians.[51] But as has been seen, Indochina, at least after 1885, became a garrison of choice, with enough distractions to adjourn thoughts of suicide except among those most inclined toward self-destruction. No comparative statistics exist for Algeria, which was a far less attractive garrison. However, Savelli seemed to agree with the second perception, that suicides declined on campaign, citing as his evidence that only one legionnaire committed suicide during the grueling, and apparently hopeless, defense of Tuyen Quang. Likewise, the regimental diaries for Tonkin in 1885 and Dahomey in 1892 make no mention of suicides, nor do the memoirs mention any.

The Legion battalion in the light column counted six suicides, and it appears that eleven of the sixteen suicides that occurred in the Algerian regiment during the campaign were in the Legion. And while this is certainly not catastrophic, other suicides might have passed unnoticed among the thirty-three legionnaires listed as "missing" from the light column.[52] There are perhaps three explanations of why Madagascar appears to have produced the exception to the general rule that suicides in the Legion declined on campaign. One, of course, is that the evidence is too fragmentary to draw a firm conclusion, that there were suicides in Tonkin in 1885 and during the Dahomey expedition of 1892 that were not recorded. However, the common sense explanation would suggest that suicides in those two campaigns were too rare to be considered worthy of mention.

A second reason why Madagascar may have produced so many suicides was simply that it was an extremely difficult campaign. Many men were obviously pushed to the brink of their physical and mental endurance, felt that they could not cope and preferred simply to do themselves in. A third reason was that, once they began, they became difficult to stop. Legion officers generally agreed that suicide, like desertion, was contagious. Once it had introduced itself into a unit, especially one whose morale was stretched as thin as that of the Legion in Madagascar, it could spread dangerously.[53] "I know nothing which makes more of an impression than these suicides," Langlois noted during the spate of suicides in the Legion. "A sort of derangement takes over the brain. You ask yourself with disquiet if this destructive fever is not going to seize you from one moment to another."[54]

Therefore, it was a great relief when the Legion marched out of camp on the 22nd because, Langlois hoped, "the march forward will perhaps chase away the black thoughts which have begun to affect us."[55] The route carried them beneath the rock cliffs of Angavo and into a broad valley where the red earthen village of Ambatohazano rose up like a red island amidst a green, segmented sea of rice fields. The column then climbed some chalk slopes to the plain of Ankazobe, which stretched, dusty and monotonous, to the horizon. "Our men must really have a stout spirit to make these long and tiring marches, pack on the back, without the slightest complaint," Langlois concluded.[56] Unfortunately, not all of them did. One legionnaire committed suicide during the night, while another shot himself in the leg, explaining to the doctor, "I can no longer march. Now you will have to carry me on a stretcher." Unfortunately, he died of blood loss. A third simply died in his bedroll, his pipe still in his mouth. The cadavers were laid out in a shallow ravine. "We no longer bury," Langlois noted.[57]

As the legionnaires pushed further toward Tananarive, they entered a countryside that was almost European—villages with wide streets, pitched-roof houses, some of which had balconies and verandas, even high steepled churches. Duchesne feared that the many villages left in the rear and to the flanks might become redoubts of Malagasy resistance, and ordered his column to march in a tighter formation.[58] But the evidence of Hova panic was all about. The hedge-lined lanes were strewn with the debris of a retreating, even a routed, army, including two cannon that had been pitched into a ravine. At least this allowed the French to advance almost without a fight, which was just as well because many of the legionnaires were on their last legs. Each morning the doctors judged a parade of unimaginable sores, bloody feces and general debilitation, a competition whose dubious winners climbed smiling onto one of the few mule-borne stretchers. On September 24, a small group of "tired legionnaires" was formed under a lieutenant. The ration of sixteen hardtack "biscuits" per soldier per day was reduced to eight, and then to four. "Those with a hearty appetite ate their day's ration with their morning coffee," noted Reibell. These biscuits sold for ten francs each in the light column, and sick legionnaires handed them over to those who would perform their fatigue duties for them.[59]

The number of men simply unable to continue the march grew daily. Others fell by the wayside and never reappeared: "They were very probably massacred by the inhabitants," the regimental diary recorded laconically.[60] This was no fantasy—E. F. Knight saw a swarm of Hova men and women set upon an Algerian prisoner, probably a straggler, hack him to pieces and then parade his remains through the streets of Tananarive. "This was no isolated case," Knight reported, "and it appears that two other wounded men were captured by the Hovas on the same day, and treated in like fashion."[61] Hova prisoners of the French seemed to have fared better—Langlois's legionnaires impressed some of them to carry their packs.[62] Knight was told by a Hova captured after a fight that the French simply disarmed them, gave them food, patted them on the back and told them "to be off to their homes."[63]

On the morning of September 26, the column climbed the slopes of Alakamisy mountain in staggering heat and looked out over the high tableland of central Madagascar to Tananarive about fifteen miles distant. "We are all crazy with joy," Langlois wrote. "We laugh, we cry, we embrace each other without being able to stop ourselves from shouting: 'Tananarive! Tananarive!' "[64] Admittedly, from a distance the city, bathed in sunlight, appeared as magical and welcome as the onion-domed silhouette of Moscow had been to Napoleon's soldiers in 1812. Large walled buildings, which included the palaces of the queen and the prime minister, the royal observatory and the royal hospital, saddled a ridge 4,700 feet high, their towers and cupolas thrusting skyward as if in competition with the numerous church spires. The ruddy-colored houses interspersed with the deep green of the tropical foliage spilled down the mountainside toward a broad valley dappled with rice fields and herds of sheep.

The Algerians drove the Hovas from the neighboring peaks at the cost of one killed and seven wounded. Duchesne ordered the column to bivouac for a well-needed rest before the final push to Tananarive, to permit the convoy to catch up and, finally, to allow the general to devise his plan of attack.[65] When he marched out of camp on September 28, it was to make a large turning movement to the northwest of the capital, so as to avoid throwing his troops single file across the dikes of the rice fields and up the steep slope of the Tananarive mountain. The appearance of the French, the lights of whose camp were clearly visible from Tananarive, dispelled the rumors that they had been defeated. The Hova soldiers threw up earthworks while their officers argued about the defense of the capital, and many women scurried away toward the southeast, their belongings balanced precariously upon their heads.

Yet it appeared as if the defense of Tananarive would be purely pro forma. As the legionnaires marched around Tananarive on September 28, the villagers came out to offer them food and fruit. Langlois wondered what impression the unshaven legionnaires, virtually barefoot and their clothes in tatters, must have made on the well-fed Hovas.[66] From the vantage point of the British vice-consulate, Knight observed "a ridiculous pretense of defense," fully worthy of the Grand Old Duke of York:

Bodies of men were marched up hills and then marched down again. I saw 1,000 Betsileo spearmen rush up a height at the back of the hospital; having reached the summit they waved their spears and raised a great shout, and then they quietly came down again, soon to recommence the same performance on some other height. . . . As soon as reality approached, as soon as the defenders found themselves within range of the French shells, and even before that, they bolted to some other position, where they could make another demonstration of battle without incurring any personal risk. It was not war, and it was not magnificent.[67]

This was not quite true, for a vigorous attack against the Legion in the rear guard left six legionnaires wounded.[68]

On the morning of the 29th, the French could look out over the two ridges that still separated them from Tananarive, "like two monstrous waves, that the very white lines of the enemy army fringe like foam," wrote Langlois, "and behind rises the imposing mass of Tananarive with its monumental palaces, its thousand little red houses, its tortuous streets where huddles a white, tumultuous and agitated crowd."[69] On the morning of September 30, the French crowned the ridge line barely three miles from Tananarive. The day opened with an artillery barrage. The Algerians and Malagasy troops descended into the valley and then up the opposite slope. Most of the Hova troops fled in panic, but some of the guard regiments put up a fairly stiff fight defending their mountain peaks. Now only a valley stood between Duchesne and the Hova capital. Duchesne sited his artillery facing Tananarive across the valley. The French guns began to bombard the town as the infantry prepared for an assault, one to be led by the Legion. The shells knocked off a corner of the queen's palace, and the Hova spectators cleared the vantage points of the town. Just as the order for the assault was about to be given, a white flag appeared above the palace.

The French soldiers filed down from their heights, across the narrow valley and into the town. The Legion was ordered to remain with the guns. Indeed, Langlois was furious when his soldiers were refused entry into Tananarive: "One was probably afraid that this troop of brigands called the Legion would compromise the peaceful work so happily begun," he wrote bitterly. "Poor Legion, how badly they understand you."[70] His disappointment could have been only temporary, however, for the Legion was given a prominent role in the pacification of Tananarive, including mounting guard on the queen's palace. "Many of them could scarcely crawl along, some lay down in the streets to die, and pitiable spectacles were often to be seen," Knight wrote of the soldiers who marched into the capital. "I met, for example, a straggler tottering into the city, almost bent double, his knapsack on his back, his rifle on his shoulder, while from the top of his helmet down to his feet he was covered with a black mass of flies, clustering on him as if he were already a corpse." Nor was their situation improved by the neglect of many basic hygienic rules, so that in the days after the capture, burial parties were a common sight in the garrison.[71]

THE OBVIOUS QUESTION to ask is, how important was the Legion's contribution to the two major campaigns of the 1890s in Dahomey and Madagascar? Legion historians are fond of quoting General Duchesne's remarks made to Legion officers at the end of the campaign, that "it is assuredly due to you, gentlemen, that we are here. If I ever have the honor to command another expedition, I will want to have at least one battalion of the Foreign Legion with me."[72] However, one must be cautious of such statements, made in the way of thanks, or as a morale-boosting exercise. It is obviously true that the Legion played an active, even a central role in the French penetration of Tonkin, Dahomey and Madagascar. Their strength, the argument goes, was that they were better disciplined than the native troops, and more resistant than the other white troops. On the face of it, this argument seems valid. Certainly, Legion appreciations of the lack of discipline of Tonkinese or black troops reflect a sense of racial superiority and regimental pride. However, even the most avid partisans of native troops conceded that they were often recruited in haste and poorly trained, and were not disciplined to European standards—for instance, the battalion of black troops sent to Madagascar were raw recruits armed and trained on board the transports sailing to Majunga.[73]

The problem for the Legion, as for other white troops in the Madagascar campaign, was not their discipline, but their ability to endure the debilitating tropical climates. Contemporaries noted that sickness rates in the Legion were lower than for those in other white regiments, an assessment with which historians have concurred. "The legionnaires have especially drawn attention to themselves in our recent colonial campaigns, by their endurance," General Joseph Galliéni announced soon after the Madagascar campaign. "Their solidity under fire is equal to that of French troops, and, as their physical resistance has proven superior, they have, in reality, played a more effective role than [French troops] in the principal actions of war which have taken place during these expeditions."[74] In Tonkin, Dahomey and Madagascar, the superior endurance of legionnaires, which was attributed to the fact that most of their men were over twenty-five years old and therefore less susceptible to disease than were the generally younger soldiers in the marines or metropolitan units, gave rise to the saying, "When a French soldier goes to the hospital, it's to be repatriated, a tirailleur to be cured, and a legionnaire to die."

But while concentrating on the superior endurance of the Legion to other white troops in these campaigns, historians have failed to ask two questions. First, could the losses to sickness and fatigue have been reduced? And, second, might the French have established better and less costly principles upon which to establish their colonial expeditions? For while the Legion suffered less than other white troops, they suffered nevertheless, seriously enough to jeopardize their military performance. This author has discovered no reliable statistics for the Dahomey campaign. However, both Silbermann and Martyn had the impression that sickness reduced Legion strength by about 25 percent. The memory of so many friends left behind in Dahomey caused Silbermann to break into tears as he stepped off the ship at Oran, an event an observant journalist put down to his joy at seeing Algeria again.[75] Those who survived the campaign were often no better off—Martyn reported that five of the 219 legionnaires evacuated from Cotonou on Christmas Day 1892 died on the return trip to Algeria, and that 69 had to be carried off on stretchers at Oran.[76] In the autumn of 1893, as the French prepared to track down Behanzin, it was reported that so many men were sick that "the Legion could with two companies organize at best one able to campaign."[77] And this occurred when General Dodds planned his campaign so as best to preserve the health of his troops.

The losses to sickness in Madagascar were quite simply catastrophic: Fully 4,614 soldiers died there, roughly a third of the original 15,000 men of the expedition, and a far higher proportion than that of the white troops, plus 1,143 Algerian mule drivers, who had been shamefully neglected.[78] These high casualty rates were quite rightly blamed on the poor organization of the Madagascar campaign, especially to the decision to build the wagon road from Majunga. Yet more might have been done to lessen casualties. Knight believed that the French "neglected the most ordinary hygienic precautions" in their camps in Tananarive. He was also appalled by the "execrable" conditions in which sick men were repatriated on the ships sailing to France, where they were confined to suffocating holds. Indeed, Reibell recorded that fully 554 soldiers died on the return trip to France, and a further 348 in France:[79] "I was astonished to find that with few exceptions, the officers seemed indifferent to the comfort of their men, and rarely visited the fetid den in which they lay,"[80] wrote Knight.

While Dodds certainly prescribed very strict hygienic precautions for the Dahomey campaign, it is possible that French officers, including those in the Legion, were insufficiently rigorous in enforcing them. Officers cannot be blamed for malarial mosquitoes, which were responsible for 71 percent of the deaths in the expedition.[81] But they might have taken more care to see that their men were supplied with quinine and that they took it. In March 1893, for instance, the doctor complained that the troops in Dahomey had not received quinine.[82] In Madagascar, Reibell complained that quinine was in short supply because it had been loaded into the transports first and therefore could not be retrieved until the ships were entirely unloaded.[83] Also, the debilitating cases of typhoid, which caused 12 percent of the deaths, and dysentery, which caused 8 percent, were largely the products of impure water and filthy utensils.[84] Therefore, French officers, including those in the Legion, might have increased the efficiency of their forces by paying more attention to the health and well-being of their troops. But poor hygiene was a problem throughout the French army, and not simply in the colonies.

However, given the high casualty rates of white troops even under the best conditions, would it not have been wiser for the French to campaign exclusively with native troops? For, after all, whatever these soldiers lacked in fire discipline, they more than made up in physical resistance. "My turcos [*tirailleurs*] have resisted more energetically the fatigues and privations than has the Legion, whose true effectives are now far below those of my battalion," Lentonnet recorded on September 1, 1895. And this even though, he claimed, the *tirailleurs* had borne a larger burden in combat and fatigue.[85] The question is, how far was Lentonnet's pride in his Algerians and his belief that they had been far more efficient than the legionnaires in Madagascar justified?

Statistics on losses in the campaign are often confusing, but the diary of the *régiment d'Algérie* conserved in the war archives at Vincennes appears to bear out Lentonnet's claims: During the march of the "light column," one battalion of legionnaires accounted for 104 casualties, all but 14 of them suicides, missing and hospitalized, compared to 34 casualties for the two battalions of Algerian *tirailleurs,* all but one a combat casualty.[86] Therefore, the Legion, which made up one-third of the regiment, accounted for three-quarters of its casualties in the light column. In the overall comparison of deaths, however, the margin of Algerian superiority is not so obvious. Duchesne reported that the Algerian regiment counted 326 deaths in course of the campaign, the vast majority due to disease, although his final report listed 604 deaths.[87] How many of these were legionnaires is not spelled out. Sergeant Georges d'Ossau of the Legion historical service wrote in 1957 that the Legion suffered 226 deaths in Madagascar, five of which were in combat.[88] This makes a 23 percent death rate for the battalion plus reinforcements of 1,000 legionnaires, and, based upon the figure of 604 deaths in the *régiment d'Algérie,* means that the Legion, with roughly one-third of the regiment's strength, suffered 37 percent of its deaths. This would seem to indicate that the Legion fared little worse than did the Algerians.

But these figures do not include sickness, nor legionnaires who died after evacuation. The Algerians also remained longer in Madagascar than did the Legion. The figures for the light column together with the memoir evidence suggest that Legion effectiveness was severely diminished in Madagascar. And the Legion was relatively well off compared to other white units, especially the 200th Infantry, which captured the prize with 1,039 deaths.

Therefore, one might draw several conclusions from a study of these colonial campaigns of the 1890s. The first is that Legion efficiency could have been improved if French officers had paid more attention to logistics and the sanitary conditions of their troops. While the legionnaires perhaps won top prize among white troops for stamina, in the opinion of Captain F. Hellot, "had the courage of the rebels [Hovas] been as great as their mobility," then the expedition would have been seriously embarrassed.[89] The second follows on from the first, that given the generally poor quality of the enemy opposition, these imperial expeditions could have been carried out far more effectively using a greater percentage, even the exclusive use, of native infantry. The Legion no doubt provided the most solid contingent in the Dahomey campaign. They, together with the marines, certainly held the line effectively at Dogba. However, there is no evidence that native troops would not have performed well enough to thwart that attack, or that the outcome of the campaign would have been any different without Legion participation. The conquest of the Western Sudan was carried out almost exclusively by black troops. The two units that contributed most to the success of the Madagascar campaign were the Algerian *tirailleurs,* who emerged as the backbone of the infantry there, and the artillery, whose bombardment of the queen's palace at Tananarive provoked the Hova surrender.

Commanders of colonial expeditions continued to request the participation of the Legion because, when properly selected and led, they made excellent soldiers. But a second important reason for the inclusion of white troops in these expeditions, at least outside of Tonkin, was not that native soldiers were skittish and lacked solidity, as was often claimed, but that their French officers did not entirely trust their native troops. Therefore, the task of legionnaires and marines was to solidify discipline within these expeditions as well as to fight the enemy. Of course, it is fair to point out that this was not an exclusively French practice, but one initiated by the British as well following the Indian Mutiny of 1857. But it was a costly task. In the final analysis, then, one must modify not only the claims of Legion historians based upon Duchesne's praise that the Legion's contribution to the capture of Tananarive was crucial. The old cliché might also be amended in the light of the Madagascar campaign to read, "Metropolitan troops and legionnaires go to the hospital to die. Tirailleurs just do not go to hospital."

Chapter 14

THE MONASTERY
OF THE UNBELIEVERS

BETWEEN 1900 AND the outbreak of World War I, the Legion lived what might be called its High Renaissance, a period when its peculiar culture flourished to the extent that it bequeathed an indelible image of the Legion to subsequent generations. Crocodiles of legionnaires in their white kepis, blue greatcoats, white trousers and blue waistbands marching out of fortresses of dried mud to do battle with those recalcitrant inhabitants of North Africa who perversely refused to be drawn into the expanding frontiers of the French empire was to become a cliché of popular fiction and the cinema in the years between the two world wars. Why the post–World War I generation found this image of the Legion impossibly seductive will be discussed in a subsequent chapter. What is important to note here is that it is in this pre-1914 period that the Legion's self-image as a band of hardened but sentimental outcasts became cast in concrete, a self-image that it would battle to preserve in the changing conditions of the twentieth century.

The affirmation of the Legion's image in the decade or so before the outbreak of World War I was encouraged by the Franco-German confrontation over Morocco. In 1900, Morocco had so far avoided annexation for one simple reason—the imperial powers had yet to decide who was to claim it as a prize. Therefore, while the attentions of Europe, especially of France and Germany, would focus upon Morocco for the next fourteen years (indeed, on three occasions they would almost go to war over it), the conquest of Morocco would be a far different affair than earlier imperial campaigns. The grand invasions of the nineteenth century were inappropriate, even dangerous, in this atmosphere of international distrust, and so were replaced by campaigns of stealth and limited operations cunningly designed to allay diplomatic suspicions, to avoid protests that might force a choice between retreat or war, and even to escape notice in Europe altogether. Therefore, the actual problems posed by the conquest of Morocco were more political than military.

It was precisely the complicated political issues that shrouded the Moroccan conquest which would cause the Legion to have such a prominent role in it. Because between 1905 and the Franco-German accords of 1911 the primary opposition to the French conquest came from Germany, and because the Foreign Legion contained so many German nationals, the existence of the Legion became a major source of conflict between the two countries. The polemical tone of these debates, as well as the public profile of the Legion in France and abroad, was raised by authors like Premschwitz, Rosen, Béric and others who offered an unflattering image of the Legion as a desert Bastille where adventurous and naïve recruits were pitched in with the scrapings of humanity and brutalized by a discipline of almost penal severity. It is an image of the Legion that has survived down to our own day, despite the best efforts of Legion apologists to counter it. For the first time, then, the conditions of service in the Legion, indeed its legal right to exist, became issues of public debate serious enough to strain relations between two major powers. Therefore, the quality of Legion life in the decade or so before the outbreak of World War I, its recruitment and discipline, its peculiar *moeurs de garnison* became issues that concerned not only its military efficiency but also the international image of the Legion, and by extension that of France.

Recruitment to the Legion has already been discussed in some detail. Although heterogeneous, it was far from being a rabble of hopeless men with little military potential. There were enough recruits who sought a military vocation, or for whom life in the Legion, for whatever reason, was an attractive, even if temporary, alternative to what they had known before, to build the elements of a proficient force. However, by the turn of the century, subtle changes in Legion recruitment began to take place that had some Legion officers worried. The most noticeable change was a decline in the number of recruits from the "lost provinces" of Alsace-Lorraine. Their increasing absence was particularly regretted by French officers. They had formed an important element in the pre-1870 army, where their strong sense of patriotism and preference for military careers had made them greatly admired. Their willingness to cross the frontier and enlist in the Legion after 1871 in defiance of German law was viewed as an expression of the continued attachment of these annexed areas to France. So prized had these former French citizens become as a political symbol that between 1871 and 1880 the Legion was legally, though not in practice, closed to everyone except men from Alsace-Lorraine and Switzerland.[1] Indeed, before the doubling of Legion strength in 1884, the Legion was sometimes referred to as *le régiment d'Alsace-Lorraine.*

Legion Captain Abel Clément-Grandcourt believed that in 1885 fully 45 percent of the legionnaires were from Alsace-Lorraine,[2] although how many of these were Germans who had claimed to be from Alsace to curry favor with recruiting sergeants, or simply to be enlisted, is impossible to know. The numbers must have been fairly substantial, for, as has been seen, the desire to avoid the disorganization of units by eliminating legionnaires from Alsace-Lorraine before the campaigns of the 1890s had been a major argument in favor of retaining the system of the *bataillon de marche.*[3] Nevertheless, their numbers had declined to an estimated 22 percent by 1897. And while there appears to have been a minor surge in enlistments around the turn of the century,[4] by 1904 the war ministry estimated that only 5.3 percent of legionnaires were from Alsace-Lorraine. Indeed, so worried was the Legion by the virtual disappearance of these men from Legion ranks that they even considered creating separate units for Alsace-Lorrainers, an option eventually rejected both because national battalions had caused problems in the past (and would do so again in the future), and also because there were simply not enough of these men to make such a solution practical.[5] By 1913, 6.7 percent of legionnaires, according to one source, claimed to be from Alsace-Lorraine.[6]

Why were these men, once a mainstay of Legion recruitment, staying away in droves by 1904? Gaston Moch suggested that an 1889 law that allowed Alsace-Lorrainers to declare French nationality and proceed into the regular French army was one explanation,[7] although if this diverted large numbers of these men away from the Legion, officers did not appear to be aware of it. Another reason, of course, was that recruitment from Alsace-Lorraine was bound to dry up as memories of the *"année terrible"* of 1870–71 receded into the distant past. Clément-Grandcourt believed that the German government had made special efforts to entice men from the recently annexed provinces into the German army, although none had yet penetrated the officer corps. Recruitment was also influenced by news of a campaign—for instance, Madagascar, as dreadful as that campaign was, produced a surge in recruits, as would the Casablanca troubles of 1907–08.[8]

But Clément-Grandcourt believed that these external factors alone could not account for the shortfall of recruits from Alsace-Lorraine. Quite the contrary, the Legion was itself to blame because the word was out in Alsace-Lorraine that service in the Legion meant high mortality rates, especially from typhoid in Algeria, tough discipline and "rough punishments." The spectacle of those returning in the inelegant civilian suit given to departing legionnaires, emaciated and yellow with fever—"In what a state we send them back!"—had served to drive that message home.[9] Clément-Grandcourt's views were shared by Raoul Béric, who in a 1907 novel, *Les routiers,* traced the fortunes of Otto Weiss, a native of Lorraine who, after swearing on the grave of his grandfather, a much-decorated soldier of France, that he will remain loyal to his true native country, joins the Foreign Legion. But he is quickly disillusioned by the brutality of Legion life, by the drunkenness and homosexuality, by the stealing and lack of solidarity. Above all, he is disgusted by the absence of patriotism, by the Germans who "... sing in thick voices the 'Wacht am Rhein' to insult the country which they serve." After his release, he tries to settle in Nancy, only to discover that service in the Legion "is not a reference." So he returns to occupied Lorraine, and to his grandfather's grave to weep, "Grandfather! Grandfather! What must you think of me!"[10]

Of course, it would have been utterly counterproductive for this internationally recruited service to make patriotism an essential element in its ideology. But the complaints about the Legion ran deeper than that. Nor were they confined to pan-Germanists and antimilitarists. French officers, too, observed that the quality of recruitment to the Legion had reached such a nadir that the more decent soldiers, those for instance who might be motivated by patriotism, found the atmosphere of the Legion uncongenial, even hostile. In 1905, Colonel Boutegourd looked back nostalgically to the decade after the Franco-Prussian War when the Legion was composed mainly of Poles, Swiss and Alsace-Lorrainers, when courts-martial were few and usually involved an old soldier enlisted before 1870.[11] The better discipline of these men may well have disguised a lack of training and an absence of dynamic leadership during that decade. However, the situation in the Legion was so serious that even ministerial interest was aroused, and in May 1905, the colonels of the two Legion regiments were asked to list measures that would bring about an improvement in service conditions. The infantry director insisted in 1905 that the bad recruits had driven out the good: "The presence of this sort of bandit ... has sent away the honest people from the Legion, those from Alsace-Lorraine in particular, who are not, like many foreigners, men who have lost hope."[12] Clément-Grandcourt also believed that the tragedy of those from Alsace-Lorraine was that many came over the frontier at a young and impressionable age to avoid service in the German army, only to be thrown in with a rabble that quickly introduced them to drink, or worse.[13] These complaints became all too common after 1900, and agreement virtually unanimous that recruitment to the Legion was *incontestablement en décadence*.[14] "Even for the least informed observer," wrote General Trumelet-Faber in 1913, "this magnificent unit is degenerating and soon will resemble the *Bataillons d'Afrique*."[15]

The problem, everyone agreed, was that the traditional sources of Legion recruitment were drying up, only to be replaced by a less desirable sort of soldier. The increasing reluctance of men from Alsace-Lorraine to enlist was soon matched by that of the Germans. In 1905, Captain C. Mangin reported that the number of Germans in the Legion was declining because wars in German colonies had siphoned off potential recruits, and because of an active propaganda campaign in Germany against the Legion. But also, a crackdown on NCO brutality in the German army had reduced the flow of deserters seeking refuge in France.[16] It appears that the percentage of Germans in the Legion declined from 34 percent in 1904 to around 16 or 17 percent just before the outbreak of World War I in 1914.[17] One of the results was fewer volunteers: For instance, recruits for the 1er *étranger* dropped from 1,612 in 1903 to only 800 in 1904, and the total strength of the Legion dipped from 12,000 to 11,000 men after 1900.[18] And while the events of 1907–08 brought in a slight influx of recruits, it was fairly short lived, for strength hovered below 11,000 men until the outbreak of war in 1914.[19] In 1913, General Antoine Drude, commander of the Oran division, complained that the 1er *étranger* was 1,000 men short while the 2e *étranger* needed 500 men to fill out its ranks.[20] It was the shortage of men, especially of good men, that helped to abort demands for the creation of a cavalry regiment and an artillery battalion in the Legion after the turn of the century.[21]

Faced with falling enlistment, the Legion was forced to take recruits where it could get them, and that too often meant enlisting increasing numbers of Frenchmen. Of course, as has been seen, the fact that Frenchmen joined the Legion was hardly new—Frenchmen appear to account for between 25 and 30 percent of legionnaires in the 1880s and 1890s. After 1900, however, fully 45 percent of legionnaires appear to have been French,[22] and this may have been an underestimate. Nor might the numbers of Frenchmen coming into the Legion have been a bad thing in itself— but what Frenchmen! Jacques Weygand was told by his sergeant in the interwar years: "The French are all good, or all bad, but in every case *des grandes gueules* [loudmouths]."[23] Before 1914, it was the bad sort who preoccupied officers. Already in 1905 the infantry director complained that the Legion "is being invaded by the sweepings of our nationals."[24] General Herson, commander of the Oran division, agreed: "We throw them out the door, and they climb back in through the window," he wrote in 1905. "We can only gain by getting rid of the bad elements which encumber the Legion and of which the largest part, I am sad to say, are French nationals."[25]

Why was the Legion attracting so many bad French recruits? The shortfall in recruitment that caused the Legion to be less selective offers one reason. However, the real problem occurred because the Legion after 1900 increasingly became the dumping ground for rejects from other corps. Joseph Ehrhart offers but one example of a man directed into the Legion because his conscript military record was so bad that the metropolitan army would not reenlist him.[26] Around 1900 the marines also appear to have begun to squeeze out the less desirable elements, who came to the Legion to complete the fifteen years service that would make them eligible for a pension. Also, the left-wing Waldeck-Rousseau government of 1899, and its reforming war minister, General Louis André, sought to end criticism of the penal *Bat d'Af* by retaining only the most hardened criminals there. Those whose records suggested a glimmer of rehabilitation were often deposited into the Legion. General Trumelet-Faber was of the opinion that the Legion had been corrupted by these men: ". . . today it has become the refuge of all the outcasts of the *Bataillons d'Afrique*, of the *armée coloniale* and of the *tirailleurs algériens* who, because of their deplorable records, were refused reenlistment in their original corps."[27] Clément-Grandcourt agreed in a 1913 report that bad French were chasing out good Swiss, Germans and Alsace-Lorrainers.[28]

The influx of bad elements into the Legion was made worse by the fact that many of the best legionnaires, in particular those who opted for French nationality after five years' service, which made them eligible to serve in French units, were departing for other corps where the moral tone was superior and the career prospects brighter. This was not a new phenomenon, but one that had affected the Legion from its early days in Algeria for the simple reason that, in career terms, the Legion was frequently seen as a stepping-stone to something better.

Before the Franco-Prussian War, something better usually meant the *zouaves*, whose prestige peaked during the Second Empire. Although in 1904 the German Raimond Premschwitz reported that the *zouaves* were "the pride of France,"[29] in fact their prestige rapidly declined after 1870. This occurred because they became a corps of European and Jewish conscripts from Algeria whose service obligation of only one year, until 1905 when it was raised to two, made them even less professional than metropolitan conscripts. When, soon after the turn of the century, the *zouaves* arrived by train for an important review by the president of the French Republic in western Algeria, legionnaires and *tirailleurs* who had marched for several days with full kit to get there expressed their contempt by bombarding the *zouaves* with their tent pegs. Dangy believed that the *zouaves* only appeared in dangerous areas "to show off. They are well looked after perhaps because in the past they did some good work, and since then they have rested on their laurels."[30] This was not quite true—the *zouaves* had performed well during the Bou Amama uprising of 1881–82 in Algeria, had fought in Tonkin and were included in the China expedition of 1900. However, they had certainly lost their edge after 1871. Silbermann, who saw them in China, believed that their uniform of turban, short jacket and Turkish trousers was not only impractical, but also gave them "the appearance of an eccentric woman. . . . In China, the uniform of the zouaves provoked general hilarity among the troops of foreign nations," he wrote. "Even the Chinese roared with laughter to see them walk past."[31]

After the turn of the century, the character of the *zouaves* as a regiment of North African *pied noir* (settler) conscripts became even more evident. "In the zouaves there are some local chaps who are loaded," Flutsch was told by an ex-*zouave*. "They always splash it around right under your nose

. . . and you who don't have a penny to your name, that cheeses you off. In the Legion, you don't have to worry about that. Everybody's broke." Thoroughly alienated, Flutsch's friend decided to desert the *zouaves* and enlist in a more masculine organization after he witnessed a legionnaire single-handedly hold off a barroom full of policemen. "A zouave isn't dangerous, you know."[32] Less than dangerous, they had become in the eyes of some legionnaires almost timid. "The legionnaire hates a *zouave* more than he hates an Arab," English legionnaire A. R. Cooper wrote in 1933.[33] When a young *zouave* appeared in a bar in Morocco in the interwar years, legionnaire Jean Martin and a few other "old soldiers began, at his expense, to make the classic jokes about the zouaves, 'Lyautey's little girls'. But the recruit—I couldn't believe it!—smiled without understanding anything." "La mère Simon," the bar owner, jumped out from behind her bottles: " 'What are you doing here, kid?' she screamed at him. Then she grabbed him by the arm: 'Go, go! Get out of here! Don't stay with the legionnaires, you're too young. Don't you see they are going to hurt you, little fool?' "[34]

But if the Legion had outlasted competition from the *zouaves,* they discovered in the 1880s that *la coloniale* had relegated them to second place in the pecking order of colonial regiments. Backed by a strong colonial lobby, the marines ensured themselves a pay scale and promotion system far superior to that of the Legion. In Tonkin and Madagascar, where both marines and legionnaires served, Leon Randin claimed that the former took advantage of their "prime garrisons" in the rear to intercept the gifts of food and tobacco sent by the charitable *"Dames de France,"* which never reached the Legion's posts lost in the bush.[35] And even though, as has been seen, the performance, certainly the endurance, of the Legion during these colonial expeditions was generally superior to that of the marines, who included too many young volunteers in their ranks, they still continued to look down upon the Legion.

In 1839 the Legion was deliberately excluded from the organization of the marines, for it was felt that its reputation for getting out of hand would compromise the task of pacifying native peoples.[36] The superior attitude of the marines toward the Legion was obvious to Legion Lieutenant Langlois in Madagascar when a marine captain said, " 'Monsieur, you must learn,' he told me, completely out of the blue by the way, 'that when troops belonging to the war ministry march with marines, they must display the good taste to remain to the rear.' "[37] In 1908, Legion Captain Met was denounced by a marine officer in Tonkin when he sent his trumpeters to play in a church service.[38] This incident had its origins in the tense political atmosphere following the Dreyfus affair and the separation of church and state in 1905. But it also demonstrated the rivalry between the two corps that continues today. Despite this rivalry, however, the attractions of marine service were only too obvious to underpaid legionnaires—both Dangy and Silbermann enlisted in the marines after completing their tours in the

Legion. Legionnaire Lucien Jacqueline even called upon the help of the deputy for his native Calvados to get into the marines after his five years of Legion service expired in 1907.[39]

It would have been remarkable if this decline in quality recruitment was without consequence for the Legion. And indeed, one of the first results was a discipline crisis that began to shake the Legion in the new century. The infantry director complained in 1905 that ". . . for the last few years, too many unstable and vicious people had joined who do no service. The scenes of indiscipline have multiplied to the extent that, the commanding general of the Oran division, in a special report, 10 April 1905, no. 1641J, had to ask for new disciplinary powers to use against the soldiers of the Foreign Legion."[40] Colonel Désorthès of the *2ᵉ étranger* at Saïda complained that punishments of thirty to sixty days in prison had been inflicted in his regiment on 1,482 occasions in 1905, together with 370 discipline councils and 334 courts-martial.[41] General Herson reported that the selling or destruction of equipment and the smashing up of the barracks had reached epidemic proportions.[42]

Flutsch's colonel agreed that things had gone too far when he could hand out a quarter-century's worth of confinements in one day and when 20 percent of his soldiers were behind bars: "If I can congratulate you on your combative qualities," he told his assembled legionnaires,

you should realize that I am far less proud to think that, in my one regiment, there are more men under lock and key than in the 163 regiments of the metropolitan army. I don't hope to change things. It was like this before I came. It will be like this after I leave.[43]

He was certainly correct about that. In March 1912, General Trumelet-Faber complained that the Legion was going through (yet another) discipline crisis:

Bad soldiers congregate [in the Legion] more than before, punishments are at once more numerous and less effective, and the more or less incorrigible soldiers who encumber this splendid regiment are a constant source of worry for the command and absorb a disproportionate amount of its attention to the detriment of its military mission."[44]

Not only was its military mission at risk, its social mission as an institution of rehabilitation was also placed in jeopardy. This was of more than passing importance, for the rehabilitative mission, together with military efficiency, formed the twin pillars of the Legion's *raison d'être*. The rehabilitative mission was a necessary myth, at once an institutional justification, a basis for self-confidence and a guarantee of survival. Without it, the Legion was disarmed in the face of charges of exploitation leveled by its many critics. Martin called Legion life *"misérable et magnifique."*[45] But one depended upon the other—without suffering and sacrifice, there was no redemption. The religious parallels were obvious. Gaston Moch compared the Legion to the crusading orders of the Middle Ages, Knights Templar and Teutonic, an "inviolate asylum . . . a moral repose" whose "moral grandeur" resided in the fact that it put men "on the road to salvation."[46] Flutsch, too, found parallels, although more prosaic ones than Moch, between the religious life and that of the Legion. "The Legion is a little like a cloister," Flutsch wrote. "It's the monastery of the unbelievers. In fact, the rules of silence and chastity are fairly well observed."[47] Some monastery! "The Legion must not become what many mistakenly believe it is, the receptacle of the rabble of the world's races," Trumelet-Faber continued. "If this conception is realized, it will soon lose its character and its worth."[48] Just before the outbreak of the war, Moch estimated that 48 percent of legionnaires reenlisted. However, from 18 to 36 percent could not reenlist because they had died in service, become infirm, deserted, been punished and "above all" because they had been discharged for disciplinary infractions.[49]

But why all the hand-wringing, one may ask? After all, the Legion should have been able to take a few discipline problems in its stride, for this must have been an occupational hazard for a unit that traditionally asked no more searching questions of its recruits than age, nationality and the name one cared to travel under. The Legion's reputation for strict, even ferocious, discipline must eventually tame even the most recalcitrant recruit. For, to the old standbys like *le tombeau, le silo,* and the *crapaudine,* which, by the way, were common throughout the *Armée d'Afrique,* or the exhausting gymnastics with a rock-filled pack in the *"pelote,"* the Legion could add punishments that demonstrated commendable imagination as, in Tonkin, tying a legionnaire found drunk on duty to a tree next to a water hole frequented by a tiger.[50]

However, the truth was that the Legion was ill-equipped to deal with its increasing discipline problems. In the first place, it was desperately short of officers and NCOs. The Legion regiments contained twice the number of battalions as a line infantry regiment. While a metropolitan infantry company counted 148 men (and was usually closer to 120), a Legion company almost always numbered over 200 and might even reach 300, yet be restricted to the same maximum complement of three officers, six sergeants and eleven corporals, and was denied the "complementary cadres" of supernumerary officers and NCOs retained in France to staff reservists upon mobilization. Furthermore, while a line regiment would usually share a common garrison, the requirement for the Legion's two regiments to furnish small detachments for posts throughout Algeria, Madagascar, Tonkin and, from 1907, Morocco dispersed its scarce cadres still further, even more so as they were entitled to a six-month convalescent leave at the end of each two-year tour east of Suez. General Dautelle, commander of the 3rd Infantry Brigade at Mascara in Algeria, complained in 1910 that a

Legion battalion counted only five or six officers, and each company one or two sergeants.[51] General Maurice Bailloud noted that in the 1910 maneuvers, some Legion companies had only one officer and two or three NCOs,[52] which probably helps to account for the complaint of some legionnaires that officers were virtually invisible in the life of the regiment.[53]

Not only were the numbers of cadres in the Legion insufficient, but also their quality was sometimes suspect. While the Legion certainly attracted some good officers in this period, its eccentric reputation, the remoteness of its garrisons and the lack of career advantages meant that the officer corps was uneven. "GM" complained in 1903 that Legion officers had the worst of both worlds, denied the career advantages of marine officers and the comfortable garrisons of the metropolitan corps.[54] In 1896, Legion Colonel de Villebois-Mareuil had lamented the fact that foreign officers with inadequate military knowledge, and French reserve officers seeking to be reintegrated into the regular army *"à titre étranger,"* were dumped into the Legion,[55] a complaint echoed by General Bailloud in 1910: "Sometimes the officer is a foreigner who does not have the knowledge, nor the authority, required to hold such a command," he reported after watching the Legion in autumn maneuvers.[56]

General Trumelet-Faber repeated the litany that the Legion required a special type of officer, "a bachelor with the temperament of a condottiere, dreaming of action, whose only possessions are his African footlocker and who is only happy on bivouac."[57] The quality of the officer corps was especially important in the Legion, according to the colonel of the *2ᵉ étranger,* because

depending upon the direction which he is given, the legionnaire can be the best soldier in the world or the worst of brutes, which makes him capable of the most heroic and even the most noble actions, or the most degrading. Officers who are badly prepared for this mission will only obtain bad results. And all the rigors of disciplinary or judicial action will be without effect when a word going right to their hearts will transform them into soldiers who are disciplined and devoted till death.[58]

While there were certainly a number of officers who spent most of their careers in the Legion, Trumelet-Faber complained that there were also a number who were merely passing through, especially those who "to be able to say they are legionnaires . . . come for a few months," an indication that the Legion's outlaw reputation was even beginning to work its magic on the French officer corps—up to a point.[59] The most difficult task of any new officer was to establish his authority over legionnaires who were naturally skeptical. While legionnaires seldom engaged in open revolt, they were quite capable of practicing what a British trade unionist would call a "go slow": "If you only knew how they are distant and cool, how their looks are hard," laments a young Legion lieutenant in André Raulet's novel on Legion life in the interwar years. "Never do they take the slightest initiative. I find no devotion in them, no good will, and I am obliged to explain exactly what I want from A to Z. If not, they stop in their tracks."[60] Good officers who were able to demonstrate that they were prepared to command could overcome this initial opposition. However, temporary Legion officers were almost never able to establish their authority. They not only destroyed any attempt at creating an atmosphere of trust in their unit, but also they were openly scorned by the troops because they were not true "legionnaires."[61]

The problems of the officers were compounded by those of Legion NCOs. "The task of Legion officers is complicated," de Villebois-Mareuil believed, "not only by the nature and the number of men under their orders, but also by the numerical, military and moral poverty of the NCOs at his command."[62] The problems with finding good NCOs have already been discussed. No doubt some of them depended upon brutality to enforce their authority, a brutality that caused discipline problems. But the view of the Legion NCO as the half-mad sadist of anti-Legion lore needs to be rectified. Frederic Martyn admitted that there was a "certain amount of petty tyranny" from NCOs who could push men whose nerves were on edge too far.[63] Rosen claimed that a favorite trick of NCOs was to give orders to drunken legionnaires and punish them severely if they disobeyed. He also noted that it was useless to appeal to an officer, for the NCOs kept them in ignorance of what was going on in the company.[64]

Certainly it would have been the height of folly to put oneself on the wrong side of a Legion sergeant. Yet Flutsch claimed that this was seldom the case: "In the Legion, the NCOs are tough but they don't bother you," he was told.

If there were one who was a nuisance, we would make him suffer, we would play games with him, we would make a fool of him. And if the captain tried anything, he would be fed up quick enough when his entire company is in prison, all for different reasons: There would be one who would black his face with boot polish for the morning inspection, another would run away when he shouted "Attention!" You know, ideas are never lacking in the Legion when one needs to play the fool. You will see. It's better than on civvy street.[65]

But this was seldom necessary: "In fact, the NCOs almost never intervened," Flutsch wrote. "The officers were invisible and the NCOs appeared only to give out general orders without making individual observations unless it was a serious case, to limit damage which would have caused a death or led to a loss of equipment."[66] Le Poer reported that his NCOs were strict, "but the punishments were not too severe. The favorite one was to keep you altogether in the barrack and compel you to sleep during the night in your ordinary uniform on a plank bed in the guard room. That was the worst of it."[67]

According to Le Poer, the retribution reserved for overly unpopular superiors might not stop at harmless barrack antics, and a corporal in his company was killed because he persisted in harassing his men after duty hours. This might be an extreme case, but Le Poer claimed that on the first exercise in which live ammunition was issued, the captain cautioned them against "accidents. . . . He quoted a passage from the Bible, for God's sake, which speaks of an eye for an eye, a tooth for a tooth! The old soldiers understood immediately, and by the time we arrived at the first stop, we new troops understood as well as they." While such things were possible in any army, Le Poer believed that the intense personal enmities that could build up in the Legion, especially against unpopular officers and NCOs, might lead to murder: "During combat this sort of thing happens more often than most people would believe," he wrote. "Even after combat when all the rifles are dirty and a cartridge casing can be ejected, without danger, immediately after the shot is fired, a stray bullet can pierce a tent and strike the detested man who believes he is safe."[68] Pfirmann also saw a sergeant who was badly wounded by legionnaires in a discipline company after he had treated them badly.[69]

While Legion officers and NCOs would have been fools to ignore the fact that excesses of discipline might bring on unwanted health problems, there is no evidence to suggest that this intimidated or deterred them from imposing an iron rule when necessary—or even when it was not necessary. Jacques Weygand recorded that the only thing worse than overzealousness in the eyes of legionnaires was to be considered a soft touch, so that *"mieux vache que con"*—better a swine than a fool—was the law that guided officer conduct in matters of discipline.[70] But generally the scale of punishments—*"le tarif"*—was clearly spelled out and had only to be applied automatically to a fairly predictable list of Legion misdemeanors. Flutsch claimed that this led to a Legion society in which "the definition of individual liberty corresponded to an exact reality: do what you like so long as you do not infringe the liberty of others." And while he felt that some of the punishments exceeded the severity of the crime, they were applied without favoritism and therefore aroused few feelings of resentment.[71] Silbermann heard legionnaires who claimed that the severity of Legion discipline paled in comparison to that of the German army.[72] Even some of the critics of the Legion agreed that many small infractions that would have invoked punishment in fussy line units were winked at in the Legion.[73] Influential officers might also impose "moral sanctions," like refusing to use the familiar *"tu"* when addressing legionnaires, or making them guard the mules on a march.[74] Merolli observed officers reduce Legion delinquents, sentimental men all, to tears by scolding them that their mothers would be ashamed of their misconduct.[75]

Does this mean that the Legion's reputation for strict, even brutal, discipline was totally without foundation? Not exactly. The problem, at least in the pre-1914 era, came not so much from brutal NCOs as from brutal legionnaires who were overly represented. Merolli complained that the rejects from other corps who enlisted under false names to escape detection caused a constant headache, always talking back, frequently drunk and "capable of a thousand stupidities." An NCO who did not dominate them lost all authority.[76] Flutsch, too, noted that there was a class of legionnaire who was simply not amenable to discipline, who regarded with "indifference" the prospect of spending sixty days in a pestilential cell without wine, coffee or tobacco, days spent in aimless exercises and nights sleeping on boards or floors of beaten earth.[77] "Most of the soldiers did not mind prison," Maurice Magnus reported. "On the contrary, they were rather proud of it and it was proverbial that a man who had not been in prison often was not a good soldier.[78]

These men simply ignored the consequences of their actions, especially when drink was involved. On the contrary, they regarded drunkenness as a way to make a personal statement whose significance was underlined by the fact that they were punished for it. "I was possessed by this stupid rage of a melancholy legionnaire who wants to be punished at any price," Martin remembered of his mental state after a drinking bout, "as if this should be something very significant, and particularly hurtful toward the object of his melancholy."[79] The fact that these men were treated in a manner that might not match the guidelines laid down by Amnesty International would not demoralize a unit, however. On the contrary, strict discipline was welcomed because it gave men without a strong sense of limits certain guidelines of behavior (even if they took it as a challenge to overstep them), while it also protected the good soldiers from the thugs and those who preferred to take the law into their own hands."[80]

The problem of the Legion was what to do with these men. Grouping them in discipline sections had led to "scandalous scenes" and even collective rebellion.[81] The obvious course of action was simply to throw them out of the Legion. Incredibly, until 1906 there was no legal way to do this. On the contrary, days spent in prison were not counted against the five-year enlistment, so that bad soldiers actually served longer than good ones. Three decrees of 1906, 1908 and 1912 gave the Legion the right to nullify the enlistment contracts of chronic discipline problems. But the procedure was fairly bureaucratic even by the baroque standards of French administration.[82] Besides, the expelled soldier would simply reenlist under a false name, or have someone else enlist for him and substitute himself at the last minute: "As candidates for the Legion need no identity papers, they can always bluff their way in," Trumelet-Faber complained, adding that the Legion needed to shed five hundred bad elements, "and we would have excellent regiments."[83]

The last recourse, especially in the field, was to utilize punishments outlawed by the French army, the most notorious being the *crapaudine,* allegedly introduced into the Legion by Négrier in 1881: "This is how it was done," Le Poer reported of a soldier who had got into an argument with his corporal during a route march.

First his hands were pinioned behind his back, then his ankles were shackled tightly to each other, afterwards the fastenings of his wrists were bound closely to the ankle bonds, so that he was compelled to remain in a kneeling posture with his head and body drawn back. After some time pains began to be felt in the arms, across the abdomen, and at the knees and ankles. These pains increased rapidly, and at last became intolerable. . . . This poor devil did not get much punishment. I think he was en crapaudine *for only an hour or so, but, take my word for it, if you place a man in that position for four, five, or six hours, he will be in no hurry to get himself into trouble again.*[84]

Although the *crapaudine* caused great pain, in many respects it demonstrated the Legion's preference for short, sharp punishments which, once accomplished, wiped the slate clean. Martyn saw this "barbarous" punishment applied only once during his Legion career to a legionnaire who had struck an NCO. And although he disapproved of it, "It must be remembered that in most armies he would have been tried by drumhead court-martial and shot."[85] Dr. Alcide Casset, who shared a garrison with the Legion in the Sud Oranais at the century's end, reported that the *crapaudine* was in fairly common use in the remote garrisons of southern Algeria, especially with men for whom "violence is part of their temperament; they have nothing to fear and nothing to lose."[86]

Flutsch saw the *crapaudine* as indicative of the Legion's rather indulgent attitude toward the misdemeanors of legionnaires, one of whom appeared drunk before the tent of his lieutenant and insulted him "with an accent of profound conviction and in a high voice. . . . When the lieutenant judged that the number had lasted long enough, he designated, according to the size and strength of the actor, two, three, or four spectators—'OK, knock him down and put on the *crapaudine*.' " The braying legionnaire was tied up "like a sack of potatoes and left on his stomach until the officer, judging that the man had calmed down, ordered him untied and allowed him to go to his tent. Of course, that was the end of it and nothing more was said."[87]

Therefore, the Legion certainly had a discipline problem before 1914, but it was probably less severe than statistics might suggest. In the first place, the serious discipline problems could be sent to discipline sections, or left behind in the depots. This is not to argue that they ceased to cause disruption in both places, especially in the depots, where they threatened to corrupt the new recruits. But at least they could be fairly well contained. Second, even those who complained that the Legion was perhaps not altogether a credit to France, that it was sinking to the level of the *Bats d'Af,* also were quick to point out that the Legion's problems had not affected its combat efficiency: ". . . its worth under fire has remained intact, as we have seen in Morocco," wrote Clément-Grandcourt.[88]

But this was not invariably the case, especially during the Casablanca expedition of August 1907. Hardly had the Legion arrived in the town, whose inhabitants had revolted against the increasing numbers of Europeans who had settled there, than the naval commander wired Paris asking to get up a permanent court-martial and return "a certain number" of legionnaires to Algeria because of "cases of indiscipline in the Foreign Legion."[89] Ehrhart, who landed with the Legion in Casablanca, admitted that they finished off some of the wounded and pillaged fairly extensively: "In the afternoon, one could see the legionnaires carrying the most diverse things, putting one thing down to pick up another," he wrote. "I contented myself with a pair of bronzed slippers, a white shirt and a blue sweater. Then a hundred francs in Hassani duros. One also saw drunken legionnaires." The commanding general withdrew the Legion from the town and forced them to surrender their pillage. However, legionnaires continued to break up the stalls of the Jewish merchants who quickly moved in to serve the expedition and to steal their merchandise, imposing a sort of rough justice because they judged that the Jews were selling pillaged goods at excessive prices.[90]

Legion discipline was fragile at Casablanca in part because the expedition was organized in haste and the usual selection process did not have time to operate. Therefore, the Legion went into battle with men whom they would probably have eliminated had they been given time. However, it may be equally true that the Legion behaved no worse in Casablanca than they had at other times. Protestant Pastor J. Pannier noted the tendency of newly arrived Legion drafts to take Hanoi by storm,[91] while young Legion lieutenant Paul Rollet arrived in Madagascar in 1902 to take charge of a contingent, nine of whose legionnaires had just run amok in the native village and raped the women.[92] On the other hand, it may have been that the Legion behaved no worse than other units, indeed sometimes better. But their reputation for slipping the leash meant that they received far more attention than other units. When, for instance, the 150 Legion replacements arrived by ship in Majunga in 1895 in the company of conscript volunteers destined for the ill-fated 200th Infantry Regiment, it was the conscripts who "immediately distinguished themselves by going that very evening to assault the neighboring village of Makoas to take off their women."[93] The difference most probably lay with the fact that the Casablanca invasion had attracted international attention, and therefore the high command felt obliged to make the Legion behave for the benefit of the world press.

The last, and perhaps most important, thing to note about the Legion's discipline crisis was that much of the indiscipline was more apparent than real, part of a cultural manifestation that was indelibly bound up with the character of legionnaires. Flutsch discovered that the indiscipline that usually kept forty men per company occupied pacing the prison yard was often a creative act, if not of artistic quality at least of a highly individualistic nature, *"des actes fantaisistes"* motivated by the legionnaire's need to assert himself, to make a personal statement.[94] Punishments, especially those inflicted for alcohol-induced infractions or for fighting, demonstrated masculine aggressiveness, which was much prized by the organization. In fact, the Legion's attitude toward punishment was highly ambivalent. Even Flutsch's colonel, while he admonished his men to try to behave during a five-day route march, felt obliged to add that "I don't expect my legionnaires to transform themselves into cowering *lignards* [line infrantrymen] and cease to send men to the cells at a rate much inferior to twenty percent of strength."[95]

And while the Legion punished indiscipline to a point, it also rewarded it: "If you have not been in jail, when they organize an operation . . . you'll be left behind," Flutsch was told. "When they need men, officers prefer those who have been in the box. Don't need pretty-pretties for tough jobs. You need chaps who aren't afraid to tell you to get stuffed!" Flutsch promptly deserted, marched as far as he could, mainly at night, to exhibit his stamina, and turned himself in after seven days so he could be selected for campaign, and at the same time demonstrate "an act of independence which would give me new rights to the esteem of my entourage."[96] Indiscipline, at least in moderation, demonstrated a willingness to take risks, to *"faire la bombe,"* to do something slightly mad.

The basic point to be made is that indiscipline in the Legion was a relative concept, and not at all an indication that legionnaires were intrinsically bad soldiers. On the contrary, for the Legion, soldiering was about being able to do what was required when called upon. S. L. A. Marshal, in his well-known, if flawed, study of GIs in World War II, also found that

Some of the most gallant single handed fighters I encountered in World War II had spent most of their time in the guardhouse. . . . Fire wins wars, and it wins the skirmishes of which war is composed. Toss the willing fighters out of an action and there can be no victory. Yet, company by company, we found in our work that these were men who had been consistently bad actors in the training period, marked by faults of laziness, unruliness, and disorderliness, who just as consistently became lions on the battlefield, with all of the virtues of sustained aggressiveness, warm obedience, and thoughtfully planned action. When the battle was over and time came to coast, they almost invariably relapsed again. They could fight like hell, but they couldn't soldier.[97]

Merolli agreed that men who caused the most problems in garrison invariably were the best to have on campaign.[98] Therefore, it seems that the Legion was able to institutionalize the notion of "bad soldier but good fighter," thereby making a virtue of defying the petty restrictions of garrison life, even basic good manners, to the point that the Legion's deplorable barracks behavior became an integral part of its *esprit de corps* and combat effectiveness.

But there were limits—when a campaign was in the offing and the competition for selection keen, legionnaires could transform themselves into choirboys lest incarceration in the cells eliminate them from consideration.[99] The shortage of officers and NCOs, the fact that Legion life was not highly structured or controlled by the military hierarchy but rather the tone was set according to the values of the inmates, that behavior condemned in a more traditional military milieu was actually honored in the Legion, simply served to confirm the opinion of its officers, who insisted, sometimes with despair, that the Legion was "different"—"Each day it is more clearly apparent that a legion of mercenaries does not act, and is not commanded, like a regiment of good troops from France," General Dautelle wrote in 1910.[100] But indiscipline Legion-style must not be taken to mean that the Legion teetered on the brink of moral collapse. At the very least, it demonstrated an *insouciance,* a taste for risk and a defiance of the consequences, invaluable attributes in men whose *métier* was to fight their way out of tight corners. At its best, it slipped over into the performing arts.

But even assuming that the discipline crisis that hit the Legion before 1914 was in part a cultural illusion, it worried commanders and did threaten both its military efficiency and what it argued, with some credibility, to be its rehabilitative mission. The question then becomes, what might the Legion have done to improve the situation? The first problem to attack was that of recruitment, where the Legion should have exercised greater selectivity. The problems caused by the fact that the Legion did not altogether control its recruitment, and the difficulty of keeping out the worst soldiers who returned when expelled, have already been discussed. However, at least three things might have been done to filter out the least desirable legionnaires. First, the system of depositing poor soldiers into depots and discipline sections indicates that the Legion might have trimmed its strength by at least a quarter and still have counted enough men to meet its responsibilities. The other two reforms are in fact practiced by the Legion today: a more complete interrogation and background check of recruits before allowing them to enlist, and, last, the possibility of terminating the contract by either party within four months of enlistment. This was already the practice in certain native corps in the French army, so the precedent existed.

More selective recruitment would have gone some way toward curing the second Legion problem—that of indiscipline. The influence of a few bad soldiers was probably out of all proportion to their numbers because they tended to congregate in the depots, where they influenced the new recruits, and because they found a more receptive audience for their bad habits among the disoriented, the stateless, the young, and those without strong character. But there were other things that could have been done to lessen the cases of indiscipline.

It was axiomatic among connoisseurs of Legion behavior that legionnaires must be kept active: "The legionnaire, to demonstrate his qualities, needs frequent change, constant action, suffering to endure, sacrifices," wrote Merolli. "If he is left for too long in garrison, he becomes drunken, quarrelsome, a scrounger and insufferable."[101] What was true for all troops was probably especially the case for the Legion because of their recruitment and their alcoholic habits. Unfortunately for the Legion, the command more often used it as a work crew in this period than as a fighting unit. Despite the fact that officers often praised the virtues of empire building, legionnaires appear to have been rather less enthusiastic about the "civilizing mission," which for them usually translated into hard labor. Morale was the first casualty: "[The legionnaire] is an outlaw who has fled a society where he felt uncomfortable, who needs to run risks," GM argued.[102] But these camps offered few risks for men who, after all, had enlisted to see action.

Béric believed that this, together with the aimless monotony of these posts, had blunted the Legion's fighting edge as well as its morale. "Never an exercise, never firing practice, never an armed reconnaissance around the camp," Béric complained of one of these interminable assignments building walls and tearing them down again to rebuild them better. "Thus, these camps in the Sud Oranais were like a prison into which were thrown passionate souls, where fragile spirits were corrupted, where energies were wasted. . . . Was it prudent to let such arms rust away?"[103] Boredom fostered the *"cafard,"* a state of depression which led to other problems that might quickly contaminate an entire unit. "[The captain] knew by long experience, how the contagion of evil is active among men who are bored."[104]

This was a poor state of affairs, especially because, as already seen, these were among the most stable and dependable legionnaires, the worst having already been left behind in the depots. That said, however, the Legion might have undertaken more vigorous efforts to maintain *esprit de corps* in these isolated outposts through exercises and training. It is possible that there were not enough officers and NCOs to do this. But the more likely explanation is that it was not part of their military culture. Officers seemed to rely on periodic bouts of drunkenness as a way of allowing legionnaires to let off steam. As a last resort, the legionnaires might be encouraged to organize a *grande fête*. The results surprised Béric, who expected a raucous and ribald production. On the contrary, "the program was chaste and tearful"; skits based on banal romances alternated with songs that reflected deep melancholy, homesickness, and perhaps regret for a misspent life.[105] Indeed, one may well wonder if, in the long run, such thespian exercises did morale more harm than good.

The fact that legionnaires were paid next to nothing has already been noted. However, what has not been discussed is how low pay contributed to the Legion's discipline problems. "In the final analysis, the legionnaire is a mercenary," General Herson wrote in 1905. "As in all troops of this type, the question of money plays a capital role."[106] One role the Infantry Director believed that it played was in attracting recruits—he attributed the dropoff in recruitment to the Legion in 1905 to the fact that the Dutch colonial army and the American and German navies were a better financial proposition.[107] However, it is unlikely that higher pay would have attracted more recruits, or a better class of recruit—the pay seems to have been the last thing on the minds of most legionnaires when they enlisted, although some did volunteer for the regular meals. But better pay would have helped solve many endemic problems that ultimately affected morale and efficiency, the first of which was the enormous number of problems associated with drunkenness.

Alcohol and the Legion were virtually inseparable. Merolli, who was very upbeat about the Legion, called drunkenness the unit's one great defect.[108] Even in an era when alcoholism was a serious social problem, the Legion's addiction to drink was regarded as extravagant. Premschwitz found it to be the Legion's "favorite vice,"[109] while Private Dangy was advised by his corporal at Saïda that "You must always be prepared to take a drink wherever you find it."[110] It was advice that legionnaires took to heart. The "collective drunk" became a tradition in the field—for instance, Flutsch's detachment of 120 men consumed seven hundred liters of wine in a matter of minutes. "There is only one place in the world where life is 'drinkable,' " one of his comrades noted. "In the Legion!"[111] Pastor J. Pannier attributed 75 percent of the courts-martial in the Legion to the effects of drink.[112] Alcohol was often the cause of many of the fights that punctuated Legion life, especially the devastating ones between sections and companies that occurred on paydays. "When I have my pay," a Belgian legionnaire told Pannier, "I can't keep from drinking."[113]

Drink also helped to undermine efficiency. One of Flutsch's comrades got drunk on guard duty and forgot the password: "It's always the same thing," he confessed. "When I'm smashed I do anything and I never remember."[114] Legionnaire L. Wagner was summoned to the officers' mess at eleven forty-five one morning in 1908 to prepare lunch after the company doctor discovered the cook passed out on the kitchen floor.[115] Flutsch was impressed for guard duty late on payday night because the entire guard room was paralytic.[116] Dangy substituted at the last moment in an operation in Morocco because so many of the legionnaires selected were too drunk to march.[117] During the Bou Amama revolt of 1881, Charles des Ecorres saw some legionnaires become uncontrollable, assault the brandy barrel and eventually fall down drunk after the Arabs had successfully pillaged the convoy,[118] perhaps a small preview of the drunkenness observed among some legionnaires during the retreat from Lang Son in 1885, and at Casablanca in 1907. Opinion was divided on why legionnaires were so addicted to alcohol. Some said it was caused by the "*cafard*," the wave of depression that periodically descended upon those in the colonies, while others believed that drink brought on low spirits. Pannier was told that legionnaires drank to forget,[119] but they seldom forgot to drink. The psychologist Roger Cabrol believed that alcohol facilitated communication in the polyglot Legion world, and perhaps, too, masked a number of psychological problems among legionnaires.[120] Paul Rollet conceded that the "sensational drunks" of legionnaires were often criticized, but he excused them as perhaps the last relaxation of men who led a dangerous life.[121]

For whatever reason, heavy drinking was part of the Legion culture. As usual, the Legion attempted to make a virtue of necessity. Legionnaires advanced the opinion, unsupported by any shred of medical evidence, that alcohol prevented disease.[122] Officers sometimes lamented the discipline problems caused by excessive drinking—"When I get the order to pay them, I am tempted to transfer to the infantry," Flutsch's Lieutenant Leclerc told him after an evening spent quelling drunken legionnaires. "At Géryville they must say to themselves when they sign the order, 'It's Leclerc's turn tomorrow.' "[123] Nevertheless, received wisdom held that a good hangover was preferable to the *cafard*.

However, quite apart from the discipline problems caused by excessive drinking, the major drawback of the immoderate consumption of alcohol was that legionnaires seldom had any money to pay for it. The only obvious source of cash for the excessively thirsty was to sell equipment or uniform parts. This practice drove the French command to distraction, and they reacted by imposing draconian penalties for this offense. However, when the idea of a collective, or even a solitary, drinking spree was in the air, this deterred no one.

To get money for drink, the legionnaire had two options: Either steal someone else's equipment, or sell his own. "In matters of stealing, the Legion draws the line very sharply," Rosen wrote. "The theft of equipment, to replace lost or stolen parts, was considered absolutely respectable and gentleman-like. There was no other remedy, as the man who loses something is punished severely."[124] Not only did this create an atmosphere of "each man for himself," but it also set men on a cycle of punishment that, once begun, was difficult to break. Often entire sections would decide to sell equipment to get money to have a monumental binge, absolutely heedless of the consequences. When Flutsch's section decided to sell their drawers to get money for drink, ". . . I declared that wine did not sit well with me and I couldn't drink with them but I did not mean to break the laws of solidarity. I therefore threw my underpants on the pile which was already formed. This gesture was fully appreciated and I had only to do everything to calm my reason which violently disagreed."[125] One can only wonder how many potentially good soldiers were lost in this way.

Of course, the counterargument would be that the more legionnaires were paid, the more they would drink. This is possibly true—when Legion pay was raised after World War I, most of the extra cash was invested in alcohol. But the fact remains that they would not have had to steal and face years in discipline sections from which they returned—if they returned—thoroughly corrupted and as men lost to decent soldiering. The reports for the interwar years do not list the selling of equipment as a problem in the Legion. A. R. Cooper wrote in 1933 that the selling of pieces of kit continued, however, but usually during a campaign when they were traded to Arabs for scarce food and when the loss was less likely to be noticed, could more easily be explained away or could be replaced by stealing from the dead.[126] Indeed, although Flutsch held himself to be a sterling example of the redemptive qualities of Legion service, the fact remains that twice he was saved after he had sold uniform parts by sergeants who forced the clothes merchants to give back their purchases—"If [Sergeant] Siegel had not figured out what you did at Zouireg," his lieutenant told Flutsch, "your goose was cooked, my boy! It would have been too bad, perhaps, but you were cooked!"[127] Others were not so lucky. This was a real injustice of Legion service in this period, not merely because it exploited legionnaires for low pay, but especially because it helped lend credence to Clément-Grandcourt's assertion that the Legion spoiled more recruits than it redeemed. There was probably little the Legion could do about their soldiers' endemic alcoholism. Indeed, they took the view, largely against the evidence, that these periodic binges were essentially therapeutic exercises for men denied all other pleasures. Yet they might have helped legionnaires to avoid some of the dire consequences of their acts.

The denial of these "other pleasures" was also a consequence of low pay. In North Africa no woman with a reasonable hope of marriage or even aspirations, however remote, of social respectability would be seen dead with men so degraded as legionnaires. "A question asked of a woman by a legionnaire never received a reply, whatever the question was," Flutsch recorded. "The woman took on an offended air as if she asked herself what in her attitude or in her dress could have encouraged this man to ask that question, even if it was simply the time of day."[128] Therefore, outside of Indochina and in the days before the BMC [Bordel Militaire Contrôlé], young and virile men found few outlets for their sexual energies. Flutsch was advised to masturbate "when it itches too much. . . . It isn't with your daily pay, which you need just to pay for your soap, that you are going to treat yourself to a harem." There was a rather robust Toulousaine well past her prime at Géryville willing to copulate for a legionnaire's modest pay.[129] However, Merolli claimed that prostitutes attracted only a few "old hands not too careful about their health."[130] Even the establishment of the BMC in the interwar years was a dubious perk that in no way substituted for higher pay. Any resemblance between a visit to the plump and overage North African women who inhabited the BMC and sexual gratification was purely coincidental. On payday especially, the emphasis was definitely placed on volume rather than customer satisfaction: "Come on, you! Your turn! Give duro [money]! Hurry! Not here to waste time!" Those who turned to the girls of the casbahs ran "terrible dangers," Martin believed. "All or almost all were rotten to the bottom of their carcasses. And then in Islam, jealousy is not a literary concept. A knife in the back cuts short grand debates of conscience." Still, he admitted that when legionnaires returned from a column, they tended not to be too fussy.[131]

Flutsch believed that enlistment in the Legion was the surest way to avoid an amorous adventure.[132] This was not quite true. One of the consequences of the absence of women was homosexuality. This was not a major problem in the Legion, but it did contribute to the lower moral tone about which there were many complaints. Some confirmed homosexuals came into the Legion from the penal units after 1900, and these could be vicious. Flutsch was warned to watch out for them in the depot at Saïda,[133] where they were generally known as "musicians."[134] Béric believed that homosexuality was most common in the remote posts of the Sud Oranais where "inaction and boredom stimulate the force of desire; promiscuity facilitates approaches; ambient immorality excuses it." The young soldiers—*"les girons"* or pretty boys—were the usual victims. Most legionnaires, he believed, who indulged in homosexual practices were pushed to it by force of circumstance. But it created a bad atmosphere, broke up friendships and "gave birth to sentiments of distrust and disgust" that could lead to desertion and even suicide."[135] Premschwitz claimed that homosexual couples were common and that a Legion corporal in southern Algeria committed suicide "because his darling cheated on him."[136]

In short, higher pay would have gone a long way toward improving the discipline and the moral health of the Legion, and by extension its combat performance. It might also have improved its image, for Rosen believed that it was the legionnaires themselves who, exaggerating the difficulties of service in their letters home, were in part responsible for the poor opinion of the Legion in the public mind.[137] But there was little chance that Legion pay would be raised by a parsimonious government that probably calculated—correctly—that it would increase expenses while making no difference to recruitment. The colonialists, the very people who should have represented Legion interests in this matter, were no doubt sensitive to complaints of the cost of empire and the diversion of defense funds away from the metropolitan army. They had also put their parliamentary and journalistic influence behind the marines, which, as has been seen, actually benefited from the poor conditions of service in the Legion. Clément-Grandcourt added that a raise in pay would make for bad public relations, because the enemies of the Legion would claim that they were bought men,[138] a rather perverse argument as at the very least a decent wage would disarm those like Rosen who complained that the Legion was a speculation in human misery.

In the end, the verdict on the Legion before World War I must be one that combines admiration, horror and ambivalence in almost equal measure. Admiration because of those salvaged by the Legion, for its unique asylum, for the sense of dignity and purpose it gave to the lives of outcasts and exiles, men who believed that "I never slept with lady luck."[139] Generally speaking, its discipline was strict but fair and more easily understood than some of the impersonal forces that appeared to control their lives on the outside. Legion life sometimes made extraordinary physical demands on its soldiers, but then European working-class life was no bed of roses either before World War I. Flutsch found that his comrades had "the spontaneity of children" and "a certain rectitude which guides them. Here, there are no intrigues like everywhere else. If they never drank wine, they would always be very good company."[140]

But it is difficult to know if drink was a cause or simply a symptom of a deeper institutional malaise that showed the Legion's dark side. Asylum and rehabilitation there were, perhaps, for those who had the strength of character and the desire and capability to better themselves. For those lacking these basic qualities—which, unfortunately, was most of them—the Legion too often presented a smorgasbord of temptation, an atmosphere detrimental to the very rehabilitation it claimed to offer, which was not offset by the moral leadership of officers and NCOs in sufficient numbers and quality. Even officers who knew and admired the Legion—and here was the horror—admitted that it shattered as many lives as it saved, perhaps more. At its worst, the Legion might become a maw that too often mangled good intentions and condemned potentially excellent soldiers to years in discipline sections through neglect or because they were not paid enough money to afford simple human pleasures. And there were enough legionnaires who were, in Frederic Martyn's view, "queer in the upper story"[141] to make the Legion at times even a dangerous place to be, especially for those less well able to defend themselves. Even Flutsch, who, of all authors, gives the most sensitive appreciation of the Legion before 1914, had to admit that he led something of a charmed life, without which he might easily have come to harm.

For these reasons, the ambivalence follows quite naturally. For those who best knew them, legionnaires possessed an almost schizophrenic personality—aggressive yet sentimental, intemperate yet generous and sociable, men deeply wounded by life, in constant need of comfort and companionship, but who at the same time "ignore fear and know how to die, because they scorn life."[142] Flutsch argued that each regarded his softness as a character defect and did his best to hide it: "Each one wore a mask of indifference or of hardness which veiled an acute sensitivity, something to be hidden at all cost," he wrote of his comrades. "In their view, only the less virile could be moved by suffering or a fall from grace, be touched by remorse or regret."[143]

Yet this was the hand the Legion had been dealt. In the absence of reforms that might have improved the quality of recruitment and discipline, the Legion still had one arrow in its operational quiver—the mounted companies.

Chapter 15

THE MOUNTED
COMPANIES

THE MOUNTED COMPANIES provided a solution to some of the Legion's problems, the most obvious being those caused by the uneven quality of Legion recruitment. Aristide Merolli believed that the soldiers of the mounted companies were *"l'élite de la Légion . . . a very severe choice, a true selection . . . vigor, endurance, good conduct are rigorously required."*[1] Legionnaire Jean Martin had certainly found the mounted companies difficult to penetrate in 1931. Kept back at Sidi-bel-Abbès to train recruits, his repeated requests to be transferred to a mounted company had been refused. He could escape from the training unit only by threatening to commit a punishable offense. But life in a field company at Colomb-Béchar in the Sud Oranais, though better than square-bashing at Bel-Abbès, hardly fulfilled his dreams of touring the bleak frontier regions between Algeria and Morocco on muleback. Instead, the monotonous routine of the work-site was broken only by evenings spent drinking small glasses of stiff Algerian rosé *"Chez La Mère Rachel"* or in one of the town's other bars, until one day he learned that the latest reinforcement for the mounted companies was a few men light. He hurried to the company office and cajoled the corporal into placing his name on the waiting list. Within what seemed only hours, he was bouncing about in the back of a lorry traveling east to Bou-Denib, the Moroccan post that guarded the arid eastern foothills of the High Atlas.

The first day out had been a test. The mounted section, composed of a lieutenant, two sergeants, four corporals (of which Martin was one) and fifty-five legionnaires, had covered over fifty miles, changing places every hour on their twenty-nine mules. The second day had been a relatively short hike of thirty miles, almost a day off by the mounted company standards, but the lingering fatigue of the first day had made it an ordeal for Martin. The third day had been bearable, but it took almost three hours to find the well among the shifting sand dunes. "You've seen nothing yet," the veteran Corporal Leroux explained. "Wait till you see tomorrow's march . . . 24 hours without water. . . . Night march over the hammada."

As the single file of men and mules climbed the steep paths worn by goats, Martin could only think of the high, arid plateau, the redoubtable Hammada of the Guir, that he was about to cross. "When you've crossed the hammada," it was said, "you can call yourself a veteran of the mounted company." By the time the group emerged onto the summit, the sun was a blood-red trace on the horizon whose light was reflected in the crescent moon that glowed out of a blackening sky. But even in this failing light that briefly warmed the earth to the color of faint pink, the hammada appeared bald, brooding and inhospitable as it stretched limitless as a desiccated sea to the horizon. The march slowed to avoid damaging the hoofs of the mules on the large ink-black stones. The men on foot, their rifles strapped across their backs, moved to the sides of the column to avoid the dust kicked up by the animals and carried by a wind that now rose cold out of the dark plain. Those on muleback swayed in a fitful slumber, virtually immured among the sacks of oats, cooking pots and tents arranged across the backs of their mules. Every hour a whistle followed by the command "*changez-montez!*" caused a brief halt as a new rider mounting from the right extended his hand to be pulled into the Arab saddle by his partner from the mule's opposite side.

At midnight, the "*grande halte*" was called. Each man contributed some of his water to make coffee, which soon brewed over small fires that had constantly to be blown into flame. The mules were unsaddled only after an hour to avoid chills and allowed to remain unsaddled for an hour before the march resumed. Soon the sun rose into a sky bleached of color, which rapidly became so heavy with heat that it seemed to hang menacingly over the heads of the silent soldiers. Those on foot moved forward with stiff, wooden steps that betrayed increasing fatigue. At every command of "*changez-montez!*" they drew long draughts from their canteens, if, that is, they were not already empty. A mule faltered and had to be unsaddled and left behind. Before the day was out, four others were abandoned in the same way. The weariness felt by the legionnaires was more than physical. The hammada cast a spell of profound melancholy. It offered no concessions to the senses, nothing upon which the eye could rest—no wisp of gray vegetation, no fold of ground—nothing but a lugubrious plain over which stones lay sprinkled like peppercorns on an enamel plate. Martin moved forward with difficulty, his mind obsessed with a vision of a glass of cold beer, which was at least as real as the lakes that appeared on the horizon only to vanish when approached.

Near midday a veteran spied the small pyramid that marked the point of descent. As they reached the edge of the plateau and stared down over a landscape that, though brown and uninviting by European standards, appeared positively idyllic to these legionnaires, every eye searched out the small spot of greenery that marked the wells of Berbatine. Alas, the only water there proved to be a small puddle of green liquid upon which floated the bodies of dead rats—it was so repulsive that even the few horses in the section, less resistant to thirst than the mules, refused to drink. The lieutenant called a two-hour halt. The last water reserve was poured into the cooking pots. Martin was so exhausted that he collapsed onto the ground. Meridja was still over twenty miles away. He did not know if he could make it, especially after dining on salted "monkey meat" and sweet coffee. But, dismounted like everyone else, he plodded through the valley of the Wadi Guir, sinking up to his ankles in sand with each step, his throat on fire. He now regretted pouring the remaining drops from his canteen—the last of the parsimonious allocation of two liters of water per man per day—between the lips of his mule. He had been half-moved by pity for the poor beast, whose face was almost as contorted from suffering as his own, and half-motivated by a desire to play the hardened veteran.

By sundown, the group mercifully had moved out of the sand onto firm ground—at least they could mount up again. "After we cross that hill, it is only one more hour to the post," someone said. One more hour! Martin felt he could not last one more minute—the straps of his Arab sandals cut into his feet, and his throat was so parched that words, even sounds, no longer came from it. The stumbling of the mule was sheer torture. Martin took a cartridge out of his belt and fiercely, almost uncontrollably, stabbed his mule in the back of the head with the pointed end. The stumbling drove him mad. He was no longer capable of pity. A martyr himself, he sought to martyr the poor beast who shared his agony.

Finally a flare shot skyward, arched back toward the earth and exhausted itself. At the foot of a gara—a low, flat-topped hill—that marked the end of the valley, Martin could just discern the square silhouette of Meridja. He was feverish, his back and neck stiff, and he felt as if he carried a cannonball upon his shoulders. Nevertheless, Martin rejected an offer from another corporal to oversee the watering of the mules. He could not speak; he could hardly stand. Yet he could not report to the infirmary, for that would eliminate him for sure. "Come on! Let's have a drink!" One of the veterans was looking at him. "You're OK. You're just tired. It'll pass. You held your own pretty well for a greenhorn." "Don't stuff yourself with quinine." A second veteran was talking to him. "Take some aspirin, drink some hot wine and go to bed. Sweat it out, get a good night's sleep and tomorrow you'll feel better." They did not have to say more. Martin knew that he had made it, that he now belonged to the "tribe."[2]

*   *   *

THE SECOND SET of problems that the mounted companies helped to solve was the tactical one posed by fighting in North Africa. "For a long time now, experience has taught us that the principal factor in the success of our colonial wars is the rapidity of movement," wrote Captain Hélo.[3] But although the problems may have been obvious, the solution was often less so, especially in the bleak frontier regions between Algeria and Morocco where Arab horsemen moved like quicksilver, evading almost all attempts of the more ponderous French to entrap them. Rapid marches by the infantry were exhausting and often even counterproductive. The cavalry had two choices—either utilize their mobility to the full by moving beyond infantry support and thereby inviting destruction, or play it safe by staying close to home and relinquishing the initiative to the enemy. Earlier attempts to organize mounted infantry in Algeria to bridge the tactical gap between infantry and cavalry had foundered basically on a lack of sustained interest. For this reason, the conquest of Algeria had been transformed essentially into a war of attrition where the native Algerians had been hammered and starved into submission.

However, in the Sud Oranais this tactic was less effective. In the first place, the population of Arabs and Berbers was largely nomadic and offered targets that usually moved too fast for the French to hit them. Second, if pressed, they need only drop back into the quasi-security offered by Morocco. Pursuing French columns, even if they chose to violate Moroccan territory, were usually fractured by the most effective of all enemy arms—the sand seas of dunes, waterless valleys and featureless hammadas of the Sud Oranais. The shortcomings of French forces hit home hard in 1881 with the Bou Amama revolt. French columns sent to apprehend the holy man struck into thin air—most of the time. On May 19, 1881, a column that included a battalion of the Legion discovered dismounted Arabs holding a pass five hundred meters wide between two rocky hills. The infantry, including the Legion, rushed forward to attack it, leaving the convoy guarded by three squadrons of *Chasseurs d'Afrique*. The ruse of counting for success upon the impetuosity of the French worked to perfection. The Arab horsemen then swarmed upon the convoy, killing most of the *Chasseurs* and pillaging with commendable thoroughness. By the time the infantry could fight their way back, the convoy was a wreck, seventy-two French soldiers were dead, twelve were missing and fifteen were wounded.[4]

What became known as the Battle of Moualok or Chellala, though a fairly minor skirmish, was to have fairly profound consequences for the Legion. The battle drove home the by-now obvious conclusion that cavalry unsupported by infantry was vulnerable. Apart from the loss of the *Chasseurs,* the major criticism leveled at the French methods was their overdependence upon native horsemen organized as *goums* to provide the main cavalry cover. These *goumiers* were of such volatility that it was simply dangerous to rely upon them for anything except small scouting parties. When challenged by Bou Amama's horsemen, they rushed back toward the convoy with such speed that they helped to disorganize its defense. Furthermore, the inexperienced eyes of European troops were unable to distinguish friend from foe amidst the swirl of native horsemen—the enemy simply mixed in with the *goum* and in this way were able to reach their objective virtually uncontested. Even after the fighting was finished, and "the Legion had stacked arms and were congratulating themselves by smoking cigarettes, a group of dissidents led by Bou Amama himself walked through the camel convoy," read a report to the 19th Army Corps. On the day following the battle, two-thirds of the *goumiers* were sent home.[5] However, commanders were henceforth increasingly reluctant to risk their remaining cavalry by flinging them too far afield,[6] leaving their columns "sightless" and decreasing their effectiveness still further. Therefore, something clearly had to be done to provide support for the cavalry; otherwise, the French would continue to be condemned to frustration by their more agile opponents.

The second important result of Moualok and of the subsequent French paralysis in the Sud Oranais was that the man capable of providing the solution to the French problem was actually dispatched to the Sud Oranais—Colonel François-Oscar de Négrier. An 1859 graduate of Saint-Cyr, veteran of the Franco-Prussian War, where he was wounded at the battle of Saint-Privat and escaped from the subsequent German siege of Metz, de Négrier enjoyed the well-deserved reputation of being one of the army's most brilliant officers. He required every ounce of his imagination to solve the problem of immobility that afflicted the French in the Sud Oranais. De Négrier's solution did not spring full blown, but evolved gradually from December 1881. Initially, he divided the hitherto unitary columns marching in a square formation into an articulated force composed of a convoy proper with its own defense, and a "maneuver echelon" or light group composed of the most mobile forces, whose task was to attack the enemy. Companies assigned to the convoy no longer marched in a square formation, very fatiguing in broken country, but by sections on the flanks. "What a radical change!" Legion Captain Armengaud wrote, noting that this made for a more supple march order and caused far less confusion for departures and camping.[7]

The problem, of course, was the "maneuver echelon." Initially it operated close to the column. However, this structure simply offered a better method of convoy defense and still relinquished the initiative to the enemy. The problem was how to free the maneuver echelon as much as possible from the convoy to give it an independent operational task and a greater range of action. Until this was done, the maneuverability of the French would continue to be determined by the speed, or rather lack thereof, of the heavy convoy. The convoy must cease to be the focus of an operation, but serve merely as a mobile base, a sort of milk cow in the desert, to which the maneuver echelon would return periodically to re-supply.

This was easier said than done. It escaped the attention of no one that the real problem was how to provide long-range infantry support for the maneuver echelon. "The problem is not to move faster," de Négrier wrote. "But to go further for longer. . . . Fire fights are rare here. We fight with volleys of kilometers. You have to march."[8] De Négrier's first experiment with the mounted forces appears to have been a rather timid organization of fifty-four legionnaires chosen from among the best shots, mounted on Arab mules, who followed the *goum* and a squadron of *Chasseurs d'Afrique* as they ranged beyond the immediate vicinity of the convoy to provide fire support should they run into trouble.[9] But it worked. Covering 120 miles in two days, this small command fell upon a tribe that little expected the hitherto plodding French to appear out of the blue, burning their tents and making off with four thousand sheep. The column moved to collect them like an aircraft carrier sailing toward the target to gather in its flights, auctioned off the sheep and distributed fifteen francs in proceeds to every legionnaire.[10]

The experiment caught on, was imitated and expanded by other com-manders, especially after an even more successful *razzia* or raid near the Chott Tigri netted eighteen thousand sheep, six hundred camels, thirty-six horses and a number of tents and rugs in late January 1882. However, disaster befell a Legion mounted section in April 1882 while it served as an escort for a mapping party operating in the Chott Tigri—cut off from the main body, it tried to fight on muleback and was cut off and massacred.[11] This defeat for the mounted companies settled the debate between officers who argued that one mule per man increased mobility, and those who believed that such lavishness simply encouraged mounted infantry to be-have like cavalry. If half the force of a mounted company were on foot, then the other half would be forced to dismount.[12] The mounted compa-nies were set at 215 men, later raised to 230, with a little over half as many mules and horses for the officers. Other units like the *tirailleurs* and *zou-aves*, and even a few line regiments called in to help quell the revolt, imitated this experiment with mounted formations. However, after the Bou Amama rebellion died out in 1883, they were quietly disbanded in other regiments, leaving the Legion with a mounted company monopoly.[13] Lyau-tey justified retaining the mounted companies in the Legion because the European soldier

cannot endure excessive fatigue. In a word, one has to handle him care-fully. That is why one can only require of him great efforts of marching by putting him in special conditions. . . . The native soldier, used to the coun-try, acclimatized, hardened to heat, having far fewer needs, above all if one reacts against the unfortunate tendency to Europeanize him, is capable of furnishing on foot, in any terrain, a superior effort, as long as his load is light. . .

By creating mounted companies in the *tirailleurs,* "one gave to this unit more than was required."[14]

NIGHT MARCHES WERE always disliked. The only thing more disagreeable than the hours spent on foot when sandals did little to protect the feet from unseen rocks, thorns and tufts of thyme were those spent on muleback. The forced immobility was especially trying in the hours just before dawn, when a cold wind left the legionnaires shivering in a drowsy discomfort. In this critical period, with nerves sharpened by fatigue, the last thing one needed was for a mule to go down in the middle of the track. Martin stopped to help the rider bring his prostrate animal to its feet. But the beast, part of the machine gun section, refused to get up, even though he only carried a pack of 180 pounds, about thirty-five pounds under the burden, minus rider, carried by the other mules. There was no choice but to unload him, stand him up and reload him once again. The company filed by to the left and right and soon disappeared into the darkness. *"Dégagez la piste!"*—"Clear the track!"—a lieutenant from the light group of Algerian *tirailleurs* who followed yelled from a distance. "Can't!" Martin shouted, as he pulled furiously at the tangle of straps and equipment that lay under the mule. "I can't move. I've got a mule down, and I can't get him up." "I don't give a damn!" shouted the officer. "I'm ordering you to . . ." But before the words were out of his mouth, Martin cursed him as another legionnaire struck his horse across the withers, sending the lieutenant galloping involuntarily up the trail, his swearing becoming less audible as he vanished into the blackness. In garrison this would have earned Martin a few days in prison. But once the lieutenant's anger subsided, he probably realized that everyone's nerves were on edge, and did not bother to locate the legionnaire who had insulted him.[15]

A THIRD PROBLEM to which the mounted companies offered a solution was the high dropout rate on the march, which had diminished Legion effectiveness in other campaigns. The problem of the Legion was not their fighting qualities: "In full force," General Trumelet-Faber wrote in 1913, "the Legion shows its superiority." As usual, the problem was to get it to the battlefield in something like full strength. The Legion was solid under fire and, above all, "she furnishes a considerable moral support to native troops." But the blistering route marches under staggeringly heavy loads were more than many legionnaires could bear, despite a "constant and excessive pride" that drove legionnaires to overreach themselves in the presence of Arab troops.[16] Yet before the mounted companies could solve this or any other of the Legion's problems, it had to be properly employed.

The Legion's retention of the mounted companies after 1883 may well have had more to do with tradition, to which that corps was becoming firmly attached, than with any clear idea of tactical needs. There were attempts to use mounted companies in the Western Sudan in 1892-93 and in Madagascar in 1895. In Madagascar, the attempt to improvise a mounted company got off on the wrong foot: "Nothing more picturesque than this departure," wrote Lieutenant Langlois.

The mules, realizing that they are required to make a new effort, are uncooperative. They stop, bray, refuse to advance, while their unfortunate riders, who are not especially enthusiastic about this night ride, swear at them in the most diverse languages. All finally disappeared in a cloud of dust, and the camp returned to calm.

But not for long, for during the next day riders without mules and mules without riders trickled back, and the idea was abandoned.[17]

In North Africa, where the mounted companies had been born, a shift in strategy had brought about a profound change in their status. After the end of the Bou Amama rebellion, the French adopted a defensive posture on the Algerian/Moroccan frontier that consisted of holding a series of posts manned principally by infantry whose purpose was to prevent incursion by raiders out of Morocco. The mounted companies, originally conceived as a force of pursuit and reconnaissance, were assigned principally the task of escorting convoys between these posts. One of these half-companies was ambushed on September 2, 1903, near a place called El Moungar, as it escorted a convoy southward toward the garrison of Taghit. Those who escaped death in the initial fusillade fought on valiantly all day until rescued by a detachment from Taghit, but not before losing thirty-five killed and forty-eight wounded. Although, as usual, the Legion made a virtue of necessity by hailing the defense of El Moungar as a second Camerone,[18] the reports laid the blame for the defeat squarely at the feet of the detachment commander, Captain Vauchez, who was said to be insufficiently vigilant, had chosen his ground badly and had placed virtually his entire escort in the *avant-garde*.[19]

The disaster at El Moungar, like that of Moualok, was paradoxically to revive the fortunes of the mounted companies, perhaps because the defeat brought out their critics. Opponents of mounted companies argued that the enormous amounts of water consumed by the mules, the high price they fetched in North Africa, a price that made them an especially attractive target to the Moroccans, and the fact that, once in combat, the mules were actually a great encumbrance limited their flexibility and meant that the costs of the mounted companies exceeded their military value.[20] Defenders countered that they were perhaps expensive, but less so than a battalion of infantry, which was the alternative, and a less effective one at that.[21] One of the ways to answer these criticisms was to free the mounted companies from their role as convoy escorts and restore their tactical mobility. But the essential precondition for this was change of strategy, a requirement fulfilled by the arrival of Colonel Hubert Lyautey as commander of the Sud Oranais in the autumn of 1903.

Lyautey had served as chief of staff to Colonel, later General, Joseph Galliéni in Tonkin and Madagascar, where he had helped to apply Galliéni's *"tache d'huile,"* or "oil spot," methods of pacification. An ardent imperialist, Lyautey was firmly convinced of the need to absorb Morocco into the French orb, and believed that the *"tache d'huile,"* hitherto a pacification technique, could also be adapted to one of conquest in the turbulent and ill-defined conditions of eastern Morocco. Lyautey arranged his forces into three categories: The "mobile elements" were composed essentially of *goums* led by French officers whose task was to pursue raiders into Morocco and to provide reconnaissance and distant security for posts that Lyautey began surreptitiously to create inside the frontiers claimed, but not occupied, by the Sultan. The Legion mounted companies and "lightened *tirailleur"* units composed the second-echelon "support elements," while regular Legion and *tirailleur* units occupied the bases at Aïn Sefra, Béchar and Ras-el-Aïn (Berguent) from which these units scrambled.[22] In this way, Lyautey rescued the mounted companies, and perhaps in the process the military reputation of the Legion before World War I.

Lyautey made great claims for the success of his "system," which combined these innovative tactics with economic incentives calculated to draw the dissident Moroccans into the markets he set up in his posts. Unfortunately for the French, Lyautey's reforms did not work well, at least not as planned. His *goumiers,* recruited mainly from the sedentary tribes of Géryville, lacked the mobility and ferocity of the Moroccan raiders, who almost invariably escaped to the Tafilalt in Morocco. Reduced to virtual impotence by lack of intelligence and mobility, virtually the only option open to the French was to carry out reprisal raids upon nomadic *douars* in Morocco. Lyautey's economic reforms fared no better—the Moroccans saw no contradiction in trading with the French one minute and plundering them the next. What was more, by drawing trade away from traditional interests in Fez and Marrakesh, as well as through his policies of encroachment into the Sultan's territories, the French reaped a whirlwind of rebellion in 1908.[23] Ironically, perhaps, this allowed the mounted companies to come into their own, but in ways that were not foreseen by the tactical theories of de Négrier and Lyautey.

In the spring of 1908, a large *harka* or war party of Moroccans organized in Eastern Morocco. French forces, divided into three columns, marched out of Algeria to converge on the *harka* from three different directions before it could strike at Béchar, its intended target. On April 14, 1908, the 24th Mounted Company of the *1er étranger,* accompanied by a small contingent of native spahis, settled into the small oasis of Menabha, in the valley of the Guir, about eight miles from the position of the *harka*. Menabha was pleasant enough by the standards of the Sud Oranais— plenty of water, a few palm trees and an abundance of stones that the legionnaires immediately began arranging into a defensive wall, taking care to avoid the scorpions that invariably lurked beneath, in preparation for the arrival of the column. Around five o'clock in the evening, the legionnaires on foot, *tirailleurs, zouaves,* a battery of small 80-mm mountain guns and a convoy of eight hundred camels filed into the camp to await the order to attack, which would come as soon as the other columns were in position.

However, the *harka* hardly intended to leave the initiative to the French—at ten minutes past five o'clock on the morning of April 16, Legion Sergeant Charles Lefèvre of the mounted company was awakened by shots fired at a distance from the camp. Instinctively he slipped from his tent to join a line of legionnaires who lay prone along one face of the camp square. Almost immediately a heavy fire erupted from the hill overlooking the camp. Fortunately, in the predawn obscurity it was aimed at the line of white tents behind them. Nevertheless, a few legionnaires began to groan as bullets struck them. As the legionnaires lay on the ground staring outward into the darkness, they could hear a loud clamor behind them. But before they had time to react, a line of ghostly white figures began to appear to their front. Soon the camp was overrun with Moroccans. In the pandemonium, Lefèvre rushed back to his tent to rescue his savings account book. He passed through the line of dead, dying and panic-stricken mules to join a redoubt organized by the mounted company behind their feed sacks. The lieutenant ordered him to carry a wounded legionnaire to the aid station, which he did, dodging through a hail of bullets to the ambulance, which itself was in the center of the fighting—a Moroccan who had been shooting the wounded through a tear in the tent had just been killed.

When Lefèvre joined his section, which was engaged in a lively bayonet drill with the enemy, he could see in the growing light that the face of the square occupied by Algerian troops had been completely broken (to be fair, a section held by forty-seven legionnaires of the *2e étranger* had also been submerged and forced to retreat into the camp), admitting a torrent of Moroccans. This situation was salvaged by two initiatives. First, a section of seventy-five legionnaires from the mounted company, supported by the artillery, assaulted the hill overlooking the camp. Although they were subsequently given high marks for excellent fire control and good use of ground, the crest was taken only after ten legionnaires were killed and seventeen wounded, largely because they had been so heavily outnumbered.[24] Second, in the camp, the Moroccans allowed their pillaging instincts to get the better of their discipline. This took the pressure off the defenders, who retired to organize a counterattack that succeeded in driving the Moroccans from the camp, but only after the sun was well up. "Our aggressors now flee in front of us, and we kill them at point blank range," Lefèvre recorded in his diary.

The chase continues for about two kilometers from the camp. All around one only sees the white burnouses billowing in the wind in a desperate flight. We shoot many of them by adjusting our distances just like on the firing range. The wounded get no quarter. They are mercilessly finished off with a bullet in the head or a bayonet thrust in the chest. In any case, they await death with a fatalism which characterizes them. . . . Pity is absent from our hearts at this moment.

They then sat down among the cadavers to have some breakfast.[25]

Lefèvre called Menabha a victory, which it undoubtedly was in the narrow sense that Moroccan losses had been estimated at over 100 men. Still, the French had been utterly surprised even though they knew they were in the presence of a superior force. Their failure to secure the high ground above the camp with anything greater than a small post cost them dearly—Lefèvre estimated French losses at 50 dead and 120 wounded. The mounted company alone counted 19 dead, mostly from the assault on the hill outside the camp. And while they had covered themselves with glory—indeed, the column commander announced to the captain commanding the mounted company that "It was your company that saved the situation"[26]—this was hardly the task for which they had been designed. Besides, the losses in mules had been substantial, while the Moroccans returning to their villages and *douars* laden with pillage propagated the view that they had actually won a great victory, and this swelled the support for those who preached a holy war against the French.

In any case, the Moroccans were not defeated, and as they reformed at Bou Denib in early May, the French moved to attack them. Lefèvre found the valley of the Guir, through which the 24th Mounted Company marched on May 13 as flank guard for the French column, rich by the standards of Eastern Morocco. Small fields of wheat and barley grew beside the broad bed of the wadi, while *ksour*—fortified villages shaped and squared like medieval fortresses—lay barely visible behind groves of deep green date palms. To the south, the Hammada of the Guir rose up like a high wall. By midafternoon, the French came in sight of the camp of the *harka* at the large palm oasis of Beni Ouzien. After a preliminary artillery bombardment, the 24th was flung into an attack on the Moroccans who occupied the palm grove. However, once beneath the trees, they could no longer be supported by their artillery. "We had to carry on by ourselves, or beat a retreat, which didn't cross our minds," Lefèvre recounted. "Numerous enemy bodies lay on the ground and money spilled out of their bags which we don't even have time to pick up." Toward evening, they were withdrawn from the grove. "Moroccan losses must be considerable," Lefèvre believed, "because at this late hour of the night one hears from all points on the plain the lamentations of the wounded and of the survivors looking for corpses."[27]

General Bailloud, the commander of the 19th Corps, severely criticized this action as another example of a lack of interarm cooperation that was in evidence at Menabha, and of a lack of a methodical battle plan. The French commander, General Vigy, had become "hypnotized" by the struggle of the 24th Mounted Company, and had engaged in a battle beneath the palm trees where his 75-mm artillery pieces could not be brought into action.[28] One might also add that, once again, the mounted company had been used as élite assault troops when there had been plenty of infantry available to undertake such actions. In the process, the mounted company had lost fifteen dead, including its interim commander. For this reason, the 24th was held in reserve on the following day when the *Ksar* of Bou Denib was first bombarded and then attacked by the French. However, they participated in full measure in the pillage of the town that soon began. "Our mounts are laden as much as possible with dates, barley, flour, burnouses and arms," Lefèvre wrote. Outside the town, five hundred men and three hundred women were under guard. "One of [the women] makes me understand that she has lost her child in the fight and pleads with me to find it. I am lucky enough to put my hands on it and bring it to her. She makes me a gift of her glass necklace from the Sudan."[29]

Though the Moroccans had been badly mauled at Bou Denib in May, they had not yet been so badly defeated that they had given up. The mobile troops organized to pursue the retreating *harka* failed to find it. Therefore, the French could not have been surprised when it reappeared before Bou Denib in August. From the Moroccan viewpoint, however, it proved to be a mistake. Assaults upon the *Ksar* of Bou Denib, newly fortified and garrisoned by the 24th and supported by artillery, and upon an outlying blockhouse also held by legionnaires, were costly failures. The arrival of a relief column allowed the French to march out of Bou Denib on the night of September 6–7 with five thousand men and eighteen artillery pieces onto the Plain of Djorf, where the *harka* had made camp. "The sunrise offers an impressive spectacle," wrote Lefèvre. "Before us stretching for at least six kilometers are all the tents of the *harka*."[30] What followed was a massacre. The Moroccans attacked the French square and were blasted from a distance by the artillery, which, after a time, then turned on the camp, which disappeared in pillars of smoke. The Moroccans, or rather those still alive, fled up the pass that led out of the plain, pushing donkeys laden with what they could salvage of their possessions. The mounted company was launched in pursuit and discovered a trail of wounded and dying, "lying in every corner and we still find human debris at more than ten kilometers from the battlefield." The scene at Bou Denib was worse, where the inhabitants had been impressed to bury the dead, "but the job was carried out too quickly, for one sees feet, hands and heads sticking out. . . . Pestilential odors permeate everything."[31]

The performance of the mounted companies at Menabha, Bou Denib and Djorf in 1908 considerably strengthened their reputation, even though, as seen, there they had been used as line infantry rather than in reconnaissance and cavalry support roles. This reputation was enhanced still further in 1910, when a mounted company singlehandedly held off a furious Moroccan attack on the Moulouya River in Eastern Morocco. Such was the performance of the mounted companies that in 1913 General Trumelet-Faber could report that ". . . this unit occupies almost by itself half the history of the Regiment in the pacification of the Sud Oranais."[32]

In fact, Trumelet-Faber was so enthusiastic about the mounted companies that he believed that they should form the basis for a complete reorganization of the Legion. "Mounting the entire Legion would perhaps be going too far," he believed, but he suggested that each battalion could furnish a 200-man mounted company and three "light companies" of 150 men each. A mounted company came fresh into combat, and could put 160 rifles on line (discounting the 40 men detailed to hold the mules): "One must witness the agility and vigor with which the 160 men come into action. These 160 rifles have a first class aggressive capacity." Furthermore, it would allow the French to cut down the number of European troops used on campaign, because the mobility of the mounted companies and their lower rate of attrition permitted them to support four times their number of native troops. Trumelet-Faber cited the Moulouya campaign of May–October 1912 as proof of the endurance of the mounted companies, when only 12.9 percent or 29 of 225 men dropped out, compared to 23.5 percent or 129 of 548 men lost to sickness and exhaustion in the Legion infantry battalion that took part.[33]

But this solution to the high attrition rate in the Legion was perhaps not as simple as Trumelet-Faber believed. In the first place, despite double pay and an aggressive, elite image, volunteers failed to come forward in large numbers for the mounted companies. Raimond Premschwitz believed that "One does not go willingly into the mounted company, because one has no rest and is always on the road."[34] And those who did volunteer seldom planned to make it a career. In 1902, General Fernand O'Connor agreed that the mounted companies were indeed an elite, but no one was willing to serve in them for longer than a year.[35] When Lyautey came to the Sud Oranais in 1903, he discovered that so great was the turnover in the mounted companies that they were completely disorganized for a great part of the year. One of his first reforms was to stagger the replacement schedule to limit the effects of this periodic disorganization.[36]

The high turnover in the mounted companies came as a great shock to General Bailloud when, in September 1910, he sought out the 24th Mounted Company to congratulate those who had fought so bravely two years earlier, only to discover that none were left: "There had been a *complete turnover* in two years," he reported.[37] However, he simply betrayed how little he understood the mentality of the mounted companies.

When, in September 1908, Lefèvre was sent back to Algeria, he announced that "I left the infected post of Bou Denib with no regrets. For with the glory of our arms we have above all collected misery. Often, not to say always, badly fed, badly quartered, paying top price for everything with no compensation, that's OK for awhile. But one ends up by becoming fed up, and we are all very tired."[38] English legionnaire A. R. Cooper, who served in the mounted companies in the interwar years, found the life desperately hard: "The officers of the mounted company were old legionnaires and very severe," he wrote. "The hardships and monotony of life were terrible. It was perhaps my hardest time in the Legion. I lost all count of time and did not care about anything, least of all what happened to me. I was hopeless and desperate." Even in garrison, there was nothing to do but "stare at sand and grumble."[39]

So while the attrition rate on campaign in the mounted companies was less than in regular infantry units, legionnaires did not therefore prefer to serve on muleback, at least not indefinitely. The mounted companies owed their lower attrition to a more rigorous selection and to the fact that the men were not obliged to carry heavy packs. Nevertheless, the fact remained that the long route marches, while punishing, occurred only periodically in the infantry, and alternated with perhaps tedious but not especially oner-ous garrison duty elsewhere in Algeria, Tonkin or Madagascar. The mounted companies, by contrast, were given little leisure, which made them an unattractive prospect for many.

And while those legionnaires who longed for the active life, who dis-liked the monotony and petty restrictions of the barracks, sought out the mounted companies, even they found the life too rigorous to endure in-definitely. Already the shortage of volunteers for the mounted companies had forced the Legion to designate the unwilling, so that Trumelet-Faber's plans to expand them would have met resistance, and probably a higher attrition rate. Also, there were already complaints that, as in the Legion overall, there were simply not enough officers and NCOs to staff the mounted companies as constituted, much less in an expanded version.[40]

It is also perhaps ironic that at almost the very moment that Trumelet-Faber was suggesting an expansion of the mounted companies, other gen-erals, including Lyautey, were debating whether to withdraw them from the Sud Oranais. The reason for this was simple—desertion had become a serious problem in the mounted companies there. In fact, in the decade before World War I, desertion had become a serious problem in the Legion generally. Of course, the problem was not a new one—desertion in Mexico and during the passage to the Far East has already been discussed. But the question of desertion in the Legion became a far more important one with the approach of World War I for two reasons: first, because it became a serious issue that sharpened tensions between France and Germany before the war. And second, because it caused many French officers to doubt the loyalty of legionnaires and consequently discouraged operational and tactical experimentation in the Legion.

The main problem lay with the perception of what desertion in the Legion was about, and what was really behind it. As was suggested in the chapter on Mexico, much desertion was on impulse, not surprising given the nomadic disposition of many legionnaires. French psychologist Roger Cabrol found that each legionnaire harbored "the almost permanent intention [to desert] whatever his seniority," even though they seldom acted on it. Legionnaires were inherently unstable men. As their enlistment was an expression of a desire to travel, "to purify themselves," to "find a new beginning," so desertion was a continuation of the same quest for change.[41] General Daudignac agreed that desertion was inherent in the nature of Legion recruitment, "troubled spirits, wanderers motivated by the taste for adventure, the thirst for money or the need to change." Whenever he asked legionnaires why they deserted, he always received the same answer: "To see some country. There is nothing else to do here."[42] Merolli pointed out that many deserters had already deserted from the German army, and so found it easier to desert a second time.[43]

"One could see very clearly how the men who assembled [in the Legion] behaved," Junger wrote.

Hardly had they achieved this goal, often at the price of great difficulties, than their covetousness gave way to an equally acute disillusion, and they set out with an equal determination, to flee again. All had sought something very vague, perhaps a place where there was no law, perhaps a fabulous world, or even equally an island of forgetfulness. But they quickly saw the absurdity of their attempt, and homesickness took over like a breakdown of the spirit.[44]

Desertion might be triggered by thoughts of home, by resentment caused by the use of the Legion as a work detail rather than as a fighting unit, or simply by the feeling among legionnaires that youth and opportunity were passing them by.[45]

The Legion expected that many young recruits would attempt to desert, quickly rounded them up and, after fifteen days in the cells, put them back on the barrack square. "Desertion is more common among young soldiers who, homesick, regret their enlistment," General Muteau wrote in 1910.[46] But by the turn of the century, if not before, desertion had become such an integral part of the Legion experience that it was considered almost a rite of passage for a new recruit. Ernst Junger found that desertion was a sort of Legion game at which he resolved to demonstrate his mastery: ". . . I imagined that I only came here to show the others how such an enterprise should be carried out."[47] Both Flutsch and Premschwitz discovered that they were much better accepted by older comrades after they had attempted to desert.[48]

In fact, the point of desertion was not so much to succeed, but to make a personal statement, usually in the most imaginative way possible. Desertion was part of a legionnaire's existential search for satisfaction, a flight from reality, encouraged by the tendency of legionnaires to fantasize, something that the mournful garrisons of southern Algeria probably did little to hold in check. Flutsch met a legionnaire who attempted to enlist him in a plan to escape *en masse* from Algeria and march across Morocco to Agadir on the Atlantic coast, where they would hijack a boat and sail to Malaysia. "As long as the mother of fools is not dead," Flutsch was told by one of his more experienced comrades, "the one that dreamed that one up won't be an orphan."[49] But the mother of fools had other, more successful offspring in the Legion: On December 13, 1908, fifty German legionnaires of the *2e étranger*, led by a Bavarian named Pal, commandeered a train at Aïn-el-Hadjar in the Sud Oranais and tried to get to the coast. They were stopped, and surrendered quietly. The investigation discovered that Pal had already deserted from the *1er étranger*, where he had served under the name of Kadur. He had convinced the legionnaires that he was a member of Prussian war minister Count von Waldersee's staff and had been sent on an official mission to get them to Tangier. He confessed that his escapade had been inspired by a report in a German newspaper in which a worker disguised as a captain had ordered the military guard to arrest the mayor of a small town and had made off with the municipal strongbox. Pal was given twenty years hard labor.[50]

In this situation of instability, fantasy and regret, it might take little to trigger a departure *"en bombe"*—bad news from home or a rough word from a superior that might normally be taken in stride—among an assemblage of men already predisposed toward dramatic gestures.[51] The problem this caused for the Legion was that, on the outside, desertion was attributed to the brutal conditions of Legion service. The Legion argued that, on the contrary, the sense of loyalty to the Legion sprang from a stern but fair discipline, a comprehensible set of rules that contrasted sharply with what legionnaires perceived to be the arbitrary, often unjust, nature of the life that most had experienced before enlistment. Yet the fairness of Legion discipline was not universally acknowledged. Trumelet-Faber complained that many punishments in the Legion sprang from the fact that foreigners, Germans especially, did not understand orders and were punished when they were slow to carry them out.[52] For instance, Pfirmann was given a hefty fifteen days in the cells after he mistakenly signed a chit ordering eight coffee rations when there were only seven men present in the room: "I did not speak enough French to justify myself," he wrote.[53] And while this certainly did not produce desertion in his case, in men less well disposed, confronted with more weighty cases of injustice or an accumulation of smaller examples of arbitrary or unfair discipline, the cards in the Legion might appear to be as stacked against them as they had been on the outside, perhaps more so. Indeed, the complaint about Legion punishments was not so much their severity, but their frequency. The tendency of Legion NCOs to distribute days in the cells for the most minor infractions could, and indeed did, create an atmosphere of unfairness, especially among foreigners.

This was important, for, as has been argued, the traditional notion of morale and discipline as something defined and imposed by the military hierarchy upon the ranks fails to take into account the role played by legionnaires in delineating their own definitions of permissible behavior. It is fairly clear that legionnaires considered desertion under certain circumstances to be acceptable conduct, a viable remedy for depression or injustice, real or imagined, and that this behavior was tolerated within limits by the military hierarchy. It was a recognition of the special psychology of their men, and the character of the regiment.

Although desertion became almost a hallmark of the Legion, it was seldom a problem in Algeria. For instance, desertion statistics for the 2e *étranger* for the first decade of the twentieth century show that, in Algeria, between 108 and 219 men deserted each year, a small percentage of regimental strength.[54] Yet the primary reason that the desertion rate was so low in Algeria was that there was simply no place to desert to. To get out of Algeria successfully, a deserter invariably had to have money to buy civilian clothes and a ticket out. Rosen claimed to have pulled it off because, riding first class in a new suit of clothes bought with money sent by his girlfriend, he looked too much the gentleman to be taken for a legionnaire, and therefore no one asked to see his passport.[55] Flutsch was told that Jews, because they would be given aid by their numerous co-religionists in North Africa, and madmen, because the Arabs treated the deranged with great reverence, enjoyed the greatest success rate: "Don't you worry about him," Flutsch was told of an Italian who escaped completely naked from the hospital where he had been confined for strange behavior. "He can go without problem from douar to douar, from Morocco to Tunisia. He speaks Arab. He's loony. They will treat him everywhere like he was Mohammed. Anyone who can play the fool will be listened to on all fours, and will never lack for couscous or grilled mutton."[56] Most deserters, like Ernst Junger, were rounded up in a matter of days, if not hours, walking down the high road or following the railroad tracks between Sidi-bel-Abbès and Oran, so that they might not even have the six days' absence required to be classified as a deserter.[57]

However, the association between desertion and the Legion inevitably led to accusations of brutality and harsh treatment of those caught. Like many, indeed most, deserters, Premschwitz was arrested by native Algerians, who surrendered him to kindly French gendarmes for the twenty-five-franc reward normally handed out for deserters. However, he considered himself "divinely blessed," as, he claimed, many deserters were simply killed, or returned to the Legion in desperate condition after having been dragged behind the horses of the native police.[58] The French writer Hubert-

Jacques ridiculed the accusations common in the German press before World War I of brutal treatment inflicted upon deserters.[59] However, Doctor Alcide Casset, who served in the Sud Oranais toward the end of the century, agreed that the *goumiers* sent on the trail of deserting legionnaires with orders to bring them back

"dead or alive" seldom troubled to encumber themselves with exhausted men: They are always brought back "dead." In effect, the reward they are paid is the same. They find it infinitely simpler and more rapid to kill the man and bring back only his head. . . . I was called upon to verify their deaths by looking at the heads. In these conditions, no fear of making a diagnostic error.[60]

This appears to have been the case on the wild frontier because it was a war zone and therefore desertion, especially with arms, was considered a serious offense. It was also severely punished during World War I, when the French were seldom prepared to treat desertion with indulgence—Colonel Xavier Derfner reported that four German deserters returned by *goumiers* were summarily shot: "The next day, their bodies were exposed beside the track, so that the column marching to El-Bordy, and the legionnaires in particular, would note that it was not easy to desert."[61]

Some legionnaires, especially those armed and prepared to defend themselves, might also have to be overcome by force. However, in the more settled regions of Algeria where desertion was a less desperate act, its policing was less harsh and far more routine. Junger was captured after only one day by an entire Arab village, which, he was later told, regularly found Legion deserters hiding in their haystacks, which were one day's march from Sidi-bel-Abbès. The native police who took them to jail consoled them by saying that they would have their wives prepare "a nice little soup" for them. "Here there is a relationship established between the hunter and his game," he concluded.[62] Nor must it be assumed that the *goumiers* who came to claim their reward, saddlebags filled with heads, did so at Legion posts, for they surely would have been murdered. For instance, Flutsch was told of an incident in which a Legion sergeant severely thrashed a sergeant of the *Bats d'Af* after he delivered a Legion deserter whom he had forced to march without shoes.[63] In fact, outside of war zones, the Legion was very tolerant of desertion, and punished it severely only after the fourth attempt.

This is not to say that desertion could not pose problems for the Legion, for when the Legion arrived at a place that offered the possibility of a successful escape, then "Katie bar the door!" The Suez Canal, as has been seen, was one such place. Even Galliéni, who requested six hundred legionnaires for Madagascar so that, if necessary, he could *"mourir convenablement"* [die decently], believed that desertion could in certain conditions seriously compromise Legion performance. "A clever enemy who will make them promises and will keep them could certainly provoke desertions which not only could weaken our numbers at a time when they could not be reinforced," he wrote in 1900, "but even more could give the adversary intelligence on our military situation . . . with [legionnaires], the spirit of adventure dominates the sentiment of discipline and professional pride."[64]

It may well be that the "clever enemy" that Galliéni feared was present in Casablanca in 1908. In the years before World War I, an active campaign against the Legion was carried out in Germany by pan-Germanists, army and navy leagues, and specialist organizations such as "The German Protection League against the Foreign Legion" in Munich and "The Association to Combat the Enslavement of Germans in the Foreign Legion."[65] But while this was limited mainly to hostile propaganda whose goal was to discourage Germans from enlisting in the Legion, French soldiers long believed in the existence of German-run "desertion agencies." On September 25, 1908, their suspicions were confirmed when five legionnaires in the company of the German consul were shouted at by a French lieutenant in charge of the port guard as they attempted to row to a German freighter standing off Casablanca. The Moroccan oarsmen panicked and plunged into the sea. The surf caught the small boat and capsized it, allowing the French to arrest the five waterlogged legionnaires on the beach.[66] A sixth legionnaire was arrested in the company of the Austrian consul thirty minutes later. The German consul protested that, as he had given them a *laisser-passer,* they fell under his jurisdiction according to treaties arranged with the Moroccan Sultan. The French countered that the deserters were under contract to the French army, and steadfastly refused to release the legionnaires and apologize, as the Germans demanded.

In the atmosphere of growing national tension, which had been heightened by what the Germans saw as a high-handed French encroachment into Morocco, the *"affaire"* of the Casablanca deserters practically brought the two nervous governments, goaded by their respective jingoistic presses, to blows. However, both Berlin and Paris realized soon enough that the legal status of six legionnaires hardly offered a cause worthy of unleashing a general European war. On November 24, 1908, the two governments agreed to offer mutual excuses and refer the matter to the International Court at The Hague, which ruled that French jurisdiction over those who enlisted in the Legion was binding.

What became known as "the affair of the Casablanca deserters" served to underscore Galliéni's fears that Legion desertion not only could in certain circumstances undermine fighting strength and perhaps morale, but also made the employment of the Legion in politically sensitive areas like Morocco a hazardous undertaking. A report of October 1, 1908, said that 217 legionnaires had deserted in Casablanca in a little over a year, or roughly *30 percent of the effectives.*[67] A November 1907 letter to the war minister from Corporal Benedittini of the *2ᵉ étranger* claimed that these "numerous desertions," as well as the large number of courts-martial in Casablanca, could be traced to the brutality of Legion NCOs: "The foreigners arrive in the corps, above all the young ones, being treated as I have just described to you, soon learn to hate the name of French," he wrote.[68] This might possibly be true in certain cases, but brutality does not suffice to explain the fever of desertion that struck the Legion at Casablanca. The more likely explanation is that legionnaires were exercising their God-given right to take French leave.

Yet the large number of desertions in Casablanca demonstrated that there were some theaters in which the employment of the Legion was politically dangerous and where its military effectiveness might be brought under serious strain. But more, it showed a dark side of the Legion's policy of efficiency built upon selection. The problem was summed up succinctly by General Dautelle, commander of the 3rd Infantry Brigade, in September 1910: "The best soldiers of the Foreign Legion, the most physically robust, are generally the foreigners," he wrote. "It is also they who desert most easily." The French did not desert because "coming often with a troubled past, they look to acquire in the Legion a retirement pension with the minimum of effort and fear neither discipline nor prison."[69] The desertion statistics of the *1er étranger* for the first eight months of 1910 bear out Dautelle's observations—only 11 of 168 deserters were French, and most of these had not returned from a home leave.[70] The French reported on October 1, 1908, that of 217 desertions in the Legion in Casablanca, 114 were German, 80 were Austrian and only one was French.[71]

This dilemma confronting Legion officers—choosing good soldiers who were potential deserters, or bad soldiers—was especially acute in the mounted companies. The Legion, indeed, the entire *Armée d'Afrique*, was deeply shocked in July 1910, when eighteen soldiers of the 3rd Mounted Company of the *1er étranger* fled into Morocco.[72] "One mustn't believe that it is the bad soldiers who abandon their regiment," Colonel Girardot of the *1er étranger* reported of these men. "Many of these deserters were excellent soldiers. Among those of the 3rd Mounted Company, a large number had no, or only minor, punishments. One must keep in mind that many foreigners who enlist with us have already deserted their flag."[73] Captain Met, who investigated this desertion, blamed it on the fact that the company simply was at the end of its tether because of constant campaigning. This certainly seems to have been a contributory factor. However, in this case, as perhaps in others where nerves were on edge, an act of misplaced severity on the part of an NCO appears to have pushed the men over the brink: A sergeant forced legionnaire Weinrock, whom he suspected of malingering, to miss several turns on muleback. The sick Weinrock subsequently fell behind the column and was murdered by an Arab. This certainly triggered the exodus.[74]

Also in July 1910, several soldiers of the 5th Mounted Company deserted because they believed they were less than twenty-five kilometers from the Spanish enclave of Melilla.[75] The *1er étranger* reported that of 160 desertions from that regiment between January and September 1910, 105 had occurred in the frontier region.[76] Desertions in the mounted companies were especially galling because these were picked troops, and as they were mounted, they had the best chance of making good their escape. Legion desertion had become pervasive enough by the summer of 1910 that the army seriously considered withdrawing the Legion into the interior of Algeria.

However, for several reasons they were obliged to accept Legion desertion as an occupational hazard. In the first place, they simply did not have enough white troops, and given the colonial calculus that required at the very least one white soldier for every two native rifles, the Legion was indispensable. General Bailloud wrote at the height of the desertion crisis in 1910 that the only other available white troops in North Africa, the *zouaves,* were full of conscripts, half-trained and unable to endure the climate. "In an Arab country, we cannot leave only the tirailleurs in contact with the natives." Given the alternatives, he believed that a few desertions among legionnaires were *"pas grave."*[77]

A second reason why Legion desertion did not worry the high command unduly was that it tended to be a cyclical phenomenon. Lyautey believed in 1910 that the Legion's problems "Are today visible and acute in a way which is unfortunately glaringly obvious." But he also believed that desertion would dry up because "The murder by the Riffians of most of the deserters has produced the most salutary effect which will certainly discourage desertions."[78] General Dautelle argued that it was not even necessary to advertise the fate of deserters who fell into Moroccan hands, which the Legion systematically did. Rather, desertions, always frequent when the Legion arrived in a new desertable location, subsided as it settled in. "Once sent out, he continues like a horse that does not stop until he crosses the finish line," Dautelle reported. "Then, curiosity is extinguished and after a while desertions drop off."[79]

But while Legion desertion was not a catastrophic problem in a strictly military sense, it was nevertheless a serious embarrassment that could help to undermine efficiency. The problem of desertion in the mounted companies highlighted the reluctance of the Legion to create a cavalry regiment in the pre-1914 period. While lack of manpower and cadres probably formed the main reason why these attempted reforms remained a dead letter, when questioned on the creation of a cavalry regiment in 1902, the colonel of the *2e étranger* believed that this would simply raise the scale of the Legion's problems to a new level: Legion cavalrymen could desert more easily, while their access to saddles would make the selling of equipment profitable enough to finance weeks of revelry.[80]

General Dautelle believed that the number of deserters, though small, was important: "It is nevertheless true that there is a net loss, moral and material, with each desertion," he wrote.[81] The problem was that it gave a poor impression of the solidity of French strength in native eyes, which could tempt them into rebellion, and it also could be exploited by the Spanish, who were pushing their own claims to Morocco.[82] It also served to discredit the Legion, and as a consequence the entire French imperial enterprise, in the eyes of France and of the world. The French military attaché in Berlin, Colonel Pellé, complained that desertions in the Legion gave credence to charges by ex-legionnaires like Erwin Rosen, whose book had enjoyed immense success in Germany, and outbursts by deputies in the Reichstag that the Legion "is unworthy of a country which has pretensions to the title of a civilized nation." Writing at the height of the third Moroccan crisis of 1911, which came barely three years after that of the Casablanca deserters, Pellé wrote: "This is how that one will justify one day a war against our country, as a great cause of civilization."[83]

In the end, the Reich did not require the Legion as an excuse to declare war. But France would need the Legion to fight it.

Chapter 16

1914

THE PERFORMANCE OF the Foreign Legion on the Western Front in World War I ranked among the best in the French army. The conduct of the *régiment de marche de la Légion étrangère,* the celebrated RMLE, at such spots as Carency, Navarin Farm, Belloy-en-Santerre, Verdun and the Bois de Hangard made it one of two regiments in the French army to earn the double fourragère that combined the colors of the Legion of Honor and the *Croix de Guerre 1914–1918,* one of five regiments to have earned the *médaille militaire,* and one of nineteen to be awarded the cross of the Legion of Honor. In all, the RMLE was cited nine times in army orders, which placed it second behind the *régiment d'infanterie coloniale du Maroc,* whose ten citations made it the most decorated unit in the French army. Even today, soldiers of the *3e étranger,* heir to the titles of the RMLE, carry enough rope on their shoulders to furnish a lynch mob with the wherewithal to bring a substantial party of outlaws to rough justice.

World War I posed a serious challenge to the Legion's self-image and consequently to its fighting efficiency, for it created a tension between the Legion's traditional role as a mercenary corps experienced in colonial welfare and its legal mission to integrate those foreigners who volunteered for the French army. The groundswell of support for France from young men, many of whom were patriotic, middle-class, and often politicized, was matched only by the deception of most at being placed in a unit whose atmosphere and values were diametrically opposed to their own. How did the Legion resolve this tension? By remaining faithful to its "traditions," according to the regimental history of the RMLE. "From 1914 to 1918, the Legion, despite everything and despite everyone, *continued on its road,*" it recorded, "reinforced by thousands of brave hearts, troubled in the beginning, that it knew how to conquer"—the combination of experienced Legion cadres and the elimination of those lukewarm on the idea of serving in the Legion allowed the RMLE to realize its heroic deeds.[1] This is essentially correct. However, by defining—or redefining—its personality as an elite, professional, even colonial unit, it limited its utility to France because it deliberately squandered or eliminated important sources of recruitment.

The First World War provided a real moment of truth for the Legion, for it had to deal with a recruitment crisis that, in retrospect, was even more serious than the one that had occurred after the turn of the century. The situation may be summed up succinctly as follows: At the beginning of the war, the Legion was swamped with more recruits, and, from a traditional standpoint, many recruits of the wrong sort, than it could efficiently digest. However, by the last months of the war, it faced a dearth of recruits serious enough to jeopardize the Legion's continued presence on the Western Front, and from the point of view of its commander, even the Legion's existence as a unit. Why did this occur? Basically because the Legion reflected and was forced to pay the price for the ambiguous attitude of France to foreigners, for the French government's desire to "ghettoize" them in a unit perceived to be—to put it kindly—a holding pen for marginal social elements. In the long run, the mishandling of the initial wave of volunteers by the government, the sinister reputation of the Legion, and the spread of the conflict to countries that otherwise might have furnished recruits for the Legion, not to mention the fact that before 1914 between a fifth and a quarter of Legion strength had been furnished by France's major enemies, combined almost to scupper the RMLE.

The Amalgamation

The indelible image of August 1914 is that of the nations of Europe marching to war fairly quivering with popular enthusiasm. Such ardor could not fail to have repercussions for the Legion, especially as French law forbade foreigners from serving in the ranks of the regular French army. As early as July 30, 1914, a manifesto called upon Italians living in Paris to support France in the coming conflict. It touched a responsive chord among those for whom the memory of the Garibaldi Legion, which had fought for France in 1870, was still fairly recent history.[2] On August 1, the day that general mobilization was declared, a group of foreign intellectuals led by the Swiss writer Blaise Cendrars announced that "The hour is grave. Every man worthy of this name must act today, must forbid himself to remain inactive in the midst of the most formidable conflagration that history has ever experienced."[3] Left-wing Russian expatriates began spontaneously to drill in a cinema they hired on the rue de Tolbiac, despite protests from fellow refugees that this represented a betrayal of socialist pacifism.[4]

The many Jews who had fled to Paris in the 1890s to escape the pogroms of Eastern Europe and their descendants were equally enthusiastic—in the heavily Jewish quarter of Montmartre, a Jewish butcher rode a horse decorated with the French tricolor and placards urging Jews to enlist. A group of Jews paraded through the Place de la Bastille carrying banners in support of France, while the Jewish poet Sholem Schwartzbard composed a song that compared Jewish volunteers to the Maccabees. Rumanian Jews calling themselves the *Groupe de volontaires Juifs Russo-Roumains du 18e* opened a recruiting office in a cafe on the rue Marcadet and launched a manifesto that reminded "Fellow Jews" that "France . . . the first country in the world to grant Jews the Rights of Man—this dear country where we and our families have found sanctuary" now required their services. Groups of Russian-Jewish refugees from Switzerland arrived in Paris to offer their services to the French army, while in Brussels 82 Jews presented themselves at the French consulate with an offer to enlist.[5]

British residents of Paris were invited to call by the Imperial Club for a meeting whose purpose was the "formation of a British volunteer corps, and to offer its services to the French War Minister. . . . God save the King! Vive la France!"[6] Similar *frissons* of patriotic fervor were detected among Spanish, Luxemburgers, Portuguese, Czechs, Ruthenians, Croats, Serbs, Armenians, Syrians, Greeks and others. Even eight hundred subjects of the German and Austrian monarchies allegedly offered their services to France. On August 5, an appeal was made to American residents of Paris by René Phélizot of Chicago and others to support France, while in faraway Atlanta, Georgia, Kiffin and Paul Rockwell, both college students, had already contacted the French consul in New Orleans—by August 7, they were aboard a steamer bound for France.[7]

Cendrars complained that the French government was extremely dilatory in dealing with this surge of foreign support for France:

It had taken a good month of discussions with the Minister of War before he would accept this enormous mass of men of good will, and admit into the [recruitment] bureaux this army of foreign volunteers which furnished the world's best propaganda for the French cause (the Boches [a pejorative term for Germans] would have understood immediately. They were wild not to have us.)[8]

In fact, the French government appears to have been less slow off the mark than Cendrars believed. On August 8, the *Journal officiel* published a decree of August 3 that allowed these foreign volunteers to enlist from August 21 "for the duration of the war." There was, however, one important proviso that was to cause the French no end of trouble—these enlistments must be in the Foreign Legion.

Many of the enthusiastic recruits filled the time between the general mobilization of August 1 and their reporting dates drilling under the direction of their members with previous military experience: The Americans in the gardens of the Palais Royal, the British in the "Magic City" amusement park, the Russians in their cinema. By the last week in August, the volunteers began to report in national groups to the Hôtel des Invalides on the Left Bank, where they were given a physical and signed their enlistment papers. According to Blaise Cendrars, who reported on September 3, the scene in the stately courtyard of the Invalides was fairly chaotic, and he even met a Canadian volunteer who appeared with three hundred "semi-wild" horses that he had brought over at his own expense from Canada.[9] The formalities completed, the volunteers were marched behind their national flags to the railway stations that disbursed them to the designated training areas across France. On August 25, the American contingent, about fifty strong, followed an American flag carried alternately by Phélizot and ex-Harvard undergraduate Alan Seeger through cheering crowds up the avenue de l'Opéra and the rue Auber to the cavernous Gare Saint-Lazare to entrain for Toulouse via Rouen.[10]

In recent years, historians have challenged the notion that France went gladly, almost gaily, into war in 1914.[11] It is also possible that a desire to portray a world eager to rally to the defense of France has also caused a similar confusion about the numbers and motives of the foreign volunteers who offered their services to France in World War I. The spectacle of foreign support certainly offered a welcome boost to French morale, especially after the catastrophic early "Battles of the Frontiers," and gave her the moral high ground in the propaganda war against the Central Powers—the conservative Catholic deputy Albert de Mun boasted before the French chamber that "France has foreign volunteers, while Germany has only deserters!"[12] But exactly how many foreign volunteers she had is not clear.[13] Some of the individual national statistics appear impressive—almost 5,000 Italians volunteered, enough to form their own *régiment de marche* with an Italian commander, which fought bravely in the Argonne in December 1914 and January 1915. V. Lebedev claimed that 4,000 Russians were in French uniform by December 1, 1914,[14] although many of these "Russians" were Poles or Jews who formed their separate contingents—Jewish historian Zosa Szajkowski estimated the number of Jewish volunteers at 4,000.[15] A battalion of 928 Greeks was constituted in the spring of 1915 as the *bataillon de marche étranger d'Orient,* as was another of 948 Montenegrins, while a detachment of 53 Japanese offered themselves as a group to France.[16]

Legion statistics show that 42,883 foreigners enlisted during the course of the First World War,[17] although, as will be argued, not all of these men served in Legion units. According to figures gleaned from the various *journaux de marche,* the Legion went from 10,521 men in 1913 to 17,147 in 1914 and peaked at 21,887 in 1915, after which it declined substantially.[18]

In other words, Legion strength increased by 11,366 men in the first year, probably in the first nine months, of the war.[19] Therefore, the number of foreign volunteers for the French cause, while substantial, appears to have been less than the propaganda of the time would seem to suggest.

What motivated these foreigners to offer themselves to the French army? Again, propaganda and popular memory suggest that love for France and a desire to defend the Allied cause were behind the surge of enlistments, and this was certainly true in many cases. Cendrars's manifesto was addressed to "all foreign friends of France,"[20] as were those of other national groups. The Polish Jew Pierre Goldfarb enlisted because "France was for me a friend. This is why I defend her with the greatest courage and if I remain here, I will tell my parents: victim of his duty!"[21] The Americans Alan Seeger and Henry Farnsworth attributed their enlistments to love for France and devotion to the Allied cause,[22] as did many of the Eastern Europeans. And, as has already been noted, many Jews identified the cause of French democracy with the interests of their people—V. Lebedev was told by one enlistee that he fought "For the Jewish people!"[23] Cendrars was more prosaic—he enlisted, he said, because *"je déteste les Boches."*[24]

Therefore, patriotism, love for France and ideology were strong among those in the first wave of enlistments. However, together with these sentiments, often mixed in with them, were others. Obviously, many men of military age did not want to be left out of the first major European war in forty years, especially as it was meant to be a short one. Many of the Americans who enlisted in August 1914 were of French extraction. However, others like "Percy and Scanlon . . . both good Southern Negroes who had followed Jack Johnson to France" were drifters and adventurers who happened to be traveling in Europe,[25] and could have possessed only the vaguest notions of the larger political and strategic issues of the war. In September 1916, Seeger confessed in his diary that "it is for the glory alone that I engaged."[26] It is also clear that Seeger harbored ambitions of being a war correspondent, which he hoped his enlistment would further. Rockwell also accused fellow American Edward Morlae, who "claimed to have been everywhere and to have done everything," of only seeking "cheap notoriety," a claim that seems to have been substantiated in part when Morlae deserted in 1915 and presented himself as something of a war hero in New York.[27] Others had joined after the general closedown of factories on mobilization threw them out of work.

Nevertheless, the men who came forth to offer their services to France, though heterogeneous, were not your typical Legion recruits. Paul Rockwell noted that the *3e régiment de marche,* which was recruited among foreigners resident in Paris (although it appears that the government also profited from the mobilization to exile a number of petty criminals into the Legion), was composed in the main of men who "belonged to the most sedentary professions."[28] "As for the Legion, as far as I have seen it, it is not much like its reputation," wrote Farnsworth, himself a graduate of

Groton School and Harvard, in January 1915, after five days in the barracks of Reuilly in Paris. "Many of the men are educated, and the very lowest is of the high-class workman type." His corporal was a "militant socialist" who often engaged those from a business background in heated political discussions of the sort that were seldom heard in Sidi-bel-Abbès.[29]

"We were all foreigners, or certainly sons of foreigners, but, with few exceptions, those who held the limelight were Parisian born," wrote Cendrars of his new comrades.

There was not a single peasant among us, nothing but small tradesmen from the suburbs: tailors, furriers, upholsterers, leather-gilders, sign-writers, coach-painters, goldsmiths, and concierges, night-club musicians, racing cyclists, pimps and pick-pockets, the grandsons of the revolutionaries of 1848 who came from all corners of Europe to man the July barricades, or those of the last of the journeymen doing their Tour de France, and who settled in Paris because they were skilled workers, earned a good living and had found wives there; also a few sons of noblemen, such as the Pole, the knight of Przybyszewski [nephew of the celebrated decadent writer], or the Peruvian, de Bengoechea [killed north of Arras], son of the most eminent banker in Lima, plus a few intellectuals from Montparnasse who, like me, were enchanted by the obscene language of these exhilarating companions and their enchanting exuberance.[30]

Quite naturally, a group of volunteers motivated in great part by a love for France, or a desire to see the triumph of democracy, which they identified with the Allied cause, and which contained many intellectuals and middle-class or "high class workman types," were rather disturbed by the prospect of being deposited into a unit with the reputation of the Foreign Legion. Some protested openly at being pitched into a regiment of "outcasts from society and fugitives from justice."[31] A Jewish volunteer wrote that, "As I am a soldier and am fighting for France, it will make me happy to be called soldier and not legionnaire; and when I will go through the campaign one could not tell me that I served in a regiment which has no flag."[32] Cendrars complained that he and the other leaders of his movement had been repeatedly assured that, although the law required them to enlist as *volontaires étrangers*,

there was never any question of our being automatically enlisted in the Foreign Legion, or so we had been given to understand, and formally promised, by the highly placed persons in political, literary and artistic circles whom Canudo and I had urged to appeal to the War Ministry and the President on behalf of our recruiting movement.[33]

The American Maurice Magnus was reluctant to volunteer for the Legion, but the American consul in Algiers assured him in 1916 that the composition of the corps had been completely altered by the influx of patriotic recruits:

He told me what I had heard before, that since the war had broken out, the Legion was entirely different from what it used to be, that the traditional Legion had been cleared out and that it was made up of enthusiasts for the Allied Cause. By traditional Legionary he meant the professional soldier, adventurer, deserter. "The Legion is now a clean, healthy place," he said, "with men who have ideals, and there is an American contingent, in fact several hundred Americans. At the present moment several thousand Americans are fighting in France." This sounded very encouraging, and I felt that I had chosen the right course.[34]

Therefore, the new volunteers were rather apprehensive when they learned that they were, in fact, legionnaires. When the war broke out, the Legion counted four battalions in Algeria, three in Tonkin and five in Morocco. The Algerian battalions were ordered to send half of their strength, or about one-sixth of prewar Legion strength to France to incorporate the new recruits. Together, this would constitute four new Legion regiments: the *2ᵉ*, *3ᵉ* and *4ᵉ régiments de marche* of the *1ᵉʳ étranger* and the *2ᵉ régiment de marche* of the *2ᵉ étranger*. Legionnaires from the *1ᵉʳ étranger*, minus its Germans, Austrians and others who declined to fight the Central Powers, left Sidi-bel-Abbès on August 28 and stopped in Avignon to collect the large number of Italian volunteers before proceeding north.[35] Those from the *2ᵉ étranger* called at Toulouse to incorporate the volunteers, including most of the Americans, who had assembled there.

The first impressions were not invariably unfavorable: The volunteers at Toulouse gawked with admiration as the *2ᵉ étranger* marched smartly behind their band into the Pérignon barracks.[36] Henry Farnsworth found the legionnaires from Africa far more professional than the Paris firemen who had provided most of the cadres for the *3ᵉ régiment de marche*—one old legionnaire called *le Père Uhlin* was especially useful in showing the new recruits the ropes, quite literally. "There is an official string provided to tie the tent pegs to the outside of the sack," Farnsworth wrote. "He has at least 27 uses to which it might be put. All in his slow Alsatian legionary *argot*." He was also happy when they received a veteran Legion NCO: "It will be a comfort to have a man who knows his business over us. The firemen from Paris may be good drill-masters, but as campaign leaders they are nothing but a nuisance."[37]

But the outlook, mentality and social backgrounds of the "Africans" were so radically different from that of the new men that the amalgamation promised to be a stormy one. Lebedev explained that the training of the Eastern Europeans was going fairly well until the old Legion arrived, "people from another world, with the ideas and habits of mercenaries of the Middle Ages. It is difficult for a socialist to get used to serving with them."

Sections were "constantly divided into two hostile clans. For one found, in almost equal numbers, real legionnaires, real roisterers from Africa, and Russian volunteers who did not speak French."[38] Cendrars recorded that the arrival of the legionnaires caused a morale crisis. The Americans, he believed, took it especially hard, "for the Legion's reputation on the other side of the Atlantic was extremely sinister, and I knew more than one American who had comported himself bravely until this time, and now, secretly dreamed of deserting."[39] American legionnaire David King agreed that "The old *Légionnaires* were made of quite different stuff and were in it for reasons ranging from man-slaughter to unrequited love. It struck me as strange, at first, that there were even Germans and Turks among the *anciens*."[40] Rockwell recorded that the friction between the two groups created an atmosphere of "each man for himself and his particular group of friends."[41]

Dissension between the Americans and the old legionnaires deepened in March 1915, when two veterans made scathing comments about Americans in general and Phélizot in particular while the unit was resting behind the lines. Phélizot challenged them to a fight, and, a fair man with his fists, had the better of his opponents when, according to Rockwell, a third legionnaire arrived and, in a thumping demonstration of the Legion philosophy that the only fair fight is the one you win, smashed Phélizot from behind with a two-liter bottle of wine, knocking him unconscious. Phélizot twice reported to the infirmary complaining of severe headaches. However, the Legion doctor, working on the principle that treatment was "civilian medicine" and that his task was to "conserve the effectives,"[42] sent him back to his unit. On his return from the second visit, he collapsed by the roadside and died from a fractured skull.[43]

Seeger believed that the Legion should have been thrown into action immediately rather than allow friction between the two groups to grow, for

> . . . it must be admitted that here discontent has more than the usual to feed upon, where a majority of men who engaged voluntarily were thrown in a regiment made up almost entirely of the dregs of society, refugees from justice and roughs, commanded by sous-officiers who treated us all without distinction in the same manner that they were habituated to treat their unruly brood in Africa.[44]

Zosa Szajkowski argues that Jewish volunteers were the special objects of scorn of these old legionnaires, who taunted them that they had only come for the *gamelle,* or the mess tin.[45] The Swiss Jean Reybaz complained that the veteran legionnaires who arrived at the Avignon depot where he had been sent stole the new recruits blind.[46]

The presence of so many relatively well-off recruits also presented veterans with a golden opportunity to separate them from their cash— Magnus, who dined conspicuously every night in the best hotel in Sidi-bel-

Abbès, in this way singled himself out as a target for NCOs and even legionnaires short of cash, which, "if you did not lend, they got nasty."[47] However, David King found that, even though there was little chance of recovering principal, much less interest, loans could prove a good investment: "Non-commissioned officers were forbidden to borrow money from their subordinates, but most of them did, especially the corporals," he wrote. "It was not bad policy to lend, even if you never expected to see the money back. They rarely borrowed twice from the same man, and it certainly greased the wheels."[48]

Nor was the unfriendly reception of the "volunteers for the duration" confined to the Legion in France—"A fact that I could never properly understand was the undying hatred and jealousy that existed between the old Legionnaires and the volunteers for the war," wrote John Barret, a graduate of Trinity College, Dublin, who volunteered in August 1914, but who subsequently was sent to the Legion in Morocco. "The feeling was even more bitter on the part of the officers and non-coms."[49]

The obvious explanation for this hostile reception is that the mentality and outlook of the two groups were so radically different, similar to the problems that caused friction between the Paris firemen cadres and the Legion volunteers noted by Cendrars:

They felt out of place among us, understanding nothing of our mentality of foreign volunteer enlistees whom they considered as a collection of "bouffeurs de gamelle" [mess tin guzzlers], treating us badly, abusing us and ragging those among us who had money, that they took for the heirs of rich families or madmen. . . . It was completely beyond their understanding that all these men could come to fight gratuitously. They could not believe it. And if that flabbergasted them, they looked for shameful reasons, demeaning motives and were not far from considering us as criminals. They were different from us and cordially detested.[50]

Maurice Magnus was also told by his sergeant to request a transfer to France from Sidi-bel-Abbès because "no one is going to believe that you have come here for idealistic purposes of doing your share to aid the Allies. They could not understand that. . . . Besides, the greatest objection they will have always is that you are not one of themselves."[51]

The Bulgarian Kosta Todorov recorded the shock waves sent out by this collision of two worlds: "Idealists who had come to defend the principles of the French Revolution marched in the same ranks with professional soldiers indifferent to all ideals and values save one—the honor of the Legion and its fighting prestige," he wrote. " 'Fools! So you've come to fight for freedom and civilization? Words, empty words!' " he was told by his sergeant.

"Then why are you here?" I asked him. "Orders, of course. We're professional soldiers. We don't give a damn what we fight for! It's our job. We've

nothing else in life. No families, no ideals, no loves." Others, like Rouanet who was tattooed all over with obscene pictures, considered us rank amateurs who had no right to the glorious name of legionnaire. To earn that, one had to live through the grueling African school of desert outposts, hunger, and thirst. They all drank heavily, talked their own colonial slang, knew the field-service regulations by heart, were crack marksmen, bore up easily under prolonged marches, and had as much contempt for other regiments as for civilians. On their pre-Legion past they kept silent, but their military records could be read from their medals—China, Indo-china, Madagascar, Morocco . . .[52]

The mixing of veterans and foreign volunteers in the Foreign Legion was to have at least three unfortunate consequences. The first was that quality leadership was difficult to come by. The Legion in Africa was already short of cadres, and ill-equipped to handle the flood of volunteers that more than doubled the size of the unit. This was all the more true because a number of Legion officers, fearing that the Legion would not be sent to France, which meant that they would miss out on the war, which was expected to be nasty, brutish and short, successfully obtained transfers to line units. Some of the foreign contingents, the Italians in particular, were allowed to name some of their own cadres. Others had to be scraped up by the government from the territorial army—that is, the second-echelon reserve made up of men over thirty years old. It was to the territorial reserve that the government turned to staff the *3ᵉ régiment de marche*. However, "apart from ten or so," these men refused "to take their places in a regiment which was obviously to play an active role, but invoked as a pretext the foreign origins of the men."[53] Therefore, the Paris fire brigade, a regular army unit, was designated to furnish cadres for the volunteers of the *3ᵉ régiment de marche*. But Cendrars was categorical that even these professional soldiers saw their assignment to the Legion as an "unmerited insult."[54]

This was to have two results: The first was that the demands by the cadres to be transferred out led to a constant turnover of training personnel. "They left us one after the other during the first months, and I believe that there was not a single original instructor who remained of these men who should have set an example . . . ," wrote Cendrars.[55] Second, those who did remain often made poor leaders, either because as veteran legionnaires they lacked the experience and tact to deal with men whose backgrounds and motivations were usually far different from those of the pre-1914 vintage, or because, as Frenchmen, often reservists or territorials, sent to the Legion by default and usually against their will, they despised their men. With the exception of his captain, whom he believed "a brave man," Cendrars showered contempt upon most of his leaders, from colonel to corporal. The colonel, "a decrepit old man sent from the army geographical service, a bureaucrat, with a lorgnette and ideas from another era," obliged them to march from Paris to the front, although a train was available. His captain, whom the men nicknamed *"Plein-de-Soupe"* (Fatass), was a reserve officer who in civilian life was a judicial functionary in a Norman market town. "He believed himself to be of superior quality, and looked upon us as a collection of delinquents." The NCOs from the Paris fire brigade were sticklers for parade-ground discipline, "but as trainers of men, they were hopeless, because there is a great distance between theory and practice. . . . Not one of them fancied having their hide riddled with us." Both the lieutenant and the company sergeant were relieved after they were discovered cowering in a dugout during their first night in the trenches, leaving their men to fend for themselves.[56] Farnsworth was favorably impressed by his captain, who, a veteran of 1870, must nevertheless have been too old for the job. His fireman NCOs were "nothing but a nuisance." "We were disreputably officered in the *3me de marche,*" the American Victor Chapman concluded after the unit was amalgamated with the *1er étranger* in August 1915.[57]

Poor leadership quite naturally translated into poor morale, a second negative consequence of this unimaginative handling of the foreign volunteers. This would have serious enough implications for the fighting efficiency of the Legion. But more, it was to have a long-term effect upon the Legion's strength. The initial apprehension that many foreigners felt at being incorporated into the Legion seemed to be confirmed by the actual conditions in the regiments. Those who could began to request more congenial surroundings—the English and Belgians were allowed to transfer to their national armies, while in the spring the Italians were released to go home after Italy joined the Allies. This began a stampede to be released or transferred from the Legion, which, as will be seen, reached the point of mutiny in some units of foreign volunteers by the summer of 1915. "Every man was finding fault, grumbling, making all the possible steps to get out of the Legion into French regiments," Victor Chapman wrote.[58] Alan Seeger certainly spoke for them when he wrote in September 1915, "I feel more and more the need of being among Frenchmen, where the patriotic and military tradition is strong, where my good will may have some recognition, and where the demands of a sentimental and romantic nature like my own may be gratified," he wrote, after noting that the departure of the Russians and the Belgians in July 1915 had reduced regimental strength by almost two-thirds.[59]

The discontent among the foreign volunteers inside the Legion was reflected as well on the outside, a third consequence of the French government's policy of incorporating all foreign volunteers into the Legion. This made for bad publicity. It tarnished the propaganda victory that France had been handed by the influx of volunteers at the beginning of the war—the fact that the French government had required foreign volunteers to join the Legion was a forceful component of anti-French propaganda in neutral countries, a parliamentary committee led by the eminent French sociologist

*General Bernelle
commanded the Legion
in Spain in 1835–36.*

*Colonel Conrad, killed
at Barbastro in 1837.*

Combat in the streets of Constantine. (From Histoire de L'Algérie contemporaine *by Charles-André Julien)*

Marshal Bugeaud, commander-in-chief in Algeria in the 1840s, who doubted the Legion's ability to adapt to his counter-insurgency methods in Algeria and called for its abolition.

Abd el-Kader, leader of the Algerian resistance against the French.

Legionnaires around 1840.

Marshals of France who served with the Legion (clockwise from top left): Saint-Arnaud, MacMahon, Canrobert and Bazaine. Despite the famous officers who had served in its ranks, the Legion was eclipsed in prestige before the Franco-Prussian War of 1870–71 by the zouaves. (Saint-Arnaud, from Le Maréchal de Saint-Arnaud *by Quatrelles L'Épine)*

Colonel Carbuccia, who commanded the Legion during the 1849 siege of Zaatcha. He died of cholera during the Crimean expedition of 1854.

Colonel Viénot commander of the 1er étranger, killed in the Crimea in 1854. The Legion headquarters at Sidi-bel-Abbès and later at Aubagne in the south of France bear his name.

The death of Colonel de Chabrière, commander of the 2ᶜ étranger, at the Battle of Magenta, painted by P. Benigni.

A modern painting of the 2ᶜ étranger at the battle of Ischeriden (June 24, 1857). This painting was part of a campaign between the two world wars to reinstate the white kepi, the potent symbol of Legion particularism.

Captain Danjou, who
perished with most of
his small detatchment
of legionnaires in the
heroic defense of
Camerone in Mexico on
April 30, 1863.
Camerone became the
Legion's most powerful
legend, and Danjou's
wooden hand its most
celebrated relic. Today,
Legion recruits sign
their enlistment papers
beneath Beaucé's
painting of the fight.

The last moments of the Siege of Camerone, as painted by J.-A. Beaucé.

LEGION ETRANGER

84. Pose après la Boxe

5. SAIDA — Caserne de la Légion

DÈS. — Le déjeuner du corps de garde à l'entrée de la caserne du 1ᵉʳ Étranger

Scenes of regimental life around the turn of the century: pose *après la boxe;* Saïda; *washing clothes; guard meal; siesta.*

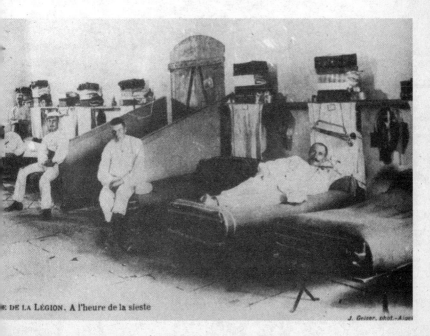

DE LA LÉGION. A l'heure de la sieste

General de Négrier, father of the mounted companies. He commanded Legion units in Algeria in 1881 and during the Lang Son expedition in 1885.

A Legion mounted company. Originally designed as a cavalry support unit in 1881, the mounted companies, operating two men to a mule, gradually assumed more independent roles in North Africa.

Emperor Behanzin of Dahomey.

Les amazones

"*Amazons.*"

General Dodds, who commanded the 1892 invasion of Dahomey.

General Duchesne, commander of the Madagascar expedition of 1895, who ordered his troops to "march or die."

A supply barge in Madagascar.

Foreign volunteers for the French army in front of the Gare Saint-Lazare, Paris, August 25, 1914.
(From American Fighters in the Foreign Legion *by Paul A. Rockwell)*

Legion volunteers with their national flags in September 1914. (From American Fighters in the
Foreign Legion *by Paul A. Rockwell)*

Legionnaires preparing to go over the top near Belloy-en-Santerre, July 4, 1916. (From American Fighters in the Foreign Legion by Paul A. Rockwell)

A Legion machine-gun company moves forward near Verdun on August 20, 1917.

The flag of the RMLE, which received the medaille militaire in 1919, making it the second most decorated unit in the French army.

General Paul Rollet, known as the "Father of the Legion," assiduously stood guard over its public image in the interwar years.

Marshal Hubert Lyautey, Resident General of Morocco between 1912 and 1925 and an avid patron of the Legion.

For the general public, the Legion's dual image of mystery and brutality proved irresistible. Georges d'Esparbès's 1912 book portrayed legionnaires as men with interesting pasts to whom the Legion offered a second chance.

LES MYSTÈRES DE LA LÉGION ÉTRANGÈRE PAR G. D'ESPARBÈS

Prix: 95 Centimes

PARIS
E. FLAMMARION, Éditeur.

GEGEN DIE DEUTSCHE SCHMACH

INTERNATIONALER VÖLKERRECHTS-BUND ZUR BEKÄMPFUNG D. FREMDENLEGION

In Germany, authorities tried to staunch the flow of young men into the Legion through such organizations as the "International Human Rights League in Opposition to the Foreign Legion," which urged their countrymen "to resist the degradation of Germans." (Edimedia)

Beau Geste. *(Photofest)*

Laurel and Hardy lampooned the myth that behind every legionnaire stood a tragic love affair by having all the men, including the rebel Arab chief, carry a picture of the same woman. (Photofest)

An allegorical painting that depicts Rollet, standing before the Legion monument with the flag of the 3ᶜ étranger, receiving the salutes of past generations.

A Legion post in the Rif War.

Sick call in the Moroccan Atlas in 1934. Medical visits offered a battle of wits between doctors ordered to maintain unit strength and legionnaires eager to escape fatigues or punishments.

Inspection of the guard at Sidi-bel-Abbès around 1930.

The midday break on the march.

The Legion was often used as a construction unit, which could lower morale and combat readiness.

The Legion created both cavalry and artillery units in the interwar years, despite fears expressed by Rollet and Lyautey that desertion and rebellion made such innovations dangerous.

The Legion shows the flag before a limited but appreciative audience in Morocco in 1936.

A sergeants' mess in Morocco.

Elements of the 13ᵉ DBLE fighting with the British 8th Army in the Western Desert in 1942. (ECP Armées—France)

The flag of the 3e étranger, *successor to the RMLE, in enemy hands in January 1943. (Editions Tallandier)*

The Gaullist 13e DBLE parading before their leader in Rome in 1944 in their Narvik berets rather than in white kepis, regarded as a pro-Vichy symbol.

"Crab" units of the REC in the Plaine des Joncs.

Legion infantry in the Tonkin delta.

Legionnaires near Hoa Binh in February 1952.

A Legion patrol.

Général de Lattre de Tassigny.

General Salan.

Legion paras drop near Lang Son during Operation Hirondelles, July 17, 1953.

A legionnaire prepares a fire to heat rations at Dien Bien Phu. The shallow trench, the lack of camouflage and the obvious profusion of equipment, not to mention the smoke he is about to make, would have struck a World War I veteran as suicidal behavior.

1ᵉʳ *REP marches through Bône on May 8, 1958, led by Colonel Pierre Jeanpierre.*
(ECP Armées—France)

A helicopter guides elements of the 1ᵉʳ REP as they clear a djebel of "fellaghas."
(ECP Armées—France)

Major Hélie de Saint-Marc and officers of the 1ᵉʳ REP during the Algiers putsch of 1961. (Editions Tallandier)

Legionnaires interrogate FLN prisoners. (From Legionnaire by Simon Murray)

The Legion departs Sidi-bel-Abbès on September 29, 1962, for Aubagne in the south of France, preceded by the hand of Danjou, the ashes of Legionnaire Moll of Chicago, and the caskets of General Rollet, Prince Aage and Legionnaire Zimmerman.

Emile Durkheim discovered in 1916.[60] It is also possible that it actually cost France some manpower, because those already in the Legion chafed to get out while those still on the sidelines were made more reluctant to enlist.

The evil reputation of the Legion and the low morale of those who had offered their services to France could not long be kept secret. As early as November 30, 1914, the French military attaché in London received a letter from "a former MP for Dartford" complaining about the treatment given his nephew, "a British subject for many years resident in Paris, and has therefore as strong an attachment to France as he has to his own country," in the *2ᵉ étranger*.

The composition and character of this regiment is only too well known. I feel sure that it could not be the desire of the French government to place young men of good character amongst the scum of Europe. My nephew writes that he is willing to fight to give his life if needs be amongst French or English Regulars, but that existence is "hell upon earth" in the midst of bad characters by whom he and his comrades are surrounded ... They don't ask to be relieved of their military duties, but to be treated as men and not outcasts.[61]

The important socialist daily *L'Humanité* complained on July 1, 1915, that some of the Russian refugees "who could have formed entire battalions" were so put off by the "arbitrary, brutal, authoritative discipline and mechanical submission" required of them that some had actually taken the, for them, risky option of returning home to Russia. Even the conservative popular weekly *Petit Parisien* published a letter on June 27, 1915, from the president of the Society of Jewish Merchants complaining that stories of "crude" treatment of Jews at the hands of officers in the Legion were such common currency "that their friends and coreligionists in Paris were deterred from joining the Legion."[62]

Of course, one must be careful to place the Legion's problems in context. The efficiency and morale of many French units suffered in 1914 from the large influx of recruits and reservists, which the cadres were hard-pressed to assimilate and lead effectively into combat, and from the high losses of the war's opening weeks.[63] Yet this cannot disguise the fact that the French government displayed a great lack of imagination in dealing with the foreign volunteers of 1914–15. The obvious course was simply to integrate most of these foreigners into regular line regiments, as most nations like the United States, Canada and Great Britain did as a matter of course, and as France eventually was obliged to do.

This would have offered several advantages: It would have attracted and conserved larger numbers of men for a French army that was heavily outnumbered by its German rival. It would have improved the morale of these volunteers by providing an atmosphere more sympathetic to their ideals and backgrounds. Last, it would have lessened the spread of resentment, which quickly took over in many of the more nationally homogeneous groups of foreign volunteers. Even a cursory reading of Legion history should have warned the war ministry that the grouping of nationalities was bound sooner or later to lead to discipline problems. "The New York papers do not exaggerate when they say this Legion is a fighting crowd," wrote Russell Kelly, a graduate of the Virginia Military Institute, in March 1915. "There are just enough of each nationality so that one country fights another."[64]

Why the government waited until the problems of the Legion had reached crisis proportions to disperse the foreigners throughout the army is an interesting one. They were well aware of the poor reputation of the Legion, and if they had forgotten, the volunteers themselves constantly reminded them of this fact. Yet at first the government stuck to the letter of a law that was an expression ultimately of a distrust of foreigners, of a reluctance to assimilate them. How could many of the volunteers have failed to resent being lumped into this category by a country they had volunteered to serve out of love, loyalty and devotion, rather than because it offered an asylum, perhaps a chance for rehabilitation, a profession, or a livelihood?

This was even more the case as it became obvious that the Legion was unprepared to make any concessions to the ideals and attitudes of the volunteers. Sergeant Max Niclot, serving with the *tirailleurs tunisiens* in Morocco, witnessed a striking demonstration of the Legion's attitude toward patriotism on August 4, 1914, when the order of general mobilization was read out before a mounted company of the *2e étranger*—a Frenchman in the ranks who greeted the news with an enthusiastic shout of *"Vive la France!"* was immediately slapped with thirty days in the cells.[65] As has been seen, this was the attitude that African legionnaires brought with them back to France. Even General Joseph Galliéni, military governor of Paris in 1914, appears to have assumed that these fresh volunteers could be motivated in the same way as their African counterparts. "I knew, by the services that the Foreign Legion had rendered in our colonial expeditions, what one could make of these troops, generally animated by vibrant traditions," he wrote after a visit to *3e régiment de marche,* that of Cendrars, at the Reuilly barracks in Paris on September 9, 1914.[66] The collision of two ideals, one patriotic and idealistic, the other professional and mercenary, was a recipe for trouble.

The first Legion unit to see action was the *4e bataillon de marche* of the *1er étranger,* a three-battalion regiment entirely made up of Italians, including its cadres, commanded by Lieutenant Colonel Giuseppe Garibaldi. At three o'clock on the morning of December 26, 1914, the regiment was awakened and each man given a ration of *eau de vie.* The night was clear but bitterly cold as the men filed stiffly toward the jump-off point before the Bois de Bolante in the Argonne. Flares sent up from the German positions threw macabre shadows, while artillery rumbled ominously in the distance. Soon flashes appeared on the neighboring hills as the bombardment picked up intensity and acrid, throat-scalding smoke drifted over the Italian legionnaires. Packs were thrown off, and the soldiers filed into the advanced trenches, the officers exhorting their men to uphold the honor of Italy, as German shells began to explode around them.

The French artillery fell silent. A blast of bugles, followed by a collective shout—*"Avanti! Avanti! Viva l'Italia! Italia! Italia!"*—mingled with *"Vive la République! Vive la France!"* The legionnaires helped each other out of the trenches and ran toward the German lines. Nature appeared to be self-destructing around them as bark flew in the air and small trees fell as if snapped by an invisible hand. Soon cries of agony went up, and even the bugle call was cut short by a bullet that entered the horn and severed the throat of the bugler. The first men reached the German barbed wire only to find that the artillery had failed to cut it. This stopped the first wave, or what was left of it, as the men tore at the wire. Soon the second and third waves appeared out of the smoke and twisted through the wire and toward the trenches, some of whose occupants could be seen fleeing to the rear. The legionnaires cleaned out those who remained. The German fire seemed to slacken as the seventh wave of legionnaires arrived. The survivors busied themselves preparing for the inevitable counterattack, collected the considerable number of wounded, and returned to retrieve the packs while German shells sprinkled over the position. After an hour, the Italians were ordered back to their starting point.[67]

In January 1915, the Italians were thrown into a second attack. On the 5th, two battalions assaulted German lines at Courtes Chausses after eight mines were detonated beneath the German positions. The Garibaldians seized two trench lines and a number of prisoners. The regiment continued to battle on the 7th, 8th and 9th in the Bois de Bolante. But total Italian losses in December and January amounted to 429 men. In March, the unit was dissolved, and the legionnaires enlisted in the Italian army. The first entry of the Legion into the war had been a bloody one, an experience that was to be repeated by the other Legion units.

Chapter 17

1915—TRENCH
WARFARE AND MUTINY

UNLIKE THE ITALIANS in the *4ᵉ bataillon de marche,* who were pitched into a major offensive virtually straight out of training, the introduction of most legionnaires to trench warfare was a more gradual one. Valbonne, a small village about twenty miles from Lyon, eventually became the center of Legion training. Even by the standards of wartime improvisation, everyone agreed that it was a desperately uncomfortable place—rows of huts in an open field that in winter became a quagmire. Magnus found that the barracks of Sidi-bel-Abbès offered first-class accommodation compared to the lice-infested shacks at Valbonne, and the civilian population that ran the small bars and shops at the edge of the camp were even more rapacious, if that were possible, than their counterparts in the Legion's home town.

Magnus was also of the opinion that Valbonne offered "absolutely no instruction in anything that could be useful to defend one's life at the front."[1] And while Magnus was so soured on the Legion that he cannot be relied upon as a completely unbiased witness, he may not have been too far wrong. Much time was spent in long marches and in target practice, which might have helped except that the rifle, especially the cumbersome standard-issue Lebel, had been superseded in lethality by the artillery and the machine gun. "The Lebel is an excellent rifle but it is worthless in the trenches," Cendrars wrote in 1915. "Mud, a grain of sand will block the mechanism and it is far too cumbersome. . . . We went out [on patrol] like poor idiots with our one-shot popguns and this ridiculous metallic scabbard for the bayonet which bothers you in all your movements, gets stuck between the legs when one crawls, rings like a sleigh-bell on the smallest pebble and gives you away with each step."[2] Indeed, trench humor held that while the Lebel was utterly useless in the front lines, it was indispensable in the rear areas, where supervision of its care and cleaning provided employment for NCOs with time on their hands.

Legion training was complicated by the usual language problems. Russell Kelly reported that during a night maneuver to take a fort, "The sergeant in command was a Frenchman with no knowledge of any language except French, so he had great difficulty in explaining the tactic to us."[3] Magnus complained that the language problem was compounded when, out of frustration, many foreign NCOs began to shout at their charges, transforming their already heavily accented French into complete gibberish.[4] The difficulties of making oneself understood were complicated by a constant turnover of training personnel,

so that, as each one has his own ideas as to the proper way to do things, we men, having learnt at the hands of one man how to use our bayonets, for example, would have to unlearn all we had learnt, and do the same thing in a way that better pleased a new arrival, and this ad libitum,

wrote American volunteer Algernon Sartoris. "It was exercise, however."[5] Cendrars complained that this turnover extended to the front lines: "[Officers] passed through the Legion because that counted as combat duty, but they stayed only fifteen days, three weeks, just to lead a trench raid and try to win a citation."[6] This was perhaps because it was French practice to award a *croix de guerre* to all members of a trench raid that brought back prisoners,[7] a prospect alluring enough to tempt some staff officers briefly out of their comfortable chateaus well to the rear.

Nor were the officers always tactful. American legionnaire Kiffin Rockwell, who later became one of the heroes of the *Escadrille Lafayette,* was incensed when he saw a French major at Valbonne insult a group of legionnaires who had been seriously wounded at the front and as a result were being invalided out:

He told them they were not worth a damn, that they disgraced the Legion, and that they only came here for la gamelle. *Now, we have heard that from sergeants and such all the time. But for a commandant to tell men who have ruined themselves for life out of love for France and the principles she is fighting for, I think it is going a little too far. . . . Yet I see these things every day. . . . It is such a disgrace to France for such things to happen that I wish something could be done to stop it.*[8]

As a consequence, legionnaires who went into the trenches, especially in the early days, had little idea what to expect, a condition they shared with soldiers of all armies. In the late autumn of 1914, veteran Legion

NCOs ordered their men to sleep with their boots on and tie their rifles to their wrists in the North African manner, and shouted *aux armes* each time a few bullets zinged overhead, which was frequently.[9] However, they quickly discovered that artillery bombardments posed a far greater threat than marauding Arabs, so that digging became essential. Command posts and kitchens also had to be moved far to the rear after German shells unsportingly disturbed more than one staff conference or adjourned preparations for dinner.[10] Cendrars's first encounter with the trenches, which typically took place at night, was a memorable, but altogether typical, one:

We waded in mud up to the ankles, even to the knees, and glutinous clods, which detached themselves from the lips of the trench when we brushed by them, slid disagreeably down our necks. And, as in a nightmare, we were impeded at every step. One man's Lebel got stuck across the passage, the kit bag of another caught on a splinter-proof shield. These shields formed an obstacle every ten yards. They were invisible in the dark and we banged straight into them. The men were falling about, slithering, swearing, colliding with one another, amidst a great clatter of hardware and mess-tins. It was a case of two steps forward and one back.

The rain fell, the trenches smelled of "chemicals and carrion," and the lieutenant urged them forward: *"Serrez! Serrez!"* (Close up!) ". . . It was delicious to feel our feet melt, sink into the soft, freezing mud, but when you couldn't move you got scared. Men stopped every ten meters to piss. The column was straggling, dislocated." Suddenly they heard noises on the far side of the shield.

A galloping, a tremendous thundering of boots coming straight at us. Voices. A crush of bodies. And suddenly appeared a group of men who pushed us out of the way. No, it was not the Boches! "Move over, you idiots," they shouted, crushing us against the sides of the trench, hitting us with their rifles and tent poles and poking the handles of their entrenching tools in our eyes. "You bastards the relief? We've been waiting for over two hours for you. We're off. Make yourself at home."

Home proved to be

a chewed-up terrain full of mine-holes and shell-craters, collapsing dugouts, crumbling parapets, disemboweled and scattered sandbags, tangled links of barbed wire, and the shallow beginnings of slimy nauseating trenches. Where were we? There was a terrible stink of shit. . . . "Lie down", I told my men. . . . "You're a nice chap, corporal. But this place is full of shit!" "It brings good luck! Get some sleep."[11]

The senses struggled to adjust to the eerie confusion of flares, the high whine of artillery shells passing overhead and the muffled thud of explosions in the communications trenches to the rear. Somewhere down the line a cry of *"Aux armes! Aux tranchées!"* went up, followed by the crackling of a fusillade. A few bullets sang overhead, or thumped into the damp earth of the trench. The newcomers threw themselves down. Some began firing into the blackness, blindly, holding their rifles over their heads. The example was contagious—soon the entire trench was blazing away, wildly, into the air, to the front, the rear (after all, who knew where the Germans were?). The officers and NCOs struggled to regain control of their troops. "Keep your heads down! Don't shoot! Quit firing, damn it!" The shooting slowly died out as the tensions were released, and the new legionnaires realized that their lives were not in immediate danger. Groups of sentries were posted in small trenches to the front. The rest of the night was spent trying to stay awake, and to stay warm. Somewhere in the blackness, a machine gun clanked and sputtered, and the low thunder of artillery rolled as if a storm was brewing over the horizon.

Life in the trenches hardly lived up to the romantic image of battle that most legionnaires brought with them. But it was not too bad, once one got used to the random explosion of shells and learned to avoid the dips in the parapet where the appearance of a cloth kepi was bound to attract the bullet of an alert German sniper. In many respects, daylight was the most trying time, when the men descended into the black dugouts, jostling and arguing as they settled on the damp straw. Some smoked a cigarette, others ate a piece of bread left over from the evening meal. Most simply huddled elbow to elbow, heads swathed in Balaklava helmets and legs wrapped in blankets, staring at the walls, casually scratching those spots where the vermin were beginning to make their presence felt, "like an animal in a burrow," wrote Seeger.[12] (Later, they would have to get used to sleeping in gas masks.)

The logs and wattle matting that made up the dugout roof gave off a strong and pleasant odor of wood, almost like Christmas, until a shell shrieked close and exploded, bouncing pieces of stone and shrapnel off the cover above, like a quick splattering of raindrops on a housetop, and filling the hole with the acrid odor of cordite. Gradually the talking subsided, and the men fell asleep, completely oblivious to the shelling outside and to the drone of aircraft above. However, as soon as darkness returned, the troglodytes reemerged and began to crawl over the churned and shattered landscape that sequestered two invisible armies in its folds and crevices. Men set off to fetch the evening soup through communications trenches that often had been obliterated by enemy shelling, while others repaired the wire or slithered out to patrol no man's land. Those on guard stared into the blackness, trying to distinguish movement amidst a chaos of dark forms and indistinct shapes.

The first meeting between these new legionnaires and the Germans was a salutary one. Quite apart from a poverty of shells and bullets, which often kept the French lines silent while the German ones were crackling with fireworks, Cendrars discovered that "in the little cowboy and indian war which we carried on in the midst of the factory war," the Germans also had the upper hand. "The German patrols had a lot of bite, being better equipped than ours"—parabellums, grenades, electric torches, rubber truncheons, and flares, all of which were highly prized by the French when they could capture them.[13] Seeger agreed that in trench warfare, "the Germans are marvelous."[14] Marvelous, indeed. Kiffin Rockwell confessed that the first encounter between the Germans and a small American contingent of legionnaires did not reflect great credit upon the latter. Guarding a small *avant poste* situated in the ruins of a chateau with Alan Seeger in early January 1915, Rockwell heard something sputter at his feet:

We each said: "What's that?" I reached down and picked it up, when [Seeger] said: "Good God! It's a hand grenade!" I threw it away and we both jumped to attention, asking each other what to do, and finally decided for Seeger to go to the petit poste *for the corporal, while I watched. Just as he and the corporal came running up, the corporal called, "Garde à vous, Rockwell," and another grenade fell at my feet. I jumped over the ladder toward the corporal and as I reached his side the bomb exploded. We both called out "Aux armes!" We had no more than done this, when the door gave in and a raiding party entered the side of the opening.*

Rockwell and the corporal bolted for safety, but German bullets brought down the corporal. The Germans stripped the corporal of his rifle and equipment, and then knocked off the top of his skull with the butts of their rifles. "The affair was rather a disgrace for all of us," Kiffin Rockwell confessed. Nor were the Germans prepared to let them forget it. "About two hours after all this happened, there came from the German trenches the most diabolical yell of derision I ever heard. It was mocking Weidemann's last words, his call '*Aux armes!*' and it froze my blood to hear it."[15] Seeger also remembered the German taunts: "from far up on the hillside, a diabolical cry came down, more like an animal's than a man's, a blood-curdling yell of mockery and exultation."[16]

Yet despite these early confrontations—indeed, in part because of them—legionnaires began to modify their patrol tactics. It was a demonstration that these new legionnaires, like their prewar counterparts in North Africa, were learning how to impose their outlooks on their commanders. Seeger confessed in April 1915 that the patrols into no man's land tried to avoid "useless collisions" with the Germans that only provoked reprisals. One patrol left a POW menu on the German wire as an invitation to desert, only to return on a later night to discover in the same spot a basket of sandwiches, two bottles of Munich beer, cigarettes and chocolate with letters in excellent French to their "Dear Comrades" in the opposing trenches thanking them for their invitation but explaining that they had plenty to eat. Seeger concluded that violence between the two sides had greatly subsided and that he had

no doubt if we were to remain here much longer under the same conditions that there would be a kind of tacit understanding not to fire at outposts and that there would even develop neutral zones and surreptitious commerce between the sentinels, as I have heard from veterans was the case in the latter years of our civil war.[17]

Of course, this was the trend all along the front lines in the winter of 1914–15, and had led to the famous Christmas truce, a spontaneous fraternization that occurred on some parts of the front.[18] Cendrars too demonstrates that these legionnaires were imposing their own rules of engagement in the trenches that might not always reflect their commanders' wishes. His squad arranged an ambush to frighten their lieutenant, who planned to discipline them for looting, so that he would cease to visit them in the front lines.[19] And when the fireman sergeants tried to have Cendrars punished for fraternization with the Germans, the legionnaire explained that there was a large pile of coal between the lines where both French and German patrols came to provision themselves. At first these meetings erupted into fire fights,

but later, under pressure of circumstances, the different regiments in the sector came in turns, and the Boches also. This happened quite naturally, without prearrangement, without talks or an understanding. The Boches come every other day. Tonight's our turn. Tomorrow's their's. . . . The men come with sacks. They aren't armed. But as you never know, they carry grenades in their pockets. The Boches do the same thing. . . . They are cold just like us, and it is really not worth getting killed for coal, don't you agree? Better to form a queue.

Cendrars also admitted that each side often left cigarettes and newspapers for the other to pick up, but denied that this was fraternization.[20] On the contrary, the implication of Cendrars's testimony was that he was quite prepared to fight so long as it contributed to victory. However, the legionnaires had concluded that, at this stage of the war, at any rate, aggression for its own sake was actually counterproductive, especially as the Germans were so much better armed and equipped.

This appears to be supported by the first offensives into which the new Legion was hurled in the summer of 1915. Seeger was at least half correct when he divined as early as October 1914 that

The Germans, as far as I can see, occupy all the territory they have coveted and all that they would keep in the event of their ultimate victory. It is my

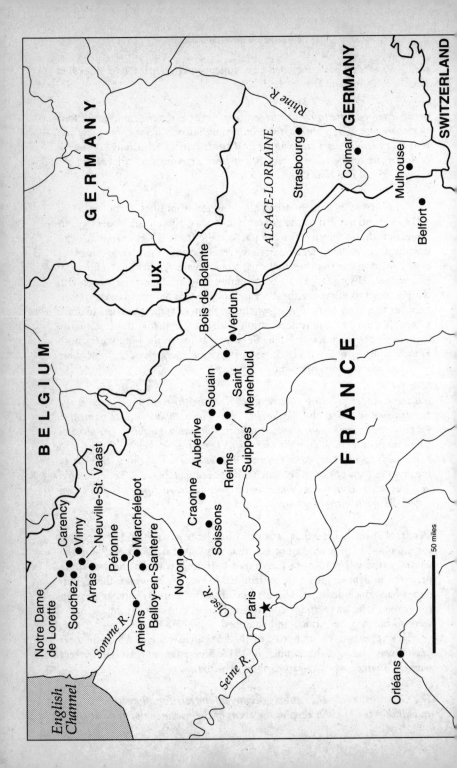

idea that they will now wage a defensive war entirely, limiting themselves to holding what they have.[21]

Apart from their attacks at Verdun in 1916, that is precisely what the Germans did in the West between the opening Battle of the Marne in 1914 and the Michael offensives of 1918. A defensive stance on the Western Front freed troops to seek a decisive victory in the East. Therefore, if there was to be fighting on the Western Front, then it was the Allies—and in 1915 this meant essentially the French—who had to initiate it.

French commander-in-chief Joseph Joffre prepared to launch a series of assaults on the German western wall from May 1915 that were meant to crack open the front and allow the Allies to flow into the German heartland. Unfortunately for the French, this task would prove beyond reach, for several reasons. In the first place, the French were desperately short of materiel, especially of heavy artillery, needed to pound the German lines into submission. The 75-mm gun was a marvelous field piece, but it lacked the range to hit the German reserve trenches, especially the heavy batteries well to the rear that could continue to punish French attackers with little risk to themselves. It was essentially a direct fire weapon, which meant that it lacked a curved trajectory that made it able to hit enemy positions masked by hills, so that the Germans learned to site their defenses whenever possible out of direct view. The absence of trench mortars and a sufficient number of high-impact shells to smash the German defenders in their deep dugouts meant that French attacks, until the summer of 1917, would lack punch.

This defect, while important, might not have been fatal had the French been able to develop flexible tactics that minimized the importance of firepower—tactics that, for instance, relied upon short, violent hurricane barrages and surprise for success. Unfortunately, this was not easy for any army to achieve, least of all that of France. The uncoordinated attacks of the opening weeks of the war, attacks that had cost the French heavily during the Battles of Frontiers in August and on the Marne in early September, had made generals reluctant to concede too much initiative to subordinate commanders. Battle, it was believed, must be tightly controlled and closely managed. Assault waves leapfrogged through the lines of German trenches following a prearranged schedule of barrages. No adjustments could be made that took account of changed local circumstances or the unexpected. Artillery support stopped periodically so that the short-ranged 75s could move into more forward positions to support the attack on the next trench line, forfeiting valuable time, which allowed the Germans to organize counterattacks. And last, the preparations for these offensives, the stockpiling of material and gathering of men behind the lines for weeks in advance, telegraphed the intentions of the Allied planners, making surprise virtually impossible to achieve.

Therefore, when historians speak of the difficulties encountered by

Legion attacks, it must be remembered that the entire French army was making war on a shoestring, pushed into premature offensives by commanders who were under pressure to attack from politicians and allies whose own instincts told them that to hesitate would leave the initiative to the Germans, and who argued that the technological balance favored the defensive more each day. Therefore, to postpone an attack was merely to make it more costly in the long run.

However, few of these broad considerations could have been of much consolation to the legionnaires brought in to attack Hill 140, which was in fact a shoulder of the Vimy Ridge in the Artois sector, on May 9, 1915. After a preliminary artillery barrage lasting four hours, four battalions of the *2ᵉ régiment de marche* of the *1ᵉʳ étranger* were launched at Hill 140. The first German line was quickly reached, but the climb to the summit was undertaken in a murderous fire that killed most of the cadres, including three of the battalion commanders and many of the company commanders. The regimental commander was also wounded. On the right, the attack of the 156th Infantry Regiment stalled, exposing the attackers to a costly flanking fire. Nevertheless, the legionnaires charged on, companies and battalions mixed and often leaderless, to the top of the hill. However, reinforcements failed to arrive despite urgent appeals from legionnaires. The brigade commander, a much-respected veteran of North Africa, Colonel Theodore Pein, went forward to organize the defensive positions and was brought down by a German sniper. A counterattack supported by heavy artillery fire drove the legionnaires from the hill some time after three o'clock in the afternoon, although they did not surrender all of their gains.

The attack on Hill 140, the second serious offensive in which the Legion participated in World War I, has rightly been hailed by Legion historians as a great demonstration of courage. Despite a murderous fire, a fire that took out most of the cadres, the legionnaires pressed on to the objective on their own initiative,[22] a great demonstration of commitment from the volunteers for which the regiment was awarded a *croix de guerre*. Even those battalions that had not received a large leavening of veteran legionnaires, the Czechs, Poles and Greeks who formed autonomous units with their national flags, appear to have fought as well as the others, a demonstration, perhaps, that the offensive is an option of choice with less experienced troops.

For their part, the Germans attributed the Legion success to the fact that their attack fell upon a weakly held sector which, without natural defense obstacles, had been badly churned by the French artillery. The *Berliner Tageblatt* exulted that the counterattack, which drove the Legion from Hill 140, had been spearheaded by a unit of Alsatians who had "in this way inflicted the recompense due to these men without a fatherland."[23]

Yet the inexperience of these Legion units proved costly: 1,889 legionnaires, or almost 50 percent of strength, had fallen on May 9 alone.[24] A first criticism was that the Legion attack was carried out almost as if it were a private battle, with little concern with what went on on its flanks. "The history of the 2ᵉ régiment de marche does not mention during these combats, any liaison, any exchange of information with the neighboring regiments," read an after-action critique. This was especially important as the 156th Infantry Regiment on its right flank had been assigned "the formidable center of resistance of Neuville-St. Vaast," against which it failed to advance. However, had the 156th maneuvered to cover the Legion's flank, "it is probable that these would have had far fewer casualties; B battalion [of the Legion] could have operated to its front; Neuville would have fallen through encirclement," wishful thinking perhaps, as Neuville only fell in June 1915 to the crack 5th Infantry Division after fierce house-to-house fighting. In other words, the organization was not supple enough to react to opportunities and changes that occurred in the course of the battle. Lack of liaison also accounted for the failure of reinforcements to arrive once the Legion reached the top of Hill 140, so that they were eventually driven from the crest by a German counterattack.[25] Other mistakes made by the attackers included the fact that they rolled over successive German positions in the short space of two hours without stopping to clear them out, so that the Germans emerged from their dugouts and often shot the legionnaires from behind. The death of most of the cadres made it difficult to organize the defense of Hill 140 properly once the legionnaires had seized it. The presence of more machine guns would also have helped the defenders thwart the German counterattack.[26]

Some of these defects were rectified on June 16 when the Legion was again in action before Souchez in the same sector. The attacked jumped off just after noon, the Legion in the second wave behind the Algerians, and crossed the Souchez ravine at the foot of Hill 119, which was traversed by a murderous machine-gun fire. The hill was seized. But a German counterattack that smashed into the zouaves to the Legion's left at eight o'clock in the evening forced a slight readjustment of the lines. The next morning, a German bombardment of such intensity rained down upon the Legion lines that the hill was abandoned. Unfortunately, the retreat through the Souchez ravine proved to be as costly as the attack, costing the Legion more troops including a battalion commander.

The Souchez action showed that the Legion had profited from their mistakes on May 9. For instance, each squad detailed trench cleaners with knives and ample supplies of grenades. However, the inability to regulate artillery fire meant that French soldiers again ran under their own shells during their advance. Lack of liaison again meant that reinforcements were slow to arrive, so that the Legion and other units of the Moroccan Division had to hold the terrain for most of the night against German barrages and counterattacks. They also appear to have been slow to reorganize the German trenches, which were "facing" the wrong way.[27] Reybaz confessed of this attack that "the utilization of terrain was with us . . . a science which was still largely ignored."[28]

Rockwell reported that the June 16 action was more costly for the Legion than that of May 9.[29] However, although the American contingent suffered considerable losses for the first time, the regimental diary of the *2ᵉ régiment de marche* of the *1ᵉʳ étranger* does not support Rockwell's contention—45 *legionnaires* were killed, 320 wounded, and 263 listed as missing, including Russell Kelly, out of an attacking force of 67 officers and 2,509 men. This makes for a casualty rate of 24 percent, substantial certainly, but less than half that of the May 9 attack. Furthermore, the casualty rate among officers was 34 percent, which was less devastating than on May 9.

Nevertheless, although the Legion had covered itself with glory in Artois, the attack of June 16 brought the problems of the Legion to a head. Already in April, friction between veterans and Russian "Republicans" had led to forty-two of the Russians being sent to the rear, apparently in disgrace. After protests, the forty-two Russians were allowed to transfer to line regiments.[30] However, this was merely a minor incident compared to what even the quasi-official history of the RMLE refers to as *"l'affaire du 16 juin 1915."*[31] Poor relations combined with the enormous casualties of the May 9 battle obviously had sapped morale. Probably the critical factor, one that helps to explain the great bravery of legionnaires on May 9, and the reluctance some of them subsequently showed for battle, was the fact that they no longer believed a breakthrough possible. Quite naturally, the first manifestations of this occurred in the more nationally homogeneous units, among men who shared a common language and could therefore more easily make a common cause against their French commanders. Ordered into the attack on June 16, the Greeks in C battalion refused to charge, an even more forceful demonstration of how these new legionnaires no longer shared the command's view of what was achievable in the battlefield conditions of the early summer of 1915. The regimental commander, Lieutenant Colonel Cot, rushed over to them, only to be told that they had enlisted to fight Turks, not Germans. Cot apparently promised to send them to the Dardanelles, which, combined with the arrival of a wave of Algerian *tirailleurs*, bayonets fixed, behind them, induced them to attack.[32]

The regimental diary of the *2ᵉ régiment de marche* confessed that the attitude of the Greeks during the June 16 attack was "hardly edifying." "Following the explosion of a shell in the trench," read the regimental diary,

a certain number of Greeks flee to the rear, and the energetic intervention of several officers is required to return them to their place. The effervescence caused by this incident is however sufficient to cause the brigade colonel to demand the relief of the battalion to the rear where it is in the process of being reorganized.

This conduct apparently earned for them "the reprobation of the other legionnaires." On June 19, the colonel was again forced to intervene to quell a demonstration of Greek legionnaires, who two days later were sent away "to be reorganized and given the training which they are totally lacking."[33]

Lieutenant Gustave Marolf, a Swiss, saw his Greek legionnaires scramble for the rear when ordered into the attack: "A wave of terror ran through my Greeks," he wrote to his brother of the events of June 16.

Part of them had run away, probably terrified by the barrage of which they were the target. As for the NCOs, all gone! I shout in Greek: "Forward! Forward!" with all my force. But, of four sections, I only see a few men. The rest had evaporated! My beautiful company, in which I thought I could have complete confidence, had broken, the victim of fear!

Marolf was at once "humiliated" by the defection of his men—"And my promotion, what will become of it after this brilliant success?"—and relieved that the Germans did not transform their flight into a "catastrophe." Returning to the rear, he discovered them hiding in trenches and shell holes. "I am furious, but I don't have the energy to horsewhip them." The NCOs were broken, and Marolf acquitted of responsibility by a court-martial.[34] The Greek battalion was disbanded and its legionnaires subsequently dispatched to the eastern Mediterranean, some to operate unsuccessfully in irregular formations that were broken up because of indiscipline, while others were sent to reinforce the Legion battalion in the Dardanelles. In fact, as a group the Greeks did not do well in Legion service in the First World War—a *bataillon de marche d'Orient* attached to the *1er étranger* and made up of Greeks from Turkish territories was disbanded after six months because of indiscipline.[35]

But these problems could not have been confined only to the Greeks, for at the same time those from Alsace-Lorraine who had not signed the declaration of a desire to serve against Germany were also sent away from the front.[36] These departures, combined with the losses of May 1915, reduced the *2e régiment de marche* from four battalions on May 9 to two battalions by August. On July 1, the regimental diary complained that morale, which had been high before May 9, "and brought to a state of exhilaration worthy of the handsome results achieved during the recent combats, has fallen rather low following the departure of the Italians and the incorporation of Greek elements always ready to carry out acts of collective indiscipline."

This scramble to exit the Legion proved to be contagious. "The removal of [the Greeks] did nothing to calm the malaise, the trouble which reigned in the spirits of those who remained," the diary continues. "For this reason, the Russians also made the necessary requests to obtain the cancellation of their contracts and passage into a metropolitan regiment."[37] "Made the necessary requests" is putting it mildly. Many of the "Russians" appear to have been Parisian Jews of Russian extraction who simply refused to return to the front from the rear cantonments. However, apparently unlike the other groups, between seven and eleven of these rebels were court-martialed and shot.[38]

According to legionnaire Sholem Schwartzbard, this did not end the trouble. The existence of a circular allowing "Russians" to transfer to the Russian army or to French regiments was made known between the attacks of May 9 and June 16, 1915. When, however, the requests to transfer were ignored and the legionnaires were told to prepare for a new attack, a number of Jewish legionnaires assembled in a wood and demanded to know why they were not allowed to transfer. When the colonel explained that Russia and France were fighting the same enemy, he was told, "But not in the Foreign Legion." They were locked up in a large barn guarded by Senegalese troops, and eventually decided to rejoin their unit.[39]

Szajkowski charges that the harsh treatment of the Jews was the result of anti-Semitism, and that news of the executions stimulated a campaign by anti-Semitic groups in France to force those foreign-born Jews who had not yet enlisted to join the Legion. These had become even less eager to step forward for service after the news of the executions reached the Jewish community in Paris.[40] As this author was refused permission to consult the justice records for the Legion in World War I, it is impossible to know for certain if the Jews of the Legion suffered more as a group than did others, such as the Greeks, for instance. Nor can one know for sure the motives of the protesters. Schwartzbard recorded that French officers blamed the protests upon Jewish revolutionaries, when in fact they had been motivated simply by a desire to transfer out of the Legion. According to the antimilitarist journal *Le Crapouillot,* which claimed to base its figures upon official statistics, 442 French soldiers were executed by firing squads in 1915, higher than for any other year of the war except for 1917, the year of the great mutinies in the French army, when 528 were shot.[41] Therefore, seven or eleven men shot out of one battalion would appear to be very high and suggest that the Jews were indeed treated with particular harshness— for instance, American historian Leonard V. Smith, who has studied the justice records for the 5th Infantry Division in World War I, discovered only five executions in the entire division of almost ten thousand men between the outbreak of war and the mutinies of 1917.[42]

There is also anecdotal evidence that anti-Semitism was prominent in the Legion and that it distorted perceptions about the causes of the 1915 mutiny. Part of this, as noted, was a product of North Africa, where popular anti-Semitism was endemic. The experience of the Dreyfus Affair also did little to ease acceptance of the Jews in the military environment, a condition that became more evident after 1914 when the army was removed from the restraints of diplomatic behavior imposed in peacetime. However, even many new Legion recruits, including the Americans, appear to have disliked the Jews. This came in part, no doubt, from the fact that many of them spoke Yiddish, which was taken for German by the uninitiated, and therefore made them suspect in this period of exalted anti-German feeling. Some were also part of the intellectual diaspora from Russia, and therefore were confirmed political radicals. However, the major charge against the Jewish legionnaires was that they had enlisted to avoid being sent to internment camps and having their goods sequestered. This appears to be the commonly accepted motive for the enlistment of many of the Jews by legionnaires who subsequently castigated them because they served indifferently. "The Second Foreign Regiment was afflicted with a battalion composed almost entirely of Russian Jews and political exiles, which was permeated from the start with a spirit of revolt and anarchy," Rockwell wrote. "Many of its members had enlisted with no idea of ever going to the front."[43] Even the *Historique* of the RMLE claimed that many volunteers had only come into the Legion "to save the furniture."[44]

The charges against the Jews appear to be largely unfair. Perhaps some, even most, of those whose situation as foreign residents opened them to the threat of internment camps and the sequestration of their goods did join to avoid these fates. But coercion was the major source of recruitment for all European armies in this period—after all, without conscription, how would armies have amassed huge numbers of soldiers? The atmosphere of chauvinistic hysteria that gripped France, as well as other belligerent countries in World War I, forced groups of foreign nationals who otherwise slipped through the conscription net into uniform. No doubt some of them did make indifferent soldiers. According to Cendrars, the Jews tried to be included with the Polish formations of the Legion, but when the Poles rejected this, ". . . they started to intrigue to be posted to the rear, and those who had no contacts began all sorts of tricks to get out."[45] But in this they were not alone. Indeed, few national groups appear to have been exempt from this, including the French. Cendrars noted that the first "deserters" and those who set the worst example were the French cadres, especially the Paris firemen, who fairly bolted for the exit when they learned that the Legion was to be sent to the front.[46] When those from Alsace-Lorraine were given the opportunity of volunteering for the heavy artillery, "which sent them for several months far to the rear for their classes in the training camps and which exempted them forever from returning to the front lines," few turned it down.[47] If the Jews pushed to be released from the Legion, they were in numerous company, for everyone, including most of the Americans who were allowed to transfer into metropolitan regiments in 1915, petitioned to get out.

Nor is there any evidence that they faltered in battle, as did the Greeks, for instance. Therefore, the "mutiny" of the Jewish legionnaires cannot be put down to the fact that they were battle-shy from the beginning. On the contrary, when considered in the context of the large-scale discontent that churned the Legion in June 1915, the mutiny appears to be the result of the fact that foreign volunteers were consigned to the Legion in the first place and that they were poorly treated when they arrived there, and as a protest against the high command's wasteful methods of making war.

Therefore, on the surface at least, it appears as if the Legion were going through a major crisis on the Western Front in the summer of 1915, and that this crisis occurred because legionnaires had begun to thwart the wishes of the command, whose goals they no longer shared. But evidence of low morale was lacking when the Legion was pitched into Joffre's September offensives in Champagne. Beneath a heavy rain, the Legion attacked the Butte de Souain on September 25. The *2ᵉ régiment de marche* of the *2ᵉ étranger* seized a battery of German 77-mm guns and several machine guns before allowing successive attack waves to pass through it. That night, it heard a confusion to its front and prepared to receive a German counterattack, only to discover that the noise was that of French troops who had panicked. The sight of the legionnaires with fixed bayonets convinced the Frenchmen to return to their forward positions.

On September 28, two Legion regiments participated in the attack on the strongly fortified Navarin Farm. "Making such time as we could, we finally arrived at the summit of the little ridge," American legionnaire Edward Morlae wrote of this battle.

Then we left the cover of the trench, formed in Indian file, fifty meters between sections, and, at the signal, moved forward swiftly and in order. It was a pretty bit of tactics and executed with a dispatch and neatness hardly equalled on the drill-ground. The first files of the sections were abreast, while the men fell in, one close behind the other; and so we crossed the ridge, offering the smallest possible target to the enemy's guns.[48]

The most difficult thing to explain is why the Legion waited until Navarin Farm to employ this particular tactic, as according to Seeger this had been practiced in training as early as October 1914.[49] Possibly the rapid turnover of cadres helps to explain it. However, its effect was somewhat spoiled, according to Morlae, by the insistence of his captain that the file progress at the regulation 180 steps per minute, despite the desperately heavy shelling.[50] Morlae also suggests that the Legion, as well as other units, had learned from the experience on Hill 140 that their first task on taking the forward German line must be to reverse the trench: "In what seemed half a minute we had formed a continuous parapet, twelve to fourteen inches in height," he wrote.

. . . Next, each man proceeded to dig his little individual niche in the ground, about a yard deep, twenty inches wide, and long enough to lie down in with comfort. Between each two men there remained a partition wall of dirt, from ten to fifteen inches thick, the usefulness of which was immediately demonstrated by a shell which fell into Blondino's niche, blowing him to pieces without injuring either of his companions to the

right or the left. . . . Soon the order came down the line to deepen the trenches. It seemed we were to stay there until night.[51]

But they were still two hundred yards short of the main German position, which continued to shower them with machine-gun bullets and artillery. The battle at the Navarin Farm was a costly one for the Legion. But their frontal assault, while unsuccessful, was credited with allowing other French units to take the position from the rear. Both regiments were cited in army orders.

The Champagne offensive was the final event that forced the Legion to restructure. Many of its recruits of the first year of the war had either been released to their national armies, redistributed to metropolitan units or to North Africa or were pushing up poppies. The *4ᵉ régiment de marche*, made up of Italians, had been dissolved on March 5, 1915. The *3ᵉ de marche* had followed in July 1915. The *2ᵉ de marche* went down from four to two battalions after cannibalizing all available troops from the *3ᵉ*. The Champagne offensive had reduced numbers still further. On November 11, 1915, what was left of the Legion in France was fused into the *régiment de marche de la Légion étrangère*. Therefore, Legion strength plummeted from a high in early 1915 of 21,887 men to 10,683 by 1916, of which 3,316 served on the Western Front.[52]

Of course, this hemorrhage of soldiers out of the Legion in 1915 was not invariably caused by discontent. Part of the crush to get out was motivated by a desire to stay alive, to put distance between themselves and the front lines as much as to escape from the Legion per se. Also, these transfers probably expressed a desire common among soldiers to change, a belief that things might be better elsewhere. The army might also have done much to lessen the discontentment: Quite apart from the constant turnover and often poor quality of cadres assigned to the Legion, Cendrars complained that low morale came from the policies of constantly rotating soldiers to different sections of the line, after they had learned the lay of the land and put their trenches and dugouts in order. The filthy state of the cantonments, which, though in the rear, were often still within artillery range, also upset the men, and became a major complaint of the French army mutineers of 1917.[53] But the combination of high casualties and widespread discontent in the Legion would force it not only to restructure, but also to reforge an identity more in keeping with the traditions of the regiment. This would transform the Legion on the Western Front from a gathering of reluctant foreigners to an elite regiment.

Chapter 18

"THE GREATEST GLORY
WILL BE HERE"

IN ONE RESPECT, the crisis, both in manpower and morale, that the Legion weathered in the summer of 1915 proved a great blessing. The Legion had never been comfortable in its role of assimilating large numbers of reluctant foreigners. Though its courage on the battlefield had been exemplary, it was apparent that many of its soldiers no longer shared the goals of their commanders and were ill at ease in the hard-bitten atmosphere of a mercenary unit. This caused many to flee the Legion, and had even led to mutiny in June 1915. However, this crisis, once surmounted, allowed the Legion to put its house in order. The cumbersome and nationally organized units of 1914–15 gave way to a leaner, more homogeneous organization much more in the old style of the Legion.

Even before this reorganization took place, however, it was apparent that a Legion mentality was beginning to emerge among those eager to legitimize themselves as "real" legionnaires. Those who elected to remain in the Legion on the whole did so voluntarily, which suggests that among these men an amalgamation was beginning to take place between veteran legionnaires and new recruits, and a glimmer of regimental pride had taken hold. Seeger, who had seriously considered transferring to a French regiment, in the end elected to remain with the Legion in part because "I am content and have good comrades," but basically because the Legion's performance meant that it had acquired "a wonderful reputation, and that we are ranked now with the best." He argued that, despite everything, "Our chance, now that we are with the Moroccan division, of seeing great things is better than ever . . . perhaps the greatest glory will be here, and it is for glory alone that I engaged."[1] The successes in Artois had much to do with the decision of Henry Farnsworth to remain. Although he had not taken part in these attacks, they had reflected glory upon the entire regiment: "Think only that, when all the other troops said the thing was impossible, the Legion took not one line, as planned, but four, and was not stopped then, though more than half the officers and men were down at the taking of Souchez." In an August 1915 letter to his parents, he contrasted the military bearing and professionalism of the Legion with a neighboring regiment of territorials, honest men all no doubt, but who were slovenly and bolted into their dugouts at the first explosion of a shell from "miserable 77's." In September he castigated French regulars for surrendering terrain that even "our old *3ᵉ régiment de marche* . . . never considered as a very remarkable outfit," would not have given up in an attack. And the legionnaires adopted expressions common to the Legion in North Africa.[2]

The feeling of being part of an elite unit made itself felt in other ways. Reybaz found the unit of Provençaux next to which he served very generous with their wine and good hunters, but afraid to crawl out of the trenches to fetch the birds they brought down between the lines, so that this task invariably fell to the legionnaires, who refused their offers of money but went "for the pleasure of playing with danger."[3] When the American Algernon Sartoris reported to Valbonne in December 1916, his hut erupted into a brawl between the Spanish and the rest almost as soon as he set foot in the door. "It was a near call and might have been a nasty business," he wrote.

I began to wonder if I had not taken more on my shoulders than I could carry, but little [Gaston] Mayer [another American] reassured me, said I would gradually get used to it and comforted me in general. Among the other men, too, I found a certain rough kindliness.[4]

As late as November 1917, the American Ivan Nock passed up the chance to transfer to the American army because "I'm pretty sure no U.S. regiment will ever be as distinguished as the *Légion Etrangère*. Besides, I'm beginning to think I'm a Frenchman."[5]

However, it was Cendrars, a man especially concerned when his group of foreign intellectuals were directed into the Legion, who embraced the Legion's prewar mystique most enthusiastically. In part, he too was impressed by the regiment's ferocious reputation, which he discovered was actually of practical value—during the battle of May 9, groups of German soldiers surrendered to them, and

they did not need to be told twice, preferring to run all the risks of crossing the open battlefield with their hands in the air rather than remain another minute in the hands of the chaps from the Legion. "Die Fremdenlegion!"

They were scared as hell of us. And to be truthful, we were not a pretty sight.[6]

Perhaps this was an indication that the anti-Legion campaign mounted by Germany before the war had actually backfired by inflating its violent reputation. But even more than this, Cendrars seems to have been seduced by the very North African romanticism of the Legion that had so revolted some of the more respectable volunteers.

The first inkling of his new prestige came during his first leave when he found that his Legion uniform—the Moroccan Division had been fitted out in colonial khaki in 1915—earned him great success in the Paris brothels.[7] But the Legion experience offered him more than that, he claimed: "Legion or no Legion. Personally I did not care," he wrote.

I do not attach too much attention to words. I enlisted, and as several times already in my life, I was prepared to follow the consequences of my action. But I did not realize that the Legion would make me drink this chalice to the dregs and that these dregs would make me drunk, and that by taking a cynical pleasure in discrediting and debasing myself, I would end up by breaking free of everything to conquer my liberty as a man. To be. To be a man. And discover solitude. That is what I owe to the Legion, and to the old lascars of Africa, soldiers, NCOs, officers, who came to lead us and mix with us as comrades, these desperados, these survivors of God knows what colonial epics, but who were all men, all. And that made it well worth the risk of death to meet these damned souls, who smelled of the galleys and were covered with tattoos. None of them ever let us down and each one was willing to sacrifice himself, for nothing, for kudos, because he was drunk, for a challenge, for a laugh, to stick it to someone, by God. . . . They were tough and their discipline was of iron. These were professionals. And the profession of a man of war is an abominable thing and leaves scars, like poetry. You have it or you don't. One cannot cheat because nothing wears out the soul more and stigmatizes the face (and secretly the heart) of man and is more vain than to kill, and to begin again.[8]

Therefore, while the Legion was seriously reduced in strength, it improved in efficiency. The *Historique* probably put it correctly, although not exactly diplomatically, when it concluded that, "Slight reduction in numbers, but serious improvement in the worth of the remainder, this was the result of the filtering of enlistees: The rejection of scum is not a loss."[9] Of course, it was entirely disingenuous of the Legion to blame their problems entirely upon reluctant recruits—as has been seen, the ferocious and unsavory reputation of the Legion, the often hostile reception given to the volunteers by the veterans of Africa and the poor quality of many of the temporary cadres all contributed to the Legion's problems.

The restructuring of the Legion came at a time when the French high command was rethinking its strategic options. The offensives in Artois and Champagne in the summer of 1915 were critical in the strategic shift on the Western Front from breakthrough to attrition—what Joffre called *"grignotage,"* or "nibbling." On one hand, one might view the distinction as an artificial one, for the high command hoped that attrition would lead to breakthrough. On the other, it is possible to see it as a compromise between a high command committed to an *offensive à outrance* (an all-out offensive) and soldiers on the ground who realized that this was utterly unrealistic. The point of the 1917 mutinies was not that they were the result of socialism and subversion. Rather, they were a protest by the soldiers against the wasteful offensive strategy of the high command, and this protest actually forced the high command to adopt the more cautious, more defensive (or, at least, limited offensive) strategy of Pétain.[10]

American historian Leonard V. Smith has argued that, in the case of the 5th Infantry Division, this process did not begin in 1917, but was a slow one that saw the soldiers imposing their own norms on battle as early as September 1914.[11] It was the soldiers themselves who were responsible for Joffre's conversion to a "nibbling" strategy by their actions in the summer offensives of 1915. This thesis would seem to be supported by the Legion's history of this period. The revolts of June 1915 in the Legion were ostensibly protests against insensitive treatment of the foreign volunteers and against having been placed in the Legion in the first place. While in the absence of archives more detailed than the *journaux de marche* it is impossible to ascertain how far they were also protests against a certain way of making war, as were those that erupted in 1917 in other French units, coming in the wake of the failure of the April–May 1917 offensives, it is entirely possible that they were. The Legion had imported fresh, unblooded troops for the September offensives at Souain and Navarin Farm. However, it is fairly clear that on the ground level, the task demanded by the high command came to be considered quite impossible. The regimental diary of the *2e régiment de marche* of the *2e étranger* praised the conduct of the men during the attack of September 25 when, despite heavy losses, it continued to attack and even to rally troops of the 171st Infantry, which had broken.[12]

Three days later, on September 28, it was the turn of the *2e régiment de marche* of the *1er étranger* to attack the strongly held German reserve trenches at Navarin Farm. Companies were compelled to break off attacks after heavy losses when they discovered that German wire had not been cut nor machine gun nests destroyed by the French barrages. With 608 *hors de combat* out of 2,003 officers and men, or a 30 percent casualty rate, Lieutenant Colonel Cot asked that the attack be abandoned and the regiment be withdrawn to the rear. The resolution of the attackers had not faltered—Cot blamed their failure on the formidable German defenses and the fact that most of the officers and NCOs were killed.[13] But the cadres had disappeared in puffs of smoke on May 9 also, and still the legionnaires had thrust forward, despite higher casualty figures than in September. While their courage was still intact, what appears to have changed was their belief that these attacks would deliver victory. The action of these legionnaires, like that of other troops such as those in the 5th Infantry Division, sent a strong signal to the high command that, in the opinion of the men on the ground, there was a serious gap between the strategic goals of the high command and the ability of the French army to achieve them.

1916, when much of the French army was involved in fighting the mammoth battle of Verdun, was a fairly quiet year for the Legion, spent mainly in calm sectors and training camps. It did participate in the Somme campaign, designed at least in part to draw pressure away from Verdun, and there distinguished itself on July 4 when, despite insufficient artillery support, the Legion charged over two hundred yards of open ground toward the heavily fortified village of Belloy-en-Santerre. Seeger's company was in the vanguard: "His tall silhouette stood out on the green of the cornfield," Seeger's friend Rif Baer wrote to the poet's parents. "He was the tallest man in his section. His head erect, and pride in his eye, I saw him running forward, with bayonet fixed. Soon he disappeared and that was the last time I saw my friend."[14] The first Legion wave had been cut down by German machine guns. The second crawled forward past the wounded men, one of whom was Seeger, through the field of wheat. A final bound behind a hail of grenades, and they were in the village, which they seized after two hours of house-to-house fighting. The legionnaires then installed themselves at the edge of the town, which by now was in ruins, and all night held off repeated counterattacks from German reinforcements who disembarked from trucks only a few hundred meters away. When they were finally relieved on the morning of July 6, their bag included 750 German prisoners. The Legion lost in killed, wounded and missing 25 officers and 844 soldiers, including Alan Seeger, of 62 officers and 2,820 cadres who participated in the attack, or a 30 percent casualty rate, in an action considered one of the most glorious in Legion history.[15]

1917 proved to be a more exciting, and more costly, year for the Legion. This was in part because trench raids had assumed a new importance on both sides, and a new dimension with the addition of artillery support. However, the Legion also participated in the ill-fated Nivelle offensives of April, calculated to break through the German lines by attacking on a narrow front on the Chemin des Dames west of Reims along the Aisne. Although his general plan failed, Nivelle continued a series of limited offensives, including those calculated to seize the heights of Moronvilliers in the chalk ridges east of Reims.

The Legion's contribution to the Nivelle offensive was an assault upon the village of Aubérive. Despite seven days of artillery preparation that reduced the woods on the Moronvilliers heights to matchsticks, when the legionnaires jumped off at four-fifty on the morning of April 17 in appalling weather, the clanking of numerous German machine guns announced that the enemy had lain untouched in their deep, concrete-reinforced bunkers. The attack waves were splintered, and men pressed into the mire to avoid the heavy German fire. Unable to advance according to the timetable, groups of legionnaires formed around officers or NCOs and moved forward, infiltrating the German positions. Over the next four days, the battle became a series of disjointed skirmishes between small groups of Germans and legionnaires who fought through over seven miles of trenches with grenades and bayonets. One group of ten legionnaires under an *adjudant-chef* (sergeant-major) seized a position which contained a battery of heavy artillery guarded by an infantry company. On April 20, the heavy fortified German reserve position fell to a grenade assault.

Legion losses had been heavy, and included the regimental commander, Lieutenant Colonel Duriez, and nine officers. One battalion had been reduced from almost 800 to 275 men. The fighting had been made all the more difficult by the terrible weather, and because the legionnaires were insufficiently supplied with grenades: "Only the lack of grenades stopped them. One saw them crying with rage, their hands powerless," the regimental diary recorded.[16] Legionnaire Casimir Pruszkowski, wounded in the action, confirmed in an official report (an encouraging, perhaps rare, example of senior officers soliciting the opinions of intelligent front-line troops) that rifle grenades gave the Germans tremendous advantages in trench fighting. He also noted that lookouts offered Germans the most vulnerable targets, that the legionnaires were still too heavily laden for attacks, and that infantry-artillery liaison still left much to be desired.[17] To this, one might add new German defensive methods that relied upon lightly held front lines so as to avoid excessive casualties in initial artillery bombardments, combined with carefully coordinated counterattacks from secure positions in the rear, all of which made it a costly business for the Legion.[18] For all of these reasons, the Legion's fifth citation had been well merited.

The failure of the Nivelle offensive dashed the high hopes of the French army in a breakthrough and produced a series of mutinies that appear not to have infected the Legion.[19] The most important reason why the Legion avoided the morale crisis, which affected about one-third of French army units in 1917, including elite ones, was that their problems had been largely resolved by the restructuring that occurred after the summer of 1915. Admittedly, the evidence is limited to Cot's explanation in the regimental diaries for the failure of the 1915 attacks, and to Cendrars's comments about organizing a live-and-let-live system in the trenches, but one might conclude that in the RMLE, officers and men had come to share a common assessment of what it was possible to achieve in the conditions of trench warfare. At the very least, those who remained in the Legion were volunteers whose mentality was closer to that of professional soldiers than to conscripts. Also, the Legion was simply less heavily engaged in 1916 and

1917 than it had been in 1915, so that discontentment over the way the war was being conducted—apparently the main motive for the mutinies—was less developed in the Legion. In fact, the Legion was counted among the reliable troops who were used to seal off the roads and return the mutineers to the front.[20]

The strategy of the new commander-in-chief, Philippe Pétain, was generally a defensive one. He acknowledged that France had wasted her strength in attempting to achieve victory before she had accumulated the necessary materiel and before her British allies had been fully mobilized. For this reason, she risked defeat from sheer exhaustion. Therefore, his slogan was *"attendre les chars et les américains"*—wait for the tanks and the Americans. However, in order to restore morale and rebuild the confidence of his army, he ordered a limited offensive against a salient in the German lines near Verdun in August, for the first time massing vast quantities of heavy artillery. Dazed by the tremendous artillery barrage, the Germans put up little resistance as the Legion surged forward for over two miles. The Legion's trophies included 680 prisoners and sixteen artillery pieces, including a large French naval gun recaptured from the Germans and a large quantity of machine guns. The cost to the Legion was the fairly minor bill of 53 killed and 271 wounded and missing. On July 14 the RMLE was awarded the yellow and green *fourragère* of the *médaille militaire,* especially created for it by Marshal Pétain. On September 27, the flag of the RMLE was awarded the Legion of Honor, with the promise of a second, red *fourragère.*

The year 1918 would be critical for the Legion on the Western Front, the most critical since 1915. However, it entered the year with several strengths—a fairly homogeneous organization, a solid battlefield reputation and a commander prepared to act as a forceful—even fanatical—spokesman for the RMLE. When Lieutenant Colonel Paul Rollet arrived in May 1917 to replace Lieutenant Colonel Duriez, killed at Aubérive in May, "He fell upon us like a meteor," remembered Captain Fernand Maire. "Small, thin, nervous, a lined face from which shone, beneath thick arching brows, two transparent blue eyes. . . . He suddenly restored to us a strong odor of Africa."[21] Although Maire had not met Rollet, his reputation as a captain of *la montée* before the war had preceded him. Born in 1875, son of an officer, Rollet had the Legion in his blood. In December 1899, barely four years out of Saint-Cyr, where he had graduated 311th in a class of 587, he tired of the monotonous existence of a line infantry regiment in the Ardennes in eastern France and requested transfer to the Legion. By 1914, he had seen service in Madagascar, Algeria and Morocco, where he had distinguished himself as an indefatigable marcher and an officer who had inherited in full measure his father's often irreverent attitude toward superiors. Although he had a reputation as a strict disciplinarian, Rollet earned the loyalty of his legionnaires by the sartorial liberties he took with the uniform—during the war, for instance, he insisted on wearing his kepi through the most ferocious bombardments, and only consented to wear the regulation helmet for the 1919 victory parade—and by the tenacity with which he defended his men when he believed they had been mishandled by a higher authority who did not understand the special rules of the Legion. "He understood his men, even their need of wine—he was not indifferent to a glass himself," wrote English legionnaire A. R. Cooper. "And if one could go to him direct, one was sure of a fair hearing and understanding."[22]

In 1914, Rollet had abandoned the Legion for a line command in France. However, the death of Duriez returned him to his regiment and to what became for him a mission in life. After the war especially, Rollet was to stamp his personality on the Legion to the point that he earned the nickname of "Father of the Legion." Few who served under him, even future deserters like the American Bennett Doty, could fail to be impressed: "He came down the line," Doty wrote, "a little broadshouldered man with a spade beard and fiercely turned-up mustache streaked with gray, and a nose like an eagle's beak."[23] Unfortunately, the respect of legionnaires for the regiment's father was not extended to its "mother," Rollet's wife, whom he married in 1925 and who became known to a generation of postwar legionnaires as "Nénette." Rollet frequently asked for men to help Nénette around the house, but only the newest arrivals volunteered: "The men who knew Nénette used to say they would rather be sent to court martial than work for her," Cooper wrote.[24] In 1918, however, Rollet would have his hands full preserving the RMLE as a fighting unit.

For France, 1918 would also be a crisis year. The collapse of the Eastern Front allowed the Germans to shift their armies west, where, for the first time in the war, they would actually enjoy a numerical advantage. Therefore, the only thing secret about the German offensive of 1918 was when and where they planned to attack. "We expect a German offensive and perhaps a breakthrough. We will do our best," Rollet wrote in February 1918. And despite his insistence that Legion morale was "very high" in the winter of 1917–18, and that the Legion was "an incomparable instrument of war without peer in any army," the challenges were all too obvious.

The first was that by 1918 the Legion in France was being seriously squeezed for recruits. While Legion strength stood at over twelve thousand men in 1917 (excluding the battalion in the *armée d'Orient*) and 1918, it had steadily reduced its commitment in the colonies. In 1915 and 1916, its strength in Tonkin had plunged from three battalions to one company, and while it had continued to maintain five battalions in Morocco, strength there had been seriously reduced. Cadres also had to be provided for a *Légion d'Orient* made up of Armenians and Syrians operating in the Levant in 1917 and 1918. All of this left only three battalions for the Western Front. For obvious reasons, most German and Austrian subjects had been left behind in North Africa in 1914. This made for a very curious atmosphere in the Legion there. According to Joseph Ehrhart, who was in Morocco when the war broke out, strict measures were taken "to avoid unfortunate incidents between German and Austrian legionnaires and French. Newspapers were forbidden and communiques were not read out." Apart from an attempt by five Germans to hand over a blockhouse to the Moroccans and a knife fight between a French and a German legionnaire, "in general, everything passed off alright."[25]

However, other sources suggest that the national divisions intensified in the Legion after the outbreak of war. The Irishman John Barret, one of the "volunteers for the duration" sent in 1914 to Morocco, discovered that "Every solitary man of these [Germans, Austrians and a Turk in his company] hoped for the victory of the German armies and openly voiced their opinions, particularly when they were a little drunk, which happened rather often." German legionnaires deserted daily to the Moroccans, according to Barret, and when his unit was sent to reinforce the Moroccan garrison at Khenifra after a French column of over three hundred men had been massacred there,[26] "I remember how sick I felt when I saw that the men I was compelled to call comrades were delighted at the French disaster, although they themselves wore (or rather disgraced) the French uniform." The old German and Austrian veterans who had been marooned in North Africa by the war "hated" their compatriots who enlisted in the Legion "instead of returning to Germany and Austria to fight for the Fatherland." Still, he noted that, despite the incongruous and, for him, distasteful spectacle of the Legion marching against the Moroccans singing the *"Wacht am Rhein,"* "the unit had great esprit de corps."[27] In 1916, Magnus discovered at Sidi-bel-Abbès "a German regiment of the lowest type transplanted to Africa," many of whose members were openly disloyal:

They read the papers ardently, and were delighted at the French set-back at Verdun and the German victories. Their idea was that no one but a German could be a good soldier. And often I heard: "Look at them—they call themselves soldiers, and think they can beat our well-trained German army?"[28]

A second group who could not be sent to France were those who had elected not to fight the Germans, or who had been sent there because they were wounded or considered in some other way unfit for active service— Magnus wrote that his captain was nicknamed "the telephone captain" or "Captain Hallo-Hallo," because it was rumored that at Gallipoli he rushed into the dugout on the pretext of calling headquarters each time there was any danger.[29] Ehrhart recorded that the Legion in Morocco received reinforcements of Polish POWs who enlisted on the condition that they would serve in Morocco, and Italian volunteers who presumably had no desire to serve in their own army.[30] However, Magnus speaks highly, for instance, of the Spanish soldiers at Sidi-bel-Abbès who might have been dispatched to the Western Front, as well as other odds and ends like Danes.[31]

A second impediment to the reinforcement of the RMLE was the attitude of the Moroccan resident general, Hubert Lyautey. In August 1914 he had been ordered to withdraw to a few coastal enclaves and repatriate most of the troops in Morocco to France. Lyautey disobeyed these orders and instead pushed his troops out to the periphery of the conquered areas on the theory—the correct one as it transpired—that by holding the frontiers strongly he could maintain control of those areas already pacified. And while he claimed to have repatriated more troops to France than the government actually requested, on August 16 he "protested formally against sending the Legion to France." On August 20, 1914, the war ministry compromised and decided to retain the Legion in Morocco, but ordered each of the four battalions in Algeria to send a half-battalion to France.[32]

While it is certainly true that most of the Legion in North Africa was unsuitable for service on the Western Front, even when Lyautey could have contributed to the strength of the RMLE, he proved reluctant to do so. On November 9, 1916, Lyautey wrote that he did not want to send the Czechs and Poles to France because this would open the door for the departure of the French and those from Alsace-Lorraine as well, "so that the Legion would no longer have sufficient cadres and I cannot do without it."[33] In this respect, at least, Lyautey appears to have been more concerned with securing his precarious colony than with doing all he could to help the salvation of France. By 1917, large numbers of contracts of German and Austrian legionnaires who had enlisted before the outbreak of war in 1914 were beginning to expire, and many chose internment in France, where they were allowed to work for wages inflated by the war. Furthermore, they encouraged their former comrades whose enlistments were coming to an end to do the same, which further depleted regimental strength. On September 4, 1917, Lyautey wrote to the war minister to request urgent measures to allow the "Austro-Germans" to reenlist for the duration of the war, for which they would be given a twenty-five-franc bonus and an extra twenty centimes a day, ". . . always with the goal in mind of preserving the battalions of the Legion which form the best of my white troops whose existence is my primary preoccupation."[34] But these incentives, if implemented, were hardly competitive with wages on the outside. Also, some of these men must have had a bad conscience about serving in a French unit while France was at war with their country.

For these reasons, on December 15, 1917, Lyautey floated a sterner proposal that special "concentration camps" be created in Algeria where "the life of ex-legionnaires who have been interned is rendered less soft and above all by abolishing their salary." However, this appears to have fallen on deaf ears, for on March 16, 1918, the commander of the 1st Battalion of the *1er étranger* reported that foreigners were not reenlisting because the wages paid to internees in France and Algeria were superior. The following month he complained that his companies were down to one hundred men, that the "enormous majority" preferred internment and that the only reenlistments were among men in trouble with the law. By the summer of 1918, the five Legion battalions in North Africa had seen their strength considerably diminished. So desperate was the situation that Lyautey had been forced to impress men from the transportation corps, who made terrible legionnaires. A note of June 9, 1918, proposed that legionnaires whose contracts had expired be offered the choice of a five-hundred-franc reenlistment bonus or being sent to Corsica, because they posed a threat to the security of North Africa.[35]

The situation in France was hardly better, and the RMLE struggled to maintain a fighting strength—indeed, it struggled to remain in existence. The basic problem, in some ways the irony, for the Legion was that in the situation of a world war, recruits were hard to come by. The feast of recruits in 1914–15 had turned to famine by 1918. Rollet summed up the Legion's situation succinctly in July 1918:

Since the entry of Belgium, Italy, Portugal, America and Greece into the war, since the creation of the Polish, Czechoslovakian and Armenian national armies, the Legion has lost many of its best soldiers and has seen its sources of recruitment dry up. Only the Swiss and Spanish continue to enlist. (Their numbers vary from 80 to 100 a month—totally insufficient to keep up strength.)[36]

Furthermore, the poor treatment of many volunteers in the war's opening weeks made the government wary of sending some men to the Legion. This, combined with the expansion of the artillery under Pétain, meant that foreigners volunteering for service might be enlisted in the Legion *pro forma* and then sent to a regular French unit. For instance, there were still a small but important number of Americans who were willing to enlist because they wished to get into action quickly and avoid being sent back to the United States for prolonged training. This is precisely what happened to the American Julian Green, who left the Ambulance Corps to see more active service. "As a foreigner, I could not be allowed to join the French army, but this difficulty was neatly got around by first having me sign up in the Foreign Legion (in which I remained for the space of an hour), and then transferring me from the Legion into the regular army."[37] The Legion career of Cole Porter appears to have been identical to that of Green, and certainly too short to have served as inspiration for any of his music— enlisted in the Legion on April 20, 1918, assigned to the 3rd Artillery Regiment and sent to the artillery school at Fountainebleau.[38]

The British offering their services to the Legion, if the archives of the French military attaché in London are anything to go by, were unpromising material. They included H. D. Baird of County Wexford, who could not join the British army because "owing to an accident . . . I am compelled to wear a rubber tube inserted in my side (it was my side that was injured)"; a retired Indian army major—"I speak Hindustani"; a veteran of Egypt,

South Africa and the Sudan—"although I am a little over 60, I am as good as most men of 40"; another "from a good family well known in Norfolk" who claimed to see very well with glasses and wanted to know if he could join when he turned 18; an American married to "a French lady—and a better wife no man could wish for"; a lieutenant cashiered from the British army because "he took no interest in his work"; a seventeen-year-old schoolboy; a Portuguese whose father did not want him to go to the front "and risk my life" but who was "ready to join any branch of the said legion, such as garrison duty, or any other work as a soldier"; four American Rhodes Scholars studying at Oxford; and so on.[39] In short, there was nothing that looked very promising there. The only slightly mitigating factor in all of this, if mitigating it was, was that regular units were also scraping the bottom of the recruitment barrel.

The recruitment crisis was serious because of large defections that continued to deplete Legion ranks in 1918. The Czechs were allowed to form their own army in 1918, and this cost Rollet 1,020 men.[40] Lyautey protested loudly when two Czechs departed Morocco to join their own army, which was forming at Cognac, because soon others would ask to do the same thing.[41] The problem for the Legion was not simply finding bodies, but men who would make good soldiers. Rollet complained that the Czechs, like the Poles and Armenians before them, had left the Legion under great pressure, "under the menace of being considered as shirkers refusing to defend their national cause."[42] He reported in July 1918 that the only replacements he had for the departing Czechs were 150 wounded legionnaires still on convalescent leave and a group of 694 Russians, "265 of whom declared they do not want to fight."

In the wake of the Revolution, the Russians were a risky proposition—already in September 1917, three battalions of Russians sent to France to participate on the Western Front had mutinied at the camp of La Courtine. At first, the Legion incorporated the reluctant Russians anyway, but this had produced numerous desertions. However, those Russians who had not deserted had fought very well in April, May and June 1918. Therefore, a further 375 Russians willing to fight were sent to the front in June and July. They did not desert, according to Rollet, "but the conduct under fire of these Russians was not brilliant—as soon as they were under a violent artillery barrage, they found a shell hole and remained there all day, allowing their neighbors to attack by themselves. Their comrades, old legionnaires, because of this are very angry with them." As a consequence, they were worse than useless—they could not be trusted with automatic weapons, "the soul of a combat group" and were too unreliable to bring up ammunition, and their lack of French excluded their use as telephonists or runners. He noted that of 300 Russians in the regiment, eighty had deserted or were awaiting a court-martial. He thought that the maximum number of Russian replacements the regiment could absorb was 180, "chosen among the best" of the training camp, who would be distributed 15 to a company.

"To go beyond this number would be dangerous and risk a disaster," he concluded, and suggested that the rest be sent to North Africa or to the Russian Legion.[43]

Desperate for men—indeed, apparently on the verge of panic—Rollet suggested three recruitment sources: The first was to seek volunteers among French regiments. Calls for old legionnaires to return had produced only mediocre results, "old territorials, NCOs for the most part." But if each French regiment furnished only two volunteers, this could give him six to seven hundred men. "The Foreign Legion has always contained, in peacetime, 40 per cent French," he wrote. "It would be a good thing to return to this wise tradition." Second, he believed that a recruiting drive among "Yugoslavians" captured by the Serbs and placed in POW camps in Corsica would net a further hundred. Last, as a measure of his desperation, he was even prepared to take German and Austrian legionnaires from Morocco—"Some Legion officers have received letters on this subject. One could call upon this category of excellent legionnaires. One could certainly obtain 100 volunteers in this way." He castigated the refusal of Morocco to send reinforcements, arguing that repatriated French POWs could replace vacancies there.

This report is a curious one for several reasons. In the first place, 905 Frenchmen, by far the largest national contingent, were already serving in the RMLE by June 1918.[44] Also, while spending much ink on the possibility of enlisting a dollop of Germans and Yugoslavs, Rollet apparently ignored the assignment to artillery units of foreigners like Julian Green and Cole Porter who were enlisting in the Legion. Perhaps he was not aware that this was going on. More likely, as will be seen later, he was not interested in enlisting foreigners from countries with political clout. In July 1918, an American citizen, Frank S. Butterworth, proposed the recruitment of a "regiment" for the French Foreign Legion in the United States, but was refused permission by the Secretary of War.[45] Also, a small unit of legionnaires was dispatched to the United States in September 1918 to tour the country in support of liberty loans. However, this does not seem to have produced any American recruits for the Legion.[46] Nor does Rollet appear to have considered the possibility of incorporating into the Legion some of the large numbers of native troops from the colonies who were flowing into the French army by 1918, even as a temporary measure to replace casualties and departures. This can only be explained as part of the colonial mentality, when, even on the Western Front and in a unit serving as part of the Moroccan Division that contained Moslem units, Rollet obviously believed the Legion should retain its character as a *troupe blanche*. In this, Rollet only reflected the tradition of the French army, which, as in the British and American armies in this period, was to maintain separate regiments.

Rollet ended with a desperate plea for the Legion, which he appears to believe was in serious danger of being disbanded. In the process, he demonstrated his budding talent as a public relations expert, which he would use in the interest of the Legion so effectively in the interwar years: *"A regiment with such tradition and such a history must not die,"* he appealed.

It must live until the end of the war, even if one must increase strength through levies on French regiments. This would be an excellent source—to transfer around 500 soldiers from infantry regiments to the Legion would create in several days 500 heroes. One must add that if the Regiment of the Legion was dissolved during the War, it would not be possible to reconstitute it in peacetime (just remember the attacks of the foreign press between 1900 and 1914). And so would vanish this excellent school of energy, of will, of courage which formed the heart and character of ardent young officers full of fire who would go afterward into the regiments in settled garrisons, animated with sacred fire and maintain the good and healthy traditions—It would not be a simple unit which would disappear with the Legion, but a notable part of the worth of the French army.[47]

Why Rollet was so worked up about the disbandment of the Legion is difficult to imagine. According to Elisabeth Erulin's figures, the Legion counted 12,687 men in 1918.[48] Legally all foreigners in the French army were required at least to pass through it. It was an internal part of imperial defense in North Africa and Indochina. If it were disbanded, France would have to intern most of the foreigners serving in North Africa. Therefore, for both practical and legal reasons, the Legion appeared in no real danger of disappearing in 1918. However, the RMLE was very much under threat, all the more so because it was taking terrific losses in the fighting that raged in France in the spring and summer of 1918.

The Legion was not involved in the initial fighting touched off by the Michael Offensives launched principally at the British lines around Saint-Quentin on March 21. However, by late April the Germans were threatening to seize the strategically significant communications center of Amiens. On April 26, the RMLE together with English troops was ordered to occupy the Hangard Wood, which lay just north of the Amiens-Noyon highway. Despite support from rolling barrages and tanks, the fighting was desperate in the open conditions of the "war of movement," where front lines were not well defined by trench lines as they had been for almost four years. German machine-gun teams infiltrated into the porous lines between the advanced posts and wrought havoc among legionnaires who attempted to advance in a thick fog.

The rolling barrage, developed for the static conditions of 1916 and 1917, proved to be too imprecise in conditions of fluid fighting. Legionnaires who attempted to advance behind the British tanks were cut down, so that the attack faltered after it had gone barely seven hundred yards. A German counterattack drove the Allies out of the wood, but they returned to establish a precarious dominance. The day cost the RMLE 120 men killed, 497 wounded and 205 missing. The 1st Battalion was down to 1 officer and 187 legionnaires. The Legion continued to hold the wood under a drizzle, sometimes a downpour, of harassing artillery and isolated attacks by German patrols until relieved on May 6. "The attack of 26 April has permitted once again to demonstrate that valorous troops will always know how to make up for insufficient support by their devotion and their heroism," the regimental diary concluded.[49]

Although the German offensive stalled before Amiens, Ludendorff and Hindenburg held a surprise up their sleeve. May 27 was the turn of the French on the Chemin des Dames west of Reims, the very area where the Nivelle offensive had faltered barely a year earlier. Despite directives from Pétain insisting that the French lines be organized for a defense in depth, the French sector commander placed the bulk of his forces in the forward trenches, where many fell victim to the initial German barrage. By May 30, the RMLE together with the entire Moroccan Division had been bussed to the *Montagne de Paris* just west of Soissons to make a stand.

The German attack began at nine o'clock in the morning. Using infiltration techniques and supported by artillery, the Germans gradually pushed back the Legion first line, which also suffered from a lack of munitions. However, once they arrived at the main position, the enemy could advance no further, either then or on the following day, when the regimental diary declared triumphantly: "The question is answered—the Boches even when numerous, will not pass in front of the Legion." Although the Legion suffered only 42 men killed during the two days of fighting, 219 were wounded and 70 missing.[50] The Legion continued to fight around Soissons over the next few days, taking a minor but steady drain of losses, many to gas shells. On the 12th it withstood a violent German attack supported by artillery at a cost of 36 dead, 94 wounded and 5 missing. The forward elements were praised for their skill and open fighting and in holding steady despite the German barrage. However, the diary notes that the regiment had lost 1,250 men since Hangard Wood and that these had not been replaced. These losses were severely felt, for it had exhausted its reserves and managed to hold on the 12th because it had been reinforced by two rifle companies and a machine-gun company from the 7th *tirailleurs*.

The Moroccan Division was called upon to spearhead Foch's offensive of July 18 against the salient created by the German advance south of Soissons. The attack, preceded by tanks and a rolling barrage, was considered one of the most brilliant tactical actions of the Legion during the war, despite the fact that the barrage often outran the infantry, which had to halt to clear up machine-gun nests. In less than two hours, the Legion had overrun the German positions and taken a large number of prisoners. The commander of the Moroccan Division believed that one reason that the results of his troops were superior to that of others was that his division had shed its field packs and therefore could move forward quickly. The

Germans counterattacked three times behind a heavy artillery barrage July 20. Despite heavy losses, the Legion held their positions, and the German attacks exhausted themselves. Nevertheless, while praising the operation, the division commander believed that the advance might have been greater on the first day had the liaisons between the command posts and the front lines been more effective. He also pointed out that infantry–artillery liaison left much to be desired,[51] demonstrating that the French had yet to achieve the flexibility to allow them to deal with unforeseen developments that departed from the prearranged battle plan. The three days of combat had again cost the Legion heavily—780 men—and provoked Rollet's fears for the future of the RMLE.

And those fears were well founded, for the Legion was again thrown into the line near Soissons on September 1 and charged with pursuing the Germans, who were making a fighting retreat to the north. On September 2 it took the villages of Terny and Sorny after two days of attacks by American troops had faltered before it. But the countryside around Terny and Sorny was heavily defended by machine-gun nests, against which the Legion advanced, using infiltration tactics, only with great difficulty. Despite heavy losses that had reduced many Legion companies to fifty men, the Moroccan Division, including the Legion, was thrown at the Hindenburg Line on September 14. Legionnaires in the battalion under the command of Major Fernand Maire captured double their numbers in German prisoners. The Germans reposted with counterattacks and gas shells, which increased the fatigue of fighting in gas masks. The Hindenburg Line had been pierced, but the fighting had cost the Legion 10 officers and 275 legionnaires killed and 1,118 wounded.[52] September 14 became the *fête du régiment* for the *3e étranger*. So decorated was the RMLE already that a third *fourragère* combining the colors of the *Légion d'honneur* and the *croix de guerre* had to be invented for it.

However, the decorations showered upon the RMLE in themselves would cause controversy, for they led to accusations that the foreigners had been employed as cannon fodder, and that the Legion was a sacrificial corps. In some ways the Legion contributed (and continues to contribute) to the credibility of these charges by its insistence that it always asks for the most difficult tasks, those considered beyond the capabilities of other units. The American Legionnaire Bennett Doty wrote of the Legion in World War I,

In its first action, charging in the face of machine gun fire, across trenches and barbed wire, it had been virtually annihilated. Recruited up to strength again, it had gone on thus through the entire war, depleting almost to nothing over and over again—a sort of sacrificial corps, ever at the worst place.[53]

Some estimates put Legion casualties during the war as high as 31,000 of the 44,150 men who served in the Legion, a catastrophic 70 percent casualty rate.[54]

doubt that the Legion, especially as part of the Moroccan
[ ] ven some difficult missions during the war. However, when
[ ] ntext of the entire war, it appears that to call it a "sacrificial
[ ] e going too far. It missed the early battles of August—
[ ] 14 that were so costly to the French. And while the Legion
suffered heavily in Artois and Champagne in 1915, so did the entire French
army, taking over 102,500 casualties in the May 9–June 18 offensives, and
more than 143,500 in those of September 25–30 in Champagne.[55] And
while the attack on Belloy-en-Santerre in 1916 has sometimes been described as a suicide mission, the number of officers and legionnaires actually killed or missing on July 4 and 5, 1916, was less than 9 percent of
strength.[56] Furthermore, this was the only significant action of the RMLE
in a year when the French and German armies were battering themselves to
pulp at Verdun and the British army was slogging forward at significant
cost on the Somme. In 1917, a year of heavy fighting for the British, the
Legion was only twice seriously engaged, the second time at Verdun where
French casualties were comparatively light. 1918 was a tough year for the
Legion, but so was it for everybody else. Therefore, in terms of the missions
assigned to it, to call the Legion a "sacrificial corps" is certainly an exaggeration.

Nor does the number of Legion casualties appear to justify this accusation. Charges that 35,000 legionnaires died in the war appear to be
wildly out of line. The Legion estimates its dead on the Western Front at
4,116 officers and men,[57] and its overall casualties there at around
11,000.[58] Another 1,200 died in other theaters, particularly in the Dardanelles. Of course, the numbers might be substantially increased if one
includes volunteers who subsequently transferred out of the Legion and
who became casualties while fighting in other units or perhaps men who,
while officially registered in the Legion, never actually served there. The
Historique of the RMLE claims that Legion losses were actually fewer than
those of many line regiments, that the effectives of the RMLE were only
renewed three times while some French regiments "renewed their effectives
eight or ten times." This relatively low casualty rate is attributed to "the
exceptional quality of the cadres."[59] It is not really clear how much this
argument is worth. In the first place, many of the "renewals" of line regiments were probably the result of transfers, an option denied to most
legionnaires after the autumn of 1915. Second, while the Legion did eventually build up what appear to be excellent cadres, it was certainly not the
case for the most part through the Artois offensives of 1915. Third, while
it would certainly be unfair to claim that the Legion had an easy war, it saw
only restricted, if briefly violent, action for three years of the war—1914,
1916 and 1917.

Legion histories usually concentrate on the successes of the RMLE on
the Western Front, and there can be no doubt that these were quite spectacular. This success was undoubtedly one of the accomplishments of Le-

gion Lieutenant Colonel Cot, who was able to preside over the restoration of the morale and professional character of the regiment after the unhappy experiment with the "volunteers for the duration." The Legion also contributed contingents to the Dardanelles and subsequently the Macedonian campaigns and helped to maintain France's North African empire. However, in a sense it was the triumph of the professional, elite character of the Legion that also pointed up its limitations, the first of which was its failure to integrate the initial wave of patriotic and idealistic volunteers who rallied to France in 1914–15. Of course, this failure was not entirely of Legion making—the great expansion had forced it to accept cadres who were simply substandard, and it was poorly equipped to handle these men. However, the "volunteers for the duration" appear on the whole to have received little better treatment from veteran legionnaires, who made it quite clear that men of their background and ideals had no place there. In other words, they had to adapt to the Legion—the Legion made no effort to adapt to them.

In terms of their battlefield success, it can be argued that the Legion made the correct decision by fighting to retain its prewar personality, by insisting upon its elite, professional, even colonial character in the midst of the war between nations in arms. However, paradoxically, by increasing its efficiency, it limited its utility. The Legion deliberately denied itself, or squandered, important sources of recruitment in the war's opening months. And while some of those recruitment sources would have dried up in any case as more nations joined the war and reclaimed their nationals, the departure might neither have been so brusque nor so traumatic had a greater effort been made to reconcile these volunteers to the Legion and project an elite, but less cutthroat, image. In this way, the Legion imposed limits on its growth. And because it elected to remain small, it placed limits on its overall utility.

Most legionnaires, for one reason or another, simply could not be assigned to the Western Front. And while one could argue, as did Lyautey, that the Legion provided a useful function in holding and even extending conquests in Morocco, it is difficult to see how the fighting there contributed in any significant way to the victory over the Central Powers. In the end, the Legion in North Africa, which was most of the Legion, served as a sort of holding pen for hostile foreign nationals, which at least denied their services to the enemy even if this was only a small gain for France. The final months of the war also demonstrated the recruitment difficulties faced by this international force in a world war, even though it had elected to remain small. Rollet continued to conjure up recruits, the majority probably among Frenchmen. Nevertheless, it must have come as a great relief to Rollet, who feared that the Legion would not survive the war, to be able to return to North Africa and the old business of colonial soldiering. But even there, life for the Legion would never be the same.

Chapter 19

NEW LEGION, "OLD LEGION"

THE LEGION AFTER the close of World War I suffered an acute identity crisis. This is hardly surprising, for it was a crisis shared with most of Europe. The war's enormous bloodletting, followed by the political chaos and economic dislocation of the interwar years, translated into a breakdown of faith in many of the values that had guided the prewar world. It was the dissolution of these moral certainties that left much of European society rudderless in an age complicated by fresh, uncompromising political ideologies and economic uncertainties, which historians blame for the "political squalor" of the interwar years—a confusion and lack of resolve in the chancelleries of Europe that eventually allowed Hitler to tip the world into a second global conflict.

Such a profound shock in Europe's equilibrium was bound to have repercussions for the Legion. Once the dust of the European conflict had settled, it became clear that what was already being called the "Old Legion" had perished in the trenches of Northern France. While the prestige of the Legion at the close of World War I was immense, so immense in fact that the Spanish government sent lieutenant Colonel José Millan Astray to Sidi-bel-Abbès in 1919 to prepare for the creation of the *Tercio extranjero* in the Spanish army the following year and in 1922 the president of the French Republic, Alexandre Millerand, paid a special visit to Legion headquarters, the cost of the war had been great. "The losses of the 'Old Legion' during the war are not compensated for by the glory of the RMLE!" Paul Rollet wrote soon after the war's end.[1] For Rollet, the Legion had to be rebuilt from the ground up, for everywhere he saw problems. If the "Old Legion" had disappeared, he believed, then it fell to its surviving alumni to "recreate" it, as part of a process designed to give the Legion stability and secure its future.

This was especially critical because the Legion would shoulder a far greater role in colonial defense than had fallen to it before 1914. As early as June 1919, General Jean Mordacq, who had served in the prewar Legion and had risen to the post of *chef de cabinet* for Prime Minister Georges Clémenceau, began to lay plans to rebuild and restructure the Legion. "I had great plans and I believed that the time had come, no longer to have foreign regiments, but foreign divisions, including troops of the three arms (infantry, cavalry, artillery—and even engineers)," he wrote.[2] In November 1919, the resident general of Morocco, Hubert Lyautey, called for thirty thousand white troops in Morocco, most of whom were to be provided by an expanded Legion whose recruitment should be carried out "with method and tenacity."[3] In 1920, decrees organized cavalry and artillery regiments in the Legion. And although that on the artillery was never completely applied, it did mark the end of the Legion as an exclusively infantry formation.

The postwar Legion was expanded, restructured and assigned new homes. Sidi-bel-Abbès remained the headquarters for the *1er étranger*, which became essentially an administrative center and basic training camp, over the protests of Paul Rollet, who wanted to abandon Algeria altogether and group the Legion in Morocco—in retrospect an ironic proposal coming from a man who later was to transform "Bel-Abbès" into the Legion's shrine and holy city. However, the bulk of the Legion shifted to Morocco. In most respects, this made sense. Not only did the remaining pockets of "dissidence" in the Atlas remain to be dealt with, a task completed only in 1933.[4] But also the turbulence in the Spanish zone posed a continued threat to the French protectorate, and in 1925 the Rif War would spill over into the French zone. However, the political advantages offered the Legion in Morocco were probably as attractive as the strategic ones were logical. A protectorate ruled with great flair—and great independence—by Lyautey, Morocco presented the Legion a unique opportunity to gain greater autonomy (and better pay!).

The *2e étranger* left Saïda for its new garrison at Meknès. The RMLE became the *3e étranger* under Rollet quartered at Fez from January 1921, while in December 1920 the *4e étranger* was created at Meknès before it eventually settled in Marrakesh in southern Morocco. In 1922, the *régiment étranger de cavalerie* (REC) was organized with its headquarters at Sousse in Tunisia. By 1929, the Legion counted eighteen battalions of infantry, six cavalry squadrons, five mounted companies, and four companies of sappers. In 1930, the three Legion battalions in Indochina, nominally part of the *1er étranger,* were elevated to the status of the *5e étranger,* while in 1939 three battalions from the *1er étranger* and one battalion from the 2e étranger were fused to form the 6e étranger for service in Syria. A 2e régiment étranger de cavalerie was created in 1939, while artillery batteries were progressively organized in the 1930s.

While the Legion would eventually swell to include over thirty-three thousand men by 1933, the process was a gradual one. Initially, the creation of new units consisted in the main of a reordering of an unwieldy prewar administrative structure of detached companies and battalions. One of the problems of the Legion was that until the Depression brought in an enormous influx of recruits, the new units were chronically understaffed.[5] More serious in Rollet's view, however, was the disappearance of most of the veterans after 1919: "The post-war Legion, with too few veterans, is difficult to get into shape," he wrote.[6] Colonel Boulet-Desbareau, commanding the 1er étranger, agreed in December 1920 that the absence of NCOs was a problem, especially as 72 percent of the recruits "come from nationalities who have made war against us." Yet, he reported, "discipline is perfect. In the opinion of the veteran officers of the Legion, it is better than before. There are far fewer drunks."[7] The "Moroccans," however, saw it differently. Rollet complained bitterly to Lyautey, in what were obviously shots fired in his war to group the Legion in Morocco, that Sidi-bel-Abbès was creaming off the best recruits for the depot and dispatching to the Legion in Morocco too many discipline cases amnestied at the end of the war and "orientals" from Asia Minor who made bad soldiers. All the recruits were badly trained, while he had been given neither corporals nor musicians.[8] Lyautey agreed on December 27, 1920, that, while he was a great partisan of using the Legion to save French lives, the postwar Legion was not the equal of its predecessor, in great part because its troops were "physically depressed or insufficiently developed."[9]

The opinion was unanimous that the atmosphere in the postwar Legion had altered for the worse. The regimental diarist of the 2e étranger recorded in 1921 that the legionnaires, 52 percent of whom were Germans,

do not seem to have come to the Legion in search of new adventures. The struggle which has overturned Europe since 1914 has sufficiently satisfied the seekers of strong emotions, and the desire to live peacefully while waiting for better times seems to be the main motivating force for numerous enlistments. The legionnaires of this epoch are different from those before the war. They seem more malleable, less drunken, but also more thin-skinned. Their mentality for the moment seems to be that of "transplants," while before the war we had the "uprooted." Apart from the food, they are largely indifferent to their surroundings. The rather large number of letters that they write and receive show that they have not broken with their old countries. That is why we receive frequent requests to annul enlistments coming from parents of young legionnaires less than twenty years old.[10]

Jacques Lauzière, a French officer assigned to the Legion in the immediate postwar period, expected to rub shoulders with the bronzed lascars described by pre-1914 writers like Grisot, Roger de Beauvoir and Georges d'Esparbès. Instead he was set to command a collection of "adolescents . . . with hardly any fuzz on their chin," psychologically unstable, a quarter of whom admitted to being less than twenty years old, and 64 percent of whom were under twenty-five. 73 percent claimed to have exercised a manual trade, 7 percent to have been farmers and 13 percent "intellectuals," artists or employed in offices. The few old veterans occupied the sedentary jobs in the unit, or spent their time drinking and attempting to sabotage the leadership of the many new officers with no prior Legion experience who, in their view, were applying inappropriate leadership techniques designed for French conscripts, not true legionnaires.[11] Indeed, so serious was the recruitment situation that one Legion battalion commander even went so far as to suggest in 1923 that the Legion's sacred five-year enlistment be reduced to three years to draw in "the hesitant, whom the prospect of five years hold back."[12]

The Englishman A. R. Cooper, who had enlisted in the Legion in 1914 and fought in the Dardanelles before transferring to the British army for the remainder of the war, found the atmosphere of the Legion greatly altered upon his reenlistment in 1919. "I soon began to realize that I had made a terrible mistake in coming back," he wrote. "That conditions were not the same as they had been during the war, and that I had been too young to realize what life in the Legion meant." Cooper blamed the change in atmosphere principally upon the influx of Russians, refugees from the White Russian armies defeated in the Civil War, who were "bad soldiers, insubordinate, not good fighters, lacking *esprit de corps*."[13] The Russian recruits may have been poor soldiers,[14] but they were credited with one cultural innovation in the postwar Legion—the game of "*coucou*." Apparently imported from Czarist army messes, *coucou* was a variation upon Russian roulette with the odds of survival greatly reduced. The rules required one legionnaire chosen by lot to step outside while his comrades arranged themselves around the walls of a completely darkened room. The single legionnaire then reentered the room and said "*coucou*," while, one imagines, simultaneously taking violent evasive action as his comrades took this as a cue to fire their revolvers in his general direction.[15]

The change of atmosphere noted in the post-1918 Legion cannot be blamed entirely upon the Russians, however, who did not begin to appear in significant numbers until 1921, and were only a dominant nationality in the REC, where by 1925 they made up 82 percent of strength. In 1921, for instance, only 12 percent of the legionnaires were Russians.[16] However, Cooper's perspective was not a solitary one. Even Rollet advanced what was on the face of it the curious complaint that the problem with the postwar Foreign Legion was that it contained too many foreigners: "The proportion of French is extremely insufficient," he wrote. "In the *3ᵉ étranger*, 9 per cent at present," against a prewar rate that he placed as high as 50 percent.[17] Why an officer of the "old Legion" should lament the absence of large numbers of French is puzzling at first, because by common consent Frenchmen made the worst legionnaires before 1914.[18] However, as will be seen, after 1920 Rollet might be forgiven for waxing nostalgic about men who seldom deserted and whose loyalty was never in question. Colonel Marty, commander of the *2ᵉ étranger* in 1924, agreed that Frenchmen made the least good legionnaires, but "these French form by the qualities of race, by the obligatory attachment to 'their army', a counterweight to foreign influences which the preponderance can in certain cases bring about grave consequences (affair Pahl)."[19] In fact, throughout the interwar years, the Legion continued to favor Frenchmen in promotion, an indication that loyalty was a primary concern. For instance, in 1934, while only 16 percent of legionnaires claimed French nationality, fully 35 percent of corporals and NCOs were French. The Germans, who accounted for 44.5 percent of all legionnaires in that year, provided only 21 percent of corporals and NCOs. By 1939, the percentage of German corporals and NCOs equaled their strength in the corps—21 percent. But 30 percent of French legionnaires had claimed 41 percent of corporals and NCO slots.[20]

On the surface, at least, the induction process resembled that of the prewar period, with the difference that the physical examination had been substantially stiffened. Nevertheless, Legion officers complained that the physical examination was carried out by doctors in France "who do not know the Legion and ignore its needs and desires." As a result, many veteran legionnaires were eliminated while "this filtering allowed doubtful but physically fit elements through, which the regulations concerning annulment of enlistments do not permit us to eliminate."[21] Excessive attention was perhaps paid to the quality of eyesight and especially of teeth, although how rigorously this was enforced is not clear. When the Englishman Brian Stuart appeared for his physical, the sergeant told him he would be rejected as soon as the doctor saw his glasses, but that the sergeant could "square" it for five francs. "I produced the five francs, at the same time wondering whatever kind of doctor could be 'squared' with that sum." In fact, the sergeant "squared" the corporal, who whispered to Stuart the letters as they were pointed to on the eye chart.[22] Ferri-Pisani saw a Belgian legionnaire with ten years' service refused re-enlistment because he was missing a number of teeth: "They blame me," the old legionnaire complained bitterly. "*They* pulled my molars *themselves* at the beginning of my second enlistment before I left for Tonkin. . . . I've made them a present of my ten years!" "Try Versailles," another counseled. "They are much easier than Paris."[23] A report of the colonel of the *4ᵉ étranger* in 1933 suggested that a physical examination failed to eliminate unfit recruits who *rapidly show themselves incapable of enduring the rough life of the* bled, *missing teeth, used up, psychological misfits, who burden the hospitals and reduce the actual strength, a strength already diminished by the number of men taken away for the benefits of support services.*[24]

While there is no reason to doubt this assessment, Brian Stuart believed that the Legion might have recuperated more of these men had they adopted a graduated approach to training. Instead, Legion training was, in his view, of the "kill or cure" variety—many push-ups, running up and down sand dunes, "doubling" while carrying a heavier man and the traditional long marches in the intense Algerian heat. This was especially hard on those who had been deprived of regular nutrition at critical times in their childhood, particularly in Central and Eastern Europe during the war when rationing had reached near-starvation levels, or during the Depression when men had eaten only irregularly or insufficiently for months before enlistment.[25]

Certain aspects of Legion life remained unchanged, or almost unchanged, from the pre-1914 era. Sidi-bel-Abbès had gained little in charm. What had altered was the ability of fresh legionnaires to savor the few cultural embellishments that did exist. Recruits were given an enlistment bonus followed by an additional sum upon completion of basic training. Englishman Brian Stuart witnessed what was for many their first encounter with cash for some time—one legionnaire, obviously an ex-waiter, slipped the sum deftly into his trouser pocket, saluted and bowed, muttering, "*Merci bien, m'sieu.*" Two Russians "grabbed the money like hungry wolves." Some men broke into tears, others froze in place as if bereft of movement and had to be helped from the room, while one man rushed through the door clutching his cash close to his breast "as though the Devil was after him." Few kept it for long. Turned loose on the town feeling very rich indeed and smartly turned out in their new red and blue kepis, the admonition of the sergeant to "Beware of the Old Soldier! Don't drink with him and above all, don't lend him money!" was quickly forgotten. After decades of trying unsuccessfully to keep its soldiers out of the *village nègre,* the Legion finally bestowed its seal of approval upon three establishments: Le Moulin Rouge, Au Palmier and Le Chat Noir. Stuart found the Moulin Rouge less intimidating, for unlike the other brothels, the completely naked hostesses did not swarm over the customers but remained in the far corner of the room until summoned upon the completion of negotiations between the Madame and the legionnaire.[26]

The "old Legion," or what was left of it, was universally unhappy about the atmosphere of the immediate postwar corps. Georges Manue, who joined in 1921, catalogued the complaints of the veterans, at the top of which was the fact that the *bleus* held their elders in insufficient esteem, a fact they put down to an unfortunate lapse of standards during the war. In their view, the Legion *has its tacit laws which it must do its utmost to uphold. These are: the respect for seniority, the concern for the community, sharing, mutual aid, teaching the young ones through rough jokes which they were wrong to forbid. It is only right that the* bleu *defers to the veteran.*

The new recruits only dreamed of "towns and women," while the veterans spent their time in the canteen and disdained "civilian life, which is for them something very distant, improbable, like another planet." An old sergeant told him: "Do like me, never put on a hat. Snuff it in the Legion. Civvy street's not worth a damn. You're never at ease, never free." But this new breed of legionnaire only bided their time until their enlistments terminated—they wandered aimlessly about their Moroccan garrison towns neglecting to salute superiors. "[The officers] do not react, because the few who are shocked by this *laisser-aller* feel helpless to correct it."[27] Stuart also experienced the dislike of veterans for new recruits when one legionnaire with twenty years' service refused to salute him after he was promoted to corporal, which was perhaps just as well, as the veteran had an obscenity tattooed on the palm of his right hand.[28]

In view of many, including Rollet, if the atmosphere of the postwar Legion had deteriorated, then the cadres were as much at fault as the recruits. The renewal of the Legion after the war had caused a bonanza of promotion for the newly enlisted. Indeed, it was possible to go from private to sergeant in the early 1920s in one year,[29] a rapidity unprecedented in the Legion with the possible exception of the Tonkin and Formosa campaigns of 1885. Young, often inexperienced, the NCOs exercised less authority over their men, relied less upon "informal sanctions" like the beating Flutsch received from his sergeant when he sold his equipment, and rather more upon regulations than had their prewar counterparts. This produced complaints of a "new inflexibility brought to the regulations by a cadre which does not realize what a delicate instrument it has in its hands."[30]

Nor in the view of officers with experience of the pre-1914 Legion were the right men being promoted. Rollet noted that, because few of the foreign recruits spoke French, the requirements of command and administration favored French legionnaires, who "as a result received promotion which was almost unmerited."[31] Military headquarters in Rabat complained in 1924 that corporals and sergeants were selected too often on the basis of university diplomas, theoretical knowledge of regulations or their command of the French language, rather than on their "qualities of character," and ordered this to stop.[32] The absence of experienced NCOs was also a concern for Colonel Boulet-Desbareau of the *1er étranger* in that year because of the large number of politicized recruits from Eastern and Central Europe: "A strong discipline has always been required in the Legion," he wrote.

Today it is more necessary than ever because of the numerous elements who took refuge there in the post-war period and who must be closely watched (German nationalists or Spartakists, Russian communists, Hungarians, Bulgarians, Rumanians, etc.)[33]

The disappearance of the prewar NCO class was matched by that of the prewar class of officers. After 1918, the army instituted a system called TOE (*théâtre des opérations extérieures*), which rotated officers from France on two-year tours abroad. This broke up in great part the prewar arrangement where an officer who joined a corps like the Legion tended to remain with it until promotion, extremely slow before 1914, or retirement took him away. Some of these temporary Legion officers, like Jacques Lauzière, found the methods of the old guard of legionnaires decidedly backward and poorly adapted to the new type of Legion recruit, who needed teachers and mentors. Instead, officers lived in the closed circle of the mess, treated like Arab potentates—the "*caïd*"—by their batmen, who fussed after their comfort, content to strike poses and to increase automatically arbitrary punishments inflicted by the NCOs. For their part, old Legion hands condemned the newcomers as having little understanding of the needs of a mercenary corps of foreigners. Rollet believed that "the situation was worse than average for the French army," and that the Legion was sent ex-POWs, who still harbored bitter resentments against Germans, and men at the end of their careers, "who only dreamed of their liberation." A three-month course was organized at Sidi-bel-Abbès to initiate new officers into the Legion's mysteries. But Rollet complained that this had actually done more harm than good, for "until now, no one at Bel-Abbès has proven capable of giving to the new [officers] the slightest useful advice about the duties which will fall upon them in Morocco," and charged that Bel-Abbès was creaming off the best officers.[34]

Of course, Rollet, who wished to group the Legion in Morocco, was no friend of the *1er étranger* until 1925, when he became its commander.[35] However, similar grumbles about the postwar officer corps of the Legion were heard from others of the old guard keen that the Legion reforge its pre-1914 character rather than be seduced by a liberal concept of discipline. Lieutenant Colonel Martin, commander of the *2e étranger*, wrote in 1923 that

There exists at the present moment at the 1er étranger *a category of officer that I can only compare to officers of the "National Guard"; They do not move from the Algerian garrisons and let their men go to Morocco or elsewhere without them. On the other hand, the officers and French NCOs only pass through the units in Morocco to the greatest detriment to the moral worth of the soldiers. We will never reconstitute an elite troop in these conditions.*[36]

Legion veteran Major de Corta wrote in an undated memorandum that lieutenants were sent from Saint-Cyr to command an isolated garrison of thirty legionnaires, a tour of duty something like "fortress arrest." Too many captains were prewar NCOs, a situation not unique to the Legion,

without much education, incapable of leading the officers, and above all young officers, ready to be enthused by a dynamic, intelligent and educated leader . . . prepared to disdain an aged, unintelligent, and poorly educated man, who cuts his bread on his thumb without elegance. In short, conditions have changed, and I believe that it would render a very bad service to the best school graduates to send them upon their graduation, into the posts currently occupied by the Legion in Morocco, where they would be completely deprived of intelligent and sympathetic direction.[37]

French army headquarters in Rabat dispatched a lengthy report in 1924 lamenting the absence of majors with Legion experience, the poor quality of captains and the youth and inexperience of the subalterns.[38] In June 1924, Rollet complained bitterly of several of his lieutenants in the *3e étranger*: one, "a liar, and lazy, whose incompetence caused the death of 10 legionnaires"; a second, "worn out by alcohol, an unfortunate example to his young comrades and for his subordinates"; and a number of officers "who manifestly cannot bring themselves to accord their confidence to the soldiers a majority of whom are our enemies of yesterday." He also noted that the detachment of officers in isolated posts had made it difficult to rebuild the solidarity of the prewar Legion officer corps.[39] In 1926, Rollet reported that these officers were finding it difficult in isolated Moroccan posts to command legionnaires who preferred to listen to their NCOs.[40]

Therefore, if the reports are an accurate reflection of reality, then the postwar Legion appeared to be passing through a period of adjustment. Of course, war weariness and demobilization led to a running down of all armies after 1919. This decline in morale and discipline was perhaps especially acute in the French army in North Africa. When fresh Second Lieutenant André Beaufre reported to the 5th *tirailleurs* in Algeria in 1923, he discovered that the regiment he had selected with enthusiasm in an impressive graduation ceremony at Saint-Cyr only days before was poorly led and organized. ". . . The troops were occupied in guard duties and trivial chores, instruction was reduced to a useless routine quite out of touch with what I had been taught at Saint-Cyr," he wrote. "I tried in vain to introduce a few indispensable reforms (for instance, dividing the company into platoons). But the company commander, who never left his office, said it was hopeless because the sergeant-major was against it. . . . For a time I lost interest in my job . . ."[41]

A situation like that described by Beaufre appeared as dispiriting to a keen young officer as to surviving veterans of the prewar Legion, who retained golden memories of the "old corps" and who nurtured ambitions for the Legion to become the elite professional component of an overwhelmingly conscript army. "The Legion, of all the French army, is now the only troop which is truly and purely a 'professional unit', the only one which escapes the crisis (not only 'periodic' but 'continuous') of the incorporation and training of the [conscript] class," Major Poirmeur wrote in 1923. "More than the native regiments, more than the colonial [marine] units, it is a separate entity, and must be treated as such."[42]

On the face of it, there seems to have been a contradiction between the ambitions of Legion officers to expand to fill a gap left by the retraction of the old overseas forces after 1918, and their contention that the type of recruit, of NCO, and especially of officer required to people this reconstituted Legion were as rare as hens' teeth in the postwar world. But while the architects of the postwar Legion were well aware that the process of re-forging the Legion would take some time, they appear to have underestimated the difficulties: "When, in March 1920, I took command of the 2ᵉ *étranger,* it had to be rebuilt from the ground up," wrote Lieutenant Colonel Martin in March 1923. ". . . Everyone set to work with a will to reconstitute the 'Old Legion'. I believed that two years would suffice, but alas, we are far from our goal at the present time."[43]

The problems of the postwar Legion were particularly serious given the ambitions harbored by many of an expanded Legion role in imperial defense.[44] General Mordacq's 1919 proposal to create a Legion "division" met opposition, and not just in parliament, where French deputies balked at the prospect of an autonomous unit of foreign mercenaries within an army to be composed of short-service conscripts. The major concern of professional soldiers who knew the Legion well, even of those who loved it, was that to organize cavalry and especially artillery units was to court major, potentially even disastrous, problems. The commander of the 19th Army Corps in Algiers, General Niessel, complained in July 1920 that mounting legionnaires would simply facilitate desertion, a warning echoed by General Cottez, who wrote to Lyautey of the "disagreeable complications which would follow the desertions which would inevitably occur" in a Legion cavalry unit.[45]

Even Rollet appears to have adopted a remarkably conservative position on the creation of a Legion division. His objections were due in part to a lack of cadres and cash to staff the units already in place, much less to form new ones of other arms. Also, he worried that the creation of units whose cadres were drawn from arms other than the infantry would threaten the cohesion of the corps. The "true Legion," he argued, was "infantry, in its daily work of conquest, pacification, and colonization." However, the problem of desertion was also on his mind. The creation of a Legion cavalry regiment in Tunisia, which, in 1920, was agitated by anti-French riots, he argued, would raise the "probability of desertions to Tripolitania." One also suspects that the creation of a cavalry regiment in Tunisia also complicated Rollet's plans for the creation of a central Legion command in Morocco.

The hottest opposition was reserved for the idea of transforming le-

gionnaires into artillerymen. Rollet declared this an "error" as "the legion-
naire, rather 'hot headed', does not have the qualities of an artilleryman."[46]
Lyautey went even further in his objections—for the same reason that the
British learned not to assign natives to artillery units following the 1857
Indian Mutiny, Lyautey pointed out that desertion with arms of Legion
artillerymen could cause serious problems. Citing the 1908 case when fifty
German deserters hijacked a train in the Sud Oranais, he queried the war
minister:

*And I ask myself if the famous escapade of this company of Legion recruits
who took to the* bled *with arms and equipment under the command of a
German officer in the Oran Division, would have ended so easily had they
disposed of a modern tractor pulled battery? I believe therefore in conclusion, that the true, the only normal utilization of the Legion is in the
infantry (including mounted infantry). There she is really the queen of
colonial battle, the incomparable troop, who never lets down the leader
who knows how to command it, employ it, the last reserve which holds
when all else fails and whose morale is sheltered from all depressing influences. . . . On the other hand we have excellent horsemen and brave artillerymen, and the increase of force which a few legion squadrons or batteries
will bring should really not be considered.*[47]

In other words, the problem of Legion desertion, and of Legion loyalty,
caused some of its commanders to doubt its potential for flexibility and
organizational adaptability.

Opponents of the creation of units other than infantry in the Legion
did not entirely win their argument. Taking advantage of the defeat of the
White Russian armies, whose remnants, many of them Cossacks, began to
filter through Constantinople from November 1920, the government ordered a cavalry regiment formed for service in Tunisia—the *régiment
étranger de cavalerie* (REC), which was officially constituted in 1922. It
was thought necessary to create a dependable unit of cavalry to replace the
Tunisian spahis regiments disbanded after they were contaminated by nationalist agitation.[48] Four companies of sappers were also organized, and
some Legion infantry battalions were given their own organic artillery
batteries.

Desertion, or the threat of desertion, compromised the ability of the
command to constitute battle-worthy units in the immediate postwar years.
Unlike the prewar years, legionnaires now began to desert in small but
significant numbers to the dissident Moroccan tribes. This appears to have
been a new phenomenon, not a prolongation of desertion during the war.
The problem of legionnaires taking to the hills in Algeria and Morocco
during World War I does not appear to have been a great one—indeed,
Lyautey's worries in those years, as far as one is able to tell by the archives,
had not been about desertion but that Germans from the "Old Legion"

preferred internment camps to reenlistment. Albert Bartels, a German businessman living in Rabat in 1914, claimed to have escaped internment and fought the French through the war at the head of various native tribes with the aid of three German deserters from the Legion.[49] On February 12, 1921, Major de Corta reported that of around twenty-five Legion deserters living with the marauding tribes in the Tafilalt in southeastern Morocco, five had been there since the war.[50]

In the immediate postwar years, the Legion appears to have suffered a rash of desertions, attempted desertions or desertion conspiracies in Morocco. Jacques Weygand recorded a conversation with Rollet in which the general claimed to have put down a 1919 mutiny in a Legion detachment by shooting every tenth legionnaire drawn by lot.[51] General Aubert, commander of the Taza subdivision, complained in 1920 that each Legion battalion in his sector counted between thirty and forty deserters.[52] One hundred legionnaires deserted from one battalion stationed at Ouezzane near the Rif in 1920.[53] Worse, rather than simply disappear into the night, many of these deserters were actually fleeing to the enemy, where, de Corta claimed, they were given food, sometimes women and "a facile existence," in return for "leading frequent raids." Unfortunately, these raids were often directed against their former Legion comrades: "Hospitably welcomed and well treated, they are organized and equipped and told to lead the attacks against our posts, detachments, convoys, *groupes mobiles* and to encourage new desertions."[54] One such attack occurred on the night of January 31, 1921, when Legion deserters led by a former German sergeant-major named Fister, armed with automatic rifles taken in their departure, attacked "in a European manner" an isolated worksite in eastern Morocco, killing a Legion corporal, two legionnaires and three Moroccans.

But these attacks were merely symptomatic of a general discipline problem. De Corta reported at the same time that a

general desertion movement was announced in two companies on the [River] Ziz. These were instantly assembled and sent to the rear at Bou Denib under the surveillance of reliable native units. The ten most dangerous ringleaders were sent under special escort, but they mutinied and trying to escape, were shot. Now, this was the best commanded battalion and the one in which I had the most confidence.

After fourteen desertions in a Legion company at Midelt on the upper Moulouya, an investigation uncovered a massive desertion plot "and a state of mind which obliged us to withdraw it from contact with the dissidents and move it to the rear." Even west of the Atlas near Kasba Tadla, an investigation following several desertions uncovered an

entente between legionnaires and dissidents to make themselves masters of the post by a coup de force and make common cause with the rebels. . . .

One must remark that most of the ringleaders discovered after investigation gave the impression of being good soldiers without punishments.[55]

A 1923 report speaking of these desertions concluded that they "were the result of a skillful propaganda carried out in the interior of the units by a certain number of legionnaires of German origin, acting in connivance with the Moroccan dissidents, with a view to acquire the leadership which they lacked."[56] Manue believed that many who deserted were enticed away by the stories of dissidents giving deserting legionnaires women in return for leading raids.[57] Major Maire's battalion was withdrawn from near the Spanish zone in 1924 after a corporal and sixteen legionnaires disappeared. He ordered a forced march, with spahis shadowing his force to pick up any other deserters, to get as far away as possible from the tempting frontier on the first day.[58] De Corta complained that "the lack of experienced NCOs and of reliable veteran legionnaires, makes it particularly difficult to know and observe" what was going on in the units.[59]

The army took a very serious view of these desertions to the enemy. General Poeymirau, commander of the Meknès region, concluded in 1921 that

it will probably become difficult . . . to use the units of the Foreign Legion in the first line, in immediate contact with the rebels, and this will require a general reorganization. . . . This is an absolutely new situation for, if until now we have had to fear desertions in contact with Europeans, never did we have them in contact with native dissidents. Now, it seems that today these dissidents are sufficiently in touch with the general situation to organize near them desertion agencies, to provoke [legionnaires] and count upon them.[60]

On February 13, 1921, Lyautey ordered that the Legion be pulled back from the "front" and that Legion units should never be used alone.[61]

The apparently large number of desertions in the Legion in 1920 and 1921 were due to exceptional circumstances, caused by the immediate problems of restructuring the postwar Legion, and reinforced by the strong anti-German sentiments in the victorious Allied countries evident at the Versailles Peace Conference.[62] The fact that the Legion had begun an aggressive policy of recruiting through military attachés and consuls in foreign countries could hardly have helped matters. Not only did it raise questions about dubious recruiting methods[63] and give rise to adverse comment on the Legion in foreign countries.[64] But also, from the perspective of desertion and the creation of solid units, the practice of snatching men from their home towns in foreign lands meant that the Legion was bound to get a large number of recruits who had not made the psychological break from their countries, cultures, even their families, a process that the requirement to travel to France to enlist would at least have initiated.

Instead, they must have collected many who enlisted on a whim, possibly the very young, or even those like London stockbroker Brian Stuart, who, after seeing a film about the Foreign Legion, rushed out of the cinema to enlist,[65] which was possible to do at the French consulate on Brompton Road.

The trip to Algeria gave the new recruits ample time to reflect upon their folly. Lieutenant Colonel Maurel of the *4e étranger* recorded that those enlisted in Germany were sent to barracks in Belfort or Nancy, where they were treated, "without indulgence and with disdain. After this, they are sent to Marseille and I would not say received but tolerated at Fort Saint-Jean. As for the crossing, it is better not to speak of it." Sidi-bel-Abbès was overcrowded, so that training was badly carried out. "He becomes discouraged, feels alone—because those who surround him will be sent elsewhere. He is in a state to listen to bad advice." This, according to Maurel, was the source of desertions, which were often led, as in 1908, by German ex-officers and NCOs able to fill a vacuum left by the absence of strong leadership and morale in the Legion.[66] Indeed, in 1920, the war minister warned the prime minister to give instructions not to enlist ex-officers or NCOs from the German army in the Legion.[67]

Desertion problems on this scale probably did not linger beyond 1921. Certainly a report from the war minister on September 3, 1923, in response to a request by the German Ambassador for information about a German who disappeared into the Legion, spoke of the 1921 wave of desertions as if they were ancient history.[68] In January 1922, General Cottez wrote to the war minister that desertion had greatly diminished in the Legion, and blamed the problem on the postwar practice of paying legionnaires an enlistment bonus after four months' service, which "is the cause of numerous desertions." Nevertheless, he recommended taking the Legion away from the Spanish zone, which offered a sanctuary too tempting for potential deserters.[69]

It was good advice—in 1924, complaints began to filter in of desertions from the Legion, even from the mounted companies ("These units had however been selected as being reliable"), to Abd el-Krim, the rebel leader. The numbers that appear in the archives, while admittedly fragmentary, seem to suggest a problem less disastrous than in 1920–21—seventeen deserters from Maire's battalion and twelve from a mounted company. Nevertheless, they were a solid propaganda victory for Abd el-Krim, who openly courted world public opinion during The Rif War (1921–26) by presenting himself as the leader of a beleaguered nation fighting for its rightful independence: "These desertions are grave at the moment," read a 1924 report. "Abd el-Krim, in speaking of these Legion deserters, declared that civilization came to him and that we would be left only with negroes and Jews. And more the deserters serve as machine gunners with Abd el-Krim."[70] But while it is possible that desertion from the Legion during the Rif War was significant, its propaganda value was far greater than its actual military contribution to the rebellion. Abd el-Krim claimed to have no more than fifty deserters in his army, Germans for the most part, although it is not clear if most came from the Spanish or the French Legion. "More, I will confess to you that I did not trust them," the rebel chief told the French writer J. Roger-Mathieu after the war. "If I allowed them to go to battle, it was only after having them observed for a long time by my men, so much did I fear to see these chaps betray me like they betrayed you or like they betrayed the Spanish."[71].

The Legion provided Abd el-Krim with his most celebrated deserter— Joseph Klems, who told the American journalist Vincent Sheean that he had deserted around 1920 after a drunken French officer had called him a *"boche."*[72] A 1924 report acknowledged that the rebel chief used Legion deserters to man telephones, construct bunkers and as machine gunners, and concluded that "one can use the Legion for a *baroud* [a fight] on condition that it is not left there afterwards."[73] Certainly, Abd el-Krim openly encouraged Legion desertion with leaflets printed in German— "Why do you fight with the French?" one sample ran.

Abd el-Krim means freedom. Come into the Rif with your arms, and if you do not want to continue fighting, you will be repatriated through Tangier. Lt. Klems will help you. At Ajdir, we make war the modern way, and you, Germans, will understand. You have been with the French for adventure. . . . Abd el-Krim fights for an ideal, to defend his native land.[74]

A. R. Cooper claimed that the 3rd battalion of the *1er étranger* was denied active service in 1926 and withdrawn to Aïn Sefra in Algeria because of desertion.[75] The desertion of legionnaires to the enemy in Morocco appears to have lasted as long as the fighting. Jean Martin wrote that as late as the seizure of the Djebel Sagho in 1933, the last strongly defended area of the Atlas to submit to the French, deserters shouted insults in German at the attacking legionnaires:

There were numerous deserters among these last dissidents, gone over to the enemy several years earlier, some thirty years ago, who could not surrender, knowing full well that they would be executed. They were the most ferocious of these last rebels. We still found them in the Atlas during the summer.[76]

While the number of deserting legionnaires, at least after 1921, though significant, was probably never catastrophic, and while they never contributed significantly to the military success of the dissident tribes, that is not to say that Legion desertion had no military effect. As has been noted, desertion made the army reluctant to station the Legion close to dissident areas, especially near the Spanish zone. The fear of desertion contributed directly to the initial success of Abd el-Krim against the French, for despite the worsening situation in 1924 and 1925, commanders held the Legion, regarded as their most solid troops, back from the Spanish zone.[77]

1925 proved the most challenging year for the Legion in the interwar period, when it had to confront both the Rif rebellion and the Druse revolt in the Levant. The Rifian leader Abd el-Krim was the most remarkable and talented leader faced by the colonizing powers in Morocco. Born around 1882 at Ajdir near Alhucemas Bay in Northern Morocco, Krim's father moved the family to Tetouan in 1892. Very ambitious for his son, Krim's father placed him in a Spanish school where he received an education far superior to that of most of his contemporaries, whose learning seldom extended beyond memorization of Koranic texts. After perfecting his Moslem education in the celebrated Qarawiyin *medersa* in Fez, the twenty-four-year-old Krim took his first job as the editor of the Arabic supplement of *El Telegrama del Rif,* the Spanish newspaper in Melilla. He soon combined this editorial post with an important position in the Bureau of Native Affairs, as well as serving as a *cadi,* or Moslem judge. However, Krim became increasingly disenchanted with the inequality and corruption of Spanish rule. In 1917, Krim was imprisoned by the Spaniards for his outspokenly nationalist, pro-German and anti-French statements. Released in 1918, he resumed his job at *El Telegrama del Rif.* But when the Spanish authorities began extraditing Moroccan refugees in Melilla who had been fighting against the French to the French zone, Krim began to fear for his own safety. In January 1919, he took a twenty-day leave from his job and never returned.

In the mountains, Krim, together with his father and younger brother, began to recruit support for a rebellion. By the spring of 1921, he had succeeded in organizing the tough but notoriously faction-ridden Rifians into something resembling an army of between three thousand and six thousand men, accumulate supplies and weapons, and even establish a diplomatic corps to plead his cause abroad. His plan was to draw the Spaniards out of their bases at Tetouan and Melilla, cause them to extend their supply lines, and use the superior mobility and knowledge of terrain of the Rifians to defeat them piecemeal. This was a sound conception, for at that very moment the Spanish commander General Manuel Silvestre was pushing his troops west from Melilla toward Alhucemas Bay in an attempt to extend Spanish control over the Rif, only one-third of which they effectively occupied. By May 1921, Silvestre's twenty-five thousand men were scattered in 144 small blockhouses and outposts that ran west from Melilla for thirty-five miles, terminating at the garrisons of Anual and Meyan, into which he had crowded eight hundred men each.

While on the surface Krim appeared to be hopelessly outnumbered, when on July 17, 1921, his Rifians struck all along the Spanish line, both the morale and efficiency of the Spanish army proved to be shockingly low. When one of the outer garrisons of Anual was overrun after three days of fighting, Silvestre ordered a general evacuation. However, what should have been an orderly retreat was overtaken by contagious panic. All down the line, poorly disciplined Spanish soldiers threw down their weapons, abandoned their posts and began running for Melilla through the hot, dusty mountains. Most failed to arrive—between thirteen thousand and nineteen thousand soldiers, including Silvestre, were hacked down by Rifians. The victorious rebels reached the outlying suburbs of Melilla, but Krim declined to take the town although it was defended by only one thousand eight hundred poorly trained Spanish conscripts. Subsequent attempts by the Spanish to make headway against a rebellion of what was considered the toughest and most resilient portion of tough and resilient people foundered upon the poor morale of Spanish conscripts and military leadership of more than ordinary incompetence. After more than three years of indecisive campaigning, in November 1924, the Spanish again met disaster when they abandoned Chaouen in the central Rif. Although he had only seven thousand troops, Krim was able to strike successfully at the forty thousand Spaniards extended along the crude track that wound through the mountain defiles between Chaouen and the Mediterranean coast. When the Spanish rear guard commanded by Francisco Franco finally stumbled into Tetouan on December 13, between seventeen thousand and twenty thousand of their comrades lay dead behind them.

For the first four years of the rebellion, the French remained passive, but not disinterested, onlookers from their southern zone. In May 1924, the French crossed the Ouerrha River into territory claimed, but not occupied, by Spain and proceeded to establish a series of blockhouses running along a seventy-five-mile front from Biban north of Fez to Kifan above Taza, blockhouses they garrisoned with Algerian and Senegalese troops. The French justified their grab for territory by saying that the Rifians were pillaging the Beni Zerwal tribe, meant to be under French protection. Not all of the tribesmen welcomed the French advance, especially after a French native affairs officer beat a *caïd* and shot thirteen others, allegedly for plotting with Abd el-Krim, and they petitioned Krim for deliverance.

The French move was probably not calculated to start a war with Abd el-Krim, who had insisted throughout that he had no quarrel with France. Although the establishment of an independent Moslem republic in the Rif was not in French interest, the French sought to strengthen their control over tribes who had proved restive during World War I and who might prove so again. The question is, why did Abd el-Krim react to the provocation by attacking the French? It is possible that Krim believed his prestige threatened by the French move. His food supply certainly was, as the Ouerrha Valley was a major breadbasket for the Rif. His success against the Spanish may have caused him to underestimate the French. Still, the decision to attack south was a fairly desperate one for the rebel chief. He was already engaged in a war on two fronts against Spanish forces, and hardly needed to add a third front against the better-organized and numerous French. His only hope of victory was to provoke a general uprising in the French zone, where admittedly he enjoyed some sympathy. But this hope was a fairly remote one—the French had disarmed the tribes and kept a watchful eye on them through a network of native affairs officers. Krim lacked the men to seize and hold territory, especially politically significant objectives like Fez. Besides, the military success of his forces rested upon their dispersion and mobility. To concentrate them at key points was simply to offer the French a target against which they could concentrate their superior firepower. Furthermore, the sultan, a holy figure in Morocco whose attitude was critical to any popular uprising, was very much the creature of the French.

Despite these considerations, on April 13, 1925, Abd el-Krim threw five *harkas* or war parties comprising a total of perhaps four thousand men, with another four thousand in reserve, at the French lines. Although forewarned of the attack, the French remained confident—with some justification, they attributed Rifian successes since 1921 to Spanish incompetence, and remained firm in the belief that their roughly sixty thousand troops in Morocco, backed by modern artillery and air support and their defense line on the Ouerrha heights, would offer a sufficient deterrent. They learned a hard lesson—by June, less than three months after the beginning of Krim's offensive, forty-four of sixty-six French posts had been cut off and overwhelmed, usually because the French found it difficult to reinforce them over the roadless terrain. At Aulai, the French garrison held out for twenty-two days under sustained mortar fire until it could be rescued. But the rescue came too late for outlying blockhouse Number 7—its thirty-man garrison was overwhelmed, their bodies mutilated and thrown onto the wire of the French position, where they decomposed gently in the Moroccan summer.

The Legion distinguished itself in the bitter fighting around the post of Biban, which changed hands at least four times, on the third occasion falling to a Legion grenade attack that succeeded at the cost of 103 dead and 300 wounded. But on June 5, the Rifians overwhelmed the garrison and held the post until the end of September.[78] At Beni Derkul, a few miles from Biban, Lieutenant Pol Lapeyre blew himself up with his few surviving Senegalese after withstanding a two-month siege. Many posts were abandoned without a fight, while those that held out suffered great deprivation despite the best efforts of Captain Jean de Lattre de Tassigny to organize airlifts of ice and medals, meant to raise morale, for the beleaguered garrisons. Abd el-Krim's offensive drove to within twenty miles of Fez. In the process he captured fifty-one cannon, two hundred machine guns, five thousand rifles and around two thousand prisoners and inflicted numerous casualties on the French.[79]

How well did the Legion perform in these wars? It is difficult to know exactly, as many of the accounts of battles are written very much in the heroic style. Also, they tend to reflect the European obsession with seizing positions, which, the post of Biban apart, the Rifians had little interest in defending—their intention was to inflict casualties, not defend ground. This is not to say that there were not heroic moments in the campaigns of 1925, for there certainly were. One of the most celebrated, if catastrophic, fights occurred on June 10 when forty legionnaires of the 6th battalion of the *1ᵉʳ étranger* volunteered to lead a night raid to break the siege of the post of Mediouna and return its garrison of Senegalese to the French lines. The Rifians had surrounded the post with two siege lines that had already thrown back two French rescue attempts, and the garrison signaled that they would blow themselves up on the following day if no help arrived. The group, under the command of two officers, left at eleven o'clock at night armed with rifles, grenades and dynamite. Boots had been discarded in favor of slippers or puttees wrapped around the feet. Two lieutenants managed to include themselves by mingling with the group as it filed forward under the silent gaze of the remainder of the battalion, which was to walk forward in close support. The first obstacle was the Wergha River, which the group crossed with difficulty. But in the unfamiliar country at night, the attacking group became separated from the remainder of the battalion.

The legionnaires crawled forward through the last ravine that separated them from the outer Rifian siege trenches, taking care not to dislodge rocks, which would wake the sentries. What happened next is not clear. Legionnaire A. R. Cooper claimed that the entire party reached the fort undetected.[80] But another report stated that the legionnaires had to fight their way through the siege trenches.[81] A group of ten under the command of a lieutenant got into the French post, hoping to hold out. But the post commander, warned of the rescue by an air-dropped message, had mined it and was prepared to break out. The French-led soldiers charged out into a swarm of alerted Rifians, but the battle was an unequal one. Small groups exhausted their grenades and munitions before being overwhelmed by the rebels. By the next morning, only three legionnaires had found their way back to base, in an action that earned the battalion a citation in army orders.[82]

The Legion together with the remainder of the French army in North Africa had its hands full in 1925. Despite his relatively small force, Abd el-Krim was able to gain and maintain a psychological advantage over his French opponents, who often found it difficult to adapt to the special conditions of warfare in the Rif, conditions very different from those of European war. "This Riff campaign of May 1925 in the Wergha Valley was exceptionally hard," wrote André Beaufre. "Newcomers like myself did not realize this, but Moroccan veterans shook their heads: We were up against trained fighters who manoeuvred skillfully."[83] As noted, the Rifians were not defensive fighters and seldom attempted to hold what they had seized, which made them elusive targets. The searing heat of the summer of 1925, with temperatures reaching 130 degrees Fahrenheit, caused great suffering, especially as Moroccan scouts sometimes sought to make extra cash by refusing to divulge water sources unless bribed.[84] The remoteness of the battlefields made them difficult to supply, while the broken, boulder-strewn terrain offered excellent cover for the mobile Rifians and reduced the value of artillery and machine guns. Air power, upon which the French had placed great faith, failed them badly. Planes could not reprovision the isolated posts. Nor was their bombing of great utility—Cooper complained that the planes bombed targets "with the usual lack of cooperation,"[85] a complaint echoed by Legion officers in Syria.[86] Legion veteran and Notre Dame alumnus Charles Sweeny organized the *escadrille Chérifienne* out of American flyers, which flew 470 missions during the Rif campaign. However, it was broken up in November 1925, under pressure from the American government.

One of the results of the enemy's mobility was to force the French to tighten their formations on the march, which lessened their mobility. The *"groupe mobile,"* developed before 1914 from the mounted companies, and which in the interwar years evolved into mobile formations of Legion or North African infantry, cavalry, artillery and engineers, "moves like a monstrous hedgehog," wrote Lieutenant Colonel Lorillard, evoking the same problems faced by the French in North Africa since Bugeaud and de Négrier. ". . . The *groupe mobile* must constantly present a cuirass without a break, constituted by the breasts, bayonets and eventually bullets. All other considerations must give way to the requirement to maintain the block constantly intact, which considerably slows the march of the G.M."[87] Quite naturally, this formation, developed for the open spaces of the hammada of southeastern Morocco, was less useful in the mountainous areas (and eventually in Indochina).

Beaufre, whose *tirailleurs* campaigned with the Legion in one of these formations, found it a particularly unrewarding way to make war: "This human square, alone in hostile territory, kept its formation up hill and down dale—the baggage following the track while the flank guards plodded on endlessly under a blazing sky," he wrote.

. . . We the regulars, plodded on over the uneven ground, through scrub and meager corn and soya fields, worn out by the heat of the sun and the draining of constant perspiration, the men bowed under the weight of their kit and ammunition, their feet agonized in their heavy boots which filled up with water every time we forded a stream. Not in the best of condition to start with, we were soon at the last limits of exhaustion.

Finally, the enemy was located:

Then the column halted at the foot of a hill from which the partisans [goums] had just withdrawn. The advance guard had made contact. The hills ahead of us appeared deserted, but soon the air was filled with shrill cries which echoed from rock to rock, and sporadic firing broke out. In

*front a battalion of the Legion in their white képis deployed as regularly as
though they were on an exercise. The artillery (four 65 mm. mountain
guns!) opened up. We had to attack through the legionaries. We clambered
over rocks and through olive trees, bullets whistling past us; then there was
nothing except a few dead Riffs lying in their holes. We climbed on, out of
breath. Then a deserted village—a poor village smelling of rancid oil, the
sole sign of life a flurry of scrawny chickens destined for the pot that night.
We reached the crest, regrouped and called the roll: a handful of wounded,
one man killed.*

After a night of sleep broken by constant sniper fire and cries of *"aux
armes"* in anticipation of an attack, they broke camp just before dawn:
"Exhausted, pulling our swollen feet back into our boots, we drank scald-
ing coffee, buckled our equipment, loaded the animals, folded the tents,
stowed the kit and, as the day broke, set off on another day just like the
last."[88]

Beyond the immense difficulties of the fighting, it also appears that the
postwar changes made it difficult for the Legion to adapt to the style of
warfare in the Rif, which placed a premium on individual skills. Lieutenant
Colonel Buchsenschutz anticipated problems in September 1924 when he
noted that

*the present recruitment which brings a large proportion of young foreign-
ers does not give us the same resources as before when we received older
men who had exercised a trade. . . . It is absolutely vital that, more than
ever, the officers are able to be leaders in all branches, even those which are
outside their skills as infantry officers.*

Not only did officers appear deficient in knowledge of road building and
fortifications, traditional Legion specialties, but even "practical knowledge" of mortars and mountain guns, grenades, automatic rifles and machine guns eluded some of them, "so that a stoppage does not leave him
disarmed, and that he knows not only *as much* but more than his men. The
example of the columns of 1923 prove that this is not always the case. . . .
In a word, one must not have the 'officer spectator.' "[89] A. R. Cooper
complained that the officers were trained for European war: "If they are
obstinate and stand on their dignity, they make terrible and costly mistakes," he wrote. "If they are sensible, they rely on their sergeants and
corporals who know the game."[90] Rollet complained that it was precisely
because officers were relying too much on their NCOs that they failed to
establish their authority.[91]

The poor preparation of officers certainly lowered the combat efficiency of the Legion. Cooper attributed the disaster at Mediouna in part to
the fact that the officers lacked experience in the irregular fighting in Morocco. On May 23, 1925, he claimed that a surprise attack that broke over

his battalion as they were preoccupied helping themselves to oranges created utter panic: "Ordinarily there would have been a steady retreat in echelon formation," he wrote.

But we had been taken unawares. Masses of Riffs were already upon us and a wave of panic swept through the soldiers who, moments before, had been happily sucking oranges. "Sauve-qui-peut!" a voice screamed. Men rolled helter-skelter down the steep hill into the river, where they wallowed helplessly as an enfilade attack spat bullets into our ranks from end to end. . . . It was a desperate struggle to get across the waist-high torrent before we were mown down by the hidden tribesmen. Shots came at us from the front, sides and rear as we fought inch by inch up the wooded slope on the far side. For a hundred yards I played hide-and-seek between the trees with a tribesman who had singled me out. It was a question of who was the better marksman. My Legion training paid its reward, and I turned to see if I was in danger from behind. Far below me about a hundred Riffs emerged from a ravine to pounce upon twenty Legionnaires who were urging mules through the water. It was a terrible sight. The tribesmen were lashing out with long knives, cutting off the Legionnaires' heads before hacking the bodies to pieces.[92]

Major Zinovi Pechkoff, in whose battalion Cooper was serving, gives a less dramatic account of this retreat. While admitting that the battalion's escape was a narrow one, he claimed that the rear guard held its own, and that the situation was salvaged, "Thanks to the solidity and the discipline of the legionnaires."[93]

According to Cooper, on June 14, after fighting bravely but with heavy losses for several weeks, his battalion had exhausted its psychological capital and broke in the face of a Rifian attack:

The Arabs . . . came behind us shouting: "You want some chickens? You want some eggs?" while shooting at us. This is the only time that I saw the Legion run. The men could no longer resist. One had demanded too much of the battalion. I even saw men stay behind deliberately and let the enemy kill them without offering any resistance. . . . The officers were very prudent and did not breathe a word of the conduct of the Legion on that day. Major Casaban inflicted no punishments. . . .

That night, a grenade was thrown into the sergeants' quarters, wounding three of them. "I even believe that some of the officers who died that night were killed inside the post."[94]

The situation in Cooper's battalion was perhaps exceptional, but probably not, as the great success of the Rifians in throwing the French on the defensive in the summer of 1925 with very few troops can be explained only by low French morale, made lower still by fatigue and apparently indecisive fighting. Beaufre's *tirailleurs*, who appear to have been joined in the same *groupe mobile* with Cooper's legionnaires, endured the same decline of morale. According to Beaufre, officers in his *tirailleur* battalion also lost their heads during the evacuation of a post in the summer of 1925, and turned a withdrawal into a headlong flight during which even the wounded were abandoned to the Rifians. Beaufre was left lying on a piece of canvas, stark naked and with a bullet wound in his stomach, only to be rescued by three *goumiers* who had lingered behind to strip the dead. "What, they are abandoning their officers now!" one of them said. "How low can you get?"[95]

It is probable, even logical, that the Legion adjusted with difficulty to the conditions of mountain warfare in Morocco. The commander of the 2nd battalion of the *1er étranger* wrote on June 12, 1925, that his men did not use ground well, bunched too closely together and were too slow to fire at a target when one appeared, which was not often. He also urged a more rapid march upon objectives, which were seldom defended tenaciously, better arrangements for securing newly taken ground, including rigorous fire plans, and "as fatigue is great, one should not dream of sleeping without building defenses."[96] In a repetition of the complaints heard before 1914, critics charged that Legion units were too heavy: "Their exterior action is weak—except by artillery," wrote Lieutenant Colonel Buchsen-schutz in September 1924. "It is 'heavy' line infantry ill adapted to guerrilla warfare. Besides, its weak effectives oblige it to stay put, and it even suffers rather frequently from losses through ambushes organized by dissidents against the obligatory fatigue parties—water, wood, supply, etc.," which he argued were expensive, not only in manpower but also in monetary terms.[97]

The suggestion was that inflexibility was built into the Legion system, a condition required by the heterogeneous nature of Legion recruitment, the lack of any obvious common bonds of loyalty and by the need to operate by example. This is hinted at by Beaufre's observation that "the Legion deployed as if they were on an exercise." Beaufre was an outsider. But legionnaire Jean Martin agreed: "It is in these *grandes affaires* that one discovers the beauty of a Legion combat," he wrote.

> ... *The most prodigious, the most surprising, was the spectacle of this formidable troop under control, maneuvering under fire as in training, poised, tranquil, concerned only with doing its work well and not to make a mistake, as if the most important thing at the moment was to obey the regulations and not to bring down the ire of the sergeant. We had been well trained! Such an atmosphere makes cowardice impossible.*[98]

But while the ability to operate with almost machinelike efficiency made the Legion a formidable foe in set-piece operations, and belied to a certain extent the charge that legionnaires were badly trained, it also suggests a weakness and lack of flexibility against an enemy that was expert at infiltration tactics and night operations. Rollet noted that guard and outpost duty was a particularly unnerving experience in Morocco: "Often the dissident throws rocks to oblige the sentinel to show himself," he warned. "During this time a second Moroccan shoots without missing."[99] The ability of the Rifians especially to murder sentries and attack isolated parties caused posts to shut up at night, a tactic Legion Lieutenant Lacour blamed for the "half-surprise" at Musseifré in Syria: "If we had not observed so strictly the rules of Moroccan warfare," he reported, then he would have sent out "advanced sentinels, mobile and fixed patrols, etc."[100]

Abd el-Krim's offensive, while impressive, was condemned to failure once he rejected a Franco-Spanish peace offer that stopped short of complete recognition of an autonomous Rif republic. In June 1925, Paris and Madrid began talks on joint military action, and in July Marshal Philippe Pétain arrived in Morocco to take command. By the end of the summer, the French had concentrated 160,000 troops there, and the Spanish 200,000. Furthermore, the Rifians had been weakened by poor harvests and by a typhus epidemic that swept through the mountains. In mid-September, Pétain launched a drive that recaptured Biban and reclaimed all the territory lost since April. This was coordinated with an amphibious landing at Alhucemas Bay by the Spaniards, which advanced slowly against ferocious Rifian resistance. General advances became easier to organize as the French realized that the Moroccans usually retired at night to caves and villages, leaving positions undefended. Therefore, after losing men to costly daylight attacks, the French soon worked out the technique of advancing at night and throwing up walls of rock and concertina wire around a piece of high ground.

To prevent sniping and attacks from concealed positions at close range in which the curved Moroccan knives tended to have the better of the cumbersome bayonets of the Legion, swarms of "partisans" or Moroccan irregulars recruited by the French were thrown out to keep the enemy at bay. Sometimes these men preferred to come to some arrangement with the dissidents, which might even go so far as selling them their rifles and ammunition.[101] But they were credited for spearheading the French advance in the Taza region under the leadership of the charismatic Colonel Henri de Bournazel.[102] "I can still see the partisans wheeling round us, the caïds at their head, uttering shrill cries as they galloped past, then climbing up to the crests of the hills," Beaufre remembered of the summer of 1925. "They employed the traditional Moroccan tactics, setting fire to the villages after a few shots, looting quickly and withdrawing equally quickly."[103]

After a winter respite, French and Spanish forces coordinated offensives into the central Rif in April and May 1926. On May 27, Abd el-Krim surrendered to the French and, to the bitter indignation and fury of the Spaniards, was exiled to a comfortable estate on the island of Réunion with an annual pension of one hundred thousand francs. In 1947, the French government decided to transfer Krim and forty-two members of his entourage to an even more elegant and opulent exile on the French Riviera. On May 31, when the ship carrying him to France called briefly at Port Said, Krim, in an act worthy of a legionnaire, slipped his surveillance and was granted asylum in Egypt, where he died in 1963.

The Rif campaign helped to encourage a Druse rebellion in Syria in the summer of 1925. The Druse, a religious sect that broke away from Islam in the eleventh century, had seen their powerful political position in the Levant under The Ottoman Empire erode in favor of the Christian Maronites once the French took control at the end of World War I. The Syrian fighting kicked off with a similar catastrophe for French arms there when a three-thousand-man column composed of Malagasy and Syrian troops was devastated by a Druse attack, requiring the dispatch of a Legion battalion there. Bennett Doty, a native of Demopolis, Alabama, and sometime student at Vanderbilt and the University of Virginia, endured an uncomfortable and tedious voyage from Sidi-bel-Abbès to Syria with legionnaires who were constantly drunk and fighting among themselves, to the point that they turned what was meant to be a formal dockside sendoff in Tunis into a drunken fiasco.

On September 10, 1925, Doty's unit, the 8th Battalion of the *1er étranger,* together with a squadron from the REC, occupied a dilapidated collection of flat-roofed houses organized around a mosque called Musseifré. The cavalry occupied the village, while the infantry constructed six small fortified camps around the perimeter of the town. Six days of building walls and clearing the inevitable landing strip on a limited ration of stinking water had most legionnaires in a foul mood. On the 15th, a reconnaissance sent out by the garrison met strong resistance from a Druse force and had one sergeant killed. Nevertheless, when the heliograph signaled strong forces advancing on Musseifré on the evening of the 16th, many were disinclined to believe it. However, at around three o'clock on the morning of September 17, shots were fired and the French sent up flares that revealed a swarm of men advancing upon the camp.

At first light, it became apparent that many of the attackers had slipped between the posts into the town, where they had captured many of the REC's horses and attempted to ride out between the infantry posts. It proved good sport for the legionnaires, who first shot down the horses and then killed the riders as they sprinted toward safety. After a lull, another attack poured down the hill toward the posts. Legionnaires, firing from loopholes they had scraped out of the walls, shot into the howling crowd of Druse. "Time and time again the fringe of the charge died within a few feet of the walls," wrote Doty. "I fired till my rifle was hot and steamed in my hands. Then I threw grenades. Then I fired again."[104] Several of the machine guns jammed, while a grenade badly thrown by a legionnaire in one company silenced a defensive position. This allowed more Druse to infiltrate past the posts into the village, where they began to snipe at the legionnaires from the housetops.

To Doty, the legionnaires whom he had found quarrelsome and boorish company in peacetime were magnificent under fire, stripped to the waist, cigarettes dangling from their lips, kepis pushed back on their heads, firing their rifles until the attackers reached the wisps of barbed wire strung out before the wall and then pitching grenades into the screaming hordes: "I could hardly believe the change," he wrote. "It was not only that they were brave, fighting with utmost heroism. But they were patient and enduring, full of devotion and self-sacrifice, helpful to everyone, and obeying every order, not only without a murmur but with a sort of self-immolating alacrity." His lieutenant walked from man to man, automatic pistol in hand, pointing toward targets and, when the legionnaires hit them, would pat them on the shoulder and congratulate them on their marksmanship.[105]

By the end of the afternoon, the lack of munitions obliged the outposts to slow their rate of fire. The legionnaires began to count the minutes when, by their calculation, relief must arrive. Although the ground was covered with Druse corpses, the attackers still approached, but cautiously, in short rushes from boulder to boulder. By the end of the afternoon, the last cartridges were distributed. "A word went around the wall, passed from man to man," wrote Doty. " 'Keep a last cartridge for yourself.' " The legionnaires waited for the last charge, which, miraculously, did not materialize. Then the sound of bugles, "as if from the insides of a closed victrola," could be heard in the distance. The Druse became agitated, and a hail of shells began to slam into the camp, followed by a charge of Algerian *tirailleurs* in extended order, who swept into the village. The legionnaires fired the remainder of their ammunition into the fugitives who fled the town. "We opened the gates of our redoubt," concluded Doty, "and strolled out with hands in our pockets."[106]

Musseifré and the siege of Rachaya, which followed on November 19, 1925, when a squadron of the REC made a similar defensive stand against a Druse attack, were certainly heroic actions in the best of the Legion tradition. However, in the end, their success depended upon the enemy attacking entrenched legionnaires. In mobile warfare, the Legion was often less effective, often treated essentially as a backup force. This had been the case in the Sud Oranais before 1914, where even the mounted companies had been developed, in theory at least, as support units for *goums*. While the Legion certainly saw action in the interwar years, it was not always the unit of choice for commanders.

On December 20, 1933, one of the best-known Legion officers of the interwar years, Zinovi Pechkoff, wrote to Rollet that he had transferred from Morocco to Syria because "during this entire campaign my battalion was never engaged and neither my officers, nor my NCOs, nor my men, nor me, ever had a chance [to demonstrate] the qualities of the battalion in combat." While he considered this a personal affront, it also seemed to reflect upon the combat performance of the entire Legion: "I realized that, having been warned against me, my superiors accorded no confidence in my battalion—a situation as unjust as unjustified."[107] A report from the *3e étranger* in that year noted that everyone "was a little disappointed to see during these operations that the Legion was given what was in effect only a secondary role, while in the offensives, the Moroccan or Algerian ti-railleurs were always in the first echelon," an observation that seems to confirm Beaufre's account of his experiences in the Rif. The legionnaires "would have preferred taking a more active part in the *baroud*," although it acknowledged that its attrition rate on the campaign was one-fifth of the effectives, many of them discipline problems who sought sanctuary in the hospital rather than face a punishment.[108] As late as October 1933, the military governor of Paris, General Henri Gouraud, wrote to Rollet,

You know that in the fighting this year in Morocco, in the Meknès region, a battalion of the Legion was surprised and lost one or two machine guns or automatic rifles. The officers from Morocco told me that this was not the first time this has happened, and none of them conclude that the Legion at present is worth the old Legion. I protested, but I would be happy to have your opinion.[109]

Rollet's reply is not recorded.

The verdict on Legion performance was not uniformly uncompli-mentary—Lieutenant Colonel de Tscharner of the *4e étranger* praised his NCOs in 1933 for their high *esprit de corps* and for their conduct under fire, which was "often brilliant, always perfect."[110] However, a 1934 re-port stated that Legion performance in Morocco was below par, and put it down to the fact that away from the front Legion units were broken up and distributed among various garrison duties. "It is impossible to get the units back in trim, training is neglected. When operations recommence, the units have lost their maneuverability. This is certainly the cause of the exagger-ated losses suffered in certain combats."[111] Therefore, the much-praised *"oeuvre pacifique de la Légion,"* which included the construction of the "Legionnaire's Tunnel" in Morocco and other public works projects to which the Legion pointed with pride, actually contributed to a diminution of the corps' combat performance, and gave rise to the ironic observation among legionnaires that their unit was merely a uniformed public works company.

The morale and combat performance of the Legion in the interwar years appear to have been uneven. While the Legion overcame the serious crisis of the immediate postwar years, it continued to be plagued by prob-lems of recruitment and the formation of adequate cadres. Lyautey had written in 1924 that the Legion must have officers *who have the love of the Legion in their blood, to electrify and enflame the lower cadres . . . those who have the sacred fire and who alone will be the administrators, men of action, leaders of the band and psychologists. Let us place at the head of the regiments and the battalions men of this steel and who shine out, and the Legion will be reborn.*[112]

They had achieved this to a certain extent, especially in the higher commands. But the system of TOE continued to send into the Legion men poorly prepared to lead units of foreign professionals. "The tool has no bite," Rollet noted in the early 1920s. "Necessary to reshape and reforge this 'tool.' "[113] He and the alumni of the "Old Legion" had succeeded in this task to a large degree. But the Legion machine often proved ponderous and inflexible, able to adapt to the demands of mobile warfare only with difficulty.

The point to make is not that the Legion was an inefficient fighting unit in the interwar years, that legionnaires lacked bravery or even an *esprit de corps*. Rather, what becomes clear is that, even in the estimation of many of its leaders, the postwar Legion was going through a period of adjustment, of which recouping its military reputation was only one aspect. Its place in the firmament of French regiments, which had seemed settled before 1914, had been called into question. "The Legion, of all the French army, is at the present time the only troop which is purely professional," the commander of the 2e *étranger* had noted in 1923.[114] This was both a source of professional pride as well as a potential source of weakness. Hostility from left-leaning governments toward the French army in general in this high renaissance of the "nation-in-arms" was to be expected. However, this hostility extended to the war ministry, which saw the Legion's independent inspectorate abolished after Rollet's retirement in 1935. "This hostility [to the Legion] is obvious in the smallest things as in the most important," one of Rollet's correspondents complained. "It is distressing."[115]

If all of this were not bad enough, the anti-Legion campaign, which came out of Germany before the war, and which had made such an impression upon Rollet, now spread through sensational novels and films to all countries, including allied ones like America and Great Britain. It threatened even to taint France. The best way to strengthen discipline and morale, as well as to counter an unfavorable Legion image, was to strengthen "traditions," and to create a public relations network to defend its interests without. Those tasks fell to Paul Rollet.

Chapter 20

THE INVENTION
OF TRADITION

IN 1932, A SLIGHTLY nervous Second Lieutenant Marcel Blanc climbed from the train at the Sidi-bel-Abbès station to begin his statutory three months' Legion apprenticeship. As he walked toward the barracks in the company of the half-dozen lieutenants who had been dispatched to greet him, he quickly formed the impression that this was a town fighting for its Frenchness. At first view, the Boulevard de la République, which led to the public gardens, appeared to be merely an exotic, palm-bordered artery of any small French provincial city. This walk took the young officer past the municipal theater, the law courts, the town hall and the obligatory *monument aux morts,* modest memorials to civic pride built to the baroque specifications of official Third Republic architecture or, in the case of the new law courts, in an austere classical style perhaps more in keeping with the artistic tastes of the many inhabitants of Spanish origin. The slap of wine bottles upon the zinc-covered bars and exuberant Mediterranean greetings echoed out of the darkened, cavernous cafes that lined the streets near the Place Carnot. Inside, the inhabitants played dominoes, discussed the fortunes of the local football club, which had defeated Philippeville for the North African championship a decade earlier, or discussed the recent disaster at Turenne between Tlemcen and Marnia in which 57 legionnaires had died and another 220 had been injured when their troop train plunged into a ravine.

But the European activity and architecture of the city center disguised, Potemkin-like, a reality altogether African. The Avenue de la Fontaine

Romaine was perhaps an attempt to conjure up a classical, pre-Arab past in the way of justifying the French-led European *reconquista* of the Maghreb. But the uniformed tourist was invariably disappointed to discover that the avenue led to no Roman fountain at all—in fact, the only structure that predated the French foundation of 1847 was the small *kouba,* or tomb, of the eighteenth-century Moslem holy man who gave his name to the town. The true cosmopolitan character of Bel-Abbès was revealed on the market day, when native Algerians, members of the town's large Jewish community and Bel-Abbèsiens of European extraction, many of them speaking Spanish, jostled and bargained with the keepers of the temporary stalls set up beneath canvas awnings on the Rue de Montagnac.

Those disappointed that a town whose name was linked with the exotic image of the French Foreign Legion offered the banal appearance of any subprefecture in France had only to venture north of the grid of streets that formed the European heart of Sidi-bel-Abbès to the section known officially as the *"faubourg Bugeaud,"* but popularly as the *"village nègre."* There, between the barracks of the *gendarmerie nationale* and the Wadi Mekerra, the streets smelled of kebabs and dung, Arabs hustled donkeys laden with impossible loads between the low-roofed houses, and the bleating of terrified sheep in the abattoir mingled with the raucous quarrels of prostitutes.

At the point in his march where the Rue Prudon, named for the captain of engineers who laid out the town plan, intersected the boulevard de la République, the young officer realized that he was on the Avenue de la Caserne (later Boulevard du Général Rollet), and therefore close to the object of his pilgrimage. An iron gate set in the low wall of an elongated one-story structure revealed a typical European barracks square, so typical, in fact, that the buildings could as easily have been in Paris or Bar-le-Duc as in this Arab heartland. However, in 1932 this square had an added feature seldom seen in French garrisons—a central tree-lined alleyway known as the *voie sacrée* or "sacred way," which led from the gate to a large monument. There was also evidence of much building—a new swimming pool and officers' mess, to be followed by a cinema, a sergeants' mess and other structures fashioned from the reddish stones of the four town gates, whose destruction had been ordained by the town council in 1927 to make the town center more accessible to motor traffic.

Colonel Nicolas, commander of the *1ᵉʳ étranger,* came out from behind his desk, a hint of a smile brightening his emaciated face, perhaps the first signs of the illness that would kill him two years later. Nicolas had already made his name, together with Rollet and Maire, as one of the Legion's "musketeers." Blanc thanked the colonel for his Legion assignment, a favor arranged by Blanc's father, a distant cousin of Nicolas, and expressed his eagerness to get to Morocco before the country was completely pacified. Nicolas quickly set him straight: "Well, lad, like everyone else, here you start at the bottom," he said.

Then you'll go where I send you, and we'll see soon enough. . . . Your work will consist above all of paying attention to what is going on, to impregnate yourself with the state of mind which reigns in the Legion, an essentially human, sensitive and therefore interesting world, exhilarating for an officer. You will also read everything you find in the library on Lyautey.

Blanc was then treated to a short lecture on the national peculiarities of legionnaires and of their unique psychology before he was dismissed. The young officer's initiation into the Legion's mysteries had begun.[1]

By 1932, the image of the Legion as a band of romantic outcasts was already well enough established to place Sidi-bel-Abbès on the tourist itinerary before World War I, where German and British travelers came "to contemplate these famous mercenaries about whom so many fantastic stories and legends have been written."[2] As the Legion's place in the public imagination grew in the interwar years, the mysteries that shrouded its collective character deepened. And as it became increasingly the focus of popular attention, so the process of character definition became a very self-conscious one in the Legion. The Legion's myths, heretofore an informal and half-formed collection of regimental lore and vague public perception, were collected, expanded, ritualized and given official status, while its "traditions" were not only codified and standardized, but in some instances actually invented. For this to happen required two preconditions. The first was a leader to coordinate and orchestrate what was essentially an inchoate, spontaneous movement within the Legion to reaffirm and strengthen its distinct identity. This was the role of Paul Rollet, the man often called the "Father of the Legion" because his personality so dominated the corps in the interwar years. But Rollet was more than a "father" to his corps—he was the architect of the Legion's postwar revival, at once its commanding general and its impresario.

The second factor that favored a romanticization of the Legion and a reaffirmation of its "traditions" to the point of invention was the new challenges faced by the Legion at the close of World War I. The success, even the survival, of the Legion obsessed Rollet, for everywhere he looked he saw potential for the Legion's demise. Already, as commander of the RMLE in 1918, he had feared that the absence of recruits might result in the disbandment of the Legion. The political upheavals that inundated the Legion with waves of Germans and Russians, Jews and Spaniards, whose deep nationalist antipathy for France or ideological preferences for the extreme right or left made them poor candidates for assimilation into a mercenary force, were a further concern. In the absence of the old soldiers who had played such a vital role in the socialization of the Legion's heterogeneous recruits, the entire outlook, spirit and even efficiency of the unit was under threat—one of the burning questions for soldiers in the interwar years was whether the "New Legion" was worthy of the military reputation of its pre-1914 predecessor. If this were not bad enough, Rollet was especially distressed by what he viewed as the attacks on the Legion by novelists, filmmakers and even from ex-legionnaires willing to sell memoirs made sensational for public consumption. In his view, this posed a threat more serious than the anti-Legion campaign run out of Germany before 1914, for it was a movement made for mass consumption and not confined to the narrow nationalist agenda of one country.

To counter these threats to the Legion posed by the constant changes and innovations of the postwar world, Rollet reached back into the Legion's past to resurrect, reaffirm and restructure symbols, practices and lore that would offer visible links between the historical Legion and the post-1918 corps. This would bestow legitimacy upon the Legion in the eyes of its recruits and give them a sense of continuity and communion with past generations through a set of highly symbolic and repetitive rituals, which would act as a means of inculcating values and standards of behavior in legionnaires by implying that these were the perpetuation of hallowed practices. But also, "tradition" would reaffirm the Legion's status in its own eyes as the only truly professional corps in an overwhelmingly conscript army.

Rollet's goal was to bequeath his Legion the stability of an unchanging and invariable "tradition" in a period of turbulence and change. The Legion was "a very special troop, whose worth comes from its heterogeneous composition cemented by TRADITION."[3] The commander of the *2e étranger* in 1923 agreed: "[The Legion's] reorganization is slow, too slow in my opinion, because tradition is at the base of the Legion and the measures taken often neglect the experience acquired over almost one hundred years."[4] Major Poirmeur of the *3e étranger* argued in 1924 that the Legion would recover its efficiency once it was "solidly cemented by 'tradition.' "[5] Unfortunately, in the early 1920s these "traditions" were little more than a collection of ill-defined and informal practices, many of which had fallen into abeyance during the war or remained only in the memories of those few survivors of the pre-1914 Legion (which was why Poirmeur surrounded the word in quotation marks).

The visible links that bound the new and old Legions across the chasm of World War I were tenuous ones in 1919. The most obvious one was Sidi-bel-Abbès, itself, with the regimental *"Salle d'Honneur,"* which featured the combats of Camerone and Tuyen Quang, the names of the regiment's commanders engraved in marble and the lists of Legion officers killed in combat. But *salles d'honneur* were not unique to the Legion. And, as has been seen, even Rollet had wanted to abandon Sidi-bel-Abbès after the war, so that there appears to have been no particular importance attached to the continuity provided by the Legion's long association with its primary garrison. If the Legion was forced to retain Sidi-bel-Abbès as its headquarters, it was essentially because the 19th Army Corps feared seeing the Legion disappear into the relative independence of Lyautey's Morocco. The *anonymat* persisted, but it is not clear what significance this practice held for the many adolescent recruits who joined after the war and whose experience of life, and motivations for enlistment, differed from those of their prewar counterparts. As the diarist of the 2ᵉ *étranger* noted in 1921, the prewar "adventurers" mentality seemed to be a thing of the past among the young recruits, who were "indifferent to their surroundings."[6] And, above all, the old veterans who could pass on such anecdotes as that of the "Royal Prince of Prussia," so common before the war, had become an endangered species. The Legion now had no uniform that distinguished it from other corps, which had formed such an important element of its prewar identity. Even its traditional *"Valeur et Discipline"* device on its regimental standards was replaced in 1920 by *"Honneur et Fidélité."* In other words, the Legion did not have "traditions" as such, but rather a more or less vague collection of ancestral memories that had yet to be formalized in any systematic fashion.[7]

Rollet was not alone in wanting to create a postwar image of the Legion based upon his perception of its pre-1914 personality. His contribution was to confirm and direct a movement that to a large degree was spontaneous, to formalize a series of symbols and rituals that would give to legionnaires a sense of belonging to a unique fraternity. It is in this sense that Legion "tradition" was invented, a "factitious" link between the post- and prewar Legion, a panoply of symbols and rituals whose constant repetition not only established a rhythm of regimental life, but also gave a sense of invariable constancy in a period of upheaval and change. Rollet's purpose was to teach a new generation of legionnaires to speak in a common idiom, to create a vision borrowed from myth to design a collective mentality, to formulate a common view of reality. In other words, the Legion existed as an organizational structure. Now he must make the legionnaires.

As in any army, no symbol was considered more potent than that of the uniform. While uniform details may seem arcane to some, it is clear that the Legion took the issue of the creation of a special uniform very seriously, and rightly so. A uniform confers special status, a sense of belonging to an elite, and offers an incentive to bravery. Unfortunately, the distinctive uniforms that had characterized the French army, and especially the French army abroad, before 1914 had been shed in favor of less target-worthy colors during World War I. The metropolitan troops emerged from the conflict in their "blue horizon" uniforms, while the overseas detachments finished the conflict in khaki, which had become the operational uniform for the Legion in 1907. This was not to the liking of Legion "traditionalists," especially as the *"Commission des Uniformes"* appointed in the aftermath of the war appeared intent upon recommending a single uniform for the entire army. The question was further complicated by the fact that troops in Syria and Morocco were required to use up odds and ends of surplus American stocks that remained in the warehouses at the end of the conflict.[8] The Legion command was intent upon giving the Legion a uniform which at once distinguished it from the common regimental herd, while at the same time distancing the legionnaire from "all the human contingencies which surround him."[9]

The history of Legion fashion is an intricate and sometimes hotly debated one, in part because uniform regulations changed with some frequency, and perhaps were not always enforced in remote areas. Indeed, the historian may be on shaky ground in talking of a Legion uniform at all—English journalist G. Ward-Price, who visited the Legion in Morocco in 1933, declared them to be "the untidiest soldiers I had ever seen. The stubby beards on the chins of most of the men were inevitable in a country where water was so scarce, but it was astonishing to find troops, that had only left their barracks six weeks before, in such ragged and nondescript clothes." Many of them wore sandals, and he even saw a man "on campaign in a pair of under-pants."[10] Martin also confessed that legionnaires in the field in Morocco were liable to kit themselves out in the native markets—"We had exactly the appearance, beneath our unusual clothes, of a band of partisans," he wrote. "The only part of our uniform left to us was the kepi."[11]

If on campaign the legionnaire sought to express his personality in a *clochard*-like idiom, in garrison he looked to make a more elegant sartorial statement. In fact, it was the reverse side of the same phenomenon: "One always flatters legionnaires by telling them that they are chaps different from the others," Martin wrote.[12] But the task was not as easy as all that. While before the war most of the *Armée d'Afrique* dressed as if going to a costume ball, the Legion was confined to the rather drab, certainly very common uniforms of the metropolitan army, of which it was a part. The kepi and the epaulets disappeared in 1915, the supply services could not furnish the blue waistbands, and in 1927, Rollet complained that legionnaires did not even have their own buttons emblazoned with the grenade with seven flames. Therefore, as late as 1923 there was nothing to distinguish a legionnaire from any other soldier in the French army except his stripes and the regimental number on his collar tips, which were on a green background.[13]

The campaign to gain a distinctive uniform for the Legion focused upon the kepi. In 1850, the Legion and the *Bataillons d'Afrique* had been issued kepis, with white covers that included a *"couvre-nuque"* ("neck cloth") for the summer. In 1852, the kepi became the common cap for the entire army. Pictures of legionnaires in pre-World War I North Africa show them dressed in white uniforms and white kepis. In 1907, the Legion was put in khaki campaign uniforms and the kepi was covered with a khaki cloth, which sunlight and constant washing bleached white. New legionnaires, eager to shed the status of *bleus* as quickly as possible, scrubbed their newly issued khaki covers to appear more like the *anciens*. However, during World War I, the kepi was replaced by the garrison cap.

The rehabilitation of the kepi in the Legion began in 1922, when

General Cottez requested its distribution. The following year, a stock of surplus khaki kepis was issued to legionnaires in Morocco, who quickly contrived to make them white to match the image of the prewar Legion. Thus, the "tradition" of the *képi blanc* was born. In March 1926, Rollet complained that he had written on four separate occasions to the war ministry in 1924 and 1925 to have the kepi replace the garrison cap and the pith helmet for the Legion, without results.[14] His letters must have had some effect, however, for on June 18, 1926, the Legion became the only unit in the army allowed to wear the kepi. It was only a partial victory, for the regulation permitted the prewar red kepi, rather than the white one favored by legionnaires. By the centennial of the Legion in 1931, several of the Legion regiments had taken matters into their own hands and only those of the *1er* and *4e étranger* were red.[15]

Two years later in Morocco, Martin recorded that a battle raged between legionnaires and the command over the white kepi, almost as fierce as the one fought between the Legion and Moroccans in the mountains. Upset apparently by the number of head wounds among legionnaires, the command considered distributing helmets, but abandoned this idea as a recipe for sunstroke in a Moroccan summer. Instead, they commanded the legionnaires to replace their kepis or dye them khaki. "That caused a real stink," wrote Martin. "The veterans 'had' always 'fought' in white kepis, in the toughest campaigns, and we were 'going up' in khaki?" When the order came to dye their white kepis by any means, the legionnaires obeyed, while at the same time demonstrating a flair for creative insubordination by producing a rainbow of colors running from light beige through ocher to a "delicious pale mauve" in the machine-gun section. "This went on all summer!" Martin continued. "The legionnaires were still wearing white kepis in September, despite all the orders and counter-orders, observations and punishments."[16] Bennett Doty believed that the kepi in itself represented a victory over the solar topi, especially when it was worn "at the right angle, [which] accurately expresses the half-sardonic, rough *insouciance* of the Legion."[17] The color issue was finally resolved when the Legion paraded in white kepis down the Champs Elysées on July 14, 1939.[18] "Many readers will probably be surprised to learn that the white kepi cover is very recent in the Legion, at least in a quasi-permanent status on the kepi of the legionnaire," the *Livre d'or* recorded in its 1981 edition. ". . . The vision of the legionnaire wearing an immaculately clean white cover on his kepi dates from the last fifteen years."[19] While it was clearly older than that, only in quite recent times has the white kepi taken on the importance of a quasi-religious symbol, bestowed upon legionnaires near the end of their basic training in an impressive torchlight ceremony. When Adrian Liddell Hart enlisted in 1951, he was issued a battered, secondhand kepi with a torn white cover: "No matter," he concluded philosophically. "We could now pass, at a distance, for legionnaires."[20]

Rollet and other "traditionalists" won the battle to have the Legion revive the kepi, resurrect the red and green epaulets *"dites* (so-called) *de tradition"* from November 1930,[21] and reissue the blue waistband, which had in effect disappeared from the uniform, if not from the regulations, in time for the Legion centenary in 1931. A 1934 report recorded that, while these results had been beneficial for Legion morale, they "were often the result of initiatives of the corps leaders or unit commanders, acting generally on the margins of regulations."[22] And while Rollet believed that his efforts to secure a special uniform were greatly appreciated by the legionnaires, not everyone agreed: "This dress, so appreciated by the *images d'Epinal* [a line of patriotic prints] and color magazines, was much less so by those who must exhibit it," wrote legionnaire Charles Favrel, who enlisted in 1938. In Algeria, the white kepi was reserved for the band, while the epaulets were too heavy for the shirts and sat badly on the shoulders. The puttees worn by all French soldiers, he reckoned, were a plot by military suppliers to sell off excess cloth, and he speculated that a fair portion of French POWs in 1940 owed their capture to unraveling puttees, so that "they couldn't run away fast enough." The blue waistband—all two and a half yards of it—was a complete nuisance, especially in town when one had to make a rest stop. The legionnaire was required to close one end in a door and perform a pirouette before reappearing in public. When legionnaires in his group boarded ships to be transported to France in 1940, one of their first acts, Favrel claimed, was to jettison their waistbands overboard. "But this spontaneous gesture of emancipation proved to be useless," Favrel complained, for "A stock of new waist bands caught up with us at the camp of Larzac!"

Throughout the chaos of the fall of France and the organization of the Gaullist resistance, the blue waistbands followed the Legion like a bad debt, even into the heart of the Libyan desert, where they were ordered to put them over their British-issued short trousers. When, in 1943, legionnaires were given GI clothing, the Legion retained the waistband as a distinguishing mark. However, Favrel wrote that "this carnival travesty" was finally, though only temporarily, abandoned at the insistence of Allied commanders.[23]

Rituals occupied a central place in Legion life. Blanc discovered that ceremonies began with the arrival of Colonel Nicolas at the barracks gate each morning on horseback to inspect the guard, far different from his metropolitan regiment, where the colonel arrived on his bicycle and dismounted at full tilt, leaving the guard to catch it as best he could. The daily training routines were capped by the weekly *"revue des catégories"*— officers, NCOs and legionnaires, decorations dangling from their chests, drawn up along the *voie sacrée* to hear announcements of promotions and decorations, welcome new officers, give good-conduct certificates to departing legionnaires, dispatch contingents to other garrisons, and finally to review the cases of the discipline section, which stood to the left of the formation, their blankets folded under their arms. The ceremony ended with the Legion band, whose ranks had swelled under Rollet to 180 members, in addition to a 100-strong orchestra and bands created for every other regiment, striking up the "Boudin." "It was for the newly arrived a sort of public enthronement," Blanc remembered. "The enthronement was pronounced before Tradition, before History, in front of one's Peers, a trilogy which manifested itself in the Legion monument, the *salle d'honneur*, and the Mess."[24] Ritualized, formalized, constantly repeated, Legion life was regulated by ceremonies, from the weekly dinners held by officers of each rank, to the parades on November 11, to the celebration of Christmas and the exchange of New Year's wishes between officers and legionnaires.

However, one ceremony came to occupy a central place in Legion "tradition"—that of Camerone. The institutionalization of Camerone as the preeminent celebration of the Legion occurred on April 30, 1931. For Rollet, the gigantic ceremonies that he organized at Sidi-bel-Abbès on that day were also meant to establish the formal, historical link between the "old" and the "new" Legion. The choice of April 30, rather than the Legion's birthday of March 9, was deliberate. The anniversary of the 1863 battle of Camerone in Mexico offered a far more dramatic symbol of regimental legitimization, a more potent behavioral role model and occasion for celebration, than did the signing into life of the Legion by King Louis-Philippe in 1831. In this, as in many of his innovations, Rollet played midwife to a "tradition" that had been emerging spontaneously in the Legion.

Although the fight at Camerone in 1863 was a rather marginal event in the Mexican campaign, its importance in the legitimization of the Legion in the public conscience, and in the eyes of legionnaires, was immense. Coming upon the heels of the very credible Legion performances at Sebastopol in 1854–55 and Ischeriden in 1857, Camerone conferred upon the Legion the reputation of a troop capable of making the supreme sacrifice, the beginning of the legend of the heroic desperadoes.[25] The first time that Camerone was actually celebrated appears to have been in 1906. Whether this was deliberate or the fortuitous result of a ministerial decision of February 16, 1906, to award a *Légion d'honneur* to the *1er étranger* in a ceremony that eventually took place on April 28 of that year is unclear. But legionnaires certainly saw the connection—Joseph Ehrhart, who was present at Sidi-bel-Abbès in 1906, remembered the decoration of the regimental banner as a very emotional occasion that recalled Camerone on "28 April, 1866,"[26] while in Tonkin a detachment of the *1er étranger* likewise marked the event with a review that recalled Camerone. Aristide Merolli, who joined the Legion in 1911, gives accounts of Cameron celebrated in 1913 and 1914,[27] with the reading of the account of the battle, followed by games and an alcoholic binge. However, if Camerone had been celebrated in the RMLE in World War I, one would expect it to have been commented upon by the Legion's numerous diarists and letter writers. But these "volunteers for the duration" appear to have been completely ignorant of Camerone.

The celebration of Camerone was revived in the 1920s as part of the attempt to link the "New Legion" with the old one. On April 30, 1931, numerous dignitaries, including Louis II of Monaco, Marshal Louis Franchet d'Esperey, generals, foreign officers and twenty-seven delegations of *anciens* gathered at Sidi-bel-Abbès in the presence of legionnaires of all units to watch a parade led by sappers sporting beards, wearing leather aprons and carrying hatchets. The use of the sappers to "open the route" in Legion parades was another "tradition" that had disappeared with the Second Empire in 1870 and was reinvented by Rollet to recall the sappers created by Bernelle in Spain and the beards popular in the old Legion but no longer worn after 1918. This opened a ceremony that included the recitation of an account of the battle and the appearance of the wooden hand of Captain Danjou, paraded in a glass reliquary, as the Legion band played what was now established as the official version of the Legion march, "Le Boudin." However, the legionnaires in this period do not appear to have marched with the slow elongated step that is such a distinctive feature of their march today. Newsreels show a normal, even a rapid pace, which is to a degree confirmed by Bennett Doty, who spoke of marching off to Syria in 1925 accompanied by the Legion band playing "its best pieces, its gayest, most rhythmic airs, drawing us along at the Legion's rapid marching step . . ."[28] The slow Legion march appears to be a "tradition" that dates from the post-World War II era, when it was first used for the victory parade down the Champs Elysées of June 18, 1945.[29]

The high point of the 1931 celebration came with the unveiling of the Legion monument—a large metal globe upon which Camerone is marked by a gold star, and all countries in which the Legion has campaigned highlighted in gold, sitting on a square marble base, at the four corners of which stand four statues of legionnaires representing the conquest of Algeria and the campaigns of the Second Empire, Tonkin and the RMLE. The figures were modeled upon paintings of legionnaires done by Maurice Mahut, an artist whose drawings and illustrations of legionnaires before 1914, in particular those included in d'Esparbès's *Les mystères de la Légion étrangère* in 1911, had contributed to the myth of legionnaires as men with a mysterious past.[30] This monument, as well as references to Camerone in the Legion *salle d'honneur,* offered a visible link between the Legion and its past. It became the focus of regimental ritual, a place of pilgrimage surrounded by liturgical convention—the barracks square in which it stood was christened the *voie sacrée* or "sacred way," and so transformed into a sort of sanctuary violated only during elaborate regimented ceremonies. "Its purpose is not to embellish a quarter," Major Maire said of this monument. "It is destined to be the symbol of the troop which gives asylum to those who need a refuge."[31] This was the official consecration of a heretofore informal and spontaneous collection of sagas and myths, those of the "unknown heroes," a handful of *képis blancs* whom romantic misfortune had driven into the last refuge of the Legion, and who bore the standard of European civilization to those parts of the globe ravaged by heat, disease and bloodthirsty savages. This image was too laden with drama and romance for Hollywood to ignore.

Like all faiths, the Legion required a holy city. Sidi-bel-Abbès, a town Rollet had wanted to abandon altogether in 1920, now became "the town the Legion built," *"la Maison-Mère, centre vital de la Légion,"*[32] a sort of Vatican through which all new legionnaires must pass to receive the catechism, and to which veterans return for spiritual renewal. North Africa became the Legion's "melting pot," the environment whose harshness forged regimental character, the center of its moral geography. Camerone was its holiest feast day, the promise of death without resurrection perhaps, but not without immortality. Even today, Legion recruits are aligned beneath Jean-Adolphe Beaucé's painting of Camerone and given a recitation of the battle before they proceed to sign their enlistment papers. So sacred has the scriptural version of this event become that when it was discovered only a few years ago by an Austrian archivist in the Vienna archives that the hand of Captain Danjou had not been found among the bodies by the relief as described in the *Livre d'or,*[33] but in fact had been purchased two years later by Austrian troops from a farmer who lived almost one hundred miles from the site of the battle, the new information was believed by some Legion officers to be subversive enough to warrant suppression.[34]

In the process of establishing Camerone as the central event in the Legion calendar, Rollet demonstrated his command of Legion psychology. Camerone established the cult of sacrifice, of heroic death in battle. And while evoking heroic moments in the history of the regiment is hardly unique to the Legion, the power of its message is probably unequaled. Camerone and the hand of Danjou exercised a powerful effect in a Legion recruited among the disoriented, men who verbalized little and responded best to visual symbols. It encouraged the view, quite literally, that the only good legionnaire was a dead legionnaire. *"Nous saurons bien tous périr suivant la tradition"* (We will all know how to die following tradition), the final line of the *"Boudin"* declares. French psychologist Roger Cabrol actually encountered legionnaires near the end of their careers who had a psychological crisis because they felt they had let down the institution by surviving to retirement, "legionnaires who had not succeeded in proving that they were heroes like their forbearers," he wrote. "Death and Legion, like all the recitations and the social stereotype of the Legion. The gift of the body is implied in the enlistment."[35] These are perhaps extreme examples. A. R. Cooper bailed out after twelve years precisely because he believed, or claimed to believe, that it was Legion policy not to allow men to survive until retirement. Although this was patent nonsense, having survived the Dardanelles and some of the toughest fighting of the Rif War, as well as what he describes as the transparent attempt by one of his officers to send him on suicide missions, he may perhaps be forgiven for taking early retirement.

The themes of death and sacrifice interlace Legion ritual, assurance that the Legion always stood by its own, never abandoned them, even *in extremis*. In *Les hommes sans nom* (*The Men Without Names*) Colonel de Joyeuse explains that Legion graves are always meticulously kept in the *bled,* and that no one is ever abandoned, even if extra lives are expended to retrieve the corpse.[36] As has been seen, however, the "Old Legion" made it a fairly standard practice to leave behind those unable to keep up— indeed, Legion efficiency had been based in part on their relentless march forward and refusal to be slowed by stragglers. To a large extent this had been forced upon them by circumstances, which included the lack of medical support, the remoteness of the battlefields and the fact that they were often closely pressed by the enemy, as during the retreat from the Gates of China in 1885. And while the Legion, like other corps, certainly honored their war dead, what might be described as the cult of the elaborate Legion funeral was a post-World War I invention. Flutsch was told that in Tonkin, legionnaires who could not keep up were actually shot by their own comrades, which was considered more humane than disarming and abandoning them to the not too tender mercies of the locals, which was also a common practice. During the Madagascar campaign, for instance, Legion dead were often pitched unceremoniously into ravines, perhaps rightly so in circumstances that bordered upon physical and moral collapse.[37] A. R. Cooper also claimed that bodies were left behind during the Rif campaign because it was all they could do to carry the wounded.[38] One of the greatest benefits for the Legion of Rollet's emphasis upon the elaborate celebration of sacrifice and death as part of regiment ritual was that it provided a value system and a means of socialization for men who were most susceptible to this sort of mythmaking.

Not everyone proved susceptible to the myth, however. Charles Favrel, who experienced his first Camerone in 1938, recorded that while selection to recite the account of the battle was considered a great honor, and one that usually fell to a Teutonic sergeant who read it in a high unintelligible voice, "as his audience already does not understand correct French, the incident has little importance." What legionnaires retained of Camerone was the memory of the formidable drinking that went on afterwards: "Camerone? they say shaking their head, Oh, la, la! What a drunk!"[39] The Englishman Henry Ainley, who enlisted during the Indochinese War of 1946–54, believed that the primary purpose of Camerone was to allow legionnaires to let off steam and settle scores. In any case, unpopular NCOs stayed well away from the postparade celebrations.[40]

There is other evidence that, despite the ritualistic emphasis upon Camerone and the message that legionnaires must be prepared to make the ultimate sacrifice, the "tradition" was hedged in practice. As will be seen, in January 1943 a unit of the *3e étranger* was overrun in Tunisia, in the process, almost inconceivably given the strength of "tradition," abandoning to the enemy one of the Legion's most precious relics. And in Indochina, legionnaires passed up at least two occasions to *faire Camerone*. The first came in October 1950, when the BEP (*Bataillon étranger parachutiste*) and a battalion of the *3ᵉ étranger* were cornered during the retreat from Cao Bang on Route Coloniale 4. According to Hungarian legionnaire Janos Kemencei, the idea of resistance to the death was discussed and then rejected because the legionnaires determined that they lacked the munitions and fortifications to make a proper job of a glorious last stand.[41] The second time came at Dien Bien Phu in 1954, where several thousand legionnaires surrendered only days after they had crowded around the radios in their fetid, shell-torn bunkers to hear the April 30 broadcast that reminded them that on that day in 1863, "Life rather than courage abandoned these French soldiers."[42]

The point is neither that the legionnaires had lacked courage nor that they were wrong to surrender, although in retrospect those who gave themselves up to the Viet Minh would have lost little in fighting to the death, as Viet Minh prison camps were more like Auschwitz than Colditz. Rather, legionnaires were able to draw the distinction between the myth of Camerone and its practical application on the battlefield. They also placed limits upon their willingness to sacrifice themselves. Kemencei reasoned that he was quite prepared to *faire Camerone* "to preserve the honor of the Legion." But all bets were off when the leadership, as so often in Indochina, "are incompetents, unworthy to command the men who have the misfortune to serve under their orders. . . . A decimated army is not worth much, and battles are won with the living."[43]

The 1931 celebration marked the culmination of Rollet's campaign to unite the Legion around a panoply of symbols and "traditions." It was also a bid by the Legion to define itself as France's premier regiment, justified in this view by its status as the French army's only remaining completely professional corps. In this way, Rollet cleverly sought to secure its future against possible ingratitude, xenophobia, or political pressure, either foreign or domestic. Rollet commissioned the well-known military scholar and collector Jean Brunon to compile a history of the Legion in time for the centenary. Although one of its later editors has written that the *"livre d'or de la Légion étrangère"* "has no pretensions other than to conserve the souvenir of the great moments of this institution,"[44] it was more than that. The *Livre d'or* was both a hagiography destined, like Camerone, to awe and inspire, and an attempt to reestablish the "Old Legion" as a model for the new one, as did artists commissioned by the Legion like Pierre Benigni (1878–1956), a student of the celebrated military painter of the early Third Republic Edouard Detaille, who collaborated with Jean Brunon in the publication of the *Livre d'or*. Benigni's painting of the Battle of Ischeriden in 1857, which shows legionnaires attacking in *képis blancs,* was an obvious attempt to boost the cause of the white kepi for the Legion, as there is no certainty that the Legion was wearing white covers on their kepis at the time.[45]

That Rollet commissioned a history written in a heroic mode is hardly surprising. His purpose was both to inspire and to create an image of the Legion as a corps of adventurers. However, Rollet and others conscientiously sought to define a Legion mentality. Or rather redefine it, as by common consent it had vanished in World War I. One of the most powerful arguments in favor of enhancing traditions was to bind together a corps "formed by an amalgamation coming from all the peoples of the earth; that this group of men profoundly different in race, origin, trade, religion, language and sentiments forms there a block whose elements are indissoluble."[46] Adrian Liddell Hart agreed that the Legion *kameradschaft* "arose from our very differences for, in a curious way, these differences of race and age, social background and motive, cancelled each other out."[47]

Yet how heterogeneous was the Legion? It was certainly multinational, but beneath a babble of different languages the men of the "Old Legion" had much in common, similar social origins, an inability to find satisfaction in civilian life and a sense of being in the professional military trade perhaps foremost among them. Indeed, one of the characteristics of the Legion had been its unwillingness or inability to make a niche for men whose backgrounds or motives differed from those mentioned above—patriotic Alsatians before 1914, the "temporary" volunteers of 1914–15, the influx of "transplanted," sober, largely young men in the immediate postwar years. And, as will be seen, an increase in Eastern European Jews and eventually Spanish Republicans in the ranks as World War II approached also caused problems of indigestion.

As the reaction to the volunteers of 1914 and those after 1918 had demonstrated, the Legion had a strong sense of its own personality, and a strong desire to preserve it in the face of an invasion of men who did not require the asylum the Legion offered, whose apprenticeship in the military trade was only a temporary and reluctant one, for whom *Legio Patria Nostra* ("The Legion Is Our Fatherland," another invented epigram of the interwar years) was little more than a quaint and empty slogan. Jean Brunon believed that although the character of the Legion had altered through its history, "its base rests immutable: The Legion remains therefore really what it has always been."[48] Basically, this was correct. And if it is so, it is largely because Rollet helped to define and confirm the outlook of a corps prepared to make few concessions to the idealistic, the political, the patriotic, the middle-class—in other words, those whose ideals slowed their assimilation, discouraged them from defining life in purely Legion terms, to "think Legion." Henry Ainley was of the opinion that it was "An admirable organization for the desperate—but not at all the place for those who have a certain lust for life and liberty."[49] "The day the legionnaire lost the sentiment of living on the margins of society," wrote Prince Aage, a member of the Danish royal family and descendant of Louis-Philippe who joined the Legion as an officer soon after World War I, "he lost his strength and his human worth."[50] These were precisely Cabrol's conclusions in his 1971 study of legionnaires: "One would think that the multiplicity of nations represented would cause seismic problems," he wrote. "This is not so. There is a basic personality. . . . In fact, one legionnaire resembles another, and that is a guarantee of success." Those who experienced problems in civilian life adapted especially well to the Legion "microculture because it is easy to understand and it poses no problems of socio-economic confrontation. Life is programmed, pedigreed, rhythmic."[51] In other words, what the Legion preferred was men who were dysfunctional, or at the very least unsatisfied, in traditional civilian or even traditional military society. Those in trouble with the law, so long as they were not hardened criminals, also made loyal recruits because they had no viable alternative to life in the Legion.

Therefore, the Legion and its propagandists spent much time in the interwar years defining the Legion character, or rather Legion characters. The Legion, in Rollet's view, was a sanctuary for life's tragic figures, men cast into its ranks by forces beyond their control, who then depended upon the Legion for direction and psychological well-being. It was these men who most needed "tradition": "The legionnaires need to feel protected by one hundred years of glory against the disdain and the indifference of the crowd," wrote Manue.[52] It is also they who needed the larger-than-life leaders, a clutch of great figures like Rollet, Maire, de Tscharner, de Corta, Nicolas and Aage, who served in a way as founding fathers and as the creators and custodians of tradition, dominating personalities who established themselves in Legion lore in the interwar years. For this reason, the Legion novels and sympathetic memoirs of the interwar years are peopled with stock characters—the Russian aristocrat, the Belgian sergeant-major who fled into the Legion after stealing the regimental funds, the half-mad legionnaire who tattoos obscenities on his hand to give his superiors a full frontal insult with each salute, the hopelessly alcoholic German batman who dresses up in the colonel's uniform and terrorizes subalterns, the sergeant with a dark secret who one day commits suicide and so on, men whose life is given purpose and direction by the Legion, who in heroic death actually redeem their wasted lives. Charles Favrel claimed that the legend of the Legion as a haven for criminals was so prevalent in the interwar years that prospective recruits sometimes claimed to have committed a crime because they believed this was the only way they would be accepted.[53]

This is not to say that Rollet invented these characters, or that they did not exist. On the contrary, one of the primary qualities of myth is that it has a foundation in reality. These were the men who peopled the Legion before 1914, and whom Rollet wished to entice back into the Legion. These were his ideal legionnaires for at least two reasons. The first was that, if handled properly by officers who knew what they were about, the disoriented were easy to lead, as Ernst Junger had observed in 1913, "no one allows himself to submit more easily than he who does not know what he wants."[54] The last thing that Legion officers wanted to deal with was a man who asked questions, who actually thought about life in ways that might cause him to place limits upon his loyalty to the Legion. This was why so many officers sent to the Legion on TOE after 1918 found it so difficult to adapt there, and has given rise to observations by French line officers that service as a Legion officer is really very easy, because they do not have to deal with "thinking" soldiers who want to know the reason behind an order.[55]

The second reason why Rollet and others sought out men unable to cope with the burdens of their existence was that this formed an essential precondition for the myth of redemption through Legion service. Unless a legionnaire's past concealed some dark secret, unless he had failed to make a success of his previous life, then the Legion's argument that it served a rehabilitative function lost its credibility.[56] But, as has been seen in the pre-1914 complaints by Captain Clément-Grandcourt, Raoul Béric and even by Flutsch, the counterargument was that the atmosphere of the corps was such that it took a man of great character indeed to remain on a sound moral footing in the Legion. The Legion actually encouraged a man to adopt or continue a pattern of dysfunctional behavior—drinking, fighting, and even to a point desertion—because such behavior was tolerated and even rewarded there.

Of course, a large place remained for the romanticism of the Legion, encouraged by the *anonymat*—Rollet was fond of asking legionnaires in the ranks what they had done in civilian life, and in one version of a celebrated story that is alleged to have taken place in Syria between 1921 and 1925 elicited the reply from a Russian, "*J'étais colonel, mon colonel.*" Cooper noted that this much-publicized incident became a standing joke among legionnaires, so that all Russians were said to be ex-colonels in the Czarist army and Belgians ex-sergeant-majors who had departed with the company funds, to the point that Belgians were often addressed as "sergeant-major."[57] In fact, Rollet formalized the *anonymat* further with a 1931 directive that required the company officer to ask the legionnaire, in the event of inquiries, if he were willing for his presence to be divulged, a practice subsequently undermined by agreements with the Germans in 1940, the Soviet Union in 1945 and the Americans and British in 1948 that allowed for the recovery of deserters.[58]

Prince Aage repeated the ancient belief that "a woman is behind each legionnaire," and decried the establishment of the official bordellos because they "deprive the legionnaire of his 'romantic' aspect": "One can say that, *without women, there would be no Legion* [italics in original]. . . . Woman is part even of the character of the Legion, and, without her, the legionnaire would not be what he is; an overgrown child, sensitive and complicated." He reproduced the unlikely but arresting story of an older legionnaire and a young lieutenant both killed in action who were discovered to have carried the picture of the same woman, proving that, unknown to each of them, they were father and son.[59] This myth was amusingly satirized by Laurel and Hardy in *Beau Hunks,* when all legionnaires in the company, and even the rebel Arab chief, were found to carry the picture of the same woman. Carol concluded that although legionnaires constantly talked of women, they were only an abstraction: "The real woman does not exist. The Foreign Legion is a unit without women. For starters it is too virile for them.... Outside the barracks, it is physical sexuality, mechanical, in pleasure spots. Inside, the woman remains in the idealized imagination."[60]

The problem began when the desire to preserve the romantic myths began to stand in the way of unit efficiency. When, as before 1914, complaints began to be heard about the bad characters who were enlisting in the Legion and some officers began to demand stricter recruitment controls, Georges Manue objected that whatever the Legion gained in quality, it would forfeit in mystery: "It is just that possibility to leave incognito that seduces the vanquished of life who are little troubled by showing it," he wrote. "Besides, it is to the mystery of his origins that the legionnaire owes much of his character."[61] Never mind that the upper-class romantics, the Beau Gestes, were virtually nonexistent: "I was five years in command of several different battalions, but I don't think I ever met more than twenty men that one could definitely identify as having come from the better classes of society," the British writer Ward-Price was told by a Legion officer.[62] Enough upper-class exiles had existed, or were believed to exist, to lend credence to the myth. But more to the point, by enlisting, *every* legionnaire participated to the full in the Legion's myths, wrapped himself in a cloak of mystery. "The legionnaires are mythomaniacs, inventors of fables which they are the first to believe in," wrote Manue.[63]

The fact that in the Legion, where according to Pechkoff, "each man lives with his thoughts ... each individual has his philosophy,"[64] legionnaires developed identifiable traits of a collective character appears confusing only if one assumes that, in the opinions and desires of its spokesmen, the Legion was truly a heterogeneous force. But the Legion spokesmen in the interwar years insisted that it had a collective character: "A touch of madness, chronic *cafard*, pride in the corps recreates, in these individuals who have sometimes lost it, a particular sense of honor, ticklish in the extreme, a contagion of heroism born of this *esprit de corps*," wrote Manue. "That is what gives the legionnaire a character which has no equal in any corps in the world."[65] Men with troubled pasts must be strictly disciplined or kept busy or, according to Prince Aage, "he risks to fall into the most tenacious and the most infernal regions of the *cafard*." In any case, "at the moment of death, all legionnaires, whomever they are, vomit and blaspheme their disgust for life and for men."[66]

Georges Manue, who had served in the Legion in the early 1920s when by common agreement it had been altered beyond recognition by the war and the postwar influx of poorly assimilated recruits, was somewhat iron-ically tasked with writing a piece of the *"Psychologie du Légionnaire"* for the 1958 edition of the *Livre d'or*. However, the irony ceases when one realizes that defining a Legion character was largely a work of reconstitu-tion not description, which allowed Manue to characterize legionnaires as

Ardent characters, tempted by misfortune, weak souls crushed by liberty, searching for a framework for their dreams, aristocrats or paupers, leveled by the uniform, all legionnaires are united by the same pride, the same secret aspirations, the same desires, the same needs; Pushed by the same male forces, physical and moral, they are united outside of ordinary con-ventions upon the plan of the great human laws.

Manue argued that this "immutable" Legion character had been developed during the "heroic period" before 1914, when "the units of the Legion were composed for years of the same legionnaires, and they were com-manded by the same leaders . . . creating a typical mentality." "At this time," he believed, "there existed a psychology of the legionnaire," which, despite changing recruitment patterns, had been passed onto the succeed-ing generations through tradition.[67]

Myth and legend had an important role to play in the creation of this collective mentality, for it obliged legionnaires to conform to the myths even if their pasts had nothing romantic about them. It gave them an image to live up to. Adrian Liddell Hart, the son of the well-known British mil-itary historian and critic, insisted that the tradition of asylum and ano-nymity "has inspired a legend, a moral climate affecting those who are not refugees in the legal sense." He confessed that he had been completely seduced by the romance of Legion mythology before enlistment,

the legend of anonymous characters and curious situations, the sense of order and freedom. . . . I wanted to be on the frontier and in the center; to be accepted and yet to remain an exception. "The guest of life" . . .

The legends had a leveling effect upon the character of the unit—even its discipline and fighting potential were linked to its romantic image—discipline in the Legion "depends in the last analysis on the challenge, the unexpected," he believed. The enlistment, a high individualized act, was the assumption of an obligation to participate in the legend of the Legion:

The legionnaire fights for himself—and he has identified himself with the Legion. . . . The Legion is not the protagonist of a cause. He is not essen-tially a soldier performing a duty. He is an individual true to himself.[68]

This definition of Legion character and the reaffirmation of unit loyalty were also made necessary by the attention focused upon the Legion by the cinema and by popular fiction in the interwar years. The strengthening of Legion romantic myths and the reaffirmation of "tradition" were a reply to the strong countermyth formulated by the Germans before 1914, one that portrayed the Legion as a band of criminal outcasts kept in line by brutal officers and NCOs. Rollet became concerned when this vilification of the Legion spread to other countries in the interwar years. Even in memoirs written by renegade legionnaires masquerading as accurate accounts of Legion service that carried stirring titles like *Hell Hounds of France, From the Abyss to the Foreign Legion, Twixt Hell and Allah* or *Death March in the Desert,* the Legion was stigmatized as a trap for unsuspecting or romantically naïve foreigners who had been mugged by the Legion myth, a tradition that continues in Legion memoir literature in our own day.[69]

The factors that drew so much popular attention to the Legion were not unique to the interwar years. Rather, they emerged from the heightened awareness and the broader dissemination of conflicting images of the Legion that had been apparent since at least the second half of the nineteenth century. In fact, it was the conflicting nature of those images that in many ways helped to make the Legion attractive to a larger public. In strictly literary terms, legionnaires provided many of the qualities of the heroes found in dime Western novels and low-budget films. Their mysterious origins and life of adventure made them glamorous. The fact that they were Europeans fighting in bleak foreign lands bestowed upon them the mantle of civilization conquering barbarism. Yet they were sufficiently primitive themselves to find fulfillment, even pleasure, in confronting danger, and to retain the basic survival skills that allowed them to triumph over their savage enemies. Furthermore, the Legion's reputation for brutality allowed for the literary creation of suitable villains, unsavory characters like Sergeant Lejaune in *Beau Geste* or Deucalion, a psychotic ex-officer in André Armandy's *Le renégat* who escapes into the Legion to avoid a death sentence. These were Europeans who had completely surrendered to the savagery of their environment, who added tension to the plot and whose inevitable death in the last chapter represented the triumph of civilization and moral values.

Furthermore, as the underlying theme for many of the novels and films, as for the Legion itself, was often that of sacrifice and redemption, the desert settings provided an appropriate moral geography for a story of human salvation set within the larger one of expanding European civilization and justice. Survival in the teeth of calamity was the beginning of self-respect, the recovery of identity, a reward for courage and virtue.[70] To rephrase it into the contemporary American idiom, "No pain, no gain." The institution of the Legion was sanctified by the sacrifice of legionnaires, legitimized because it was subordinated to a human ideal, although Adrian Liddell Hart believed the impulse to enlist as a requirement for the expiation of some sin was more a masochistic than a moral one. The infectious attraction of the Legion myth depended upon its conflicting images—the

Legion held out the promise that one could always break with the past and begin anew, while the suffering and danger required for this process of expiation reaffirmed the conviction that one was correct not to have done so.[71]

But one could always do so vicariously. The political and artistic conditions of the interwar years particularly favored the dissemination of these conflicting images of the Legion. The growing pacifism of the interwar years combined with protests raised in France over the Rif War to focus suspicion on the Legion as an unsavory corps in which unsuspecting recruits might come to great harm. On the other hand, in the atmosphere of economic dislocation and political confusion of the interwar years, the pre-1914 era evoked great nostalgia. The prewar world, re-created through the healing haze of memory, seemed to have been a well-ordered place where issues were simple and where everyone knew his proper place in the social order. As British film historian Jeffrey Richards has noted, the cinema of imperialism that flourished in this period in Britain and America, as well as in France, offered up prewar settings dominated by ritual and a hierarchical system. The heroes prevailed over treacherous and ungrateful natives through discipline and loyalty, reassuring those who might otherwise have begun to have doubts on that score after World War I of the superior attributes of Western culture and of the obligations imposed by the "white man's burden."[72] Furthermore, this basic message was inserted into stories with exotic settings and romantic themes that dealt with destiny, fate, loves that died at dawn, and the unfairness of life all very popular to interwar audiences.[73] Europeans wanted an escape from routine, from the life-style of the crowded industrial cities. They craved simple plots in which virtue, honesty and simplicity were rewarded. Even intellectuals saw this sort of film as a palliative for jaded and overly sophisticated tastes.[74]

Quite naturally, the Legion would be assigned a prominent place in this genre, to Rollet's deep regret. A. R. Cooper recorded that Rollet was angered by *Beau Geste* because he believed the Legion misrepresented in the novel.[75] Some films on the Legion, especially those out of Hollywood, were given venomous reviews by the Legion. *Morocco,* a 1930 production with Marlene Dietrich as a cabaret singer and Gary Cooper as Legionnaire Brown, was denounced by the *Légion étrangère,* the official magazine of the Legion, as yet another production of the "American nest, from which we rarely receive any good," which was an obvious attempt to discredit the Legion with "the habitual calumny and a complete incomprehension of the subject."[76] The production of *Le grand jeu* in 1934, which was enormously successful in France and more influential there than was *Beau Geste,* caused the Legion, through the *Amis de la Légion,* to intervene with the war minister, World War I hero Marshal Pétain, to have it censured. The president of the *Amis de la Légion,* American art dealer Philip Ortiz, objected to the depiction of legionnaires in the film as drunken, quarrelsome and generally indifferent to their military duties. He questioned the low moral tone of a story that essentially turned upon a conspiracy between a legion-naire and the wife of a cafe owner to murder her drunken husband. "One makes us live with the Legion in a vitiated, depressing, repugnant atmo-sphere," Ortiz complained. "At no time do they come to their senses. Nothing healthy, nothing invigorating. *No breath of fresh air in this film* [italics in original], nothing is presented as a sincere and authentic reflec-tion of the true life of the legionnaire."[77]

The critical success of *Le grand jeu* did not cause the Legion to retreat from what it believed to be the battle for its reputation. Protests were raised in April 1932 by Paul Rockwell over the publication of Ernst Loehndorf's *Hell in the Foreign Legion* as well as the favorable reviews accorded to Bennett Doty's *Legion of the Damned*, whose "sincerity and moral value of the book" were called into question.[78] In May 1934, the possibility of taking the BBC to court for "oral defamation" was discussed.[79] The 1926 production of *Beau Geste* was censured in France, while the celebrated 1939 version with Gary Cooper, Ray Milland and Robert Preston was forbidden altogether until 1977. *Condemned* with Ronald Colman was also banned because, like *Beau Geste,* it contained a scene of a Legion mutiny.[80] In 1936, the *Légion étrangère* complained bitterly about *Under Two Flags,* a film freely adapted from the Ouida classic, in which a former guards officer who enlists in the Legion is sent on a suicide mission by a Legion major after the major discovers that his mistress is in love with the legionnaire. "We have tried to make Hollywood understand what the Le-gion is," it editorialized in November 1936.

We have sent instructors, French observers and documentalists over there, but this has served and will serve for nothing, for the producers have their own ideas on this brilliant phalange and they want to present it to their public as they imagine it and as it is not.[81]

Defenders of the Legion, like Ortiz, in the hope of drumming up official support, claimed that unflattering films and novels about the Legion were in reality attacks upon France by Gallophobic foreigners. Ortiz begged the French government to subsidize a film on the Legion that would present a more favorable image.[82] The ministry replied on October 27, 1932, that "it seems preferable, as far as possible, to maintain a silence over the Foreign Legion."[83] A 1934 report agreed that the attacks against the Legion were "one of the manifestations of the propaganda against France abroad," and called for a government-sponsored film.[84] In 1937, the war ministry and the governor-general of Algeria subsidized the production costs of *Légions d'honneurs,* a film in which a legionnaire, an ex-officer, falls in love with his captain's wife, but chooses to seek a glorious death, for which he is awarded a Legion of Honor rather than dishonor her.

While the Legion was upset with many, perhaps most, of these films, in their essential aspects they were not at cross-purposes with the basic image that Rollet, Aage, Maire, Manue and Jean des Vallières, author of *Les hommes sans noms,* sought to project of the Legion. For instance, *Beau Geste,* which angered Rollet, supported several Legion myths. The story of three brothers who flee into the Legion, taking the blame for something they did not do, to protect the honor of their family bolstered the notion that behind every legionnaire lay a story of more than ordinary interest, suggested an upper-class presence in the ranks and delivered on the promise of redemption that Legion service was meant to bestow.

There appears to be little Rollet could quarrel with in Wren's description of Legion recruitment as

the usual sort of men of all ages whom one would see in the poorer streets of any town . . . they certainly did not look like rogues or criminals. Two or three out of a couple of dozen or so, were well-dressed and well spoken, and one of them, I felt sure, was an ex-officer of the French or Belgian army.

Wren is at pains to point out that the sadistic Sergeant Lejaune [Markoff in the 1939 film] is untypical of Legion NCOs: "Though these men were usually harsh and somewhat tyrannical martinets, they were not villainous brutes." In the film, Markoff is described as "a trifle uncouth, but the best soldier we'll ever see." The Gestes refuse to take part in the mutiny provoked by Lejaune because "to us it is unthinkable that we should stand by and see murder done, the regiment disgraced, the Flag betrayed, and the fort imperilled. . . . We are soldiers of France."

When they finally do desert, the American Buddy justifies it quite logically. First, the unit was in no danger. Second, "Hev you had a square deal in this Ma dam Lar Republic-house stunt?" he asks. "Nope. Didn't you and your brother stand by your dooty in this mutiny game? Yep. And then didn't this Lejaune guy start in to shoot you up? Shoot you up and some more. Shore. 'Taint a square deal."[85] As Jeffrey Richards concludes, *Beau Geste* "memorably dramatizes those attributes of a good public schoolboy—loyalty, comradeship, self-sacrifice, duty and honor."[86] However, perhaps Rollet realized that this subtle moral message was not invariably drawn from the material: "Had not Beau Geste established [in British eyes] the moral respectability, heroic virtue almost, of deserting from the Foreign Legion?" asked the Englishman Michael Alexander in the 1950s. "Wren went further: he made the brothers Geste desert during a military operation, wantonly set fire to valuable French government property [Fort Zinderneuf] and murder an N.C.O. *Quel geste alors!*"[87] But Wren obviously did not see his novel as an anti-Legion exposé, but merely the excuse to tell a ripping good yarn—in 1941 he wrote in the preface for Captain P.O. Lapie's *La Légion étrangère à Narvik,* "*Vive la Légion! Que son histoire vive à jamais!*"[88] "Long Live the Legion! May its history live forever!"

The themes of redemption, duty and the mysterious past were present in *Morocco,* a film apparently loathed by Rollet. The cabaret manager in Mogador in Morocco tells singer Amy Jolly not to spend time with the legionnaires at their tables, but rather to concentrate her attentions upon the officers. It is untrue that legionnaires are ex-generals or aristocrats who joined to forget the past—"At 75 centimes a day, they are nobody," he tells her. "Talk to the officers, they have the money." But she is fatally attracted to Legionnaire Brown, played by Gary Cooper, whom she attempts to entice to desert. Steeled against her considerable charms, however, Brown remains loyal to the Legion. In fact, it is Amy Jolly who deserts the cabaret circuit to become a camp follower—the final scene finds her following Brown's regiment as it marches out of the gates of Mogador and over the inevitable sand dune, still clutching her now useless high-heeled shoes. The strong message is that honor among men, especially legionnaires, is more important than the love of a woman. While one might expect Rollet to have objected to a scene in which Captain César attempts to get Brown killed but is himself shot, instead he complained of "half-naked native women," the poor marching order of the legionnaires, of legionnaires and their NCOs drinking in easy familiarity with the *"femmes du monde* in a low dance hall, and the setting of Mogador, which was far away from the actual Moroccan fighting. Rollet succeeded in having *Morocco* banned in North Africa.[89]

In the final analysis, the novels and films on the Legion relied for their success, like the Legion propagandists, on stereotyped characters, basic ideas and simplified assumptions.[90] French historian André-Paul Comor has written that once the image of the Legion was formed in the public mind, it was merely a question of "diffusing the well known clichés."[91] The depiction of the legionnaires of *Le grand jeu* as, in the words of one critic, "rather colorless marionettes" who off the battlefield appear "incapable of dominating their life"[92] is not far off that projected by pro-Legion writers. These are precisely "life's vanquished men" celebrated by Manue.[93]

The reproach against the Legion made on the outside was that the *anonymat* served as a cover for criminals, or that legionnaires were exploited by a discipline that was severe to the point of brutality, charges that Legion propagandists denied vehemently. Training and discipline were hard, but this was necessary to meld disparate elements into a solid unit. With men such as these, officers had to be understanding, paternalistic, but not weak or sentimental. "With these beings who have suffered in their past lives . . . one must destroy everything," Robert is told in Weygand's *Légionnaire.* "The principal objective is to forbid them to think . . ."[94] For the leisure to reflect inevitably brought on a bout of *cafard* in whose clutches legionnaires were capable of the most desperate and irrational acts. The Legion offered permanent custodial service with the option of rehabilitation.

For a man who commanded the summits of Legion psychology and who displayed such a deft feel for public relations, Rollet's strong objections to much of this outpouring of popular interest in the Legion is somewhat surprising. Most of it was a reflection of popular taste, rather than a specific attack on the Legion. The public wanted certain themes and plots that could be adapted just as well to a setting provided by the Legion, the Far West, or the British Empire. Nor was the message, though subtle, invariably unfavorable—quite the contrary! Even if the literary and popular image of the Legion was a contradictory one, at the very least the corps profited from the publicity. At best, the publicity was extremely positive, or at least intriguing. Each potential recruit had to reconcile the images to his own satisfaction and make the decision to enlist or stay home. But any potentially bad publicity was easily reasoned away: "I had no childish illusions," wrote Bennett Doty, who was attracted away from a boring office job in New York by colorful accounts of the Rif War. "The books I had read about the Legion were rather black ones. But I thought, 'In those there is as much apple-sauce as in the giddy romantic Ouida ones. The truth is somewhere in between and I'll soon find out.' " One thing he did discover was that Sergeant Lejaune was complete fiction: "As a matter of fact that would be impossible in the Legion. A brutal sergeant would not live long in a hard-boiled outfit like the Legion. He'd be murdered in his sleep."[95] But at the very least, some men took the depictions of Legion brutality as a challenge, and the test of taking the worst a Legion NCO like Lejaune had to throw at them as the best means of taking the measure of their toughness.

Nor did these films put off London stockbroker Brian Stuart, rather short of work in 1930: "I forget the title of the film being shown at the cinema," he wrote,

but it was of the blood, bullets, bayonets and brutality variety—with a few luscious Arab maidens here and there—dealing with the French Foreign Legion. The Mars benedictine hummed happily in my interior and the Arab maidens were very luscious indeed. The blue smoke of a Balkan Sobranie curled above my head as I descended the marble staircase and out into Charing Cross Road. I made up my mind to join the Foreign Legion.[96]

The Cork (Ireland) *Examiner* believed that *Beau Geste* had started a vogue for the Legion that had encouraged English and Irish to join.[97] A 1934 report concluded that the bad publicity had not hurt Legion recruitment, but had actually boosted it: "The campaign of defamation carried out in certain countries against the Foreign Legion is not new," it reported.

It has never compromised its recruitment. The Germans even concede bitterly that it has favored it. . . . For some time, the Legion has been à la mode with film directors, journalists and novelists. One has talked a lot, usually saying the same old thing. The Legion would gain by rediscovering the mystery of silence.[98]

The Englishman Simon Murray claimed that his decision to enlist in the Legion fresh from school at age nineteen during the Algerian War was motivated in part by his reading of *Beau Geste*: "What I did not know at the time was that Wren had painted a picture of the Legion that was not all that inaccurate," he wrote, "and I was about to step into a very hard way of life indeed for which I was totally unprepared." When things began to disappear in the barracks, he did expect the thief, once caught, to be given the "traditional" treatment *à la Beau Geste* of being laid out spread-eagle on a table with bayonets rammed through his hands, an assertion repeated as fact in a more recent Legion memoir.[99]

Successful films like *Sergent X* (1931) and *Un de la Légion,* released in 1936 and starring the popular comic actor Fernandel, and music with a Legion theme like Vincent Scotto's 1937 operetta *Ceux de la Légion,* as well as the popular songs like *Mon légionnaire* and *Le fanion de la Légion,* made immensely popular by singers like Marie Dubas and Edith Piaf in 1938, testified to a burst of popular interest in the Legion that did cause it to pay more attention to its public image. One of the most important elements of this concern, certainly in recruitment, was believed to be the impressions of their service by ex-legionnaires. According to a 1934 report, the best defense against bad publicity was to "return to civilian life Legionnaires content with their condition, proud of their years of service and these old soldiers will know themselves and better than others, once back home, how to reestablish the truth."[100] It was axiomatic in the Legion that the best recruiting propaganda was provided by ex-legionnaires. Unfortunately, many legionnaires had occasion to be bitter at the way they were treated upon liberation. Many, French and foreign, were refused work permits and even pensions because of the complicated technicalities of French administrative regulations.[101] Legionnaires repatriated after having contracted diseases in the colonies were released from the hospitals, cured or not, after a certain number of days and dumped on the streets, where they were sometimes arrested by the police for *"vagabondage"* and expelled from the country. Others might wait years for naturalization papers, and, refused passports by their consuls because they had served in the Legion, were denied work or often arrested by French police—on December 15, 1938, thirty-four ex-legionnaires were detained in the prisons of Marseille, Aix-en-Provence and Toulon because they had no papers. This shabby treatment of men who had often fought and been wounded in French service raised fears of lower recruitment.[102] "When [legionnaires] are liberated, they are thrown *without resources* into civilian life," read a 1937 report. "All sorts of difficulties await them there (in France as well as abroad) and they too often became human wrecks. *This situation furnishes to foreign propaganda its best arguments. It is paralyzing recruitment efforts.* [Italics in original]"[103]

In 1898, Colonel de Villebois-Mareuil had founded *La Légion,* a mutualist society that had around a dozen branches by the outbreak of the war. In 1919, General Mordacq had called upon the president of *La Légion* to help him pass the bill on the creation of a Legion division.[104] However, the problem in this period was to coordinate efforts to help liberated legionnaires. These efforts were hurt by a rivalry between the *Société des centres d'entr'aide aux réformés et libérés de la Légion étrangère* and the *Amis de la Légion,* organized by the American Philip Ortiz. An art dealer living in Paris, Ortiz had been horrified when his adolescent son joined the Legion, but after being treated to a personal guided tour of Sidi-bel-Abbès by none other than Rollet, he subsequently became one of its most fervent supporters.[105]

Yet despite modest, even contentious beginnings, these efforts did create a network of ex-legionnaires to defend Legion interests and keep traditions alive, even to lay the foundations for what would become a wealthy organization dedicated to the well-being of legionnaires in and out of uniform. It gave the Legion a means to formalize relationships among its old boys, to enhance the sense of fraternity through shared experiences: "Whatever their condition," wrote Jean Martin,

a porter, a retired officer, a newspaper vendor at the entrance of the metro, a businessman who stopped at the curb in a sumptuous car, a small old man who had gained weight, a German visiting Paris as a tourist, all spoke with sadness of the time spent out there, all lingered over the old memories of the bled, *and took pleasure to see and hear someone who just returned, and, to prolong the interview, all offered: "Say, let's have a drink." Even if the veteran had no money to eat.*[106]

The Legion was not entirely seduced by its own propaganda, however. As the political situation in Europe became more troubled in the 1930s, it became clear to the Legion that it might be vulnerable to political agitation. In 1933, the *Service d'immatriculation de la Légion étrangère,* which kept an eye on recruitment, complained that the large number of Italians enlisting posed a security risk in North Africa.[107] A 1934 report expressed the fear that, in the event of a European war, French, Belgians and Swiss would be dispatched to Europe, leaving North Africa in the care of its German recruits. "It would be imprudent to go by the experience of the last war," the report read,

for it is certain that in the case of a new conflict, the Legion would be much more undermined than it has ever been. The present intrigues of certain powers against our authority in North Africa leave no doubt on this subject.

This situation was especially dangerous as the only other white infantry in North Africa, the *zouaves* and the marines, were "very mediocre and their poor quality does not escape legionnaires." For these reasons, "the security of French North Africa must be confided almost uniquely to the loyalty of the Legion and the regiments of North African tirailleurs. Therefore, it is this loyalty that one must obtain and conserve intact."[108] This proved a prophetic report: In May 1936, a series of "communist and revolutionary . . . demonstrations of indiscipline in general isolated, rarely collective," occurred in the *1er étranger* "in close liaison with the political events in the metropole [a reference to the election of the left-wing Popular Front and widespread strikes], insidious and at the same time very active." Although the demonstrations, the work of "undesirable French elements of which the number does not cease to grow each month," were severely dealt with, the report recommended vigilance.[109]

This was especially true of the Germans. The number of German recruits had diminished drastically by 1936, because of the Spanish Civil War and the "draconian measures taken by the III Reich toward their nationals desiring to enlist in the Foreign Legion." Rapid German rearmament also absorbed many potential German recruits. Already the number of Germans in the Legion had dropped from 37 percent in 1934 to 19.2 percent in 1935.[110] By February 1937, only 11 percent of recruits were German.[111] A 1935 report noted that the German police confiscated the military record books, good conduct certificates and medals of legionnaires returning to Germany, and made their lives a misery as an example to young Germans who might otherwise be tempted to enlist. German legionnaires returning home were also interrogated thoroughly on their service.

Those Germans who still came forward were in the main left-wing political opponents of Hitler and many Jews, who "are not generally speaking first class military elements."[112] A 1937 report noted that German Jews were "of a generally revolutionary tendency," while even those Germans forced to return to the Legion by political harassment "look favorably upon the attempts by the Third Reich to recover its colonies and increase the force of its permanent army."[113] However, Colonel Azan, commander of the *1er étranger,* reported in the same year that the "immense majority" of legionnaires had remained indifferent to Nazi propaganda.[114]

This was not the case in the following year, when Azan wrote that, with the exception of those who had enlisted for political reasons, the *Anschluss* had been greeted with "profound joy" by Germans, Austrians and Czechs of German origin. "I no longer think of requesting French naturalization," one legionnaire wrote home, "because I am too profoundly German." Azan's remedy for this political effervescence was one of which Rollet would have approved—to increase military ceremony, "to revivify in the hearts of the veterans and above all [in those of] the young legionnaires sentiments of pride, *esprit de corps* and respect for traditions."[115] In April 1938, General Georges Catroux, an ex-Legion officer and by 1938 commanding general of the 19th Army Corps, warned that German legionnaires were "exalted" by the success of Hitler's diplomacy, especially the *Anschluss,* which had even shaken the faith of non-German legionnaires in French resolve. But he believed that Legion *esprit de corps* would successfully weather the political storm.[116]

Subversion by foreigners appears to have offered a minimal threat to Legion efficiency. Potentially more damaging was the reappearance of a situation all too familiar in the "Old Legion"—an influx of "loyal" but worthless Frenchmen, "old chasseurs of the Bataillons d'Afrique, or ex-colonials [marines]," which had been noted since 1933.[117] It was the revival of the "Old Legion" with a vengeance. Colonel Azan complained in April 1938 that recent enlistments were "very mediocre and it is not desirable to see their numbers increase."[118]

This is not to say that the Legion did not take precautions against subversion in the ranks. The first was to remove Germans from sensitive positions, like that of radio operator.[119] The second, another inspiration of Colonel Azan, was to distribute a *"Memento du Légionnaire,"* a list of duties expected of legionnaires running to sixty-two pages, which, apart from its length and rather emotional style, was similar to that issued to American soldiers following the Korean War, when the collaboration of U.S. POWs with the communists revealed that many lacked the most elementary notions of loyalty. This list stressed the individual commitment of the legionnaire to the Legion, as exemplified by the contract. The example of the *anciens* was continually cited as a model to emulate: "Like your *anciens,* you will serve with all the force of your soul, and if necessary up to the supreme sacrifice," it declared. "This LEGION is your new FATHERLAND and you will always cherish in your heart this device: 'LEGIO PATRIA NOSTRA.' " And on it went, very much in keeping with the popular and official myths, praising the essential humanity of the corps, admonishing legionnaires to "forget a doubtful or bitter past," calling upon them to give complete loyalty and confidence to their officers, even to be "passionately devoted" to them "to the point of sacrifice," as they are "your companions in suffering and in danger." (Obviously, the brochure was composed by an officer.) "It is this discipline, strict but freely accepted, that makes the strength of our 'Old Legion.' " Even leisure activities were provided for: "You must never remain deaf to cries of '*A MOI LA LEGION,*' " which was declared a "sacred call."

Those in authority were charged with being fair but firm in discipline. But more, "You will know by heart perfectly the history of our Old Legion, and inculcate with love the centenary traditions to your subordinates. You will also tell them of the countries where [the Legion] has fought and the battlefields where it made itself illustrious. You will name for them the main heroes and will comment on their acts." The objectivity of this history is thrown into serious doubt by the insistence that "Never has the enemy been able to claim that he made the Legion retreat nor resist its bayonets. Never has the Legion abandoned its dead, its wounded, its arms or its matériel to the enemy. Never has a legionnaire surrendered to the enemy."[120]

The third was to step up surveillance of legionnaires. Cooper insisted that a sort of informal secret service existed in the Legion in the early 1920s, and that he was asked to make reports on the sutlers in Morocco, many of whom were Moslems and as such were suspected of informing Moroccan dissidents of operations, of buying weapons from legionnaires, and of encouraging desertion. He was also asked to send in reports periodically on the state of morale in his company to a sergeant operating out of the hospital at Sidi-bel-Abbès.[121] Orders were sent out to each regiment in the early 1930s to "exercise surveillance over NCOs and legionnaires in their relations: with their countries of origin; with the civil population and the local communist organizations. Several elements classed as 'doubtful' have been under a particular surveillance."[122]

Finally, on February 17, 1937, "The Intelligence Service" of the Foreign Legion was formally organized. Its mission statement insisted that the Legion was a potential refuge for dangerous elements and vulnerable to foreign agents who might try to undermine its morale: "The morale of this troop can vary with the international situation . . . the attitude of certain elements and their relations with their countries of origin are worth special surveillance." It was also given the mission to seek out foreign spies planted in the Legion, or to recruit legionnaires who might spy on the enemy. It was also to centralize all information coming from Legion units and pass it on to the intelligence service of the General Staff. The Legion intelligence service included the *Bureau des statistiques de la Légion étrangère* (BSLE) at Sidi-bel-Abbès, commanded by a major, with an adjutant who spoke fluent German, and three NCOs, "preferably French, polyglot and offering all guarantees." Its job was to carry out postal censorship, centralized intelligence including that on foreign armies (presumably obtained from interrogating foreign legionnaires), and provide information on legionnaires soon to be released who might make suitable agents. Beneath the BSLE was the *Service d'immatriculation de la Légion* (SIL), whose job it was to control recruitment, "to interrogate recruits in an in-depth manner," with a view of eliminating undesirable elements. It also helped legionnaires reintegrate into civilian life.[123]

But while some sort of surveillance was no doubt necessary in a corps vulnerable to desertion and even to treason, the presence of *mouchards* or "grasses" in the ranks caused problems. "The use of these informers was notorious," wrote Liddell Hart, "and though it may have been justifiable for security reasons, the system of espionage and denunciation was abused for all kinds of personal reasons." Some flaunted their power, real or imagined, to denounce other legionnaires, which sometimes earned them beatings.[124] Simon Murray, who came from an upper-middle-class background, was told by his company sergeant that his promotion to corporal had been blocked by the BSLE because they could not figure out "who I am and what the hell I am doing here."[125] So much for *Beau Geste*!

The interwar years were decisive ones for the Legion, not the least because it pulled off a triumph of public relations in the process of confirming, once again, the unique mercenary character of the corps. If achievement can be measured against intentions, then Rollet and others who set out in 1919 to recreate the "Old Legion" may be said to have succeeded brilliantly. Although this official campaign of character affirmation was in part a response to what the Legion saw as a deliberate attempt at character assassination orchestrated by Hollywood and popular novelists, in fact the contribution of those elements was essential to the success of the Legion myth. Not only did this myth contribute to regimental cohesion and the fighting potential of the unit. It also served to bring the Legion to the attention of a broad public, to romanticize it and in the process to justify it as an institution that serves a human ideal.

The myth of the Legion, to which Hollywood and P. C. Wren contributed as well as Rollet, allowed it to survive and prosper. By codifying and dramatizing its sense of personality, the Legion was able to maintain an even keel in the treacherous waters of the interwar years and World War II. The twin functions of exile and rehabilitation made it a "natural" refuge for Nazis after 1945. Its military reputation permitted the French to cheer it on the Champs Elysées, caused Germans and other foreigners to show themselves willing to enlist and die in its service, and even pardoned the rebellion of certain of its members against President Charles de Gaulle in 1961. "Essentially the Legion is a legend, an idea," wrote Adrian Liddell Hart.

It exists in the situation of the moment; it responds to a challenge. It is influenced more by what people think it is than what it has been. . . . Its survival is due at least as much to its human mystique as to any military genius.[126]

However, the successful re-creation and institutionalization of the "Old Legion" was a weakness as well as a strength. What the myth had achieved was the triumph of an intentionally anachronistic vision, the prolongation of a nineteenth-century image of the Legion as a relatively small band of white men doing battle with people of color on the distant frontiers of the empire. It was in these conditions that the mercenary spirit best survived, when ideologies and competing group loyalties could be submerged into a common sense of being European in an alien world. Yet this corps with its obvious preference for Germans and insistence that it was a tight brotherhood with special psychological needs requiring special qualities of leadership had responded sluggishly to the challenges of integrating foreign volunteers in 1914. And while it had eventually achieved glory on the Western Front, it had also created conditions that threatened its recruitment and continued presence in France by the late summer of 1918.

In the final analysis, one may wonder if it were wise policy, and one in French interests, to define an esprit de corps for the Legion in terms that were almost defiantly anachronistic in the ideologically polarized world of the 1930s. Was this not to fit the Legion into a straitjacket of the mercenary mentality at the very moment when nations, as well as many of the Legion's recruits, were staking out their positions in even more ideological terms than in 1914? Rollet had certainly re-created the "Old Legion." But how would this revivified "Old Legion" adapt to the renewed challenges of world war? "When war breaks out between the countries: Germany, France, England, all the others, the Legion has a tough time staying herself, with the volunteers for the duration of the war," wrote legionnaire Giulio Cesare Silvagni, in terms that recalled the attitudes of veteran legionnaires of 1914. "There are some good ones. That's for sure. But they have not known the *bled*."[127]

Chapter 21

"CAUSE FOR HOPE" — THE LEGION IN THE FALL OF FRANCE, 1940

THE YEAR 1940 MARKED FRANCE'S military nadir. The collapse of an army regarded by many as the best hope for the defense of Western democracy was so stunning that even its German conquerors were caught by surprise. Paradoxically, perhaps, the Legion could look back with some satisfaction upon a year that witnessed the humiliation of the French army, for the foreigners in French service had fought well when all was collapsing around them. On the one hand, a sound battlefield performance was perhaps to be expected from a corps that took pride in its character as a professional unit in an overwhelmingly conscript force. However, one of the ironies of 1940 was that the Legion that took the field against the *Wehrmacht* was very much a modified version of the "Old Legion" that had been reconstituted so meticulously by Legion officers and propagandists from the wreckage of World War I. Many of its members were reluctant legionnaires, while the more traditional Legion formations were upstaged to a degree by the performance of a group of patriotic volunteers and political refugees hastily transformed into legionnaires.

The decision of the French government to ghettoize foreign volunteers into specially created units brought on many of the problems of adaptation, confusion and misunderstanding that had characterized the incorporation of foreign volunteers in 1914. However, the confrontation between the professional legionnaires and the volunteers for the duration of the war was more acute in 1939–40 than it had been in 1914, for at least two reasons. First, the Legion was more self-consciously "professional" by

1940, while, second, its recruits, most of whom were refugees from the ideological confrontations of the 1930s, were more aggressively political. While many of the volunteers of 1939–40 came forward to serve France as they had in 1914, many also saw enlistment in the French army as a means of continuing the struggle against fascism that they had begun elsewhere. As France was in the front line, it was the natural place to fight a war heavy with ideological and moral content.

As in 1914, this situation naturally brought about a head-on collision between the ideal of France as the standard-bearer of democracy and international justice behind which all right-thinking men should rally, and the reality that this meant service in a unit whose mercenary and even brutal image had been extended and confirmed in the popular mind in the interwar years. To be fair to France, the tradition of asylum had been placed under serious strain, especially since 1938. An avalanche of refugees from the Spanish Civil War had joined the flow of Jews and others out of Germany, which soon turned to a flood as Hitler intensified policies of political repression at home and marched his regiments into Austria and eventually Czechoslovakia. German police would often transport their Jews and political undesirables to the French frontier and fling them penniless over the border. In a country already suffering from the economic problems of the Depression, these people could not possibly be absorbed into the work force. However, gathered in internment camps such as those organized for the hundreds of thousands of Spanish refugees in the south, they cost the French government vast sums of money that it could ill afford. Furthermore, many, especially on the right, saw them as a potential security threat.

If the decision to place foreign volunteers in the Legion, or at least in separate foreign regiments, was in effect simply the continuation of a policy of nonassimilation that had been followed by the government before the war, it was to have two consequences for the Legion. The first was to introduce politics into Legion life, a process extended by the Gaullist/Vichy split in the Legion in 1940. It became difficult for the Legion to maintain its ideal of a professional force aloof from politics when many of its recruits were passionately political: "Divided between partisans and adversaries of Hitler, the Germans discovered themselves to be antagonistic brothers ready to kill each other," wrote Charles Favrel of the political debates that broke out in the barracks.

The Hitlerites said they weren't going to fight, while the "antis" declared themselves volunteers for the front and made pronouncements which would have brought tears to the eyes of President Lebrun [president of the Third Republic]. . . . The Spanish ex-militiamen stirred up the discussions by mixing in fascism and Franco, the Czechs took on the Sudeten Germans, the Poles denounced both the nazis and the reds, Hitler and Stalin, but everyone abused the two or three Italians who had not yet decided which side to be on.[1]

The second problem was in many ways a corollary of the first. While it certainly would be going too far to say that the Legion experienced discipline problems or even a crisis of morale in 1939–40, it was nevertheless true that the volunteers for the duration of the war were less amenable to traditional Legion methods of indoctrination, which they believed to be unacceptably anachronistic, regulations and practices fashioned for men of another era and another mind-set. Consequently, as in 1914, the relationship between the Legion and many of its new recruits would be marked by friction and even distrust.

LEGION TRADITIONALISTS HAD been struggling to maintain the professional equilibrium of their corps even before 1939 brought a deluge of foreign recruits into its ranks. Violent fluctuations in recruitment that began in March 1932, when the government, in the throes of the Depression and desperate to economize, ordered a 25 percent reduction in strength, made it difficult administratively to keep the corps on an even keel. By 1934, enlistments barely topped 1,000, down from a 1931 high of 7,081, and numbers had retracted from over 33,000 men in 1933 to 20,445 men by 1935. With war looming in 1938, Paris reversed its policy and began to encourage enlistments, even to the point of placing advertisements in foreign newspapers, sending money to organizations of Legion veterans abroad, alerting frontier police to be on the lookout for prime recruitment prospects. Yet Franco, Hitler, and to a lesser extent Mussolini proved to be far better recruiting agents than even the French police. By 1939, the number of German political refugees, many of them Jews or left-wing opponents of the Nazis, coming into the Legion was substantial. The end of the Spanish Civil War in that year witnessed the enlistment of 3,052 Spaniards, most of them refugees of the defeated republican armies. In March 1939, Hitler occupied Czechoslovakia, which produced 801 Czech volunteers, among them Charles Hora. "You must enlist in the Foreign Legion," the Czech military attaché in Paris told him, "because you will find no work in France. What's more, this will permit you to rejoin later the national Czech forces, when the war breaks out."[2]

The general mobilization of September 1, 1939, which coincided with the German attack upon Poland, inundated Rollet's "Old Legion" with new arrivals. Although a law of April 12, 1939, allowed foreigners resident in France for ten years to enlist in French line regiments, either many of the refugees did not qualify or the military administration chose to apply it in an eccentric and often arbitrary fashion. A further decree of December 29, 1939, permitted citizens of neutral countries to enlist in a restricted number of regular French formations,[3] another ministerial pronouncement that appears to have been dead on arrival largely because the war ministry undercut in private the pronouncements it made in public. A ministerial note of November 13, 1939, cautioned against the incorporation of "undesirable elements whose loyalties are sometimes suspect" into French regiments, and suggested that these positions should be reserved for foreigners with special skills.[4] However, even skills desperately needed by the French army were often not qualification enough to secure a place there. For instance, French intelligence officer Gustave Bertrand was forced to enlist Spanish and Polish cryptographers expert in German codes into the Foreign Legion before he could use them because "civilians were not allowed in the temple" and no other option was available to them within the French army.[5]

In 1939, as in 1914, the French again demonstrated their deeply ambivalent attitudes toward the foreigners who volunteered to defend them. "[The foreigners] invaded the recruitment bureaux, eager to join the army and defend France," wrote Joseph Ratz, a Russian emigré, who volunteered for service in 1939, only to be confronted by functionaries who "wandered among the administrative formalities, legal paragraphs and restrictions imposed upon foreigners."[6] When many Jews of Polish origin who had lived in France for years came forward to serve, they were directed toward the Polish army in exile, only to find that Jews were not welcome there.[7] Refugees of more recent date were also victims of confused policies—French police carried out frequent identity checks, and offered men of military age without enlistment papers the choice between enlistment, expulsion or internment. The internment of "undesirable aliens" was permitted from November 2, 1938, and its scope was extended in December 1939. However, many foreigners who attempted to enlist found recruitment bureaus closed to them. In part this resulted from the fact that the French army simply could not cope with the numbers of volunteers, so that refugee organizations established lists of potential recruits as a gesture of good will, as in 1914.[8] Others were declared undesirable: On September 8, 1939, the war minister ordered Germans, Austrians and Italians excluded from the French army, as well as Czechs unable to prove their nationality.[9] The ban on German and Austrian refugees was lifted in October, when they were allowed to enlist in the Legion. Also in October, the Italian consul at Toulouse complained that Italians living in the South of France were being pressured into the Legion: "It seems that a certain state of mind has caused some mayors or police to pressure several people of Italian origin to make them enlist," read a September 21, 1939, report, which pointed out that the French were upset when mobilization often forced them to close their businesses to the profit of those run by Italians. "Sometimes the population also pushed the transalpines to enlist through fear of harassment or even of violence."[10] Officially, 639 Italians enlisted in the Legion in 1939, many of whom military officials feared were communists.[11]

ON SEPTEMBER 16, 1939, the war minister decided to form special corps of foreign volunteers independent of the Foreign Legion,[12] presumably in an attempt to avoid the sort of conflicts that had occurred in 1914. To make certain that these units of foreign volunteers would be in no way confused with the "real" Legion, which wanted to distance itself from them, they were assigned numbers superior to 20 from February 1940, and so became the *21e, 22e* and *23e régiments de marche des volontaires étrangers* (RMVE). However, while the Legion in this period considered the RMVE to be entirely separate organizations, to say that the RMVE had no ties to the Foreign Legion would be inaccurate. Some cadres were furnished by the Legion in North Africa as well as Legion reservists recalled to train them, while photographs show the band of the 21e RMVE bearing the Legion crest and colors. The 21st also celebrated Camerone in 1940, a definite attempt to establish a link with the Legion.[13] In his after-action report, Major Hermann, who commanded the 22e RMVE, referred to his men as "legionnaires."[14]

The assignment of foreign volunteers, most of whom did not speak sufficient French to understand the distinction between the RMVE and the Legion or who signed their enlistment papers oblivious to the fact that they were signed on for five years or for the "duration of hostilities," appears to have depended upon the whim, fancy or ministerial directive of the over-worked recruitment bureaus. Nor were those sent to the RMVE safe from the long arm of the Legion, for in February 1940, nine hundred men were dispatched from the training camps of the RMVE to the newly created *12e étranger*. This action ignited a bureaucratic debate over whether or not they should be required to sign new contracts, which was apparently not resolved when the German offensive of May 10, 1940, ended the period of Phony War.[15] Therefore, it appears that around nine hundred RMVE volunteers actually fought in a regular Legion unit. Furthermore, the Legion has since recognized the veterans of the RMVE as bona fide *anciens combattants*. Last, if the French government could draw fine administrative distinctions between the RMVE and the Legion proper, many foreigners could not. In the minds of many, they had been assigned to the Legion. A ministerial note of October 26, 1939, echoed the concerns of 1914 when it noted that foreigners were "surprised" to be assigned to the RMVE and "showed some apprehension at serving in the Foreign Legion."[16]

The Legion (excluding the RMVE) counted the *1er, 2e, 3e, 4e, 5e* and *6e régiments étrangers* and the *1er* and *2e régiments étrangers de cavalerie* (REC) by 1939. However, the Legion in 1940, as in 1914–18, would remain essentially an imperial force. Of course, France had legitimate im-perial interests to defend, and as in the past proved reluctant to surrender their security entirely to perhaps untrustworthy indigenous levies. This is not to say that the Legion made no direct contribution to the defense of

France—quite the contrary. Merely that the Legion's contribution might have been greater and more effective had constituted Legion regiments been shipped to France and refugees and most other foreign volunteers integrated into French line regiments—all that professionalism, all that tradition carefully nurtured by Rollet, all those celebrities of the popular cinema who "smelled of warm sand," whose mere appearance on the Maginot Line would have reduced the *Wehrmacht* to jelly, left to molder in colonial outposts, or split up and showered upon hordes of European exiles for whom the attentions of these mercenary soldiers seemed at best a dubious honor, at worst an insult.

To cope with the requests by foreigners to enlist in the French army, requests that stood at sixty-four thousand by October 15, 1939, the 6e *étranger* was organized out of the Legion battalions stationed in Syria and given its own artillery; the 11e *étranger* was created in November 1939, followed by the 12e *étranger* in February 1940 to fight in France. A 13th *demi-brigade,* the Legion unit that eventually emerged as the most celebrated of World War II, was formed in February of 1940 to operate in Finland, later in Norway. Last, a *groupe de reconnaissance de division d'infanterie no.* 97 (GRD 97) was furnished by the two RECs to fight in France. A December 1939 offer by the ubiquitous Charles Sweeney, veteran of the RMLE and leader of the short-lived *escadrille chérifienne* during the Rif War, to raise a corps of American volunteers appears to have been taken seriously only in May 1940, by which time all bets were off.[17]

Not surprisingly, perhaps, the amalgamation and training of such large numbers of foreigners—by February 1940, eighty-three thousand foreigners, almost double the number to have volunteered during World War I, had asked to enlist[18]—did not go smoothly. However, the problems were not entirely logistical ones. As in 1914, "Many of these foreigners have manifested a certain apprehension at being placed in the Foreign Legion," read a January 1940 report, which admitted that many sought naturalization and a transfer to French line regiments. Not to worry, however, for "if certain foreigners pretend that they do not want to serve in the Legion, it is because they do not know the Legion." They would be swept up by its proud traditions once they had joined. "The foreign volunteers of 1914 would have accomplished nothing had they not been put into the Legion, but, through the Legion, they wrote a most splendid page of history (1914–18) for they became true legionnaires,"[19] the report asserted with great confidence.

If the foreign volunteers were apprehensive about the Legion, the Legion reciprocated with apprehensions of its own. Although many nationalities, including Afghans, Chinese and most South American nations, were represented among the volunteers, Legion officers were deeply suspicious of the two groups that furnished the lion's share of recruits—Spanish Republicans and Jews from Eastern Europe. In some respects, their fears were perfectly justified. Conventional wisdom held that the Legion functioned best when its nationalities were delicately balanced, its leadership suitably Olympian, and when regimental loyalties transcended all others. It was not that Legion methods did not work; merely, it was recognized that they did not work for everyone. And the political turmoil of the interwar years sent into the Legion recruits upon whom its regimental magic might exercise only limited powers. Eastern European refugees especially were middle class, a group traditionally able to distinguish rapidly between the romanticism and realities of Legion life. Older, often very well educated, they were deeply out of sympathy with the culture of the barracks in which social acceptance was earned after a novitiate of bullying, brawling, drinking and womanizing. For them, the Legion offered a marriage between a monastery and a penal colony. The only Legion tradition most were likely to find seductive was that of desertion.

The deep ideological divisions of interwar Europe of which most were victims also militated against the formation of a regimental spirit on the Legion model. Legion propaganda to the contrary, it was difficult to convince men who often had sacrificed much for nation, religion or political ideology to limit their horizons to the barracks square. To consign such men to the Legion was to invite incomprehension and conflict. These were temporary soldiers fighting for a cause, men with a personal stake in the war's outcome, whose attitudes differed sharply from those of the professionals who had fled into the Legion in part to escape a modern world with which they were out of sync and sympathy. For legionnaires, fighting was a *métier,* not a crusade, a contest of military skills—cool, detached, impersonal.

From the Legion's viewpoint, committed ideologists not only made poor recruits, they could also be dangerous. The official harassment of German veterans of the Legion by the Nazi government after 1934 had largely removed the threat from the right. While fears persisted that the Legion might be infiltrated by German spies, and a few German legionnaires expressed great admiration for the accomplishments of the Third Reich, Nazis of conviction were too few to disrupt regimental spirit. The same could not be said of many of the Spaniards and Jews, men of the left whose political convictions, in the eyes of many Legion officers, posed a serious threat to Legion *esprit de corps.*

A third category of men whom the Legion discovered assimilated poorly in 1939 was composed of about one thousand reservists, exlegionnaires, whom the government recalled to provide experienced cadres for the new Legion formations. Sergeant Georges Manue, reunited with his old corps fifteen years on, discovered that many of his fellow reservists were unsettled by this brutal reunion with a past that had been lived in a long-forgotten spirit of youthful fantasy. The sacred Legion fire had all but died out among those who had acquired wives and children, for whom the mere memories of Legion training made their aging bodies ache, or who, having survived the Legion once, did not feel up to an encore, especially if the Legion experience in World War I were any indication of what awaited them. " 'I don't feel ready for this job,' " Manue recalled being told, "a hundred times. 'I'm old, I've wife and child, I've earned the right to a nice, quiet regiment.' "[20]

The arrival of the Spanish in great numbers with the defeat of the Republican armies in 1939 challenged the equilibrium of the Legion to the point that some have claimed that it altered the personality of the corps in this period. This was probably an exaggeration, as even though 3,052, or 27.7 percent, of the men enlisting in the Legion in 1939 were Spanish, the corps was expanding so rapidly in that year that the Legion only counted 8.2 percent Spaniards overall.[21] Nevertheless, these numbers certainly do not include those assigned to the RMVE, whose combat elements appear to have included 2,709 Spaniards in February 1940, or about 40 percent of combat strength.[22] It is also important to note that at the time their arrival caused great consternation. Captain P. O. Lapie of the *13ᵉ demi-brigade* recorded that his fellow officers were very reticent about accepting the Spaniards, "whom they referred to *en bloc* as the communists."[23] In June 1939, the war ministry directed that the Spaniards be sent to Morocco for training, "in the southern regions as far as possible from the Spanish possessions," and be given regular Legion officers and NCOs so that they can acquire "the spirit proper to the Legion."[24]

This was easier said than done. When Legion corporal Alfred Perrot-White took delivery of a contingent of two hundred Spaniards to train in January 1939, he realized that his work was cut out for him: "We had plenty of trouble in store handling those men," he wrote.

They were for the most part sullen and ill disciplined, very sick about joining the Legion in the first place, and with only one thought in mind— that being to desert across the Franco-Spanish border of Morocco. In fact, at one time conditions became so bad that practically the whole garrison at Gérryville was used as a police force to keep the Spanish company in order. There were many fights with knives and guns, and wholesale desertions, but not one was successful. I believe more than ten men were killed in the attempt, but, as always happens in the Legion, the officers and N.C.O.s held the upper hand. Discipline began to show, and before these men finished their training, they had more or less—outwardly at least—settled down to facing the inevitable.[25]

The war minister warned against this policy of keeping Spanish recruits together, and in July 1939 called for the Spaniards to be distributed among the various foreign regiments, taking care that they did not exceed 14 percent of strength,[26] a policy that was somewhat undermined on October 5 of that year when he ordered that the Spaniards must be kept separate from the others.[27] This was the case at the training camp at Vancia, near Lyon, where "We were forbidden to fraternize with [the Spaniards], to train with them, even to speak to them," wrote Zosa Szajkowski, a volunteer in the *12ᵉ étranger.*

They were isolated in restricted areas. They were treated as criminals. They would sit in groups, singing songs that under the circumstances seemed to us to be very sad. They made us feel sick, but we were being watched and had to be careful. Sometimes the Spaniards used to sing the anthem of the short-lived Spanish Republic ["Himno de Riego"], but even this song seemed to be sad . . . whenever we could we threw them cigarettes, candy, soap, razor blades, and other things.[28]

Many blamed the problems with the Spaniards on the fact that most had volunteered simply to get out of the dreary internment camps into which they had been forced when they crossed the Pyrenees in 1939, and had no real desire to soldier for France, much less for the Legion. A. D. Printer, a volunteer for the duration who made his way to the United States after the French defeat of 1940, discovered that

even from their fellow volunteers the Spaniards met suspicion. Most of the others, having been residents or refugees in France, spoke the language and understood the people. The only French contacts the Spaniards had had before they came to the Legion were the Gardes Mobiles or the Senegalese in the concentration camps at Gurs and Le Vernet. In order not to be lonely, they formed "cells," which were against the spirit of the Legion and which isolated them still more. For the officers and for the noncoms, the Spanish legionnaires were a nuisance. They did not fit in. They had been members of a popular army; now they were subjected to the ironclad discipline of a mercenary unit. They brought with them their typical Spanish individualism. They brought, too, their great sense of personal dignity, which was constantly trampled upon in the units where German sergeants and veteran French colonials had formed the outlaws of Europe into soldiers. Most of the left-wing extremists had preferred to remain in the concentration camps. Those who joined the Legion were loyal young soldiers of the Republic, professionals of the Spanish army, a few intellectuals and tradesmen.[29]

However, the problem appears to have laid less in the Spanish attitudes to the Legion than in the inflexibility of the approaches of the "Old Legion" to men of an entirely different stamp. Conventional Legion wisdom held that these volunteers came out of a "democratic" army and needed to be instructed in the ways of professional soldiers. "To the officers of the Legion, brilliant young reactionaries from Saint Cyr and Saumur or old troopers without any political convictions at all, every Spaniard was either a Communist or an anarchist, to be handled with the same affection as a box of dynamite," wrote Printer.[30] However, the Spaniards, many of whom had enlisted in the Legion to fight fascism, must have been disappointed to find fascism in the Legion, especially in the form of German NCOs whom they identified with Nazis, backed by officers who lived in a sort of splendid isolation, far different from their military experience in Spain. "Shaped by their war, closely united by a proven political solidarity, the Spaniards were armed, not only to resist in a quasi 'syndicalist' manner methods designed to intimidate but also to rise up resolutely against all attempts to humble their personalities," wrote Charles Favrel, who served with them in the *13ᵉ demi-brigade*.

For them, the Legion had not been a choice but a requirement accepted with a heavy heart, a bad moment to get over by making common cause with their companions. Resolved to remain men, they refused therefore to allow themselves to be poured into the mold of unconditional obedience. In addition to this, their combat experience caused them to reject the traditional conceptions of the Prussian system implanted at Sidi-bel-Abbès for a century. Tenacious and courageous, reluctant to accept sacrificial missions, their idea of war was to kill and not to be killed stupidly! They were not traditional Legion timber, the docile and blind executors of the order given by the superior.

They also acquired a nasty reputation for organizing reprisals against overly zealous Legion NCOs.[31]

The meeting of the Legion and the Spanish Republicans in 1939 was certainly the clash of two military cultures, as well a rerun of the problems the Legion had experienced in incorporating a large number of recruits from another defeated Spanish army in 1839–40. Legion officers who succeeded best with the new breed of recruits had to adapt their leadership style to the personality of the legionnaires, rather than force the "volunteers for the duration" to accept a discipline that at best produced only sullen compliance. One such officer was Lieutenant Albert Brothier, who was dispatched from Sidi-bel-Abbès to take over a company of the newly formed *12ᵉ étranger* in 1940, composed in large measure of Jewish refugees and Spaniards. "We military professionals were a minority," he wrote.

The reserve cadres, who were in a majority, had no intention of transforming themselves into professionals. As for our volunteers, they enlisted with us to fight and not for anything else (and they let us know this immediately). It therefore fell to us cadres to train these individuals to become fighters, give them an individual spirit. We could not, in a few weeks, change their mentalities acquired from groups which remained homogeneous. Therefore, we made the effort to adapt ourselves to this situation to stay in control of our troop and to be the indispensable link and the cement.

And while this approach differed radically from traditional Legion methods—indeed, it virtually turned them upside down—Brothier claimed great success. "The hierarchy was never challenged," he wrote. "It was less distant, more humane, more familiar." Indeed, his Spanish batman called him "Papa," even though they were both twenty-eight years old, a nickname that soon caught on with the other Spaniards. "When I arrived in the company barracks each morning, rather than the traditional 'Attention!', I was greeted by joyous 'buenos dias papa'. And if I needed to make a little speech, the end was always punctuated by a salvo of applause." Brothier claimed that this informal discipline was accepted by everyone, and that he never inflicted a single punishment in his company.[32]

Indeed, it soon became clear that prejudice had caused the Legion seriously to underestimate the military qualities of the Spaniards. Legion *Adjudant-Chef* Mazzoni wrote from the training camp at Barcarès near the Pyrenees in January 1940 that although their "military background could cause one to doubt their loyalty, [they] seem on the contrary to show up as very good soldiers, and one can testify that, well led, these volunteers would furnish very good combatants."[33]

This is precisely what Captain P. O. Lapie of the *13e demi-brigade* discovered during the Narvik expedition of May 1940: "The Spaniards rediscovered on these abrupt slopes the hardness of their sierras," he wrote. "They jumped about like tiger cats and never tired. Those officers who had been reticent about welcoming Spanish republicans in the Legion . . . were delighted to recognize their worth in combat."[34] Printer also wrote that the prejudice against the Spaniards

changed when the officers began to appreciate the soldierly qualities of the men, and later Spaniards were chosen for the hardest tasks. These young Spanish volunteers were famous for their skill as machine-gunners and for their marching ability. They were not, as a rule, good shots with light arms, lacking the phlegm that is essential. They loved the feel of steel in their hands—their great pocket knives and the four-edged bayonets of the French army.[35]

If the Spaniards eventually earned the grudging respect of their Legion superiors, the Jews faced greater barriers to acceptance. Unlike the Spaniards, most Jewish volunteers were city bred and lacked the fitness and rusticity that made the Iberians such excellent soldiers. Captain Lapie reported that the *13e demi-brigade* was called *"la troupe des intellectuels"* because it contained so many Eastern European Jews with university diplomas, an observation that, in Legion circles, was not meant as a compliment. "They were excellent in study, in application, in calculations," Lapie wrote. "They were detestable in drill, in marching, in fatigue duties, and in discipline, always complaining."[36] The future General Jean-Pierre

Hallo, a fresh second lieutenant assigned to the Legion in 1939, found his Jewish recruits to be

men from comfortable backgrounds and most often cultivated. Their average age approached 30 years. Not very athletic in general, their sedentary life style had already caused some to grow a little thick around the waist. They would have great merit and even courage to follow the rhythm of their Spanish comrades, lean, rustic and hardened by three years of tough combat.[37]

Like the Spaniards, the Jews were also suspected of left-wing sympathies, the "political mud-scrapers and no-accounts in their own countries" whom Perrot-White's lieutenant told him to avoid.[38] While communists were certainly in a minority among Jewish volunteers, Zosa Szajkowski admitted that

There were, indeed, many Communists among us and they called themselves VF's [volontaires forcés or forced volunteers]. They were always reading newspapers, eager to find some indication of a quick end to the "imperialistic war." They held meetings and even published a mimeographed bulletin. The anti-Communists tried not to provoke them. They were afraid that the discovery of a Communist organization among the Jewish volunteers would result in arrests, perhaps even executions, most certainly in anti-Jewish propaganda. However, the Communists would constantly provoke their adversaries and even warn them that on the front line a bullet cannot always be traced to the rifle that fired it.

Quite naturally, such activity undermined attempts to establish a regimental spirit. But when a Jewish adjutant sought the names of the ringleaders, even the noncommunist Jews refused to cooperate. "We told him that as much as we disliked them the very suggestion that we play the role of informers was distasteful to us," Szajkowski wrote. In his case, however, it almost proved to be a fatal decision. Wounded during the retreat from Soissons, the communist legionnaires refused to come to his aid:

The legionnaires passed me by. I knew almost every one of them from the times when we were active in the Communist movement. But I had left the movement; I was a former Communist and I knew that they would not help me. They looked at me and continued to run toward the bridge. Not one of them stopped to help me. I could not see; my eyes were closed.

Finally, he was rescued by a career Legion sergeant who came back to drag him to safety at considerable risk to his own life.[39]

The final charge against the Jews was that they served the Legion reluctantly. *Adjudant-Chef* Mazzoni, who recognized the military value of the Spaniards in January 1940, believed that his Jews, especially those who had lived in France for years, posed no security threat. However, most only sought naturalization and transfer to French regiments. "In any case, with a few exceptions, I do not believe that we can place great hopes in this category of volunteer," he concluded.[40]

When Prince Aage received a consignment of these "volunteers for the duration" in the *3ᵉ étranger,* he was livid. Most were middle-class Jews resident in France who "were not hot to get into the struggle. . . . They hardly had the military temperament, while their assignment to the Legion, which had more or less the same reputation as Biribi [the nickname given to the penal companies in Tunisia], did not put them in a celebratory frame of mind." When Aage saw these men walk into the barracks square looking like "the Burghers of Calais marching to their hanging," he shouted, "Stick those birds in a corner. . . . I don't want to see them! They are rotting my battalion." After receiving some special attention from the German NCOs, most secured transfers to French regiments.[41]

Even Szajkowski admitted that the attitude of some Jews toward military service was very ambivalent, especially when it was learned that they were to serve in the Legion. Many were delighted when the military physician at the training camp at Vancia, a naturalized Frenchman active in the Association of Polish Jews in France and thereby keen that all Jews serve, was replaced by an anti-Semite equally keen to eliminate them. "Anyway, the Jewish captain came back and the massive rejections of Jewish volunteers were immediately stopped."[42]

Lieutenant Jacques Ragot discovered a large number of young Jews whose parents had emigrated to France in the 1930s dropped on his mounted company in Morocco in 1940: "Any other Legion unit would have been better for these poor boys than a mounted company," he wrote.

In the two mounted companies [of the 3ᵉ étranger], the discipline which existed in 1940 was the Legion discipline of 1914. . . . If the legionnaires of the mounted companies were selected for their stamina, the same could not be said for their intellectual and moral outlook. Headquarters and the battalions frequently dumped onto the distant mounted companies elements which could cause problems in the towns . . . among whom were several veterans of the "Bat d'Af" . . . who were difficult cases. I was on leave when the volunteers, young enlistees not even finished with basic training, fell innocently into this milieu.

The existence of the volunteers was eased somewhat by the fact that their extra sources of income allowed them to buy exemption from fatigue duties with bottles of wine. However, they shocked the veterans in March 1940 when the prize company pig, Adolphe, was slaughtered for Sunday lunch: *"Scandale, Mon Lieutenant!"* the cook shouted at his commanding officer. *"Légion, pas zouaves,"* he insisted, a reference to the fact that the *zouaves* contained many Algerian Jews. "There was no doubt, at least a third of what had been Adolphe lay there, uneaten, among the ashes and debris" of the rubbish heap, Ragot noted. The cook walked away unconsoled when Ragot refused to punish the Jews. "Legion, finished," the cook muttered. "Scandal. Never seen that Legion."[43]

The influx of large numbers of Jews did not please the Legion. On February 10, 1940, a report stated that the *12ᵉ étranger* and the 21ᵉ, 22ᵉ and 23ᵉ RMVE counted 300 Jews each, with 400 in training in North Africa and 1,800 in the camp at La Valbonne, also near Lyon. The report stated categorically that the Legion wanted no more Jews, and that they must be refused admission "under diverse pretexts" but in such a way that they did not seem to be "special measures for Jews." Three days later, a note stated that the Army General Staff and the general commanding North Africa "want to see Jewish candidates absolutely excluded from the Legion."[44] Why? The reluctance of many to serve in the Legion, suspicions about their loyalty, dislike of the middle-class or "intellectual" background of many of the Jewish recruits, and fears that large numbers of Jews would upset the diversity that the Legion sought to maintain probably all played a role. However, in the light of the particularly harsh treatment of what appear to have been Jewish mutineers of 1915, of the decided preference for Germans in matters of recruitment that characterized the "Old Legion," and the subsequent treatment of many Jewish volunteers after the 1940 defeat, it is difficult to escape the conclusion that anti-Semitism was the principal motivation in the Legion's desire to exclude Jews. This is not to say that in the past individual Jews had not done well in the Legion. But the rise of anti-Semitism in France since the era of the Dreyfus affair, the strong popular anti-Semitism of North Africa, and the fact that the Legion was obliged to absorb so many Jews at once made them unpopular recruits.

The elimination of all of these Jews from the foreign regiments was not possible, however. What was possible was their dispersion, some to Syria and Indochina, or to French regiments. Most continued to be suspect by the Legion commanders. However, the future General Brothier, the man who as commander of the *1ᵉʳ étranger* in 1960 caused the military feats of the RMVE to be acknowledged fully by the Legion, believed that his Jewish soldiers possessed qualities that simply did not fit into traditional military concepts. "In observing the behavior of our Jewish volunteers," he wrote, "later I better understood why, in the Israeli army, familiarity and slovenliness went so well with courage and a redoubtable efficiency."[45]

It does appear as if, in the RMVE at least, some efforts were made to accommodate the political sensibilities of these recruits—for instance, when a contingent of NCOs, some of whom were German, was dispatched from the *2ᵉ étranger* in the autumn to staff the RMVE in France, they were returned to North Africa, presumably because their nationality and command style were ill-suited to the atmosphere of the RMVE.[46] And even Szajkowski, embittered by what he saw as a pattern of injustice toward

Jews by France and the Legion in both world wars, admitted that anti-Semitism melted away at the front,

where the officers treated the Jewish volunteers as men. Perhaps the common danger of death weakened any anti-Jewish sentiments they might have had. Besides, the Jewish volunteers fought valiantly, a fact the officers frankly admitted. They often promised that after the war those who survived would be looked upon as equals in the eyes of the French and not be treated as aliens, and that families of the fallen volunteers would be similarly treated.[47]

Nevertheless, officers of a traditional stamp had every right to feel pessimistic about the prospects of the Legion making a significant contribution to the defense of France in 1940. Smart money was on the *11ᵉ étranger,* the first unit formed of 2,500 long-service legionnaires from North Africa and around 500 ex-Legion reservists, and the one that had the pick of the cadres, including its commander, the quasi-legendary Colonel Fernand Maire, which gave it in the eyes of official Legion circles "a potential greatly superior to that of the 12ᵉ REI which is 50 percent Polish."[48] It seems fair to assume that most of these "Poles" were Jews, as those from a Catholic Polish background, as the Poles who came to France in the 1920s to work in the mines of the north, could more easily find acceptance in French units or in the Polish army. Although a new formation, the *11ᵉ étranger* imported the classic personality of the Moroccan Legion into France—the battalion rather than the regiment was the focus of loyalty, a heritage of the mobile columns composed of separate battalions of Legion and *tirailleurs,* and its commanders enjoyed all of the privileges and rights of the *caïdat,* the quasi-regal status accorded to officer rank in the Legion. No time was wasted attempting to indoctrinate legionnaires of the *11ᵉ étranger* in the need to defend France or persuade them of the legitimacy of France's international position. Emotional appeals to the France of the spirit, France the mother of civilization, were left to the leaders of the "volunteers for the duration." "The theme was simple," Manue wrote of the 11th's morale-boosting techniques.

You have the honor, Messieurs, called to France, to represent on the North-eastern front your comrades of the eight regiments of Africa, the Levant, of Tonkin. You are responsible for the honor of the Legion, that is to say one hundred years of the purest glory. Therefore, you must do more than any soldier of France.

This was usually expressed in the defiant and taunting shorthand of, "Are you worthy to be a legionnaire?"[49]

The Legion influence in the other foreign regiments in France ran from pale to invisible. The 12th had a smaller contingent of around four hundred Legion cadres and was composed principally of volunteers for the duration of the war who experienced Sidi-bel-Abbès only vicariously through their regular NCOs. Complaints were also voiced that the 12th contained too many reserve officers recalled from comfortable retirements and thoroughly depressed by the spartan existence of campaign life, and foreign officers "whose military training was almost negligible," and who in combat led the retreat.[50] The military prospects of the RMVE did not appear bright—a reluctant, polyglot soldiery who, outside of a smattering of regular Legion officers and NCOs, were staffed primarily by reservists. Indeed, the only Legion formation that appeared to inspire complete confidence was the football [soccer] team, which officers wanted to hold back from a tour of duty at the front in April 1940 because "at the moment it is capable of defeating easily any French side."[51]

Making legionnaires out of this was not an easy task. At the Legion's main training center at Saïda, the "moral formation" of a number of volunteers who, according to Manue, had been identified by Legion interrogators as "tough cases"[52] "proceeded according to ancient tradition"—firing exercises, drill, marches in which the pack loads and the distances were increased each week, classes of "theory" in the shade of the eucalyptus trees beside the Wadi Saïda on the Aïn-el-Hadjar road, assaults of the peaks of the Marabout or the Sergeant, objectives never mentioned in the history books but ones probably as important to the Legion's combat success as Eton's playing fields were to Wellington. "Who does not retain the memory of these re-entries into the barracks under the midday sun," wrote General Hallo.

"Direction à gauche deux fois, compagnie halte!" and, one by one, the companies turn, break ranks, align themselves, and present arms in a mass which awaits the verdict of the lieutenant who stands rigidly at attention before them. If all was well, it's the liberating "dismissed." Otherwise, it's another command: "Port arms, by squad, double time, single file behind me!" and it's a half hour run up the slopes of the plateau de la Rencontre before going through the ceremony of the return to the barracks square beneath a blistering sun.[53]

However, most "volunteers for the duration," whether legionnaires proper or RMVE had to forego the total immersion of the Legion's North African baptism and remain content with the sprinkles of admission to the faith provided by the missionary episcopacy in the overcrowded training centers of France. The atmosphere was certainly not the same. Szajkowski confessed that many of the Jews who trained with him at Vancia spent their time awaiting naturalization papers that would allow them to transfer to line regiments, bribing sergeants for an overnight pass to visit their wives installed at extortionate wartime prices in small rooms near the camp, and fretting about bromide in the food that might diminish their performance during these nocturnal forays.[54]

In October 1939, a training camp was established at Barcarès near Perpignan close to the Spanish frontier. If Barcarès resembled a minimum-security prison rather than a military camp, that was because it had been designed to quarantine Spanish Republican refugees. Rows of tar-paper huts whose translucent window coverings cast an eerie half-light on the meager furnishings inside stretched along a spit of sand ten kilometers long but only a few hundred meters wide that separated the Mediterranean from the étang de Leucate, a brackish coastal lake. Foreign volunteers mustered, drilled or crouched to wash beneath the few water spigots in the shadeless, windblown, mosquito-infested spaces between the huts.

The French government obviously expected little of these formations, for they were given extremely low priority in weaponry—surplus Lebels from World War I, some even earlier models, and submachine guns of Rif War vintage. Heavy weapons like mortars and machine guns were either collectors' items, too few in number to allow adequate instruction, or lacking some essential feature like disassembling instructions or a sight. Regular Legion Lieutenant Georges Masselot, assigned to the *12e étranger* as heavy-weapons instructor, found that he had to write his own training manuals and return to antediluvian methods of sighting mortars with a weight on the end of a string because of the absence of sights. The breakage of a part was a major catastrophe, for replacement parts were unavailable at any price.[55] The 12th was never given any antitank weapons, a rather serious oversight given the fact that the Germans tended to rely rather heavily on the offensive strength of their panzer divisions. Only the *13e demi-brigade* appears to have been issued the much-admired infantry rifle the MAS 36 just prior to their departure for Narvik in April 1940.[56] An after-action report for the 22e RMVE noted that "the men had hardly seen mortars and 25mm cannon [antitank guns]—one cannon and two 81 mm mortars to train the three regiments in the camp. The 10th Company had only shot twice at 200 meters with automatic arms."[57] The *12e étranger* was lacking so many essential pieces of equipment that many soldiers were obliged to tie their equipment together with string, which earned them the nickname of "the string regiment" from their German opponents.

The low status accorded the Legion in 1940 meant that, apart from the *11e étranger,* which contained the highest percentage of professional le-gionnaires and which served in Lorraine in the winter and spring of 1939–40, and the *13e demi-brigade,* most of the formations remained in the training camps well away from the front almost until the German attack of May 10 forced the French high command to call up all its reserves. Manue confessed that even the *11e étranger* was "technically mediocre" and pos-sessed only minimal notions of what modern combat in Europe was to be like—it had only a nodding acquaintance with tracked vehicles and no practice with antitank weapons. And although the regiment had enormous pride, its Moroccan past was almost a liability, for it retained an anachronistic vision of war as a sort of deadly sporting event, duels of men armed with rifles shooting it out in full view of each other, not as a crushing application of firepower and technology in which men struggled almost helplessly to survive.[58]

Despite the low expectations placed on them, of the six major foreign formations (including the GRD 97 but excluding the *13ᵉ demi-brigade*) that took part in the battle for France, only the 23ᵉ RMVE, half-trained and inadequately armed and thrown into the conflict on June 5 when the battle was already lost, failed to turn in a stellar performance. (Instead, they broke and ran near Sainte-Menehould on June 13.[59]) The *11ᵉ étranger* was engaged almost from the opening attack, tenaciously defending a section of the Inor Wood north of Verdun against repeated German offensives backed by artillery. On June 11, it began a fighting retreat that, like so many regiments of the French army in that desperate summer, quickened the disintegration of the regiment. By June 18 when the commanding officer burned the flag and buried the battle streamer near the church of Crezilles in the Meurthe-et-Moselle, the 11th had lost three-quarters of its men, many in an eleventh-hour attack mounted simply to retrieve the honor of the regiment. The rest escaped encirclement and moved south to Toul.

The *12ᵉ étranger* was snatched from its main training center at La Valbonne on May 11 and after various peregrinations was ordered on May 24 to defend the town of Soissons on the Aisne River. The new legionnaires appeared reluctant to dig in, convinced perhaps by the absence of serious defenses that the high command did not intend to make a determined stand. "We were wasting our time," wrote Sergeant François of the 7th Company of the general attitude. "Either complete rest in the rear or an attack. At least a well defined task, organized and whose utility can be understood by everyone."[60] However, increasing German air activity, the sound of incessant motor traffic from the German side of the Aisne, and the appearance of German advanced elements across the river on May 31 caused a change of attitude. The legionnaires began to fashion loopholes in walls, place obstacles and barricades in the roads, and dig antitank trenches. Strangely enough, this activity conjured up for François a sense of *déjà-vu,* an image of *"La dernière cartouche"* of 1870—"One only lacks the red trousers to make the illusion complete," he wrote. "We are nervous perhaps, but resolved. We are not afraid."

Perhaps this was the courage of ignorance. On June 5, waves of Stukas began an air bombardment of the town unmolested by French fighters or antiaircraft fire. "Really, I never would have imagined such a thing," he noted in his diary. "Soon the whistling of bombs and the noise of the explosions create an hallucinating concert coming always closer to us. My men take cover where they can. Many must regret not having worked harder to create a shelter." However, the bombs caused no casualties, so that when the German artillery joined in in the afternoon, the legionnaires hardly bothered to take shelter, an indication that German airpower was not a decisive element in the 1940 campaign. By June 8, François's legionnaires definitely had the impression that they were being surrounded and cut off and soon received an order to retire. The legionnaires of the 12th joined a general flow of refugees and soldiers heading south, keeping whenever possible to the wood line to avoid enemy aircraft.[61] Not all were so lucky. Many were cut off in the Soissons pocket; others like François were killed or wounded during the retreat. The armistice found the 12th at Limoges, only three hundred men left of the original two thousand eight hundred who departed La Valbonne a few weeks earlier.

The 21e RMVE had barely taken up positions on the Maginot Line when the German offensive broke. Shifted north of Verdun at the end of May, the 21st suffered badly from German attacks on the night of June 8–9. Like the rest of the French army, the 21st joined the general retreat. Those left when the armistice was signed on June 22 were disarmed in Nancy and dispatched into captivity. Perhaps the biggest surprise of the campaign, however, was the conduct of the 22e RMVE. Shipped out of Barcarès on May 6 for the quiet of the Alsace sector, the volunteers lacked many essential elements of equipment. The seriousness of the German breakthrough caused them to be taken by train, army truck, and finally a six-day march to take up positions at the village of Marchélepot on the Somme. The unit fought a number of costly actions between May 22 and 26 before it was withdrawn. On June 5 as it prepared to attack Villers-Carbonnel near Marchélepot, the 22nd together with the 112th Infantry Regiment was hit by a massive German preemptive strike that included artillery, aircraft and tanks. Although the casualties were high, the attack was repulsed. While the claim that they were outgunned by the Germans became something of an alibi for the French high command, and one that historians have subsequently punctured, in the case of the attack upon the 22e RMVE, as elsewhere, the Germans were able to achieve local superiority by concentrating their forces.

A second attack led by what the regimental commander called "an absolute invasion of tanks like a rising tide" broke upon the defenders, supported by air power and artillery. "The only option was the struggle of an infantry regiment left on its own against an enemy admirably equipped and deploying in every area modern materiel." The commander noted that, although German artillery and air support were well coordinated with infantry attacks, the enemy consistently deployed and maneuvered in full view of the French lines. The result was that when the French could bring artillery and air support into the battle, they could produce panic among the attackers, as on the afternoon of June 5 when a bombardment of the deploying Germans by 81-millimeter mortars operating at the limit of their range coincided with a bombing run by three French planes, "which spread panic among [the Germans]. This incident raised the morale of the 22nd to the highest point and despite the presence of enemy tanks the men wanted to pursue the fleeing Germans."[62]

By nightfall on June 5, the defensive positions of the 22nd were still intact and morale was good. However, the first battalion had lost half its strength, half its automatic arms, a section of mortars and two of its antitank guns. The second battalion was reduced to two companies, while the third had also seen its numbers cut in half. Even more serious, the 22nd suffered from a complaint common to all Legion regiments in the heat of the battle in 1940—lack of munitions. Daylight on June 6 revealed fresh German preparations for an attack, which began at 4 A.M. with artillery bombardments. German infantry assaults supported by tanks were repulsed, so that the task of breaking the position was given over to the artillery and the Luftwaffe, "work which they carried out conscientiously," Hermann remarked bitterly. Finally, around six o'clock, the Germans turned the 22nd's position to the west: "We had nothing to stop such a manoeuvre. We would have needed field artillery. . . . We were reduced, due to lack of means, to allow the Germans to come within the range of our arms before we could fire and slow his advance and inflict losses."

At eight o'clock, the Germans opened a general attack along the front of the 22nd. A combination of skillful German infiltration tactics through the woods and the lack of munitions caused the 22nd to withdraw gradually around the village of Marchélepot. "The audacity of the Germans grew as our volume of fire diminished," Hermann recorded. "They profited to infiltrate everywhere and by 11 o'clock all the liaisons [between companies] were cut in the regiment." The regiment was reduced to eight light and two heavy machine guns, one 81-millimeter mortar and nine 25-millimeter antitank guns, which at least imposed prudence upon the panzers. At midday, the Germans sent in a French lieutenant who had been captured early in the morning when he attempted to make contact with division headquarters to tell them of the lack of munitions. Obviously, the message had not been received, for the car in which he had been traveling had been ambushed and he made a prisoner. Either the 22nd surrender, Hermann was informed by his subordinate, or three hundred prisoners would be shot. Hermann refused, but he had few illusions: cut off, virtually out of ammunition, he had no radio contact with his division or liaison with the units on his flanks. "It remained to us only to make the enemy pay dearly for his conquest."

That was difficult to do, for as the Germans threw themselves into the French lines or into the houses occupied by the 22nd, they confronted men who had shot their last cartridge and thrown their last grenade. The chaplain looked to the fifty wounded gathered in the cellar of the chateau of Fresnes-Mazancourt where Hermann had set up the regimental command post. German artillery continued to sprinkle the French position, and as the Germans advanced cautiously to occupy the positions of the second battalion, which had completely spent its munitions, their commander could hardly believe that so few men had held his units in check. Although Hermann claimed that 150 German tanks massed to his front, they were reluctant to advance into the village because of the French antitank guns and the presence of the Spaniards, "not ignoring the number of the regiment which held Marchélepot."

The afternoon was spent in a house-to-house battle: "This was a street battle around the command post, from the church and toward its north entrance it was defended by real demons who standing on the barricades threw their grenades until they were killed by enemy fire," Hermann wrote. "The copse destroyed by [artillery] shells, the survivors sought refuge in the command post followed by groups of the enemy. The fight continued in the courtyard of the farm behind fallen walls. There were few munitions. The end was near. Despite the grenades, the Germans penetrated into the streets and the gardens, the straw of the barns and the trucks were on fire. At 4:40 the ground floor of the command post was invaded. Resistance ended there. Several legionnaires who had kept their last bullet committed suicide rather than fall into the hands of the Germans." The 2nd Battalion continued to fight for another two hours, before they exhausted completely their munitions and surrendered. The Germans complimented Hermann on the performance of his regiment.[63] Some of the captured volunteers of German extraction were shot out of hand by their captors. It was also charged by survivors that the continued solidarity of the Spanish POWs in German captivity caused most of them to be sent to concentration camps, where they perished. Over four hundred individual citations were awarded, and the 22nd was cited in army orders and awarded the *croix de guerre* with palm. That was a regiment that understood how to *faire Camerone!* On September 20, 1985, the *croix de guerre* of the 22ᵉ RMVE was included among the battle streamers that decorated the flag of the 2ᵉ *étranger*.

The point of this brief combat sketch is to allow one to draw the conclusion that, with the possible exception of the 23ᵉ RMVE, the conduct of the Legion and the RMVE in the battle for France in 1940 ran from very credible to spectacular. What the regiments lacked in military skill they made up in courage and tenacity, and this despite the fact that most had been hastily cobbled together from very heterogeneous elements, poorly armed and given almost no air, artillery or tank support. French logistics badly failed them, and all of the regiments complained of lack of munitions, as well as an absence of adequate armament, especially of antitank weapons. Sergeant François praised the courage of the legionnaires of the 12ᵉ *étranger*: "With equal arms, we were easily worth our adversaries," he wrote,

> . . . who did not show more audacity nor more decisiveness than we. And that is magnificent when one realizes that the military training of most of us was abbreviated, that most of the cadres coming from the reserves possessed only one thing, important certainly but insufficient in itself,

"good will." And, last, do not forget that these soldiers which we fought were used to all the difficulties of combat. And despite this the 12ᵉ REI fought from the Aisne until the last day of the campaign for France, re-forming constantly and facing each day an enemy which certainly domi-nated us materially but never morally.[64]

Similar praise was lavished on the 22ᵉ RMVE from its commander, languishing in a German prisoner-of-war camp: "The short existence of the 22ᵉ RMVE ended on the Somme, barely eight months after its formation," Major Hermann concluded in the epitaph for his regiment.

At least we had the satisfaction of seeing confirmed in the last days of combat that it was worthy of its forebears because even its adversaries rendered homage to its valiance. If it had not found itself disarmed before the enemy, exhausted, it would have taken its place in a short time among the elite regiments.[65]

The obvious question, however, is how much did this performance owe to the "traditions" of the Legion, to notions of upholding the honor of the regiment, to the detachment and expertise of professional cadres? Accord-ing to Manue, the comradeship and regimental pride of the 11th more than made up for its lack of expertise in fighting a modern war. The same does not appear to apply to the other foreign formations other than the small GDR 97. As in 1914–15, for France to have ordered these volunteers into Legion regiments or at the very least regiments with Legion associations appears to have been counterproductive. The obvious conclusion to draw is that the *élan* of these regiments of foreign volunteers was the product of the anti-Nazi sentiments of many of the men, and the previous military service and cohesion especially, but not exclusively, of the Spaniards. After-action reports for the *12ᵉ étranger* concluded that "The Polish Jews, not courageous by nature, did their duty," while that of the 22ᵉ RMVE, which contained about 30 percent *"apatrides,"* or Jewish residents without French nationality, not to mention foreign Jews, asserted that "The troops fought very well whatever their origins."[66] Perhaps, too, as in the offensives of May–June 1915, the enthusiastic ignorance of men experiencing war for the first time caused them to perform beyond the limits veterans would have believed prudent.

However, this is not to say that, beyond the *11ᵉ étranger* or the GRD 97, which, outgunned like the rest of the Legion, finished the war with a most respectable record as part of the 7th North African Infantry Di-vision operating near the World War I battlefields of the Somme, the "Old Legion" made no contribution to this performance. The *12ᵉ étranger* drew about half of its cadres from the Legion, and the other half from the reserve. Colonel Besson, commander of the 12th, claimed that all of his cadres were excellent, with the exception of the German NCOs, who, "magnificent in training, were mediocre under fire (perhaps afraid of being made prisoner during the retreat)." According to Besson, it was the cadres who held the regiment together: "The soldiers lacked a little cohesion," he wrote "There were many Polish Jews (around 600) and 900 Spaniards, good but looters. All of this held together thanks to the cadres."[67]

Sergeant François confirmed that, cast into this mass of temporary volunteers, veteran legionnaires felt it their duty to set the example during the first bombardments: "We legionnaires coming from Africa had a reputation to uphold and to affirm for our comrades enlisted for the duration of the war, who watched us and who were often only as good as the example set by those whom they took to be the tough chaps," he wrote. "So we could not stop ourselves from swaggering a little and to comment a trifle too severely upon that which among young legionnaires could give rise to remarks."[68] Yet the contribution of Legion cadres could not be the entire story, for the three RMVE had very few Legion cadres. Captain de Franclieu, who commanded the Third Battalion of the 22ᵉ RMVE, described his staff as *"cadres de circonstances"* taken from everywhere, but who nevertheless performed well.[69]

How far were the men permeated with the consciousness of being legionnaires, of having the traditions and honor of the regiment to uphold? This is impossible to say. As has been seen, many were reluctant legionnaires. The fact that a majority of the volunteers for the duration belonged to one of two large blocks—Jews or Spaniards—each of which maintained its own autonomous attitudes and *esprit,* made it difficult to create a regimental spirit. Nor did most have access to the temples of indoctrination in North Africa, or the time to imbibe the regimental traditions of the Legion. Nevertheless, it would have been difficult to remain indifferent to the fact that they were considered legionnaires. Some, like the Czech Charles Hora, assigned to the *11ᵉ étranger,* were so taken by the life that they made it a career. Sergeant François noted that as the *12ᵉ étranger* moved to the front in May, they were greeted enthusiastically by the population once it realized who they were. "Going through the hamlets and villages, all the inhabitants ran to their doors, distributing drink and food to those who passed," he wrote.

In return, we give them hope, a bewildering moment at the sight of all this poor humanity fleeing in all directions, a vision aggravated by the pessimistic statement of soldiers returning from battle. THE LEGION. Does not this name sum up all the military virtues? Is not its past a guarantee for the present, for all these people, who perhaps would be afraid to billet us, but who are ready to give us credit for all the most terrifying wartime actions invented but plausible, because it's a question of the Legion, and that gave them cause for hope? To hope that the invasion would not reach them, that the enemy will stop there where we will be.[70]

But it is impossible to know how far this spirit percolated through to the ranks.

Along with these positive causes for motivation, one might include a negative one—that of executing legionnaires who defaulted in battle. It remains to future historians with access to Legion justice records to discover if Legion courts-martial were trigger-happy. However, Manue speaks of two legionnaires executed for desertion in his regiment just hours before the armistice:

For an instant I thought, "What's the use now?" The voice of a humane leader replied: "You speak of justice! And the 500 killed and wounded yesterday, what do you think of that? Dead in the line of duty and these left alive?" He was right. [In] The other war, we shot each time that Salvation required it.[71]

Favrel also claimed that he was tasked with leading two legionnaires convicted of desertion after a summary court-martial, but who claimed simply to have crawled into a house to catch some sleep, to their executions in Norway.[72] If these four executions took place, that makes exactly three more executions in the Legion in 1940 than occurred in the entire U.S. Army in World War II. Perhaps this helps to explain the contention of Lieutenant de la Rocque of the *12e étranger* that his legionnaires did not fall to pillaging during the retreat in 1940 as did much of the rest of the French army, whose discipline often collapsed.[73] What is certain is that the foreign units that fought for France in 1940, though for the most part far removed in both structure and motivation from the "Old Legion" as Rollet had conceived it, were equal to its most impressive *faits d'armes.*

Defeat would bequeath a legacy to the Legion almost as bitter as that of France. Like France, the Legion from June 1940 was split between Gaullists keen to pursue the war with the Allies, and those loyal to the Vichy government under the venerable Marshal Philippe Pétain. In this respect, the history of the Legion between the Fall of France in 1940 and the Allied victory of 1945 is that of the French army on a similar and more concentrated scale. But because the Legion relied upon foreign recruits, the conflicts between professional and political loyalties on one hand and ideological commitment on the other were often more acute there. For the next five years, the Legion struggled to maintain its professional equilibrium and military proficiency.

Chapter 22

"QUESTION OF CIRCUMSTANCES" — THE 13ᵉ DBLE

WHILE THE FRENCH army was quickly dissolving into chaos as the legions of German panzers cut swathes through its rear, an obscure action was being fought in an apparently improbable place—the fjords of northern Norway. The Narvik expedition of April–May 1940 appears in retrospect to have been a product of the sense of unreality and confused priorities that took possession of the Allied high command during the forced inactivity of the *sitzkrieg,* as the Phony War was called. The immobility of the north-eastern front through the winter of 1939–40 resulted from the absence of any obvious place for the Allies to strike at the Germans. While French Commander-in-Chief General Maurice Gamelin probably exaggerated when he stated that an assault on the Siegfried Line, which covered the common Franco-German frontier on the Saar, would merely have opened the conflict with another Verdun, it is equally true that an attack there would possibly have gained little ground at a substantial cost.[1] The obvious route into the German heartland was through Belgium. However, that country had been neutral since 1936, and a premature invasion by the Allies would have upset world opinion, as well as thrown the Belgian army, upon whose support Gamelin eventually counted, into the enemy camp. Therefore, in the north, the initiative was ceded to the Germans.

This caused the Allied commanders to look for other theaters of action. However, the question of where and against whom they should intervene was muddled by Allied hostility to the Soviet Union. The Nazi-Soviet Pact of August 1939, which threw France's significant Communist party into the pro-Hitler camp and into hiding, and the treacherous partition of Poland between the two totalitarian powers, followed by Stalin's invasion of Finland on November 30, 1939, had agitated public opinion and led to calls for reprisals against Russia. In retrospect, the idea of adding Stalin to a list of active enemies that already included Hitler, with Mussolini and Franco maintaining for the moment a menacing neutrality, appears foolhardy. Nevertheless, the Allied high command began to hatch plans for retaliation against the Soviet Union, which had been declared an "objective enemy."

After considering and rejecting an attack on the Baku oil fields on the Caspian Sea, it was decided in early January 1940 to dispatch a brigade to aid Finland, where the Red Army's winter offensive had been frozen by heroic Finnish resistance. Given the location and the climate, the Alpine troops were naturally designated for this task. In February, with unassailable bureaucratic logic, it was decided to twin a *demi-brigade* of desert warriors with the half-brigade of *chasseurs alpins*. But hardly had this rescue force been organized when Finland capitulated to the Soviets on March 12. Casting around for other areas in which to intervene, the French and British generals settled upon a strike in northern Norway. The idea was not a sign of complete lunacy, although at first appearance it might appear to be so. The Allied commanders had correctly identified the lack of raw materials as the Achilles heel of German defense, and as Swedish iron ore reached Germany through Norwegian ports, Norway offered an obvious theater for action. Furthermore, the Allies possessed the naval power to project force into those distant parts. But while French and British commanders dickered over where to invade, Hitler preempted them with an invasion of his own on April 9, 1940.

The decision to include the Legion, a force whose reputation had been carved out of the sands of the Sahara and the jungles of Africa and Indochina, in an expedition to the Arctic Circle might also count as evidence that the equilibrium of the high command had been severely shaken by the inactivity of the Phony War. However, the Legion was nothing if not versatile—after all, it had contributed a unit to the Allied incursion into Northern Russia in 1918–19. In this case, too, it rose splendidly to the occasion. By March 1, 55 officers, 210 NCOs and 1,984 corporals and legionnaires had volunteered or been volunteered from the Legion regiments in North Africa and organized into two battalions for the new unit, which on March 27 or thereabouts, was designated as the 13ᵉ DBLE. On the surface, at least, the 13ᵉ DBLE appeared to be a Legion formation in the old style of the *régiments de marche* of selected professionals, far different from the *12ᵉ étranger* or the RMVE, or even from the *11ᵉ étranger* in that it contained only a handful of reserve officers. The average age of the legionnaires hovered between twenty-six and twenty-eight years old, and most counted four to five years' service, while the NCOs had served for ten years or more. Its commander was Raoul Magrin-Vernerey, a hero of World War I, seventeen times wounded and whose career since 1924 had been spent primarily with the Legion, and its officers were professional legion-naires almost to a man.

However, despite this traditional "Old Legion" profile, the 13ᵉ was not immune from the recruitment changes that had affected the Legion since 1934, for between one-fifth and one-quarter of the regiment was Spanish.[2] However, according to Charles Favrel, who served with the 13ᵉ, this did not prevent the political refugees from exploiting the myth to the fullest in early March with the women of Marseille: "Despite a few Aryans of im-pressive stature, our reinforcement could only offer them a selection of average size, Spaniards for the most part, whose Mediterranean type added no spice to their habitual menu," he wrote. "But these frenzied women wanted to rub up against this bronzed and fabulous myth named Legion, which they now experienced in the flesh." Indeed, so successful were the legionnaires in cashing in on their myth in the deregulated free market of Phony Wartime France that their now-idle BMC (Bordel Mobile de Campagne—the unit brothel), which had followed them to France, was eventually repatriated to North Africa.[3]

The legionnaires of the 13ᵉ DBLE found the final approach to Narvik unnerving. The training at Larzac in south central France, the brilliant sendoff at Brest, the tedious voyage via Scotland in the rank holds of troopships had given way to a sense of foreboding as the flotilla of Allied ships glided through the still gray waters of the fjords. The gentle slap of water against the hull, the dull pulsating of the ships' engines, the smell of salt and grease were all as unfamiliar to legionnaires as the snow-capped peaks that rose majestically from the water's edge. The beauty of the scenery heightened the sense of unreality and the pervasive feeling of vul-nerability that came naturally to soldiers out of their element, penned in a collection of slow-moving metal hulks, obvious targets in the twilight of a polar night in May to the wings of fighters that the imagination inevitably conjured up on the horizon. Nor, after two naval battles in the waters off Narvik in early April, could the legionnaires convince themselves that the Germans would be surprised by their visit. Five thousand German troops held Narvik. True, about 1,500 were German sailors marooned from their burning ships in April. But the main force was provided by Austro-German mountain troops commanded by a specialist in mountain warfare, Lieutenant-General Dietl, the man who had organized the 1936 Winter Olympics. And while the German troops were remote from their base of supply and counted only two artillery batteries, they had more than com-pensated for this with the capture of the stores of 6th Norwegian Division. A substantial superiority in land-based aircraft also counted heavily in their favor. Against this, the Allies would bring a force of three British battalions from the 24th Brigade of Guards, two Norwegian brigades, the two French half-brigades, and a contingent of Poles.

Nineteen minutes into the morning of May 13, seven British warships opened fire on Bjerkvik, a picture-postcard fishing village that lay along a snowy shore eight miles up the Herjangs Fjord from Narvik. The village church, which the Germans had profaned as an ammunition depot, erupted, briefly painting both the snow of the 4,500-foot promontory that dominated the town and the dark waters of the fjord bright orange. More of the wooden houses on shore caught fire, sending fingers of reflected flame reaching toward the spectators on the ships. A single German plane appeared and unloaded a bomb that sent a spout of spray toward the lowering sky, before disappearing behind a mountain pursued by a clatter of antiaircraft guns that erupted from the ships like applause.

"Hurry up Frenchies! Quickly boys!" the sailors of the *Monarch of Bermuda* urged the legionnaires, who surrendered their life jackets, donned their combat gear, and climbed fully laden into the English torpedo boats moored alongside. More German fighters flew low over the convoy, ignoring the reverberating antiaircraft fire and turning the surface of the water between the ships into a chaos of geysers and waterspouts. The guns of the HMS *Resolution* sent ear-shattering volleys into the town. The legionnaires were torn between a desire to burrow for protection into the unyielding deck, and that of getting off the metal targets and onto a more familiar, if enemy-infested, element. The rifles that they had sighted, cleaned and cherished for weeks now seemed derisory elements of protection, as useful as bows and arrows amidst the whistles and screams of much more lethal ordnance, whose din rebounded off the craggy faces of the surrounding mountains. Soon a line of torpedo boats was making for the shore, black spots in the bluish Arctic dawn, drawing troop-laden whalers in their wakes—a rather primitive invasion flotilla if judged by later standards of amphibious attack. At the last minute they veered right and left to avoid the designated landing beaches, where machine-gun bullets rattled over the rocks and rippled the surface beyond.

Once on shore, the companies deployed and moved to seize the high ground to the north and south of the town, supported by three light tanks, not always an easy task as the snow was still knee-deep in places. The 2nd Battalion overran the German camp at Elvegaarden just behind the town, capturing most of the German medical staff, which had remained with the wounded, while two companies pushed their way through the ruins of Bjerkvik where the Germans fought a skillful rear guard action with carefully sighted machine-gun nests. Favrel quickly became aware that the night attack had killed far more civilians then enemy soldiers,

a horrible massacre of a humanity surprised half naked in its sleep. Rifle in hand, I had to travel over an atrocious way of the cross scattered with shredded corpses, cribs overturned upon their dead babies, wounded screaming in pools of blood.

The Germans took almost five hours to vacate the village, taking care to set booby traps as they retired. Favrel also claimed that elements of the 13^e

DBLE then brought dishonor upon the unit by looting the town, which earned the Legion a denunciation by German radio as a group of "professional bandits."[4]

Narvik proved a far tougher objective to seize. Unlike the picturesque Bjerkvik, Narvik offered a bleak industrial perspective in keeping with the severe landscape that towered above it. Scatterings of spartan houses ran down the spine of a peninsula that stabbed into the water between two deep fjords. A railway line followed the northern shore through several tunnels and looped around the end of the peninsula before it fractured into fingers of track at the harbor on the south shore. Into this small space behind bunkers and walls, the German commander had crammed an estimated 4,500 troops. For this reason, the plan, which called for 1,500 legionnaires and a battalion of Norwegians to jump off from Oijord on the north shore, cross the narrow entrance of Rombaks Fjord, and land smack in the middle of the German positions, was a risky one.

The operation, postponed several times, finally took place in the opening minutes of May 28. Two Legion companies got ashore and seized their objectives quickly. However, once the Germans recovered from their surprise, the following elements had to fight through German 77s and machine guns vomiting destruction at them from the cover of the railway tunnels and strafing by German aircraft, which obliged the supporting British ships, and therefore most of their fire support, to withdraw. The situation for the legionnaires was that of a man left suspended over a precipice, two hands on the ledge and trying to throw a leg over the top. But they managed it, although it proved a difficult task without artillery support to winkle the small groups of Germans organized around machine guns out of the tunnels and folds of earth. Lieutenant Colonel Magrin-Vernerey came forward, often to within thirty yards of the German lines, stylishly orchestrating the seizure of the German positions by pointing out the direction of attack with his walking stick.

Once on land, the 1st Battalion pushed along the north shore of the peninsula, while the 2nd moved around the south to link up with Polish troops moving along the southern shore of the Beisfjord. Narvik was in Allied hands by the end of the day, but the Germans conducted a fighting retreat, making use of the abrupt terrain, which favored the defensive. Over the next days, the Allied troops pushed along the railway lines to within ten miles of the Swedish frontier before events in France caused the operation to be cancelled. By June 7, the 13ᵉ DBLE was slipping back down the fjords to the open sea and England. Seven officers, five NCOs, and fifty-five legionnaires had been lost, most of them storming Narvik on May 28. Favrel witnessed one legionnaire shot out of hand for looting in Narvik.

Like the regiments fighting in France, the verdict on the performance of the 13ᵉ DBLE in the Narvik campaign must be a largely positive one. The legionnaires provided a constant effort, despite great fatigue caused by almost incessant daylight and the fact that there were few areas available beyond the reach of the Germans, which caused the legionnaires to attempt to sleep—without much success—upon beds constructed out of branches and leaves and laid on the snow-covered slopes. The eviction of 4,500 well-entrenched German troops from Narvik by roughly 1,500 legionnaires supported by a battalion of Norwegians was no small accomplishment. Of course, one may argue that the enemy garrison was composed essentially of shipwrecked sailors and Austrians. Nevertheless, they were well armed and well supported by artillery and air power, and as far as one can tell used natural defenses well. The fighting in some sectors was very bitter indeed, so there is no evidence that the Germans lacked heart. Also, the Legion had to overcome serious handicaps, which included poor functioning of the radios, which slowed and disarticulated maneuvers, and delayed logistical support caused by the problems of unloading the ships.[5]

Nevertheless, there was room for improvement. Legion Lieutenant Jouandon noted several defects in the 13e DBLE, some of them classic complaints of the interwar Legion: Poor training, an uneven quality of NCO, especially of many sergeants who arrived at their grade by seniority after having been promoted too rapidly to corporal, and the creaming off of the best legionnaires for specialist positions, "so that the combat sections often received only those who could do nothing else." He also noted that officers made tactical mistakes because, unlike their German counterparts, they had "neither the sense, nor the curiosity of terrain." In Jouandon's view, Legion officers required "less formalism, more initiative," an observation that applied to the French officer corps in general. Nevertheless, if many of the weaknesses of the 13e DBLE were Legion weaknesses, their strengths were also Legion strengths—a combative spirit among the officers that they succeeded in communicating to the troops, and enough experienced NCOs and legionnaires to provide leadership for the combat sections. Like their counterparts in France, the legionnaires in Norway concluded that the enemy was not composed of supermen, but in Jouandan's view they seemed "not very battle hardened. . . . In sum, for [our] troops the comparison was not unfavorable."[6]

And there the matter might have rested, a minor episode, a happy footnote in the history of the Legion written by a temporary formation amidst the cataclysmic events of 1940 in France. Yet the 13e DBLE was fated to play a larger role in the history of the Legion, and the history of France in World War II, than its obscure genealogy might have indicated. The events that transformed the 13e DBLE from an obscure and temporary formation into a symbol of duty and combative spirit for an entire nation occurred not in Norway, but in England.

By mid-June 1940, Trentham Park, a manor house near Stoke-on-Trent, hosted a camp of almost 4,500 French soldiers, refugees from Narvik and the celebrated escape from the beaches of Dunkirk, including the 1,619 survivors of the 13th. The morale that had been raised so high by Norway had plummeted when the unit had been put ashore at Brest, to witness briefly in full measure the chaos of the French defeat and to take casualties every bit as high as those of Narvik. Gathered beneath a relentless English rain in hastily erected tents, the legionnaires were asked whether they wished to continue the fight against Germany or to return to North Africa, a decision that effectively meant to stack arms, as immediate prospects for carrying on the struggle from the colonies appeared remote. It was a decision heavy with moral and political implications, and a unique one in the history of the Legion, for unlike in 1835 when the Legion had been given to Spain, each legionnaire was now asked to choose his own destiny. As might be expected, each legionnaire reasoned very much in his own terms.

The decision by the French government to capitulate to the Germans rather than fight on from North Africa, followed by Charles de Gaulle's call for continued resistance on June 18, 1940, was to disturb profoundly the cohesion of the 13^e DBLE, especially as virtually the only troops available for recruitment into the Free French were those marooned in England. Trouble began to brew in the unit almost as soon as it reached Trentham Park, brought on by low morale, which was made lower still by the confused situation in France. Not surprisingly, perhaps, the malaise was most quickly apparent among the volatile Spanish legionnaires, men who retained a mind of their own that any amount of Legion discipline seemed powerless to alter. Mutterings of discontent among the Spaniards finally broke into the open on June 25, the day the armistice between France and Germany went into effect, when twenty-nine of them at Trentham Park refused to muster and as a consequence were delivered to the British police. This provoked a larger strike by many of the remaining Spaniards in the *demi-brigade* who, responding in part to rumors that the Legion was to be dissolved, feared that they would be turned over to the Franco government. They too were delivered to the British police.[7] War weariness must also have been a strong element in their decision, for when on July 1 they were given a choice of repatriation to North Africa or fighting on with the Free French, they preferred internment in Britain.[8]

The treatment of the Spaniards hastened the collapse of the badly deteriorating relations between many officers and men, which fed upon rumor, distrust and innuendo. To this one might add the Anglophobia that was to bedevil recruitment and serve to discredit the Free French movement in the eyes of many Frenchmen from the beginning. The doubts of *Adjudant-Chef* Mary about the sincerity of his officers began with his arrival at Trentham Park. There he discovered a clutch of officers whom he had believed lost during a forward reconnaissance in Brittany already installed in the camp, but without their men. He discovered that, cut off by the Germans, the officers had told the men to make their own way to French lines, while they had "decided" to reach England. "These explanations start us thinking and from this moment we have the conviction that we had been led to England knowingly by making us believe that we will go to

North Africa," Mary reported. "We are disgusted by this procedure and this only increases the distaste which we feel for some time, without speaking of it, in the presence of the British and unfortunately of certain French." The delivery of the Spanish legionnaires, "yesterday's brothers in combat," to the British police was the last straw for Mary, who reasoned that they had no right to call upon foreigners to "render justice in the name of the Government of their Country [France] which they have renounced."[9]

Given the strong moral and political implications of the decision to fight on or return to North Africa, and the subsequent role played by the 13ᵉ DBLE as a symbol of France's, and the Legion's, fighting spirit, it is ironic perhaps that few officers made their decision on political grounds. De Gaulle's brief visit to the unit on June 30 was very low-key, even stiff, and certainly did not electrify the officers of the 13th. *Adjudant-Chef* Mary claimed that some legionnaires whose minds were already made up boycotted his visit, a futile gesture in the end because he did not seek to speak to the legionnaires,[10] some of whom appear to have been on duty outside the camp in any case. Some were perhaps influenced by Lieutenant Colonel Magrin-Vernerey, who swallowed his Anglophobia and sided with de Gaulle. Anglophobia appears to have played a principal part in the decision of Lieutenants Jouandon and Vadot, who had distinguished themselves during the battle for Narvik, to depart for North Africa.[11] Anglophobia, stimulated by Dunkirk, which the French saw as a treacherous defection rather than a miraculous escape, not to mention assorted uncomplimentary remarks upon French martial qualities by British civilians around Trentham park, made many men opt for repatriation.

Some subalterns linked by friendships going back to Saint-Cyr came to collective decisions. Many were "relieved" by the armistice, Gabriel de Sairigné noted in his diary. "Personal questions," he wrote, decided the issue for "almost everyone"—the desire to see one's family, versus the belief that they would be integrated into the detested British army. By joining de Gaulle they would boost their careers, and perhaps win the war with England, although that prospect was grimly remote, almost unimaginable in June 1940.[12] One officer was heard to remark: "I'm staying [in England]. What do you expect me to do in France or North Africa? Nothing, for the only thing I know how to do is to drive an automobile. Once discharged from the army, I would be in civilian life a failure, incapable of supporting a family."[13] Mary complained that discussions between officers who wanted to fight on and legionnaires became increasingly acrimonious, to the point that he and others considered desertion if forced to remain in England. Some officers provoked skepticism among the legionnaires by repeating as fact rumors that the Legion had been disbanded and that groups of legionnaires and *tirailleurs* were roaming North Africa and had even reached Nigeria and the Côte d'Or, committing the "worst excesses," and that the "worst reprisals" awaited those who returned to France, including repatriation of German and Italian nationals to their governments.[14]

On July 1, at six o'clock in the morning, the regiment split. Some 636 officers and men of the original 1,619 who arrived at Trentham Park boarded five trains headed to Bristol and the ship for North Africa. "Emotion at the station during the Colonel's adieux," wrote de Sairigné. "Everyone looks to make excuses. Everyone knows full well, however, that Morocco won't fight."[15] "The last minute is truly poignant," Mary recorded. "The hearts are full of emotion, then 'he' [the colonel] offers his hand, for the last time also we salute him."[16] Nevertheless, tension between the two groups mounted when an honor guard of those who had rallied to de Gaulle refused to present arms to their departing colleagues. A final episode remained to spoil the departure of those returning to North Africa—the British police delivered the three hundred Spanish legionnaires to the Bristol docks, but they lay down and refused to board.

If the 13e DBLE (renamed the 14e DBLE between July 2 and November 4, 1940, after which they reverted to their original number) entertained pretensions of rescuing the honor of France and the Legion, it appeared poorly equipped to do so. Thirty-one of the regiment's 59 officers had departed, and only around 900 legionnaires remained. De Sairigné complained soon after the split that "Discipline is terribly lax. The officers become very hard. One must constantly stay on top of demands and absurd excuses. Generous English hospitality has something to do with it; AWOL and desertions, the police are nervous." However, by August 25, when they were inspected by George VI, de Sairigné exulted, "Impeccable parade; the Legion is absolutely under control."[17] Part of that control had to do with the quality of the officer corps, which included men who would eventually rise to general rank, such as Captains Pierre Koenig and Jacques Pâris de Bollardière, and Lieutenant Bernard Saint-Hillier, to name just a few. Others, like the Georgian emigré Captain Dimitri Amilakvari and Gabriel de Sairigné, certainly would have become generals had they survived long enough. On August 1, the 14th was joined by Second Lieutenant Pierre Messmer, one of de Gaulle's future prime ministers.

The promised *"beaux voyages"* began on August 30, when 936 officers and men of the *demi-brigade* boarded ships at Liverpool for a tour of Africa and a part in the early history of the Free French movement: The failed attempt to win Dakar for the Gaullist camp, the storming of Libreville in the Gabon, and the campaign against the Italians in Eritrea from February to April 1941. The Eritrean campaign, though costing the lives of only eighteen NCOs and legionnaires, recalled those of the 1920s in Morocco, made difficult by poor logistics, heat and lack of water. Poor Italian morale and British support helped to tip the balance in the favor of the Allies. The victorious Legion seized Massaouah on April 8, 1941. When Colonel Magrin-Vernerey, now traveling under the *nom de guerre* of Monclar to protect his family in France, entered the town, the native population greeted him with fascist salutes, believing this to be a polite European salutation. Monclar immediately made his way to enemy headquarters and arrested the Italian commander, Admiral Bonetti, personally, but not before the admiral had pitched his sabre out of the window into the sea. An Italian admiral, he declared pompously, never surrenders his arm. Fortunately, one of the legionnaires had seen the saber fly into the water, waited patiently until low tide, retrieved it, and gave it to the colonel.[18] De Sairigné noted that the surrender and disarming of the Italians, which should have been a great morale booster, had only served to remind him of the confusion of defeat he had witnessed in Brittany on June 18, 1940.[19]

This tour of Africa had allowed the 13th to regain its equilibrium and begin to forge an esprit de corps. However, it would face two severe tests over the next years, one moral and the other military. The moral challenge sprang out of a confrontation with fellow legionnaires in Syria in the summer of 1941, one that reopened many of the old and badly healed wounds that resulted from the division of Trentham Park. In many respects, this made the second test, the military one against Rommel's Afrika Korps in the Western Desert, a more straightforward operation.

The situation in Syria served to point up how far the mentality of the 13e had evolved from the days of decision in June 1940, and demonstrated the full force of the difficult political choices that the 1940 defeat and de Gaulle's decision to fight on had imposed upon French officers. Unfortunately, it also demonstrated how poorly equipped many of those officers were to evaluate those choices. The 6e *étranger,* which garrisoned Syria, was considered a staunchly pro-Vichy unit. French historian A.-P. Comor has contested this view, pointing out quite rightly that there was considerable proresistance sentiment in the regiment in June 1940, which produced a movement to join the British in Palestine. However, this foundered for a variety of reasons, including divisions among the officers, the lack of vehicles to get them to the frontier with British-ruled Palestine, a mutiny among Spanish workers attached to a battalion of RMVE that took two days to suppress, and the influence of the commander-in-chief in North Africa, General Charles Noguès, upon whom the British and Free French initially had placed much hope, but who in the end threw in with Pétain. This convinced the Syrian commander, General Eugène Mittelhauser, to pledge his loyalty to Vichy.

"Personally, neither I nor most of my officers harbored any animosity against the officers of the 13e BDLE [sic]," Colonel Fernand Barre, commander of the 6e *étranger,* wrote. "If, like many of them, we had participated in the Narvik expedition, and then regrouped in England, we would have probably, like them, rallied to the FFL [Free French]. Question of circumstances."[20] Nevertheless, Barre had taken care to return any officer suspected of Gaullist sympathies to France. So by the summer of 1941 when "circumstances" offered Barre a choice, his opinions upon Free

France were well formed and staunchly negative, in large part because these colonial soldiers continued to see Britain rather than Germany as their primary enemy.

Colonel Barre's argument that "circumstances" determined who picked which side no doubt held true for 1940. The issues were horribly muddled in that terrible summer, and it is forever to the credit of Charles de Gaulle that he was able to peer through the fog of confusion, anger and recrimination of those months to chart a clear course for the recovery of France's dignity. That more people did not rally to his cause can indeed be explained in part by circumstance—even if his appeal to fight on were accepted (and it is not clear that all of those who rallied to him did so out of idealistic motives), it was not, after all, easy for those who were not championship swimmers to reach England and the Free French camp.

Yet by the summer of 1941 the reasons for French legionnaires in Syria to fight an Allied invasion in the name of the Vichy government had been reduced to three: loyalty to the established government of France, the honor of the regiment, and the fact that the Germans seemed the odds-on favorite. Loyalty to the government had been enforced by continuing conflicts with the British over their attack on the French fleet at Mers el Kébir, the port of Oran, on July 3, 1940, the Dakar expedition and the British blockade of Djibouti, acts of "piracy" against French shipping, and by indignation over British bombing of mainland France. Coming to some sort of arrangement with Germany still seemed to many French officers the best way to protect the empire. Officers suspected of Gaullist sympathies had been purged or transferred. Furthermore, French opinion was profoundly impressed by the German military successes in the Balkans and Greece in April 1941. All of which serves to demonstrate how lonely the Gaullist position was in the summer of 1941, one which would become even more forlorn with the breathtaking advances of German panzer units against the Red Army from June 22.

In the aftermath of the Syrian campaign, French officers on both sides attempted to minimize their political differences, advancing the claim that they had not really wanted to fight, and that the whole unfortunate incident might have been avoided by a *baroud d'honneur,* a sort of military compromise that allows commanders to surrender with their honor intact after a symbolic struggle. However, the conventions surrounding a *baroud d'honneur* require one side to have a clear superiority, which the Allies decidedly did not, attacking on June 7, 1941, thirty well-entrenched French battalions with only twenty of their own. Therefore, regimental pride would not allow the Vichy French to surrender to an inferior force, a fact that did not prevent the commander of French troops in southern Lebanon, General Arlabosse, from claiming subsequently that he had been defeated by a superior force backed by artillery and tanks.[21] More's the pity that general Arlabosse did not advance this claim before the battle and ask for terms. Indeed, the *baroud d'honneur* appears to have been a red herring designed to paper over differences in the French camp and throw the onus for the fight squarely on the shoulders of the British, who were blamed for refusing to commit enough troops to allow the Vichy troops to surrender with a clear conscience.

From the standpoint of patriotism and political morality, the officers of the 13e clearly believed their arguments irrefutable. By 1941, it was increasingly apparent, at least to them, that the Vichy government had become more than a hostage to Hitler; it was a willing collaborator. And nowhere was this more obvious than in Syria. De Sairigné spoke of the "profound indignation" in the 13e DBLE when it was discovered that the Germans had been allowed free use of Syria as a staging post to supply a revolt by the Iraqi nationalist Rashid Ali-al-Gaïlani against British rule in April 1941.[22] "This has a name," General Georges Catroux, commander of the Free French forces in the eastern Mediterranean, wrote in an appeal addressed to French troops in Lebanon. "It's called aiding the enemy; it's called treason! Assistance and premeditated treason which will debase and dishonor you if you do not oppose it![23]

Catroux was more correct than probably even he realized. The German use of Syria was no flash in the pan, but part of a major agreement signed between Vichy and Hitler on May 28, 1941, which included use of other French bases in north and west Africa, in return for what Vichy hoped— naïvely— would be a major renegotiation of the occupation agreement, and even of a new era of support by France for Nazi Germany.[24] This collaboration between Pétain and Hitler in Syria offered an unwelcome distraction to the British, who had been pushed out of Greece and Crete and who were threatened in Egypt. However, the principal advocate for the invasion of Syria was de Gaulle himself, who hoped among other things to recruit a number of troops from the defeated garrison. Therefore, the Allies decided upon an attack, which the hostile conduct of the Vichy government and the collaboration of the French administration there had invited, with a force that included an important contingent of Free French troops. Here were the perfect "circumstances" Barre required to change sides without losing face.

The participation of the 13^e DBLE in the operations against Syria testified to the degree of rising political commitment in the regiment by 1941. If the decision to join de Gaulle in June 1940 had often been taken for reasons of adventure or personal gain, a year of fighting as a self-conscious minority in the Allied cause had convinced many of the bankruptcy of Vichy's policies. Therefore, when it became a question of reneging on the clause in their contract that exempted them from service against fellow Frenchmen, only Colonel Monclar and one company commander refused to take part in the invasion, a selective sensitivity as blood had already been shed in this Gaullist/Vichy civil war by legionnaires of the 13e in Gabon. Unfortunately for the officers of the 13e DBLE, unanimity had also been achieved in the 6e *étranger*.

The first shots in the campaign were verbal ones—the Free French scattered leaflets and denunciations of Vichy policies in Syria, while Colonel Barre fired back with a tract entitled, "Why I Am Not a Gaullist," a diatribe that raised the tone of the debate by several decibels. Among men for whom the tradition of quiet discussion and gentle persuasion was not well developed, this had the effect of hardening opinion in both camps. Political arguments became banners beneath which each Legion regiment rallied. While the officers of the 13th reproached those of the 6th for supporting a compromised collaborationist regime, their propaganda was couched very much in Legion terms—those who had chosen Free France in 1940 had rejected defeat, traveled, found glory and were destined to be victorious over Hitler as troops equipped with the latest weapons, an obvious comment on the antiquated condition of Vichy's "Armistice Army." The alternative for legionnaires of the 6th was a return to the barracks life of North Africa, with its steady ration of road mending and *cafard*. "You are too 'legionnaire' to go over to the side of the defeated," the Free French argument concluded.[25]

Colonel Barre countered this provocation by publishing a fairly comprehensive list of grievances against the Gaullists. If in the process he exposed in full the paranoia and political and moral confusion that riddled the ranks of Vichy, not to mention a marked inability to distinguish between Churchill and Hitler, it must be remembered that French officers were still trying to come to terms with their most staggering military defeat since Waterloo. Barre's response also helps to explain why a category of French officers who were prepared to fight the Allies at every opportunity failed to lift a finger when the Germans used Syria in 1941, moved troops into Tunisia and occupied the "free" zone of Southern France in November 1942, and allowed the Japanese to occupy Indochina.

Barre countered that de Gaulle's movement was essentially an insurrection against established authority, that he represented those whose divisive policies and mismanagement had brought France to her present predicament, as spokesman for the "principles of [17]89" and the Popular Front of 1936, for the reign of Jews and Free Masons, for "these secret sects [which] will cause the rebirth of the same disorders and the same calamities." Barre reproached the Free French for helping to further English designs to take over the French empire, evoking, of all things, the "amputation" of Canada and India by the British at French expense in 1763, together with that of Egypt in 1881, not to mention Mers el Kébir, Dakar and now Syria. For Barre, the Free French were simply a collection of opportunists. "That is why I am not a Gaullist," Barre concluded.[26]

On June 8, 1941, two brigades of British troops under General Sir Henry Maitland Wilson invaded Syria from Iraq, while the 7th British Division moved up the coast from Haifa toward Beirut. The 13ᵉ DBLE, as part of the *1ᵉʳ Division Française Libre*, crossed the Syrian frontier at Dera with the 5th Indian Brigade and marched for Damascus. For the first few days of the campaign, the 13th remained in reserve. Only on June 19 did they enter the battle for the first time, thrown into an assault upon one of the peaks that dominated the village of Kissoue, key to the southern defenses of Damascus, which it took after a brief, if violent, attack that left thirteen legionnaires dead and several wounded.

That very evening, the 13th continued the advance toward Damascus. The great fear that the two regiments of the Legion would find themselves locked in head-on combat was realized on June 20, when advanced elements of the 13ᵉ clashed with a unit of the *6ᵉ étranger* that held Kadam, a southern suburb of Damascus. The opening fusillade killed a Belgian legionnaire in the 13ᵉ and wounded a corporal in the 6th. To pull in his troops, Major Amilakvari had the bugler blow the "Boudin," which was answered by the bugler from the defensive positions. Amilakvari ordered a cease-fire and approached the enemy position, which he discovered to be held by a sergeant and several legionnaires from the 6th. When the sergeant told the major that his orders were to hold his position until one o'clock in the morning, Amilakvari agreed not to advance until then.[27]

This appears to have been an isolated incident. However, it was not the only one—a report by Lieutenant Baulens of the *6ᵉ étranger* claims that a patrol of which he was part opened fire on "a column of trucks transporting legionnaires of the Gaullist battalion," at dusk on the evening of June 10 south of Damascus.[28] Therefore, legionnaire did fire upon legionnaire. Otherwise, the 6th fought stolidly, suffering 128 killed and 728 wounded, one-quarter of its strength, most of them battling the Australians in Lebanon. The 13th fought their way into Kadam against stiff opposition put up by the *29ᵉ régiment de tirailleurs algériens,* and Legion officers had their hands full preventing reprisals against the wounded. The 13th was moved through Damascus and up the road toward Homs. The armistice caught them preparing to move upon Ba'albek. The campaign cost the 13ᵉ DBLE a relatively modest 21 killed and 47 wounded.

The real confrontation between the two units of the Legion occurred not during the campaign, but afterward. According to the terms of the armistice signed at Saint-Jean d'Acre on July 14, 1941, the legionnaires of the *6ᵉ étranger* were to be offered the choice between repatriation to France or assignment to the 13ᵉ DBLE. This *"séance d'option"* was held a month later, just two days before the 6th was to embark for France. Within a large enclosed square at Camp T2 outside Beirut, the 6th was drawn up with its colonel at its head. Despite the suffocating heat, the ambiance, "more than glacial" according to de Sairigné,[29] plunged further toward a polar record when Colonel Koenig, representing the Free French, ordered Barre to leave, realizing full well that his legionnaires might be unwilling to defect in their commander's presence. Barre refused and was upheld by a large British colonel who, de Sairigné believed, appeared to be enjoying immensely this spectacle of dissension among Frenchmen. After a quiet word between the British colonel and Koenig, the legionnaires were ordered to file through a door, turning to the left if they chose to remain with the 6th, or to the right where a long line of army trucks stood ready to transport them to the 13ᵉ DBLE. The trucks went home empty: "*Oh satisfaction—immense joy—All the legionnaires* except one (a very bad subject) *turned left, without hesitating* [italics in original]," Barre remembered, obviously still deeply moved by a scene that had taken place forty years earlier. "Then all the corporals, the NCOs and the officers did the same. Finally, I went through the door myself and found my regiment reconstituted. The *clique* played the refrain of the Legion, Le Boudin, as everyone stood to attention. Then the 6ᵉ marched away behind its music."[30] De Sairigné grumbled about the "particularly lamentable attitude of Colonel Bar [*sic*],"[31] but the Gaullists could do nothing to stop the departure of the 6th.

Therefore, the repatriation of the *6ᵉ étranger* to France appeared to be a political defeat for the Gaullists in general, and for the 13ᵉ DBLE in particular. However, the rejection of the Gaullists by the Syrian garrison was less categorical than the final leavetaking between the 6th and the 13th might seem to indicate. Colonel Barre arrived in Marseille with only 1,233 of the original force of 3,344 men listed on the regimental roster on June 8, 1941. In other words, over 60 percent of his legionnaires had been left behind, and not all of them in graveyards and hospitals. Around 3,000 Vichy troops in Syria opted for the Free French. Although the regimental diary of the 13ᵉ DBLE claims the defection of 1,400 legionnaires from the 6th,[32] more realistic estimates hover between 677 and around a thousand, most of whom had enlisted from Allied POW camps or who had deserted to the 13th before August 14.[33] Some of those desertions had been provoked by legionnaires from the 13th operating in groups of four around the camps of the 6th with the mission of persuading isolated legionnaires to come over.

What all this tells us about the state of mind of the legionnaires of the 6th is not clear. It is possible that political refugees were convinced by the political arguments of fighting on. Barre complained that groups of Gaullist "solicitors" played upon the nationalism or nostalgia of isolated legionnaires, "speaking to them in their maternal language, showing them that it is their duty, now that they have fought loyally for France, to put themselves on the side of the only nation that can and wants to give them back their fatherland."[34] Legionnaires with more traditional motivations could be offered "adventure, new horizons, far off countries, *le baroud,* well being, distractions, etc.," which compared favorably with the prospect of the boring life of the barracks at Bel-Abbès.[35] The fact that the 13ᵉ DBLE belonged to a victorious force imparted the prestige necessary to attract others.

OFFICERS, HOWEVER, PROVED more difficult to persuade—97 percent of the officers of the 6th elected repatriation to France. A.-P. Comor believes that had officers from the two camps been allowed to meet in the month between the end of hostilities in Syria and the repatriation of the 6ᵉ *étranger,* more might have been won over. This is possibly true. British reluctance to take on board more Free French troops than they could train and equip, and to strengthen a movement whose leader, in their eyes, was already demonstrating a talent for intractability, offers one explanation for the failure to meet until just before departure. However, the fact remains that when officers from the two Legion camps did finally meet, their *tête-à-tête* was more like a dialogue of the deaf. When representatives from the 13ᵉ DBLE appeared to discuss changing sides with their counterparts in the 6th, they were received, according to Colonel Barre, "without friendliness, nor cordiality, but *correctly*. There was neither friction nor fighting—the discussions were sometimes lively, but without violence."[36]

This hostile reception was no doubt caused in part by jealousy provoked by the rapid promotion of those who had joined de Gaulle. But what the representatives of the 13th discovered was that the propaganda war had served to harden positions on either side rather than to persuade. To this one might add the high casualties suffered by the 6ᵉ *étranger,* which served to make defection appear as an expression of disloyalty and lack of solidarity with dead and wounded comrades.[37] This was the argument put forward by the commander of Vichy forces in Lebanon at the end of the campaign when he warned his soldiers that they would soon be "the object of solicitations by misled Frenchmen who will not lack the shame to ask you to change camps, to trample on the corpses of so many of our brave, fallen comrades faithful to their duty as a soldier."[38] But the habit of obedience to superiors was too ingrained, especially among those holding an active command, to be easily broken.

The propaganda battle between the two sides merely helped to enforce an institutionalized conformity that most officers believed vital to the preservation of discipline, group-think that swathed everyone in the security of majority sentiment and therefore helped to ensure cohesion. This pressure to conform was especially intense among Legion officers, a group with a developed sense of elite status, a self-conscious priesthood of the elect among whom any deviation was treated as heretical and disloyal behavior. The few officers whom the 13th managed to recruit from the 6th were those isolated in POW camps or hospitals, which put them beyond reach of the pressures of hierarchy and the mess, but also removed them from the responsibilities of active command. In this respect, Barre was especially active in assuring that "circumstance" played as small a role as possible in the decisions of his officers. What was more, he was transferred back to Algeria to command the *dépôt commun des régiments étrangers* (DCRE), its main training center, a post taken up on his departure by his deputy in Syria. In this way, Barre helped to set the political tone, or lower it depending upon one's point of view, of the Legion in North Africa—Syria was added to Mers el Kébir as another example of the treachery of the

English and their renegade allies in the 13e DBLE. The division of the Legion had been consummated until the end of the North African campaign on May 1943 and beyond. The 6e *étranger* would return to its passive collaboration and *cafard,* while the 13e DBLE would have the far more serious task of measuring itself against Rommel.

The next test for the 13th was a military one. And like the political test of Syria, it was a performance that earned mixed reviews. Nevertheless, in retrospect, the period between the fall of Syria in the summer of 1941 and the end of the North African campaign in May 1943 might be looked upon as the golden age of the 13^e DBLE in World War II. For the first time since 1940, the 13^e DBLE would carry the banner of the Legion into battle against the Germans. The fact that its campaign was a solitary one removed any rivals to dispute its glory. Its leadership, under newly promoted Lieutenant-Colonel Dimitri Amilakvari—Monclar was now a general— was more experienced, and possibly higher in quality than ever. The recruits from the 6e *étranger,* although fewer than hoped for, allowed the 13e DBLE to double its strength to 1,771 men, organized into three small four-company battalions of around 500 men each, redesignated as the 1er, 2e and 3e *bataillons de Légion étrangère* (BLE). The 2e and 3e BLE would fight in the Western Desert as part of the 1er *brigade française libre,* attached to the British Eighth Army. The British reequipped these legionnaires as mechanized infantry to fight in the Western Desert, which made it possibly the most modern force in the French army, certainly in the Legion. The fact that equipment was available for only two of the three battalions, so one had to be left behind, was only a slight disappointment in the burgeoning military fortunes of the 13th.

On January 20, 1942, Field Marshal Erwin Rommel attacked British positions south of Benghazi in Libya, driving them back toward Egypt. To stabilize the front, the British began preparing a series of defensive positions that stretched inland south from El Ghazalah. The southern extremity of that line was anchored by a triangle of moles and pillboxes at a place called Bir Hacheim (Bir Hakeim), an abandoned Italian desert camp that stood beside a dry well at the confluence of several desert tracks. When, on February 14, the Legion as part of the "First Free French Brigade Group" replaced the 150th Indian Brigade at Bir Hacheim, the men looked out over a sand-blown plateau decorated by a few wisps of pallid vegetation that stretched, dry as a bone, to the horizon. If the countryside was depressing, when combined with the weather, it was enough to make one suicidal—the temperature alternated between blistering days and frigid nights, with the occasional sandstorm conjured up for variety. Of more immediate worry, however, was the poor state of the defenses, which would be hard-pressed to hold out against a determined attack of camel-mounted tribesmen, much less the Afrika Korps. For the next three months, the 957 legionnaires who comprised around a third of the garrison improved the fortifications, laid minefields, and experimented with detached motorized reconnaissance formations inspired by British General Jock Campbell, and therefore baptized "Jock Columns." It was at Bir Hacheim, on this forlorn, sand-blown plateau, that the 13ᵉ DBLE would earn its enduring place in history and in the hearts of Frenchmen.

On May 26, Rommel, feinting a frontal assault, swung his forces in a southward arch to outflank the British positions, and ran into Bir Hacheim. An attack by Italian tanks early on the morning of May 27 was stopped cold, at a cost to the assailants of thirty-two tanks lost and ninety-one prisoners. "All the men and especially the anti-tank [gunners] were terrific," de Sairigné exulted in his diary. So many tanks were abandoned that several German and Italian trucks drove into the French position, believing it to be an Italian fortress.[39] As the enemy had obviously decided to bypass the defenses and strike in the British rear, General Koenig ran slash and burn raids against Rommel's overstretched supply lines as they lapped around Bir Hacheim. Within a few days, the Axis attack was running out of steam and the prognosis for an Allied victory appeared good. But on May 31, the Italians breached the British lines north of Bir Hacheim.

By June 2 Bir Hacheim was an Allied island in an advancing tide of Axis troops—two Italian officers came to the camp to ask the French to surrender and walked away with Koenig's refusal. For the next few days, the camp was under continual bombardment by artillery and bombers. On June 6, two separate combined attacks by tanks and infantry stalled at the very southwestern edge of the perimeter, mainly due to the effect of artillery and antitank fire. "Very few losses on our side," noted de Sairigné, "while the medics crisscross the battlefield on the enemy side."[40] However, on the 8th the enemy stepped up his artillery and air bombardment, mixed with an occasional probe with tanks and infantry. On the 9th, an attack that threatened to break into the position was thrown back only by a last-minute counterattack led by half-tracks. Both water and munitions were running low. The 10th opened with an infernal artillery barrage. More seriously, accurate German counterbattery fire was beginning to limit the ability of the French guns, so far the mainstay of the defense, to respond. A determined German attack at three o'clock in the afternoon swarmed over the French pillboxes taking several legionnaires prisoner before it could be repelled.

Completely out of water and ammunition for the 75-millimeter cannon, Koenig ordered a breakout. Although each battalion was given a definite role to play, the regimental diary admitted that "time was lacking to organize the planned movements, no formation is any longer imposed and some units go forward in a compact mass. The enemy positions, probably intimidated by the imposing aspect of these masses, prudently fall quiet so as not to be localized and only open firing after their passage."[41] In fact, the retreat turned into an unorganized flight, necessary perhaps, but the most costly episode of the battle for the Legion. The legionnaires and other members of the fleeing garrison, which included a small British contingent, charged the enemy positions, the Bren guns on their half-tracks blazing. The Germans lit up the night with flares, and tracer bullets knitted a linear network across the sky. Vehicles exploded into funeral pyres as they drove over mines: "Very impressive," de Sairigné wrote.

Big shambles also, and, for a few seconds, I doubt that one can regain control of the men. Finally, it more or less sorts itself out. But the plan was worked out too late, the enemy line having been revealed closer than one would have believed. Many of the arms have not been destroyed and are going to hamper considerably the vehicles.[42]

The breakout dissolved into a series of blind firefights, a *"corrida individuelle,"* wrote de Sairigné, who became separated from his company in the night, assembled a few isolated soldiers, and made his way as best he could toward the British lines eight miles away. General Koenig and Lieutenant Colonel Amilakvari, together in a car driven by Englishwoman Susan Travers, who had joined the Free French in England and been assigned to 13[e] DBLE as a driver, also wandered alone in the desert, narrowly evading German positions on several occasions. Miraculously, the flight, which had invited disaster, was only marginally catastrophic. While the days of siege had cost the Legion only 14 dead and 17 wounded, primarily because of the strength of the defensive positions, 11 legionnaires were killed, 32 were wounded, and 37 taken prisoner during the breakout. Worse, however, 152 remained unaccounted for, many in POW camps. The two battalions of the Legion at Bir Hacheim were reduced to 693 men, largely deprived of their artillery and other heavy weapons, which had been left behind in their escape.

The immediate aftermath of Bir Hacheim was undoubtedly the high point of the history of the 13[e] DBLE, and for the Legion in World War II. Though Koenig was modest about his garrison's performance, in the hands of Maurice Schumann, future French foreign minister who in 1942 was the voice of the Gaullist *Radio Londres,* Bir Hacheim became a "rendez-vous d'honneur" and a symbol of the spirit of Free French patriots, on a par with that of Verdun in 1916. There would be other combats, even other *faits d'armes,* but the solid performance of the Legion during what was called the Battle of El Ghazalah won it praise for its discipline under fire, its aggressive mastery of the Jock columns, and the damage inflicted on the German and Italian tanks by Legion artillerymen. This, like the confrontation with the *6e étranger* in the Levant, confirmed and heightened its separate Free French identity.[43] The *demi-brigade* was withdrawn to Alexandria, where it was given what the regimental diary called an "enthusiastic reception" by the French population there. "And even the English soldiers salute them with a certain respect."[44] In fact, the British were annoyed by Gaullist propaganda that portrayed Bir Hacheim holding out despite having been abandoned by the British. The Germans exploited this

Anglophobia by quoting POWs seized at Bir Hacheim who complained that the RAF had denied them air support. When, a few days later, Churchill paid a visit to the troops in the Western Desert, he neglected to call on the Free French, which Koenig considered a snub.[45]

Unfortunately, the euphoria did not last. In the autumn of 1942, British General Bernard Montgomery prepared to throw Rommel into retreat. Reequipped by the British, with strength up to 1,274 men organized into two battalions, the Legion's role was to carry out a diversionary night attack upon Axis positions at El Himeimat—a strongly fortified ridge about 1,300 feet high that overlooked the sandy depression of Quattara and anchored the extremity of Rommel's defensive lines running south from the sea at El Alamein. Several factors would make the attack a difficult one: El Himeimat was held by four hundred Italian paratroopers backed by artillery, and covered by deep minefields. Furthermore, the French lacked up-to-date intelligence on the defenses. Last, the attack had to be carried out across an open plain swept by enemy fire.

While Montgomery's plan worked, the Legion's part in it was a shambles. Problems began almost as soon as the 13th crossed the starting line at seven-fifteen on the evening of October 23. Like many night attacks, this one became difficult to control, especially after the command radio net went out. Tanks and vehicles stalled in the deep sand. Just when the engineers had cleared a path through the minefields, the enemy artillery opened up. With their radios dead, the forward observers could call up no artillery support of their own. The half-tracks began to set off the mines, while a group of German panzers intervened against the flanks, all of which caused the commander of the first battalion, Major Pâris de Bollardière, to abandon his attack. Without radio contact, however, he was unable to inform Lieutenant Colonel Amilakvari, who continued to push the second battalion forward into heavy fire.

To complicate their problems, German armored elements counterattacked as dawn broke. The French artillery fired badly and the Luftwaffe appeared in force, which forced the second battalion to withdraw to a small hill and establish a defensive position that was pounded heavily by the Germans. At nine o'clock on the morning of October 24, Koenig ordered a withdrawal. As the Legion retreated, a fragment of shell from a German 105-millimeter cannon caught Amilakvari in the head, killing him. By three o'clock in the afternoon, the 13th, or what was left of it, was back at its starting line.

The British were extremely critical of this Legion performance. In their view, the casualty figures of eleven killed, sixty-nine wounded and 10 missing for two battalions were too light to have merited a withdrawal. French General Edgard de Larminat defended his troops with a hot attack on British "bad faith," demonstrating the ticklish nature of the relations between the two allies. The British liaison officer with the French offered a more dispassionate explanation for the failure of the operation, blaming it essentially on the lack of artillery support and poor coordination caused in part by lack of radio communication. However, the French obviously had a case of bad conscience, for Koenig relieved de Bollardière.

El Himeimat was an unfortunate incident above all because it placed the 13th under something of a cloud for the remainder of the North Africa campaign. The Legion had fought poorly at El Himeimat. In its defense, it can be argued that in a night attack things often appear more confused than they actually are, especially when the radios go dead. The attack was poorly prepared, the terrain unfamiliar and difficult, and the Axis forces offered a very respectable resistance. Be that as it may, Montgomery withdrew the 13th from the front.

This exposed the fragility of French morale. The awareness that theirs was an enormous gamble whose payoff hinged upon the success of their arms, made them especially sensitive to failure. The death of Amilakvari, the temporary disgrace of de Bollardière, and Montgomery's November 14 decision to withdraw them from the front, threw them into a melancholy mood. What followed was known in regimental history as the "time of forgetfulness," one of bitterness and lassitude, of dreary bivouacs and depleted reserves. In May 1943 they were permitted to participate in the last stages of Rommel's retreat in Tunisia at Djebel Garci. But with North Africa now in the Allied Camp, the Legion could at last recover unity. Not everyone in the 13ᵉ DBLE regarded that as a happy outcome: "Our role is finished," declared de Sairigné. "We return to the ranks where fantasy will be less tolerated and where one must put up with weaklings and imbeciles."[46]

But the divisions in the Legion could not be forgotten in the euphoria of a victory parade, any more than could those between de Gaulle and his detractors in North Africa, whose quarrels were mirrored in the Legion—in the Tunis celebration to mark the defeat of the Axis in North Africa, held on May 20, 1943, de Gaulle's Free French forces marched with the British Eighth Army because the French 19th Army Corps, loyal to de Gaulle's rival General Henri Giraud, refused to accept them, and vice versa. If marriage there was to be between Gaullist and anti-Gaullist factions of the Legion, it would be at the business end of a shotgun. The remainder of the war for the 13th might be summed up as follows: The 13th and the Legion fought until the downfall of Hitler, sometimes on the same side. To understand why the divisions were so bitter, perhaps one should return to the Legion in North Africa to discover how they had fared since 1940.

Chapter 23

A FRAGILE
UNITY

The "Vichy" Legion

The defeat of France in 1940 and the restriction by the Germans of the French army to one hundred men brought to the Legion the inevitable problems of demobilization. And none was to prove more difficult to resolve than the status of those foreigners who had volunteered to serve for the duration of the war, either as legionnaires or in the RMVE. In this respect, Vichy did not mark a radical departure from the policies toward refugees of the Third republic, but a continuation and intensification of those policies. However, in the aftermath of a defeat whose roots seemed too deep to be attributed to mere military mistakes or incompetence, refugees, and especially Jewish refugees, became associated in the minds of the Vichy elite with the now-intensified problems of unemployment and the "purity" of French culture. Furthermore, their presence was an embarrassment to Vichy officials eager to prove their neutrality to their German captors. Therefore, the volunteers for the duration were demobilized, and in the process stripped of the military status that might have protected them from German reprisals. Some were simply returned to the streets, where they confronted the same problems that had bedeviled many of them before 1939—lack of working papers or a residence permit, which some Vichy prefects refused to deliver despite previous military service. Therefore, Vichy fell back on the old policy of internment.

A law of September 27, 1940, reinforced on November 28, 1941, required all those considered "superfluous to the national economy" or without evident means of support to be interned. Therefore, some volunteers never tasted the delights, however brief, of freedom following the armistice, but were simply told that they were demobilized but interned. Labor camps, known as *groupements de travailleurs étrangers* or GTE, were created in the "free" or southern zone of France not occupied by the Germans, for men between eighteen and fifty-five who had arrived in France after January 1, 1936.[1] Many did so voluntarily, including ex-volunteers for the duration, to obey the law, to avoid starvation or escape internment camps, because the promises of work and steady pay were attractive, or because the alternative was to go underground. These camps often became the first stage of deportation to Germany, especially for Jews, who began to be separated from other workers in "Palestinian" GTE groups. The massive deportation of these groups to Germany began in August 1942, not, as recent research has shown, because Germany demanded them but because French Prime Minister Pierre Laval saw this as a way to ingratiate himself with Hitler and gain concessions.

Some ex-volunteers were shipped to GTE camps in North Africa reserved for "undesirables," where they met volunteers for the duration whom the war had stranded there. These camps had no formal links to the Legion, even if some ex-Legion officers and NCOs served as cadres.[2] There were other, less formal links, however, not the least of which were the former legionnaires and volunteers for the duration there, a situation most of them regarded as a betrayal of their support for the French war effort and their Legion service. The threat of internment was also used freely by Legion commanders as a threat to force legionnaires to reenlist when their terms of service expired. A report of October 21, 1942, claimed that discharged legionnaires were even taking the extreme measure of volunteering for *Service de Travail Obligatoire* (STO), forced labor service in Germany, because their Legion commanders refused to give them the necessary support for residence papers and they feared the North African labor camps.[3]

Even the Legion intelligence service, the BSLE, recognized the moral dilemma these camps posed for the Legion, at least in part, when it protested the treatment of ex-legionnaires in a report of August 28, 1941. In the category of "undesirables" consigned to the camps were included legionnaires whose contracts had been annulled because of disciplinary infractions, legionnaires or volunteers for the duration "judged undesirable from a national point of view," Jewish legionnaires or volunteers for the duration, and German and Italian legionnaires who had asked for repatriation to their countries. There was a "grave malaise" in these camps because they were staffed by old NCOs who could find no other employment and whose pay was insufficient when it arrived at all. As for the inmates, whose nominal salary was fifty centimes (about two cents) a day, they often received no pay for up to three months at a time. The BSLE believed that the Legion had obligations toward some of those men, especially those who could not go home.[4] Last, it does appear as if the Legion were at least involved in running one of these groups, designated as the *compagnie de discipline des travailleurs,* reserved for deserters and troublemakers from the other camps. Not surprisingly perhaps, Spanish republicans were prominent among them. This was run along the lines of the famous *discipline* of the Legion at Colomb-Béchar, complete with Legion NCOs. Beatings, brutal punishments and virtual starvation were said by several witnesses to be routine.[5]

Conditions in the camps, especially those in the Sahara, created to revive the long held but elusive dream of a trans-Saharan railroad, could only be described as slave labor. The American consul in Casablanca reported that many of these ex-volunteers were kept there at the insistence of the German Armistice Commission out of fear that, if released, they would join the Allied armies. "A good deal of just indignation has been expressed in North Africa over France's treatment of these men," he wrote on May 15, 1942.

Many French military officers of superior rank have expressed their disgust, saying frankly that the maltreatment of these volunteers had been acquiesced in out of sheer servility to the Germans, that by doing so France had stained her honor and built up hatred and vindictiveness against herself in those men's countries, and above all, would hardly be able to obtain either foreign or North African volunteers in any future emergency. They also admit that there will be a heavy reckoning with the North African natives afterwards.

However, the American envoy to Algiers, Robert Murphy, reported that the Germans merely served the Vichy government as an alibi to pursue a purely French policy of internment.[6]

On a few occasions, the Vichy government did intervene in favor of the veterans of 1939–40, as in late 1942 when it pleaded for those released from German POW camps only to be rearrested by German authorities in France, and when it exempted some war veterans from deportation to death camps in Germany after mid-1942.[7] But apart from a few high-profile political refugees, the Germans did not seek repatriation of Jews and other undesirables, but were content to allow Vichy to support German interests by confining them to concentration camps, as she did by defending her colonies against the Allies.

The Germans were keen, however, to recover their nationals still serving in the Legion, the first installment of a continuing struggle throughout the war to retain legionnaires demanded by the belligerent countries. Article XIX of the Armistice Agreement of 1940 obliged the French to turn over all German nationals on French soil, whom it would designate to German authorities. General Maxime Weygand, the Vichy government's *délégué général* in North Africa, saw the ensuing "struggle for the preservation of the Foreign Legion" as part of an Axis plan to abolish the Legion, as the Italians also began to reclaim their nationals. The French tactic, Weygand decided, would be to preserve the tradition of asylum while using the German demands to shed undesirable elements. "This would give an appearance of satisfaction [while] the Legion did not suffer too much from this 'purge,' " he wrote.[8]

As Weygand suggested, the smashing German victories had left many German legionnaires impatiently marooned in North Africa, many of whom "are becoming dangerous by their propaganda, especially those from Morocco," Legion officers began to report.[9] Philip Rosenthal, a German Jewish refugee who had abandoned his Oxford studies to enlist in the Legion to fight Hitler, found that the French collapse had made the Germans in his unit contemptuous of serving in a beaten army and eager to leave.[10] In August 1940, around 320 Germans who had been removed from their regular units after having demanded repatriation, mostly to escape punishments, were "in a state of permanent mutiny" at Koléa, the Algerian internment camp where they were awaiting repatriation. Attempts by French officers to address them were drowned out by shouts of *"Heil Hitler,"* followed by "a torrent of invectives against France, her army and the Legion. . . ."[11] On September 26, and October 9, 1940, two installments totalling 996 German legionnaires were collected for repatriation.[12] After January 1941, the German-dominated Armistice Commission became more insistent, demanding names of Germans serving in the Legion, which seriously threatened to compromise the Legion tradition of asylum. This caused Weygand to send a group of German legionnaires to Tonkin and therefore out of reach of the Armistice Commission.[13] However, under increasing German pressure, the Legion "sanctuary" began to crumble as names were delivered to the Armistice Commission over the protests of General Alphonse Juin, and finally on March 31, 1942, the government ordered that all German legionnaires must be interviewed by the German military delegate even if they were not volunteers for repatriation.[14]

No doubt many Germans who wished to remain in the Legion were disguised as Czechs, Poles or Alsatians, although the Armistice Commission was not fooled by this ruse.[15] But the pressures soon began to tell—in early 1941, French authorities acting in the best traditions of creative administration invented a loophole that allowed them to give up fifty German legionnaires whom the Reich claimed were deserters, by classifying them as POWs.[16] Furthermore, although Legion authorities continued to protest that they only repatriated those Germans who requested it,[17] clearly French weakness and administrative concessions on names and interviews caused many German legionnaires to lose faith in these promises. As early as September 1940, the *2e Bureau,* French military intelligence, in Morocco noted that German legionnaires were asking to be returned to Germany often to avoid punishment, but also because they believed their status insecure under the armistice.[18] A year later, the BSLE reported that "The German legionnaires are fed up with signing declarations right and left and so many loyal legionnaires have declared, 'They'll finish by getting us too.' " Seventy-six legionnaires, including seven NCOs, asked for repatriation, "believing that it is better to volunteer now than to be forced to return later and to be opened to reprisals."[19] Enough German legionnaires were repatriated to allow the formation of the 361st Afrika Regiment, which was used as a labor unit until April 1942, when it was armed and its designation changed to the 361st Infantry Regiment. It fought with the Afrika Korps in the vicinity of Bir Hacheim in 1942.[20] Most of these men must have been legionnaires of fairly ancient vintage, as those Germans coming into the Legion after 1934 were increasingly Jews and other political refugees who would not have risked repatriation. The departure of these Germans from the Legion would indicate that the Legion traditions accentuated by Rollet in the interwar years exercised little profound influence upon these men. By serving the Afrika Korps, Goebbels declared, these German legionnaires could earn rehabilitation, which after undergoing rehabilitation in the Legion must have made them the world's most rehabilitated soldiers.

The atmosphere in the Legion in North Africa appears to have been profoundly depressing to many legionnaires. Despite claims by the BSLE in September 1941 that legionnaires in North Africa were immensely proud of the heroic resistance of the 6e étranger in Syria,[21] it could escape the attention of no one that the Legion had been left to molder on the sidelines of the greatest conflict in world history. Enlistments had declined from 5,549 in 1940 to 2,381 by 1942, and Legion strength plummeted from a 1940 high of perhaps almost 50,000 men to 18,000, excluding of course the 13e DBLE. General Juin, contemplating these large deficits, was forced to consider the abolition of some Legion units like the 4e étranger and the reduction of others to skeletal forces,[22] and this at a time when the army in North Africa as a whole was having no trouble filling vacancies with men eager to flee the dreary existence of occupied France.[23] Furthermore, most of those volunteering for the Legion were Frenchmen, generally a poor recruitment source but especially so as the BSLE estimated in 1941 that fully half of them had prison records, while almost all had been excluded from enlisting in other French corps.[24]

Although the old guard loyal to Vichy appeared to have a firm grip on the situation, clearly those legionnaires who came into the Legion to fight Hitler in 1940 were not content to be used, in the opinion of English legionnaire Anthony Delmayne,

to fight undernourished natives unable to pay their taxes . . . when there were so many Nazis to be killed. Many of us had a considerable stake in the war. . . . Rumors that Vichy was going to sell us down the river filled these men with dread, and there were riots, mutinies, fights and suicides in the fort.[25]

One such man with a stake in the war was Philip Rosenthal, future secretary of state for the Ministry of Economy and Finance of the German

Federal Republic, who was taunted by his *adjudant-chef*, "Ah, Monsieur has not left for England!" When his attempted desertion to the Spanish zone in Morocco failed, he found that his lieutenant could not comprehend any more than the *adjudant-chef* that he was not content any longer to give "good and loyal service to Hitler" by staying out of the war.

He attributed [my desertion attempt] simply to what one called a "coup de tête." Like many French officers he did not indulge in politics. He was content to obey his superior. France had ceased fighting, therefore he ceased fighting. This narrow minded loyalty explains why, in the beginning, only a relatively small number of officers rallied to de Gaulle: Not because they lacked a sense of honor, but through lack of lucidity. I tried to explain my reasons, but he interrupted me immediately: "Don't say anything that could hurt your case. I want to punish you only for illegal absence."[26]

Apparently neither man harbored any hard feelings, however, for in 1950 the lieutenant invited Rosenthal, who later successfully deserted and finished the war a major in the British army, for a drink in the officers mess at Meknès.[27]

The loss of Syria in 1941 produced much the same effect upon many army officers in North Africa as Mers el Kébir had done in the French navy. Furthermore, many of the fifteen thousand soldiers of the Syrian garrison, cleverly allowed by the Germans to return to North Africa, preached a gospel of hatred and hostility to the British and Gaullists with the fervor of men who had been martyred for the faith. The French high command became more firmly convinced than ever that France could survive only by defending her neutrality and staying out of the war.[28] But the situation was not completely under control, despite the firm grip maintained upon Sidi-bel-Abbès by the veterans of the *6e étranger*. In part, this was a product of a desire to fight among professional soldiers, so much so that Colonel Barre was forced to intervene to squelch talk among some of the cadres of volunteering for the *légion des volontaires français contre le bolchevisme* recruited to fight in the German ranks on the eastern front.

It was only too evident that many legionnaires and some young officers were growing increasingly impatient with Vichy neutrality.[29] Those who cared to think about the fact that Vichy's position required them to point their guns in the same direction as those of the Germans were increasingly discontented, especially as German demands upon the French economy grew, Vichy collaboration in supporting Rommel's campaign in the Western Desert was more obvious, the United States entered the war, and the tenacious defense of the Soviet Union increasingly gave the lie to pessimistic predictions of Moscow's imminent collapse. More, the unmistakable air of obsolescence hung heavily over a force that tinkered with its mules and continued to build roads with traditional pick-and-shovel methods while a modern, technological war swirled around it. Rosenthal recorded that there was an agitated atmosphere in his unit caused in part by the fact that no one had any reason to be loyal to Vichy—the political refugees loathed the regime, while the Germans found it insulting to serve in a defeated army. Traditional Legion methods of controlling this sort of *cafard* by keeping the men busy on road mending simply served to make the situation worse.[30] When Perrot-White was assigned to a Legion artillery battery at Port-Lyautey (Kenitra) in Morocco in August 1942, he discovered it crammed with convinced Gaullists from the commander down.[31]

When the Allied invasion began on November 8, 1942, these divisions and doubts appear to have made some difference. Perrot-White claimed that he and his "Gaullist" battery adopted a passive attitude of not firing at the American troops, or firing wide, which failed to save them from destruction by the American planes, a fate also suffered by a convoy of Legion reinforcements sent from Fez. He only agreed to drive a truck in the evacuation after he persuaded himself that it did not constitute a "combatant act." However, even he was disgusted when a group of Spaniards whom he believed to be part of the REC surrendered to the Americans without firing a shot: "This act I considered a blot upon the honour of the Legion," he wrote. "Even if they did not want to fight against the Allies, they could have done the same as we had, adopted a passive attitude and stayed where they were. Deliberately turning themselves over as prisoners was an unforgivable military crime."[32]

Not surprisingly, perhaps, given the high percentage of veterans of the *6ᵉ étranger* in residence, the attitude of the soldiers at Sidi-bel-Abbès to the news of the invasion was more decisive. Major Rouger reported that his men "left Bel-Abbès with the conviction that they were going to do some 'good work' and that the enemy would have to deal with them despite their lack of armament." However, Rouger was destined to be doubly disappointed. First, because dug in on the road between Sidi-bel-Abbès and Oran, hostilities were suspended before the fighting reached them. His only contribution to the combat that raged around Oran was to refuse to allow a convoy through whose commander, he believed, intended to defect to the Americans. News of the end to the fighting caused "consternation" and left his men crying with frustrated rage over the unavenged deaths of comrades in other regiments. His second disappointment occurred when his Legion convoy returned to Sidi-bel-Abbès to be greeted with wild enthusiasm by "a large portion of the population, especially the Jews," under the mistaken impression that they were being liberated by the Americans.[33]

The End of "Neutrality"

The successful Allied invasion did not immediately restore the Legion to its predebacle brilliance—quite the contrary. Until the end of the war, the Legion continued to be plagued by three problems: continued division between Gaullists and those who had remained loyal to Vichy, a shortfall of recruits and, finally, the problems of restoring combat efficiency. Given the bitter experience of Syria, the return of the prodigal sons of the 13e DBLE to Sidi-bel-Abbès in 1943 was hardly regarded by the *"maison-mère"* as an occasion for corporate festivity. An honor guard sent by the 13th from Tunisia to Algiers for de Gaulle was escorted back to the frontier under armed guard. The old guard continued to salute the outsized portrait of Pétain displayed prominently in the barracks for weeks after the Allied invasion, and to protest furiously the desertions from the Legion to the 13th, due no doubt to the prestige of the Free French, but attributable also to the expectation of higher pay. Nor in every case were these "desertions" spontaneous—Gaullist officers organized a network to channel "deserters" from the *1er étranger* to the 13th, an act of hostility that brought contingents from the two units to a menacing confrontation in the suburbs of Sidi-bel-Abbès during one such illicit transfer of recruits. For its part, the BSLE established a spy network in the 13th. Bad relations continued beyond the official abolition of the Free French forces on August 1, 1943, so that when the first replacements of 17 officers, 20 NCOs, and180 legionnaires arrived at the 13th from Sidi-bel-Abbès they were coolly received. Some of the replacement officers, exasperated by the frequent accusations of being "eleventh hour-joiners" flung at them, eventually transferred out.

While relations gradually improved between the 13th and Sidi-bel-Abbès, tensions between the Gaullists and the old Pétainists, many of whom switched their allegiance to de Gaulle's resistance rival General Henri Giraud after November 1942, surfaced periodically until the end of the war. The old *1er division française libre*, of which the 13e DBLE was part, despite successive name changes in 1943 and 1944, retained the Gaullist Cross of Lorraine on its shoulder patch, in contrast with the rest of the *Armée d'Afrique*, which wore a Gallic cockerel silhouetted against a sunburst as its symbol. The separate symbols were abandoned only for "Operation Anvil," the invasion of southern France in the summer of 1944. The 13th took its individualism even further, daring to distance itself from one of the most potent of Legion symbols—in Italy and later in France, the 13th continued to parade in its Narvik beret rather than the white kepi, which it finally consented to wear for the victory parade in 1945. The reequipping of the Free French troops on the American model after 1943 would also be a source of friction. While in the final campaign in the winter of 1944–45 officers of the 13th complained that they were starved of supplies and recruits to the benefit of other Legion units and were assigned the hardest fighting by ex-Vichy generals who deliberately sought their destruction, claims that appear unfounded.[34]

Recruitment posed a second problem for the Legion, and offered a repeat in many respects of its World War I experience. The shortfall of enlistments during the dark years after 1940 and the pilfering by the Armistice Commission left the Legion seriously undermanned at the very moment when the opportunity to return to the war at last presented itself. By 1943, 14,342 men remained on the Legion rolls, a number reduced further by desertions and "illegal absences," which increased in 1943 even in the 13th. This was caused in part by ten months of inactivity between the end of the North African fighting and the 13th's entry into Italy. But worse, other Allied armies where the pay and conditions of service, and less stringent discipline, not to mention the prestige, were generally higher than in the Legion exerted an often irresistible attraction—for instance, around sixty legionnaires classified as "bad elements" deserted the 13th in 1943 for the better life of the British army.[35] A report of March 14, 1943, complained of a feeling that the Legion was dying because so many legionnaires were eager to get into their national armies. The spectacle of ex-legionnaires returning as officers of the U.S. Army, complete with inflated American pay, had also increased the feeling that legionnaires were missing out on their share of wartime prosperity and prestige.[36] The Allies had picked up where the Germans left off, securing the release of Poles, Belgians, Dutch and Luxemburgers and even some Russians, which in 1945 caused Legion Lieutenant Colonel Gaultier to echo fears similar to those of Rollet in 1918 that "one risks arriving rapidly at the disappearance of the Foreign Legion."[37] The Dutch consul in Algiers was especially effective in securing the discharge of his nationals from the Legion.[38] But not all losses were due to desertions and the Allied shakeout of their nationals. The Germans, too, could take some credit for causing the Legion some manpower problems in battle, from 1943.

The problem was how to replace these departures, and here the Legion faced many obstacles, some of their own making. Few legionnaires whose enlistment contracts had terminated, especially the Spaniards, were storming the company offices to reenlist. A November 23, 1944, report from Lieutenant Colonel Tritschler of the *régiment de marche de la légion étrangère* (RMLE) complained that these men were given residence permits too easily and that they should be sent into concentration or work camps as a means of forcing them to remain, an indication that you could take the Legion out of Vichy, but it was infinitely more difficult to take Vichy out of the Legion.[39] It also appears that the Legion sometimes simply kept men beyond their legal time of service. How widespread this practice was is not clear. However, the *3ᵉ étranger* admitted in 1945 that "a notable quantity of desertions" could be attributed to the practice of keeping legionnaires beyond the expiration of their contracts.[40]

Desperate for recruits, the Legion sought out other sources, which even included those volunteers of 1939–40 whom it had demobilized, scorned and abandoned in the camps of southern Algeria and Morocco. Even though Legion recruiting officers in the camps were accused by the American Friends Service Committee, a Quaker organization active in the camps, of resorting to threats to denounce the internees to the Allies as fascists and even to imprisonment and torture, not surprisingly, few evinced any burning desire to renew their Legion experience. Some agreed to serve in the British Pioneer Corps. Most simply wanted to put as much distance between themselves, France and the Legion as possible.[41]

Legion officers complained that the government was allowing foreigners to join regular French units and the Polish forces or remain in resistance units rather than requiring them to enlist in the Legion.[42] So desperate was the Legion for soldiers that in August 1944 it even snapped up 650 Ukrainians complete with German uniforms and arms, whose defection from the 30th SS Division to the French resistance was organized by the American Office of Strategic Services. The Resistance handed them over to the Americans. Quick negotiations allowed them to be incorporated into the reinforcement-hungry 13^e DBLE, where they operated with their own officers. This was a suspension of the Legion's normal practice of mixing nationalities and can only be explained by the desperate pressure of circumstances. A second Legion practice was also suspended in the case of these men when Soviet complaints forced the French to surrender them to the certain death of Communist justice, while the remainder were pursued by Stalin into Indochina after the war.[43] Clearly, the world conflict was playing havoc with the Legion's laws of asylum.

The world conflict would also play havoc with the Legion's attempt to recover its combat efficiency, a third major problem it faced. The Allied invasion of Morocco and Algeria had demonstrated in a few brief hours of fighting that the French armistice army was hopelessly outclassed technologically by its better-armed opponents. That lesson would be driven home forcefully in the opening weeks of 1943, when both the 1er and 3e *étrangers* contributed forces to drive the Germans out of Tunisia. Unfortunately for the Allies, Rommel insisted upon a delayed departure. Two German offensives launched in January and February 1943 to drive the Allies from the approaches to Tunis savaged the Legion, as they did the U.S. Army at Kasserine Pass. That spearheaded by the 10th Panzer Division on January 18 from Pont du Fahs southwest of Tunis quickly surrounded the second battalion of the 3e *étranger* and eventually overran the position, capturing two Legion battalion commanders. According to Legion records, the legionnaires earned compliments for their resistance from the German commander.

On the 19th, the German attack pursued its relentless course to the southwest, with panzers driving along the main routes while German infantry closely supported by artillery infiltrated around French positions on the mountain paths. The French withdrew through the broken terrain, but the retreat was a costly one. Although the French claimed to have inflicted numerous casualties upon the Germans,[44] a report of March 14, 1943, noted that the 3e *étranger* lost thirty-five officers and 1,600 legionnaires in January alone.[45] What was more, the 3rd also forfeited its flag, the most decorated in the Legion, when its forward units were overrun on January 18–19. Happily for the Legion, Axis efficiency on the battlefield did not on this occasion extend to the *après-bataille*. After taking suitable pictures of Axis officers holding up their battle trophy, one of which was published in the Italian newspaper *Corriere della Sera,* the German command used the flag to decorate a meeting room in some buildings converted into a field hospital. Two French residents of Tunis discovered the flag in the back of a German ambulance during the Axis retreat in May, and gave it to General Giraud, who restored it to the Legion. Fortunately, no one seemed to notice during the Tunis victory parade of May 20, 1943, that the Legion's most celebrated flag had lost the streamers denoting its World War I decorations during its three months of captivity.[46]

While Legion histories compliment the Legion on its heroic perfor-mance in the Tunisian campaign, it was apparent that heroism by itself was insufficient against an army as efficient as the *Wehrmacht.* In the main, French units had been assigned secondary tasks of holding flanking high ground in support of major thrusts by American and British troops, where they performed yeoman service. But the ability to hold ridge lines tena-ciously in Tunisia could not overcome the poor impression made upon the British and Americans by the somewhat hoary exoticism of The *Armée d'Afrique,* which appeared to them to be a meeting between extras from a Hollywood film set and a convention of antique weapons collectors, backed by a supporting cast of mules. The rapid collapse of France in 1940; the two-year period of "neutrality" of the North African officer corps, which appeared inexplicable, if not inexcusable, in Allied eyes; the long period of bickering between the North African hierarchy and the Allied command after the November 1942 invasion, followed by the quarrels among the Gaullists and supporters of General Giraud, served to reinforce the low opinion in which the "Anglo-Saxons" held French capabilities.

Despite these reservations, the *Armée d'Afrique* fell under the tutelage of the U.S. Army's French Army Instruction and Training Corps, which undertook to reequip the tatterdemalion regiments of North Africa with modern equipment and instruct them in its use. For the Legion, this meant learning how to become mechanized infantry able to operate in conjunc-tion with tanks. Outdated French equipment gave way to jeeps, half-tracks and an array of weapons that left many veterans of "old" Legion, now told that they must "disguise themselves as Americans," bug-eyed with aston-ishment. Even though impromptu songs that compared American helmets to soup bowls and insisted that their rifles had seen service in the Civil War—in fact, they were 1917-model Garand rifles—were soon topping the concert bill on mess nights, the avalanche of ironmongery was like food placed before a claque of starving children.[47]

This is not to say that the conversion to American methods did not cause problems, foremost of which perhaps was that the unaccustomed American emphasis upon logistics forced the *Armée d'Afrique,* after much grumbling, to break up combat units for use in support roles. For the 13th especially it was a less than happy reorganization, for they exchanged their British-inspired desert mobility for a more plodding American-model battalion of 850 men organized into three rifle companies, a heavy weapons company and a machine-gun company.[48] The unit priorities for reequipment also provided yet another issue over which supporters of de Gaulle, who argued for the old Free French units, and Giraud, who championed the ex-Vichy forces, could clash, a dispute that helped to delay the arrival of the 13ᵉ DBLE in Italy until April 1944.

Italy did not prove to be one of the happiest proving grounds for Allied skills in World War II. Professor Sir Michael Howard once suggested that the Allied problems were inevitable once they decided to conquer Italy by beginning at the bottom. While the Italian campaign was a strategic success for the Allies because it tied down German divisions that Hitler might have employed more usefully elsewhere, the mountainous terrain offered the Germans ample opportunity for defense, while the limited communications network provided the largely roadbound Allied forces few attack options. Because the Allied advance in Italy was a slow and frustrating one, and because so little was expected of the French for reasons already mentioned, what British Brigadier K. W. D. Strong described as "the good French performance in Italy" came as an agreeable and welcome surprise to American and British leaders.[49]

There are several explanations for this. First must be the quality of the commander of the French Expeditionary Corps, General (later Marshal) Alphonse Juin. A veteran of North Africa, Juin possessed the diplomacy and patience to work effectively with his Allied counterparts, as well as a firm grasp of the strengths of his troops and the best way to employ them. In this way, he was able to engineer the eventual breakthrough of the Gustav Line, a series of virtually impregnable defenses that ran east to west across the peninsula through Monte Cassino. The second factor in the French performance was the troops themselves, especially, but not exclusively, the Moroccan regiments. The rusticity and backwardness of the *Armée d'Afrique,* which was initially much derided by Allied officers in 1942, in fact proved a great advantage in the rugged terrain of central Italy, which so resembled that of North Africa. Juin made certain that his men were well supplied with mules, which allowed them to move off the roads and pierce German lines at thinly defended points where attacks were least expected. The aggressive professionalism of these men often contrasted starkly with the lax, even timid, performance of British and American conscripts, although on the negative side of the ledger the Moroccans especially were often accused of being more dangerous to Italian civilians than to German soldiers.

A final factor in this superior French performance was the quality of its leadership. "Of course every division, of no matter what nationality, had its heroes . . . ," British historian of the Italian campaign John Ellis writes.

Yet one cannot but feel that the French Corps had more than its share. That there was a style of leadership there and a spirit of authentically patriotic self-sacrifice that would have seemed almost indecent in other units, particularly in the more prosaic, sometimes cynical American, British and Commonwealth ones.[50]

While Ellis is not speaking particularly of the Legion, this type of leadership was to be found there in abundance. And while this helps to explain the aggressive performance of the 13ᵉ DBLE in Italy, leadership in itself could not make Italy an entirely successful venture for the Legion.

In April 1944, when the 13th arrived in Italy, the campaign that had begun in Sicily in July of the previous year was approaching its first anniversary, and an unhappy one it would be if the Allies were still stalled before the Gustav Line. The battalions of the 13th designated as the *1ᵉʳ* and *2ᵉ bataillons de légion étrangère (BLE)*, were part of the *1ᵉ division de marche d'infanterie (1ᵉ DMI)*, the old *1ᵉ division française libre*. The attack plan was Juin's, and he assigned the 1ᵉ DMI the task of moving along the southern banks of the Liri towards San Giorgio à Liri in a move to outflank and penetrate German defenses while two divisions of Moroccans and Algerians stormed the mountains to their front.

The 13th was initially held in reserve as the attack jumped off on May 11, and immediately ran into difficulty when the failure of the Moroccans to seize the mountains opened the roadbound DMI to plunging fire from German positions above and well-laid minefields along its line of march. Only on the 17th was the 13th brought to the front lines, where it was almost immediately hit by an air attack that cost it 102 casualties. On the 21st the legionnaires joined the slow advance along the Liri, but they were thrown back by a German counterattack. Fortunately, a breakthrough by the Moroccans and *Chasseurs d'Afrique* to the south allowed the legionnaires to be placed in trucks and join the pursuit toward and around Rome, which resulted in a hard fight between legionnaires and German panzer and parachute regiments at Radicofani north of Rome on June 18. For its actions, the 1st battalion of the BLE was awarded a *croix de guerre*. In all, the Italian campaign, though brief, cost the 13th 466 casualties, or one-quarter of its strength, a severe blow when one considers the difficulty of finding replacements.[51]

Neither the Legion nor the 1ᵉ DMI of which they were part were content with their slow progress against what they conceded to be limited German strength. There were several reasons for their slowness. First, of course, one must place the difficulties of the campaign in context. The line of advance along the Liri that it had been assigned, cut by hedgerows and overlooked by steep slopes covered with boulders, thorn bushes and German bunkers, was an extremely difficult one. The rugged terrain combined with stiff German resistance had defeated the Americans and British for several months. However, that said, the 1ᵉ DMI appears to have performed less well than the other French divisions, admittedly a high standard to match. Perhaps some of the problems stemmed from the fact that all of its previous combat experience had been in the free-flowing conditions of the Western Desert. The Free French veterans were clearly less comfortable, and understandably so, cast in the role of heavy infantry slogging it out with the *Wehrmacht* in the narrow mountain valleys of Italy.

Criticisms of the DMI, though not specifically of the Legion, were that the NCOs, brave enough in the attack, failed to protect their men during the lulls in the fighting so that "we do not camouflage ourselves enough; we do not dig enough, we do not manoeuvre enough."[52] Certainly some of the blame for the failure to advance can be laid at the feet of the American armored units with whom the 1^e DMI worked, soldiers often out of sympathy with its aggressive professionalism, and who often demonstrated a preference for survival over attack. But all of the unit's problems could not be blamed on the Americans, for it was supported by French tanks as well. A major problem had been the poor response to German counterattacks, and here Legion Major de Sairigné blamed the lack of depth in the French attack formations and the dispersion of antitank weapons. In the pursuit, he believed 180-man companies too cumbersome and recommended that subordinate commanders should be allowed more initiative, a criticism of the highly centralized French command structure heard since World War I.[53]

THE LEGION'S LAST CAMPAIGN in the European theater of World War II was, appropriately, the liberation of France. For the 13e DBLE, this justified the stand that they had taken in 1940, and marked a fitting climax to a five-year journey over three continents. As in 1915–18, Sidi-bel-Abbès resurrected the RMLE, three battalions of mechanized infantry organized like the American infantry, into combat commands composed of tanks, mechanized (Legion) infantry and light artillery. The REC was also included in these arrangements. These units landed on France's south coast in the late summer of 1944, broke through a thin crust of German resistance, and raced up the Rhône Valley behind retreating Germans. However, German resistance began to stiffen in the late autumn as the Allies approached the Rhine. The fighting in Alsace was bitter in the hard winter of 1944–45, and only in the spring were the French able to drive into Germany. These final campaigns earned the praise both of contemporaries and historians, especially for their defense of Strasbourg against a formidable German counterstroke in January 1945. The combats against Germans fighting from well-fortified positions were remarkably hard, and the legionnaires sometimes demonstrated commendable creativity in dealing with their opponents.

For instance, on the night of January 11–12, 1945, a group of legionnaires surrounded in the Alsatian village of Herbsheim by a German offensive unleashed three days earlier were ordered to withdraw to French lines after an attempt to rescue them failed. Destroying their heavy weapons, and carrying their wounded on stretchers, they filtered through the first line of German defenses covered in part by the noise of a German tank operating on the road. As they approached the second line, a German-speaking legionnaire announced to the sentinel that they were the reinforcements sent to prevent the French breakout. After the sentinel obligingly answered all of the questions put to him about the number of German troops and their disposition, the legionnaires dispatched the unfortunate guard and charged through the German position, sowing death on their way to a safe escape.[54]

More than any other of its actions in World War II, perhaps even than those in World War I, this winter campaign in eastern France appeared to justify the often-repeated belief that the Legion was used as a *troupe de sacrifice* by the French high command. As early as October 1944, even before the really difficult conditions of the winter campaign set in, the ex-Free French reported that

The impression of the systematic sabotage of our units is more and more evident. . . . Cadres and soldiers are beginning to be tired of fighting in bad conditions, to liberate people who are not thankful for it. Morale is low, very low, and the responsibility for this must be laid at the feet of the high command.[55]

For its part, the high command reacted against the continual carping of the 13e DBLE and of the old Free French 1e DMI, which "pretends that their action alone saved the French army from disaster and liberated Belfort and Mulhouse. . . . Not only is this order of the day in great part in opposition with the facts, but also it testifies to a complete lack of respect and fighting comradeship toward the other large army units, which will certainly be deeply resented by all the units."

Discontent finally boiled over in the 13e DBLE in early February 1945, after taking 1,026 casualties, or 42 percent of their effectives, in the January fighting in Alsace, when two officers traveled to the war ministry in Paris to accuse de Lattre de Tassigny and their enemies at Sidi-bel-Abbès for "looking to destroy it through its perpetual engagement in new actions, [and by] filtering recruits."[56] The complaint caused the division to be shifted to the Alps in March 1945.

How justified was the accusation that the 1e DMI in general and the 13e DBLE in particular had been singled out for annihilation by ex-Vichyites bent upon revenge? Not at all, according to A.-P. Comor. All units serving in the 1st French Army under General de Lattre de Tassigny appear to have borne the burden of carnage with a commendable equality, including the RMLE, which lost 2,204 men between November 1944 and April 1945, or 70 percent of its average strength.[57] There may be several explanations why the French took such heavy casualties. The first was that de Lattre relentlessly drove his troops forward, as if attempting to compensate for his manpower shortages and for all the other intangible but potent feelings of lost prestige that flowed from the 1940 defeat. For instance, de Gaulle's decision to hold on to Strasbourg against the wishes of the Allies in the face of the January 1945 German offensive may have made political sense, but it was a logic that French troops had to pay for with a minor Verdun. The shortage of replacements has already been mentioned. In practical terms, this meant that units had to be kept longer at the front, which increased wear and tear, and consequently casualties, dramatically.

Lack of training was also a problem linked to the thirst for recruits. In practical terms, this meant that replacements were tossed into combat, often after the most perfunctory training. The complaints were that Legion units were wooden, lacked maneuverability, were unaccustomed to infiltration tactics, especially in heavily wooded terrain, and had little practice operating in conjunction with tanks.[58] A report for the RMLE complained that the legionnaires in the attack collected around the tanks, where they drew dense German fire, "absorbed losses out of proportion with the numbers placed against them, and lost part of their offensive capacity." German defensive positions were well organized, and their defensive techniques sought to disassociate the infantry from their accompanying tanks, often with success. An example was cited of an incident in the Bois de Sand in eastern France when one German tank held twelve French tanks and accompanying Legion infantry in check. Legion Captain Grand d'Esnon reserved his greatest indictment for French army training: "I saw legionnaires with more than ten years service and very adequately courageous throw their grenades in combat without pulling the pins out, because in training they had never utilized real ones," he wrote. The same was true of smokescreens, never used although all the equipment had been provided, because they had never practiced the techniques. Seldom had legionnaires ever trained with tanks, although tank/infantry combat was their *raison d'être*. "⁸/₁₀ths of losses, and I do not exaggerate, come from poor training," d'Esnon believed.

Why was training not made more realistic, d'Esnon asked? In part, this was due to "lack of character and a spirit of routine" that reigned in the French army. But in his view, the malaise ran deeper—the French were the victims of their own pride, especially where the Americans were concerned. They had been invaded by the Americans, upon whom they were dependent for arms, a tributary position many French officers accepted with difficulty. More, the price of American bounty had been paid in the form of the deep modification of a military system that was in many respects very different from that of the *Armée d'Afrique,* at least. It must have also been obvious to many French officers that the Americans especially held them in barely veiled, and unjustified, contempt, a contempt reciprocated in full measure by French *africains,* for whom an American army that relied more on firepower than personal courage, and that appeared obsessed with their creature comforts, reminded them all too much of the French conscripts whose alleged lack of fighting spirit had cost them the Fight for France in 1940. Because of all this, d'Esnon believed, the French army was quite prepared to toss out the baby with the bathwater: "It is extraordinarily humiliating to think," he wrote,

that certain particularly useful combat exercises which subsequently will prove themselves such by the need to approximate real conditions will not be carried out during the preparation for the campaign for France, because they were imposed by the Americans. The lack of military experience of [the Americans] was often generously compensated for by an exact and honest vision of the goals which made them construct an army and the results that they expected.

Therefore, the French had paid for their pride with the blood of their troops, including that of legionnaires.[59]

WHAT CAN BE the verdict on the Legion in World War II? The first thing that might be said is that much of its best military performance was turned in by units, and by legionnaires, who were not motivated by a traditional Legion outlook, especially the *12ᵉ étranger* and the RMVEs of 1940. But even the 13ᵉ DBLE, whose commander was fond of explaining that *"La Légion, c'est le détachement,"*[60] evolved in ways that increasingly distinguished it from the "old Legion." While the decision to fight on in June 1940 was often taken from a mercenary desire to continue to fight, conflict with "loyal" Vichy troops quickly provoked a politicized, even a democratic, outlook within the 13th. Its officers for a period in 1941–42 were selected by a vote of the other officers, while recruitment remained "for the duration of the war plus three months," unlike the "old Legion," which continued to insist upon a five-year commitment.

Therefore, while military theorists like S. L. A. Marshal are perhaps correct to point out that soldiers do not fight for patriotism, but out of loyalty to their comrades, the sentiment of serving a cause or a national purpose does provide a cement of regimental cohesion and fidelity. The sentiment that they were fighting on the wrong side also affected the "old Legion," at least in Morocco, where some units put up only a halfhearted resistance to the Allied invasion of November 1942. Therefore, part of the Legion was very much *engagée* in World War II, despite its "traditions." But Legion versatility has allowed it to assimilate the heroic actions of these units into regimental "tradition."

It was its continued insistence upon its mercenary character, however, that consigned the Legion to an eclipse in postwar French opinion. Major de Sairigné believed that "the French will never understand what they owe to these foreigners who fight for them with an extraordinary spirit, in unbelievable conditions."[61]

This was also the verdict of the RMLE, which complained that they had been pulled back too quickly from Germany, where they would have preferred "to profit a little longer from the legitimate satisfactions which fall to the victor," and expedited to North Africa, in part because of the revolt in the Constantinois of May 1945. France had left a bad impression, for French men and women did not appreciate the Legion, and everywhere the legionnaires had encountered "Meanness, pettiness of spirit and of acts, lack of respect for a victorious army." In the view of French officers, not the least those of the 13^e DBLE, French honor had been salvaged by her colonial army, with legionnaires in the vanguard. But an ungrateful population seemed to be preparing for "a national army profoundly linked to the people."[62] Perhaps it was slightly embarrassing for the French people to be reminded that salvation and honor had been purchased in large measure by the blood of foreigners, North Africans and mercenaries. In the first place, the professional army had been too closely associated with the now-discredited Vichy regime. Second, the inundation of British and especially of American troops, not to mention the heroic resistance of the Soviet Union, had made the French participation in the victory over Hitler appear an interesting but rather minor contribution in the grand scheme of things.

Last, in the battle of "myths," uncharacteristically perhaps, the Legion enjoyed less than complete success. Already the high command had protested the battle order issued by the 1e DMI in which it lay claim to having thwarted the German attack upon the Colmar pocket in January 1945 almost singlehandedly. This was seen as a transparent ploy by the Gaullists to seize the public relations high ground from their rivals in the *Armée d'Afrique*. But these campaigns of self-advertisement paled beside the enormous prestige of the *2e Division blindée,* which fought in the much more prestigious Normandy invasion behind the legendary General Philippe Leclerc de Hautecloque, a "Gaullist of the First Hour" who had marched his troops from Chad to Libya across the Sahara to strike a blow against the Axis. Then there were the *forces françaises de l'intérieur* (FFI), the Resistance, whose legend of heroic sacrifice was being constructed even before the liberation, encouraged both by the Communists and the Gaullists, and fed by the need for the restoration of French self-esteem. Faced with this stiff competition, the 13e DBLE finished an interesting but poor third in the battle to win public recognition as the primary heroes of the French liberation.

Not surprisingly, the great fatigue of the Legion in 1945, the dearth of recruits and the seeming indifference of the population caused some in the Legion to worry about the unit's future, much as Rollet had done in similar circumstances in 1918. "In general, the Foreign Legion is not well known, and conditions do not favor the *massive* enlistments required by her in wartime," wrote Lieutenant Colonel Gaultier of the RMLE in March 1945.

This is difficult to credit, however, given the massive publicity showered upon the Legion in the 1930s. The more logical explanation is that the Legion mystique had been dwarfed, marginalized and made unfashionable by the immensity of the war. The ministry consoled Gaultier that the war would soon be over and that the Legion could recruit in Germany,[63] a prospect that must have filled many traditional Legion officers with joyful expectation.

Clearly, while the Legion had fought bravely in World War II as in the earlier conflict, and while it could even claim a share in the redemption of French honor out of proportion to its actual numbers, large, world-scale conflicts were not its preferred milieu. The mobilization or occupation of many nations caused it to suffer a dearth of recruits, and forced it to absorb resentful refugees who slotted uncomfortably into the regimental ambience. One might also argue that the mechanized character of World War II caused the Legion problems that it never completely resolved—those of training a polyglot soldiery in forms of warfare more complex than the imperial conflicts the Legion had fought hitherto. The traditional courage and drive of the Legion often was not matched by an expertise in modern forms of warfare. In part, this was the product of a unit operating with a system, and with support services, that were not its own. But it is difficult to escape the feeling that the Legion was not altogether comfortable in the professional conditions of *La Grande Guerre*, that its reputation and its image were better fulfilled in marginal conflicts in distant lands, wars that allowed more scope for the Legion's special brand of theatrics—trials of endurance and glorious last stands amidst remote and exotic landscapes.

Happily for the Legion, as peace settled over the wreckage of Europe, it appeared as if these conditions were about to be fulfilled once again. By 1946, the Germans were coming back and the Legion was headed for Indochina, where the enemy had neither panzers nor *Luftwaffe*. It was going to be almost like old times.

Chapter 24

"MASTERS OF THE BATTLEFIELD"— THE LEGION IN INDOCHINA

Prelude to War

After a month spent in the cramped, stinking hold of the *Pasteur*, the sight of Cap Saint Jacques in the summer of 1952 should have come as a great relief to the nine hundred legionnaires, North Africans and Senegalese who milled on the decks amidst a chaos of kit bags as they prepared to transfer to a liberty ship that would take them up the Saigon River. But this fore-land of Asia, which pushed its dark green jungle into a sea as gray as the sky that lowered above it, appeared even from this distance alien and unwelcoming. Nor were spirits lifted during the eight-hour ride upriver to Saigon. The ship steamed slowly against the muddy current, through dreary marshlands that stretched off both bows as far as the eye could see. The impression of desolation was heightened by the carcasses of ships, sunk by the Japanese in 1945, that rusted against the banks. The threat of Viet Minh snipers, or a heavy downpour that blurred swamp and channel into an indistinguishable gray shadow, forced the already bad-tempered soldiers into the stifling heat of the hold, where they passed the last hours of their voyage sweating, swearing and drinking warm beer or wine soured by the heat. Finally, isolated houses began to appear, which soon became numer-ous enough to qualify as suburbs. The ship nosed between the rotting jetties and half-submerged hulks to the quayside. The legionnaires stood to attention on the deck, rainwater dripping from the bills of their kepis and soaked to the skin, as the notes of "Le Boudin" gurgled through the downpour, and an impeccably dressed staff officer delivered a speech of welcome, made unintelligible by the sound system, even had the polyglot draft of replacements for the *corps expéditionnaire français en Extrême-Orient* been able to understand French.

Saigon, the entrance to the land that was well on its way to becoming a graveyard for two modern Western armies, combined the normal frenetic pace of an oriental city with a *fin du monde* atmosphere. The wide, tree-lined boulevards were filled with a torrent of taxis, jeeps, army trucks, bicycles, pedestrians and *pousse-pousses*—pedaled or motorized rickshaws—whose drivers appeared intent upon committing either murder or suicide. Interspersed among the handsome administrative buildings were restaurants and cafés bursting with soldiers. The bar and roof garden of the Hotel Continental were the most fashionable and most popular of these spots. Here senior officers and functionaries, businessmen and journalists arranged transfers of piastres to Paris at lucrative rates of exchange, traded gossip or espionage, or basked in the company of delicious Chinese and Vietnamese "taxi girls," the side vents of whose slim dresses of bright blue, yellow or red silk reached to about mid-thigh. No one appeared to notice the distant rumble of artillery that announced that, just beyond the comfortable villas smothered in bougainvillea, a war of almost unimaginable savagery was being fought.

Soldiers in search of female company could always resort to the Buffalo Park, an army bordello whose two hundred females exhibited such predatory ferocity in the competition to drag the clients into one of the small cubicles that lined the large hall that only courageous, mad or uninformed males dared to enter. Those soldiers who preferred a leisurely selection of their companions, or who looked to have their libido rather than their survival instincts stimulated, took themselves to Cholon, a labyrinth of cooking stalls, bars, brothels, dance halls, shops and opium dens just across the river from Saigon. However, it was not considered safe to go there alone, especially after dark.

By 1952, even the dullest legionnaire was coming to realize that the Indochinese War was not going well for the French. In fact, the whole affair had rather got off on the wrong foot, although in 1946 when the war broke out there were few in the French ranks who had predicted defeat, much less disaster. The signs of imperial erosion had been evident, however, for by the interwar years this Pearl of the Orient, this jewel in the French imperial crown had already begun to demonstrate the centrifugal tendencies that were to cast it into bloody conflict. This had not prevented Indochina from remaining the Legion's preferred garrison, a prize held out to men of long service and good conduct. Life there was a tangible mirage of higher pay, comfort and facile women. After decades of tramping the jungle highlands of Tonkin, the Legion had gradually been regrouped near Tonkin's Red River delta in barracks considered sumptuous by North African standards. The barracks at Vietri, sixty miles northwest of Hanoi, which became the headquarters of the *5ᵉ étranger* when it was formed in 1930, looked more like a holiday resort than a garrison. From the large windows of the three-story barracks built in an airy colonial style, legionnaires could look out over well-tended gardens across the large lake formed by the confluence of the Red and Clear rivers to the mountains beyond. The garrison at Tong, about thirty miles from Hanoi, had a slightly more martial appearance, if only because it lay next to a training camp. However, the arcaded verandas of the two barrack buildings that faced each other across well-tended lawns telegraphed the distinct impression of a corps that had increasingly devoted itself to its own well-being.

And that well-being was immense. The higher cost of living in Tonkin, double that of North Africa, was more than compensated for by higher pay. Junior lieutenants, who could barely make ends meet in France, were able to keep at least three servants in Tonkin. This privilege was even extended to legionnaires, whose pay of twelve francs twenty-five centimes a day for those with only three years' service in 1937 was almost six times that received in North Africa. And most legionnaires in Tonkin counted over ten years' service and therefor were paid considerably more. Naturally, such wealth freed them from the fatigue duties that so reduced leisure time at Sidi-bel-Abbès—when one Legion lieutenant freshly arrived from North Africa in 1932 ordered his men down to the washhouse to clean their uniforms, he provoked gales of laughter, for in Indochina such work was done by "boys." "Boys" also did the cooking, polished boots and belts, and kept the barracks tidy for a monthly stipend that varied from twenty francs for menial duties to a top pay of two hundred francs for a really experienced *bep* or cook. So, apart from the eleven-mile march required every fifteen days, and annual maneuvers that took place in December during the *belle saison* in Tonkin, when the temperature dropped all of two degrees, there was little in the way of duties to keep the men occupied, and even those were curtailed in the monsoonal summer heat. Apart from tennis, played exclusively by officers; some hunting, which was also reserved for rank; and fishing for the men, even sports were practiced with restrained enthusiasm, in part because of the climate, but basically one suspects because legionnaires had lost their competitive edge in this atmosphere of *la dolce vita*.

This must not be taken to mean that legionnaires found nothing to occupy their time—quite the contrary. Officially, Thursday afternoons, Sundays and evenings were free. For fully half of the legionnaires in this period, these moments, as well as any others away from duties, were spent with their *congaïs*. For the modest sum of between twenty and forty piastres—two hundred to four hundred francs—a month, the *co* would accept the legionnaire as a temporary husband, provide him with a *cai-nha* or house, one meal a day, a few cigarettes and *choum* (rice alcohol), and wash his clothes. Competition was keen among legionnaires to have the most attractive *co*, to show her off at the cinema, or to invite other legionnaires "home" for an evening of cards. The sight of a legionnaire taking a Sunday turn in a *pousse-pousse*, his *co* beside him and their child balanced on his knee, was a common one. Even when legionnaires were sent to worksites elsewhere, they were inevitably accompanied by their *cos*. Quite naturally, this pervasive domesticity came as a shock to officers fresh from Morocco or Syria, where tough conditions, the absence of women, and frequent operations required a taut military posture. Those who attempted to react against this, however, got nowhere. Most sought consolation in the fact that if the Legion in Indochina did not exactly tremble with military readiness, at least it avoided the worst excesses of Legion behavior elsewhere. The *embourgeoisement* of the legionnaire translated into relative sobriety and fewer punishments, for a prolonged sentence to the cells led to a suspension of pay, which meant inevitably that the *co* was obliged to find another legionnaire to support her. The disciplinary *section spéciale* contained only twenty inmates in 1931, and desertions were infinitesimal in Tonkin in the interwar years. This was in part a reflection of the fact that legionnaires were sent to Tonkin as a reward for a good disciplinary record.[1] However, cognoscenti might be forgiven for worrying that legionnaires who had ceased to drink, fight and take up the challenges of desertion had stepped across the threshold of premature senility.

Not surprisingly, perhaps, this domesticated garrison force was ill prepared to confront the turmoil that erupted in Tonkin and northern Annam in 1930–31, the first in a series of events that were to lead to the large conflict of 1946. Rising resentment against heavyhanded methods of French imperial administration erupted on the night of February 9–10, 1930, when a group of nationalists with the connivance of some *tirailleurs tonkinois* in the garrison of Yen Bai led an insurrection. Although this revolt was quickly put down, it began several long months of agitation, which included a Communist-led revolt in the Nghe An province of northern Annam, mostly of peasants, known as the Nghe Tinh soviet movement. The Legion participated in the police actions carried out with great severity against what the French were already calling, not without justification, the "Red Terror." On September 12, 1930, planes were called in to bomb a group of twenty thousand peasants who were marching upon Vinh, the capital of Nghe An province. Unrest was not ended, however, and continued until November 1931. A May 1931 report from the 3rd (operations) bureau of the *troupes d'Indochine* reminded local commanders that soldiers were not allowed to take food from civilians without paying, install themselves at villagers' expense or force them to perform unpaid labor. Above all, it complained of summary executions of "leaders" and of an apparently widespread belief that such acts carried out in full view of the villagers "produce an effect very favorable to our cause upon the population."[2]

While this report was not directed at the Legion specifically, that corps was staking out a reputation as one of the most uncompromising in dealing with often cruel and bloodthirsty rebels. On October 5, 1930, the siege of a native police post was lifted by a Legion company that killed around one hundred rioters. Another company of legionnaires operating near Vinh left thirty-three attackers dead and took fifty-one prisoners on December 12. Other bands were summarily dispersed by Legion patrols in actions that earned the *"Ordre du Dragon d'Annam"* for the standard of the 3rd battalion of the newly created *5ᵉ étranger,* and over one hundred individual citations for its officers and men. As a consequence, a sullen and hostile crowd gathered for the parade to celebrate the centenary of the Legion on March 9, 1931, at Vinh—as the battalion marched past, agitators shouted offers of one thousand piastres for the head of the battalion commander and threw tracts into the ranks of the legionnaires. One witness described what happened next:

Furious, Major Lambert ordered a platoon with bayonets fixed to charge the Annamites massed there. The legionnaires, hitting out at random, grabbed six Annamites and, immediately lining them up near the bridge in front of the Residency, shot them. Two of these unfortunates managed to jump into the water. They were followed by shots and killed in the water.[3]

With tensions running so high, only the merest spark was required to produce an even larger conflagration. That spark was struck on May 27, 1931, when twenty-six-year-old Legion Sergeant Perrier, cycling along a road in the Vinh region and unarmed, attempted to intervene to prevent a Communist-led crowd from decapitating a village chief and his elders. Perrier was immediately set upon, cords tied to each wrist, and two groups of agitators pulled in opposite directions until his arms were torn from their sockets. After suitable mutilations, which included sticking bamboo stakes into his eyes, his lifeless body was pitched into a rich paddy. The reaction of Perrier's comrades upon the discovery of his body was fairly predictable. At the Legion post of Nam Dan, a number of prisoners were taken out of the jail and shot. In the subsequent trial of five of these legionnaires, the defense argued that the accused were merely following orders. "To avoid overcrowding, one killed prisoners every evening, even innocents," including coolies who supplied the post and who were impru-dent enough to request payment. "That was done in all the posts," includ-ing by officers who "amused themselves by cutting off heads, even with a small regulation knife." Furthermore, the legionnaires had come from Mo-rocco, where "all the dissidents are executed. One led the legionnaires arriving here to believe that it was the same in Annam." After a moving appeal by a Catholic missionary, Father Gauthier, who told the court that "Our legionnaires . . . have done good work, patriotic work, French work, and restored peace in the country," the legionnaires were acquitted.[4]

Estimates place the number of dead in the repression of the rebellions of 1930–31 at around two thousand, with up to four thousand political activists arrested. The first conclusion many Vietnamese patriots drew from the repression of the "Red Terror" of 1930–31 was that no compromise was possible with the French, and that revolution was the only course open to them. The Nationalist Party (VNQDD), which had masterminded the Yen Bai revolt and which was an important rival of the Vietnamese Communists, was destroyed as an effective force by French repression. The Communists, too, suffered greatly. But enough of them remained abroad, including Ho Chi Minh, to live to fight again another day. Above all, they had learned that revolution must be backed by sufficient military force to defend itself. Also, they collected the glory for opposing the French, which helped to give them the leadership of the nationalist movement by 1945.[5]

Nor did they forget the Legion. "The attitude of the troops and of the Legion in particular is of an odious brutality," one observer wrote on March 15, 1931.

An unbridled army rabble, giving over to all its instincts, escaping almost completely from the control of its leaders, now terrorizes the entire country. One steals, one rapes, one condemns and one executes as one pleases. The legionnaires enter the houses, take what pleases them, attack women and young girls. For no reason, without proof, men, young people, are arrested and shot in cold blood, without trial. This is a real troop of pirates in uniform which has been set loose on the country. . . . If it is by these methods that one pretends to pacify the country, one is badly mistaken. The most obvious result of all this is to excite further passions and to raise up against us the most peaceful among the Annamites. . . . If this is what we want, we'll soon be there! And the communists have really been handed a golden issue to use against us.[6]

The actions of the Legion in Annam had been spectacular enough to earn it a special mention in the convention of March 6, 1946, between Paris and the Viet Minh government installed in Hanoi—although Ho Chi Minh agreed to permit fifteen thousand French troops north of the 16th parallel, he specifically excluded the Legion from this contingent because, among other things, legionnaires had destroyed his native village in Annam.[7] Even many in the French army concluded after 1954 that the savage repression of the Yen Bai revolt, in which the Legion played a small part, and of the troubles in Annam in 1930–32, in which the Legion assumed a vanguard role, had been counterproductive, and that subsequent French policy backed everything that was moribund in the country.

The second blow to French prestige in Indochina, as elsewhere in the world, came with the French defeat of May–June 1940. The Japanese, already upset with the French for aiding the Nationalist Chinese by supplying arms through Lang Son, forced Resident General and ex-Legion officer Georges Catroux to close the frontier to war supplies destined for the Nationalist Chinese, and to accept a Japanese control commission to see that it was enforced. When the new government of Philippe Pétain learned of this, Catroux was dismissed and replaced by Admiral Jean Decoux. Like Catroux, Decoux realized that his position—90,000 troops at full stretch, of which only 14,500 were white, armed with First World War equipment, with no naval or air power to speak of it—was a weak one. He proceeded to sign an agreement with Tokyo on August 30, 1940, that accorded the Japanese certain military facilities in Tonkin in return for recognition of French sovereignty there.

As the details of this accord were being negotiated in Hanoi with a great amount of bad faith on both sides, the Japanese flung a division of thirty thousand men at Lang Son on the night of September 21–22. Although the French had been beefing up their defenses at Lang Son in the expectation of a Japanese action, the attack produced complete panic.[8] On the 25th, the French commander raised the white flag. The commander of the 2nd battalion of the *5e étranger* protested the "humiliation" of marching off into captivity "like a herd of sheep, before an enemy whom he has not even seen in front of him," but he marched off nonetheless. This is cited as the first instance of a Legion unit surrendering without a fight, although according to Alfred Perrot-White heavily Spanish units of the REC surrendered to the Americans without firing a shot during the invasion of Morocco in November 1942.[9] The Japanese separated the battalion's 179 German and Austrian legionnaires and attempted without success to enlist them in the Japanese cause. Finally, on October 5, the Japanese officially regretted the incident of Lang Son and returned the prisoners to Tonkin.[10]

Successful Japanese pressure, such as the cease-fire imposed by Japan in the Franco-Thai dispute of 1940–41, accumulated incidents that contributed to a French loss of face in the eyes of the Vietnamese. But the Japanese attacks on French prestige were not merely indirect ones. As part of her Greater Asia policy, which sought to replace European imperialism in the Far East with Japanese domination, the Japanese worked directly to undermine French control in Indochina. Japanese authorities gave direct support to the Cao Dai and Hoa Hao religious sects in the south, and prevented French attempts to smash their influence.

French weakness also permitted various national and revolutionary groups to re-form and even to infiltrate the imperial civil service, which Vichy had belatedly opened to Vietnamese recruitment. The Communists were especially active in reforming an infrastructure that had been destroyed in the repression of the early 1930s, recruiting intellectuals to their cause and organizing a panoply of apparently benign front organizations to attract adherents. Two clandestine military bases were established in the northern highlands near the Chinese border, from which the Viet Minh would eventually expand. The leader of the embryonic Vietnam Liberation Army, Vo Nguyen Giap, slowly built his force from forty-four to almost three thousand soldiers by the spring of 1945. Although most of his arms were gathered up in attacks on French posts, his military organization was given a boost in 1945 when the American Office of Strategic Services (OSS) dropped over five thousand weapons to the insurgents under the mistaken belief that they were to be used against the Japanese, whom Giap had no intention of attacking. Ho wrote enthusiastic letters to President Truman declaring that "the great American Republic is a good friend of ours."

The decisive events that were to allow the great expansion of the Viet Minh were the Japanese coup against the French of March 9, 1945, followed by their surrender in August. After 1940, the Japanese had gradually increased the numbers of their troops in Indochina to thirty thousand, stationed primarily in the cities and masking major French garrisons. The loss of Burma and the fall of the Philippines and of Iwo Jima in February 1945 caused Tokyo to fear an Allied invasion of Indochina. On the night of March 9, ironically perhaps the birthday of the Legion, the Japanese, reinforced with troops they had withdrawn from Burma, pounced on the French. The French army was in a poor position to defend itself. Although the French counted sixty-five thousand troops, many of them were unreliable native formations. The white troops had received no reinforcements of supplies for over four years. Consequently, units like the Legion had aged considerably—in one company of the *5e étranger*, the average age was thirty-seven. The lack of medical supplies had translated into an increase in malaria, dysentery and venereal disease. The climate, the isolation from France and from the war, the need to maintain the status quo with the Japanese, and the deadly routine of a garrison army in the tropics had stifled what was left of a spirit of initiative among most of the officers. Although the French had drawn up plans to counter just such a possibility, the leading generals chose to ignore intelligence reports and rumors rife in Hanoi and Saigon of an imminent Japanese strike—the two armies had lived side by side in relative harmony, and already there had been so many false alarms of Japanese movements that the top generals were not prepared to give serious credence to these latest ones. No alert was posted for the evening of March 9, and many soldiers were not even in barracks.

In these conditions, the French reaction to the Japanese surprise could only be disjointed and haphazard. Many officers were seized at home or while strolling in the streets with their wives, and a group of officers from a regiment of *tirailleurs* were inhospitably captured as they hosted an *apéritif* for their Japanese counterparts. The few garrisons that did resist, such as the legionnaires in the disciplinary section at Ha Giang, quickly exhausted their ammunition, surrendered and were brutally executed by the Japanese. The prize for resistance went to the garrison at Dang Dong near Lang Son, which did not contain any legionnaires, and held out for three days before surrendering. Another group of legionnaires at Lang Son intoned the *"Marseillaise"* before being machine-gunned to death. A column of around five thousand troops that included the remnants of the three battalions of the *5e étranger*, some *tirailleurs tonkinois* and artillerymen made a fighting retreat to China. Here, too, despite the lack of arms and supplies, and the poor physical condition of the men, the morale and cohesion of the legionnaires and the artillerymen remained superior to that of the Vietnamese troops.

The Americans did little to help this retreating column. No doubt Roosevelt had little sympathy for these tattered remnants of a colonial regime. But this Japanese action must have seemed to be a very minor incident in an obscure corner of a very large war. The Gaullists might have called attention to the plight of these retreating troops. But even they appear to have taken the view that the staunchly Vichyite loyalties of an Indochina garrison that had spent the war playing volleyball with the Japanese and inviting them to cocktail parties little qualified them for sympathy. A report of January 1, 1946, castigated French commanders for their lack of preparation and foresight, and the poor degree of professionalism of those commanders who did opt to defend themselves. Only the Legion escaped the general condemnation.[11]

Although the French emphasized the treachery of the Japanese action and the often heroic martyrdom of their soldiers, especially of the legionnaires and troops of *la Coloniale,* the inescapable fact was that the French presence in Indochina had been terminated by force. The sheer ease with which the Japanese had rounded up, butchered, dispersed, tracked down or driven from the country an army that had occupied Indochina for sixty years was a serious loss of face for the French, not only in the eyes of the population, but also in the eyes of the Allies, who no longer consulted them in deciding the fate of Indochina—the Potsdam Conference of July 1945 authorized the British to accept the Japanese surrender south of the sixteenth parallel, roughly near Tourane (Da Nang) south of Hue, while the Chinese accepted it to the north of that line. More seriously, the French departure followed by the Japanese surrender created a political vacuum that the communists were well prepared to step into—Ho Chi Minh's "August Revolution" of 1945 upon the surrender of the Japanese installed the Viet Minh in Hanoi as a prelude for the declaration of the Democratic Republic of Vietnam on September 2, 1945.

The Outbreak of War to the Fall of Cao Bang in 1950

When, on November 20, 1946, what became known as the Haiphong incident touched off a full-scale shooting war between the French and the Viet Minh, the French discovered that they entered the conflict with some serious handicaps. Their army was small, weakened by the defeat and reorganization of the war, and virtually without supplies. Its first priority was to rebuild a force to occupy Germany. Indeed, when the possibility was discussed in 1945 of reoccupying Indochina with two divisions, the only troops available were Senegalese, which the high command was reluctant to use because "The reconquest of this country with an old and refined civilization by a troop composed of a majority of blacks would risk making a bad impression." When the French finally did equip two divisions, it discovered that it lacked the means to get them there. Only in September 1945 did the first French troops land in Saigon. By February 1946, however, the garrison had been stiffened to almost fifty-six thousand soldiers. Nevertheless, the reoccupation would have to be quickly done, for the high command calculated that rotations and replacements would reduce this number to thirty-eight thousand within a year.[12]

Nor could the French economy support a substantial conflict far from home with resources that were badly needed to rebuild a country seriously debilitated following four years of German occupation and Allied invasion. French commanders must have been betting that they would not have to, for they placed the fighting qualities of the Vietnamese in the same category as those of the Malagasies—that is, near the bottom.

None of this is to say, however, that Ho Chi Minh was in a terribly strong position to resist them in 1946. The Viet Minh force of about thirty thousand soldiers at the time of the August Revolution of 1945 had perhaps doubled by the outbreak of hostilities in December of the following year, although estimates vary depending upon whether one includes Viet Minh regional forces and guerrillas in the tally. If the French troops were poorly armed by western standards, the armament of the Viet Minh was primitive. They also lacked supplies and medicines. Their commanders, including Giap, who would develop into one of the most redoubtable generals of the twentieth century, lacked experience in 1946. Furthermore, Ho Chi Minh found his control of Tonkin compromised by the Chinese Nationalists, whose occupation north of the 16th parallel was rapacious. Therefore, he had to tolerate, even to encourage, a French return to Indochina as a lever to pry the Chinese back over the border, on the theory that the French were too weak to remain over time whereas a Chinese occupation risked becoming permanent. "It is better to sniff French dung for a while than eat China's all our lives," Ho replied to critics of his March 1946 decision to permit fifteen thousand French troops (excluding the Legion) north of the 16th parallel, in return for the departure of almost 180,000 Chinese soldiers.[13]

As the political maneuvering of Ho Chi Minh in 1945–46 suggests, perhaps the greatest strength possessed by the Viet Minh was patience. In military terms, this caused the Viet Minh leaders, Giap foremost among them, to plot a war of *longue durée*. Mao Tse-tung's theories on revolutionary warfare supplied Giap with a strategic outline for his campaign against the French. According to Mao, revolutionary war passes through three phases. In the first phase, the superior strength of the enemy force causes the revolutionaries to avoid decisive combat and fall back on a strategy of small-scale raids and attacks. As the guerrillas build their strength and achieve rough parity with the enemy, then the commander can enter the second phase: a mix of conventional and guerrilla actions to keep the enemy off balance. In Indochina, this meant placing the French before a series of choices, both in terms of geography and force structure, all of which were made equally unattractive. Giap could concentrate his activity in upper Tonkin, in Laos, in the deltas around Hanoi or Saigon, in the desolate coastal areas or the remote central highlands of Annam, or in more than one of these areas simultaneously. The French had to be strong everywhere, or at the very least maintain the flexibility to intervene anywhere a serious threat materialized, while Giap could conserve and concentrate his forces in those areas where the greatest military or political advantage could be achieved. The final stage in Mao's guerrilla war occurs when the government army, like a bull confused, badly bloodied and exhausted by the matador, is forced onto the defensive. When this happens, then the revolutionaries can move to a "general counteroffensive," which will culminate in the enemy's defeat.

In other words, Giap retained the strategic initiative and controlled the tempo of the war. And here the question of French force structure became critical. For the Indochina over which the French and Viet Minh fought is a vast and extremely diverse land running from the sparsely inhabited and jungle-covered mountains of the north, to the populated rice lands along the coast, to the jungles and savannahs of the south, like the Plaine des Joncs, which creeps to the very outskirts of Saigon and becomes a shallow, reed-filled lake in the rainy seasons. The Viet Minh adapted to this diversity better than the French, for the Vietnamese Liberation Army units theoretically could fight anywhere in the country, while the French were required to develop units specializing in regional combat. Of no troop was this more true than the Legion, which supplied four regular infantry regiments for operations in the mountains and pacification duties in more populated areas, two battalions of parachutists, and the REC, which created amphibious forces for the marshes of Cochinchina as well as regular armored formations. The Legion also organized its own engineer, transport, supply, maintenance and even medical services, as well as contributed battalions to the *groupes mobiles,* inspired by tactical experiments in Morocco and imported into Indochina in 1951. Not only did this stretch available manpower and limit the ability to assign replacements, but also units developed for one area or one type of warfare frequently operated badly in a different combat environment, depriving the French of a certain degree of strategic flexibility. Frequent transfers of forces from one area to another in response to a Viet Minh initiative or a change in strategic priorities brought on by one of the many French command changes also meant that French troops seldom knew their area well.

Giap's initial task was to deny the French, as later he was to deny the Americans, the quick victory they sought. The initial French strategy was the perfectly logical one of striking at the Viet Minh while they were weak in an attempt to "decapitate" the leadership and disorganize their fledgling army. The 2e *bureau* identified a Viet Minh "National Redoubt" at Bac

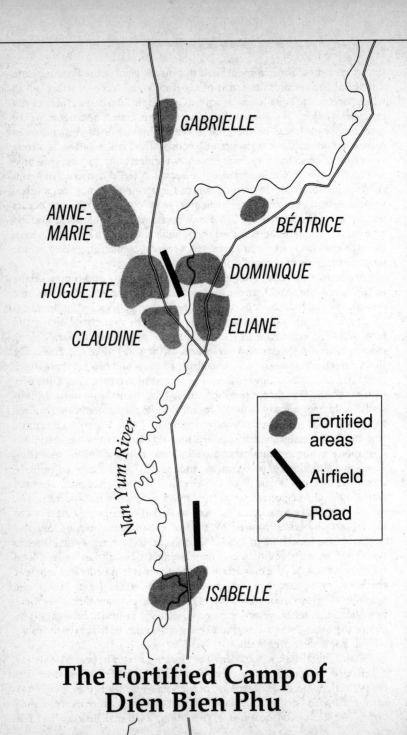

GABRIELLE

ANNE-
MARIE

BÉATRICE

HUGUETTE

DOMINIQUE

CLAUDINE

ELIANE

Nan Yum River

Fortified
areas

Airfield

Road

ISABELLE

The Fortified Camp of
Dien Bien Phu

Can, a network of workshops, depots and military headquarters in the Tonkin highlands near Tuyen Quang.

On October 7, 1947, the French paratroops floated out of the air upon Bac Can in what had been baptized "Operation Lea." While the early rumors that Ho Chi Minh had been captured in this surprise attack proved untrue, reporter and writer Bernard Fall, among others, recounted that the resistance leader had escaped in such haste that he had left behind correspondence ready to be signed on his desk.[14] French troops also captured substantial stocks of Viet Minh arms and munitions, although the rebels vanished into the jungle without a fight.

The belief that they had only narrowly failed to win the war at Bac Can encouraged the French in their belief in the utility of paratroop landings. While no unit more exemplified the taste for risk and forward combat than the Legion, the decision to transform legionnaires into paratroops had first to overcome the objections that had become customary each time the Legion wished to depart from its normal heavy infantry organization. However, when volunteers were called for in April 1948, there was no shortage of available manpower. Some may have regretted their decision when they were dropped in a tent village in the forest of Khamisis, about 13 miles south of Sidi-bel-Abbès. "How could such an attractive Mediterranean forest hide such misery!" asked Janos Kemencei, one of these first volunteers.[15] Water had to be rationed, there were no washing facilities for men or their clothes, neither beds nor mattresses, nor was there a mess tent, so that the food, abundant but insipid, was eaten standing up. One smelled the latrines long before they came into sight, and a fine dust permeated everywhere. To top it all off, the training was fairly tough, and centered on marching five miles in full combat kit in less than an hour. Those who passed these physical tests were dispatched to Philippeville to train with the *chasseurs parachutistes,* where the training was equally severe, and the punishments, which consisted of shaving the head, were frequent and usually arbitrary.

The *bataillon étranger de parachutistes* (BEP) eventually established one of the most impressive records of any unit in Indochina. Quickly recognized as one of the French army's elite corps, it was awarded the dubious honor of playing a leading role in the two great French disasters of the war—the debacle on the Route Coloniale 4 in 1950, and Dien Bien Phu. R.C. 4 linked Lang Son with That Khe, Dong Khe and Cao Bang, which guarded the strategically important Chinese frontier. For these isolated posts, crammed with legionnaires and colonial infantry, R.C. 4 was a lifeline, a slender thread that twisted, rose and tumbled through a turmoil of jagged limestone ridges and high needles of jungle-covered rock. These military camps were inserted into narrow valleys carved out of the rock by rivers made blood red by the clay of the terraced rice fields, which followed the water course until it flowed out of view behind an emerald wall of forest. These were remote approaches from China used by brigands and opium smugglers prepared to negotiate the miles of almost trackless jungle that stretched away to the south and west toward Laos or the Tonkin delta.

The 1949 Communist victory in China placed these posts on the very front line of the Indochinese War. China gave Giap a sanctuary in which to train brigade- and eventually division-size forces, which were soon well supplied, largely with American arms collected on the battlefields of Korea in the summer of 1950. Giap also recognized the vulnerability of these posts, many of whose satellites were little more than isolated long bunkers that would not have looked out of place on the American frontier three-quarters of a century earlier. As early as 1949, he began to apply pressure upon the convoys that supplied the garrisons, and soon the struggle to keep these posts alive became a murderous one. A sergeant of the *3ᵉ étranger* described one such attack, which occurred at a point where the road passed through a narrow gorge, to French journalist Lucien Bodard: "First, the Viets paralyzed the convoy," he explained.

Mines blew just behind the leading armored cars, separating them from the trucks. As soon as this happened, a dozen impregnable machine guns, perched on the limestone cliffs above, opened fire, enfilading the entire column. Then a hailstorm of grenades came down. Regulars, hidden elbow to elbow on the embankment which dominated the roadway, threw them with precision, a dozen per vehicle. It was a firestorm. Trucks burned everywhere, completely blocking the way. All of that had lasted hardly a minute.

As the Viet Minh attacked, the legionnaires jumped from their trucks and climbed the embankment through a surging tide of Vietnamese, then they grouped to defend themselves. "The Viets proceeded very methodically," the sergeant continued.

The regulars went from truck to truck picking up the abandoned arms and supplies, then they fired the vehicles. Others attacked the French who still fought on the embankment. The coolies finished off with machetes the wounded who had fallen on the roadway or at the bottom of the bank. It was hand to hand everywhere. There were hundreds of individual fights, hundreds of reciprocal exterminations. In this slaughterhouse, the political commissars, very calm, directed the work, giving orders to the regulars and the coolies which were immediately executed. . . . The red officers circulated in the middle of the battle, crying in French, "Where is the colonel? Where is the colonel?" They were looking for Colonel Simon, commander of the 3ᵉ étranger, the man who had a bullet in his head—a bullet lodged there from years ago. . . . He was in the convoy and Giap had ordered that he be taken alive.

I was in the part of the convoy which was destroyed. I was on the embankment with several legionnaires. We defended ourselves furiously there for a half hour, then we were overrun. I escaped into the forest, I hid in a thicket fifty yards from the road. Just next to me I heard several shots. It was legionnaires who blew their brains out. They had been discovered by the Viets. They didn't find me.

I don't know how this nightmare finished. It seems that Colonel Simon succeeded in assembling around him a hundred of his men. Formed in squares, they fought off the Viet waves with grenades for hours. Three hours later, reinforcements arrived—heavy rescue tanks. A few minutes before one heard the noise of their tracks, the Viets had beat it. At the beginning, to attack, they had blown the bugle charge. They gave the signal for the retreat by a new bugle call. They disappeared into the jungle in perfect order, unit after unit. Special formations of coolies took their killed, their wounded, as well as all the booty they had picked up.

We were masters of the battlefield. The road was a cemetery, a charnel house. The convoy was nothing but a tangle of disemboweled corpses and burned out machines. It already stank. The survivors reassembled. They cleared the road and collected the dead and wounded. The convoy, or what was left of it, left.

That night, at Cao Bang, everyone drank themselves into oblivion.[16]

By the summer of 1950, Giap had twenty thousand of his best-trained troops, armed with heavy weapons, posed to strike at the French on R.C. 4. The French high command, while recognizing full well the vulnerability of this finger of posts protruding northward from Lang Son, was nevertheless divided on whether to abandon or to defend them. On July 25, 1949, the *comité de défense nationale* had endorsed a recommendation by army chief of staff General Georges Revers that these posts be evacuated. However, the evacuation, already long overdue, was postponed by two events. The first was one of those bizarre scandals with which French politics appear to abound. On September 18, a fight broke out on a bus in Paris's Gare de Lyon between an ex-legionnaire, Thomas Perez, and two Indochinese students just back from the Communist-sponsored World Youth Congress in Budapest. Perez, who disappeared into the Legion, later claimed that he was hired by French intelligence to expose high level "leaks" in the French government. If that were indeed the plan, it worked, for when the two students were arrested, found in their possession was a copy of the Revers report. French security police later recovered seventy-two copies of the report in one of the students' flats, but soon discovered that so many printed copies of the Revers report existed that it had become almost the daily reading of Paris's large Vietnamese community.[17] The torturous course of what became known in France as "The Generals' Plot" need not concern us here. Its immediate result was to discredit Revers and his report, several of whose recommendations had been opposed by colonial, secret service and military interests. More important in the long run, it revealed a muddle and indecision over Indochinese policy that stretched to the highest echelons of the French Fourth Republic.

The instability and lack of direction of the government were mirrored in the army. Just at the moment when General Roger Blaizot was preparing to evacuate R.C. 4, he was replaced as commander-in-chief by General Marcel Carpentier. One of the French army's stars, who had risen from major in 1940 to lieutenant general by 1946, Carpentier nevertheless found Indochina complex and disorienting. For this reason, he deferred to the opinions of General Marcel Alessandri, who had immense experience in the Far East and who was a determined opponent of withdrawal. Alessandri offered several excellent reasons for doing the wrong thing—the victory of the Communists in China made the maintenance of the R.C. 4 "barrier" more vital than ever. Revealing a prejudice that was to afflict the French throughout the war, he believed that the Viet Minh lacked the ability to overrun these posts, especially Cao Bang. Last, evacuation would insult the memory of the comrades who had died fighting to defend and supply these garrisons.

While they dithered, Giap stepped up the pressure on the vital convoys and on some of the outlying posts, not so much with a view to overrunning them as to perfect the assault tactics of the five combat divisions of twelve thousand men each that he was training in China. At six forty-five on the morning of May 25, 1950, a violent artillery barrage suddenly rained down upon the two companies of Moroccans at Dong Khe. Unobserved by the garrisons, the Viet Minh had succeeded in hoisting five well-camouflaged 75-millimeter cannons onto the heights above the town, where for two days they "fired down the tubes" into the French post using the same techniques they were to employ later at Dien Bien Phu. On May 27, 1950, after a forty-eight-hour attack, Giap's crack 308th "Iron Brigade," soon to become the "Iron Division," overwhelmed Doug Khe in a human-wave assault. In Hanoi, Alessandri reacted immediately, collecting thirty-four aircraft to drop a battalion of French colonial paratroopers upon Dong Khe. The paras took the 308th completely by surprise as they ransacked the town, and, after fierce fighting that cost the Viet Minh three hundred dead, ejected them into the jungle. This action was important, for it confirmed French opinion that one of their para battalions was worth an entire brigade of the Iron Division.

Nevertheless, Carpentier was not blind to the danger he was running on the R.C. 4. Convoys could no longer travel beyond That Khe, leaving Dong Khe and Cao Bang as islands in a Viet Minh sea. Furthermore, since August 1949, French intelligence had been tracking Viet Minh battalions as they traveled north into China to be retrained and reequipped. French historian and veteran of the Indochina War Colonel Henri Jacquin writes that the subsequent disaster at Cao Bang did not result from a failure of

French intelligence.[18] French military archives tell a different story. In the light of the attack of North Korea on the South on June 24, 1950, Carpentier predicted on August 18 that the Viet Minh were preparing "with Chinese collaboration, on the other side of the frontier, a general counter-offensive to be carried out with numerous well-armed infantry supported by artillery and eventually by armored groups, in any case by quality fighter aircraft." The objective of the offensive would be to roll up the frontier posts from Cao Bang to Lang Son. For these reasons, the frontier posts "will be defended without thought of retreating."[19]

It is clear that French intelligence made several mistakes. First, they confess in an after-action report that, although they could track Viet Minh units to the Chinese frontiers, they had no idea what was going on once they arrived in China. Next, while on September 8 they predicted imminent attacks, they were not precise on the objectives. While they listed Dong Khe as a primary objective, That Khe was also believed to be under threat. Furthermore, Lang Son was also listed as a primary objective, a miscalculation that contributed to the evacuation in panic of that outpost. Expert concealment and camouflage of Viet Minh units caused them to underestimate seriously enemy strength: Instead of eighteen to twenty battalions including three heavy weapons battalions as predicted, the Viet Minh produced thirty to thirty-two battalions including six to seven heavy battalions and numerous artillery. Finally, intelligence like everyone else desperately underestimated the Viet Minh ability to move rapidly and maneuver, and their willingness to take heavy casualties. Carpentier confessed in a report to the French prime minister that the complete transformation of the Viet Minh "in three or four months" from a rag-tag maquis into a modern force had caught him completely by surprise.[20]

Nevertheless, growing Viet Minh strength caused Carpentier to reverse himself and to order in early September an evacuation of Cao Bang "before 15 October."[21] But even before his order was issued, it was already desperately out of date. At seven o'clock on the morning of September 16, another hail of artillery and mortar shells pummeled Dong Khe, this time held by two companies of the *3ᵉ étranger*. After the by-now familiar two days of softening up, a human-wave assault overran the post at dawn on September 18. A week later, an officer and thirty-one legionnaires appeared out of the jungle near That Khe, the only survivors of Dong Khe.

Giap had probably only wanted to put pressure on the French, to make them fight and die, gradually to weaken them. What he had not counted on was that the French command, which had declined to abandon these posts when it enjoyed the relative freedom to do so in 1949 or even early 1950, now decided to bolt in conditions that invited disaster. It no longer made any sense to evacuate the Cao Bang garrison by way of R.C. 4 with Dong Khe strongly held by the Viet Minh. It would have been logical to opt for either an air evacuation or a retreat down the R.C. 3 toward French forces moving upon Thai Nguyen from the Tonkin delta. However, Carpentier did neither. Instead, he reinforced Cao Bang by air with a *tabor*, or battalion, of North Africans while he assembled a force of three Moroccan *tabors* and the crack 1er BEP, in all about 3,500 men, at That Khe. This force, code-named Task Force Bayard, was placed under the command of Lieutenant Colonel Marcel Le Page. Carpentier's plan was for Bayard to seize Dong Khe and hold it for the Cao Bang garrison coming down the R.C. 4, although he failed to communicate this information to Le Page, or to coordinate attacks by the two columns simultaneously upon Dong Khe.

The French command contrived to turn a bad plan into a catastrophic one. The staff work was appalling, in part the product of confusion and disagreement between Carpentier and Alessandri, who exploded with rage when ordered to organize the retreat. Although the French were outnumbered almost eight to one, no one bothered to organize an intervention force of paratroopers as insurance against misfortune. La Page dithered at That Khe until September 30, when his force finally set out for Dong Khe, still without intelligence of the garrison or even aware of the aim of his mission. The coordination between the two columns was to be provided by a colonel at the end of a telephone line at Lang Son, almost a hundred miles away. Nor was either column provided with security on their flanks—the Viet Minh were only capable of guerilla action, after all![22]

The French plan called for Bayard to seize Dong Khe on October 2, the day on which Legion Lieutenant Colonel Charton, Commander at Cao Bang, would blow his magazines and strike out down the R.C. 4 to march the thirty-three miles between Cao Bang and Dong Khe. On the evening of September 30, Le Page left That Khe to march the eleven miles to Dong Khe. Surprise was his best ally. But when advanced elements of the 1er BEP hit opposition as they neared Dong Khe, Le Page rejected the furious pleas of the Legion paras that they be allowed to punch through to Dong Khe. Instead, he postponed the attack until the following morning, by which time, as the legionnaires had predicted, the Viet Minh had brought up reinforcements. As a consequence, Le Page's two-pronged advance upon Dong Khe sputtered on the limestone ridges that surrounded the town. This hardly improved the disposition of the paras, whose open contempt of Le Page's leadership and of the fighting abilities of the Moroccans, while perhaps justified, helped to undermine cohesion in a heterogeneous force whose morale was already fragile.

THIS NEED NOT have been fatal, as Charton had not yet left Cao Bang. But the French command failed to realize that the pressing need was to save their troops from catastrophe. Le Page should have withdrawn to That Khe. Instead, a letter was dropped from a plane to Le Page on the afternoon of October 2 that, for the first time, explained the purpose of his operation. Le Page was ordered to bypass Dong Khe to the west and return to the R.C. 4 at Nam Nang, about eleven miles north of Dong Khe. This order was issued in Lang Son, where it was believed that Le Page confronted only three Viet Minh battalions. Leaving a rear guard of the BEP and a *tabor* of Moroccans to hold a ridge line to prevent Viet Minh forces from advancing upon him from the east, Le Page plunged into the jungle. As he struggled through a country of tangled vegetation and limestone cliffs, the BEP and the Moroccans were hit by assault waves well supported by artillery and mortar fire. It was painfully obvious to the legionnaires in the rear guard that their commanders had underestimated the numbers, skill and quality of armament of their enemy. In fact, the French discovered to their dismay that they were outgunned by the Viet Minh.

From six o'clock on the morning of October 3, the Moroccans and the BEP began to fall back after destroying their mules and heavy equipment. Their march was a calvary. "We plunged into the mountains, on a 'trail' which was a trail only in name," wrote Kemencei.

Several of our wounded died that night. They could not take falling every ten or twenty yards with their porters. We were all beat, for we had practically not slept since we left our base. Climb, descend several times each day on these abrupt slopes loaded to the maximum with packs and equipment was backbreaking. At each stop for several minutes, everyone slept.[23]

By October 5, after great sacrifice and effort, Le Page had managed to lead his troops into the valley of Coc Xa, where they were encircled by the Viet Minh. Without food or water, almost without ammunition, Le Page settled down to await Charton. At five o'clock on the evening of October 6, Le Page made radio contact with Charton. He grasped at the prospect of a meeting with Charton as if it were salvation itself.

Charton's column, which departed Cao Bang at high noon on October 3, looked more like a gypsy migration than a military expedition. His force contained a large number of civilians, including the town's numerous prostitutes, as well as the third battalion of the *3ᵉ étranger*. This, as well as the fear of ambush, caused the column to move at a snail's pace down the R.C. 4. At ten o'clock on the morning of October 4, as the head of his column completed the eighteen miles between Cao Bang and Nam Nang, a radio message informed Charton of Le Page's failure before Dong Khe. He was ordered to move off R.C. 4 along the Quang Liet Trail, where, he was told, Le Page awaited him on the ridges to the east of Coc Xa. While the Quang Liet Trail was perhaps marked on the maps at Lang Son, it was much more difficult to locate on the ground. Local scouts discovered a track that led off into the jungle, and after blowing up their trucks and heavy equipment, the group set off along it only to discover that the trail soon vanished into thick bush. Progress became terribly slow as scouts hacked a path through the dense vegetation, and the column soon strung out over four miles.

ON OCTOBER 6, some of Charton's advanced elements pushed forward to make contact with Le Page and ran into serious Viet Minh resistance. With his etiolated column, however, Charton's ability to maneuver was severely limited. In fact, both commanders had filed into an enormous ambush— fifteen Viet Minh battalions had closed in on the beleaguered French. Before dawn on the morning of October 7, the BEP was charged with leading the breakout of Le Page's group from the valley of Coc Xa toward the approaching Charton. "We attacked several times," wrote Kemencei, who wondered why the command could not have waited until daylight and coordinated the attack with air support.

Result: the cadavers of the men of the BEP paved the passage which, despite the terrible losses, had been opened by the legionnaire parachutists. . . . I still had four full clips for my U.S. carbine. I gave two to another NCO who had none left at all. Then, with a brisk order, quick and precise, repeated several times in a ringing voice: "Forward, charge!," this group which was almost out of munitions but with bayonet or knife in the fist, threw themselves on the enemy as a single man. I followed as best I could, emptying my clips on our left flank where the murderous bursts were coming from. In this way I passed through the middle of many dying, legionnaires or Viets, some wounded by bayonets.[24]

Thanks to this attack by the BEP, regarded as one of the finest actions of the Legion, the two columns joined hands, so to speak. But the Moroccans from Le Page's column were by this time at the end of their tether. They fled over the rocks and down the cliff faces crying *"Allah-Akbar! Allah-Akbar!"* Their panic quickly spread to the North Africans with Charton, who until then had maintained their composure. Among Le Page's force, only the Legion paras, or what was left of them, kept their heads. "These men were silent and resolved. . . . Several proposed to *'faire Camerone.'* But with what fortifications and what munitions? On this terrain, the Viets would shoot us like rabbits."

At four o'clock in the afternoon, the 3rd *tabor* with Charton's force broke in the face of a feeble Viet Minh attack. The French force was dissolving into a mob. The only coherent unit was the battalion of the *3e étranger*. Charton moved south with it and about three hundred Moroccans, avoiding Viet Minh positions, until he was wounded and captured. Le Page gathered the remaining battalion commanders around him, and they took the decision to break into small groups and flee toward That Khe, twenty miles away. Most followed the Song Ky Cong River, but the bush was swarming with Viet Minh shouting, *"Rendez-vous, soldats français! Rendez-vous, vous êtes perdus!"* ("Give yourselves up, you are lost!") Twelve officers and 475 men actually made it to That Khe, including

3 officers and 21 men of the BEP. Janos Kemencei was not among them. He was hiding in a bush when a small Viet Minh soldier placed a gun barrel to his head, and said, *"lai-dai"*—"Come here."[25]

The loss of the combined Le Page and Charton columns cost the French between five thousand and six thousand men in what Bernard Fall called the greatest French colonial defeat since the fall of Quebec in 1759. Worse, news of the defeat produced utter panic in Hanoi. Both That Khe and Lang Son were abandoned in conditions of great disorder, even though neither garrison was threatened by the Viet Minh, leaving behind tons of munitions, rifles, machine guns, uniforms, gasoline and even, according to some accounts, thirteen howitzers and an airplane. The 1[er] BEP had performed with sterling courage during the retreat from Cao Bang, a courage that led to its annihilation. Reconstituted, it continued to demonstrate, together with the 2[e] BEP, which arrived in Indochina in January 1949, a developed *esprit* and high morale right through the most desperate circumstances at Dien Bien Phu. In part, this was because they received the cream of Legion officers and recruits. "Within a week volunteers for the paratroops were told to come forward," Liddell Hart wrote of his basic training. "Though they were rumored to be virtual suicide-squads the pay was considerably higher than in other arms. A large number of volunteers were forthcoming."[26]

But while the 1[er] and 2[e] BEPs, along with the colonial parachute battalions, formed the shock troops of the French army, their full potential was not always realized, nor could it be realized, by the high command in the combat conditions of Indochina. In some ways, it was curious that the French threw themselves with such enthusiasm into the formation of parachute battalions—from only a few hundred paratroops in 1946, the numbers expanded to 5,684 by 1950 and nearly doubled in the following year, with even engineer, artillery and signals units organizing airborne formations. By the end of the war the Expeditionary Force numbered six European battalions, including the two BEPs, six Vietnamese battalions, one each from Laos and Cambodia, plus the odds and ends from support units, all of which required the creation of a separate Airborne Forces Command Indochina (*Troupes Aéro portées d'Indochine* or TAPI) to organize the various bases and supply and training centers, as well as to coordinate operations.

Such a wholesale expansion was in many respects curious, as the classic role of paratroopers in World War II was to be dropped behind the lines, fix the enemy, disorganize enemy rear areas and provide centers of resistance to which advancing infantry could rally. In short, the role of the paratroopers was to get the infantry moving, essentially by providing an objective to rescue. And even then, it is possible to argue that the paratroops were a terribly overrated force in World War II, for the only successful paratroop operations were the German ones against the Belgian forts in 1940 and in Crete, although even there against largely unorganized

British resistance the German losses had been so great that they were never used again. It is difficult to detect any substantial contribution made by Allied paratroops to the Normandy invasion, except to provide an incentive for the infantry to get off the invasion beaches, and to conjure up suspenseful episodes for feature films, a class into which the "Bridge Too Far" at Arnhem also falls. Perhaps the French mania for forming paratroop battalions after 1946 can be explained in large part by the fact that they had missed out on this experience in World War II. Two small paratroop units existed in the French army in 1940. By 1944–45, the French forces counted three regiments of *chasseurs parachutistes,* which usually fought as infantry. Therefore, the French were unaware of the shortcomings of airborne troops, and were eager to prove themselves as modern and as capable as other armies in this military specialty. Paratroops also appeared to offer a solution to the lack of ground mobility in Indochina, as well as appeal to the elitist instincts of a section of the French army.

Their role in Indochina were even more obscure, for there were no front lines, and therefore no "rear" in any sense familiar to a European soldier, although many French commanders never seemed to grasp this fact. Dropping paratroops into enemy territory during Operation Lea in 1947, for the occupation of Hoa Binh in November 1951, and on Phu Doan a year later served no real purpose because the Viet Minh simply faded away rather than immediately coagulate around this para infection in their "rear." In these instances, Giap preferred to allow the French to settle into their captured possessions, string themselves out on the approach roads, and then force them to fight their way clear, as at Hoa Binh in 1951–52.

Perhaps the airborne operation with the most strategic potential was the drop on Dong Khe in 1950, which caught the Viet Minh by surprise. But the French high command squandered the opportunity when they did not evacuate the garrison at Cao Bang while the coast, in this case R.C. 4, was clear. By 1953, the French no longer possessed the capability of fighting through to isolated forces in the highlands overland, and preferred to supply them by air. This worked at Na San in 1952. They also achieved tactical surprise with an air drop on Lang Son in 1953, but this operation amounted to little more than a large raid. This classic para tactic of a deep drop in the rear, repeated at Dien Bien Phu, led to disaster. The only real role open to them was to be dropped directly onto posts threatened by Viet Minh attack, as at Dong Khe in 1950 and Nghia Lo in 1951. Generally speaking, however, the paratroopers never discovered a role for themselves, and were most often used as shock infantry.

For this reason, while the two BEPs fought very well, one may wonder if their creation was the best possible use of Legion manpower. Of course, the debate over whether one should separate out the most highly motivated men for special units or spread them throughout an army is an old one. For the Legion, as with other forces, the paras provided an extra insurance policy, a supplemental commitment on the part of those who, already volunteers for the Legion, took the extra step of volunteering for the paras. What this meant was that even if the unit did not perform well, at least its soldiers would try. But from the viewpoint of the Legion as a whole, the creation of the BEPs creamed off many of the most motivated legionnaires from its infantry units. Given their five-year enlistment and their generally higher cultural level—generally higher, that is, than that of the North Africans, Senegalese or Vietnamese serving in the French army—the army should have trained more legionnaires for armor or other technical specialties, rather than simply pushing them out of airplane doors. The chief of the armored branch actually suggested this, but to no effect. As a result, the armored/infantry ratio in the Legion remained among the lowest in the Expeditionary Corps. And in all units, the Legion continued to be desperately short of mechanics and other specialists.

This is not to say, however, that there were no tactical possibilities for the paratroopers. Yet they were definitely limited by the weather for almost three-quarters of the year, and by the fact that centers of Viet Minh mainforce resistance were concentrated in remote, jungle-covered highlands that offered few drop zones. A third limitation was that of materiel, both in aircraft and in equipment for airborne battalions. Transport aircraft were at a premium in Indochina—for instance, Operation Lea, the plan executed in October 1947 to capture the Viet Minh high command by dropping paratroops on their headquarters near Bac Can, was based on an excellent strategic assessment that by capturing the Viet Minh high command, the insurrection would be decapitated. Unfortunately, the plan was cursed by what a war college would call a strategic/tactical mismatch—that is, it failed largely because the French lacked the tactical capability to carry it out. It took three return trips and most of a day to put a mere 950 paratroopers on the objective, forfeiting the advantages of surprise, which permitted Ho Chi Minh to depart, not in undue haste as first reported, but at leisure.[27] And although after 1950 the French, with American aid, gradually built up their fleet of C47s and C-119 "Flying Boxcars" to supplement the old Junker 52s inherited in 1945, this was not accompanied by a sufficient increase in crews, mechanics and spare parts, which limited the number of aircraft available for operations.

The policy from 1952 of defending remote outposts like Nghia Lo and establishing *bases aéroterrestres* such as Na San and eventually Dien Bien Phu, which barred the route to Laos, gobbled up most of that air support for defensive, rather than offensive, operations. Indeed, during the battle of Dien Bien Phu, the massive supply organization of the Viet Minh, which depended upon Provincial Road No. 41, offered a suitable target for para disruption. But a lack of available transport aircraft caused the plan to be abandoned. Also, the uncontested air superiority enjoyed by the French at the war's beginning gradually diminished as the Viet Minh acquired effective antiaircraft protection.

The shortage, and diversity, of materiel was obvious in the airborne battalions. Not surprisingly, perhaps, for the French army in 1946 was living on half-rations. Janos Kemencei discovered material conditions at Sidi-bel-Abbès to be hardly better than in the camp for displaced persons that he had fled—uniforms were a mix-and-match of American and British castoffs, men were given neither underwear nor socks, his rifle was an 1893-model Lebel, and meals consisted essentially of boiled leeks with the occasional treat of stewed camel meat in a thin sauce. Others characterized the Legion as offering "too much music . . . not enough bread" in this period.[28]

More important, however, was the shortage of equipment, including parachutes, which meant that all had to be recovered after a drop. The Viet Minh, instantly recognizing the attention the paras gave to recuperating their parachutes, even sent women and children to destroy them during a drop. Kemencei constantly lamented the lack of equipment—especially mortars and machine guns—but even of simple items like supplemental magazines, so that ammunition for automatic rifles was carried loose in sacks and often had to be slotted into magazines during fire fights. Only in 1952 were French weapons relatively standardized with the importation of American equipment. Until then, units were armed with whatever iron-mongery had been left moldering in French arsenals or with surplus equipment that could be borrowed or even stolen. The result was a diversity of armament that taxed the ingenuity of even experienced sergeants to master. The length of the World War I–vintage Lebels and MAS 36s with which many were armed until 1950 meant that the rifles had to be parachuted in a separate bundle, and the paras jumped armed only with their knives. "As shock troops and elite troops, we were well catered for!" Kemencei remarked sardonically. Even when the 1er BEP was rearmed in 1950, he considered these "recuperated weapons . . . unworthy of us."

While these equipment shortages did not undermine morale unduly, they did compromise confidence and efficiency. Legionnaires perished because of lack of ammunition, ammunition that was badly adapted, had deteriorated from poor storage, or was sabotaged by Communist trade unionists in French factories. Kemencei noted that on the R.C. 4 in October 1950, the Rebvel 31s of the 1er BEP, designed for service on the Maginot Line, desperately heavy, and requiring the operator to kneel to fire, were far less effective in jungle combat than the latest belt-fed, 32-pound American machine guns that the Viet Minh were firing. "I think that, armed with this materiel, we would have doubled or tripled our efficiency," he concluded. ". . . I am convinced that if we had been adequately armed (. . . that is, with American and other machine guns) we would have suffered far fewer casualties, and kept many legionnaires in a state to fight. The BEP would certainly not have been wiped out."[29] "The soldiers have come to make disturbing comparisons between the accumulation and modernization of Viet Minh armament and our own," the 2e *étranger* reported in

1950. "The explanation that one can give that we are carrying out pacification while the Viet is making 'war' does not satisfy them."[30]

The BEPs remained excellent units throughout the war. However, their efficiency gradually declined. Losses were high both from combat and disease. The 1er BEP wrote in 1951 that its high sickness rate came from operating in rice paddies, bathing in water polluted by corpses, and the fact that legionnaires refused to take medicines to ward off malaria.[31] Paratroop operations in remote areas took a fearful toll, especially when prolonged beyond three weeks, which probably exceeded the psychological endurance of many men: "It's a catastrophe," the commander of the 2^e BEP wrote of one operation in 1950.

I cite the example of the last three days of operations: The strength of companies which stood at 90 to 100 fell brutally to 60. . . . The legionnaires had lost a great part of their offensive power. They marched, but . . . their fatigue prevented them from exploiting a success. A group of rebels escaped them simply because the legionnaires were unable to charge over a hundred yards (some fell down exhausted, others vomited bile).[32]

Cadres grew older and less dynamic, while replacements were often hastily trained. "I've said it. I've written it. I do not have 'fresh' cadres, 'fresh' legionnaires," the 2^e BEP again complained in March 1952. ". . . The battles are becoming constantly and rapidly harder. . . . We cannot continue for long at this pace, neither on a tactical level nor on a health level."[33] While the Viet Minh infantry continued to progress to the point where, on its home ground, it could be considered first rate, the French infantry, on the contrary, became less effective as the war continued. Even the superiority complex that characterized the paratroopers in the early days was gradually replaced in the years 1952–53 by a more subtle appreciation of their own merits and those of the enemy. "No one underestimates the worth of the enemy, who has proven himself," the commander of the 2e BEP wrote in December 1952. "But no one has developed an inferiority complex because of him either."[34] This was perhaps a tribute to strong para morale, for the third battalion of the 2e *étranger* reported after the hard fighting around Hoa Binh in 1951–52 that "there has been created in the battalion a sort of inferiority complex" *vis-à-vis* the Viet Minh.[35] Therefore, line units, too, appeared to be suffering a decline of efficiency and morale.

Chapter 25

"SQUEEZED LIKE A LEMON"— THE WAR OF ATTRITION, 1951-1954

THE PROBLEMS OF the BEPs were, if anything, magnified in the rest of the Legion, especially after the collapse on the R.C. 4. Nineteen fifty was definitely a major turning point in the war, one that in Maoist terms marked the move from purely guerrilla conflict to the "positional" phase, when strength on both sides was roughly equal and the insurgents undertook more daring, large-scale operations. It also caused the French to begin to reevaluate for the first time an enemy that so far most had not taken very seriously. In the Legion, and more particularly in the *3ᵉ étranger,* which had seen one of its battalions sacrificed with Charton, those who had so far fought only poorly armed guerrillas in the populated lowlands learned of the defeat with stunned disbelief. "The result has been a sort of distrust of our own arms, incapable of insuring victory for us in this battle," read a December 1950 report. The loss of two elite Legion battalions apparently also gave rise to disparaging comments about the Legion from those who believed them more PR than punch, which led to "fights with soldiers from neighboring units, who in their spirit have not yet been engaged in the war and who made remarks to [the legionnaires] contrary to their honor as soldiers." Nevertheless, the requests by legionnaires for prolongations of tours of duty in Indochina had dropped by 50 percent as the result of the conviction that the "real war" in the delta was about to begin, although this appears to have been only temporary.[1] In fact, Indochina remained a fairly popular posting throughout the war with many legionnaires who, despite its hardships, preferred its more relaxed atmosphere to that of North Africa.

Nevertheless, the French, including the Legion, were becoming progressively weaker as the Viet Minh gained in strength. One must make clear at the outset that the Foreign Legion furnished troops that were among the best in the French camp. The Legion's faith in their military worth was never seriously shaken, even at Dien Bien Phu: "The Legion regiments know that in Indochina they are the last purely European troops," the commander of the *3ᵉ étranger* wrote in the aftermath of the Cao Bang defeat. "They consider themselves a little like the old guard, they willingly accept that the high command demands the utmost of them . . ."[2]

Yet there were certain unmistakable signs of decline that began to affect even the Legion. The French government made the political decision to exempt French conscripts from Indochina, not surprising given the tradition of reserving colonial wars for specialized corps of professional volunteers. Unfortunately, in this age when formal imperial ties were being called into question, a decline in enthusiasm and morale was apparent in some sections of the colonial army, notably the Senegalese and North African troops, who had ceased to fight with the vigor they had displayed in World War II. And with the exception of a few units, the French never managed to instill the same fire into their Vietnamese troops as the Viet Minh were able to do. Therefore, the burden of combat increasingly fell upon the Legion and the French colonial infantry. At the height of the war in 1954, the French Expeditionary Corps numbered 235,721 officers and men, of whom 18,710, or 7.9 percent, were legionnaires. To this number can be added the 261,729 men from the "Associated States" of Vietnam, Laos and Cambodia, forces of dubious value. Therefore, while it must be kept in mind that the Legion was the cutting edge of the French expeditionary force in the Far East, it was beset by many of the same problems that reduced the effectiveness of the French forces generally.

The first perception of the Legion in the Indochinese War put forward by such misleading and inaccurate, but quite widely read, books as George Robert Elford's *The Devil's Brigade* or John Ehle's *The Survivor* was that it was composed of ex-*Wehrmacht*, and especially SS, men whose wartime formation on the Eastern Front transmitted a personality of brutal efficiency into the Legion. Certainly Germans were in the majority in the Legion—up to 60 percent of the Legion was German during the Indochinese War. How far the Legion became a refuge for war criminals or even ex-Nazi soldiers is unclear, however. Attempts by the Legion to recruit among German POWs appear to have met some success in 1945.[3] But the *3ᵉ étranger* noted in 1946 that most of its recruits were very young, barely twenty years old, far less drunken and often willing to trade their daily half-liter wine ration to an *ancien* for food,[4] no great sacrifice in Indochina after the real thing was replaced with powdered "vinogel," which even veterans whose palates had turned to wood after years of drinking Algerian plonk hesitated to touch. But it does appear to undermine the general image of the Legion flinging its doors open to seasoned veterans of the *Wehrmacht* and SS.

In fact, French policy was to exclude ex-SS soldiers, although as in many recruitment matters this may have been ignored on more than one occasion. "The physical examinations were very thorough," wrote Janos Kemencei, a Hungarian who enlisted at seventeen out of a displaced persons camp in 1946.

. . . They made us raise our left arm to reveal on the armpit the tattoo which denounced the veterans of the Waffen SS, and the blood group to which they belonged. Several among us had curious little superficial wounds precisely under this left armpit. Certain of these volunteers were rejected, others accepted. I never knew why. As for me, having no tattoos, and my scar on the neck of apparent unimportance, I passed these first tests.

In Kemencei's view, the motivation for most of the enlistees was not to find a political refuge in the Legion, but rather escape "this incredibly inhumane life of the post-war period."[5]

The shift in the military balance in 1950 came at a very bad time for the Legion. Many of its experienced soldiers began to depart once their enlistments began to run out from late 1949 on, at the very moment when Giap's forces were beginning to acquire real bite. Their replacements, while often Germans, were also young men without any previous military experience, but who lacked the guiding hand of the veterans of World War II. The Englishman Henry Ainley, who enlisted in 1950 to fight communism, discovered that "my 32 years . . . [were] ten years above average."[6] In 1951, the 5ᵉ *étranger* noted that the replacements sent from Bel-Abbès were young, while the following year an inspection of Legion units noted that recruits were "Generally young with an average training." Forty-three percent of the Germans recruited in 1953 had yet to attain their majority, a cradle-snatching policy that was a constant irritant between Paris and Bonn in the early 1950s, as it had been between Paris and Berlin thirty years earlier. But as the Legion depended upon Germans for 60 percent of their recruitment in that year,[7] they could hardly honor West German requests that these minors be released without creating serious vacancies in the ranks. But what they gained in quantity, they might have lost in quality. The 5ᵉ *étranger* was fairly scathing about its 1953 intake, which it described as "Young and poorly developed, without previous service, badly trained, badly prepared technically and physically, the recent enlistees are seldom interesting, their morality is doubtful, their honesty suspect and their loyalty does not appear assured."[8] Adrian Liddell Hart, who enlisted in 1951, discovered many of his fellow recruits to be a trifle tender for the unit's hard-boiled image: "A great many legionnaires are surprisingly well-behaved and conscientious—perhaps too well-behaved for the taste of some traditionalists," he wrote. " 'Demoiselles in képis blancs,' the colonel commandant used to remark."[9]

The Legion appears to have found it increasingly difficult to transform these men into efficient fighters after 1950. In 1946, Janos Kemencei's basic training course at Saïda lasted a grand total of thirty-five days.[10] Raised to nine weeks, the training course was reduced to as little as six weeks by 1951, when Giap's assaults on the Tonkin delta caused a great demand for replacements.

The training instruction itself was a mélange *like everything else in the Legion, corresponding to the diverse and imperative needs of the Indo-China War, to the variety and inadequacy of our equipment, and above all, to our own differences [wrote Liddell Hart]. On most days we marched in open order to the fringes of a small wooded valley half a mile from the barracks. We were supposed to look as though we were looking out for Viet-Minh.*

After a half-hour or so of gymnastics whose exercises were carried out to the accompaniment of cries of *"Vive le sport!,"* the men separated into groups that rotated through stations where they learned to break down and reassemble a machine gun, toss grenades, or write French words and their German equivalent in notebooks smudged with dirt and sweat. "All training instructions were translated into German—and when officers were not present, they were often given straight in German," Liddell Hart reported.[11] Lieutenant Basset, training with the *2ᵉ étranger* in Saïda in 1951, found it far less complicated to give his instructions in German.[12] The blowing of whistles signaled a change of station or a break, during which the recruits gathered around one or two Arabs who sold sweets, soda, sandwiches and even beer out of sacks that straddled the backs of moth-eaten donkeys. Quite a bit of time was also spent on the firing range. Second Lieutenant Pierre Sergent remembered that training centers were equipped with a *"Poste E(xtrême)-O(rient),"* replicas of Indochinese outposts where legionnaires practiced laying mines, opening roads and generally becoming familiar with the routines of camp life.[13]

Many new legionnaires went straight from basic training to Indochina, rather than serve in a North African garrison for a few months to perfect their instruction, probably because the Legion could not afford the luxury of holding back men desperately needed at the front. As early as 1949, commanders in Indochina were complaining that legionnaires lacked adequate training, "tactical training in particular," and that the demands of service and of manning many small outposts made it very difficult to organize classes to equip those selected for promotion to corporal and sergeant with "the knowledge indispensable for future NCOs."[14] The *3ᵉ étranger* reported in 1950 that the new replacements, "hardly trained," were absolutely at sea in a variety of armament "which they are not used to."[15] In early 1952, Lieutenant Colonel Raberin, commander of the *5e étranger,* railed against the recruits provided by Bel-Abbès, who "don't know anything." The majority had never shot a mortar or thrown a live grenade. What he needed was men trained in small-unit operations, able to cope in situations where they were "often isolated from their leaders and their comrades [he] needs to *know what he is doing—act by reflex*—and to demonstrate *initiative.*"[16]

The REC seemed on the verge of despair in the same year when it noted of its recruits that "their training is weak, very weak . . . [they] only seem to have learned how to shout out their matriculation number."[17] Legion deficiencies reflected those in the French army generally—lack of physical fitness, inadequate indoctrination and inability to use weapons effectively in combat. French infantry, including legionnaires, were not given enough live-fire exercises or training in close combat to develop self-confidence, and virtually no training in night fighting. This resulted in a progressive deterioration in the quality of French forces, while the Viet Minh became progressively better trained and armed, maneuvered more easily, and were lighter and more agile. In other words, Viet Minh regular formations were increasingly able to outfight the French in small-unit operations after 1950, which meant high losses, for half-trained French infantry were tossed into battle virtually right off the boat, and essentially acquired their training on the job. Those who survived the first three months had the best chance of coming out alive.

A sign of the deterioration of the fighting ability of the French infantry was the enormous increase in their dependency upon the artillery— expenditure of artillery shells doubled between 1952 and 1954. As the maneuverability of French forces declined, they increasingly relied on artillery or air support to handle situations that could have just as easily responded to small-unit tactics. Certainly, one reason why the French employed their artillery more from 1952 was because, thanks to the Americans, they actually had more artillery to fire. However, an increased dependency upon artillery did not translate into greater destructive capacity for the French. Requests were made for centers in Indochina to perfect training received in North Africa and to create specialized courses. But while commanders constantly complained of poor training, they were equally adamant that they could not fight and train at the same time. Only in the last year of the war were four such centers created, by which time even the faintest hope of victory had slipped completely from the French grasp.

Poor training might have been less important had the Legion been able to count upon solid leadership. However, as with its soldiers, the quality of the cadres was declining as the war progressed, especially after 1950 when the departure of many Germans meant, more seriously, the departure of experienced German NCOs. In some respects, the Legion was better placed to provide quality NCOs than other corps, both because they selected the best recruits for further training as *élèves caporaux* and then as *élèves sous-officiers* in North Africa, and because they maintained a regimental structure that made it easier to organize courses than could other units whose highest echelon was a battalion. But this potential was not always realized. Henry Ainley and three other legionnaires "were delighted to have a crack at getting our corporal's stripes and felt very keen and confident about our futures," when, at the end of basic training, they were selected for the corporals' training squad. But after a four-month course that made basic training look like child's play, he balked at the offer of the sergeants' training squad and requested a posting to Indochina.[18] Often a commander refused to assign his best man to special NCO training sections because they could not be spared from the day-to-day duties of the unit.

This problem was not a uniform one across the entire Legion, but varied from unit to unit, depending essentially upon the place the unit held in the unofficial Legion hierarchy. The best NCOs tended to be creamed off for the BEPs, the *groupes mobiles,* and also to a certain extent for the REC. The infantry units were least well served. In 1949, the *2ᵉ étranger* complained of the "glaring shortcomings of overall quality" in its NCOs. There were "still too many drinkers" among the veteran NCOs, while the young ones lacked experience "and sufficient authority to command with desirable firmness."[19] "The quality of the cadres of the Legion is no longer what it used to be, qualitatively or quantitatively," wrote Colonel Vallider, commander of the *zône sud du plateau* in central Vietnam, on March 15, 1951. "NCOs hastily promoted, without real training, officers who never served in the Legion and who have not volunteered to serve there. Worthwhile cadres are more and more rare, and at the same time the quality of the troops diminishes because of the needs of the Legion and the intensive recruitment of these last years which do not allow a severe selection."[20] Near the end of the campaign in 1953, the *5ᵉ étranger* lamented, "Radical measures must absolutely be taken to reconstitute the quality NCO cadres which the Legion possessed until 1946."[21]

One of those measures might have been to utilize more efficiently the talent that did exist in Legion ranks in the form of ex-NCOs and even officers from foreign armies. The *5ᵉ étranger* complained in 1953 that they were prevented from doing this by regulations that required eight years' service before promotion to *sergent-chef.*[22] The story was the same in 1954: The NCOs had "more bravery and good will than real competence," the third battalion of the *5ᵉ étranger* noted in June. "50 percent of the junior NCOs and soldiers have everything to learn: French first of all, next the techniques of the profession, and last, how to give orders without making speeches."[23]

The problem in Indochina was that there were simply not enough NCOs to go around. This was caused in part by the fact that there was also a serious deficit in the number of officers, so that NCOs often had to fill their jobs too. Commanders constantly cited their shortage of officers and their general level of fatigue, especially as the war dragged on and those who survived returned for their second and even third tours of duty. For instance, the average age of second lieutenants at the beginning of their tour of duty in early 1954 was thirty-one years old, while it was thirty-five for lieutenants, thirty-eight for captains and forty-three for battalion commanders. While there is no evidence that the Legion escaped the age problem, they do appear to have suffered less from an officer shortage than some other infantry units—for instance, on August 17, 1953, the army noted that the officer deficit in the Legion was only 12.8 percent, while it ran almost 19 percent in North African, Senegalese and Vietnamese units, which was a factor in the lower morale and sometimes poor combat performance of those units.[24] The Legion did not always appreciate this relative advantage, for it continued to complain that it was sent officers who had no Legion background, who did not understand how to lead legionnaires because they did not appreciate their special mentality. Too many were sent against their will, were not physically up to the job, and arrived "with a melancholic air, sad not to have secured their last reprieve."[25] The 5ᵉ étranger found that its draft of officers in July 1951 were all very young and could not be given weighty responsibilities.[26]

This placed immense pressure upon Legion NCOs, especially in those areas where small posts gobbled them up. An inspection carried out in the last months of 1952 noted that it was not uncommon to find a Legion company with only one officer whose men were scattered over the countryside in small posts under the command of very young sergeants who had been promoted without any additional training, and who simply could not provide the quality leadership normally furnished by a junior officer.[27] At the beginning of 1951, to note but one of many examples that fill the Legion war reports, the 5ᵉ étranger wrote that they were short seventeen adjudants-chefs, thirty-five adjudants, and seventy-one sergents-chefs. The result was that the units were run by very young lieutenants who "lack experience and administrative training when they command the companies," and young sergeants.[28] "Where are they, the adjudants-chefs and adjudants of the Legion?" the commander of the second battalion of the 5ᵉ étranger asked on June 2, 1953.[29]

How did these training and manning problems affect Legion performance in the final four years of the war? Following the collapse of Cao Bang, Giap concluded that the French were on the ropes and that the time for the final "counteroffensive" in the north had arrived. It proved a desperate miscalculation, for in Maoist terms he had skipped a stage. On the R.C. 4, he had been able to take advantage of French command mistakes to mount what was in effect a mammoth ambush. His army had begun to achieve an equilibrium of force with the French, at least in Tonkin. They had yet to achieve superiority, especially when he placed them within range of French artillery, air attacks and counteroffenses expertly orchestrated by General Jean de Lattre de Tassigny, certainly the best commander the French side produced in the war, who was dispatched in the wake of Cao Bang to salvage the situation. But even *"Roi Jean"*—King John, as his troops called him more in awe than affection—although he was able to inflict serious losses upon the troops that Giap threw at him in the Tonkin delta for much of 1951, was not strong enough to attack the Viet Minh in their highland bastions, although he attempted it by throwing a force at Hoa Binh in the mountains to the west of the Tonkin delta in late 1951 on the theory that this would cut Viet Minh north–south communications. In short, Giap, the ex-professor of history at the Lycée Thang-Hong in Hanoi, had moved from apprentice to journeyman in his new trade. He was not yet a master of the military craft.

The end of 1951 witnessed a standoff. Giap's subsequent strategy sought to confront the French with two equally unattractive choices. On the one hand, he infiltrated the Tonkin delta with guerrillas to carry out a campaign of what the French called *"pourissement"*—literally, "make rotten." To confront this, de Lattre ringed the delta with a concrete belt of blockhouses and posts, and scattered his troops over the countryside to control the population. By January 1954, 82,470 troops were immobilized behind the wire of 920 posts in the Tonkin delta alone, to control Viet Minh forces estimated at only 37,000. The same thing occurred in Cochinchina near Saigon.

At the same time, Giap kept his main forces together and threatened to strike at Laos, which for political reasons the French were forced to protect. Therefore, the French were also obliged to fight large-force actions and to do so had to abandon posts, which allowed Viet Minh *"pourissement"* to continue unchecked. It was a situation that Napoleon and Wellington would have recognized, for it was so similar to that of Spain during the Peninsula War of 1808–13. And as in Spain over almost a century and a half earlier, the French found that they could not be strong everywhere. King John might have handled it better. By the end of 1951, however, he was dying of cancer and had to be replaced. With his departure, strategic vision became a rare commodity in the upper echelons of the French command.

Probably the classic experience of a legionnaire in Indochina was the monotonous duty in the outposts and blockhouses. In theory, these posts were to be centers from which French troops spread out to control the countryside, to prevent Viet Minh infiltration. As the war progressed, however, they increasingly became prisons, inviting targets for surprise attacks, so that in most areas of the Tonkin delta by 1953, as well as elsewhere, it was the French who were "infiltrated" into Viet Minh territory. The problems of controlling the countryside from these posts were immense. There was, of course, the general political problem that most Vietnamese saw no reason to support the French, even if they did not actively oppose them.

Even the creation by the French of a friendly Vietnamese government from 1949 did not solve this political problem. The government of Emperor Bao Dai had no independence in critical areas like foreign policy, and therefore no real credibility. Furthermore, in an attempt to increase their stature in the eyes of the Vietnamese population, its officials adopted an attitude of studied neutrality to pose as a compromise between the Viet Minh and the French. They therefore failed to lend effective support to French pacification efforts. The 2ᵉ BEP complained in 1953 that their pacification operations in the Tonkin delta came to naught because they were not accompanied by political and social actions by Vietnamese authorities. The only effective authority in the countryside was the Viet Minh, who reasserted that authority as soon as the paratroops waded out of sight over the rice paddies.[30] Pacification, with no political dimension, no implantation of a viable civilian infrastructure, was doomed to failure.

These frustrating and half-understood problems were very difficult to solve by traditional military methods. In the 1940s, and even until the end of the war in some areas, patrols were fairly free to circulate in the countryside. Seldom did this pay off, however, even in military terms, for several reasons. Perhaps the most important was that the Viet Minh dominated the intelligence war from the beginning. The French were fairly proficient at "deep" or strategic intelligence, gathered mainly through radio intercepts. Local intelligence was another matter. French air reconnaissance was underdeveloped due to a shortage of aircraft generally, and after narrowly escaping capture during Operation Lea in 1947, the Viet Minh high command placed a special emphasis upon dispersion and camouflage, at which they became extremely proficient.

Unlike in North Africa, the French had never established an Indochinese equivalent of an "Arab bureau." The Japanese coup against the French of March 9, 1945, followed by the purges by the Fourth Republic of many officials who had remained loyal to Vichy, meant that the French had to begin virtually from scratch in 1946 to rebuild their knowledge of and contacts in Indochina. This was also true in the army. Many units either did not have intelligence officers, or burdened them with other duties like communications officer or even battalion executive office.[31] The battalion commander of the 3rd battalion of the 13ᵉ DBLE complained that French intelligence was badly organized at the top, with different arms and services failing to cooperate in intelligence gathering, and then refusing to pass information down to the battalion level, much less the company level where it was needed.[32] The *5ᵉ étranger* observed that there were "sometimes profound divergences" in intelligence assessments sent by the general staff and the division, so one did not know whom to believe.[33] It became very difficult for the French to establish an intelligence network once the war had already begun. Budgets to pay informers were derisively small— 1,300 francs a month for the entire regiment, the 13ᵉ DBLE observed in 1950.[34]

A dire shortage of Vietnamese interpreters made it difficult for Legion patrols to gather intelligence—for instance, the third battalion of the 13ᵉ DBLE complained in 1952 that they had only three interpreters for the entire battalion.[35] Some interpreters worked for the Viet Minh or for themselves, or simply gave garbled or inaccurate translations. An April 1951 report complained that "Some I[ntelligence] O[fficers] place too much faith in their interpreters and have a tendency to give them a free reign in interrogations, the recruitment of personnel, the manipulation of agents, etc."[36] The shortage came in great part from the fact that most could command far better pay in less dangerous civilian jobs.[37] The Viet Minh, on the other hand, were able to keep a firm grip on the population through both terror and persuasion. The French seldom could look for help there. Patrols tripped out over the paddies and jungles largely blind, often equipped with out-of-date or inaccurate maps, without benefit of air reconnaissance photographs,[38] to wander aimlessly about the countryside, inviting ambush or setting off mines. "The battalion is often badly informed" the 1ᵉ BEP complained in 1953, and had "no intelligence concerning the general situation or the particular one."[39]

On the other hand, the Viet Minh were usually well informed on French patrols or operations from several sources. Legionnaires often discussed them with their *congaïs* or in bars. The Viet Minh were also tipped off by Vietnamese militia or "auxiliaries" serving with the French, or by their Trin Sat formations, three-man units set to watch French posts constantly. "The Viet [Minh] have a spy service so remarkable that their intelligence service prefers, in the face of superior numbers, to refuse combat and take refuge in the villages friendly to them [and practically all of them are]," the 5ᵉ *étranger* reported in 1952.[40] French units, the Legion, included, also had an unfortunate tendency to broadcast in the clear on their radios.[41] This not only allowed the Viet Minh to eavesdrop, but even to broadcast contrary orders on occasion, thus increasing confusion in French ranks. At Dien Bien Phu, the Viet Minh sometimes broke into the French communications net to play revolutionary songs. Here is an area where the Legion might have used its linguistic diversities to advantage, as did for example many U.S. Marine units in World War II, by training Navahos as radio operators. Surely the Legion could have assigned teams of Serbs or Armenians to operate their radios. But this possibility never seems to have occurred to them.

Sometimes a Legion patrol might surprise a Viet Minh unit, if they ventured out during the sacrosanct early afternoon siesta or if tipped off by a rare intelligence pearl. "Unfortunately, these cases are rare," the 13ᵉ DBLE wrote in 1950. "We must admit that we are badly informed. From this come numerous operations which 'a priori' achieve no positive result and rather have unfortunate repercussions on morale." In fact, it had caused posts to avoid combat, because of the lack of intelligence.[42] Many also "buttoned up" at dusk, conceding the night to the enemy. Kemencei's paras discovered that, as a general rule of thumb, if the peasants were working happily in the rice paddies, then there were no Viet Minh or mines about, for the local population knew that French retribution would fall upon them immediately. If the fields were empty, however, trouble was near.[43] By 1953, the *2ᵉ étranger* was complaining that strength was so low that it was impossible to take advantage of good intelligence even when they were able to acquire it.[44]

The commander of the 3rd battalion of the 13ᵉ DBLE argued that the Legion was in its element in major battles, like that to keep R.C. 6 to Hoa Binh open in 1951–52. They were less effective when countering Viet Minh *"pourissement"* in populated areas. For a start, they simply did not have the skills to search Viet Minh villages, which were honeycombed with tunnels and secret hiding places.[45] Kemencei noted that in the villages,

We only found women, children and old people. It took us some time to discover that the rebels who shot at us, and whom we never managed to flush out, usually had hiding places or refuges in underground shelters organized well in advance. But it was difficult to catch them in their nests, for the entrance was too narrow for Europeans, and the hiding place usually had another exit. In one of these villages, part of the population, nobles at their head, received with us tea and chown. *But after our departure, they shot at us. This is how we had one killed and several wounded. Of course, the punishment was made to fit the crime.*[46]

It does not seem to have occurred to Kemencei that the Viet Minh probably fired on purpose precisely to provoke the sort of retaliation that would further alienate the population from the French. Henry Ainley agreed that pacification was not the Legion's *forte:* "The men of the Foreign Legion were first-class soldiers, but they had nothing whatsoever to do with a mission of pacification and political re-education," he wrote. "The Foreign Legion was brilliant at two things—killing and dying well, both of which the Légionnaires did frequently and with *éclat*. But that had little to do with protecting the quiet little yellow men who surrounded us, hated us cordially and occasionally got round to murdering us when they saw the chance."[47]

In the retrospective light of the American experience, it appears unfair to single out the Legion for poor performance in a task that U.S. forces carried out no more successfully. But while the frustrations of being unable to distinguish friend from foe were common to Western soldiers who fought in Vietnam, the hard-hitting mentality of the Legion probably made them less willing to pull their punches. Cruelty probably had several sources, which included frustration with the indecisive nature of the war, a reaction to the death of friends, especially by mines, and to the studied brutality of the Viet Minh terrorists, or a sense of racial superiority. Some of the problems probably stemmed from the recruitment of a certain number of unstable men who, in the conditions of war, might go off the rails, like the six legionnaries in Ainley's battalion who one night shot and robbed some of the local villagers.[48]

The lack of firm supervision, especially by officers and senior NCOs, also permitted irregular behavior on occasion. "I had heard many stories about the license of légionnaires on operations when women were discovered and already we had been passing the bottle of schum to keep up our spirits," wrote Adrian Liddell Hart, who served with the amphibious units of the REC in the Plaine des Joncs near Saigon. "But this was a mobile unit, and we were closely supervised. We left the women and children unmolested—squatting forlornly in the swamp amidst the shambles as we lurched away."[49]

Ainley stopped his patrol leader, an Armenian, from raping a young Vietnamese girl:

I grabbed him by the shoulder, pulled him off the girl and told him that he couldn't do that. I don't know which of the two of us was the most surprised by my outburst. Still under the influence of Africa, I realized that I had laid hands on a superior and the consequence could be terrible. Thyme was so amazed that he finally burst out laughing and in the friendliest way told me that I would soon get used to a little friendly rape. To my relief the girl had taken the opportunity to bolt off into the bush with torn clothes clasped to her. In a cowardly way I was most relieved. I didn't feel up to fighting a whole army on the question of well-established traditional sports.[50]

More shocking to him, Ainley soon discovered that "rape, beating, burning, torturing of entirely harmless peasants and villagers were of common occurrence in the course of punitive patrols and operations by French troops," and were even encouraged by officers and NCOs who reported it in anodyne language in official reports. The torture of Viet Minh "suspects" was regularly practiced by the battalion intelligence officer, who directed a *"Bande Noire"* of Vietnamese thugs and deserters. "It seemed scarcely credible that the French—after all they had suffered during the war—could tolerate such a practice," he wrote, but conceded that, in the absence of other intelligence sources, "the majority regarded the whole matter as a necessary and inevitable evil."[51]

Practices such as relieving the villages of their livestock and rounding up suspects were also encouraged by the poor material situation of the French posts. The poverty of rations, "little tins of *pâté,* little bags of bonbons, which are more suitable for a children's outing in the Bois de Boulogne than for famished légionnaires on operations," according to Liddell Hart, encouraged looting. It also made a mockery of the "Indo-Chinese version of psychological warfare" devised by the General Staff—

*The leaflets [left in the villages] showed a small chicken, presumably meant
to represent the people of Viet-Nam, being swallowed by a large fierce
snake which signified the Viet-Minh or Red China. As we were the only
people who were preying on chickens at the moment, the propaganda was
not particularly apt.*[52]

Ainley reported that cattle-rustling expeditions were organized by his company, even in friendly areas, and the animals sold to a meat merchant, to
get money for company funds. "It was accepted army practice to make off
with everything moveable and saleable that was found in the course of
patrols and operations in the non-pacified zones, but individual *razzia,* by
local commanders of small units who were short of cash, were frequently
and unofficially winked at."[53]

   As for the roundup of "suspects," this was made necessary by the
shortfall of combat strength, as well as by the notion that the Legion was
perfectly capable of providing for its own needs, even the construction of
its own posts with virtually no equipment, because its ranks were well
supplied with skilled artisans. The "POW" system was vital for the life of
the posts, for they carried out many of the fatigue and building duties. A
commission periodically passed through the posts to review the cases of the
"POWs," but some were hidden and became known as "black-market
prisoners." These were used as bearers, and if killed in action, they were
tallied with Viet Minh KIAs. When funds did occasionally come through to
hire civilian labor, the legionnaires enlisted their black-market POWs and
pocketed their pay.[54]

   Life in these posts—on average occupied by sixty to eighty men—was
depressing. Frozen in a defensive posture, at the mercy of the local Viet
Minh commander, who often had the power to overwhelm a post at will,
nerves were constantly on edge, and moral lassitude common. Ainley discovered that even Sundays gradually degenerated into debilitating monotony, as the legionnaires of his post set to guard a rubber plantation about
thirty miles from Saigon slowly became drunk in the debilitating heat of the
late morning. "Gradually the morning disintegrated and the afternoon
pattern began to form under the increasing weight of the heat," he continued.

*In the sergeants mess Smedlow, Rossini and Moineau were indulging in
their usual Sunday after-lunch fight, plates flying, bottles breaking and the
Annamite boy screaming like a stuck pig just for the fun of it. Hartz and I
sipped our brandy and ducked the flying crockery. A few huts away, in the
village, we could hear Sergeant de Perre quietly and methodically beating
up his congaie, who was crying in a soft, penetrating, brain-piercing note.
From the Captain's bungalow we could hear the Captain explaining to the
Planter's congaie how much he was loved by his men and admired by his
superiors. . . . It was just another Sunday no different to many others.*[55]

Life in these posts was not only extremely tedious, it was also exhausting, because the side that does not have the support of the population in a guerrilla war must be constantly vigilant, constantly on the move, constantly ready for action. The Viet Minh, on the other hand, were relatively safe and only fought when they were fresh, up to strength, and commanded a tactical advantage. Last, it could be dangerous. The proliferation of posts made them increasingly vulnerable because of their small garrisons and the fact that Viet Minh weaponry improved faster than did French defensive measures. Many of the posts were of log and dirt construction, which disintegrated when struck by Viet Minh mortars and recoilless rifles. The communists also became expert at striking several posts simultaneously to prevent mutual support, while concentrating their main effort on the most vulnerable. Also, often an attack was merely bait to draw out an "intervention force," which was then ambushed and seriously mauled as it raced to the rescue. As a result, these "intervention forces" increasingly refused to go out at night, so any post attacked could expect to see relief only after daybreak.

In the daytime, about one-third of the men in the posts were on guard, while up to three-quarters might be on alert at night. Insects were a constant, sleep-disturbing torment. Patrols through dense bush or jungle, legionnaires dressed in their floppy bush hats, open shirts and shorts, setting minefields, laying ambushes, often without the benefit of leave for six to eight months, gradually accumulated fatigue, which, in turn, led to mistakes in combat. Nor was morale improved by the realization that all this effort seldom prevented the sabotage of roads, the murder of friendly officials, or the passage of Viet Minh supplies. On the contrary, it created a steady drain of casualties usually caused by mines, which reduced strength further, placed greater strain upon those who remained, and discouraged offensive action. "An impression that everything we were doing, even building the post, was of the utmost futility began to settle on the company," wrote Ainley. "And the impression, like a leech, sucked away what little vitality was left in the men. Dysentery, malaria and general fatigue made the situation even more critical."[56]

The drop in numbers was critical to efficiency because it meant that no men could be spared to form the "intervention platoon" to rescue any patrols in difficulty, which made men even more reluctant to venture beyond the outpost gates. Poor medical evacuation arrangements also reduced the enthusiasm to be mentioned in dispatches, especially toward the end of the day when a wound meant an all-night wait for evacuation. The result was that they ventured out less and less—in July 1952, the 1st battalion of the 5e *étranger* reported that it simply did not have enough men to give "breathing space" to many posts that were "seriously hemmed in" by the Viet Minh: "As the absence of reserves prohibits the small operations which clear out and give room to the posts, these feel more and more isolated."[57] "I kept coming back to all the different people I had known in the Legion who had met death and disaster in various forms," wrote Ainley. "For some it had been countless attacks of malaria or dysentery which had finally led them to hospital and invaliding home. Others had gone under from the combined effects of heat and alcohol. The majority, however, had been the victims of the eternal guerrilla mine-laying activity which got them when least expected."[58]

As the war continued, despite the better armament of the Viet Minh, the percentage of casualties lost to mines actually increased—fully 75 percent of French deaths and 56 percent of the wounds in the Tonkin delta, where most French troops were concentrated, were caused by mines between September 1953 and February 1954. Lieutenant Basset, serving with the 2e *étranger* in 1951, noted that on patrol men walked with a reed held out in front. When it touched a wire and bent, then they stopped. His post reciprocated by reorganizing the minefields outside their perimeter, adding however a courteous sign in Vietnamese and French warning of the danger—then they bobby-trapped the sign.[59] "On patrol, we usually marched with our heads down, because of the mines and traps scattered on our itineraries," wrote Kemencei of the early years of the war. "The mines were mostly of local manufacture, set off by a string. They were not powerful, compared to Japanese mines. but even though they were primitive, they were enough to wound the nearest soldier by putting out an eye or breaking a leg." One of the most feared were the metal stakes that pierced the foot if stepped on and led to serious infection.[60]

The heterogeneous nature of the French Expeditionary Force made it difficult to keep posts up to strength. The French army in the colonies argued that its heterogeneity was a strength, for it allowed an amalgamation of national and ethnic talents to create a well-rounded force. However, the prolonged nature of the conflict caused the French army serious manpower strains, for it was unable to distribute replacements according to need. North African replacements could not be directed to the Legion, nor legionnaires to the Senegalese, and so on. This was a problem Giap did not have to face.

Henry Ainley complained that the replacements were picked over for the hard-hitting units in Tonkin, while the posts, especially in the south, got the rest:

The rare driblets affected to our battalion were those too old or too untried to be of any use for the heavy fighting up North, and barely covered our overall losses. Our officer situation was equally critical. At HQ we were reduced to four officers and the companies to an officer per company. The net result was an appallingly heavy increase in the responsibilities of the NCOs and a general decrease in discipline and morale of the men. . . . We were going through a very bad period in the Battalion and I had become heartily sick of the never-ending stream of rape, desertion and general indiscipline.[61]

A decline in discipline contributed to that traditional Legion problem—desertion—although desertion did not reach disturbing rates in Indochina. Desertion on the outward voyage continued, especially in Singapore, where officials refused to hand over deserters to the French after legionnaires departing before the expiration of their contracts in 1948 convinced the local press that they would be shot if returned. "The view of the coast of Sumatra with its coconut palms and its beach tempted us too much to resist escaping," one Italian legionnaire was quoted as saying. In Suez, Aden and Colombo, Sri Lanka, the British authorities continued to hand over deserters, "after having passably roughed them up."[62] Desertions were encouraged also by the appalling conditions on board most of the troopships, and the lack of interest in the comfort of their men shown by French officers, including those of the Legion.[63] In 1952, the French legation in Colombo explained "this upsurge in cases to desertion" to "disaffection with the Legion or perhaps by lack of interest in the Indochinese campaign."[64]

In Indochina, Viet Minh appeals to legionnaires, especially to those from central and eastern European countries with Communist governments, enjoyed only limited success. In 1945, five deserters from the *5e étranger* joined Giap and eventually rose to positions of responsibility in the Viet Minh organization. The following year, a dozen German legionnaires came over to Giap, but were executed after a few weeks when, disillusioned, they demanded to be sent home. This was followed by the execution of another group of Legion deserters in 1948.[65] There were a few spectacular cases, like those of two deserters named Koch and Klement, who wrote propaganda tracts directed at German legionnaires and who were even credited with the assassination of the governor's aide in Hue.[66] Stefan Kubiak, a Pole and a Communist who had deserted the Polish army after World War II and drifted into the Foreign Legion, defected to the Viet Minh in 1947. Although distrusted by them at first, he eventually earned his way into their good graces as an expert armorer, and for his courageous conduct at the Battle of Hoa Binh in 1951–52. Promoted to captain, he served with the 312th division and participated in the attack against his former Legion companions on the defensive position of Béatrice at Dien Bien Phu.[67] A German deserter named Heinrich Peters was placed in French uniform and used for assassinations of officials. Other incidents involving legionnaires, although minor, raised questions about their trustworthiness.[68]

A report of January 15, 1949, said that the Legion had registered 721 deserters since September 1945—a 3.2 percent desertion rate—the vast majority Germans. Some had returned voluntarily, sixteen had died fighting for the Viet Minh, and 530 were "presumed" still to be in rebel ranks.[69] Most probably regretted their decision, like the Pole Eugene Mazurek of the 2e BEP, who fled to the enemy in October 1951 from a discipline company. He returned to the French and reported that the life of a deserter was essentially that of a POW, distrusted, insulted, badly fed and obliged to attend interminable "re-education" sessions by the Viet Minh. "The VM know that the deserter is not dependable and, to be more precise, he's a coward who is afraid to be killed in the posts by the VM and comes over to them to rest," confessed Mazurek. Quite a few had been shot for attempting to get back to the French, he claimed. Far more important than the deserter himself were his weapons and the propaganda value the Viet Minh gained from repatriating those from Communist countries through China and the Soviet Union.[70]

Few who defected to the Viet Minh did so for political reasons. The *rapports sur le moral* written by each unit four times a year stressed that the legionnaires paid not the slightest attention to Viet Minh propaganda.[71] Most who deserted were simply demoralized by life in the isolated posts. Of twenty-three deserters from the 2nd battalion of the *5ᵉ étranger* in the first six months of 1954, ten surrendered voluntarily and only three went over to the enemy. "In the majority of cases, it is a question of flight explicable by eight months spent in the rice paddies without a single rest day and which last as long as the piasters in his possession," the battalion commander concluded.[72] Of eight desertions in the *3ᵉ étranger* in the second quarter of 1953, four were put down to "concrete"—that is, the boring life of the posts—and four to "feminine contacts."[73]

"Feminine contacts" were another possible influence on desertion. Already in 1951 the *3ᵉ étranger* had categorized Viet Minh propaganda aimed at the Legion as "badly done. But it is not the same with the verbal propaganda of the women, combined with the *coups de cafard,* which is behind a certain number of departures."[74] The *congaïs* were a factor in some desertions, although they probably prevented more than they provoked. Some legionnaires and their *congaïs* may have decided to desert for greener pastures. But as a general rule, legionnaires were only temporary husbands, while the Legion offered a permanent source of livelihood for these women. Documents captured by French intelligence revealed that the Viet Minh had failed to turn the *congaïs* against the Legion. The vast majority of *congaïs* remained loyal to their legionnaires, especially when they had children, and hesitated to betray a post. Attempts to persuade some in the revolutionary ranks to act as *congaïs* failed because they did not want to lose their chastity to the enemy, even though it was explained to them that chastity was a bourgeois notion. In the end, the Viet Minh preferred to deal through prostitutes because their attitude to intelligence and betrayal was far more businesslike.[75]

If the Legion was considered especially vulnerable to demoralization in its fixed posts, by common consent it was in its element in offensive forms of warfare. One of these was familiar to legionnaires—the *groupe mobile,* brought to Indochina by General Boyer de La Tour and developed by de Lattre to help defend the Tonkin delta in 1951. These consisted of three partially motorized battalions of different origins—Legion, North African,

Senegalese or Vietnamese—in keeping with the colonial army's views on the worth of heterogeneous formations. To these were joined an artillery battalion, or one of heavy mortars if artillery was in short supply. For larger operations, armored, engineering or amphibious units were sometimes attached. By the end of the war, the French had organized eighteen *groupes mobiles,* including Vietnamese units.

The *groupes mobiles* performed excellent service as intervention groups, especially during Giap's offensives against the Tonkin delta in 1951—already in 1951, the *3ᵉ étranger* noted that legionnaires left in posts were envious of those in mobile groups.[76] However, they did not prove to be a war-winning formula. In part, they were meant to make up for a desperate lack of French air power. They were essentially roadbound, which limited their effectiveness to those areas with developed road networks, like the Tonkin delta. Once in broken and/or forested country, with their 120 vehicles strung out along a road, they became vulnerable to ambush. This is precisely what happened to G.M. 100 when it was ordered to evacuate An Khe in the central highlands on June 24, 1954, in conditions similar to those that had prevailed four years earlier on the R.C. 4. Tipped off well in advance by its intelligence, the Viet Minh caught it in a massive ambush that destroyed all of its artillery and vehicles and 1,200 men.[77]

The complaint about the mobile groups was that they were too heavy to pursue if the enemy slipped away, and too light to fight if the Viet Minh divisions and even corps that began to challenge them by early 1953 decided to offer battle. This caused the French command to begin to organize light divisions by combining several *groupes mobiles,* but this was done too late to provide decisive results. Besides, Indochina simply did not have the road network that allowed larger groups to operate effectively. As the war progressed, the increasing strength of the Viet Minh and the lack of tanks forced the *groupes mobiles* to devote an increasing percentage of its manpower to defending its artillery and command company, which lessened its punch. While service in the *groupes mobiles* was very popular in the Legion, they suffered from the same shortage of personnel, especially NCOs and specialists, as other units. In fact, Captain Masselot of the 1st battalion of the *5ᵉ étranger* complained in November 1952 that the success of the *groupes mobiles* was bought at the expense of other Legion units who were stripped of materiel, reinforcements, specialists, even short-changed in leave and decorations, for the benefit of the more prestigious mobile sections.[78]

The effectiveness of the *groupes mobiles,* as with the rest of the French forces, gradually declined as the pace of the war, the wear and tear on equipment, and the irreplaceable loss of experienced cadres took its toll. An inspector of Legion units in November and December 1952 believed that aggressive battalion commanders were pushing their units too hard during their six months of command, and then passing on to their successors a battalion whose force had diminished. "One has the impression that some battalion commanders are in a hurry to complete their six months of command, and during this time squeeze their battalion like a lemon to extract the maximum, to their own profit of course," the inspector reported on January 12, 1953. "In this way, our battalions lose an enormous amount of their combat potential. And the troops, who see an endless parade of new commanders at their head, are less coherent, less aggressive under fire."[79]

The *5ᵉ étranger* complained in 1953 that its battalions assigned to the *groupes mobiles* "arrive on the battlefield in skeletal strength."[80] It was the same story the following year when two battalions of the *5ᵉ étranger* had to be combined to keep its *groupe mobile* up to strength. "The instrument (GM5) did not have the operational capacity corresponding to its mission," it noted. "A battalion whose *operational strength* is not 600 men is not a battalion." Two-thirds of its legionnaires were new men with less than six months' service. "The accumulated fatigue, forgetfulness or the loss by the soldiers of the most elementary reflexes translate into unnecessary losses." The *groupe mobile* had been reduced to only two battalions, which allowed it to execute only "elementary manoeuvres" and placed even more strain on the troops, whose morale nevertheless was high.[81] The commander of the 3rd battalion of the *5ᵉ étranger* believed that the Legion had become a prisoner of its myths, trying to organize units without specialists to staff them: "It is time to put an end to the LEGION prejudice which believes that for one driver's slot, we will find ten, and which nourishes itself on the illusion that every legionnaire knows how to use a trowel," he wrote in 1954. "The battalion has all it can do to utilize its materiel due to lack of competent specialists."[82]

Some of the *groupes mobiles* were also used unimaginatively. The 3rd battalion of the *3ᵉ étranger* assigned to a *groupe mobile* in 1951 complained that it had been used to build fortifications for five months, which had "diminished the combative qualities of the units, destroyed the homogeneity of the battalions, considerably undermined the spirit of discipline . . ."[83] Manning problems in the *groupes mobiles* were complicated by the decline of morale in North African and Senegalese units. Problems in the North African units had been encouraged by the reorganization of 1945, which ended the tradition of providing them with specialized Arabic-speaking officers. The friction and low morale in these units caused the principle of operational heterogeneity to be abandoned. This offered another example of how the heterogeneous nature of the French forces in a prolonged war limited the flexibility of the Expeditionary Force, and put it at a disadvantage against the homogeneous Viet Minh.

In general, the weather, the terrain and the dispersion of Viet Minh forces limited the role for armor in Indochina largely to infantry support. Therefore, few possibilities for spectacular action that tankers might find in Europe were opened for the REC. From 1953, there were attempts to organize armored task forces with organic infantry, but this was hampered by the shortage of infantry and frequent mechanical problems with the half-tracks that carried them. Like the *groupes mobiles*, the tanks were largely roadbound. Where the REC did excel was in the development of amphibious units in the south, cleverly adapting Alaskan "crabs," called weasels by the Americans, designed as support vehicles for cold-weather operations, and Mississippi Delta "alligators," of purely civilian origins, for combat use.

To understand the amphibious units developed by the REC in Cochinchina, one must first visualize the countryside in which they operated. In 1950, a narrow, potholed road ran southwest out of the Cholon district of Saigon into a waterlogged countryside of paddy fields and jungles. Every few kilometers, wooden watchtowers surrounded by sandbags stood sentinel over a humpback bridge or a small village settled on the edge of the marsh. Senegalese, Arab or Vietnamese troops casually surveyed the traffic of cars filled to axle-breaking capacity and buses painted in the yellow and scarlet colors of Vietnam, which nestled closely to any military vehicle for protection. The road entered the town of My Tho, which straddled a branch of the Mekong River. On the far side of the river, one could see the armored car that waited beneath the ubiquitous flags of France and Vietnam to escort the traffic deeper into the countryside, until, that is, a rainstorm swept in, obscuring the opposite bank from view.

The Legion camp was on the south side of the river, a collection of dilapidated stucco buildings and newer, but equally dilapidated, huts, all of which was surrounded by pillboxes, barbed wire and painted sentry boxes. The "crabs" were easy to spot—a trail of churned mud ran from the edge of the swamp to two large sheds where they were housed. A Vietnamese slum ran up to the wire on one side of the camp, while a dark wall of jungle loomed beyond two watchtowers on the other. The mosquitos were voracious. Beyond lay an expanse of reeds and islands of forest that stretched a hundred miles to Cambodia. It was in this land, where dry footage was at an absolute premium, that the Viet Minh had decided to make their headquarters in the south.

The first crab companies were organized in 1948 in the Plaine des Joncs. "The crab a was a tracked vehicle about the overall size of an average car, with thin, very thin, armour-plating," wrote Liddell Hart.

There was one bucket seat in front beside the engine for the driver. In the main body-space there was a bench for the three other members of the crew with stowage room for ammunition and arms and a mounted bracket for the machine-gun. At the rear there were several closed-in lockers for supplies and other gear, and a fixed pair of rudders were attached with which to steer the vehicle when it floated on the water and became a paddle-boat. A collapsible tarpaulin awning could be drawn over the crew space on a supporting frame.[84]

The crabs were called the "cavalry of the rice paddies," and effectively helped to drive the Viet Minh from their bases near Saigon, deeper into the Plaine des Joncs and the forests.

The increasing power of Viet Minh units caused the crab units to become more vulnerable in 1950, and sent the high command looking for ways to attach accompanying infantry. The "alligators," amphibious vehicles capable of carrying twenty-five men, proved to be the ideal solution. In the autumn of 1951, two amphibious groups of battalion strength were created in the REC, combining crabs as light reconnaissance vehicles and alligators as support. This gave the French, and the Legion in particular, an off-road capability they had seldom before enjoyed, and an ability to penetrate with relative safety deep into Viet Minh areas. By December 1951, it was possible to advance the claim that "At present, the 1er REC is more an amphibious than a land force."[85]

Unfortunately for the REC, these vehicles did not adapt as successfully to other areas—they were limited by the monsoon, which determined the water level, and the fact that the alligators could not travel on roads, and they did not work in the Tonkin delta because of the different consistency of the mud and different structure of the rice paddies.[86] Mechanical problems also limited operations, as did commanders who used them merely as floating support armor, rather than assigning them cavalry-type missions of reconnaissance and envelopment. When they were properly used in the south, they could accomplish quite decisive results, as at Tho Lao on May 17, 1952, when a large Viet Minh unit surrounded by the REC surrendered. By the end of the war, however, the situation in the south had deteriorated badly.

The most serious challenge to Legion adaptability was undoubtedly the *"jaunissement"*—literally "yellowing"—the French term for Vietnamization of the war. The continued shortfall of French troops, the reluctance of the French government to provide more soldiers for Indochina, and the ever-increasing strength of the Viet Minh caused de Lattre to press Bao Dai to augment Vietnamese participation. In early 1951, thirty thousand Vietnamese regulars and thirty-five thousand *supplétifs*, or auxiliaries, were serving with French forces. In July 1951, Bao Dai declared a "general mobilization" of the Vietnamese population. Within a year, the number of Vietnamese serving had risen to fifty-four thousand regulars and fifty-eight thousand *supplétifs*, with a further fifteen thousand men in training, the basis of an independent Vietnamese army.

The problem for de Lattre was how to train this many men. Four hundred French officers and NCOs were seconded to the fledgling Vietnamese army from units that had already stretched their manpower to the limit. The solution arrived at for whipping this new Vietnamese army into shape was to attach these recruits to established units. In March 1950 "parasite" Vietnamese battalions had already been joined to some Legion units. Now, however, the Legion was ordered to form composite battalions with a base of 534 Legion officers, NCOs and legionnaires and 292 *autochtones,* indigenous recruits. Although in theory this should have given a majority of Europeans, in practice the Vietnamese appear to have been more numerous in some of these mixed units. Each Legion regiment mothered a composite battalion, sometimes two, and Legion battalions took a mixed company under its wing. Legion units were also ordered to provide cadres for "auxiliary" Vietnamese units—a sort of Home Guard whose men served on one-year contracts.

How well did this experiment work? Overall, it can be considered a success. It certainly increased the number of troops available to the French, and by early 1952 the Vietnamese army had begun to acquire its own autonomy and personality. Its problems were essentially three. First, although numbers of men were sufficient, it lacked quality cadres, in part because Bao Dai refused to call up middle-class students who continued to sit out the war in university classrooms.

Second, it lacked political motivation and direction. This came in part from the recruitment—the French high command in Central Vietnam believed in April 1951, even before general mobilization was declared, that the recruitment pool had already been picked over by the Viet Minh, who collected the most fit and most politically motivated, leaving the dregs for the French.[87] For instance, the 1ᵉʳ BEP complained in 1953 that it received recruits who knew nothing of the war and who were often physically unfit but who had been designated by village headmen,[88] presumably under pressure to provide bodies for military service. Also, the French refused to make the political concessions to the Bao Dai government that would have allowed it real status and independence in the eyes of its people. Therefore, the attitude of benevolent neutrality in the war that permeated the Vietnamese government was mirrored by the army. This was a problem that continued into the American phase of the conflict, and was often inelegantly, but accurately, summed up by GIs with the question, "How come their gooks are so much better than our gooks?"

Last, trained by the French and equipped in part by the Americans, the new Vietnamese Army was less well adapted to the conditions of warfare in Indochina than were its Viet Minh opponents. To this might be added what became a misuse of many of these units, especially of the auxiliaries, by the French, who stuck them in isolated posts with their families in the belief that they would fight ardently to defend them. However, these posts aroused no more enthusiasm, indeed they aroused even less, among Vietnamese than they did among the French, so that morale plummeted and desertions followed. Nevertheless, many Vietnamese units turned in an honorable military performance, and although infiltrated by the Viet Minh, betrayals and desertions were not as common as they might have been.[89]

How did the Legion adapt to this task of training Vietnamese troops? Generally speaking, with bad grace, although in this they were probably no less guilty than other French units, who were very skeptical about the possibilities of transforming Vietnamese into soldiers. It is true also that this mission placed special strains upon the Legion. The Viet Minh unsportingly refused to suspend the war to allow the Legion to train their Vietnamese, so that in the battalions it was business as usual while the extra burden of digesting Vietnamese conscripts continued. For instance, the *3e étranger* created mixed units using 1,500 legionnaires and 2,500 Vietnamese in 1951. These larger numbers might have been very welcome, but they had not been accompanied by an increase in the number of NCOs, of which as has been seen there was already a serious dearth. Therefore, in the short term, the influx of Vietnamese disorganized the companies further. Training was complicated by the language problem, because many of the foreign NCOs did not speak French, much less Vietnamese, while most of the French could not be promoted to NCOs.

The real objection to training Vietnamese was spelled out by Lieutenant Colonel Pelleterat de Borde, commander of the *2e étranger,* in terms that would have been endorsed by Rollet. In a lengthy *"rapport exceptionel"* of March 28, 1951, he made the predictable argument that this was not part of the Legion's "traditions." In the first place, the legionnaires despised the Vietnamese, "whom they consider good only to carry arms or work as coolies. This mentality is perhaps regrettable, but it is nonetheless very developed among NCOs and legionnaires of German, Slavic or Hungarian origins who make up the majority." Second, the legionnaires were unstable characters who prospered only in a truly Legion milieu. To remove them from or dilute this structured environment was to invite a return "to the disorders inherent in the weakness of his nature."

The third argument maintained that the inclusion of Vietnamese would shatter the "homogeneity of a Corps which guarantees by its traditions the worth of the subdivision of the arm." The cohesion, discipline and worth in combat were ensured by the presence of a special breed of officers who understood them.

because it is a heavy troop in combat which needs to be animated to maneuver—the platoon commander must normally be an officer, for there are very few senior NCOs [and] these with a few exceptions are intellectually lazy and fall into routines. Courageous and confident in their reflexes, they do not like to think out seriously an operation or a maneuver before undertaking it.

Fourth, the combat styles of legionnaires and Vietnamese were simply incompatible—one was heavy but reliable, the other light, mobile but irresolute, "capable of slipping away if the combat gets off to a bad start." Last, he added a series of problems that would invariably follow from amalgamation, including conflicts over the Vietnamese soldiers' women, homosexual incidents between legionnaires and Vietnamese, and the possibility that Viet Minh propaganda would be more effective upon legionnaires after amalgamation. In short, the inclusion, even as a temporary training measure, of Vietnamese in the Legion would be "to the detriment of their cohesion, their leadership, their homogeneity and their traditions."[90]

There was nothing extraordinary about these attitudes, which were common in the Legion. Any combat unit will tend to resist tasks that it perceives will interfere with its elite image. The incontestable fact, as de Lattre realized, was that if the French were to hold their own in Indochina, they needed more soldiers. In the absence of French conscripts, the recruitment of Vietnamese was to be their only source, even if these men did not always inspire confidence. Also, if the Viet Minh were clearly having success in turning out solid units capable of maneuvering well, why could not the Legion do the same thing? Time for the old arguments that the Legion was fit only for certain missions because of its "traditions" had clearly passed, although it is hardly surprising that jeremiads similar to those heard in the Legion in 1914, in 1919 and 1939 were again echoed in reports.

Prejudice against Vietnamese troops and a disinclination to participate in Vietnamization died hard. The Legion being the Legion, however, the officers did not complain of the difficulties, according to the commander of the *3ᵉ étranger,* "concerned not to be suspected of being afraid," and worked honestly to make Vietnamization succeed, but "they don't believe in it."[91] The legionnaires, however, seemed to take the whole experiment in better spirits than many of their superiors obviously did, and regarded the spectacle of diminutive Vietnamese kitted out in uniforms designed for Europeans and their arrival in camp accompanied by their family entourage as highly entertaining: "They amuse the legionnaires by their look, and their slightly Courtelinesque [a reference to the French comic playwright Courteline] family *harkas,*" the *3ᵉ étranger* reported. "The legionnaires have a tendency to treat them like a new nationality of legionnaire."[92]

Despite the warnings and obvious problems, the experiment of attaching Vietnamese to Legion battalions appears, on balance, to have achieved overall success. In the *5ᵉ étranger,* the Vietnamese were told, "You are legionnaires, and you must fight and conduct yourselves as legionnaires." It found that they performed credibly in combat, but disliked intensely the manual labor of building posts.[93] The *5ᵉ étranger* declared in 1952 that its Vietnamese battalions had far fewer problems with desertion than did those with other units.[94] In May 1953, General Leblanc, the commander of central Vietnam, had to turn the 4th battalion of the *2ᵉ étranger* into a mixed battalion "because of the difficulties of recruiting legionnaires."[95] The REC integrated its crab units up to 50 percent after it discovered that its vehicles could carry more Vietnamese than Europeans, thus increasing its combat strength on operations, while the indigenous soldiers also proved more effective in searching villages. In other words, the recruitment of Vietnamese helped the Legion to attenuate their manpower shortage and probably improved efficiency.

Nevertheless, all regiments did not join into this paean of praise for the experiment. The *3e étranger* declared in December 1952 that the commanders of its two "yellowed" battalions had lost confidence in their men and wanted the percentage of white troops raised.[96] Lieutenant Basset observed that in combat, "a quarter fight, half go over to the other side, the last quarter waits to see who is the winner."[97] These problems were solved in part when these Vietnamese units were turned over to the Vietnamese army. This was not a happy occasion for everyone. Major Rambaud, who commanded 4th battalion of the *2e étranger,* reported that his Vietnamese "considered themselves to be 'regular' soldiers of the French army" and had no desire to go into the Vietnamese army.[98]

The most prolonged opposition to *jaunissement* came out of the BEPs, perhaps because they especially regarded themselves as an elite, and deeply resented having to accept recruits who never lost their "conscript mentality. They await the end of their contract like conscripts await *'la classe'* [the end of their service period]." The presence of these men "breaks the unity of this unit which must suspend belief when it sees the accumulation of wives and children with which his Vietnamese comrade burdens himself."[99] They were also upset that, whereas the infantry had gradually shed its "yellow" battalions, it had actually seen its numbers of Vietnamese increase. This caused problems in 1954 during the battle of Dien Bien Phu, when the idea of being parachuted into a battle which was already lost apparently did not strike the BEP's Vietnamese troops as the ideal spring holiday. The *2e* BEP insisted that its Vietnamese paratroopers, "the majority of whom are young in service, [were] motivated by a single desire not to fight and to go home. They hampered the battalion to the point that the commander no longer wanted them as reinforcements."[100]

If the *2e* BEP's experience with its Vietnamese recruits was disappointing, other Vietnamese paratroop units performed very credibly at Dien Bien Phu. Overall, considering the extra burden of work that this program of Vietnamization placed upon the Legion, its history of color prejudice, the obvious antipathy of many Legion officers and NCOs for this training mission, and the fact that most of the Vietnamese sent to the Legion were reluctant conscripts, the Legion's participation in *jaunissement* may be termed a qualified success.

Chapter 26

THE FINAL ACT—
DIEN BIEN PHU

WITHOUT A DOUBT, the Legion's *tour de force* in Indochina occurred at what effectively amounted to the French finale there—the battle of Dien Bien Phu. That remote valley in the highlands of Tonkin became a show-case of courage, both French and Vietnamese. Unfortunately, the courage of many of the French-led troops was not matched by the competence of their commanders. The origins of the disaster lay in the decision by the French commander-in-chief in Indochina, General Henri Navarre, to create a *base aéroterrestre* at a point that would block Viet Minh penetration of Laos. In his view, Dien Bien Phu offered the best strategic location, across an important road junction linking upper Tonkin with Laos. It was far from Viet Minh main-force units, while the existence of an airstrip dating from the Japanese occupation would give the French access by air. The successful French defense of Na San, another *base aéroterrestre* in the higlands east of Dien Bien Phu, in November–December 1952 helped to convince the French command that the Viet Minh lacked the means to overwhelm these entrenched camps.

Paratroops floated into the level valley, about thirteen miles long and seven miles wide, through which ran the Nam Yum River, on November 20, 1953, chased out the Viet Minh troops occupying it and began to establish a camp. Although the site was overlooked by mountains, the French high command calculated that they were beyond artillery range even if the mountains were occupied by the Viet Minh. Therefore, according to French thinking, the Viet Minh, inexperienced artillerymen, must bring their artillery into the valley, what little they could shift to this remote area, to make it effective, where it could be easily handled by French aviation and counterbattery fire. The French high command also chose to ignore the fact that Dien Bien Phu was at a maximum operating distance from air bases near Hanoi and that the monsoon weather sharply reduced the air support upon which the garrison depended. Viet Minh artillery and antiaircraft guns, whose appearance surprised the French command, firing from well-concealed positions did the rest.

The tactical deficiencies of the French position are well known. The network of defenses built on a series of small hills was poorly conceived. The key to the battle would be the airstrip—the French had to keep it open while Giap had to try to close it down, which he managed to do on virtually the first day of the battle. Most of the garrison was packed into central defensive positions around the airstrip—Huguette, Dominique, Claudine and Eliane. A mile and a half to the north and the northwest, Béatrice and Gabrielle, each held by a battalion, were established on two small hills overlooking the airstrip. A loosely connected series of strong points held by T'ai auxiliaries and christened Anne-Marie stretched northwest beyond Huguette. About four miles to the south, Isabelle, with two battalions and two 105 batteries under the command of Colonel André Lalande, who had fought at Narvik and throughout World War II with the 13ᵉ DBLE, was given the mission of supporting the central position with artillery fire. Béatrice and Gabrielle, obviously the weak points of the defense, were at the extreme range of Isabelle's guns. Although the defensive positions were linked by trenches, blockhouses and dugouts, protected by minefields and barbed wire, no attempt had been made to camouflage the French camp. For Viet Minh artillery observers, Dien Bien Phu held no secrets—a scrap of yellow dust, which turned to mud with the March monsoon, whose every activity was observed, recorded and fired upon. For the French, on the other hand, the activities of their foes were masked by the verdant jungle whose fringe reached to the periphery of their camp.

WHEN GIAP OPENED the battle on March 13, 1954, with an attack on the distant and fairly isolated Béatrice, the negligence of the French command as well as the poor organization of the defense was instantly revealed. Although the attack was rapidly executed, it was no surprise, for the 450 legionnaires of the 3rd battalion of the 13ᵉ DBLE who held Béatrice even knew the hour of the attack. Sergeant Kubiak, who survived Béatrice, reported that the officers were nervous, but the legionnaires considered the Viet Minh "crazy" to attempt to dislodge the Legion from their position, an indication that almost no one on the French side, from commander to private, really understood what they were now up against. In the early afternoon, a violent artillery barrage "rained down on us without stopping like a hailstorm on a fall evening," remembered Kubiak. "Bunker after bunker, trench after trench, collapsed, burying men and weapons."[1] Some of the shells struck the airfield, exploding planes, munitions and fuel. At five o'clock in the afternoon, two Viet Minh regiments leapt from their approach trenches barely two hundred yards from Béatrice. At six-thirty a Viet Minh shell took out the battalion command post, followed a few minutes later by a second round that killed the commander of the northern sector. With no one to coordinate the defense on Béatrice, the companies fought on independently. At ten-thirty that evening, the radio of the 10th company fell silent. A half-hour later the last word arrived from the 11th company that fighting had reached the command bunker. A few minutes after midnight on March 14, Sergeant Kubiak's company called down artillery on their own positions. With a handful of survivors, he slipped into the jungle and at daylight was able to regain the French lines.

The rapid fall of Béatrice was put down to one of those unfortunate "accidents of war" that can make the difference between victory or defeat—the artillery shells that had taken out the command posts, thus making it impossible for the defense to coordinate covering artillery fire. The same "accident" occurred on the following night to a battalion of Algerians on Gabrielle.[2] But some accidents are preventable. What these accidents revealed was that, in underestimating the Viet Minh, the French had failed to implement some basic precautions. The construction of defenses had been left up to the individual commanders, many of whom looked forward to mobile action and regarded time spent in constructing deep defenses as an admission of fear.[3] Their bunkers were not strong enough to stand up to Viet Minh artillery fire, or for that matter to the monsoons, nor had any effort been made to camouflage them, all of which was to leave the French garrison very vulnerable. There opening attacks had also revealed the audacity of the direct-fire techniques used by the Viet Minh, firing "down the tube" from well-camouflaged positions directly at the French as they had done at Dong Khe in 1950, rather than risk indirect fire at which they were less experienced.

The fall of Béatrice left Gabrielle dangerously exposed to a Viet Minh assault, which opened at five o'clock on the evening of March 14. The Algerians who held Gabrielle fought tenaciously for most of the night, lasting longer, as Bernard Fall notes, than had the Legion on Béatrice.[4] However, in the early morning hours Viet Minh artillery fire managed to silence most of the garrison's guns and mortars and, as on Béatrice, a shell took out the command bunker, leaving the defenders leaderless. A French attack toward Gabrielle spearheaded by a company of the 1er BEP enjoyed some success, but was compromised when French-led Vietnamese paratroops were pinned down by a Viet Minh artillery barrage. By eight o'clock on the morning of March 15 the garrison of Gabrielle began to fall back toward the center of the French camp. On Anne-Marie, the third outlying defensive position to the north, T'ai tribesmen began to disappear through the wire into the jungle.

The fall of these three outlying positions not only seriously compromised the defense of Dien Bien Phu, it also revealed that the garrison commander, Colonel Christian de Castries, was simply the wrong man for the job. A cavalryman and protégé of de Lattre with an impressive combat record, the tall, aristocratic de Castries had made his reputation conducting slashing light-armor operations. His command style was that of open warfare, Napoleonic *coup d'oeil,* the ability to take the rapid decisions that throw the enemy into disarray at the critical moment. He possessed the cavalryman's gambler mentality, prepared to risk all on a single throw of the dice. For these reasons, the high command saw him as the ideal commander for Dien Bien Phu, whose purpose in their eyes was to serve as a base for French mobile operations. Giap had other ideas, however, and transformed the French-held valley into a besieged camp. Therefore, in retrospect, the command of Dien Bien Phu should have fallen to a man more skilled in the techniques of siege warfare, one who made careful calculations, worked out his options in advance and husbanded his resources—above all, one able to withstand prolonged pressure without being overwhelmed with the prospect of defeat. In the end, de Castries' passivity, his isolation in his bunker where he continued to dine off the family silver laid out upon an immaculate white tablecloth, caused a revolt among his senior paratroop colonels, who effectively took over the direction of operations.

THE FIRST THREE DAYS of battle revealed the glaring inefficiency of de Castries' preparations, and his lack of command decision at critical moments. A counterattack to retake Béatrice was quickly organized but just as quickly turned back with withering fire. As a second counterattack was forming, de Castries accepted the Viet Minh offer of a temporary truce to collect the wounded, an uncharacteristically gallant gesture on Giap's part that can be explained as a device to give the Viet Minh the time required to recuperate their strength at this critical point. An assault to retake Gabrielle was a poorly planned and undermanned affair, without clear orders and objectives. Thus the French position at Dien Bien Phu began to unravel. The Viet Minh now had breached the defenses and commanded ground overlooking the airstrip. Morale in the French camp hit rock bottom. The French artillery commander, Lieutenant Colonel Charles Piroth, committed suicide. Airplanes burst into flames on the airstrip. The battle was lost after only three days. Everyone expected the human-wave offensive that would submerge the garrison at almost any hour.

But it did not come. For if the French were suffering, Giap too had his problems—high losses and low ammunition foremost among them. Therefore, the battle eased off for almost two weeks. This allowed French morale to improve somewhat, especially when the 1er BEP annihilated two companies of Viet Minh who held the road between the main center and

Isabelle, to register the first French victory of the battle. The price was high, however. This action alone cost the French 151 dead and 72 wounded and revealed that they could not continue to pay the high price of keeping open the road to Isabelle indefinitely. Furthermore, units that had faltered in the first days, usually Indochinese troops, were disarmed and used as coolies. Some preferred to take up residence in caves dug into the side of Dominique along the river, where they were soon joined by other deserters, especially from North African units. By the end of the battle in May, an estimated three thousand to four thousand deserters were holed up in the caves along the Nam Yum. How many of these deserters were legionnaires is not clear. For instance, the 13e DBLE listed seventy-seven deserters at Dien Bien Phu.[5] The "Rats of Nam Yum" became a real nuisance to the garrison, refusing to fight but at the same time scurrying out of their burrows at night to collect parachute-dropped supplies and thus denying them to the garrison. The French command debated whether or not to clean them out, but decided that they had enough on their hands with the Viet Minh.

As Giap had calculated, the battle of Dien Bien Phu ultimately turned into a logistical struggle. The French had bet on being able to keep their airstrip open and to interdict the Viet Minh supply routes through bombing. They lost that bet virtually from the first day. The airstrip closed by shelling, they were forced to parachute supplies and reinforcements. An inefficient method of revictualing at the best of times, the drops were made even more so by the intensity and accuracy of Viet Minh antiaircraft fire, which obliged the French to parachute from 8,500 feet into an ever-shrinking perimeter. U.S. Army logistics experts estimated that the garrison at Dien Bien Phu required at least 200 tons of supplies a day to maintain combat effectiveness. While the U.S. Army estimates are perhaps on the heavy side, it was reckoned that the French dropped no more than 120 tons a day between March 13 and May 7, 1954, about 100 tons of which the garrison was able to collect. The rest went to the Viet Minh or the Rats of Nam Yum. At the same time, Giap was able to supply a combat force of around fifty thousand troops and another forty thousand to fifty thousand logistical troops along well-camouflaged routes used by trucks and coolies, which the French were never able to sever.[6]

As Giap built up his munitions and filled out his units with reinforcements, his coolies pushed out trenches nearer the French positions. On March 30, Giap's troops leapt out of their approach trenches at French positions on Eliane and Dominique, cutting through the wire so quickly that French defensive fires fell behind them. A Legion mortar company fought to the last man, as did a company of Vietnamese paratroopers. But most of the Algerians, who made up the bulk of the garrisons, broke and made for the caves on the Nam Yum. Counterattacks by Legion paratroopers helped to retake Dominique and part of Eliane. The fighting continued until April 6, when Giap called a halt. His casualties had been devastating, and it became obvious to him that he had to adopt a more progressive, less wasteful strategy. He called in units operating in other areas, and even sent for twenty-five thousand young recruits whose training had yet to be completed. But the French, too, were suffering, with Legion battalions down to three hundred men each and the artillery counting enough munitions for one more night of battle.

Giap now abandoned human-wave assaults in favor of "siege by infiltration," the pushing forward of webs of trenches from all directions until they ensnared and effectively isolated a French strongpoint from support. This began a period of trench taking, World War I without the gas. The 2^e BEP dropped into Dien Bien Phu on April 9, and the next day were thrown into an assault on a portion of Eliane called Eliane 1, which changed hands several times before the paratroops finally secured it. The only reason that Giap did not finish off the French was that his army, too, was suffering from what he called "right-wing tendencies"—i.e., low morale caused by the estimated 6,600 killed and twelve thousand wounded, and second thoughts about the desirability of sacrificing one's life for the Revolution. To get his weary troops in shape for the final push, Giap organized lectures on agrarian reform, which seemed to produce the desired result. Giap concentrated fifteen thousand men in thirty battalions and began to entwine Huguette in a web of approach trenches.

Huguette 1 and the legionnaires who held it were submerged on the night of April 22–23. De Castries, promoted to brigadier general, made the controversial decision to retake it over the objections of two of his senior colonels. The attack, led by the 2^e BEP, jumped off at two o'clock on the afternoon of April 23 behind a heavy French artillery barrage. But as the legionnaires moved over the blistering metal plates of the now-disused airstrip in small commando groups, they came under intense Viet Minh artillery and machine-gun fire. Unfortunately, their cries for help went unheeded by the battalion commander who, buried deep in his bunker, did not have his radio tuned to the proper frequency. The attack was called off, but not before the 2^e BEP took 150 casualties. The battalion commander was relieved of command, and the remnants of the two BEPs merged into a *bataillon de marche, BEP.*

By the end of April, the Viet Minh occupied the airstrip. Of the sixteen thousand men who had been thrown into the battle since March 13, the French were down to three thousand combatants in the central position, and a further 1,200 on Isabelle, which had yet to be seriously threatened. Indeed, another of de Castries' controversial decisions was to leave the Isabelle garrison, and especially its battalion of legionnaires, on the margins of the battle when they could have been of far more use defending the main position. Apparently he reasoned that the troops on Isabelle would have to leave their two howitzer batteries behind in a withdrawal, and therefore forfeit artillery support that he felt he could not do without.[7] One thousand men lay wounded in the underground hospital. Moreover, the monsoon had begun to fall from March 30, collapsing the already fragile bunkers and turning the trenches into troughs. Indeed, the Viet Minh artillerymen now slammed the French garrison with 105 shells captured from French parachute drops, while in some of the final attacks the Viet Minh troops assaulted the French wire while dressed in camouflaged paratroop uniforms and steel helmets provided courtesy of French air drops.

Despite the obviously deteriorating situation, or perhaps because of it, the Legion behaved like a drunk man with a credit card, calling for volunteers in units already stretched to the breaking point to be parachuted into a battle that was already lost, as if some morbid fascination with reediting Camerone on a grand scale had taken hold of their imaginations. During night guard, Janos Kemencei, who had been wounded and captured at Cao Bang and subsequently released as a "humanitarian gesture," now at Dien Bien Phu, found that men were continually floating out of the dark sky.[8] The 1st battalion of the *3e étranger* found 120 volunteers for Dien Bien Phu.[9] The *5e étranger,* in a report that complained bitterly that it barely had enough troops to put its *groupe mobile* into action, announced proudly that 207 officers and NCOs had volunteered to be parachuted into Dien Bien Phu.[10] This offered proof of high morale rather than sensible thinking. This was the conclusion of the 13e DBLE, which had to prevent men from volunteering for Dien Bien Phu to keep up unit strength.[11]

On May 4, the Legion paras on Huguette were finally submerged by the 308th "Iron Division." On the morning of May 7, all the points on Eliane fell into Viet Minh hands. Giap took advantage of his momentum to overrun the rest of the French positions. At five-forty that afternoon, de Castries, impeccably dressed in a clean uniform and wearing his red spahis cap, and his staff were captured in his command bunker. At six o'clock, Janos Kemencei's 1er BEP, or what was left of it, was approached by a line of pajama-clad Viet Minh, young, thin, trembling, who ordered them out of their trenches. He was tired, discouraged and humiliated, especially when he saw the POW column joined by hundreds of men who obviously had not suffered too greatly from the siege. His paratroopers were in rags, many had no boots and were wounded. Where had all these men been when the call had gone out to organize counterattacks? Clearly, the fighting at Dien Bien Phu had been done by a handful of men, paratroopers and legionnaires among them. That night, Isabelle exploded into geysers of mud as Viet Minh artillery pounded it into oblivion before swarming over what remained. The French role in Indochina had effectively ended.

Many of the survivors of the battle would not survive the war, however, for the death march that the Viet Minh now imposed upon them killed far more of the French troops than the entire battle ever had. French and Legion POWs, roughly 60 percent of whom perished in captivity, suffered more than Senegalese and North Africans, but less than captured Vietnamese, 90 percent of whom failed to return. Why this was true is not entirely clear. Many of the losses occurred because many began their captivity wounded and in a state of advanced exhaustion, so that legionnaires frequently collapsed by the wayside during the forty-day, six-hundred-kilometer march to the camps. Legionnaires also appear to have been more susceptible to malaria and amebiasis than other troops. However, it also appears that they were less willing to help each other than were French and North African troops.[12]

How does one evaluate the performance of the Legion in Indochina? Certainly, most commentators consider the legionnaires and paratroopers to have been the most solid in the French camp.[13] This is no doubt correct. In its own estimation, the 2e BEP was "worth its weight in gold."[14] The strength of the Legion lay in the obvious courage of its troops, as demonstrated at Dien Bien Phu, and the quality of its best officers. That the Legion, indeed any French troops, were able to maintain morale at all in the atmosphere of indifference, even outright hostility, of France to the war, a hostility that translated into poor armaments and even sabotaged equipment, is in itself a tribute to a strong esprit de corps: "All [the officers] feel painfully the heavy sacrifices undergone for such a result," the 13e DBLE reported in the aftermath of the battle, "and note with bitterness the guilty indifference exhibited by our country toward the Expeditionary Corps. This is all the more evident as some have tried to blame the incompetence and the weaknesses of the soldiers for the unfortunate evolution of the Indochinese battles."[15] Many must have reasoned out this situation like Lieutenant Basset of the *2e étranger*, who felt by 1952 that

after all, I am beginning not to care, I fight the war like a game. I like combat, the risk, like others enjoy bowls or fishing. I fight for myself, for my legionnaires, for the Legion—France??? Yes, I believed when I was younger, but the mentality of most of the French is so rotten that I cannot pretend to fight for them.[16]

This wartime environment had special consequences for the Legion. In part, the impression of Legion solidity was a relative one, the result of the fact that so many other units, especially the imperial troops, did not perform well. The Legion also produced what one might term a pyramid performance, with the BEPs at the top, the GMs and the REC in the middle, and the infantry, especially the static units, occupying the base. At Dien Bien Phu, the Legion fought with great courage and tenacity. Its two lapses were the failure to retake Huguette 1 on April 23, for which the battalion commander was relieved, and the accusation that legionnaires on Isabelle were largely idle spectators to the battle. Neither accusation appears to be entirely justified. Huguette 1 was strongly held and the failure to seize it was no disgrace, even if the battalion commander was asleep at the switch. And while it is certainly possible that the garrison at Isabelle could have been employed more usefully in the main position, they vigorously defended their redoubt against Viet Minh encroachment.

So, while it was a defeat for France, Dien Bien Phu was paradoxically a sort of victory for the Legion. But in a way the Legion was in its element there, engaged in a head-butting contest against Viet Minh units that were rushing it head on. The heroic resistance at Dien Bien Phu became a necessary myth for the army generally as well as for the Legion, for it disguised some serious professional shortcomings, the inability, or unwillingness, to construct viable defense works among them. In more open warfare, the criticism was that the Legion had lost much of its flexibility and ability to maneuver. It also suffered from a lack of technical specialists. Its high casualty rate, which the Legion places at 10,483 officers and men,[17] higher than for any other period including that of the two world wars, can be attributed in large part to the fact that the Legion maintained an average of twenty thousand men in Indochina, who fought intensively over eight years. However, the reports reveal that inadequate training and inexperienced leadership also played a part in this high casualty figure.

As in both world wars, Indochina demonstrated the difficulty of sustaining Legion quality and numbers during a prolonged conflict. Legion number peaked in 1953 at 36,312,[18] which rivaled its strength in 1939–40, although some of these were Vietnamese being trained for their own army. In a way it gained an advantage in this period from the dissolution of the German army, which eliminated competition for recruits in that country, despite a campaign by the German Social Democratic Party against the Legion's recruitment of Germans that began in 1949. Yet it did not organize itself to take as full an advantage of these numbers as it might have done. The Legion could have increased its efficiency had it run fewer units at full strength, and trained its soldiers longer, and if possible in Indochina, before sending them into combat.

Many of these solutions may have been out of its hands. But it seems to suggest that the Legion was ideal for short, sharp conflicts that did not place too much strain on its manpower, "come as you are" operations of the sort it fought before 1914, or as after reorganization in 1915 as the RMLE or in Morocco in the interwar years, drawing a relatively small amount of fighting strength from a fairly large manpower pool. Forcing it to place too many men in the field invariably led to problems of staffing, training and replacements, which compromised efficiency to a greater or lesser extent depending upon the unit. The superior performance of the BEPs and the *groupes mobiles* was bought at the expense of line infantry units. Poor training and low numbers increasingly told as the Viet Minh regular battalions grew stronger. The Legion fought less well because they were tired, because they usually did not have enough men to engage and maneuver against the enemy, and because they invariably could not take all of their heavy weapons on an operation due to lack of strength or a lack of specialists to operate them.

The Legion was also hurt by the gradual erosion of the French imperial military system, and its final collapse at Dien Bien Phu. One of the cornerstones of this system had been a faith in the value of the heterogeneity of its troops, a division of labor among them according to the racial characteristics and combat qualities ascribed to each type of unit. As has been seen, this had already been called into question in the interwar years, when the absence of Frenchmen had led to the creation of the REC and eventually even of Legion artillery batteries, over the protests of some like Rollet and Lyautey. Likewise, the creation of the BEP caused some to resurrect the old arguments about legionnaires being fit only for heavy infantry.

But the steady deterioration of many of the imperial formations imposed extra combat burdens, and required a variety of missions from the Legion such as pacification or the training of Vietnamese troops. As in Mexico, discipline in sedentary Legion units began to fray around the edges when they were scattered in isolated posts, often under the command of young and inexperienced NCOs. The Legion was special, its officers repeated *ad nauseam*. Its personality, its character, its traditions required that legionnaires become paratroopers, fight in *groupes mobiles* or mobile infantry formations, even hold doomed fortresses like Dien Bien Phu. "The majority [of Legion officers] believe that the pressing interest of France is in Africa," the 13ᵉ DBLE declared in the aftermath of Dien Bien Phu. "But also everyone would like to find elsewhere missions more in keeping with the nature of a troop like the Foreign Legion."[19] In Algeria, the Legion would be able to return to its "traditions."

Chapter 27

"PRIESTS OF A DEAD GOD" — THE WAR IN ALGERIA, 1954-1956

THE LEGION RETURNED from Indochina to an Algeria already in rebellion in a somber mood. The shock of the humiliation and loss of face at Dien Bien Phu had already begun to create great holes in the regimental memory banks even before the terrible year of 1954 was out. The cease-fire had precipitated a morale crisis, the 13ᵉ DBLE reported in December 1954: "They have suffered the humiliation of giving way before an adversary who could never, to tell the truth, break them," its colonel wrote. "For the *anciens,* it was the requirement to treat on an equal footing an adversary who they always dominated, which brought on the crisis."[1]

As thirty-two-year-old Captain Hélie de Saint Marc of the 1ᵉʳ BEP, a veteran of the French Resistance and Buchenwald as well as three tours in Indochina, watched the Viet Minh troops clad in their loose black uniforms and sun helmets march over the Doumer Bridge to a rapturously contrived popular welcome in Hanoi, he thought to himself that it would be nice to be on the winning side for once.[2] Janos Kemencei was made to sign a declaration of thanks to Ho Chi Minh for his humane treatment, given a new shirt, trousers and a belt, and on August 27, 1954, handed over to French sailors who took him down the Red River to Hanoi, one of the eleven thousand POWs released by the Viet Minh. Although all were suffering desperately from malnutrition and various tropical diseases, they were the lucky ones—twenty-six thousand POWs had died in communist care. Planes of the SDECE, the French secret service, repatriated them quietly to Algeria via France, to avoid publicity. Upon arrival, Kemencei discovered that the food allowance of the POWs had been deducted from their back pay upon the infallible bureaucratic logic that they had been fed by the Viet Minh during captivity and therefore were not entitled to it.[3]

For men who were frustrated and bitter in 1954, memories, even the most recent ones, tended to be selective. The years of fighting in Indochina had been heavy with personal dramas and sacrifices, leaden with the remembrance of dead comrades whose graves were already disappearing beneath the tropical vegetation, troubled by the spectacle of shoals of refugees swimming to French ships departing Haiphong to beg for rescue. Almost unanimously, they transferred this frustration onto their government and their countrymen. Kemencei blamed the Paris "intelligentsia" for having handed to the enemy "the keys of his victory." Even the colossal military blunders of R.C. 4 and Dien Bien Phu, not to mention the poor logistics, lack of intelligence, lack of an infrastructure, desperate underestimation of the enemy and so many other military failures and shortcomings, could be laid at the feet of the miserable republic, which appointed generals who were "incompetent, unworthy of commanding men who have the misfortune to serve under their orders."[4] Lieutenant Colonel de Boissieu, commanding the *5e étranger,* wrote that

A parallel is easily established for those who fought and suffered in this country since 1946, between our loss of prestige in Vietnam and the outbreak of the present rebellions in North Africa. This region in which all have served, where they will continue to serve, and which is the cradle of the Legion, is particularly dear to them. The policies followed disturb them greatly; even the more so as there again, as before in Vietnam, the origin of the directives, the place of indoctrination and the refuge of certain leaders, even treasons, come from the metropole.[5]

The republic was not blameless—far from it. But for French soldiers who already viewed their profession as a calling, a national priesthood, it was but one easy step to interpret their ordeal in Indochina as a martyrdom imposed by national neglect, indifference and even sedition. "The inconsistency of the IVth Republic, upon whom we had a tendency to blame Dien Bien Phu, led us to believe that the army was the ultimate rampart of the country's honor," wrote General Jacques Massu, commander of the crack 10th Parachute Division in Algeria.[6]

The French forces in the colonies in general, and the Legion in particular, was an army increasingly cut off from its political base. Therefore, the Algerian War would begin in an atmosphere of mistrust between a portion of the army and the French IVth Republic, a mistrust that only deepened when the republic placed Tunisia and Morocco on the road to independence in the wake of Dien Bien Phu. Deeply colonialist, profoundly anti-communist, the veterans of Indochina accepted, albeit with bad grace, the release of Algeria's two North African neighbors because these were protectorates. Compromise on the autonomy of Algeria, French since 1834 when a smallpox of enclaves on the North African coast had been declared "Possessions françaises du Nord de l'Afrique," and considered an integral part of metropolital France, was quite impossible.

And in no military unit was this uncompromising attitude more developed than in the Legion. While the Legion prided itself upon the professional detachment with which it fought its wars, Algeria offered a conflict to which legionaires were sentimentally bonded from the outset. Why this was so can be traced directly to its "traditions" as embellished by Rollet in the interwar years, when Sidi-bel-Abbès became the bastion of Legion ritual—the quartier Viénot with its voie sacrée and museum, which enclosed the corps' most sacred relics, sat like some miniature Vatican surrounded by the modest military capital of "Bel-Abbès." The shadows of thousands of legionnaires who had caroused in its village nègre or listened to the Sunday concerts of the Legion band at the foot of the bandstand on the Place Carnot hovered there, as they did across the hinterland of the Oranais beyond the seat of its retirement home, La Maison du Légionnaire, and its cemetery. This was the Legion's terre d'élection, the epicenter of its geographical and spiritual existence, whose unforgiving landscape and raging sun were the grindstones of the legionnaire's suffering and redemption, without which there could be no Legion. The Legion's myths, its history and the recession of France's imperium after 1954 had carved out of Algeria a psychological world that became at once the Legion's temple and its prison. Algeria and "Bel-Abbès" formed components of the Legion's personality, like Camerone and the képi blanc. These could not be relinquished without enormous anguish and trauma.

Nor was the Legion unique in this attitude. The republic, too, discovered its ability to maneuver, to take initiatives and make compromises that might have limited what became the vast tragedy of the Algerian conflict, compromised by a second group who held French Algeria dear—the pieds noirs. Algeria in 1954 contained over one million people of European extraction who were very much in the driver's seat there. Most had arrived between 1872 and 1914 from Sicily, Malta and Spain as well as France, when the phylloxera epidemic had wiped out French vineyards, thereby boosting Algerian wine production, and when wheat began to be grown profitably in the broad, dry valleys of the north. Emigration virtually ceased with the First World War, the pied noir birthrate leveled off, and most of their smallholders surrendered their unequal struggle against an unyielding countryside to move into Algiers, Oran, Constantine and Bône. There they lived as modest merchants, artisans or tributaries of the French state, whose contracts, subsidies and civil service jobs breathed faint life into a stillborn economy.

An amalgamation of heterogeneous elements of which only 20 percent were reckoned to be of French origins, the pieds noirs—literally, "black feet," a reference to the high black boots worn by many of the early settlers that had so impressed the Arabs—were gradually melded into a fairly coherent expatriate culture by their common sense of isolation and foreignness in Africa. They spoke French with a voluble accent that mainlanders immediately recognized as white North African, produced their own comedians and musicians, and shared their sense of superiority over their Jewish and especially their Moslem neighbors. This deeply ingrained sense of racial and social superiority had political consequences, for it had resulted in an almost total political disenfranchisement of Moslem Algerians, who were subjects, but not citizens, of the French state. Attempts in 1936 to extend French citizenship to a mere twenty-five thousand select Moslems collapsed on *pied noir* opposition, as did post–World War II reforms that sought to enfranchise Moslems in a meaningful way.

The bomb blasts coordinated by the *Front de Libération Nationale* (FLN) that signaled the beginning of the Algerian War on All Saints Day of 1954 came at the worst possible time for the left-leaning government of Pierre Mendès-France. The prime minister had already expended his government's political capital to purchase support for the break with Indochina and the granting of "internal autonomy" to Tunisia as a prelude to complete independence in 1956. The prime minister's well-publicized attempts to get the French to drink more milk had set a substantial posse of wine growers, alcohol merchants and café owners howling for his scalp, and earned him the derisive popular nickname of "Mendès Lolo," or "Mendès Milk." The votes of the twenty deputies of the Algerian lobby were vital to his government's survival in the fragmented, undisciplined and unstable French National Assembly of the 1950s. This was especially true because the *pieds noirs,* for reasons both historic and economic, were a mainstay of support for the parties that sat to the left in the Assembly—even Sidi-bel-Abbès had a Communist mayor in this period. In practical terms, this meant that the left-of-center parties that attempted to father reforms that might have made French rule more acceptable to the 90 percent of the Algerian population made up of Moslems became the hostages of the roughly ten percent of *pied noir* Algerians.

For this reason, on November 12, 1954, Mendès-France declared solemnly to the Assembly that "*L'Algérie, c'est la France*. And who among you . . . would hesitate to employ every means to preserve France?"[7] To ensure his parliamentary majority, Mendès-France was forced to insist that repression of the rebellion must come before any concessions could be made to the terrorists. This declaration demonstrated less imagination even than the Indochinese policy of too little too late, for under its blinkered directives virtually no political concessions at all could be offered to the Moslem population to give them an incentive for supporting France. In this way, a combination of government instability, which gave inordinate parliamentary power to a clutch of *pieds noirs* deputies, and the inflexible credo of *L'Algérie, c'est la France* was to tie France and Algeria together in a Gordian knot of war that was finally sliced, rather than untied, by Charles de Gaulle.

If the French dated the beginning of the Algerian War from November 1, 1954, Moslem Algerians remembered May 8, 1945, as the war's birthday. A VE Day celebration in the town of Sétif, whose bleak streets etched a rectilinear pattern on a dusty plateau eighty miles west of Constantine, turned nasty when Moslems transformed what was meant to be a wreath-laying at the *monument aux morts* into a demonstration for Algerian independence. Shots were fired, touching off a frenzy of rape and killing by Moslems that lasted five days, butchered over one hundred Europeans and left many others wounded. Government repression, when it came, was brutal. "Sovereignty columns" made up of legionnaires and Senegalese combed the Constantine region imposing order and exacting retribution, backed up by dive bombers and even French naval gunnery, which indiscriminately shelled villages along Algeria's eastern Mediterranean coast. Also, the political crackdown fell most heavily upon moderate Moslems who were most likely to come to some sort of compromise with Paris. While the number of Moslems killed during the repression was greatly exaggerated by Moslem opinion makers, and was probably more like six thousand rather than the fifty thousand claimed by Arab nationalists,[8] Sétif was Yen Bai all over again, and many Algerians never forgot it, including the *tirailleurs* returning from their distinguished service in Italy and France. One of them, Sergeant Ahmed Ben Bella, was convinced by tales of the French repression that Algeria must be ruled by Algerians.

The sheer savagery of the conflict on both the French and Moslem sides was to polarize the two communities and cause any sort of political compromise to recede out of reach. Already, a century and a quarter of French rule had done much to reduce viable Moslem intermediaries to a mere handful. French policy toward the Moslem population traditionally had been to break up the large families of Algeria and rule through French-appointed *caïds*, men who had no real following in the population and who were often corrupt. Some Frenchmen realized that the intentional breakup of traditional Algerian social and political structures by the conquerors had reduced Moslems in Algeria, in the opinion of nineteenth-century French statesman Jules Cambon, to "a sort of human dust over whom we have no influence." When Hubert Lyautey became resident general of Morocco upon the French conquest of that country in 1912, he sought to avoid the mistakes of Algeria and preserve the native elite there, so long as they remained loyal to him. French arrests and harassment of moderate Algerian nationalists in 1945, the capitulation of successive French governments before *pieds noirs* pressure, FLN assassination of those Algerians who cooperated with the French, and torture and indiscriminate reprisals carried out by the French in reaction to FLN outrages did the rest. One had to choose between the French and the revolution. Compromise became effectively impossible. In these ways, the trench of bitterness and racial hatred that had traditionally existed between the communities was widened by the war into an unbridgeable gulf.

This digression into the political background of the war is necessary, for without it one is able to evaluate neither the methods used by the elite French soldiers who fought the war, including the Legion, nor the reasons and ideals of those officers led by Legion paras who sparked a revolt against the government of Charles de Gaulle in April 1961. "Together with most of my contemporaries, I sincerely believed that, even if the prophecies of Lyautey and of [Charles de] Foucauld were correct (that it is more difficult to hold a colony than to conquer it), France could not leave the southern shores of the Mediterranean without dangerously weakening herself, and running mortal risks," wrote General Massu. Nevertheless, in 1954 it appeared that, compared to Indochina, the pacification of Algeria would prove to be a piece of cake: ". . . The effort required of us so close to the metropole, in an incomparably easier terrain and climate, seemed to us easy enough . . ."[9]

Massu might have gone even further, for the FLN, called into being in August 1955, had great weaknesses, especially when compared with the dedication, political and military organization and ideological homogeneity of the Viet Minh. Its leadership in 1954 was small and virtually unknown. Throughout the war and even into independence it would be split by rivalries and divisions that would bring it to the brink of self-destruction. Its unity was largely a negative one, brought about by a sense of the injustice of French rule and dedication to Algerian nationalism and the Moslem religion. It lacked leaders of the stature of Ho Chi Minh and Giap, as well as the guiding hand of Marxist ideology and the Maoist theory of war that had supplied the Viet Minh with both a blueprint for fighting the war and a rigid discipline, almost a messianic fervor, that sprang from a sense of serving the "Cause of History." Although many French officers saw the FLN as yet another manifestation of the international Communist conspiracy, support from the Eastern Bloc was largely rhetorical, as was that of Nasser, the high priest of Arab nationalism in Cairo. Even the French Communist Party was for once obliged to mute the tone of its strident anticolonialism because of its electoral support among *pieds noirs*.

Militarily, the Armée de Libération Nationale (ALN) was never able to achieve a modicum of the success enjoyed by the Viet Minh. Although it grew steadily in numbers and skill, especially after it gained sanctuaries in Tunisia and Morocco in March 1956, the ALN seldom operated in anything above *katiba* or company strength lest a larger body of men attract the attention of French bombers and intervention forces of paras and legionnaires. To the end, the shotgun remained a standard weapon in their armory. In Maoist terms, the ALN was never able to move their war beyond the opening stage of guerrilla war and terrorism.

Indeed, a particularly vicious devotion to terrorism was to characterize the FLN, both because sadists and thugs were well represented in its ranks, and because terrorism paid off in political terms. The alacrity with which ALN operatives sliced off the noses and upper lips of Arab "collaborators," and even wiped out whole families, both Moslem and *pied noir,* down to babes in arms, often after mutilating their victims in the most grisly and obscene ways, sent shudders of horror and rage through all who witnessed such spectacles. One such witness was Janos Kemencei, in Philippeville on the Mediterranean coast north of Constantine in August 1955 to complete the six annual jumps required to retain his para status when he was requisitioned to restore order in the outlying village of El Hallia. "On the side of the road, near me, a horrible vision froze me," he wrote.

Women and men were shouting their heads off—yes, shouting, over-whelmed with an indescribable hopelessness. . . . A baby and a very young girl were impaled in the vines, on metal spikes on the side of the road. Dead. Their parents, deranged with grief, cried out their distress. A little further on, I saw other small bloody silhouettes lying on stretchers. Nearly 80 children, men and women, without defense, had been massacred, torn limb from limb in this little village, by Arabs who until then had lived on good terms with their victims. After that, I understood the furor of some soldiers, who administered their own justice by liquidating without mercy these assassins, sending them—but cleanly—into another world. [10]

Kemencei got one detail wrong, for most of the assassins had long since departed, so that French retribution generally fell upon the Moslem civilians, precisely as the FLN had calculated. The French became convinced that every Moslem was a potential enemy, and pointed to the savagery of FLN terror to justify their own repressive measures. Even Algerian Governor-General Jacques Soustelle, who came out with the intention of pursuing genuine reform for the benefit of the Moslem population, was so sickened and outraged by the Philippeville massacres that he abandoned all thoughts of conciliation and compromise until the war had been won. In this way, the Philippeville massacres became a victory for the FLN, for they served to separate further the two communities and adjourn the possibility of compromise. [11]

The optimism with which the French initially tackled the Algerian pacification slowly hardened into a more realistic assessment of their opponents after the FLN managed to survive their first grim winter in the mountains of the Aurès and the Kabylia. In Moslem eyes, the fact that they had survived at all bestowed the *baraka*—literally "the gift" from God—upon them, which brought in recruits, including a number of deserters from the *tirailleurs.* When the rebellion broke out, the French had less than forty thousand soldiers in Algeria. And while those numbers increased to four hundred thousand by the end of 1956, the French discovered belatedly that they were poorly organized to deal with the Algerian revolt. In the first place, Dien Bien Phu had been the last gasp of the old *Armée d'Afrique.*

The Sétif massacres of 1945 had already destroyed much of the esteem in which many Moslems had held the army until then, a respect that had caused so many of them to add to its glory in Italy and France in World War II. Indochina, following upon the heels of the campaigns of 1943–45, had created a break between the *Armée d'Afrique* and its traditional homeland. For the *tirailleurs,* this translated into an increasing disaffection with a war to impose French sovereignty upon Asian peoples. For the Moslem mind, much impressed with force, the stunning defeat of the French in that forlorn valley in upper Tonkin was a sign that the *baraka* had abandoned their colonial masters. Perhaps this feeling was most developed among Moslem POWs, who received a special anticolonial "disintoxication" at the hands of the Viet Minh. This did not make them Communists, but it did in many cases seriously undermine loyalty to the French.

The second casualty of this long separation between the *Armée d'Afrique* and the Maghreb was the officer corps. The last campaigns of conquest in Morocco had closed off in 1934, and the number of officers with practical experience of North Africa had steadily diminished. A few old North Africa hands were still to be found in the upper ranks, but an entire generation of younger officers who normally would have served their apprenticeship in the Maghreb had been shunted off to Europe and Indochina. With them had disappeared a body of men whose deep experience of Algeria, whose contacts with its people and knowledge of their psychology, although often summary and cliché-ridden, were irreplaceable. "The requirements of the Indochinese War have caused great misery in the *Armée d'Afrique,*" General de Monsabert told the National Assembly on November 23, 1954. "The local command cannot respond to surprises. One must restore the primacy of the infantry and troop training, give preference to native regiments whose presence alone will suffice to avoid trouble."[12] Toward the end of the war, the French were to use native formations, usually irregular ones, very effectively. But the brunt of the war would have to be shouldered by conscripts and reservists imported from mainland France. However, the lack of motivation, poor training and usually inadequate leadership of these men often limited their usefulness to garrison and other static duties, and meant that the hard fighting in the inaccessible hinterland fell to an elite of paratroopers, legionnaires, and a handful of other first-echelon units.

The outbreak of the Algerian War caught the Legion, like the rest of the French army, quite literally, on the hop. The only Legion units in Algeria in 1954 were the *1er étranger* and the *depôt commun de la Légion étrangère* at Sidi-bel-Abbès, both essentially training and administrative formations. Most of the other Legion regiments were wrapping up last-minute affairs in Indochina. The *2e étranger* disembarked in Tunis in 1955, and then shifted to Morocco, where it remained until 1956, in the company of the *4e étranger,* re-created in 1955, which did not arrive in Algeria until 1957. The *3e étranger* returned from Indochina in late 1954, the *13e* DBLE in

May 1955 and the *5ᵉ étranger* not until February 1956. The BEPs became the 1ᵉʳ and 2ᵉ REP, operational from early 1956, while a 2ᵉ REC had also been re-created in 1946 to accompany the 1st Foreign Cavalry Regiment. All of this meant that the response to the rebellion in the early days was very much an improvised one, even in the BEPs. Kemencei, repatriated from a Viet Minh prison camp in a very fragile physical state, was flung together with a number of recuperating prisoners into action almost immediately, with the predictable result that the operation had to be called off because many of the men simply could not keep up.

Kemencei realized the sad truth that the French army in the spring of 1955 was hardly better prepared to take on its Algerian role than it had been in Indochina in 1946, or 1950 for that matter. When he was distributed his equipment in March 1955 just before a jump with the 3ᵉ BEP into the Hodna plain, equipment that included puttees and World War I surplus tents together with other odds and ends utterly unsuited to airborne operations, "It was only with difficulty that I could overcome my anger." And while the equipment gradually improved, Legion paras preferred to purchase surplus U.S. boots and down sleeping bags with their own pay rather than utilize stiff French-issue hobnail boots and sleeping bags that were not moisture-proof. Conditions in the base camps at Batna and Biskra were primitive, with four or five water faucets and one open-air latrine for a five-hundred-man battalion: "These overcrowded installations hardly improved morale," Kemencei wrote, "and rather than a well earned rest of a few hours, this promiscuity produced belligerence and even fights." Daily rations on operation were totally inadequate, a serious situation because, unlike in Indochina where it was common practice to live off the country, "here, in Algeria, we were totally dependent upon official and regulation rations." Daily rations consisted of a two-and-a-quarter-pound tin of green beans to be shared among four men, a pound of corned beef for three, sardines, Gruyère, a crust of dry bread and the ubiquitous *vinogel,* all often eaten cold because the men were usually forbidden to light fires on operation. And even then, on one operation in the Aurès, his commander decided to increase mobility by undertaking a five-day operation with only two days' worth of food and water. "What good could these imbecile maneuvers do," questioned Kemencei, "except weaken the physical and moral resistance of the combatants before the battle?" In any case, it simply caused the legionnaires to purchase their own rations.[13]

Even in 1960, Simon Murray found conditions in the Legion para training camp at Sully, a disaffected farm about ten miles south of Sidi-bel-Abbès, below the standards one would expect to be laid on for elite soldiers:

The dormitories are enormous converted barns, the lavabo *is a horse trough in the open yard outside the barracks, and the* réfectoire *is in a loft above disused wine vats. . . . There are no lavatories as such, but a trench three hundred yards from the barracks represents the facilities; we share them with the flies. We don't have plates to eat off as in Mascara, so we have to use our tin gamelles, which substantially reduce appetite—like drinking Dom Pérignon out of a dirty coffee cup. All in all this is a hole and I don't like the look of it one little bit. . . . The food here is unbelievable; almost inedible after Mascara . . . and there is insufficient fresh water. It has to be brought each day in a cistern from Bel-Abbès. By lunchtime it's already warm and undrinkable.[14]*

The tactics employed in the early days appear to have been little better than the equipment. Until the Philippeville massacres of August 1955, the war was treated as a police action in every sense of the word, with gendarmes taken along on operations and FLN suspects hauled before justices of the peace, who often released them for lack of evidence. "My indignation was immense when I realized that several times 'fellaghas' [FLN guerrillas; proper plural is *fellouze*] arrested on one day with arms in their hands, reappeared the next day in town scoffing at us," Kemencei wrote.[15] After one such operation in which several *fellouze* were killed and others captured, gendarmes appeared at the hospital to interview wounded paras of the 1er REP to ask if they wanted to "file a charge" against the FLN prisoners.[16] Nevertheless, although Legion paras at first made fun of the attempts by unfit policemen to maintain the blistering pace of operations through the hills, they were much missed when they were withdrawn because, as Arabic-speaking *pieds noirs,* they were useful for interrogations.

"*Bouclage*" or "*quadrillage,*" a counterguerrilla technique used as early as the suppression of the Chouan revolt in the West of France during the French Revolution, was applied initially. This consisted of several units, usually of conscripts or even police, sealing off a section of terrain while a mobile unit, acting as beaters, sought to drive the rebels toward the blocking force. But while the guerrillas often suffered in these operations, largely because it forced them to keep on the move, it failed to eradicate them, for several reasons. The French were often operating on the basis of stale or inaccurate intelligence. They knew the impossible rugged terrain far less well than the rebels, who were usually able to slip away at night because the blocking troops were tired, inattentive, unable to read maps properly or too slow to get into position. And while Legion units often turned in very respectable lists of "fells" killed or captured and numbers of weapons seized, in fact much energy was expended for small results. The FLN was able to replace its losses faster than the French could kill them.

"For all these reasons . . . these operations are not worth it," Captain Pierre Sergent of the 1er REP believed. "How much wasted energy! And also, how many losses sustained when a cornered enemy decides to use his arms."[17] Captain Antoine Ysquierdo of the 1er REP discovered that Algeria was "exactly like Indochina," minus the monsoons.

The supposedly innocent inhabitants know everything, say nothing or tell you that they have never seen the fellouze, *when they are sitting on an arms cache. Everyone works for the rebels. The most insignificant shepherd knows everything. But to capture the bands, that is another story! . . . We have sent out 5,000 to 6,000 men and who knows how much materiel to kill a dozen poor fools and recuperate a pile of rusty shotguns, some semolina and cans of sardines. . . . But then, to track down the real* fel-louze, *those who slit the throats of the civilians in the bus the other day, nothing, zero! Impossible to keep an operation like this secret when it has been prepared for months by 36 chaps and in which participates a bunch of good for nothing soldiers.*[18]

There were some bright spots in these early days, which, when expanded, served as the basis for more successful policies in later times. One was the creation of the *Sections Administratives Spécialisées* (SAS) officers, an initiative of Soustelle. The task of these officers was to live in the villages, usually alone and at great personal risk, to bolster the authority of the traditional *djemmas* or councils, ward off FLN intimidation and call in military intervention when necessary. This was one of the more successful French initiatives of the war, and one that earned for them a good international press. Yet they never realized their full potential because they were too few and because their programs were underfinanced. French mistrust of Moslems caused them to hesitate to give them rifles to defend themselves. The critics of the SAS also found them to be very paternalistic, more interested in ensuring the docility of the Moslem populations than in understanding them. Nor was their work of pacification always advanced by the attitude of French units. One of the SAS officers, Captain Helmut Ontrup, echoed complaints heard in Indochina that, while incomparable in open combat, the Legion performed pacification duties poorly: "The Legion . . . does not worry about the fine points and subtleties of a guerrilla [war]," he wrote. "A static unit in a sector which must win the heart of a Moslem population can never be the Legion. . . . The 3ᵉ REI remained a deaf and blind giant!"[19] Also, a *ratissage,* or sweep, by a mobile group like the paras keen to increase their score in dead *fellouze* and none too refined in their methods of interrogation could undo in a few minutes the patient pacification work of several years.

A second innovation pioneered in the Constantine region by General André Beaufre, a *tirailleur* officer and veteran of Indochina, was that of *regroupement.* A student of Mao, Beaufre's aim was to separate the population from the guerrillas by relocating them into *zones de pacification* that were watched over by sedentary conscript units, while mobile forces harassed FLN rebels in the *zones d'opérations.* During the war, over two million Moslems were resettled and 1,840 fortified villages created. The success of this policy has been hotly debated. Defenders of *regroupement* point out that it removed the source of support for the FLN and eased the problems of operations elsewhere. It also diverted the flight of Moslems from the countryside toward the horrid conditions of the *bidonvilles* that sprung up around the major cities, and placed them where they could take advantage of French medical services.[20]

Its critics do not dispute that it hurt the FLN, but argue that *regroupement* did little to win the population over to the French side, and instead caused at the least great resentment at the uprooting and, at worst, provoked flight into Tunisia or Morocco into the arms of the FLN. Because the French often allocated too few troops to guard these camps, which could number thousands of refugees, the policy often resulted in a French-FLN condominium. Perhaps its greatest weakness, however, was that, like so many other military tactics employed in Algeria, *regroupement* became extremely controversial. Like the scandal that broke out in Great Britain when Kitchener first used "concentration camps" in the Boer War, popular opinion in France and elsewhere, including the French army, was disturbed by revelations of ghastly conditions of filth, malnutrition and general neglect that prevailed in many of these camps.[21] Nevertheless, Beaufre was the first French commander in the war to show some military success against the FLN.[22]

The mobile war in the *bled,* in which the Legion was involved, lost nothing in harshness and cruelty, especially after the Philippeville massacres. In part this sprung from natural fear, suspicion and hatred, of the sort that erupted in 1956 when a company of the 1ᵉʳ REP descended upon an Arab village in the Nementchas after one of its sergeants had been knifed by an Arab, slaughtered sixty-four people with submachine guns and bayonets and set fire to the village.[23] This is not to say that the Legion was necessarily more savage than other French units, all of whom were liable to act in this way. A great part of the problem sprang from the policy of "collective responsibility," of the sort applied by a Legion unit that shot nine farm workers near Sidi-bel-Abbès after two *fellouze* were discovered hiding in a barn. Again, it must be stressed that there is no evidence that the Legion was more guilty of this than other French units, or the FLN for that matter. But it did not escape the attention of many that it was this sort of conduct that had caused a number of German officers to be hanged as war criminals at the close of World War II, not to mention the baleful effect it had on the Moslem population.[24]

That said, however, it is possible that the Legion was particularly liable to behave in a harsh and ruthless manner. This sprang in part from its tradition of unquestioned obedience to superiors and the unit's sense of racial separateness, especially its dislike of Arabs. The high morale and sense of solidarity in Legion para units possibly made them more likely to fly off the handle when provoked. Certainly their training, described by Simon Murray as a tough, no-holds-barred affair, far more intense than his basic training at Mascara, appears calculated to harden sensibilities as well as bodies. Close-combat instruction was carried out on concrete slabs rather than in pits of sand or sawdust to soften falls, and anyone who pulled his punches became the object of the special attentions of a German sergeant, a veteran of Monte Cassino, who demonstrated the correct method, on at least one occasion breaking the leg of his unfortunate victim. In fact, Murray, certainly no enemy of the Legion as he is generally enthusiastic about his time there, discovered that a "meaningless barbarism" permeated his Legion para training, with beatings and savage application of *pelote* or punishment gymnastics common. For committing small lapses in training,

the punishment is to stand the man to attention with his hands behind his back and then thump him with every ounce of strength, deep in the solar plexus. Nobody survives. The body folds into a crumpled form, sags to the ground and is left writhing and gasping in agony with the lungs screaming for air, like a pole-axed ox. Lustig enjoys inflicting this kind of pain.

While Murray gave the tactical training high marks, the frequent, arbitrary and apparently meaningless punishments destroyed morale:

There is no camaraderie. . . . We are fed up with being pushed around by these second-rate N.C.O.s, particularly the corporals who have no fire in their bellies, no enthusiasm, no sense of humor, and are quite incapable of generating any kind of spirit in the section. There is no direction and sense of purpose. We are just drifting. There is no focal point on which to concentrate; there are no objectives at which to aim. It's as stagnant as a blocked drain.

The officer in charge of training was "totally wet and completely overshadowed by his N.C.O.s. He has no discernible qualities of leadership, in fact he has no discernible qualities at all." By comparison with Sully, the army para training camp at Blida where everyone was sent to carry out the jumps was "a dream world" of luxurious surroundings and good food. But above all, the NCOs, "known as *moniteurs,* are great guys, full of humor, without all the endless forced toughness that Legion N.C.O.s wear as part of their uniform."[25]

Such an atmosphere does not condemn the Legion out of hand. Torture and the *corvée de bois,* the practice of telling a prisoner that he was free to go and then shooting him in the back as he walked away, were not Legion monopolies. The American experience in Vietnam also proved that conscript units were very capable of getting out of hand, as at My Lai. But retaliation does seem to have been part of a policy vigorously applied by elite units in Algeria,[26] as Simon Murray discovered in the Aurès Mountains in August 1961: "The normal course of events in these villages which are supporting the fellagha is for the legionnaires to wring the necks of the chickens and stuff them into their *musettes,*" he wrote.

Livestock are set free and the mechtas *[houses] are then burned to the ground. The order to burn the huts came in each case from a captain of the Deuxième Bureau who was with us and presumably knew that these were the dwellings either of fellagha themselves or sympathizers. . . . Just before noon we came across some* mechtas, *and this time the men had not had time to flee. Under questioning by the officer of the Deuxième they refused to admit that they had any dealings with the fell and in fact they had very little to say at all. This all changed when they were put inside one of the huts and it was set ablaze. They started to scream blue murder and when we let them out we couldn't stop them talking.*

One of them was finally elected as spokesman and he said he could lead us to a cache that was filled with arms, and so off we set. We followed him over hills and plains and valleys for about fifteen miles, at the end of which time he said he couldn't find it. We had all stopped and were lying about waiting for the order to move on while the Arab explained his problems to the Deuxième captain. I was sitting just above the Arab who was jabbering away to the officer and waving his arms around in desperation. They were below me on the side of a small valley with a dried-out stream bed at the bottom.

Suddenly the officer grabbed a sub-machine-gun off a legionnaire standing near him and as the Arab started to scream in protest he kicked him in the side and sent him rolling down the hill. The machine-gun came quickly to the officer's shoulder and he squirted bullets into the writhing body of the Arab as he rolled down into the dried bed of the stream. When he reached the bottom he was as dead as the stones around him. We left him. We had a long walk back and in between us and our lorries was a mountain barrier 5,000 feet high. Nobody mourned the Arab—it was too hot and we were too tired.

We have no souls, we have no feelings, our senses are dead—dead like the dead corpse in the stream. Is this really me?[27]

Not surprisingly, perhaps, the frustrations and inconclusive nature of this sort of warfare caused French soldiers to welcome the Suez expedition of November 1956. The reasons for the invasion of Egypt by a joint Anglo-French force, in conjunction with an offensive by the Israeli army, are complex, but illustrate well the observation that though allies fight on the same side, they do not necessarily fight for the same goals. The Israelis were fighting for what they believed to be their survival, while the British, angered by Nasser's nationalization of the canal, feared a threat to their interests east of Suez. Why the French became involved is not clear. It appears that the French Socialist prime minister Guy Mollet was passionately pro-Israel, both because he regarded her as a pioneer socialist country and because he believed she needed to be defended from Nasser, who, like British Prime Minister Anthony Eden, he saw as a nascent Hitler in the Near East. Those involved in the Algerian War, including the officers of the 1er

REP who were dropped on Port Saïd on November 5, believed that the fall of Nasser would decapitate the FLN by depriving them of their most fervent supporter. That this view was naïve both because it gave Nasser far too much credit for FLN success and because it ignored most of the factors that had encouraged the Algerian uprising in the first place goes without saying.

None of this prevented disappointment from being all the more poignant and bitter when objections by the United States and the Soviet Union caused the operation to be canceled after only forty hours. For the French paras, who had scattered the Egyptians like rabbits and displayed a sort of raw efficiency that left their British counterparts blinking with disbelief, this was yet one more example of betrayal, by the "Anglo-Saxons," by the West, by the IVth Republic. The FLN took heart from the tremendous propaganda windfall and even collected arms left behind by the hastily withdrawn allied armies. For the passionately anticommunist Hungarian Janos Kemencei, the simultaneous defeats in November 1956 of the Hungarian revolution and of the French at Suez were deeply felt: "I no longer had any faith," he wrote. "My professionalism remained intact. But I no longer wanted to fight for causes lost in advance, like here in Algeria." For Kemencei, Suez brought to the surface a general discontentment with the poor conditions of the service in the Legion, as well as with the attitudes of the French soldiers whom he had been detached from the Legion to train. "Then our old fashioned and even frankly bad logistics did not encourage me to waste my health any longer. To support an intemperate climate without appropriate materiel, support the constant absence of hygiene, swallow on operations execrable food, all of this had literally disgusted me with the army." He was saved from resignation only by a providential posting to Madagascar.[28]

For many officers, the sense of betrayal was so profound that their loyalty to their government was shaken. Massu's paras obeyed the cease-fire order of November 6 with "rage in the heart . . . when Cairo seems to us just around the corner, with no serious obstacle to prevent our advance." On his return to Algiers, he discovered that the FLN had transformed "Nasser's unexploited defeat" into

a triumphal victory. Not only do its faithful take heart, but those who had given over to panic want to reaffirm their loyalty. . . . Our hearts are heavy. The deception runs through all of my beautiful division so ready to carry out a task worthy of it! We chew over without end this senseless story which has deprived us not only of a glorious victory, to which a soldier cannot remain indifferent, but also the beginning of a solution to the Algerian affair, which we are now confronting once again.[29]

Chapter 28

THE BATTLE OF
ALGIERS

MASSU'S PARAS HAD little time to brood, however, for they were ordered almost immediately to undertake what was to become one of the most publicized and controversial operations of the war—the Battle of Algiers. In January 1957, when Massu's 10th Para Division was called in to establish order in the second city of France, Algiers was a town of almost nine hundred thousand people that spilled across a ribbon of hills separating the Mediterranean from the rich agricultural plain of the Mitidja. From the sea, the triangular shape of the old city enclosed within its crumbling walls and watchtowers was plainly visible, its mosques and houses tightly layered upon the hillside like kernels of an albino pine cone. This was the Moslem heart of *"Alger la blanche,"* a teaming labyrinth of torturous alleys, stairways and cul-de-sacs that smelled of dung and urine, which outsiders found both disorienting and intimidating. It was here that many of Algiers's four hundred thousand Moslems crowded into houses that were vertical cubes of masonry, bolted and blind against the dark, narrow streets, but whose central courtyards rose to flat-roofed terraces that opened onto breathtaking views of the harbor and the azure Mediterranean beyond. This was to be the stronghold of the FLN in the Battle of Algiers, the one that the paras had to dominate to be victorious.

Although the escalating brutality of the confrontation between the paras and FLN terrorists caused each to blame the other for initiating the skirmish, it appears that it had its origins in a major conference of FLN leaders held in August 1956 under the very noses of the French in the

Soummam valley, which separates the Greater and Lesser Kabylia. This conference defined a military command structure for the ALN and greatly strengthened the organization of the FLN. More important, perhaps, it defined the organization's war aims, something successive French governments were never able to do in Algeria, which made their policies appear weak and vacillating next to the coherent demands of the nationalists. It also took the decision that there was to be no cease-fire before a complete recognition of Algerian independence had been achieved, a policy upon which de Gaulle's peace initiatives would eventually founder. It was also at Soummam that the FLN decided to open a major front in Algiers.

Violence in Algiers began to escalate in the summer of 1957 with random assassinations by the FLN, which provoked a reprisal bombing by *pied noir* extremists on August 10 of Moslem dwellings in the Casbah that left seventy dead. Under the direction of twenty-year-old Saadi Yacef, the FLN had established a network of operatives fourteen hundred strong that included several revolutionary Moslem women. On September 30, 1956, Yacef handed three of these girls bombs and instructed them to plant them in the Milk-Bar and the Cafétéria, both frequented by *pied noir* youth. The carnage, and sense of outrage, caused by the explosions was predictable. A third placed in the hall of the Air France terminal failed to detonate. These bombings were followed by a wave of assassinations of French officials, which provoked predictably violent reactions by the *pieds noirs, ratonades,* or random assaults, that, because FLN operatives took care to remain behind closed doors, fell upon innocent Moslems who were beaten and even killed. It was at this point that the governor-general called in General Massu.

By January 1957, the reputation as the elite of French forces that the paras had already tailored for themselves was approaching mythical proportions. Their heroic conduct in Indochina under a clutch of flamboyant and aggressive commanders had made them the darlings of the army, and any young man with a military vocation believed his *curriculum vitae* incomplete without a *brevet de parachutiste.* Of no unit was this more true than Jacques Massu's 10th Para Division, which included the 1er REP. Its commanders, around whom lingered a strong odor of Indochina to the point that they continued to refer to the FLN as the "Viets," cultivated a very macho command style, energetic, tough, suicidally brave. Top Saint-Cyr graduates jostled to be taken by the Legion, and the best of these sought out the REPs, pitying their less fortunate classmates condemned to serve in regiments of "voters" as conscripts were derisively called. (And in this way ignoring that equally efficient and elite colonial and *chasseur* paratroop regiments were one-half to three-quarters conscripts.) The Legion even creamed off their best men to go into the REPs—Simon Murray was called into his lieutenant's office at three o'clock in the morning and told to sign a form volunteering for the REP. "I refused initially, but after he implied that I was scared—which I am—I finally said I would go and signed the paper. This is all unsatisfactory as I am not keen on heights at all. There is no justice in the world—or is it just here?"[1] As has been noted, this sense of elite status had been heightened by the tactical scheme in Algeria that made the Legion and the 10th and 25th Para Divisions the firemen of the war for whom was reserved a lion's share of the hard action. In this way, the paras became symbols of force and violence, and their colonels took on the status of saints in a hierarchy of the elect.

The French writer Jean Lartéguy, whose Algerian war novels explore the para myth, defined the popular version of the collective para personality:

A simple, rather pathetic lot, anxious to be loved and delighting in contempt for their company, capable of energy, tenacity, courage, but also inclined to abandon everything for a girl, a smile or the prospect of a good adventure. . . . Vain, disinterested, thirsting for knowledge but adverse to instruction, sick at heart at being unable to follow a big, unjust and generous leader and being forced to attribute their reason for fighting to some political or economic theory . . . to take the place of the leader they haven't been able to find. . . . Pathetic and at the same time exasperating. . . . Ubu [The imaginary king of Alfred Jarry's Ubu Roi] turned hero. . . . They're on the lookout for a master who would know how to break them and at the same time cover them with glory, inflict on them the discipline they're longing for and give them back the admiration of the people which they feel they are being denied.[2]

It is possible to argue that without the hard-hitting military capabilities of the paras the French army in Algeria would have turned in a plodding performance. However, leaving aside for the moment the question of the controversial antiguerrilla tactics of the paras, the "para myth" was to have at least two negative consequences for the French army in Algeria. The first was that, as in Indochina, the indiscriminate expansion of the paras came about at the expense of the other units, and ultimately created a cleavage with the remainder of the army. Officers in "classical" units found their resentment rising at the increasingly cavalier attitude taken by para units toward military regulations, regarded as having been conceived for the "lead asses" in line units. They also disliked the fact that para companies counted their full complement of five officers, and might even include officers *à la suite* waiting for a vacancy, while line companies were run by one regular lieutenant or a passed-over captain and two conscript *"aspirants,"* men preparing for commissions as reserve second lieutenants, and some platoons were even led by corporals.

"To begin with, the paratroops were a wonderful myth, a story to enthrall every schoolboy in France," Lartéguy's Captain Naugier explains to Colonel Raspéguy.

But instead of spreading it throughout the army, and growing bigger and bigger, the myth has shrunk, as you've seen for yourself, and now it's turning to vinegar. . . . We have created a sect of fighters apart from the army, but that's not the way you win a war like the Algerian war, or remake a country. All you do is get yourself hated.[3]

To be hated by the enemy is one thing. However, the para myth also gave rise to resentment in the French army toward the paras, and in particular toward the 10th Para Division. This was an important factor in the so-called revolt of the conscripts against the generals' putsch of April 1961, spearheaded by the 1[er] REP. "A growing hatred for the 'paras,' " according to Jean Planchais, the defense correspondent for the prestigious French daily *Le Monde* during the Algerian War, found despised "lead ass" officers in line units telephoning Paris to say "that they were ready to come with their men to sort out the problem."[4]

The second problem with the para myth is that it helped to politicize them. The Battle of Algiers played a very important role in the formation of this political outlook, for, to borrow Lartéguy's imagery, it turned them from centurions into the praetorian guard of *Algérie française*. The spectacle of Massu, his jaw locked into an expression of unbending professional determination above stalactites of metals, marching into Algiers at the head of his immaculate division, like the new marshal and his deputies come to clear the town of desperadoes, left the *pied noir* population limp with exhilaration. This adulation was only increased by the paras' remarkable success in crushing the FLN network in Algiers. But it had a negative side, for it encouraged their narcissism, stimulated their sense of elite status, fostered their feeling that long-accepted military and even political conventions did not apply to them. Their colonels increasingly came to believe in their own legends, and treated their regiments as if they were their personal property, reviving in a way the proprietorial attitudes of the *ancien régime* army. This was encouraged by the fact that the Algerian War was essentially one fought on the regimental level, with generals appearing as distant and remote figures far up the hierarchy. The Battle of Algiers deepened their political commitment to French Algeria by casting them in the role of the people's tribunes: "Fear has made film-stars out of us, and that's not what we wanted." Lartéguy's Captain Naugier remarks. "So, of course, one shoots a line, squares one's shoulders and draws one's stomach in, but we feel like crying. Here we are, turned into praetorians for having wished too strongly to be soldiers of the people, and into bogeymen for wanting to be loved."[5]

The victory of the 10th Para Division over the FLN in Algiers was above all a victory of intelligence and energy. Employing a system that Massu called *quadrillage offensif*, Algiers was divided into squares, an elaborate system of files established for each person, with neighborhood and household heads required to be accountable for their residents. An

FLN general strike called for January 28, 1957, was broken by paras, who literally ripped the shutters off of the closed shops, obliging shopkeepers to emerge to protect their exposed goods. The FLN retaliated with more bomb outrages. But the paras located the bomb factory on February 19 through the expedient of establishing a list of unemployed Moslem masons and interrogating them until they discovered the one who had constructed it. Then they turned to breaking up the remainder of the FLN network. In this, Massu claimed, they were aided by FLN weaknesses. One of the most flagrant security breaches was created by the FLN's tendency, curiously bureaucratic for a clandestine organization, to generate tremendous amounts of paper—reports on meetings or of operations in which the names of those who had performed especially well were cited for special recognition. As education in written Arabic had been utterly neglected in French schools, or because the FLN was divided between Berbers and Arabs, their common language of correspondence was French, which provided the paras with easy-to-read lists of suspects to be arrested and interrogated. The often-bitter divisions and rivalries within the FLN—personal, political, friction between Arab and Berber, or in one instance a scorned wife whose FLN husband had taken a mistress—also played into French hands, and on occasion led a suspect to spill the beans on his colleagues.[6] Feeling the noose grow tighter around their organization, some of the FLN leaders fled Algiers. Although under pressure, however, Yacef's operatives were not yet out, and in early June more bombings of *pied noir* haunts were carried out.

The final dismantling of the FLN network resulted from a tactic known as *"la bleuite,"* that is, employing FLN turncoats who, dressed in common blue workingman's coveralls, mingled with the revolutionaries and pinpointed their hideouts. Yacef countered this tactic to a point by supplying French intelligence with his own "turncoats," who could for a time throw them off the scent. But by August 1957, even he realized that the paras were closing in. The honor of taking the last and most sought-after leaders of the Algiers FLN fell to the 1er REP. On September 23, Yacef's main runner was picked up by the paras, and under interrogation revealed his bosses' hideout at 3 Rue Canton, a narrow impasse in the Casbah. At five o'clock in the morning, Lieutenant Colonel Pierre Jeanpierre's 1er REP blocked off their lodgings. Yacef and his principal bomb carrier, Zohra Drif, had just enough time to slip into a cache constructed between the bathroom and a staircase. Trained to search for such hiding places by now, the Legion paras located it by tapping on the wall, and opened a hole with a pickaxe. Yacef threw a grenade that wounded three paras as well as the lieutenant colonel. However, when he was told that an explosive charge had been set to go off in ten minutes, he climbed, half-naked and coughing from the effects of the smoke of his burning papers, from his crevice.

In their jubilation at the capture of Yacef and Zohra Drif, the Legion paras neglected to check 4 Rue Canton, where one of the primary FLN hit men, an ex-pimp and petty criminal, Ali la Pointe, was hiding. It was not until October 8 that the REP tracked him down. When Ali la Pointe, Yacef's twelve-year-old nephew known as Petit Omar, and another FLN operative repeatedly refused summonses to emerge from their hiding place, the legionnaires placed a small charge meant to blow a hole in the wall. The resulting explosion, which apparently ignited Ali la Pointe's hidden bomb store, not only killed the fugitives and injured four paras, but also resulted in the deaths of seventeen Moslems in three neighboring houses that the legionnaires had neglected to evacuate.

The death of Ali la Pointe ended the Battle of Algiers. It was a stunning victory for the paras, whose popularity soared to new heights among the *pieds noirs,* who could now go to the cinemas, shop and sit in the cafés along the chic Rue Michelet and attend sporting events free from the lingering fear of assassination. The FLN, having lost much ground among increasingly war-weary Moslems, was forced to abandon urban terrorism to go for victory in the countryside, even outside of Algeria. The defeat also placed strains upon their leadership, fractious at the best of times. Yet the defeat of the FLN was more apparent than real, for the methods employed by the paras to win the battle had probably done more than anything to discredit the cause of *Algérie française* in the eyes of both French and world opinion. For the issue upon which the swarms of journalists who had covered the Battle of Algiers for the world press had concentrated upon was that of torture.

As has been seen, the use of torture by the army had been widespread in Indochina, as Massu admitted, although he claimed that it had been applied mainly by Vietnamese interpreters working for the French, using "ancient methods practiced among them, such as suspension by the wrists, perhaps followed by forced swallowing of water."[7] In 1949, the left-wing Catholic journal *Témoignage chrétien* called attention to the frequent use of electric-shock tortures by French officers there, and expressed concern that "It is permitted, recognized, and no one complains." This caused a brief outcry in Christian Democratic circles, the Mouvement Républicain Populaire (MRP), but was forgotten in the debacle on the R.C. 4 and the advent of de Lattre.[8] The use of torture in Algeria before 1957 was widespread enough to come to the attention of both Governor-General Marcel-Edmond Naegelen in 1949 and Jacques Soustelle in 1955, who expressly forbade it.

But for the paras in Algiers in 1957, torture appeared to offer a quick and effective way to break up the FLN infrastructure. "In Algeria, the problem was completely different [than in Indochina]," Massu claimed in the defense of his command's methods.

It was imperative that we obtain urgent operational intelligence, upon which depended the lives of innocent human beings, deliberately sacrificed by the F.L.N. to gain its objectives. *Such cruelty did not inspire one with the desire to spare those whose confessions could interrupt a fatal course of events. Therefore, practically speaking, if to make them "cough up" it was necessary "to rough 'em up a bit," the interrogators were obliged to submit suspects to physical pain, whose violence was graduated to achieve the confession.*

While Massu conceded that accidents could happen,

this was nothing more than a physical pressure, even violent, used to get quick information and which did not degrade the individual. . . . The procedure most often employed, beyond slaps, was electricity, by using the generators of field radios . . . and the application of electrodes on different points of the body. I experimented on myself . . . and most of my officers did so as well.

Massu required unit commanders to exercise a close surveillance because torture *"was a morally dangerous practice and one which could not be carried out for long. Also, I quickly understood that one must not prolong the tours of regiments in Algiers, but turn them over alternating with a tour [of operations] in the countryside."*[9] In the 1er REP, Lieutenant Colonel Jeanpierre, who had survived deportation to Mauthausen during the German occupation of France, rejected the suggestions of an old comrade that the paras were performing the same role as that once played in France by the Gestapo, and insisted that his duty was to prevent terrorist attacks by any means. He offered any officer who objected to torture the possibility of leaving the regiment, but none did. Even the para chaplain, Father Delarue, defended the practice as necessary to save lives: "There is no clean war," he claimed, pointing to the Allied use of terror bombing in World War II. "Sometimes it is a combat of one good against another good, if not an evil against another evil."[10]

The arguments made by the para officers in defense of their use of torture appear fairly compelling, especially when placed in the context of the atmosphere of fear and retribution of Algiers in 1957. Not only did torture work as a military tactic, but also the casual brutality of the FLN entitled them to no sympathy from anyone with a hint of civilized standards. Only left-wing intellectuals were capable of performing the required moral gymnastics to justify FLN excesses while at the same time condemning French countermeasures. Massu and others realized the importance of the Battle of Algiers as a test of power with the FLN. Certainly, had the FLN managed to dominate Algiers, it would have gained enormous prestige and reaped a bumper harvest of recruits throughout Algeria. Without torture, Massu and others claimed, the FLN network there could not have been broken. Torture, in fact, won the Battle of Algiers. However, two questions have been asked of the paras' methods: First, was torture in fact effective? And second, what were its long-term consequences?

Albert Camus, himself a *pied noir,* believed that the usually indiscriminate way in which the paras rounded up suspects and tortured them to find *"un bon,"* one real FLN runner or money collector, often created more terrorists than it snagged in the long run, men who would simply kill another time. While one will never know how many FLN activists the French actually created by torturing innocent people, at the very least one may conclude that such methods earned them little sympathy from the Moslem population. Even from his perspective as a Legion private, Simon Murray noted in his diary in August 1960 that the policies of *regroupement* and torture, about which he had heard "terrible stories,"

must have lost them many friends. . . . With all the good results . . . [there] was a steady build-up of hatred against the French—a hatred that comes from living in fear and terror. And this antagonism drew the Arabs, so often before divided among themselves, into a common cause; it made them feel the necessity of combining for survival and it made them finally aware of their own strength. The French became the foreign intruder and the concept of nationalism was born in the Arabs, which was never there before. . . . We mercenaries fight for a lost cause—a cause that will be buried in the French political arena, not here. The heap of dead bodies gets higher each day and the white crosses mark the pathway to the inevitable end; for the end is inevitable. . . . I wonder how many more crosses must be struck before the end comes—the end for the French, when a new nation will be born, conceived entirely through French misunderstanding.[11]

A second objection to torture is that, for the most part, it simply produces a plethora of false information, men talking to stop the pain. Such had obviously been the case with the Arab killed by Simon Murray's Legion paras—faced with the possibility of immediate death in a flaming *mechta,* and that of prolonging life with the possibility of escape by claiming to know the location of an arms cache, the Arab, obviously, offered to talk. But all the paras got out of his confession was a long hike and a pointless death, one more small tack pushed into the coffin of French rule. Antoine Ysquierdo of the 1er REP obviously had similar experiences. In his novel about the war, an Arab tells his captors, "Captain, if you hit me, I talk because I am afraid . . . but what I say is not true, because I know nothing . . ."[12] Certainly, torture did produce some useful information. But most positive intelligence appears to have come out of the *bleuite,* the use of turned FLN operatives, than out of torture. Indeed, one of the greatest successes of the war was achieved by French intelligence in 1958–59 when, through planted documents, they managed to convince the leaders of three *wilayas*—ALN regional commands—that they had been seriously contaminated by the *bleuite.* This set them on a reign of terror during which they tortured confessions of guilt out of perhaps thousands of their innocent followers.[13] It is possible that in the purges that followed the suspicious FLN leaders murdered up to four thousand of their own *fellouze*.

The worst aspect of torture from Massu's point of view was that, even if it gained a temporary tactical advantage for the French in Algiers, ultimately it contributed to the loss of the war. And here the moral question became a primary one. For when the news broke in France about the widespread use of torture, the conscience especially of the important and vocal French intellectual community was deeply disturbed. For a country whose memories of the German occupation were barely a decade old, stories of the death of Ben M'hidi, the first important FLN leader to be captured in Algiers, in mysterious circumstances in March, followed by the disappearance of Maurice Audin, a young Algiers University lecturer and militant Communist, in the hands of the paras in June, brought unpleasant memories surging back. Quite predictably, the intellectual left, led by Jean-Paul Sartre and Simone de Beauvoir, condemned it in no uncertain terms. This came as no surprise to the army, and could be dismissed by them as the bleatings of intellectuals who traditionally opposed any military enterprise. In the eyes of the military, the fact that these protesters opposed *Algérie française* in any case made their condemnation of torture appear a tactic rather than a legitimate expression of moral concern.

But the moral concern was real, the feeling that all means were not justified to achieve even the laudable ends of extinguishing FLN terrorists, that restraints must be exercised even in a war as angry as that in Algeria. The sad fact was that the objections to torture met with incomprehension in an army at least part of which had been cut off from its parent society for almost a generation, which had grown apart from its values, aspirations and even ethical standards. This became apparent when protests began to be heard from others who could not be dismissed as opponents of the army. General Jacques de Bollardière, sector commander at Blida in 1956, who as a captain had fought with the 13e DBLE at Narvik and remained with the Gaullists throughout the war, confronted Massu personally over the methods used by his men. When this failed to produce any concessions from Massu, de Bollardière wrote a blistering letter on March 27, 1957, denouncing torture and protesting the Moslems who had "disappeared in the night" after being arrested by Massu's paras, that was published in the widely read French weekly *L'Express*. This earned for de Bollardière a posting back to France, a punishment of sixty days "fortress arrest," and provoked his eventual resignation from the army. De Bollardière's protest was followed by the resignation of Paul Teitgen, a devout Catholic and resistance hero, from his post of secretary-general of the Algiers Prefecture, where his special duties included supervision of the Algiers police. Teitgen resigned, he said, because he no longer exercised the power to prevent what he called Massu's "war crimes."

Perhaps the most agonized and thoughtful condemnation of torture came from French writer Pierre-Henri Simon. Writing as a French patriot,

Simon acknowledged that the French army in Algeria was not dealing with "the disciples of Ghandi, the apostles of non-violence," but very brutal and vicious men. He fully understood the enraged reaction of a unit ambushed with the connivance of the local population, or whose members had been murdered and savagely mutilated by the *fellouze*. Nevertheless, to Massu's defense that the vicious atrocities of FLN terrorists were far worse than a little gentle persuasion practiced by the paras, Simon countered that basic humanity must be preserved, especially in the face of the brutal provocations of the FLN: "If really we are capable of a moral reflex which our adversary has not, this is the best justification for our cause, and even for our victory." He chided the army for abandoning the "hearts and minds" traditions of Galliéni and Lyautey, which they claimed to hold dear. "Even if the torture of an Arab paid off," he believed, "I would still say that it was criminal," a spot on the honor of France and of the army, and a moral defeat.[14]

The issue of torture was to have two long-term consequences. First, the realization that the paras were willing to sacrifice legality for expediency did much to contribute to the loss of faith in France in the war, and, because this was carried out before the world press, it also helped to undermine the French position in international opinion. It was proof, once again, of the Clausewitzian dictum that military action cannot be divorced from its political context. In a country that was growing increasingly war-weary, that was disturbed and frustrated by the lack of any apparent solution in Algeria and by the increasing turmoil that the war visited upon French political institutions, whose reluctant conscripts and reservists longed to return home and resume their normal existence, torture added yet another dimension of distaste. While perhaps only a minority were genuinely concerned about the moral implications of torture, the publicity given to its existence dampened further what little enthusiasm the French public still retained for the war. It meant that, even though the FLN in the end would lose its military battles against the French army, it would be victorious on the most important front—the political one. Paul Teitgen was of the opinion that Massu won the Battle of Algiers, "but that meant losing the war." Rather, with the advantage of hindsight, it was the FLN who emerged as the real winner of the Battle of Algiers.[15]

The second consequence of the debate over torture was that it was one more issue that contributed to the alienation of the paras from the government and from important sections of French public opinion. "After this brutal and difficult episode followed by the quasi-general disapproval of 'The Ladies of Public Opinion and the safeguard committee,' the press stepped up its campaign of systematic denigration of the soldiers and their action in Algiers," wrote the 1er REP's Antoine Ysquierdo.

Each one could spit its venom upon the army with impunity with nothing being done to limit this campaign of defamation, cleverly supported and orchestrated to achieve a definite goal. This was the only resource which the rebellion and its sympathizers possessed to thwart as far as possible, that is morally, the consistent and intolerable pressure of the parachutists. There were no more assassination attempts, the happiest escapees from the network were in prison or fleeing toward the refuges in the maquis *where they had not seen the last of us!*[16]

The War in the Bled

This, however, was not apparent in the autumn of 1957. Forced out of Algiers, the FLN had to do battle with the French army in open country, where they proved no more of a match for the Legion and paras than they had been in the city. The first threat posed by the French to the FLN was the Morice Line. Completed in September 1957, the Morice Line threw up a barrier between the FLN sanctuary in Tunisia and Algeria. The barrier was a stretch of electrified barbed wire running some two hundred miles from the Mediterranean to the *erg* or sea of sand dunes that separated Algeria and Tunisia further south. A similar barrier separated Algeria and Morocco. Captain Charles Hora, who served with the *3ᵉ étranger* on the Morice Line, categorized it as no more than a glorified cow hedge. But no cow could survive its five thousand volts of electricity, even if it managed to negotiate its concertina wire and deep minefields to either side of the fence. In fact, despite its rather fragile and primitive appearance, the Morice Line was a fairly sophisticated piece of military technology. A series of electrical stations were able to detect instantly any attempt to breach the line, which brought down a hail of preregistered artillery fire followed by the arrival of assault groups, at first along the road that paralleled the line, and eventually by helicopter. Nor were attempts to go around it to the south successful, for air reconnaissance would invariably pick out the groups of *fellouze* slogging over the dunes at first light and strafe and bomb them, leaving the *méharist,* or camel, units, or in some cases paras eager to practice their airborne skills, to clean up the rare survivors.

The Morice Line posed a serious threat to the FLN, for it cut off their ability to resupply and reinforce their *wilayas*—regional commands—in Algeria from their growing army in Tunisia. On occasion it was possible for isolated groups to slip through a depression beneath the line caused by a wadi, to tunnel under the line, or even to slip concrete pipes beneath the wire. But the breach would be discovered by patrols on the following day. This caused the FLN to mount ever-larger assaults upon the line, massing their groups near the frontier while specialists cut a path through the wire with insulated wire cutters or even blew their way through with bangalore torpedoes. As many of their soldiers would rush through as could before the inevitable arrival of the intervention group, often Legion or paras. They tried diversionary tactics, such as feinting a crossing in one area to draw the intervention group, and then mounting their major breakthrough elsewhere.

One of their most successful devices was a rubber sheath placed over the wire, which insulated it but did not alert the electrical stations to the crossing because the current continued to flow. Nevertheless, the crossing was detected by patrols at first light, and as the rebels were on foot and therefore could not travel far, French forces would begin to comb the hills looking for them. Once located, a bitter battle would ensue at point-blank range with submachine guns, grenades and even knives, against rebels well-hidden in the boulders and crevices of the arid hills and resolved to *faire Camerone,* which caused high casualties on both sides. It was in one of these confrontations between legionnaires and *fellouze* on the Morice Line in 1958 that Colonel Jeanpierre of the 1ᵉʳ REP was killed—many believe unnecessarily and in typical Legion fashion—when he ordered his helicopter to assault an FLN position in an attempt to neutralize its fire upon his advancing legionnaires.[17] But despite heavy Legion losses, the result, Legion critics assert, of neglect of elementary caution and a traditional Legion delight in frontal assaults unsupported by artillery or air strikes, those of the FLN were infinitely worse, especially after they elected to mount a major assault on the Morice Line just east of Souk-Ahras on April 27–30, 1958, in a desperate attempt to get reinforcements to their *wilayas* in Algeria. In the resulting battle, one of the largest of the war, the FLN suffered crippling casualties.

Nineteen fifty-eight proved a very successful year for the Legion in another respect—it was awarded a Certificate of Merit for Distinguished Service by the American Society for the Prevention of Cruelty to Animals and a similar recognition from the RSPCA in London, after a legionnaire of the 13ᵉ DBLE rescued a starving donkey and returned it to his base where, renamed Bambi, it served the unit as a mascot. Interest was pricked among the "Anglo-Saxons" after London's *Daily Mail* carried a photo of the donkey being carried on the back of a legionnaire. Attempts to award the Certificate of Merit to the generous legionnaire foundered upon the *anonymat.* However, the Chief Secretary of the RSPCA was informed by the Legion that numerous mascots, "running from the bear to the lizard, passing through monkeys, sand foxes, storks and other birds, hedgehogs, without forgetting of course the multitude of dogs and cats follow each unit in its movements. In certain [units], the number of animals is greater than the strength in manpower." Especially gratifying was the knowledge that Bambi "at the present time is enjoying an enviable destiny and that he is sharing the life of our legionnaires and even . . . their beer."[18] In light of these considerations, the award became a collective one.

In any case, Bambi's fate was certainly more enviable than that of the mule discovered by Murray's section of the 2ᵉ REP in September 1961.

"We had been out all day and the rain had not ceased for a second, and as the light was failing and we were coming down into a valley, there was the mule," he wrote.

It looked like the loneliest thing in the world. Benoît tried to kill it with his pistol and Hirschfeld joined in with his sub-machine-gun. I was seventy yards away and yelled at them in vain to shoot it behind the ear. Stupid ignorant bastards—they just kept firing at it, and a guffaw of laughter went up as each burst of bullets hammered into the poor brute's side. It staggered around in bewildered agony, groping for life and stubbornly refusing to die. Finally it fell and with a little twitch it breathed its last and lay still—food for the jackals that night. We continued on our way leaving behind a little incident that left a monument of something shabby and dirty in my mind.

Nor were the beloved mascots invariably safe—Murray stared in disbelief as a drunken legionnaire in a cold rage strangled, bayoneted and crushed the skull of his pet cat with the heel of his boot after it had eaten his dinner.[19]

The Morice Line proved to be one of the most successful strategies followed by the French during the war, for it forced the FLN to operate in conventional, large-scale units before they were ready,[20] a tactic that cost them an estimated six thousand casualties and 4,300 weapons. Unfortunately, as in the Battle of Algiers, the soldiers tended to mar this impressive and hard-earned military victory with a political defeat when they mounted an unauthorized raid upon an FLN training center at Sakiet in Tunisia. The resulting international outcry and political prevarication in Paris and Algiers added further to their growing disenchantment with the way the war was being handled by their political leaders. Therefore, when *pieds noirs* in Algiers and other cities began a series of massive strikes in March and April 1958 that culminated in open revolt on May 13, fueled by Paris's plan to push through reforms to benefit the Moslem population and set the stage for some sort of negotiated settlement, the government discovered that its soldiers were no longer prepared to defend it.

The actual occasion for the revolt was the execution by the FLN of three French POWs, an event that put the army in a filthy mood, and offered further proof to *pied noir* intransigents that Paris was intent on doing a deal with criminals. Ceremonies to honor the dead soldiers escalated into riots and then to revolution. Led by Massu, officers throughout Algeria "boarded the moving train" of *pied noir* resistance to Paris. The paras looked on indulgently as the offices of the governor-general were sacked by a *pied noir* mob. In France, there was little public enthusiasm outside the parties of the left to preserve a republic that was perceived to be geriatric and incompetent. Hurried negotiations in Paris and Algiers produced the only political solution that seemed acceptable to all sides—

the recall of Charles de Gaulle out of retirement to preside over the dismantling of the IVth Republic and the inception of the Vth.

With the border effectively sealed from FLN incursions and a new government in Paris allegedly committed to *Algérie française,* the army moved to place victory out of reach for the FLN. 1959 would be hailed as the "brilliant year" of the French army in Algeria, when the *wilayas* of the interior, already struggling for breath, would be reduced to the status of military quadriplegics. Ironically, perhaps, as this was primarily an army operation, its impresario would be an air force general, Maurice Challe, who replaced General Raoul Salan as commander-in-chief in Algeria. An airman who had achieved fame in the French resistance for having purloined the Luftwaffe order of battle just prior to the Normandy invasion of 1944, Challe combined an outspoken frankness with good sense and solidity, an impression fostered by his round, good-humored face and bourgeois habit of smoking a pipe. Challe was set the task of mounting an offensive that would reduce the *wilayas* to isolated bands of ragged fugitives.

For de Gaulle, the political objectives of the Challe offensive were twofold: convince the FLN that military victory was impossible and that they must come to terms with Paris, and get the army out of the cities like Algiers where Massu and others had become too closely involved in the *pied noir* political games and occupy them with the sort of healthy outdoor activity for which they had been trained. De Gaulle's critics claim that the Challe offensive came a year too late to finish off the FLN when they had been knocked seriously off-balance by their defeat on the Morice Line, by the near self-destruction of several *wilayas* provoked by the *bleuite,* and by the political confusion into which the surprising emergence of de Gaulle had momentarily cast them. One might also add that the Challe offensive came too late to entice a section of the army, notably the 1er REP, away from their interest in politics.

Despite the military successes against the FLN, Challe believed that the French strategy of spreading its static forces thinly across Algeria while hitting the rebels with its mobile troops of legionnaires and paras had proved a haphazard and wasteful one. The French could not be strong everywhere, and with up to eighty thousand troops concentrated on the Morice Line in 1957–58, this gave the *katibas* a great degree of freedom of movement to blow up electricity pylons, assassinate Moslems loyal to France, attack isolated farms, mine roads and ambush French patrols. The intervention forces contained no more than fifteen thousand men, were often employed on the frontiers, and were simply too few, too badly informed and too ponderous to operate effectively over the length and breadth of Algeria. Through the system of *quadrillage,* Algeria had been divided into seventy-five different sectors. As operations were seldom coordinated between neighboring sectors, when pressured in one area the *katibas* had merely to slip into another sector to find relative calm, leaving

the French to comb, shell and strafe the now empty *djebels,* or hills. When
the French departed, the FLN returned.

Challe's new tactics included two components. The first was to create
commandos de chasse, to be accompanied by scout units of Moslem *harkis.*
The job of these units was to live in the *djebel,* to mark and pin down the
FLN units and then call in the paras, legionnaires and other units of the
new, concentrated general reserve, which formed his second innovation.
These troops were ferried into an area by helicopter to set up a perimeter
often as large as ten miles in diameter, which was gradually contracted to
corner the rebel units. Sometimes a unit of paras might be helicoptered into
the center of the perimeter to draw out the enemy. When this was done, air
and artillery strikes would be called in, after which the "general reserve"
forces would move in to finish the job. However, now, rather than move on
after having inflicted heavy casualties, the units would continue to track
and harass FLN units until they had been destroyed as effective forces.

Challe first tried out his new techniques near the old Legion stronghold
of Saïda. There the countryside was less broken than in the Aurès or the
Kabylia, although it had been dominated for years by the *katibas* of *wilaya*
5. Using the 10th Para Division and legionnaires as his general reserve, in
a matter of weeks he managed to kill over 1,600 FLN and capture 460
more. Although the FLN had not been destroyed in the Saïda-Mascara
sector, he felt that the garrison forces could maintain control. "Opération
Courroie," which took place in April 1959 in the more difficult terrain of
the Ouarsenis in the Algiers hinterland, enjoyed less success because the
FLN forces there proved to be more elusive. Part of the French problem was
that they were only beginning to work out their helicopter tactics. Although the first French helicopter raid dated from 1955, helicopters became available in quantity only from 1957, and only gradually were they
released from the command echelon to be used by assault forces. The
French soon learned to move their intervention forces as far forward as
possible to the battle zone by motor transport, and then use helicopters to
shuttle troops to the objectives and blocking positions. At first the helicopters landed directly upon the enemy position. But as soon as the rebels
recovered from their surprise and began to shoot back, it was found more
prudent to land four hundred to eight hundred yards from the objective.
The absence of armaments as heavy as even a 50-calibre machine gun in the
FLN camp, together with the rebels' ignorance of such defensive techniques
as lead firing, left the helicopters fairly safe so long as they maintained their
distance. Nevertheless, the French did develop a more heavily armored
helicopter, the Pirate, for use in close in fighting.[21]

As spring turned to summer, the *harkis* units, which Challe had expanded from a handful to fully sixty thousand men, were beginning to
come into their own. In July, Challe concentrated twenty-five thousand
troops in the FLN stronghold of the Kabylia for "Opération Jumelles,"
using all of his new techniques including a strong dose of *bleuite* to instruct

local villagers in the dangers of aiding the FLN. While "Jumelles" did not destroy the FLN, it caused it to break up into small bands, and substantially loosened its hold on the population. For legionnaires, these operations, carried out at altitudes as high as six thousand feet, were exhausting, much like that undertaken by Simon Murray in November 1960. Gasping for breath in the oxygen-thin atmosphere, legs and back aching after days of clambering over jagged faces of mountains, baked by the heat in the day, yet too frozen to sleep at night, they gradually accumulated fatigue until the hours passed in a daze of careless exhaustion. The sergeant's nerves were perpetually on edge, which caused him to kick and swear at laggards. Finally, shots were heard as a company of Legion paras stumbled into an FLN position, losing twenty men in an instant.

The "fells," though still invisible, were located on a ridgeline to the front. The sky suddenly filled with helicopters that tried to land on the rebel position but swooped away when the first helicopter to touch down was riddled with fire. The air rippled with heat as the paras pounded the position with their mortars and machine guns, to no apparent effect. But fast-moving "Pirates" moved back and forth over the ridge, raking it with bullets and causing a net diminution in the rebel rate of fire. *"Sacs à terre! Montez à l'assaut!"* It was four o'clock. Two companies of paras moved in a line up the side of the ridge, the legionnaires bobbing and darting from bush to boulder, pausing quickly to catch their breath and then moving forward again, their bodies bent against the slope, as fire from supporting companies made the *fellagha* position look like an erupting volcano. The first legionnaires in their green berets crested the ridge, squirting clips of bullets into trenches and dropping grenades into holes. Fifty-three "fells" lay dead in a matter of minutes. There were no prisoners.

Hardly had the bodies been aligned and counted, however, than the paras charged off down the hill in pursuit of another group of "fells" signaled by a helicopter. As they struggled cautiously through the valley, each legionnaire feeling extremely alone as the men in the line to the left and right were usually invisible among the bush and stones, someone suddenly shouted *"Attention!"* Bullets flew overhead as the legionnaires, flat on their stomachs, poured rounds into the gray-green foliage to the front. *"Grenade!"* The firing stopped, heads went down with eyes covered, and in an instant there was a tremendous explosion. *"En avant! En avant!"* The charge overran three dead "fells" as riddled as Swiss cheese, equipped with two British Enfields, a Sten gun, binoculars, compasses, good boots, shaving kits, toothbrush and a blanket each.

When they reached the bivouac they were to share with the 13ᵉ DBLE, which had acted as the blocking force, a *Deuxième bureau* officer ordered Murray and another legionnaire to return to the cadavers and retrieve their heads for identification as possible *harki* deserters. It was grisly work severing the heads in the fading light with a penknife. They placed two dripping heads in their sacks and headed back to camp, Murray covering his equipment and rations with blood in the process. "The third head we left, because it was no longer recognizable behind the mask of bullet holes." The intelligence officer took photographs of the heads, and then told Murray to dispose of them, which he did by grabbing them by the blood-soaked hair and tossing them into the bushes. Later that evening, some of the Spaniards in one section had pooled their rations to make a soup.

The équipe had eaten and there appeared to be a considerable amount left in the pot, so they called over a German and invited him to fill his tin mug. Just as he was about to put the cup full of soup to his lips one of the Spaniards, with a mighty guffaw, reached his hand into the cauldron and pulled out by the hair one of the Arab heads, which he had retrieved from the bushes. On looking up at the noise, one could see the scene and follow the story at a glance—the Spaniard stood there with the ghastly head dripping soup, dangling by the hair from his outstretched hand, while the German stood aghast, white as a sheet, frozen for a second, and then promptly turned and threw up. This gave rise to another guffaw from the Spaniard and his chums. . . . I must confess at the time I laughed like hell; so did we all—that is, except the fellow who had received the soup.[22]

When Challe was recalled to France in April 1960, the only area that had yet to submit to the full force of his tactics was the Aurès. His plan appeared to have delivered quite spectacular results: FLN casualties had exceeded French ones by a ratio of ten to one, large numbers of arms had been recovered, and the proportion of prisoners to killed had risen from 27 to 42 percent, a sure sign of growing FLN demoralization. The FLN command structure had been seriously disrupted. "The military phase of the rebellion is terminated in the interior," Challe could proclaim proudly. Army engineers moved in to construct roads, schools and clinics in areas that had been "no-go" zones for the French for five years. The army began to take great pride in its military accomplishments, came to feel a close identity of purpose with the mission of improving conditions in the Moslem communities, and developed a sense of proprietorial interest in the *harkis* who had played such an active role in its victories. The army, especially those "general reserve" forces of paras and legionnaires, believed that it had achieved victory, and for this reason was all the more baffled and then angered when de Gaulle appeared to throw away at the conference table the gains they had won with so much blood on the battlefield. This was at the heart of the rift between de Gaulle and his praetorians in April 1961.

A more detached view of the situation in Algeria in the spring of 1960 following the Challe offensives was less rosy from the French perspective. In part, Challe's successes, while substantial, had been achieved because the FLN had simply not contested his offensives. Attacks upon the Morice Line the previous year had proved too costly. Had they elected to mount such offensives again, they might certainly have relieved some of the pressure on the *wilayas* by diverting French troops to the frontiers. But FLN headquarters in Tunis had largely written off the forces of the interior, and instead had elected to husband the army in their Tunisian sanctuary to serve as an effective symbol of continued resistance for the Moslem population within Algeria. Indeed, one of the paradoxical consequences of the Challe offensives was to settle the often-murderous power struggles in FLN ranks in favor of the hardliners. Inside Algeria, Challe had inflicted severe damage upon the FLN, but he had not destroyed it, and it remained, dormant and in embryo, awaiting more favorable times. Nor did the Challe offensives convince France that the war was won. One of the corollary operations had been a stepping-up of *regroupement,* with inhabitants of the operational zones uprooted and placed in resettlement camps in appalling conditions, which, when revealed by the conservative newspaper *Le Figaro* in July 1959, provoked an uproar across the political spectrum. Also, these operations again raised the specter of the use of torture, a revival of a controversial practice that elicited a rebuke from the Gaullist government. In short, military victory could not be an end in itself. It was obvious to de Gaulle that a political accommodation with the rebellion must be found.

Chapter 29

THE ROAD
TO REBELLION

SOME SORT OF confrontation between de Gaulle and the paras was probably unavoidable, given the bitter memories of defeat and abandonment of
allies in Indochina, the belief widespread within the sharp edge of the
French army that the prestige and the future of France were bound up with
the retention of Algeria, and that they had achieved "victory" there. However, the pill of Algerian independence might have been less bitter for them
had France not turned over the store lock, stock and barrel to the FLN,
although as has been suggested the paras proved to be fairly effective
recruiting agents for the FLN and played their part in narrowing the political options for the Moslems. Nevertheless, the politicians, including de
Gaulle, must accept a great deal of the blame for the outcome. The fall of
the government of Mendès-France in 1955 removed the last politician of
stature in the IVth Republic who might have been able to find a compromise with moderate Algerians. De Gaulle, too, failed to move quickly in
1958 to capitalize on the hope that his arrival in power raised among
Moslems that a compromise peace might be reached. It appears likely that
as early as 1957, de Gaulle concluded that Algerian integration into the
French political system would unleash an avalanche of Moslem immigrants
onto the French mainland, so that his retreat at Colombey-les-Deux-Eglises
might become Colombey-les-Deux-Mosquées. The General appeared to
believe that time was on his side, that his prestige would be enough, when
required, to persuade the Moslem majority to accept his terms. He also
underestimated the singleminded commitment of the FLN to complete

victory, assuming that the Challe offensives would convince the rebels of the futility of continued resistance, and persuade them to accept a negotiated peace.

The combination of these factors made some sort of political collision likely, because the army was at first baffled and then increasingly angered by de Gaulle's outreach to the FLN. His trips to Algeria in June and July 1958 when he shouted *"Je vous ai compris"* ("I have understood you") and *"Vive l'Algérie française"* to frenzied *pied noir* crowds at first assured his military supporters of his commitment to their procolonial views. However, doubts soon began to set in. His first political initiative came on October 3, 1958, with the Constantine Plan, which promised economic revitalization of Algeria and a large increase in Moslem representation in the French National Assembly as part of the full integration of Algeria into France. At the same time he made a direct appeal to the FLN, calling for a cease-fire, a *paix des braves*. All the FLN had to do was to wave "the white flag of truce." These initiatives backfired badly. In France, those who began to do their sums realized that the full economic and political integration of Algeria would not only seriously retard improvements in the French standard of living, but would also swamp the Assembly with seventy-five Moslem deputies, therefore delivering to them the balance of power in a fragmented French assembly. For the *pieds noirs,* of course, "integration" meant a continuation of the *status quo ante,* or something fairly close to it. For the Moslems, after years of disappointments, "integration" was in the words of English historian Alistair Horne "at best a romantic delusion, at worst a confidence trick."[1]

With his offer of a *paix des braves,* the Chief of State succeeded in infuriating both the army and the FLN—the army because it meant a recognition of and negotiations with terrorists who, in any case, were on the verge of defeat. The FLN, which two weeks before had established a government in exile, and their allies on the French left, led by Simone de Beauvoir, claimed that it was tantamount to capitulation before any of their political goals had been met, and especially resented the reference to the "white flag," which they chose to interpret as a call to surrender rather than a truce. To emphasize their rejection, the FLN opened a new wave of terrorism.

De Gaulle's next initiative came on September 16, 1959, in the midst of Challe's "Opération Jumelles," when he promised self-determination for Algeria:

In the name of France and of the republic, by virtue of the power granted to me by our constitution to consult its citizens . . . I commit myself to ask, on the one hand, of the Algerians in their twelve departments, what it is they finally wish to be and, on the other hand, of all Frenchmen to endorse their choice.

The menu offered the three choices of "secession," "integration . . . France [from] Dunkirk to Tamanrasset," or an association between France and a federal Algerian state in which all of its communities would be represented.[2] Challe was enraged and wrote that, "One does not propose to soldiers to go and get killed for an imprecise final objective."[3] What de Gaulle had done was to hand the FLN a political victory—that is, placing the possibility of Algerian independence on the table—at the very moment that their *katibas* were being chewed into small fragments by the paras. Now all the FLN had to do was to ensure that they became the only recognized representatives of the Algerian Moslems. For Captain Pierre Sergent of the 1er REP, on September 16, "France just lost the chance to be a great nation." He announced to his colonel that, "FOR ME, THE FLAG OF THE FLN FLIES OVER ALGIERS FROM THIS MOMENT. Algeria will be independent. . . . Only a revolution could reverse the course of events. . . . On 16 September 1959, I felt like a very old citizen of a very old country."[4]

With the tension mounting between Paris and military and *pied noir* circles in Algiers, it required only one spark to set off some sort of confrontation. This was provided by Massu, who in an interview with a German newspaper announced that "I, and the majority of the officers in a position of command, will not execute unconditionally the orders of the Head of State." Massu was yanked out of Algiers and given a personal dressing down by the Head of State in Paris before being sent to his new posting in Metz in Eastern France. For Massu, the war was over. Challe, too, offered his resignation over the Massu disgrace.

In Algiers, militant *pieds noirs* used the *bombe Massu* as an excuse to activate a prepared rebellion, which, they assumed naïvely, would spread to Paris. On January 24, 1960, they took to the streets. Challe called out the two regiments of paras, including the 1er REP, who with the police were given the task of driving the demonstrators out of their positions in the center of town. As the gendarmes approached at six o'clock on the evening of January 24, the *pieds noirs* demonstrators ambushed them with a deadly hail of rifle bullets and homemade bombs. The 1er REP, barely six hundred yards away, did not lift a finger to help the police, a lapse that provoked a heated exchange between Lieutenant Colonel Henri Dufour of the Legion paras and the "gendarmerie" commander, one that has never received a satisfactory explanation. The most likely is that the paras' well-known sympathy and even open contacts with the militants of *Algérie française* made them disinclined to intervene.

This is certainly the attitude they adopted subsequently, with the commanders of most of the other units informing Challe that they had no intention of breaking down the barricades thrown up by the students. On the contrary, there were scenes of fraternization, with Captain Sergent assuring the activists that his men would never fire on them. De Gaulle decided to wait them out, allowing the demonstrators to tire and drift off and French public opinion gradually to demonstrate their support for his firm stance against the agitators. Finally, on the night of January 29, de Gaulle went on television to declare that he would never abandon the "Frenchmen of Algeria" and remind them that "It is I who bear the country's destiny. I must therefore be obeyed. . . . Law and order must be re-established . . . your duty is to bring this about. I have given, and am giving, this order." Hardly had he gone off the air than declarations of loyalty were pouring in from army units offering to crush the rebellion. Sergent tried to convince his colonel to order the 1er REP to join the insurgents, but he refused. "I hesitated to act against the opinion of my superior, but, finally, I thought it impossible to be more *Algérie française* than he and all the colonels who, for six days, fought for her. I backed down." The colonels began to discuss what they would do if ordered to attack the barricades. Colonel Favreau of the 5e *étranger* suggested marching forward, the band in the front and rifles pointed toward the ground, convinced that the militants "would never fire on the Legion."[5] In the end, they did not have to. Under conditions negotiated by Lieutenant Colonel Dufour, the insurgents were allowed to march out of their bastion with their arms, and were accorded full military honors by the 1er REP.

The military supporters of *Algérie française* realized that they had missed a golden opportunity to attempt a putsch. Moreover, they had revealed for all to see a yawning rift in the French camp. The FLN was strengthened at a time when their military fortunes were in steep decline, because they could calculate that de Gaulle had to choose between negotiating with them or caving in to the "ultras" on the right. De Gaulle began to transfer those who seemed most reluctant to follow his orders back to France, including Challe.

In Algeria, however, things went from bad to worse. In the spring of 1960, the commander of *wilaya* 4, Colonel Si Salah, contacted the French to say that he was willing to negotiate with them on the basis of de Gaulle's call for a *paix des braves*. After talks in Algeria, Si Salah and two of his staff were flown to Paris on June 9 for a meeting with de Gaulle. It came to naught. On June 14, de Gaulle made a direct appeal to the FLN government-in-exile. The Algerians returned to their *wilaya*, where they were purged by FLN headquarters in Tunis, who apparently learned of their treachery from a leak in the French government. Alistair Horne speculates that de Gaulle used the threat of treating with Si Salah to get the FLN to the negotiating table.[6] If so, it did not work, because brief talks held between the FLN and the French at Melun on June 25–29 quickly collapsed. De Gaulle had been outmaneuvered, for he had sacrificed Si Salah while at the same time recognizing the FLN as the *de facto* spokesmen of the Moslem community in Algeria. Whether or not Si Salah could have become the nucleus of a viable "Third Force" in Algeria has been hotly debated. What is important is that military leaders, especially General Challe, saw de Gaulle's failure to do business with Si Salah as the great missed opportunity of the war and as nothing short of the betrayal of the army.

Nowhere had the resentment against de Gaulle achieved a more con-centrated force than in the 1er REP. Their enthusiasm for the fight with the FLN declined proportionately with their increasing political activism. While operating on the Morice Line in 1960, Sergent's company was pre-vented by higher authority from pursuing and destroying an FLN force it had driven back over the Tunisian border. In disgust, he refused to carry out an order for a subsidiary and useless operation: "For the first time in my career, I refused to obey," Sergent wrote.[7] At the same time, the com-mander of the 1er REP, Lieutenant Colonel Henri Dufour, a legionnaire of the old school who had served his apprenticeship fresh out of Saint-Cyr in 1934 in the *3e étranger* under the redoubtable Lieutenant Colonel Maire, made contact with General André Zeller, a retired chief of staff of the armed forces and a fierce partisan of *Algérie française,* to propose that the 1er REP capture the Delegate General and his entourage as it marched past the reviewing stand on July 14. This was to be coordinated with the im-prisonment of de Gaulle and his government by troops marching down the Champs Elysées in Paris. On July 13, Dufour received word from Zeller that things were not prepared in Paris, so the plan was abandoned.

The conspiracies continued, however. On November 14 a funeral at Zéralda, the 1er REP's base about twenty miles from Algiers, for ten paras killed on operation turned into an emotional political demonstration. "Fol-lowing the tradition," Sergent wrote, "the colonel bade a last adieu to his men: 'It is not possible that your sacrifice was in vain. It is not possible that our compatriots in the metropole remain deaf to our cries of anguish.' " Father Delarue, divisional chaplain of the 10th Paras, declared: "You die at a time when, if we believe in the speeches we hear, we no longer know why we die." This funeral led to Dufour's recall to France. But Dufour conspired with the militant officers in his regiment, led by Sergent, to go into hiding, stealing the regimental standard in the process so that the transfer of com-mand to a new colonel could not take place, and he would remain, in Sergent's words, *"le patron moral"* of the 1er REP.[8]

The paras were clearly not prepared to write off Algeria as they had Indochina, as another unfortunate accident of policy on the way to com-plete decolonization. Algeria had witnessed no Dien Bien Phu, the FLN had been virtually pushed out of Algeria, but despite all this, de Gaulle ap-peared intent upon giving away the store. To prevent this, Sergent and General Edmond Jouhaud, a die-hard *pied noir* who had commanded the air force in Indochina before becoming air force chief of staff, conspired with the colonels of the *18e* and the *14e régiments de chasseurs para-chutistes* (RCP), who like the 1er REP were stationed around Algiers, to take advantage of the massive demonstration planned by *Algérie française* militants during de Gaulle's visit to Algeria in December. The plan was vague at best, which was just as well because the results of de Gaulle's visit were completely unforeseen.

Pied noir militants set off their demonstrations, which quickly turned to riots in Algiers and Oran. The first thing that went wrong for the conspirators was that de Gaulle avoided Algiers altogether, and by changing his itinerary managed to evade at least four assassination attempts that had been laid for him. The second miscalculation of the *Algérie française* "ultras" was that their anti-Gaullist demonstrations produced a massive Moslem backlash. Prompted by the FLN, which had managed successfully to reconstruct its network in Algiers, Moslems poured out of the Casbah waving green and white FLN flags, chanting, *"Algérie algérienne! Algérie musulmane!"* and, whipped up by the ululations of their veiled women, began to clash with the *pieds noirs*. Violence was also visited on the Jewish community, and some pro-French Arabs were assassinated.

Faced with this growing disorder, Sergent was deeply disappointed with the reluctance of the conspirators to act. Two of the para colonels hesitated to take the lead. Only Colonel Georges Masselot of the 18ᵉ RCP, a *pied noir,* offered his unequivocal support to Jouhaud. Sergent believed that Jouhaud failed to rise to the occasion, for instead of pumping up their morale with a blistering speech on the necessity to keep Algeria French, in the manner of a Legion recruiting sergeant, he merely told them to reflect before taking a final decision and give their answer to Sergent in the morning. Having slept on it, even Masselot decided that "the general situation is not favorable, we think that France is not ready and that Paris will react badly. We think that neither the navy nor the air force is with us, and that all this is an adventure which will lead to nothing." When Sergent carried this news to Jouhaud, the general thanked him. "We must wait for another occasion," he said.[9]

At last the military conspirators had been handed their Dien Bien Phu in Algeria. These Moslem counterdemonstrations, whose apparent spontaneity and size surprised even the FLN, which had orchestrated them, made a deep impression on the United Nations, which had begun to debate the Algerian question on December 6. The contention of the army and the *pieds noirs* that the demands for Algerian independence were the work of only a handful of Moslem militants was scuppered without a trace. The FLN saw December 1960 as the major turning point in the war. Not only did it show that de Gaulle no longer retained the power to make peace in Algeria, but also the United Nations on December 20 recognized Algeria's right "to self-determination and independence," an important political victory in a recognized forum of international opinion.

These demonstrations also revealed the contradictions and naïve assumptions upon which the conspirators, led by Sergent, had founded their faith in *Algérie française.* Their support of French Algeria can certainly be explained in professional terms—a desire to conserve the first significant victory for French arms since 1918, or loyalty to dead comrades. A feeling that they had given their word to loyal Moslems that France would remain also played an important role. Strategic considerations, the fear that "Africa is at stake, decolonization is the tactic," and more specifically that the important naval station at Mers el Kébir would become a Soviet base also played a large part. Yet their commitment to *Algérie française* was also philosophical and moral. Most were profoundly colonialist and could not imagine French greatness without colonies. Sergent believed that what was required was an assimilation of French culture by the Moslem elite, combined with a massive program of economic reform, *"des solutions d'avant-garde,"* which would benefit the lower classes.[10] This was, in retrospect, a rather ironic championship of Franco-Algerian integration, as in the 1980s Sergent became one of the main standard-bearers of the National Front, whose main platform is opposition to Moslem immigration into France.

Even putting aside the question of whether a Moslem elite cared to turn its back on a rich Islamic and Maghrebian heritage to embrace a French one, or whether France was prepared to make the substantial economic sacrifice required to bring the Maghreb into the twentieth century, the flaw in the conspirators' plans remained the *pieds noirs*. The Algerians of European extraction had no desire to grant the Moslems equality, which was one reason why Algeria had reached its political impasse. What they wanted was a Maghrebian South Africa under French protection. Indeed, according to one account, the possibility of a "Mexican" solution—giving the Legion to a quasi-independent Algeria under *pieds noir* leadership—was also discussed in late 1960.[11] The military conspirators could not both make plans against de Gaulle with the ultras of *Algérie française* and also hope to win over the Moslem community. The Moslem backlash of December 1960 forced them to make a choice between the *pieds noirs* and the Moslems, a dilemma Masselot realized when he told a militant *pied noir* leader calling for military intervention, "I too am a *pied noir,* and get it into your head that there cannot be any *Algérie française* without the Arabs!" In the end, they chose the *pieds noirs,* who ceased their attacks on the police and, together with the paras, defended their property and lives against the Moslem insurrection.[12]

Government retribution following the December demonstrations fell especially heavy upon the 1er REP, which it realized was a principal hotbed of ultra sentiment in the army. All the company officers were returned to France, including Pierre Sergent, who was sent to cool his passions in Chartres. Sergent, far from contrite, discovered that his new military colleagues were completely out of sympathy with his devotion to French Algeria, insisting that the future of France lay in Europe and that of the army with modernization, not in continuing to fight a low-tech war to retain a backward country. But for Sergent this simply confirmed his belief in their lack of vision and essentially philistine outlook, and he continued to plot. While his fellow conspirators were not to be found exclusively in the 1er REP, that regiment furnished a solid core of military plotters led by Sergent, Dufour, Lieutenant Colonel Hélie de Saint Marc and Lieutenant Roger Degueldre. It would also prove to be the regiment that offered the most solid support to the "Generals' Putsch" of April 22–26, 1961.

Why was the unprecedented fury against the government so strong in the 1er REP? The legionnaires of the 1er REP had probably seen more of the fighting than men in other regiments because it was forbidden to rotate to France, and because it experienced far less personnel turnover even than other para regiments, which were half to three-quarters made up of short-service conscripts. Some Legion officers had been in combat almost constantly since 1940, while the presence in the ranks of legionnaires like Janos Kemencei who had battled through Indochina and Algeria were not uncommon. The scars left by that fighting, both physical and psychological, were only too apparent—memories of lost battles, dead comrades, loyal Indochinese abandoned to the mercies of the Viet Minh, French indifference and governmental betrayal. That fighting had also included the politically controversial Battle of Algiers. In fact, the regiment's headquarters at Zéralda placed it in permanent contact with the overheated political climate of the first city of Algeria. Legionnaires and their officers fraternized in the cafés of the Rue Michelet with *pied noir* militants, inhaling the city's atmosphere, which was thick with revolutionary defiance.

This would have been a heavy historical and psychological legacy for any group to digest, especially when the arrival of de Gaulle conjured up a strong feeling of déjà vu among veterans of Indochina. However, the members of the 1er REP, especially its officers, were probably less able than others to adjust to the loss of Algeria. For generations the Legion, in common with other colonial regiments, had offered an attractive career option for men who not only sought a life of adventure, but who also were out of step and unsympathetic with republican institutions and practices, as well as some of the ideologies and attitudes of their countrymen. Many of these men, like Hélie de Saint Marc or Pierre Sergent, boasted a very strict moral sense, a tendency to see issues very much in clear-cut black-and-white terms.

Claude Paillat, who covered the Challe offensive for the magazine *Paris-Match*, found that the officers of the 10th Para Division, led by Saint Marc,

made me think of the children of the French Revolution: they bring liberty, they were going to regenerate people. They saw themselves as pure, a little like American missionaries in China, sometimes naïve, but fantastically generous. They came out of the shadows and said: We are going to remake a society different from these slightly rotten colonies. They had an unthinkable, superhuman dream. French society got a sense of them, but did not understand. They fell into an adventure that crushed them.[13]

Indeed, their singleminded adherence to an ethical code at the top of which were courage, loyalty and honor, notions uncontaminated by political realities, was one of the elements that made them such redoubtable warriors. For them, the Legion offered a refuge, an environment sympathetic to their outlook and prejudices, a world of manly sentiments and uncomplicated emotions.

While such attitudes were to be found elsewhere in the forces, especially in the paras and commando units, the fact that the Legion was a corps of foreign mercenaries served to insulate these men even more from the world of practical politics. Already the Legion possessed a developed sense of its separate identity. This had continued to grow in Algeria, as the Legion was able to measure itself both professionally and in its attitudes toward the war against the units of conscripts next to which it served. Perhaps the most obvious indication that the Legion's notion of superior status had achieved dangerous proportions came during the installation of Lieutenant Colonel Dufour as head of the 1er REP on May 1, 1959. In the traditional change-of-command ceremony, the inspector general of the Legion, General Paul Gardy, who was to play an active role in the April 1961 Generals' Putsch, altered the address traditionally delivered on this occasion—instead of instructing legionnaires to obey their new commander "in the interest of the service, the execution of military regulations and the respect for the laws," Gardy replaced the final clause with "the interests of the Foreign Legion." When this was pointed out to him, he merely replied in a dismissive manner, "Oh! You know, the respect for the laws!"[14]

The high monastic walls thrown up by the Legion's sense of corporate identity and professionalism made that unit especially attractive to a certain type of personality. The Legion, while hard physically, was intellectually the easiest of worlds, one where orders were obeyed without question by slightly inscrutable but unquestionably loyal legionnaires. The peace of their barracks was never troubled by discussions or even debates with a rank and file of "electors" who needed to be persuaded about the utility of France's Algerian policy. Even commanders of other para units that participated in the putsch or who were sympathetic to it, like Masselot of the 18^e RCP, discovered that their conscript soldiers were not prepared to follow them into rebellion.[15]

Nor does this growing indignation among Legion officers over de Gaulle's Algerian policy ever seem to have been shaken by the intellectual challenges of French military education, which appears to have reserved no place in its curriculum for a discussion of the function of the army within the state. These men seemed to have no real notion of strategy in a Clausewitzian sense, that the purpose of the armed forces was to serve the policy of the government (granted, that policy was often confused, nebulous or even nonexistent). It is also true that French professionals had every right to feel that they had done everything expected of them in a military sense, and that the government was in the process of squandering their hardearned military victories in the political arena. But de Gaulle had to remind them in his Olympian manner on more than one occasion that it was not "their" war, that they had no proprietorial claim to the Algerian conflict merely because they fought and died in it. The function of the forces was to serve the interests of the state as defined by its political leaders.

But this view sold poorly in the Legion, where officers had never grasped the advantages of being able to see both sides of a question. To do so could, in fact, become dangerous because it could threaten sacrosanct regimental solidarity. The strong opinions of men like Sergent, Degueldre, or Dufour certainly dominated discussion in the mess. However, those of Saint Marc, who was interim commander of the 1er REP in April 1961, were critical in throwing a divided regiment into the opposition camp. Saint Marc had earned immense respect in the 1er REP for the almost priestly purity of his views. Once he opted to join the General's Putsch, all discussion ceased: "It was Hélie who led and ennobled the movement," one officer testified. "Thanks to him, the putsch became a moral leap." Two of the seven company commanders in the 1er REP had serious reservations about the decision to join the putsch.[16] But once the regimental consensus had been reached, it was considered the height of disloyalty to opt out, to express a dissenting view, to elect a different course of action. This attitude had exercised a strong influence on the decisions of the officers of the 6e *étranger* in Syria to remain loyal to Vichy in 1941. It also played a role in keeping Legion officers who had reservations about torture during the Battle of Algiers in line, even though in theory Jeanpierre had offered the option of leaving. But requesting a transfer out of the 1er REP, probably the most prestigious regiment in the French army, was unthinkable.

Antoine Ysquierdo recounted the delicate manner with which the issue of torture had been treated by "Colonel Gypey," his character modeled upon Jeanpierre: "I give you eight days to flush out something for me," the colonel tells his assembled company commanders.

I know that some among you dislike this "dirty job," or that they consider it such. Know that, as far as I'm concerned, I consider this a mission like any other, that we must complete efficiently and in a very short time. Each officer must be devoted to intelligence gathering; if it were otherwise, I would consider that some have no place in my regiment and that they are unworthy to command men like ours. No questions? . . . You're free to go![17]

This solidarity was deepened by the Legion cult of the *anciens* and loyalty to, even veneration of, dead comrades. *"Mon Colonel,"* Massu had uttered at the burial of Jeanpierre, killed in action in May 1958, "we swear to you that we will die rather than abandon *Algérie française*."[18] This helps to explain why the funeral for the ten dead paras at Zéralda in November 1960 became such an emotional event.

As it increasingly appeared that Algeria would be cut free from France, unit loyalty and solidarity became an important factor in determining attitudes, foremost among them the feeling that without Algeria there could be no Legion. As has been noted, Algeria and Sidi-bel-Abbès had certainly not been considered sacred ground by Rollet in 1919. However, the official consecration of Sidi-bel-Abbès as the *ville sainte* of the Legion in 1931, followed by the withdrawal in 1956 from Tunisia and especially from Morocco, led many to cling to *Algérie française* as the only way to guarantee the survival of the Legion. One such man was Charles Hora: "I was for *Algérie française* with all my heart," he wrote, "because the Legion could only disappear with its disappearance."[19] And while ultras could be found in many regiments, their professional reasons for supporting *Algérie française* were seldom as strong as those of the legionnaires. Loyalty to a numbered regiment was, after all, only temporary, and even regular para officers could envision the possibility, however impoverished, of life after Algeria. The spirit and continuity of the once-proud *Armée d'Afrique* had been interrupted in 1940 and had declined seriously after 1945. Besides, units in France could be designated to "carry on the traditions" of the *zouaves* or spahis. Even *"la coloniale,"* never historically a North African formation in any case, could avoid undue psychological trauma in the postcolonial world by returning to its original title of *"infanterie de marine."*

But in its own mind, one softened and shaped by its rich mythology, the unique spirit of the Legion might never survive the emigration from Algeria. In November 1961, following the failed *coup* of April, the commander of the *1er étranger* reported that morale had been seriously undermined by fears for the future of the Legion.[20] Before 1962, imaginations vivid enough to visualize the Legion adapting to the cramped barracks life of *"la régulière"* in Nîmes, Orange or Castelnaudary, carrying out with dignity and solemnity the ceremonies of Camerone in a Marseille bedroom community, or repatriating their dead saints Rollet and Aage to a corner of a municipal cemetery in the shadow of Mont Saint-Victoire near Aix-en-Provence simply did not exist. North Africa was considered the only stage sufficiently grand to contain such a distinguished troop of players. The irony was that through their attempts to preserve the Legion by challenging de Gaulle over Algeria, they furnished the best arguments possible for its abolition.

Therefore, to many legionnaires for whom the Legion offered a career and even a lifetime, Algeria appeared to be the last throw of the dice. They had nothing to lose, and men with a gambler's mentality were not lacking in the Legion, especially in the 1er REP, which was composed entirely of men whose *métier* was to take risks. These challenges also appealed to a small thug element in the regiment, most prominent among whom was Lieutenant Roger Degueldre. Degueldre, a huge, square-jawed rock of a man, had worked his way through the ranks in Indochina, where he distinguished himself at Tra Vinh, Cochinchina, on January 21, 1950, by saving a wounded Captain Hervé de Blignières who, through Degueldre's influence, became one of the link men in the military conspiracy against de Gaulle. Degueldre deserted when he was transferred from the 1er REP to the *4ᵉ étranger,* although some of the para officers continued to hide him while he helped to found the *Organisation Armée Secrète,* which announced its presence on January 25, 1961, with the assassination of the liberal *pied noir* lawyer Maître Pierre Popie. Degueldre continued to carve out a reputation as a particularly vicious terrorist as head of the OAS's Delta Force until he was dispatched, not without difficulty, by a French firing squad at Paris's Fort d'Ivry on June 28, 1962.

What the plotters who gathered in Algiers from April 20, 1961, under the leadership of none other than Maurice Challe, perhaps required was less moral purity and rather more hardheaded planning. Because Generals Challe, Jouhaud and Zeller were indignant about de Gaulle's abdication in Algeria to the FLN, they assumed incorrectly that their indignation was widely shared. Challe, who enjoyed a reputation as a left-leaning republican, was most out of place with the odd assortment of muddled military intellectuals from the army's counterinsurgency *5ᵉ bureau,* hardened Legion paras trembling with readiness for adventure, spiritual advocates of Franco-Moslem unity and quasi-fascist *pied noir* mob orators, but he seemed to believe that a decisive demonstration of military discontent would cause a change of policy in Paris. He was dead wrong. Why Challe and his fellow conspirators who had so loathed the pusillanimous IVth Republic expected de Gaulle to react in a crisis with the same lack of backbone as most politicians of that little-regretted régime is not clear. As a man with some experience of de Gaulle, he should have realized that when challenged, the general simply dug his heels in deeper.

In the very early hours of April 22, 1961, Sergent, given his old company by Saint Marc, drove at breakneck speed from Zéralda to Algiers, brushing aside police roadblocks but stopping long enough to detail his legionnaires to arrest the commander-in-chief in Algeria, General Fernand Gambiez, when he attempted to stop the REP convoy. Once in Algiers, Sergent managed to talk the officer of the guard into opening the gate to army headquarters, which was seized by the paras. Although Sergent insisted that the coup had been minutely planned,[21] in practice there were remarkable lapses. Not only was there no coordination with Oran and Constantine, whose commanders reaffirmed their loyalty to Paris, but even in Algiers the navy and air force commanders managed to shut themselves off from the plotters. Perhaps the most egregious lapse occurred at the Palais d'Eté, where Robert Buron, the minister of public works, was in residence. The paras arrested him and confined him to his room. However, they failed to cut off his telephone, which allowed him to alert Paris of the events in Algiers.

At seven o'clock in the morning of April 22, Algiers awoke to the news that "The army has seized control of Algeria and the Sahara . . . *Algérie française* is not dead." The streets filled with *pieds noirs* delirious with joy, beating out *"Al-gé-rie fran-çaise"* on their car horns. But in the plotters' command post, the early euphoria quickly began to wear off. General

Zeller's researchers had discovered enough supplies to keep Algeria going for about three weeks, and the vaults of the Algiers branch of the Bank of France virtually empty. The navy would have nothing to do with the conspiracy, while from throughout the country commanders who apparently had given warm assurances of support after a few glasses of wine sobered up quickly when presented with their portion of the bill to pay—"Like to, of course. . . . Agree with you entirely. . . . Give me a little time to think about it."

Perhaps the greatest disappointment came when the retired inspector-general of the Legion, General Gardy, visited Sidi-bel-Abbès only to receive a frosty reception from his old command. General de Pouilly, the commander of the Oran military division, admitted that the attitude of Sidi-bel-Abbès worried him immensely, for given the central place Rollet had created for Bel-Abbès in the Legion psychology, many Legion units were likely to take their cue from Colonel Albert Brothier, the commander of the 1er étranger. Brothier, son of a gendarme, began his Legion career in 1940 with the 22e RMVE. After five years as a POW in Germany, in 1946 he joined the 13e DBLE in Indochina. As a major in 1953, he was seriously wounded leading the 1er BEP, but survived to take over the 1er REP upon the death of Jeanpierre in 1958. The following year, he took command of the *maison mère* at Sidi-bel-Abbès. Brothier appears to have played a curious double role, but ultimately one that benefited de Gaulle. Already, in December 1960, he had refused Dufour's request to help in the capture of de Gaulle during his visit to Algeria. At the same time, according to French historian Henri Le Mire, he maintained contacts with Salan in his Madrid exile. He appears to have continued to play both sides of the street during the putsch, sending two companies of legionnaires from Sidi-bel-Abbès to Oran to support de Pouilly, while the Legion band quietly connected Radio Oran with Algiers so that eastern Algeria could receive the broadcasts of the putschists.[22]

While Paris appears to have ignored warnings of the planned *coup d'état*, warnings that came from the FLN among others, it moved fairly quickly to isolate the plotters. De Gaulle declared a state of emergency, surrounded the National Assembly with tanks (although some were so broken down they had to be towed into place), and arrested a few officers thought to be in cahoots with the plotters. In Paris and other French cities, the trade unions called a very successful one-hour strike to protest the action in Algiers. At the same time, the plotters had their hands full consolidating their toehold in Algiers. The 14e RCP was proving remarkably squeamish when told to seize the naval base at Mers-el-Kébir, while in Oran de Pouilly told Challe in no uncertain terms that if his paras appeared there it would spark off civil war. Strains and dissension were also evident at the highest echelons in the camp of the plotters—General Salan, once commander-in-chief both in Indochina and Algeria, flew in from Madrid, where he reigned over a court of *pied noir* exiles, to an outwardly polite welcome. However, Challe was less than overjoyed at the sight of the shifty "Mandarin," while the appearance of OAS "assassins" in Salan's wake caused the saintly Saint Marc to have second thoughts about the purity of the putschists' motives.

The decisive strike against the conspiracy came at eight o'clock on the evening of April 23. De Gaulle appeared on television, dressed in his brigadier's uniform, to give what became perhaps the most celebrated speech of his career: "In the name of France," he commanded, "I order that all means, I repeat *all means,* be employed to block the road everywhere to those men. . . . I forbid every Frenchman, and above all every soldier, to execute any of their orders. . . . *Françaises! Français! Aidez-moi!*" This speech, followed by one by Premier Michel Debré that conjured up flocks of volunteers to defend France against an expected invasion of Legion paras, struck at the heart of the coup's support in the army, in what came to be called the "victory of the transistors." Fence-sitting officers in Algeria now had a clear line to follow. Those who were still leaning toward the putschists were given a decisive impetus by their conscript soldiers, some of whom took matters into their own hands by seizing depots, imprisoning their commanders and establishing soldiers' committees.

But mostly the resistance was passive—when Saint Marc visited the barracks of the *zouaves* to convince its commander to rally to the revolt, he was met at the gate by sentries who announced, "You cannot come in here. This is the legal army of the French republic." When he finally did gain access to the commander, he was told, "There are soldiers' committees. They only half obey me. I support you with all my heart, but I can do nothing." Saint Marc concluded that the conscripts provided officers disinclined to intervene in any case with a perfect alibi.[23] This was not entirely true, for even in regiments where the officers had joined the revolt, such as the 14e and 18e RCP, or where the putsch counted many sympathizers, as in the 2e, 3e and 8e *régiments de parachutistes d'infanterie de marine* and the 9e RCP, the troops took de Gaulle's speech of April 23 very much to heart.[24]

At Sidi-bel-Abbès, Brothier came down firmly on the side of legality. Legion units from all over Algeria telephoned him for direction, to be told, "We cannot take the risk of seeing the Germans fire upon Frenchmen. The putsch is a French affair; it is unthinkable that foreigners should become mixed up in it."[25] That decision, seconded by the intervention of Defense Minister and ex-captain of the 13e DBLE Pierre Messmer, no doubt saved the Legion, whose abolition had been sought by a number of left-wing politicians and was apparently seriously considered by de Gaulle.

Nevertheless, small tremors of revolt rattled both the 1er REC and the 2e REP at Philippeville. As the 2e REP drove west toward Algiers through crowds of cheering *pieds noirs,* Simon Murray thought that "The entrance of the Allies into Paris at the end of the war could not have received a more enthusiastic welcome." Still, it was not clear to him "which side are we really on?" That question should have been answered when they were ordered to occupy an air base held by a unit of conscript marines,

and they weren't having any of it. So we were given wooden batons, heavy, with sharp points, and in one long line we slowly eased into the marines, pushing them forward like bolshie rams. They frequently turned and attacked with aggression. This was met in many cases with savage beatings and it became a sad and shoddy business. Marine officers were pushed around by our officers—there were scenes of officers yelling at each other with questions of loyalty and accusations of traitor and so on. L'Hospitallier [the company commander, Lhopitallier] bust [sic] his baton on the head of one of the marines. Gradually they were herded out of the airport premises and we were in control of the base from which we will apparently make the drop on Paris.[26]

But that was not to be, as the massive Noratlas transport planes had already slipped quietly back across the Mediterranean. "This news provoked a shock," Sergent confessed. "We are already without the Navy. What will we do if the aviation abandons us? It will mean isolation." Sergent believed that the desertion of the air force caused an even more important psychological blow to air force general Challe than the resistance of the conscripts.[27] It was apparent even to *légionnaire 2e classe* Murray that "The army is completely divided and we appear to be very much a minority. . . . I wonder what will happen if this *putsch* does not succeed and what our own position will be—perhaps we'll be disbanded and all sent home. Nice thought to sleep on!"[28] Rather than a springboard to power in France, Algeria increasingly appeared to have become the conspirators' prison.

By Tuesday, April 25, Challe had lost heart. A mountain of militants led by Sergent and Degueldre contemplated deposing, even assassinating, the too-polite-by-half air force general and replacing him with a committee of public safety under Salan, whom they believed prepared to risk civil war and even a clash with army units loyal to de Gaulle. However, Challe was cajoled into soldiering on for *Algérie française* for the rest of the day. That night, however, he drove to Zéralda with the intention of giving himself up. Zeller, Salan and Jouhaud put on civilian clothes and disappeared. Saint Marc placed his Legion paras in their trucks and led them back to Zéralda, not without difficulty, for some were reluctant to return.

On the morning of April 26, the Legion camp awoke to find themselves surrounded by heavily armed police and army units, with helicopters buzzing overhead. In the mess, some officers talked of fighting it out, proposals that fortunately came to nothing. A colonel appeared to fetch a pale Challe. Saint Marc turned out an honor guard for the general as he disappeared out the gate and into captivity. In Algiers, Lieutenant Colonel Guiraud, who had been on leave when his regiment had been hijacked by Saint Marc, was convoked before Defense Minister Messmer and forced to watch as he dictated orders dissolving the 1ᵉʳ REP and the 14ᵉ and 18ᵉ RCP.

In Zéralda, the legionnaires began smashing up the barracks and burning archives as tremendous explosions tore through the three magazines. And to think that, in the old days, they received up to five years in the *section spéciale* for selling their underwear! They boarded trucks, many tearing off their decorations and shooting their submachine guns into the air, as some of their officers bitterly taunted journalists. As they awaited departure, legionnaires in one of the trucks began to sing Edith Piaf's *"Je ne regrette rien,"* which was soon picked up by others. Throwing out defiant *bras d'honneur* to all and sundry, they disappeared through the gates to the applause of a local crowd. "It was the most magnificent *quartier* in the French army," Murray recorded, "which they built themselves from scratch, brick by brick, in the tradition of the Legion." The 2ᵉ REP paid for the gesture, for upon returning to their barracks they found it occupied. "It was probably feared that we also would blow the place to pieces." Camerone 1961 was the most sober since the original event almost a century earlier. "No passes were issued so we just sat in misery on the hill and guzzled the extra food and beer that was issued to cheer our sinking spirits."[29]

In subsequent trials, Challe and Zeller were sentenced to fifteen years' prison, Hélie de Saint Marc to ten years, and Colonels Lecomte and Masselot of the 14ᵉ and 18ᵉ RCP to eight years apiece. Saint Marc's crime was considered especially heinous because, in the opinion of *Le Monde*'s defense correspondent Jean Planchais, he commanded a Legion of foreigners, "that is to say, men whose loyalty is to their superiors. To use that loyalty which is essential to enlist in the Legion in an internal French affair was a very grave gesture."[30] Kemencei, although he disapproved of the *coup*, agreed that in the place of the paras, he would have done the same thing.

The legionnaires of these two great and prestigious units [the 1ᵉʳ REP and the 1ᵉʳ REC] who joined the insurgents obeyed their officers, as all legionnaires have always obeyed their superiors. If I had been in their place, I would have also followed the orders to the "letter". . . . And even today, I find that my comrades were right to have confidence in their officers: They never received the order to shoot at Frenchmen! Never on any Frenchman! And this intangible fact, this honor was never shared with certain other corps constituted and armed during these unfortunate events.[31]

Kemencei ignores how close the *coup* came to provoking a civil war in which the legionnaires would certainly have been ordered to fire upon Frenchmen. This was prevented only by Challe's unwillingness to do so. Had events been dominated by Salan, or had Sergent or Degueldre had more influence, they certainly would have been ordered to fire upon Frenchmen. This is not to forget that the criteria for criminal behavior is determined in large measure by the victor—after all, the fact that legionnaires had fired on Frenchmen, like much of the rest of the French army, during the Commune of 1871 had not made them criminals from the government's viewpoint. Nor did this prevent over one hundred legionnaires from murdering Frenchmen as part of the OAS. Those who had absconded, including Generals Salan, Jouhaud and the ex-inspector of the Legion, General Gardy, were sentenced to death *in absentia*. All of the convicted were amnestied by de Gaulle in 1968, following the large-scale opposition to his régime in May of that year, possibly as a condition laid down by Massu, who was then commanding French troops in Germany and to whom de Gaulle turned for support.

The *coup* attempt had several unfortunate results. The first was that, as in December 1961, efforts by partisans of *Algérie française* to secure their future merely served to hasten their defeat, because they had seriously weakened the French negotiating position in Algeria. It became clear that de Gaulle had to pull out of Algeria, and the FLN simply had to wait him out. Over the next weeks, position after position defended by French negotiators collapsed in the face of FLN intransigence. The *coup* attempt also divided and demoralized the army. With three of the army's best units disbanded outright, and others transferred, decapitated or kept short of fuel to prevent any extracurricular activity, army morale bottomed out, its officers still split over where the true course of "duty" and "honor" lay. At Sidi-bel-Abbès a few days after the attempted *coup,* Colonel Brothier assembled the NCOs of the 1er REP "to tell us that the Foreign Legion had no business intervening in a politico-military conflict," Janos Kemencei remembered. "He was applauded by almost everyone."[32] Nevertheless, the commander of the *1er étranger* reported in November 1961 that NCOs from the 1er REP had been "sensitized to the maximum, they have a special spirit, and one must admit are profoundly politicized."[33]

The Legion officer corps became a primary target of a government housecleaning. According to Kemencei, the Legion was inundated with officers who not only lacked professionalism, but who also came with a definite political mission: "And you, the rebel. . . . Shut up!" a drunken officer newly assigned to the Legion shouted at him in a bar. "We'll tame all of you, the anti-Gaullists, OAS and all that. We'll show you our Republican metal." "Alas," Kemencei wrote, "this was not a solitary case."[34] In early May, a helicopter swooped down on the 2^e REP in the middle of an operation to take away two senior officers sympathetic to the putschists: "It circled round and round above us as we stood to attention at 'present arms' in farewell and then it hovered for a second and was gone. Sad, because of what they represent to us as officers, and very fine officers the Legion has always had." Two days later the colonel was replaced by an officer who "is viewed with some suspicion as he is obviously a Gaullist and therefore a potential enemy."[35]

Morale in the Legion plummeted following the events of April. The commander of the 1er *étranger* reported in November 1961 that

The successive spectacle of generals arrested by their subordinates, then junior officers tried and thrown out of the army for having executed the orders of their superiors has profoundly troubled the spirit of discipline. . . . As far as the Legion is concerned, the dissolution of the 1er REP, the momentary suspension of recruitment, then its difficult reinstitution, and finally the impression that the Legion was made the scapegoat of this affair by the atmosphere of distrust and general suspicion of which it is the object, all this has provoked bitterness and a defensive reaction which consists of enclosing oneself in the attitude of an outcast.

He complained that the government appeared intent upon "disabling the Legion by breaking its officer corps." The fact that the failure of the *coup* had led to a renewal of FLN activity and the prospect of having to deal with the *pied noir* population also had depressed morale, because "all of this throws an honorable outcome to the conflict in doubt."[36]

French Algeria was finished. On March 18, 1962, representatives of France and the FLN agreed to a cessation of hostilities on the basis of Algerian self-determination. Attempts by the OAS under the direction of Salan and Degueldre to delay the inevitable through terror built up so much animosity between the Moslem and *pied noir* communities that it became impossible for those of European extraction to remain after independence, even had they elected to do so. The summer of 1962 witnessed a mass exodus of *pieds noirs* from Algeria. Crowded into airports and docks, each person clutching the two suitcases allowed by officials, some departed for Spain, Canada or Israel. But most sailed for France, where they would form pockets of deeply bitter anti-Gaullist emigrés scattered mostly throughout the south, "half-French and half-Algerian," Albert Camus's widow lamented, "and, in truth, dispossessed in both countries."[37] Behind them lay the empty European quarters of Algiers and Oran, the ashes of their possessions, which many had burned in the streets before departure, still smoldering and the walls of the eerily empty buildings scrawled with fading OAS slogans.

They were the lucky ones. What the soldiers who had witnessed the final agony of Indochina had predicted actually came to pass. As the FLN government moved in from Tunis to take over from the departing French and their *katibas* flocked down from the *djebels,* the barely veiled splits within the FLN burst into the open. Throughout the summer of 1962, factions of the victorious FLN engaged in a civil war that raised the war's death toll substantially. However, the most intense retribution was reserved for the *harkis* and other Moslems who had fought with the French. About fifteen thousand of the quarter-million who had served in French ranks escaped to France. Between 30,000 and as many as 150,000 of the rest—as well as their families—were massacred in the most atrocious and brutal fashion by the FLN. In France, retribution was more measured. Captured, Salan and Jouhaud were retried. Jouhaud was again condemned to death but escaped the firing squad after Salan, immaculate in his uniform, drew only a life sentence from a jury swayed by the purity of his motives and his prior service to the state, much to de Gaulle's anger. Only Degueldre of the leaders, dressed in his Legion para uniform and singing the *"Marseillaise,"* paid for the crimes of the OAS, although it took the sergeant of the firing squad fully five *coups de grâce* to finish him off.

France could now turn a new page. So could the Legion. "The oldest veterans of the Legion who have for 40 years traversed with it many depressing periods, are still able to see beyond the present situation and believe that the Legion will find its place by having the necessary resilience to cross over a difficult period," wrote Colonel Vaillant of the *1er étranger* in November 1961.[38] It had been extremely difficult for the Legion to remain true to its professional character, to maintain its mercenary "detachment" in the face of the successive crises of defeat and division that had stalked France, and the Legion, since 1940. That some Legion units succumbed to the temptation of rebellion was due in part to the narcissism of the corps, its sense of a separate, elite status fostered by a generation of myth making, and the betrayal of the strictly professional outlook of the Legion by some of its officers, too long exiles from French political realities. At least some of its leaders now realized that to survive, the Legion must rebuild its professional character. In December 1962, the inspector general of the Legion informed the legionnaires of the 2e REP that the Legion was to diversify its combat skills and clean up its public image to become a crack multipurpose force. "The message has been well received," Murray recorded. "Morale has in one stroke been given a gigantic shot in the arm. We're back in business. Somebody thinks we can do more than just build bloody roads all day. Suddenly the mountain of the next two years diminishes, there is a feeling of moving forward again."[39] There would be, after all, life after Algeria.

Chapter 30

THE
BALANCE SHEET

THE HISTORY OF the Legion is a remarkable story, both of survival and success. While the Legion's most impressive victories in the twentieth century have been scored on the battlefields of public relations, the cinema and popular fiction, its achievements are neither contrived nor illusory. There can be few, if any, units that have produced such a sustained record of combat performance, in which its members have every right to feel a legitimate pride.

That reputation was upheld on May 19, 1978, when 650 paras of the 2^e REP dropped over the copper-mining town of Kolwezi in Zaire's Shaba province. A week earlier, Cuban-supported soldiers of the Congolese National Liberation Front (FLNC) had invaded Kolwezi, ejected the Zairian garrison and seized a large number of hostages from among the population of European technicians and their families. President Joseph Mobutu appealed for foreign aid, a call answered by France, Belgium and the United States, which provided 18 C-141 Starlifters to support the operation. At the last minute, however, the Belgians hesitated to commit their paratroops, leaving the Legion to parachute alone into the rebel-held town against odds estimated at ten to one.

The rebel soldiers appear to have been taken completely by surprise, largely because they were busy running amok in the town. While some made a tough stand at the Kolwezi police station, most fled in panic back toward Angola in civilian cars looted from the town. But the battle, while one-sided, gave little cause for celebration—the FLNC troops left behind the bodies of 190 massacred whites and 200 black civilians, some of them horribly mutilated. Another 40 white hostages taken by the retreating soldiers were later found murdered. For their part, the paras killed an estimated 250 rebel soldiers at a cost of five legionnaires dead and 25 wounded.

This goes a long way toward answering one of the questions posed by this book—has the Legion performed efficiently as a military organization? The answer must be yes, although not an unequivocal yes. Its exemplary combat record was based upon its generally superior cadres and upon the practice of selecting out its best troops, those men with a genuinely military vocation, for regiments or *bataillons de marche*. While this practice was often criticized in forces engaged in major conflicts because it shattered the personal relationships built up in the sections upon which loyalty and combat efficiency depend and deprived units of their best combatants, it seems to have worked well for the Legion for at least two reasons. The first is that most of the campaigns of imperial conquest required only periodic bursts of energy from which the entire Legion did not suffer because some of its best legionnaires had been selected out to fight.

Second, while the Legion tends to blame any blemish on its record upon poor or substandard recruitment, and attribute its successes to its unique *esprit de corps,* this explanation does contain an element of truth. The Legion, like any army or military subgroup, counted a number of men whom it was just as well to leave behind in rear areas because they would have performed poorly. This was obvious to Simon Murray even when he reported to the elite 2^e REP in Algeria in 1960: "The *quartier* is occupied by the base company, which is apparently full of the most worthless members of the regiment," he wrote. "The appearance of those present here would seem to confirm this."[1] This was in part because it had only limited control over its recruitment and was obliged to take men whom French police or politicians desired to expedite to North Africa, or because, once it had enlisted a man who proved unsuitable, during a large portion of the Legion's history it was virtually impossible to get rid of him. The requirement to keep the Legion up to strength to occupy numerous small and scattered garrisons caused it to enlist a number of men, especially French denied enlistment in regular units, who made poor soldiers. Nor were enough experienced and motivated cadres capable of commanding legionnaires always available.

This helps to explain in part the contradictory image of the Legion, on the one hand praised as among the steadiest soldiers in the pre-1914 campaigns of imperial conquest such as Tonkin in 1885, Dahomey, Madagascar or Morocco, or even in World War I when only relatively limited numbers of its troops were employed outside of North Africa after 1915. And on the other hand, it was decried as an assemblage of jail bait. The point is that it was both. Nor did it always prove possible to leave the poorest soldiers behind, for the Legion's relatively high dropout rates on the march, especially compared to North African units, were often put down to "bad characters" who lacked motivation or who preferred to hobble into the hospital to avoid a punishment. The problem for the Legion, as for any mercenary force, has been that the numbers of men with a truly military vocation have been limited. The Legion's ability to transform into elite soldiers many of its other recruits, especially young ones who enlist with naïvely romantic ideas of soldiering or who join simply to earn the years necessary for a pension, has been limited. For this reason, combat performance diminished when the Legion was forced to fling open the doors of the recruitment bureaus and actually use a large percentage of its legionnaires, as in Mexico or in Indochina after World War II. And even there the image of success could be maintained by selecting out mounted, mobile and para formations, or by placing legionnaires in situations where they could *faire Camerone*. Nevertheless, these periods also reveal weaknesses in training, a defect the Legion shared with the French army generally, but that was intensified by the reluctance of the best officers and NCOs to be assigned to troop training. Indeed, complaints that the Legion spends more time teaching its members to sing than to develop individual combat skills are still heard in the modern Legion.[2]

A final element of Legion success has been its high degree of unit loyalty. That a polyglot, multinational force whose members have almost nothing in common, including a language or a sense of humor, would be able to form a coherent unit appears at first sight to pose an enigma. However, in this as in other areas, the Legion has proved able to transform its apparent liabilities into assets. Morale and motivation were maintained by competition among nationalities, with the Germans usually setting the pace in the race not to be outdone in skills or courage by legionnaires from other countries. Regimental loyalty was also nurtured by "sacred" rituals that revolved around the regimental standard and the celebration of Camerone. The fame of the Legion, its romantic, even cutthroat reputation, has meant that many legionnaires, especially those who were disenchanted with life or who in some other way failed to find satisfaction outside the Legion, draw a large amount of their psychological capital from their membership in the corps.

The Legion was usually able to maintain its morale with great success. But morale in a mercenary force is often very fragile, vulnerable to, among other things, the erratic and unstable nature of its recruitment. The evolution of the political situation in Europe on occasion brought an influx of a large number of men from one country, as with the Germans after World War I or the Spaniards in 1939. Such conditions might eliminate the delicate national balance that stimulated emulation. It could give rise to a feeling (real or supposed) among a large mass of men cocooned in their own language and who had often developed parallel hierarchies of their own beneath German former officers and NCOs of being exploited by the French military system. Indeed, one of the characteristics of legionnaires historically is that they have often been anti-French—contemptuous of France's army and her political system. "Take the French for what they are, a bunch of Frogs," American legionnaire William Brooks was told in 1973 by a fellow legionnaire, demonstrating that this attitude continued into the post-Algerian Legion. "Hang out with the Germans or the Francos [Spanish fascists]. They won't let you down. The French Foreign Legion is only as good as its worst German Legionnaire."[3] This situation might seriously compromise discipline, especially if Legion officers and NCOs reacted to it with a lack of understanding and diplomacy, which was sometimes the case.

It was just such a breakdown of morale in the Legion, encouraged in large part by the influx of Germans after World War I, that caused Rollet to place the revival and even creation of regimental ritual and "tradition" on the front burner of his concerns. This did not prove a sure-fire guarantee of success, however. "Tradition" and regimental loyalty were not like a vaccination that, once administered, warded off all infection for the lifetime of enlistment. Rather, they required a slow process of indoctrination that presupposed a psychological need on the part of the apprentice legionnaire, a void in his life that could be filled by inculcating a strong sense of regimental loyalty. In the view of the Legion, this transformation was best realized in the arid open spaces of North Africa and in the shadow of the *maison mère* at Sidi-bel-Abbès. When the Legion was not at home, not *chez eux,* as during the Mexican campaign when most of its recruits were trained at Aix-en-Provence, or during both world wars, then the vaccination was liable to be less successful.

While the development of tradition was an important element in fostering unit cohesion and especially in projecting a positive image of the Legion as an elite fighting force before the general public, it was also a double-edged sword. Men attracted by the romantic image of the Legion, especially the young and the middle-class, could be destined for disappointment when confronted by the hard realities of Legion service. Tradition, especially as defined by Rollet and others in the interwar years, also froze out several categories of men. This was done quite intentionally. The outlaw image of the Legion, its racism, anti-Semitism and anti-intellectualism, its aggressive, hard-drinking and brothel-crawling culture were attractive to many and formed a common basis for sympathy among men of different nationalities. Therefore, the heterogeneity of the Legion was more apparent than real, for legionnaires shared a common background and attitudes, even certain psychological traits. Again, it must be stressed that the panoply of Legion attitudes and prejudices was not exceptional, but was fairly common in French right-wing and military circles generally, as well as reflecting North African and many working-class social realities. But they did contribute to make assignment to the Legion purgatory for some who found its atmosphere and traditions unsympathetic or even disreputable.

This was especially true of those foreigners sent there in the two world wars. Because many were middle-class, Jewish, politicized or men who out of patriotic devotion to France wanted integration into regular French regiments, not confinement to a military ghetto whose supervisors were outspokenly unsympathetic to their sensibilities, their religion or their opinions, the Legion assimilated them badly. These may be considered small imperfections in a long Legion record of military success. Indeed, one of the reasons for the Legion's survival and remarkable cohesion was that it obstinately refused to allow politics and ideology, even sentiment, to compromise its personality as an elite, professional force. Nevertheless, it was unfortunate that the Legion proved to be so inflexible on these occasions, both because France, twice invaded, especially required the goodwill and the manpower that these volunteers represented, and because these men fought as bravely for France and for their ideals as did any "real" legionnaires, in 1915 and 1940 winning battle honors that contributed to the Legion's martial reputation.

Indeed, the Legion's preferences in recruitment were put succinctly by Captain Fiore of the *8ᵉ compagnie mixte montée* of the *3ᵉ étranger* in 1943, when a shortfall in enlistment caused him to suggest signing up Axis POWs in Tunisia: "Avoid all intellectuals, argumentative people, persuasive speakers able to influence opinion," he wrote on June 28.

Give preference to farm workers, day laborers and all other manual trades, men with little education, hardly able to read and write, even better if they are illiterate, in general those who appear to have no political opinions, simple men.[4]

In these conditions, no wonder educated, patriotic, politicized recruits found the Legion atmosphere uncongenial.

Beneath the decorations, the lists of battles won, the history of imperial conquests, the Legion did demonstrate weaknesses in the eyes of some of its commanders. The first complaint against it was that, though solid and courageous, the Legion was sluggish and lacked maneuverability. This stemmed from the polyglot character of the Legion, which deprived it of the ability to respond rapidly to commands, and a general inertia and lack of initiative beyond a literal obedience to orders, which required exceptional officers to animate it in action. This translated into a preference for last stands and frontal assaults, which, although costly, were acceptable because the Legion was made up of foreigners who did not vote. While one may assume that the officers who commanded the Legion knew what they were about, it is also apparent that legionnaires did prove capable of performing roles beyond which some of its leaders thought it capable. Even some of the Legion's most avid supporters like Lyautey and Rollet believed it futile and even dangerous to use the Legion as anything but heavy infantry. Once this view became accepted as gospel, it discouraged, but did not prevent, more imaginative use of legionnaires as cavalrymen, artillerymen, or paratroops, even though they performed more than adequately in all of those roles. This prejudice against more diversified specialties sprang in part from a tendency to assign qualities to troops in the colonial army and the *Armée d'Afrique* according to the role each was expected to play. There was also a fear that a multiplicity of Legion specialties would compromise its ability to carry out its basic infantry role.

A final objection that prevented experimentation with Legion formations was concerns over their ultimate loyalty. Few aspects of Legion life have been more notorious, and perhaps more open to misinterpretation, than desertion. Desertion was endemic in the Legion, as it had been in the mercenary armies of eighteenth-century Europe. Outside of the Legion, and especially outside of France, desertion has been interpreted as an indictment of the brutal and barbarous life of the Legion, an impression that Legion deserters themselves have been in no hurry to correct. Some could convince themselves that they had been treated unjustly, because the Legion had failed to live up to their expectations or because leadership there was often very negative. Once disillusion set in, it became easy to interpret an event that would before have been taken in stride as sufficient reason for desertion.

In reality, however, desertion from the Legion has had a far more complicated set of motivations. The Legion defense that desertion had nothing to do with brutality or injustice but stems from the psychological instability and picaresque outlook of many legionnaires has much to recommend it. Desertion is characteristic of mercenary forces, whose troops often lack an overriding sense of loyalty to the unit. Recruitment patterns could also influence attitudes and provoke desertion, especially in an atmosphere of national and political tensions, which inevitably rose to the surface when a large percentage of legionnaires were of one nationality or were politically motivated. Simple homesickness or depression accounted for a number of desertions. But the most important point is that desertion became institutionalized as part of Legion life. Many legionnaires saw desertion as a challenge, a gesture, a personal statement that was part of the process of becoming a legionnaire. It was usually impulsive. The point was not that the desertion should succeed, but that it should be dramatic. One can suppose that many deserters were actually perplexed by the unexpected success of their enterprise, which is why some of them took the first opportunity to reenlist under another name. Despite all this, desertion was seldom a problem that seriously eroded combat performance. In most cases, the Legion campaigned in areas too remote or the enemy was simply too ferocious to make departure from the unit a viable option. Nor was desertion, especially in small doses, necessarily a bad thing, as it allowed the Legion to shed discontented or marginal elements. Unfortunately for the Legion, the soldiers it most needed to get rid of—poor French recruits—proved to be the most loyal.

This is not to say, however, that desertion was an exaggerated or unimportant aspect of Legion life. On occasion it might seriously undermine performance, especially if there were a place to desert to, as in Mexico, in Casablanca in 1907–08, in Morocco immediately following World War I, possibly in the Rif War, and at certain times during World War II. But the most negative effects of desertion lay elsewhere. It provided a constant source of diplomatic friction, especially between France and Germany until well after World War II, which in 1908 led the two countries perilously close to war. It was a small, but persistent, source of bad publicity for France. Moreover, desertion or the threat of desertion exercised a direct influence upon the employment of the Legion, as in the Rif in 1925, when withholding the Legion from the frontier with the Spanish zone contributed to the initial success of Abd el-Krim's offensive. Fear of desertion also influenced Legion organization, for it caused French generals to be reluctant to expand the Legion beyond its basic heavy infantry role. Lyautey objected that turning legionnaires into artillerymen could be suicidal for the French if these men revolted, while others forecasted that Legion cavalrymen would simply be able to desert at speeds and in numbers hitherto unknown there. The Legion never fully trusted its soldiers, an extension of French suspicion of foreigners that caused that country to place them in a separate corps in the first place, and took elaborate steps from the 1920s to create a secret service whose primary mission was to oversee the loyalties of its own troops.

While sluggishness and desertion were peculiar to the Legion, its other weaknesses were common enough in line units, although they might assume a more exaggerated form in the Legion. In theory, infantry units especially should be versatile, able to turn their hands to a variety of tasks that war requires of them, from conventional conflict to what today are euphemistically called "low-intensity operations." In practice, however, units prefer to carve special niches for themselves that correspond to a carefully nurtured self-image. The Legion was no exception to this rule. Traditionally it proved poor at "pacification," which it saw as a mission in opposition to its elite combat image. While it was frequently used to build roads and other structures as part of the imperial *"mission civilisatrice,"* any contact between the Legion and the local population was liable to result in a public relations disaster. The cohesiveness of the Legion, its racism, its elite combat image, the preference of its commanders for strongarm solutions to problems of colonial agitation and its recruitment made it especially useful to support a shoot-first policy. One of the criticisms of the 2ᵉ REP in the Kolwezi operation was that they were trigger-happy and killed far more people than necessary.[5] Nor was a didactic role such as Vietnamization in Indochina encouraged by regimental preference for action, although legionnaires often performed better at this than many of its officers predicted.

Like other units, the Legion also performed less well when shattered into minute groups in small scattered garrisons, as in Mexico, in Morocco in the interwar years or in Indochina. This practice weakened regimental spirit and the influence of the command upon the legionnaires. All soldiers tend to go to pot in garrison. However, the diversions of bored legionnaires might assume stunning proportions. It was a cliché that legionnaires had to be kept occupied; otherwise, drunkenness, fighting, *cafard,* desertion and even suicide would inevitably follow. It is also likely that the weakened influence of the command upon small, isolated units contributed to excesses of indiscipline, such as those committed by legionnaires in Northern Annam in 1930–31.

Legion efficiency was also hampered by the French military system, which, in the colonies especially, was notoriously parsimonious. Weapons, uniforms and equipment that were often badly adapted to the climate and the requirements of combat; inadequate transport that, quite literally, placed an enormous burden on the shoulders of the legionnaire; miserly rations; and usually inadequate medical support all contributed to transform difficult campaign conditions into very arduous ones. While the Legion attempted to supplement this through training for long marches and selection, the result was excessive fatigue, high drop-out rates, and fewer rifles on line. While an inadequate military system hurt all French imperial forces, it did not hurt all of them equally. Native regiments could survive on slim rations and "requisitions," and demonstrated far more resilience than white troops on long marches. If so many Legion campaigns from the early conquests in Algeria to Dien Bien Phu read like an unrelieved narrative of suffering and sacrifice, it is largely because the combination of terrain, inadequate logistics and armaments and poor senior leadership often proved more pernicious enemies for the legionnaires than did the enemy. Therefore, as Janos Kemencei realized, the real injustice of Legion service was that good troops too often failed to realize their true potential because they were inadequately trained, armed, led and supplied.

If the Legion has carved for itself a reputation as an elite force, this has not been because it has functioned as part of a modern military system. On the contrary, many legionnaires with experience in other armies have considered the Legion very backward in several respects, a criticism that continues in the post-Algerian War force.[6] When American legionnaire William Brooks heard a French general insist to a group of Legion NCOs in Djibouti in the mid-1970s that " 'The Legion will always be a modern arm within a modern army,' ... I was dumbfounded," he wrote.[7] This attitude was dangerous because it encouraged the Legion to undertake missions beyond its capabilities. "They just kept harping about how modern they were," Brooks recorded. "I don't think they read anything that wasn't published by their own propaganda press. But they believed it and it made them special." The elite status claimed by the Legion has nothing to do with its modernity. Rather, the Legion is entitled to that status because *a very high percentage of its members have suicidal tendencies. James Jones once wrote that an elite unit is only elite when the majority of its members consider themselves already dead. That is the full evolution of the soldier. I believe legionnaires think they are already dead. Dying is what the Legion is all about.*[8]

A second problem of the Legion that this work has attempted to resolve is that of the myth versus the countermyth of the Legion—the Legion as a vehicle of salvation, a second chance of redemption for disoriented souls, or as an instrument of exploitation and brutality for the naïve, unsuspecting or down-and-out. The problem is not an easy one to resolve, largely because the evidence tends to be very partisan. The countermyth, that charges the Legion with brutality and exploitation, invites suspicion for a variety of reasons. Its main propagandists were Germans who had a vested interest in attacking a French military employer of many of their nationals, or the left, which saw the Legion as an agent of exploitation and oppression of both the working classes and of colonial peoples.

Like most myths, the charge that the Legion treats the recruits with a brutality that would be unacceptable in a national army has a basis in reality. Brutal NCOs can be found in almost any military environment. They are not the norm, but they are more likely to flourish in the Legion for several reasons. First, NCOs have enjoyed an elevated status in the Legion, which made them virtually unaccountable for their actions, least of all to French officers, who traditionally held aloof from the day-to-day running of their units. This gave rise to occasional abuses. Furthermore, a legionnaire who felt that he had been treated unfairly by an NCO discovered early on that it was useless, even counterproductive, to complain to higher authority—the practice was to submit to the punishment, and then remonstrate, if one still felt after a *quinze dont huit* (fifteen days of punishment, eight of which were spent in the cells) that there was anything left to be gained from it. Also, in a nonverbal environment like the Legion, points can be forced home more easily with fists than through persuasion.

However, blanket charges of brutality leveled at the Legion are exaggerated. As has been seen, desertion, often cited as the major product of excessive Legion discipline, was more often the product of other causes. There were certain punishments that continued to be practiced in the Legion long after they were outlawed in the army—the *tombeau*, the *crapaudine*, the *pelote* (still authorized today), or the *silo*. The justifications for their survival were several: they were not a Legion monopoly but were practiced throughout the *Armée d'Afrique;* short, sharp punishments were in effect more humane and more efficient than a prolonged jail sentence, which deprived a unit of a man's services and stained his service record; and, finally, given the nature of Legion recruitment, the good legionnaires needed to be protected from the minority of bullies and thugs.

As for the sadistic Legion NCO, he was much more likely to be found in fiction than in reality, like Sergeant Lejaune in *Beau Geste*. In fact, before 1914 NCOs often impinged very little on the life of the legionnaires, basically because they were few and usually remote figures. Squads tended to be largely self-governing organizations, with the corporal reaching a *modus vivendi* with his messmates. Deep animosities certainly existed, especially in a milieu where NCOs were quick to use their fists. But unpopular NCOs or corporals might consider taking out an extra life insurance policy, especially in combat conditions. NCOs could be perceived to be unjust, as was the sergeant who ordered legionnaire Weinrock to miss his turns on muleback in the Sud Oranais in 1910, a punishment that eventually resulted in his death. But NCO brutality, as far as it existed, appears to be a more modern phenomenon associated especially with training.[9]

It is also true that brutality or excessive discipline is a relative concept, and one that has changed over time. In the first half of the nineteenth century when the Legion was founded, the recruits do not appear to have been subjected to the sort of humiliation that became the norm in basic training later on. As the nineteenth century evolved into the twentieth, the idea of breaking down the recruit and then building him up in a way in which he identified closely with the military organization became more common. In the early days of the corps, a new legionnaire was liable to be given only minimal training—upon reporting to the Legion in 1840, the German Clemens Lamping was asked if he could handle a musket, and when replying in the affirmative was sent straight to his unit.[10] Lamping found the Legion to be a rough crowd, as did Antoine Sylvère in 1905. The corporal exerted his authority on the first day by beating up a legionnaire who talked back to him. But most of the violence appears to have been traded among legionnaires rather than handed down by the hierarchy.

In any case, Legion life was almost a bed of roses compared to that of the building site where Flutsch had worked before his enlistment. Even Maurice Magnus, who was almost paralytic with indignation over Legion training during World War I, discovered that the violence of his superiors was more verbal than physical. Only once did he actually witness a legionnaire knocked unconscious by a corporal, and that legionnaire was an Arab and therefore was probably considered out of place in the Legion.[11] In general, Legion recruits appear to have been given enormous leeway outside of training hours to wander into town and dispose of their time as they wished as far as duties and finances would allow. This was very different from the experience of Simon Murray in 1960, who discovered that legionnaires were subject to constant humiliation and physical abuse during basic training, and especially during airborne training, restricted to the barracks for weeks or given passes only to see them revoked for some trivial reason. "What kind of bastards are we dealing with?" he asked. "They think it spells discipline, but in my book it spells horse shit."[12]

In other words, although abuses of authority can be found in any age, legionnaires who came out of the rough working-class or peasant world of nineteenth-century Europe found what was often denounced by middle-class observers of the Legion as an excessively harsh or even brutal existence to be nothing out of the ordinary. But this changed as standards of living, of education and of public conduct improved. Then the attitudes and methods of some NCOs appeared increasingly at odds with public notions of permissible behavior and positive leadership. And while it must be stressed that this evolution in the attitude of military organizations to recruit training was a general one in the West, it is likely that they found a more extreme expression in the Legion for reasons already mentioned. But at the time that the accusation of brutality began to be heard, that is, before the turn of the century, there is no evidence that authority was exercised any more harshly in the Legion than in a French line regiment, or in a German or Russian one for that matter.

Did the Legion exploit its soldiers? The answer to this question depends in part upon one's point of view. If one opposed the French colonial enterprise or the contributions of foreigners to French military strength, then any effort expended in Legion service could be counted as exploitation. Nevertheless, to accept this argument today is to bring an especially harsh retroactive judgment to a historical enterprise that had validity in its own era. France had the right to defend herself and to enlist foreigners to defend her foreign policy and imperial interests. Service in the Legion was frequently difficult, sometimes fatal. However, recruits balanced this possibility with the advantages of service when they enlisted. The Legion argued that its recruits came of their own free will, which was certainly true for the greatest number of them. Recruitment bureaus were difficult to locate, especially if one spoke no French, and recruiting officers and sergeants gave the potential recruit every opportunity to change his mind before he signed.

But, the argument may be made, these people did not know what they were getting into when they enlisted. The lure of adventure, the romantic image that the Legion cultivated, and which was cultivated for it in popular fiction and cinema, was in fact an enormous swindle that enticed young men into a service that subsequently exploited them. One Legion deserter has claimed in a recent memoir that he and others, "were victims of the Legion misinformation service. They had believed everything they had heard and had been taken in by it."[13] But this argument appears to have little validity. Much of the public image of the Legion in the last one hundred or so years has been extremely negative. If one chose to enlist in any case, it was often because he found the prospect of serving under Sergeant Lejaune at Fort Zinderneuf attractive and regarded the alleged brutality and tough service of the Legion as a challenge, as a way to test his own ruggedness.

How one reacted to the realities of Legion service depended largely upon one's expectations. Those who held a romanticized view of soldiering as a bold adventure in exotic settings were bound to be disappointed, as were those who came to serve France out of loyalty or patriotism. Middle-class recruits quickly came to wonder if the investment of five years of their lives was worth the anticipated dividend of appearing interesting at dinner parties upon their return to civilization. They also discovered that adaptation to barracks culture required a fairly radical downward adjustment of behavior. Others who fled into the Legion as a last opportunity to force order onto lives fallen into squalid disarray were simply too far gone to make a comeback, but seized the opportunity to lay the blame for their own failures and shortcomings upon the Legion.

The problem of exploitation was not so much that the Legion recruit risked humiliation, hard service, death or disability in the company of rogues for discredited causes. While the Legion saw some very tough fighting, the notion, as exemplified in the celebrated statement of General de Négrier, that legionnaires had enlisted to die and that therefore their lives served merely as stepping-stones to promotion or preferment by ambitious French officers was exaggerated. In fact, legionnaires much admired officers who displayed this sort of reckless courage and were usually eager to follow them. The greatest disappointment of Legion service that gave rise to feelings of shattered expectations which could lead to desertion was not combat, but boredom, especially when they discovered that they were used primarily as a construction unit. Therefore, the much-publicized *mission civilisatrice* of the Legion actually diminished its morale and combat performance. As far as legionnaires were concerned, the element of exploitation contained in Legion service was not that they were sent to fight, but that they were sent to fight with inadequate resources. The lack of foresight and planning of the high command, and the parsimonious French parliaments meant low pay, poor food, appalling logistics, understaffed medical services and many unnecessary deaths in imperial campaigns. The conditions in which many legionnaires were dispatched to fight in 1940 and in Indochina after 1946 bordered upon criminal neglect.

The barbarism of Legion justice, or rather the absence of justice in the Legion, also agitated critics of the Legion. About this, however, they were often misinformed or given to sensationalism. Early breaches of conduct were treated rather leniently. Only those who overstepped the rules repeatedly or who committed some heinous offense like deserting with arms might merit a sentence to the infamous *"Discipline"* at Colomb-Béchar. The rhythm of existence there was very much of the kill-or-cure variety, a philosophy of punishment that seems to be enjoying a renaissance in some civilian circles. Like any army, the Legion took a dim view of deserting in a battle zone, especially with arms, and the culprit might expect the harshest of penalties, but not always. The major complaint against Legion justice was not that it was brutal, but that it was inconsistent, a complaint heard especially from Germans used to a truly rigorous set of rules. Nor were native police in North African frontier areas liable to be accused of treating deserters, or their severed heads, with undue tenderness.

This brings us to the Legion myth, the justification of its existence as an enterprise of social redemption and rehabilitation. Evidence for the validity of this view is strong. Legion service was hard, Rollet was fond of pointing out, but it was fair. That was precisely Flutsch's conclusion when he discovered that the Legion operated by a set of easily comprehensible rules that, if obeyed, made life in its ranks much less turbulent, more organized and more equitable than on the outside, an oasis of order in an often confused and unjust world. Legion service allowed Flutsch time to think out his situation, and gave him the self-assurance to return to face the consequences of his, albeit fairly minor, crime. Flutsch discovered the Legion to be a refuge, an almost monastic retreat, for men ill-equipped for life in a *laissez-faire* world. For twenty-two-year-old Joseph Ehrhart, refused reenlistment in the French army because of a poor service record and reduced to sleeping rough and scrounging a living in Paris train stations, the Legion offered a lifeline. The same could be said for numerous refugees, men uprooted by Europe's perpetual political turbulence, who discovered in the Legion a stepping-stone to a new life as French citizens or even a permanent stopping place. The fact that reenlistment rates were reasonably high served as evidence that Legion life was not all that unattractive.

While attractive for public consumption, this myth had its limits. In the first place, the Legion's *métier* was combat, not to provide an outdoor counseling service for the troubled male population of Europe. Men who failed to adapt to its functions could not expect sympathetic treatment. That said, however, anyone prepared to cooperate with the system might easily discover a fairly comfortable niche in it. "No one in the Legion was 'punching tickets' [as in the U.S. Army] or phoning their congressman," wrote William Brooks. "If you didn't make the grade then you got the shit kicked out of you. Of course, this also got misused."[14] But together with the men successfully redeemed through Legion service must be counted those for whom the Legion provided a very unsympathetic environment because of their politics or their religion. Nor must one neglect the unredeemable—drunken, lazy, and turbulent elements, jailbait or bums on the outside who discovered in the Legion a perfect support system. While the Legion can be assigned no blame for the attitudes of these men, by tolerating them, by allowing them to congregate around the depots where new recruits reported and even by making a virtue of some of their more extravagant behaviors like drunkenness, in the belief that it allowed them to let off steam or that it was a sign of aggressiveness, they were in effect permitted an influence upon the social atmosphere of the Legion out of proportion to their numbers.

In this way, the Legion contributed to a situation that helped to undermine its own myth of salvation, for the pressure upon legionnaires to conform to a hard-drinking culture, with its inevitable result of a high rate of punishment and even of desertion, was immense. Legion life actually encouraged this sort of dysfunctional behavior. Critics even within the

army could argue that the Legion lost as many men as it redeemed. Therefore, if the Legion did, in fact, offer salvation, it was to those whose
characters and sense of priorities were already powerful enough to avoid
the worst temptations that Legion life placed before them. The Legion
provided the cover of the *anonymat*. Beyond that, the major concern was
that the legionnaire be on line when required.

Also, to many foreigners especially, the Legion could seem more tough
than fair, because they were operating in a military and bureaucratic culture,
and in a language, that they did not understand. During service this could
translate into many incomprehensible decisions for foreigners, like that
which caused Charles Hora's Korean batman to desert. Told that the Legion
did not accept enlistments from "peoples of color," but that Filipinos were
acceptable, "Chang the Korean" enlisted as a Filipino. With his false name
and nationality, he earned several decorations. However, when after the regulation three years he sought a *rectification d'identité*, he could produce no
papers proving that he was "Chang the Korean." Therefore, he was not allowed to wear his decorations, for French law forbade wearing decorations
under a false identity. He found the explanation that in the Legion, "medals
are not decorations of pride, but reflections of great memories" unacceptable, and subsequently deserted.[15] More important were men who found it
impossible to collect the pensions owed them after Legion service because
they could produce no papers, which Communist and fascist bureaucracies
refused to forward, or because they came from countries where bureaucracies were too inefficient, like Italy, or too primitive to match the impressive
levels of paperwork required by the French administration. If justice is a
question of perception, then it may be argued that, in the eyes of legionnaires
like those pushed to desertion in 1910 over the unfair treatment of Private
Weinrock, the Legion was always hard, but it was not always fair.

Perhaps the greatest limiting factor of the myth of salvation was that
the Legion succumbed to its own public relations campaign. It formed an
official stereotype of its legionnaires as men with mysterious and troubled
pasts who required the firm guiding hand of Legion discipline, with a touch
of tolerance and even indulgence. It was not that this attitude was inhumane. But it created an image of the individual legionnaire that hovered
between arrested adolescence and advanced schizophrenia. It was a comfortable myth, because it allowed officers to form an image of themselves
as a priesthood ministering to a flock of social and psychological misfits in
need of firm guidance. But it prepared them poorly to deal with legionnaires who did not fit into this mold, especially those who arrived in both
world wars. Too often these men were treated with suspicion and were
insulted, and quickly became disgusted with their decision to serve France.
All in all, the myth of salvation was one more element in sealing off the
world of the Legion from reality, increasing the monastic quality of its
life-style and outlook, deepening its sense of estrangement from *la régulière*
and even from France.

All of which raises a final question—how beneficial has the Legion been for France? In a way, this is a superfluous question, for the existence of the Legion is itself a reflection of French attitudes toward foreigners. It testifies to the view that France must always pay some price for the political turbulence of Europe in the form of refugees, because the attractions of her universal culture at the center of which stands Paris, her democratic institutions and her traditions of asylum have made her an obvious destination for the uprooted. An immigrant country like the United States has been forced to make a virtue of necessity by taking pride in its heterogeneous culture. France, on the other hand, like most ancient nations with a well-defined history, adopted the attitude that the arrival of these waves of outsiders posed a threat to her cultural and linguistic integrity. What was more, foreigners might threaten her political stability, either because of the ideas they imported and their attachment to revolutionary groups, or because they were a potential source of sedition. For these reasons, it seemed logical to round up as many of these men as possible and get them out of the country. Those who were serious about acquiring French nationality could earn it by serving in the hard school of the colonies.

When measured by these standards, in the Legion the French have gotten what they wanted, and probably more. For together with ridding France of some of her foreigners, the Legion has policed her colonies and fought her wars, while at the same time earning fame as a crack unit with an international reputation for military efficiency. In this way the Legion has occupied a vital place in French defense, for it has become a cliché of Legion apologists that every dead legionnaire has spared the life of a Frenchman.

This is a role that continues today. The 1er *étranger* at Aubagne, a suburb of Marseille, serves as the Legion's main induction and administrative center. Recruits are trained by the 4e *étranger* at Castelnaudary in southern France, and then distributed to one of the Legion's other units— the 1er REC in Orange, the 2e REP in Corsica, the 2e *étranger* in Nîmes, the 3e *étranger*, which trains in jungle warfare in French Guiana, or the 5e *étranger*, the old Indochina regiment, which now operates largely as a labor battalion on the Mururoa atoll in the Pacific where the French carry out their nuclear testing. The 13e DBLE, still proudly wearing its Gaullist Cross of Lorraine, provides the garrison for Djibouti in the Horn of Africa, while a small Legion detachment occupies the island of Mayotte in the Comoro Islands in the Indian Ocean. Recently, the 6e *étranger* has been resurrected as an engineer regiment.

Far from appearing as a quaint anachronism, the future of the Legion appears bright now that it has become obvious that the Socialist government elected in 1982 has no intention of carrying out its electoral pledge to abolish the Legion. The progressive reduction of conscript service to nine months has actually increased the value of the Legion to the French military. The appeal of the Legion is buoyant enough to allow the Legion to accept, according to its calculations, only one in six volunteers and still maintain a strength of ten thousand. As in the past, most of the nations of Europe are represented in its ranks, with Germans and French predominating. The 1980s witnessed an unprecedented influx of English recruits, caused by a combination of the Falklands War and the appearance on British television of a program on the Legion narrated by Simon Murray. With these men, the Legion provides elements for France's *force d'action rapide,* designated to operate on Europe's central front. The easing of tensions in Europe may even increase the usefulness of a corps whose traditional role has been to fight outside of Europe. Legion units were dispatched to Lebanon in recent years. The Legion also plays a central role in France's strong presence in Africa. Quite apart from the 1978 intervention of the 2^e REP in Zaire, the Legion frequently trains in the Central African Republic and provides elements to support French policy in Chad. At the time of this writing, Legion units are also serving with the multinational force in the Persian Gulf.

Last, the Legion's reputation for tough efficiency continues to make it the unit of choice for many of the French army's best officers. At this level, the Legion practices a sort of no-nonsense professionalism: "The Legion had functional inspections," wrote William Brooks of his experience in the 1970s. "Was the equipment clean, and did it work? The thought of eye wash (as in the U.S. Army) never entered anyone's mind." Once, on a training exercise, his platoon leader pitched an inoperable machine gun into the brush and left it there.

When we arrived back on base, he told the armorer to go get it. Jesus, can you see a lieutenant in the American armed forces doing that? He also told the armorer that if the gun refused to work next time he would kick his ass! God, I loved it! That was the kind of personal initiative taught in the Legion, but you were not privy to it until you earned it; i.e., NCO rank.[16]

Yet the Legion ledger has a debit side. One of the complaints against it traditionally has been that it draws off quality cadres that could have been better utilized to improve the quality of *la régulière.* Therefore, the combat record achieved by the Legion has been accomplished to an extent at the expense of the rest of the army and of French military efficiency generally. The cutthroat reputation of the Legion has also brought France much unfavorable publicity, much of it uninformed or politically motivated certainly, but plausible. Its brutal reputation, and on occasion its excessive behavior, helped to give French colonialism a poor image abroad. And while the Legion played a central role in imperial conquest, it proved less effective in incorporating the men who came to serve France out of loyalty and patriotism in the two world wars.

This helps to undermine the argument that every dead legionnaire represents a French life saved. Not only is it likely that France would have enticed more foreign volunteers into her ranks when national survival was really at stake in the two wars had she incorporated them into the regular army, but also she would have utilized more of them. For despite the heroic conduct of legionnaires in both 1915–18 and 1940, the fact remains that probably no more than a quarter to a third, possibly less, of Legion manpower was ever used on the critical front in those periods. Compare this, for instance, to the two-thirds of Legion manpower employed at any one time in Indochina between 1946 and 1954. In fact, the Legion served principally as a great colonial internment camp for foreigners in the two world wars.[17] The conclusion toward which one is invariably led is that France did not really want to utilize these men because she suspected their loyalty, and preferred to fight her national wars without them. As for the colonial wars, the government was extremely reluctant to send Frenchmen to the colonies in any case. Without foreign and native volunteers, the French, like the British, would have had no empire. So the number of French lives economized by the Legion in its main role of imperial warfare can only be a matter of conjecture, especially as at times the Legion counted up to 40 percent Frenchmen in its ranks.

A final drawback for France in its decision to collect foreigners into a unit that cultivated an aggressively mercenary mentality was that its loyalty was never fully assured. It is curious that the French government has tolerated the existence of a corps that has placed loyalty to the regiment higher on its standard of values than loyalty to France, and whose very motto, *Legio Patria Nostra,* is a declaration of circumscribed allegiance. Indeed, this has helped to make the Legion a magnet for officers and soldiers out of sympathy with many of the values of Republican France. Rollet must bear much of the blame—or the credit, depending on one's point of view—for this state of affairs, for by inventing and amplifying Legion traditions in the interwar years he intensified the separateness of the corps, its feelings of self-sufficiency, its belief that it existed only for itself and to glorify its own myths. He succeeded far too well, for the rebellion of important segments of the Legion in Algeria was due in part to the fact that the Legion had become a prisoner of its own myths, too attached to its moral geography and *"ville sainte"* to remember that its function was to carry out government policy, however distasteful. The Legion today is as much a "monastery of the unbelievers," perhaps even more so, as in Flutsch's time.

All these arguments, however, appear prosaic and unconvincing when placed beside the unique panache of the Legion and the colorful role it has played in the history of French imperialism and the French army. Besides, in the Legion France has gotten what it wants. The Legion, the saying goes, has become French by the blood it has shed. But it has also become French because it is tightly bound up with French prejudices and with French vanity. When France applauds the Legion loudly on Bastille Day, the enthusiasm is self-congratulatory. France believes that she has been endowed with a special gift, even a genius, for organizing foreigners to fight and die for her. This is a reaffirmation of France's special role as a *terre d'asile* (land of asylum), the regenerator of the exiles of mankind. For this reason, Legion propagandists have had little trouble in convincing their country-men that criticism of the Legion abroad is in reality an indirect attack upon France. "This splendid troop . . . has always provoked jealousy, envy and denigration among all foreign peoples," Colonel Louis Berteil insisted.[18] Its elite image and ferocious military reputation are also necessary for French *amour propre,* for it helps to rehabilitate the military honor of an army whose record over the past two centuries has been an uneven one.

For all of these reasons, the Legion has survived in a form and with a mentality long extinct in the armies of other nations. As dinosaurs go, however, it is a lively and colorful one. To watch the Legion parade down its *voie sacrée* before the monument commissioned by Rollet (which, like other Legion relics, has been transferred to Aubagne near Marseille), its bearded sappers, axes on their shoulders, opening the march with their slow elongated step, followed by legionnaires in their white kepis, red and green epaulets and blue sashes, is to glimpse its irresistible mystique. It takes only a small leap of the mind to imagine that the bleak, boulder-strewn peaks of southern Provence that tower over the museum to the Legion's past glories, which contains the crypt with the wooden hand of Captain Danjou, are those of the Kabylia or the Rif. For if the Legion is a uniquely French creation, it has become an international property. The Legion expresses some essential need of the human spirit, the belief that one can break with life and begin again, that salvation is to be found in the quest for danger and suffering.[19] As long as there are people who believe that, then the Legion will have a bright future, as well as an interesting past.

ACKNOWLEDGMENTS

LIKE ALL AUTHORS, I owe a great debt of gratitude to the many people whose encouragment, cooperation and support helped to nudge this book toward completion. John Keegan first suggested that I write on the Foreign Legion, an idea endorsed with enthusiasm and much helpful advice by my agents Gill Coleridge and Michael Congdon. Bill Fuller offered many valuable insights and suggestions during long and pleasant conversations at the Naval War College. My colleagues at The Citadel have provided the congenial atmosphere and, in the case of Larry Addington, Bill Gordon and Joe Tripp, the expertise that helped me to resolve many teasing questions. Even the impatience expressed by my Citadel cadets at not seeing the work completed, as well as their infallible ability to rescue themselves from the bleak prospect of a lecture on the Reformation or the Industrial Revolution by a few well-placed questions about the Legion, lubricated the process. I am also most grateful for the generous support of The Citadel Development Foundation, which funded the vital research visits to France. Finally, I must thank my editor, M. S. Wyeth, who patiently imposed order upon what was at times a rebellious script.

In France, my primary gratitude must go to the Legion itself, which proved unstintingly helpful and hospitable, especially A/c Tibor Szecsko, Adjutant Yann Cuba, and S/c Hugues Rivière. Visits to the 2ᵉ REI under the command of Colonel François provided a memorable view of the vitality of the modern Legion. As usual, the staff of the *Service historique de l'Armée de terre* at Vincennes proved immensely helpful. Colonels Pierre Carles and

Henry Dutailly made enlightening comments on portions of the manuscript, while Raymond Guyader and André-Paul Comor patiently answered my many queries. However, my special thanks must go to Richard Mahaud, whose close reading of my manuscript saved me from many errors of fact and interpretation. I, of course, accept full responsibility for any that remain.

It remains for me to thank my family. My parents-in-law, Charles and Thérèse Lamoureux, provided generous hospitality between bouts of research in Paris and Aubagne. My wife, Françoise, and my son, Charles, heroically endured this writer's fits of frustration and bad temper. Finally comes my daughter, Olivia, who provided excellent company during a blistering Charleston summer while I completed the manuscript, and to whom this book is dedicated.

The Citadel
Charleston, May 1990

SOURCE NOTES

PREFACE

1. John R. Elting, *Swords Around the Throne: Napoleon's Grande Armée* (New York: The Free Press, 1988), 355.

2. Lucien Bodard, *The Quicksand War: Prelude to Vietnam* (Boston and Toronto: Little Brown, 1967), 240.

3. Service historique de l'Armée de terre [SHAT], 3H 148, 19 June 1913.

4. Ernest Junger, *Jeux africains* (Paris: Gallimard, 1970), 172.

5. Daniel Pipes, *Slave Soldiers and Islam: The Genesis of a Military System* (New Haven and London: Yale University Press, 1981), 87, 89, 91.

6. Felix Gilbert, "Machiavelli: The Renaissance of the Art of War," in Peter Paret (ed.), *The Makers of Modern Strategy* (Princeton, N.J.: Princeton University Press, 1987), 26. For a more positive view of the *condottiere*, see Michael E. Mallet, *Mercenaries and Their Masters* (London, 1974).

7. Gunther Rothenburg, "Maurice of Nassau, Gustavus Adolphus, Raimondo Montecuccoli, and the 'Military Revolution' of the Seventeenth Century," in Paret (ed.), *Makers*, 47.

8. R. R. Palmer, "Frederick the Great, Guibert, Bulow. From Dynastic to National War," in Paret (ed.), *Makers*, 92–4, 99, 108.

9. André Corvisier, *Armies and Societies in Europe, 1494–1789* (Bloomington, Ind., and London: Indiana University Press, 1976), 135–6.

10. Samuel F. Scott, *The Response of the Royal Army to the French Revolution: The Role and Development of the Line Army, 1757–1763* (Oxford: Oxford University Press, 1978), 6, 12–14. Scott's calculations disagree with those of John R. Elting, *Swords*, p. 10, who places the number of foreign regiments in 1790 at twenty-three. While Swiss regiments in French service were about one-quarter non-Swiss, only a few hundred French subjects gained admittance to them. In the ninety-one line infantry regiments of the Royal Army, less than eight percent of the soldiers were foreigners. About one-half of the men serving in the

army's eight German regiments were from Lorraine or, especially, Alsace. The three Irish regiments were about three-quarters foreign, mostly from the Low Countries, whose inhabitants also furnished the majority of a Liégeois regiment. About one-third of the foreigners in the line infantry served in French regiments. The percentage of foreigners in the army's twelve light infantry battalions, formed in 1788, was about the same as for the line infantry, although many were northern Italians serving in the *Chasseurs Royaux-Corses* and the *Chasseurs Corses*, where Italian was the language of command. Only three percent of the cavalry was made up of foreigners, mostly Germans, who served in the Royal Allemand Cavalry and other units composed of men from Alsace and Lorraine, where the language of command was German. Six percent of the men in the hussar regiments were foreigners. The artillery remained the most exclusively French arm in the army.

11. Scott, *Response,* 154–55.

12. Scott, *Response,* 166–67.

13. For a full treatment of foreign troops in French service under Napoleon, see Elting, *Swords,* Chapter XVIII.

14. For a discussion of French attitudes toward imperial expansion in the nineteenth century, see Christopher Andrew and A. S. Kanya-Forstner, *France Overseas* (London: Thames and Hudson, 1984).

15. Douglas Porch, "Bugeaud, Galliéni, Lyautey. The Development of French Colonial Warfare," in Paret (ed.), *Makers,* 388–95. Algeria was considered part of metropolitan France after 1870, while Tunisia and, from 1912, Morocco were protectorates under the jurisdiction of the French Foreign Ministry. Sub-Saharan Africa, Madagascar and Indochina fell under the navy, before being passed on eventually to the colonial ministry.

16. Jules Richard, *La jeune armée* (Paris: La Librairie Illustrée, nd [1890]), 132.

17. Perhaps it is appropriate at this point to interject a word about sources. One of the problems that a study of the Legion poses for the historian is the often wildly diverse, even contradictory nature of the evidence. That men reacted in different ways to their Legion experiences is hardly surprising given different circumstances, outlooks and expectations. A more difficult problem arises, however, in dealing with official assessments of Legion shortcomings, especially those spelled out in the monthly *"rapport sur le moral,"* which became institutionalized in Legion units in the 1920s. Some historians in France have suggested to this author that criticisms of Legion morale and performance in these reports must not be taken at face value, but viewed in the context of bureaucratic infighting between command and field or staff echelons in the army. They provided a means for unit commanders, men who in the Legion are not usually known for their reluctance to mince words, to let off steam against a headquarters that they perceived as remote, unrealistic or simply unconcerned.

There may be something to be said for this interpretation. After all, in the Western Desert in 1942 Rommel often exaggerated his difficulties as a means to gain more materiel from Berlin. However, as a general observation I believe that there are two things wrong with the supposition that reports that point out problems in the Legion must not be taken at face value. The first is that it runs counter to the operational norms of a bureaucracy, especially a military bureaucracy, in which the promotion or other rewards sprinkled over the lower echelons depend upon the good will of and good working relations with superiors. On the whole, military commanders prefer positive attitudes in their subordinates that demonstrate a willingness to take up challenges and enhance the organization's morale and efficiency, and hence their own reputations as leaders. Critics and complainers are regarded as poor team players, even as disruptive elements, messengers who risk being shot. It is to the advantage of the subordinate commander to present his unit as one that functions efficiently. A second point to make is that the reports are frequently very upbeat, even unrealistically so, which rather undermines the argument that they served as a vehicle for protest.

18. See in this regard André-Paul Comor, *L'image de la Légion étrangère à travers la littérature française, 1900–1970* (Aix-en-Provence: mémoire de maîtrise [master's thesis], Aix-en-Provence, 1971), 23.

19. Antoine Sylvère, *Le légionnaire Flutsch* (Paris: Plon, 1982).

CHAPTER 1

1. Douglas Porch, *Army and Revolution: France 1815–1848* (London: Routledge & Kegan Paul, 1977), 121–2.

2. Porch, *Army,* 31–6.

3. Porch, *Army,* 31.

4. Felix Tavernier, "Le régiment de Hohenlohe et la Révolution de 1830 à Marseille," *Vert et rouge,* no. 105 (1956): 14–17.

5. André Corvisier, "Le recrutement et la promotion dans l'armée française du XVII siècle à nos jours. Rapport sur les études faites par le groupe de travail"; Jean Vidalenc, "Une contre-épreuve de l'insoumission. Les engagements volontaires sous la monarchie constitutionnelle (1814–1848)"; Henri Dutailly, "Quelques aspects du recrutement de l'armée d'Afrique sous la Monarchie de Juillet," *Revue internationale d'histoire militaire,* no. 37 (fascicule 2) (1976): 31–2, 55–71, 73–5.

6. SHAT, 5 March 1831, Xb 725.

7. Colonel Paul Azan, *L'armée d'Afrique, 1830 à 1852* (Paris: Plon, 1936), 124.

8. SHAT, Xb 725, 5 March 1831.

9. SHAT, Xb 725, 7 and 22 March 1831.

10. SHAT, Xb 725, 16 July 1831.

11. Porch, *Army,* 49.

12. J. Vidalenc, *Les demi-soldes* (Paris: Librairie Marcel Rivière 1955).

13. G. Bapst, *Le Maréchal Canrobert. Souvenirs d'un siècle* (Paris: Plon, 1909–13), Vol. I, 132.

14. Porch, *Army,* 49.

15. SHAT, Xb 725, 26 August 1831.

16. SHAT, Xb 726, inspection report for 1833.

17. SHAT, Xb 726, 30 June 1831.

18. SHAT, Xb 726, 29 August 1831.

19. SHAT, Xb 726, 30 August 1831.

20. SHAT, Xb 726, 31 March and 23 September 1831.

21. Henry Dutailly, *Les officiers servant à titre étranger, 9 mars 1831–31 décembre 1903* (mémoire de maîtrise, Aix-en-Provence, 1969), 16.

22. SHAT, Xb 725, 22 August 1831. Until the major reforms of the post-1870 era, the Staff Corps formed a separate arm in the French army. Its officers were criticized for being excessively bureaucratic and out of touch with troop command, which they never exercised.

23. SHAT, Xb 725, 22 August 1831.

24. SHAT, Xb 725, 5 May 1831. An exception perhaps was Edouard-August Cousandier, ex-NCO in the Swiss regiments under the Restoration, who appears to have taken the post as paymaster at Langres on 12 March 1831. I thank Mr. Richard Mahaud for this information.

25. SHAT, Xb 725, 20 March 1831.

26. SHAT, Xb 725, 19 May 1831.

27. SHAT, Xb 725, 11 July 1831.

28. SHAT, Xb 725, 19 May 1831.

29. SHAT, Xb 725, 26 August 1831.

30. SHAT, Xb 725, 26 August 1831.

31. SHAT, Xb 725. "Note sur quelques faits relatifs au commandement et à l'administration de la Légion étrangère."

32. SHAT, Xb 725, 19 May 1831.

33. SHAT, Xb 725, 4 May 1831.

34. SHAT, Xb 725, 4 June 1831.

35. H. Dutailly, "Chronique de l'ancienne Légion," *Képi blanc,* no. 278 (June 1970).

36. SHAT, Xb 725, 20 November 1831.

37. Louis Lamborelle, *Cinq ans en Afrique: Souvenirs militaires d'un Belge au service de la France* (Brussels: 1862), 11.

38. Lamborelle, *Cinq ans,* 18.

39. C.-A. Julien, *Histoire de l'Algérie contemporaine: Conquête et colonisation* (Paris: PUF, 1964), 86.

40. Julien, *Algérie*, 80, 85.

41. Azan, *Armée d'Afrique*, 49.

42. Azan, *Armée d'Afrique*, 47.

43. SHAT, Xb 726, 1834 inspection.

44. SHAT, E4 45. Cited in J.-C. Jauffrey, *L'idée d'une division de Légion étrangère et le premier régiment étranger de cavalerie, 1836–1940* (Montpellier: thèse pour le doctorat de 3ᵉ cycle, Université Paul Valéry, 1978), 31.

45. H. Dutailly, "Le 6ᵉ bataillon de l'ancienne Légion étrangère (1831–1835) était-il belge?" *Revue militaire belge*, XX-8 (December 1974): 692–3.

46. SHAT, Xb 725, 1 December 1832.

47. Azan, *Armée d'Afrique*, 80–1.

48. Azan, *Armée d'Afrique*, 50.

49. Paddy Griffith, *Military Thought in the French Army, 1815–1851* (Manchester and New York: Manchester University Press, 1989), 78–9, 128–9.

50. SHAT, Xb 726, 1833 inspection.

51. SHAT, Xb 726, 1 January 1834.

52. Azan, *Armée d'Afrique*, 81; Grisot, General and Coulombon, *La Légion étrangère de 1831–1887* (Paris: Berger-Levrault, 1888), 10. I also thank Richard Mahaud for much of this information.

53. Dutailly, "Chronique," October, November, December 1970.

54. Dutailly, "Chronique," October 1970.

55. Dutailly, "Chronique," October 1970.

56. Azan, *Armée d'Afrique*, 81.

57. Julien, *Algérie contemporaine*, 89–92.

58. Dutailly, "Chronique," September 1970.

59. Dutailly, "Chronique," September 1970.

60. "Chronique," September 1970; Grisot and Coulombon, *La Légion étrangère.* Page 12 points out that the 66th Infantry Regiment also shared some of these undesirable posts with the Legion. However, the 66th, made up from the remnants of the ex-Royal Guards of the Bourbons, was sent to Algeria, via Ancona, as a punishment after it refused to oppose a November 1831 workers' insurrection in Lyon. See Porch, *Army and Revolution*, 52, 54–5, 58–60.

61. Dutailly, "Chronique," September 1970; Grisot, *Légion*, 97. Dutailly notes the error of date in Grisot, and questions the assertion that the two dead legionnaires were Germans. One was named Pierre Masse, and the second was never positively identified because he had been decapitated by the Arabs on the previous day.

62. Julien, *Algérie contemporaine*, 272.

63. Grisot, *Légion*, 17.

64. SHAT, Xb 725, 22 September, 1831.

65. SHAT, Xb 726, 1 January 1834 inspection report.

66. Bernelle and de Colleville, *Histoire de l'ancienne Légion étrangère* (Paris: E. Marc-Aurèle, 1850), 78.

67. Bernelle and de Colleville, *Histoire de l'ancienne Légion étrangère*, 72–84; Grisot, *La Légion étrangère*, 20–25; Colonel Azan, "Les unités polonaises de la Légion," *Vert et rouge*, no. 21 (1949), 18.

68. Grisot, *Légion*, 32; Dutailly, "Chronique," November 1970.

69. SHAT, Xb 725.

70. Grisot, *Légion*, 32, who dates the amalgamation from August 19, is out by two days.

CHAPTER 2

1. John F. Cloverdale, *The Basque Phase of Spain's First Carlist War* (Princeton, N.J.: Princeton University Press, 1984), 170–88, 196–202.

2. J-C Jauffret, "M. Thiers, l'Espagne et la Légion étrangère, 1835–1837," *Revue*

historique des armées, no. 3 (1979, spécial): 145–72; J. P. T. Bury and R. P. Tombs, *Thiers, 1797–1877. A Political Life* (London: Allen & Unwin, 1986), 57–60.

3. Jauffret, "Thiers," 151.

4. Paul Azan, *Armée d'Afrique*, 162.

5. SHAT, Xb 776, 1835.

6. SHAT, Xb 776, 1835; Grisot and Coulombon, *La Légion étrangère de 1831 à 1887*, 26–8.

7. SHAT, Xb 776, 22 December 1838.

8. Grisot, *Légion*, 29.

9. Paul Azan, *La Légion étrangère en Espagne, 1835–1839* (Paris: Charles-Lavauzelle, 1906), 407–11.

10. SHAT, Xb 776, 26 December 1838.

11. G. von Rosen, *Bilder aus Spanien und der Fremdenlegion, Erster Band* (Kiel: Bunsow, 1843), 48.

12. SHAT, Xb 776, December 1838. Reproduced in Azan, *Légion*, 581–95. The assessment categories are my own.

13. SHAT, Xb 725, 1834.

14. H. Dutailly, "Le 6ᵉ bataillon de l'ancienne Légion étrangère," 687–98.

15. SHAT, fonds privés, 1K 256; Abel Galant, *Précis historique de la Légion étrangère en Espagne* (unpublished manuscript, no page numbers).

16. Azan, *Légion*, 140, 142–3, 177, 649.

17. Galant, *Précis*.

18. Azan, *Légion*, 177.

19. Galant, *Précis*.

20. Azan, *Légion*, 141.

21. Edward M. Spiers, *Radical General: Sir George de Lacy Evans, 1787–1870* (Manchester, England: Manchester University Press, 1983), 5, 69.

22. Galant, *Précis*.

23. Paul Azan, "La Légion étrangère en Espagne d'après les lettres du sous-lieutenant Jean-Jacques Azan, 1836–1838," *Carnet de la sabretache*, no. 167 (November 1906): 648, 650 (henceforth "Lettres").

24. See Cloverdale, Chapter 10, for the ultimate fate of the Carlist movement.

25. Azan, *Légion*, 166.

26. Cloverdale, *Carlist War*, 188, 202–3.

27. Spiers, *Evans*, 93, 96–7, 99–100.

28. Azan, *Légion*, 223–4.

29. J.-C. Jauffret, *L'idée d'une division de Légion étrangère*, 33.

30. Azan, *Légion*, 224–6; F-H Bernelle, "Le général Joseph Bernelle," *Vert et rouge*, mai–juin, juillet–août 1943: 10–14, 14–17.

31. Azan, "Lettres," 654.

32. SHAT, Xb 776, Bernelle report 19 April 1836. Bernelle refers to the action being fought at Lescaros. However, Azan believes that the fight took place at "Leranos." Azan, *Légion*, 431.

33. SHAT, Xb 776, Bernelle report; Azan, *Légion*, 170–71.

34. SHAT, E4 45, April 1836.

35. Azan, *Légion*, 174.

36. Azan, *Légion*, 179–81.

37. Azan, *Légion*, 177–78.

38. SHAT, E4 44 & 45, eighty-three deserters from August 1835 to April 1836.

39. Von Rosen, *Blinder . . .* , 46.

40. Azan, *Légion*, 256.

41. Azan, *Légion*, 230–2.

42. *Mémoires de Madame Dosne, l'égérie de M. Thiers* (Paris: Plon, 1928), Vol. 1, 131–32.

43. Comte Pelet de la Lozère, "Souvenirs du roi Louis-Philippe," *Revue universelle*, LXII, no. 7 (1 July 1935): 6–29.

44. SHAT, E4 44, 25 August 1836.

45. Azan, *Légion*, 247–8.

46. Azan, *Légion*, 251–2.

47. Azan, *Légion*, 251.

48. SHAT, E4 45, 26 December 1836.

49. SHAT, E4 45.

50. SHAT, E4 45, 3 January 1837.

51. SHAT, E4 45, 9 February 1837.

52. Azan, *Légion*, 288.

53. For strength see SHAT, Xb 776, "Etat présentant l'éffectif de la Légion . . . jusqu'au 30 juin 1837."

54. Quoted in Azan, *Légion*, 539.

55. Azan, *Légion*, 621.

56. Azan, *Légion*, 299.

57. Azan, *Légion*, 622.

58. Azan, *Légion*, 304. Galant, *Précis*, gives the number of casualties as four officers dead, eight wounded, and eighty legionnaires killed or missing.

59. Azan, *Légion*, 633.

60. Azan, *Légion*, 266.

61. Azan, *Légion*, 274.

62. Azan, *Légion*, 307.

63. Galant, *Précis*.

64. Wilhelm von Rahden, *Wanderungen eines alten Soldaten*, vol. 3 (Berlin: 1851), 251. Quoted in Azan, *Légion*, 327.

65. Azan, *Légion*, 523.

66. Azan, *Légion*, 323.

67. V. Doublet, *Vie de Don Carlos V de Bourbon, roi d'Espagne* (Bourges: Pornin, 1842), 103.

68. Azan, *Légion*, 373. See also SHAT Xb 776, 1838, which gives the number of those eligible for repatriation at seventy-two officers and 199 men.

69. Germain Bapst, *Le Maréchal Canrobert*, Vol. I, 356–7.

70. Galant, *Précis*.

CHAPTER 3

1. Grisot and Coulombon, *La Légion étrangère de 1831 à 1887*, 51.

2. Charles-André Julien, *Histoire de l'Algérie contemporaine*, 140.

3. "1837, l'assaut de Constantine," *Vert et rouge*, no. 20 (1949): 17–18.

4. SHAT 1H 52, Valée report, 26 October 1837.

5. SHAT, 1H 52, Valée report, 26 October 1837.

6. Jean Brunon, "Le centenaire de la prise de Constantine et la mort du colonel Combe," *Vert et rouge*, no. 3 (August 1937): 5.

7. SHAT, 1H 52, Valée report.

8. SHAT, 1H 52, Valée report.

9. SHAT, 1H 52, Valée report.

10. Saint-Arnaud, Achille, *Lettres du Maréchal de Saint-Arnaud, 1832–1854*, 2 vols. (Paris: Calmann-Lévy, 1864), 136.

11. Louis de Charbonnières, *Une grande figure. Saint-Arnaud, Maréchal de France* (Paris: Nouvelles editions latines, 1960), 30.

12. Saint-Arnaud, *Lettres*, 152.

13. Saint-Arnaud, *Lettres*, 138, 155–6.

14. SHAT, 1H 52, Valée report.

15. Saint-Arnaud, *Lettres*, 138–9.

16. Saint-Arnaud, *Lettres*, 139.

17. Saint-Arnaud, *Lettres*, 140–1.

18. Saint-Arnaud, *Lettres*, 141–42.

19. Saint-Arnaud, *Lettres*, 145.

20. Saint-Arnaud, *Lettres*, 142.

21. Saint-Arnaud, *Lettres*, 147–48.

22. Saint-Arnaud, *Lettres*, 147.

23. Saint-Arnaud, *Lettres*, 147.

24. Saint-Arnaud, *Lettres*, 131.

25. Saint-Arnaud, *Lettres*, 143.

26. Lady Duff Gordon, *The French in Algiers* (London: John Murray, 1855), 23.

27. Saint-Arnaud, *Lettres*, 125.

28. SHAT, Xb 727, 1841.

29. I thank Colonel Henri Dutailly for this information.

30. SHAT, Xb 727, 1841.

31. SHAT, Xb 726, 10 November 1838.

32. SHAT, Xb 726, 1837.

33. H. Dutailly, "Chronique de l'ancienne Légion," July 1970, 280.

34. SHAT, Xb 727, 18 November 1843.

35. SHAT, Xb 726, 10 November 1838.

36. SHAT, Xb 726, October 1840.

37. SHAT, Xb 727, 18 November 1845.

38. SHAT, Xb 727. See, for instance, the inspection reports of the 1st regiment for 1843: 1,280 literate for 2,482 men; 2nd regiment, 20 September 1844: 1,113 literate for 2,726 men; November 1845: 1,307 literate for 3,285 men.

39. Gordon, *The French*, 76–7.

40. Germain Bapst, *Le maréchal Canrobert*, Vol. 1, 361.

41. Guy de Miribel, *Mémoires du maréchal de Mac-Mahon, duc de Magenta: Souvenirs d'Algérie* (Paris: Plon, 1932), 173.

42. SHAT, Xb 727, 19 November 1844.

43. SHAT, Xb 727, 1842.

44. Saint-Arnaud, *Lettres*, 224.

45. Miribel, *Mac-Mahon*, 172–3.

46. SHAT, H86 Alger, 22 October 1842. The letter is a copy of Soult's letter sent to General de Négrier, commander of the Constantine division, upon whose territory the abuses took place.

47. P. Christian, *L'Afrique française, l'empire du Maroc et les déserts du Sahara* (Paris: Barbier, nd [1846]), 446.

48. SHAT, Xb 727, October 1840.

49. Bapst, *Canrobert*, Vol 1, 358. See also Maréchal Boniface de Castellane, *Journal du Maréchal de Castellane, 1804–1862* (Paris: Plon, 1896), Vol. III, 223–27.

50. Saint-Arnaud, *Lettres*, 223–24.

51. Captain Blanc, *Types militaires d'antan. Généraux et soldats d'Afrique* (Paris: Plon, 1885), 208–9.

52. SHAT, Xb 726, 1836.

53. Statistics derived from SHAT, Xb 726 & 727.

54. Hew Strachan, *Wellington's Legacy. The Reform of the British Army, 1830–1854* (Manchester: Manchester University Press, 1984), 89.

55. SHAT, Xb 696, inspection reports for the 2e régiment d'infanterie légère.

56. SHAT, Xb 723 *zouaves*.

57. SHAT, H 86 Alger, 22 October 1842.

58. P. de Castellane, *Souvenirs de la vie militaire en Afrique* (Paris: Calmann-Lévy, 1879), 149.

59. Miribel, *MacMahon*, 173.

60. SHAT, Xb 727, 20 September 1844.

61. Captain Forey, *Campagnes d'Afrique, 1835–1848: Lettres adressées au maréchal de Castellane par le captaine Forey* (Paris: Plon, 1898), 103. This was a fate that Captain Forey of the 2nd Light Infantry Regiment wished for one of his superiors: "We all however await with

anxiety the promotion to lieutenant colonel for a certain M. de la Torre, who had the talent to make himself abhorred by everyone," he wrote on August 11, 1837. "They are at this moment organizing two battalions of the Foreign Legion. That is just the place for him."

62. Bapst, *Canrobert*, Vol. I, 359.

63. Figures compiled by the author from inspection reports in SHAT:

	Hospital	Died	Desertions
1836	284/39.4%	134/18.6%	105/14.6%
1837	—	286/13.6%	226/10.7%
1838 (Nov)	221/8%	102/3.7%	221/8%
1839 (Oct)	427/14.9%	256/8.9%	232/8.1%
0 (Oct)	1,016/24.4%	136/3.2%	283/6.8%
1841	639/22.9%	204/7.3%	292/10.5%
1842 (Nov) 1st reg.	273/11.2%	177/7.2%	291/11.9%
1843 (Nov) 1st reg.	347/13.9%	156/6.2%	292/11.7%
1st reg.	245/8.8%	—	287/10.3%
1844 (Sept) 2nd reg.	294/10.7%(1,482 fever)	—	151/5.5%
1845 (Sept) 1st reg.	290/9.2%	—	199/6.3%
1845 (Nov) 2nd reg.	261/7.9% (2,046 fever)	—	184/5.6%

64. Julien, *L'Algérie contemporaine*, 272.

65. Saint-Arnaud, *Lettres*, 190. See also Lady Duff Gordon, "The Prisoner of Abd el-Kader," *The French in Algiers*, 93–176.

66. P. de Castellane, *Souvenirs de la vie militaire en Afrique*, 3ᵉ édition, 92–3.

67. Bapst, *Canrobert*, Vol. 1, 360–1. The date of the massacre was, in fact, November 8, 1836. I thank Mr. Richard Mahaud for this information.

68. SHAT, Xb 726, October 1840.

69. Captain Emile Froelicher, *Le siège de Milianah, ses ravitaillements* (Paris: Charles-Lavauzelle, 1889), 9–34.

70. Gordon, *The French*, 23.

71. Bapst, *Canrobert*, Vol. 1, 257.

72. See SHAT, Xb 726, 10 November 1838 and October 1840.

73. General Paul Azan, *Conquête et pacification de l'Algérie* (Paris: Librairie de France, 1929), 503–4.

74. SHAT, Xb 726, October 1840.

75. SHAT, Xb 727, 20 September 1844.

76. SHAT, Xb 727, 15 November 1842. See also SHAT, Xb 726, 1837 and 10 November 1838.

77. SHAT, Xb 727, October 1840. In 1837, General Rullière found that the weapons of the Legion were "generally badly maintained" and that the overcoats of the NCOs and soldiers "are not in good repair" (Xb 726). "The training of legionnaires needs to start again at the beginning," wrote General Dampierre in November 1838. "The Legion is weak in evolutions and maneuvers because it is rarely exercised." It had neither a drill field nor a firing range, while its frequent service in the *"avants postes"* was not only "very difficult" and the cause of the high sickness rates in the Legion, but also further undermined training (10 November 1838 and October 1839, Xb 727). General de Négrier also criticized the inadequate preparation of legionnaires in 1842 (Xb 727, 1842).

78. Gordon, *The French*, 18.

CHAPTER 4

1. Julien, *l'Algérie contemporaine*, 173.

2. Gordon, *The French*, 36.

3. Anthony Thrall Sullivan, *Thomas-Robert Bugeaud: France and Algeria, 1784–*

1849: Power, Politics and the Good Society (Hamden, Conn.: Archon Books, 1983), 69–70.

4. For more details on Bugeaud's life, see H. d'Ideville, *Le maréchal Bugeaud, d'après sa correspondance intime et des documents inédits, 1784–1882* (Paris: Firmin-Didot, 1881–82).

5. Bapst, *Le maréchal Canrobert*, I, 258–9.

6. Julien, *L'Algérie contemporaine*, 171.

7. T-R Bugeaud, *Par l'épée et par la charrue: Ecrits et discours de Bugeaud* (Paris: Presses Universitaires de France, 1948), 289–91.

8. Bapst, *Canrobert*, I, 264–70.

9. Bapst, *Canrobert*, I, 264–70.

10. Lamborelle, *Cinq ans en Afrique*, 47.

11. Gordon, *The French*, 25.

12. Gordon, *The French*, 43–4. In fact, the number of legionnaires ambushed was forty-five.

13. *Archives d'outre-mer*, Aix-en-Provence, 18 mi 1, 28 December 1840 and 19 January 1841.

14. Gordon, *The French*, 78.

15. *Archives d'outre-mer*, 18 June 1842.

16. I thank Richard Mahaud for this information.

17. *Archives d'outre-mer*, 18 June 1842.

18. Bapst, *Canrobert*, I, 255.

19. Paul Azan, *Conquête et pacification*, 375.

20. Jacques de la Faye, *Souvenirs du général Lacretelle* (Paris: Emile Paul, 1907), 2–3.

21. Lamborelle, *Cinq ans*, 109–10.

22. Lamborelle, *Cinq ans*, 115.

23. Lamborelle, *Cinq ans*, 111–12.

24. Gordon, *French*, 52.

25. Lamborelle, *Cinq ans*, 118–19.

26. Gordon, *French*, 52.

27. Lamborelle, *Cinq ans*, 120.

28. Gordon, *French*, 51.

29. Lamborelle, *Cinq ans*, 122.

30. de la Faye, *Lacretelle*, 3.

31. SHAT, Xb 727, 21 January & 15 November 1842.

32. SHAT, Xb 727, 18 November 1845.

33. de la Faye, *Lacretelle*, 2.

34. Lamborelle, *Cinq ans*, 258.

35. Miribel, *MacMahon*, 176.

36. Gordon, *The French*, 54, 60, 69

37. Letter of September 29, 1843, in the private collection of M. Raymond Guy-ader.

38. Gordon, *French*, 53.

39. A. K. Koch, "Relation de l'expédition dans le sud de la province d'Oran en 1849," *Spectateur militaire*, 1949: 662.

40. Lamborelle, *Cinq ans*, 262.

41. Lamborelle, *Cinq ans*, 198.

42. Gordon, *French*, 26.

43. Lamborelle, *Cinq ans*, 199.

44. Gordon, *French*, 26.

45. Lamborelle, *Cinq ans*, 151.

46. Gordon, *French*, 26.

47. Lamborelle, *Cinq ans*, 151.

48. Gordon, *French*, 62–3.

49. Blanc, *Types militaires d'antan*, 234–36.

50. Gordon, *French*, 84.

51. Lamborelle, *Cinq ans*, 157.

52. Lamborelle, *Cinq ans*, 82–3.

53. Lamborelle, *Cinq ans*, 85.

54. Lamborelle, *Cinq ans*, 194.

55. de la Faye, *Lacretelle*, 4.

56. *Archives d'outre mer*, 18 mi 1, 28 February 1841.

57. SHAT, Xb 727, 15 November 1842.

58. de la Faye, *Lacretelle*, 1–2.

59. SHAT, Xb 727, 20 September 1844.

60. SHAT, Xb 727, 19 September 1845.

61. SHAT, Xb 727, 20 September 1844.

62. SHAT, Xb 727, 1843.

63. Julien, *L'Algérie contemporaine*, 272.

64. Lamborelle, *Cinq ans*, 42.

65. SHAT, Xb 726, October 1840.

66. Lamborelle, *Cinq ans*, 42.

67. Miribel, *MacMahon*, 177–78.

68. Jean Brunon et al., *Le livre d'or de la Légion étrangère, 1831–1976* (Paris: Charles-Lavauzelle, 1981), 423.

69. SHAT, Xb 726, October 1840.

70. Lamborelle, *Cinq ans*, 188, 262.

71. SHAT, Xb 727, 18 November 1845.

72. General F. C. du Barail, *Mes souvenirs* (Paris: Plon, 1894–96), Vol. I, 226.

73. Miribel, *MacMahon*, 183–84.

74. SHAT, Xb 727, 18 November 1845.

75. Miribel, *MacMahon*, 183–84.

76. Lamborelle, *Cinq ans*, 37.

77. Lamborelle, *Cinq ans*, 85.

Chapter 5

1. Douglas Porch, *The Conquest of the Sahara* (New York: Knopf, 1984).

2. Emile Herbillon, *Quelques pages d'un vieux cahier: Souvenirs du général Herbillon, 1794–1866* (Paris: Berger-Levrault, 1928), 128.

3. Edouard Collineau, "Un soldat de fortune. Notes et souvenirs du général Collineau," *Carnet de la Sabretache*, no. 288 (March–April 1924), 140–41.

4. Julien, *L'Algérie contemporaine*, 383–84.

5. Bapst, *Canrobert*, I, 461.

6. P-N Bonaparte, *Un mois en Afrique* (Paris: Pagnerrre, 1850), 22.

7. Bonaparte, *Un mois*, 21–28; E. Herbillon, *Relation du siège de Zaatcha* (Paris: J. Dumaine, 1863), 15. For a view more favorable to the French see Charles Boucher, "Le siège de Zaatcha," *Revue des Deux Mondes*, 1 April, 1851: 70–100; Félix Mornaud, "La guerre dans les oasis," *L'Illustration*, nos. 350, 351, 352 & 354 (10, 17, 24 November and 8 December 1849). Reports on how much taxes were raised by Saint-Germain vary, but all agree that they were substantial.

8. Herbillon, *Relation*, 17–18. A second version of these events, provided by *L'Illustration* reporter Félix Mornaud, held that Bouzian mounted his mule and was riding out of Zaatcha with Sekora when some of the spahis began joking that, "If he had seen the Prophet in a dream, he would soon see him in person as the intention of the commander was to split open his head as soon as he dismounted." Bouzian took fright and attempted to flee. The spahis began to beat him with the flats of their swords, his rosary broke, one of his sons began to fire upon the spahis, and a general melée ensued ("La guerre," no. 351, 17 November 1849, 190).

9. Herbillon, *Relation*, 18–19. See also SHAT, H 211, "Histoire de la campagne du Ziban. Siège et prise de Zaatcha, 1849," manuscript, no author, nd, no pp.

10. Herbillon, *Relation*, 20.

11. Herbillon, *Relation*, 27.

12. Herbillon, *Relation*, 28–32.

13. Herbillon, *Relation*, 31–2.

14. Herbillon, *Relation*, 28.

15. Bonaparte, *Un mois*, 20.

16. SHAT, H 263, "Carnet de correspondance du ministre de la guerre relative à l'Algérie. 12 juin 1848 à 7 juin 1850," 22 August 1849.

17. Grisot and Coulombon, *La Légion étrangère*, 109, 145.

18. Bonaparte, *Un mois*, 19.

19. du Barail, *Mes souvenirs*, I, 367–8.

20. Camille Rousset, *La conquête de l'Algérie* (Paris: Plon, 1889), II, 244.

21. Herbillon, *Relation*, 33–4. Grisot, *Légion*, 149–50, lists sixty-two of the Ouled-Sahnoun killed to two attackers, with 1,400 camels and 5,000 sheep captured.

22. SHAT, H 263, "Carnet," 10 August 1849.

23. Herbillon, *Relation*, 34.

24. "L'insurrection des Zibans, 1849," *Légion étrangère*, no. 12 (December 1931) gives the date as 1833. This is also the date favored by Collineau, "Un soldat de fortune," 152, who says that the attack was carried out by the Bey of Tunis. However, Herbillon, *Relation*, insists that this occurred in 1831.

25. SHAT, H 263, "Carnet," 10 August 1849.

26. SHAT, H 211, "Histoire."

27. SHAT, H 211, "Colonne expéditionnaire du Hodna et du Sahara. Journal de marche du chef d'état-major," 16 July 1849.

28. Herbillon, *Relation*, 35.

29. SHAT, H 211, "Colonne."

30. SHAT, H 263, "Carnet," 10 August 1849.

31. SHAT, H 263, 4 & 7 September 1849.

32. Grisot, *Légion*, 151.

33. Collineau, "Un soldat de fortune," 151.

34. See SHAT, H 263, "Correspondance du Général Herbillon," 25 September 1849, for the most complete description of Seriana. See also Herbillon, *Pages*, 133.

35. Herbillon, *Relation*, 47.

36. SHAT, H 263, "Carnet," 4 & 22 September 1849.

37. SHAT, H 263, "Carnet," 4 September.

38. Miribel, *MacMahon*, 175.

39. SHAT, H 263, "Carnet," 30 September.

40. SHAT, H 263, "Carnet," 4 September.

41. SHAT, H 263, "Carnet," 22 September.

42. SHAT, H 263, "Carnet," 5 November.

43. SHAT, H 263, "Carnet." On August 10 Rullière wrote to the governor-general following the failure of Carbuccia's July attack, "It is up to you, General, to control the ardor of this colonel whose excessive ambition has sometimes got the better of his judgment and his intelligence."

44. Jean-Jacques Pélissier, *Aspects de la vie politique et militaire en France à travers la correspondance reçue par le maréchal Pélissier (1828–1864)* (Paris: Bibliothèque nationale, 1968), 290–1.

45. SHAT, H 263, "Carnet," 4 & 22 September, 5 November.

46. Herbillon, *Relation*, 55.

47. Herbillon, *Relation*, 57.

48. Herbillon, *Relation*, 57–8.

49. Charles Boucher, *Lettres et récits militaires* (Paris: Calmann-Lévy, 1897), 11–12.

50. Herbillon, *Relation*, 70.

51. Herbillon, *Relation*, 63.

52. Herbillon, *Relation*, 70.

53. Pélissier, *Aspects de la vie politique et militaire*, 148.

54. Herbillon, *Relation,* 75. Other sources say five killed and twenty-five wounded.

55. Herbillon, *Relation,* 73–4.

56. SHAT, H 263, "Carnet," 10 November 1849.

57. Herbillon, *Relation,* 74.

58. Herbillon, *Relation,* 77–8.

59. Herbillon, *Relation,* 80–1.

60. Herbillon, *Relation,* 81.

61. SHAT, H 263, "Carnet," 27–29 September.

62. Herbillon, *Pages,* 138.

63. Herbillon, *Relation,* 97–8.

64. Grisot, *Légion,* 153.

65. Herbillon, *Relation,* 101–2.

66. Herbillon, *Pages,* 140. SHAT, H 211, "Journal," two companies of legionnaires and a battalion of the 43rd.

67. Herbillon, *Relation,* 103; SHAT, H 211, "Journal," 20 October. In his *Souvenirs,* however, Herbillon wrote that "At first sight, I realized that it was not prudent to attempt a new assault" (139).

68. Herbillon, *Relation,* 107; SHAT, H 211, "Journal," obviously incomplete, gives thirty-five dead, 137 wounded and ten "concussed."

69. SHAT, H 263, "Carnet," 22 September & 10 November.

70. Herbillon, *Relation,* 108–10; Bonaparte, *Un mois,* 72.

71. Herbillon, *Pages,* 141.

72. Bonaparte, *Un mois,* 44, 67; Jean de la Rocca, *Pierre-Napoléon Bonaparte. Sa vie et ses oeuvres,* 3ᵉ édition éditée par le journal *L'Avenir de la Corse* (Paris: nd [1867]).

73. Bonaparte, *Un mois,* 46–8.

74. SHAT, H 263, "Carnet," 22 September.

75. Bonaparte, *Un mois,* 46, 58.

76. Herbillon, *Relation,* 122, SHAT, H 211, "Journal," 25 October.

77. Herbillon, *Pages,* 142–3.

78. Bonaparte, *Un mois,* 50–1, 53, 72.

79. Herbillon, *Pages,* 145–7.

80. SHAT, H 263, "Carnet," 24 December.

81. Maréchal Victor de Castellane, *Journal du Maréchal de Castellane, 1804–1862* (Paris: Plon, 1896), 198.

82. Bonaparte, *Un mois,* 97, 104–5, 111–12.

83. Bapst, *Canrobert,* I, 479.

84. Bapst, *Canrobert,* I, 480–1.

85. Bapst, *Canrobert,* I, 484.

86. Herbillon, *Relation,* 200–1.

87. Julien, *Histoire de l'Algérie,* 304–5.

88. Figures taken from SHAT, H 211, "Journal," September–November 1849.

89. Bapst, *Canrobert,* I, 478.

90. Herbillon, *Relation,* 101–2, 119.

91. Bonaparte, *Un mois,* 43.

92. Herbillon, *Pages,* 156.

Chapter 6

1. Louis de Massol, *France, Algérie, Orient* (Versailles: Beau, 1860), 44.

2. Othon Patrick Kremar, *Sidi-bel-Abbès et les Bel-Abbèsiens. Une ville française, 1843–1962* (Montpellier: Africa Nostra, 1962); *Képi blanc,* special (September 1979), on Sidi-bel-Abbès; General Charles-Jules Zédé, "Souvenirs de ma vie," *Carnet de la Sabretache,* September-October 1933: 429–31.

3. Edouard Collineau, "Notes et souvenirs du général Collineau," *Carnet de la Sabretache,* no. 288 (March-April 1924), 172.

4. A. Rastoul, *Le maréchal Randon (1795–1871), d'après ses mémoires et des documents inédits. Etude militaire et politique* (Paris: Firmin-Didot, 1890), 82.

5. Gordon, *The French*, 18.

6. Massol, *France*, 6.

7. William Stammer, *Recollections of a Life of Adventure* (London: Hurst & Blackett, 1866). 77.

8. G.-W. Diesbach de Torny, *Notes et souvenirs*, unpublished manuscript, ALE Aubagne, 119, 127.

9. "La Légion étrangère," *La revue d'infanterie*, no. 524 (1 May 1936): 810.

10. Antoine Camus, *Les bohèmes du drapeau. 2ème série. La Légion étrangère* (Paris: Brunet, 1864), 1.

11. Gordon, *French*, 23.

12. Zédé, "Souvenirs," no. 366, 435, 438–49.

13. Camus, *Bohèmes*, 3.

14. Stammer, *Recollections*, 105.

15. Camus, *Bohèmes*, 11.

16. Massol, *France*, 271.

17. Zédé, "Souvenirs," no. 366, 438.

18. Paul de Choulot, *Mes souvenirs pour servir à l'histoire du 1er régiment de la Légion étrangère* (Paris: Dumaine, 1864), 4.

19. Grisot and Coulombon, *La Légion étrangère*, 173–74.

20. SHAT, Xb 778, inspection of the *1er étranger*, 1861.

21. Zédé, "Souvenirs," no. 366, 433.

22. Diesbach, *Notes*, 1–2.

23. Zédé, "Souvenirs," no. 367, 494–95.

24. Pélissier, *Aspects de la vie politique*, 289.

25. Louis Noia, *Campagne de Crimée* (Clichy: Imprimerie Loignon, nd), 245.

26. Grisot, *Légion*, 565–70.

27. Zédé, "Souvenirs," no. 368, 45.

28. Zédé, "Souvenirs," no. 368, 46.

29. Zédé, "Souvenirs," no. 368, 48–50; "La Légion étrangère en Italie," *Vert et rouge*, September-October 1942, 4–8.

30. M. Kamienski, *La mort d'un soldat* (Paris: 1960), 14.

31. Zédé, "Souvenirs," no. 368, 51. Grisot, *Légion*, p. 252, lists 41 killed and 119 wounded; however, he passes over a number of missing and prisoners in silence.

32. Zédé, "Souvenirs," no. 369, 51.

33. *1er régiment étranger (Suisse)*, journal de marche, manuscript, ALE Aubagne, 23. See also Patrick Turnbull, *Solferino. The Birth of a Nation* (New York: Saint Martin's, 1985), 107–9.

34. Emile Carrey, *Récits de Kabylie* (Paris: Calmann-Lévy, 1876).

35. Zédé, "Souvenirs," no. 369, 120.

36. Stammer, *Recollections*, 78.

37. Zédé, "Souvenirs," no. 371, 256, 261. These precautions were taken in part because an earlier boatload of *zouaves* had created serious disturbances in Fort-de-France.

38. Camus, *Bohèmes*, 3–5, 10–11.

39. Henry Dutailly, "Le 2e étranger," *Képi blanc*, nos, 332, 333, 334 (1975).

40. Stammer, *Recollections*, 106–7.

41. "Lettres du caporal Fijalkowski," ALE Aubagne, manuscript, 18 May & 7 May 1859.

42. Eugène Amiable, *Légionnaire au Mexique* (Brussels: Charles Dessart, 1942), 52, 96. An interesting memoir but one that must be used cautiously because it contains numerous errors and inconsistencies.

43. Massol, *France*, 273–87.

44. Zédé, "Souvenirs," no. 369, 128; no. 367, 496; no. 368, 49.

45. Fijalkowski, "Lettres," 1 October, 1856.

46. Amiable, *Légionnaire*, 53, 104.

47. Amiable, *Légionnaire*, notes, 148, 150.

48. Grisot, *Légion*, 354, 358–59.

49. Massol, *France*, 6.

50. Fijalkowski, "Lettres," 18 May, 1859; 1 October, 1856.

51. Camus, *Bohèmes*, 5.

52. Massol, *France*, 277.

53. SHAT, Xb 778, inspection of the *1er étranger*, 1861.

54. Grisot, *Légion*, 174, 176, 191, 195.

55. "*1er régiment étranger*, 1856–1862," ALE, Aubagne.

56. Th. Pruvost, *Le général Deplanque, 1820–1889* (Paris: Charles-Lavauzelle, 1902), 61.

57. SHAT, Xb 778.

58. *Contrôle de troupe: Légion étrangère, 1868–1870*, SHAT.

Chapter 7

1. Lieutenant Colonel Morel, *La Légion étrangère* (Paris: Chapelot, 1912), 45–47.

2. Zédé, "Souvenirs," no. 371, 764.

3. Diesbach, *Notes*, 17.

4. Diesbach, *Notes*, 91–2.

5. Zédé, "Souvenirs," no. 371, 271.

6. Zédé, "Souvenirs," no. 371, 266.

7. Zédé, "Souvenirs," no. 372, 378. See also *Légion étrangère. Historique sommaire du corps*, ALE manuscript. The entry for October 31, 1863, lists losses as eight hundred legionnaires and eleven officers. These include those killed in combat.

8. Diesbach, *Notes*, 133, 169.

9. Amiable, *Légionnaire*, 145.

10. Diesbach, *Notes*, 50.

11. Danjou had not lost his hand in the Crimea, as is often written.

12. For Maine's testimony, see "*Dossier Camerone*," ALE.

13. "*Dossier Camerone*."

14. Diesbach, *Notes*, 91.

15. Etienne Micaud, *La France au Mexique*, (Paris: Editions du monde moderne, 1927), 156–60.

16. Zédé, "Souvenirs," no. 371, 258–59.

17. Jack Audrey Dabbs, *The French Army in Mexico, 1861–1867: A Study in Civil-Military Relations* (The Hague: Mouton, 1963), 129, 114, 70–1, 65; "Les indiens à la Légion étrangère (Mexique 1863–64)," *Légion étrangère*, no. 64 (April 1936): 5.

18. H. Spinner, *Souvenirs d'un vieux soldat* (Neuchâtel: Messeiller, 1906), 136.

19. Diesbach, *Notes*, 193–95.

20. Zédé, "Souvenirs," no. 373, 55.

21. SHAT, 1K 198, fonds privés Dupin.

22. Zédé, "Souvenirs," no. 373, 56.

23. SHAT, 1K 198, fonds Dupin.

24. Amiable, *Légionnaire*, 105–6.

25. André Castelot, *Maximilien et Charlotte du Mexique: La tragédie de l'ambition* (Paris: Librairie académique Perrin, 1977), 278–79.

26. Amiable, *Légionnaire*, note 106.

27. Dabbs, *French Army*, 267.

28. *Légion étrangère. Historique sommaire du corps*, ALE, manuscript, October 1863.

29. *Historique sommaire*, April 1864.

30. Zédé, "Souvenirs," no. 373, 455.

31. Pierre Sergent, *Camerone* (Paris: Fayard, 1980), 408. Louis Leconte in the

preface to Amiable, *Légionnaire,* 13, casts doubt on Amiable's claims to have belonged to the Legion cavalry.

32. Amiable, *Légionnaire,* 94, 103–5.

33. Sergent, *Camerone,* 393.

34. Grisot, *Légion,* 300, 303, 304, 306. Other sources suggest eighteen killed.

35. P. Guinard, "Cavaliers de la Légion étrangère au Mexique," *Carnet de la Sabretache,* no. 389 (July–August 1937): 323 note 5. It is not clear whether this figure includes the company of "mounted partisans," which numbered three officers and 124 men on that date. See note 2, 323.

36. ALE, L2.

37. Grisot, *Légion,* 309.

38. Amiable, *Légionnaire,* 169.

39. Grisot, *Légion,* 309–11.

40. Grisot, *Légion,* 306. See also Paul Gaulot, *L'expédition du Mexique (1861–1867): D'après les documents et souvenirs de Ernest Louet* (Paris: Nouvelle édition, 1908), II, 318–19.

41. Diesbach, *Notes,* 96.

42. Amiable, *Légionnaire,* 98.

43. Zédé, "Souvenirs," no. 366, 435.

44. Zédé, "Souvenirs," no. 366, 434.

45. Ghislain de Diesbach, *Service de France* (Paris: Emile-Paul, 1972), 275.

46. Zédé, "Souvenirs," no. 366, 428.

47. Zédé, "Souvenirs," no. 366, 435.

48. Gustave Derudder, *Vie du commandant Clemmer: Un soldat d'Afrique.* (Calais: Imprimerie des Orphelins, 1889), 96–7.

49. Camus, *Bohèmes,* 13.

50. Zédé, "Souvenirs," no. 366, 435.

51. *Dossier Camerone,* ALE.

52. Derudder, *Clemmer,* 97.

53. W. Serman, *Les officiers français dans la nation, 1848–1914* (Paris: Aubin, 1982), 139–42.

54. Sergent, *Camerone,* 390.

55. Sergent, *Camerone,* 207–8.

56. Amiable, *Légionnaire,* 153–55.

57. Sergent, *Camerone,* 394.

58. ALE L2, 93.

59. ALE L2, 94–104.

60. Amiable, *Légionnaire,* 129–30.

61. Grisot, *Légion,* 221.

62. SHAT, Xb 778, 1863.

63. SHAT, Xb 778, 1864.

64. SHAT, Xb 778, 1866.

65. Amiable, *Légionnaire,* note 165.

66. Dabbs, *French Army,* 230, 268.

67. Amiable, *Légionnaire,* note 143; Dabbs, *French Army,* 158.

68. General Daudignac, "La Légion étrangère," *La nouvelle revue,* tome IX (1 March 1909): 7; Dabbs, *French Army,* 226.

69. Etienne Micaud, *La France au Mexique* (Paris: Editions du monde moderne, 1927), 177–213.

70. *Papiers et correspondance de la famille impériale saisis aux Tuileries* (Paris: Imprimerie Nationale, 1871–72), II, 98–99.

71. Dabbs, *French Army,* 230.

72. Sergent, *Camerone,* 247.

73. SHAT, Xb 778, 1866.

74. SHAT, G7 92, 29 March 1865.

75. SHAT, G7 92, 31 March 1865.

76. SHAT, G7 92, 11 April 1865.

77. SHAT, G7 92, 12 April 1865.

78. SHAT, G7 92, January 1865.

79. SHAT, G7 92, 14 July 1865.

80. SHAT, G7 92, 6 February 1867.

81. *Papiers et correspondance de la famille impériale saisis au Tuileries*, II, 216.

82. Grisot, *Légion*, 573.

83. Amiable, *Légionnaire*, note 136.

84. Dabbs, *French Army*, 171.

85. Dabbs, *French Army*, 142.

86. Diesbach, *Notes*, 208–10.

87. Amiable, *Légionnaire*, 150–51.

88. Amiable, *Légionnaire*, 165.

89. Daudignac, "La Légion étrangère," 7.

90. Gaulot, *L'expédition du Mexique*, II, 187–89.

91. Grisot, *Légion*, 309.

92. Zédé, "Souvenirs," no. 373, 46, 53–4, 64.

93. Derruder, *Clemmer*, 240.

94. Diesbach, *Notes*, 129, 137.

95. General Penette and Captain Castaingt, *La Legión Extranjera en la Intervención Francesa, 1863–1867* (Mexico City: Sociedad Mexicana de Geografía y Estadística, 1962), 101–113.

96. Amiable, *Légionnaire*, note 143.

97. Derudder, *Clemmer*, 240.

98. Amiable, *Légionnaire*, 142.

99. *Papiers et correspondance*, 110.

100. Amiable, *Légionnaire*, note 136, note 143.

101. Anthony Kellet, *Combat Motivation. The Behavior of Soldiers in Battle* (Boston, the Hague, London: Kluwer Nijoff, 1982), 107–9.

Chapter 8

1. Grisot and Coulombon, *La Légion étrangère de 1831 à 1887*, 317–26.

2. Henry Dutailly, "1871. Au combat dans le Loiret," *Historia*, no. 414 bis—spécial: *"La Légion étrangère. 150ᵉ anniversaire"* (2nd trimester 1981), 40.

3. Auguste Boucher, *Récits de l'invasion. Journal d'un bourgeois d'Orléans pendant l'occupation prussienne* (Orléans: Herluison, 1871), 168–200.

4. V.-R. Aubin, *La Touraine pendant la guerre de 1870–1871* (Paris and Lille: Taffin-LeFort, 1893), 60–1.

5. Grisot, *Légion*, 338.

6. Grisot, *Légion*, 346.

7. Roger de Beauvoir, *La Légion étrangère* (Paris: Firmin-Didot, 1897), 105–8.

8. Grisot, *Légion*, 358.

9. ALE A2, *1ᵉʳ régiment étranger, 1867–1872*.

10. ALE A2, *1ᵉʳ régiment étranger, 1867–1872*.

11. ALE A2, *1ᵉʳ régiment étranger, 1867–1872*, 28 May 1871.

12. Grisot, *Légion*, 365.

Chapter 9

1. J. N. Gung'l, "La Légion il y a quarante ans," *Légion étrangère*, 1 February 1914: 34.

2. Erwin Rosen, *In the Foreign Legion* (London: Duckworth & Co., 1910), 13.

3. Sylvère, *Flutsch* (Paris: Plon, 1982), 250.

4. Frederic Martyn, *Life in the Legion from a Soldier's Point of View* (New York: Scribner's, 1911), 15.

5. John Patrick Le Poer, *A la légion étrangère: Journal d'un Irlandais* (Paris: Juven, 1906), 13.

6. Ernst Junger, *Jeux africains* (Paris: Gallimard, 1970), 63.

7. Martyn, *Life in the Legion*, 14.

8. Martyn, *Life in the Legion*, 46.

9. Rosen, *In the Foreign Legion*, 41.

10. Charles Poimiro, *La légion étrangère et le droit international* (Paris: Berger-Levrault, 1913), 225–6.

11. Rosen, *In the Foreign Legion*, 9.

12. Le Poer, *A la légion*, 21.

13. Rosen, *In the Foreign Legion*, 16–17.

14. Le Poer, *A la légion*, 22. Joseph Ehrhart met a similar reception from an uncle whom he stopped off to see in Dijon on his way to Algeria in 1906: "He belonged to those uninitiated who used to confuse the Legion with the Bataillon d'Afrique and the discipline companies." Joseph Ehrhart, *Mes treize années de Légion étrangère* (unpublished manuscript, ALE, no page numbers), Chapter I.

15. Rosen, *In the Foreign Legion*, 22.

16. Junger, *Jeux africains*, 138.

17. Martyn, *Life in the Legion*, 51.

18. Ehrhart, *Mes treize années*, Chapter I.

19. Junger, *Jeux africains*, 141.

20. Rosen, *In the Foreign Legion*, 29.

21. Ehrhart, *Mes treize années*, Chapter I.

22. Ehrhart, *Mes treize années*, Chapter I.

23. Sylvère, *Flutsch*, 72.

24. Martyn, *Life in the Legion*, 70.

25. Aristide Merolli, *La grenade héroique: Avant la tourmente* (Casablanca-Fez: Editions Moynier, 1937), 79–80.

26. Rosen, *In the Foreign Legion*, 128.

27. Ehrhart, *Mes treize années*, Chapter I.

28. Luc Dangy, *Moi, légionnaire et Marsouin: Algérie, Nouvelle-Calédonie—Nouvelles-Hébrides, 1902–1913* (Paris: Eugène Figuière, 1932), 30.

29. Gung'l, "La Légion," 34.

30. Martyn, *Life in the Legion*, 87.

31. Jean Pfirmann, *Sergent Pfirmann*, unedited manuscript, ALE, 8.

32. Martyn, *Life in the Legion*, 86.

33. Rosen, *In the Foreign Legion*, 46

34. Merolli, *La grenade*, 86.

35. Ehrhart, *Mes treize années*, Chapter I.

36. Junger, *Jeux africains*, 153–68.

37. Ehrhart, *Mes treize années*, Chapter I.

38. André-Paul Comor, *L'image de la légion étrangère à travers la littérature française, 1900–1970* (Aix-en-Provence: thèse de maîtrise, Université de Provence, 1971), 23.

39. Sylvère, *Flutsch*, 119.

40. Rosen, *In the Foreign Legion*, 46.

41. Dangy, *Moi, légionnaire*, 63.

42. Martyn, *Life in the Legion*, 10.

43. Leon Randin, *A la légion étrangère* (Nêuchatel: Delachaux et Niestlé; and Paris: Fischbacher, 1906), 9.

44. Jean Martin, *Je suis un légionnaire* (Paris: Fayard, 1938), 7.

45. Sylvère, *Flutsch*, 265.

46. Zédé, "Souvenirs de ma vie," no. 366, 439.

47. Georges d'Esparbès, *La légion étrangère* (Paris: Flammarion, 1900), 32–3.

48. Hubert-Jacques, *L'Allemagne et la légion étrangère* (Paris: Chapelot, 1914), 49; Gaston Moch, *La question de la légion étrangère* (Paris: Bibliothèque Charpentier, 1914), 198–9.

49. Merolli, *La grenade héroique*, 33.

50. Rosen, *In the Foreign Legion*, 28.

51. J. Pannier, *Trois ans en Indochine: Notes de voyage* (Toulouse: Société des publications morales et réligieuses, 1906), 157.

52. Ehrhart, *Mes treize années*, Chapter I.

53. Ernst Junger, *Jeux africains*, 172, 176.

54. Roger Cabrol, *L'adaptation à la légion étrangère: Etude socio-psycho-pathologique* (Bordeaux: Thèse pour le doctorat en médecine, Université de Bordeaux II, 1971), 90–2, 111.

55. Sylvère, *Flutsch*, 65.

56. Martyn, *Life in the Legion*, 110–11.

57. Ehrhart, *Mes treize années*, Chapter I.

58. Merolli, *La grenade*, 105, 108–9.

59. Randin, *A la légion*, 10.

60. Ehrhart, *Mes treize années*, Chapter I.

61. Geoffrey Parker, *The Army of Flanders and the Spanish Road* (Cambridge, England: Cambridge University Press, 1972), 41.

62. Martyn, *Life in the Legion*, 17.

63. Martyn, *Life in the Legion*, 11.

64. Gung'l, *"La Légion,"* 35–6.

65. Rosen, *In the Foreign Legion*, 39–40. Junger too noted that the elation of a new life soon gave way to depression, "for, to burn all your boats behind you, you must be a Cortez." *Jeux africains*, 176.

66. Rosen, *In the Foreign Legion*, 53.

67. Charles des Ecorres, *Au pays des étapes: Notes d'un Légionnaire* (Paris: Lavauzelle, 1892), 53.

68. Le Père Pralon, *Lionel Hart, engagé-volontaire sous-officier à la Légion étrangère glorieusement tombé au Tonkin, à 20 ans* (Paris: Retaux-Bray, 1888).

69. Le soldat Silbermann, *Cinq ans à la légion étrangère, dix ans dans l'infanterie de marine: Souvenirs de campagne* (Paris: Plon, 1910), 6.

70. Dangy, *Moi, légionnire*, 53. These exact words could not have been said in 1902, as the Spanish Legion was created only in 1920.

71. Sylvère, *Flutsch*, 82.

72. Des Ecorres, *Au pays*, 268.

73. GM, *La Légion étrangère et les troupes coloniales* (Paris: Chapelot, 1903), 5.

74. Abel Clément-Grandcourt, "Les Alsaciens-Lorrains et la légion étrangère," *Feuilles d'histoire*, 1 June 1910: 556; SHAT, 1H 1015, Desorthès report, December 1908.

75. GM, *La Légion*, 9.

76. Sylvère, *Flutsch*, 79.

77. Randin, *A la légion*, 10.

78. Sylvère, *Flutsch*, 70.

79. SHAT, 3H 148, Trumelet-Faber report, March 1912.

80. Dangy, *Moi, légionnaire*, 30–31.

81. Sylvère, *Flutsch*, 73.

82. Sylvère, *Flutsch*, 248.

83. Sylvère, *Flutsch*, 73–5.

84. Ehrhart, *Mes treize années*, Chapter I.

85. Martyn, *Life in the Legion*, 95.

86. Merolli, *La grenade*, 89.

87. Sylvère, *Flutsch*, 109, 161.

88. Raimund Anton Premschwitz, *Mes aventures à la Légion étrangère*, 62, manuscript preserved in SHAT, 1H 1015. The original German title is *Meine Erlebnisse als Fremdenlegioner in Algerien* (Metz: Muller, 1904). All numbers are from the manuscript.

89. Roger de Beauvoir, *La Légion étrangère*, 8–9.

90. Le Poer, *A Modern Legionary*, 24.

91. Rosen, *In the Foreign Legion*, 78.

92. Merolli, *La grenade héroique*, 99.

93. Cabrol, *L'adaptation à la légion étrangère*, 96.

94. Sylvère, *Flutsch*, 79–80.

95. Rosen, *In the Foreign Legion*, 81–2.

96. Rosen, *In the Foreign Legion*, 103.

97. Sylvère, *Flutsch*, 143–4.

98. Rosen, *In the Foreign Legion*, 277, 248.

99. SHAT, 3H 1015, 20 November 1905.

100. Rosen, *In the Foreign Legion*, 105.

101. Rosen, *In the Foreign Legion*, 59–60

102. Rosen, *In the Foreign Legion*, 108–9.

103. M.M., *Memoirs of the Foreign Legion* (New York: Knopf, 1925), 187.

104. Ehrhart, *Mes treize années*, Chapter I.

105. M.M., *Memoirs*, 127.

106. Rosen, *In the Foreign Legion*, 85.

107. Ehrhart, *Mes treize années*, Chapter I.

108. Sylvère, *Flutsch*, 78–9.

109. Martyn, *Life in the Legion*, 112–13.

110. Junger, *Jeux africains*, 173.

111. Ehrhart, *Mes trêize années*, Chapter I.

112. Martyn, *Life in the Legion*, 113.

113. Premschwitz, *Mes aventures à la légion étrangère*, 55.

114. Martyn, *Life in the Legion*, 113.

115. Rosen, *In the Foreign Legion*, 159.

116. Dangy, *Moi, légionnaire*, 72.

117. Premschwitz, *Mes aventures*, 124.

118. Sylvère, *Flutsch*, 99–100.

119. Pralon, *Engagé-volontaire*, 146–7.

120. Premschwitz, *Mes aventures*, 144–5.

121. Rosen, *In the Foreign Legion*, 166–9.

122. Ehrhart, *Mes treize années*, Chapter IV.

123. Rosen, *In the Foreign Legion*, 164–5.

124. Sylvère, *Flutsch*, 101–2.

125. Sylvère, *Flutsch*, 68.

126. Sylvère, *Flutsch*, 68.

127. Jean-Louis Armengaud, *Le Sud oranais: Journal d'un légionnaire. Treize mois de colonne pendant l'insurrection des Ouled-sidi-cheik soulevés par le Marabout Bou-Amama, 1881–82* (Paris: Charles-Lavauzelle, 1893), 57.

128. Sylvère, *Flutsch*, 93.

129. Premschwitz, *Mes aventures*, 107; Merolli, *La grenade*, 88–9.

130. Richard Holmes, *Acts of War. The Behavior of Men in Battle* (New York: Free Press, 1986), 45–6.

131. Pfirmann, *Sergent Pfirmann*, 7.

132. Premschwitz, *Mes aventures*, 62–3.

133. Merolli, *La grenade*, 99–100.

134. Le comte de Villebois Mareuil, "La légion étrangère," *Revue des Deux Mondes*, 15 April 1896: 886–7.

135. Pralon, *Engagé-volontaire*, 156.

136. Pfirmann, *Sergent Pfirmann*, 56, 73.

137. Pfirmann, *Sergent Pfirmann*, 56.

138. Hubert-Jacques, *L'Allemagne et la légion étrangère*, 146–7.

139. Villebois Mareuil, "La Légion étrangère," 887.

140. Sylvère, *Flutsch*, 66.

141. GM, *La légion étrangère et les troupes coloniales*, 16–17.

142. Villebois Mareuil, "La légion étrangère," 886.

143. SHAT, 7N 106.

144. Martyn, *Life in the Legion*, 281.

145. Clément-Grandcourt, "Les Alsaciens-Lorrains et la légion étrangère," 561.

146. Sylvère, *Flutsch*, 69–70. The discipline companies were established in 1875. They were distinct from the *Bats d'Af*, the penal units into which young men who had civilian criminal records were sent to do their military service.

147. SHAT, 1H 1015, 10 March 1906.

148. Dangy, *Moi, légionnaire*, 47.

149. Rosen, *In the Foreign Legion*, 93–4.

150. Premschwitz, *Mes aventures*, 113.

151. Richard Holmes *Acts of War*, 40–3.

152. Sylvère, *Flutsch*, 115.

153. Martin, *Je suis légionnaire*, 113.

154. Dangy, *Moi, légionnaire*, 127–45.

155. Rosen, *In the Foreign Legion*, 96.

156. Rosen, *In the Foreign Legion*, 93–4.

157. Sylvère, *Flutsch*, 85–6.

158. Dangy, *Moi, légionnaire*, 49–50.

159. Le Poer, *A la légion*, 65.

160. Rosen, *In the Foreign Legion*, 61.

161. Sylvère, *Flutsch*, 145.

162. Jean Martin, *Je suis un légionnaire*, 114.

163. Sylvère, *Flutsch*, 67. Dangy believed that fighting was the way in which men who were unable to confide in anyone protected their privacy: "This demonstration of their physical vigor allows them to remain alone with their conscience and their soul." Dangy, *Moi, légionnaire*, 49–50.

164. Sylvère, *Flutsch*, 206.

165. Le Poer, *A la légion*, 196.

166. Le Poer, *A Modern Legionary*, 23.

167. Sylvère, *Flutsch*, 158–9.

168. Le Poer, *A la légion*, 106–12.

169. Martin, *Je suis un légionnaire*, 115.

170. Raoul Béric, *Les Routiers. La légion étrangère: Source d'admiration et de pitié* (Paris: L'édition moderne, 1907), 65.

171. Le Poer, *A Modern Legionary*, 23.

172. Dangy, *Moi, légionnaire*, 45.

173. Rosen, *In the Foreign Legion*, 124.

174. Merolli, *La grenade*, 92, 119.

175. Des Ecorres, *Au pays*, 335–6.

176. Le Poer, *A la légion*, 54.

177. Dangy, *Moi, légionnaire*, 51.

178. Béric, *Les routiers*, 158.

CHAPTER 10

1. Charles Meyer, *La vie quotidienne des français en Indochine, 1860–1910* (Paris: Hachette, 1985), 153.

2. Henry McAleavy, *Black Flags in Vietnam: The Story of a Chinese Intervention. The Tonkin War of 1884–85* (New York: Macmillan, 1968), 242; A. Thomazi, *La conquête de l'Indochine* (Paris: Payot, 1934), 196, lists twenty-one dead, seventy-one killed and two missing.

3. McAleavy, *Black Flags*, 256; Thomazi, *La conquête de l'Indochine*, 214.

4. McAleavy, *Black Flags*, 257–8.

5. Pralan, *Lionel Hart*, 189.

6. For a discussion of the Formosa campaign, see Captain Garnot, *L'expédition française de Formose, 1884–1885* (Paris: Delagrave, 1894).

7. Bôn-Mat, *Souvenirs d'un légionnaire* (Paris: Albert Messein, 1914), 23.

8. L. Huguet, *En colonne. Souvenirs d'extrême-Orient* (Paris: Flammarion, nd), 26–7.

9. Martyn, *Life in the Legion*, 148.

10. L. Huguet, *En colonne*, 25–27, 73.

11. Dick de Lonlay, *Au Tonkin, 1883–1885. Récits anecdotiques* (Paris: Garnier, 1886), 499.

12. Le Poer, *A Modern Legionary*, 118.

13. Bernard Savelli, *La Légion étrangère au Tonkin: des origines à 1914* (Aix-en-Provence: mémoire de maîtrise, 1971), 38.

14. A.-P. Maury, *Mes campagnes au Tonkin* (Lyon: Vitte et Perrussel, 1888), 77, 211–12.

15. Bôn-Mat, *Souvenirs*, 173–4.

16. Pralan, *Lionel Hart*, 214.

17. Le Poer, *A Modern Legionary*, 133–4.

18. Maury, *Mes campagnes*, 95.

19. Maury, *Mes campagnes*, 228.

20. Pralan, *Lionel Hart*, 128.

21. Charles Des Ecorres, *Au pays des étapes*, 261.

22. Le Poer, *A la Légion*, 158.

23. Captain G. Prokos, *Opérations coloniales. Tactique des petits détachements. Vol. II. Chine et Indochine* (Paris: Charles-Lavauzelle, nd), 35.

24. Le Poer, *A Modern Legionary*, 173.

25. Le Poer, *A Modern Legionary*, 113–14, 138, 166.

26. Louis Carpeaux, *La chasse aux pirates* (Paris: Grasset, 1913), 165.

27. Le Poer, *A Modern Legionary*, 134–5.

28. Le Poer, *A Modern Legionary*, 143.

29. Martyn, *Life in the Legion*, 167.

30. Huguet, *En colonne*, 35–43.

31. Bôn-Mat, *Souvenirs*, 142.

32. Bôn-Mat, *Souvenirs*, 147–8.

33. *Notes sur la campagne du 3ᵉ bataillon de la Légion étrangère au Tonkin* (Paris and Limoges: Charles-Lavauzelle, 1888), 13–15.

34. Bôn-Mat, *Souvenirs*, 149.

35. *Notes . . . du 3ᵉ bataillon*, 20.

36. Hubert Lyautey, *Lettres du Tonkin et de Madagascar, 1894–1899* (Paris: Armand Colin, 1942), 90.

37. Grisot and Coulombon, *La Légion étrangère de 1831 à 1887*, 447.

38. Captain Champs, *Le siège de Tuyen-Quan. Récit anecdotique par un témoin oculaire* (Verdun: Freschard, 1902), 5.

39. Theophile Boisset, *Tuyen-Quan pendant le siège* (Paris: Fischbacher, 1885), 7.

40. Boisset, *Tuyen-Quan*, 23.

41. Grisot, *Légion étrangère*, 449; Edmond Marc Dominé, *Journal du siège. Place de Tuyen-Quan* (manuscript, ALE, 22–23 February 1885. The published edition was printed by Charles-Lavauzelle, Paris, 1885.).

42. Dominé, *Journal*, 28 February.

43. Dominé, *Journal du siège de Tuyen-Quan.* See also Théophile Boisset, *Tuyen-Quan pendant la guerre* (Paris: Fischbacher, 1885), 23. Boisset was the Protestant pastor attached to the Legion at Tuyen Quang.

44. Huguet, *En colonne*, 97.

45. Boisset, *Tuyen-Quan*, 28–9.

CHAPTER 11

1. Louis Carpeaux, *La chasse aux pirates*, 5. Carpeaux's souvenirs were based upon his experiences in 1894–1895 when he was serving as a Legion sergeant in the Lao Kay region of Tonkin. They were first published under the pseudonym Henri Niéllé, "La chasse aux pirates. Souvenirs d'une expédition au Tonkin," *Le Journal des voyages*, numbers of 5 August–26 September 1906.

2. L. Huguet, *En colonne*, 48–9.

3. Huguet, *En colonne*, 109.

4. Frederic Martyn, *Life in the Legion*, 122–3.

5. Sergeant Ernest Bolis, *Mémoires d'un sous-officier. Mes campagnes en Afrique et en Asie de 1889–1899* (Châlon-sur-Saône: Imprimerie du Courrier de Saône-et-Loire, 1905), 61.

6. Charles Meyer, *La vie quotidienne*, 179.

7. Colonel Tournyol du Clos, "La Légion étrangère au Tonkin (1883–1932). Le siège de Tuyen-Quan (20 janvier–3 mars 1885)," *La revue d'infanterie*, no. 525, vol. 89 (1 May 1936): 859.

8. Le Poer, *A la Légion étrangère*, 44–5.

9. John Le Poer, *A Modern Legionary* (New York: Dutton, 1905), 91.

10. "Notes d'un sergent de la vieille légion," *Vert et rouge*, no. 83 (1952): 31.

11. Leon Randin, *A la Légion étrangère*, 214–16.

12. SHAT, 7N 100.

13. SHAT, 7N 106, 1909 report.

14. Joseph Erhart, *Mes treize années*, Chapters IV & V.

15. Ehrhart, *Mes treize années*, Chapter V.

16. Ehrhart, *Mes treize années*, Chapter V.

17. Ernest Junger, *Jeux africains*, 126.

18. Meyer, *La vie quotidienne*, 265, 267.

19. Ehrhart, *Mes treize années*, Chapter V.

20. Bôn-Mat, *Souvenirs d'un légionnaire*, 130.

21. Meyer, *Vie quotidienne*, 259.

22. Junger, *Jeux africains*, 128.

23. Silbermann, *Cinq ans à la Légion*, 132.

24. Bôn-Mat, *Souvenirs*, 93, 101, 169.

25. Ehrhart, *Mes treize années*, Chapter V.

26. Meyer, *Vie quotidienne*, 262–3.

27. Martyn, *Life in the Legion*, 120.

28. Bolis, *Mémoires*, 14.

29. Correspondence of Lucien Jacqueline, 1902–1907, papers in the possession of Richard Mahaud, letter of 15 October 1906.

30. Bolis, *Mémoires*, 14.

31. Martyn, *Life in the Legion*, 122–3.

32. Pralan, *Lionel Hart*, 174–5.

33. Bolis, *Mémoires*, 17.

34. Martyn, *Life in the Legion*, 124.

35. *Notes sur la campagne du 3ᵉ bataillon*, 5–7.

36. Pralan, *Lionel Hart*, 178–80.

37. Silbermann, *Cinq ans à la Légion*, 85.

38. Lieutenant Colonel A. Ditte, *Observations sur la guerre dans les colonies. Organisation—exécution. Conférences faites à l'école supérieure de la guerre* (Paris: Charles-Lavauzelle, 1905), 355.

39. Junger, *Jeux africains*, 125.

40. Evelyn Waugh, *When the Going Was Good* (London: Penguin, 1975), 74.

41. Silbermann, *Cinq ans à la Légion*, 85.

42. Pralan, *Lionel Hart*, 174–5.

43. Le Poer, *A Modern Legionary*, 101–2.

44. Le Poer, *A Modern Legionary*, 104–5.
45. *Notes, ... du 3ᵉ bataillon*, 10.
46. Martyn, *Life in the Legion*, 126–8.
47. Pfirmann, *Le sergent Pfirmann*, 181.
48. Le Poer, *A Modern Legionary*, 107–10. As stated previously Le Poer's work contains inaccuracies, and the sequence of events is sometimes confused. This has caused one Legion scholar to express doubts to this author upon its authenticity as a source. The confusions are probably due to the fact that Le Poer enlisted at age sixteen and compiled his memoirs some twenty years after the events described. It is also possible that it was ghost-written, as Le Poer had little formal schooling, and given a dramatic conclusion to make it more marketable. However, Le Poer obviously served in Tonkin in this period. The sentiments and attitudes of Le Poer appear perfectly plausible ones to this author, even if the detail of events recounted is sometimes muddled.
49. Lyautey, *Lettres du Tonkin*, 73.
50. Lyautey, *Lettres du Tonkin*, 78.
51. Lyautey, *Lettres de Tonkin*, 74.
52. Bôn-Mat, *Souvenirs*, 91.
53. A.-P. Maury, *Mes campagnes au Tonkin*, 73.
54. Martyn, *Life in the Legion*, 131–2.
55. J. Pannier, *Trois ans en Indochine*, 131.
56. McAleavy, *Black Flags*, 271–2.
57. SHAT, 10H 3, 18 March 1885 report.
58. Dick de Lonlay, *Au Tonkin*, 514–15.
59. Bôn-Mat, *Souvenirs*, 168, 171–2.
60. Bôn-Mat, *Souvenirs*, 165–6, 171.
61. Le Poer, *A Modern Legionary*, 143–4.
62. McAleavy, *Black Flags*, 274.
63. Philippe Franchini, *Les guerres d'indochine* (Paris: Pygmalion, 1988), Vol. 1, 104.
64. McAleavy, *Black Flags*, 273.
65. SHAT, 3H 10, 22 April 1885 Négrier report.
66. SHAT, 3H 10, Négrier report.
67. Maury, *Mes campagnes*, 193–4.
68. Maury, *Mes campagnes*, 194–6.
69. Bôn-Mat, *Souvenirs*, 177, 179.
70. Le Poer, *A Modern Legionary* 145.
71. See SHAT, 10H 19 for an account of the battle.
72. Bôn-Mat, *Souvenirs*, 181.
73. ALE A4, 1ᵉʳ régiment étranger d'infanterie, "Historique des faits," 24 March 1885.
74. *Notes*, 44.
75. Bôn-Mat, *Souvenirs*, 188–9.
76. SHAT, 10H 16, *"Rapport sur l'évacuation et la retraite de Lang-son à Chu,"* 14 April 1885.
77. SHAT, 10H 16, Diguet's report.
78. Maury, *Mes campagnes*, 215–17.
79. Le Poer, *A Modern Legionary*, 160.
80. McAleavy, *Black Flags*, 264–277.
81. The case against Herbinger's decision to retreat rested essentially upon two arguments. The first is that the Chinese had been so badly defeated before Lang Son that, according to Négrier, ". . . the enemy no longer wants to attack and it is useless to evacuate" (SHAT, 3H 10). As proof, Négrier cited the fact that the French retreat was not pressed by the Chinese. However, Major Schaeffer, commander of the 3rd Battalion of the Legion, reported that, although driven back, "[the enemy] had shown his great numbers and had demonstrated a great energy in the attack of the fort. It was obvious that he would begin again the next day and with fresh troops taken from his reserves." As proof of this, the

Chinese had left their flags planted on the crests of the hills (SHAT, 3H 10, Schaeffer report, 4 April 1885). And in Hanoi, General Brière de l'Isle sent a telegram of panic to Paris insisting that the Chinese were on the offensive and had a strategic plan to invest the delta (McAleavy, *Black Flags*, 272).

The second argument concentrates on the ability of the garrison to withstand a second attack and/or a siege. Captain R. Carteron insisted that there was plenty of food and munitions at Lang Son (*Souvenirs de la campagne du Tonkin*, Paris: L. Baudoin, 1891, note 219, 293). However, the garrison had been on half-rations for some days, the artillery shells were virtually exhausted, and, according to Dick de Lonlay, the soldiers were down to seventeen bullets per man (*Au Tonkin*, 531). If this were true, then a second determined Chinese attack against the 3,700-man garrison would have succeeded. The least that can be said is that there was utter confusion over the state of supplies and munitions at Lang Son, that the French had encountered immense logistical problems in the campaign, and that they might have experienced extreme difficulty in extricating a besieged garrison before it succumbed.

Herbinger's real problem appears to have been his unpopularity among colonial officers in Tonkin, for whom he was a "metropolitan" outsider and a professor to boot, men whom they contemptuously dismissed as "mandarins." This view seems to have been typified by General Gustave Borgnis-Desbordes, who described the retreat from Lang Son as "the unorganized flight of a brigade left in the hands of a very knowledgeable man, an ex-professor of the *école de guerre*, certainly intelligent, with a laudable theoretical knowledge of his profession, but absolutely losing his head on the spot in practical war conditions which are not books. . . . When General Brière [de l'Isle] told me on the evening of the 28th that the brigade was retreating under the command of Colonel Herbinger . . . an ex-professor at the *école de guerre*, I told him: 'Then we're buggered,' and I was right." (Marcel Blanchard, "La correspondance de Félix Faure touchant les affaires coloniales, 1882–98." *Revue d'histoire des colonies françaises*, vol. 42, no. 147 [1955], 159.)

82. Franchini, *Les guerres*, 105.
83. G. Prokos, *Opérations coloniales*, II, 164.
84. Pfirmann, *Le Sergent Pfirmann*, 59–60.
85. Martyn, *Life in the Legion*, 176–7.
86. Carpeaux, *La chasse aux pirates*, 114–15, 270.
87. Commandant Chabrol, *Opérations militaires au Tonkin* (Paris: Charles-Lavauzelle, 1896), 267.
88. Carpeaux, *La chasse aux pirates*, 34–35.
89. Martyn, *Life in the Legion*, 130–31.
90. Chabrol, *Opérations*, 269.
91. Carpeaux, *La chasse aux pirates*, 180.
92. Carpeaux, *La chasse aux pirates*, 53.
93. Martyn, *Life in the Legion*, 170.
94. Le soldat Silbermann, *Cinq ans à la Légion*, 143.
95. Lyautey, *Lettres du Tonkin et de Madagascar*, 259.
96. Bôn-Mat, *Souvenirs d'un légionnaire*, 138–9.
97. Carpeaux, *La chasse aux pirates*, 64–5.
98. A.-P. Maury, *Mes campagnes*, 178.
99. Chabrol, *Opérations*, 18.
100. Pfirmann, *Le Sergent Pfirmann*, 157.
101. Carpeaux, *La chasse*, 37.
102. Le Poer, *A Modern Legionary* 182.
103. Martyn, *Life in the Legion*, 171–2.
104. Pfirmann, *Le Sergent Pfirmann*, 69, 74, 82–3.
105. Carpeaux, *La chasse*, 94–5, 185–6.
106. Prokos, *Opérations coloniales*, II, 134.
107. Sylvère, *Flutsch*, 64.
108. Colonel Tournyol du Clos, "La Légion étrangère au Tonkin (1883–1932)," 859–60.

109. Chabrol, *Opérations militaires*, 297–304.
110. Lyautey, *Lettres de Tonkin*, 182.
111. Carpeaux, *La chasse aux pirates*, 84.
112. Le Poer, *A Modern Legionary* 127.
113. Carpeaux, *La chasse aux pirates*, 46–9.
114. Sylvère, *Flutsch*, 64.
115. Le Poer, *A Modern Legionary* 127.
116. Carpeaux, *La chasse aux pirates*, 42, 215–16.
117. Chabrol, *Opérations*, 19.
118. Carpeaux, *La chasse aux pirates*, 100.
119. Carpeaux, *La chasse aux pirates*, 238–39.
120. Prokos, *Opérations coloniales*, II, 138, 167–8.
121. Chabrol, *Opérations*, 196–200.
122. Claude Farrère, *Extrême-Orient* (Paris: Flammarion, 1934), 55–57.
123. Carpeaux, *La chasse aux pirates*, 201, 203, 213.

CHAPTER 12

1. Martyn, *Life in the Legion*, 184–5.
2. Captain Jacquot, *Mon Journal de Marche du Dahomey, 1892–1893*, unpublished manuscript in possession of the author. No page numbers, 20–21 July 1892.
3. SHAT, 10H 3.
4. General Viscount Wolseley, *The Soldier's Pocket-Book for Field Service* (London: Macmillan and Co., 1886), 414–15.
5. SHAT, 10H 3.
6. SHAT, Dahomey carton 1, 13 April 1892.
7. Henri Paul Lelièvre, *Campagne du Dahomey, 2 août 1892 au 6 novembre 1892*, unedited manuscript, ALE Aubagne, 98–98bis.
8. Lieutenant Colonel A. Ditte, *Observations sur la guerre*, 40–1.
9. Jean-Louis Lentonnet, *Carnet de campagne du lieutenant-colonel Lentonnet* (Paris: Plon, 1899), 140.
10. A. S. Kanya-Forstner, *The Conquest of the Western Sudan: A Study in French Military Imperialism* (Cambridge, England: Cambridge University Press, 1969), 272. Kanya-Forstner continues: "The dreary lines of chained bearers which accompanied the Voulet-Chanoine expedition were the same as those which followed the armies of Samori. The much vaunted *villages de liberté,* supposedly the Military's chief contribution to the fight against the slave trade, were little more than a means of alleviating the labour shortage along the supply lines. Freed slaves who were not sent to the villages where they could be used as porters were usually conscripted into the *tirailleurs* just as prisoners had been drafted into the armies of Umar" (272–3).
11. Charles Balesi, *From Adversaries to Comrades-in-Arms: West Africans and the French Military, 1885–1918* (Waltham, Mass.: Press Crossroads, 1986), 41.
12. Kanya-Forstner, *Western Sudan*, 228.
13. André Lebon, *La Pacification de Madagascar, 1896–1898* (Paris: Plon, 1928), 242.
14. See Porch, *The Conquest of the Sahara*, Chapter XII.
15. The military and administrative dividing lines in the French colonies were enough to confuse Frenchmen, let alone foreigners. The French essentially had two colonial armies. The *Armée d'Afrique,* which included the Legion, nominally made up the 19th Corps metropolitan army. However, its responsibilites were for North Africa. The *armée coloniale,* the old *troupes de marine,* belonged to the navy until 1900, when it was transferred to the war ministry. These marines provided regiments of white volunteers as well as white officers and NCOs for native regiments raised in sub-Saharan Africa, Indochina and eventually Madagascar. A number of marine regiments made up principally of conscripts also served in France.

Administrative divisions were equally confusing. Algeria, considered part of metropolitan France, fell under the jurisdiction of the Ministry of the Interior. Tunisia and Morocco were protectorates, and therefore overseen by the *quai d'Orsay*, the French foreign ministry. France's remaining possessions were administered by the navy until a colonial ministry was finally created.

16. Martyn, *Life in the Legion*, 186–7.

17. "O it's Tommy this, an' Tommy that, an 'Tommy go away'; / But it's 'Thank you Mister Atkins,' when the band begins to play."

18. Martyn, *Life in the Legion*, 188. According to Alexandre d'Albeca, *La France au Dahomey* (Paris: Hachette, 1895), the second ship was named simply the "Saint-Nicolas."

19. Jacquot, *Mon journal*, 27 August 1892.

20. Martyn, *Life in the Legion*, 192.

21. Lelièvre, *Campagne*, 9.

22. Martyn, *Life in the Legion*, 192–3.

23. Jacquot, *Mon journal*, 31 August 1892.

24. Lelièvre, *Campagne au Dahomey*, 20–1.

25. Commandant Grandin, *A l'assault du pays des noirs: Le Dahomey* (Paris: René Haton Librairie, 1895), I, 25–6.

26. "*Rapport sur les opérations du corps expéditionnaire du Dahomey en 1892,*" SHAT, Dahomey carton 2. See also *La Légion étrangère au Dahomey. Resumé très succinct des motifs de notre intervention,*" ALE Aubagne, L4.

27. Alfred Barbou, *Histoire de la guerre au Dahomey* (Paris: Librairie Duquesne, 1893), 30.

28. R. A. Kea, "Firearms and Warfare in the Gold Coasts from the 16th to the 19th Centuries," *Journal of African History*, 12 (1971): 185–213.

29. David Ross, "Dahomey," in Michael Crowder (ed.), *West African Resistance: The Military Response to Colonial Occupation* (New York: Africana, 1972), 147.

30. Ross, "Dahomey," 154–6.

31. On the "Race for Lake Chad," see Porch, *The Conquest of the Sahara*, Chapter XIII.

32. Kanya-Forstner, *The Conquest of the Western Sudan*, 239.

33. Martyn, *Life in the Legion*, 195.

34. Jacquot, *Mon journal*, 2 September 1892.

35. Lelièvre, *Campagne*, 21–3.

36. Lelièvre, *Campagne*, 37.

37. Jacquot, *Mon journal*, 19 September.

38. Martyn, *Life in the Legion*, 196.

39. Lelièvre, *Campagne*, 62.

40. J. Bern, *L'expédition du Dahomey: Notes éparses d'un volontaire* (Sidi-bel-Abbès: Lavenue, 1893), 145.

41. Martyn, *Life in the Legion*, 196.

42. Lelièvre, *Campagne*, 63.

43. Jacquot, *Mon journal*, 19 October.

44. Martyn, *Life in the Legion*, 197.

45. Lelièvre, *Campagne*, 64. Two officers and three soldiers were killed, and nine soldiers wounded ("La Légion étrangère au Dahomey," ALE, A4, 28).

46. Martyn, *Life in the Legion*, 198.

47. Jacquot, *Mon journal*, 19 September.

48. Jacquot, *Mon journal*, 19 September.

49. Lelièvre, *Campagne*, 66, 68.

50. Jacquot, *Mon journal*, 19 September.

51. Jacquot, *Mon journal*, 19 September.

52. Lelièvre, *Campagne*, 72.

53. Martyn, *Life in the Legion*, 203.

54. Jacquot, *Mon journal*, 21 September.

55. Lelièvre, *Campagne*, 74–6.

56. "La Légion étrangère au Dahomey: Resumé très succinct," 26–27.

57. Martyn, *Life in the Legion*, 206.

58. Lelièvre, *Campagne*, 93.

59. Martyn, *Life in the Legion*, 206–7.

60. J. Bern, *Expédition*, 187.

61. Lelièvre, *Campagne*, 94–5.

62. Jacquot, *Mon journal*, 4 October.

63. Jacquot, *Mon journal*, 4 October.

64. Lelièvre, *Campagne*, 97.

65. Martyn, *Life in the Legion*, 211.

66. Martyn, *Life in the Legion*, 212.

67. Jacquot, *Journal*, 6 October.

68. *Rapport sur les opérations du corps expéditionnaire du Dahomey en 1892,* SHAT, Dahomey carton 1, 42–4.

69. Lelièvre, *Campagne*, 110.

70. *Rapport*, 45–6.

71. Martyn, *Life in the Legion*, 218.

72. Jacquot, *Mon journal*, 14 October.

73. Jacquot, *Mon journal*, 14 October.

74. Martyn, *Life in the Legion*, 226.

75. Michael Crowder, *West African Resistance*, 161.

76. Jacquot, *Mon journal*, 21 October.

77. Martyn, *Life in the Legion*, 214.

78. Jacquot, *Mon journal*, 1 November.

79. *Rapport*, 63.

80. Ed. Aublet, *La guerre au Dahomey, 1888–1893* (Paris: Berger-Levrault, 1894), 320–21.

81. Jules Poirier, *Conquête de Madagascar, 1895–1896* (Paris: Charles-Lavauzelle, nd), 121–2.

82. Aublet, *La guerre au Dahomey*, 326.

83. Ross, "Dahomey," 162–4.

CHAPTER 13

1. General Reibell, *Le calvaire de Madagascar: Notes et souvenirs de 1895* (Paris: Berger-Levrault, 1935), 50.

2. G. Hanotaux, *L'affaire de Madagascar* (Paris: Calmann-Lévy, 1896), 190.

3. Reibell, *Le calvaire*, 48–9.

4. Poirier, *Conquête*, 121–2.

5. Reibell, *Le calvaire*, 100.

6. Reibell, *Le calvaire*, 39.

7. Poirier, *Conquête*, 117–120.

8. E. F. Knight, *Madagascar in Wartime* (London: Longmans Green & Co., 1895), 162.

9. Knight, *Madagascar*, 209–10.

10. Bennet Burleigh, *Two Campaigns: Madagascar and Ashantee* (London: T. Fisher Unwin, 1896), 173.

11. Knight, *Madagascar*, 210.

12. Silbermann, *Cinq ans à la Légion*, 88.

13. Knight, *Madagascar*, 188.

14. Knight, *Madagascar*, 229.

15. Lieutenant Langlois, *Souvenirs de Madagascar* (Paris: Charles-Lavauzelle, 1897), 76–7, 89.

16. Lieutenant Colonel Jean-Louis Lentonnet, *Carnet de campagne du Lieutenant-colonel Lentonnet* (Paris: Plon, 1899), 66–7.

17. SHAT, Madagascar carton 7, *"Rapport sur l'organisation du service de santé."*

18. Lentonnet, *Carnets,* 68.

19. Reibell, *Calvaire,* 86.

20. Colonel X . . . , *La vérité sur la guerre de Madagascar* (Toulouse: Berthoumieu, 1896), 94.

21. Silbermann, *Le soldat Silbermann,* 204–5.

22. Langlois, *Souvenirs,* 34.

23. Langlois, *Souvenirs,* 97.

24. Reibell, *Calvaire,* 85.

25. Langlois, *Souvenirs,* 114.

26. Reibell, *Calvaire,* 83.

27. Reibell, *Calvaire,* 119.

28. Ditte, *Observations,* 35–6.

29. Reibell, *Calvaire,* 83.

30. Lentonnet, *Carnet de campagne,* 60, 109.

31. Langlois, *Souvenirs,* 96–7.

32. Reibell, *Calvaire,* 115–16.

33. Aublet, *La guerre au Dahomey,* 193, 197.

34. Reibell, *Calvaire,* 115.

35. Langlois, *Souvenirs,* 100.

36. *"Rapport d'ensemble sur l'expédition de Madagascar (1895–1896),"* *Journal officiel,* 12 September 1896, 5113. Published by Berger-Levrault, Paris and Nancy, 1897.

37. Reibell, *Calvaire,* 104.

38. Langlois, *Souvenirs,* 116.

39. *"Rapport d'ensemble,"* 14 September 1896, 5158.

40. Langlois, *Souvenirs,* 117–18.

41. Langlois, *Souvenirs,* 123–4. See also SHAT, Madagascar carton 19, Duchesne report, 54–5.

42. Langlois, *Souvenirs,* 134.

43. *"Rapport d'ensemble,"* 14 September 1896, 5161.

44. Knight, *Madagascar in Wartime,* 238, 249, 250–1, 264, 266.

45. Langlois, *Souvenirs,* 114, 141.

46. Lentonnet, *Carnet,* 102, 138.

47. Langlois, *Souvenirs,* 140.

48. R. A. Premschwitz, *Mes aventures;* Sylvère, *Flutsch,* 282.

49. Martyn, *Life,* 286.

50. Jacques Weygand, *Légionnaire* (Paris: Flammarion, 1951), 206–7.

51. Bernard Savelli, *La Légion étrangère au Tonkin,* 111.

52. SHAT, Madagascar carton 7, *Journal de marche, 1ᵉ et 2ᵉ régiments d'Algérie,* 62. See also carton 19, Duchesne report.

53. Weygand, *Légionnaire,* 216.

54. Langlois, *Souvenirs,* 140.

55. Langlois, *Souvenirs,* 141.

56. Langlois, *Souvenirs,* 143.

57. Langlois, *Souvenirs,* 144.

58. *"Rapport d'ensemble,"* 5161.

59. Reibell, *Calvaire,* 119.

60. SHAT, Madagascar carton 7, *Journal de marche,* 53.

61. Knight, *Madagascar,* 282–3.

62. Langlois, *Souvenirs,* 159–60.

63. Knight, *Madagascar,* 284.

64. Langlois, *Souvenirs,* 160.

65. *"Rapport d'ensemble,"* 5162.

66. Langlois, *Souvenirs,* 163–4.

67. Knight, *Madagascar,* 281.

68. *"Rapport d'ensemble,"* 5163.

69. Langlois, *Souvenirs*, 168.
70. Langlois, *Souvenirs*, 178.
71. Knight, *Madagascar*, 303–4.
72. Tony Geraghty, *March or Die: France and the Foreign Legion* (London: Grafton, 1986), 114; Philippe Cart-Tanneur and Tibor Szecske, *Le premier étranger* (Paris: Sterling, 1986), 39. Langlois, who claims to have been present when these remarks were made, reproduces an effusive, but slightly less categorical, version of Duchesne's remarks (*Souvenirs*, 186–8).
73. Balesi, *From Adversaries to Comrades-in-Arms*, 41.
74. Ditte, *Observations*, 354–5.
75. Silbermann, *Le soldat Silbermann*, 74–5.
76. Martyn, *Life in the Legion*, 247, 249.
77. SHAT, Dahomey carton 1; Alfred Barbou, "*Histoire de la guerre au Dahomey*," manuscript 14.
78. Duchesne, *Rapport*, 401–2.
79. Reibell, *Calvaire*, 174.
80. Knight, *Madagascar*, 304, 334.
81. Reibell, *Calvaire*, Annex IV.
82. SHAT, Dahomey carton 1, March 7, 1893.
83. Reibell, *Calvaire*, 122.
84. Reibell, *Calvaire*, Annex IV.
85. Lentonnet, *Carnet*, 121.
86. SHAT, Madagascar carton 7, *Journal de marche*, vol. I, 62.
87. SHAT, Madagascar carton 19, Duchesne's report. Compare with *Rapport*, 401.
88. *Képi blanc*, no. 125 (September 1957), 56–9.
89. Sonia Howe, *The Drama of Madagascar* (London: Methuen, 1938), 320.

CHAPTER 14

1. Moch, *La question*, 164. See also Grisot, *Légion*, 579–81, for texts.
2. Clément-Grandcourt, "*Les Alsaciens-Lorrains et la Légion étrangère*," 556.
3. SHAT, 10H 3.
4. Clément-Grandcourt, "*Les Alsaciens-Lorrains*," 556.
5. SHAT, 1H 1015, 20 November 1905 report.
6. Henri Dugard, *La Légion étrangère* (Paris: Les Marches de l'Est, 1914), 139.
7. Moch, *La question*, 164.
8. Clément-Grandcourt, "*Les Alsaciens-Lorrains*," 557.
9. Clément-Grandcourt, "*Les Alsaciens-Lorrains*," 559–60.
10. Béric, *Les routiers*, 59, 274.
11. SHAT, 1H 1015, 31 May 1905.
12. SHAT, 1H 1015, 20 November 1905.
13. Clément-Grandcourt, "*Les Alsaciens-Lorrains*," 560.
14. SHAT, 3H 148, 1913.
15. SHAT, 3H 148, 25 February 1913.
16. SHAT, 1H 1015, Mangin report.
17. Elisabeth Erulin, *Les nationalités à la Légion étrangère* (Paris: Mémoire DESS de Défense, Université de Paris II, 1982–83), 6/A. See also Dugard, *La Légion étrangère*, 139, who says that in 1913 17.6 percent of legionnaires were German.
18. SHAT, 1H 1015, 20 November 1905 report.
19. Erulin, *Les nationalités à la légion étrangère*, 2/F.
20. SHAT, 3H 148, 12 March 1913. Moch, *La question*, 146–8, disputes these figures, arguing that the official figures count only reenlistments in France, ignoring the strength of cadres and those enlisting in North Africa. The true numbers in the Legion, he claims, were between thirteen and fourteen thousand.
21. SHAT, 7N 100, letter from War Minister General Louis André of 18 March

1902, and reply of 15 April from colonel of the *2ᵉ étranger*. See also Moch, *La question*, 302, on the 1908 Senate bill to create a cavalry regiment in the Legion; Jean-Charles Jauffret, *L'idée d'une division*, 51, 53–63. Jauffret cites the costs as the major reason for the failure of the 1908 Senate bill.

22. Erulin, *Les nationalités*, 6/A. Dugard, *La Légion étrangère*, 139, places the percentage of Frenchmen in 1913 at 45.2.

23. Weygand, *Légionnaire*, 72.

24. SHAT, 1H 1015, 20 November 1905.

25. SHAT, 1H 1015, 12 June 1905.

26. Ehrhart, *Mes treize années*.

27. SHAT, 3H 148, Trumelet-Faber report, March 1912, 20–1.

28. SHAT, 3H 148, 19 June 1913.

29. Premschwitz, *Mes aventures*, 130.

30. Dangy, *Moi, légionnaire*, 79–80.

31. Silbermann, *Cinq ans à la Légion étrangère*, 212.

32. Sylvère, *Le légionnaire Flutsch*, 55–6.

33. Adolphe Richard Cooper, *Twelve Years in the Foreign Legion* (Sydney, Australia: Angus & Robertson, 1933), 86.

34. Martin, *Je suis un légionnaire*, 198–9.

35. Randin, *A la Légion étrangère*, 217.

36. Savelli, *La Légion étrangère au Tonkin*, 72.

37. Lieutenant Langlois, *Souvenirs de Madagascar*, 106.

38. *Le journal de marche de Colonel Met*, ALE, 1908, no page numbers.

39. *Correspondance du légionnaire Lucien Jacqueline, 1902–1907*, letter of 27 March 1907.

40. SHAT, 1H 1015, 20 November 1905.

41. SHAT, 1H 1015, December 1905.

42. SHAT, 1H 1015, Herson report, nd.

43. Sylvère, *Flutsch*, 93.

44. SHAT, 3H 148, Trumelet-Faber report, March 1912.

45. Martin, *Je suis légionnaire*, 106.

46. Moch, *La question*, 181, 186.

47. Sylvère, *Flutsch*, 168.

48. SHAT, 3H 148, Trumelet-Faber report, March 1912.

49. Moch, *La question*, 147–8.

50. d'Esparbès, *Les mystères de la Légion étrangère*, 36.

51. SHAT, 9N 6, 28 September 1910.

52. SHAT, 9N 6, 24 October 1910.

53. "We scarcely knew them": Rosen, *In the Foreign Legion*, 92. "We lived for ourselves, among ourselves, far from our officers who hardly knew us and whom we rarely saw": Dangy, *Moi, légionnaire*, 146. "Very rarely did I see Legion officers carry out their duties; they were usually hunting or engaged in sports": Premschwitz, *Mes aventures*, 106–7.

54. GM, *La Légion étrangère et les troupes coloniales*, 89–90.

55. Villebois-Mareuil, "La Légion étrangère," 885.

56. SHAT, 9N 6, 24 October 1910.

57. SHAT, 3H 148, 25 February 1913.

58. SHAT, 7N 100, 15 April 1902.

59. SHAT, 3H 148, Trumelet-Faber, 25 February 1913.

60. André Raulet, *Légion uber alles! Souvenirs de la Légion étrangère* (Paris: Lavauzelle, 1934), 10–11.

61. Sylvère, *Flutsch*, 115.

62. Villebois-Mareuil, "La Légion étrangère," 886–7.

63. Martyn, *Life in the Legion*, 32.

64. Rosen, *In the Foreign Legion*, 207, 254.

65. Sylvère, *Flutsch*, 54.

66. Sylvère, *Flutsch*, 115.

67. Le Poer, *A Modern Legionary* 24.

68. Le Poer, *A la Légion*, 43, 75–6.

69. Pfirmann, *Le sergent Pfirmann*, 190–1.

70. Weygand, *Légionnaire*, 102–3.

71. Sylvère, *Flutsch*, 115.

72. Silbermann, *Cinq ans*, 6.

73. Béric, *Les routiers*, 281.

74. Moch, *La question*, 213–14.

75. Merolli, *La grenade*, 175.

76. Merolli, *La grenade*, 214, 216.

77. Sylvère, *Flutsch*, 244.

78. M.M., *Memoirs of the Foreign Legion*, 155.

79. Martin, *Je suis légionnaire*, 228–9.

80. Kellet, *Combat Motivation*, 134.

81. SHAT, 1H 1015, 15 December 1906.

82. Moch, *La question*, 131–33.

83. SHAT, 3H 148, 1913.

84. Le Poer, *A Modern Legionary*, 33–4.

85. Martyn, *Life in the Legion*, 215.

86. A. Casset, *Dans le "Sud Oranais"* (Paris: 1911), 55, 58.

87. Sylvère, *Flutsch*, 160–2.

88. Clément-Grandcourt, "La situation actuelle dans la Légion étrangère," *Bulletin du comité de l'Afrique française*, October 1909, 337.

89. SHAT, 3H 23, 11 August 1907.

90. Ehrhart, *Mes treize années*.

91. Pannier, *Trois ans en Indochine*, 131.

92. Rollet papers, ALE.

93. Reibell, *Le calvaire de Madagascar*, 104.

94. Sylvère, *Flutsch*, 244.

95. Sylvère, *Flutsch*, 93.

96. Sylvère, *Flutsch*, 184, 188.

97. S. L. A. Marshal, *Men Against Fire* (New York: William Morrow, 1947), 60–1.

98. Merolli, *La grenade*, 214.

99. Merolli, *La grenade*, 218.

100. SHAT, 9N 6, 28 September 1910.

101. Merolli, *La grenade*, 34.

102. GM, *La Légion étrangère*, 67.

103. Béric, *Les routiers*, 123, 126.

104. Béric, *Les routiers*, 146.

105. Béric, *Les routiers*, 150.

106. SHAT, 1H 1015, 12 June 1905.

107. SHAT, 1H 1015, 20 November 1905.

108. Merolli, *La grenade*, 143.

109. Premschwitz, *Mes aventures*, 96.

110. Dangy, *Moi, Légionnaire*, 34.

111. Sylvère, *Flutsch*, 171. *"Buvable,"* which is actually a pun on "bearable" and "drinkable."

112. Pannier, *Trois ans*, 303.

113. Pannier, *Trois ans*, 303.

114. Sylvère, *Flutsch*, 86.

115. L. Wagner, *Carnet de route d'un légionnaire au Maroc, 1907–1908* (Casablanca: Imprimeries réunies de la vigie marocaine et du petit marocain, 1938), 114.

116. Sylvère, *Flutsch*, 169.

117. Dangy, *Moi, légionnaire*, 88.

118. Des Ecorres, *Au pays des étapes*, 223.

119. Pannier, *Mes trois ans*, 74.
120. Roger Cabrol, *L'adaptation*, 100–1.
121. Martin, *Jes suis un légionnaire*, 9.
122. Premschwitz, *Mes aventures*, 49.
123. Sylvère, *Flutsch*, 171.
124. Rosen, *In the Foreign Legion*, 59–60.
125. Sylvère, *Flutsch*, 260.
126. Cooper, *Twelve Years*, 185–6.
127. Sylvère, *Flutsch*, 171.
128. Sylvère, *Flutsch*, 117.
129. Sylvère, *Flutsch*, 67, 233.
130. Merolli, *La grenade*, 159.
131. Martin, *Je suis un légionnaire*, 105–6, 192.
132. Sylvère, *Flutsch*, 117.
133. Sylvère, *Flutsch*, 67, 69–70.
134. Dangy, *Moi, légionnaire*, 64.
135. Béric, *Les routiers*, 127–9.
136. Premschwitz, *Mes aventures*, 96.
137. Rosen, *In the Foreign Legion*, 108–9.
138. SHAT, 3H 148, 19 June 1913.
139. Sylvère, *Flutsch*, 208, 220.
140. Sylvère, *Flutsch*, 154–5.
141. Martyn, *Life in the Legion*, 255.
142. Raoul Brice, *Un Lorrain à la légion étrangère* (Paris: Edition moderne, nd [1914]), 48.
143. Sylvère, *Flutsch*, 228.

CHAPTER 15

1. Merolli, *La grenade héroique*, 165.
2. Based upon Martin, *Je suis un légionnaire*, 19–28, 31–55.
3. Captain Hélo, *L'infanterie montée dans le Sud Algérien et dans le Sahara* (Paris: Charles-Lavauzelle, nd [1895]), 7.
4. Armengaud, *Le Sud Oranais*, 18–21.
5. ALE, report of 12 June 1902.
6. Hélo, *L'infanterie montée*, 43.
7. Armengaud, *Le Sud Oranais*, 68.
8. See de Négrier's notes, N 22, Musée de L'Empéri, Salon-de-Provence. Quoted in J.-C. Jauffret and George Gugliotta, *Les compagnies montées de la Légion étrangère* (Aix-en-Provence: Mémoire de Maîtrise, Institut d'études politiques, Université d'Aix-en-Provence), 29.
9. Hélo, *L'infanterie montée*, 48.
10. Armengaud, *Le Sud Oranais*, 75–6.
11. "1882: Le sanglant combat de chott Tigri," *Vert et rouge*, no. 25 (1949), 40–3.
12. Captain Maurel, *Les compagnies montées du Sud Oranais* (Paris: Chapelot, 1913), 13–14.
13. Jauffret and Gugliotta, *Les compagnies montées*, 32.
14. General Hubert Lyautey, "La Protection du Sud-Oranais," *Revue de Cavalerie*, vol. XLIII (April–September 1906), 332–37.
15. Martin, *Je suis légionnaire*, 122–4.
16. SHAT, 3H 148, *"Rapport sur la nécessité de rendre les troupes de la Légion plus mobiles,"* 11 February 1913.
17. Langlois, *Souvenirs de Madagascar*, 46–7.
18. This event is still commemorated by the *2ᵉ étranger*, to which this mounted company belonged.

19. For a description of the battle, see Douglas Porch, *The Conquest of Morocco* (New York: Knopf, 1982), 71–3. For tactical criticisms of Vauchez, see SHAT, 1H 1034.

20. Captain Coipel, "Opérations dans le Sud-Oranais en 1903," *Revue militaire générale,* 1 February 1908, 205–18.

21. SHAT, 7N 100, Report of General O'Connor, 13 May 1902.

22. Maurel, *Les compagnies montées,* 38.

23. For a discussion of Lyautey's methods, see Porch, *The Conquest of Morocco,* 122–36, 183–99. Ross E. Dunn, *Resistance in the Desert. Moroccan Responses to French Imperialism, 1881–1912* (London: Croom Helm, and Madison, Wisconsin: University of Wisconsin Press, 1977), discusses how Lyautey's military and economic policies contributed to the 1908 confrontations.

24. ALE, A 29, report of General Bailloud to war minister.

25. *Les mémoires du sergent Lefèvre à la Légion étrangère, 1907–1909* (unedited manuscript, ALE, no page numbers), portions of which were published in *Képi blanc* in 1956–57. For the official report of Menabha, see SHAT, 3H 565.

26. "*Rapport du Captaine Maury commandment la 24ᵉ compagnie du 1ᵉʳ Régiment étranger, sur la part prise par cette unité au Combat de Menabha, le 16 avril 1908,*" ALE, A 29, 6.

27. Lefèvre, *Mémoires.*

28. ALE, A 29, Bailloud report.

29. Lefèvre, *Mémoires.*

30. Lefèvre, *Mémoires.*

31. Lefèvre, *Mémoires.* See also SHAT, 3H 565, *Journal de marche de la colonne du Haut-Guir;* ALE, A 30, report of Colonel Alix.

32. SHAT, 3H 148, "*Rapport sur la nécessité de rendre les troupes de la Légion plus mobiles,* 11 February 1913.

33. SHAT, 3H 148, "*Rapport.*"

34. Premschwitz, *Mes aventures,* 139.

35. SHAT, 7N 100, 13 May 1902.

36. Musée de l'Empéri, Salon-de-Provence, N22, General Herson to colonel of *1ᵉʳ étranger,* 13 December 1904.

37. SHAT, 9N 6, 26 September 1910.

38. Lefèvre, *Mémoires.* 18 September 1908.

39. Cooper, *Twelve Years,* 95.

40. SHAT, 9N 6, Bailloud report, 24 October 1910.

41. Cabrol, *L'adaptation,* 77, 86–9, 111.

42. General Daudignac, "La Légion étrangère," 7.

43. Merolli, *La grenade,* 105.

44. Junger, *Jeux africains,* 172.

45. See, for example, Bennett Doty, *Legion of the Damned* (Garden City, N.Y.: Garden City Publishing Company, 1928), 216. See also Simon Murray, *Legionnaire. My Five Years in the French Foreign Legion* (New York: Times Books, 1978), 195, 210.

46. SHAT, 9N 6, 26 September 1910.

47. Junger, *Jeux africains,* 184–5.

48. Sylvère, *Le légionnaire Flutsch,* 203; Premschwitz, *Mes aventures,* 103–4.

49. Sylvère, *Flutsch,* 140–2.

50. Daudignac, "La Légion étrangère," 11–14. See also *Le Petit Parisien* and *Le Petit Journal,* January 1909.

51. Béric claimed that desertion was rarely thought out, but was ignited by a fit of depression, sometimes caused by homosexual love affairs, but more likely during an alcoholic binge (Béric, *Les routiers,* 128, 280). At other times, a drunk legionnaire might pass out, wake up after the "all in" and, afraid to face punishment, desert. This certainly typified the attitude of Martin who, after drinking all night, calculated that he was bound to receive 15 days in the cells, while the maximum he could get was sixty days if he stayed away for a "five-twenty-three" (5 days, 23 hours), "which means that the longer absence is less expensive" (Martin, *Je suis un légionnaire,* 230). Merolli was of the opinion that desertions

were most numerous in the spring: "It is perhaps the renewal of nature, the blood which flows quicker, more generously in the veins, the great desire for a different life, which pushes men toward *le cafard*." But he also cautioned that old soldiers favored the spring because it was easier to find food and work as an agricultural laborer (Merolli, *La grenade,* 172). In Tonkin, the *congaïs* were often accused, with some justification, of stimulating desertion.

52. SHAT, 3H 148, 25 February 1913.

53. Pfirmann, *Sergeant Pfirmann,* 13.

54. SHAT, 9N 6, "*2ᵉ régiment étranger. Etat numérique des désertions du 1 janvier 1900 au 1 septembre 1910.*"

55. Rosen, *In the Foreign Legion,* 268–73.

56. Sylvère, *Flutsch,* 187.

57. Junger, *Jeux africains,* 196–217.

58. Premschwitz, *Mes aventures,* 82.

59. Hubert-Jacques, *L'Allemagne et al Légion,* 61–107.

60. Casset, *Dans le "Sud Oranais,"* 57, 59.

61. Colonel Xavier Derfner, *Les mémoires d'un légionnaire garibaldien* (Bordeaux: Impr. Delmas, 1961), 68.

62. Junger, *Jeux africains,* 213–14.

63. Sylvère, *Flutsch,* 203.

64. Ditte, *Observations sur la guerre,* 355. British writer Tony Geraghty attempts to portray Legion desertion as part of a larger problem in the French army in *March or Die,* 129. In fact, there was no relationship between the two, neither in the perceptions of people at the time nor in reality. Contemporaries charged that the deserters were socialists and pacifists who refused to defend France. However, most of the "desertions" in the French army were reservists who failed to report for their annual training periods, often because they were no longer resident in France. When war broke out in 1914, the number who failed to report was infinitesimal.

65. Comor, *L'image de la Légion étrangère,* 60–71; Erulin, *Les nationalités à la Légion étrangère,* section 7.

66. SHAT, 3H 77.

67. SHAT, 3H 77, 1 October 1908. See also the report of General d'Amade of the same date, which says desertions number 114. The figure of 30 percent is based upon the strength of the Legion in Casablanca on 21 November 1908 of 707 men.

68. SHAT, 3H 72, letter of 24 November 1907 and subsequent investigation.

69. SHAT, 9N 6, 28 September 1910.

70. SHAT, 9N 6, "*Désertions au 1ᵉʳ R.E., 1ᵉʳ janvier—31 août 1910.*" This is contrary to the opinion expressed by Benedittini's captain, who reported in 1907 that "the deserters from the central portion [Saïda] are almost all French, rogues or jail bait" (SHAT, 3H 72). But this report provides no statistics. Nor does it stand to reason, as the problem with the "rogues and jail bait" of French nationality was how to get rid of them, not how to keep them from deserting.

71. SHAT, 3H 77, 1 October 1908. Again, d'Amade gives different statistics on 30 September, but the deserters are overwhelmingly German, with only five French.

72. SHAT, 1K 205, Aïn-Sefra, 17–26 July 1910.

73. SHAT, 9N 6, 17 September 1910.

74. *Journal de marche du Colonel Met,* ALE, no page numbers.

75. SHAT, 9N 6, 26 September 1910.

76. SHAT, 9N 6, "*Désertions au 1ᵉʳ R.E. . . .*"

77. SHAT, 9N 6, 24 October 1910.

78. SHAT, 9N 6, note attached to Dautelle report.

79. SHAT, 9N 6, 28 September 1910.

80. SHAT, 7N 100, 15 April 1902. He also wondered how cavalry who spoke no French were to be used effectively as reconnaissance and scouts.

81. SHAT, 9N 6, 28 September 1910.

82. SHAT, 9N 6, 24 October 1910.

83. SHAT, 7N 110, 5 March 1911.

CHAPTER 16

1. *Historique du Régiment de marche de la Légion étrangère: 3ᵉ régiment étranger d'infanterie* (Paris: Berger-Levrault, 1926), 41–3.

2. Captain Camillo Marabini, *Les Garibaldiens de l'Argonne* (Paris: Payot, 1917), 26–41.

3. M.-C. Poinsot, *Les volontaires étrangers enrôlés au service de la France en 1914–1915* (Paris: Berger-Levrault, nd), 12–13.

4. V. Lebedev, *Souvenirs d'un volontaire Russe dans l'Armée française* (Paris: Librairie académique, 1917), 68–9.

5. Zosa Szajkowski, *Jews and the French Foreign Legion* (New York: KTAV Publishing House, 1975), 25.

6. Poinsot, *Les volontaires*, 18–19.

7. Paul Rockwell, *American Fighters in the Foreign Legion, 1914–1918* (Boston and New York: Houghton Mifflin, 1930), 5.

8. Blaise Cendrars, *La main coupée* (Paris: Folio, 1974), 141. The work was first published by Denoël, Paris, in 1946. An abridged translation in English exists under the title *Lice* (London: New English Library, 1973).

9. Cendrars, *La main coupée*, 143–48.

10. Rockwell, *Americans*, 8.

11. Jean-Jacques Becker, *1914: Comment les français sont entrés dans la guerre* (Paris: Presses de la Fondation nationale des sciences politiques, 1977), 574–5, 577.

12. Rockwell, *Americans*, 6.

13. Poinsot, *Les volontaires étrangers*, 77. See also Franc-Nohain and Paul Delay, *Histoire anecdotique de la guerre de 1914–1915*. Fascicule 3, *"Les Alsaciens-Lorrains et les étrangers au service de la France"* (Paris: Lethielleux, April 1915), 123–34, lists 32, 296 foreigners enlisted between 21 August 1914 and 1 April 1915:

Alsatians-Lorrainers	6,500	Greeks	1,380	Diverse	4,254
Belgians	1,462	Luxemburgers	591	Germans	1,027
British	379	Spanish	969	Austro-Hungarians	1,369
Russians	3,393	Swiss	1,867	Turks	592
Italians	4,913	North Americans	600		

Cendrars, *La main coupée*, 140–1, claims that 88,000 foreigners volunteered in 1914 alone.

14. Lebedev, *Souvenirs*, 41.

15. Szajkowski, *Jews*, 30.

16. Erulin, *Les nationalités à la Légion étrangère*, figures in bibliography.

17. *Historique du régiment de marche*, 159–162.

18. Erulin, *Les nationalités*, 2/F. It is possible that there was a slight rise in recruitment in 1917–18. But the way in which Erulin's figures are presented leaves some doubt as to whether she includes the RMLE in the general total or counts that regiment separately.

19. It is, of course, possible that the figure could be higher if one assumes that roughly 2,000 of the 10,521 legionnaires serving in 1913 would be at the end of their enlistment. However, after August 1914, legionnaires from countries at war with France were not released, but offered the choice of internment or reenlistment in the Legion. Also, the figure is close to the 11,854 enlistments "for the duration of the war" that Poinsot claims were officially produced by the ministry at the end of 1914 (Poinsot, *Les volontaires étrangers*, 77).

20. Cendrars, *La main coupée*, 141.

21. Szajkowski, *Jews*, 29.

22. Alan Seeger, *Letters and Diary of Alan Seeger* (New York: Scribner's, 1917), 141, 144; Henry Farnsworth, *Letters of Henry Weston Farnsworth of the Foreign Legion* (Boston: privately published, 1916), 177.

23. Lebedev, *Souvenirs*, 35, 57.

24. Cendrars, *La main coupée*, 378.

25. Rockwell, *Americans,* 8–11.
26. Seeger, *Letters and Diary,* 154.
27. Rockwell, *Americans,* 10, 60.
28. Rockwell, *Americans,* 94.
29. Farnsworth, *Letters,* 94, 99.
30. Cendrars, *La main coupée,* 31–2.
31. Rockwell, *Americans,* 54.
32. Szajkowski, *Jews,* 29.
33. Cendrars, *La main coupée,* 148.
34. M.M., *Memoirs of the Foreign Legion,* 106.
35. SHAT, 26N 861.
36. Rockwell, *Americans,* 13–14.
37. Farnsworth, *Letters,* 117, 139.
38. Lebedev, *Souvenirs,* 44, 72.
39. Cendrars, *La main coupée,* 61, 152.
40. David Wooster King, *"L. M. 8046." An Intimate Story of the Foreign Legion* (New York: Duffield, 1927), 18.
41. Rockwell, *American Fighters,* 54.
42. Albert Erlande, *En campagne avec la Légion étrangère* (Paris: Payot, 1917), 67–8.
43. King, *"L.M. 8046,"* 60–3.
44. Seeger, *Letters and Diary,* 153.
45. Szajkowski, *Jews,* 28.
46. Jean Reybaz, *Le 1ᵉʳ Mystérieux. Souvenirs de guerre d'un légionnaire suisse* (Paris: André Barry, 1932), 16–17.
47. M.M., *Memoirs,* 171.
48. King, *"L.M. 8046,"* 17.
49. Rockwell, *Americans,* 240.
50. Cendrars, *La main coupée,* 154.
51. M.M., *Memoirs,* 198. In the preface to "M.M.'s" memoirs, D. H. Lawrence, who knew Magnus well, cautions against the tone of righteous indignation that permeates the book. Magnus, whose mother was believed to have been an illegitimate daughter of the Kaiser, was an impecunious, high-class social parasite. "The Legionaries must have been gentlemen, that they didn't kick him every day to the lavatory and back," he writes on page 78.
52. Kosta Todorov, *Balkan Firebrand* (Chicago and New York: Ziff Davis, 1943), 50.
53. SHAT, 26N 861, *3ᵉ régiment de marche du 1ᵉ régiment étranger,* 6 September 1914.
54. Cendrars, *La main coupée,* 154.
55. Cendrars, *La main coupée,* 154–5.
56. Cendrars, *La main coupée,* 73, 98–9, 138–9, 153–4.
57. Farnsworth, *Letters,* 102–3, 139, 206.
58. Farnsworth, *Letters,* 206–7.
59. Seeger, *Letters and Diary,* 131, 154.
60. Szajkowski, *Jews,* 34–5.
61. SHAT, 7N 1287.
62. Szajkowski, *Jews,* 33.
63. Guy Pedroncini, *Les mutineries de 1917* (Paris: Presses Universitaires de France, 1967), 20–26.
64. Russell A. Kelly, *Kelly of The Foreign Legion: Letters of Légionnaire Russell A. Kelly* (New York: Mitchell Kennerley, 1917), 46.
65. Max Niclot, "Le 4 août dans le bled marocain," *Almanach du Combattant,* XXXVe année (1964), 61–2.
66. Joseph Galliéni, *Mémoires du Maréchal Galliéni: Défense de Paris, 25 août–11 septembre 1914* (Paris: Payot, 1926), 175–76.
67. Marabini, *Les Garibaldiens de l'Argonne,* 141–8.

CHAPTER 17

1. M.M., *Memoirs*, 240–4, 250.
2. Cendrars, *La main coupée*, 198–9.
3. Russell Kelly, *Letters*, 26.
4. M.M., *Memoirs*, 168.
5. Rockwell, *Americans*, 213.
6. Cendrars, *La main coupée*, 156.
7. Rockwell, *Americans*, 283.
8. Rockwell, *Americans*, 141.
9. King, "*L.M. 8046*," 30.
10. Rockwell, *Americans*, 29, 39.
11. Cendrars, *La main coupée*, 80–87.
12. Seeger, *Letters and Diary*, 29.
13. Cendrars, *La main coupée*, 198–9.
14. Seeger, *Letters and Diary*, 72.
15. Rockwell, *Americans*, 47–9.
16. Seeger, *Letters and Diary*, 69.
17. Seeger, *Letters and Diary*, 98–100.
18. See in this context Tony Ashworth, *Trench Warfare, 1914–1918: The Live and Let Live System* (New York: Holmes & Meier, 1980).
19. Cendrars, *La main coupée*, 182–4.
20. Cendrars, *La main coupée*, 312–14.
21. Seeger, *Letters and Diary*, 5–6.
22. For descriptions of the May 9 offensive, see *Légion étrangère*, January–February 1939, 14–17; *Historique du régiment de marche*, 50–2; SHAT, 26N 861, *Journal de marche du 2ᵉ régiment de marche du 1ᵉʳ étranger*.
23. SHAT, 19 N 1567.
24. SHAT, 26 N 861, *Journal de marche du 2ᵉ régiment de marche du 1ᵉʳ étranger*, 10 May 1915.
25. SHAT, 6N 861, "*Attaque du 9 mai 1915 par le 2ᵉ régiment de marche du 1ᵉʳ étranger.*"
26. SHAT, 6N 861, "*Attaque.*"
27. Most of these suggestions are gleaned from testimony provided by Rockwell, *Americans*, 80–91.
28. Reybaz, *Le 1ᵉʳ mystérieux*, 76.
29. Rockwell, *Americans*, 83.
30. Lebedev, *Souvenirs*, 80–5.
31. *Historique*, 49.
32. Rockwell, *Americans*, 84.
33. SHAT, *2ᵉ régiment de marche*, 19 June 1915.
34. Alphonse Marolf, *Gustave Marolf: Capitaine mitrailleur au 1ᵉʳ étranger, 1884–1916. Léttres, récits, souvenirs* (Geneva: Imprimerie Centrale, 1943), 80–81.
35. *Les armées françaises dans la grande guerre* (Paris: Service Historique de l'Etat Major de l'Armée, Ministère de la Guerre, 1923), tome VIII, 1ᵉʳ volume, 29–30, 104–5.
36. SHAT, 26N 861, *2ᵉ régiment de marche*, 21 June 1915.
37. SHAT, 26N 861, *2ᵉ régiment de marche*, 1 July 1915.
38. Szajkowski, *Jews*, 31; Rockwell, *Americans*, 102; Leon Poliakov, *Histoire de l'Antisemitisme. L'Europe suicidaire, 1870–1933*. (Paris: Calmann-Lévy 1977), 294. Poliakov says that seven Jews were executed and that they died shouting, "Vive la France! Vive l'Armée! A bas [down with] la Légion!"
39. Sholem Szwartzbard, *In krig mit zikh aleyn* (Chicago: 1933), 87–93; Szajkowski, *Jews*, 31.
40. Szajkowski, *Jews*, 31–2.
41. *Le Crapouillot*, August 1934, 49: 216 in 1914, 315 in 1916 and 136 in 1918, for a total of 1,637 men.

42. Leonard V. Smith, "The Evolution of Military Justice, September 1914–April 1917: The Case of the Fifth Infantry Division." Unpublished paper delivered at the 1988 meeting of the Society for French Historical Studies, 10 (forthcoming in the *Journal of Military History*).

43. Rockwell, *Americans*, 102.

44. *Historique*, 42.

45. Cendrars, *La main coupée*, 61.

46. Cendrars, *La main coupée*, 153–4.

47. Cendrars, *La main coupée*, 60.

48. Edward Morlae, *A Soldier of the Legion* (Boston and New York: Houghton Mifflin, 1916), 46.

49. Seeger, *Diary and Letters*, 16.

50. Morlae, *A Soldier*, 91.

51. Morlae, *A Soldier*, 51–4.

52. Erulin, *Les nationalités*, 2/F.

53. Cendrars, *La main coupée*, 214–15.

CHAPTER 18

1. Seeger, *Letters and Diary*, 152, 154, 173.

2. Farnsworth, *Letters*, 176, 193–4, 200; Seeger, *Letters*, 213.

3. Reybaz, *Le 1er mystérieux*, 29.

4. Rockwell, *Americans*, 212.

5. Rockwell, *Americans*, 283.

6. Cendrars, *La main coupée*, 120.

7. Cendrars, *La main coupée*, 151.

8. Cendrars, *La main coupée*, 157–9.

9. *Historique*, 43.

10. Pedroncini, *Les mutineries*, 310–11.

11. Leonard V. Smith, *Command Authority in the French Army: The Case of the 5e Division d'Infanterie* (New York: Ph.D dissertation, Columbia University, 1989).

12. SHAT, 26N 861, *journal de marche, 2e Régiment de marche du 2e étranger*.

13. SHAT, 26N 861, *journal de marche du 2e Régiment de marche du 1e étranger*.

14. Seeger, *Letters*, 214–15.

15. SHAT, 2N 862. Losses reported by the brigade were 741 casualties among the troops and twenty-two officers.

16. SHAT, 24N 2912; RMLE, 23 April 1917, 12.

17. SHAT, 24N 2912, letter of 2 May 1917.

18. "La bataille des Monts," *Légion étrangère*, no. 7 (1938), 10–14.

19. Pedroncini, *Les mutineries*, does not list the Legion as one of the regiments touched by these mutinies, which affected about one-third of French units.

20. Jean-Pierre Dorian, *Le colonel Maire: Un héros de la Légion* (Paris: Albin Michel, 1939), 137–42.

21. Dorian, *Le colonel Maire*, 136–7.

22. Cooper, *Twelve Years in the Foreign Legion*, 236.

23. Doty, *Legion of the Damned*, 28.

24. Cooper, *Twelve Years*, 238.

25. Ehrhart, *Mes treize années*, Chapter VII.

26. For the disaster of Khenifra in December 1914, see Porch, *The Conquest of Morocco*, 284–8.

27. Rockwell, *Americans*, 238–42.

28. M.M., *Memoirs*, 153.

29. M.M., *Memoirs*, 150–1.

30. Ehrhart, *Mes treize années*, Chapter VII.

31. M.M., *Memoirs*, 155.

32. SHAT, 7N 2119.

33. SHAT, 3H 93.

34. SHAT, 5N 213.

35. SHAT, 3H, 93.

36. ALE, Rollet papers, report of 26 July 1918.

37. Julian Green, *Memoirs of Happy Days* (New York and London: Harper & Brothers, 1942), 182–3.

38. See ALE, file on Cole Porter. The author also knew a man in his home town who joined the French artillery in 1918, presumably also passing through the Legion.

39. SHAT, 7N 1287.

40. ALE, Rollet report.

41. SHAT, 3H 93, 29 August 1918.

42. Rollet papers, ALE, no date but summer 1918.

43. Rollet papers, ALE, 28 July 1918 report.

44. Rockwell, *Americans,* 331, provides figures for nationalities.

45. Szajkowski, *Jews,* 53.

46. See papers in ALE. Also, "A nous la Légion! Ou quand nous allions au secours de l'Amérique," *Képi blanc* (August 1967), 38–45.

47. ALE, Rollet papers, 26 July 1918 report.

48. Erulin, *Les nationalités,* 2/F.

49. RMLE, journal de marche, ALE R12.

50. RMLE, journal de marche, ALE R12.

51. "*Observations sur les attaques du 18 au 20 juillet 1918*" and "*Liaison infanterie—artillerie,*" Rollet papers, ALE.

52. SHAT, 26N 862, "*Journal de marche et opérations. Régiment de marche de la Légion étrangère,*" 14 September 1918. The *Livre d'Or* lists fifteen officers and 1,158 legionnaires wounded, 188.

53. Doty, *La légion des damnés* (Paris: Librairie Stock, nd), 46–7. Walter Kanitz writes that, "This is a good description of the part the Legion played in both the great wars: A sort of sacrificial corps, ever at the worst place!" *The White Kepi. A Casual History of the French Foreign Legion* (Chicago: Henry Regnery Company, 1956), 94.

54. Charles Mercer, *The Foreign Legion. The Vivid History of a Unique Military Tradition* (London: Arthur Barker Limited, 1964), 228. See also Szajkowski, *Jews,* 27; Geraghty, *March or Die,* 150.

55. Arthur Banks, *A Military Atlas of the First World War* (London: Heinemann, nd), 144.

56. Percentage based on figures taken from the *journal de marche,* SHAT, 26N 862, which gives two different sets of figures, but ones that are close enough for a general observation.

57. Jean Brunon et al, *Le livre d'or de la Légion étrangère, 1831–1981* (Paris: Charles-Lavauzelle, 1981), 389.

58. *Historique,* 163.

59. *Historique,* 164.

Chapter 19

1. ALE, "*La pacification du 'Maroc utile,'* " Rollet papers, n/d.

2. General Mordacq, *Le ministère Clémenceau. Journal d'un témoin* (Paris: Plon, 1931), vol. III, 328.

3. SHAT, 3H 95, letters of 4 November 1919 and 4 November (year illegible).

4. General Cottez wrote in August 1920 that, "The work to be accomplished in Morocco reposes essentially upon the use of the native regiments and the Foreign Legion." SHAT, 3H 95, 16 August 1920.

5. In 1923, for instance, the Legion counted 13,469 men, not excessive growth considering that it counted three new regiments. Indeed, Rollet complained in an undated

memo written in the early 1920s that the Legion did not have enough men to fill their new units (SHAT, 9N 123, *"Situation des effectifs présents à la Légion étrangère de 1919 à 1939"*). In fact, the official organization of 10 January 1921, which established four infantry regiments each consisting of five battalions of 500 men and two mounted companies of 250 men each, plus an administrative and training center at Sidi-bel-Abbès through which all recruits and even all Legion officers would pass before assignment to a field unit, required an effective of 18,000 men for the infantry alone (Commandant Lambert, *La Légion étrangère*, [Paris: Charles-Lavauzelle, 1923]), 102–103.

6. ALE, Rollet papers, *"La Légion,"* nd.

7. ALE, *"1er régiment étranger. Rapport sur l'état d'esprit,"* 26 December 1920.

8. ALE, Rollet papers, reply of Major Riet, 4 March 1920.

9. SHAT, 3H 697, 27 December 1920.

10. SHAT, 34N 310, *Historique du régiment de 1921 à 1934.*

11. Jacques Lauzière, "La nouvelle Légion étrangère," *Le Mercure de France*, no. 619 (35ᵉ année, 1 April 1924), 56–78.

12. SHAT, 3H 697, 24 January 1923, Major Poimeur of the *3e étranger*. "Numbers would not suffer," he wrote. "Those legionnaires worthy of the name would remain after their three years. The others would not be missed. Their departure would be that of the malcontents, the worthless, pillars of the prison or of the hospital, who weigh down our strength, undermine the moral health of the troops and their efficiency." Unfortunately, it was precisely the "pillars of the prison and the hospital" who often chose to remain, because the Legion guaranteed them a quality of life unmatched on the outside.

13. Cooper, *Twelve Years*, 72, 91.

14. Even Major Pechkoff, the son of writer Maxim Gorky who had joined the Legion during World War I and who subsequently became one of its most distinguished officers, admitted that his countrymen made poor NCOs, "because the Russian hesitates and, even when he tries, does not have the authority over his men.... He hesitates when he commands. He is not firm and sure of himself at all." Zinovi Pechkoff, *La Légion étrangère au Maroc 1923–1925* (Paris: Marcelle Lesage, 1929), 25.

15. Weygand, *Légionnaire*, 218–19.

16. Erulin, *Les nationalités*, section 6, "Les russes."

17. ALE, Rollet papers, undated memorandum, *"La Légion."*

18. In 1924, Rollet admitted that this was still the case: "The French contingent has an average moral value inferior to that of the foreign contingent," he wrote. "With few exceptions, the following serve *à titre français*: 1. A small number are foreigners naturalized Frenchmen. 2. NCOs assigned exceptionally to the Legion [by virtue of a March 1921 decree which allowed NCOs to transfer to the Legion for one year]. 3. Men who have not satisfied their military obligations and who are, either absentees, or the very young who have enlisted to escape their families or justice." SHAT, 3H 697, 22 September 1924.

19. SHAT, 3H 697, 2 August 1924. The Pahl (or Pal) affair is a reference to the attempted desertion *en masse* of fifty German legionnaires in 1908 in the Sud Oranais.

20. Figures based upon numbers provided in SHAT 9N 123, "Repartition des légionnaires par grades et origines nationales pour années 1934 et 1939."

21. ALE, 7 March 1934, 6–7.

22. Brian Stuart, *Adventure in Algeria* (London: Herbert Jenkins, 1936), 31.

23. Ferri-Pisani, *Avec ceux de la légion* (Paris: Editions de France, 1932), 8–11.

24. ALE, *"Rapport du Colonel Conte, Commandant le 4e Régiment Etranger d'Infanterie sur l'état d'esprit du Régiment,"* 2 December 1933. A 1934 report noted that, since the war, the Legion had recruited between four and seven thousand men each year. "But, if one examines the conditions in which this recruitment was carried out, one realizes that we limited ourselves to opening the doors of the recruiting bureaus more or less widely depending on the circumstances, the needs or the possibilities," it read. "It does not appear that we profited from this considerable influx of candidates to carry out a judicious selection of recruits." ALE, 7 March 1934, 6–7.

25. Stuart, *Adventures in Algeria*, 63–4.

26. Stuart, *Adventures in Algeria*, 43–50.

27. G.-R. Manue, *Têtes brûlées. Cinq ans de Légion* (Paris: La nouvelle société d'édition, 1929), 61, 100, 206, 208, 242.

28. Stuart, *Adventures in Algeria*, 70–1.

29. Manue, *Têtes brûlées*, 205.

30. Manue, *Têtes brûlées*, 61.

31. SHAT, 3H 697, 22 September 1924.

32. SHAT, 3H 697, September 1924.

33. ALE, *"Rapport sur l'état d'esprit,"* 31 May 1924.

34. ALE, Rollet papers, undated memorandum, *"La Légion."*

35. Rollet's early complaints about Bel-Abbès were ironic, for when he became commander of the 1er *étranger* in 1925, he reported that he was unable to retain good officers at Sidi-bel-Abbès, which "must remain the cradle where one shapes up, acquires a taste for this element, for its particular lifestyle, for its command in wartime," because of the potent attraction for officers of combat pay in Morocco. SHAT, 3H 697, *"Rapport du Colonel Rollet . . . au sujet de la suppression de l'indemnité de fonctions pour les cadres de la Légion étrangère en service en Algérie,"* 1926.

36. SHAT, 3H 697, Martin report, 23 March 1923.

37. SHAT, 3H 697.

38. SHAT, 3H 697, September 1924.

39. SHAT, 3H 697, 1 June 1924.

40. SHAT, 3H 697, *"Rapport de Colonel Rollet . . . au sujet du stage des officiers . . . ,"* 1926.

41. André Beaufre, *1940. The Fall of France* (New York: Knopf, 1968), 19.

42. 3H 697, 24 January 1923.

43. SHAT, 3H 697, 23 March 1923.

44. Jauffret, *L'idée d'une division*, 64–81.

45. SHAT, 3H 697, July 1920 letter, and 15 July 1920.

46. ALE, Rollet papers, undated memorandum, *"La Légion."*

47. 3H 697, 22 July 1920.

48. Jauffret, *L'idée d'une division*, 86.

49. Albert Bartels, *Fighting the French in Morocco* (London: Alston Rivers, 1932).

50. SHAT, 3H 95, 12 February 1921.

51. Weygand, *Légionnaire*, 235. Although ostensibly a novel, Weygand's book is closely autobiographical.

52. SHAT, 3H 259, 23 February 1920.

53. SHAT, 3H 697, *"Questions relatives à la Légion étrangère."*

54. SHAT, 3H 95, 12 February 1921.

55. SHAT, 3H 95, 13 February 1921.

56. SHAT, 3H 95, 3 September 1923.

57. Manue, *Têtes brûlées*, 163.

58. Maire, *Nouveaux souvenirs sur la Légion étrangère*, 55–6.

59. SHAT, 3H 95, 13 February 1921.

60. SHAT, 3H 95, 13 February 1921.

61. SHAT, 3H 95.

62. "If the legionnaire at present has the defects of his predecessors," the 1er *étranger* reported in March 1921, "he differs from them by the passionate interest he brings to contemporary events. One must at all costs prevent him from being influenced by the political action of agitators sent from abroad. . . . Domestic politics do not interest the legionnaire. On the other hand, he follows closely foreign events. The advance of the Allies on the right bank of the Rhine impressed the Germans. Some among them believed that this would bring on a new war." ALE, *"Rapport sur l'état d'esprit,"* 1er *étranger*, March 1921.

63. Lieutenant Colonel Martin, commander of the 2e *étranger*, spoke out against this practice in March 1923, because "one has seen the rebirth of the old methods of crimping of past centuries." SHAT, 3H 697, 23 March 1923.

64. Lyautey also blasted the practice because it "raised many diplomatic difficulties

and discussions even in the most friendly foreign parliaments (Yugoslavia—Denmark)....
I do not mention the others." SHAT, 3H 697, 12 May 1924.

65. Stuart, *Adventures in Algeria*, 18.

66. SHAT, 3H, 17 January 1921.

67. SHAT, 3H 259, 29 December 1920.

68. SHAT, 3H 95, 3 September 1923.

69. SHAT, 3H 697, January 1922.

70. SHAT, 3H 697, *"Questions relatives à la Légion étrangère,"* 1924.

71. Colonel Pierre Carles in an interview with the author recounted that many
veterans of the Rif still serving when he joined the Legion after 1945 spoke of numerous
desertions during the Rif War. J. Roger-Mathieu, *Mémoires d'Abd el-Krim* (Paris: Librairie
des Champs-Elysées, 1927), 146–7.

72. Vincent Sheean, *An American among the Riffi* (New York and London: The
Century Company, 1926), 260.

73. SHAT, 3H 697, 1924.

74. Rudyers Pryne, *War in Morocco* (Tangier: 1927), 217.

75. Cooper, *Twelve Years*, 223.

76. Martin, *Je suis un légionnaire*, 151.

77. Manue, *Têtes brûlées*, 224.

78. David S. Woolman, *Rebels in the Rif: Abd el-Krim and the Rif Rebellion*
(Stanford, Calif.: Stanford University Press, 1968), 176–77.

79. Woolman, *Rebels in the Rif*, 183.

80. Cooper, *Born to Fight*, 173.

81. "La tragédie de Médiouna, 10 et 11 juin 1925," *Vert et Rouge*, no. 28 (1950),
40–5.

82. "La tragédie de Médiouna, 40–45.

83. Beaufre, *1940*, 22–3.

84. A.R. Cooper, *Douze ans à la Légion étrangère* (Paris: Payot, 1934), 178.

85. Cooper, *Twelve Years*, 161.

86. "Unfortunately, . . . the pilots . . . launched their bombs uselessly on the cadavers strewn in front of us on the plain, while they would have done such good work on
the village (which was in the hands of the Druses)." ALE, *"Relation du combat de Musseifré
par un officier y ayant pris part* [Lt. Lacour]."

87. Lieutenant Colonel Lorillard, *La guerre au Maroc* (Paris: Charles-Lavauzelle,
1934), 27.

88. Beaufre, *1940*, 21–2.

89. SHAT, 3H 697, 11 September 1924.

90. Cooper, *Twelve Years in the Foreign Legion*, 130.

91. Officers were "distrusted by their subordinates, or on the contrary too dependent on their NCOs whose advice they ask. As a result they fail to establish their authority,
or they get off on the wrong foot." SHAT, 3H 697, 1926.

92. Cooper, *Born to Fight*, 165–6.

93. Pechkoff, *La Légion étrangère au Maroc*, 185–19 for the 1927 edition, 203–
16 for the 1929 edition. Pechkoff places this action on May 22. See also his *The Bugle Sounds*
(New York: Appleton, 1926), 217–222.

94. Cooper, *Douze ans*, 172–3, 185–6.

95. Beaufre, *1940*, 26.

96. SHAT, 34N 310, *journal d'opérations*, 2nd battalion of the 1er REI, 12 June
1925.

97. SHAT, 3H 697, *"Quelques chiffres au sujet de l'emploi de la Légion,"* 12
September 1924.

98. Martin, *Je suis un légionnaire*, 93.

99. ALE, Rollet papers, November 1922.

100. ALE, *"Relation du combat de Musseifré."*

101. G. Ward-Price, *In Morocco with the Legion* (London: The Beacon Library,
1937), 105–8.

102. In Jacques Weygand's strongly autobiographical novel *Légionnaire,* the legendary leader of *goums,* Colonel Henri de Bournazel, tells the hero Robert that the Legion had not seen much action in Morocco, not because the Moroccans feared the Legion and therefore avoided attacking them, but because, "The command hesitates to use you. Your units are too heavy, your formations too rigid" for a country where "everything is a question of suppleness and subtlety." Weygand, *Légionnaire,* 181.

103. Beaufre, *1940,* 21.

104. Doty, *Legion of the Damned,* 90.

105. Doty, *Legion of the Damned,* 97, 101.

106. Doty, *Legion of the Damned,* 111–15.

107. ALE, Rollet papers.

108. ALE, "Rapport annuel sur l'état d'esprit," 3ᵉ REI, 1933.

109. ALE, Rollet papers, 24 October 1933.

110. ALE, "Rapport confidentiel," 4ᵉ étranger, 31 January 1933.

111. ALE, report of 7 March 1934.

112. SHAT, 3H 697, 12 May 1924.

113. ALE, Rollet papers, "La pacification du 'Maroc utile.' "

114. SHAT, 3H 697, 23 March 1923.

115. A/C André Gandelin, "Le général Rollet, un homme de coeur, de caractère et d'idéal," *Revue historique des armées, no. spécial 1981, La Légion étrangère, 1831–1981,* 133. See also ALE, Rollet papers, letter of 1 April 1934.

CHAPTER 20

1. *Képi blanc spécial—Septembre 1979,* no. 382 bis, 23.

2. Louis Rousselet, *Sur les confins du Maroc, d'Oudjda à Figuig* (Paris: Hachette, 1912), 27.

3. ALE, Rollet papers, "La Légion," nd.

4. SHAT, 3H 697, 23 March 1923.

5. SHAT, 3H 697, 24 January 1924.

6. SHAT, 34N 310, *Historique du régiment de 1921 à 1934.*

7. For a discussion of "invented" tradition, see Eric Hobsbawm, "Introduction: Inventing Traditions," in Eric Hobsbawn and Terence Ranger (eds.), *The Invention of Tradition* (Cambridge, England: Cambridge University Press, 1983), 1–14.

8. "The legionnaire wants his uniform to be different from that of other corps," General Cottez reported in January 1922, calling for a kepi and a blue waistband (SHAT, 3H 697), a statement Rollet endorsed completely. "This question [of the uniform] is not a negligible detail, in particular in the Legion, where the *esprit de corps* is very developed," read a 1934 report, which warned that "the legionnaires are as badly dressed as the other soldiers in the French army and soon nothing will distinguish them." ALE, 7 March 1934.

9. Brunon et al., *Le Livre d'or,* 225.

10. Ward-Price, *In Morocco with the Legion,* 131.

11. Martin, *Je suis un légionnaire,* 176, 178.

12. Martin, *Je suis un légionnaire,* 178.

13. Raymond Guyader, "Le Légionnaire des années 1919 à 1927," *Képi blanc,* no. 449 (July 1985).

14. SHAT, 3H 697, 14 March 1926.

15. Jean Brunon, "Essai sur le folklore de la Légion étrangère," *Vert et rouge,* no. 19 (1948): 30.

16. Martin, *Je suis un légionnaire,* 177–8.

17. Doty, *Legion of the Damned,* 62.

18. ALE, Georges d'Ossau, "Le Képi-blanc," typed memo.

19. Brunon et al., *Livre d'or,* 225.

20. Adrian Liddell Hart, *Strange Company* (London: Weidenfeld and Nicolson, 1953), 33.

21. Guyader, "Le légionnaire des années 1927 à 1935"; Brunon et al., *Livre d'or*, 225.

22. ALE, report of 7 March 1934. Nor were the regulations always honored: the *4ᵉ étranger* complained in December 1933 that their uniforms were impractical, of poor quality and utterly lacking in elegance. ALE, 4ᵉ REI, 2 December 1933.

23. Charles Favrel, *Ci-devant légionnaire: La vraie légende de la Légion* (Paris: Presses de la Cité, 1963), 58–9.

24. *Képi blanc, spécial—Septembre 1979*, no. 382 bis, 23.

25. *L'Illustration,* a popular newspaper, consecrated a large article to the battle with an engraving in its 18 July 1863 issue. The survivors of Danjou's 3rd Company were decorated, the first medals awarded to French troops in the Mexican campaign, and a memorial plaque was ordered placed in the Invalides, although this was done only in 1949. Napoleon III granted the request of Colonel Jeanningros that "Camerone" be inscribed upon the standard of the *"Régiment étranger,"* and the official artist of the expedition, Jean-Adolphe Beaucé, was commissioned to paint a scene of the last moments of Camerone. The painting was shown in the Salon of 1869, purchased by the state, and disappeared from view until discovered at the Musée de Tours and given to the Legion in 1952. After 1871, Camerone occasionally surfaced in literature calculated to intensify the spirit of patriotic revanchism—an article about the battle appeared in the prestigious literary magazine *Revue des Deux Mondes* in 1878, and in 1889 a small brochure written by General Alexis de la Hayrie, who had been a battalion commander in the *Régiment étranger* in Mexico, was published in Lille. Abbé Lanusse, chaplain at Saint-Cyr who had been present in Mexico, produced *Les héros de Camaron, 30 avril 1863* in 1891, as the title suggests, written in prose calculated to inspire his future officers. The following year a monument was built at the scene of the battle.

26. Ehrhart, *Mes treize années de Légion étrangère,* Part I.

27. Merolli, *La grenade héroique,* 307, 332.

28. Doty, *Legion of the Damned,* 43.

29. *Képi blanc,* no. 501, May 1990, 37.

30. Georges d'Esparbès, *Les mystères de la Légion étrangère* (Paris: Flammarion, 1912). This was a re-edition of *La Légion étrangère,* first published as a series of articles in 1898 and then in book form in 1901. The 1912 edition was enriched by the drawings of Maurice Mahaut. D'Esparbès proved to his satisfaction that the Legion recruited principally among Europe's uprooted middle classes, men whose lives contained some terrible secret that they interred for the Legion. Unfortunately, his research methods, which consisted principally of lingering about the wine shops of Sidi-bel-Abbès buying drinks for legionnaires as long as they remained willing—or capable—of recounting their life stories, would strike modern investigators as suspect, for the inventiveness of legionnaires probably ran as deep as Monsieur d'Esparbès's pockets. The cover of *Les mystères de la Légion étrangère* was decorated with a drawing of a legionnaire in full combat kit, but wearing a mask. The device at the beginning of the first chapter declared, *"Ma vie a son secret."* Already before World War I, the *1ᵉʳ étranger* had earned the nickname of the *"1ᵉʳ mystérieux,"* because the pasts of its inmates were alleged to be shrouded in mystery.

31. *Képi blanc, spécial—Septembre 1979*, no. 382 bis, 10.

32. Brunon et al., *et al., Livre d'or,* 454.

33. Brunon et al., *Le Livre d'or,* 107.

34. Pierre Sergent, "Du nouveau sur le combat de Camerone," *Revue historique des armées, numéro spécial 1981, La Légion étrangère, 1831–1981:* 86–8. The reaction of some officers to the publication of this new information was recounted to the author by Legion archivist Tibor Szecsko.

35. Roger Cabrol, *L'adaptation,* 104–5.

36. Jean des Vallières, *Les hommes sans nom* (Paris: Albin Michel, 1933), 231–2.

37. Lieutenant Langlois, *Souvenirs de Madagascar* (Paris: Charles-Lavauzelle, nd), 144.

38. A. R. Cooper, *Born to Fight* (Edinburgh and London: Blackwood, 1969), 166. But even when the Legion had the leisure to pay their respects in an appropriate manner, it is not always clear that they did so—Magnus describes the funeral of a legionnaire at Bel-Abbès in 1916 that in his view was carried out with indecent haste.

39. Charles Favrel, *Ci-devant légionnaire*, 45.

40. Henry Ainley, *In Order to Die: With the Foreign Legion in Indo-China* (London: Burke, 1955), 19.

41. Janos Kemencei, *Légionnaire en avant!* (Paris: Jacques Gracher, 1985), 207.

42. Kemencei, *Légionnaire*, 269.

43. Kemencei, *Légionnaire*, 291–92.

44. Colonel Pierre Carles, "Survol de l'histoire du sous-officier de la Légion étrangere 1831–1981," *Revue historique des armées, Numéro spécial 1981, La Légion étrangère 1831–1981:* 24.

45. Communication from M. Raymond Guyader to the author. Benigni was made an honorary legionnaire during the celebration of Camerone in 1933 and served on the editorial committee of *La Légion étrangère* and of its post-1945 successor, *Vert et rouge*. In more recent years, Andreas Rosenberg, an Austrian who served in the Legion from 1939 to 1944, and as *peintre aux armées* in 1944–45, has been commissioned by the Legion to produce watercolors that evoke the prominent campaigns of the Legion but that especially portray legionnaires as tough but fundamentally human characters.

46. Jean Brunon, "Essai sur le folklore de la Légion étrangère," *Vert et rouge*, no. 19 (1948): 30.

47. Liddell Hart, *Strange Company*, 57.

48. Brunon, "Folklore," 30.

49. Ainley, *In Order to Die*, 223.

50. Prince Aage de Denmark, *Mes souvenirs de la Légion étrangère* (Paris: Payot, 1936), 106.

51. Cabrol, *L'adaptation*, 106–7.

52. Manue, *Têtes brûlées*, 244.

53. Favrel, *Ci-devant légionnaire*, 25.

54. Junger, *Jeux africains*, 172.

55. These observations have been made to the author by regular French officers.

56. Such was the case with a Hungarian intellectual in Pechkoff's battalion who gained an entirely new perspective on life in the Legion: "This rigid and severe discipline is a salutary thing for those who cannot discipline themselves, nor discipline others." Pechkoff, *La Légion étrangère au Maroc*, 200. Manue also congratulated the Legion for turning a Parisian *apache* or delinquent and an anarchist into useful citizens because of "the disciplined life they were forced to lead." Manue, *Têtes brûlées*, 251.

57. Cooper, *Twelve Years in the Foreign Legion*, 72–3.

58. Liddell Hart, *Strange Company*, 49.

59. Prince Aage, *Mes souvenirs*, 99, 104, 154.

60. Cabrol, *Adaptation*, 105–6.

61. Manue, *Têtes brûlées*, 245.

62. Ward-Price, *In Morocco*, 217.

63. Manue, *Têtes brûlées*, 107.

64. Pechkoff, *La Légion*, 202.

65. Manue, *Têtes brûlées*, 10–11.

66. Aage, *Mes souvenirs*, 108, 113.

67. Brunon et al., *Le livre d'or*, 431–6.

68. Liddell Hart, *Strange Company*, 29–30, 50, 84, 173.

69. See, for instance, Christian Jennings, *A Mouthful of Rocks: Modern Adventures in the French Foreign Legion* (New York: The Atlantic Monthly Press, 1989). "Most people who joined up, trained keenly and were posted to a good regiment, yet still deserted, were victims of the Legion misinformation service," Jennings writes. "They had believed everything they had heard and had been taken in by it" (181).

70. For an explanation of these themes, see Ray Allen Billington, *Land of Savagery, Land of Promise: The European Image of the American Frontier* (London and New York: Norton, 1981), 151–2; Simon Schama, *An Embarrassment of Riches: An Interpretation of Dutch Culture in the Golden Age* (New York: Knopf, 1987), 24–5.

71. Liddell Hart, *Strange Company*, 206.

72. Jeffrey Richards, *Visions of Yesterday* (London: Routledge and Kegan Paul, 1973), 46.

73. Pierre Boulanger, *Le cinéma colonial de "L'Atlantide" à "Lawrence d'Arabie"* (Paris: Seghers, 1975), 105.

74. Billington, *Land of Savagery*, 320.

75. Cooper, *Twelve Years*, 237.

76. *Légion étrangère*, no. 10 (October 1931), 24–5.

77. ALE, Rollet papers, 3 May 1934. Ortiz's letter had some effect, for certain portions of the film, such as the line, "They [the Moroccans] defend their land," were cut. However, *Le grand jeu* was a critical success—even the royalist newspaper *Action française* approved of it because "from these vulgar heroes is born a poetry, the poetry of luck and of death." Boulanger, *Cinéma colonial*, 105. Indeed, as in the quasi-official Legion portraits of itself, it is the very weaknesses of the characters that humanizes them.

78. *Légion étrangère*, 17 May 1932, 151; 19 July 1932, 244.

79. ALE, Rollet papers, May 1934.

80. *Légion étrangère*, December 1934, 419. I also thank Richard Mahaud for some of this information.

81. *Légion étrangère*, no. 71 (November 1936).

82. Indeed, several proposed film scripts remain in the Rollet papers at Aubagne.

83. ALE, Rollet papers, 27 October 1932.

84. ALE, 7 March 1933 report, 16.

85. P. C. Wren, *Foreign Legion Omnibus: Beau Geste, Beau Sabreur, Beau Ideal*. (New York: Grosset & Dunlap, 1928), 207–8, 218, 274, 371.

86. Richards, *Visions of Yesterday*, 159.

87. Michael Alexander, *The Reluctant Legionnaire: An Escapade* (London: Rupert Hart-Davis, 1956), 19.

88. P.O. Lapie, *La Légion étrangère à Narvik* (London: John Murray, 1941), xii.

89. Boulanger, *Cinéma colonial*, 84–5. Boulanger cites these as Rollet's objections to the 1926 version of *Beau Geste*. However, the film he describes is *Morocco*.

90. Richards, *Visions*, 44.

91. Comor, "L'image de la Légion étrangère," 159.

92. Boulanger, *Cinéma colonial*, 8.

93. Manue, *Têtes brûlées*, 245.

94. Weygand, *Légionnaire*, 78.

95. Doty, *Legion of the Damned*, 6–7.

96. Stuart, *Aventure in Algeria*, 18.

97. *Légion étrangère*, no. 27 (March 1933), 94.

98. ALE, SIL report 7 March 1934, 16.

99. Murray, *Légionnaire*, 12, 60; Jennings, *A Mouthful of Rocks*, 191.

100. ALE, 1934 report.

101. ALE, Rollet papers, 13 March 1935. Even pensions were refused because legionnaires, allowed to enlist without papers, were required to produce them for a pension, which was often impossible for Germans and Russians whose governments refused to send them, or for Italians whose hopelessly inefficient administrations were often unable to locate them.

102. ALE, Rollet papers, 12 March 1936 letter; *"Le problème des libérés de la Légion étrangère,"* nd, probably 1938.

103. SHAT, 9N 123, 25 March 1927.

104. Mordacq, *Le ministère Clémenceau*, 330.

105. Rivalries and politics also plagued the *Société d'entr'aide*—the director complained in 1936 that "the mentality is distressing: Pettiness, spitefulness, hatreds, bitterness, and insatiable appetites for personal satisfaction." ALE, Rollet papers, see letter of 28 April 1933 and 12 March 1936. A June 1938 report suggested that the "spectacle of disunion" created by three rival societies in Marseille "does not encourage foreigners to serve under our flag." SHAT, 9N 123, 30 April 1938.

106. Martin, *Je suis un légionnaire*, 295–6.

107. Italian recruits were "small, without energy, dirty, badly dressed," mediocre soldiers who deserted often. SHAT, 9N 123, 1933.

108. ALE, 7 March 1934 report.

109. ALE, *"Etat d'esprit—Propagande communiste et révolutionnaire,"* nd.

110. SHAT, 9N 123, *"Répartition par nationalités des engagés volontaires en 1934 et 1935."*

111. ALE, *"Etat d'esprit,"* nd but obviously 1937.

112. ALE, SIL, *Rapport Annuel,* 1935.

113. ALE, *"Etat d'esprit,"* nd.

114. ALE, *"Etat d'esprit,"* 1937.

115. SHAT, 9N 123, 1 April 1938.

116. SHAT, 9N 123, 21 April 1938.

117. ALE, *"Rapport annuel sur l'état d'esprit,"* 3ᵉ REI 1933.

118. SHAT, 9N 123, 1 April 1938.

119. ALE, *"Etat d'esprit,"* nd, probably 1937.

120. "Les devoirs du légionnaire," *Vert et rouge,* no. 9 (1946): 22–4.

121. Cooper, *Twelve years,* 181, 259.

122. ALE, *5ᵉ régiment étranger,* nd.

123. SHAT, 9N 123.

124. Liddell Hart, *Strange Company,* 176–77, 180–1.

125. Murray, *Legionnaire,* 167.

126. Liddell Hart, *Strange Company,* 48.

127. Giulio Cesare Silvagni, *La peau des mercenaires* (Paris: Gallimard, 1954), 305.

CHAPTER 21

1. Favrel, *Ci-devant légionnaire,* 93.

2. Charles Hora, *Mon tour du monde en quatre-vingts barouds* (Paris: La Pensée Moderne, 1961), 39.

3. SHAT, 7N 2475, 25 September 1939.

4. SHAT, 7N 2475, 13 November 1939.

5. Gustave Bertrand, *Enigma ou la plus grand énigme de la guerre, 1939–1945* (Paris: Plon, 1973), 72.

6. Joseph Ratz, *La France que je cherchais: Les impressions d'un Russe engagé volontaire en France* (Limoges: Imprimerie Bontemps, 1945), 65–66.

7. Szajkowski, *Jews,* 60.

8. Szajkowski, *Jews,* 60–1.

9. SHAT, 7N 2475, 8 September 1939.

10. SHAT, 7N 2475, 21 September 1939.

11. ALE, *"Note sur les variations d'effectifs de la Légion étrangère depuis 1900,"* Service d'information, 8 June 1961. SHAT, 7N 2475, 7 November 1939.

12. SHAT, 7N 2475, 16 September 1939.

13. *Képi blanc,* no. 490 (May 1989), 40, 43.

14. SHAT, 34H 319, 39.

15. SHAT, 34N 317.

16. SHAT, 7N 2475, 26 October 1939.

17. SHAT, 7N 2475, December 1939.

18. SHAT, 7N 2475, 17 February 1940.

19. SHAT, 7N 2475, 18 January 1940.

20. G-R Manue, *Vu du rang* (manuscript, ALE), 10–11. This work was published as *Sous la grenade à sept flammes. Comment on a creé un corps d'élite, 1939–1940* (Paris: Sequana, 1941). Page numbers are from the original manuscript.

21. André-Paul Comor, *L'Epopée de la 13ᵉᵐᵉ demi-brigade de Légion étrangère, 1940–1945* (Paris: Nouvelles éditions latines, 1988), 29.

22. SHAT, 7N 2475, *"Situation des effectifs des unités de marche de volontaires étrangers à la date du 10 février 1940."*

23. Lapier, *La Légion étrangère à Narvik*, 30.

24. SHAT, 9N 123, 8 June 1939.

25. Alfred Perrott-White, *French Legionnaire* (London: John Murray, 1953), 128–9.

26. SHAT, 9N 123, 19 July 1939.

27. SHAT, 7N 2475, 5 October 1939.

28. Szajkowski, *Jews*, 69–70.

29. A.D. Printer, "Spanish Soldiers in France," *Nation*, vol. clv (1943): 489–90. Quoted in Szajkowski, *Jews*, 101–2.

30. Printer, "Spanish Soldiers in France," 489–90.

31. Favrel, *Ci-devant légionnaire*, 53, 222–3.

32. *Képi blanc,* no. 490 (May 1989), 47.

33. SHAT, 7N 2475, 25 January 1940.

34. Lapie, *La Légion étrangère à Narvik,* 30.

35. Printer, "Spanish Soldiers," 489–90.

36. Lapie, *La Légion étrangère à Narvik,* 34.

37. *Képi blanc,* no. 490 (May 1989), 28.

38. Perrott-White, *French Legionnaire,* 81.

39. Szajkowski, *Jews,* 64, 74–5.

40. SHAT, 7N 2475, 25 January 1940.

41. Favrel, *Ci-devant légionnaire,* 93–4.

42. Szajkowski, *Jews,* 64–5.

43. Jacques Ragot, *De Gaulle, la Légion, l'Algérie: Souvenirs d'un officier* (La Teste: Chez l'auteur, 1984), 50–56.

44. SHAT, 7N 2475, 10 and 13 February 1940.

45. *Képi blanc,* no. 490 (May 1989), 47.

46. SHAT, 7N 2475, 22 November 1939.

47. Szajkowski, *Jews,* 72.

48. SHAT, 7N 2475, 10 November 1939.

49. Manue, *Vu du rang,* 34–5.

50. SHAT, 34N 317, 11 February 1941.

51. SHAT, 9N 123, 20 April 1940.

52. Manue, *Vu du rang,* 10.

53. *Képi blanc,* no. 490 (May 1989), 28.

54. Szajkowski, *Jews,* 65.

55. *Képi blanc,* no. 490 (May 1989), 37.

56. Favrel, *Ci-devant légionnaire,* 119.

57. SHAT, 7N 2475, *"Extraits de fiches de renseignements établis après l'armistice par le commandant Jacquot."*

58. Manue, *Vu du rang,* 12–13, 46.

59. Roger Bruge, *Les combattants du 18 juin. Tome I. "Le sang versé"* (Paris: Fayard, 1982), 113–14.

60. SHAT, 34N 317, *"Journal de marche du sergent François de la 7ᵉ cie du 12ᵉ R.E.I.,"* 29 May.

61. SHAT, 34N 317, *"Journal de marche du sergent François."*

62. SHAT, 3H 319, report of Chef de bataillon Hermann, 25.

63. SHAT, 34H 319.

64. SHAT, 34N 317, *"Journal de marche du sergent François."*

65. SHAT, 34H 319.

66. SHAT, 7N 2475, *"Extraits de fiches."*

67. SHAT, 7N 2475, *"Extraits de fiches de renseignements."*

68. SHAT, 34N 317, *"Journal de marche du sergent François."*

69. SHAT, 7N 2475, *"Extraits."*

70. SHAT, 34N 317, *"Journal de marche du sergent François."*

71. Manue, *Vu du rang*, 53.

72. Favrel, *Ci-devant légionnaire*, 164.

73. SHAT, 34N 317, 11 February 1941 report.

CHAPTER 22

1. Some historians believe that Gamelin missed an opportunity to attack in September 1939 while the cream of the Wehrmacht was occupied in Poland and the Siegfried Line was manned by second-echelon German units.

2. Comor, *L'Epopée*, 40.

3. Favrel, *Ci-devant légionnaire*, 117–18.

4. Favrel, *Ci-devant légionnaire*, 140, 145–6.

5. Comor, *L'Epopée*, 70–1.

6. SHAT, 34N 318, "*Observations faites lors la campagne de Norvège.*"

7. SHAT, 34N 318, report of S/c Niederhauser; also that of A/c Mary, 55.

8. Comor, *L'Epopée*, 85.

9. SHAT, 34N 318, Mary report, 51–2.

10. SHAT, 34N 318, Mary report, 65.

11. Comor, *L'Epopée*, 95.

12. ALE, "*Carnet de route du Lieutenant Gabriel de Sairigné,*" unpublished diary, 22 June, 1 July 1940.

13. SHAT, 34N 318.

14. SHAT, 34N 318, Mary report, 56; report of Lieutenant Laborde.

15. Sairigné, "*Carnet de route,*" 1 July.

16. SHAT, 34N 318, Mary report, 66.

17. Sairigné, "*Carnet de route,*" 7–14 July, 25 August.

18. ALE, "*Résumé du journal des marches et opérations, 13ᵉ DBLE, 20 February, 1940–19 February, 1949,*" 47.

19. Sairigné, "*Carnet de route,*" 8 April 1941.

20. ALE, letter of Colonel Barre, 1 October 1981.

21. ALE, "*Troupes du Levant. Ordre général no. 14,*" 13 July 1941.

22. De Sairigné, "*Carnet de route,*" 7 June 1941.

23. ALE, "*Officiers, Sous-Officiers, Soldats du Levant,*" 14 May 1941.

24. Robert O. Paxton, *Vichy France: Old Guard and New Order, 1940–1944* (London: Barry & Jenkins, 1972), 117–24.

25. Comor, *L'Epopée*, annexe 18, "*Lègionnaires du Levant!*"

26. Comor, *L'Epopée*, annexe 19, "*Je ne suis pas Gaulliste . . . Pourquoi?*", 341.

27. Comor, *L'Epopée*, 154.

28. ALE, "*Récit du Lieutenant Baulens.*"

29. De Sairigné, "*Carnet de route,*" 14 August 1941.

30. ALE, letter of 10 January 1981.

31. De Sairigné, "*Carnet de route,*" 14 August 1941.

32. ALE, *Résumé du journal des marches et opérations, 13ᵉ DBLE*, 50.

33. Comor, *L'Epopée*, 161–2.

34. Michel-Christian Davet, *La double affaire de Syrie* (Paris: 1967), 197.

35. ALE, Barre letter, 10 January 1981.

36. ALE, Barre letter, 10 January 1981.

37. Comor, *L'Epopée*, 158–62. Officers have told this author that the issue of repatriation was embittered by the fact that the Australians shot many prisoners of the 6ᵉ *étranger* out of hand.

38. ALE, "*Troupes du Levant: Ordre Général no. 14,*" 13 July 1941.

39. De Sairigné, "*Carnet de route,*" 27 May 1942.

40. De Sairigné, "*Carnet de route,*" 6 June.

41. ALE, *Résumé du journal des marches et opérations, 13ᵉ DBLE*, 71–2.

42. De Sairigné, "*Carnet de route,*" 11 June 1942.

43. Comor, *L'Epopée*, 202–3.

44. ALE, *Résumé*, 75.

45. Henri Amouroux, *La grande histoire des français sous l'occupation, Vol. IV: Le peuple révellé* (Paris: Laffont, 1979), 268–69.

46. De Sairigné, *"Carnet de route,"* 3 June 1943.

CHAPTER 23

1. Michael R. Marrus and Robert O. Paxton, *Vichy France and the Jews* (New York: Basic Books, 1981), 67–9.

2. OSS report, National Archives, RG 226, no. 2160. Quoted in Szajkowski, *Jews*, 108.

3. SHAT, 1P 2229, 21 October 1942.

4. SHAT, 12P 84, 28 August 1941.

5. Szajkowski, *Jews*, 94, 98, 102.

6. National Archives, RG59, 85IT, Transah./30 & 27. Quoted in Szajkowski, *Jews*, 93–4, 98–9.

7. Marrus and Paxton, *Vichy France and the Jews*, 86, 257.

8. General Maxime Weygand, *Mémoires, vol. III, "Rappelé au Service"* (Paris: Flammarion, 1950), 390–91.

9. SHAT, 1P 2229, 26 October 1940 and 28 April 1941.

10. Philip Rosenthal, *Il était une fois un légionnaire* (Paris: Albin Michel, 1981), 120.

11. Louis Berteil, *L'armée de Weygand* (Paris: Albatros, 1975), 51–55.

12. SHAT, 1P 2229, 26 October 1940.

13. SHAT, 1P 2229, 21 May 1941.

14. SHAT, 1P 2229, 30 January & 31 March 1942.

15. SHAT, 4H 274, 10 & 14 February 1941.

16. SHAT, 1P 2229, 28 April 1941.

17. SHAT, 1P 2229, 20 April 1941.

18. SHAT, 1P 2229, 10 September 1940.

19. SHAT, 12P 84, 8 September 1941.

20. Paul Carell, *Afrika Korps* (Paris: J'ai Lu, 1963), 278.

21. SHAT, 12P 84, 8 September 1941.

22. Comor, *L'Epopée*, 241–2.

23. Robert O. Paxton, *Parades and Politics at Vichy: The French Officer Corps under Marshal Pétain* (Princeton, N.J.: Princeton University Press, 1966), 327.

24. SHAT, 12P 84, 21 July & 22 September 1941.

25. Mercer, *The Foreign Legion*, 267.

26. Rosenthal, *Il était une fois*, 118–19.

27. Ragot, *De Gaulle, La Légion, l'Algérie*, 62–63.

28. Paxton, *Parades and Politics*, 246.

29. Comor, *L'Epopée*, 240–1.

30. Rosenthal, *Il était une fois*, 120.

31. Perrott-White, *French Legionnaire*, 179.

32. Perrott-White, *French Legionnaire*, 182–97.

33. SHAT, 12P 82, 8 February 1943.

34. Comor, *L'Epopée*, 239–45, photo 26 between 256–7, 300–1, 305, 311.

35. Comor, *L'Epopée*, 251, 245.

36. SHAT, 12P 82, 14 March 1943.

37. SHAT, 12P 83, 10 March 1945.

38. SHAT, 12P 83, 23 November 1944.

39. "Spanish revolutionary propaganda is making itself felt more and more in our ranks," Tritschler wrote. "It tends to create among these young legionnaires [about to terminate their five years] a feverous atmosphere, a slackness, which translates into individ-

ual desertions at a slow but regular pace." However, the Legion insisted upon maintaining the five-year enlistment: "The formula 'Enlisted for the duration of the war' is contrary to the Legion spirit and assimilates him to a reservist," Tritschler insisted. This statement must be seen as a not-so-veiled criticism of the 13ᵉ DBLE, which enlisted recruits for the duration of hostilities, in contrast to the "regular" Legion, and therefore had a more "political" orientation than the "Old Legion." SHAT, 12P 83, 23 November 1944. Lieutenant Colonel Gaultier of the RMLE admitted in March 1945 that the five-year enlistment contract was a great impediment to enlistment. SHAT, 12P 83, 10 March 1945.

40. SHAT, 12P 82, June 1945. It is possible that this was the result of the *rabiot,* the practice of deducting time spent in punishment from legal service time, but adding it onto the end of the period of enlistment as a sort of *service non compris.* Charles Favrel insisted that he had no *rabiot* to serve when his colonel refused to release him upon the expiration of his contract in March 1943. When he hired a lawyer and threatened to sue his commander, he was immediately transferred to a mounted company, and gained his release only by a personal appeal to the Minister of Defense in Algiers. Favrel, *Ci-devant légionnaire,* 227–30.

41. Szajkowski, *Jews,* 172–77.

42. SHAT, 12P 83, 10 March 1945.

43. Comor, *L'Epopée,* 285–7.

44. Général Jean Compagnon, "La Légion étrangère dans la campagne de Tunisie, 1942–1943," *Revue historique des armées,* no. spécial 1981, La Légion étrangère, 1831–1981: 185–216.

45. SHAT, 12P 82, 14 March 1943. Major Louis Rouger who commanded the 1ᵉʳ bataillon of the *1ᵉʳ étranger* confessed that training "was not emphasized because of duties," before being sent to Tunisia. The armament was poor, many trucks had to be abandoned, and the officers, while good, were too few. "Soldiers, good but need discipline, as always in the Legion, to avoid useless casualties." SHAT, 12P 82, 8 February 1943.

46. SHAT, 12P 82, "*Journal de Marche du 3ᵉ REI, décembre 1942/avril 1943,*" 12. "*L'Aventure du Drapeau du 3ᵉ Etranger. Tunisie 19 janvier–12 mai 1943.*"

47. Général Jean-Pierre Hallo, "Le Régiment de marche de la Légion étrangère, 1943–1945," *Revue historique des armées,* no. spécial 1981, La Légion étrangère: 223

48. Comor, *L'Epopée,* 246–7.

49. John Ellis, *Cassino: The Hollow Victory* (New York: McGraw-Hill, 1984), 45.

50. Ellis, *Cassino,* 347.

51. Comor, *L'Epopée,* 265.

52. Ellis, *Cassino,* 364.

53. Comor, *L'Epopée,* 267–9.

54. ALE, de Sairigné, "*Carnet de route,*" 12 January 1945.

55. Comor, *L'Epopée,* 282.

56. Comor, *L'Epopée,* 301.

57. Comor, *L'Epopée,* 300–1.

58. Comor, *L'Epopée,* 299.

59. SHAT, 12P 83, "*Observations sur l'infanterie blindée à la suite des opérations du RMLE en 1944–45.*"

60. Lapie, *La Légion étrangère à Narvik,* 23.

61. De Sairigné, "*Carnet de route,*" 28 January 1945.

62. SHAT, 12P 82, 3ᵉ REI, June 1945.

63. SHAT, 12P 83, 10 March 1945.

CHAPTER 24

1. Tibor Szecsko, *Implantation et engagement de la Légion étrangère au Tonkin, 1914–1941* (Montpellier: Doctorat d'université d'histoire, Université Paul Valéry—Montpellier III, September 1987), 131–9, 150–4, 169–73.

2. SHAT, 10H 77, 20 May 1931.

3. Andrée Viollis, *Indochine S.O.S.* (Paris: Gallimard, 1935), 159.

4. Szecsko, *Implantation*, 271–8; Viollis, *Indochine S.O.S.*, 146–7, 153. See also Claude Paillat, *Dossiers secrets de la France contemporaine, Vol. III, La guerre à l'horizon, 1930–1938* (Paris: Robert Laffont, 1981), Chapters 31, 32, and 34.

5. James P. Harrison, *The Endless War: Vietnam's Struggle for Independence* (New York: Columbia University Press, 1989), Chapter 2.

6. Viollis, *Indochine S.O.S.*, 158–9.

7. Gilbert Bodinier, *1945–1946: Le retour de la France en Indochine. Textes et documents* (Vincennes: SHAT, 1987), 228.

8. Franchini, *Les guerres d'Indochine*, vol. I, 153–6.

9. Perrot-White, *French Legionnaire*, 194.

10. Szecsko, *Implantation*, 304–16.

11. Franchini, *Les guerres d'Indochine*, vol. I, 183–8; "La résistance du 5ᵉ étranger," *Vert et rouge*, no. 10 (1947): 14–25; Colonel Henri Dutailly, *"La retraite de Chine: Résistance militaire et comportement du combattant dans une unité isolée,"* unpublished conference at the Ecole d'état major, in SHAT, 10H 80. See also SHAT, 10H 79, report of Lieutenant Colonel Quilichini, 1 January 1946, and 12P 82 for the events of the *coup* of 9 March 1945.

12. Bodinier, *1945–1946*, 28, 32–3, 66–9.

13. Harrison, *The Endless War*, 109.

14. Yves Gras, *Histoire de la guerre d'Indochine* (Paris: Plon, 1979), 190.

15. Kemencei, *Légionnaire en avant!*, 155.

16. Lucien Bodard, *La guerre d'Indochine: L'enlisement* (Paris: Gallimard, 1963), 406–9.

17. Henri Jacquin, *Guerre secrète en Indochine* (Paris: Olivier Orban, 1979), 197–98.

18. Jacquin, *Guerre secrète en Indochine*, 201–4.

19. SHAT, 10H 1142, 18 August 1950.

20. SHAT, 10H 1142, October 1950, Carpentier report to prime minister, no date.

21. SHAT, 10H 1142. 3ᵉ *bureau*, FAEO, 14 October 1950.

22. Gras, *Histoire de la guerre d'Indochine*, 330–1.

23. Kemencei, *Légionnaire en avant!* 201.

24. Kemencei, *Légionnaire en avant!*, 205–11.

25. Kemencei, *Légionnaire en avant!*, 205–11.

26. Liddell Hart, *Strange Company*, 35.

27. Gras, *Histoire de la guerre d'Indochine*, 190.

28. Claude Paillat, *Dossier secret de l'Indochine* (Paris: Presses de la Cité, 1964), 18.

29. Kemencei, *Légionnaire en avant!*, 142–3, 176, 191, 207.

30. SHAT, 10H 375, 2ᵉ REI, 1950. Sergeant Stojkiewitch of the 3ᵉ *étranger*, who was wounded during the Cao Bang retreat, reported that the Viet Minh possessed more grenades than the Legion, the same number of machine guns, but fewer light automatic weapons. 10H 1142.

31. SHAT, 10H 376, 1951.

32. SHAT, 10H 376, 2ᵉ BEP 1950.

33. SHAT, 10H 376, 2ᵉ BEP, August 1951–March 1952.

34. SHAT, 10H 376, 2ᵉ BEP, 9 December 1952.

35. SHAT, 10H 375, 2ᵉ REI 1952.

CHAPTER 25

1. SHAT, 10H 375, *"Rapport sur le moral,"* 3ᵉ REI, 4th trimestre 1950.

2. SHAT, 10H 375, *"Rapport sur le moral,"* 4th trimester 1950.

3. Erulin, *Les nationalités à la Légion étrangère*, 6/A.

4. Paillat, *Dossier secret*, 20.

5. Kemencei, *Légionnaire en avant!*, 137. A 15 December 1947 report provoked by a Tass article claiming that the Legion was enlisting ex-SS in Germany and Austria

reiterated that ex-German soldiers and NCOs could be enlisted, but excluded enlistment of ex-SS, who must be identified by their tattoos, and ex-officers of the Wehrmacht because they were "unassimilatable." SHAT, 10H 184, 15 December 1947.

6. Henry Ainley, *In Order to Die*, 17.

7. Erulin, *Les nationalités*, 6/A.

8. SHAT, 10H 375, 1st semester 1951; 10H 2262, 12 January 1953; 10 H 374, 1st semester 1953.

9. Liddell Hart, *Strange Company*, 77.

10. Kemencei, *Legionnaire en avant!*, 141.

11. Liddell Hart, *Strange Company*, 62–4.

12. Lieutenant Basset, *Journal de Marche, Indochine 1951–54* (Nîmes: unpublished manuscript, Salle d'honneur, 2ᵉ REI), 3–4.

13. Pierre Sergent, *Ma peau au bout de mes idées* (Paris: La Table Ronde, 1967), 89.

14. ALE, 2ᵉ REI, "Rapport sur le Moral et l'état d'esprit: 4ᵉ trimestre 1949," 4.

15. SHAT, 10H 375, 3ᵉ REI, 3rd semester, 1950.

16. SHAT, 10H 375, 5ᵉ REI, 1st semester, 1952.

17. 10H 376, REC, 1st semester 1953. In 1953, the commander of a Legion engineering section stated that he had men "who do not even know how to shoot a rifle" because their engineer training did not include this rather essential detail. SHAT, 10H 378, génie, 1st semester 1953. Indeed, this author was told by Legion veterans of Indochina that some recruits were sent to Indochina with no training whatsoever.

18. Ainley, *In Order to Die*, 17–20.

19. SHAT, 10H 375, 2ᵉ REI, 3ᵉ trimester 1949.

20. SHAT, 10H 3174, 15 March 1951. See also 10H 2262, 12 January 1953.

21. SHAT, 10H 375, 5ᵉ REI and GM 3, 1954.

22. SHAT, 10H 375, 5ᵉ REI, 1st semester 1953.

23. SHAT, 10H 375, III/5ᵉ REI, 6 June 1954.

24. SHAT, 10H 2262, 17 August 1953.

25. SHAT, 10H 375, 5ᵉ REI, 1st semester 1953.

26. SHAT, 10H 375, 5ᵉ REI, July 1951.

27. SHAT, 10H 2262, 12 January 1953.

28. SHAT, 10H 375, 5ᵉ REI, 1st and 2nd semesters 1951.

29. SHAT, 10H 375, II/5ᵉ REI, 2 June 1953.

30. SHAT, 10H 376, 2ᵉ BEP, 2nd semester 1953.

31. SHAT, 10H 375, 3ᵉ REI, 1st semester 1951.

32. SHAT, 10H 376, 13ᵉ DBLE, 26 May 1952, and 1954.

33. SHAT, 10H 375, 5ᵉ REI, 1954.

34. SHAT, 10H 376, 13ᵉ DBLE 1950.

35. SHAT, 10H 375, 1952.

36. SHAT, 10H 2262, 12 April 1951.

37. SHAT, 10H 376, 13ᵉ DBLE 1950.

38. SHAT, 10H 375, 13ᵉ DBLE 1950 & 5ᵉ REI, 6 June 1954.

39. SHAT, 10H 376, 1ᵉ BEP, 2nd semester 1953.

40. SHAT, 10H 375, 5ᵉ REI, 1st semester 1952.

41. SHAT, 10H 376, 13ᵉ DBLE, 26 May 1952.

42. SHAT, 10H 376, 13ᵉ DBLE, 1950.

43. Kemencei, *Légionnaire en avant!*, 174.

44. SHAT, 10H 375, 2ᵉ REI, 1st semester 1953.

45. SHAT, 10H 376, III/13ᵉ DBLE, 1st semester 1952.

46. Kemencei, *Légionnaire en avant!*, 174.

47. Ainley, *In Order to Die*, 222.

48. Ainley, *In Order to Die*, 144–5.

49. Liddell Hart, *Strange Company*, 138.

50. Ainley, *In Order to Die*, 42–3.

51. Ainley, *In Order to Die*, 29, 37.

52. Liddell Hart, *Strange Company*, 138–40.

53. Ainley, *In Order to Die*, 56, 218.

54. Ainley, *In Order to Die*, 103–4.

55. Ainley, *In Order to Die*, 115–16.

56. Ainley, *In Order to Die*, 188.

57. SHAT, 10H 375, 1 July 1952.

58. Ainley, *In Order to Die*, 188, 221.

59. Lieutenant Basset, *Journal de Marche, Indochine 1951–54*, 49, 60.

60. Kemencei, *Légionnaire en avant!*, 174.

61. Ainley, *In Order to Die*, 146, 153. Several Legion commanders complained that the shortage of NCOs had led to a decline in efficiency and to "serious crimes," including rape, desertion, drunkenness and refusal to obey orders. See SHAT, 10H 3174, 10 August 1950 and 20 March 1951; also 10H 375, 24 February 1950.

62. See SHAT, 10H 184 for a rather lengthy correspondence on this issue.

63. The captain of the *Joffre* wrote in March 1949 that "the general insubordination of the troops and the lack of authority of the officers are the cause of the repeated incidents and a source of disorder on board" (SHAT, 10H 184, 1 March 1949). See also Liddell Hart, *Strange Company*, 186–94, on the utter lack of concern of Legion officers for the comfort of their men on the return journey. He was also scandalized by the inedible food and "openly communist" crew members.

64. SHAT, 10H 184, 27 September 1952.

65. Pierre Sergent, *Un étrange Monsieur Frey* (Paris: Fayard, 1982), 255.

66. SHAT, 10H 3239, 10 October 1951. See also Jacques Doyon, *Les soldats blancs de Ho Chi Minh* (Paris: Fayard, 1973).

67. Bernard Fall, *Hell in a Very Small Place* (New York and Philadelphia: J. B. Lippincott, 1967), 269–70.

68. See SHAT, 10H 3239 for several incidents. Ainley wrote that two legionnaires in his company helped the Viet Minh blow up an ammunition dump. *In Order to Die*, 205–6. Sgt. Stojkiewitch of the II/3ᵉ REI, taken prisoner at Cao Bang, was interrogated by two Legion deserters, a German and a Hungarian. SHAT, 10H 1142.

69. SHAT, 10H 184, 15 January 1949.

70. SHAT, 10H 3239.

71. SHAT, 10H 375, 5ᵉ REI, 2nd semester 1952 & 1953.

72. SHAT, 10H 375, II/5ᵉ REI, June 1954.

73. SHAT, 10H 375, 3ᵉ REI, 2nd semester 1953.

74. SHAT, 10H 375, 3ᵉ REI, 1st semester 1951.

75. SHAT, 10H 2262, 3 December 1953.

76. SHAT, 10H 375, 3ᵉ REI, 1st semester 1951.

77. Gras, *Histoire de la guerre d'Indochine*, 572.

78. SHAT, 10H 375, I/5ᵉ REI, 12 November 1952.

79. SHAT, 10H 2262, 12 January 1953.

80. SHAT, 10H 375, 2nd semester 1953.

81. SHAT, 10H 375, 5ᵉ REI, 1954.

82. SHAT, 10H 375, III/5ᵉ REI, 6 June 1954.

83. SHAT, 10H 375, 3ᵉ REI, 1st semester 1951.

84. Liddell Hart, *Strange Company*, 131.

85. SHAT, 10H 376, 1ᵉ REC, December 1951.

86. Hubert Ivanoff, *Le Premier régiment étranger de cavalerie en Indochine, 1947–1956* (Montpellier: mémoire de maîtrise, Université Paul Valéry, 1982), 119–23.

87. SHAT, 10H 3174, 10 April 1951.

88. SHAT, 10H 376, 1ᵉʳ BEP, 1st semester 1953.

89. Gras, *Histoire de la guerre d'Indochine*, 444; Franchini, *Les guerres d'Indochine*, II, 64–5.

90. SHAT, 10H 3174, Pelleterat de Borde, "*Rapport exceptionel*," 28 March 1951.

91. SHAT, 10H 375, 3ᵉ REI, 1st semester 1951. See also 10H 375, 5ᵉ REI, 2nd semester 1951, and 10H 3174, 15 March 1951, for similiar complaints about Vietnamization in the Legion.

92. SHAT, 10H 375, 3ᵉ REI, 1st semester 1951.
93. SHAT, 10H 375, 5ᵉ REI, 1st semester 1952.
94. SHAT, 10H 375, 5ᵉ REI, 1st semester 1952.
95. SHAT, 10H 3174, 17 May 1953.
96. SHAT, 10H 375, 3ᵉ REI, December 1952.
97. Basset, *Journal de marche, Indochine 1951–54*, 31.
98. SHAT, 10H 3174, 29 May 1951.
99. SHAT, 10H 376, August 1951–March 1952; 2nd semester 1954.
100. SHAT, 10H 376, 2ᵉ BEP, 1st semester 1954.

Chapter 26

1. Kubiak, "Opération Castor . . . Verdun 1954," *Képi blanc*, October 1962: 36.
Quoted in Bernard Fall, *Hell in a Very Small Place*, 137.
2. Gras, *Histoire de la guerre d'Indochine*, 546–7.
3. Bernard Fall, *Hell in a Very Small Place*, 281.
4. Fall, *Hell in a Very Small Place*, 147.
5. SHAT, 10H 376, 13ᵉ DBLE, 15 December 1954.
6. Philip B. Davidson, *Vietnam at War: The History 1946–1975* (Novato, Calif.:
Presidio Press, 1988), 214–20.
7. Fall, *Hell in a Very Small Place*, 272.
8. Kemencei, *Légionnaire en avant!*, 268.
9. SHAT, 10H 375, 3ᵉ REI, May 1954.
10. SHAT, 10H 375, 5ᵉ REI and GM3, 1954.
11. SHAT, 10H 376, 13ᵉ DBLE, May 1954.
12. Robert Bonnafous, "Les Prisonniers du corps expéditionnaire français dans les
camps Viêt-Minh (1945–1954)," *Guerres mondiales*, no. 147 (1987): 94, 102.
13. Gras, *Histoire de la guerre d'Indochine*, 512.
14. SHAT, 10H 376, 2ᵉ BEP, 2nd semester 1953.
15. SHAT, 10H 376, 13ᵉ DBLE, 15 December 1954.
16. Basset, *Journal de marche, Indochine 1951–54*, 61.
17. Brunon et al., *Livre d'or de la Légion étrangère*, 389.
18. Erulin, *Les nationalités à la Légion étrangère*, 2/F.
19. SHAT, 10H 376, 13ᵉ DBLE, 15 December 1954.

Chapter 27

1. SHAT, 10H 376, 13ᵉ DBLE, 15 December 1954.
2. Laurent Beccaria, *Hélie de Saint Marc* (Paris: Perrin, 1988), 148.
3. Kemencei, *Légionnaire en avant!*, 286–7; Beccaria, *Saint Marc*, 148–9 and
note.
4. Kemencei, *Légionnaire*, 291–2.
5. ALE, "Rapport sur le Moral," 1st semester 1955, 5ᵉ REI.
6. Jacques Massu, *La vraie bataille d'Alger* (Paris: Plon, 1971), 55.
7. Alistair Horne, *A Savage War of Peace: Algeria 1954–1962* (London: Macmillan, 1977), 98–9.
8. Henri Le Mire, *Histoire militaire de la guerre d'Algérie* (Paris: Albin Michel,
1982), 16, estimates that 3,000 Moslems were killed. Horne, *A Savage War of Peace*, 27,
gives a more detached discussion of figures, pointing out that even if one accepts the very
lowest estimates of 1,200 Moslems killed, they exceeded in any case the deaths of Europeans
by a ratio of twelve to one.
9. Massu, *La vraie bataille d'Alger*, 54.
10. Kemencei, *Légionnaire en avant!*, 301–2.
11. Horne, *A Savage War of Peace*, 122–3.

12. Jean Planchais, *Une histoire politique de l'armée. Vol 2: 1940–1962. de De Gaulle à de Gaulle* (Paris: Le Seuil, 1967), 274–6.

13. Kemencei, *Légionnaire en avant!*, 297–8, 303–4.

14. Murray, *Legionnaire*, 54, 56.

15. Kemencei, *Légionnaire en avant!*, 298.

16. Antoine Ysquierdo, *Une guerre pour rien* (Paris: La Table Ronde, 1966), 43.

17. Sergent, *Ma peau au bout de mes idées*, 96–7.

18. Ysquierdo, *Une guerre pour rien*, 53–4.

19. Le Mire, *Histoire militaire*, 288.

20. Le Mire, *Histoire militaire*, 139–42.

21. Peter Paret, *French Revolutionary Warfare from Indochina to Algeria: The Analysis of a Political and Military Doctrine* (New York: 1964), 44–5, 50–1; Horne, *A Savage War of Peace*, 221.

22. Horne, *A Savage War of Peace*, 165–6.

23. Horne, *A Savage War of Peace*, 171.

24. Horne, *A Savage War of Peace*, 115.

25. Murray, *Legionnaire*, 55–74.

26. Jean Feller, *Le Dossier de l'armée française: La Guerre de "Cinquante Ans." 1914–1962* (Paris: Librairie Académique Perrin, 1966), 475.

27. Murray, *Legionnaire*, 158–9.

28. Kemencei, *Légionnaire en avant!*, 318.

29. Massu, *La vraie bataille d'Alger*, 28–9.

CHAPTER 28

1. Murray, *Legionnaire*, 48–9.

2. Jean Lartéguy, *The Centurions* (New York: Dutton, 1962), 417–18.

3. Jean Lartéguy, *The Praetorians* (New York: Dutton, 1963), 50, 54.

4. Planchais, *Une histoire politique de l'armée*, Vol. 2, 352.

5. Lartéguy, *The Praetorians*, 54.

6. Massu, *La vraie bataille d'Alger*, 135–40.

7. Massu, *La vraie bataille d'Alger*, 164.

8. Planchais, *Histoire politique*, Vol. 2, 302–3.

9. Massu, *La vraie bataille d'Alger*, 164–6.

10. Beccaria, *Hélie de Saint Marc*, 174–7.

11. Murray, *Legionnaire*, 67–8.

12. Ysquierdo, *Une guerre pour rien*, 93.

13. Horne, *A Savage War of Peace*, 322–3.

14. Henri-Paul Simon, *Contre la torture* (Paris: Le Seuil, 1957), 95–6, 121–2.

15. Horne, *A Savage War of Peace*, 195–207.

16. Ysquierdo, *Une guerre pour rien*, 76.

17. Hora, *Mon tour du monde*, 183–4.

18. ALE, letters of 1 and 8 October 1958, and certificate.

19. Murray, *Legionnaire*, 160, 196.

20. Paret, *French Revolutionary Warfare*, 34–5.

21. J. Duncan Love et al., *Helicopter Operations in the French-Algerian War* (McLean, VA: Research Analysis Corporation, 1965), 16–35.

22. Murray, *Legionnaire*, 95–102.

CHAPTER 29

1. Horne, *A Savage War of Peace*, 305–7.

2. Horne, *A Savage War of Peace*, 344–5.

3. Horne, *A Savage War of Peace*, 347.

4. Sergent, *Ma peau au bout de mes idées*, 172–3.
5. Sergent, *Ma peau au bout de mes idées*, 193–4.
6. Horne, *A Savage War of Peace*, 393–4.
7. Sergent, *Ma peau*, 164.
8. Sergent, *Ma peau*, 215.
9. Sergent, *Ma peau*, 216–25.
10. Sergent, *Ma peau*, 154–6, 242.
11. J. R. Tournoux, *Jamais Dit* (Paris: Plon, 1971), 242–3.
12. Horne, *A Savage War of Peace*, 432, 545.
13. Beccaria, *Saint Marc*, 203.
14. Pierre Sergent, *Je ne regrette rien* (Paris: Fayard, 1972), 458.
15. Le Mire, *Histoire militaire*, 348.
16. Beccaria, *Saint Marc*, 221–2.
17. Ysquierdo, *Une guerre pour rien*, 102.
18. Beccaria, *Saint Marc*, 221–2.
19. Hora, *Mon tour*, 208.
20. ALE, *Rapport sur le morale*, 1er REI, 21 November 1961.
21. Sergent, *Ma peau*, 253.
22. Le Mire, *Histoire militaire*, 343.
23. Beccaria, *Saint Marc*, 227–8.
24. Le Mire, *Histoire militaire*, 348.
25. Le Mire, *Histoire militaire*, 343.
26. Murray, *Legionnaire*, 137–8.
27. Sergent, *Ma peau*, 274–5.
28. Murray, *Legionnaire*, 138.
29. Murray, *Legionnaire*, 139–41.
30. Beccaria, *Saint Marc*, 246.
31. Kemencei, *Légionnaire en avant!*, 336.
32. Kemencei, *Légionnaire en avant!*, 336.
33. ALE, *Rapport sur le moral*, 1er REI, 21 November 1961.
34. Kemencei, *Légionnaire en avant!*, 338–9.
35. Murray, *Legionnaire*, 142.
36. ALE, *Rapport sur le moral*, 1er REI, 21 November 1961.
37. Horne, *A Savage War of Peace*, 542.
38. ALE, *Rapport sur le moral*, 1er REI, 21 November 1961.
39. Murray, *Legionnaire*, 211.

Chapter 30

1. Murray, *Legionnaire*, 80.
2. William Brooks, "The French Foreign Legion Today: An American 82nd Airborne Vet Provides an Inside Look," Part One, *Soldier of Fortune*, Vol. 3 No. 4 (July 1978), 64–6.
3. Brooks, "The French Foreign Legion Today," Part Two, *Soldier of Fortune*, Vol. 3 No. 5 (September 1978), 39.
4. SHAT, 12P 82, 28 June, 1943.
5. Brooks, "The French Foreign Legion Today," Part Three, *Soldier of Fortune*, Vol. 3 No. 6 (November 1978), 70. This view has also been expressed to the author by French officers, although they concede that the operation was well executed.
6. Jennings, *A Mouthful of Rocks*, 156.
7. Brooks, "The French Foreign Legion Today," Part Three, 76–7.
8. Letter to the author from William Brooks.
9. Christian Jennings claimed that, "Three people I had met had been completely prepared to kill various Sergeants or Corporals because of the treatment they had received from them." Jennings, *A Mouthful of Rocks*, 109–10.

10. Gordon, *The French in Algiers,* 18.

11. M. M., *Memoirs of the Foreign Legion,* 168–9.

12. Murray, *Legionnaire,* 63.

13. Jennings, *A Mouthful of Rocks,* 181.

14. Letter to the author from William Brooks.

15. Hora, *Mon tour du monde,* 202.

16. Letter to the author from William Brooks.

17. Some of them were enemy nationals who were used profitably to police French colonial possessions. Others were also Jews whose capture by the Germans might have caused them serious problems, although it is not certain that this is why they were excluded from service at the front. But many were perfectly valid fighters, like a battalion of *volontaires étrangers* sent to Syria in 1940, composed mainly of Spaniards.

18. Berteil, *L'Armée de Weygand,* 51.

19. Liddell Hart, *Strange Company,* 206–7.

SELECTED BIBLIOGRAPHY

Books

Aage de Denmark, Prince. *Mes souvenirs de la Légion étrangère*. Paris: Payot, 1936.

Ainley, Henry. *In Order to Die: With the Foreign Legion in Indo-China*. London: Burke, 1955.

D'Albeca, Alexandre. *La France au Dahomey*. Paris: Hachette, 1895.

Alexander, Michael. *The Reluctant Legionnaire: An Escapade*. London: Rupert Hart-Davis, 1956.

Allainmat, Henry. *L'épreuve: Le "bagne" de la Légion*. Paris: Balland, 1977.

Amiable, Eugène. *Légionnaire au Mexique*. Brussels: Charles Dessart, 1942.

Anderson, Roy C. *Devils, Not Men: The History of the French Foreign Legion*. London: Robert Hale, 1987.

Andrew, Christopher, and Kanya-Forstner, A.S. *France Overseas*. London: Thames and Hudson, 1984.

Anonymous, *Pages de gloire de la division marocaine (1914–1918)*. Paris: Chapelot, nd.

———. *Reconnaissance du groupe mobile de Berguent, du 23 au 30 janvier 1906*. Paris: Berger-Levrault, 1906.

Armandy, André. *Les réprouvés*. Paris: Editions de France, 1930.

Armengaud, Captain Jean-Louis. *Le Sud-Oranais: Journal d'un légionnaire: Treize mois de colonne pendant l'insurrection des Oulad-Sidi-Cheikh soulevés par le Marabout Bou-Amama, 1881–1882*. Paris: Charles-Lavauzelle, 1893.

———. *Lang-son. Journal des opérations qui ont précédé et suivi la prise de cette citadelle*. Paris: Chapelot, 1901.

Armstrong, James Mackinley, and Elliott, William J. *Legion of Hell*. New York and London: Appleton, 1936.

Ashworth, Tony. *Trench Warfare, 1914–1918: The Live and Let Live System*. New York: Holmes & Meier, 1980.

Aubin, V.-R. *La Touraine pendant la guerre de 1870–1871*. Paris and Lille: Taffin-LeFort, 1893.

Aublet, Ed. *La guerre au Dahomey, 1888–1893.* Paris: Berger-Levrault, 1894.

Augustin, L. E. *Sur le Front français, 1917–1918: Combattant volontaire suisse au régiment de marche de la Légion étrangère.* Lausanne, Switzerland: Imprimerie centrale, 1934.

Azam, Captain Henri. *La Légion étrangère: ses règles particulières.* Sidi-bel-Abbès: Presses du *Képi blanc*, 1951.

Azan, Paul. *La Légion étrangère en Espagne, 1835–1839.* Paris: Charles-Lavauzelle, 1906.

———. *Conquête et pacification de l'Algérie.* Paris: Librairie de France, 1929.

———. *L'armée d'Afrique, 1830 à 1852.* Paris: Plon, 1936.

Azeau, Henri. *Révolte militaire. Alger, 22 avril 1961.* Paris: Plon, 1961.

Babin, Gustave. *La Légion étrangère: Petit historique du Régiment de marche de 1914 à 1917.* Paris: Berger-Levrault, nd.

Balesi, Charles. *From Adversaries to Comrades-in-Arms: West Africans and the French Military, 1885–1918.* Waltham, Mass.: Press Crossroads, 1986.

Banks, Arthur. *A Military Atlas of the First World War.* London: Heinemann, nd.

Bankwitz, Philip. *Maxime Weygand and Civil-Military Relations in France.* Cambridge, Mass.: MIT Press, 1967.

Bannerman, W. B. *Death March in the Desert: The Story of Mervyn Pellew, Ex-Légionnaire 8901.* London: Samson Low, nd.

Bapst, Germain. *Le Maréchal Canrobert: Souvenirs d'un siècle.* Paris: Plon, 1909–13, 6 vols.

du Barail, General F. C. *Mes souvenirs.* 3 vols. Paris: Plon, 1894–96.

Barbou, Alfred. *Histoire de la guerre au Dahomey.* Paris: Librairie Duquesne, 1893.

Bardanne, Jean. *Le légionnaire espion.* Paris: Baudinière, 1933.

Bartels, Albert. *Fighting the French in Morocco.* London: Alston Rivers, 1932.

Basset, Lieutenant. *Journal de marche, Indochine 1951–54.* Unpublished manuscript, 2e REI, Nîmes.

Beaufre, General André. *1940: The Fall of France.* New York: Knopf, 1968.

Beauvoir, Roger de. *La Légion étrangère.* Paris: Firmin Didot, 1897.

Beccaria, Laurent. *Hélie de Saint Marc.* Paris: Perrin, 1988.

Becker, Jean-Jacques. *1914: Comment les français sont entrés dans la guerre.* Paris: Presses de la Fondation nationale des sciences politiques, 1977.

Bergès, Maxime. *La Colonne de Marach et quelques autres récits de l'armée du Levant.* Paris: La Renaissance du Livre, nd.

Bergot, Erwan. *2e classe à Dien Bien Phu.* Paris: La Table Ronde, 1964.

———. *La Légion.* Paris: Balland, 1972.

———. *La Légion au combat: Narvik—Bir-Hakeim—Dien-Bien-Phu, la 13e Demi-Brigade de la Légion étrangère.* Paris: Presses de la Cité, 1975.

———. *Les 170 jours de Dien-Bien-Phu.* Paris: Presses de la Cité, 1979.

———. *Régiment de marche de la Légion.* Paris: Presses de la Cité, 1984.

Béric, Raoul. *Les routiers: La Légion étrangère: Source d'admiration et de pitié.* Paris: Edition Moderne, 1907.

Bern, J. *L'expédition du Dahomey: Notes éparses d'un légionnaire.* Sidi-Bel-Abbès: La-venue, 1893.

Bernelle, General Joseph, and de Colleville, Auguste. *Histoire de l'ancienne Légion étrangère.* Paris: E. Marc-Aurèle, 1850.

Berteil, Louis. *L'armée de Weygand.* Paris: Albatros, 1975.

Betrand, Gustave. *Enigma ou la plus grande énigme de la guerre, 1939–1945.* Paris: Plon, 1973.

Billington, Ray Allen. *Land of Savagery, Land of Promise: The European Image of the American Frontier.* London and New York: Norton, 1981.

Blackledge, W. J. *The Legion of Marching Madmen.* London: Samson Low, nd.

Blanc, Captain Alphonse Michel. *Types militaires d'antan: Généraux et soldats d'Afrique.* Paris: Plon, 1885.

———. *La Légion étrangère.* Paris: Téqui, 1890.

Blond, Georges. *La Légion étrangère.* Paris: Stock, 1964.

Bocca, Geoffrey. *La Legion! The French Foreign Legion and the Men Who Made it Glorious.* New York: Thomas Y. Crowell, 1964.

Bodard, Lucien. *La guerre d'Indochine: L'enlisement.* Paris: Gallimard, 1963. (*The Quick-sand War: Prelude to Vietnam.* Boston and Toronto: Little Brown, 1967.)

Bodinier, Gilbert. *1945–1946: Le retour de la France en Indochine. Textes et documents.* Vincennes: SHAT, 1987.

Boisset, Théophile. *Tuyen-Quan pendant la guerre.* Paris: Garnier, 1889.

———. *Tuyen-Quan pendant la siège.* Paris: Fischbacher, 1885.

Bolis, Sergeant Ernest. *Mémoires d'un sous-officier: Mes campagnes en Afrique et en Asie de 1889–1899.* Chalons-sur-Saône: Imprimerie du Courrier de Saône-et-Loire, 1905.

Bonaparte, Pierre-Napoléon. *Un mois en Afrique.* Paris: Pagnerre, 1850.

Bôn-Mat. *Souvenirs d'un légionnaire.* Paris: Messein, 1914.

Bonnecarrère, Paul. *Par le Sang Versé: La Légion étrangère en Indochine.* Paris: Fayard, 1968.

Boucher, Auguste. *Récits de l'invasion: Journal d'un bourgeois d'Orléans pendant l'occupation Prussienne.* Orleans: H. Herluison, 1871.

Boucher, Charles. *Lettres de Crimée: Souvenirs de guerre.* Paris: Calmann Lévy, 1877.

———. *Lettres et récits militaires.* Paris: Calmann-Lévy, 1897.

Boulanger, Pierre. *Le cinéma colonial de "L'Atlantide" à "Lawrence d'Arabie."* Paris: Seghers, 1975.

Brice, Raoul. *Un Lorrain à La Légion étrangère.* Paris: Edition moderne, nd.

Bruge, Roger. *Les combattants du 18 juin.* Paris: Fayard, 1982.

Brunon, Jean. *Camerone et l'aigle du Régiment étranger (1862–1870).* Marseille: Imprimerie Méridionale, 1935.

———. *Camerone.* Paris: France-Empire, 1963.

———, et al. *Le livre d'or de la Légion étrangère, 1831–1981.* Paris: Charles-Lavauzelle, 1981.

Bugeaud, T.-R. *Par l'épée et par la charrue: Ecrits et discours de Bugeaud.* Paris: Presses Universitaires de France, 1948.

Burleigh, Bennet. *Two Campaigns, Madagascar and Ashantee.* London: T. Fisher Unwin, 1896.

Bury, J. P. T., and Tombs, R. P. *Thiers, 1797–1877: A Political Life.* London: Allen & Unwin, 1986.

Cabrol, Roger. *"L'adaptation à la légion étrangère: Etude socio-psychopathologique."* Thèse pour le doctorate en médecine, Université de Bordeaux II, 1971.

Cameron, Ian. *Murder in the Legion.* London: Samson Low, nd.

Camps, Captain. *Le siège de Tuyen-Quan: Récit anecdotique par un témoin oculaire.* Verdun: 1902.

Camus, Antoine. *Les bohèmes du drapeau; 2ᵉ série: La Légion étrangère.* Paris: Brunet, 1864.

Carles, Pierre. *Des millions de soldats inconnus. La vie de tous les jours dans les armées de la IVᵉᵐᵉ République.* Paris: Charles-Lavauzelle, 1982.

Carpeaux, Louis. *La chasse aux pirates.* Paris: Grasset, 1913.

Carré, Lieutenant Colonel Albert. *Les engagés volontaires Alsaciens-Lorrains pendant la guerre.* Paris: Flammarion, 1923.

Carrel, Paul. *Afrika Korps.* Paris: J'ai Lu, 1963.

Carrey, Emile. *Récits de Kabylie.* Paris: Calmann-Lévy, 1876.

Cart-Tanneur, Philippe and Szecsko, Tibor. *Le premier étranger.* Paris.

Carteron, Captain R. *Souvenirs de la campagne du Tonkin.* Paris: Baudoin, 1891.

Casset, A. *Dans le "Sud Oranais."* Paris, 1911.

de Castellane, Comte P. *Souvenirs de la vie militaire en Afrique.* Paris: Calmann-Lévy, 1879.

de Castellane, Maréchal Victor. *Journal du maréchal de Castellane, 1804–1862.* Paris: Plon, 1895–97.

Castelot, André. *Maximilien et Charlotte du Mexique: La tragédie de l'ambition.* Paris: Librairie académique Perrin, 1977.

Cendrars, Blaise. *Bringolf.* Paris: Au Sans Pareil, 1930. (*I Have No Regrets: The Strange Life of a Diplomat-Vagrant being the Memoirs of Lieutenant Bringolf.* London: Dutton, 1932.)

————. *La main coupée*. Paris: Denoel, 1946. (*Lice*. London: New English Library, 1973.)

Chabrol, Emmanuel Commandant. *Opérations militaires au Tonkin*. Paris: Charles-Lavauzelle, 1896.

Champs, Captain. *Le siège de Tuyen-Quan par un témoin oculaire*. Verdun: Freschard, 1902.

de Charbonnières, Louis. *Une grande figure: Saint-Arnaud, maréchal de France*. Paris: Nouvelles éditions latines, 1960.

Charton, Colonel Pierre. *R.C. 4: Indochine 1950*. Paris: Société de Production Littéraire, 1975.

Christian, P. *L'Afrique française: l'empire du Maroc et les déserts du Sahara*. Paris: Barbier, nd.

de Choulot, P. *Souvenirs pour servir à l'histoire du 1er régiment de la Légion étrangère*. Paris: Dumaine; Bourges: J. Bernard, 1864.

Claton, Anthony. *France, Soldiers and Africa*. London and New York: Brassey's, 1988.

Clément-Grandcourt, Captain Abel. *Croquis marocains, sur la Moulouya*. Paris: Chapelot, 1913.

Cloverdale, John F. *The Basque Phase of Spain's First Carlist War*. Princeton, N.J.: Princeton University Press, 1984.

Combe, Doctor Louis. *Le soldat d'Afrique. Vol. 2: Le légionnaire, le tirailleur*. Paris: Charles-Lavauzelle, 1921.

Comor, André-Paul. *L'image de la Légion étrangère á travers la littérature française, 1900–1970*. Mémoire de maîtrise, Université de Provence, 1971.

————. *L'épopée de la 13ème demi-brigade de Légion étrangére, 1940–1945*. Paris: Nouvelles éditions latines, 1989.

Cooper, Adolphe Richard. *Twelve Years in the Foreign Legion*. Sydney, Australia: Angus & Robertson, 1933. Reissued as *Born to Fight*. Edinburgh and London: William Blackwood, 1969.

————. *Douze ans à la Légion étrangère*. Paris: Payot, 1934.

Corvisier, André. *Armies and Societies in Europe, 1494–1789*. Bloomington, Ind. and London: Indiana University Press, 1976.

Coupin, Luce. *Vainqueurs quand même: Le 11e de Légion étrangère au feu, 1939–1940*. Draveil: Luce Coupin, 1972.

Couvert, Léon. *En flanant dans l'Oasis: Une vie légionnaire*. Paris: Dervy-livres, nd.

Cranton, Captain Victor. *Keepers of the Desert*. London: Samson Low, nd.

Croizat, V.J. *Lessons from the War in Indochina*. Rand, May 1967.

Crowder, Michael (ed.). *West African Resistance: The Military Response to Colonial Occupation*. New York: Africana, 1972.

Dabbs, Jack Audrey. *The French Army in Mexico, 1861–1867: A Study in Civil-Military Relations*. The Hague: Mouton, 1963.

Dalloz, Jacques. *La guerre d'Indochine, 1945–1954*. Paris: Seuil, 1987.

Dangy, Luc. *Moi, légionnaire et marsouin: Algérie, Nouvelle-Calédonie—Nouvelles-Hébrides, 1902–1913*. Paris: Eugène Figuière, 1932.

Davet, Michel-Christian. *La double affaire de Syrie*. Paris: Fayard, 1967.

Davidson, General Philip B. *Vietnam at War: The History 1946–1975*. Novato, Ca.: Presidio Press, 1988.

Dejean, Georges. *La confession d'un légionnaire*. Paris: Albin Michel, 1919.

Delay, Paul. *Histoire anecdotique de la guerre de 1914–1915*. Paris: Lethielleux, 1915.

Dem, Marc. *Mourir pour Cao Bang: Le drame de la Route Coloniale n. 4*. Paris: Albin Michel, 1978.

Depew, Albert N. *Gunner Depew*. Chicago: Reilly & Britton, 1918.

Derfner, Colonel Xavier. *Les mémoires d'un légionnaire garibaldien*. Bordeaux: Impr. Delmas, 1961.

Derudder, Gustave. *Vie du commandant Clemmer: un soldat d'Afrique*. Calais: Imprimerie des Orphelins, 1889.

Des Ecorres, Charles. *Au pays des étapes: Notes d'un légionnaire*. Paris: Charles-Lavauzelle, 1892.

Des Vallières, Jean. *Sous le drapeau de la Légion étrangère: Les hommes sans noms.* Paris: Albin Michel, 1933.

———. *Sa grandeur l'Infortune.* Paris: Albin Michel, 1945.

———. *Et voici la Légion étrangère.* Paris: André Bonne, 1963.

de Diesbach, Ghislain. *Service de France.* Paris: Emile-Paul, 1972.

Diesbach de Torny, Gabriel, Captain. *Notes et souvenirs.* Unpublished manuscript, ALE.

Ditte, Lieutenant Colonel A. *Observations sur la guerre dans les colonies: Organisation—exécution. Conférences faites à l'école supérieur de la guerre.* Paris: Charles-Lavauzelle, 1905.

Dominé, Edmond Marc. *Journal du siège de Tuyen-Quan.* Paris: Charles-Lavauzelle, 1885.

Dorian, Jean-Pierre. *Souvenirs du colonel Maire, de la Légion étrangère.* Paris: Albin Michel, 1939.

———. *Le colonel Maire: Un héros de la Légion.* Paris: Albin Michel, nd.

Dosne, Madame. *Mémoires de Madame Dosne, l'égérie de M. Thiers.* 2 vols. Paris: Plon, 1928.

Doty, Bennett. *Legion of the Damned.* Garden City: Garden City Publishing Company, 1928. (*La légion des damnés.* Paris: Stock, nd.)

Doublet, V. *Vie de Don Carlos V de Bourbon, roi d'Espagne.* Bourges: Pornin, 1842.

Doyon, Jacques. *Les soldats blancs de Hô Chi Minh.* Paris: Fayard, 1973.

Duchesne, General Jacques. *Rapport sur l'expédition de Madagascar.* Paris and Nancy: Berger-Levrault, 1897.

Dugard, Henry. *La Légion étrangère.* Paris: Les Marches de l'Est, 1914.

Dunn, Ross E. *Resistance in the Desert: Moroccan Responses to French Imperialism, 1881–1912.* London: Croom Helm; Madison, Wis.: University of Wisconsin Press, 1977.

Duplesis, E. *The Cohort of the Damned: From "Bleu" to Captain.* London: Samson Low, nd.

Durel, Pétrus. *Le colonel Combe.* Lyon: Waltener, 1899.

Dutailly, Lieutenant Colonel Henry. *Les officiers servant à titre étranger, 9 mars 1831–31 décembre 1903.* Mémoire de maîtrise, Université d'Aix-en-Provence, 1969.

Ehle, John. *The Survivor: The Story of Eddy Hukov.* New York: Henry Holt, 1958.

Ehrhart, Joseph. *Mes treize années de Légion étrangère.* Unpublished manuscript, ALE.

Elford, George Robert. *Devil's Guard: The Incredible Story Behind the French Foreign Legion's Nazi Battalion in Indochina.* New York: Delacorte Press, 1971.

Elliott, William S. *The Tiger of the Legion: Being the Story of "Tiger" O'Reilly.* London: Samson Low & Marston, nd.

Ellis, John. *Cassino: The Hollow Victory.* New York: McGraw-Hill, 1984.

Elting, John R. *Swords Around the Throne: Napoleon's Grande Armée.* New York: The Free Press, 1988.

Erlande, Albert. *En campagne avec la Légion étrangère.* Paris: Payot, 1917.

Erulin, Elisabeth. *Les nationalités à la Légion étrangère.* Paris: Mémoire DESS de Défense, Université de Paris II, 1982–83.

d'Esparbès, Georges. *La Légion étrangère.* Paris: Flammarion, 1900.

———. *Les Mystères de la Légion étrangère.* Paris: Flammarion, 1912. Reissue of the 1900 volume.

Ex-Legionnaire 1384. *The Son of Allah.* London: Rich & Cowan, 1937.

———. *The Arab Patrol.* London: Samson Low, nd.

———. *Hell Hounds of France.* London: Samson Low, nd.

———. *Legion of the Lost.* London: Samson Low, nd.

———. *Spies of the Sahara.* London: Samson Low, nd.

Fall, Bernard. *Hell in a Very Small Place.* New York and Philadelphia: J. B. Lippincott, 1967.

Farale, Dominique. *La Légion a la peau dure.* Paris: France-Empire, 1964.

Farnsworth, Henry. *Letters of Henry Weston Farnsworth of the Foreign Legion.* Boston: 1916.

Farrère, Claude. *Extrême-Orient.* Paris: Flammarion, 1934.

Favrel, Charles. *Ci-devant légionnaire: La vraie légende de la Légion.* Paris: Presses de la Cité, 1963.

de la Faye, Jacques. *Souvenirs du Général Lacretelle.* Paris: Emile Paul, 1907.

Feller, Jean. *Le dossier de l'Armée française: La guerre de "Cinquante Ans." 1914–1962.* Paris: Perrin, 1966.

Ferri-Pisani. *Avec ceux de la Légion.* Paris: Editions de France, 1932.

Fieffé, Eugène. *Histoire des troupes étrangères au service de la France.* 2 vols. Paris: Dumaine, 1854.

Fleury, Georges. *Mourir à Lang Son: 9 mars 1945 les Nippons attaquent en Indochine.* Paris: Grasset, 1985.

Fontelroye, Jacques. *Des morts au soleil.* Paris: Calmann-Lévy, 1926.

Forbes, Reginald R. *Red Horizon.* London: Samson Low, nd.

Forey, Captain Elie Frédéric. *Campagnes d'Afrique, 1835–1848: Lettres adressées au maréchal de Castellane par le captaine Forey.* Paris: Plon, 1898.

Franchini, Philippe. *Les guerres d'Indochine.* 2 vols. Paris: Pygmalion, 1988.

Froelicher, Captain Emile. *Le siège de Milianah, ses ravitaillements.* Paris: Charles-Lavauzelle, 1889.

G. M. (G. Morel). *La Légion étrangère et les troupes coloniales.* Paris: Chapelot, 1903.

Galant, Abel. *Précis historique de la Légion étrangère en Espagne.* Unpublished manuscript, SHAT.

Galli, H. *Carnet de campagne du lieutenant-colonel Lentonnet.* Paris: Plon, 1899.

Galliéni, Joseph. *Trois colonnes au Tonkin (1894–1895).* Paris: Chapelot, 1899.

———. *Mémoires du Maréchal Galliéni: Défense de Paris, 25 août—11 septembre 1914.* Paris: Payot, 1926.

Gandy, Alain. *Royal étranger: Légionnaires cavaliers au combat 1921–1984.* Paris: Presses de la Cité, 1985.

Garnot, Captain. *L'expédition française de Formose, 1884–1885.* Paris: Delagrave, 1894.

Gaudron, Max. *Légionnaire au Nord du Tonkin: La Légion en Indochine, 1949–1950.* Paris: Copernic, 1980.

Gaulot, Paul. *L'expédition du Mexique (1861–1867): D'après les documents et souvenirs de Ernest Louet.* Paris: Nouvelle édition, 1906.

Gaultier, General Louis, and Jacquot, Colonel Charles. *C'est la Légion.* 3 vols. Marseilles: Les Impressions Françaises, 1963.

Geraghty, Tony. *March or Die: France and the Foreign Legion.* London: Grafton, 1986.

Gordon, Lady Duff. *The French in Algiers.* London: John Murray, 1855.

Grandin, Commandant Léonce. *A l'assaut du pays des noirs: Le Dahomey.* Paris: René Haton Librairie, 1895.

———. *Mémoires d'un chef de Partisans: De Vera-Cruz à Mazatlan.* Paris: Zolra, 1895.

de Grandmaison, Captain L. *En territoire militaire.* Paris: Plon, 1898.

Gras, General Yves. *Histoire de la guerre d'Indochine.* Paris: Plon, 1979.

———. *La 1ère DFL; Les Français libres au combat.* Paris: Presses de la Cité, 1983.

Green, Julian. *Memoirs of Happy Days.* New York and London: Harper & Brothers, 1942.

Grenest, Eugène Désiré Edouard. *L'armée de la Loire. Relation anecdotique de la campagne de 1870–71.* Paris: Garnier, 1893.

Griffith, Paddy. *Military Thought in the French Army, 1815–1851.* Manchester, England, and New York: Manchester University Press, 1989.

Grisot, General Paul Adolphe, and Coulombon, Lieutenant Ernest. *La Légion étrangère de 1831 à 1887.* Paris: Berger-Levrault, 1888.

Hanotaux, Gabriel. *L'Affaire de Madagascar.* Paris: Calmann-Lévy, 1896.

Harrison, James P. *The Endless War: Vietnam's Struggle for Independence.* New York: Columbia University Press, 1989.

Harvey, John. *With the Foreign Legion in Syria.* London: Hutchinson, nd.

de la Hayrie, General. *Le combat de Camerone, 30 avril 1863.* Lille: Danel, 1889.

Hélo, Captain. *L'infanterie montée dans le Sud Algérien et dans le Sahara.* Paris: Charles-Lavauzelle, 1895.

Herbillon, Emile. *Relation du siège de Zaatcha.* Paris: J. Dumaine, 1863.

———. *Quelques pages d'un vieux cahier. Souvenirs du général Herbillon, 1794–1866.* Paris: Berger-Levrault, 1928.

Historia, spécial: 150ᵉ anniversaire, La Légion étrangère. Paris: Tallandier, 1981.

Historique des unités de la Légion étrangère pendant la guerre 1914–1918, Maroc et Orient. Oran: Heinz, 1922.

Historique du 1er bataillon formant corps du 1er régiment étranger et du 1er bataillon du 4e régiment de la Légion étrangère. Marrakech: Hébréard, nd.

Historique du 2e bataillon formant corps du 1er régiment étranger. Casablanca: Mercié, nd.

Historique du régiment de marche de la Légion étrangère: 3e régiment étranger d'infanterie. Paris: Berger-Levrault, 1926.

Hobsbawm, Eric, and Ranger, Terrance (eds.). *The Invention of Tradition.* Cambridge, England: Cambridge University Press: 1983.

Holmes, Richard. *Acts of War: The Behavior of Men in Battle.* New York: Free Press, 1986.

Hora, Charles. *Mon tour du monde en quatre-vingts barouds.* Paris: Pensée Moderne, 1961.

Horne, Alistair. *A Savage War of Peace, Algeria 1954–1962.* London: Macmillan, 1977.

Howe, Sonia. *The Drama of Madagascar.* London: Methuen, 1938.

Huart, Abel. *D'une démission à une réinstallation ou trois années d'entr'acte au Mexique et en Afrique.* Orléans: Georges Micau, 1890.

————. *Souvenirs de la guerre du Mexique (1862–1867).* Orléans: Auguste Goût, 1906.

Hubert-Jacques. *L'Allemagne et la Légion étrangère.* Paris: Chapelot, 1914.

Huguet, L. *En colonne: Souvenirs d'extrême-Orient.* Paris: Flammarion, nd.

Huot, Dr. Louis, and Voivenel, Dr. Paul. *Le Cafard.* Paris: Bernard Grasset, 1918.

Huré, General R. *L'Armée d'Afrique, 1830–1962.* Paris: Charles-Lavauzelle, 1977.

d'Ideville, Comte H. *Le maréchal Bugeaud: d'après sa correspondance intime et des documents inédits, 1784–1882.* Paris: Firmin-Didot, 1881–82.

Ivanoff, Hubert. *Le Premier régiment étranger de cavalerie en Indochine, 1947–1956.* Mémoire de maîtrise, Université Paul Valéry, 1982.

Jacqueline, Lucien. *Correspondance.* Unpublished letters in the collection of Richard Mahaud.

Jacquin, Henri. *Guerre Secrète en Indochine.* Paris: Olivier Orban, 1979.

Jacquot, Captain. *Mon Journal de Marche du Dahomey, 1892–1893.* Unpublished manuscript in possession of the author.

Jauffret, J.-C., and Gugliotta, Georges. *Les compagnies montées de la Légion étrangère, 1881–1950.* Mémoire de maîtrise, l'Institut d'études politiques d'Aix-en-Provence, 1973.

Jauffret, J.-C. *L'idée d'une division de Légion étrangère et le premier régiment étranger de cavalerie, 1836–1940.* Thèse pour le doctorat de 3e cycle, Université Paul Valéry, 1978.

Jennings, Christian. *A Mouthful of Rocks: Modern Adventures in the French Foreign Legion.* New York: The Atlantic Monthly Press, 1989.

Joffé, Constantin. *We Were Free.* New York: Simon & Durrell, 1943.

Joliet, Captain. *Historique de la 2e compagnie montée du 1er régiment étranger pendant la guerre 1914–1918.* Paris: Charles-Lavauzelle, 1920.

Julien, Charles-André. *Histoire de l'Algérie contemporaine: Conquête et colonisation.* Paris: Presses Universitaires de France, 1964.

Junger, Ernst. *Jeux africains.* Paris: Gallimard, 1970.

Junod, Edouard. *Lettres et souvenirs.* Paris: Georges Crès, 1918.

Kamienski, Miccilas. *Souvenirs.* Paris: Librairie nouvelle, 1861.

————. *Mort d'un soldat.* Paris: 1960.

Kanitz, Walter. *The White Kepi: A Casual History of the French Foreign Legion.* Chicago: Henry Regnery Company, 1956.

Kanya-Forstner, A. S. *The Conquest of the Western Sudan: A Study in French Military Imperialism.* Cambridge, England: Cambridge University Press, 1969.

Kellett, Anthony. *Combat Motivation: The Behavior of Soldiers in Battle.* Boston, The Hague, London: Kluwer Nijoff, 1982.

Kelly, Russell A. *Kelly of the Foreign Legion: Letters of Légionnaire Russell A. Kelly.* New York: Mitchell Kennerley, 1917.

Kemencei, Janos. *Légionnaire en avant!* Paris: Jacques Gracher, 1985.

King, David Wooster. *"L.M. 8046": An Intimate Story of the Foreign Legion.* New York: Duffield, 1927.

Kirwan, Captain M. W. *Reminiscences of the Franco-German War, by Captain Kirwan, Late Captain Commanding the Irish Legion During the War of 1870–71.* London: Simpkin, 1873.

Knight, E. F. *Madagascar in Wartime.* London: Longmans Green, 1896.

Koenig, General Pierre. *Ce jour-là: Bir Hakeim.* Paris: Robert Laffont, 1971.

Kremar, Othon Patrick. *Sidi-bel-Abbès et les Bel-Abbèsiens: Une ville française, 1843–1962.* Montpellier: Africa Nostra, 1962.

Krop, Pascal. *Les socialistes et l'armée.* Paris: Presses Universitaires de France, 1983.

Labeur, François. *Jean Klein, Légionnaire.* Paris: Grasset, 1912.

Laffin, John. *The French Foreign Legion.* London: Dent, 1974.

Lambert, Commandant. *La Légion étrangère.* Paris: Charles-Lavauzelle, 1923.

Lamborelle, Louis. *Cinq ans en Afrique: Souvenirs militaires d'un Belge au service de la France.* Brussels: 1862.

Langlois, Lieutenant Gustave Léon. *Souvenirs de Madagascar.* Paris: Charles-Lavauzelle, 1897.

Lanusse, L'abbé. *Les Héros de Camaron, 30 avril 1863.* Paris: Marmon et Flammarion, 1891.

Lapie, Pierre-Olivier. *La Légion étrangère à Narvik.* London: John Murray, 1941; Paris: Flammarion, 1945.

de la Rocca, Jean. *Pierre-Napoléon Bonaparte: Sa vie et ses oeuvres.* Paris: Au bureau du journal de l'*Avenir de la Corse*, 1867.

Lartéguy, Jean. *The Centurions.* New York: Dutton, 1962.

———. *The Praetorians.* New York: Dutton, 1963.

Lebedev, V. *Souvenirs d'un volontaire Russe dans l'Armée française.* Paris: Librairie académique, 1917.

Lebon, André. *La pacification de Madagascar, 1896–1898.* Paris: Plon, 1928.

Lechartier, Captain Georges Germain Félix. *Colonne du Haut-Guir en septembre 1908.* Paris: Chapelot, 1908.

Lefèvre, G. *Les Mémoires du sergent Lefèvre à la Légion étrangère, 1907–1909.* Unpublished manuscript, ALE.

Lelièvre, Henri Paul. *Campagne du Dahomey, 2 août 1892 au 6 novembre 1892.* Unedited manuscript, ALE.

Le Mire, Henri. *Histoire de la Légion de Narvik à Kolwesi.* Paris: Albin Michel, 1978.

———. *Histoire militaire de la guerre d'Algérie.* Paris: Albin Michel, 1982.

Lentonnet, Jean-Louis. *Carnet de campagne du lieutenant-colonel Lentonnet.* Paris: Plon, 1899.

Le Page, Colonel Marcel. *Cao Bang: La tragique épopée de la colonne Le Page.* Paris: Nouvelles Editions Latines, 1981.

Le Poer, John Patrick. *A Modern Legionary.* New York: Dutton, 1905. (*A la Légion étrangère: Journal d'un Irlandais.* Paris: Juvens, 1905.)

Liddell Hart, Adrian. *Strange Company.* London: Weidenfeld and Nicolson, 1953.

Löhndorff, Ernst F. *Hell in the Foreign Legion.* New York: Greensberg, 1932.

de Lonlay, Dick. *Au Tonkin, 1883–1885: Récits anecdotiques.* Paris: Garnier, 1886.

———. *Le siège de Tuyen-Quan (du 24 novembre 1884 au 3 mars 1885).* Paris: Garnier, 1889.

Lorillard, Lieutenant Colonel Paul Joseph. *La guerre au Maroc.* Paris: Charles-Lavauzelle, 1934.

Love, J. Duncan, et al. *Helicopter Operations in the French-Algerian War.* McLean, Va.: Research Analysis Corporation, 1965.

Lyautey, Hubert. *Lettres du Tonkin et de Madagascar, 1884–1899.* Paris: Armand Colin, 1942.

M. M. *Memoirs of the Foreign Legion.* New York: Knopf, 1925.

Mac Leave, Hugh. *The Damned Die Hard: The Colorful, True Story of the French Foreign Legion.* New York: Saturday Review Press, 1973.

Mac-Orlan, Pierre. *Légionnaires: La Légion étrangère espagnole, la Légion étrangère française.* Paris: Editions du Capitole, 1930.

Mac Swiney, Terence. *Extrême-Sud: Sous le drapeau de la Légion étrangère.* Geneva: Editions du Mont-Blanc, 1947.

Maire, Colonel Fernand. *Nouveaux souvenirs sur la Légion étrangère.* Paris: Fayard, 1948.

Maldan, Captain P. *Le général Espinasse.* Paris: Cosson, nd.

Mannington, G. *A Soldier of the Legion or an Englishman's Adventures Under the French Flag in Algeria and Tonkin.* London: John Murray, 1907.

Manue, G. -R. *Têtes brûlées: Cinq ans à la Légion.* Paris: Nouvelle Société d'édition, 1929.

———. *Sur les marches du Maroc insoumis.* Paris: Gallimard, 1930.

———. *La retraite au désert. Récit.* Paris: A. Redier, 1932.

———. *Sous la grenade à sept flammes: Comment on a créé un corps d'élite, 1939–1940.* Paris: Sequana, 1941. Manuscript version entitled *Vu du rang.* ALE.

Marabini, Captain Camillo. *Les Garibaldiens de l'Argonne.* Paris: Payot, 1917.

Maradan, Evelyne. *Les suisses et la Légion étrangère de 1831 à 1861.* Mémoire de licence, Université de Fribourg, 1987.

Marches et chants de la Légion étrangère. Aubagne: Presses du *Képi blanc,* nd.

Marolf, Alphonse. *Gustave Marolf: Capitaine mitrailleur au 1er étranger, 1884–1916. Léttres, récits, souvenirs.* Geneva: Imprimerie central, 1943.

Marrus, Michael R. and Paxton, Robert O. *Vichy France and the Jews.* New York: Basic Books, 1981.

Marshal, S.L.A. *Men Against Fire.* New York: Morrow & Co., 1947.

Martin, Jean. *Je suis un légionnaire.* Paris: Fayard, 1938.

Martyn, Frederic. *Life in the Legion from a Soldier's Point of View.* New York: Scribner's, 1911.

de Massol, Marquis Louis. *France, Algérie, Orient.* Versailles: Beau, 1860.

Massu, Jacques. *La vraie bataille d'Alger.* Paris: Plon, 1971.

Mathias, Jean. *Bir-Hackeim.* Paris: Editions de Minuit, 1955.

Mattéi, Antoine. *Tu survivras longtemps: Les baroudeurs de la Légion en Indochine.* Paris: Olivier Orban, 1975.

Maurel, Captain. *Les compagnies montées du Sud-Oranais.* Paris: Chapelot, 1913.

Maury, A.-P. *Mes campagnes au Tonkin.* Lyon: Vitte et Peyrussel, 1888.

———. *La Légion étrangère.* Paris: Flammarion, 1933.

McAleavy, Henry. *Black Flags in Vietnam: The Story of a Chinese Intervention. The Tonkin War of 1884–85.* New York: Macmillan, 1968.

McLean, Angus. *Vive la Legion.* London: Samson Low, nd.

Mémento du légionnaire du Régiment de marche de la Légion étrangère, 1943–1945, et du 3e Régiment étranger, 1945. Paris: Guy Le Prat, nd.

Mémento du soldat de la Légion étrangère. Sidi-Bel-Abbès: Presses du 1er étranger, 1937.

Mercer, Charles. *The Foreign Legion: The Vivid History of a Unique Military Tradition.* London: Arthur Barker, 1964.

Merolli, Aristide. *La grenade héroïque: Avant la tourmente.* Casablanca-Fez: Editions Moynier, 1937.

———, and Nadau, Lieutenant. *Une visite à la salle d'honneur.* Sidi-Bel-Abbès: Presses du 1er Régiment étranger, 1930.

Meyer, Charles. *La vie quotidienne des Français en Indochine, 1860–1910.* Paris: Hachette, 1985.

Micaud, Etienne. *La France au Mexique.* Paris: Editions du monde moderne, 1927.

Ministère de la guerre. *Les Armées françaises dans la Grande Guerre.* Tome VIII, 1er volume. Paris: Service historique de l'état major de l'Armée, 1923.

de Miribel, Guy. *Mémoires du maréchal de Mac-Mahon, duc de Magenta: Souvenirs d'Algérie.* Paris: Plon, 1932.

Moberg, Gôsta. *La Légion étrangère et son pays d'élection.* Paris: Charles-Lavauzelle, 1956.

Moch, Gaston. *La question de la Légion étrangère.* Paris: Bibliothèque Charpentier, 1914.

Mordacq, General J. J. H. *Le ministère Clémenceau: Journal d'un témoin, vol. 3, Novembre 1918–juin 1919.* Paris: Plon, 1931.

Mordal, Jacques. *Bir-Hackeim.* Paris: Amiot-Dumont, 1952.

Morel, Lieutenant Colonel Paul Emile Gustave. *La Légion étrangère, recueil de documents concernant l'historique, l'organisation et la législation spéciale des régiments étrangers.* Paris: Chapelot, 1912.

Morlae, Edward. *A Soldier of the Legion.* Boston and New York: Houghton Mifflin, 1916.

Murray, Simon. *Legionnaire: My Five Years in the French Foreign Legion.* New York: Times Books, 1978.

Navarre, Henri. *Agonie de l'Indochine (1953–1954).* Paris: Plon, 1956.

Noia, Louis. *Campagne de Crimée.* Clichy: Imprimerie Loignon, nd.

Noland, Emile. *Le Conquérant.* Paris: Calmann-Lévy, nd.

Notes sur la campagne du 3ᵉ bataillon de la Légion étrangère au Tonkin. Paris and Limoges: Charles-Lavauzelle, 1888.

O'Ballance, Edgar. *The Story of the Foreign Legion.* London: Faber and Faber, 1961.

Operator 1384. *The Devil's Diplomat.* London: Hutchinson, nd.

Orléans, Duc d'. *Campagnes d'Afrique, 1835–1839.* Paris: Michel Lévy, 1870.

Paillat, Claude. *Dossiers secrets de la France contemporaine, vol. III: La guerre à l'horizon, 1930–1938.* Paris: Robert Laffont, 1981.

———. *Dossier secret de l'Indochine.* Paris: Presses de la Cité, 1964.

Pannier, J. *Trois ans en Indochine: Notes de voyage.* Toulouse: Société des publications morales et religieuses, 1906.

Papiers et correspondance de la famille impériale saisis aux Tuileries. Paris: Imprimerie Nationale, 1871–72.

Paret, Peter. *French Revolutionary Warfare from Indochina to Algeria: The Analysis of a Political and Military Doctrine.* New York: Praeger, 1964.

———, (ed.). *The Makers of Modern Strategy.* Princeton, N.J.: Princeton University Press, 1987.

Parker, Geoffrey. *The Army of Flanders and the Spanish Road.* Cambridge, England: Cambridge University Press, 1972.

Paxton, Robert O. *Parades and Politics at Vichy: The French Officer Corps under Marshal Pétain.* Princeton, N.J.: Princeton University Press, 1966.

———. *Vichy France: Old Guard and New Order, 1940–1944.* London: Barry & Jenkins, 1972.

———, and Marrus, Michael R. *Vichy France and the Jews.* New York: Basic Books, 1981.

Pechkoff, Zinovi. *The Bugle Sounds.* New York: Appleton, 1926.

———. *La Légion étrangère au Maroc, 1923–1925.* Paris: Marcelle Lesage, 1929.

Pedroncini, Guy. *Les mutineries de 1917.* Paris: Presses Universitaires de France, 1967.

Pélissier, Jean-Jacques. *Aspects de la vie politique et militaire en France à travers la correspondance reçue par le maréchal Pélissier (1828–1864).* Paris: Bibliothèque nationale, 1968.

Penette, General Marcel, and Castaingt, Captain Jean. *La Legión Extranjera en la Intervención Francesa, 1863–1867.* Mexico City: Sociedad Mexicana de Geografía y Estadística, 1962.

Perrott-White, Alfred. *French Legionnaire.* London: John Murray, 1953.

Pfirmann, Jean. *Le sergent Pfirmann.* Unpublished manuscript, ALE.

Pipes, Daniel. *Slaves, Soldiers and Islam: The Genesis of a Military System.* New Haven and London: Yale University Press, 1981.

Planchais, Jean. *Une histoire politique de l'armée, vol. 2, 1940–1962: De de Gaulle à de Gaulle.* Paris: Le Seuil, 1967.

Poimiro, Charles. *La Légion étrangère et le droit international.* Paris: Berger-Levrault, 1913.

Poinsot, M.-C. *Les volontaires étrangers enrôlés au service de la France en 1914–1915.* Paris: Berger-Levrault, nd.

Poirier, Jules. *Conquête de Madagascar, 1895–1896.* Paris: Charles-Lavauzelle, nd.

Poliakov, Léon. *Histoire de l'Antisemitisme. L'Europe suicidaire. 1870–1933.* Paris: Calmann-Lévy, 1977.

Porch, Douglas. *Army and Revolution: France 1815–1848.* London: Routledge & Kegan Paul, 1977.

———. *The March to the Marne: The French Army, 1871–1914.* Cambridge, England: Cambridge University Press, 1981.

————. *The Conquest of Morocco*. New York: Knopf, 1982.

————. *The Conquest of the Sahara*. New York: Knopf, 1984.

Poirmeur, H. *Notre vieille Légion*. Paris: Berger-Levrault, 1931.

Pouliot, Henri. *Légionnaire! . . . Histoire véridique et vécue d'un Québecois simple soldat à la Légion étrangère*. Quebec: Le Soliel, 1931.

Pralon, Le Père. *Lionel Hart, engagé volontaire, sous-officier à la Légion étrangère, glorieusement tombé au Tonkin à vingt ans*. Paris: Retaux-Bray 1888.

Premschwitz, Raimund Anton. *Meine Erlebnisse als Fremdenlegioner in Algerien. Ein Warnungsruf an Wehrpflichtige von Raimund Anton Premschitz*. Metz: Müller, 1904.

Prêtre, Elysée. *Les cafardeux. (Ceux de la Légion)*. Paris: La Renaissance moderne, 1929.

Prokos, Captain G. *Opérations coloniales: Tactique des petits détachements. Vol. II. Chine et Indochine*. Paris: Charles-Lavauzelle, nd.

Pruvost, Th. *Le général Deplanque, 1820–1889*. Paris: Charles-Lavauzelle, 1902.

Pryne, Rudyers. *War in Morocco.*Tangier: 1927.

Querle, Anthony James. *"Allah Il Allah."* London: Samson Low, nd.

Quris, Bernard. *L'aventure légionnaire*. Paris: France-Empire, 1971.

Ragot, Jacques. *De Gaulle, la Légion, l'Algérie: Souvenirs d'un officier*. La Teste: 1984.

Randin, Léon. *A la Légion étrangère*. Paris: Fischbacher; Neuchâtel: Delachaux et Niestlé, 1906.

Rankin, Reginald. *In Morocco with General d'Amade*. London: John Lane the Bodley Head, 1931.

Rastoul, A. *Le maréchal Randon (1795–1871), d'après ses mémoires et des documents inédits: Etude militaire et politique*. Paris: Firmin-Didot, 1890.

Ratz, Joseph. *La France que je cherchais: Les impressions d'un Russe engagé volontaire en France*. Limoges: Imprimerie Bontemps, 1945.

Raulet, André. *Légion uber alles! Souvenirs de la Légion étrangère*. Paris: Charles-Lavauzelle, 1934.

Reibell, General Emile. *Le calvaire de Madagascar: Notes et souvenirs de 1895*. Paris: Berger-Levrault, 1935.

Revue Historique des Armées. No. spécial 1981, *La Légion étrangère*. Vincennes: 1980.

Reybaz, Jean. *Le 1er Mystérieux: souvenirs de guerre d'un légionnaire suisse*. Paris: André Barry, 1932.

Richard, Jules. *La jeune armée*. Paris: La librairie illustrée, 1890.

Richards, Jeffrey. *Visions of Yesterday*. London: Routledge and Kegan Paul, 1973.

Rockwell, Paul Ayres. *American Fighters in the Foreign Legion (1914–1918)*. Boston and New York: Houghton Mifflin, 1930.

Rocolle, Pierre. *Pourquoi Dien Bien Phu?* Paris: Flammarion, 1968.

Roger-Mathieu, J. *Mémoires d'Abd el-Krim*. Paris: Librairie des Champs-Elysées, 1927.

Rosen, Erwin. *In the Foreign Legion*. London: Duckworth, 1910.

Rosenthal, Philip. *Il était une fois un légionnaire*. Paris: Albin Michel, 1982.

Roucaute, Yves. *Le PCF et l'armée*. Paris: Presses Universitaires de France, 1983.

Roullet, Jacques. *Le légionnaire: Drame en quatre actes & cinq tableaux*. Paris: C. Joubert, 1924.

Rousselet, Louis. *Sur les confins du Maroc, d'Oudjda à Figuig*. Paris: Hachette, 1912.

Rousset, Camille. *La conquête de l'Algérie*. Paris: Plon, 1889.

Roy, Jules. *The Battle of Dien Bien Phu*. New York: Carroll & Graf, 1984.

Saint-Arnaud, Achille de. *Lettres du maréchal de Saint-Arnaud*. 2 vols. Paris: Calmann-Lévy, 1864.

de Sairigné, Gabriel. *Carnet de route de Lieutenant Gabriel de Sairigné*. Unpublished diary, ALE.

Savelli, Bernard. *La légion étrangère au Tonkin des origines à 1914*. Mémoire de maîtrise, Faculté de lettres, Aix-en-Provence, 1971.

Schama, Simon. *An Embarrassment of Riches: An Interpretation of Dutch Culture in the Golden Age*. New York: Knopf, 1987.

Scott, Samuel F. *The Response of the Royal Army to the French Revolution: The Role and*

Development of the Line Army, 1787–1793. Oxford, England: Oxford University Press, 1978.

Seeger, Alan. *Letters and Diary of Alan Seeger.* New York: Scribner's, 1917.

de Segura, A. *Des volontaires étrangers.* Unpublished manuscript, ALE.

Séreau, Raymond. *L'éxpedition de Norvège 1940.* Baden-Baden: Régie Autonome des publications officielles, 1949.

Sergent, Pierre. *Ma peau au bout de mes idées.* Paris: La Table Ronde, 1967.

———. *Je ne regrette rien.* Paris: Fayard, 1972.

———. *Les Maréchaux de la Légion.* Paris: Fayard, 1977.

———. *Camerone.* Paris: Fayard, 1980.

———. *Un étrange Monsieur Frey.* Paris: Fayard, 1982.

Serman, W. *Les officiers français dans la nation, 1848–1914.* Paris: Aubin, 1982.

Sheean, Vincent. *An American among the Riffi.* New York and London: Century, 1926.

Silbermann, Le Soldat. *Cinq ans à la Légion étrangère, dix ans dans l'infanterie de marine: Souvenirs de campagne.* Paris: Plon, 1910.

Silvagni, Giulo Cesare. *La peau des mercenaires.* Paris: Gallimard, 1954.

———. *La Légion marche sur Rome.* Paris: Gallimard, 1961.

Simon, Pierre-Henri. *Contre la torture.* Paris: Le Seuil, 1957.

Smith, Leonard V. *Command Authority in the French Army: The Case of the 5ᵉ Division d'Infanterie.* Ph.D. diss., Columbia University, 1989.

Snaith, J. C. *Surrender: A Most Impressive Story About Two Deserters from the Foreign Legion.* London: Hodder and Stoughton, nd.

Souriau, Marcel. *De la bäionette à l'épée.* Paris: Eugène Figuière, 1934.

Spiers, Edward M. *Radical General: Sir George de Lacy Evans, 1787–1870.* Manchester, England: Manchester University Press, 1983.

Spinner, Henri. *Souvenirs d'un vieux soldat.* Neuchâtel: Messeiller, 1906.

Stammer, William. *Recollections of a Life of Adventure.* London: Hurst & Blackett, 1866.

Strachan, Hew. *Wellington's Legacy: The Reform of the British Army, 1830–1854.* Manchester, England: Manchester University Press, 1984.

Stuart, Brian. *Adventures in Algeria.* London: Herbert Jenkins, 1936.

Sullivan, Anthony Thrall. *Thomas-Robert Bugeaud: France and Algeria, 1784–1849. Power, Politics and the Good Society.* Hamden, Conn.: Archon Books, 1983.

Swiggett, Howard. *March or Die: The Story of the French Foreign Legion.* New York: Putnam, 1953.

Sylvère, Antoine. *Le légionnaire Flutsch.* Paris: Plon, 1982.

Szajkowski, Zosa. *Jews and the French Foreign Legion.* New York: KATV, 1975.

Szecsko, Tibor. *Implantation et engagement de la Légion étrangère au Tonkin, 1914–1941.* Doctorat d'université d'histoire, Université Paul Valéry—Montpellier III, 1987.

Szwartzbard, Sholem. *In krig mit zikh aleyn.* Chicago: 1933.

Talbott, John. *The War Without a Name: France in Algeria, 1954–1962.* New York: Knopf, 1980.

Thirion, Commandant Paul. *L'expédition de Formose: Souvenirs d'un soldat.* Paris: Charles-Lavauzelle, 1897.

Thomazi, A. *La conquête de l'Indochine.* Paris: Payot, 1934.

Todorov, Kosta. *Balkan Firebrand.* Chicago and New York: Ziff Davis, 1943.

Tombs, Richard. *The War Against Paris.* Cambridge, England: Cambridge University Press, 1981.

Tournoux, J.-R. *Jamais dit.* Paris: Plon, 1971.

Townsend, John. *The Legion of the Damned.* London: The Adventurers Club, 1963.

Turnbull, Patrick. *Solferino: The Birth of a Nation.* New York: Saint Martin's, 1985.

Vandenberg, Charles. *La Légion étrangère, à propos du combat d'El-Moungar.* Paris: Chapelot, 1904.

Van der Smissen, General Alfred Louis Adolphe Graves. *Souvenirs du Mexique, 1864–1867.* Brussels: J. Lebègue, 1892.

Vidalenc, J. *Les demi-soldes.* Paris: Librairie Marcel Rivière, 1955.

Viollis, Andrée. *Indochine S.O.S.* Paris: Gallimard, 1935.

Virès, Paul. *Souvenirs de la Légion étrangère.* Geneva: Centre d'Education Ouvrière, 1928.

Von Rahden, Wilhelm. *Wanderungen eines alten Soldaten.* Berlin: 1851.

Von Rosen, G. *Bilder aus Spanien und der Fremdenlegion, Erster Band.* Kiel: Bunsow, 1843.

Wagner, L. *Carnet de route d'un légionnaire au Maroc, 1907–1908.* Casablanca: Imprimeries réunies de la vigie marocaine et du petit marocain, 1938.

Ward-Price, G. *In Morocco with the Legion.* London: Anchor Press, 1934. (*Au Maroc avec la Légion.* Paris: Payot, 1933.)

Waterhouse, Francis A. *Five Sous a Day.* London: Samson Low, nd.

———. *Twixt Hell and Allah.* London: Samson Low, nd.

Waugh, Evelyn. *When the Going Was Good.* London: Penguin, 1975.

Wellard, James. *The French Foreign Legion.* Boston and Toronto: Little, Brown and Company, 1974.

Weygand, Jacques. *Légionnaire.* Paris: Flammarion, 1951.

Weygand, General Maxime. *Mémoires.* Paris: Flammarion, 1950.

Windrow, Martin. *The French Foreign Legion: Airfix Magazine Guide 13.* London: Patrick Stephens, 1976.

Woolman, David S. *Rebels in the Rif: Abd el-Krim and the Rif Rebellion.* Stanford, Ca.: Stanford University Press, 1968.

Wolseley, General Viscount, *The Soldier's Pocket-Book for Field Service.* London: Macmillan Co., 1886.

Wren, P. C. *Foreign Legion Omnibus: Beau Geste, Beau Sabreur, Beau Ideal.* New York: Grosset & Dunlap, 1928.

———. *Sowing Glory: The Memoirs of "Mary Ambree" the English Woman-Legionary.* New York: Frederick A. Stokes, 1931.

———. *Port of Missing Men: Strange Tales of the Foreign Legion.* Philadelphia: Macrae-Smith, 1943.

———. *Stories of the Foreign Legion.* London: John Murray, 1947.

Wylie, I. A. R. *The Foreign Legion.* New York: Grosset & Dunlap, nd.

Ysquierdo, Antoine. *Une guerre pour rien.* Paris: La Table Ronde, 1966.

X . . . , Colonel. *La vérité sur la guerre de Madagascar.* Toulouse: Berthoumieu, 1896.

ARTICLES AND CHAPTERS

———. "A nous la Légion! ou quand nous allions au secours de l'Amérique." *Képi blanc,* August 1967: 38–45.

Colonel Azan. "Les unités polonaises de la Légion." *Vert et rouge,* no. 21 (1949).

Paul Azan. "La Légion étrangère en Espagne d'après les lettres de sous-lieutenant Jean-Jacques Azan, 1836–1838." *Carnet de la sabretache,* no. 167 (November 1906), 641–57.

F. -H. Bernelle. "Le général Joseph Bernelle," *Verte et rouge,* mai–juin 1943, 10–14; juillet-août 1943, 14–17.

Marcel Blanchard (ed.). "La correspondance de Félix Faure touchant les affaires coloniales, 1882–98." *Revue d'histoire des colonies françaises* 42, no. 147 (1955).

Colonel Robert Bonnafous. "Les Prisonniers du corps expéditionnaire français dans les camps Viêt-Minh (1945–1954)," *Guerres mondiales,* no. 147 (1987), 81–104.

Charles Boucher. "Le siège de Zaatcha." *Revue des Deux Mondes,* 1 April 1851: 70–100.

William Brooks. "The French Foreign Legion Today." *Soldier of Fortune* 3, no. 4 (July 1978), no. 5 (September 1978), no. 6 (November 1978).

Jean Brunon. "Le Colonel Conrad, 1788–1837." *La Légion étrangère,* no. 2 (July 1937): 14–16.

———. "Le centenaire de la prise de Constantine et la mort du Colonel Combe." *Vert et rouge,* no. 3 (August 1937): 5.

———. "Le Maréchal de Mac-Mahon. Lieutenant-colonel à la Légion étrangère (1843–1845." *Vert et rouge,* February–March 1944: 20–23.

————. "Essai sur le folklore de la Légion étrangère." *Vert et rouge,* no. 19 (December 1948): 29–31.

Colonel Pierre Carles. "Survol de l'histoire du sous-officier de la Légion étrangère (1831–1981)." *Revue historique des armées,* no. spécial 1981, "La Légion étrangère, 1831–1981": 23–50.

Captain Abel Clément-Grandcourt. "La situation actuelle dans la Légion étrangère." *Bulletin du comité de l'Afrique française,* October 1909, 336–8.

————. "Les Alsaciens—Lorrains et la Légion étrangère." *Feuilles d'histoire,* 1 June, 1910, 550–69.

Captain Coipel. "Opérations dans le Sud-Oranais en 1903." *Revue militaire générale,* 1 February 1908.

Edouard Collineau. "Un soldat de fortune. Notes et souvenirs de général Collineau." *Carnet de la Sabretache,* no. 288 (March–April 1924).

André-Paul Comor. "L'image de la Légion étrangère à travers la littérature française." *Revue Historique des Armées,* no. 3 (1981), 157–78.

General Jean Compagnon. "La Légion étrangère dans la campagne de Tunisie, 1942–1943." *Revue historique des armées,* no. spécial 1981, "La Légion étrangère, 1831–1981": 185–216.

André Corvisier. "Le recrutement et la promotion dans l'armée française du XVII siècle à nos jours. Rapport sur les études faites par le groupe de travail." *Revue internationale d'histoire militaire,* no. 37 (fascicule 2, 1976).

General Daudignac. "La Légion étrangère." *La nouvelle revue,* IX (1 March 1909): 1–14.

Henry Dutailly, "Chronique de l'ancienne Légion." *Képi blanc,* nos. 278–284 (June–December 1970); 287 (March 1971), 290 (June 1971).

————. "Les enfants de troupe à la Légion." *Képi blanc,* no. 292 (August 1971).

————. "Le 6ᵉ bataillon de l'ancienne Légion étrangère (1831–1835) était-il belge?" *Revue militaire belge,* XX-8 (December 1974) 687–98.

————. "Le 2ᵉ étranger." *Képi blanc,* nos. 332, 333, 334 (1975).

————. "Quelques aspects du recrutement de l'armée d'Afrique sous la Monarchie de Juillet." *Revue internationale d'histoire militaire,* no. 37 (fascicule 2, 1976).

————. "1871. Au combat dans le Loiret." *Historia,* no. 414 bis-spécial, "La Légion étrangère. 150ᵉ anniversaire" (2ᵉ trimestre 1981).

M. Ferron. "La Légion étrangère à Pau en 1836." *La Légion étrangère,* no. 30 (April–May 1942): 12–15.

A/C André Gandelin. "Le Général Rollet, un homme de coeur, de caractère et d'idéal." *Revue historique des armées,* no. spécial 1981, "La Légion étrangère, 1831–1981": 121–141.

G. Gugliotta and J.-C. Jauffret. "Des unités de légende. Les compagnies montées, 1881–1981." *Revue historique des armées,* no. spécial 1981, "La Légion étrangère, 1831–1981."

P. Guinard. "Cavaliers de la Légion étrangère au Mexique." *Carnet de la Sabretache,* no. 389 (July–August 1937), 321–29.

J. N. Gung'l. "La Légion il y a quarante ans." *Légion étrangère,* 1 January 1914, 6–8; 1 February 1914, 34–7; 1 March, 1914, 38–40.

"L'Assaut de Constantine." *Vert et rouge,* no. 20 (1949): 17–18.

"La bataille de Monts." Légion étrangère, no. 7 (1938): 10–14.

Raymond Guyader. "Le Légionnaire des années 1919 à 1927." *Képi blanc,* no. 449 (July 1985).

General Jean-Pierre Hallo. "Le Régiment de marche de la Légion étrangère, 1943–1945." *Revue historique des armées,* no. spécial 1981, "La Légion étrangère, 1831–1981": 217–241.

J.-C. Jauffret. "M. Thiers, l'Espagne et la Légion étrangère, 1835–1837." *Revue historique des armées,* no. 3 (1979): 145–72.

R. A. Kea. "Firearms and Warfare in the Gold Coasts from the 16th to the 19th Centuries." *Journal of African History* 12 (1971): 185–213.

A. K. Koch. "Relation de l'expédition dans le sud de la province d'Oran en 1849." *Spectateur militaire,* 1949.

Sergent Kubiak. "Operation Castor . . . Verdun 1954." *Képi blanc,* (October 1962).

"La Légion étrangère." *La revue d'infanterie.* (1 May 1936).

"La Légion étrangère en Italie." *Vert et rouge.* (September–October 1942): 4–8.

"La résistance du 5ᵉ étranger." *Vert et rouge,* no. 10 (1947): 14–25.

Jacques Lauzière. "La nouvelle Légion étrangère." *Le Mercure de France,* no. 619 (1 April 1924): 56–78.

"Le Deuxième régiment de marche du 1ᵉ étranger dans la deuxième Bataille de l'Artois [attaque du 9 mai 1915]." *Légion étrangère,* (January–February 1939): 14–17.

"Le sanglant combat de chott Tigri." *Vert et rouge,* no. 24 (1949), 40–3.

"Les devoirs du légionnaire." *Vert et rouge,* no. 9 (1946): 22–4.

"Les Indiens à la Légion étrangère." *Légion étrangère,* no. 64 (April 1935): 5–6.

"L'Insurrection des Zibans, 1849." *Légion étrangère.* 12 December 1931, 11–18; 13 January 1932, 12–21; 14 February, 1932, 46–51; 15 March 1932, 88–95.

General Hubert Lyautey. "La Protection du Sud-Oranais." *Revue de Cavalerie,* XLIII (April–September 1906): 332–37.

Félix Mornaud. "La guerre dans les oasis." *L'Illustration,* nos. 350, 351, 352 & 354 (10, 17, 24 November & 8 December, 1849).

Max Niclot. "Le 4 août dans le bled marocain." *Almanach du Combattant,* XXXVe année (1964).

General A. Niessel. "La Légion au combat. Le blocus de Milianah en 1840." *Vert et rouge,* no. 97: 14–20.

"Notes d'un sergent de la vieille légion." *Vert et rouge,* no. 84 (1952).

Comte Pelet de la Lozère. "Souvenirs du roi Louis-Philippe." *Revue universelle* LXII, no. 7 (1 July 1935): 6–29.

A. D. Printer. "Spanish Soldiers in France." *Nation,* clv (1943).

Pierre Sergent. "Du nouveau sur le combat de Camerone." *Revue historique des armées,* no. spécial 1981, "La Légion étrangère, 1831–1981": 73–89.

Felix Tavernier. "Le régiment de Hohenlohe et la Révolution de 1830 à Marseille." *Vert et rouge,* no. 105 (1956): 14–17.

Colonel Tournyol du Clos. "La Légion étrangère au Tonkin (1883–1932). Le siège de Tuyen-Quan (20 janvier–3 mars 1885)." *La revue d'infanterie,* 89, no. 525 (1 May 1936).

Jean Vidalenc. "Une contre-épreuve de l'insoumission. Les engagements volontaires sous la monarchie constitutionnelle (1815–1848)." *Revue internationale d'histoire militaire,* no. 37 (fascicule 2, 1976).

Comte de Villebois Mareuil. "La Légion étrangère." *Revue des Deux Mondes,* 15 April, 1896.

Charles-Jules Zédé. "Souvenirs de ma vie," *Carnet de la Sabretache,* no. 366 (September–October 1933): 426–41; no. 367 (November–December 1933): 481–504; no. 371 (July–August 1934): 254–76; no. 373 (November–December 1934): 445–59; no. 374 (January–February 1935): 33–74.

INDEX